Reasonableness

P.C.   Warrant   Other
                   (means/method
                    of execution)

search the
person

search the
immediate
area

INTRUSIVENESS
OF ACTIVITY

Nonintrusion   nothing   "stop"   "arrest"   Complete Deprivation

0 |——————————————————————————————————————| 100

                      R.S.   P.C.

TERRY

                          seized person

4th Amendment
safeguards

TERRY   Intrusiveness

9 OCT 01

Forms of   { stop; r.s. — limited detention < time
seizure   {   space
            { arrest — complete detention
            { p.s.   of indefinite
                        duration

frisk – limited
intrusion of privacy

definition: whereas
by physical force
or show of authority
police have restricted
freedom of movement

23 OCT

1. unconseled   10 days in jail
2. unconseled   no jail
3. cannot charge w/ DUI third
   offense
4. can charge w/ DUI second
   offense

CRIMINAL PROCEDURE AND THE CONSTITUTION

LEADING SUPREME COURT CASES AND INTRODUCTORY TEXT

2001 EDITION

By

Jerold H. Israel

*Ed Rood Eminent Scholar in Trial Advocacy and Procedure,
University of Florida, College of Law
Alene and Allan F. Smith Professor of Law Emeritus,
University of Michigan*

Yale Kamisar

*Clarence Darrow Distinguished University Professor of Law,
University of Michigan*

Wayne R. LaFave

*Professor Emeritus in the College of Law
and Center for Advanced Study,
University of Illinois*

AMERICAN CASEBOOK SERIES®

WEST GROUP

A THOMSON COMPANY

ST. PAUL, MINN., 2001

American Casebook Series and the West Group symbol
are registered trademarks used herein under license.

ISBN 0–314–25456–0

*TEXT IS PRINTED ON 10% POST
CONSUMER RECYCLED PAPER*

∞

Preface

This collection of leading Supreme Court cases is designed for those instructors who want to cover a wide range of criminal procedure topics but have available only a limited amount of time. In the main, the cases in this book were selected because of their substantial contemporary significance; they reflect the Supreme Court's current position on issues of major importance regarding the operation of our federal and state criminal justice systems. But we have also included some venerable cases that contribute significantly to an understanding of current trends and developments.

These materials differ in important ways from our three other sets of teaching materials in this field, *Modern Criminal Procedure (Modern)*, *Basic Criminal Procedure (Basic)* and *Advanced Criminal Procedure (Advanced)*. Those materials also include a goodly number of lower court cases, many of which focus on state law developments, and contain many authors' Notes and Questions and extracts from books, reports, articles, model codes, and proposed standards. By contrast, the present book is limited to the Supreme Court decisions themselves.

We have, of course, relied on and profited by the rich literature in this field in the course of preparing the introductory comments that appear at the outset of each chapter and at the beginning of most sections of each chapter. But this introductory text does not explore any particular issue in depth. Nor is it contentious, as are many of the law review articles extracted in our other books. The brief introductory comments, rather, are designed only to place the selected cases that follow in general historical and doctrinal perspective.

Although the topics covered in *Basic* are treated in considerable depth, the scope of that book is quite limited. *Basic*'s major emphasis is on police practices, e.g., arrest, search and seizure, police interrogation and confessions, and pre-trial identification procedures; no attention is given to the more formal phases of the criminal process (which are treated separately in *Advanced*). The present volume, on the other hand, not only gives issues involving the police considerable attention but covers a number of other aspects of the criminal process, e.g., criminal discovery, double jeopardy, fair trial/free press, plea bargaining, and the trial. Our "big book," *Modern*, also covers a wide range of topics, but because it explores these topics in much greater depth it is about twice the size of this book. (There is, of course, no law prohibiting an instructor from dipping into *Modern* in order to enrich class discussion of one or more of the issues raised by the materials in this book.)

As is apparent from these comparisons, we envision this collection of leading cases as being used in a course of a distinctly different character than the various possibilities we contemplated with respect to either *Modern* or *Basic*. This book is especially suited to a survey course having as its purpose a critical examination of how the United States Supreme Court has grappled with a range of basic and highly controversial issues that arise at various stages of the criminal process—issues as diverse as when the police should be permitted to "search" or "seize" without prior judicial approval or traditional "probable cause," how far a secret government agent may go in "encouraging" a person to commit a crime or "tricking" him into making an incriminating statement, when a defense lawyer's performance is so "ineffective" as to vitiate a conviction, when a prosecutor must disclose information in his files, and when a defendant must endure a second trial for the same or a related offense.

In *Modern, Advanced,* and *Basic,* our hope and expectation has been that a student working with those materials descry not only the forest (or in the case of *Advanced* and *Basic,* at least a good-sized grove), but also the trees. Here, by contrast, the emphasis is decidedly sylvan.

It is possible, of course, to produce a thin volume of teaching materials by collecting snippets of many opinions. This approach has been emphatically rejected. The modest size of this volume has been attained, rather, by the judicious selection of leading cases. Those cases that have been selected are set forth at considerable length.

Moreover, because the use of these materials will mark many students' first real exposure to the U.S. Supreme Court as an institution, we have resisted the temptation to delete, or even to summarize, concurring and dissenting opinions. Instead, we have taken pains to set forth the views of *all* members of the Court at considerable length in such cases as *Leon, Mapp* and *Miranda.*

In the main, we have followed a chronological approach in ordering the cases which appear in this book. Following the introductory materials, which include an overview of the criminal justice system and a general consideration of due process, the criminal justice system is examined from arrest and search and "on the street" questioning all the way through to the decision on guilt and imposition of sentence.

We have occasionally departed from the chronological scheme when it seemed appropriate to do so. For example, the right to counsel, "the most pervasive right" of an accused, is first considered in advance of the confession and lineup chapters so that the Court's reliance on the right to counsel in those contexts may be better understood. (Other aspects of the right to counsel, such as the necessary character and quality of representation at trial and in preparing for trial, are considered later in the book.) So too, post conviction review is considered in the context of the review of particular claims rather than in a separate chapter on habeas corpus.

The cases in this book have been edited with the above-stated purposes in mind. We have tried hard—indeed, it would not be an exaggeration to say that we have made heroic efforts—to keep these materials lean and manageable. We have also tried to ensure that within the confines of particular cases the student's attention is focused upon the broader themes and issues.

Case citations and footnotes have been eliminated from the judicial opinions without so specifying. When three asterisks appear, this designates omission of a portion of the opinion deemed inessential to an understanding and appraisal of the issues and holding in that case.

Numbered footnotes are from the original materials; lettered footnotes are ours. We would call particular attention to those lettered footnotes which contain summaries of Supreme Court decisons related to the major cases presented in this book. These footnotes often indicate how the Court later dealt with a problem alluded to in the principal case, or how a comment in the principal case later came to have importance regarding a related issue.

To make our sentence structure as short and direct as possible, we often have not used the phrases "he or she" or "his or her." Where we have used the masculine or feminine pronoun alone, consistent with the traditional rules of construction in legal texts, the pronoun should be read to encompass both male and female actors unless the context clearly indicates otherwise.

The cut-off print for inclusion of Supreme Court cases in this volume was the end of the Court's 2000–2001 term. Citations are to the United States Reports, unless the case had not yet appeared in those reports. In that event, we have used the Supreme Court Reporter citation (if available).

Experience has taught us that there will undoubtedly be some typographical errors in a publication of this length. We would appreciate your calling such errors to our attention, so they can be corrected in the next printing. We would, of course, also appreciate hearing from readers who have criticisms or suggestions regarding the substantive content of the volume.

We are most appreciative of the able secretarial assistance provided, too often under great stress, by Millie Arthur, Carol Haley, Mary Lebert and Carolyn Lloyd, in the preparation of the first edition of this volume.

JEROLD H. ISRAEL
YALE KAMISAR
WAYNE R. LaFAVE

July, 2001

Editors' Note

We have placed *Dickerson v. United States*, the case that reaffirms *Miranda,* at the end of Ch. 6, § 3. However, some instructors may want to postpone treatment of *Dickerson* until the end of § 4, after the students have discussed *New York v. Quarles, Oregon v. Elstad,* and *Withrow v. Williams.*

*

Summary of Contents

Table of Contents

*

Table of Cases

The principal cases are in bold type. Cases cited or discussed
in the text are roman type. References are to pages.

TABLE OF CASES   **XXV**

Stone v. Powell, 428 U.S. 465, 96 S.Ct. 3037, 49 L.Ed.2d 1067 (1976), 78, 414, 415, 417, 418, 420, 428, 691

Stoner v. State of Cal., 376 U.S. 483, 84 S.Ct. 889, 11 L.Ed.2d 856 (1964), 89, 263, 264

Stovall v. Denno, 388 U.S. 293, 87 S.Ct. 1967, 18 L.Ed.2d 1199 (1967), 438, 439, 445, 447, 448, 449, 450, 451, 452

Strauder v. State of West Virginia, 100 U.S. 303, 10 Otto 303, 25 L.Ed. 664 (1879), 541, 542, 647

Strickland v. Washington, 466 U.S. 668, 104 S.Ct. 2052, 80 L.Ed.2d 674 (1984), 544, 577, 578, 690, 691, 692, **693,** 702, 705, 707, 708, 709, 713, 783

Sturges, United States ex rel. Kirby v., 510 F.2d 397 (7th Cir.1975), 445

Swain v. Alabama, 380 U.S. 202, 85 S.Ct. 824, 13 L.Ed.2d 759 (1965), 637, 638, 639, 640, 641, 643, 644, 882

Tateo, United States v., 377 U.S. 463, 84 S.Ct. 1587, 12 L.Ed.2d 448 (1964), 833, 834

Taylor v. Illinois, 484 U.S. 400, 108 S.Ct. 646, 98 L.Ed.2d 798 (1988), 573

Taylor v. Kentucky, 436 U.S. 478, 98 S.Ct. 1930, 56 L.Ed.2d 468 (1978), 727, **760,** 763

Taylor v. Louisiana, 419 U.S. 522, 95 S.Ct. 692, 42 L.Ed.2d 690 (1975), 621, **625,** 633, 647

Taylor v. United States, 414 U.S. 17, 94 S.Ct. 194, 38 L.Ed.2d 174 (1973), 725

Tennessee v. Garner, 471 U.S. 1, 105 S.Ct. 1694, 85 L.Ed.2d 1 (1985), 136, 153, **160**

Terry v. Ohio, 392 U.S. 1, 88 S.Ct. 1868, 20 L.Ed.2d 889 (1968), 135, 143, 144, 146, 147, 148, 190, 202, 210, **211,** 214, 215, 217, 218, 220, 221, 223, 224, 225, 226, 227, 228, 229, 230, 231, 239, 240, 241, 242, 243, 372

Texas v. Cobb, ___ U.S. ___, 121 S.Ct. 1335, 149 L.Ed.2d 321 (2001), 390

Texas v. McCullough, 475 U.S. 134, 106 S.Ct. 976, 89 L.Ed.2d 104 (1986), 528

Townsend v. Sain, 372 U.S. 293, 83 S.Ct. 745, 9 L.Ed.2d 770 (1963), 772, 773, 780, 781

Trupiano v. United States, 334 U.S. 699, 68 S.Ct. 1229, 92 L.Ed. 1663 (1948), 172

Tucker, United States v., 404 U.S. 443, 92 S.Ct. 589, 30 L.Ed.2d 592 (1972), 839

Tumey v. State of Ohio, 273 U.S. 510, 47 S.Ct. 437, 71 L.Ed. 749 (1927), 534, 542

Turner v. Murray, 476 U.S. 28, 106 S.Ct. 1683, 90 L.Ed.2d 27 (1986), 621, **628,** 872, 882

Turner v. Pennsylvania, 338 U.S. 49, 69 S.Ct. 1357, 93 L.Ed. 1801 (1949), 320

Twining v. State of N.J., 211 U.S. 78, 29 S.Ct. 14, 53 L.Ed. 97 (1908), 33, 35, 36, 40, 41, 42, 47, 48

Ullmann v. United States, 350 U.S. 422, 76 S.Ct. 497, 100 L.Ed. 511 (1956), 468, 479, 847

Ungar v. Sarafite, 376 U.S. 575, 84 S.Ct. 841, 11 L.Ed.2d 921 (1964), 693

United States v. _____ (see opposing party)

United States ex rel. v. _____ (see opposing party and relator)

Ursery, United States v., 518 U.S. 267, 116 S.Ct. 2135, 135 L.Ed.2d 549 (1996), 814, 816

Vale v. Louisiana, 399 U.S. 30, 90 S.Ct. 1969, 26 L.Ed.2d 409 (1970), 166, **176,** 179

Valenzuela–Bernal, United States v., 458 U.S. 858, 102 S.Ct. 3440, 73 L.Ed.2d 1193 (1982), 577, 700, 756

Vandercomb, King v., 168 Eng.Rep. 455 (K.B. 1796), 793, 800

Vasquez v. Hillery, 474 U.S. 254, 106 S.Ct. 617, 88 L.Ed.2d 598 (1986), 534, **540,** 549, 580

Vernonia School Dist. 47J v. Acton, 515 U.S. 646, 115 S.Ct. 2386, 132 L.Ed.2d 564 (1995), **243,** 247, 248

Vignera v. New York, 384 U.S. 436, 86 S.Ct. 1602, 16 L.Ed.2d 694 (1966), 333, 337, 346, 349, 351

Village of (see name of village)

Villamonte–Marquez, United States v., 462 U.S. 579, 103 S.Ct. 2573, 77 L.Ed.2d 22 (1983), 151

Virginia, Ex parte, 100 U.S. 339, 10 Otto 339, 25 L.Ed. 676 (1879), 882

Wade v. Hunter, 336 U.S. 684, 69 S.Ct. 834, 93 L.Ed. 974 (1949), 827

Wade, United States v., 388 U.S. 218, 87 S.Ct. 1926, 18 L.Ed.2d 1149 (1967), 257, 435, 436, **437,** 440, 444, 445, 446, 447, 449, 451, 452, 535, 536, 538

Wainwright v. Sykes, 433 U.S. 72, 97 S.Ct. 2497, 53 L.Ed.2d 594 (1977), 745

Wainwright v. Torna, 455 U.S. 586, 102 S.Ct. 1300, 71 L.Ed.2d 475 (1982), 690

Waller v. Georgia, 467 U.S. 39, 104 S.Ct. 2210, 81 L.Ed.2d 31 (1984), 684, 685

Walton v. Arizona, 497 U.S. 639, 110 S.Ct. 3047, 111 L.Ed.2d 511 (1990), 856, 859, 861, 862

Ward v. State of Texas, 316 U.S. 547, 62 S.Ct. 1139, 86 L.Ed. 1663 (1942), 308

Ward, United States v., 448 U.S. 242, 100 S.Ct. 2636, 65 L.Ed.2d 742 (1980), 813, 817

Warden, Md. Penitentiary v. Hayden, 387 U.S. 294, 87 S.Ct. 1642, 18 L.Ed.2d 782 (1967), 462, 488

Wardius v. Oregon, 412 U.S. 470, 93 S.Ct. 2208, 37 L.Ed.2d 82 (1973), 570

Washington v. Texas, 388 U.S. 14, 87 S.Ct. 1920, 18 L.Ed.2d 1019 (1967), 44, 726, 757

Washington, United States v., 431 U.S. 181, 97 S.Ct. 1814, 52 L.Ed.2d 238 (1977), 391, 476

Watson, United States v., 423 U.S. 411, 96 S.Ct. 820, 46 L.Ed.2d 598 (1976), **136,** 166, 168, 169, 170, 196, 534

Watts v. State of Ind., 338 U.S. 49, 69 S.Ct. 1357, 93 L.Ed. 1801 (1949), 320

Watts v. State of Ind., 338 U.S. 49, 69 S.Ct. 1347, 93 L.Ed. 1801 (1949), 309, 311, **317,** 321, 351

Watts, United States v., 519 U.S. 148, 117 S.Ct. 633, 136 L.Ed.2d 554 (1997), 841

Wayte v. United States, 470 U.S. 598, 105 S.Ct. 1524, 84 L.Ed.2d 547 (1985), 518, 881

Weatherford v. Bursey, 429 U.S. 545, 97 S.Ct. 837, 51 L.Ed.2d 30 (1977), 568

CRIMINAL PROCEDURE AND THE CONSTITUTION

*

Chapter 1

AN OVERVIEW OF THE CRIMINAL JUSTICE PROCESS

SECTION 1. INTRODUCTION

The Limits of an Overview. This book presents a collection of leading Supreme Court decisions in the field of "constitutional criminal procedure"—that is, decisions dealing with the application of the United States Constitution to what is commonly described as the "criminal justice process." The criminal justice process consists of that series of procedures through which this country's criminal laws (those laws defining criminal acts and providing for the punishment of offenders) are enforced. In this chapter, we will present a brief introduction to the most important of those procedures and to the persons responsible for their administration. Our overview is designed to provide some general background information that should assist in your reading of the collected cases. In particular, it hopefully will give you some sense of the place of the individual procedure discussed in a particular case as that procedure relates to the overall process.

An overview of a process as complex as the criminal justice process necessarily requires a certain degree of overgeneralization. There is no single set of criminal justice procedures uniformly used throughout the United States. Each of the 50 states and the federal government has enacted its own criminal code applicable within the general reach of its laws.[1] Just as there is diversity among those 51

---

1. The criminal laws of a state are limited in application to offenses that occurred in their entirety or in part within that state. The federal criminal law, in contrast, has a territorial reach that extends throughout the United States and its territories. However, the federal government, unlike the state governments, cannot declare an action to be criminal simply because it is contrary to the public welfare. The federal government's regulatory authority in the criminal field, as in other fields, is limited to those subjects as to which the federal constitution grants Congress legislative authority, such as interstate and foreign commerce, and the maintenance of national services (e.g., the postal service and the armed forces).

Viewed by reference to their relationship to particular areas of federal authority, federal crimes tend to fall into three categories. First, there are those crimes that interfere with the performance of basic functions of the federal government (e.g., espionage or bribery of federal officials). A second, closely related group of federal offenses seeks to protect certain private facilities in which the federal government has a special interest as a result of its close regulation or financial involvement (e.g., robbery of federally insured banks). A third category of federal offenses are those based upon Congress' specific regulatory powers, such as its authority over interstate commerce. These include crimes involving the use of the interstate communications facilities, actions of state officials that violate rights guaranteed under the Fourteenth Amendment, and even prostitution when the participants move in interstate commerce.

For those criminal activities relating to unique federal governmental functions (e.g., coining money), federal criminal statutes are the primary (and sometimes exclusive) source jurisdictions in their definition of crime, there is diversity as well in the processes they use to enforce their criminal laws. Each jurisdiction's procedures must comply with the federal constitution, but those constitutional limitations, as will be seen, allow the individual jurisdictions considerable leeway in shaping many elements of their criminal justice process.

While the diversity among the jurisdictions must be kept in mind, there is sufficient similarity in the basic structure of the process among the different jurisdictions—provided in part by the common heritage of the English common law—to make helpful a description of the process that largely ignores state-by-state variations. Our overview seeks to provide such a description, concentrating on the sequence of procedures commonly applied in most of the 51 jurisdictions. It notes only a few of the many variations, concentrating on those variations that are fundamental and are followed in a substantial group of jurisdictions.

To assist you in following the overview, it should be helpful at the outset if you would carefully examine the chart at page 32. Note that the chart follows the flow of the criminal justice process through a horizontal line which starts at the point of the commission of the crime and continues through to the sentencing of the convicted offender. The thickness of this horizontal line gradually narrows to indicate the decreasing number of cases involved at each succeeding stage of the process. The various lines pointing upward or downward indicate cases leaving the process. The process has a "sieve effect," constantly sifting cases out of the criminal justice system before they complete all of the stages in the process.[2] You also will note that the horizontal line eventually divides into three major prongs. The first division occurs quite early in the process and notes the beginning of the separate treatment of juveniles through the juvenile justice process. The deci-

of prosecution. For most types of criminal activity, however, even where both federal and state laws apply (as in gambling and narcotics), the vast majority of all prosecutions are brought under state law. Thus, overall, over 95% of all prosecutions for felony offenses are brought under state law, and most of the major industrial states individually have more felony prosecutions each year than does the whole federal government. When consideration is given as well to misdemeanor prosecutions, which outnumber felony prosecutions by a ratio of roughly 9 or 10 to 1, the federal criminal justice process accounts for less than 1% of all criminal prosecutions.

2. Thus, there is a progressive reduction in the volume of cases as one moves from the beginning to the end of the process. More persons are investigated than are arrested, more arrested than charged, more charged than tried, and more tried than convicted. Consider, for example, the following model which approximates the distribution found in several urban communities. Start with 5,000 possible felonies that come to the attention of the police either through citizen complaint or officer observations. Because many of these reported offenses cannot be solved, the police investigation of those crimes is likely to result in the arrest of no more than 1,500 persons. Out of this group of arrestees, approximately 400 will be juveniles, who will be transferred to the juvenile process. After the police and pros-

ecutor have reviewed the case against the remaining 1100 arrestees, about 250 will be released without any charges being pressed. In an additional 100 cases, the charges will immediately be reduced to misdemeanors. Thus, of 1,500 felony arrestees, only 750 actually will have felony charges filed against them. The 750 felony charges will then be screened at preliminary hearings or grand jury proceedings, and will be subject to challenge by defense motions of various sorts. These procedures are likely to result in the dismissal of roughly 50 cases. Still another 100 cases may be dismissed by the prosecutor as a result of postcharge screening. Of the 600 felony cases that are left, approximately 500 will be resolved by guilty pleas. Perhaps 20% of those pleas will be to misdemeanor charges, and the others will be to the felony charged or to a lesser felony. There remain roughly 100 felony cases that will go to trial. Approximately 70 of the trials will result in convictions, although not necessarily for felonies. In the end, approximately 460 of the original group of adult arrestees will be convicted on a felony charge (including felonies lesser than that originally charged) and 210 will be convicted of misdemeanors. As many as 450 of the 670 convicted persons will receive a sentence that includes some incarceration, but for most of the 450, incarceration will be limited to a short jail term, typically combined with probation. Approximately 150 of those convicted (all for felonies) will be sentenced to prison terms.

sions in this book do not deal with that process, which traditionally is separated in goals and procedures from the criminal justice process. Farther along in the flow of the criminal process itself, the horizontal line again divides as felonies and misdemeanors are separated.[3] We will concentrate in our overview primarily on the processing of felony cases since felonies are more serious crimes and require more complex procedures than misdemeanors. Along the way (primarily in footnotes), we will note most of the key distinctions in the processing of misdemeanors.[4] Most of the leading decisions included in this volume deal with felonies.

Ongoing Procedures. Both the chart on page 32 and our overview present the various procedures in the process in the chronological order in which they commonly occur. By and large, each procedure constitutes a separate stage in the criminal justice process that follows upon the completion of a prior procedure. There are certain procedures, however, that tend to be ongoing. The investigatory process, for example, starts at an early stage but may continue on through to the time of trial. Similarly, the prosecutor's decision to charge is subject to an ongoing opportunity for review at various points throughout the process. The judge's review of the evidence before the jury is another step that is ongoing as it may be repeated at various points during the trial. Generally, we will discuss these ongoing procedures only at the point at which they first arise and will not consider them again at later points at which they may be repeated. Our discussion of the investigatory process will be split, however, to consider separately pre-arrest and post-arrest investigations, since investigatory procedures may be somewhat different at these two stages of the process.

Functions of the Process. Although the interrelationship of the different procedures is suggested by the chronological development of the process, it might be helpful in this connection also to identify several basic functions that will be achieved during the course of the process. Those functions are: (1) determining whether a crime has been committed, (2) detecting the possible offender, (3) apprehending that person, (4) providing for a review of the evidence by the prosecutor to determine whether the case against the alleged offender merits prosecution, (5) providing for a review of the prosecutor's decision by an independent agency, such as a magistrate or grand jury, (6) providing for a determination by a jury or judge as to the alleged offender's guilt, and (7) setting the punishment where the alleged offender has been found guilty. Almost every one of the

---

3. American jurisdictions commonly use either of two different standards in distinguishing between felonies and misdemeanors. Some classify as felonies all crimes punishable by a maximum term of imprisonment of more than one year; crimes punishable by imprisonment for one year or less are then misdemeanors. Other jurisdictions look to the location of the possible imprisonment: if the crime is punishable by incarceration in a penitentiary, it is a felony; if punishable only by a jail term, it is a misdemeanor. As a matter of practice, both dividing lines frequently produce the same result since state correction codes commonly provide for imprisonment in the penitentiary if a sentence exceeds one year and for imprisonment in jail if the sentence is for one year or less.

4. Our discussion of the prosecutorial and judicial processing of misdemeanors excludes the ordinary traffic violation. In many jurisdictions, all but the most serious traffic violations (e.g., driving while intoxicated) have been decriminalized. Indeed, even in those jurisdictions in which all traffic violations are technically misdemeanors, the less serious traffic offenses often are governed by somewhat different adjudication procedures than misdemeanors generally. On the other hand, our discussion does encompass city ordinance violations in those jurisdictions in which ordinances largely duplicate in substance and penalty state misdemeanor provisions governing such offenses as assault, petty theft, etc. Such ordinances commonly are used as a basis for prosecution in lieu of the state misdemeanor provisions (often because the fines collected for ordinance violations go to the city). In jurisdictions of this type, the procedure applied to ordinance violations is basically the same as that applied to misdemeanors punishable by state law.

procedures discussed in the next section will contribute to the performance of at least one of these functions. In some instances, the procedure will serve more than one function, and in most instances, performance of the function will be dependent upon the effectiveness of more than one procedure. Variations in the process will often be explained by a jurisdiction's choice between alternative procedures aimed at achieving the same basic function.

SECTION 2.   THE PROCESSING OF A FELONY CASE—THE STEPS IN THE PROCESS

1. *Commission of the Crime.* Note that the flow line in our chart has its greatest thickness at the first stage, the commission of crime, and then narrows sharply at the next stage, the investigation of crime. Many crimes are never reported to the police, and thus there are far fewer crimes investigated than committed.[5] Where a possible crime comes to the attention of the police, that usually occurs, as the chart indicates, after the crime has been completed. In a limited number of situations, however, police may initiate an investigation of a crime even before it is completed. Thus, in the investigation of crimes between willing participants—so called "victimless crimes," such as gambling or narcotics distribution—police often use undercover agents and other investigative techniques aimed more at trapping potential offenders as they move into the criminal activity than the investigation of completed crimes.

2. *Pre-arrest Investigation.* Once the police became aware of the possible commission of a crime, they then must determine (1) whether the crime actually was committed and (2) if it was committed, whether there is sufficient information pointing to the guilt of a particular person to justify arresting that person. Pre-arrest investigation is aimed primarily at making these determinations. The degree of investigation needed will, of course, vary with the circumstances. Where a police officer observes a crime being committed in his presence, that officer usually can make an arrest "on the spot." In such a situation, the pre-arrest investigation will have consisted of no more than the officer's initial observation. Where the officer observes suspicious activity, but is uncertain as to exactly what has occurred, he may stop the suspect on the street and briefly question him before deciding whether to make an arrest. In this type of case, the pre-arrest investigation will have consisted of the officer's observations, some interrogation (i.e., questioning), and possibly a frisk (i.e., a "pat-down") to ensure that the suspect is not carrying a weapon. Where the suspicious activity is combined with driving that constitutes a traffic violation, the officer may utilize a traffic stop. If the traffic violation is one that permits an arrest (rather than simply the issuance of a citation), the officer may arrest the driver and search both his person and the automobile (see step 3 infra). If an arrest is not permitted, the investigation will be similar to a street stop, but a search of the car may result if the driver gives consent or the officer observes contraband within the car.

Where the officer does not observe the commission of the crime, the pre-arrest investigation often is more complex. Initially, the officer will obtain a statement

---

5. A typical breakdown of reported crimes would be 60% property offenses (e.g., theft, burglary), 10% assaults of various types, 10% offenses relating to alcohol and drugs, and the remaining 20% distributed among a variety of crimes, with less than 5% involving the most serious violent crimes (robbery, rape, and murder). Because some crimes are far less likely to be reported than others, the mix of crimes actually committed is somewhat different. Crimes between willing participants, for example, are rarely reported unless observed by the officer. On the other side, thefts of motor vehicles are almost always reported as such a report is needed to collect insurance.

from the person who reports the crime and from any bystanders.[6] Any physical evidence left at the scene of the crime may be removed and examined, sometimes by the police laboratory. Potential suspects may be visited at their homes or stopped on the street and questioned. Here too, where the crime being investigated involved violence, the officer may frisk the suspect to ensure that he is not carrying a weapon. If a suspect makes a statement, it may be verified through interviews with other persons, such as employers or friends. If the officer has reason to believe that evidence of the crime can be found in a particular location (e.g., a car or a home), a search of that location may be conducted. This usually will be done pursuant to a "search warrant" (a court order authorizing the search) where the place searched is a home, but it will be done without a warrant when the place searched is a car. In unusual cases, the police may place a suspect under surveillance or utilize the services of an undercover agent to obtain information from the unwitting suspect. In other cases, a wiretap or other form of electronic surveillance will be instituted pursuant to a court order. In still others, the prosecutor may be asked to obtain a court order requiring a suspect to produce for examination certain documents or records.[7]

Among the various pre-arrest investigatory procedures discussed above, the most common procedures are the personal observation by the officer, the questioning of witnesses, and the questioning of the suspect. Even in serious felony cases, procedures such as the search of the suspect's home, wiretapping, surveillance, and scientific examination of evidence are used in only a small percentage of investigations.

3. *The Arrest.* The term "arrest" has various definitions, and discussions of arrest practices often are confused because of the failure of the discussants to agree on the meaning of that term. For the purpose of this overview, we will use a common statutory definition of "arrest"—the taking of a person into custody for the purpose of charging him with a crime. This ordinarily involves the officer's exercise of physical control over the suspect for the purpose of first transporting him to a police facility and then requesting that felony charges be filed against him.[8] To make an arrest the officer must have reasonable grounds ("probable cause") to believe that a crime was committed and that the person to be arrested was the offender.

Where there is no immediate need to arrest a suspect, an officer may first seek a court order, commonly called an arrest warrant, which authorizes the officer to make the arrest. The arrest warrant is issued by a magistrate upon a finding of probable cause and offers the advantage of prior judicial approval of the arrest. In the vast majority of felony cases, however, the officer will act without a

---

6. For those offenses not likely to be observed by the police officer or to involve an offender known to the victim, there tends to be a much lower likelihood of a successful investigation that results in a "clearance," even as measured simply by an arrest (i.e., without regard to whether there eventually is a conviction). Thus, burglary, a crime that typically falls in this category, commonly has a clearance rate within the range of 10–20% (as opposed to over 60% for aggravated assault).

7. In a small percentage of cases, the pre-arrest investigation will be conducted primarily by the prosecuting attorney rather than the police. The prosecuting attorney's primary means of investigation is the grand jury. While the most noted function of the grand jury is to review the sufficiency of the evidence

supporting a criminal charge (see step 11), the grand jury also has authority to obtain information concerning possible criminal activities. The grand jury investigation, which operates through the use of the subpoena (a court order issued on behalf of the grand jury), is described in Chapter 8.

8. In the case of a misdemeanor, the arrested person may not be transported to the police facility, but instead may simply be released on the street after the officer has given him a citation (similar to a traffic ticket). The citation will direct the individual to appear in court on a certain day to answer charges specified in the citation. His failure to do so will result in a court order directing his arrest (a "bench warrant").

warrant and will make the arrest as soon as he is convinced that he has sufficient grounds to lawfully do so. The arrest made without a court order commonly is described as a "warrantless" arrest.

Typically, contemporaneously with the arrest, the officer will search the arrestee and remove any weapons, contraband, or evidence of the crime found on his person. If the person is arrested in a car or was carrying packages, the passenger compartment of the car and those packages readily opened may be searched for the same purposes.

After being taken into custody, the arrestee will be transported to a police precinct station, a centrally located jail, or some similar police facility. If the officer should determine, however, that the arrestee is young enough to be a juvenile under state law, he will take the arrestee directly to a juvenile facility. The description of the process from this point on assumes that the arrestee is not a juvenile.

4. *Booking.* Once the arrestee arrives at the police facility, he will be "booked." Booking is the clerical process by which an administrative record is made of the arrest. The arrestee's name, time of arrival, and the offense involved are listed on the police "blotter" or "log" as an official record of the arrest. As part of the booking process, the arrestee ordinarily will be photographed and his fingerprints will be taken.

While at the police facility, the arrestee typically will be given the right to make a telephone call and will be informed of the charge on which he has been booked. He then will be placed in a "holding" unit, usually a cell in the station or a nearby jail, where he will await his presentation before a magistrate. Ordinarily, the arrestee will be searched before being placed in this facility, and that search will be more thorough than the search conducted by the officer contemporaneously with the arrest. This second search is designed primarily to make an inventory of the individual's personal belongings and to prevent the introduction of contraband into the holding unit.

5. *Post-arrest Investigation.* Whether there will be significant post-arrest investigation will vary with the fact situation. In some cases, such as where the arrestee has been caught "red-handed," there will be little post-arrest investigation. In other situations, the post-arrest investigation will involve many of the same kinds of investigative activities as could have been performed before the arrest, such as witness interviews, search of the suspect's home, viewing the scene of the crime, etc. Where the officer has sufficient grounds to justify an arrest without the evidence that might be obtained through such investigative techniques, he may use those techniques at his convenience, either before or after the arrest.

Post-arrest investigation does offer one investigative source that ordinarily is not available prior to the arrest—the person of the arrestee (who is now in custody). Thus the arrestee may be placed in a lineup where he can be viewed by witnesses, or he may be required to provide handwriting or voice samples. The arrestee also may be interrogated after having been warned of his rights. Although we do not have precise data on the extent of these post-arrest procedures, the best available estimates indicate that they are not utilized for the vast majority of arrestees.

6. *The Decision to Charge.* Sometime between the booking of the arrestee and his presentation before a magistrate (see step 9), there will be a review of the decision to press charges, first by the police and then by the prosecutor.[9] The

9. In those cases where the arrest is made   pursuant to an arrest warrant, the available review procedure varies considerably from jurisdiction to jurisdiction, both as to the participants involved and the standards they apply. Ordinarily, it starts with an arrest report that will be filled out by the arresting officer. The officer's report will contain a narrative account of the crime and the circumstances of the arrest. It commonly will include a brief description of all evidence then available (e.g., witnesses, seized contraband). A higher ranking officer, such as a "desk sergeant" or precinct duty officer, then will review the report to decide whether the case should be approved for prosecution. In many instances, this officer may reduce a recommended felony charge to a misdemeanor charge or direct that the arrestee be released. The arrestee's release may be ordered because the evidence is insufficient to support a criminal charge or because the police department has a policy against pressing charges under the special circumstances of the case (e.g., an intrafamily assault). When the arrestee is released because the available evidence is insufficient, there may be a follow-up investigation and the individual may later be rearrested.

Assuming that the higher ranking officer has approved the charge, the next step in the review process is the presentation of the case to the prosecutor's office. In some jurisdictions, the review of the case by a prosecuting attorney commonly does not occur until sometime after the arrestee's initial appearance before a magistrate (see step 9). In such jurisdictions, the complaint (see step 7) will be prepared and filed by the police without the prior approval of the prosecutor. In most jurisdictions, however, the prosecutor will review the case before the arrestee's initial appearance, and a complaint will be filed only upon review (and approval) of the prosecutor. The information considered by the prosecuting attorney in reviewing the proposed charge will vary according to local practice. In some communities, the prosecutor's review ordinarily is limited to the police report. In others, the prosecuting attorney also will interview the arresting officer, the victim, or some other eyewitness.[10]

The prosecuting attorney must decide whether the arrestee should be charged and, if so, whether the charge should be that recommended by the police. Of course, the prosecutor must consider the strength of the evidence. If it is not sufficient to support the proposed charge, then the arrestee must be released or, if the evidence does support a lesser charge, the charge must be reduced. The prosecutor also may consider various other factors, besides the weight of the evidence, in determining whether to proceed. Thus, consideration will be given to the amount of harm caused by the crime, the victim's attitude (and willingness to testify), the criminal record of the arrestee, and the adequacy of any alternative remedies that may be utilized without invoking the criminal process. Such factors are weighed because the prosecutor has responsibilities beyond avoiding the prosecution of the innocent. Even though the individual clearly is guilty and that guilt can be proven, the prosecuting attorney may decide that the prosecution

evidence often will be reviewed prior to obtaining the warrant and a subsequent review of the decision to charge will be unnecessary. We assume from this point on that the arrest in the case we are following was made without a warrant.

10. Though we can hardly characterize any particular pre-charge screening program as typical of most jurisdictions, a fairly common pattern is found as to the end result of the overall governmental screening conducted throughout the process (that is the combination of pre-charge police and prosecutor screen-

ing and post-charge prosecutorial screening, carried on up to the point of trial). Quite commonly, the cases against a substantial percentage of all adult felony arrestees (e.g., 30–45%) will be dropped as a result of such screening. Thus, far more felony arrests do not reach the point of conviction because of police and prosecutor screening than because of the combination of all other screens, i.e., the rejection of charges by independent screening agencies (the grand jury or the magistrate), successful pretrial legal challenges, or acquittals at trial.

recommended by the police would not serve the ends of justice or would be inappropriate considering limited prosecutorial resources.[11]

7. *Filing the Complaint.* Assuming the prosecutor decides to proceed, the next step is the formal initiation of criminal prosecution through the filing of a "charging" document before a court. A charging document accuses the arrestee of committing a crime, and its filing officially makes him a "defendant" in a criminal case. The most common titles for the charging documents used in the criminal law are the "complaint," the "information" and the "indictment." Although they differ in other respects, each of these documents is similar in its basic statement of the charge.

In most felony cases, the initial charging document is the complaint, which will be filed with the magistrates court prior to the arrested person's initial appearance (see step 9).[12] At later stages in the process, an indictment or information will replace the complaint as the charging document.[13] The complaint ordinarily will set forth facts alleging that the accused, at a particular time and place, committed specified acts that constitute a violation of a particular criminal statute. The complaint must be signed by a "complainant," a person who swears under oath that he believes the facts alleged in the complaint to be true. Ordinarily, the complainant will be either the victim of the crime or the investigating officer. The prosecuting attorney, in the course of reviewing the decision to charge, will make certain that the complaint is properly prepared. Once the complaint is completed and approved, it is filed with the local magistrates court, before which the arrestee will soon be presented.

8. *Magistrate Review of the Complaint.* Although the complaint is filed with the magistrates court, that court does not have authority to hold a trial in a felony case. Its function is only to handle several preliminary tasks before transferring the felony case to a trial court of general jurisdiction. The first of these tasks is to determine whether there is a sufficient legal basis to support the arrest under which the defendant is being held in custody. The magistrate is, in effect, reviewing the judgment of the police and prosecutor that the accused could properly be arrested and charged with the offense alleged in the complaint. This determination, usually made at or shortly before the defendant's first appearance, is an *ex parte* determination (that is, a determination made on the presentation of the prosecution alone, without the participation of the defense). The magistrate's decision ordinarily is based on facts presented in either the complaint itself, a supporting affidavit, or a brief oral statement given by the victim or arresting officer. To sustain the arrest, the magistrate need only find that the officer had probable cause to believe that the arrestee committed the crime charged. However, if the magistrate finds that the facts alleged do not establish probable cause, he must dismiss the complaint and the arrestee must be released.

9. *The First Appearance.* After the complaint has been filed and presented for magistrate review, the defendant is taken from the holding facility and

11. Many prosecutors have developed pre-charge "diversion programs" that provide a formal structure for the prosecutor's refusal to charge notwithstanding sufficient evidence. Under these programs, certain types of charges (usually misdemeanors) will not be prosecuted if the arrestee agrees to comply with specified "rehabilitative conditions" (e.g., making restitution to the victim, maintaining regular employment, etc.). Other prosecutors prefer not to tie the decision to charge to such conditions. They will bring charges and then seek to have the rehabilitative conditions imposed as conditions of probation following conviction.

12. The magistrates court is described at page 26 infra.

13. In misdemeanor cases which are tried before the magistrate, the complaint ordinarily is the only charging instrument used in the case. The substitution of an indictment or information for the complaint only occurs when a case is taken before the general trial court, as in a felony case (see step 12).

brought before the magistrate. This first appearance of the defendant in court is the next major step in the criminal justice process. It usually is described simply as the "first appearance," but some jurisdictions refer to it as the "initial presentment" or the "arraignment on the complaint (or arrest warrant)."[14]

All jurisdictions have a requirement that an arrested person be presented before the magistrate without unnecessary delay. In most communities, the time consumed in booking, transportation, police and prosecutor review of the decision to charge, preparation of the complaint, and performing other preliminary matters will delay the first appearance for several hours. Indeed, in many places, unless the individual is arrested in the early morning hours, his case will not be ready for presentation to the magistrate until after the courts have closed for that day. If the community does not have a "night court," the arrested person will have to spend the night in jail before being presented the next morning. While many jurisdictions impose a 24 hour limit on pre-appearance detention that requires the magistrate court to conduct sessions on weekends, others do not, and here a person arrested on a weekend may be detained up to 48 hours before being presented before a magistrate.[15]

The first appearance itself often is quite brief. Initially, the magistrate will make certain that the person before him is, in fact, the person whose name is stated in the complaint as the defendant. The magistrate then will inform the defendant of the charge set forth in the complaint. The magistrate also will inform the defendant of various rights that he has under the law. The scope of this advice varies from state to state. Ordinarily, the magistrate will at least inform the defendant of his right to remain silent and warn him that anything he says in court or to the police may be used against him at trial.

The defendant also will be told that he has a right to be assisted by counsel and that counsel will be appointed at the expense of the state if he is indigent (i.e., he cannot afford to hire an attorney).[16] Although the timing varies, most jurisdictions at least initiate the appointment process at the first appearance. The magistrate will determine if the defendant is financially eligible and desires the assistance of appointed counsel. The magistrate then will either make the appointment himself or notify the judge in charge of making such appointments. In many communities, lawyers employed by the office of the public defender will automatically represent almost all indigent defendants. They often begin that representation shortly after the indigent is arrested and thus are present when he appears before the magistrate. In those jurisdictions where the appointed counsel is selected from the "private bar" (i.e., those lawyers who are self-employed), the appointment process often is not completed until after the first appearance. The appointed lawyer will be available to the defendant, however, before the next stage in the process, the preliminary hearing on the complaint (see step 10).

Perhaps the most important function performed by the magistrate at the first appearance is the "setting of bail",—that is, the determination of those conditions that the defendant will have to meet to gain his release from custody pending his trial. The term "bail" referred originally to cash or other property that a

---

14. This is to be distinguished from the later "arraignment" at the trial court stage (see step 13), where the defendant must enter a plea to the felony charge.

15. For misdemeanors, the arrestee may be able to obtain his release on "stationhouse" bail, i.e., by posting cash as a security deposit with the police and promising to appear before the magistrate on a specific date.

16. Appointed counsel will not necessarily be provided in misdemeanor cases, as jurisdictions are not constitutionally required to appoint counsel to assist indigent defendants where conviction for a misdemeanor does not result in incarceration (see Ch. 5, § 1).

defendant had to deposit with the court to obtain his release from custody. The property served as a guarantee that the defendant would appear at trial. If he failed to do so (i.e., "skipped bail"), his property would be forfeited to the state. The most common form of bail gradually became the secured bond (the "bail-bond") purchased from a professional bondsman, rather than the cash deposit. Today, however, bail also can take several other forms, as described in the introduction to Chapter Nine. In many situations, no posting of cash or a bailbond will be required. The individual will be released upon his own recognizance (i.e., a personal promise to appear) or a condition that he comply with certain requirements (e.g., stay in the community). Under special circumstances, the law of the particular jurisdiction may even allow the magistrate to simply refuse to set bail because of the likelihood of the accused's flight or danger to the community if released. Although bail setting practices vary widely, in a fairly typical jurisdiction, roughly 25–40% of all felony defendants will not gain their pretrial release either because the magistrate found the circumstances to justify a refusal to set bail or because the defendant was unable to post a bailbond or meet other conditions required by the magistrate.

Other aspects of the first appearance are likely to depend upon whether the defendant is charged with a felony or misdemeanor. In the felony case, the magistrate will advise the defendant of the next step in the process, the preliminary hearing, and will set a date for that hearing unless the defendant desires to waive it. If the defendant is charged with a misdemeanor, he will not be entitled to a preliminary hearing (or a subsequent grand jury review). The misdemeanor charge is triable to the magistrate,[17] and the magistrate therefore can proceed with a misdemeanor case in the same fashion as would a general trial court receiving a felony case. For the misdemeanor, the first appearance becomes an arraignment on the complaint, equivalent to the arraignment on the information or indictment in a felony case (see step 12).

10. *Preliminary Hearing.* The next step in the processing of a felony case often is the preliminary hearing. The preliminary hearing is one of three independent "screening" processes that may be available in a felony case. Each involves a review of the prosecution's evidence to safeguard against unwarranted prosecutions. They are described as "screening" procedures because they operate like a sieve to "screenout" those prosecutions that lack substantial evidentiary support. The first of these screens is the magistrate's ex parte review of the arrest, described previously in step 8. The second screening is the preliminary hearing, which also is conducted by the magistrate, and the third is the grand jury's review of the evidence (see step 11). The availability of the preliminary hearing and of grand jury review varies from state to state. Only about twenty states regularly provide grand jury review. Many more states regularly provide a preliminary hearing. Almost all states provide one or the other and some utilize both.

The magistrate's task at the preliminary hearing is to determine whether there is sufficient evidence supporting the charge. The standard for testing the sufficiency of the evidence is one of probable cause, considerably less than the burden the prosecution must bear in establishing guilt at trial. If probable cause is found, the case is "boundover" (i.e., sent forward) either to the grand jury or directly to the trial court, depending on whether the state also requires grand jury

---

17. In some jurisdictions, the magistrate's trial jurisdiction does not extend to all misdemeanors, but only those punishable by no more than a certain term of imprisonment. See p. 27 infra. For the sake of brevity, our discussion will assume a dividing line between the trial authority of the magistrates court and the general trial court that coincides with the division between misdemeanors and felonies.

review. If the evidence is found insufficient, the charges are dismissed and the defendant is released from jail or from any bail restrictions. The magistrate can also reduce the charge where the evidence is found sufficient only to support a lesser charge. If the charge is reduced to a misdemeanor, it will then be set for later trial before the magistrates court itself.

Unlike the magistrate's initial screening of the complaint prior to the first appearance, the preliminary hearing is an "adversary proceeding"—that is, both sides are represented. The defendant is there with counsel and is entitled to challenge the prosecution's evidence and introduce his own evidence. As a result, the preliminary hearing sometimes resembles a mini-trial. (It is at the preliminary hearing, not the trial, that television's Perry Mason wins all of his cases). The prosecutor ordinarily will rely on live witnesses, rather than affidavits, in presenting the state's evidence. Those witnesses are then subject to cross-examination by the defense counsel, and the defense may also introduce its own witnesses.

11. *Grand Jury Review.* The function of the grand jury, like that of the preliminary hearing, is to screen out those cases in which there is insufficient evidence to continue the prosecution. The standard of proof applied by the grand jury is very much like the probable cause standard applied at the preliminary hearing, but the two screening procedures are quite different in other respects. The grand jury is composed of a group of private citizens (from 16 to 23 in the federal system), who are selected to review cases for a term of one to several months. Unlike the magistrate at the preliminary hearing, which is a public proceeding, the grand jury hears evidence in secret. Moreover, the evidence it hears is only that presented by the prosecutor. The defendant is not present and the defense has no opportunity to present evidence or cross-examine the prosecution's witnesses. After the grand jury has heard the prosecutor's evidence, it receives from the prosecutor a proposed "indictment." The indictment is the document which will replace the complaint at the trial level as the formal charging document in the case (see step 12). The grand jury votes on the proposed indictment, with the majority prevailing. If the majority concludes that there is sufficient evidence for the prosecution to proceed, the indictment is approved by the grand jury as a "true bill." If the grand jury majority concludes that the prosecution should not proceed, then the complaint must be dismissed and the defendant released from jail or from any bail restrictions.

12. *Filing of the Indictment or Information.* Assuming that the case has survived the screening of the preliminary hearing or the grand jury (or both, in some jurisdictions), it is now ready for presentation before the trial court. The next step is the filing of a new charging document with that court. If the case was reviewed and approved by the grand jury, that document will be the indictment noted previously. In states where grand jury review is not required and the case moves directly from the preliminary hearing to the trial court, the charging document is signed by the prosecutor alone. It is then referred to as an "information." The information or indictment will be similar in substance to the complaint. It will set forth the time, date, and place of the alleged criminal act as well as the nature of the act. This charging document will not be signed by the complainant, but by the prosecutor (information) or the prosecutor and the grand jury foreman (indictment). Ordinarily the offense alleged will be the same as that alleged in the complaint, but sometimes the precise charge will have been changed as a result of evidence brought out at the preliminary hearing or the grand jury review.

13. *Arraignment on the Information or Indictment.* Shortly after the information or indictment is filed with the trial court, the defendant is "arraigned" before that court. The arraignment is a brief process designed to serve two purposes: (1) to inform the defendant of the specific charge against him, and (2) to permit him to answer that charge by pleading not guilty, guilty, or *nolo contendere* (no-contest). At the arraignment the court will first read the information or indictment to the defendant and then ask him how he pleads. The defendant, ordinarily attended by his counsel, will then enter his plea. If defendant pleads not guilty, the case is set for trial. If the defendant pleads guilty or no-contest, the case is then set for sentence. The no-contest plea largely has the impact of a guilty plea, but does not require the defendant to admit his guilt.

Although the trial is, in many respects, the capstone of the criminal justice system, most of the cases reaching the trial court will be disposed of by a guilty plea rather than a trial. Many of those guilty pleas are a product of a negotiated agreement between prosecutor and defense under which the defendant receives some concession in exchange for his guilty plea. This process of negotiation is commonly called "plea-bargaining" and the resulting guilty pleas are commonly described as "negotiated pleas." Plea bargaining varies in both form and availability from one community to another. Some prosecutors' offices rarely will offer concessions for a guilty plea; others do so regularly. As discussed in Chapter 14, the exchange for the plea may be a reduction of the charge, the dismissal of possible additional charges, a recommendation as to sentence, or a specific sentence approved by the trial court.

14. *Pre-trial Procedures.* Assuming that the defendant pleads not guilty at the arraignment, there are a series of procedures that may then be utilized prior to the scheduled trial. Perhaps the most significant of these is the process by which each side will learn about the evidence to be presented by the other side (a process commonly described as "discovery"). Another major pretrial procedure is the defendant's presentation of various legal challenges to the prosecution. Most of these challenges are based on alleged violations of state law or the federal constitution. One such challenge may be the claimed denial of a speedy trial through delay in bringing the case to trial. Another pretrial challenge may not seek to bar the entire prosecution, but to bar certain evidence (e.g., a confession) that the prosecution intends to use but the defense believes to be inadmissible. Often, without such evidence, the prosecution's case may be too weak to proceed. The pretrial challenges are presented to the trial judge and are decided after a hearing before that judge.

15. *The Trial.* The trial is a fact-finding process aimed at determining whether the defendant is guilty or innocent of the offense charged. It is an adversary proceeding in which each side produces its evidence and argument. A neutral fact-finder then determines the facts and reaches a conclusion as to guilt or innocence based upon an application of the substantive criminal law to those facts. The defendant is entitled to have a jury sit as that neutral fact-finder, although he ordinarily can waive his right to a jury and have the trial judge sit as the finder of fact. In most states, juries in felony cases are composed of twelve persons.[18]

18. The situation in misdemeanor cases may differ. In some jurisdictions, the defendant does not have a right to a jury trial in minor misdemeanor cases. This is particularly true in those states that utilize magistrate courts that are not of record and provide a trial de novo before a general trial court (see page 27 infra). In those jurisdictions providing for jury trials in magistrates courts, the juries usually are composed of six persons rather than twelve.

At the trial, each side has the opportunity to make an opening statement (explaining its case) and a closing statement (reviewing the strength of the evidence it has presented), to present its own witnesses and to cross-examine the opposing witnesses. The evidence introduced at trial must meet legal standards designed in large part to assist the jury in making an accurate factual determination. In particular, hearsay evidence—statements made out of court and introduced to establish the truth of the contents of the statement—may be used only under limited circumstances. A very important exception to the general bar against hearsay allows the prosecution to use incriminating statements made by the defendant, including those given to the police. The defendant may testify at trial, but he also has the right not to do so, with no negative inference to be drawn from the exercise of that right.

After the jury has heard the evidence, the judge will explain to the jury the substantive law governing the crimes charged. The judge also will explain the jury's duty to assess the facts in accordance with the legal standard that permits it to find the defendant guilty only if the prosecution has established that guilt beyond a reasonable doubt. The jury will reach its conclusions through its private deliberations. In most jurisdictions, the jury's final decision of guilty or not-guilty (the jury's "verdict") must be agreed upon by all of the jurors.

A jury that cannot reach a unanimous verdict is known as a "hung jury." Where the jury "hangs," it is dismissed and the case ordinarily is retried before a new jury. In the vast majority of trials, however, the jury will reach a verdict of either guilty or not-guilty. If the jury finds the defendant not-guilty (i.e., "acquits" the defendant), the charges against the defendant are dismissed and he can never again be prosecuted on the same charges. If, on the other hand, the defendant is found guilty, he will then move to the next stage of the criminal justice process, the imposition of sentence. In most jurisdictions at least two thirds of the felony defendants who go to trial will be convicted on at least one of the charges brought against them. The rate of conviction at trial typically is even higher in misdemeanor cases.

16. *Sentencing.* Once guilt is determined, either through a trial or the entry of a guilty plea, the trial judge is obligated to impose a sentence in accordance with the statute under which defendant was convicted. State law often will allow the judge a choice between imposing a sentence of probation or imprisonment. If probation is used, the court must select appropriate standards of conduct (probation "conditions") which the defendant must adhere to while on probation. For some offenses imprisonment will be required, and for others the judge will chose imprisonment over probation. Here, if the jurisdiction uses what is described "indeterminate sentencing," the judge ordinarily will have considerable discretion in setting the sentence within a wide range allowed by law. The judge sets a maximum and minimum sentence and the parole board determines the actual length of the sentence within those limits. In some jurisdictions, specific guidelines direct the judge's discretion in setting maximum and minimum sentences. Departures from the guidelines are permitted only upon a judicial finding of specific justification. Where the state uses what is described as presumptive-determinate sentencing, the judge is given less discretion. The judge sets a single fixed term of imprisonment which must fall within a narrow range set by the legislature for the particular crime, with the judge directed to look to specified aggravating or mitigating circumstances to either add to or deduct from the middle of the range set by the legislature.[19] Other jurisdictions utilize determi-

---

19. In misdemeanor cases, the magistrate ordinarily is given discretion to impose a flat sentence of imprisonment not to exceed a specified maximum of a certain number of days or nate sentences combined with guidelines. Determinate sentencing structures do not provide for early release on determination of a parole board; the defendant serves the full sentence, minus a possible minor discount (e.g., 10%) earned for good behavior during incarceration.

The procedure followed in imposing felony sentences will vary from state to state, but certain basic features are quite common. Ordinarily, felony sentencing will not be undertaken immediately upon a finding of guilt, but will be delayed for a week or more to permit the collection of information relevant to determining the proper sentence. That information ordinarily will be brought together in a presentence report prepared by a probation officer. The prosecution and the defense also may call to the court's attention any information that it views as relevant to sentencing. There will not be a trial-type hearing, however. Witnesses will not be called, and the judge may consider information that would not be admissible at trial.[20]

17. *Appeals.* Following the imposition of sentence, defendant may appeal his conviction.[21] In most jurisdictions, defendant is given an automatic right to have his conviction reviewed by an appellate court. The function of the appellate court is to provide a higher court review of the legal rulings made by the trial court. If the appellate court finds no substantial legal error in the trial court proceedings, the conviction will be affirmed. For most types of error (but not for certain constitutional violations), the appellate court may find that, though the trial court erred, the error was so unlikely to have affected the outcome of the case that the error may be deemed "harmless" (i.e., not substantial). If the appellate court finds a substantial legal error was committed, the conviction will be reversed. Subsequent proceedings will then depend upon the basis for the reversal. If the appellate court relied on a ground establishing a total lack of authority to convict (e.g., no crime was committed), a new trial will not be permitted. On the other hand, if the reversal was based on an error that could be avoided in a new trial (e.g., an improper restriction of cross-examination), a new trial will be permitted.

18. *Collateral Challenges to the Conviction.* If the defendant's appeal is unsuccessful, there may be a remaining avenue for challenging his conviction. In order to ensure full consideration of possible fundamental defects in the process, the federal government and many states have provided systems for a collateral challenge to a conviction. The challenge is viewed as "collateral" because it does not flow out of the direct appellate process. Collateral challenges take many forms. The most common (and most famous) is the writ of habeas corpus, a directive of the court (to the jailer) to bring the prisoner forward so it can consider the legality of his continued detention. Collateral challenges may present only the most basic legal errors (e.g., certain constitutional defects).[22] To ensure enforcement of federal constitutional limitations on state procedure, Congress has provided since shortly after the Civil War a federal writ of habeas corpus through which state prisoners may seek relief in the federal courts.

months in jail. The judge is likely to impose that sentence immediately upon a finding of guilt, although the defense will be given an opportunity to present any information it views as relevant to sentencing.

20. The procedure for the death penalty is quite different, as discussed in Chapter 20.

21. As to the prosecution's more limited right of appeal, see page 29 infra and Chapter 19, § 3.

22. All states also have separate postconviction procedures for presenting newly discovered evidence, but relief will not be provided unless it is quite clear that, if the new evidence had been presented at trial, defendant would have been acquitted.

19. *Administering the Sentence.* The sentence imposed by the trial court ordinarily must be administered (assuming that the defendant's conviction is not reversed on appeal or collateral attack). If the defendant is placed on probation, he will be subject to certain conditions that must be enforced. If sentenced to imprisonment, his incarceration must be managed, and if subsequently released on parole, supervision of that status is required. Although some commentators view the administration of the sentence as part of the criminal justice process, we have not treated it as such. Sentence administration commonly is governed by a separate body of laws and is primarily the responsibility of a separate group of officials working in the field of corrections (primarily probation officers, prison officials, and parole officers).

It should be noted, however, that there are instances in which the police, prosecutors, and courts may be involved in the administration of corrections. A probationer or parolee who violates a condition of probation or parole is subject to arrest and the subsequent initiation of a proceeding to revoke his probation or parole. Ordinarily, these matters are left to the discretion of the probation or parole officer, but the police or prosecutor may also be involved, particularly where the action that violates probation or parole is itself a crime. The probation revocation hearing itself is commonly conducted by the trial court. Parole revocation, in contrast, ordinarily is decided by the parole board, but the board's decision to revoke may then be challenged in the courts. So too, incarceration practices may be challenged in the courts on the ground that they violate state law or the constitutional prohibition against cruel and unusual punishment. Not surprisingly, there are many leading Supreme Court decisions dealing with various aspects of sentence administration, but because our concern is with the criminal justice process itself, we have not included any of those decisions in this volume.

SECTION 3. THE PARTICIPANTS IN THE ADMINISTRATION OF THE PROCESS

Throughout the Supreme Court opinions reprinted in this volume you will find references of a generic nature to "police," "prosecutors," "defense counsel" and "judges." These are the groups primarily responsible for the administration of the criminal justice process, and many of the Supreme Court opinions in this volume will be dealing with the question of whether to impose certain obligations or restrictions on persons in these positions. In this section, we will briefly introduce some of the more significant aspects of the institutional settings within which these persons perform their respective roles. As will be seen, there are certain institutional factors that extend across the board to all persons occupying the particular position, but there is also variety in the institutional settings which can lead one to distinguish between different types of police, prosecutors, defense counsel, and judges.[23]

POLICE AGENCIES

Fragmentation. The police agencies constitute the largest of the four major groups involved in the administration of the criminal justice system. They also have the greatest volume of work, the most diverse range of functions, and the

---

23. Of course, there is even more variety within each group because of differences among individuals. Since there is considerable discretion involved in the exercise of each of these roles, the values of the particular individual will also contribute significantly to the shaping of the individual's performance in his or her position.

most complex organizational structure. The key element of that structure is the fragmentation of police authority among a large number of separate units of government. Over 18,000 different governmental agencies in the United States can be classified as "police" agencies in that (1) they have been given primary responsibility for the enforcement of one or more criminal statutes, and (2) at least some of their employees have been given the special enforcement authority (e.g., special arrest powers) that distinguishes the police officer from the private citizen. The vast majority of these 18,000 governmental agencies are units of local government (counties, cities, townships), although close to a thousand are part of a state government and about fifty are part of the federal government.

Most of the agencies at the state and federal levels are "specialized" police agencies; they have authority to enforce only a limited group of criminal laws (as in the case of state conservation officers) or to deal with offenses committed within a special geographic enclave (as in the case of the National Park Rangers). However, the vast majority of all police agencies, including almost all of those that are part of local governments, are "general" police agencies. Such agencies have authority to enforce the total range of criminal laws throughout the geographical limits of their particular unit of government.

At the federal level, the primary general police agency is the Federal Bureau of Investigation.[24] At the state level, the key general agency is the state police (in those jurisdictions in which the responsibility of the state police extends beyond traffic control). At the county level, the primary local police agency is the sheriff's department. While sheriff's departments in some states are limited to administering the county jail and serving process, most states grant those departments full law enforcement responsibilities. To avoid overlap, sheriff's deputies commonly concentrate their efforts in those communities that lack their own police departments (usually villages and sometimes townships). Far out-numbering the 3,000 sheriff's departments are the local police agencies (over 13,500) found at the city and township level. Over 90% of all municipalities with a population of 2,500 or more have their own police force. As might be expected, most of those police agencies have small staffs. Close to three-fourths have less than 25 sworn officers, and over one-fourth employ less than 5 officers. Standing in sharp contrast to the typical small municipal department are the roughly 80 local departments employing more than 500 sworn officers, with the largest, the New York City police department, having over 38,000 officers.

The fragmentation of police agencies means that in any particular community more than one agency will have the authority to enforce at least some criminal laws. Indeed, in any single metropolitan area, several dozen different police agencies are likely to be actively exercising law enforcement authority. In the tri-county area of metropolitan Detroit, for example, over 125 police agencies are separately engaged in the investigation of crime. Initially, over a dozen federal agencies have agents assigned to the area. The state adds several agencies, including the state police. Each of the three counties contributes its sheriff's

24. Although considered a general agency because its enforcement responsibilities extend to almost all major areas of federal criminal law, the F.B.I. is quite unlike any local or state general police agency. With over 11,500 agents, it is larger than any other police agency except for the police departments of New York and Chicago. It insists upon educational prerequisites for its agents (generally a law degree or a bachelor's degree with expertise in accounting or other specialized field) that go beyond those found in any local or state agency. The mix of the crimes it investigates is substantially different from those found in any other jurisdiction, with a much smaller portion of typical "street crimes" and a much higher portion of white collar offenses. Finally, and most significantly, the F.B.I. does not bear the general peacekeeping, traffic control, and social service functions that occupy so much of the effort of general police agencies at the state and local levels.

department. Finally, over 100 cities and townships provide their own police departments.

The wide distribution of police authority in the United States stands in sharp contrast to the national police force found in many countries. In this country, such a centralized police force would be viewed with deep suspicion, for fear that it could be misused by any leader seeking an authoritarian regime. Just as our political philosophy looks to federalism as a means of protecting individual liberty, it also looks to the decentralization of police authority as a safeguard against the subversion of democracy. Quite obviously, however, the dangers thought to inhere in a centralized police force could be avoided without the extreme diffusion of police authority that we have in this country. That aspect of the fragmentation of police authority reflects the additional goal of maintaining local community control over the administration of the criminal law. Each community may exercise its own influence in the shaping of the police agency predominantly responsible for law enforcement in that community.

Although it has its benefits, the fragmentation of police agencies also has its law enforcement costs. The proliferation of agencies can result in considerable duplication of effort, a rivalry between departments that is not always healthy, and even spillover tactics by which an agency in one community tends to shift certain policing problems to agencies in neighboring communities. As criminal enterprises often extend beyond community borders, an effective law enforcement response requires a degree of coordination among different agencies that extensive fragmentation often makes difficult to arrange. Fragmentation necessarily also produces less uniformity and more inequality in police enforcement. This is particularly true for those aspects of police administration in which discretion plays a large role (e.g., the treatment of intrafamily assaults), but it also arises where the law itself is ambiguous and therefore subject to varying interpretation by different departments. Attempts to impose minimal standards of police administration (as in many of the Supreme Court rulings presented in this book) also face obstacles due to fragmentation, as there is no single executive authority in the police world that can assume responsibility for implementing those standards.

Perhaps the most significant cost of fragmentation stems from the large number of police agencies thought to be too small to be fully effective in the investigation of crime. Departments without at least 50 sworn officers generally are too small to create the specialized units that may be more effective in dealing with particular types of crimes (e.g., tactical patrol units, vice squads, robbery investigative teams) or to make use of sophisticated criminal investigative techniques drawing on the use of laboratories and computers. Proponents of small departments maintain, however, that those departments have a closer relationship to the community that more than offsets such disadvantages, as the most critical factor in criminal investigation will often be the cooperation of victims, witnesses, and other citizens who have relevant information. They also note that small departments can turn to the state police for assistance on such matters as laboratory analysis of physical evidence, and can develop joint investigative task forces with neighboring communities to deal with offenses such as narcotics distribution.[25]

25. Another obstacle faced by small departments—and one not readily remedied by efforts at coordination and cooperation—is the high employee turnover rate. Whereas the rate of voluntary resignations is quite low for larger departments (particularly after officers have gone beyond the probationary stage and their retirement benefits are building), the rate of annual voluntary resignation in departments of 25 officers or less can readily be as high as 25%. Police departments almost invariably recruit at the lowest rank and pro-

Multiple Functions. Although we refer to the police as "law enforcement" officers, the enforcement of the criminal law (i.e., the investigation of crime and the apprehension of criminals) is only one of several tasks allocated to a local police department. The professional roles of that department also include the providing of basic social services, the maintenance of order, and the prevention of crime.

In the area of social services, a primary police responsibility is to help people who need emergency assistance, whether that is providing emergency first aid, assisting a person stuck in an elevator, comforting lost children, or rescuing a cat stuck in a tree. Typically, over 50% of the telephone calls to the police requesting assistance will involve such social service functions, as compared to the less than 20% relating to the reported commission of a crime. Among the local department's order maintenance functions are traffic control, crowd control, resolving domestic and streetcorner disputes, and moving panhandlers or prostitutes from the streets. While the officers here often are responding to activities that constitute minor crimes, the focus of order maintenance is on reaching a solution that preserves the public peace rather than the enforcement of the law. The appropriate order-maintenance solution may be the making of an arrest, but it quite often will be some less formal action (e.g., merely getting the illegal panhandler to move on). Finally, even in the area of crime control, the prevention of crime exists alongside the investigation of completed crime. Indeed, the prevention of crime involves the most time consuming of police activities—the patrol of the community—which ideally provides a police presence that will deter would be criminals and provide assurance to shopkeepers and residents.

The varied responsibilities of the police tend to restrict, in several ways, police effectiveness in investigating serious crime. First and foremost, the limited resources available to the police must be spread over a broad range of activities, many of which are only remotely related to investigation of felonies and the apprehension of felons. The traditional image of police work—the image conveyed over the years in countless television dramas, comic strips, and newspaper articles—is that of the officer who outwits, outshoots, and outwrestles a dangerous criminal in the course of investigating a serious crime. In fact, even in a major metropolitan area (where the rate of serious crime is likely to be highest), roughly half of the officers in the local department probably will not have made a felony arrest during the past year, and the total annual rate of weapon discharges per hundred officers (excluding the shooting range) is likely to have been in the range of 2 to 6. With their multiple functions, patrol officers, who represent the vast bulk of the sworn force, are likely to have spent less than 30% of their time on activities directly related to investigating felonies. As a result, although patrol officers are responsible for the first line of investigation, which will largely determine whether the criminal will be identified,[26] many are involved in felony investigations so infrequently as to be relatively inexperienced. Indeed, even the detectives (who represent only a small portion of the total force), while assigned basically to the investigation of crime, spend a substantial portion of their time on other matters, such as simply closing out files on cases that obviously cannot be solved or arranging for the presentation of evidence at trial in cases that have been solved.

---

mote from within the system, and smaller departments simply offer less room for promotion (as well as, in many cases, less competitive salaries).

26. The two most important determinations of whether a crime will be solved are (1)

whether the police are able to arrive on the scene so promptly as to arrest the felon contemporaneously with the crime, and (2) whether the victim or other witnesses furnish the investigating patrol officer with sufficient information to identify the offender.

The diversity of police responsibilities also has a bearing on the police department's law enforcement capacity by pushing the department to adopt a broader perspective in the selection of officers. The qualities needed in criminal investigation are not necessarily the same qualities required to perform other police functions. It often is difficult, for example, to find people who will act effectively and courageously in apprehending a felon, yet have the ability to endure the long periods of monotony involved in routine patrol. Similarly, the social service functions may require officers inclined toward a generally informal and flexible approach that would pose for them difficulties in adhering to the formalistic legal requirements typically imposed in the area of criminal investigation.[27]

The diverse responsibilities of the local police agency may also detract from the agency's law enforcement function by pushing the department in other directions when formulating policies for activities that serve multiple functions. A prime example is in the area of patrol, where commentators have identified three departmental patrol styles that guide officers in their choices among patrol tasks and in their handling of similar incidents. Arguably, from the viewpoint of law enforcement alone, the most effective patrol style is that of an aggressive, proactive patrol. The approach here is to make all traffic stops legally permissible (meanwhile gaining the opportunity to check the driver for outstanding warrants and to observe the interior of the car), to make all permissible arrests for minor crimes (allowing for the incidental search of the person), to stop and interrogate persons behaving suspiciously, and to employ intensive patrolling in high crime areas (so as to facilitate an immediate response to alarms or calls reporting serious crime). Such tactics, by maximizing interventions and observations, increase the likelihood that the police will interrupt serious crimes in progress, which remains the very best method of solving offenses such as burglary and robbery. Another style of patrol (sometimes described as the "watchman" style) puts greater emphasis on the maintenance of order. Here the police focus primarily on responding to disturbances and potential disturbances, utilizing informal, non-arrest sanctions where the offenses are minor. A third patrol style, operating in the most direct conflict with aggressive patrolling, is a service oriented patrol. Here high priority is given to citizen requests for assistance and police are advised against unnecessarily utilizing their authority in non-threatening citizen interactions. Under this style of patrol, police are less likely to be in a position where they will come across a crime in progress, although some contend that that weakness is more than offset by the building of solid community support that produces more leads from citizens.

Autonomy. Three aspects of police autonomy also have a bearing upon the institutional setting in which police operate. First, there is the independence of the police from the political forces in the community and from the community in general. Second, there is the independence of the individual officer within the department, the leeway that he or she is offered under departmental policy in taking law enforcement actions. Finally, there is the independence of the police agency from the prosecutor, who will be using the agency's product in bringing

---

27. The two major developments in police recruiting over the last few decades may both be seen as looking especially to the non-investigative aspects of police functions. Initially, there was a focus on raising educational levels, employing a higher percentage of recruits with some college education, although studies indicate that college educated officers, at least at the patrolman level, are not generally more effective except in reducing the number of citizen complaints. Second, starting in the 1960's, in recognition of the diverse roles of police and special sensitivity of policing minority neighborhoods, there has been a greater emphasis on having a more pluralistic police force, with greater numbers of females and minorities.

prosecution. This aspect of police autonomy is discussed in the next section in connection with our description of the setting within which prosecutors operate.

A major problem that plagued law enforcement for many decades was the political dominance of local police. In large cities, in particular, political machines controlled the filling of police positions, high and low, and thus made the police departments primarily responsible to the needs of the politicians in gaining reelection. During the early and middle 1900's, a strong reform movement instituted various measures designed to free the police from the role of politics. A primary component of that reform was the placing of police employment under civil service, thereby both guaranteeing officer tenure and ensuring that tests and other standardized measures would be used in both selecting recruits and making promotions. While civil service did not apply to the very top positions, so sheriffs were still elected and the local department chiefs were still appointed by elected officials, professional qualifications tended to be given greater emphasis in the selection process even at that level. Indeed, in some communities, special commissions or administrative boards were created to stand as a buffer between the appointed chiefs and the elected officials. The basic reform model also stressed the professionalization of the police department. The emphasis was on efficiency, objectivity, and integrity, achieved through a tight quasi-military structure, higher recruitment standards, a statutorily prescribed minimum period of preservice training (typically mandating at least 200 hours of classroom training and some period of field training), and taking full advantage of new technology.

During the 1960s and 1970s, there was widespread reexamination of what the earlier reforms had produced with respect to the accountability of police departments to civil authority. That reexamination was the product of concerns arising out of several professional and social developments; those included a sharp rise in crime, the demands imposed on police in dealing with racial tensions, riots, and demonstrations, the problems connected with the enforcement of drug laws (including police corruption), and the increased influence of police unions in the shaping of police policies. Subjected to unprecedented public scrutiny and debate were such police practices as the use of deadly force, the stopping, questioning, and frisking of "suspicious" persons, the surveillance of "radical" groups, and the use of informants and undercover agents. Police departments were criticized as having grown too distant from local government and local needs, as the critics rhetorically posed the question: "Who will police the police"? The increased influence of the courts, as illustrated by the cases reprinted in this volume, arguably reflected the judiciary's response to that criticism. Other responses came from the police departments themselves and from elected officials in local government. Efforts were made to expand the influence of elected officials on major issues of police administration (with those officials at least offering "advice," and sometimes legislating, on such issues as the use of chokeholds in making arrests and the proper police response to incidents of domestic violence), to make more effective use of internal police disciplinary procedures in dealing with citizen complaints, and to gain the input of community representatives through such structures as Civilian Review Boards and community liaison officers.

Today, many local departments, responding to community concerns, have adopted administrative guidelines governing the officer's use of various aspects of police authority. Notwithstanding such guidelines and extensive reporting requirements for certain actions (e.g., weapons discharges), the individual officer, particularly on patrol, remains largely autonomous. Police departments do not impose highly routinized protocols such as those applied to other public employees (e.g., bus drivers). The incidents faced by the police are viewed as too varied to be governed by a series of set procedures. Police officers, the departments note, must be given sufficient flexibility to shape their response to the incident.   They must be allowed the freedom to fashion a quick, sometimes intuitive response, as well as to develop the distinct style (in light of individual strengths) that makes the particular officer most effective.   In sum, police work is viewed as a craft, not readily subjected to bureaucratic controls.[28]

PROSECUTORS

Although the British common law tradition was one of private prosecution (i.e., the complainant hired private counsel to press the prosecution), Americans had established an office of public prosecutor even before the Revolution.   In most of the colonies, public prosecution was originally superimposed upon a system of private prosecution, but private prosecution was eventually seen as impracticable, too often subject to abuse, and inconsistent with the view that crimes were "acts against the state" and not simply wrongs inflicted upon an individual victim.   As the office of public prosecutor grew in status and prosecutors became elected officials (a product of the Jacksonian reform movement), the public prosecutor was gradually given a virtual monopoly over criminal prosecutions, with extensive discretion over both the filing and selection of criminal charges.

Fragmentation.   As in the case of police power, the authority of the public prosecutor has not been centralized, but divided among a group of officials. Initially, there is the division between state officials responsible for prosecutions under state laws (the vast majority of all prosecutions), and federal officials responsible for prosecutions under federal laws.   The Attorney General of the United States is the chief federal prosecutor, but federal prosecutorial authority has long been delegated to the various United States Attorneys, who are ultimately responsible to the Attorney General.   There are 94 United States Attorneys, one for each federal judicial district, and their offices range in size from one or two assistants to over 50 in the large urban districts.   They receive further assistance from the Criminal Division in the Department of Justice, and that Division itself initiates prosecutions in several fields (e.g., organized crime, public corruption), operating in part through special strike forces.

Ordinarily, the official with primary responsibility for prosecutions under state law is the local prosecuting attorney (also called the "district attorney," "county attorney," or "state's attorney").   The local prosecutor is selected either from a single county or from a group of counties that are combined to form a prosecutorial district in a sparsely populated area.   The local prosecutor has the primary responsibility for bringing prosecutions for all violations of state law committed within his county or district.   In many states, the local prosecutor's prosecutions are subject, at least theoretically, to the superceding authority of the state attorney general.   Some states allow the attorney general on his own initiative to replace the prosecuting attorney in any pending prosecution, while certain other states permit the attorney general to intervene in a pending prosecution only upon direction of the governor.   In practice, such intervention or replacement is rare.   In still other states, the attorney general's office may initiate prosecution itself.   Most often, attorneys general use their power to initiate prosecutions with respect only to a limited class of offenses, such as tax fraud and

---

28.   Indeed, there are those who question whether such controls could readily be imposed even if police departments were more willing to adopt them.   There tends to be a strong subculture among police officers that emphasizes mutual support and resistance to outside influence.   When this is combined with the obvious difficulty of supervising persons in the field, the end result is that departmental regulations, where simply adopted in response to political forces or community pressures and lacking support of the rank and file, are likely to have only a limited impact upon the street behavior of police.

criminal antitrust violations, where local prosecutors are likely to lack sufficient expertise. In a few states, there are no locally selected prosecutors and the attorney general is responsible for all prosecutions under state law.[29]

The fragmentation of prosecutorial authority is designed, as with the fragmentation of police authority, to ensure local community responsiveness, a matter of extreme importance for an office expected to exercise considerable discretion. Prosecutors are elected officials and thought therefore to take into consideration the values of the community in their decisions as to whether or not to charge, in their selection of charges, in their offering of plea concessions to defendants, and in their recommendations on sentence.[30] The other side of the coin, however, is a loss of consistency in the statewide application of the criminal law. Different prosecutors in different counties can follow quite different policies on such matters as the decision to charge, the use of diversion programs, plea bargaining, and the discretionary employment of various pretrial and trial procedures. To achieve closer communications among local prosecutors, state prosecuting attorneys associations and some state attorneys general have established special programs designed to keep local prosecutors informed of the various policies being followed across the state.[31] While such efforts have helped to lessen the differences in the policies followed by the various prosecutors, those policies still remain far from uniform—particularly with respect to plea negotiation.

Another problem presented by the fragmentation of prosecuting authority is that many offices are too small to be efficient. Again, state attorneys general and prosecuting attorney associations have sought to offset this deficiency by providing various support services to the smaller offices, such as legal research assistance, office management programs, and shared use of computer facilities. Also, almost a third of the states have moved to a district selection system, which permits them to create multiple county districts large enough to support a full-time prosecutor with part-time assistants in each county. These reforms have been only partially successful, however, and the inefficiency of the smaller offices remains a major difficulty in most states.

Local Prosecutors: The Urban and Large Suburban Office. Prosecuting attorneys in metropolitan districts not uncommonly have a larger legal staff than even the largest of the private law firms in the community. Los Angeles County, for example, has over 1100 assistant prosecutors. Notwithstanding their size, these offices commonly have extraordinarily heavy caseloads per prosecutor. Assistants handling felony cases may receive as many as 250 cases per year and assistants responsible for misdemeanors may receive several times that number of cases. To assist the local prosecutor in handling that caseload, some counties have relieved the prosecutor's office of most of its civil responsibilities, or have provided a separate staff for civil cases. Prosecutors in metropolitan areas are also provided with various support services, including special investigators, librarians, record control clerks, and where the office is large enough to support an

29. The prosecuting attorney and the attorney general ordinarily are the only officials with authority to prosecute violations of state law. Public attorneys at other levels of government, such as a city or township attorney, cannot enforce state provisions. Those attorneys may, however, bring prosecutions to enforce local ordinances, and such ordinances frequently duplicate state misdemeanors both in substance and authorized punishments. See note 4 supra.

30. In the federal system, the U.S. Attorneys, while not elected, are appointees of the president currently in office. When a president of a different political party takes office, tradition dictates that the U.S. Attorney resign.

31. United States Attorneys are directed by an extensive set of guidelines issued by the Attorney General, and for the exercise of certain types of authority, must receive approval from the Attorney General or an Assistant Attorney General.

automated case tracking system, computer programmers and systems analysts. Large offices may also support a substantial diversion program staffed by a director and several counselors. All of these procedures help, but the caseload remains too heavy to take every felony charge through each stage in the process. Some cases must be disposed of by dismissals or by negotiated pleas of guilty.

Large offices also face serious obstacles in seeking to achieve consistency in the exercise of discretion by assistants. Some seek to maintain consistency by assigning experienced assistants to major areas of discretionary decisionmaking (e.g., charging and plea negotiation) and relying upon those deputies to provide direction to the prosecutors under their supervision. Other offices utilize detailed guidelines and require assistants to justify their decision in writing by reference to those guidelines. Spot checks and statistical analysis are also utilized to ensure that all prosecutors are adhering basically to the same policies. Even with such controls, however, individual prosecutors retain considerable flexibility, particularly in evaluating the factual elements of the case.

Local Prosecutors: The Rural and Small Suburban Office. The public image of the prosecutor's office has been shaped largely by the big city office, but this single image largely ignores the tremendous variety in the setting and size of local prosecutor's offices. There are over 2,300 such offices in the United States, and a substantial majority represent districts with populations under 60,000. In contrast to large urban or suburban offices, many prosecutors in these districts operate without even one full time assistant. Indeed, half of all local prosecutor's offices have three or fewer assistants. In districts with an especially small population, the prosecutor is likely to be a part-time official, maintaining a private practice in addition to his public office.

The problems faced in small offices tend to be quite different from those presented in the larger offices. The criminal caseload in small districts often is fairly light, particularly as to felonies. Solo prosecutors may process no more than two felonies per month. The difficulties presented in handling such caseloads stem from the presence of other responsibilities and limited flexibility in assignments. In most small districts, the prosecutor's responsibility is not limited to criminal prosecution. The prosecutor also handles juvenile cases and often has extensive civil responsibilities. Where prosecutors are part-time employees, there is also the draw of private practice. Moreover, while resources may be adequate to handle the typical case, there is not likely to be available the extra manpower needed for the time consuming complicated fraud or homicide case that will produce a lengthy trial. The limited range of felonies typically presented also makes it likely that the assistants will not have the expertise needed to deal with the exceptional case. Very often the answer here will be to turn to the state attorney general's office for special assistance.

Small prosecutor offices have no need for a complicated bureaucratic structure to ensure consistency. The assistants, if any, work closely with the prosecutor and should fully understand his prosecutorial policies. Dealings with defense counsel, who are likely to be known socially as well as professionally, require no formal guidelines. There is neither the resources nor the need for highly structured internal programs governing matters such as diversion, which tend instead to be handled informally.

Local Prosecutors: Selection. Whether the offices are large or small, a major problem in prosecutor's offices is the high rate of turnover. As elected officials, local prosecutors know that their tenure is always subject to the whims of the electorate. While the incumbent usually has a very good chance of being reelected, elections for this post often attract a fair degree of voter attention due to the centrality of the crime issue. In part because of their limited job security, most local prosecutors do not view their office as a career position. Many see it as a stepping stone to higher political office and others view it as an opportunity to make a reputation and gain contacts that will later be helpful in private practice. Thus, studies of prosecutor career patterns report that 50% of the prosecutors in a particular state are likely to be serving their first term and close to 50% may have a current interest in seeking another government position. Of course, there are exceptions to the general pattern. In almost every state, one can find local prosecutors who have remained in office for twenty to thirty years, rejecting numerous opportunities to become judges or enter private practices.

In most offices, the assistant prosecutors also have a fairly short tenure. Estimates of the annual turnover rate throughout the country range as high as 25–33%. Like the prosecuting attorney, the assistants generally do not view themselves as occupying a career position. In some jurisdictions, the process of their selection is so highly political that assistants are likely to lose their positions, or at least be demoted from supervisory positions, if the prosecutor hiring them is succeeded in office by a candidate from another party. Prosecutors in most larger counties, however, tend to hire on a nonpartisan, merit-oriented basis (as do United States Attorneys). While the assistants in such offices are not protected by civil service, they do have substantial job security. Nevertheless, their turnover rate also tends to be substantial. The assistants commonly are hired at an early stage in their legal careers, often immediately upon their graduation from law school. They stay for a few years, gaining considerable practical experience at a relatively low pay. They then leave to enter various fields of private practice (including criminal defense work) where their experience in litigation will be most valuable. Various prosecutor's offices, in an effort to produce more career professionals, have sought to establish salaries for higher ranked, experienced assistants at a level only slightly below that of a trial judge.

Local Prosecutors: Prosecutor/Police Relations. Another problem facing prosecutors' offices is the limited means available for imposing the policies of the office (which often are derived from the desire to avoid legal difficulties) upon the police. The local prosecutor is commonly characterized as the "chief law enforcement officer" of the local district, but this does not mean that the prosecutor has the authority to simply order the police to engage or not engage in certain investigative practices as he so directs. Police departments usually do follow the legal advice of the prosecutor but they do so because the interaction of police and prosecutor make cooperation necessary, not because they are legally required to do so. The local prosecutor and the local police are separate agencies, often receiving their funding from separate sources. Unlike the federal system, where the U.S. Attorney and F.B.I. are both subject to the supervisory power of the Attorney General, the local police and local prosecutor are not subject to the higher authority of a single executive. Short of threatening to withdraw his power to prosecute, the prosecutor must rely on his power of persuasion to gain any changes in police practices thought to be desirable.

A complete breakdown in prosecutor/police relations is rare, but various studies have found more tensions and conflict than one might initially expect, considering the shared interest of prosecutor and police in law enforcement. The lack of smoother prosecutor/police relations may often be a product of inadequate communication, but it also is attributable to the different vantage points from which police and prosecutor view the same event. Unlike the prosecutor, police see crime as it is committed in the streets rather than as reported in a law office. They are more likely to be influenced in their appraisal of a case by the extent of the victim's suffering, by the accused's subsequent reaction to his criminal behavior, and by the officer's own peril in making the arrest. Although both prosecutor and police officer are interested in effective law enforcement, their immediate goals and interests also tend to differ. The police are concerned primarily with their responsibility for keeping the streets safe, while the prosecutor is focusing upon his role as the legal representative of the state, the need to keep the court process moving, and his participation in the courtroom "work group" of prosecutor, defense counsel, and judge.

DEFENSE COUNSEL

Counsel for the Indigent. In most jurisdictions, 70–80% of all felony defendants are "indigent" in the sense that they lack the funds to hire defense counsel. The percentage of misdemeanor defendants who are indigent usually is somewhat lower, but it can easily fall in the range of 30–50%. As will be seen in Chapter Five, indigent felony defendants are constitutionally entitled to defense representation paid for by the state. Indigent misdemeanor defendants have a similar right only when sentenced to incarceration, but many jurisdictions provide free representation for all indigent misdemeanor defendants charged with a misdemeanor or ordinance violation that carries a potential sentence of imprisonment.

A majority of local judicial districts provide counsel for the indigent defendant through an assigned counsel system; the court makes individual appointments of private practitioners who receive compensation from the state for the work done in the particular case, usually at a rate somewhat lower than that which would be earned in private practice. In the more heavily populated districts, however, a public defender agency is likely to be the primary provider of counsel for the indigent. In most of these districts, defender agencies are the almost exclusive provider of representation for the indigent, with private counsel being assigned only to avoid potential conflicts in cases of jointly charged codefendants. In other districts, a "mixed system" is used, with the defender agency and appointed counsel each representing a substantial portion of the indigents (although the defender agency usually has the larger group). Still other districts add a contract system, with a law firm or nonprofit association agreeing to provide representation for a specified portion of the indigent caseload for a set fee.

In many respects, local defender agencies or local branches of statewide defender agencies present a mirror image of a local prosecutor's office. Individual offices range in size from a single part-time defender to a staff of more than 200 lawyers. Larger offices are likely to include such support personnel as investigators and paralegals. However, lawyers in these offices are also likely to have very heavy caseloads (e.g., in excess of 250 cases per year for a deputy handling felonies, and over 500 for the misdemeanor deputy). While most offices assign each client to a single lawyer, some use a horizontal assignment system similar to that found in prosecutor's offices. Separate deputies may handle the first appearance, preliminary hearing, pretrial motions, and the trial.

As with local prosecutor's offices, defender offices tend to hire young and relatively inexperienced attorneys and have a high employee turnover. Large offices, in particular, face a substantial problem of "burnout." Young lawyers enter the office filled with idealism and enthusiasm but frequently leave it disillusioned and cynical. Faced with a heavy caseload, judges who sometimes force them to take a backseat in scheduling to private practitioners, clients who sometimes misuse them and often suspect their motives (or at least view them as second-rate attorneys), and cases requiring infrequent use of their trial skills, deputy defenders often are ready to give up on defense work after only a few years (turning instead to a private civil practice or to the prosecutor's office). Thus, a nationwide survey found that only about one-third of the deputies had more than four years service with their agency.

Retained Counsel. The representation of criminal defendants able to afford counsel comes largely from a small segment of the private bar. A good many general practitioners, particularly in smaller communities, will handle a few criminal cases each year. Corporate practitioners from some of the largest firms will occasionally find themselves involved in a narrow segment of the criminal caseload—the white collar crime cases often tried in federal courts. A small cadre of the most highly publicized and highly skilled trial lawyers are available primarily to defendants able to pay large fees (although such lawyers not infrequently will take on other cases with special appeal). For the general run of criminal defendants who can retain counsel (most of whom are just barely above the line of indigency), at least in medium and large cities, the private bar makes available primarily a small group of attorneys who specialize in handling a high volume of criminal cases.[32]

Why do a substantial majority of all lawyers either never take a criminal case or do so only on rare occasions? These lawyers commonly view criminal defense work as one of the least desirable fields of specialization. Compensation tends to be lower than that for practitioners in other fields, and collection of the fee is often a difficult task (leading many defense lawyers to insist upon an "up-front" payment). Perhaps even more important, the working conditions are decidedly unappealing, at least to the typical member of the private bar. The defense counsel must expect to spend most of his time in police stations, jails, and the crowded (and often hectic) misdemeanor courts. His clients generally will be people who have committed acts which he views as questionable at best. He must be reconciled to the fact that, no matter how great his ability, he will "lose" most of his cases (in the sense that his clients will be convicted). Finally, as compared to lawyers in other fields, the defense specialist is likely to rank low in public esteem and in reputation among fellow-lawyers. Of course, many very good lawyers do make criminal law their specialty, but most lawyers with other options prefer those alternatives.

THE JUDICIARY

All of the opinions contained in this volume are opinions of the Supreme Court of the United States. Through the reading of those opinions, you will surely gain an understanding of the institutional setting in which that court operates. Our discussion here is limited to the lower courts. These are the magistrates and trial judges who are given front line responsibility for administering most of the standards set forth in those Supreme Court rulings and the state appellate courts whose rulings are being reviewed by the Supreme Court.

Magistrates Courts. The courts of first instance in the administration of the criminal justice process ordinarily are the courts of "limited jurisdiction"—that is, courts lacking authority to try the most serious criminal cases, but given more

---

32. These specialists tend to come from two groups—the young lawyers who also are relying upon court appointments (in jurisdictions without public defenders) to provide a steady monetary base in the building of their practices, and the so-called "courthouse regulars" (usually having offices in a "down on the heels" district located close to the courthouse, and commonly described as the "bar" of that district, as in Detroit's "Clinton Street Bar"). The latter group of more experienced lawyers usually rely on a private clientele developed through direct solicitation of unrepresented defendants awaiting court appearances and through contacts with bail bondsmen and others who might recommend them to prospective clients.

limited functions. These courts are known in different states as "magistrates courts," "justice of the peace courts," "municipal courts," "district courts," "police courts," and "recorder's courts."[33] We will refer to them as magistrates courts because the judges of these courts are commonly described in judicial opinions as magistrates. The magistrates courts traditionally have trial jurisdiction only over some or all misdemeanors. Where their jurisdiction does not extend to all misdemeanors, the dividing line is usually determined by the maximum punishment for the offense (e.g., the magistrates court will have trial jurisdiction over misdemeanors punishable by 90 days imprisonment or less). In addition to their trial jurisdiction, magistrates courts play an important role in the processing of felonies (and any misdemeanors that are beyond their trial authority). Cases involving those offenses are brought before the magistrates court for preliminary processing before being sent to the courts of "general" jurisdiction where they can be tried. The preliminary matters that may be handled by the magistrate include: (i) the issuance of search and arrest warrants; (ii) the first appearance of the arrested person before a court; (iii) the setting of bail; (iv) the appointment of counsel for indigent defendants; and (v) the preliminary hearing for felony cases.

The structure and staffing of magistrates courts differ considerably from state to state. Perhaps the greatest variation is found in the drawing of the judicial districts served by the magistrates courts. Some states have divided the state into uniform districts with the same type of magistrates court for each district. Others have districts that coincide with different political subdivisions (city, township, village, etc.). In these states, there may be several different types of magistrates courts, each with different limits on its trial jurisdiction, different qualifications required for its judges, and even different procedures for review of its decisions.

Almost all states permit judges in at least some magistrates courts to serve as part-time jurists. Where those judges are lawyers, state law commonly restricts their private practice to avoid a conflict of interest with their judicial duties. In approximately 30 states, judges in at least some magistrates courts need not be lawyers. Typically, a state will require that judges of magistrates courts in metropolitan areas be lawyers and serve full-time, while judges in rural magistrate courts may be nonlawyers and may serve part-time. Magistrates courts with lay judges commonly are treated as courts "not of record." Misdemeanor convictions in such courts are subject to retrial before a general trial court (a trial *de novo*) rather than simply the normal appellate review on the record of the earlier trial. This trial *de novo* procedure is made available out of concern that a person convicted of a misdemeanor be entitled to a more formal and thorough trial than typically is provided in courts not of record. Magistrates who are not lawyers sometimes follow the traditional rules governing trials only in a rather loose fashion, but many defendants, though convicted, view that as sufficient and do not seek a trial *de novo*.

Over the years, national and local commissions examining the judicial system have repeatedly cited the importance of the magistrates courts to the administration of justice (for most people, these are the only courts in which they will ever appear) and the need for improvement in the structure and administration of those courts. Magistrates courts in the rural areas, staffed by non-lawyer judges,

---

33. In the federal system, there is not a separate magistrates court, but basically the same functions as performed by magistrates courts are delegated by the District Court to United States Magistrates (court officers appointed by the district judges). Several states similarly do not have separate magistrates courts, but assign to a division of the general trial court the functions of those courts.

have been criticized for their lack of legal competency and the lack of dignity and decorum in their courtrooms. Lay judges, it has been argued, too often ignore the law and reflect a local bias rather than the "good common sense" that is allegedly their strong point. Complaints as to the lack of dignity and decorum have also been leveled at the magistrates courts in metropolitan areas, where a form of "assembly line justice" too frequently prevails. In those courts, it is reported, judges tend to place greater emphasis on the speedy disposition of cases than on ensuring that the correct result is attained in each and every case. With their crowded facilities, lack of adequate staffing, and routinized procedures, big city magistrates courts create an atmosphere, critics contend, that is more appropriate for a supermarket than a court of justice.

State legislatures have sought to respond to such criticism in various ways. Lay judges have been required to participate in training programs, and even to pass examinations testing their legal knowledge. Magistrates courts have been required to extend their hours so that defendants arrested on weekends may be promptly presented. Various measures have been adopted to provide some relief from the pressure of the tremendously heavy caseloads typically borne by the urban courts. Traffic cases have either been removed from the court's jurisdiction or largely assigned to court personnel other than the judges. To reduce the civil docket, more cases have been brought within the range of the small claims division of the court. Decriminalization of public drunkenness (which otherwise might constitute as much as 15–20 percent of the misdemeanor docket) has also helped to reduce the court's docket. Even with such reforms, however, the caseload per judge, including misdemeanors, minor civil cases, and preliminary proceedings in felony cases, can easily reach 2,000 cases a year in a busy urban court.

Trial Courts of General Jurisdiction. The courts that try felony cases (and any misdemeanors beyond the magistrates court's trial jurisdiction) are commonly described as the trial courts of "general" (i.e., not limited) jurisdiction. In the federal system, that general trial court is the United States District Court. In the state system, that court is commonly called the "superior court," "circuit court," or "district court." In addition to its felony trial jurisdiction, this court will also provide the first level of appellate review for misdemeanors tried in the magistrates court.

Although the general trial court is responsible for both criminal and civil cases, the criminal portion of its docket is sufficiently significant so that even those trial judges who had no previous experience with the criminal field as practicing lawyers quickly gain considerable familiarity with the criminal process. Criminal cases commonly constitute anywhere from 15–40% of the general trial court's docket, with the lower figure applicable primarily where that docket includes juvenile and probate cases in addition to the traditional civil cases. Moreover, when caseloads are weighted according to the time spent on the particular type of case, the significance of the criminal caseload increases at least twofold. Although, as we have seen, only a small percentage of felony cases actually go to trial, that rate is still much higher than the trial rate in civil cases. Thus, even where criminal cases constitute no more than 25% of the court's total docket, those cases can readily provide over 50% of all jury trials.

Appellate Courts. In roughly three-fourths of the states, there are two levels of appellate courts: first, an intermediate court of appeals, and then the highest state court (commonly called that state's supreme court). In the remainder of the states, there is a single appellate court, the state supreme court. In the federal system, appeals are taken initially to the federal intermediate appellate court, the

United States Court of Appeals, and then to the Supreme Court of the United States.

A convicted felony defendant ordinarily will have an automatic right to have his conviction reviewed by the first level appellate court. This means that defendant will have an automatic appeal to the intermediate court where the state has two levels of review or to the state supreme court where it has only one. Any further appellate review generally lies in the discretion of the higher appellate court. Thus, a defendant whose conviction is affirmed by the state intermediate appellate court can only obtain review from the state supreme court if he can convince that court that issues posed by his case are of sufficient general importance to merit its attention.

The state supreme court will be the court of last resort in state criminal cases unless a federal constitutional issue is presented. Where such an issue is posed, the defendant can seek further review of that issue from the Supreme Court of the United States. The Supreme Court's appellate jurisdiction is largely discretionary, and the defendant seeks such review through a "petition for certiorari." The Supreme Court also has discretionary appellate jurisdiction over federal criminal cases coming from the United States Court of Appeals, but here its reviewing authority is total; that is, it can review any issue posed in the case, not simply those involving the interpretation of the federal constitution. The Supreme Court annually grants review in only a small number (typically, about 175) of the several thousand cases, civil and criminal, in which petitions for certiorari are filed.[34]

Most criminal cases reviewed by an appellate court come to that court after a conviction at the trial level. The defendant can appeal a conviction, but the prosecution cannot appeal an acquittal. Indeed, the prosecution's initial right of appeal is limited to certain rulings issued before trial that either result in the dismissal of charges or hold inadmissible evidence that the prosecution deems critical to its case. Where the defendant appeals following a conviction and that appeal is successful (i.e., the conviction is reversed), the prosecution can then seek the discretionary review of any higher appellate court in the state system. If the conviction was reversed by the state court on the basis of a federal constitutional ruling, the prosecution can then seek review by the Supreme Court through a petition for certiorari.

Those state appellate courts to which the defendant has an automatic right to review generally spend a considerable portion of their efforts on criminal cases. For such a court, often more than half of its docket consists of criminal appeals. In anywhere from 80 to 90% of those cases, the defendant's claim is likely to be rejected and the conviction affirmed. Where the appellate court has discretion as to which cases it will review, the proportion of criminal cases heard will be much lower, but the percentage of reversals is likely to be higher. This is because discretionary review permits the appellate court to screen out the many cases in which the convicted defendant does not have a strong claim, but appeals nonetheless because there is nothing to lose by seeking appellate review. In some states, as many as 90% of the felony defendants who were both convicted after a trial and sentenced to imprisonment will exercise their right to automatic review by the first level appellate court.

Selection. At least since the Jacksonian era, what constitutes the best method for selecting judges has been a matter of considerable controversy and division among the states. Basically five different procedures are used in this

---

34. Whereas the Supreme Court decision on the merits of any appeal is determined by a majority vote (5 out of 9, where all Justices are sitting), certiorari will be granted where at least 4 Justices desire to review the case.

country to select judges: (1) partisan elections (i.e., candidates running as nominees of political parties); (2) nonpartisan elections (i.e., all candidates running as independents); (3) appointment by the chief executive, with the consent of the legislature; (4) election by the legislature; and (5) the Missouri Plan, a system that includes the selection of a panel of several nominees by an independent commission, appointment of one of those nominees by the chief executive, a probationary period of judicial service, and the subsequent retention or rejection of the appointed judge in an election in which the judge runs unopposed.[35]

The division among the states in choosing one selection system over another has rested in part upon a disagreement as to what qualities are most needed in judges. In particular, there is a disagreement as to the significance of the candidate's political philosophy, including both the candidate's basic value judgments and his or her view of the rule of the judiciary. Some contend that, assuming there exists the qualities that are a prerequisite for any public office (e.g., integrity), judicial philosophy is the most critical factor. Judges are said to have broad discretion in shaping the law and it is therefore important that they reflect the value judgments and perspectives of the communities that they serve. This may require, it is argued, that the judicial selection process take into consideration, to some extent, such factors as gender, race, ethnic and socio-economic background, and previous experiences that might assist one in understanding all elements of a diverse society.

A contrary view acknowledges that at the level of the Supreme Court, and perhaps the highest state appellate courts, the judge's basic value judgments play an important role in judicial lawmaking (although it may be argued that even here, legal methodology significantly restricts the judge's discretion). The judge's value system is viewed as far less significant, however, in selecting judges of other courts. Here, the legal issues presented to the judge are said to be controlled largely by prior decisions of higher courts, except for unusual cases. The critical qualities are those that enable judges to apply that law and to make fair and accurate factfinding determinations. These qualities, sometimes described as "professional qualifications," are said to include an ability to carefully analyze statutes and high court rulings, a capacity to carefully evaluate facts, and an understanding of human nature.

Of course, desirable professional qualifications and a desired political philosophy are not mutually exclusive criteria. The division arises over which should be given the greater emphasis in the selection of judges. Supporters of the first view often prefer the popular election of judges both because it provides community control over the initial selection process [36] and because it keeps the judge attuned

---

35. The characterization of a state's system as fitting into one category or another is likely to be quite rough. Initially, some states do not adhere to the basic elements of any single selection system, but have what may best be described as a hybrid system. Thus, a state may initially use a nonpartisan election, but then, borrowing from the Missouri Plan, have the judge run for reelection unopposed, in what is described as a "retention election." Secondly, even though a jurisdiction adheres to the basic elements of one of the five systems, it is likely to have adopted significant variations within that structure. Perhaps the single most significant variant within any one structure will be the length of the judicial term for which the judge is selected. Federal judges and the judges of a few states are given the

security (and independence) of lifetime tenure or tenure up to a mandatory retirement age. The remaining states use terms varying from four years to sixteen years. Another problem presented in categorizing jurisdictions is the use of different methods to select judges at different levels of the judicial hierarchy. Gubernatorial appointment, legislative election, and the Missouri Plan are all too time consuming for the high-level officials responsible for the selection to apply those methods of selection to magistrates. Accordingly, jurisdictions that otherwise use those methods commonly select magistrates through a local election or appointment by a lower-level official (e.g., the city council in the case of a municipal court).

36. In practice, however, the elective system commonly produces a substantial number to community values by requiring that he or she run for reelection every several years. Proponents of executive appointment with legislative approval (as in the federal system), or the less common legislative election system, also tend to emphasize the judge's philosophy, but argue that judges representative of the populace and possessing adequate professional qualifications are more likely to be produced by those systems than the rarely illuminating election campaign. Supporters of the Missouri Plan tend to give greater weight to professional qualifications, although some prefer that selection system primarily because it eliminates considerations of partisan politics.

of judges who are selected initially by appointment. When a vacancy occurs during a judicial term, usually due to the sitting judge's death or retirement, it is the governor who appoints an interim successor. While that person must stand for election in the next regularly scheduled election, he or she will be listed on the ballot as the incumbent, which will greatly aid in gaining election. Surveys of sitting judges in several elective jurisdictions found that more than half of those judges were initially selected by the governor to fill a vacancy, and that incumbents have a reelection record of better than 95%.

A general view of The Criminal Justice System

This chart seeks to present a simple yet comprehensive view of the movement of cases through the criminal justice system. Procedures in individual jurisdictions may vary from the pattern shown here. The differing weights of line indicate the relative volumes of cases disposed of at various points in the system, but this is only suggestive since no nationwide data of this sort exists.

Source: Adapted from *The challenge of crime in a free society,* President's Commission on Law Enforcement and Administration of Justice, 1967.

Chapter 2

THE NATURE AND SCOPE OF FOURTEENTH AMENDMENT DUE PROCESS; THE APPLICABILITY OF THE BILL OF RIGHTS TO THE STATES

SECTION 1. THE "FUNDAMENTAL RIGHTS" (OR "ORDERED LIBERTY") AND "INCORPORATION" THEORIES

The first eight amendments were enacted as limitations solely upon the federal government. But some argued that the Fourteenth Amendment had "totally incorporated" all the provisions of the Bill of Rights, i.e., made them fully applicable to the states. As it had done earlier (see *Twining v. New Jersey,* 211 U.S. 78 (1908)), in *Palko v. Connecticut* and *Adamson v. California,* the two cases set forth in this section, the Court emphatically rejected the "total incorporation" view of the history of the Fourteenth Amendment—a view which has never commanded a majority.

Instead, the Court in *Palko* and *Adamson* (as well as other cases) adopted what has been called the "fundamental rights" or "ordered liberty" interpretation of the Fourteenth Amendment's due process clause, an approach that prevailed until the early 1960s. This approach finds no necessary relationship between the content of the Fourteenth Amendment and the guarantees of the Bill of Rights. It regards the due process clause as simply incorporating all principles of justice "implicit in the concept of ordered liberty" or "so rooted in the traditions and conscience of our people as to be ranked as fundamental." As applied to criminal procedure, this approach requires, but requires only, that the state afford a defendant "that fundamental fairness essential to the very concept of justice." If the presence of a specific Bill of Rights guarantee is not decisive under this approach, neither is its absence. A particular practice may violate "fundamental fairness" even though it is not specifically prohibited by the Bill of Rights. Under this approach, the Due Process Clause of the Fourteenth Amendment, as Justice Frankfurter emphasized in his *Adamson* concurring opinion, "has an independent potency."

The cases applying the "fundamental rights" approach recognized the possibility that some of the personal rights safeguarded by the first eight Amendments against federal action may also be protections against state action, because a denial of them would be a denial of due process. Thus, the Court held in *Powell v. Alabama* (1932) (discussed in Chapter Five) that, under the circumstances of the case, defendants charged with and convicted of capital offenses were denied Fourteenth Amendment Due Process when a state did not afford them the effective assistance of counsel. "The logically critical thing, however," pointed out Justice Harlan years later (dissenting in *Duncan v. Louisiana,* set forth in the next section), "was not that the rights had been found in the Bill of Rights but that they were deemed [to] be fundamental."

If *Powell v. Alabama* did not hold that the right to counsel was fully "incorporated into" or implicit in Fourteenth Amendment Due Process, neither did *Palko* hold that the prohibition against double jeopardy was completely "out" of the Fourteenth Amendment. As *Palko* illustrates, the Court often had to pass on state procedures transgressing the "outer edges," rather than the basic concept, of a particular Bill of Rights guarantee. It seems most doubtful that in sustaining such challenged procedures the Court was authorizing the states to abolish completely—or to avoid the "hardcore" of—e.g., the protection against double jeopardy, or the privilege against self-incrimination, or the right to trial by jury in criminal cases.

Rather the Court probably meant that the state rule in question did not violate the Fourteenth Amendment because the specific provision of the Bill of Rights invoked by the defendant did not apply to the states *to the full extent* it applied to the federal government. To hold that a particular Bill of Rights guarantee is not *totally* "incorporated," i.e., not binding on the states *in its entirety,* is not to say it is completely "out" of the Fourteenth Amendment.

The total incorporation position received its strongest support in the *Adamson* dissents, especially Justice Black's memorable dissent. But the *Adamson* case also produced the most powerful rejection of the total incorporation theory—and perhaps the most famous articulation of the "ordered liberty"-"fundamental fairness" approach—concurring Justice Frankfurter's response to the *Adamson* dissenters.

PALKO v. CONNECTICUT

302 U.S. 319, 58 S.Ct. 149, 82 L.Ed. 288 (1937).

JUSTICE CARDOZO delivered the opinion of the Court. * * *

Appellant was indicted for the crime of murder in the first degree. A jury found him guilty of murder in the second degree, and he was sentenced to confinement in the state prison for life. Thereafter the State of Connecticut [appealed, pursuant to a state statute permitting appeals "upon all questions of law arising on the trial of criminal cases, [with] the permission of the presiding judge"]. [T]he Supreme Court of Errors reversed [finding] error of law to the prejudice of the state [in excluding certain evidence and] in the instructions to the jury as to the difference between first and second degree murder.

* * * Before a jury was impaneled [defendant unsuccessfully objected] that the effect of the new trial was to place him twice in jeopardy for the same offense, and in so doing to violate the Fourteenth Amendment. [The] jury returned a verdict of murder in the first degree, and the court sentenced the defendant to the punishment of death. The Supreme Court of Errors affirmed.

[The] argument for appellant is that whatever is forbidden by the Fifth Amendment is forbidden by the Fourteenth also. [To] retry a defendant, though under one indictment and only one, subjects him, it is said, to double jeopardy in violation of the Fifth Amendment, if the prosecution is one on behalf of the United States. From this the consequence is said to follow that there is a denial of life or liberty without due process of law.

[Appellant's] thesis is even broader. Whatever would be a violation of the original bill of rights (Amendments 1 to 8) if done by the federal government is now equally unlawful by force of the Fourteenth Amendment if done by a state. There is no such general rule.

The Fifth Amendment provides, among other things, that no person shall be held to answer for a capital or otherwise infamous crime unless on presentment or indictment of a grand jury. This court has held that, in prosecutions by a state, presentment or indictment by a grand jury may give way to informations at the instance of a public officer. *Hurtado v. California,* 110 U.S. 516 (1884). The Fifth Amendment provides also that no person shall be compelled in any criminal case to be a witness against himself. This court has said that, in prosecutions by a state, the exemption will fail if the state elects to end it. *Twining v. New Jersey,* 211 U.S. 78 (1908). The Sixth Amendment calls for a jury trial in criminal cases and the Seventh for a jury trial in civil cases at common law where the value in controversy shall exceed $20. This court has ruled that consistently with those amendments trial by jury may be modified by a state or abolished altogether. * * *

On the other hand, the due process clause of the Fourteenth Amendment may make it unlawful for a state to abridge by its statutes the freedom of speech which the First Amendment safeguards against encroachment by the Congress; or the like freedom of the press; or the free exercise of religion; or the right of peaceable assembly. [In] these and other situations immunities that are valid as against the federal government by force of the specific pledges of particular amendments have been found to be implicit in the concept of ordered liberty and thus through the Fourteenth Amendment, become valid as against the states.

The line of division may seem to be wavering and broken if there is a hasty catalogue of the cases on the one side and the other. Reflection and analysis will induce a different view. There emerges the perception of a rationalizing principle which gives to discrete instances a proper order and coherence. The right to trial by jury and the immunity from prosecution except as the result of an indictment may have value and importance. Even so, they are not of the very essence of a scheme of ordered liberty. To abolish them is not to violate a "principle of justice so rooted in the traditions and conscience of our people as to be ranked as fundamental." Few would be so narrow or provincial as to maintain that a fair and enlightened system of justice would be impossible without them. What is true of jury trials and indictments is true also, as the cases show, of the immunity from compulsory self-incrimination. This too might be lost, and justice still be done. Indeed, today as in the past there are students of our penal system who look upon the immunity as a mischief rather than a benefit, and who would limit its scope, or destroy it altogether. No doubt there would remain the need to give protection against torture, physical or mental. Justice, however, would not perish if the accused were subject to a duty to respond to orderly inquiry. The exclusion of these immunities and privileges from the privileges and immunities protected against the action of the States has not been arbitrary or casual. It has been dictated by a study and appreciation of the meaning, the essential implications, of liberty itself.

We reach a different plane of social and moral values when we pass to the privileges and immunities that have been taken over from the earlier articles of the Federal Bill of Rights and brought within the Fourteenth Amendment by a process of absorption. These in their origin were effective against the federal government alone. If the Fourteenth Amendment has absorbed them, the process of absorption has had its source in the belief that neither liberty nor justice would exist if they were sacrificed. *Twining.* This is true, for illustration, of freedom of thought and speech. Of that freedom one may say that it is the matrix, the indispensable condition, of nearly every other form of freedom. * * * Fundamental too in the concept of due process, and so in that of liberty, is the thought that condemnation shall be rendered only after trial. The hearing, moreover, must be a real one, not a sham or a pretense. For that reason, ignorant defendants in a capital case were held to have been condemned unlawfully when in truth, though not in form, they were refused the aid of counsel. *Powell v. Alabama* [discussed in Ch. 5.] The decision did not turn upon the fact that the benefit of counsel would have been guaranteed to the defendants by the provisions of the Sixth Amendment if they had been prosecuted in a federal court. The decision turned upon the fact that in the particular situation laid before us in the evidence the benefit of counsel was essential to the substance of a hearing.

Our survey of the cases serves, we think, to justify the statement that the dividing line between them, if not unfaltering throughout its course, has been true for the most part to a unifying principle. On which side of the line the case made out by the appellant has appropriate location must be the next inquiry and the final one. Is that kind of double jeopardy to which the statute has subjected him a hardship so acute and shocking that our polity will not endure it? Does it violate those "fundamental principles of liberty and justice which lie at the base of all our civil and political institutions"? The answer surely must be "no." What the answer would have to be if the state were permitted after a trial free from error to try the accused over again or to bring another case against him, we have no occasion to consider. We deal with the statute before us and no other. The state is not attempting to wear the accused out by a multitude of cases with accumulated trials. It asks no more than this, that the case against him shall go on until there shall be a trial free from the corrosion of substantial legal error. [This] is not cruelty at all, nor even vexation in any immoderate degree. If the trial had been infected with error adverse to the accused, there might have been review at his instance, and as often as necessary to purge the vicious taint. A reciprocal privilege, subject at all times to the discretion of the presiding judge [has] now been granted to the state. There is here no seismic innovation. The edifice of justice stands, its symmetry, to many, greater than before. * * *

The judgment is affirmed.[a]

JUSTICE BUTLER dissents.

ADAMSON v. CALIFORNIA

332 U.S. 46, 67 S.Ct. 1672, 91 L.Ed. 1903 (1947).

JUSTICE REED delivered the opinion of the Court.

The appellant, Adamson, a citizen of the United States, was convicted without recommendation for mercy, by a jury [of] murder in the first degree [and sentenced to death]. The provisions of California law which were challenged in the state proceedings as invalid under the Fourteenth Amendment * * * permit

a. *Palko* was later overruled in *Benton v. Maryland*, 395 U.S. 784 (1969), which found that "the double jeopardy prohibition of the Fifth Amendment represents a fundamental ideal in our constitutional heritage, and that it should apply to the States through the Fourteenth Amendment."

the failure of a defendant to explain or to deny evidence against him to be commented upon by court and by counsel and to be considered by court and jury. The defendant did not testify. [T]he trial court gave its instructions and the District Attorney argued the case in accordance with the [California] provisions just referred to * * *.

We shall assume, but without any intention thereby of ruling upon the issue, that state permission by law to the court, counsel and jury to comment upon and consider the failure of defendant "to explain or to deny by his testimony any evidence or facts in the case against him" would infringe defendant's privilege against self-incrimination under the Fifth Amendment if this were a trial in a court of the United States under a similar law. Such an assumption does not determine appellant's rights under the Fourteenth Amendment. It is settled law that the clause of the Fifth Amendment, protecting a person against being compelled to be a witness against himself, is not made effective by the Fourteenth Amendment as a protection against state action on the ground that freedom from testimonial compulsion is a right of national citizenship, or because it is a personal privilege or immunity secured by the Federal Constitution as one of the rights of man that are listed in the Bill of Rights. * * *

Appellant secondly contends [that] the privilege against self-incrimination [to] its full scope under the Fifth Amendment, inheres in the right to a fair trial. A right to a fair trial is a right admittedly protected by the due process clause of the Fourteenth Amendment. [The] due process clause of the Fourteenth Amendment, however, does not draw all the rights of the federal Bill of Rights under its protection. That contention was made and rejected in *Palko* [which] held that such provisions of the Bill of Rights as were "implicit in the concept of ordered liberty," became secure from state interference by the clause. But it held nothing more. * * *

Generally, comment on the failure of an accused to testify is forbidden in American jurisdictions. This arises from state constitutional or statutory provisions similar in character to the federal provisions. California, however, is one of a few states that permit limited comment upon a defendant's failure to testify. That permission is narrow. The California law authorizes comment by court and counsel upon the "failure of the defendant to explain or to deny by his testimony any evidence or facts in the case against him." This does not involve any presumption, rebuttable or irrebuttable, either of guilt or of the truth of any fact, that is offered in evidence. It allows inferences to be drawn from proven facts. Because of this clause, the court can direct the jury's attention to whatever evidence there may be that a defendant could deny and the prosecution can argue as to inferences that may be drawn from the accused's failure to testify. * * * However sound may be the legislative conclusion that an accused should not be compelled in any criminal case to be a witness against himself, we see no reason why comment should not be made upon his silence. It seems quite natural that when a defendant has opportunity to deny or explain facts and determines not to do so, the prosecution should bring out the strength of the evidence by commenting upon defendant's failure to explain or deny it. * * *

Appellant sets out the circumstances of this case, however, to show coercion and unfairness in permitting comment. [His] argument here is that he could not take the stand to deny the evidence against him because he would be subjected to a cross-examination as to former crimes to impeach his veracity and the evidence so produced might well bring about his conviction. * * *

It is true that if comment were forbidden, an accused in this situation could remain silent and avoid evidence of former crimes and comment upon his failure to testify. We are of the view, however, that a state may control such a situation in accordance with its own ideas of the most efficient administration of criminal justice. The purpose of due process is not to protect an accused against a proper conviction but against an unfair conviction. When evidence is before a jury that threatens conviction, it does not seem unfair to require him to choose between leaving the adverse evidence unexplained and subjecting himself to impeachment through disclosure of former crimes. Indeed, this is a dilemma with which any defendant may be faced. If facts, adverse to the defendant, are proven by the prosecution, there may be no way to explain them favorably to the accused except by a witness who may be vulnerable to impeachment on cross-examination. The defendant must then decide whether or not to use such a witness. The fact that the witness may also be the defendant makes the choice more difficult but a denial of due process does not emerge from the circumstances. * * *

Affirmed.

JUSTICE FRANKFURTER (concurring).

* * * Only a technical rule of law would exclude from consideration that which is relevant, as a matter of fair reasoning, to the solution of a problem. Sensible and just-minded men, in important affairs of life, deem it significant that a man remains silent when confronted with serious and responsible evidence against himself which it is within his power to contradict. The notion that to allow jurors to do that which sensible and rightminded men do every day violates the "immutable principles of justice" as conceived by a civilized society is to trivialize the importance of "due process."

[For] historical reasons a limited immunity from the common duty to testify was written into the Federal Bill of Rights, and I am prepared to agree that, as part of that immunity, comment on the failure of an accused to take the witness stand is forbidden in federal prosecutions. It is so, of course, by explicit act of Congress. But to suggest that such a limitation can be drawn out of "due process" in its protection of ultimate decency in a civilized society is to suggest that the Due Process Clause fastened fetters of unreason upon the States. * * *

Between the incorporation of the Fourteenth Amendment into the Constitution and the beginning of the present membership of the Court—a period of 70 years—the scope of that Amendment was passed upon by 43 judges. Of all these judges only one, who may respectfully be called an eccentric exception, ever indicated the belief that the Fourteenth Amendment was a shorthand summary of the first eight Amendments theretofore limiting only the Federal Government, and that due process incorporated those eight Amendments as restrictions upon the powers of the States. [To] suggest that it is inconsistent with a truly free society to begin prosecutions without an indictment, to try petty civil cases without the paraphernalia of a common law jury, to take into consideration that one who has full opportunity to make a defense remains silent is, in de Tocqueville's phrase, to confound the familiar with the necessary.

The short answer to the suggestion that the [Due Process Clause] of the Fourteenth Amendment * * * was a way of saying that every State must thereafter initiate prosecutions through indictment by a grand jury, must have a trial by a jury of 12 in criminal cases, and must have trial by such a jury in common law suits where the amount in controversy exceeds $20, is that it is a strange way of saying it. It would be extraordinarily strange for a Constitution to convey such specific commands in such a roundabout and inexplicit way. * * * Those reading the English language with the meaning which it ordinarily conveys, those conversant with the political and legal history of the concept of due process, those sensitive to the relations of the States to the central government as well as the relation of some of the provisions of the Bill of Rights to the process of justice, would hardly recognize the Fourteenth Amendment as a cover for the various explicit provisions of the first eight Amendments. Some of these are enduring reflections of experience with human nature, while some express the restricted views of Eighteenth–Century England regarding the best methods for the ascertainment of facts. The notion that the Fourteenth Amendment was a covert way of imposing upon the States all the rules which it seemed important to Eighteenth Century statesmen to write into the Federal Amendments, was rejected by judges who were themselves witnesses of the process by which the Fourteenth Amendment became part of the Constitution. Arguments that may now be adduced to prove that the first eight Amendments were concealed within the historic phrasing of the Fourteenth Amendment were not unknown at the time of its adoption. A surer estimate of their bearing was possible for judges at the time than distorting distance is likely to vouchsafe. Any evidence of design or purpose not contemporaneously known could hardly have influenced those who ratified the Amendment. [A]t the time of the ratification of the Fourteenth Amendment the constitutions of nearly half of the ratifying States did not have the rigorous requirements of the Fifth Amendment for instituting criminal proceedings through a grand jury. It could hardly have occurred to these States that by ratifying the Amendment they uprooted their established methods for prosecuting crime and fastened upon themselves a new prosecutorial system.

Indeed, the suggestion that the Fourteenth Amendment incorporates the first eight Amendments as such is not unambiguously urged. [There] is suggested merely a selective incorporation of the first eight Amendments into the Fourteenth Amendment. Some are in and some are out, but we are left in the dark as to which are in and which are out. Nor are we given the calculus for determining which go in and which stay out. If the basis of selection is merely that those provisions of the first eight Amendments are incorporated which commend themselves to individual justices as indispensable to the dignity and happiness of a free man, we are thrown back to a merely subjective test. The protection against unreasonable search and seizure might have primacy for one judge, while trial by a jury of 12 for every claim above $20 might appear to another as an ultimate need in a free society. In the history of thought "natural law" has a much longer and much better founded meaning and justification than such subjective selection of the first eight Amendments for incorporation into the Fourteenth. If all that is meant is that due process contains within itself certain minimal standards which are "of the very essence of a scheme of ordered liberty," *Palko v. Connecticut,* putting upon this Court the duty of applying these standards from time to time, then we have merely arrived at the insight which our predecessors long ago expressed.

* * * The [Fourteenth] Amendment neither comprehends the specific provisions by which the founders deemed it appropriate to restrict the federal government nor is it confined to them. The Due Process Clause of the Fourteenth Amendment has an independent potency, precisely as does the Due Process Clause of the Fifth Amendment in relation to the Federal Government. It ought not to require argument to reject the notion that due process of law meant one thing in the Fifth Amendment and another in the Fourteenth. The Fifth Amendment specifically prohibits prosecution of an "infamous crime" except upon indictment; it forbids double jeopardy; it bars compelling a person to be a witness against himself in any criminal case; it precludes deprivation of "life, liberty, or property, without due process of law." Are Madison and his contemporaries in the framing of the Bill of Rights to be charged with writing into it a meaningless clause? * * *

A construction which gives to due process no independent function but turns it into a summary of the specific provisions of the Bill of Rights * * * would deprive the States of opportunity for reforms in legal process designed for extending the area of freedom. It would assume that no other abuses would reveal themselves in the course of time than those which had become manifest in 1791. Such a view not only disregards the historic meaning of "due process." It leads inevitably to a warped construction of specific provisions of the Bill of Rights to bring within their scope conduct clearly condemned by due process but not easily fitting into the pigeonholes of the specific provisions.

* * * Judicial review of [the Due Process Clause] of the Fourteenth Amendment inescapably imposes upon this Court an exercise of judgment upon the whole course of the proceedings in order to ascertain whether they offend those canons of decency and fairness which express the notions of justice of English-speaking peoples even toward those charged with the most heinous offenses. These standards of justice are not authoritatively formulated anywhere as though they were prescriptions in a pharmacopoeia. But neither does the application of the Due Process Clause imply that judges are wholly at large. The judicial judgment in applying the Due Process Clause must move within the limits of accepted notions of justice and is not to be based upon the idiosyncracies of a merely personal judgment. The fact that judges among themselves may differ whether in a particular case a trial offends accepted notions of justice is not disproof that general rather than idiosyncratic standards are applied. An important safeguard against such merely individual judgment is an alert deference to the judgment of the State court under review.

Justice Black, dissenting.

* * * In my judgment [the Fourteenth Amendment's] history conclusively demonstrates that the language of the first section of the Fourteenth Amendment, taken as a whole, was thought by those responsible for its submission to the people, and by those who opposed its submission, sufficiently explicit to guarantee that thereafter no state could deprive its citizens of the privileges and protections of the Bill of Rights. Whether this Court ever will, or whether it now should, in the light of past decisions, give full effect to what the Amendment was intended to accomplish is not necessarily essential to a decision here. However that may be, our prior decisions, including *Twining,* do not prevent our carrying out that purpose, at least to the extent of making applicable to the states, not a mere part, as the Court has, but the full protection of the Fifth Amendment's provision against compelling evidence from an accused to convict him of crime. And I further contend that the "natural law" formula which the Court uses to reach its conclusion in this case should be abandoned as an incongruous excrescence on our Constitution. I believe that formula to be itself a violation of our Constitution, in that it subtly conveys to courts, at the expense of legislatures, ultimate power over public policies in fields where no specific provision of the Constitution limits legislative power. And my belief seems to be in accord with the views expressed by this Court, at least for the first two decades after the Fourteenth Amendment was adopted. * * *

I cannot consider the Bill of Rights to be an outworn 18th Century "strait jacket" as the *Twining* opinion did. Its provisions may be thought outdated abstractions by some. And it is true that they were designed to meet ancient evils. But they are the same kind of human evils that have emerged from century to century wherever excessive power is sought by the few at the expense of the many. In my judgment the people of no nation can lose their liberty so long as a Bill of Rights like ours survives and its basic purposes are conscientiously interpreted, enforced and respected so as to afford continuous protection against old, as well as new, devices and practices which might thwart those purposes. I fear to see the consequences of the Court's practice of substituting its own concepts of decency and fundamental justice for the language of the Bill of Rights as its point of departure in interpreting and enforcing that Bill of Rights. If the choice must be between the selective process of the *Palko* decision applying some of the Bill of Rights to the States, or the *Twining* rule applying none of them, I would choose the *Palko* selective process. But rather than accept either of these choices, I would follow what I believe was the original purpose of the Fourteenth Amendment—to extend to all the people of the nation the complete protection of the Bill of Rights. To hold that this Court can determine what, if any, provisions of the Bill of Rights will be enforced, and if so to what degree, is to frustrate the great design of a written Constitution.

Conceding the possibility that this Court is now wise enough to improve on the Bill of Rights by substituting natural law concepts for the Bill of Rights, I think the possibility is entirely too speculative to agree to take that course. I would therefore hold in this case that the full protection of the Fifth Amendment's proscription against compelled testimony must be afforded by California. This I would do because of reliance upon the original purpose of the Fourteenth Amendment.

It is an illusory apprehension that literal application of some or all of the provisions of the Bill of Rights to the States would unwisely increase the sum total of the powers of this Court to invalidate state legislation. The Federal Government has not been harmfully burdened by the requirement that enforcement of federal laws affecting civil liberty conform literally to the Bill of Rights. Who would advocate its repeal? It must be conceded, of course, that the natural-law-due-process formula, which the Court today reaffirms, has been interpreted to limit substantially this Court's power to prevent state violations of the individual civil liberties guaranteed by the Bill of Rights. But this formula also has been used in the past and can be used in the future, to license this Court, in considering regulatory legislation, to roam at large in the broad expanses of policy and morals and to trespass, all too freely, on the legislative domain of the States as well as the Federal Government.

Since *Marbury v. Madison* was decided, the practice has been firmly established for better or worse, that courts can strike down legislative enactments which violate the Constitution. This process, of course, involves interpretation, and since words can have many meanings, interpretation obviously may result in contraction or extension of the original purpose of a constitutional provision thereby affecting policy. But to pass upon the constitutionality of statutes by looking to the particular standards enumerated in the Bill of Rights and other parts of the Constitution is one thing; to invalidate statutes because of application of "natural law" deemed to be above and undefined by the Constitution is another. "In the one instance, courts proceeding within clearly marked constitutional boundaries seek to execute policies written into the Constitution; in the other they roam at will in the limitless area of their own beliefs as to reasonableness and actually select policies, a responsibility which the Constitution entrusts to the legislative representatives of the people." *Federal Power Commission v. Natural Gas Pipeline Co.*, 315 U.S. 575 (1942).[a]

---

a. In *Rochin v. California,* 342 U.S. 165 (1952), the famous "stomach-pumping" case, Justice Black also criticized what he called the majority's use of a due process test that "empowers this Court to nullify any state law if its application 'shocks the conscience,' offends 'a sense of justice' or runs counter to the 'decencies of civilized conduct.' "

Justice Douglas joins in this opinion. * * *

Justice Murphy, with whom Justice Rutledge concurs, dissenting.

While in substantial agreement with the views of Mr. Justice Black, I have one reservation and one addition to make.

I agree that the specific guarantees of the Bill of Rights should be carried over intact into the first section of the Fourteenth Amendment. But I am not prepared to say that the latter is entirely and necessarily limited by the Bill of Rights. Occasions may arise where a proceeding falls so far short of conforming to fundamental standards of procedure as to warrant constitutional condemnation in terms of a lack of due process despite the absence of a specific provision in the Bill of Rights.

That point, however, need not be pursued here inasmuch as the Fifth Amendment is explicit in its provision that no person shall be compelled in any criminal case to be a witness against himself. That provision, as Mr. Justice Black demonstrates, is a constituent part of the Fourteenth Amendment. * * *

Much can be said pro and con as to the desirability of allowing comment on the failure of the accused to testify. But policy arguments are to no avail in the face of a clear constitutional command.[b]

* * *

Rochin was suspected of selling narcotics. When the police burst into his room, he swallowed two capsules. He was then handcuffed and taken to a hospital where, at the direction of the police, "a doctor forced an emetic solution through a tube into Rochin's stomach against his will." This "stomach pumping" produced vomiting—and two capsules that proved to contain morphine. The Court, per Frankfurter, J., ruled that the morphine should have been excluded from evidence because the methods used by the police to obtain it violated Fourteenth Amendment Due Process:

"This is conduct that shocks the conscience. * * * [T]his course of proceeding by agents of government to obtain evidence is bound to offend even hardened sensibilities. They are methods too close to the rack and the screw to permit of constitutional differentiation."

Concurring Justice Black criticized the "nebulous" and "accordion-like" quality of the majority's approach and maintained that "faithful adherence to the specific guarantees in the Bill of Rights ensures a more permanent protection of individual liberty." In a separate concurring opinion, Justice Douglas also criticized the majority's approach: "[W]e cannot in fairness free the state courts from [the specific restraints of the Fifth Amendment privilege against self-incrimination] and yet excoriate them for flouting the 'decencies of civilized conduct' when they admit the evidence. This is to make the rule turn not on the Constitution but on the idiosyncracies of the judges who sit here."

The "conduct that shocks the conscience" test did not prevent the admission of the evidence in *Irvine v. California*, 347 U.S. 128 (1954), despite the fact that "few police measures have come to [the Court's] attention that more flagrantly, deliberately, and persistently violated the fundamental principle declared by the Fourth Amendment." In *Irvine* the police had surreptitiously entered the home of a suspected bookmaker, installed a concealed microphone in a bedroom, and listened to the conversations of the occupants for over a month.

Because of the "aggravating" and "repulsive" police misconduct in *Irvine,* dissenting Justice Frankfurter insisted that *Rochin* was controlling. But Justice Jackson, who announced the judgment of the Court and wrote the principal opinion, responded: "However obnoxious are the facts in the case before us, they do not involve coercion, violence or brutality to the person [as did *Rochin*], but rather a trespass to property, plus eavesdropping."

According to some commentators, the demonstrated incapacity of the *Rochin* test to deal with the problem of egregious police misconduct was a major reason the Court overruled *Wolf v. Colorado,* 338 U.S. 25 (1949), and held in *Mapp v. Ohio,* 367 U.S. 643 (1961), that the federal exclusionary rule in search and seizure cases was binding on the states via the Due Process Clause of the Fourteenth Amendment. See generally Ch. 3.

b. The position taken in *Twining* and *Adamson*—that the Fifth Amendment privilege against self-incrimination was not incorporated in the Fourteenth—was rejected in *Malloy v. Hogan* (1964), discussed in Ch. 6, § 3. *Griffin v. California,* 380 U.S. 609 (1965), then applied *Malloy* to overrule the specific holdings of *Twining* and *Adamson,* which had permitted comment on a state defendant's failure to take the stand.

SECTION 2.   THE MODERN APPROACH: THE SHIFT TO "SELECTIVE INCORPORATION"

Although the Court has remained unwilling to accept the total incorporationists' reading of the Fourteenth Amendment, in the 1960's it "selectively" "incorporated" or "absorbed" more and more of the specific provisions of the Bill of Rights into the Fourteenth Amendment. "Selective incorporation" combines aspects of both the "fundamental rights" and "total incorporation" approaches. It accepts the basic premise of the fundamental rights proponents that the Fourteenth Amendment encompasses only rights that are "of the very essence of the scheme of ordered liberty." It also recognizes that not all rights enumerated in the Bill of Rights are necessarily fundamental and that other rights may be fundamental even though not found in the first eight Amendments. But the "selective incorporation" approach rejects the fundamental rights interpretation insofar as that view emphasizes the "totality of the circumstances" in the particular case.

In determining whether an enumerated right is "fundamental," therefore, the selective incorporation doctrine requires that the Court look at the total right guaranteed by the particular Bill of Rights provision, not merely at a single aspect of that right nor the application of that aspect in the case before it. If a particular guarantee is determined to be "fundamental," that provision is incorporated into the Fourteenth Amendment and applied to the states *to the same extent* that it applies to the federal government—or, as critics of this approach expressed it, applied "jot-for-jot and case-for-case" (Harlan, J., joined by Stewart, J., concurring in *Duncan v. Louisiana,* infra); "bag and baggage, however securely or insecurely affixed they may be by law and precedent to federal proceedings" (Fortas, J., concurring in *Duncan*).

Although strongly criticized as an artificial compromise between the fundamental rights and total incorporation approaches, and lacking even the "internal consistency" of the total incorporation view of the Fourteenth Amendment (Harlan, J., dissenting in *Duncan*), selective incorporation gained the ascendancy in the 1960's. The adoption of this position was accompanied by a movement towards a broader view of the nature of "fundamental procedural rights."

As Justice White pointed out for the Court in *Duncan,* the question asked was no longer whether the procedural safeguard at issue was "of the very essence of a scheme of ordered liberty" or required by "the 'immutable principles of justice' as conceived by a civilized society" or whether "a civilized system could be imagined" without it. Instead, the Court inquired whether the procedural safeguard in question was "fundamental to the American scheme of justice" or "necessary" or "fundamental" "in the context of the criminal process maintained by the American states."

By the time *Duncan* reached the Court the following Bill of Rights guarantees had been "selectively incorporated" (and thus held enforceable against the states according to the same standards that protect these rights against federal encroachment):

> the freedom from unreasonable searches and seizures and the right to have excluded from criminal trials any evidence obtained in violation thereof, *Mapp v. Ohio,* (1961) (set forth in Ch. 3) and *Ker v. California,* 374 U.S. 23 (1963);

the prohibition against cruel and unusual punishment, *Robinson v. California,* 370 U.S. 660 (1962);

the right to the assistance of counsel, *Gideon v. Wainwright,* (1963) (set forth in Ch. 5);

the privilege against compelled self-incrimination, *Malloy v. Hogan,* 378 U.S. 1 (1964);

the right to confront opposing witnesses, *Pointer v. Texas,* 380 U.S. 400 (1965);

the right to a speedy trial, *Klopfer v. North Carolina,* 386 U.S. 213 (1967); and

the right to compulsory process for obtaining witnesses, *Washington v. Texas,* 388 U.S. 14 (1967).[a]

These developments did not escape Justice Black. Concurring in *Duncan,* he reaffirmed his belief in the "total incorporation" theory, but expressed his willingness to support the "selective incorporation" doctrine "as an alternative": "[I]t keeps judges from roaming at will in their own notions of what policies outside the Bill of Rights are desirable and what are not. And, most importantly for me, the selective incorporation process has the virtue of having already worked to make most of the Bill of Rights protections applicable to the States."

DUNCAN v. LOUISIANA

391 U.S. 145, 88 S.Ct. 1444, 20 L.Ed.2d 491 (1968).

JUSTICE WHITE delivered the opinion of the Court.

[Appellant] was convicted of simple battery [which under Louisiana law] is a misdemeanor, punishable by two years' imprisonment and a $300 fine. Appellant sought trial by jury, but because the Louisiana Constitution grants jury trials only in cases in which capital punishment or imprisonment at hard labor may be imposed, the trial judge denied the request. Appellant was convicted and sentenced to serve 60 days in the parish prison and pay a fine of $150.

* * * Because we believe that trial by jury in criminal cases is fundamental to the American scheme of justice, we hold that the Fourteenth Amendment guarantees a right of jury trial in all criminal cases which—were they to be tried in a federal court—would come within the Sixth Amendment's guarantee.[14] Since we

a. In addition, *Duncan,* infra, held the right to jury trial applicable to the states and, a year later, *Benton v. Maryland,* 395 U.S. 784 (1969) made the prohibition against double jeopardy binding on the states. The only guarantees addressed specifically to criminal procedure not held applicable to the states are the Eighth Amendment prohibition against excessive bail and the Fifth Amendment requirement of prosecution of infamous crimes by grand jury indictment. The Supreme Court has not yet ruled directly on the bail clause, but the Court's characterization of that clause is *Schilb v. Kuebel,* 404 U.S. 357 (1971), suggests that it would qualify for protection under the Fourteenth Amendment Due Process Clause, too, if the issue were squarely presented. Still on the books, however, is *Hurtado v. California,* 110 U.S. 516 (1884), declining to apply to the states the indictment by grand jury requirement. That decision continues to be followed as valid precedent and appears unlikely to be overruled. See Ch. 11.

14. In one sense recent cases applying provisions of the first eight amendments to the States represent a new approach to the "incorporation" debate. Earlier the Court can be seen as having asked, when inquiring into whether some particular procedural safeguard was required of a State, if a civilized system could be imagined that would not accord the particular protection. [The] recent cases, on the other hand, have proceeded upon the valid assumption that state criminal processes are not imaginary and theoretical schemes but actual systems bearing virtually every characteristic of the common-law system that has been developing contemporaneously in England and in this country. The question thus is whether consider the appeal before us to be such a case, we hold that the Constitution was violated when appellant's demand for jury trial was refused.

[B]y the time our Constitution was written, jury trial in criminal cases had been in existence in England for several centuries and carried impressive credentials traced by many to Magna Carta. Its preservation and proper operation as a protection against arbitrary rule were among the major objectives of the revolutionary settlement which was expressed in the Declaration and Bill of Rights of 1689. * * *

Jury trial came to America with English colonists, and received strong support from them. Royal interference with the jury trial was deeply resented. Among the resolutions adopted by the First Congress of the American Colonies (the Stamp Act Congress) on October 19, 1765—resolutions deemed by their authors to state "the most essential rights and liberties of the colonists"—was the declaration: "That trial by jury is the inherent and invaluable right of every British subject in these colonies."

[The] constitutions adopted by the original States guaranteed jury trial. Also, the constitution of every State entering the Union thereafter in one form or another protected the right to jury trial in criminal cases. * * *

Jury trial continues to receive strong support. The laws of every State guarantee a right to jury trial in serious criminal cases; no State has dispensed with it; nor are there significant movements underway to do so. * * *

We are aware of prior cases in this Court in which the prevailing opinion contains statements contrary to our holding today that the right to jury trial in serious criminal cases is a fundamental right and hence must be recognized by the States as part of their obligation to extend due process of law to all persons within their jurisdiction. Louisiana relies especially on *Maxwell v. Dow*; *Palko;* and *Snyder v. Massachusetts,* 291 U.S. 97 (1934). None of these cases, however, dealt with a State which had purported to dispense entirely with a jury trial in serious criminal cases. * * *

The guarantees of jury trial in the Federal and State Constitutions reflect a profound judgment about the way in which law should be enforced and justice administered. A right to jury trial is granted to criminal defendants in order to prevent oppression by the Government. Those who wrote our constitutions knew

given this kind of system a particular procedure is fundamental—whether, that is, a procedure is necessary to an Anglo–American regime of ordered liberty. [Of] immediate relevance for this case are the Court's holdings that the States must comply with certain provisions of the Sixth Amendment, specifically that the States may not refuse a speedy trial, confrontation of witnesses, and the assistance, at state expense if necessary, of counsel. Of each of these determinations that a constitutional provision originally written to bind the Federal Government should bind the States as well it might be said that the limitation in question is not necessarily fundamental to fairness in every criminal system that might be imagined but is fundamental in the context of the criminal processes maintained by the American States.

When the inquiry is approached in this way the question whether the States can impose criminal punishment without granting a jury trial appears quite different from the way it appeared in the older cases opining that States might abolish jury trial. See, e.g., *Maxwell v. Dow,* 176 U.S. 581 (1900). A criminal process which was fair and equitable but used no juries is easy to imagine. It would make use of alternative guarantees and protections which would serve the purposes that the jury serves in the English and American systems. Yet no American State has undertaken to construct such a system. Instead, every American State, including Louisiana, uses the jury extensively, and imposes very serious punishments only after a trial at which the defendant has a right to a jury's verdict. In every State, including Louisiana, the structure and style of the criminal process—the supporting framework and the subsidiary procedures—are of the sort that naturally complement jury trial, and have developed in connection with and in reliance upon jury trial.

from history and experience that it was necessary to protect against unfounded criminal charges brought to eliminate enemies and against judges too responsive to the voice of higher authority. The framers of the constitutions strove to create an independent judiciary but insisted upon further protection against arbitrary action. Providing an accused with the right to be tried by a jury of his peers gave him an inestimable safeguard against the corrupt or overzealous prosecutor and against the compliant, biased, or eccentric judge. If the defendant preferred the commonsense judgment of a jury to the more tutored but perhaps less sympathetic reaction of the single judge, he was to have it. Beyond this, the jury trial provisions in the Federal and State Constitutions reflect a fundamental decision about the exercise of official power—a reluctance to entrust plenary powers over the life and liberty of the citizen to one judge or to a group of judges. Fear of unchecked power, so typical of our State and Federal Governments in other respects, found expression in the criminal law in this insistence upon community participation in the determination of guilt or innocence. The deep commitment of the Nation to the right of jury trial in serious criminal cases as a defense against arbitrary law enforcement qualifies for protection under the Due Process Clause of the Fourteenth Amendment, and must therefore be respected by the States.

Of course jury trial has "its weaknesses and the potential for misuse." We are aware of the long debate, especially in this century, among those who write about the administration of justice, as to the wisdom of permitting untrained laymen to determine the facts in civil and criminal proceedings. Although the debate has been intense, with powerful voices on either side, most of the controversy has centered on the jury in civil cases. Indeed, some of the severest critics of civil juries acknowledge that the arguments for criminal juries are much stronger. In addition, at the heart of the dispute have been express or implicit assertions that juries are incapable of adequately understanding evidence or determining issues of fact, and that they are unpredictable, quixotic, and little better than a roll of dice. Yet, the most recent and exhaustive study of the jury in criminal cases concluded that juries do understand the evidence and come to sound conclusions in most of the cases presented to them and that when juries differ with the result at which the judge would have arrived, it is usually because they are serving some of the very purposes for which they were created and for which they are now employed.

The State of Louisiana urges that holding that the Fourteenth Amendment assures a right to jury trial will cast doubt on the integrity of every trial conducted without a jury. Plainly, this is not the import of our holding. * * *

We would not assert [that] every criminal trial—or any particular trial—held before a judge alone is unfair or that a defendant may never be as fairly treated by a judge as he would be by a jury. Thus we hold no constitutional doubts about the practices, common in both federal and state courts, of accepting waivers of jury trial and prosecuting petty crimes without extending a right to jury trial. However, the fact is that in most places more trials for serious crimes are to juries than to a court alone; a great many defendants prefer the judgment of a jury to that of a court. Even where defendants are satisfied with bench trials, the right to a jury trial very likely serves its intended purpose of making judicial or prosecutorial unfairness less likely.

Louisiana's final contention is that even if it must grant jury trials in serious criminal cases, the conviction before us is valid and constitutional because here the petitioner was tried for simple battery and was sentenced to only 60 days in the parish prison. We are not persuaded. It is doubtless true that there is a category of petty crimes or offenses which is not subject to the Sixth Amendment jury trial provision and should not be subject to the Fourteenth Amendment jury trial requirement here applied to the States. [But] the penalty authorized for a particular crime is of major relevance in determining whether it is serious or not and may in itself, if severe enough, subject the trial to the mandates of the Sixth Amendment. [In] the case before us the Legislature of Louisiana has made simple battery a criminal offense punishable by imprisonment for two years and a fine. The question, then is whether a crime carrying such a penalty is an offense which Louisiana may insist on trying without a jury. * * *

In determining whether the length of the authorized prison term or the seriousness of other punishment is enough in itself to require a jury trial, we are counseled [by precedent] to refer to objective criteria, chiefly the existing laws and practices in the Nation. In the federal system, petty offenses are defined as those punishable by no more than six months in prison and a $500 fine. In 49 of the 50 States crimes subject to trial without a jury, which occasionally include simple battery, are punishable by no more than one year in jail. Moreover, in the late 18th century in America crimes triable without a jury were for the most part punishable by no more than a six-month prison term * * *. We need not, however, settle in this case the exact location of the line between petty offenses and serious crimes. It is sufficient for our purposes to hold that a crime punishable by two years in prison is, based on past and contemporary standards in this country, a serious crime and not a petty offense. Consequently, appellant was entitled to a jury trial and it was error to deny it. * * *

JUSTICE BLACK, with whom JUSTICE DOUGLAS joins, concurring.

* * * I said in *Adamson* that while I would "extend to all the people of the nation the complete protection of the Bill of Rights," that "[i]f the choice must be between the selective process of the *Palko* decision applying some of the Bill of Rights to the States, or the *Twining* rule applying none of them, I would choose the *Palko* selective process." And I am very happy to support this selective process through which our Court has since the *Adamson* case held most of the specific Bill of Rights' protections applicable to the States to the same extent they are applicable to the Federal Government. * * *

All of these holdings making Bill of Rights' provisions applicable as such to the States mark, of course, a departure from the *Twining* doctrine holding that none of those provisions were enforceable as such against the States. The dissent in this case, however, makes a spirited and forceful defense of that now discredited doctrine.

[In] addition to the adoption of Professor Fairman's "history," the dissent states that "the great words of the four clauses of the first section of the Fourteenth Amendment would have been an exceedingly peculiar way to say that 'The rights heretofore guaranteed against federal intrusion by the first eight amendments are henceforth guaranteed against State intrusion as well.'" In response to this I can say only that the words "No State shall make or enforce any law which shall abridge the privileges or immunities of citizens of the United States" seems to me an eminently reasonable way of expressing the idea that henceforth the Bill of Rights shall apply to the States.[1] What more precious "privilege" of American citizenship could there be than that privilege to claim the protections of our great Bill of Rights? * * *

While I do not wish at this time to discuss at length my disagreement with Brother Harlan's forthright and frank restatement of the now discredited *Twin-*

---

1. My view has been and is that the Fourteenth Amendment, *as a whole,* makes the Bill of Rights applicable to the States. This would certainly include the language of the Privileges and Immunities Clause, as well as the Due Process Clause.

ing doctrine, I do want to point out what appears to me to be the basic difference between us. His view, as was indeed the view of *Twining,* is that "due process is an evolving concept" and therefore that it entails a "gradual process of judicial inclusion and exclusion" to ascertain those "immutable principles [of] free government which no member of the Union may disregard." Thus the Due Process Clause is treated as prescribing no specific and clearly ascertainable constitutional command that judges must obey in interpreting the Constitution, but rather as leaving judges free to decide at any particular time whether a particular rule or judicial formulation embodies an "immutable principl[e] of free government" or is "implicit in the concept of ordered liberty," or whether certain conduct "shocks the judge's conscience" or runs counter to some other similar, undefined and undefinable standard.[a] Thus due process, according to my Brother Harlan, is to be a phrase with no permanent meaning, but one which is found to shift from time to time in accordance with judges' predilections and understandings of what is best for the country. If due process means this, the Fourteenth Amendment, in my opinion, might as well have been written that "no person shall be deprived of life, liberty or property except by laws that the judges of the United States Supreme Court shall find to be consistent with the immutable principles of free government." It is impossible for me to believe that such unconfined power is given to judges in our Constitution that is a written one in order to limit governmental power.

Another tenet of the *Twining* doctrine as restated by my Brother Harlan is that "due process of law requires only fundamental fairness." But the "fundamental fairness" test is one on a par with that of shocking the conscience of the Court. Each of such tests depends entirely on the particular judge's idea of ethics and morals instead of requiring him to depend on the boundaries fixed by the written words of the Constitution. Nothing in the history of the phrase "due process of law" suggests that constitutional controls are to depend on any particular judge's sense of values. * * *

Finally I want to add that I am not bothered by the argument that applying the Bill of Rights to the States "according to the same standards that protect those rights against federal encroachment," interferes with our concept of federalism in that it may prevent States from trying novel social and economic experiments. I have never believed that under the guise of federalism the States should be able to experiment with the protections afforded our citizens through the Bill of Rights. [It] seems to me totally inconsistent to advocate on the one hand, the power of this Court to strike down any state law or practice which it finds "unreasonable" or "unfair," and on the other hand urge that the States be given maximum power to develop their own laws and procedures. Yet the due process approach of my Brothers Harlan and Fortas (see other concurring opinion) does just that since in effect it restricts the States to practices which a majority of this Court is willing to approve on a case-by-case basis. No one is more concerned than I that the States be allowed to use the full scope of their powers as their citizens see fit. And that is why I have continually fought against the expansion of this Court's authority over the States through the use of a broad, general interpretation of due process that permits judges to strike down state laws they do not like.

In closing I want to emphasize that I believe as strongly as ever that the Fourteenth Amendment was intended to make the Bill of Rights applicable to the States. I have been willing to support the selective incorporation doctrine,

a. Although Justice Black cites no case at this point, this appears to be a reference to the famous "stomach-pumping" case of *Rochin v.* *California,* discussed in *Adamson* supra at note a.

however, as an alternative, although perhaps less historically supportable than complete incorporation. The selective incorporation process, if used properly, does limit the Supreme Court in the Fourteenth Amendment field to specific Bill of Rights' protections only and keeps judges from roaming at will in their own notions of what policies outside the Bill of Rights are desirable and what are not. And, most importantly for me, the selective incorporation process has the virtue of having already worked to make most of the Bill of Rights' protections applicable to the States.

Justice Fortas, concurring * * *

[A]lthough I agree with the decision of the Court, I cannot agree [that] the tail must go with the hide: that when we hold, influenced by the Sixth Amendment, that "due process" requires that the States accord the right of jury trial for all but petty offenses, we automatically import all of the ancillary rules which have been or may hereafter be developed incidental to the right to jury trial in the federal courts. I see no reason whatever, for example, to assume that our decision today should require us to impose federal requirements such as unanimous verdicts or a jury of 12 upon the States. We may well conclude that these and other features of federal jury practice are by no means fundamental—that they are not essential to due process of law—and that they are not obligatory on the States.

I would make these points clear today. Neither logic nor history nor the intent of the draftsmen of the Fourteenth Amendment can possibly be said to require that the Sixth Amendment or its jury trial provision be applied to the States together with the total gloss that this Court's decisions have supplied. The draftsmen of the Fourteenth Amendment intended what they said, not more or less: that no State shall deprive any person of life, liberty, or property without due process of law. It is ultimately the duty of this Court to interpret, to ascribe specific meaning to this phrase. There is no reason whatever for us to conclude that, in so doing, we are bound slavishly to follow not only the Sixth Amendment but all of its bag and baggage, however securely or insecurely affixed they may be by law and precedent to federal proceedings. To take this course, in my judgment, would be not only unnecessary but mischievous because it would inflict a serious blow upon the principle of federalism. The Due Process Clause commands us to apply its great standard to state court proceedings to assure basic fairness. It does not command us rigidly and arbitrarily to impose the exact pattern of federal proceedings upon the 50 States. On the contrary, the Constitution's command, in my view, is that in our insistence upon state observance of due process, we should, so far as possible, allow the greatest latitude for state differences. It requires, within the limits of the lofty basic standards that it prescribes for the States as well as the Federal Government, maximum opportunity for diversity and minimal imposition of uniformity of method and detail upon the States. Our Constitution sets up a federal union, not a monolith.

This Court has heretofore held that various provisions of the Bill of Rights such as the freedom of speech and religion guarantees of the First Amendment, the prohibition of unreasonable searches and seizures in the Fourth Amendment, the privilege against self-incrimination of the Fifth Amendment, and the right to counsel and to confrontation under the Sixth Amendment "are all to be enforced against the States under the Fourteenth Amendment according to the same standards that protect those rights against federal encroachment." I need not quarrel with the specific conclusion in those specific instances. But unless one adheres slavishly to the incorporation theory, body and substance, the same conclusion need not be superimposed upon the jury trial right. I respectfully but urgently suggest that it should not be. Jury trial is more than a principle of justice applicable to individual cases. It is a system of administration of the business of the State. * * * We should be ready to welcome state variations which do not impair—indeed, which may advance—the theory and purpose of trial by jury.

JUSTICE HARLAN, whom JUSTICE STEWART joins, dissenting.

Every American jurisdiction provides for trial by jury in criminal cases. The question before us is not whether jury trial is an ancient institution, which it is; nor whether it plays a significant role in the administration of criminal justice, which it does; nor whether it will endure, which it shall. The question in this case is whether the State of Louisiana, which provides trial by jury for all felonies, is prohibited by the Constitution from trying charges of simple battery to the court alone. In my view, the answer to that question, mandated alike by our constitutional history and by the longer history of trial by jury, is clearly "no." * * *

The Court's approach to this case is an uneasy and illogical compromise among the views of various Justices on how the Due Process Clause should be interpreted. The Court does not say that those who framed the Fourteenth Amendment intended to make the Sixth Amendment applicable to the States. And the Court concedes that it finds nothing unfair about the procedure by which the present appellant was tried. Nevertheless, the Court reverses his conviction: it holds, for some reason not apparent to me, that the Due Process Clause incorporates the particular clause of the Sixth Amendment that requires trial by jury in federal criminal cases—including, as I read its opinion, the sometimes trivial accompanying baggage of judicial interpretation in federal contexts. * * *

A few members of the Court have taken the position that the intention of those who drafted the first section of the Fourteenth Amendment was simply, and exclusively, to make the provisions of the first eight amendments applicable to state action. This view has never been accepted by this Court. In my view [the] first section of the Fourteenth Amendment was meant neither to incorporate, nor to be limited to, the specific guarantees of the first eight amendments. The overwhelming historical evidence marshalled by Professor Fairman demonstrates, to me conclusively, that the Congressmen and state legislators who wrote, debated, and ratified the Fourteenth Amendment did not think they were "incorporating" the Bill of Rights and the very breadth and generality of the Amendment's provisions suggests that its authors did not suppose that the Nation would always be limited to mid–19th century conceptions of "liberty" and "due process of law" but that the increasing experience and evolving conscience of the American people would add new "intermediate premises." In short, neither history, nor sense, supports using the Fourteenth Amendment to put the States in a constitutional straitjacket with respect to their own development in the administration of criminal or civil law.

Although I therefore fundamentally disagree with the total incorporation view of the Fourteenth Amendment, it seems to me that such a position does at least have the virtue, lacking in the Court's selective incorporation approach, of internal consistency: we look to the Bill of Rights, word for word, clause for clause, precedent for precedent because, it is said, the men who wrote the Amendment wanted it that way. For those who do not accept this "history," a different source of "intermediate premises" must be found. The Bill of Rights is not necessarily irrelevant to the search for guidance in interpreting the Fourteenth Amendment, but the reason for and the nature of its relevance must be articulated.

Apart from the approach taken by the absolute incorporationists, I can see only one method of analysis that has any internal logic. That is to start with the words "liberty" and "due process of law" and attempt to define them in a way that accords with American traditions and our system of government. This approach, involving a much more discriminating process of adjudication than does "incorporation," is, albeit difficult, the one that was followed throughout the Nineteenth and most of the present century. It entails a "gradual process of judicial inclusion and exclusion," seeking, with due recognition of constitutional tolerance for state experimentation and disparity, to ascertain those "immutable principles of justice which inhere in the very idea of free government which no member of the Union may disregard." * * *

The relationship of the Bill of Rights to this "gradual process" seems to me to be twofold. In the first place it has long been clear that the Due Process Clause imposes some restrictions on state action that parallel Bill of Rights restrictions on federal action. Second, and more important than this accidental overlap, is the fact that the Bill of Rights is evidence, at various points, of the content Americans find in the term "liberty" and of American standards of fundamental fairness.

[In *Gideon v. Wainwright* (1963), set forth in Ch. 5, and other cases], the right guaranteed against the States by the Fourteenth Amendment was one that had also been guaranteed against the Federal Government by one of the first eight amendments. The logically critical thing, however, was not that the rights had been found in the Bill of Rights, but that they were deemed, in the context of American legal history, to be fundamental. * * *

Today's Court still remains unwilling to accept the total incorporationists' view of the history of the Fourteenth Amendment. This, if accepted, would afford a cogent reason for applying the Sixth Amendment to the States. The Court is also, apparently, unwilling to face the task of determining whether denial of trial by jury in the situation before us, or in other situations, is fundamentally unfair. Consequently, the Court has compromised on the ease of the incorporationist position, without its internal logic. It has simply assumed that the question before us is whether the Jury Trial Clause of the Sixth Amendment should be incorporated into the Fourteenth, jot-for-jot and case-for-case, or ignored. Then the Court merely declares that the clause in question is "in" rather than "out."

The Court has justified neither its starting place nor its conclusion. If the problem is to discover and articulate the rules of fundamental fairness in criminal proceedings, there is no reason to assume that the whole body of rules developed in this Court constituting Sixth Amendment jury trial must be regarded as a unit. The requirement of trial by jury in federal criminal cases has given rise to numerous subsidiary questions respecting the exact scope and content of the right. It surely cannot be that every answer the Court has given, or will give, to such a question is attributable to the Founders; or even that every rule announced carries equal conviction of this Court; still less can it be that every such subprinciple is equally fundamental to ordered liberty.[18]

Examples abound. I should suppose it obviously fundamental to fairness that a "jury" means an "impartial jury." I should think it equally obvious that the

---

18. The same illogical way of dealing with a Fourteenth Amendment problem was employed in *Malloy v. Hogan* [discussed in Ch. 5, § 3], which held that the Due Process Clause guaranteed the protection of the Self-Incrimination Clause of the Fifth Amendment against state action. I disagreed at that time both with the way the question was framed and with the result the Court reached. I consider myself bound by the Court's holding in *Malloy* with respect to self-incrimination. I do not think that *Malloy* held, nor would I consider myself bound by a holding, that every question arising under the Due Process Clause shall be settled by an arbitrary decision whether a clause in the Bill of Rights is "in" or "out."

rule, imposed long ago in the federal courts, that "jury" means "jury of exactly twelve," is not fundamental to anything: there is no significance except to mystics in the number 12. Again, trial by jury has been held to require a unanimous verdict of jurors in the federal courts, although unanimity has not been found essential to liberty in Britain, where the requirement has been abandoned. * * *

Even if I could agree that the question before us is whether Sixth Amendment jury trial is totally "in" or totally "out," I can find in the Court's opinion no real reasons for concluding that it should be "in." The basis for differentiating among clauses in the Bill of Rights cannot be that only some clauses are in the Bill of Rights, or that only some are old and much praised, or that only some have played an important role in the development of federal law. These things are true of all. The Court says that some clauses are more "fundamental" than others, but it turns out to be using this word in a sense that would have astonished Mr. Justice Cardozo and which, in addition, is of no help. The word does not mean "analytically critical to procedural fairness" for no real analysis of the role of the jury in making procedures fair is even attempted. Instead, the word turns out to mean "old," "much praised," and "found in the Bill of Rights." The definition of "fundamental" thus turns out to be circular.

Since, as I see it, the Court has not even come to grips with the issues in this case, it is necessary to start from the beginning. When a criminal defendant contends that his state conviction lacked "due process of law," the question before this Court, in my view, is whether he was denied any element of fundamental procedural fairness. Believing, as I do, that due process is an evolving concept and that old principles are subject to re-evaluation in light of later experience, I think it appropriate to deal on its merits with the question whether Louisiana denied appellant due process of law when it tried him for simple assault without a jury. * * *

The argument that jury trial is not a requisite of due process is quite simple. The central proposition of *Palko,* a proposition to which I would adhere, is that "due process of law" requires only that criminal trials be fundamentally fair. [A]part from the theory that it was historically intended as a mere shorthand for the Bill of Rights, I do not see what else "due process of law" can intelligibly be thought to mean. If due process of law requires only fundamental fairness, then the inquiry in each case must be whether a state trial process was a fair one. The Court has held, properly I think, that in an adversary process it is a requisite of fairness, for which there is no adequate substitute, that a criminal defendant be afforded a right to counsel and to cross-examine opposing witnesses. But it simply has not been demonstrated, nor, I think, can it be demonstrated, that trial by jury is the only fair means of resolving issues of fact.

The jury is of course not without virtues. It affords ordinary citizens a valuable opportunity to participate in a process of government, an experience fostering, one hopes, a respect for law. It eases the burden on judges by enabling them to share a part of their sometimes awesome responsibility. A jury may, at times, afford a higher justice by refusing to enforce harsh laws (although it necessarily does so haphazardly, raising the questions whether arbitrary enforcement of harsh laws is better than total enforcement, and whether the jury system is to be defended on the ground that jurors sometimes disobey their oaths). And the jury may, or may not, contribute desirably to the willingness of the general public to accept criminal judgments as just.

It can hardly be gainsaid, however, that the principal original virtue of the jury trial—the limitations a jury imposes on a tyrannous judiciary—has largely disappeared. We no longer live in a medieval or colonial society. Judges enforce laws enacted by democratic decision, not by regal fiat. They are elected by the people or appointed by the people's elected officials, and are responsible not to a distant monarch alone but to reviewing courts, including this one.

The jury system can also be said to have some inherent defects, which are multiplied by the emergence of the criminal law from the relative simplicity that existed when the jury system was devised. It is a cumbersome process, not only imposing great cost in time and money on both the State and the jurors themselves, but also contributing to delay in the machinery of justice. Untrained jurors are presumably less adept at reaching accurate conclusions of fact than judges, particularly if the issues are many or complex. And it is argued by some that trial by jury, far from increasing public respect for law, impairs it: the average man, it is said, reacts favorably neither to the notion that matters he knows to be complex are being decided by other average men, nor to the way the jury system distorts the process of adjudication.

That trial by jury is not the only fair way of adjudicating criminal guilt is well attested by the fact that it is not the prevailing way, either in England or in this country. * * *

In the United States, where it has not been as generally assumed that jury waiver is permissible, the statistics are only slightly less revealing. Two experts have estimated that, of all prosecutions for crimes triable to a jury, 75% are settled by guilty plea and 40% of the remainder are tried to the court. In one State, Maryland, which has always provided for waiver, the rate of court trial appears in some years to have reached 90%. The Court recognizes the force of these statistics in stating, "We would not assert, however, that every criminal trial—or any particular trial—held before a judge alone is unfair or that a defendant may never be as fairly treated by a judge as he would be by a jury." I agree. I therefore see no reason why this Court should reverse the conviction of appellant, absent any suggestion that his particular trial was in fact unfair, or compel the State of Louisiana to afford jury trial in an as yet unbounded category of cases that can, without unfairness, be tried to a court.

Indeed, even if I were persuaded that trial by jury is a fundamental right in some criminal cases, I could see nothing fundamental in the rule, not yet formulated by the Court, that places the prosecution of appellant for simple battery within the category of "jury crimes" rather than "petty crimes."

[The] point is not that many offenses that English-speaking communities have, at one time or another, regarded as triable without a jury are more serious, and carry more serious penalties, than the one involved here. The point is rather that until today few people would have thought the exact location of the line mattered very much. There is no obvious reason why a jury trial is a requisite of fundamental fairness when the charge is robbery, and not a requisite of fairness when the same defendant, for the same actions, is charged with assault and petit theft. The reason for the historic exception for relatively minor crimes is the obvious one: the burden of jury trial was thought to outweigh its marginal advantages. Exactly why the States should not be allowed to make continuing adjustments, based on the state of their criminal dockets and the difficulty of summoning jurors, simply escapes me.

In sum, there is a wide range of views on the desirability of trial by jury, and on the ways to make it most effective when it is used; there is also considerable variation from State to State in local conditions such as the size of the criminal caseload, the ease or difficulty of summoning jurors, and other trial conditions bearing on fairness. We have before us, therefore, an almost perfect example of a situation in which the celebrated dictum of Mr. Justice Brandeis should be invoked. It is, he said, "one of the happy incidents of the federal system that a single courageous state may, if its citizens choose, serve as a laboratory * * *." *New State Ice Co. v. Liebmann,* 285 U.S. 262 (1932) (dissenting opinion). This Court, other courts, and the political process are available to correct any experiments in criminal procedure that prove fundamentally unfair to defendants. That is not what is being done today: instead, and quite without reason, the Court has chosen to impose upon every State one means of trying criminal cases; it is a good means, but it is not the only fair means, and it is not demonstrably better than the alternatives States might devise. * * * b

b. Post–*Duncan* jury trial cases arguably seemed to confirm Justice Harlan's warning that "selective incorporation" might lead to *dilution in federal cases* of Bill of Rights "specifics." In *Williams v. Florida,* 399 U.S. 78 (1970), the Court reconsidered the scope of the right to jury trial, concluded that the fact "that [the] jury at common law was composed of precisely 12 is an historical accident, unnecessary to effect the purposes of the jury system," and concluded that the Sixth Amendment permitted six-person juries in state *or federal* noncapital felony cases. Concurring in the result, Justice Harlan charged that "before today it would have been unthinkable to suggest that the Sixth Amendment's right to a trial by jury is satisfied by a jury of six, or less, as is left open, [or] by less than a unanimous verdict, a question also reserved in today's decision."

The issues left open in *Duncan*—whether the jury could be less than 6 and whether a verdict could be less than unanimous—were decided in cases discussed in Chapter 15, § 1. One of those cases, *Apodaca v. Oregon,* 406 U.S. 404 (1972), produced a result inconsistent with *Duncan*'s selective incorporation analysis although a clear majority favored that analysis. In *Apodaca,* eight members of the Court—all but newly appointed Justice Powell—adhered to the *Duncan* approach that each element of

the Sixth Amendment Jury Trial Clause applies to the states to the same extent it applies to the federal government, but these eight Justices split 4–4 over whether the Sixth Amendment *did require* unanimity in federal criminal cases. The deadlock was broken by Justice Powell, but broken *in two different directions.* He read the Sixth Amendment to require unanimity *in federal cases,* but concluded that *this feature* of the Jury Trial Clause is not "so fundamental to the essentials of jury trial" as to require unanimity in state cases as a matter of Fourteenth Amendment Due Process. Justice Powell reached these positions by adopting a Harlan-type approach to Fourteenth Amendment Due Process: "Although it is perhaps late in the day for an expression of my views, I [believe] that, at least in defining the elements of the right to jury trial, there is no sound basis for interpreting the Fourteenth Amendment to require blind adherence by the States to all details of the federal Sixth Amendment standards." Thus, *Apodaca* produced an 8–1 majority reaffirming the view that the Jury Trial Clause is to be enforced against the states to the same extent it applies to the federal government, a 5–4 majority that would hold that the Sixth Amendment does require a unanimous verdict in federal criminal trials, and a 5–4 majority that upheld a less than unanimous verdict (10–2) in a state case.

Chapter 3

ARREST, SEARCH AND SEIZURE

SECTION 1. THE EXCLUSIONARY RULE

The Fourth Amendment to the United States Constitution reads: "The right of the people to be secure in their persons, houses, papers, and effects, against unreasonable searches and seizures, shall not be violated, and no Warrants shall issue, but upon probable cause, supported by Oath or affirmation, and particularly describing the place to be searched, and the persons or things to be seized." The Amendment says nothing about how it is to be enforced, a matter which has been the subject of vigorous debate for a good many years. Most of this debate has focused upon the wisdom of and constitutional necessity for the so-called exclusionary rule, whereunder evidence obtained in violation of the Fourth Amendment is ordinarily inadmissible in a criminal trial. This exclusionary rule has existed in the federal criminal justice system for nearly 75 years, but has been mandated at the state level not nearly as long. In the first two cases in this section, *Wolf v. Colorado* and *Mapp v. Ohio,* we see the Court first rejecting and then accepting the notion that this exclusionary rule is constitutionally required in the state courts.

Mapp by no means ended the argument, though in more recent years much of the debate has centered upon the proper scope of the exclusionary rule. If, as the Supreme Court often indicated, a primary purpose of the rule is deterrence of the police, then precisely when is exclusion appropriate in the sense that it will likely have such a deterrent effect? The Court gives some answers to this question in *United States v. Leon* and *Pennsylvania Board of Probation and Parole*, the final two cases in this section.

WOLF v. COLORADO

338 U.S. 25, 69 S.Ct. 1359, 93 L.Ed. 1782 (1949).

JUSTICE FRANKFURTER delivered the opinion of the Court.

The precise question for consideration is this: Does a conviction by a State court for a State offense deny the "due process of law" required by the Fourteenth Amendment, solely because evidence that was admitted at the trial was obtained under circumstances which would have rendered it inadmissible in a prosecution for violation of a federal law in a court of the United States because there deemed to be an infraction of the Fourth Amendment? * * *

The security of one's privacy against arbitrary intrusion by the police—which is at the core of the Fourth Amendment—is basic to a free society. It is therefore

55

implicit in "the concept of ordered liberty" and as such enforceable against the States through the Due Process Clause. * * *

Accordingly, we have no hesitation in saying that were a State affirmatively to sanction such police incursion into privacy it would run counter to the guaranty of the Fourteenth Amendment. But the ways of enforcing such a basic right raise questions of a different order. How such arbitrary conduct should be checked, what remedies against it should be afforded, the means by which the right should be made effective, are all questions that are not to be so dogmatically answered as to preclude the varying solutions which spring from an allowable range of judgment on issues not susceptible of quantitative solution.

In *Weeks v. United States,* 232 U.S. 383 (1914), this Court held that in a federal prosecution the Fourth Amendment barred the use of evidence secured through an illegal search and seizure. This ruling * * * was not derived from the explicit requirements of the Fourth Amendment; it was not based on legislation expressing Congressional policy in the enforcement of the Constitution. The decision was a matter of judicial implication. Since then it has been frequently applied and we stoutly adhere to it. But the immediate question is whether the basic right to protection against arbitrary intrusion by the police demands the exclusion of logically relevant evidence obtained by an unreasonable search and seizure because, in a federal prosecution for a federal crime, it would be excluded. As a matter of inherent reason, one would suppose this to be an issue as to which men with complete devotion to the protection of the right of privacy might give different answers. When we find that in fact most of the English-speaking world does not regard as vital to such protection the exclusion of evidence thus obtained, we must hesitate to treat this remedy as an essential ingredient of the right. The contrariety of views of the States is particularly impressive in view of the careful reconsideration which they have given the problem in the light of the *Weeks* decision.

* * * As of today 30 States reject the *Weeks* doctrine, 17 States are in agreement with it. * * * Of 10 jurisdictions within the United Kingdom and the British Commonwealth of Nations which have passed on the question, none has held evidence obtained by illegal search and seizure inadmissible. * * *

The jurisdictions which have rejected the *Weeks* doctrine have not left the right to privacy without other means of protection. Indeed, the exclusion of evidence is a remedy which directly serves only to protect those upon whose person or premises something incriminating has been found. We cannot, therefore, regard it as a departure from basic standards to remand such persons, together with those who emerge scatheless from a search, to the remedies of private action and such protection as the internal discipline of the police, under the eyes of an alert public opinion, may afford. Granting that in practice the exclusion of evidence may be an effective way of deterring unreasonable searches, it is not for this Court to condemn as falling below the minimal standards assured by the Due Process Clause a State's reliance upon other methods which, if consistently enforced, would be equally effective. * * * There are, moreover, reasons for excluding evidence unreasonably obtained by the federal police which are less compelling in the case of police under State or local authority. The public opinion of a community can far more effectively be exerted against oppressive conduct on the part of police directly responsible to the community itself than can local opinion, sporadically aroused, be brought to bear upon remote authority pervasively exerted throughout the country.

We hold, therefore, that in a prosecution in a State court for a State crime the Fourteenth Amendment does not forbid the admission of evidence obtained by an unreasonable search and seizure. * * *

JUSTICE BLACK, concurring.

* * * I agree with what appears to be a plain implication of the Court's opinion that the federal exclusionary rule is not a command of the Fourth Amendment but is a judicially created rule of evidence which Congress might negate. * * *

JUSTICE MURPHY, with whom JUSTICE RUTLEDGE joins, dissenting.

[T]here is but one alternative to the rule of exclusion. That is no sanction at all.

* * * Little need be said concerning the possibilities of criminal prosecution. Self-scrutiny is a lofty ideal, but its exaltation reaches new heights if we expect a District Attorney to prosecute himself or his associates for well-meaning violations of the search and seizure clause during a raid the District Attorney or his associates have ordered. But there is an appealing ring in another alternative. A trespass action for damages is a venerable means of securing reparation for unauthorized invasion of the home. Why not put the old writ to a new use? When the Court cites cases permitting the action, the remedy seems complete.

But what an illusory remedy this is, if by "remedy" we mean a positive deterrent to police and prosecutors tempted to violate the Fourth Amendment. The appealing ring softens when we recall that in a trespass action the measure of damages is simply the extent of the injury to physical property. If the officer searches with care, he can avoid all but nominal damages—a penny, or a dollar. Are punitive damages possible? Perhaps. But a few states permit none, whatever the circumstances. In those that do, the plaintiff must show the real ill will or malice of the defendant, and surely it is not unreasonable to assume that one in honest pursuit of crime bears no malice toward the search victim. If that burden is carried, recovery may yet be defeated by the rule that there must be physical damages before punitive damages may be awarded. In addition, some states limit punitive damages to the actual expenses of litigation. * * * Even assuming the ill will of the officer, his reasonable grounds for belief that the home he searched harbored evidence of crime is admissible in mitigation of punitive damages. * * * The bad reputation of the plaintiff is likewise admissible. * * * If the evidence seized was actually used at a trial, that fact has been held a complete justification of the search, and a defense against the trespass action. * * * And even if the plaintiff hurdles all these obstacles, and gains a substantial verdict, the individual officer's finances may well make the judgment useless—for the municipality, of course, is not liable without its consent. Is it surprising that there is so little in the books concerning trespass actions for violation of the search and seizure clause? * * *

JUSTICE DOUGLAS, dissenting.

* * * I agree with Justice Murphy that * * * in absence of [an exclusionary] rule of evidence the Amendment would have no effective sanction. * * *

MAPP v. OHIO

367 U.S. 643, 81 S.Ct. 1684, 6 L.Ed.2d 1081 (1961).

JUSTICE CLARK delivered the opinion of the Court. * * *

On May 23, 1957, three Cleveland police officers arrived at appellant's residence in that city pursuant to information that "a person [was] hiding out in the home who was wanted for questioning in connection with a recent bombing, and that there was a large amount of policy paraphernalia being hidden in the home." Miss Mapp and her daughter by a former marriage lived on the top floor of the two-family dwelling. Upon their arrival at that house, the officers knocked on the door and demanded entrance but appellant, after telephoning her attorney, refused to admit them without a search warrant. * * *

The officers again sought entrance some three hours later when four or more additional officers arrived on the scene. When Miss Mapp did not come to the door immediately, at least one of the several doors to the house was forcibly opened and the policemen gained admittance. Meanwhile Miss Mapp's attorney arrived, but the officers, having secured their own entry, and continuing in their defiance of the law, would permit him neither to see Miss Mapp nor to enter the house. [When the officers broke into the hall, Miss Mapp] demanded to see the search warrant. A paper, claimed to be a warrant, was held up by one of the officers. She grabbed the "warrant" and placed it in her bosom. A struggle ensued in which the officers recovered the piece of paper and as a result of which they handcuffed appellant because she had been "belligerent" in resisting their official rescue of the "warrant" from her person. * * * Appellant, in handcuffs, was then forcibly taken upstairs to her bedroom where the officers searched a dresser, a chest of drawers, a closet and some suitcases. * * * The search spread to the rest of the second floor * * *. The basement of the building and a trunk found therein were also searched. The obscene materials for possession of which she was ultimately convicted were discovered in the course of that widespread search.

At the trial no search warrant was produced by the prosecution, nor was the failure to produce one explained or accounted for. At best [as the Ohio Supreme Court, which affirmed the conviction, expressed it], "there is, in the record, considerable doubt as to whether there ever was any warrant for the search of defendant's home." * * *

The State says that even if the search were made without authority, or otherwise unreasonably, it is not prevented from using the unconstitutionally seized evidence at trial, citing *Wolf v. Colorado*, * * *. On this appeal, * * * it is urged once again that we review that holding. * * *

The Court in *Wolf* first stated that "[t]he contrariety of views of the States" on the adoption of the exclusionary rule of *Weeks* was "particularly impressive" * * *. While in 1949, prior to the *Wolf* case, almost two-thirds of the States were opposed to the use of the exclusionary rule, now, despite the *Wolf* case, more than half of those since passing upon it, by their own legislative or judicial decision, have wholly or partly adopted or adhered to the *Weeks* rule. * * * Significantly, among those now following the rule is California which, according to its highest court, was "compelled to reach that conclusion because other remedies have completely failed to secure compliance with the constitutional provisions * * *." In connection with this California case, we note that the second basis elaborated in *Wolf* in support of its failure to enforce the exclusionary doctrine against the States was that "other means of protection" have been afforded "the right to privacy." The experience of California that such other remedies have been worthless and futile is buttressed by the experience of other States.

Likewise, time has set its face against what *Wolf* called the "weighty testimony" of *People v. Defore*, 1926, 242 N.Y. 13, 150 N.E. 585. There Justice (then Judge) Cardozo, rejecting adoption of the *Weeks* exclusionary rule in New York, had said that "[t]he Federal rule as it stands is either too strict or too lax." However the force of that reasoning has been largely vitiated by later decisions of this Court. These include the recent discarding of the "silver platter" doctrine, *Elkins v. United States;* [a] the relaxation of the formerly strict requirements as to standing to challenge the use of evidence thus seized, * * * and finally, the formulation of a method to prevent state use of evidence unconstitutionally seized by federal agents, *Rea v. United States.*[b] * * *

It, therefore, plainly appears that the factual considerations supporting the failure of the *Wolf* Court to include the *Weeks* exclusionary rule when it recognized the enforceability of the right to privacy against the States in 1949, while not basically relevant to the constitutional consideration, could not, in any analysis, now be deemed controlling.

* * * Today we once again examine *Wolf's* constitutional documentation of the right to privacy free from unreasonable state intrusion, and, after its dozen years on our books, are led by it to close the only courtroom door remaining open to evidence secured by official lawlessness in flagrant abuse of that basic right, reserved to all persons as a specific guarantee against that very same unlawful conduct. We hold that all evidence obtained by searches and seizures in violation of the Constitution is, by that same authority, inadmissible in a state court.[c]

a. 364 U.S. 206 (1960). Under the "silver platter" doctrine, evidence of a federal crime seized by state police in the course of an illegal search while investigating a state crime could be turned over to federal authorities and used in a federal prosecution so long as federal agents had not participated in the illegal search but had simply received the evidence on a "silver platter." In rejecting the doctrine, the Court pointed out that the determination in *Wolf* that Fourteenth Amendment Due Process prohibited illegal searches and seizures by state officers, marked the "removal of the doctrinal underpinning" for the admissibility of state-seized evidence in federal prosecutions.

b. 350 U.S. 214 (1956), where the Court held that a federal law enforcement agent who seized evidence on the basis of an invalid search warrant should be enjoined from turning over such evidence to state authorities for use in a state prosecution and from giving testimony concerning the evidence: "The District Court is not asked to enjoin state officials nor in any way to interfere with state agencies in enforcement of state law. * * * The only relief asked is against a federal agent, who obtained the property as a result of the abuse of process issued by a United States Commissioner. * * * In this posture we have then a case that raises not a constitutional question but one concerning our supervisory powers over federal law enforcement agencies."

c. Although an illegal arrest or other unreasonable seizure of the person is itself a violation of the Fourth and Fourteenth Amendments, the *Mapp* exclusionary sanction comes into play only when the police have obtained evidence as a result of the unconstitutional seizure. Such is the case when, for example, the police make an illegal arrest and then conduct a fruitful search which is "incident to" that arrest and thus dependent upon the lawfulness of the arrest for its legality. Such may also be the case when the connection between the illegality and the evidence is less

apparent, and even when the evidence is verbal, such as a confession obtained from a defendant some time after his illegal arrest. As explained in *Wong Sun v. United States,* 371 U.S. 471 (1963), not "all evidence is 'fruit of the poisonous tree' simply because it would not have come to light but for the illegal actions of the police. Rather, the more apt question in such a case is 'whether, granting establishment of the primary illegality [the evidence] has been come at by exploitation of that illegality or instead by means sufficiently distinguishable to be purged of the primary taint.'" In making that judgment, the "temporal proximity of the arrest and the confession, the presence of intervening circumstances and, particularly, the purpose and flagrancy of the official misconduct, are all relevant. The voluntariness of the statement is a threshold requirement." *Brown v. Illinois,* 422 U.S. 590 (1975).

In *United States v. Crews,* 445 U.S. 463 (1980), the Court held that an illegally arrested defendant "is not himself a suppressible 'fruit' and the illegality of his detention cannot deprive the Government of the opportunity to prove his guilt through the introduction of evidence wholly untainted by the police misconduct." Moreover, it is no defense to a state or federal criminal prosecution that the defendant was illegally arrested or forcibly brought within the jurisdiction of the court. The trial of such a defendant violates neither Fifth nor Fourteenth Amendment due process. As explained in *Frisbie v. Collins,* 342 U.S. 519 (1952), this rule rests "on the sound basis that due process of law is satisfied when one present in court is convicted of crime after having been fairly apprized of the charges against him and after a fair trial in accordance with constitutional procedural safeguards. There is nothing in the Constitution that requires a court to permit a guilty person rightfully convicted to escape justice because he was brought to trial against his will." The Court added that even

Since the Fourth Amendment's right of privacy has been declared enforceable against the States through the Due Process Clause of the Fourteenth, it is enforceable against them by the same sanction of exclusion as is used against the Federal Government. Were it otherwise then just as without the *Weeks* rule the assurance against unreasonable federal searches and seizures would be "a form of words," valueless and undeserving of mention in a perpetual charter of inestimable human liberties, so too, without that rule the freedom from state invasions of privacy would be so ephemeral and so neatly severed from its conceptual nexus with the freedom from all brutish means of coercing evidence as not to merit this Court's high regard as a freedom "implicit in 'the concept of ordered liberty.' "

* * * [I]n extending the substantive protections of due process to all constitutionally unreasonable searches—state or federal—it was logically and constitutionally necessary that the exclusion doctrine—an essential part of the right to privacy—be also insisted upon as an essential ingredient of the right newly recognized by the *Wolf* case. In short, the admission of the new constitutional right by *Wolf* could not consistently tolerate denial of its most important constitutional privilege, namely, the exclusion of the evidence which an accused had been forced to give by reason of the unlawful seizure. To hold otherwise is to grant the right but in reality to withhold its privilege and enjoyment. Only last year the Court itself recognized that the purpose of the exclusionary rule "is to deter—to compel respect for the constitutional guaranty in the only effectively available way—by removing the incentive to disregard it."

Indeed, we are aware of no restraint, similar to that rejected today, conditioning the enforcement of any other basic constitutional right. The right to privacy, no less important than any other right carefully and particularly reserved to the people, would stand in marked contrast to all other rights declared as "basic to a free society." * * * [N]othing could be more certain than that when a coerced confession is involved, "the relevant rules of evidence" are overridden without regard to "the incidence of such conduct by the police," slight or frequent. Why should not the same rule apply to what is tantamount to coerced testimony by way of unconstitutional seizure of goods, papers, effects, documents, etc.? We find that, as to the Federal Government the Fourth and Fifth Amendments and, as to the States, the freedom from unconscionable invasions of privacy and the freedom from convictions based upon coerced confessions do enjoy an "intimate relation" in their perpetuation of "principles of humanity and civil liberty * * *." They express "supplementing phases of the same constitutional purpose—to maintain inviolate large areas of personal privacy." The philosophy of each Amendment and of each freedom is complementary to, although not dependent upon, that of the other in its sphere of influence—the very least that together they assure in either sphere is that no man is to be convicted on unconstitutional evidence.

Moreover, our holding * * * is not only the logical dictate of prior cases, but it also makes very good sense. There is no war between the Constitution and common sense. Presently, a federal prosecutor may make no use of evidence illegally seized, but a State's attorney across the street may, although he supposedly is operating under the enforceable prohibitions of the same Amendment. Thus the State, by admitting evidence unlawfully seized, serves to encourage disobedience to the Federal Constitution which it is bound to uphold. * * *

There are those who say, as did Justice (then Judge) Cardozo, that under our constitutional exclusionary doctrine "[t]he criminal is to go free because the

if the conduct in obtaining defendant's presence violated the federal kidnapping statute the result would be the same, for Congress had not included a bar to prosecution as an available sanction under that law.

constable has blundered." *People v. Defore.* In some cases this will undoubtedly be the result. But, as was said in *Elkins,* "there is another consideration—the imperative of judicial integrity." The criminal goes free, if he must, but it is the law that sets him free. Nothing can destroy a government more quickly than its failure to observe its own laws, or worse, its disregard of the charter of its own existence. As Mr. Justice Brandeis, dissenting, said in *Olmstead v. United States,* 277 U.S. 438 (1928): "Our government is the potent, the omnipresent teacher. For good or for ill, it teaches the whole people by its example. * * * If the government becomes a lawbreaker, it breeds contempt for law; it invites every man to become a law unto himself; it invites anarchy." Nor can it lightly be assumed that, as a practical matter, adoption of the exclusionary rule fetters law enforcement. Only last year this Court expressly considered that contention and found that "pragmatic evidence of a sort" to the contrary was not wanting. * * *. The Court noted that:

> "The federal courts themselves have operated under the exclusionary rule of *Weeks* for almost half a century; yet it has not been suggested either that the Federal Bureau of Investigation has thereby been rendered ineffective, or that the administration of criminal justice in the federal courts has thereby been disrupted. Moreover, the experience of the states is impressive * * *. The movement toward the rule of exclusion has been halting but seemingly inexorable."

The ignoble shortcut to conviction left open to the State tends to destroy the entire system of constitutional restraints on which the liberties of the people rest. Having once recognized that the right to privacy embodied in the Fourth Amendment is enforceable against the States, and that the right to be secure against rude invasions of privacy by state officers is, therefore, constitutional in origin, we can no longer permit that right to remain an empty promise. Because it is enforceable in the same manner and to like effect as other basic rights secured by the Due Process Clause, we can no longer permit it to be revocable at the whim of any police officer who, in the name of law enforcement itself, chooses to suspend its enjoyment. Our decision, founded on reason and truth, gives to the individual no more than that which the Constitution guarantees him, to the police officer no less than that to which honest law enforcement is entitled, and, to the courts, that judicial integrity so necessary in the true administration of justice. * * *

Reversed and remanded.

JUSTICE BLACK, concurring. * * *

I am still not persuaded that the Fourth Amendment, standing alone, would be enough to bar the introduction into evidence against an accused of papers and effects seized from him in violation of its commands. For the Fourth Amendment does not itself contain any provision expressly precluding the use of such evidence, and I am extremely doubtful that such a provision could properly be inferred from nothing more than the basic command against unreasonable searches and seizures. Reflection on the problem, however, in the light of cases coming before the Court since *Wolf,* has led me to conclude that when the Fourth Amendment's ban against unreasonable searches and seizures is considered together with the Fifth Amendment's ban against compelled self-incrimination, a constitutional basis emerges which not only justifies but actually requires the exclusionary rule. * * *

JUSTICE DOUGLAS, concurring.

* * * I believe that this is an appropriate case in which to put an end to the asymmetry which *Wolf* imported into the law. * * *

Memorandum of JUSTICE STEWART.

* * * I express no view as to the merits of the constitutional issue which the Court today decides. * * *

JUSTICE HARLAN, whom JUSTICE FRANKFURTER and JUSTICE WHITTAKER join, dissenting.

* * * I would not impose upon the States this federal exclusionary remedy. The reasons given by the majority for now suddenly turning its back on *Wolf* seem to me notably unconvincing.

First, it is said that "the factual grounds upon which *Wolf* was based" have since changed, in that more States now follow the *Weeks* exclusionary rule than was so at the time *Wolf* was decided. While that is true, a recent survey indicates that at present one half of the States still adhere to the common-law non-exclusionary rule, and one, Maryland, retains the rule as to felonies. * * * But in any case surely all this is beside the point, as the majority itself indeed seems to recognize. Our concern here, as it was in *Wolf*, is not with the desirability of that rule but only with the question whether the States are Constitutionally free to follow it or not as they may themselves determine, and the relevance of the disparity of views among the States on this point lies simply in the fact that the judgment involved is a debatable one. Moreover, the very fact on which the majority relies, instead of lending support to what is now being done, points away from the need of replacing voluntary state action with federal compulsion.

The preservation of a proper balance between state and federal responsibility in the administration of criminal justice demands patience on the part of those who might like to see things move faster among the States in this respect. Problems of criminal law enforcement vary widely from State to State. One State, in considering the totality of its legal picture, may conclude that the need for embracing the *Weeks* rule is pressing because other remedies are unavailable or inadequate to secure compliance with the substantive Constitutional principle involved. Another, though equally solicitous of Constitutional rights, may choose to pursue one purpose at a time, allowing all evidence relevant to guilt to be brought into a criminal trial, and dealing with Constitutional infractions by other means. Still another may consider the exclusionary rule too rough and ready a remedy, in that it reaches only unconstitutional intrusions which eventuate in criminal prosecution of the victims. Further, a State after experimenting with the *Weeks* rule for a time may, because of unsatisfactory experience with it, decide to revert to a non-exclusionary rule. And so on. * * * For us the question remains, as it has always been, one of state power, not one of passing judgment on the wisdom of one state course or another. In my view this Court should continue to forbear from fettering the States with an adamant rule which may embarrass them in coping with their own peculiar problems in criminal law enforcement. * * *

* * * Our role in promulgating the *Weeks* rule and its extensions * * * was quite a different one than it is here. There, in implementing the Fourth Amendment, we occupied the position of a tribunal having the ultimate responsibility for developing the standards and procedures of judicial administration within the judicial system over which it presides. Here we review State procedures whose measure is to be taken not against the specific substantive commands of the Fourth Amendment but under the flexible contours of the Due Process Clause. I do not believe that the Fourteenth Amendment empowers this Court to mould state remedies effectuating the right to freedom from "arbitrary intrusion by the police" to suit its own notions of how things should be done * * *.

Finally, it is said that the overruling of *Wolf* is supported by the established doctrine that the admission in evidence of an involuntary confession renders a state conviction constitutionally invalid. Since such a confession may often be entirely reliable, and therefore of the greatest relevance to the issue of the trial, the argument continues, this doctrine is ample warrant in precedent that the way evidence was obtained and not just its relevance, is constitutionally significant to the fairness of a trial. I believe this analogy is not a true one. The "coerced confession" rule is certainly not a rule that any illegally obtained statements may not be used in evidence. I would suppose that a statement which is procured during a period of illegal detention is, as much as unlawfully seized evidence, illegally obtained, but this Court has consistently refused to reverse state convictions resting on the use of such statements. * * *

The point, then, must be that in requiring exclusion of an involuntary statement of an accused, we are concerned not with an appropriate remedy for what the police have done, but with something which is regarded as going to the heart of our concepts of fairness in judicial procedure. The operative assumption of our procedural system is that "ours is the accusatorial as opposed to the inquisitorial system. * * *." * * * The pressures brought to bear against an accused leading to a confession, unlike an unconstitutional violation of privacy, do not, apart from the use of the confession at trial, necessarily involve independent Constitutional violations. What is crucial is that the trial defense to which an accused is entitled should not be rendered an empty formality by reason of statements wrung from him, for then "a prisoner * * * [has been] made the deluded instrument of his own conviction." That this is a *procedural right,* and that its violation occurs at the time his improperly obtained statement is admitted at trial, is manifest. * * *

This, and not the disciplining of the police, as with illegally seized evidence, is surely the true basis for excluding a statement of the accused which was unconstitutionally obtained. In sum, I think the coerced confession analogy works strongly *against* what the Court does today. * * *

UNITED STATES v. LEON

468 U.S. 897, 104 S.Ct. 3405, 82 L.Ed.2d 677 (1984).

JUSTICE WHITE delivered the opinion of the Court. * * *

This case presents the question whether the Fourth Amendment exclusionary rule should be modified so as not to bar the use in the prosecution's case-in-chief of evidence obtained by officers acting in reasonable reliance on a search warrant issued by a detached and neutral magistrate but ultimately found to be unsupported by probable cause. * * *

The Fourth Amendment contains no provision expressly precluding the use of evidence obtained in violation of its commands, and an examination of its origin and purposes makes clear that the use of fruits of a past unlawful search or seizure "work[s] no new Fourth Amendment wrong." The wrong condemned by the Amendment is "fully accomplished" by the unlawful search or seizure itself, and the exclusionary rule is neither intended nor able to "cure the invasion of the defendant's rights which he has already suffered." The rule thus operates as "a judicially created remedy designed to safeguard Fourth Amendment rights generally through its deterrent effect, rather than a personal constitutional right of the person aggrieved."

Whether the exclusionary sanction is appropriately imposed in a particular case, our decisions make clear, is "an issue separate from the question whether the Fourth Amendment rights of the party seeking to invoke the rule were violated by police conduct." Only the former question is currently before us,[a] and it must be resolved by weighing the costs and benefits of preventing the use in the prosecution's case-in-chief of inherently trustworthy tangible evidence obtained in reliance on a search warrant issued by a detached and neutral magistrate that ultimately is found to be defective.

The substantial social costs exacted by the exclusionary rule for the vindication of Fourth Amendment rights have long been a source of concern. "Our cases have consistently recognized that unbending application of the exclusionary sanction to enforce ideals of governmental rectitude would impede unacceptably the truth-finding functions of judge and jury." An objectionable collateral consequence of this interference with the criminal justice system's truth-finding function is that some guilty defendants may go free or receive reduced sentences as a result of favorable plea bargains.[6] Particularly when law enforcement officers have acted in objective good faith or their transgressions have been minor, the magnitude of the benefit conferred on such guilty defendants offends basic concepts of the criminal justice system. Indiscriminate application of the exclusionary rule, therefore, may well "generat[e] disrespect for the law and the administration of justice." Accordingly, "[a]s with any remedial device, the application of the rule has been restricted to those areas where its remedial objectives are thought most efficaciously served."

Close attention to those remedial objectives has characterized our recent decisions concerning the scope of the Fourth Amendment exclusionary rule. The Court has, to be sure, not seriously questioned, "in the absence of a more efficacious sanction, the continued application of the rule to suppress evidence from the [prosecution's] case where a Fourth Amendment violation has been substantial and deliberate * * *." Nevertheless, the balancing approach that has evolved in various contexts—including criminal trials—"forcefully suggest[s] that the exclusionary rule be more generally modified to permit the introduction of evidence obtained in the reasonable good-faith belief that a search or seizure was in accord with the Fourth Amendment." * * *

a. A large quantity of drugs were suppressed on the ground the warrant had not issued on probable cause, in that the affidavit reported only the allegations of an untested informant and limited corroboration by police surveillance of events themselves "as consistent with innocence as * * * with guilt." The Court earlier noted that whether this warrant would pass muster under the intervening and less demanding test of *Illinois v. Gates*, § 3 infra, "has not been briefed or argued," and thus chose "to take the case as it comes to us."

6. Researchers have only recently begun to study extensively the effects of the exclusionary rule on the disposition of felony arrests. One study suggests that the rule results in the non-prosecution or nonconviction of between 0.6% and 2.35% of individuals arrested for felonies. Davies, *A Hard Look at What We Know (and Still Need to Learn) About the "Costs" of the Exclusionary Rule: The NIJ Study and Other Studies of "Lost" Arrests*, 1983 A.B.F.Res.J. 611, 621. The estimates are higher for particular crimes the prosecution of which depends heavily on physical evidence.

Thus, the cumulative loss due to nonprosecution or nonconviction of individuals arrested on felony drug charges is probably in the range of 2.8% to 7.1%. Davies' analysis of California data suggests that screening by police and prosecutors results in the release because of illegal searches or seizures of as many as 1.4% of all felony arrestees, id., at 650, that 0.9% of felony arrestees are released because of illegal searches or seizures at the preliminary hearing or after trial, id., at 653, and that roughly 0.5% of all felony arrestees benefit from reversals on appeal because of illegal searches. * * *

Many of these researchers have concluded that the impact of the exclusionary rule is insubstantial, but the small percentages with which they deal mask a large absolute number of felons who are released because the cases against them were based in part on illegal searches or seizures. * * * Because we find that the rule can have no substantial deterrent effect in the sorts of situations under consideration in this case, we conclude that it cannot pay its way in those situations.

Only [when a warrant is grounded upon an affidavit knowingly or recklessly false] has the Court set forth a rationale for suppressing evidence obtained pursuant to a search warrant; [b] in the other areas, it has simply excluded such evidence without considering whether Fourth Amendment interests will be advanced. To the extent that proponents of exclusion rely on its behavioral effects on judges and magistrates in these areas, their reliance is misplaced. First, the exclusionary rule is designed to deter police misconduct rather than to punish the errors of judges and magistrates. Second, there exists no evidence suggesting that judges and magistrates are inclined to ignore or subvert the Fourth Amendment or that lawlessness among these actors requires application of the extreme sanction of exclusion.[14]

Third, and most important, we discern no basis, and are offered none, for believing that exclusion of evidence seized pursuant to a warrant will have a significant deterrent effect on the issuing judge or magistrate. Many of the factors that indicate that the exclusionary rule cannot provide an effective "special" or "general" deterrent for individual offending law enforcement officers apply as well to judges or magistrates. And, to the extent that the rule is thought to operate as a "systemic" deterrent on a wider audience, it clearly can have no such effect on individuals empowered to issue warrants. Judges and magistrates are not adjuncts to the law enforcement team; as neutral judicial officers, they have no stake in the outcome of particular criminal prosecutions. The threat of exclusion thus cannot be expected significantly to deter them. Imposition of the exclusionary sanction is not necessary meaningfully to inform judicial officers of their errors, and we cannot conclude that admitting evidence obtained pursuant to a warrant while at the same time declaring that the warrant was somehow defective will in any way reduce judicial officers' professional incentives to comply with the Fourth Amendment, encourage them to repeat their mistakes, or lead to the granting of all colorable warrant requests.[18]

If exclusion of evidence obtained pursuant to a subsequently invalidated warrant is to have any deterrent effect, therefor, it must alter the behavior of individual law enforcement officers or the policies of their departments. One could argue that applying the exclusionary rule in cases where the police failed to demonstrate probable cause in the warrant application deters future inadequate presentations or "magistrate shopping" and thus promotes the ends of the Fourth Amendment. Suppressing evidence obtained pursuant to a technically defective warrant supported by probable cause also might encourage officers to scrutinize more closely the form of the warrant and to point out suspected judicial errors. We find such arguments speculative and conclude that suppression of evidence obtained pursuant to a warrant should be ordered only on a case-by-case basis and

b. The reference is to *Franks v. Delaware*, 438 U.S. 154 (1978), where the Court declared "it would be an unthinkable imposition upon [the magistrate's] authority if a warrant affidavit, revealed after the fact to contain a deliberately or recklessly false statement, were to stand beyond impeachment."

14. Although there are assertions that some magistrates become rubber stamps for the police and others may be unable effectively to screen police conduct, we are not convinced that this is a problem of major proportions.

18. Limiting the application of the exclusionary sanction may well increase the care with which magistrates scrutinize warrant applications. We doubt that magistrates are more desirous of avoiding the exclusion of evidence obtained pursuant to warrants they have issued than of avoiding invasions of privacy.

Federal magistrates, moreover, are subject to the direct supervision of district courts. They may be removed for "incompetency, misconduct, neglect of duty, or physical or mental disability." 28 U.S.C. § 631(i). If a magistrate serves merely as a "rubber stamp" for the police or is unable to exercise mature judgment, closer supervision or removal provides a more effective remedy than the exclusionary rule.

only in those unusual cases in which exclusion will further the purposes of the exclusionary rule.[19]

We have frequently questioned whether the exclusionary rule can have any deterrent effect when the offending officers acted in the objectively reasonable belief that their conduct did not violate the Fourth Amendment. "No empirical researcher, proponent or opponent of the rule, has yet been able to establish with any assurance whether the rule has a deterrent effect * * *." But even assuming that the rule effectively deters some police misconduct and provides incentives for the law enforcement profession as a whole to conduct itself in accord with the Fourth Amendment, it cannot be expected, and should not be applied, to deter objectively reasonable law enforcement activity. * * * [20]

This is particularly true, we believe, when an officer acting with objective good faith has obtained a search warrant from a judge or magistrate and acted within its scope. In most such cases, there is no police illegality and thus nothing to deter. It is the magistrate's responsibility to determine whether the officer's allegations establish probable cause and, if so, to issue a warrant comporting in form with the requirements of the Fourth Amendment. In the ordinary case, an officer cannot be expected to question the magistrate's probable-cause determination or his judgment that the form of the warrant is technically sufficient. "[O]nce the warrant issues, there is literally nothing more the policeman can do in seeking to comply with the law." Penalizing the officer for the magistrate's error, rather than his own, cannot logically contribute to the deterrence of Fourth Amendment violations.[22]

We conclude that the marginal or nonexistent benefits produced by suppressing evidence obtained in objectively reasonable reliance on a subsequently invalidated search warrant cannot justify the substantial costs of exclusion. We do not suggest, however, that exclusion is always inappropriate in cases where an officer has obtained a warrant and abided by its terms. [T]he officer's reliance on the magistrate's probable-cause determination and on the technical sufficiency of the

---

19. Our discussion of the deterrent effect of excluding evidence obtained in reasonable reliance on a subsequently invalidated warrant assumes, of course, that the officers properly executed the warrant and searched only those places and for those objects that it was reasonable to believe were covered by the warrant. * * *

20. We emphasize that the standard of reasonableness we adopt is an objective one. Many objections to a good-faith exception assume that the exception will turn on the subjective good faith of individual officers. "Grounding the modification in objective reasonableness, however, retains the value of the exclusionary rule as an incentive for the law enforcement profession as a whole to conduct themselves in accord with the Fourth Amendment." The objective standard we adopt, moreover, requires officers to have a reasonable knowledge of what the law prohibits. As Professor Jerold Israel has observed:

"The key to the [exclusionary] rule's effectiveness as a deterrent lies, I believe, in the impetus it has provided to police training programs that make officers aware of the limits imposed by the fourth amendment and emphasize the need to operate within those limits.

[An objective good-faith exception] * * * is not likely to result in the elimination of such programs, which are now viewed as an important aspect of police professionalism. Neither is it likely to alter the tenor of those programs; the possibility that illegally obtained evidence may be admitted in borderline cases is unlikely to encourage police instructors to pay less attention to fourth amendment limitations. Finally, [it] * * * should not encourage officers to pay less attention to what they are taught, as the requirement that the officer act in 'good faith' is inconsistent with closing one's mind to the possibility of illegality."

22. * * * Our cases establish that the question whether the use of illegally obtained evidence in judicial proceedings represents judicial participation in a Fourth Amendment violation and offends the integrity of the courts "is essentially the same as the inquiry into whether exclusion would serve a deterrent purpose." * * * Absent unusual circumstances, when a Fourth Amendment violation has occurred because the police have reasonably relied on a warrant issued by a detached and neutral magistrate but ultimately found to be defective, "the integrity of the courts is not implicated."

Reliance must be reasonable

warrant he issues must be objectively reasonable,[23] and it is clear that in some circumstances the officer [24] will have no reasonable grounds for believing that the warrant was properly issued.

Suppression therefore remains an appropriate remedy if the magistrate or judge in issuing a warrant was misled by information in an affidavit that the affiant knew was false or would have known was false except for his reckless disregard of the truth. The exception we recognize today will also not apply in cases where the issuing magistrate wholly abandoned his judicial role in the manner condemned in *Lo–Ji Sales, Inc. v. New York,* 442 U.S. 319 (1979); [c] in such circumstances, no reasonably well-trained officer should rely on the warrant. Nor would an officer manifest objective good faith in relying on a warrant based on an affidavit "so lacking in indicia of probable cause as to render official belief in its existence entirely unreasonable." Finally, depending on the circumstances of the particular case, a warrant may be so facially deficient—i.e., in failing to particularize the place to be searched or the things to be seized—that the executing officers cannot reasonably presume it to be valid.[d]

* * * The good-faith exception for searches conducted pursuant to warrants is not intended to signal our unwillingness strictly to enforce the requirements of the Fourth Amendment, and we do not believe that it will have this effect. As we have already suggested, the good-faith exception, turning as it does on objective reasonableness, should not be difficult to apply in practice. When officers have acted pursuant to a warrant, the prosecution should ordinarily be able to establish objective good faith without a substantial expenditure of judicial time.

Nor are we persuaded that application of a good-faith exception to searches conducted pursuant to warrants will preclude review of the constitutionality of the

23. [O]ur good-faith inquiry is confined to the objectively ascertainable question whether a reasonably well-trained officer would have known that the search was illegal despite the magistrate's authorization. In making this determination, all of the circumstances—including whether the warrant application had previously been rejected by a different magistrate—may be considered.

24. References to "officer" throughout this opinion should not be read too narrowly. It is necessary to consider the objective reasonableness, not only of the officers who eventually executed a warrant, but also of the officers who originally obtained it or who provided information material to the probable-cause determination. Nothing in our opinion suggests, for example, that an officer could obtain a warrant on the basis of a "bare bones" affidavit and then rely on colleagues who are ignorant of the circumstances under which the warrant was obtained to conduct the search.

c. There the magistrate was held not to have "manifest[ed] that neutrality and detachment demanded of a judicial officer when presented with a warrant application," where he went to the scene and made judgments there about what should be seized as obscene, as he "allowed himself to become a member, if not the leader of the search party which was essentially a police operation."

d. Compare the companion case of *Massachusetts v. Sheppard,* 468 U.S. 981 (1984), where a detective prepared an affidavit for a search warrant to search for various specified items of evidence of a homicide but, because it was Sunday, could only find a warrant form for controlled substances. He presented his affidavit and that form to a judge at his home and pointed out the problem to him, and the judge, unable to locate a more suitable form, told the detective that he would make the necessary changes to make it a proper warrant. He made some changes, but failed to change that part of the warrant which authorized a search only for controlled substances and related paraphernalia. The detective took the two documents and he and other officers then executed the warrant, seizing evidence of the homicide. That evidence was suppressed in the state court because the warrant failed to particularly describe the items to be seized, as required by the Fourth Amendment. The Supreme Court, per White, J., held this situation fell within *Leon* because "there was an objectively reasonable basis for the officers' mistaken belief" that "the warrant authorized the search that they conducted." As for defendant's objection that the detective knew when he went to the judge that the warrant was defective, the Court stated: "Whatever an officer may be required to do when he executes a warrant without knowing beforehand what items are to be seized, we refuse to rule that an officer is required to disbelieve a judge who has just advised him, by word and by action, that the warrant he possesses authorizes him to conduct the search he has requested."

search or seizure, deny needed guidance from the courts, or freeze Fourth Amendment law in its present state.[25] There is no need for courts to adopt the inflexible practice of always deciding whether the officers' conduct manifested objective good faith before turning to the question whether the Fourth Amendment has been violated. * * *

If the resolution of a particular Fourth Amendment question is necessary to guide future action by law enforcement officers and magistrates, nothing will prevent reviewing courts from deciding that question before turning to the good-faith issue.[26] Indeed, it frequently will be difficult to determine whether the officers acted reasonably without resolving the Fourth Amendment issue. Even if the Fourth Amendment question is not one of broad import, reviewing courts could decide in particular cases that magistrates under their supervision need to be informed of their errors and so evaluate the officers' good faith only after finding a violation. In other circumstances, those courts could reject suppression motions posing no important Fourth Amendment questions by turning immediately to a consideration of the officers' good faith. We have no reason to believe that our Fourth Amendment jurisprudence would suffer by allowing reviewing courts to exercise an informed discretion in making this choice. * * *

In the absence of an allegation that the magistrate abandoned his detached and neutral role, suppression is appropriate only if the officers were dishonest or reckless in preparing their affidavit or could not have harbored an objectively reasonable belief in the existence of probable cause. Only respondent Leon has contended that no reasonably well-trained police officer could have believed that there existed probable cause to search his house; significantly, the other respondents advance no comparable argument. Officer Rombach's application for a warrant clearly was supported by much more than a "bare bones" affidavit. The affidavit related the results of an extensive investigation and, as the opinions of the divided panel of the Court of Appeals make clear, provided evidence sufficient to create disagreement among thoughtful and competent judges as to the existence of probable cause. Under these circumstances, the officers' reliance on the magistrate's determination of probable cause was objectively reasonable, and application of the extreme sanction of exclusion is inappropriate.[e]

25. The argument that defendants will lose their incentive to litigate meritorious Fourth Amendment claims as a result of the good-faith exception we adopt today is unpersuasive. Although the exception might discourage presentation of insubstantial suppression motions, the magnitude of the benefit conferred on defendants by a successful motion makes it unlikely that litigation of colorable claims will be substantially diminished.

26. It has been suggested, in fact, that "the recognition of a 'penumbral zone,' within which an inadvertent mistake would not call for exclusion, * * * will make it less tempting for judges to bend fourth amendment standards to avoid releasing a possibly dangerous criminal because of a minor and unintentional miscalculation by the police."

e. Prior to *Leon*, the Supreme Court had often applied the exclusionary rule even when the police acted in reliance upon a subsequently invalidated statute conferring authority to search. But when confronted with such a situation once again in *Illinois v. Krull*, 480 U.S. 340 (1987), the Court, 5–4, ruled otherwise. Blackmun, J., reasoned for the majority: "The approach used in *Leon* is equally applicable to the present case. The application of the exclusionary rule to suppress evidence obtained by an officer acting in objectively reasonable reliance on a statute would have as little deterrent effect on the officer's actions as would the exclusion of evidence when an officer acts in objectively reasonable reliance on a warrant. Unless a statute is clearly unconstitutional, an officer cannot be expected to question the judgment of the legislature that passed the law." The Court in *Krull* further reasoned that there was no "evidence to suggest that legislators 'are inclined to ignore or subvert the Fourth Amendment'" or "to indicate that applying the exclusionary rule to evidence seized pursuant to the statute prior to the declaration of its invalidity will act as a significant additional deterrent" of legislators.

O'Connor, J., for the dissenters, emphasized: (1) "The distinction drawn between the legislator and the judicial officer is sound" because "a legislature's unreasonable authorization of

Accordingly, the judgment of the Court of Appeals is reversed.

JUSTICE BLACKMUN, concurring.

[A]ny empirical judgment about the effect of the exclusionary rule in a particular class of cases necessarily is a provisional one. * * * If it should emerge from experience that, contrary to our expectations, the good faith exception to the exclusionary rule results in a material change in police compliance with the Fourth Amendment, we shall have to reconsider what we have undertaken here. The logic of a decision that rests on untested predictions about police conduct demands no less. * * *

JUSTICE BRENNAN, with whom JUSTICE MARSHALL joins, dissenting. * * *

[The majority's reading of the Fourth Amendment] appears plausible, because, as critics of the exclusionary rule never tire of repeating, the Fourth Amendment makes no express provision for the exclusion of evidence secured in violation of its commands. A short answer to this claim, of course, is that many of the Constitution's most vital imperatives are stated in general terms and the task of giving meaning to these precepts is therefore left to subsequent judicial decision-making in the context of concrete cases. The nature of our Constitution, as Chief Justice Marshall long ago explained, "requires that only its great outlines should be marked, its important objects designated, and the minor ingredients which compose those objects be deduced from the nature of the objects themselves."

A more direct answer may be supplied by recognizing that the Amendment, like other provisions of the Bill of Rights, restrains the power of the government as a whole; it does not specify only a particular agency and exempt all others. The judiciary is responsible, no less than the executive, for ensuring that constitutional rights are respected.

When that fact is kept in mind, the role of the courts and their possible involvement in the concerns of the Fourth Amendment comes into sharper focus. Because seizures are executed principally to secure evidence, and because such evidence generally has utility in our legal system only in the context of a trial supervised by a judge, it is apparent that the admission of illegally obtained evidence implicates the same constitutional concerns as the initial seizure of that evidence. Indeed, by admitting unlawfully seized evidence, the judiciary becomes a part of what is in fact a single governmental action prohibited by the terms of the Amendment. Once that connection between the evidence-gathering role of the police and the evidence-admitting function of the courts is acknowledged, the plausibility of the Court's interpretation becomes more suspect. Certainly nothing in the language or history of the Fourth Amendment suggests that a recognition of this evidentiary link between the police and the courts was meant to be foreclosed. It is difficult to give any meaning at all to the limitations imposed by the Amendment if they are read to proscribe only certain conduct by

searches may affect thousands or millions" and thus "poses a greater threat to liberty." (2) "[L]egislators by virtue of their political role are more often subjected to the political pressures that may threaten Fourth Amendment values than are judicial officers." (3) "Providing legislatures a grace period during which the police may freely perform unreasonable searches in order to convict those who might have otherwise escaped creates a positive incentive to promulgate unconstitutional laws."

Yet another *Leon*-style opinion is *Arizona v. Evans,* 514 U.S. 1 (1995), where the defendant was arrested on the basis of an erroneous computer indication of an outstanding warrant attributable to a court clerk's failure to advise the police that the warrant had been quashed. In concluding the exclusionary rule should not apply to this type of Fourth Amendment violation, the Court reasoned (i) that the arresting officer acted reasonably in relying on the computer record and thus was not in need of deterrence; and (ii) that exclusion would not deter such errors by court clerks, who "have no stake in the outcome of particular criminal prosecutions."

the police but to allow other agents of the same government to take advantage of evidence secured by the police in violation of its requirements. The Amendment therefore must be read to condemn not only the initial unconstitutional invasion of privacy—which is done, after all, for the purpose of securing evidence—but also the subsequent use of any evidence so obtained. * * *

Such a conception of the rights secured by the Fourth Amendment was unquestionably the original basis of what has come to be called the exclusionary rule when it was first formulated in *Weeks v. United States.* * * *

[T]he question whether the exclusion of evidence would deter future police misconduct was never considered a relevant concern in the early cases * * *. In those formative decisions, the Court plainly understood that the exclusion of illegally obtained evidence was compelled not by judicially fashioned remedial purposes, but rather by a direct constitutional command. * * *

* * * Indeed, no other explanation suffices to account for the Court's holding in *Mapp,* since the only possible predicate for the Court's conclusion that the States were bound by the Fourteenth Amendment to honor the *Weeks* doctrine is that the exclusionary rule was "part and parcel of the Fourth Amendment's limitation upon [governmental] encroachment of individual privacy."

Despite this clear pronouncement, however, the Court * * * has gradually pressed the deterrence rationale for the rule back to center stage. The various arguments advanced by the Court in this campaign have only strengthened my conviction that the deterrence theory is both misguided and unworkable. First, the Court has frequently bewailed the "cost" of excluding reliable evidence. In large part, this criticism rests upon a refusal to acknowledge the function of the Fourth Amendment itself. If nothing else, the Amendment plainly operates to disable the government from gathering information and securing evidence in certain ways. In practical terms, of course, this restriction of official power means that some incriminating evidence inevitably will go undetected if the government obeys these constitutional restraints. It is the loss of that evidence that is the "price" our society pays for enjoying the freedom and privacy safeguarded by the Fourth Amendment. Thus, some criminals will go free *not,* in Justice (then Judge) Cardozo's misleading epigram, "because the constable has blundered," but rather because official compliance with Fourth Amendment requirements makes it more difficult to catch criminals. Understood in this way, the Amendment directly contemplates that some reliable and incriminating evidence will be lost to the government; therefore, it is not the exclusionary rule, but the Amendment itself that has imposed this cost.

In addition, the Court's decisions over the past decade have made plain that the entire enterprise of attempting to assess the benefits and costs of the exclusionary rule in various contexts is a virtually impossible task for the judiciary to perform honestly or accurately. Although the Court's language in those cases suggests that some specific empirical basis may support its analyses, the reality is that the Court's opinions represent inherently unstable compounds of intuition, hunches, and occasional pieces of partial and often inconclusive data. * * * To the extent empirical data is available regarding the general costs and benefits of the exclusionary rule, it has shown, on the one hand, as the Court acknowledges today, that the costs are not as substantial as critics have asserted in the past, and, on the other hand, that while the exclusionary rule may well have certain deterrent effects, it is extremely difficult to determine with any degree of precision whether the incidence of unlawful conduct by police is now lower than it was prior to *Mapp.* The Court has sought to turn this uncertainty to its advantage by casting the burden of proof upon proponents of the rule. "Obviously," however, "the assignment of the burden of proof on an issue where evidence does not exist and cannot be obtained is outcome determinative. [The] assignment of the burden is merely a way of announcing a predetermined conclusion."

By remaining within its redoubt of empiricism and by basing the rule solely on the deterrence rationale, the Court has robbed the rule of legitimacy. A doctrine that is explained as if it were an empirical proposition but for which there is only limited empirical support is both inherently unstable and an easy mark for critics. The extent of this Court's fidelity to Fourth Amendment requirements, however, should not turn on such statistical uncertainties. * * *

Even if I were to accept the Court's general approach to the exclusionary rule, I could not agree with today's result. * * *

At the outset, the Court suggests that society has been asked to pay a high price—in terms either of setting guilty persons free or of impeding the proper functioning of trials—as a result of excluding relevant physical evidence in cases where the police, in conducting searches and seizing evidence, have made only an "objectively reasonable" mistake concerning the constitutionality of their actions. But what evidence is there to support such a claim?

Significantly, the Court points to none, and, indeed, as the Court acknowledges, recent studies have demonstrated that the "costs" of the exclusionary rule—calculated in terms of dropped prosecutions and lost convictions—are quite low. Contrary to the claims of the rule's critics that exclusion leads to "the release of countless guilty criminals," these studies have demonstrated that federal and state prosecutors very rarely drop cases because of potential search and seizure problems. For example, a 1979 study prepared at the request of Congress by the General Accounting Office reported that only 0.4% of all cases actually declined for prosecution by federal prosecutors were declined primarily because of illegal search problems. If the GAO data are restated as a percentage of *all* arrests, the study shows that only 0.2% of all felony arrests are declined for prosecution because of potential exclusionary rule problems.[11] Of course, these data describe only the costs attributable to the exclusion of evidence in all cases; the costs due to the exclusion of evidence in the narrower category of cases where police have made objectively reasonable mistakes must necessarily be even smaller. The Court, however, ignores this distinction and mistakenly weighs the aggregated costs of exclusion in *all* cases, irrespective of the circumstances that led to exclusion, against the potential benefits associated with only those cases in which evidence is excluded because police reasonably but mistakenly believe that

---

11. In a series of recent studies, researchers have attempted to quantify the actual costs of the rule. A recent National Institute of Justice study based on data for the four year period 1976–1979 gathered by the California Bureau of Criminal Statistics showed that 4.8% of all cases that were declined for prosecution by California prosecutors were rejected because of illegally seized evidence. However, if these data are calculated as a percentage of all arrests that were declined for prosecution, they show that only 0.8% of all arrests were rejected for prosecution because of illegally seized evidence.

In another measure of the rule's impact—the number of prosecutions that are dismissed or result in acquittals in cases where evidence has been excluded—the available data again show that the Court's past assessment of the rule's costs has generally been exaggerated. For ex-

ample, a study based on data from 9 mid-sized counties in Illinois, Michigan and Pennsylvania reveals that motions to suppress physical evidence were filed in approximately 5% of the 7,500 cases studied, but that such motions were successful in only 0.7% of all these cases. The study also shows that only 0.6% of all cases resulted in acquittals because evidence had been excluded. In the GAO study, suppression motions were filed in 10.5% of all federal criminal cases surveyed, but of the motions filed, approximately 80–90% were denied. Evidence was actually excluded in only 1.3% of the cases studied, and only 0.7% of all cases resulted in acquittals or dismissals after evidence was excluded. And in another study based on data from cases during 1978 and 1979 in San Diego and Jacksonville, it was shown that only 1% of all cases resulting in nonconviction were caused by illegal searches.

their conduct does not violate the Fourth Amendment. When such faulty scales are used, it is little wonder that the balance tips in favor of restricting the application of the rule.

What then supports the Court's insistence that this evidence be admitted? Apparently, the Court's only answer is that even though the costs of exclusion are not very substantial, the potential deterrent effect in these circumstances is so marginal that exclusion cannot be justified. The key to the Court's conclusion in this respect is its belief that the prospective deterrent effect of the exclusionary rule operates only in those situations in which police officers, when deciding whether to go forward with some particular search, have reason to know that their planned conduct will violate the requirements of the Fourth Amendment.

* * * But what the Court overlooks is that the deterrence rationale for the rule is not designed to be, nor should it be thought of as, a form of "punishment" of individual police officers for their failures to obey the restraints imposed by the Fourth Amendment. Instead, the chief deterrent function of the rule is its tendency to promote institutional compliance with Fourth Amendment requirements on the part of law enforcement agencies generally. Thus, as the Court has previously recognized, "over the long term, [the] demonstration [provided by the exclusionary rule] that our society attaches serious consequences to violation of constitutional rights is thought to encourage those who formulate law enforcement policies, and the officers who implement them, to incorporate Fourth Amendment ideals into their value system." It is only through such an institution-wide mechanism that information concerning Fourth Amendment standards can be effectively communicated to rank and file officers.[13]

If the overall educational effect of the exclusionary rule is considered, application of the rule to even those situations in which individual police officers have acted on the basis of a reasonable but mistaken belief that their conduct was authorized can still be expected to have a considerable long-term deterrent effect. If evidence is consistently excluded in these circumstances, police departments will surely be prompted to instruct their officers to devote greater care and attention to providing sufficient information to establish probable cause when applying for a warrant, and to review with some attention the form of the warrant that they have been issued, rather than automatically assuming that whatever document the magistrate has signed will necessarily comport with Fourth Amendment requirements.

After today's decision, however, that institutional incentive will be lost. Indeed, the Court's "reasonable mistake" exception to the exclusionary rule will tend to put a premium on police ignorance of the law. Armed with the assurance provided by today's decision that evidence will always be admissible whenever an officer has "reasonably" relied upon a warrant, police departments will be encouraged to train officers that if a warrant has simply been signed, it is reasonable, without more, to rely on it. Since in close cases there will no longer be any incentive to err on the side of constitutional behavior, police would have every reason to adopt a "let's-wait-until-its-decided" approach in situations in which there is a question about a warrant's validity or the basis for its issuance.[14]

13. * * * A former United States Attorney and now Attorney General of Maryland, Stephen Sachs, has described the impact of the rule on police practices in similar terms: "I have watched the rule deter, routinely, throughout my years as a prosecutor * * *. [P]olice-prosecutor consultation is customary in all our cases when Fourth Amendment concerns arise * * *. In at least three Maryland jurisdictions, for example, prosecutors are on twenty-four hour call to field search and seizure questions presented by police officers."

14. The authors of a recent study of the warrant process in seven cities concluded that application of a good faith exception where an officer relies upon a warrant "would further

Although the Court brushes these concerns aside, a host of grave consequences can be expected to result from its decision to carve this new exception out of the exclusionary rule. A chief consequence of today's decision will be to convey a clear and unambiguous message to magistrates that their decisions to issue warrants are now insulated from subsequent judicial review. Creation of this new exception for good faith reliance upon a warrant implicitly tells magistrates that they need not take much care in reviewing warrant applications, since their mistakes will from now on have virtually no consequence: If their decision to issue a warrant was correct, the evidence will be admitted; if their decision was incorrect but the police relied in good faith on the warrant, the evidence will also be admitted. Inevitably, the care and attention devoted to such an inconsequential chore will dwindle. Although the Court is correct to note that magistrates do not share the same stake in the outcome of a criminal case as the police, they nevertheless need to appreciate that their role is of some moment in order to continue performing the important task of carefully reviewing warrant applications. Today's decision effectively removes that incentive.

Moreover, the good faith exception will encourage police to provide only the bare minimum of information in future warrant applications. The police will now know that if they can secure a warrant, so long as the circumstances of its issuance are not "entirely unreasonable," all police conduct pursuant to that warrant will be protected from further judicial review. The clear incentive that operated in the past to establish probable cause adequately because reviewing courts would examine the magistrate's judgment carefully, has now been so completely vitiated that the police need only show that it was not "entirely unreasonable" under the circumstances of a particular case for them to believe that the warrant they were issued was valid. The long-run effect unquestionably will be to undermine the integrity of the warrant process. * * *

JUSTICE STEVENS, * * * dissenting * * *.

* * * It is probable, though admittedly not certain, that the Court of Appeals would now conclude that the warrant in *Leon* satisfied the Fourth Amendment if it were given the opportunity to reconsider the issue in the light of *Gates*. Adherence to our normal practice following the announcement of a new rule would therefore postpone, and probably obviate, the need for the promulgation of the broad new rule the Court announces today.

[W]hen the Court goes beyond what is necessary to decide the case before it, it can only encourage the perception that it is pursuing its own notions of wise social policy, rather than adhering to its judicial role. I do not believe the Court should reach out to decide what is undoubtedly a profound question concerning the administration of criminal justice before assuring itself that this question is actually and of necessity presented by the concrete facts before the Court. * * *

PENNSYLVANIA BOARD OF PROBATION AND PAROLE v. SCOTT

524 U.S. 357, 118 S.Ct. 2014, 141 L.Ed.2d 344 (1998).

JUSTICE THOMAS delivered the opinion of the Court. * * *

Respondent Keith M. Scott pleaded nolo contendere to a charge of third-degree murder and was sentenced to a prison term of 10 to 20 years, beginning on March 31, 1983. On September 1, 1993, just months after completing the mini-

encourage police officers to seek out the less inquisitive magistrates and to rely on boiler-plate formulae, thereby lessening the value of search warrants overall. * * *

mum sentence, respondent was released on parole. One of the conditions of respondent's parole was that he would refrain from "owning or possessing any firearms or other weapons." The parole agreement, which respondent signed, further provided:

> "I expressly consent to the search of my person, property and residence, without a warrant by agents of the Pennsylvania Board of Probation and Parole. Any items, in [sic] the possession of which constitutes a violation of parole/reparole shall be subject to seizure, and may be used as evidence in the parole revocation process."

About five months later, after obtaining an arrest warrant based on evidence that respondent had violated several conditions of his parole by possessing firearms, consuming alcohol, and assaulting a co-worker, three parole officers arrested respondent at a local diner. Before being transferred to a correctional facility, respondent gave the officers the keys to his residence. The officers entered the home, which was owned by his mother, but did not perform a search for parole violations until respondent's mother arrived. The officers neither requested nor obtained consent to perform the search, but respondent's mother did direct them to his bedroom. After finding no relevant evidence there, the officers searched an adjacent sitting room in which they found five firearms, a compound bow, and three arrows.

At his parole violation hearing, respondent objected to the introduction of the evidence obtained during the search of his home on the ground that the search was unreasonable under the Fourth Amendment. The hearing examiner, however, rejected the challenge and admitted the evidence. As a result, the Pennsylvania Board of Probation and Parole found sufficient evidence in the record to support the weapons and alcohol charges and recommitted respondent to serve 36 months' backtime.

The Commonwealth Court of Pennsylvania reversed and remanded, holding, inter alia, that the hearing examiner had erred in admitting the evidence obtained during the search of respondent's residence. The court ruled that the search violated respondent's Fourth Amendment rights because it was conducted without the owner's consent and was not authorized by any state statutory or regulatory framework ensuring the reasonableness of searches by parole officers. The court further held that the exclusionary rule should apply because, in the circumstances of respondent's case, the deterrence benefits of the rule outweighed its costs.

The Pennsylvania Supreme Court affirmed. The court stated that respondent's Fourth Amendment right against unreasonable searches and seizures was "unaffected" by his signing of the parole agreement giving parole officers permission to conduct warrantless searches. It then held that the search in question was unreasonable because it was supported only by "mere speculation" rather than a "reasonable suspicion" of a parole violation. Carving out an exception to its per se bar against application of the exclusionary rule in parole revocation hearings, the court further ruled that the federal exclusionary rule applied to this case because the officers who conducted the search were aware of respondent's parole status. The court reasoned that, in the absence of the rule, illegal searches would be undeterred when officers know that the subjects of their searches are parolees and that illegally obtained evidence can be introduced at parole hearings.

We granted certiorari to determine whether the Fourth Amendment exclusionary rule applies to parole revocation proceedings.

We have emphasized repeatedly that the State's use of evidence obtained in violation of the Fourth Amendment does not itself violate the Constitution . .

Rather, a Fourth Amendment violation is " 'fully accomplished' " by the illegal search or seizure, and no exclusion of evidence from a judicial or administrative proceeding can " 'cure the invasion of the defendant's rights which he has already suffered.' " The exclusionary rule is instead a judicially created means of deterring illegal searches and seizures. As such, the rule does not "proscribe the introduction of illegally seized evidence in all proceedings or against all persons," but applies only in contexts "where its remedial objectives are thought most efficaciously served." Moreover, because the rule is prudential rather than constitutionally mandated, we have held it to be applicable only where its deterrence benefits outweigh its "substantial social costs."

deterrence

balancing

Recognizing these costs, we have repeatedly declined to extend the exclusionary rule to proceedings other than criminal trials For example, in *United States v. Calandra*, [414 U.S. 338 (1974)] we held that the exclusionary rule does not apply to grand jury proceedings; in so doing, we emphasized that such proceedings play a special role in the law enforcement process and that the traditionally flexible, nonadversarial nature of those proceedings would be jeopardized by application of the rule. Likewise, in *United States v. Janis*, [428 U.S. 433 (1976)] we held that the exclusionary rule did not bar the introduction of unconstitutionally obtained evidence in a civil tax proceeding because the costs of excluding relevant and reliable evidence would outweigh the marginal deterrence benefits, which, we noted, would be minimal because the use of the exclusionary rule in criminal trials already deterred illegal searches. Finally, in *INS v. Lopez-Mendoza*, 468 U.S. 1032 (1984), we refused to extend the exclusionary rule to civil deportation proceedings, citing the high social costs of allowing an immigrant to remain illegally in this country and noting the incompatibility of the rule with the civil, administrative nature of those proceedings.

GRAND JURY

CIVIL TAX

CIVIL DEPORTATION

As in *Calandra*, *Janis*, and *Lopez-Mendoza*, we are asked to extend the operation of the exclusionary rule beyond the criminal trial context. We again decline to do so. Application of the exclusionary rule would both hinder the functioning of state parole systems and alter the traditionally flexible, administrative nature of parole revocation proceedings. The rule would provide only minimal deterrence benefits in this context, because application of the rule in the criminal trial context already provides significant deterrence of unconstitutional searches. We therefore hold that the federal exclusionary rule does not bar the introduction at parole revocation hearings of evidence seized in violation of parolees' Fourth Amendment rights.

Because the exclusionary rule precludes consideration of reliable, probative evidence, it imposes significant costs: it undeniably detracts from the truthfinding process and allows many who would otherwise be incarcerated to escape the consequences of their actions. Although we have held these costs to be worth bearing in certain circumstances, our cases have repeatedly emphasized that the rule's "costly toll" upon truth-seeking and law enforcement objectives presents a high obstacle for those urging application of the rule.

COSTS

The costs of excluding reliable, probative evidence are particularly high in the context of parole revocation proceedings. Parole is a "variation on imprisonment of convicted criminals," in which the State accords a limited degree of freedom in return for the parolee's assurance that he will comply with the often strict terms and conditions of his release. In most cases, the State is willing to extend parole only because it is able to condition it upon compliance with certain requirements. The State thus has an "overwhelming interest" in ensuring that a parolee complies with those requirements and is returned to prison if he fails to do so. The exclusion of evidence establishing a parole violation, however, hampers the

State's ability to ensure compliance with these conditions by permitting the parolee to avoid the consequences of his noncompliance. The costs of allowing a parolee to avoid the consequences of his violation are compounded by the fact that parolees (particularly those who have already committed parole violations) are more likely to commit future criminal offenses than are average citizens. Indeed, this is the very premise behind the system of close parole supervision.

The exclusionary rule, moreover, is incompatible with the traditionally flexible, administrative procedures of parole revocation. Because parole revocation deprives the parolee not "of the absolute liberty to which every citizen is entitled, but only of the conditional liberty properly dependent on observance of special parole restrictions." States have wide latitude under the Constitution to structure parole revocation proceedings.[5] Most States, including Pennsylvania, have adopted informal, administrative parole revocation procedures in order to accommodate the large number of parole proceedings. These proceedings generally are not conducted by judges, but instead by parole boards, "members of which need not be judicial officers or lawyers." And traditional rules of evidence generally do not apply. Nor are these proceedings entirely adversarial, as they are designed to be " 'predictive and discretionary' as well as factfinding."

Application of the exclusionary rule would significantly alter this process. The exclusionary rule frequently requires extensive litigation to determine whether particular evidence must be excluded. Such litigation is inconsistent with the nonadversarial, administrative processes established by the States. Although States could adapt their parole revocation proceedings to accommodate such litigation, such a change would transform those proceedings from a "predictive and discretionary" effort to promote the best interests of both parolees and society into trial-like proceedings "less attuned" to the interests of the parolee. We are simply unwilling so to intrude into the States' correctional schemes. Such a transformation ultimately might disadvantage parolees because in an adversarial proceeding, "the hearing body may be less tolerant of marginal deviant behavior and feel more pressure to reincarcerate than to continue nonpunitive rehabilitation." And the financial costs of such a system could reduce the State's incentive to extend parole in the first place, as one of the purposes of parole is to reduce the costs of criminal punishment while maintaining a degree of supervision over the parolee.

The deterrence benefits of the exclusionary rule would not outweigh these costs. As the Supreme Court of Pennsylvania recognized, application of the exclusionary rule to parole revocation proceedings would have little deterrent effect upon an officer who is unaware that the subject of his search is a parolee. In that situation, the officer will likely be searching for evidence of criminal conduct with an eye toward the introduction of the evidence at a criminal trial. The likelihood that illegally obtained evidence will be excluded from trial provides deterrence against Fourth Amendment violations, and the remote possibility that the subject is a parolee and that the evidence may be admitted at a parole revocation proceeding surely has little, if any, effect on the officer's incentives.

The Pennsylvania Supreme Court thus fashioned a special rule for those situations in which the officer performing the search knows that the subject of his search is a parolee. We decline to adopt such an approach. We have never suggested that the exclusionary rule must apply in every circumstance in which it

---

5. We thus have held that a parolee is not entitled to "the full panoply" of due process rights to which a criminal defendant is entitled, *Morrissey v. Brewer*, 408 U.S. 471 (1972), and that the right to counsel generally does not attach to such proceedings because the introduction of counsel would "alter significantly the nature of the proceeding," *Gagnon v. Scarpelli*, 411 U.S. 778 (1973).

might provide marginal deterrence. Furthermore, such a piecemeal approach to the exclusionary rule would add an additional layer of collateral litigation regarding the officer's knowledge of the parolee's status.

In any event, any additional deterrence from the Pennsylvania Supreme Court's rule would be minimal. Where the person conducting the search is a police officer, the officer's focus is not upon ensuring compliance with parole conditions or obtaining evidence for introduction at administrative proceedings, but upon obtaining convictions of those who commit crimes. The non-criminal parole proceeding "falls outside the offending officer's zone of primary interest." Thus, even when the officer knows that the subject of his search is a parolee, the officer will be deterred from violating Fourth Amendment rights by the application of the exclusionary rule to criminal trials.

Even when the officer performing the search is a parole officer, the deterrence benefits of the exclusionary rule remain limited. Parole agents, in contrast to police officers, are not "engaged in the often competitive enterprise of ferreting out crime"; instead, their primary concern is whether their parolees should remain free on parole. Thus, their relationship with parolees is more supervisory than adversarial. It is thus "unfair to assume that the parole officer bears hostility against the parolee that destroys his neutrality; realistically the failure of the parolee is in a sense a failure for his supervising officer." Although this relationship does not prevent parole officers from ever violating the Fourth Amendment rights of their parolees, it does mean that the harsh deterrent of exclusion is unwarranted, given such other deterrents as departmental training and discipline and the threat of damages actions. Moreover, although in some instances parole officers may act like police officers and seek to uncover evidence of illegal activity, they (like police officers) are undoubtedly aware that any unconstitutionally seized evidence that could lead to an indictment could be suppressed in a criminal trial. In this case, assuming that the search violated respondent's Fourth Amendment rights, the evidence could have been inadmissible at trial if respondent had been criminally prosecuted.

We have long been averse to imposing federal requirements upon the parole systems of the States. A federal requirement that parole boards apply the exclusionary rule, which is itself a "grudgingly taken medicant," would severely disrupt the traditionally informal, administrative process of parole revocation. The marginal deterrence of unreasonable searches and seizures is insufficient to justify such an intrusion. We therefore hold that parole boards are not required by federal law to exclude evidence obtained in violation of the Fourth Amendment. Accordingly, the judgment below is reversed, and the case is remanded to the Pennsylvania Supreme Court. * * *

JUSTICE STEVENS, dissenting.

JUSTICE SOUTER has explained why the deterrent function of the exclusionary rule is implicated as much by a parole revocation proceeding as by a conventional criminal trial. I agree with that explanation. I add this comment merely to endorse Justice Stewart's conclusion that the "rule is constitutionally required, not as a 'right' explicitly incorporated in the fourth amendment's prohibitions, but as a remedy necessary to ensure that those prohibitions are observed in fact."

JUSTICE SOUTER, with whom JUSTICE GINSBURG and JUSTICE BREYER join, dissenting.

* * * The exclusionary rule does not * * *, mandate the exclusion of illegally acquired evidence from all proceedings or against all persons, and we have made

clear that the rule applies only in "those instances where its remedial objectives are thought most efficaciously served." * * *

Because we have found the requisite efficacy when the rule is applied in criminal trials, the deterrent effect of the evidentiary limitation upon prosecution is a baseline for evaluating the degree (or incremental degree) of deterrence that could be expected from extending the exclusionary rule to other sorts of cases. * * *

In *Janis*, for example, we performed incremental benefit analysis by focusing on the two classes of law enforcement officers affected. We reasoned that when the offending official was a state police officer, his "zone of primary interest" would be state criminal prosecution, not federal civil proceedings; accordingly, we said, "common sense dictates that the deterrent effect of the exclusion of relevant evidence is highly attenuated when the 'punishment' imposed upon the offending criminal enforcement officer is the removal of that evidence from a civil suit by or against a different sovereign." *Stone v. Powell*[, 428 U.S. 465 (1976)] was another variant on the same theme, where we looked to the collateral nature of the habeas proceedings in which the rule might be applied: "The view that the deterrence of Fourth Amendment violations would be furthered rests on the dubious assumption that law enforcement authorities would fear that federal habeas review might reveal flaws in a search or seizure that went undetected at trial and on appeal." And in *United States v. Calandra* we observed that excluding such evidence from grand jury proceedings "would deter only police investigation[s] consciously directed toward the discovery of evidence solely for use in a grand jury investigation"; an investigation so unambitious would be a rare one, we said, since prosecutors are unlikely to seek indictments in the face of dim prospects of conviction after trial.

In a formal sense, such is the reasoning of the Court's majority in deciding today that application of the exclusionary rule in parole revocation proceedings would have only an insignificant marginal deterrent value, "because application of the rule in the criminal trial context already provides significant deterrence of unconstitutional searches." In substance, however, the Court's conclusion will not jibe with the examples just cited, for it rests on erroneous views of the roles of regular police and parole officers in relation to revocation proceedings, and of the practical significance of the proceedings themselves.

As to the police, the majority say that regular officers investigating crimes almost always act with the prospect of a criminal prosecution before them. Their fear of evidentiary suppression in the criminal trial will have as much deterrent effect as can be expected, therefore, while any risk of suppression in parole administration is too unlikely to be on their minds to influence their conduct.

The majority's assumption will only sometimes be true, however, and in many, or even most cases, it will quite likely be false. To be sure, if a police officer acts on the spur of the moment to seize evidence or thwart crime, he may have no idea of a perpetrator's parole status. But the contrary will almost certainly be the case when he has first identified the person he has his eye on: the local police know the local felons, criminal history information is instantly available nationally, and police and parole officers routinely cooperate.

As [many] cases show, the police very likely do know a parolee's status when they go after him, and (contrary to the majority's assumption) this fact is significant for three reasons. First, and most obviously, the police have reason for concern with the outcome of a parole revocation proceeding, which is just as foreseeable as the criminal trial and at least as likely to be held. Police officers, especially those employed by the same sovereign that runs the parole system, therefore have every incentive not to jeopardize a recommitment by rendering evidence inadmissible. Second, as I will explain below, the actual likelihood of trial is often far less than the probability of a petition for parole revocation, with the consequence that the revocation hearing will be the only forum in which the evidence will ever be offered. Often, therefore, there will be nothing incremental about the significance of evidence offered in the administrative tribunal, and nothing "marginal" about the deterrence provided by an exclusionary rule operating there. Finally, the cooperation between parole and police officers, as in the instances shown in the cases cited above, casts serious doubt upon the aptness of treating police officers differently from parole officers, doubt that is confirmed by the following attention to the Court's characterization of the position of the parole officer.

The Court recalls our description of the police as "engaged in the often competitive enterprise of ferreting out crime," which raises the temptation to cut constitutional corners (which in turn requires the countervailing influence of the exclusionary rule). As against this picture of the police, the Court paints the parole officer as a figure more nearly immune to such competitive zeal. * * * This view of the parole officer suffers, however, from its selectiveness. Parole officers wear several hats; while they are indeed the parolees' counselors and social workers, they also" often serve as both prosecutors and law enforcement officials in their relationship with probationers and parolees." Indeed, a parole officer's obligation to petition for revocation when a parolee goes bad is presumably the basis for the legal rule in Pennsylvania that "state parole agents are considered police officers with respect to the offenders under their jurisdiction."

Once, in fact, the officer has turned from counselor to adversary, there is every reason to expect at least as much competitive zeal from him as from a regular police officer. If he fails to respond to his parolee's further criminality he will be neglecting the public safety, and if he brings a revocation petition without enough evidence to sustain it he can hardly look forward to professional advancement. And as for competitiveness, one need only ask whether a parole officer would rather leave the credit to state or local police when a parolee has to be brought to book.

The Court, of course, does not mean to deny that parole officers are subject to some temptation to skirt the limits on search and seizure, but it believes that deterrents other than the evidentiary exclusion will suffice. The Court contends that parole agents will be kept within bounds by "departmental training and discipline and the threat of damages actions." The same, of course, might be said of the police, and yet as to them such arguments are not heard, perhaps for the same reason that the Court's suggestion sounds hollow as to parole officers. The Court points to no specific departmental training regulation; it cites no instance of discipline imposed on a Pennsylvania parole officer for conducting an illegal search of a parolee's residence; and, least surprisingly of all, the majority mentions not a single lawsuit brought by a parolee against a parole officer seeking damages for an illegal search. In sum, if the police need the deterrence of an exclusionary rule to offset the temptations to forget the Fourth Amendment, parole officers need it quite as much.[1]

---

1. While it is true that the Court found in *INS v. Lopez–Mendoza* that the deterrence value of applying the exclusionary rule in deportation proceedings was diminished because the INS "has its own comprehensive scheme for deterring Fourth Amendment violations by its officers, and "alternative remedies for institu-

tional practices by the INS that might violate Fourth Amendment rights" were available, these two factors reflected what was at least on the agency's books and, in any event, did not stand alone. The Court in that case found that as a practical matter "it is highly unlikely that any particular arrestee will end up challenging

Just as the Court has underestimated the competitive influences tending to induce police and parole officers to stint on Fourth Amendment obligations, so I think it has misunderstood the significance of admitting illegally seized evidence at the revocation hearing. On the one hand, the majority magnifies the cost of an exclusionary rule for parole cases by overemphasizing the differences between a revocation hearing and a trial, and on the other hand it has minimized the benefits by failing to recognize the significant likelihood that the revocation hearing will be the principal, not the secondary, forum, in which evidence of a parolee's criminal conduct will be offered.

The Court is, of course, correct that the revocation hearing has not only an adversarial side in factfinding, but a predictive and discretionary aspect in addressing the proper disposition when a violation has been found. And I agree that open-mindedness at the discretionary, dispositional stage is promoted by the relative informality of the proceeding even at its factfinding stage. That informality is fostered by limiting issues so that lawyers are not always necessary, and by appointing lay members to parole boards. There is no question, either, that application of an exclusionary rule, if there is no waiver of Fourth Amendment rights, will tend to underscore the adversary character of the factfinding process. This cannot, however, be a dispositive objection to an exclusionary rule. Any revocation hearing is adversary to a degree: counsel must now be provided whenever the complexity of fact issues so warrant, and lay board members are just as capable of passing upon Fourth Amendment issues as the police, who are necessarily charged with responsibility for the legality of warrantless arrests, investigatory stops, and searches.

As to the benefit of an exclusionary rule in revocation proceedings, the majority does not see that in the investigation of criminal conduct by someone known to be on parole, Fourth Amendment standards will have very little deterrent sanction unless evidence offered for parole revocation is subject to suppression for unconstitutional conduct. It is not merely that parole revocation is the government's consolation prize when, for whatever reason, it cannot obtain a further criminal conviction, though that will sometimes be true. What is at least equally telling is that parole revocation will frequently be pursued instead of prosecution as the course of choice, a fact recognized a quarter of a century ago when we observed in *Morrissey v. Brewer* [408 U.S. 471 (1972),] that a parole revocation proceeding "is often preferred to a new prosecution because of the procedural ease of recommitting the individual on the basis of a lesser showing by the State."

The reasons for this tendency to skip any new prosecution are obvious. If the conduct in question is a crime in its own right, the odds of revocation are very high. Since time on the street before revocation is not subtracted from the balance of the sentence to be served on revocation, the balance may well be long enough to render recommitment the practical equivalent of a new sentence for a separate crime. And all of this may be accomplished without shouldering the burden of proof beyond a reasonable doubt; hence the obvious popularity of revocation in place of new prosecution.

The upshot is that without a suppression remedy in revocation proceedings, there will often be no influence capable of deterring Fourth Amendment violations when parole revocation is a possible response to new crime. Suppression in the revocation proceeding cannot be looked upon, then, as furnishing merely incremental or marginal deterrence over and above the effect of exclusion in criminal

the lawfulness of his arrest in a formal deportation proceeding." As the instant case may suggest, there is no reason to expect parolees to be so reticent.

prosecution. Instead, it will commonly provide the only deterrence to unconstitutional conduct when the incarceration of parolees is sought, and the reasons that support the suppression remedy in prosecution therefore support it in parole revocation. * * *

Because the search violated the Fourth Amendment, and because I conclude that the exclusionary rule ought to apply to parole revocation proceedings, I would affirm the decision of the Supreme Court of Pennsylvania.

SECTION 2. PROTECTED AREAS AND INTERESTS

If certain police activity is neither a "search" nor a "seizure" in the Fourth Amendment sense, then quite obviously the protections of the Amendment are inapplicable. Deciding just what constitutes a "search" has been especially troublesome. In the leading case (and the first case in this section) of *Katz v. United States,* holding electronic eavesdropping is governed by the Fourth Amendment, the Court decided a search could occur without a physical intrusion into a constitutionally protected area. By requiring instead an infringement upon a justified expectation of privacy, *Katz* unquestionably broadened the scope of the Fourth Amendment. But the Court has since taken a rather narrow view of what privacy expectations are in fact "justified," as is illustrated by the next two cases, *California v. Greenwood* and *Florida v. Riley,* dealing, respectively, with examination of garbage and aerial surveillance. The next two cases in this section, *United States v. Karo* and *Kyllo v. United States*, dealing respectively with use of electronic tracking devices and thermal imagers, concern the Fourth Amendment's application to sense enhancing devices. The meaning of *Katz* is also explored in *United States v. White,* concerning the troublesome question of whether it is a search or seizure for an undercover agent secretly to record or transmit the conversations he has with others.

Those objecting to police search activity have sometimes relied upon constitutional protections in addition to those in the Fourth Amendment. The claim that the Fifth Amendment privilege against self-incrimination bars a search for or seizure of private papers was rejected in *Andresen v. Maryland,* 427 U.S. 463 (1976). Distinguishing the situation discussed in Chapter Eight (§ 2), the Court in *Andresen* concluded that "although the Fifth Amendment may protect an individual from complying with a subpoena for the production of his personal records in his possession because the very act of production may constitute a compulsory authentication of incriminating information, a seizure of the same materials by law enforcement officers differs in a crucial respect—the individual against whom the search is directed is not required to aid in the discovery, production, or authentication of incriminating evidence." The claim that the First Amendment freedom of the press is violated by the search of the office of a newsgathering organization is considered in *Zurcher v. Stanford Daily,* the final case in this section.

KATZ v. UNITED STATES
389 U.S. 347, 88 S.Ct. 507, 19 L.Ed.2d 576 (1967).

JUSTICE STEWART delivered the opinion of the Court.

The petitioner was convicted [of] transmitting wagering information by telephone from Los Angeles to Miami and Boston in violation of a federal statute. At trial the Government was permitted, over the petitioner's objection, to introduce evidence of the petitioner's end of telephone conversations, overheard by FBI agents who had attached an electronic listening and recording device to the outside of the public telephone booth from which he had placed his calls. In affirming his conviction, the Court of Appeals rejected the contention that the recordings had been obtained in violation of the Fourth Amendment, because "[t]here was no physical entrance into the area occupied by [the petitioner]." We granted certiorari in order to consider the constitutional questions thus presented.

The petitioner has phrased those questions as follows:

> "A. Whether a public telephone booth is a constitutionally protected area so that evidence obtained by attaching an electronic listening recording device to the top of such a booth is obtained in violation of the right to privacy of the user of the booth.

> "B. Whether physical penetration of a constitutionally protected area is necessary before a search and seizure can be said to be violative of the Fourth Amendment to the United States Constitution."

We decline to adopt this formulation of the issues. In the first place the correct solution of Fourth Amendment problems is not necessarily promoted by incantation of the phrase "constitutionally protected area." Secondly, the Fourth Amendment cannot be translated into a general constitutional "right to privacy." That Amendment protects individual privacy against certain kinds of governmental intrusion, but its protections go further, and often have nothing to do with privacy at all. Other provisions of the Constitution protect personal privacy from other forms of governmental invasion. But the protection of a person's *general* right to privacy—his right to be let alone by other people—is, like the protection of his property and of his very life, left largely to the law of the individual States.

Because of the misleading way the issues have been formulated, the parties have attached great significance to the characterization of the telephone booth from which the petitioner placed his calls. The petitioner has strenuously argued that the booth was a "constitutionally protected area." The Government has maintained with equal vigor that it was not. But this effort to decide whether or not a given "area," viewed in the abstract, is "constitutionally protected" deflects attention from the problem presented by this case. For the Fourth Amendment protects people, not places. What a person knowingly exposes to the public, even in his own home or office, is not a subject of Fourth Amendment protection. * * * But what he seeks to preserve as private, even in an area accessible to the public, may be constitutionally protected. * * *

The Government stresses the fact that the telephone booth from which the petitioner made his calls was constructed partly of glass, so that he was as visible after he entered it as he would have been if he had remained outside. But what he sought to exclude when he entered the booth was not the intruding eye—it was the uninvited ear. He did not shed his right to do so simply because he made his calls from a place where he might be seen. No less than an individual in a business office, in a friend's apartment, or in a taxicab, a person in a telephone booth may rely upon the protection of the Fourth Amendment. One who occupies it, shuts the door behind him, and pays the toll that permits him to place a call, is surely entitled to assume that the words he utters into the mouthpiece will not be broadcast to the world. To read the Constitution more narrowly is to ignore the vital role that the public telephone has come to play in private communication.

The Government contends, however, that the activities of its agents in this case should not be tested by Fourth Amendment requirements, for the surveillance technique they employed involved no physical penetration of the telephone booth from which the petitioner placed his calls.

* * * [A]lthough a closely divided Court supposed in *Olmstead* [*v. United States,* 277 U.S. 438 (1928),] that surveillance without any trespass and without the seizure of any material object fell outside the ambit of the Constitution, we have since departed from the narrow view on which that decision rested. Indeed, we have expressly held that the Fourth Amendment governs not only the seizure of tangible items, but extends as well to the recording of oral statements overheard without any "technical trespass under * * * local property law." Once this much is acknowledged, and once it is recognized that the Fourth Amendment protects people—and not simply "areas"—against unreasonable searches and seizures it becomes clear that the reach of that Amendment cannot turn upon the presence or absence of a physical intrusion into any given enclosure.

(handwritten: NO LONGER GOOD LAW)

We conclude that the underpinnings of *Olmstead* have been so eroded by our subsequent decisions that the "trespass" doctrine there enunciated can no longer be regarded as controlling. The Government's activities in electronically listening to and recording the petitioner's words violated the privacy upon which he justifiably relied while using the telephone booth and thus constituted a "search and seizure" (a) within the meaning of the Fourth Amendment. (b) The fact that the electronic device employed to achieve that end did not happen to penetrate the wall of the booth can have no constitutional significance.

a. This does not mean that privacy is the *only* interest protected by the Fourth Amendment, or that the Amendment comes into play *only* if there is both a "search" and a "seizure." The Fourth Amendment also protects the interests in possession of property and liberty of person, as in *United States v. Place,* § 7 infra (detention of traveler's luggage 90 minutes was an unreasonable seizure in two respects, as it constituted a deprivation of defendant's "possessory interest in his luggage" and his "liberty interest in proceeding with his itinerary"). In *Soldal v. Cook County,* 506 U.S. 56 (1992), where sheriff's deputies knowingly participated in an unlawful eviction which involved hauling the plaintiff's trailer home off the landlord's property, the court of appeals ruled that the Fourth Amendment offers no protection where, as here, the intrusion upon a possessory interest was unaccompanied by an intrusion upon a privacy interest. A unanimous Supreme Court reversed, holding "that seizures of property are subject to Fourth Amendment scrutiny even though no search within the meaning of the Amendment has taken place."

b. More precisely, it could be said that if the government's activities have violated *anyone's* justified expectation of privacy, then that activity constitutes a Fourth Amendment search. However, it has long been established that a defendant in a criminal case who is seeking the suppression of evidence on Fourth Amendment grounds may invoke the violation of his own rights but not the rights of third parties; this concept has traditionally been referred to as "standing." In more recent years the *Katz* analysis has been utilized on that issue: a defendant has standing only if the government violated the privacy on which

(handwritten: STANDING)

he (as opposed to some other person) justifiably relied. Illustrative is *Rakas v. Illinois,* 439 U.S. 128 (1978), holding that passengers in a car who did not challenge the stopping of the vehicle in which they were riding but only the subsequent search under the seat and in the glove compartment lacked standing to challenge that search; because they asserted no property or possessory interest in the automobile searched or in the property seized, they had not shown they had a legitimate expectation of privacy in the places searched.

(handwritten: ∆ax had no possessory interest.)

Indeed, the Court in *Rakas* suggested that separate treatment of standing was no longer necessary. The Court saw no "useful analytical purpose" in considering the defendant's victim-status as a matter "apart from the merits of the defendant's Fourth Amendment claim." The appropriate question, the Court noted, is whether the "disputed search infringed an interest of the defendant which the Fourth Amendment was designed to protect." This was more direct, it reasoned, than asking whether the defendant's alleged standing is based on his own rights or those of a third party. The Court acknowledged, however, that looking directly at the merits would not alter the results in past cases or make the issue any easier to resolve. Perhaps because the Court foresaw some confusion between the question asked in determining whether there was a search (did the police intrude upon *anyone's* justified expectation of privacy) and the question traditionally labeled as one of standing (did the police intrude upon *this defendant's* expectation of privacy), the Court's subsequent opinions have not totally discarded the practice of referring to the latter issue as one of standing.

The question remaining for decision, then, is whether the search and seizure conducted in this case complied with constitutional standards. In that regard, the Government's position is that its agents acted in an entirely defensible manner: They did not begin their electronic surveillance until investigation of the petitioner's activities had established a strong probability that he was using the telephone in question to transmit gambling information to persons in other States, in violation of federal law. Moreover, the surveillance was limited, both in scope and in duration to the specific purpose of establishing the contents of the petitioner's unlawful telephonic communications. The agents confined their surveillance to the brief periods during which he used the telephone booth, and they took great care to overhear only the conversations of the petitioner himself.

Accepting this account of the Government's actions as accurate, it is clear that this surveillance was so narrowly circumscribed that a duly authorized magistrate, properly notified of the need for such investigation, specifically informed of the basis on which it was to proceed, and clearly apprised of the precise intrusion it would entail, could constitutionally have authorized, with appropriate safeguards, the very limited search and seizure that the Government asserts in fact took place. * * * ꜛc

The Government * * * urges the creation of a new exception to cover this case. It argues that surveillance of a telephone booth should be exempted from the usual requirement of advance authorization by a magistrate upon a showing of probable cause. We cannot agree. Omission of such authorization "bypasses the safeguards provided by an objective predetermination of probable cause, and substitutes instead the far less reliable procedure of an after-the-event justification for the * * * search, too likely to be subtly influenced by the familiar shortcomings of hindsight judgment." And bypassing a neutral predetermination of the *scope* of a search leaves individuals secure from Fourth Amendment violations "only in the discretion of the police."

These considerations do not vanish when the search in question is transferred from the setting of a home, an office, or a hotel room, to that of a telephone booth. Wherever a man may be, he is entitled to know that he will remain free from unreasonable searches and seizures. The government agents here ignored "the procedure of antecedent justification * * * that is central to the Fourth Amend-

---

c. The Court went on to distinguish the present situation from the kind of electronic surveillance possible under a New York statute which was invalidated in *Berger v. New York,* 388 U.S. 41 (1967), as a "blanket grant of permission to eavesdrop * * * without adequate supervision or protective procedures." That statute, the Court explained in *Berger,* (1) permitted a court order to issue merely on reasonable grounds to believe that evidence of crime may be obtained, without specifying what crime has been or is being committed and without describing what conversations are to be overheard, thus failing to "particularly [describe] the place to be searched, and the person or things to be seized," as required by the Fourth Amendment; (2) permitted installation and operation of surveillance equipment for 60 days, "the equivalent of a series of intrusions, searches and seizures pursuant to a single showing of probable cause"; (3) permitted renewal of the order on the basis of the original

grounds on which the initial order was issued, deemed "insufficient without a showing of present probable cause for continuance of the eavesdrop"; (4) placed no termination on the eavesdrop once the conversation sought is seized, as "this is left entirely to the discretion of the officer"; and (5) did not provide for a return on the warrant, "thereby leaving full discretion in the officer as to the use of seized conversations of innocent as well as guilty parties."

Nonconsensual electronic surveillance is authorized in limited circumstances by Title III of the Omnibus Crime Control and Safe Streets Act of 1968, 18 U.S.C.A. §§ 2510–2520. Although the Supreme Court has never passed upon the Act, it has been consistently upheld by the lower courts. Consequently, the focus of litigation in recent years has been upon whether particular wiretapping and electronic eavesdropping activities conform to the requirements of the Act.

ment," procedure that we hold to be a constitutional precondition of the kind of electronic surveillance involved in this case.   * * *

Judgment reversed.[d]

JUSTICE HARLAN, concurring.

* * * As the Court's opinion states, "The Fourth Amendment protects people, not places." The question, however, is what protection it affords to those people. Generally, as here, the answer to that question requires reference to a "place." My understanding of the rule that has emerged from prior decisions is that there is a twofold requirement, first that a person have exhibited an actual (subjective) expectation of privacy and, second, that the expectation be one that society is prepared to recognize as "reasonable." Thus a man's home is, for most purposes, a place where he expects privacy, but objects, activities, or statements that he exposes to the "plain view" of outsiders are not "protected" because no intention to keep them to himself has been exhibited. On the other hand, conversations in the open would not be protected against being overheard, for the expectation of privacy under the circumstances would be unreasonable.   * * *

The critical fact in this case is that "[o]ne who occupies it, [a telephone booth] shuts the door behind him, and pays the toll that permits him to place a call, is surely entitled to assume" that his conversation is not being intercepted. The point is not that the booth is "accessible to the public" at other times, but that it is a temporarily private place whose momentary occupants' expectations of freedom from intrusion are recognized as reasonable.   * * *

JUSTICE BLACK, dissenting.

* * * Tapping telephone wires, of course, was an unknown possibility at the time the Fourth Amendment was adopted. But eavesdropping (and wiretapping is nothing more than eavesdropping by telephone) was "an ancient practice which at common law was condemned as a nuisance. In those days the eavesdropper listened by naked ear under the eaves of houses or their windows, or beyond their walls seeking out private discourse." There can be no doubt that the Framers were aware of this practice, and if they had desired to outlaw or restrict the use of evidence obtained by eavesdropping, I believe that they would have used the appropriate language to do so in the Fourth Amendment. They certainly would not have left such a task to the ingenuity of language-stretching judges.   * * *

* * * By clever word juggling the Court finds it plausible to argue that language aimed specifically at searches and seizures of things that can be searched and seized may, to protect privacy, be applied to eavesdropped evidence of conversations that can neither be searched nor seized. Few things happen to an individual that do not affect his privacy in one way or another. Thus, by arbitrarily substituting the Court's language, designed to protect privacy, for the Constitution's language, designed to protect against unreasonable searches and seizures, the Court has made the Fourth Amendment its vehicle for holding all laws violative of the Constitution which offend the Court's broadest concept of privacy.   * * *

The Fourth Amendment protects privacy only to the extent that it prohibits unreasonable searches and seizures of "persons, houses, papers and effects." No general right is created by the Amendment so as to give this Court the unlimited power to hold unconstitutional everything which affects privacy. Certainly the Framers, well acquainted as they were with the excesses of governmental power,

d. The concurring opinions of Justice Douglas and Justice White are omitted. Jus- tice Marshall did not participate.

did not intend to grant this Court such omnipotent lawmaking authority as that. The history of governments proves that it is dangerous to freedom to repose such powers in courts. * * *

CALIFORNIA v. GREENWOOD

486 U.S. 35, 108 S.Ct. 1625, 100 L.Ed.2d 30 (1988).

JUSTICE WHITE delivered the opinion of the Court. * * *

In early 1984, Investigator Jenny Stracner of the Laguna Beach Police Department received information indicating that respondent Greenwood might be engaged in narcotics trafficking. * * *

On April 6, 1984, Stracner asked the neighborhood's regular trash collector to pick up the plastic garbage bags that Greenwood had left on the curb in front of his house and to turn the bags over to her without mixing their contents with garbage from other houses. The trash collector cleaned his truck bin of other refuse, collected the garbage bags from the street in front of Greenwood's house, and turned the bags over to Stracner. The officer searched through the rubbish and found items indicative of narcotics use. She recited the information that she had gleaned from the trash search in an affidavit in support of a warrant to search Greenwood's home.

Police officers encountered both respondents at the house later that day when they arrived to execute the warrant. The police discovered quantities of cocaine and hashish during their search of the house. Respondents were arrested on felony narcotics charges. They subsequently posted bail.

The police continued to receive reports of many late-night visitors to the Greenwood house. On May 4, Investigator Robert Rahaeuser obtained Greenwood's garbage from the regular trash collector in the same manner as had Stracner. The garbage again contained evidence of narcotics use.

Rahaeuser secured another search warrant for Greenwood's home based on the information from the second trash search. The police found more narcotics and evidence of narcotics trafficking when they executed the warrant. Greenwood was again arrested.

The Superior Court dismissed the charges against respondents on the authority of *People v. Krivda,* 5 Cal.3d 357, 96 Cal.Rptr. 62, 486 P.2d 1262 (1971), which held that warrantless trash searches violate the Fourth Amendment and the California Constitution. The court found that the police would not have had probable cause to search the Greenwood home without the evidence obtained from the trash searches.

The Court of Appeal affirmed. * * *

The California Supreme Court denied the State's petition for review of the Court of Appeal's decision. We granted certiorari, and now reverse.

The warrantless search and seizure of the garbage bags left at the curb outside the Greenwood house would violate the Fourth Amendment only if respondents manifested a subjective expectation of privacy in their garbage that society accepts as objectively reasonable. Respondents do not disagree with this standard.

They assert, however, that they had, and exhibited, an expectation of privacy with respect to the trash that was searched by the police: The trash, which was placed on the street for collection at a fixed time, was contained in opaque plastic bags, which the garbage collector was expected to pick up, mingle with the trash of others, and deposit at the garbage dump. The trash was only temporarily on the street, and there was little likelihood that it would be inspected by anyone.

It may well be that respondents did not expect that the contents of their garbage bags would become known to the police or other members of the public. An expectation of privacy does not give rise to Fourth Amendment protection, however, unless society is prepared to accept that expectation as objectively reasonable.

Here, we conclude that respondents exposed their garbage to the public sufficiently to defeat their claim to Fourth Amendment protection. It is common knowledge that plastic garbage bags left on or at the side of a public street are readily accessible to animals, children, scavengers, snoops,[4] and other members of the public. Moreover, respondents placed their refuse at the curb for the express purpose of conveying it to a third party, the trash collector, who might himself have sorted through respondents' trash or permitted others, such as the police, to do so. Accordingly, having deposited their garbage "in an area particularly suited for public inspection and, in a manner of speaking, public consumption, for the express purpose of having strangers take it," respondents could have had no reasonable expectation of privacy in the inculpatory items that they discarded.

Furthermore, as we have held, the police cannot reasonably be expected to avert their eyes from evidence of criminal activity that could have been observed by any member of the public. Hence, "[w]hat a person knowingly exposes to the public, even in his own home or office, is not a subject of Fourth Amendment protection." *Katz v. United States.* We held in *Smith v. Maryland,* 442 U.S. 735 (1979), for example, that the police did not violate the Fourth Amendment by causing a pen register to be installed at the telephone company's offices to record the telephone numbers dialed by a criminal suspect. An individual has no legitimate expectation of privacy in the numbers dialed on his telephone, we reasoned, because he voluntarily conveys those numbers to the telephone company when he uses the telephone. Again, we observed that "a person has no legitimate expectation of privacy in information he voluntarily turns over to third parties."

* * *

Our conclusion that society would not accept as reasonable respondents' claim to an expectation of privacy in trash left for collection in an area accessible to the public is reinforced by the unanimous rejection of similar claims by the Federal Courts of Appeals. In addition, of those state appellate courts that have considered the issue, the vast majority have held that the police may conduct warrantless searches and seizures of garbage discarded in public areas.

* * *a

JUSTICE BRENNAN, with whom JUSTICE MARSHALL joins, dissenting. * * *

The Framers of the Fourth Amendment understood that "unreasonable searches" of "paper[s] and effects"—no less than "unreasonable searches" of "person[s] and houses"—infringe privacy. * * * In short, so long as a package is "closed against inspection," the Fourth Amendment protects its contents, "wher-

---

4. Even the refuse of prominent Americans has not been invulnerable. In 1975, for example, a reporter for a weekly tabloid seized five bags of garbage from the sidewalk outside the home of Secretary of State Henry Kissinger. Washington Post, July 9, 1975, p. A1, col. 8. A newspaper editorial criticizing this journalistic "trashpicking" observed that "[e]vidently . . .

'everybody does it.'" Washington Post, July 10, 1975, p. A18, col. 1. We of course do not, as the dissent implies, "bas[e] [our] conclusion" that individuals have no reasonable expectation of privacy in their garbage on this "sole incident."

a. Justice Kennedy took no part in the consideration or decision of this case.

ever they may be," and the police must obtain a warrant to search it just "as is required when papers are subjected to search in one's own household." * * *

Our precedent, therefore, leaves no room to doubt that had respondents been carrying their personal effects in opaque, sealed plastic bags—identical to the ones they placed on the curb—their privacy would have been protected from warrantless police intrusion. * * *

Respondents deserve no less protection just because Greenwood used the bags to discard rather than to transport his personal effects. Their contents are not inherently any less private, and Greenwood's decision to discard them, at least in the manner in which he did, does not diminish his expectation of privacy.[2]

A trash bag, like any of the above-mentioned containers, "is a common repository for one's personal effects" and, even more than many of them, is "therefore * * * inevitably associated with the expectation of privacy." * * * * A single bag of trash testifies eloquently to the eating, reading, and recreational habits of the person who produced it. A search of trash, like a search of the bedroom, can relate intimate details about sexual practices, health, and personal hygiene. Like rifling through desk drawers or intercepting phone calls, rummaging through trash can divulge the target's financial and professional status, political affiliations and inclinations, private thoughts, personal relationships, and romantic interests. It cannot be doubted that a sealed trash bag harbors telling evidence of the "intimate activity associated with the 'sanctity of a man's home and the privacies of life,'" which the Fourth Amendment is designed to protect.

The Court properly rejects the State's attempt to distinguish trash searches from other searches on the theory that trash is abandoned and therefore not entitled to an expectation of privacy. As the author of the Court's opinion observed last Term, a defendant's "property interest [in trash] does not settle the matter for Fourth Amendment purposes, for the reach of the Fourth Amendment is not determined by state property law." In evaluating the reasonableness of Greenwood's expectation that his sealed trash bags would not be invaded, the Court has held that we must look to "understandings that are recognized and permitted by society." Most of us, I believe, would be incensed to discover a meddler—whether a neighbor, a reporter, or a detective—scrutinizing our sealed trash containers to discover some detail of our personal lives. That was, quite naturally, the reaction to the sole incident on which the Court bases its conclusion that "snoops" and the like defeat the expectation of privacy in trash. When a tabloid reporter examined then-Secretary of State Henry Kissinger's trash and published his findings, Kissinger was "really revolted" by the intrusion and his wife suffered "grave anguish." N.Y. Times, July 9, 1975, p. A1, col. 8. The public response roundly condemning the reporter demonstrates that society not only recognized those reactions as reasonable, but shared them as well. Commentators variously characterized his conduct as "a disgusting invasion of personal privacy," Flieger, Investigative Trash, U.S. News & World Report, July 28, 1975, p. 72 (editor's page); "indefensible * * * as civilized behavior," Washington Post,

2. Both to support its position that society recognizes no reasonable privacy interest in sealed, opaque trash bags and to refute the prediction that "society will be shocked to learn" of that conclusion, the Court relies heavily upon a collection of lower court cases finding no Fourth Amendment bar to trash searches. But the authority that leads the Court to be "distinctively unimpressed" with our position, is itself impressively undistinguished. Of 11 Federal Court of Appeals cases cited by the Court, at least two are factually or legally distinguishable, and seven rely entirely or almost entirely on an abandonment theory that the Court has discredited. A reading of the Court's collection of state-court cases reveals an equally unimpressive pattern.

July 10, 1975, p. A18, col. 1 (editorial); and contrary to "the way decent people behave in relation to each other," ibid. * * *

That is not to deny that isolated intrusions into opaque, sealed trash containers occur. When, acting on their own, "animals, children, scavengers, snoops, [or] other members of the general public," *actually* rummage through a bag of trash and expose its contents to plain view, "police cannot reasonably be expected to avert their eyes from evidence of criminal activity that could have been observed by any member of the public."

Had Greenwood flaunted his intimate activity by strewing his trash all over the curb for all to see, or had some nongovernmental intruder invaded his privacy and done the same, I could accept the Court's conclusion that an expectation of privacy would have been unreasonable. Similarly, had police searching the city dump run across incriminating evidence that, despite commingling with the trash of others, still retained its identity as Greenwood's, we would have a different case. But all that Greenwood "exposed * * * to the public" were the exteriors of several opaque, sealed containers. * * *

The mere *possibility* that unwelcome meddlers *might* open and rummage through the containers does not negate the expectation of privacy in its contents any more than the possibility of a burglary negates an expectation of privacy in the home; or the possibility of a private intrusion negates an expectation of privacy in an unopened package; or the possibility that an operator will listen in on a telephone conversation negates an expectation of privacy in the words spoken on the telephone. "What a person * * * seeks to preserve as private, *even in an area accessible to the public,* may be constitutionally protected." *Katz.* We have therefore repeatedly rejected attempts to justify a State's invasion of privacy on the ground that the privacy is not absolute. See *Chapman v. United States,* 365 U.S. 610 (1961) (search of a house invaded tenant's Fourth Amendment rights even though landlord had authority to enter house for some purposes); *Stoner v. California,* 376 U.S. 483 (1964) (implicit consent to janitorial personnel to enter motel room does not amount to consent to police search of room); *O'Connor v. Ortega,* 480 U.S. 709 (1987) (a government employee has a reasonable expectation of privacy in his office, even though "it is the nature of government offices that others—such as fellow employees, supervisors, consensual visitors, and the general public—may have frequent access to an individual's office"). * * *

Nor is it dispositive that "respondents placed their refuse at the curb for the express purpose of conveying it to a third party, * * * who might himself have sorted through respondents' trash or permitted others, such as police, to do so." In the first place, Greenwood can hardly be faulted for leaving trash on his curb when a county ordinance commanded him to do so and prohibited him from disposing of it in any other way. * * * More importantly, even the voluntary relinquishment of possession or control over an effect does not necessarily amount to a relinquishment of a privacy expectation in it. Were it otherwise, a letter or package would lose all Fourth Amendment protection when placed in a mail box or other depository with the "express purpose" of entrusting it to the postal officer or a private carrier; those bailees are just as likely as trash collectors (and certainly have greater incentive) to "sor[t] through" the personal effects entrusted to them, "or permi[t] others, such as police to do so." Yet, it has been clear for at least 110 years that the possibility of such an intrusion does not justify a warrantless search by police in the first instance. * * *

[handwritten margin note: letter analogy]

FLORIDA v. RILEY

488 U.S. 445, 109 S.Ct. 693, 102 L.Ed.2d 835 (1989).

JUSTICE WHITE announced the judgment of the Court and delivered an opinion, in which THE CHIEF JUSTICE, JUSTICE SCALIA and JUSTICE KENNEDY join.

On certification to it by a lower state court, the Florida Supreme Court addressed the following question: "Whether surveillance of the interior of a partially covered greenhouse in a residential backyard from the vantage point of a helicopter located 400 feet above the greenhouse constitutes a 'search' for which a warrant is required under the Fourth Amendment and Article I, Section 12 of the Florida Constitution." The court answered the question in the affirmative, and we granted the State's petition for certiorari challenging that conclusion. * * *

We agree with the State's submission that our decision in *California v. Ciraolo*, 476 U.S. 207, 106 S.Ct. 1809, 90 L.Ed.2d 210 (1986), controls this case. There, acting on a tip, the police inspected the back yard of a particular house while flying in a fixed-wing aircraft at 1,000 feet. With the naked-eye the officers saw what they concluded was marijuana growing in the yard. A search warrant was obtained on the strength of this airborne inspection, and marijuana plants were found. The trial court refused to suppress this evidence, but a state appellate court held that the inspection violated the Fourth and Fourteenth Amendments of the United States Constitution and that the warrant was therefore invalid. We in turn reversed, holding that the inspection was not a search subject to the Fourth Amendment. We recognized that the yard was within the curtilage of the house, that a fence shielded the yard from observation from the street and that the occupant had a subjective expectation of privacy. We held, however, that such an expectation was not reasonable and not one "that society is prepared to honor." * * * "In an age where private and commercial flight in the public airways is routine, it is unreasonable for respondent to expect that his marijuana plants were constitutionally protected from being observed with the naked eye from an altitude of 1,000 feet. The Fourth Amendment simply does not require the police traveling in the public airways at this altitude to obtain a warrant in order to observe what is visible to the naked eye."

We arrive at the same conclusion in the present case.[a] * * *

Nor on the facts before us, does it make a difference for Fourth Amendment purposes that the helicopter was flying at 400 feet when the officer saw what was growing in the greenhouse through the partially open roof and sides of the structure. We would have a different case if flying at that altitude had been contrary to law or regulation. But helicopters are not bound by the lower limits of the navigable airspace allowed to other aircraft. Any member of the public could legally have been flying over Riley's property in a helicopter at the altitude of 400 feet and could have observed Riley's greenhouse. The police officer did no more. This is not to say that an inspection of the curtilage of a house from an aircraft will always pass muster under the Fourth Amendment simply because the

a. In *Bond v. United States*, 529 U.S. 334 (2000), involving the question of whether the squeezing of soft luggage passengers had placed in the overhead rack of a bus was a search, the Court rejected the government's reliance upon *Ciraolo* and *Riley*, stating that "[p]hysical invasive inspection is simply more intrusive than purely visual inspection." The Court then concluded: "When a bus passenger places a bag in an overhead bin, he expects that other passengers or bus employees may move it for one reason or another. Thus, a bus passenger clearly expects that his bag may be handled. He does not expect that other passen- gers or bus employees will, as a matter of course, feel the bag in an exploratory manner. But this is exactly what the agent did here. We therefore hold that the agent's physical manip- ulation of petitioner's bag violated the Fourth Amendment." Two dissenters in *Bond* objected that the squeezing did not "differ from the treatment that overhead luggage is likely to receive from strangers in a world of travel that is somewhat less gentle than it used to be," and that whether "tactile manipulation * * * is more intrusive or less intrusive than visual observation * * * necessarily depends on the particular circumstances."

plane is within the navigable airspace specified by law. But it is of obvious importance that the helicopter in this case was *not* violating the law, and there is nothing in the record or before us to suggest that helicopters flying at 400 feet are sufficiently rare in this country to lend substance to respondent's claim that he reasonably anticipated that his greenhouse would not be subject to observation from that altitude. Neither is there any intimation here that the helicopter interfered with respondent's normal use of the greenhouse or of other parts of the curtilage. As far as this record reveals, no intimate details connected with the use of the home or curtilage were observed, and there was no undue noise, no wind, dust, or threat of injury. In these circumstances, there was no violation of the Fourth Amendment. * * *

[handwritten margin notes: - lawful flight; - normal flight; - no interference w/ use; - no intimate details; - no nuisance]

JUSTICE O'CONNOR, concurring in the judgment. * * *

In determining whether Riley had a reasonable expectation of privacy from aerial observation, the relevant inquiry after *Ciraolo* is not whether the helicopter was where it had a right to be under FAA regulations. Rather, consistent with *Katz*, we must ask whether the helicopter was in the public airways at an altitude at which members of the public travel with sufficient regularity that Riley's expectation of privacy from aerial observation was not "one that society is prepared to recognize as 'reasonable.'" * * *

Because there is reason to believe that there is considerable public use of airspace at altitudes of 400 feet and above, and because Riley introduced no evidence to the contrary before the Florida courts, I conclude that Riley's expectation that his curtilage was protected from naked-eye aerial observation from that altitude was not a reasonable one. However, public use of altitudes lower than that—particularly public observations from helicopters circling over the curtilage of a home—may be sufficiently rare that police surveillance from such altitudes would violate reasonable expectations of privacy, despite compliance with FAA air safety regulations.

JUSTICE BRENNAN, with whom JUSTICE MARSHALL and JUSTICE STEVENS, join, dissenting.

* * * Under the plurality's exceedingly grudging Fourth Amendment theory, the expectation of privacy is defeated if a single member of the public could conceivably position herself to see into the area in question without doing anything illegal. It is defeated whatever the difficulty a person would have in so positioning herself, and however infrequently anyone would in fact do so. In taking this view the plurality ignores the very essence of *Katz*. * * *

It is a curious notion that the reach of the Fourth Amendment can be so largely defined by administrative regulations issued for purposes of flight safety. It is more curious still that the plurality relies to such an extent on the legality of the officer's act, when we have consistently refused to equate police violation of the law with infringement of the Fourth Amendment.[3] But the plurality's willingness to end its inquiry when it finds that the officer was in a position he had a right to be in is misguided for an even more fundamental reason. Finding determinative the fact that the officer was where he had a right to be is, at bottom, an attempt to analogize surveillance from a helicopter to surveillance by a police officer standing on a public road and viewing evidence of crime through an open window or a gap in a fence. In such a situation, the occupant of the home

[handwritten margin note: curtilage, with diagram]

---

3. In *Oliver v. United States*, 466 U.S. 170, 104 S.Ct. 1735, 80 L.Ed.2d 214 (1984), for example, we held that police officers who trespassed upon posted and fenced private land did not violate the Fourth Amendment, despite the fact that their action was subject to criminal sanctions. We noted that the interests vindicated by the Fourth Amendment were not identical with those served by the common law of trespass.

may be said to lack any reasonable expectation of privacy in what can be seen from that road—even if, in fact, people rarely pass that way.

The police officer positioned 400 feet above Riley's backyard was not, however, standing on a public road. The vantage point he enjoyed was not one any citizen could readily share. His ability to see over Riley's fence depended on his use of a very expensive and sophisticated piece of machinery to which few ordinary citizens have access. In such circumstances it makes no more sense to rely on the legality of the officer's position in the skies than it would to judge the constitutionality of the wiretap in *Katz* by the legality of the officer's position outside the telephone booth. The simply inquiry whether the police officer had the legal right to be in the position from which he made his observations cannot suffice, for we cannot assume that Riley's curtilage was so open to the observations of passersby in the skies that he retained little privacy or personal security to be lost to police surveillance. The question before us must be not whether the police were where they had a right to be, but whether public observation of Riley's curtilage was so commonplace that Riley's expectation of privacy in his backyard could not be considered reasonable. * * *

What separates me from Justice O'Connor is essentially an empirical matter concerning the extent of public use of the airspace at that altitude, together with the question of how to resolve that issue. I do not think the constitutional claims should fail simply because "there is reason to believe" that there is "considerable" public flying this close to earth or because Riley "introduced no evidence to the contrary before the Florida courts." * * * I think we could take judicial notice that, while there may be an occasional privately owned helicopter that flies over populated areas at an altitude of 400 feet, such flights are a rarity and are almost entirely limited to approaching or leaving airports or to reporting traffic congestion near major roadways. And, as the concurring opinion agrees, the extent of police surveillance traffic cannot serve as a bootstrap to demonstrate public use of the airspace.

If, however, we are to resolve the issue by considering whether the appropriate party carried its burden of proof, I again think that Riley must prevail. Because the State has greater access to information concerning customary flight patterns and because the coercive power of the State ought not be brought to bear in cases in which it is unclear whether the prosecution is a product of an unconstitutional, warrantless search, the burden of proof properly rests with the State and not with the individual defendant. The State quite clearly has not carried this burden. * * *

JUSTICE BLACKMUN, dissenting.

[B]ecause I believe that private helicopters rarely fly over curtilages at an altitude of 400 feet, I would impose upon the prosecution the burden or proving contrary facts necessary to show that Riley lacked a reasonable expectation of privacy. Indeed, I would establish this burden of proof for any helicopter surveillance case in which the flight occurred below 1000 feet—in other words, for any aerial surveillance case not governed by the Court's decision in *California v. Ciraolo.*

In this case, the prosecution did not meet this burden of proof, as Justice Brennan notes. This failure should compel a finding that a Fourth Amendment search occurred. But because our prior cases gave the parties little guidance on the burden of proof issue, I would remand this case to allow the prosecution an opportunity to meet this burden. * * *

UNITED STATES v. KARO

468 U.S. 705, 104 S.Ct. 3296, 82 L.Ed.2d 530 (1984).

JUSTICE WHITE delivered the opinion of the Court.

In *United States v. Knotts,* 460 U.S. 276 (1983), we held that the warrantless monitoring of an electronic tracking device ("beeper")[1] inside a container of chemicals did not violate the Fourth Amendment when it revealed no information that could not have been obtained through visual surveillance. In this case, we are called upon to address two questions left unresolved in *Knotts:* (1) whether installation of a beeper in a container of chemicals with the consent of the original owner constitutes a search or seizure within the meaning of the Fourth Amendment when the container is delivered to a buyer having no knowledge of the presence of the beeper, and (2) whether monitoring of a beeper falls within the ambit of the Fourth Amendment when it reveals information that could not have been obtained through visual surveillance.

In August 1980 Agent Rottinger of the Drug Enforcement Administration (DEA) learned that respondents James Karo, Richard Horton, and William Harley had ordered 50 gallons of ether from government informant Carl Muehlenweg of Graphic Photo Design in Albuquerque, New Mexico. Muehlenweg told Rottinger that the ether was to be used to extract cocaine from clothing that had been imported into the United States. The Government obtained a court order authorizing the installation and monitoring of a beeper in one of the cans of ether. * * *

At about 6:00 p.m. on February 6, * * * two vehicles were under both physical and electronic surveillance. When the vehicles arrived at a house in Taos rented by Horton, Harley, and Michael Steele, the agents did not maintain tight surveillance for fear of detection. When the vehicles left the Taos residence, agents determined using the beeper monitor that the beeper can was still inside the house. Again on February 7, the beeper revealed that the ether can was still on the premises. * * * On February 8, the agents applied for and obtained a warrant to search the Taos residence based in part on information derived through use of the beeper. The warrant was executed on February 10, 1981, and Horton, Harley, Steele, and Evan Roth were arrested, and cocaine and laboratory equipment were seized.

* * * The District Court granted respondents' pre-trial motion to suppress the evidence seized from the Taos residence on the grounds that the initial warrant to install the beeper was invalid and that the Taos seizure was the tainted fruit of an unauthorized installation and monitoring of that beeper. The United States appealed but did not challenge the invalidation of the initial warrant. The Court of Appeals affirmed, holding that a warrant was required to install the beeper in one of the 10 cans of ether and to monitor it in private dwellings and storage lockers. The warrant for the search in Taos and the resulting seizure were tainted by the prior illegal conduct of the Government. * * *

Because the judgment below in favor of Karo rested in major part on the conclusion that the installation violated his Fourth Amendment rights and that any information obtained from monitoring the beeper was tainted by the initial

---

1. "A beeper is a radio transmitter, usually battery operated, which emits periodic signals   that can be picked up by a radio receiver."

illegality, we must deal with the legality of the warrantless installation. It is clear that the actual placement of the beeper into the can violated no one's Fourth Amendment rights. The can into which the beeper was placed belonged at the time to the DEA, and by no stretch of the imagination could it be said that respondents then had any legitimate expectation of privacy in it. The ether and the original 10 cans, on the other hand, belonged to, and were in the possession of, Muehlenweg, who had given his consent to any invasion of those items that occurred. Thus, even if there had been no substitution of cans and the agents had placed the beeper into one of the original 10 cans, Muehlenweg's consent was sufficient to validate the placement of the beeper in the can.

* * * The mere transfer to Karo of a can containing an unmonitored beeper infringed no privacy interest. It conveyed no information that Karo wished to keep private, for it conveyed no information at all. To be sure, it created a *potential* for an invasion of privacy, but we have never held that potential, as opposed to actual, invasions of privacy constitute searches for purposes of the Fourth Amendment. * * *

We likewise do not believe that the transfer of the container constituted a seizure. A "seizure" of property occurs when "there is some meaningful interference with an individual's possessory interests in that property." Although the can may have contained an unknown and unwanted foreign object, it cannot be said that anyone's possessory interest was interfered with in a meaningful way. At most, there was a technical trespass on the space occupied by the beeper. The existence of a physical trespass is only marginally relevant to the question of whether the Fourth Amendment has been violated, however, for an actual trespass is neither necessary nor sufficient to establish a constitutional violation. * * *

In *United States v. Knotts,* law enforcement officials, with the consent of the seller, installed a beeper in a five-gallon can of chloroform and monitored the beeper after delivery of the can to the buyer in Minneapolis, Minnesota. Although there was partial visual surveillance as the automobile containing the can moved along the public highways, the beeper enabled the officers to locate the can in the area of a cabin near Shell Lake, Wisconsin, and it was this information that provided the basis for the issuance of a search warrant. As the case came to us, the installation of the beeper was not challenged; only the monitoring was at issue. The Court held that since the movements of the automobile and the arrival of the can containing the beeper in the area of the cabin could have been observed by the naked eye, no Fourth Amendment violation was committed by monitoring the beeper during the trip to the cabin. In *Knotts,* the record did not show that the beeper was monitored while the can containing it was inside the cabin, and we therefore had no occasion to consider whether a constitutional violation would have occurred had the fact been otherwise.

Here, there is no gainsaying that the beeper was used to locate the ether in a specific house in Taos, New Mexico, and that that information was in turn used to secure a warrant for the search of the house. * * *

At the risk of belaboring the obvious, private residences are places in which the individual normally expects privacy free of governmental intrusion not authorized by a warrant, and that expectation is plainly one that society is prepared to recognize as justifiable. Our cases have not deviated from this basic Fourth Amendment principle. Searches and seizures inside a home without a warrant are presumptively unreasonable absent exigent circumstances. In this case, had a DEA agent thought it useful to enter the Taos residence to verify that the ether was actually in the house and had he done so surreptitiously and without a warrant, there is little doubt that he would have engaged in an unreasonable search within the meaning of the Fourth Amendment. For purposes of the Amendment, the result is the same where, without a warrant, the Government surreptitiously employs an electronic device to obtain information that it could not have obtained by observation from outside the curtilage of the house. The beeper tells the agent that a particular article is actually located at a particular time in the private residence and is in the possession of the person or persons whose residence is being surveilled.[a] Even if visual surveillance has revealed that the article to which the beeper is attached has entered the house, the later monitoring not only verifies the officers' observations but also establishes that the article remains on the premises. Here, for example, the beeper was monitored for a significant period after the arrival of the ether in Taos and before the application for a warrant to search. * * *

We cannot accept the Government's contention that it should be completely free from the constraints of the Fourth Amendment to determine by means of an electronic device, without a warrant and without probable cause or reasonable suspicion, whether a particular article—or a person, for that matter—is in an individual's home at a particular time. Indiscriminate monitoring of property that has been withdrawn from public view would present far too serious a threat to privacy interests in the home to escape entirely some sort of Fourth Amendment oversight.

We also reject the Government's contention that it should be able to monitor beepers in private residences without a warrant if there is the requisite justification in the facts for believing that a crime is being or will be committed and that monitoring the beeper wherever it goes is likely to produce evidence of criminal activity. Warrantless searches are presumptively unreasonable, though the Court has recognized a few limited exceptions to this general rule. * * *

If agents are required to obtain warrants prior to monitoring a beeper when it has been withdrawn from public view, the Government argues, for all practical purposes they will be forced to obtain warrants in every case in which they seek to use a beeper, because they have no way of knowing in advance whether the beeper will be transmitting its signals from inside private premises. The argument that a warrant requirement would oblige the Government to obtain warrants in a large number of cases is hardly a compelling argument against the requirement. It is worthy of note that, in any event, this is not a particularly attractive case in which to argue that it is impractical to obtain a warrant, since a warrant was in fact obtained in this case, seemingly on probable cause.

---

a. Compare *United States v. Place,* 462 U.S. 696 (1983), dealing with a temporary seizure of luggage at an airport so that it could be brought into contact with a drug detection dog. The majority declared "that a person possesses a privacy interest in the contents of personal luggage that is protected by the Fourth Amendment. A 'canine sniff' by a well-trained narcotics detection dog, however, does not require opening the luggage. It does not expose noncontraband items that otherwise would remain hidden from public view, as does, for example, an officer's rummaging through the contents of the luggage. Thus, the manner in which information is obtained through this investigative technique is much less intrusive than a typical search. Moreover, the sniff discloses only the presence or absence of narcotics, a contraband item. Thus, despite the fact that the sniff tells the authorities something about the contents of the luggage, the information obtained is limited. This limited disclosure also ensures that the owner of the property is not subjected to the embarrassment and inconvenience entailed in less discriminate and more intrusive investigative methods.

"In these respects, the canine sniff is *sui generis.* We are aware of no other investigative procedure that is so limited both in the manner in which the information is obtained and in the content of the information revealed by the procedure. Therefore, we conclude that the particular course of investigation that the agents intended to pursue here—exposure of respondent's luggage, which was located in a public place, to a trained canine—did not constitute a 'search' within the meaning of the Fourth Amendment."

[handwritten in margin: particularity requirement]

We are also unpersuaded by the argument that a warrant should not be required because of the difficulty in satisfying the particularity requirement of the Fourth Amendment. The Government contends that it would be impossible to describe the "place" to be searched, because the location of the place is precisely what is sought to be discovered through the search. However true that may be, it will still be possible to describe the object into which the beeper is to be placed, the circumstances that led agents to wish to install the beeper, and the length of time for which beeper surveillance is requested. In our view, this information will suffice to permit issuance of a warrant authorizing beeper installation and surveillance.

In sum, we discern no reason for deviating from the general rule that a search of a house should be conducted pursuant to a warrant.[5]

[But] it is clear that the warrant affidavit, after striking the facts about monitoring the beeper while it was in the Taos residence, contained sufficient untainted information to furnish probable cause for the issuance of the search warrant. The evidence seized in the house should not have been suppressed with respect to any of the respondents. * * *

JUSTICE O'CONNOR, with whom JUSTICE REHNQUIST joins, concurring in part and concurring in the judgment. * * *

[A] privacy interest in the location of a closed container that enters a home with the homeowner's permission cannot be inferred mechanically by reference to the more general privacy interests in the home itself. The homeowner's privacy interests are often narrower than those of the owner of the container. A defendant should be allowed to challenge evidence obtained by monitoring a beeper installed in a closed container only if (1) the beeper was monitored when visual tracking of the container was not possible, so that the defendant had a reasonable expectation that the container's movements would remain private, and (2) the defendant had an interest in the container itself sufficient to empower him to give effective consent to a search of the container. A person's right not to have a container tracked by means of a beeper depends both on his power to prevent visual observation of the container and on his power to control its location, a power that can usually be inferred from a privacy interest in the container itself. One who lacks either power has no legitimate expectation of privacy in the movements of the container. * * *

JUSTICE STEVENS, with whom JUSTICE BRENNAN and JUSTICE MARSHALL join, concurring in part and dissenting in part. * * *

The attachment of the beeper, in my judgment, constituted a "seizure." The owner of property, of course, has a right to exclude from it all the world, including the Government, and a concomitant right to use it exclusively for his own purposes. When the Government attaches an electronic monitoring device to that property, it infringes that exclusionary right; in a fundamental sense it has converted the property to its own use. Surely such an invasion is an "interference" with possessory rights; the right to exclude, which attached as soon as the can respondents purchased was delivered, had been infringed.[2] That interference

---

5. The United States insists that if beeper monitoring is deemed a search, a showing of reasonable suspicion rather than probable cause should suffice for its execution. That issue, however, is not before us. The initial warrant was not invalidated for want of probable cause, which plainly existed, but for misleading statements in the affidavit. The Government did not appeal the invalidation of the warrant and as the case has turned out, the Government prevails without a warrant authorizing installation. It will be time enough to resolve the probable cause-reasonable suspicion issue in a case that requires it.

2. It makes no difference in this case that when the beeper was initially attached, the can had not yet been delivered to respondents.

is also "meaningful"; the character of the property is profoundly different when infected with an electronic bug than when it is entirely germ free. * * *

The Court recognizes that concealment of personal property from public view gives rise to Fourth Amendment protection when it writes: "Indiscriminate monitoring of property that has been withdrawn from public view would present far too serious a threat to privacy interests in the home to escape entirely some sort of Fourth Amendment oversight." This protection is not limited to times when the beeper was in a home. The beeper also revealed when the can of ether had been moved. When a person drives down a public thoroughfare in a car with a can of ether concealed in the trunk, he is not exposing to public view the fact that he is in possession of a can of ether; the can is still "withdrawn from public view" and hence its location is entitled to constitutional protection. * * *

KYLLO V. UNITED STATES

___ U.S. ___, 121 S.Ct. 2038, ___ L.Ed.2d ___ (2001).

JUSTICE SCALIA delivered the opinion of the Court. * * *

In 1991 Agent William Elliott of the United States Department of the Interior came to suspect that marijuana was being grown in the home belonging to petitioner Danny Kyllo, part of a triplex on Rhododendron Drive in Florence, Oregon. Indoor marijuana growth typically requires high-intensity lamps. In order to determine whether an amount of heat was emanating from petitioner's home consistent with the use of such lamps, at 3:20 a.m. on January 16, 1992, Agent Elliott and Dan Haas used an Agema Thermovision 210 thermal imager[a] to scan the triplex. Thermal imagers detect infrared radiation, which virtually all objects emit but which is not visible to the naked eye. The imager converts radiation into images based on relative warmth—black is cool, white is hot, shades of gray connote relative differences; in that respect, it operates somewhat like a video camera showing heat images. The scan of Kyllo's home took only a few minutes and was performed from the passenger seat of Agent Elliott's vehicle across the street from the front of the house and also from the street in back of the house. The scan showed that the roof over the garage and a side wall of petitioner's home were relatively hot compared to the rest of the home and substantially warmer than neighboring homes in the triplex. Agent Elliott concluded that petitioner was using halide lights to grow marijuana in his house, which indeed he was. Based on tips from informants, utility bills, and the thermal imaging, a Federal Magistrate Judge issued a warrant authorizing a search of petitioner's home, and the agents found an indoor growing operation involving more than 100 plants. Petitioner was indicted on one count of manufacturing marijuana, in violation of 21 U.S.C. § 841(a)(1). He unsuccessfully moved to suppress the evidence seized from his home and then entered a conditional guilty plea[, and the court of appeals affirmed]. * * *

It would be foolish to contend that the degree of privacy secured to citizens by the Fourth Amendment has been entirely unaffected by the advance of technology. For example, * * * the technology enabling human flight has exposed to public

Once the delivery had been effected, the container was respondents' property from which they had the right to exclude all the world. It was at that point that the infringement of this constitutionally protected interest began.

a. As the Court later elaborated, "the District Court found that the Agema 210 'is a nonintrusive device which emits no rays or beams and shows a crude visual image of the heat being radiated from the outside of the house'; it 'did not show any people or activity within the walls of the structure'; '[t]he device used cannot penetrate walls or windows to reveal conversations or human activities'; and '[n]o intimate details of the home were observed.' "

view (and hence, we have said, to official observation) uncovered portions of the house and its curtilage that once were private. See *Ciraolo*, [Ch. 3, § 2]. The question we confront today is what limits there are upon this power of technology to shrink the realm of guaranteed privacy.

The *Katz* test—whether the individual has an expectation of privacy that society is prepared to recognize as reasonable—has often been criticized as circular, and hence subjective and unpredictable. While it may be difficult to refine *Katz* when the search of areas such as telephone booths, automobiles, or even the curtilage and uncovered portions of residences are at issue, in the case of the search of the interior of homes—the prototypical and hence most commonly litigated area of protected privacy—there is a ready criterion, with roots deep in the common law, of the minimal expectation of privacy that exists, and that is acknowledged to be reasonable. To withdraw protection of this minimum expectation would be to permit police technology to erode the privacy guaranteed by the Fourth Amendment. We think that obtaining by sense-enhancing technology any information regarding the interior of the home that could not otherwise have been obtained without physical "intrusion into a constitutionally protected area" constitutes a search—at least where (as here) the technology in question is not in general public use. This assures preservation of that degree of privacy against government that existed when the Fourth Amendment was adopted. On the basis of this criterion, the information obtained by the thermal imager in this case was the product of a search.[2]

The Government maintains, however, that the thermal imaging must be upheld because it detected "only heat radiating from the external surface of the house." The dissent makes this its leading point, contending that there is a fundamental difference between what it calls "off-the-wall" observations and "through-the-wall surveillance." But just as a thermal imager captures only heat emanating from a house, so also a powerful directional microphone picks up only sound emanating from a house—and a satellite capable of scanning from many miles away would pick up only visible light emanating from a house. We rejected such a mechanical interpretation of the Fourth Amendment in *Katz*, where the eavesdropping device picked up only sound waves that reached the exterior of the phone booth. Reversing that approach would leave the homeowner at the mercy of advancing technology—including imaging technology that could discern all human activity in the home. While the technology used in the present case was relatively crude, the rule we adopt must take account of more sophisticated systems that are already in use or in development.[3] * * *

2. The dissent's repeated assertion that the thermal imaging did not obtain information regarding the interior of the home is simply inaccurate. A thermal imager reveals the relative heat of various rooms in the home. The dissent may not find that information particularly private or important, but there is no basis for saying it is not information regarding the interior of the home. The dissent's comparison of the thermal imaging to various circumstances in which outside observers might be able to perceive, without technology, the heat of the home—for example, by observing snow-melt on the roof—is quite irrelevant. The fact that equivalent information could sometimes be obtained by other means does not make lawful the use of means that violate the Fourth Amendment. The police might, for example, learn how many people are in a particular house by setting up year-round surveillance; but that does not make breaking and entering to find out the same information lawful. In any event, on the night of January 16, 1992, no outside observer could have discerned the relative heat of Kyllo's home without thermal imaging.

3. The ability to "see" through walls and other opaque barriers is a clear, and scientifically feasible, goal of law enforcement research and development. The National Law Enforcement and Corrections Technology Center, a program within the United States Department of Justice, features on its Internet Website projects that include a "Radar–Based Through-the-Wall Surveillance System," "Handheld Ultrasound Through the Wall Surveillance," and a "Radar Flashlight" that "will enable law officers to detect individuals

The Government also contends that the thermal imaging was constitutional because it did not "detect private activities occurring in private areas." * * * The Fourth Amendment's protection of the home has never been tied to measurement of the quality or quantity of information obtained. * * * Thus, in *Karo*, [Ch. 3, § 2], the only thing detected was a can of ether in the home; and in *Arizona v. Hicks*, 480 U.S. 321 (1987), the only thing detected by a physical search that went beyond what officers lawfully present could observe in "plain view" was the registration number of a phonograph turntable. These were intimate details because they were details of the home, just as was the detail of how warm—or even how relatively warm—Kyllo was heating his residence.

Limiting the prohibition of thermal imaging to "intimate details" would not only be wrong in principle; it would be impractical in application, failing to provide "a workable accommodation between the needs of law enforcement and the interests protected by the Fourth Amendment." To begin with, there is no necessary connection between the sophistication of the surveillance equipment and the "intimacy" of the details that it observes—which means that one cannot say (and the police cannot be assured) that use of the relatively crude equipment at issue here will always be lawful. * * * We * * * would have to develop a jurisprudence specifying which home activities are "intimate" and which are not. And even when (if ever) that jurisprudence were fully developed, no police officer would be able to know in advance whether his through-the-wall surveillance picks up "intimate" details—and thus would be unable to know in advance whether it is constitutional.

The dissent's proposed standard—whether the technology offers the "functional equivalent of actual presence in the area being searched"—would seem quite similar to our own at first blush. The dissent concludes that *Katz* was such a case, but then inexplicably asserts that if the same listening device only revealed the volume of the conversation, the surveillance would be permissible. Yet if, without technology, the police could not discern volume without being actually present in the phone booth, Justice Stevens should conclude a search has occurred.* * * The same should hold for the interior heat of the home if only a person present in the home could discern the heat. Thus the driving force of the dissent, despite its recitation of the above standard, appears to be a distinction among different types of information—whether the "homeowner would even care if anybody noticed." The dissent offers no practical guidance for the application of this standard, and for reasons already discussed, we believe there can be none. The people in their houses, as well as the police, deserve more precision.[6]

We have said that the Fourth Amendment draws "a firm line at the entrance to the house." That line, we think, must be not only firm but also bright—which requires clear specification of those methods of surveillance that require a warrant. While it is certainly possible to conclude from the videotape of the thermal imaging that occurred in this case that no "significant" compromise of the

through interior building walls." www.nlectc.org/techproj/ (visited May 3, 2001). Some devices may emit low levels of radiation that travel "through-the-wall," but others, such as more sophisticated thermal imaging devices, are entirely passive, or "off-the-wall" as the dissent puts it.

6. The dissent argues that we have injected potential uncertainty into the constitutional analysis by noting that whether or not the technology is in general public use may be a factor. That quarrel, however, is not with us but with this Court's precedent. See *Ciraolo* ("In an age where private and commercial flight in the public airways is routine, it is unreasonable for respondent to expect that his marijuana plants were constitutionally protected from being observed with the naked eye from an altitude of 1,000 feet"). Given that we can quite confidently say that thermal imaging is not "routine," we decline in this case to reexamine that factor.

homeowner's privacy has occurred, we must take the long view, from the original meaning of the Fourth Amendment forward. * * *

Since we hold the Thermovision imaging to have been an unlawful search, it will remain for the District Court to determine whether, without the evidence it provided, the search warrant issued in this case was supported by probable cause—and if not, whether there is any other basis for supporting admission of the evidence that the search pursuant to the warrant produced. * * *

JUSTICE STEVENS, with whom THE CHIEF JUSTICE, JUSTICE O'CONNOR, and JUSTICE KENNEDY join, dissenting. * * *

While the Court "take[s] the long view" and decides this case based largely on the potential of yet-to-be-developed technology that might allow "through-the-wall surveillance," this case involves nothing more than off-the-wall surveillance by law enforcement officers to gather information exposed to the general public from the outside of petitioner's home. All that the infrared camera did in this case was passively measure heat emitted from the exterior surfaces of petitioner's home; all that those measurements showed were relative differences in emission levels, vaguely indicating that some areas of the roof and outside walls were warmer than others. As still images from the infrared scans show, no details regarding the interior of petitioner's home were revealed. Unlike an x-ray scan, or other possible "through-the-wall" techniques, the detection of infrared radiation emanating from the home did not accomplish "an unauthorized physical penetration into the premises," nor did it "obtain information that it could not have obtained by observation from outside the curtilage of the house."

Indeed, the ordinary use of the senses might enable a neighbor or passerby to notice the heat emanating from a building, particularly if it is vented, as was the case here. Additionally, any member of the public might notice that one part of a house is warmer than another part or a nearby building if, for example, rainwater evaporates or snow melts at different rates across its surfaces. Such use of the senses would not convert into an unreasonable search if, instead, an adjoining neighbor allowed an officer onto her property to verify her perceptions with a sensitive thermometer. Nor, in my view, does such observation become an unreasonable search if made from a distance with the aid of a device that merely discloses that the exterior of one house, or one area of the house, is much warmer than another. Nothing more occurred in this case. * * *

Notwithstanding the implications of today's decision, there is a strong public interest in avoiding constitutional litigation over the monitoring of emissions from homes, and over the inferences drawn from such monitoring. Just as "the police cannot reasonably be expected to avert their eyes from evidence of criminal activity that could have been observed by any member of the public," *Greenwood*, [9th ed., p. 159], so too public officials should not have to avert their senses or their equipment from detecting emissions in the public domain such as excessive heat, traces of smoke, suspicious odors, odorless gases, airborne particulates, or radioactive emissions, any of which could identify hazards to the community. In my judgment, monitoring such emissions with "sense-enhancing technology," and drawing useful conclusions from such monitoring, is an entirely reasonable public service.

On the other hand, the countervailing privacy interest is at best trivial. After all, homes generally are insulated to keep heat in, rather than to prevent the detection of heat going out, and it does not seem to me that society will suffer from a rule requiring the rare homeowner who both intends to engage in uncommon activities that produce extraordinary amounts of heat, and wishes to conceal that production from outsiders, to make sure that the surrounding area is well insulated. * * *

Despite the Court's attempt to draw a line that is "not only firm but also bright," the contours of its new rule are uncertain because its protection apparently dissipates as soon as the relevant technology is "in general public use." Yet how much use is general public use is not even hinted at by the Court's opinion, which makes the somewhat doubtful assumption that the thermal imager used in this case does not satisfy that criterion.[5] In any event, putting aside its lack of clarity, this criterion is somewhat perverse because it seems likely that the threat to privacy will grow, rather than recede, as the use of intrusive equipment becomes more readily available.

It is clear, however, that the category of "sense-enhancing technology" covered by the new rule is far too broad. It would, for example, embrace potential mechanical substitutes for dogs trained to react when they sniff narcotics. But in *United States v. Place,* [9th ed., p.168], we held that a dog sniff that "discloses only the presence or absence of narcotics" does "not constitute a 'search' within the meaning of the Fourth Amendment," and it must follow that sense-enhancing equipment that identifies nothing but illegal activity is not a search either. Nevertheless, the use of such a device would be unconstitutional under the Court's rule, as would the use of other new devices that might detect the odor of deadly bacteria or chemicals for making a new type of high explosive * * *.

Because the new rule applies to information regarding the "interior" of the home, it is too narrow as well as too broad. Clearly, a rule that is designed to protect individuals from the overly intrusive use of sense-enhancing equipment should not be limited to a home. If such equipment did provide its user with the functional equivalent of access to a private place—such as, for example, the telephone booth involved in *Katz,* or an office building—then the rule should apply to such an area as well as to a home. * * *

The two reasons advanced by the Court as justifications for the adoption of its new rule are both unpersuasive. First, the Court suggests that its rule is compelled by our holding in *Katz,* because in that case, as in this, the surveillance consisted of nothing more than the monitoring of waves emanating from a private area into the public domain. Yet there are critical differences between the cases. In *Katz,* the electronic listening device attached to the outside of the phone booth allowed the officers to pick up the content of the conversation inside the booth, making them the functional equivalent of intruders because they gathered information that was otherwise available only to someone inside the private area; it would be as if, in this case, the thermal imager presented a view of the heat-generating activity inside petitioner's home. By contrast, the thermal imager here disclosed only the relative amounts of heat radiating from the house; it would be as if, in *Katz,* the listening device disclosed only the relative volume of sound leaving the booth, which presumably was discernible in the public domain. * * *

Second, the Court argues that the permissibility of "through-the-wall surveillance" cannot depend on a distinction between observing "intimate details" such as "the lady of the house [taking] her daily sauna and bath," and noticing only

---

5. The record describes a device that numbers close to a thousand manufactured units; that has a predecessor numbering in the neighborhood of 4,000 to 5,000 units; that competes with a similar product numbering from 5,000 to 6,000 units; and that is "readily available to the public" for commercial, personal, or law enforcement purposes, and is just an 800–number away from being rented from "half a dozen national companies" by anyone who wants one. Since, by virtue of the Court's new rule, the issue is one of first impression, perhaps it should order an evidentiary hearing to determine whether these facts suffice to establish "general public use."

"the nonintimate rug on the vestibule floor" or "objects no smaller than 36 by 36 inches." This entire argument assumes, of course, that the thermal imager in this case could or did perform "through-the-wall surveillance" that could identify any detail "that would previously have been unknowable without physical intrusion." In fact, the device could not and did not enable its user to identify either the lady of the house, the rug on the vestibule floor, or anything else inside the house, whether smaller or larger than 36 by 36 inches. * * *

Although the Court is properly and commendably concerned about the threats to privacy that may flow from advances in the technology available to the law enforcement profession, it has unfortunately failed to heed the tried and true counsel of judicial restraint. Instead of concentrating on the rather mundane issue that is actually presented by the case before it, the Court has endeavored to craft an all-encompassing rule for the future. It would be far wiser to give legislators an unimpeded opportunity to grapple with these emerging issues rather than to shackle them with prematurely devised constitutional constraints. * * *

UNITED STATES v. WHITE

401 U.S. 745, 91 S.Ct. 1122, 28 L.Ed.2d 453 (1971).

[On numerous occasions a government informer, carrying a concealed radio transmitter, engaged defendant in conversations which were electronically overheard by federal narcotics agents. The conversations in a restaurant, defendant's home and in the informer's car were overheard by the use of radio equipment. A number of conversations in the informer's home were not only electronically overheard by an agent stationed outside the house but by another agent who, with the informer's consent, concealed himself in the latter's kitchen closet. At no time did the agents obtain a warrant or court order. The informer was not produced at the trial, but the testimony of the "eavesdropping" agents was admitted and led to defendant's conviction of narcotics violations. The Court of Appeals Circuit read *Katz* as prohibiting testimony about the electronically overheard statements.]

JUSTICE WHITE announced the judgment of the Court and an opinion in which THE CHIEF JUSTICE, JUSTICE STEWART, and JUSTICE BLACKMUN join. * * *

Hoffa v. United States, 385 U.S. 293 (1966), which was left undisturbed by *Katz,* held that however strongly a defendant may trust an apparent colleague, his expectations in this respect are not protected by the Fourth Amendment when it turns out that the colleague is a government agent regularly communicating with the authorities. In these circumstances, "no interest legitimately protected by the Fourth Amendment is involved," for that amendment affords no protection to "a wrongdoer's misplaced belief that a person to whom he voluntarily confides his wrongdoing will not reveal it." * * *

Concededly a police agent who conceals his police connections may write down for official use his conversations with a defendant and testify concerning them, without a warrant authorizing his encounters with the defendant and without otherwise violating the latter's Fourth Amendment rights. For constitutional purposes, no different result is required if the agent instead of immediately reporting and transcribing his conversations with defendant, either (1) simultaneously records them with electronic equipment which he is carrying on his person, (2) or carries radio equipment which simultaneously transmits the conversations either to recording equipment located elsewhere or to other agents monitoring the transmitting frequency. If the conduct and revelations of an agent operating without electronic equipment do not invade the defendant's constitutionally justifiable expectations of privacy, neither does a simultaneous recording of the same conversations made by the agent or by others from transmissions received from the agent to whom the defendant is talking and whose trustworthiness the defendant necessarily risks.

Our problem is not what the privacy expectations of particular defendants in particular situations may be or the extent to which they may in fact have relied on the discretion of their companions. Very probably, individual defendants neither know nor suspect that their colleagues have gone or will go to the police or are carrying recorders or transmitters. Otherwise, conversation would cease and our problem with these encounters would be nonexistent or far different from those now before us. Our problem, in terms of the principles announced in *Katz,* is what expectations of privacy are constitutionally "justifiable"—what expectations the Fourth Amendment will protect in the absence of a warrant. * * * If the law gives no protection to the wrongdoer whose trusted accomplice is or becomes a police agent, neither should it protect him when that same agent has recorded or transmitted the conversations which are later offered in evidence to prove the State's case.

Inescapably, one contemplating illegal activities must realize and risk that his companions may be reporting to the police. If he sufficiently doubts their trustworthiness, the association will very probably end or never materialize. But if he has no doubts, or allays them, or risks what doubt he has, the risk is his. In terms of what his course will be, what he will or will not do or say, we are unpersuaded that he would distinguish between probable informers on the one hand and probable informers with transmitters on the other. Given the possibility or probability that one of his colleagues is cooperating with the police, it is only speculation to assert that the defendant's utterances would be substantially different or his sense of security any less if he also thought it possible that the suspected colleague is wired for sound. At least there is no persuasive evidence that the difference in this respect between the electronically equipped and the unequipped agent is substantial enough to require discrete constitutional recognition, particularly under the Fourth Amendment which is ruled by fluid concepts of "reasonableness."

Nor should we be too ready to erect constitutional barriers to relevant and probative evidence which is also accurate and reliable. An electronic recording will many times produce a more reliable rendition of what a defendant has said than will the unaided memory of a police agent. It may also be that with the recording in existence it is less likely that the informant will change his mind, less chance that threat or injury will suppress unfavorable evidence and less chance that cross-examination will confound the testimony. Considerations like these obviously do not favor the defendant, but we are not prepared to hold that a defendant who has no constitutional right to exclude the informer's unaided testimony nevertheless has a Fourth Amendment privilege against a more accurate version of the events in question.

It is thus untenable to consider the activities and reports of the police agent himself, though acting without a warrant, to be a "reasonable" investigative effort and lawful under the Fourth Amendment but to view the same agent with a recorder or transmitter as conducting an "unreasonable" and unconstitutional search and seizure. * * *

No different result should obtain where, as in the instant case, the informer disappears and is unavailable at trial; for the issue of whether specified events on a certain day violate the Fourth Amendment should not be determined by what later happens to the informer. His unavailability at trial and proffering the testimony of other agents may raise evidentiary problems or pose issues of prosecutorial misconduct with respect to the informer's disappearance, but they do not appear critical to deciding whether prior events invaded the defendant's Fourth Amendment rights.

The Court of Appeals was in error for another reason. In *Desist v. United States,* 394 U.S. 244 (1969), we held that our decision in *Katz v. United States* applied only to those electronic surveillances that occurred subsequent to the date of that decision. Here the events in question took place in late 1965 and early 1966, long prior to *Katz.* * * *

The judgment of the Court of Appeals is reversed.

JUSTICE BLACK * * * concurs in the judgment of the Court for the reasons set forth in his dissent in *Katz v. United States.*

JUSTICE BRENNAN, concurring in the result.

I agree that *Desist* requires reversal of the judgment of the Court of Appeals. * * * [I]t is my view that current Fourth Amendment jurisprudence interposes a warrant requirement not only in cases of third-party electronic monitoring (the situation in this case) but also in cases of electronic recording by a government agent of a face-to-face conversation with a criminal suspect. * * *

JUSTICE DOUGLAS, dissenting.

* * * Monitoring, if prevalent, certainly kills free discourse and spontaneous utterances. Free discourse—a First Amendment value—may be frivolous or serious, humble or defiant, reactionary or revolutionary, profane or in good taste; but it is not free if there is surveillance. Free discourse liberates the spirit, though it may produce only froth. The individual must keep some facts concerning his thoughts within a small zone of people. At the same time he must be free to pour out his woes or inspirations or dreams to others. He remains the sole judge as to what must be said and what must remain unspoken. This is the essence of the idea of privacy implicit in the First and Fifth Amendments as well as in the Fourth. * * *

JUSTICE HARLAN, dissenting.

* * * Since it is the task of the law to form and project, as well as mirror and reflect, we should not, as judges, merely recite the expectations and risks without examining the desirability of saddling them upon society. The critical question, therefore, is whether under our system of government, as reflected in the Constitution, we should impose on our citizens the risks of the electronic listener or observer without at least the protection of a warrant requirement.

This question must, in my view, be answered by assessing the nature of a particular practice and the likely extent of its impact on the individual's sense of security balanced against the utility of the conduct as a technique of law enforcement. For those more extensive intrusions that significantly jeopardize the sense of security which is the paramount concern of Fourth Amendment liberties, I am of the view that more than self-restraint by law enforcement officials is required and at the least warrants should be necessary.

The impact of the practice of third-party bugging, must, I think, be considered such as to undermine that confidence and sense of security in dealing with one another that is characteristic of individual relationships between citizens in a free society. * * * The argument of the plurality opinion, to the effect that it is irrelevant whether secrets are revealed by the mere tattletale or the transistor, ignores the differences occasioned by third-party monitoring and recording which insures full and accurate disclosure of all that is said, free of the possibility of error and oversight that inheres in human reporting.

Authority is hardly required to support the proposition that words would be measured a good deal more carefully and communication inhibited if one suspected his conversations were being transmitted and transcribed. Were third-party bugging a prevalent practice, it might well smother that spontaneity—reflected in frivolous, impetuous, sacrilegious, and defiant discourse—that liberates daily life. Much offhand exchange is easily forgotten and one may count on the obscurity of his remarks, protected by the very fact of a limited audience, and the likelihood that the listener will either overlook or forget what is said, as well as the listener's inability to reformulate a conversation without having to contend with a documented record. All these values are sacrificed by a rule of law that permits official monitoring of private discourse limited only by the need to locate a willing assistant.

* * * The interest [the plurality] fails to protect is the expectation of the ordinary citizen, who has never engaged in illegal conduct in his life, that he may carry on his private discourse freely, openly, and spontaneously without measuring his every word against the connotations it might carry when instantaneously heard by others unknown to him and unfamiliar with his situation or analyzed in a cold, formal record played days, months, or years after the conversation. Interposition of a warrant requirement is designed not to shield "wrongdoers," but to secure a measure of privacy and a sense of personal security throughout our society. * * *

JUSTICE MARSHALL, dissenting.

I am convinced that the correct view of the Fourth Amendment in the area of electronic surveillance is one that brings the safeguards of the warrant requirement to bear on the investigatory activity involved in this case. In this regard I agree with the dissents of Justice Douglas and Justice Harlan.

ZURCHER v. STANFORD DAILY

436 U.S. 547, 98 S.Ct. 1970, 56 L.Ed.2d 525 (1978).

JUSTICE WHITE delivered the opinion of the Court.

[Nine policemen were injured by demonstrators at Stanford University Hospital. Two days later the Stanford Daily carried articles and photos devoted to the demonstration and attack; the photos by a staff member indicated he had been located where he could have photographed the assailants. A warrant was obtained to search the Daily's offices for negatives, film and pictures relevant to identification of the assailants. Executing officers searched photo labs, filing cabinets and desks, but found no evidence. The Daily later brought a civil action in district court, where declaratory relief was granted. That court held (i) that the Fourth Amendment forbade the issuance of a warrant to search for materials in the possession of one not suspected of crime except upon a showing of probable cause a subpoena *duces tecum* would be impracticable; and (ii) that the First Amendment bars search of newspaper offices except upon a clear showing that important materials would otherwise be destroyed or removed and that a restraining order would be futile.]

It is an understatement to say that there is no direct authority in this or any other federal court for the District Court's sweeping revision of the Fourth Amendment. Under existing law, valid warrants may be issued to search *any* property, whether or not occupied by a third party, at which there is probable cause to believe that fruits, instrumentalities, or evidence of a crime will be found. Nothing on the face of the Amendment suggests that a third-party search warrant should not normally issue.   * * *

Against this background, it is untenable to conclude that property may not be searched unless its occupant is reasonably suspected of crime and is subject to arrest.   * * *   The Fourth Amendment has itself struck the balance between privacy and public need, and there is no occasion or justification for a court to revise the Amendment and strike a new balance by denying the search warrant in the circumstances present here and by insisting that the investigation proceed by subpoena *duces tecum,* whether on the theory that the latter is a less intrusive alternative, or otherwise.   * * *

In any event, the reasons presented by the District Court and adopted by the Court of Appeals for arriving at its remarkable conclusion do not withstand analysis. First, as we have said, it is apparent that whether the third-party occupant is suspect or not, the State's interest in enforcing the criminal law and recovering the evidence remains the same; and it is the seeming innocence of the property owner that the District Court relied on to foreclose the warrant to search. But as respondents themselves now concede, if the third party knows that contraband or other illegal materials are on his property, he is sufficiently culpable to justify the issuance of a search warrant. Similarly, if his ethical stance is the determining factor, it seems to us that whether or not he knows that the sought-after articles are secreted on his property and whether or not he knows that the articles are in fact the fruits, instrumentalities, or evidence of crime, he will be so informed when the search warrant is served, and it is doubtful that he should then be permitted to object to the search, to withhold, if it is there, the evidence of crime reasonably believed to be possessed by him or secreted on his property, and to forbid the search and insist that the officers serve him with a subpoena *duces tecum.*

Second, we are unpersuaded that the District Court's new rule denying search warrants against third parties and insisting on subpoenas would substantially further privacy interests without seriously undermining law enforcement efforts. As the District Court understands it, denying third-party search warrants would not have substantial adverse effects on criminal investigations because the non-suspect third party, once served with a subpoena, will preserve the evidence and ultimately, lawfully respond. The difficulty with this assumption is that search warrants are often employed early in an investigation, perhaps before the identity of any likely criminal and certainly before all the perpetrators are or could be known. The seemingly blameless third party in possession of the fruits or evidence may not be innocent at all; and if he is, he may nevertheless be so related to or so sympathetic with the culpable that he cannot be relied upon to retain and preserve the articles that may implicate his friends, or at least not to notify those who would be damaged by the evidence that the authorities are aware of its location. In any event, it is likely that the real culprits will have access to the property, and the delay involved in employing the subpoena *duces tecum,* offering as it does the opportunity to litigate its validity, could easily result in the disappearance of the evidence, whatever the good faith of the third party.   * * *[8]

---

8. It is also far from clear, even apart from the dangers of destruction and removal, whether the use of the subpoena *duces tecum* under circumstances where there is probable cause to believe that a crime has been committed and that the materials sought constitute evidence of its commission will result in the production of evidence with sufficient regularity to satisfy the public interest in law enforcement. Unlike the individual whose privacy is invaded by a search, the recipient of a subpoena may assert the Fifth Amendment privilege against self-incrimination in response to a summons to produce evidence or give testimony. This priv-

We are also not convinced that the net gain to privacy interests by the District Court's new rule would be worth the candle.[9] In the normal course of events, search warrants are more difficult to obtain than subpoenas, since the latter do not involve the judiciary and do not require proof of probable cause. Where, in the real world, subpoenas would suffice, it can be expected that they will be employed by the rational prosecutor. On the other hand, when choice is available under local law and the prosecutor chooses to use the search warrant, it is unlikely that he has needlessly selected the more difficult course. His choice is more likely to be based on the solid belief, arrived at through experience but difficult, if not impossible, to sustain a specific case, that the warranted search is necessary to secure and to avoid the destruction of evidence.

[The Framers] did not forbid warrants where the press was involved, did not require special showings that subpoenas would be impractical, and did not insist that the owner of the place to be searched, if connected with the press, must be shown to be implicated in the offense being investigated. Further, the prior cases do no more than insist that the courts apply the warrant requirements with particular exactitude when First Amendment interests would be endangered by the search. As we see it, no more than this is required where the warrant requested is for the seizure of criminal evidence reasonably believed to be on the premises occupied by a newspaper. Properly administered, the pre-conditions for a warrant—probable cause, specificity with respect to the place to be searched and the things to be seized, and overall reasonableness—should afford sufficient protection against the harms that are assertedly threatened by warrants for searching newspaper offices.

[handwritten margin note: STANDARDS FOR SEARCH WARRANT]

There is no reason to believe, for example, that magistrates cannot guard against searches of the type, scope, and intrusiveness that would actually interfere with the timely publication of a newspaper. Nor, if the requirements of specificity and reasonableness are properly applied, policed, and observed, will there be any occasion or opportunity for officers to rummage at large in newspaper files or to intrude into or to deter normal editorial and publication decisions. The warrant issued in this case authorized nothing of this sort. Nor are we convinced, * * * that confidential sources will disappear and that the press will suppress news because of fears of warranted searches. Whatever incremental effect there may be in this regard if search warrants, as well as subpoenas, are permissible in proper circumstances, it does not make a constitutional difference in our judgment.

The fact is that respondents and *amici* have pointed to only a very few instances in the entire United States since 1971 involving the issuance of warrants for searching newspaper premises. This reality hardly suggests abuse; and if abuse occurs, there will be time enough to deal with it. Furthermore, the

---

ilege is not restricted to suspects. We have construed it broadly as covering any individual who might be incriminated by the evidence in connection with which the privilege is asserted. The burden of overcoming an assertion of the Fifth Amendment privilege, even if prompted by a desire not to cooperate rather than any real fear of self-incrimination, is one which prosecutors would rarely be able to meet in the early stages of an investigation despite the fact they did not regard the witness as a suspect. Even time spent litigating such matters could seriously impede criminal investigations.

9. We reject totally the reasoning of the District Court that additional protections are required to assure that the Fourth Amendment rights of third parties are not violated because of the unavailability of the exclusionary rule as a deterrent to improper searches of premises in the control of nonsuspects. * * * It is probably seldom that police during the investigatory stage when most searches occur will be so convinced that no potential defendant will have standing to exclude evidence on Fourth Amendment grounds that they will feel free to ignore constitutional restraints. * * *

[handwritten: people's rights impede criminal investig.]

press is not only an important, critical, and valuable asset to society, but it is not easily intimidated—nor should it be. * * *

JUSTICE BRENNAN took no part in the consideration or decision of this case.

JUSTICE POWELL, concurring.

* * * Even aside from the difficulties involved in deciding on a case-by-case basis whether a subpoena can serve as an adequate substitute,[1] I agree with the Court that there is no constitutional basis for such a reading. * * *

JUSTICE STEWART, with whom JUSTICE MARSHALL joins, dissenting.

* * * It seems to me self-evident that police searches of newspaper offices burden the freedom of the press. The most immediate and obvious First Amendment injury caused by such a visitation by the police is physical disruption of the operation of the newspaper. Policemen occupying a newsroom and searching it thoroughly for what may be an extended period of time will inevitably interrupt its normal operations, and thus impair or even temporarily prevent the processes of newsgathering, writing, editing, and publishing. By contrast, a subpoena would afford the newspaper itself an opportunity to locate whatever material might be requested and produce it.

But there is another and more serious burden on a free press imposed by an unannounced police search of a newspaper office: the possibility of disclosure of information received from confidential sources, or of the identity of the sources themselves. Protection of those sources is necessary to ensure that the press can fulfill its constitutionally designated function of informing the public, because important information can often be obtained only by an assurance that the source will not be revealed. * * *

Today the Court does not question the existence of this constitutional protection, but says only that it is not "convinced . . . that confidential sources will disappear and that the press will suppress news because of fears of warranted searches." This facile conclusion seems to me to ignore common experience. It requires no blind leap of faith to understand that a person who gives information to a journalist only on condition that his identity will not be revealed will be less likely to give that information if he knows that, despite the journalist's assurance his identity may in fact be disclosed. And it cannot be denied that confidential information may be exposed to the eyes of police officers who execute a search warrant by rummaging through the files, cabinets, desks and wastebaskets of a newsroom. Since the indisputable effect of such searches will thus be to prevent a newsman from being able to promise confidentiality to his potential sources, it seems obvious to me that a journalist's access to information, and thus the public's will thereby be impaired.

A search warrant allows police officers to ransack the files of a newspaper, reading each and every document until they have found the one named in the warrant,[7] while a subpoena would permit the newspaper itself to produce only the

---

1. For example, respondent had announced a policy of destroying any photographs that might aid prosecution of protestors. While this policy probably reflected the deep feelings of the Vietnam era, and one may assume that under normal circumstances few, if any, press entities would adopt a policy so hostile to law enforcement, respondent's policy at least illustrates the possibility of such hostility. Use of a subpoena, as proposed by the dissent would be of no utility in face of a policy of destroying

evidence. And unless the policy were publicly announced, it probably would be difficult to show the impracticality of a subpoena as opposed to a search warrant.

7. The Court says that "if the requirements of specificity and reasonableness are properly applied, policed, and observed" there will be no opportunity for the police to "rummage at large in newspaper files." But in order to find a particular document, no matter how specifically it is identified in the warrant, specific documents requested. A search, unlike a subpoena, will therefore lead to the needless exposure of confidential information completely unrelated to the purpose of the investigation. The knowledge that police officers can make an unannounced raid on a newsroom is thus bound to have a deterrent effect on the availability of confidential news sources. The end result, wholly inimical to the First Amendment, will be a diminishing flow of potentially important information to the public. * * *

JUSTICE STEVENS, dissenting.

* * * [Before 1967] warrants were used to search for contraband, weapons and plunder, but not for "mere evidence." The practical effect of the rule prohibiting the issuance of warrants to search for mere evidence was to narrowly limit not only the category of objects, but also the category of persons and the character of the privacy interests that might be affected by an unannounced police search.

Just as the witnesses who participate in an investigation or a trial far outnumber the defendants, the persons who possess evidence that may help to identify an offender, or explain an aspect of a criminal transaction, far outnumber those who have custody of weapons or plunder. Countless law abiding citizens—doctors, lawyers, merchants, customers, bystanders—may have documents in their possession that relate to an ongoing criminal investigation. The consequences of subjecting this large category of persons to unannounced police searches are extremely serious. The *ex parte* warrant procedure enables the prosecutor to obtain access to privileged documents that could not be examined if advance notice gave the custodian an opportunity to object. The search for the documents described in a warrant may involve the inspection of files containing other private matter. The dramatic character of a sudden search may cause an entirely unjustified injury to the reputation of the persons searched. * * *

A showing of probable cause that was adequate to justify the issuance of a warrant to search for stolen goods in the 18th century does not automatically satisfy the new dimensions of the Fourth Amendment [whereunder a warrant may issue for "mere evidence"]. The only conceivable justification for an unannounced search of an innocent citizen is the fear that, if notice were given, he would conceal or destroy the object of the search. Probable cause to believe that the custodian is a criminal, or that he holds a criminal's weapons, spoils, or the like, justifies that fear, and therefore such a showing complies with the Clause. But if nothing said under oath in the warrant application demonstrates the need for an unannounced search by force, the probable cause requirement is not satisfied. In the absence of some other showing of reasonableness, the ensuing search violates the Fourth Amendment. * * *

SECTION 3. PROBABLE CAUSE

Because the warrant clause of the Fourth Amendment provides that "no Warrants shall issue, but upon probable cause," it is apparent that a valid arrest warrant or search warrant may issue only upon a showing of probable cause to the issuing authority. In the many instances in which police may arrest and search without first obtaining a warrant, their conduct is governed by the other half of the Amendment, which declares the right of the people to be secure "against unreasonable searches and seizures." But such an arrest or search is unreason-

the police will have to search every place where it might be—including, presumably, every file in the office—and to examine each document they find to see if it is the correct one. I thus fail to see how the Fourth Amendment would provide an effective limit to these searches.

able unless based upon probable cause; as stated in *Wong Sun v. United States*, 371 U.S. 471 (1963), were the requirements less stringent when a warrant is obtained, then "a principal incentive now existing for the procurement of * * * warrants would be destroyed."

When the police arrest or search without a warrant, they initially make the probable cause decision themselves. But upon a motion to suppress evidence found in the arrest or search (or, sometimes, pursuant to efforts to justify continued custody of the arrestee) there will occur a subsequent judicial determination of the probable cause issue. When the police arrest or search with a warrant, the probable cause determination is made by a magistrate in the first instance. But his decision is not final; subject to the *Leon* "good faith" limitation, the defendant on a motion to suppress may still seek exclusion of evidence on the ground that the warrant was not in fact issued upon probable cause.

The two cases in this section, *Spinelli v. United States* and *Illinois v. Gates*, reflect how the Supreme Court's approach to the probable cause issue has changed in recent years as the Court shifted to a less structured "totality of the circumstances" test.

SPINELLI v. UNITED STATES

393 U.S. 410, 89 S.Ct. 584, 21 L.Ed.2d 637 (1969).

JUSTICE HARLAN delivered the opinion of the Court.

William Spinelli was convicted * * * of traveling to St. Louis, Missouri, from a nearby Illinois suburb with the intention of conducting gambling activities proscribed by Missouri law. At every appropriate stage in the proceedings in the lower courts, the petitioner challenged the constitutionality of the warrant which authorized the FBI search that uncovered the evidence necessary for his conviction. * * * Believing it desirable that the principles of [*Aguilar v. Texas*, 378 U.S. 108 (1964)] should be further explicated, we granted certiorari * * *.

In *Aguilar*, a search warrant had issued upon an affidavit of police officers who swore only that they had "received reliable information from a credible person and do believe" that narcotics were being illegally stored on the described premises. While recognizing that the constitutional requirement of probable cause can be satisfied by hearsay information, this Court held the affidavit inadequate for two reasons. First, the application failed to set forth any of the "underlying circumstances" necessary to enable the magistrate independently to judge of the validity of the informant's conclusion that the narcotics were where he said they were. Second, the affiant-officers did not attempt to support their claim that their informant was " 'credible' or his information 'reliable.' " The Government is, however, quite right in saying that the FBI affidavit in the present case is more ample than that in *Aguilar*. Not only does it contain a report from an anonymous informant, but it also contains a report of an independent FBI investigation which is said to corroborate the informant's tip. We are, then, required to delineate the manner in which *Aguilar's* two-pronged test should be applied in these circumstances.

In essence, the affidavit * * * contained the following allegations:

    1. The FBI had kept track of Spinelli's movements on five days during the month of August 1965. On four of these occasions, Spinelli was seen crossing one of two bridges leading from Illinois into St. Louis, Missouri, between 11 a.m. and 12:15 p.m. On four of the five days, Spinelli was also seen parking his car in a lot used by residents of an apartment house at 1108

Indian Circle Drive in St. Louis, between 3:30 p.m. and 4:45 p.m. On one day, Spinelli was followed further and seen to enter a particular apartment in the building.

2. An FBI check with the telephone company revealed that this apartment contained two telephones listed under the name of Grace P. Hagen, and carrying the numbers WYdown 4–0029 and WYdown 4–0136.

3. The application [*warrant*] stated that "William Spinelli is known to this affiant and to federal law enforcement agents and local law enforcement agents as a bookmaker, an associate of bookmakers, a gambler, and an associate of gamblers."

4. Finally, it was stated that the FBI "has been informed by a confidential reliable informant that William Spinelli is operating a handbook and accepting wagers and disseminating wagering information by means of the [*NO WEIGHT*] telephones which have been assigned the numbers WYdown 4–0029 and WYdown 4–0136."

There can be no question that the last item mentioned, detailing the informant's tip, has a fundamental place in this warrant application. Without it, probable cause could not be established. The first two items reflect only innocent-seeming activity and data. Spinelli's travels to and from the apartment building and his entry into a particular apartment on one occasion could hardly be taken as bespeaking gambling activity; and there is surely nothing unusual about an apartment containing two separate telephones. Many a householder indulges himself in this petty luxury. Finally, the allegation that Spinelli was "known" to the affiant and to other federal and local law enforcement officers as a gambler and an associate of gamblers is but a bald and unilluminating assertion of suspicion that is entitled to no weight in appraising the magistrate's decision. *Nathanson v. United States*, 290 U.S. 41 (1933).

So much indeed the Government does not deny. Rather, following the reasoning of the Court of Appeals, the Government claims that the informant's tip gives a suspicious color to the FBI's reports detailing Spinelli's innocent-seeming conduct and that, conversely, the FBI's surveillance corroborates the informant's tip, thereby entitling it to more weight. * * * We believe, however, that the "totality of circumstances" approach taken by the Court of Appeals paints with too broad a brush. Where, as here, the informer's tip is a necessary element in a finding of probable cause, its proper weight must be determined by a more precise analysis.

The informer's report must first be measured against *Aguilar's* standards so that its probative value can be assessed. If the tip is found inadequate under *Aguilar*, the other allegations which corroborate the information contained in the hearsay report should then be considered. At this stage as well, however, the standards enunciated in *Aguilar* must inform the magistrate's decision. He must ask: Can it fairly be said that the tip, even when certain parts of it have been corroborated by independent sources, is as trustworthy as a tip which would pass *Aguilar's* tests without independent corroboration? * * * [*1ST measure using Aguilar standards*]

Applying these principles to the present case, we first consider the weight to be given the informer's tip when it is considered apart from the rest of the affidavit. It is clear that a Commissioner could not credit it without abdicating his constitutional function. Though the affiant swore that his confidant was "reliable," he offered the magistrate no reason in support of this conclusion. Perhaps even more important is the fact that *Aguilar's* other test has not been satisfied. The tip does not contain a sufficient statement of the underlying circumstances from which the informer concluded that Spinelli was running a bookmaking operation. We are not told how the FBI's source received his information—it is not alleged that the informant personally observed Spinelli at work or that he had ever placed a bet with him. Moreover, if the informant came by the information indirectly, he did not explain why his sources were reliable. In the absence of a statement detailing the manner in which the information was gathered, it is especially important that the tip describe the accused's criminal activity in sufficient detail so that the magistrate may know that he is relying on something more substantial than a casual rumor circulating in the underworld or an accusation based merely on an individual's general reputation.

The detail provided by the informant in *Draper v. United States*, 358 U.S. 307 (1959), provides a suitable benchmark. While Hereford, the FBI's informer in that case, did not state the way in which he had obtained his information, he reported that Draper had gone to Chicago the day before by train and that he would return to Denver by train with three ounces of heroin on one of two specified mornings. Moreover, Hereford went on to describe, with minute particularity, the clothes that Draper would be wearing upon his arrival at the Denver station. A magistrate, when confronted with such detail, could reasonably infer that the informant had gained his information in a reliable way. Such an inference cannot be made in the present case. Here, the only facts supplied were that Spinelli was using two specified telephones and that these phones were being used in gambling operations. This meager report could easily have been obtained from an off-hand remark heard at a neighborhood bar.

Nor do we believe that the patent doubts *Aguilar* raises as to the report's reliability are adequately resolved by a consideration of the allegations detailing the FBI's independent investigative efforts. At most, these allegations indicated that Spinelli could have used the telephones specified by the informant for some purpose. This cannot by itself be said to support both the inference that the informer was generally trustworthy and that he had made his charge against Spinelli on the basis of information obtained in a reliable way. Once again, *Draper* provides a relevant comparison. Independent police work in that case corroborated much more than one small detail that had been provided by the informant. There, the police, upon greeting the inbound Denver train on the second morning specified by informer Hereford, saw a man whose dress corresponded precisely to Hereford's detailed description. It was then apparent that the informant had not been fabricating his report out of whole cloth; since the report was of the sort which in common experience may be recognized as having been obtained in a reliable way, it was perfectly clear that probable cause had been established.

We conclude, then, that in the present case the informant's tip—even when corroborated to the extent indicated—was not sufficient to provide the basis for a finding of probable cause. * * * The judgment of the Court of Appeals is reversed * * *.

JUSTICE WHITE, concurring.

* * * The tension between *Draper* and the *Nathanson–Aguilar* line of cases is evident from the course followed by the majority opinion. * * * Since [the informant's] specific information about Spinelli using two phones with particular numbers had been verified, did not his allegation about gambling thereby become sufficiently more believable if the *Draper* principle is to be given any scope at all? I would think so, particularly since the information from the informant which was verified was not neutral, irrelevant information but was material to proving the gambling allegation: two phones with different numbers in an apartment used

away from home indicates a business use in an operation, like bookmaking, where multiple phones are needed. The *Draper* approach would reasonably justify the issuance of a warrant in this case, particularly since the police had some awareness of Spinelli's past activities. The majority, however, while seemingly embracing *Draper*, confines that case to its own facts. Pending full scale reconsideration of that case, on the one hand, or of the *Nathanson–Aguilar* cases on the other, I join the opinion of the Court and the judgment of reversal especially since a vote to affirm would produce an equally divided Court.[a]

ILLINOIS v. GATES

462 U.S. 213, 103 S.Ct. 2317, 76 L.Ed.2d 527 (1983).

JUSTICE REHNQUIST delivered the opinion of the Court.

* * * A chronological statement of events usefully introduces the issues at stake. Bloomingdale, Ill., is a suburb of Chicago located in DuPage County. On May 3, 1978, the Bloomingdale Police Department received by mail an anonymous handwritten letter which read as follows:

> "This letter is to inform you that you have a couple in your town who strictly make their living on selling drugs. They are Sue and Lance Gates, they live on Greenway, off Bloomingdale Rd. in the condominiums. Most of their buys are done in Florida. Sue his wife drives their car to Florida, where she leaves it to be loaded up with drugs, then Lance flys down and drives it back. Sue flys back after she drops the car off in Florida. May 3 she is driving down there again and Lance will be flying down in a few days to drive it back. At the time Lance drives the car back he has the trunk loaded with over $100,000.00 in drugs. Presently they have over $100,000.00 worth of drugs in their basement.
>
> They brag about the fact they never have to work, and make their entire living on pushers.
>
> I guarantee if you watch them carefully you will make a big catch. They are friends with some big drugs dealers, who visit their house often.
>
> Lance & Susan Gates
>
> Greenway
>
> in Condominiums"

The letter was referred by the Chief of Police of the Bloomingdale Police Department to Detective Mader, who decided to pursue the tip. Mader learned, from the office of the Illinois Secretary of State, that an Illinois driver's license had been issued to one Lance Gates, residing at a stated address in Bloomingdale. He contacted a confidential informant, whose examination of certain financial records revealed a more recent address for the Gates, and he also learned from a police officer assigned to O'Hare Airport that "L. Gates" had made a reservation on Eastern Airlines flight 245 to West Palm Beach, Fla., scheduled to depart from Chicago on May 5 at 4:15 p.m.

Mader then made arrangements with an agent of the Drug Enforcement Administration for surveillance of the May 5 Eastern Airlines flight. The agent later reported to Mader that Gates had boarded the flight, and that federal agents in Florida had observed him arrive in West Palm Beach and take a taxi to the

a. The separate dissents of Black, Fortas, and Stewart, JJ., are omitted. Marshall, J., did not participate.

nearby Holiday Inn. They also reported that Gates went to a room registered to one Susan Gates and that, at 7:00 a.m. the next morning, Gates and an unidentified woman left the motel in a Mercury bearing Illinois license plates and drove northbound on an interstate frequently used by travelers to the Chicago area. In addition, the DEA agent informed Mader that the license plate number on the Mercury registered to a Hornet station wagon owned by Gates. The agent also advised Mader that the driving time between West Palm Beach and Bloomingdale was approximately 22 to 24 hours.

Mader signed an affidavit setting forth the foregoing facts, and submitted it to a judge of the Circuit Court of DuPage County, together with a copy of the anonymous letter. The judge of that court thereupon issued a search warrant for the Gates' residence and for their automobile. The judge, in deciding to issue the warrant, could have determined that the *modus operandi* of the Gates had been substantially corroborated. As the anonymous letter predicted, Lance Gates had flown from Chicago to West Palm Beach late in the afternoon of May 5th, had checked into a hotel room registered in the name of his wife, and, at 7:00 a.m. the following morning, had headed north, accompanied by an unidentified woman, out of West Palm Beach on an interstate highway used by travelers from South Florida to Chicago in an automobile bearing a license plate issued to him.

At 5:15 a.m. on May 7th, only 36 hours after he had flown out of Chicago, Lance Gates, and his wife, returned to their home in Bloomingdale, driving the car in which they had left West Palm Beach some 22 hours earlier. The Bloomingdale police were awaiting them, searched the trunk of the Mercury, and uncovered approximately 350 pounds of marijuana. A search of the Gates' home revealed marijuana, weapons, and other contraband. The Illinois Circuit Court ordered suppression of all these items, on the ground that the affidavit submitted to the Circuit Judge failed to support the necessary determination of probable cause to believe that the Gates' automobile and home contained the contraband in question. This decision was affirmed in turn by the Illinois Appellate Court and by a divided vote of the Supreme Court of Illinois.

The Illinois Supreme Court concluded—and we are inclined to agree—that, standing alone, the anonymous letter sent to the Bloomingdale Police Department would not provide the basis for a magistrate's determination that there was probable cause to believe contraband would be found in the Gates' car and home. The letter provides virtually nothing from which one might conclude that its author is either honest or his information reliable; likewise, the letter gives absolutely no indication of the basis for the writer's predictions regarding the Gates' criminal activities. Something more was required, then, before a magistrate could conclude that there was probable cause to believe that contraband would be found in the Gates' home and car.

The Illinois Supreme Court also properly recognized that Detective Mader's affidavit might be capable of supplementing the anonymous letter with information sufficient to permit a determination of probable cause. In holding that the affidavit in fact did not contain sufficient additional information to sustain a determination of probable cause, the Illinois court applied a "two-pronged test," derived from our decision in *Spinelli v. United States*. The Illinois Supreme Court, like some others, apparently understood *Spinelli* as requiring that the anonymous letter satisfy each of two independent requirements before it could be relied on. According to this view, the letter, as supplemented by Mader's affidavit, first had to adequately reveal the "basis of knowledge" of the letter writer—the particular means by which he came by the information given in his report. Second, it had to provide facts sufficiently establishing either the "veracity" of the affiant's informant, or, alternatively, the "reliability" of the informant's report in this particular case.

The Illinois court, alluding to an elaborate set of legal rules that have developed among various lower courts to enforce the "two-pronged test,"[4] found that the test had not been satisfied. First, the "veracity" prong was not satisfied because, "there was simply no basis [for] * * * conclud[ing] that the anonymous person [who wrote the letter to the Bloomingdale Police Department] was credible." The court indicated that corroboration by police of details contained in the letter might never satisfy the "veracity" prong, and in any event, could not do so if, as in the present case, only "innocent" details are corroborated. In addition, the letter gave no indication of the basis of its writer's knowledge of the Gates' activities. The Illinois court understood *Spinelli* as permitting the detail contained in a tip to be used to infer that the informant had a reliable basis for his statements, but it thought that the anonymous letter failed to provide sufficient detail to permit such an inference. Thus, it concluded that no showing of probable cause had been made.

We agree with the Illinois Supreme Court that an informant's "veracity," "reliability" and "basis of knowledge" are all highly relevant in determining the value of his report. We do not agree, however, that these elements should be understood as entirely separate and independent requirements to be rigidly exacted in every case, which the opinion of the Supreme Court of Illinois would imply. Rather, as detailed below, they should be understood simply as closely intertwined issues that may usefully illuminate the common sense, practical question whether there is "probable cause" to believe that contraband or evidence is located in a particular place.

This totality of the circumstances approach is far more consistent with our prior treatment of probable cause than is any rigid demand that specific "tests" be satisfied by every informant's tip. Perhaps the central teaching of our decisions bearing on the probable cause standard is that it is a "practical, nontechnical conception." "In dealing with probable cause, * * * as the very name implies, we deal with probabilities. These are not technical; they are the factual and practical considerations of everyday life on which reasonable and prudent men, not legal technicians, act." Our observation regarding "particularized suspicion," is also applicable to the probable cause standard:

> The process does not deal with hard certainties, but with probabilities. Long before the law of probabilities was articulated as such, practical people formulated certain common-sense conclusions about human behavior; jurors as factfinders are permitted to do the same—and so are law enforcement officers. Finally, the evidence thus collected must be seen and weighed not in terms of library analysis by scholars, but as understood by those versed in the field of law enforcement.

As these comments illustrate, probable cause is a fluid concept—turning on the assessment of probabilities in particular factual contexts—not readily, or even

---

4. In summary, these rules posit that the "veracity" prong of the *Spinelli* test has two "spurs"—the informant's "credibility" and the "reliability" of his information. Various interpretations are advanced for the meaning of the "reliability" spur of the "veracity" prong. Both the "basis of knowledge" prong and the "veracity" prong are treated as entirely separate requirements, which must be independently satisfied in every case in order to sustain a determination of probable cause. Some ancillary doctrines are relied on to satisfy certain of the foregoing requirements. For example, the "self-verifying detail" of a tip may satisfy the "basis of knowledge" requirement, although not the "credibility" spur of the "veracity" prong. Conversely, corroboration would seem not capable of supporting the "basis of knowledge" prong, but only the "veracity" prong. * * *

usefully, reduced to a neat set of legal rules. Informants' tips doubtless come in many shapes and sizes from many different types of persons. * * * Rigid legal rules are ill-suited to an area of such diversity. "One simple rule will not cover every situation." [7]

Moreover, the "two-pronged test" directs analysis into two largely independent channels—the informant's "veracity" or "reliability" and his "basis of knowledge." There are persuasive arguments against according these two elements such independent status. Instead, they are better understood as relevant considerations in the totality of circumstances analysis that traditionally has guided probable cause determinations: a deficiency in one may be compensated for, in determining the overall reliability of a tip, by a strong showing as to the other, or by some other indicia of reliability.

If, for example, a particular informant is known for the unusual reliability of his predictions of certain types of criminal activities in a locality, his failure, in a particular case, to thoroughly set forth the basis of his knowledge surely should not serve as an absolute bar to a finding of probable cause based on his tip. Likewise, if an unquestionably honest citizen comes forward with a report of criminal activity—which if fabricated would subject him to criminal liability—we have found rigorous scrutiny of the basis of his knowledge unnecessary. Conversely, even if we entertain some doubt as to an informant's motives, his explicit and detailed description of alleged wrongdoing, along with a statement that the event was observed firsthand, entitles his tip to greater weight than might otherwise be the case. Unlike a totality of circumstances analysis, which permits a balanced assessment of the relative weights of all the various indicia of reliability (and unreliability) attending an informant's tip, the "two-pronged test" has encouraged an excessively technical dissection of informants' tips, with undue attention being focused on isolated issues that cannot sensibly be divorced from the other facts presented to the magistrate. * * *

7. The diversity of informants' tips, as well as the usefulness of the totality of the circumstances approach to probable cause, is reflected in our prior decisions on the subject. In *Jones v. United States*, 362 U.S. 257 (1960), we held that probable cause to search petitioners' apartment was established by an affidavit based principally on an informant's tip. The unnamed informant claimed to have purchased narcotics from petitioners at their apartment; the affiant stated that he had been given correct information from the informant on a prior occasion. This, and the fact that petitioners had admitted to police officers on another occasion that they were narcotics users, sufficed to support the magistrate's determination of probable cause.

Likewise, in *Rugendorf v. United States*, 376 U.S. 528 (1964), the Court upheld a magistrate's determination that there was probable cause to believe that certain stolen property would be found in petitioner's apartment. The affidavit submitted to the magistrate stated that certain furs had been stolen, and that a confidential informant, who previously had furnished confidential information, said that he saw the furs in petitioner's home. Moreover, another confidential informant, also claimed to be reliable, stated that one Schweihs had stolen the furs. Police reports indicated that petitioner had been seen in Schweihs' company and a third informant stated that petitioner was a fence for Schweihs.

Finally, in *Ker v. California*, 374 U.S. 23 (1963), we held that information within the knowledge of officers who searched the Ker's apartment provided them with probable cause to believe drugs would be found there. The officers were aware that one Murphy had previously sold marijuana to a police officer; the transaction had occurred in an isolated area, to which Murphy had led the police. The night after this transaction, police observed Ker and Murphy meet in the same location. Murphy approached Ker's car, and, although police could see nothing change hands, Murphy's *modus operandi* was identical to what it had been the night before. Moreover, when police followed Ker from the scene of the meeting with Murphy he managed to lose them after performing an abrupt U-turn. Finally, the police had a statement from an informant who had provided reliable information previously, that Ker was engaged in selling marijuana, and that his source was Murphy. We concluded that "To say that this coincidence of information was sufficient to support a reasonable belief of the officers that Ker was illegally in possession of marijuana is to indulge in understatement."

We also have recognized that affidavits "are normally drafted by non-lawyers in the midst and haste of a criminal investigation. Technical requirements of elaborate specificity once exacted under common law pleading have no proper place in this area." Likewise, search and arrest warrants long have been issued by persons who are neither lawyers nor judges, and who certainly do not remain abreast of each judicial refinement of the nature of "probable cause." The rigorous inquiry into the *Spinelli* prongs and the complex superstructure of evidentiary and analytical rules that some have seen implicit in our *Spinelli* decision, cannot be reconciled with the fact that many warrants are—quite properly—issued on the basis of nontechnical, common-sense judgments of laymen applying a standard less demanding than those used in more formal legal proceedings. Likewise, given the informal, often hurried context in which it must be applied, the "built-in subtleties" of the "two-pronged test" are particularly unlikely to assist magistrates in determining probable cause.

Similarly, we have repeatedly said that after-the-fact scrutiny by courts of the sufficiency of an affidavit should not take the form of *de novo* review. A magistrate's "determination of probable cause should be paid great deference by reviewing courts." "A grudging or negative attitude by reviewing courts toward warrants" is inconsistent with the Fourth Amendment's strong preference for searches conducted pursuant to a warrant "court should not invalidate * * * warrant[s] by interpreting affidavit[s] in a hypertechnical, rather than a common-sense, manner."

If the affidavits submitted by police officers are subjected to the type of scrutiny some courts have deemed appropriate, police might well resort to warrantless searches, with the hope of relying on consent or some other exception to the warrant clause that might develop at the time of the search. In addition, the possession of a warrant by officers conducting an arrest or search greatly reduces the perception of unlawful or intrusive police conduct, by assuring "the individual whose property is searched or seized of the lawful authority of the executing officer, his need to search, and the limits of his power to search." Reflecting this preference for the warrant process, the traditional standard for review of an issuing magistrate's probable cause determination has been that so long as the magistrate had a "substantial basis for * * * conclud[ing]" that a search would uncover evidence of wrongdoing, the Fourth Amendment requires no more. We think reaffirmation of this standard better serves the purpose of encouraging recourse to the warrant procedure and is more consistent with our traditional deference to the probable cause determinations of magistrates than is the "two-pronged test."

Finally, the direction taken by decisions following *Spinelli* poorly serves "the most basic function of any government": "to provide for the security of the individual and of his property. The strictures that inevitably accompany the "two-pronged test" cannot avoid seriously impeding the task of law enforcement. If, as the Illinois Supreme Court apparently thought, that test must be rigorously applied in every case, [anonymous tips would be] of greatly diminished value in police work. Ordinary citizens, like ordinary witnesses, generally do not provide extensive recitations of the basis of their everyday observations. Likewise, as the Illinois Supreme Court observed in this case, the veracity of persons supplying anonymous tips is by hypothesis largely unknown, and unknowable. As a result, anonymous tips seldom could survive a rigorous application of either of the *Spinelli* prongs. Yet, such tips, particularly when supplemented by independent police investigation, frequently contribute to the solution of otherwise "perfect crimes." While a conscientious assessment of the basis for crediting such tips is required by the Fourth Amendment, a standard that leaves virtually no place for anonymous citizen informants is not.

For all these reasons, we conclude that it is wiser to abandon the "two-pronged test" established by our decisions in *Aguilar* and *Spinelli*.[11]   In its place we reaffirm the totality of the circumstances analysis that traditionally has informed probable cause determinations.   The task of the issuing magistrate is simply to make a practical, common-sense decision whether, given all the circumstances set forth in the affidavit before him, including the "veracity" and "basis of knowledge" of persons supplying hearsay information, there is a fair probability that contraband or evidence of a crime will be found in a particular place.   And the duty of a reviewing court is simply to ensure that the magistrate had a "substantial basis for * * * conclud[ing]" that probable cause existed.   We are convinced that this flexible, easily applied standard will better achieve the accommodation of public and private interests that the Fourth Amendment requires than does the approach that has developed from *Aguilar* and *Spinelli*.

Our earlier cases illustrate the limits beyond which a magistrate may not venture in issuing a warrant.   A sworn statement of an affiant that "he has cause to suspect and does believe that" liquor illegally brought into the United States is located on certain premises will not do.   *Nathanson v. United States*.   An affidavit must provide the magistrate with a substantial basis for determining the existence of probable cause, and the wholly conclusory statement at issue in *Nathanson* failed to meet this requirement.   An officer's statement that "affiants have received reliable information from a credible person and believe" that heroin is stored in a home, is likewise inadequate.   *Aguilar v. Texas*.   As in *Nathanson*, this is a mere conclusory statement that gives the magistrate virtually no basis at all for making a judgment regarding probable cause.   Sufficient information must be presented to the magistrate to allow that official to determine probable cause; his action cannot be a mere ratification of the bare conclusions of others.   In order to ensure that such an abdication of the magistrate's duty does not occur, courts must continue to conscientiously review the sufficiency of affidavits on which warrants are issued.   But when we move beyond the "bare bones" affidavits present in cases such as *Nathanson* and *Aguilar*, this area simply does not lend itself to a prescribed set of rules, like that which had developed from *Spinelli*.   Instead, the flexible, common-sense standard articulated in *Jones* [and other cases] better served the purposes of the Fourth Amendment's probable cause requirement.

Justice Brennan's dissent suggests in several places that the approach we take today somehow downgrades the role of the neutral magistrate, because *Aguilar* and *Spinelli* "preserve the role of magistrates as independent arbiters of probable cause * * *."   Quite the contrary, we believe, is the case.   Nothing in our opinion in any way lessens the authority of the magistrate to draw such reasonable inferences as he will from the material supplied to him by applicants for a warrant; indeed, he is freer than under the regime of *Aguilar* and *Spinelli* to draw such inferences, or to refuse to draw them if he is so minded.

The real gist of Justice Brennan's criticism seems to be a second argument, somewhat at odds with the first, that magistrates should be restricted in their

11. * * * Whether the allegations submitted to the magistrate in *Spinelli* would, under the view we now take, have supported a finding of probable cause, we think it would not be profitable to decide.   There are so many variables in the probable cause equation that one determination will seldom be a useful "prece-dent" for another.   Suffice it to say that while we in no way abandon *Spinelli's* concern for the trustworthiness of informers and for the principle that it is the magistrate who must ultimately make a finding of probable cause, we reject the rigid categorization suggested by some of its language.

authority to make probable cause determinations by the standards laid down in *Aguilar* and *Spinelli* and that such findings "should not be authorized unless there is some assurance that the information on which they are based has been obtained in a reliable way by an honest or credible person." However, under our opinion magistrates remain perfectly free to exact such assurances as they deem necessary, as well as those required by this opinion, in making probable cause determinations. Justice Brennan would apparently prefer that magistrates be restricted in their findings of probable cause by the development of an elaborate body of case law dealing with the "veracity" prong of the *Spinelli* test, which in turn is broken down into two "spurs"—the informant's "credibility" and the "reliability" of his information, together with the "basis of knowledge" prong of the *Spinelli* test. That such a labyrinthine body of judicial refinement bears any relationship to familiar definitions of probable cause is hard to imagine. * * *

Justice Brennan's dissent also suggests that "words such as 'practical,' 'nontechnical,' and 'common sense,' as used in the Court's opinion, are but code words for an overly permissive attitude towards police practices in derogation of the rights secured by the Fourth Amendment." * * * "Fidelity" to the commands of the Constitution suggests balanced judgment rather than exhortation. The highest "fidelity" is achieved neither by the judge who instinctively goes furthest in upholding even the most bizarre claim of individual constitutional rights, any more than it is achieved by a judge who instinctively goes furthest in accepting the most restrictive claims of governmental authorities. The task of this Court, as of other courts, is to "hold the balance true," and we think we have done that in this case.

Our decisions applying the totality of circumstances analysis outlined above have consistently recognized the value of corroboration of details of an informant's tip by independent police work.

Our decision in *Draper v. United States,* however, is the classic case on the value of corroborative efforts of police officials. There, an informant named Hereford reported that Draper would arrive in Denver on a train from Chicago on one of two days, and that he would be carrying a quantity of heroin. The informant also supplied a fairly detailed physical description of Draper, and predicted that he would be wearing a light colored raincoat, brown slacks and black shoes, and would be walking "real fast." Hereford gave no indication of the basis for his information.[12]

On one of the stated dates police officers observed a man matching this description exit a train arriving from Chicago; his attire and luggage matched Hereford's report and he was walking rapidly. We explained in *Draper* that, by this point in his investigation, the arresting officer "had personally verified every facet of the information given him by Hereford except whether petitioner had accomplished his mission and had the three ounces of heroin on his person or in his bag. And surely with every other bit of Hereford's information being thus personally verified, [the officer] had 'reasonable grounds' to believe that the remaining unverified bit of Hereford's information—that Draper would have the heroin with him—was likewise true."

---

12. The tip in *Draper* might well not have survived the rigid application of the "two-pronged test" that developed following *Spinelli*. The only reference to Hereford's reliability was that he had "been engaged as a 'special employee' of the Bureau of Narcotics at Denver for about six months, and from time to time gave information to [the police] for small sums of money, and that [the officer] had always found the information given by Hereford to be accurate and reliable." Likewise, the tip gave no indication of how Hereford came by his information. At most, the detailed and accurate predictions in the tip indicated that, however Hereford obtained his information, it was reliable.

The showing of probable cause in the present case was fully as compelling as that in *Draper*. Even standing alone, the facts obtained through the independent investigation of Mader and the DEA at least suggested that the Gates were involved in drug trafficking. In addition to being a popular vacation site, Florida is well-known as a source of narcotics and other illegal drugs. Lance Gates' flight to Palm Beach, his brief, overnight stay in a motel, and apparent immediate return north to Chicago in the family car, conveniently awaiting him in West Palm Beach, is as suggestive of a prearranged drug run, as it is of an ordinary vacation trip.

In addition, the magistrate could rely on the anonymous letter, which had been corroborated in major part by Mader's efforts—just as had occurred in *Draper*.[13] The Supreme Court of Illinois reasoned that *Draper* involved an informant who had given reliable information on previous occasions, while the honesty and reliability of the anonymous informant in this case were unknown to the Bloomingdale police. While this distinction might be an apt one at the time the police department received the anonymous letter, it became far less significant after Mader's independent investigative work occurred. The corroboration of the letter's predictions that the Gates' car would be in Florida, that Lance Gates would fly to Florida in the next day or so, and that he would drive the car north toward Bloomingdale all indicated, albeit not with certainty, that the informant's other assertions also were true. "Because an informant is right about some things, he is more probably right about other facts," *Spinelli*, supra (White, J., concurring)—including the claim regarding the Gates' illegal activity. This may well not be the type of "reliability" or "veracity" necessary to satisfy some view of the "veracity prong" of *Spinelli*, but we think it suffices for the practical, common-sense judgment called for in making a probable cause determination. It is enough, for purposes of assessing probable cause, that "corroboration through other sources of information reduced the chances of a reckless or prevaricating tale," thus providing "a substantial basis for crediting the hearsay."

Finally, the anonymous letter contained a range of details relating not just to easily obtained facts and conditions existing at the time of the tip, but to future actions of third parties ordinarily not easily predicted. The letter writer's accurate information as to the travel plans of each of the Gates was of a character likely obtained only from the Gates themselves, or from someone familiar with their not entirely ordinary travel plans. If the informant had access to accurate information of this type a magistrate could properly conclude that it was not unlikely that he also had access to reliable information of the Gates' alleged illegal activities.[14] Of course, the Gates' travel plans might have been learned from a

---

13. The Illinois Supreme Court thought that the verification of details contained in the anonymous letter in this case amounted only to "the corroboration of innocent activity," and that this was insufficient to support a finding of probable cause. We are inclined to agree, however, with the observation of Justice Moran in his dissenting opinion that "In this case, just as in *Draper*, seemingly innocent activity became suspicious in the light of the initial tip." And it bears noting that *all* of the corroborating detail established in *Draper*, supra, was of entirely innocent activity—a fact later pointed out by the Court in both *Jones v. United States*, and *Ker v. California*.

This is perfectly reasonable. As discussed previously, probable cause requires only a probability or substantial chance of criminal

activity, not an actual showing of such activity. By hypothesis, therefore, innocent behavior frequently will provide the basis for a showing of probable cause; to require otherwise would be to *sub silentio* impose a drastically more rigorous definition of probable cause than the security of our citizens demands. We think the Illinois court attempted a too rigid classification of the types of conduct that may be relied upon in seeking to demonstrate probable cause. In making a determination of probable cause the relevant inquiry is not whether particular conduct is "innocent" or "guilty," but the degree of suspicion that attaches to particular types of non-criminal acts.

14. The dissent seizes on one inaccuracy in the anonymous informant's letter—its statement that Sue Gates would fly from Florida to talkative neighbor or travel agent; under the "two-pronged test" developed from *Spinelli*, the character of the details in the anonymous letter might well not permit a sufficiently clear inference regarding the letter writer's "basis of knowledge." But, as discussed previously, probable cause does not demand the certainty we associate with formal trials. It is enough that there was a fair probability that the writer of the anonymous letter had obtained his entire story either from the Gates or someone they trusted. And corroboration of major portions of the letter's predictions provides just this probability. It is apparent, therefore, that the judge issuing the warrant had a "substantial basis for * * * conclud[ing]" that probable cause to search the Gates' home and car existed. The judgment of the Supreme Court of Illinois therefore must be reversed.

JUSTICE WHITE, concurring in the judgment.[a]

* * * Although I agree that the warrant should be upheld, I reach this conclusion in accordance with the *Aguilar–Spinelli* framework.

For present purposes, the *Aguilar–Spinelli* rules can be summed up as follows. First, an affidavit based on an informer's tip, standing alone, cannot provide probable cause for issuance of a warrant unless the tip includes information that apprises the magistrate of the informant's basis for concluding that the contraband is where he claims it is (the "basis of knowledge" prong), *and* the affiant informs the magistrate of his basis for believing that the informant is credible (the "veracity" prong).[20] Second, if a tip fails under either or both of the

Illinois, when in fact she drove—and argues that the probative value of the entire tip was undermined by this allegedly "material mistake." We have never required that informants used by the police be infallible, and can see no reason to impose such a requirement in this case. Probable cause, particularly when police have obtained a warrant, simply does not require the perfection the dissent finds necessary.

Likewise, there is no force to the dissent's argument that the Gates' action in leaving their home unguarded undercut the informant's claim that drugs were hidden there. Indeed, the line-by-line scrutiny that the dissent applies to the anonymous letter is akin to that we find inappropriate in reviewing magistrate's decisions. The dissent apparently attributes to the magistrate who issued the warrant in this case the rather implausible notion that persons dealing in drugs always stay at home, apparently out of fear that to leave might risk intrusion by criminals. If accurate, one could not help sympathizing with the self-imposed isolation of people so situated. In reality, however, it is scarcely likely that the magistrate ever thought that the anonymous tip "kept one spouse" at home, much less that he relied on the theory advanced by the dissent. The letter simply says that Sue would fly from Florida to Illinois, without indicating whether the Gates' made the bitter choice of leaving the drugs in their house, or those in their car, unguarded. The magistrate's determination that there might be drugs or evidence of criminal activity in the Gates' home was well-supported by the less speculative theory, noted in text, that if the informant could pre-

dict with considerable accuracy the somewhat unusual travel plans of the Gates, he probably also had a reliable basis for his statements that the Gates' kept a large quantity of drugs in their home and frequently were visited by other drug traffickers there.

a. In an omitted portion of his opinion, Justice White argued for adoption of a "good-faith" exception to the exclusionary rule.

20. The "veracity" prong is satisfied by a recitation in the affidavit that the informant previously supplied accurate information to the police, or by proof that the informant gave his information against his penal interest, see *United States v. Harris*, 403 U.S. 573 (1971) (plurality opinion). [Editor's Note: In *Harris*, the informant said that he had purchased illicit whiskey from defendant for two years, most recently within the past two weeks, and had often seen defendant get the whiskey for him and others from a certain building. The plurality opinion concluded that because "people do not lightly admit a crime and place critical evidence in the hands of the police in the form of their own admissions," such admissions "carry their own indicia of credibility—sufficient at least to support finding of probable cause to search" when, as here, the basis of knowledge is also indicated (as almost inevitably will be the case when there is such an admission). The four dissenters objected that "the effect of adopting such a rule would be to encourage the Government to prefer as informants participants in criminal enterprises rather than ordinary citizens, a goal the Government specifically eschews in its brief in this case upon the explicit premise that such persons are often less reliable than those who two prongs, probable cause may yet be established by independent police investigatory work that corroborates the tip to such an extent that it supports "both the inference that the informer was generally trustworthy and that he made his charge on the basis of information obtained in a reliable way." In instances where the officers rely on corroboration, the ultimate question is whether the corroborated tip "is as trustworthy as a tip which would pass *Aguilar's* tests without independent corroboration."

In the present case, it is undisputed that the anonymous tip, by itself, did not furnish probable cause. The question is whether those portions of the affidavit describing the results of the police investigation of the respondents, when considered in light of the tip, "would permit the suspicions engendered by the informant's report to ripen into a judgment that a crime was probably being committed." * * *

In my view, the lower court's characterization of the Gates' activity here as totally "innocent" is dubious. In fact, the behavior was quite suspicious. I agree with the Court that Lance Gates' flight to Palm Beach, an area known to be a source of narcotics, the brief overnight stay in a motel, and apparent immediate return North, suggest a pattern that trained law-enforcement officers have recognized as indicative of illicit drug-dealing activity.

Even, however, had the corroboration related only to completely innocuous activities, this fact alone would not preclude the issuance of a valid warrant. The critical issue is not whether the activities observed by the police are innocent or suspicious. Instead, the proper focus should be on whether the actions of the suspects, whatever their nature, give rise to an inference that the informant is credible and that he obtained his information in a reliable manner.

Thus, in *Draper v. United States* an informant stated on Sept. 7 that Draper would be carrying narcotics when he arrived by train in Denver on the morning of Sept. 8 or Sept. 9. The informant also provided the police with a detailed physical description of the clothes Draper would be wearing when he alighted from the train. The police observed Draper leaving a train on the morning of Sept. 9, and he was wearing the precise clothing described by the informant. The Court held that the police had probable cause to arrest Draper at this point, even though the police had seen nothing more than the totally innocent act of a man getting off a train carrying a briefcase. As we later explained in *Spinelli*, the important point was that the corroboration showed both that the informant was credible, i.e. that he "had not been fabricating his report out of whole cloth," and that he had an adequate basis of knowledge for his allegations, "since the report was of the sort which in common experience may be recognized as having been obtained in a reliable way." The fact that the informer was able to predict, two days in advance, the exact clothing Draper would be wearing dispelled the possibility that his tip was just based on rumor or "an off-hand remark heard at a neighborhood bar." Probably Draper had planned in advance to wear these specific clothes so that an accomplice could identify him. A clear inference could therefore be drawn that the informant was either involved in the criminal scheme himself or that he otherwise had access to reliable, inside information.[22]

obey the law."] The "basis of knowledge" prong is satisfied by a statement from the informant that he personally observed the criminal activity, or, if he came by the information indirectly, by a satisfactory explanation of why his sources were reliable, or, in the absence of a statement detailing the manner in which the information was gathered, by a de-

scription of the accused's criminal activity in sufficient detail that the magistrate may infer that the informant is relying on something more substantial than casual rumor or an individual's general reputation.

22. Thus, as interpreted in *Spinelli*, the Court in *Draper* held that there was probable cause because "the kind of information related

As in *Draper*, the police investigation in the present case satisfactorily demonstrated that the informant's tip was as trustworthy as one that would alone satisfy the *Aguilar* tests. The tip predicted that Sue Gates would drive to Florida, that Lance Gates would fly there a few days after May 3, and that Lance would then drive the car back. After the police corroborated these facts, the magistrate could reasonably have inferred, as he apparently did, that the informant, who had specific knowledge of these unusual travel plans, did not make up his story and that he obtained his information in a reliable way. It is theoretically possible, as respondents insist, that the tip could have been supplied by a "vindictive travel agent" and that the Gates' activities, although unusual, might not have been unlawful. But *Aguilar* and *Spinelli*, like our other cases, do not require that certain guilt be established before a warrant may properly be issued. "[O]nly the probability, and not a prima facie showing, of criminal activity is the standard of probable cause." I therefore conclude that the judgment of the Illinois Supreme Court invalidating the warrant must be reversed.

The Court agrees that the warrant was valid, but, in the process of reaching this conclusion, it overrules the *Aguilar–Spinelli* tests and replaces them with a "totality of the circumstances" standard. As shown above, it is not at all necessary to overrule *Aguilar–Spinelli* in order to reverse the judgment below. Therefore, because I am inclined to believe that, when applied properly, the *Aguilar–Spinelli* rules play an appropriate role in probable cause determinations, and because the Court's holding may foretell an evisceration of the probable cause standard, I do not join the Court's holding.

The Court reasons that the "veracity" and "basis of knowledge" tests are not independent, and that a deficiency as to one can be compensated for by a strong showing as to the other. Thus, a finding of probable cause may be based on a tip from an informant "known for the unusual reliability of his predictions" or from "an unquestionably honest citizen," even if the report fails thoroughly to set forth the basis upon which the information was obtained. If this is so, then it must follow *a fortiori* that "the affidavit of an officer, known by the magistrate to be honest and experienced, stating that [contraband] is located in a certain building" must be acceptable. It would be "quixotic" if a similar statement from an honest informant, but not one from an honest officer, could furnish probable cause. But we have repeatedly held that the unsupported assertion or belief of an officer does not satisfy the probable cause requirement. Thus, this portion of today's holding can be read as implicitly rejecting the teachings of these prior holdings.

by the informant [was] not generally sent ahead of a person's arrival in a city except to those who are intimately connected with making careful arrangements for meeting him." *Spinelli* (White, J., concurring). As I said in *Spinelli*, the conclusion that *Draper* itself was based on this fact is far from inescapable. Prior to *Spinelli*, *Draper* was susceptible to the interpretation that it stood for the proposition that "the existence of the tenth and critical fact is made sufficiently probable to justify the issuance of a warrant by verifying nine other facts coming from the same source." *Spinelli* (White, J., concurring). But it now seems clear that the Court in *Spinelli* rejected this reading of *Draper*.

Justice Brennan erroneously interprets my *Spinelli* concurrence as espousing the view that "corroboration of certain details in a tip may be sufficient to satisfy the veracity, but not the basis of knowledge, prong of *Aguilar*." I did not say that corroboration could *never* satisfy the basis of knowledge prong. My concern was, and still is, that the prong might be deemed satisfied on the basis of corroboration of information that does not in any way suggest that the informant had an adequate basis of knowledge for his report. If, however, as in *Draper*, the police corroborate information from which it can be inferred that the informant's tip was grounded on inside information, this corroboration is sufficient to satisfy the basis of knowledge prong. *Spinelli* (White, J., concurring). The rules would indeed be strange if, as Justice Brennan suggests, the basis of knowledge prong could be satisfied by detail in the tip alone, but not by independent police work.

The Court may not intend so drastic a result. Indeed, the Court expressly reaffirms the validity of cases such as *Nathanson* that have held that, no matter how reliable the affiant-officer may be, a warrant should not be issued unless the affidavit discloses supporting facts and circumstances. The Court limits these cases to situations involving affidavits containing only "bare conclusions" and holds that, if an affidavit contains anything more, it should be left to the issuing magistrate to decide, based solely on "practical[ity]" and "common-sense," whether there is a fair probability that contraband will be found in a particular place.

Thus, as I read the majority opinion, it appears that the question whether the probable cause standard is to be diluted is left to the common-sense judgments of issuing magistrates. I am reluctant to approve any standard that does not expressly require, as a prerequisite to issuance of a warrant, some showing of facts from which an inference may be drawn that the informant is credible and that his information was obtained in a reliable way. The Court is correctly concerned with the fact that some lower courts have been applying *Aguilar–Spinelli* in an unduly rigid manner. I believe, however, that with clarification of the rule of corroborating information, the lower courts are fully able to properly interpret *Aguilar–Spinelli* and avoid such unduly-rigid applications. I may be wrong; it ultimately may prove to be the case that the only profitable instruction we can provide to magistrates is to rely on common sense. But the question whether a particular anonymous tip provides the basis for issuance of a warrant will often be a difficult one, and I would at least attempt to provide more precise guidance by clarifying *Aguilar–Spinelli* and the relationship of those cases with *Draper* before totally abdicating our responsibility in this area. Hence, I do not join the Court's opinion rejecting the *Aguilar–Spinelli* rules.

JUSTICE BRENNAN, with whom JUSTICE MARSHALL joins, dissenting.

Although I join Justice Stevens' dissenting opinion and agree with him that the warrant is invalid even under the Court's newly announced "totality of the circumstances" test, I write separately to dissent from the Court's unjustified and ill-advised rejection of the two-prong test for evaluating the validity of a warrant based on hearsay announced in *Aguilar v. Texas*, and refined in *Spinelli v. United States*.

* * * In *Spinelli*, the Court reviewed a search warrant based on an affidavit that was "more ample" than the one in *Aguilar*. The affidavit in *Spinelli* contained not only a tip from an informant, but also a report of an independent police investigation that allegedly corroborated the informant's tip. Under these circumstances, the Court stated that it was "required to delineate the manner in which *Aguilar's* two-pronged test should be applied * * *."

The Court held that the *Aguilar* test should be applied to the tip, and approved two additional ways of satisfying that test. First, the Court suggested that if the tip contained sufficient detail describing the accused's criminal activity it might satisfy *Aguilar's* basis of knowledge prong. Such detail might assure the magistrate that he is "relying on something more substantial than a casual rumor circulating in the underworld or an accusation based merely on an individual's general reputation." Although the tip in the case before it did not meet this standard, "[t]he detail provided by the informant in *Draper v. United States* provide[d] a suitable benchmark" because "[a] magistrate, when confronted with such detail, could reasonably infer that the informant had gained his information in a reliable way."

Second, the Court stated that police corroboration of the details of a tip could provide a basis for satisfying *Aguilar*. The Court's opinion is not a model of clarity on this issue since it appears to suggest that corroboration can satisfy both the basis of knowledge and veracity prongs of *Aguilar*. Justice White's concurring opinion, however, points the way to a proper reading of the Court's opinion. After reviewing the Court's decision in *Draper v. United States,* Justice White concluded that "[t]he thrust of *Draper* is not that the verified facts have independent significance with respect to proof of [another unverified fact]." In his view, "[t]he argument instead relates to the reliability of the source: because an informant is right about some things, he is more probably right about other facts, usually the critical, unverified facts." Justice White then pointed out that prior cases had rejected "the notion that the past reliability of an officer is sufficient reason for believing his current assertions." Justice White went on to state:

> "Nor would it suffice, I suppose, if a reliable informant states there is gambling equipment in Apartment 607 and then proceeds to describe in detail Apartment 201, a description which is verified before applying for the warrant. He was right about 201, but that hardly makes him more believable about the equipment in 607. But what if he states that there are narcotics locked in a safe in Apartment 300, which is described in detail, and the apartment manager verifies everything but the contents of the safe? I doubt that the report about the narcotics is made appreciably more believable by the verification. The informant could still have gotten his information concerning the safe from others about whom nothing is known or could have inferred the presence of narcotics from circumstances which a magistrate would find unacceptable."

I find this reasoning persuasive. Properly understood, therefore, *Spinelli* stands for the proposition that corroboration of certain details in a tip may be sufficient to satisfy the veracity, but not the basis of knowledge, prong of *Aguilar*. As noted, *Spinelli* also suggests that in some limited circumstances considerable detail in an informant's tip may be adequate to satisfy the basis of knowledge prong of *Aguilar*. * * *

In rejecting the *Aguilar–Spinelli* standards, the Court * * * relies on * * * the "practical, nontechnical" nature of probable cause.

[O]ne can concede that probable cause is a "practical, nontechnical" concept without betraying the values that *Aguilar* and *Spinelli* reflect. As noted, *Aguilar* and *Spinelli* require the police to provide magistrates with certain crucial information. They also provide structure for magistrates' probable cause inquiries. In so doing, *Aguilar* and *Spinelli* preserve the role of magistrates as independent arbiters of probable cause, insure greater accuracy in probable cause determinations, and advance the substantive value of precluding findings of probable cause, and attendant intrusions, based on anything less than information from an honest or credible person who has acquired his information in a reliable way. Neither the standards nor their effects are inconsistent with a "practical, nontechnical" conception of probable cause. Once a magistrate has determined that he has information before him that he can reasonably say has been obtained in a reliable way by a credible person, he has ample room to use his common sense and to apply a practical, nontechnical conception of probable cause. * * *

The Court also insists that the *Aguilar–Spinelli* standards must be abandoned because they are inconsistent with the fact that non-lawyers frequently serve as magistrates. To the contrary, the standards help to structure probable cause inquiries and, properly interpreted, may actually help a non-lawyer magistrate in making a probable cause determination. * * *

At the heart of the Court's decision to abandon *Aguilar* and *Spinelli* appears to be its belief that "the direction taken by decisions following *Spinelli* poorly serves 'the most basic function of any government: to provide for the security of the individual and of his property.' " This conclusion rests on the judgment that *Aguilar* and *Spinelli* "seriously imped[e] the task of law enforcement," and render anonymous tips valueless in police work. Surely, the Court overstates its case. But of particular concern to all Americans must be that the Court gives virtually no consideration to the value of insuring that findings of probable cause are based on information that a magistrate can reasonably say has been obtained in a reliable way by an honest or credible person. * * *

The Court's complete failure to provide any persuasive reason for rejecting *Aguilar* and *Spinelli* doubtlessly reflects impatience with what it perceives to be "overly technical" rules governing searches and seizures under the Fourth Amendment. Words such as "practical," "nontechnical," and "commonsense," as used in the Court's opinion, are but code words for an overly permissive attitude towards police practices in derogation of the rights secured by the Fourth Amendment. Everyone shares the Court's concern over the horrors of drug trafficking, but under our Constitution only measures consistent with the Fourth Amendment may be employed by government to cure this evil. We must be ever mindful of Justice Stewart's admonition that "[i]n times of unrest, whether caused by crime or racial conflict or fear of internal subversion, this basic law and the values that it represents may appear unrealistic or 'extravagant' to some. But the values were those of the authors of our fundamental constitutional concepts." * * *

Rights secured by the Fourth Amendment are particularly difficult to protect because their "advocates are usually criminals." But the rules "we fashion [are] for the innocent and guilty alike." By replacing *Aguilar* and *Spinelli* with a test that provides no assurance that magistrates, rather than the police, or informants, will make determinations of probable cause; imposes no structure on magistrates' probable cause inquiries; and invites the possibility that intrusions may be justified on less than reliable information from an honest or credible person, today's decision threatens to "obliterate one of the most fundamental distinctions between our form of government, where officers are under the law, and the police-state where they are the law."

JUSTICE STEVENS, with whom JUSTICE BRENNAN joins, dissenting.

* * * The informant had indicated that "Sue drives their car to Florida *where she leaves it to be loaded up with drugs * * *. Sue flies back after she drops the car off in Florida.*" (emphasis added). Yet Detective Mader's affidavit reported that she "left the West Palm Beach area driving the Mercury northbound."

The discrepancy between the informant's predictions and the facts known to Detective Mader is significant for three reasons. First, it cast doubt on the informant's hypothesis that the Gates already had "over $100,000 worth of drugs in their basement." The informant had predicted an itinerary that always kept one spouse in Bloomingdale, suggesting that the Gates did not want to leave their home unguarded because something valuable was hidden within. That inference obviously could not be drawn when it was known that the pair was actually together over a thousand miles from home.

Second, the discrepancy made the Gates' conduct seem substantially less unusual than the informant had predicted it would be. It would have been odd if, as predicted, Sue had driven down to Florida on Wednesday, left the car, and flown right back to Illinois. But the mere facts that Sue was in West Palm Beach with the car,[1] that she was joined by her husband at the Holiday Inn on Friday,[2]

---

1. The anonymous note suggested that she was going down on Wednesday, but for all the officers knew she had been in Florida for a month.

and that the couple drove north together the next morning [3] are neither unusual nor probative of criminal activity.

Third, the fact that the anonymous letter contained a material mistake undermines the reasonableness of relying on it as a basis for making a forcible entry into a private home.

Of course, the activities in this case did not stop when the magistrate issued the warrant. The Gates drove all night to Bloomingdale, the officers searched the car and found 400 pounds of marijuana, and then they searched the house. However, none of these subsequent events may be considered in evaluating the warrant, and the search of the house was legal only if the warrant was valid. I cannot accept the Court's casual conclusion that, *before the Gates arrived in Bloomingdale*, there was probable cause to justify a valid entry and search of a private home. No one knows who the informant in this case was, or what motivated him or her to write the note. Given that the note's predictions were faulty in one significant respect, and were corroborated by nothing except ordinary innocent activity, I must surmise that the Court's evaluation of the warrant's validity has been colored by subsequent events. * * *

SECTION 4. SEARCH WARRANTS

As the cases in the three sections following this one illustrate, there are many instances in which the police may seize or search on probable cause without first obtaining a warrant. However, the obtaining and executing of search warrants is nonetheless a common means for obtaining evidence of crime, for with rare exceptions extended searches of premises may be conducted only pursuant to a warrant. The Fourth Amendment sets out several requirements for warrants, stating that "no Warrants shall issue, but upon probable cause, supported by Oath or affirmation, and particularly describing the place to be searched, and the persons or things to be seized."

The first case in this section, *Maryland v. Garrison*, considers the meaning and significance of the particular description requirement. *Garrison*, together with the other case included here, *Richards v. Wisconsin*, also explores what it takes for the execution of a valid search warrant to be reasonable, still another requirement under the Fourth Amendment.

MARYLAND v. GARRISON

480 U.S. 79, 107 S.Ct. 1013, 94 L.Ed.2d 72 (1987).

JUSTICE STEVENS delivered the opinion of the Court.

Baltimore police officers obtained and executed a warrant to search the person of Lawrence McWebb and "the premises known as 2036 Park Avenue third

---

2. Lance does not appear to have behaved suspiciously in flying down to Florida. He made a reservation in his own name and gave an accurate home phone number to the airlines. And Detective Mader's affidavit does not report that he did any of the other things drug couriers are notorious for doing, such as paying for the ticket in cash, dressing casually, looking pale and nervous, improperly filling out baggage tags, carrying American Tourister luggage, not carrying any luggage, or changing airlines en route.

3. Detective Mader's affidavit hinted darkly that the couple had set out upon "that interstate highway commonly used by travelers to the Chicago area." But the same highway is also commonly used by travelers to Disney World, Sea World, and Ringling Brothers and Barnum and Bailey Circus World. It is also the road to Cocoa Beach, Cape Canaveral, and Washington, D.C. I would venture that each year dozens of perfectly innocent people fly to Florida, meet a waiting spouse, and drive off together in the family car.

floor apartment." When the police applied for the warrant and when they conducted the search pursuant to the warrant, they reasonably believed that there was only one apartment on the premises described in the warrant. In fact, the third floor was divided into two apartments, one occupied by McWebb and one by respondent Garrison. Before the officers executing the warrant became aware that they were in a separate apartment occupied by respondent, they had discovered the contraband that provided the basis for respondent's conviction for violating Maryland's Controlled Substances Act. The question presented is whether the seizure of that contraband was prohibited by the Fourth Amendment.

The trial court denied respondent's motion to suppress the evidence seized from his apartment, and the Maryland Court of Special Appeals affirmed. The Court of Appeals of Maryland reversed and remanded with instructions to remand the case for a new trial.

There is no question that the warrant was valid and was supported by probable cause. The trial court found, and the two appellate courts did not dispute, that after making a reasonable investigation, including a verification of information obtained from a reliable informant, an exterior examination of the three-story building at 2036 Park Avenue, and an inquiry of the utility company, the officer who obtained the warrant reasonably concluded that there was only one apartment on the third floor and that it was occupied by McWebb. When six Baltimore police officers executed the warrant, they fortuitously encountered McWebb in front of the building and used his key to gain admittance to the first-floor hallway and to the locked door at the top of the stairs to the third floor. As they entered the vestibule on the third floor, they encountered respondent, who was standing in the hallway area. The police could see into the interior of both McWebb's apartment to the left and respondent's to the right, for the doors to both were open. Only after respondent's apartment had been entered and heroin, cash, and drug paraphernalia had been found did any of the officers realize that the third floor contained two apartments. As soon as they became aware of that fact, the search was discontinued. All of the officers reasonably believed that they were searching McWebb's apartment. No further search of respondent's apartment was made.

The matter on which there is a difference of opinion concerns the proper interpretation of the warrant. A literal reading of its plain language, as well as the language used in the application for the warrant, indicates that it was intended to authorize a search of the entire third floor. This is the construction adopted by the intermediate appellate court, and it also appears to be the construction adopted by the trial judge. One sentence in the trial judge's oral opinion, however, lends support to the construction adopted by the Court of Appeals, namely, that the warrant authorized a search of McWebb's apartment only. Under that interpretation, the Court of Appeals concluded that the warrant did not authorize the search of respondent's apartment and the police had no justification for making a warrantless entry into his premises. * * *

In our view, the case presents two separate constitutional issues, one concerning the validity of the warrant and the other concerning the reasonableness of the manner in which it was executed. We shall discuss the questions separately.

I

The Warrant Clause of the Fourth Amendment categorically prohibits the issuance of any warrant except one "particularly describing the place to be searched and the persons or things to be seized." The manifest purpose of this particularity requirement was to prevent general searches. By limiting the authorization to search to the specific areas and things for which there is probable cause to search, the requirement ensures that the search will be carefully tailored to its justifications, and will not take on the character of the wide-ranging exploratory searches the Framers intended to prohibit. Thus, the scope of a lawful search is "defined by the object of the search and the places in which there is probable cause to believe that it may be found. Just as probable cause to believe that a stolen lawnmower may be found in a garage will not support a warrant to search an upstairs bedroom, probable cause to believe that undocumented aliens are being transported in a van will not justify a warrantless search of a suitcase."

In this case there is no claim that the "persons or things to be seized" were inadequately described or that there was no probable cause to believe that those things might be found in "the place to be searched" as it was described in the warrant. With the benefit of hindsight, however, we now know that the description of that place was broader than appropriate because it was based on the mistaken belief that there was only one apartment on the third floor of the building at 2036 Park Avenue. The question is whether that factual mistake invalidated a warrant that undoubtedly would have been valid if it had reflected a completely accurate understanding of the building's floor plan.

Plainly, if the officers had known, or even if they should have known, that there were two separate dwelling units on the third floor of 2036 Park Avenue, they would have been obligated to exclude respondent's apartment from the scope of the requested warrant. But we must judge the constitutionality of their conduct in light of the information available to them at the time they acted. Those items of evidence that emerge after the warrant is issued have no bearing on whether or not a warrant was validly issued. Just as the discovery of contraband cannot validate a warrant invalid when issued, so is it equally clear that the discovery of facts demonstrating that a valid warrant was unnecessarily broad does not retroactively invalidate the warrant. The validity of the warrant must be assessed on the basis of the information that the officers disclosed, or had a duty to discover and to disclose, to the issuing Magistrate.[10] On the basis of that information, we agree with the conclusion of all three Maryland courts that the warrant, insofar as it authorized a search that turned out to be ambiguous in scope, was valid when it issued.

II

The question whether the execution of the warrant violated respondent's constitutional right to be secure in his home is somewhat less clear. We have no

---

10. Arguments can certainly be made that the police in this case should have been able to ascertain that there was more than one apartment on the third floor of this building. It contained seven separate dwelling units and it was surely possible that two of them might be on the third floor. But the record also establishes that Officer Marcus made specific inquiries to determine the identity of the occupants of the third-floor premises. The officer went to 2036 Park Avenue and found that it matched the description given by the informant: a three-story brick dwelling with the numerals 2–0–3–6 affixed to the front of the premises. The officer "made a check with the Baltimore Gas and Electric Company and discovered that the premises of 2036 Park Ave. third floor was in the name of Lawrence McWebb." Ibid. Officer Marcus testified at the suppression hearing that he inquired of the Baltimore Gas and Electric Company in whose name the third floor apartment was listed: "I asked if there is a front or rear or middle room. They told me, one third floor was only listed to Lawrence McWebb." The officer also discovered from a check with the Baltimore Police Department that the police records of Lawrence McWebb matched the address and physical description given by the informant. The Maryland courts that are presumptively familiar with local conditions were unanimous in concluding that the officer reasonably believed McWebb was the only tenant on that floor. Because the evidence supports their conclusion, we accept that conclusion for the purpose of our decision.

difficulty concluding that the officers' entry into the third-floor common area was legal; they carried a warrant for those premises, and they were accompanied by McWebb, who provided the key that they used to open the door giving access to the third-floor common area. If the officers had known, or should have known, that the third floor contained two apartments before they entered the living quarters on the third floor, and thus had been aware of the error of the warrant, they would have been obligated to limit their search to McWebb's apartment. Moreover, as the officers recognized, they were required to discontinue the search of respondent's apartment as soon as they discovered that there were two separate units on the third floor and therefore were put on notice of the risk that they might be in a unit erroneously included within the terms of the warrant. The officers' conduct and the limits of the search were based on the information available as the search proceeded. While the purposes justifying a police search strictly limit the permissible extent of the search,[a] the Court has also recognized the need to allow some latitude for honest mistakes that are made by officers in the dangerous and difficult process of making arrests and executing search warrants.

In *Hill v. California,* 401 U.S. 797 (1971), we considered the validity of the arrest of a man named Miller based on the mistaken belief that he was Hill. The police had probable cause to arrest Hill and they in good faith believed that Miller was Hill when they found him in Hill's apartment. As we explained: "The upshot was that the officers in good faith believed Miller was Hill and arrested him. They were quite wrong as it turned out, and subjective good-faith belief would not in itself justify either the arrest or the subsequent search. But sufficient probability, not certainty, is the touchstone of reasonableness under the Fourth Amendment and on the record before us the officers' mistake was understandable and the arrest a reasonable response to the situation facing them at the time."

While *Hill* involved an arrest without a warrant, its underlying rationale that an officer's reasonable misidentification of a person does not invalidate a valid arrest is equally applicable to an officer's reasonable failure to appreciate that a valid warrant describes too broadly the premises to be searched. Under the reasoning in *Hill,* the validity of the search of respondent's apartment pursuant to a warrant authorizing the search of the entire third floor depends on whether the officers' failure to realize the overbreadth of the warrant was objectively understandable and reasonable. Here it unquestionably was. The objective facts available to the officers at the time suggested no distinction between McWebb's apartment and the third-floor premises.[12]

---

a. Relying upon this principle from *Garrison,* the Court in *Wilson v. Layne,* 526 U.S. 603 (1999), involving police execution of an *arrest* warrant while accompanied by a newspaper reporter and photographer, held that "it is a violation of the Fourth Amendment for police to bring members of the media or other third parties into a home during the execution of a warrant when the presence of the third parties in the home was not in aid of the execution of the warrant." To emphasize that the presence of a third party is not always improper, the Court commented: "Where the police enter a home under the authority of a warrant to search for stolen property, the presence of third parties for the purpose of identifying the stolen property has long been approved by this Court and our common-law tradition."*Wilson*

was a § 1983 case and thus involved no exclusionary rule issue, and the Court dropped this footnote: "Even though such actions might violate the Fourth Amendment, if the police are lawfully present, the violation of the Fourth Amendment is the presence of the media and not the presence of the police in the home. We have no occasion here to decide whether the exclusionary rule would apply to any evidence discovered or developed by the media representatives."

12. Nothing McWebb did or said after he was detained outside 2036 Park Avenue would have suggested to the police that there were two apartments on the third floor. McWebb provided the key that opened the doors on the first floor and on the third floor. The police

For that reason, the officers properly responded to the command contained in a valid warrant even if the warrant is interpreted as authorizing a search limited to McWebb's apartment rather than the entire third floor. Prior to the officers' discovery of the factual mistake, they perceived McWebb's apartment and the third-floor premises as one and the same; therefore their execution of the warrant reasonably included the entire third floor.[13] Under either interpretation of the warrant, the officers' conduct was consistent with a reasonable effort to ascertain and identify the place intended to be searched within the meaning of the Fourth Amendment.

The judgment of the Court of Appeals is reversed, and the case is remanded for further proceedings not inconsistent with this opinion.

It is so ordered.

JUSTICE BLACKMUN, with whom JUSTICE BRENNAN and JUSTICE MARSHALL join, dissenting. * * *

I

* * * I conclude that the search of respondent's apartment was improper. The words of the warrant were plain and distinctive: the warrant directed the officers to seize marijuana and drug paraphernalia on the person of McWebb and in McWebb's apartment, i.e., "on the premises known as 2036 Park Avenue third floor apartment." As the Court of Appeals observed, this warrant specifically authorized a search only of McWebb's—not respondent's—residence. In its interpretation of the warrant, the majority suggests that the language of this document, as well as that in the supporting affidavit, permitted a search of the entire third floor. It escapes me why the language in question, "third floor apartment," when used with reference to a single unit in a multiple-occupancy building and in the context of one person's residence, plainly has the meaning the majority discerns, rather than its apparent and, indeed, obvious signification—one apartment located on the third floor. Accordingly, if, as appears to be the case, the warrant was limited in its description to the third floor apartment of McWebb, then the search of an additional apartment—respondent's—was warrantless and is presumed unreasonable "in the absence of some one of a number of well defined 'exigent circumstances.'" Because the State has not advanced any such exception to the warrant requirement, the evidence obtained as a result of this search should have been excluded.

II

* * * Even if one accepts the majority's view that there is no Fourth Amendment violation where the officers' mistake is reasonable, it is questionable whether that standard was met in this case. * * *

The efforts of Detective Marcus, the officer who procured the search warrant, do not meet a standard of reasonableness, particularly considering that the detective knew the search concerned a unit in a multiple-occupancy building. Upon learning from his informant that McWebb was selling marijuana in his

could reasonably have believed that McWebb was admitting them to an undivided apartment on the third floor. When the officers entered the foyer on the third floor, neither McWebb nor Garrison informed them that they lived in separate apartments.

13. We expressly distinguish the facts of this case from a situation in which the police know there are two apartments on a certain floor of a building, and have probable cause to believe that drugs are being sold out of that floor, but do not know in which of the two apartments the illegal transactions are taking place. A search pursuant to a warrant authorizing a search of the entire floor under those circumstances would present quite different issues from the ones before us in this case.

third-floor apartment, Marcus inspected the outside of the building. He did not approach it, however, to gather information about the configuration of the apartments. Had he done so, he would have discovered, as did another officer on the day of executing the warrant, that there were seven separate mailboxes and bells on the porch outside the main entrance to the house. Although there is some dispute over whether names were affixed near these boxes and bells, their existence alone puts a reasonable observer on notice that the three-story structure (with, possibly, a basement) had seven individual units. The detective, therefore, should have been aware that further investigation was necessary to eliminate the possibility of more than one unit's being located on the third floor. Moreover, when Detective Marcus' informant told him that he had purchased drugs in McWebb's apartment, it appears that the detective never thought to ask the informant whether McWebb's apartment was the only one on the third floor. These efforts, which would have placed a slight burden upon the detective, are necessary in order to render reasonable the officer's behavior in seeking the warrant.

Moreover, even if one believed that Marcus' efforts in providing information for issuance of the warrant were reasonable, I doubt whether the officers' execution of the warrant could meet such a standard. In the Court's view, the "objective facts" did not put the officers on notice that they were dealing with two separate apartments on the third floor until the moment, considerably into the search after they had rummaged through a dresser and a closet in respondent's apartment and had discovered evidence incriminating him, when they realized their "mistake." The Court appears to base its conclusion that the officers' error here was reasonable on the fact that neither McWebb nor respondent ever told the officers during the search that they lived in separate apartments.

In my view, however, the "objective facts" should have made the officers aware that there were two different apartments on the third floor well before they discovered the incriminating evidence in respondent's apartment. Before McWebb happened to drive up while the search party was preparing to execute the warrant, one of the officers, Detective Shea, somewhat disguised as a construction worker, was already on the porch of the row house and was seeking to gain access to the locked first-floor door that permitted entrance into the building. From this vantage point he had time to observe the seven mailboxes and bells; indeed, he rang all seven bells, apparently in an effort to summon some resident to open the front door to the search party. A reasonable officer in Detective Shea's position, already aware that this was a multiunit building and now armed with further knowledge of the number of units in the structure, would have conducted at that time more investigation to specify the exact location of McWebb's apartment before proceeding further. For example, he might have questioned another resident of the building. * * *

Moreover, a reasonable officer would have realized the mistake in the warrant during the moments following the officers' entrance to the third floor. The officers gained access to the vestibule separating McWebb's and respondent's apartments through a locked door for which McWebb supplied the key. There, in the open doorway to his apartment, they encountered respondent, clad in pajamas and wearing a half-body cast as a result of a recent spinal operation. Although the facts concerning what next occurred are somewhat in dispute, it appears that respondent, together with McWebb and the passenger from McWebb's car, were shepherded into McWebb's apartment across the vestibule from his own. Once again, the officers were curiously silent. The informant had not led the officers to believe that anyone other than McWebb lived in the third-floor apartment; the search party had McWebb, the person targeted by the search warrant, in custody when it gained access to the vestibule; yet when they met respondent on the third floor, they simply asked him who he was but never where he lived. Had they done so, it is likely that they would have discovered the mistake in the warrant before they began their search.

Finally and most importantly, even if the officers had learned nothing from respondent, they should have realized the error in the warrant from their initial security sweep. Once on the third floor, the officers first fanned out through the rooms to conduct a preliminary check for other occupants who might pose a danger to them. As the map of the third floor demonstrates, the two apartments were almost a mirror image of each other—each had a bathroom, a kitchen, a living room, and a bedroom. Given the somewhat symmetrical layout of the apartments, it is difficult to imagine that, in the initial security sweep, a reasonable officer would not have discerned that two apartments were on the third floor, realized his mistake, and then confined the ensuing search to McWebb's residence.

Accordingly, even if a reasonable error on the part of police officers prevents a Fourth Amendment violation, the mistakes here, both with respect to obtaining and executing the warrant, are not reasonable and could easily have been avoided.

I respectfully dissent.

RICHARDS v. WISCONSIN

520 U.S. 385, 117 S.Ct. 1416, 137 L.Ed.2d 615 (1997).

JUSTICE STEVENS delivered the opinion of the Court.

In *Wilson v. Arkansas*, 514 U.S. 927 (1995), we held that the Fourth Amendment incorporates the common-law requirement that police officers entering a dwelling must knock on the door and announce their identity and purpose before attempting forcible entry. At the same time, we recognized that the "flexible requirement of reasonableness should not be read to mandate a rigid rule of announcement that ignores countervailing law enforcement interests," and left "to the lower courts the task of determining the circumstances under which an unannounced entry is reasonable under the Fourth Amendment."

In this case, the Wisconsin Supreme Court concluded that police officers are never required to knock and announce their presence when executing a search warrant in a felony drug investigation. * * * We disagree * * *.

On December 31, 1991, police officers in Madison, Wisconsin obtained a warrant to search Steiney Richards' hotel room for drugs and related paraphernalia. The search warrant was the culmination of an investigation that had uncovered substantial evidence that Richards was one of several individuals dealing drugs out of hotel rooms in Madison. The police requested a warrant that would have given advance authorization for a "no-knock" entry into the hotel room, but the magistrate explicitly deleted those portions of the warrant.

The officers arrived at the hotel room at 3:40 a.m. Officer Pharo, dressed as a maintenance man, led the team. With him were several plainclothes officers and at least one man in uniform. Officer Pharo knocked on Richards' door and, responding to the query from inside the room, stated that he was a maintenance man. With the chain still on the door, Richards cracked it open. Although there is some dispute as to what occurred next, Richards acknowledges that when he opened the door he saw the man in uniform standing behind Officer Pharo. He quickly slammed the door closed and, after waiting two or three seconds, the officers began kicking and ramming the door to gain entry to the locked room. At trial, the officers testified that they identified themselves as police while they were kicking the door in. When they finally did break into the room, the officers caught Richards trying to escape through the window. They also found cash and cocaine hidden in plastic bags above the bathroom ceiling tiles.

Richards sought to have the evidence from his hotel room suppressed on the ground that the officers had failed to knock and announce their presence prior to forcing entry into the room. The trial court denied the motion, concluding that the officers could gather from Richards' strange behavior when they first sought entry that he knew they were police officers and that he might try to destroy evidence or to escape. * * * Richards appealed the decision to the Wisconsin Supreme Court and that court affirmed.

The Wisconsin Supreme Court did not delve into the events underlying Richards' arrest in any detail, but [instead] found it reasonable—after considering criminal conduct surveys, newspaper articles, and other judicial opinions—to assume that all felony drug crimes will involve "an extremely high risk of serious if not deadly injury to the police as well as the potential for the disposal of drugs by the occupants prior to entry by the police." Notwithstanding its acknowledgment that in "some cases, police officers will undoubtedly decide that their safety, the safety of others, and the effective execution of the warrant dictate that they knock and announce," the court concluded that exigent circumstances justifying a no-knock entry are always present in felony drug cases. * * * Accordingly, the court determined that police in Wisconsin do not need specific information about dangerousness, or the possible destruction of drugs in a particular case, in order to dispense with the knock-and-announce requirement in felony drug cases. * * *

We recognized in *Wilson* that the knock-and-announce requirement could give way "under circumstances presenting a threat of physical violence," or "where police officers have reason to believe that evidence would likely be destroyed if advance notice were given." It is indisputable that felony drug investigations may frequently involve both of these circumstances. The question we must resolve is whether this fact justifies dispensing with case-by-case evaluation of the manner in which a search was executed.

The Wisconsin court explained its blanket exception as necessitated by the special circumstances of today's drug culture, and the State asserted at oral argument that the blanket exception was reasonable in "felony drug cases because of the convergence in a violent and dangerous form of commerce of weapons and the destruction of drugs." But creating exceptions to the knock-and-announce rule based on the "culture" surrounding a general category of criminal behavior presents at least two serious concerns.

First, the exception contains considerable overgeneralization. For example, while drug investigation frequently does pose special risks to officer safety and the preservation of evidence, not every drug investigation will pose these risks to a substantial degree. For example, a search could be conducted at a time when the only individuals present in a residence have no connection with the drug activity and thus will be unlikely to threaten officers or destroy evidence. Or the police could know that the drugs being searched for were of a type or in a location that made them impossible to destroy quickly. In those situations, the asserted governmental interests in preserving evidence and maintaining safety may not outweigh the individual privacy interests intruded upon by a no-knock entry. Wisconsin's blanket rule impermissibly insulates these cases from judicial review.

A second difficulty with permitting a criminal-category exception to the knock-and-announce requirement is that the reasons for creating an exception in one category can, relatively easily, be applied to others. Armed bank robbers, for example, are, by definition, likely to have weapons, and the fruits of their crime may be destroyed without too much difficulty. If a per se exception were allowed for each category of criminal investigation that included a considerable—albeit hypothetical—risk of danger to officers or destruction of evidence, the knock-and-announce element of the Fourth Amendment's reasonableness requirement would be meaningless.

Thus, the fact that felony drug investigations may frequently present circumstances warranting a no-knock entry cannot remove from the neutral scrutiny of a reviewing court the reasonableness of the police decision not to knock and announce in a particular case. Instead, in each case, it is the duty of a court confronted with the question to determine whether the facts and circumstances of the particular entry justified dispensing with the knock-and-announce requirement.

In order to justify a "no-knock" entry, the police must have a reasonable suspicion that knocking and announcing their presence, under the particular circumstances, would be dangerous or futile, or that it would inhibit the effective investigation of the crime by, for example, allowing the destruction of evidence. This standard—as opposed to a probable cause requirement—strikes the appropriate balance between the legitimate law enforcement concerns at issue in the execution of search warrants and the individual privacy interests affected by no-knock entries. Cf. *Maryland v. Buie* [Ch. 3, § 6]; *Terry v. Ohio* [Ch. 3, § 8]. This showing is not high, but the police should be required to make it whenever the reasonableness of a no-knock entry is challenged.[a]

Although we reject the Wisconsin court's blanket exception to the knock-and-announce requirement, we conclude that the officers' no-knock entry into Richards' hotel room did not violate the Fourth Amendment. We agree with the trial court, and with Justice Abrahamson, that the circumstances in this case show that the officers had a reasonable suspicion that Richards might destroy evidence if given further opportunity to do so.

The judge who heard testimony at Richards' suppression hearing concluded that it was reasonable for the officers executing the warrant to believe that Richards knew, after opening the door to his hotel room the first time, that the men seeking entry to his room were the police. Once the officers reasonably believed that Richards knew who they were, the court concluded, it was reasonable for them to force entry immediately given the disposable nature of the drugs.

In arguing that the officers' entry was unreasonable, Richards places great emphasis on the fact that the magistrate who signed the search warrant for his hotel room deleted the portions of the proposed warrant that would have given the officers permission to execute a no-knock entry. But this fact does not alter the reasonableness of the officers' decision, which must be evaluated as of the time they entered the hotel room. * * *

a. In *United States v. Ramirez*, 523 U.S. 65 (1998), the Court held that whether this reasonable suspicion test has been met "depends in no way on whether police must destroy property in order to enter," and then concluded no Fourth Amendment violation had occurred in the instant case, where police executing a search warrant authorizing entry to seize a wanted person broke a garage window in order to deter the occupants of the premises (who thereafter exited and surrendered) from entering the garage to obtain weapons: "A reliable confidential informant had notified the police that Alan Shelby might be inside respondent's home, and an officer had confirmed this possibility. Shelby was a prison escapee with a violent past who reportedly had access to a large supply of weapons. He had vowed that he would 'not do federal time.' The police certainly had a 'reasonable suspicion' that knocking and announcing their presence might be dangerous to themselves or to others."

SECTION 5. WARRANTLESS ARREST AND SEARCH OF PERSONS

The Supreme Court has long expressed a strong preference for the use of arrest warrants and search warrants. As the Court has indicated in a host of cases, resort to the warrant process is preferred because it "interposes an orderly procedure" involving "judicial impartiality" whereby "a neutral and detached magistrate" can make "informed and deliberate determinations" on the issue of probable cause. To leave such decisions to the police would allow "hurried actions" by those "engaged in the often competitive enterprise of ferreting out crime." Yet, as the cases in this section and the two following—dealing, respectively, with search of premises and search of vehicles—clearly demonstrate, there are a great many exceptions to the warrant requirement. When the Court approves warrantless activity, it is typically because of a view that the police (1) were acting in exigent circumstances, (2) were intruding upon lesser Fourth Amendment interests, or (3) were otherwise not involved in activity as to which before-the-fact judicial scrutiny would be useful.

The first case in this section, *United States v. Watson*, explains why it is that no warrant is required to make an arrest. The next case, *United States v. Robinson*, addresses warrantless search of the person incident to arrest. *Robinson* gave rise to two significant issues, later addressed in the next two cases, *Whren v. United States* and *Atwater v. City of Lago Vista*, respectively: whether an arrest or other Fourth Amendment seizure made on probable cause may nonetheless be "unreasonable" because of the officer's ulterior motives or his departure from usual practice (e.g., as set out in police regulations); and whether an arrest on probable cause may nonetheless be "unreasonable" because releasing the offender on a citation would have sufficed. The final case in this section, *Tennessee v. Garner*, teaches that sometimes an arrest will be "unreasonable" in a Fourth Amendment sense because of the amount of force used in making it.

UNITED STATES v. WATSON

423 U.S. 411, 96 S.Ct. 820, 46 L.Ed.2d 598 (1976).

JUSTICE WHITE delivered the opinion of the Court.

[Reliable informant Khoury told a federal postal inspector that Watson had supplied him with a stolen credit card and had agreed to furnish additional cards at their next meeting, scheduled for a few days later. At that meeting, which occurred in a restaurant, Khoury signaled the inspector that Watson had the cards, at which point the inspector arrested Watson without a warrant, as he was authorized to do under 18 U.S.C. § 3061 and applicable postal regulations. The court of appeals held the arrest unconstitutional because the inspector had failed to secure an arrest warrant although he concededly had time to do so, and this was a significant factor in the court's additional holding that Watson's consent to a search of his car was not voluntary.]

* * * Section 3061 represents a judgment by Congress that it is not unreasonable under the Fourth Amendment for postal inspectors to arrest without a warrant provided they have probable cause to do so. This was not an isolated or quixotic judgment of the legislative branch. Other federal law enforcement officers have been expressly authorized by statute for many years to make felony arrests on probable cause but without a warrant. * * *

Because there is a "strong presumption of constitutionality due to an Act of Congress, especially when it turns on what is 'reasonable,' * * * [o]bviously the

Court should be reluctant to decide that a search thus authorized by Congress was unreasonable and that the Act was therefore unconstitutional." Moreover, there is nothing in the Court's prior cases indicating that under the Fourth Amendment a warrant is required to make a valid arrest for a felony. Indeed, the relevant prior decisions are uniformly to the contrary. * * *

* * * Just last Term, while recognizing that maximum protection of individual rights could be assured by requiring a magistrate's review of the factual justification prior to any arrest, we stated that "such a requirement would constitute an intolerable handicap for legitimate law enforcement" and noted that the Court "has never invalidated an arrest supported by probable cause solely because the officers failed to secure a warrant." *Gerstein v. Pugh,* 420 U.S. 103 (1975).[a]

The cases construing the Fourth Amendment thus reflect the ancient common-law rule that a peace officer was permitted to arrest without a warrant for a

a. The Supreme Court in *Gerstein* went on to say:

"Under this practical compromise, a policeman's on-the-scene assessment of probable cause provides legal justification for arresting a person suspected of crime, and for a brief period of detention to take the administrative steps incident to arrest. Once the suspect is in custody, however, the reasons that justify dispensing with the magistrate's neutral judgment evaporate. There no longer is any danger that the suspect will escape or commit further crimes while the police submit their evidence to a magistrate. And, while the State's reasons for taking summary action subside, the suspect's need for a neutral determination of probable cause increases significantly. The consequences of prolonged detention may be more serious than the interference occasioned by arrest. Pretrial confinement may imperil the suspect's job, interrupt his source of income, and impair his family relationships. Even pretrial release may be accompanied by burdensome conditions that effect a significant restraint of liberty. When the stakes are this high, the detached judgment of a neutral magistrate is essential if the Fourth Amendment is to furnish meaningful protection from unfounded interference with liberty. Accordingly, we hold that the Fourth Amendment requires a judicial determination of probable cause as a prerequisite to extended restraint of liberty following arrest."

In *County of Riverside v. McLaughlin,* 500 U.S. 44 (1991), the Court, 5–4, concluded "that a jurisdiction that provides judicial determinations of probable cause within 48 hours of arrest will, as a general matter, comply with the promptness requirement of *Gerstein.* For this reason, such jurisdictions will be immune from systematic challenges.

"This is not to say that the probable cause determination in a particular case passes constitutional muster simply because it is provided within 48 hours. Such a hearing may nonetheless violate *Gerstein* if the arrested individual can prove that his or her probable cause determination was delayed unreasonably. Ex-

amples of unreasonable delay are delays for the purpose of gathering additional evidence to justify the arrest, a delay motivated by ill will against the arrested individual, or delay for delay's sake. In evaluating whether the delay in a particular case is unreasonable, however, courts must allow a substantial degree of flexibility. Courts cannot ignore the often unavoidable delays in transporting arrested persons from one facility to another, handling late-night bookings where no magistrate is readily available, obtaining the presence of an arresting officer who may be busy processing other suspects or securing the premises of an arrest, and other practical realities.

"Where an arrested individual does not receive a probable cause determination within 48 hours, the calculus changes. In such a case, the arrested individual does not bear the burden of proving an unreasonable delay. Rather, the burden shifts to the government to demonstrate the existence of a bona fide emergency or other extraordinary circumstance. The fact that in a particular case it may take longer than 48 hours to consolidate pretrial proceedings does not qualify as an extraordinary circumstance. Nor, for that matter, do intervening weekends. A jurisdiction that chooses to offer combined proceedings [e.g., incorporating the probable cause determination with arraignment] must do so as soon as is reasonably feasible, but in no event later than 48 hours after arrest."

In *Powell v. Nevada,* 511 U.S. 79 (1994), holding *McLaughlin* retroactive to that case, the Court noted: "It does not necessarily follow, however, that Powell must 'be set free' or gain other relief, for several questions remain open for decision on remand," including "the appropriate remedy for a delay in determining probable cause (an issue not resolved by *McLaughlin*)." In *Powell,* an untimely probable cause determination was made four days after defendant's arrest, shortly after he gave the police an incriminating statement. The Court declared that "whether a suppression remedy applies in that setting remains an unresolved question."

misdemeanor or felony committed in his presence as well as for a felony not committed in his presence if there was reasonable grounds for making the arrest. This has also been the prevailing rule under state constitutions and statutes. * * *

Because the common-law rule authorizing arrests without warrant generally prevailed in the States, it is important for present purposes to note that in 1792 Congress invested United States Marshals and their deputies with "the same powers in executing the laws of the United States, as sheriffs and their deputies in their several states have by law, in executing the laws of their respective states." The Second Congress thus saw no inconsistency between the Fourth Amendment and giving United States Marshals the same power as local peace officers to arrest for a felony without a warrant. * * *

The balance struck by the common law in generally authorizing felony arrests on probable cause, but without a warrant, has survived substantially intact. It appears in almost all of the States in the form of express statutory authorization. * * *

This is the rule Congress has long directed its principal law enforcement officers to follow. Congress has plainly decided against conditioning warrantless arrest power on proof of exigent circumstances. Law enforcement officers may find it wise to seek arrest warrants where practicable to do so, and their judgments about probable cause may be more readily accepted where backed by a warrant issued by a magistrate. But we decline to transform this judicial preference into a constitutional rule when the judgment of the Nation and Congress has for so long been to authorize warrantless public arrests on probable cause rather than to encumber criminal prosecutions with endless litigation with respect to the existence of exigent circumstances, whether it was practicable to get a warrant, whether the suspect was about to flee, and the like. * * *

Reversed.

JUSTICE STEVENS took no part in the consideration or decision of this case.

JUSTICE POWELL, concurring.

* * * On its face, our decision today creates a certain anomaly. There is no more basic constitutional rule in the Fourth Amendment area than that which makes a warrantless search unreasonable except in a few "jealously and carefully drawn" exceptional circumstances. * * * In short, the course of judicial development of the Fourth Amendment with respect to searches has remained true to the principles so well expressed by Mr. Justice Jackson:

> "Any assumption that evidence sufficient to support a magistrate's disinterested determination to issue a search warrant will justify the officers in making a search without a warrant would reduce the Amendment to a nullity and leave the people's homes secure only in the discretion of police officers. * * * When the right of privacy must reasonably yield to the right of search is, as a rule, to be decided by a judicial officer, not by a policeman or Government enforcement agent."

Since the Fourth Amendment speaks equally to both searches and seizures, and since an arrest, the taking hold of one's person, is quintessentially a seizure, it would seem that the constitutional provision should impose the same limitations upon arrests that it does upon searches. Indeed, as an abstract matter an argument can be made that the restrictions upon arrest perhaps should be greater. A search may cause only annoyance and temporary inconvenience to the law-abiding citizen, assuming more serious dimension only when it turns up evidence of criminality. An arrest, however, is a serious personal intrusion regardless of whether the person seized is guilty or innocent. Although an arrestee cannot be held for a significant period without some neutral determination that there are grounds to do so, no decision that he should go free can come quickly enough to erase the invasion of his privacy that already will have occurred. Logic therefore would seem to dictate that arrests be subject to the warrant requirement at least to the same extent as searches.

But logic sometimes must defer to history and experience. The Court's opinion emphasizes the historical sanction accorded warrantless felony arrests. * * *

The historical momentum for acceptance of warrantless arrests, already strong at the adoption of the Fourth Amendment, has gained strength during the ensuing two centuries. * * * Given the revolutionary implications of such a holding, a declaration at this late date that warrantless felony arrests are constitutionally infirm would have to rest upon reasons more substantial than a desire to harmonize the rules for arrest with those governing searches.

Moreover, a constitutional rule permitting felony arrests only with a warrant or in exigent circumstances could severely hamper effective law enforcement. Good police practice often requires postponing an arrest, even after probable cause has been established, in order to place the suspect under surveillance or otherwise develop further evidence necessary to prove guilt to a jury. Under the holding of the Court of Appeals such additional investigative work could imperil the entire prosecution. Should the officers fail to obtain a warrant initially, and later be required by unforeseen circumstances to arrest immediately with no chance to procure a last-minute warrant, they would risk a court decision that the subsequent exigency did not excuse their failure to get a warrant in the interim since they first developed probable cause. If the officers attempted to meet such a contingency by procuring a warrant as soon as they had probable cause and then merely held it during their subsequent investigation, they would risk a court decision that the warrant had grown stale by the time it was used.[5] Law enforcement personnel caught in this squeeze could ensure validity of their arrests only by obtaining a warrant and arresting as soon as probable cause existed, thereby foreclosing the possibility of gathering vital additional evidence from the suspect's continued actions. * * *[6]

JUSTICE MARSHALL, with whom JUSTICE BRENNAN joins, dissenting. * * *

The signal of the reliable informant that Watson was in possession of stolen credit cards gave the postal inspectors probable cause to make the arrest. This probable cause was separate and distinct from the probable cause relating to the offense six days earlier, and provided an adequate independent basis for the arrest. Whether or not a warrant ordinarily is required prior to making an arrest, no warrant is required when exigent circumstances are present. When law enforcement officers have probable cause to believe that an offense is taking place in their presence and that the suspect is at that moment in possession of the evidence, exigent circumstances exist. Delay could cause the escape of the suspect or the destruction of the evidence. Accordingly, Watson's warrantless arrest was valid under the recognized exigent circumstances exception to the warrant re-

---

5. The probable cause to support issuance of an arrest warrant normally would not grow stale as easily as that which supports a warrant to search a particular place for particular objects. This is true because once there is probable cause to believe that someone is a felon the passage of time often will bring new supporting evidence. But in some cases the original grounds supporting the warrant could be disproved by subsequent investigation that at the same time turns up wholly new evidence supporting probable cause on a different theory. In those cases the warrant could be stale because based upon discredited information.

6. Justice Stewart's opinion concurring in the result is omitted.

quirement, and the Court has no occasion to consider whether a warrant would otherwise be necessary. * * *

Since, for reasons it leaves unexpressed, the Court does not take this traditional course, I am constrained to express my views on the issues it unnecessarily decides. The Court reaches its conclusion that a warrant is not necessary for a police officer to make an arrest in a public place, so long as he has probable cause to believe a felony has been committed, on the basis of its views of precedent and history. As my Brother Powell correctly observes, the precedent is spurious. None of the cases cited by the Court squarely confronted the issue decided today. * * *

The Court next turns to history. It relies on the English common-law rule of arrest and the many state and federal statutes following it. There are two serious flaws in this approach. First, as a matter of factual analysis, the substance of the ancient common-law rule provides no support for the far-reaching modern rule that the Court fashions on its model. Second, as a matter of doctrine, the longstanding existence of a Government practice does not immunize the practice from scrutiny under the mandate of our Constitution.

* * * Only the most serious crimes were felonies at common law, and many crimes now classified as felonies under federal or state law were treated as misdemeanors. * * * To make an arrest for any of these crimes at common law, the police officer was required to obtain a warrant, unless the crime was committed in his presence. Since many of these same crimes are commonly classified as felonies today however, under the Court's holding a warrant is no longer needed to make such arrests, a result in contravention of the common law.

* * * As a matter of substance, the balance struck by the common law in accommodating the public need for the most certain and immediate arrest of criminal suspects with the requirement of magisterial oversight to protect against mistaken insults to privacy decreed that only in the most serious of cases could the warrant be dispensed with. This balance is not recognized when the common-law rule is unthinkingly transposed to our present classifications of criminal offenses. Indeed, the only clear lesson of history is contrary to the one the Court draws: the common law considered the arrest warrant far more important than today's decision leaves it.

I do not mean by this that a modern warrant requirement should apply only to arrests precisely analogous to common-law misdemeanors, and be inapplicable to analogues of common-law felonies. Rather, the point is simply that the Court's unblinking literalism cannot replace analysis of the constitutional interests involved. * * *

Lastly, the Court relies on the numerous state and federal statutes codifying the common-law rule. But this, too, is no substitute for reasoned analysis. * * *

The Court has typically engaged in a two-part analysis in deciding whether the presumption favoring a warrant should be given effect in situations where a warrant has not previously been clearly required. Utilizing that approach we must now consider (1) whether the privacy of our citizens will be better protected by ordinarily requiring a warrant to be issued before they may be arrested; and (2) whether a warrant requirement would unduly burden legitimate governmental interests.

The first question is easily answered. Of course the privacy of our citizens will be better protected by a warrant requirement. We have recognized that "the Fourth Amendment protects people, not places." Indeed, the privacy guaranteed by the Fourth Amendment is quintessentially personal. Thus a warrant is required in search situations not because of some high regard for property, but because of our regard for the individual, and *his* interest in his possessions and person. * * *

The Government's assertion that a warrant requirement would impose an intolerable burden stems, in large part, from the specious supposition that procurement of an arrest warrant would be necessary as soon as probable cause ripens. There is no requirement that a search warrant be obtained the moment police have probable cause to search. The rule is only that present probable cause be shown and a warrant obtained before a search is undertaken. The same rule should obtain for arrest warrants, where it may even make more sense. Certainly, there is less need for prompt procurement of a warrant in the arrest situation. Unlike probable cause to search, probable cause to arrest, once formed will continue to exist for the indefinite future, at least if no intervening exculpatory facts come to light.

This sensible approach obviates most of the difficulties that have been suggested with an arrest warrant rule. Police would not have to cut their investigation short the moment they obtain probable cause to arrest, nor would undercover agents be forced suddenly to terminate their work and forfeit their covers. Moreover, if in the course of the continued police investigation exigent circumstances develop that demand an immediate arrest, the arrest may be made without fear of unconstitutionality, so long as the exigency was unanticipated and not used to avoid the arrest warrant requirement. Likewise, if in the course of the continued investigation police uncover evidence tying the suspect to another crime, they may immediately arrest him for that crime if exigency demands it, and still be in full conformity with the warrant rule. This is why the arrest in this case was not improper.[15] Other than where police attempt to evade the warrant requirement, the rule would invalidate an arrest only in the obvious situation: where police, with probable cause but without exigent circumstances, set out to arrest a suspect. Such an arrest must be void, even if exigency develops in the course of the arrest that would ordinarily validate it; otherwise the warrant requirement would be reduced to a toothless prescription. * * *

It is suggested, however, that even if application of this rule does not require police to secure a warrant as soon as they obtain probable cause, the confused officer would nonetheless be prone to do so. If so, police "would risk a court decision that the warrant had grown stale by the time it was used." (Powell, J., concurring). This fear is groundless. First, as suggested above, the requirement that police procure a warrant before an arrest is made is rather simple of application. Thus, there is no need for the police to find themselves in this "squeeze." Second, the "squeeze" is nonexistent. Just as it is virtually impossible for probable cause for an arrest to grow stale between the time of formation and the time a warrant is procured, it is virtually impossible for probable cause to become stale between procurement and arrest. Delay by law enforcement officers in executing an arrest warrant does not ordinarily affect the legality of the arrest. * * *

15. Although the postal inspectors here anticipated the occurrence of the second crime, they could not have obtained a warrant for Watson's arrest for that crime until probable cause formed, just moments before the arrest. A warrant based on anticipated facts is premature and void.

UNITED STATES v. ROBINSON

414 U.S. 218, 94 S.Ct. 467, 38 L.Ed.2d 427 (1973).

JUSTICE REHNQUIST delivered the opinion of the Court.

Respondent Robinson was convicted in United States District Court for the District of Columbia of the possession and facilitation of concealment of heroin. * * * [T]he Court of Appeals *en banc* reversed the judgment of conviction, holding that the heroin introduced in evidence against respondent had been obtained as a result of a search which violated the Fourth Amendment to the United States Constitution.

On April 23, 1968, at approximately 11 o'clock p.m., Officer Richard Jenks, a 15-year veteran of the District of Columbia Metropolitan Police Department, observed the respondent driving a 1965 Cadillac near the intersection of 8th and C Streets, Southeast, in the District of Columbia. Jenks, as a result of previous investigation following a check of respondent's operator's permit four days earlier, determined there was reason to believe that respondent was operating a motor vehicle after the revocation of his operator's permit. This is an offense defined by statute in the District of Columbia which carries a mandatory minimum jail term, a mandatory minimum fine, or both.

Jenks signaled respondent to stop the automobile, which respondent did, and all three of the occupants emerged from the car. At that point Jenks informed respondent that he was under arrest for "operating after revocation and obtaining a permit by misrepresentation." It was assumed by the majority of the Court of Appeals, and is conceded by the respondent here, that Jenks had probable cause to arrest respondent, and that he effected a full custody arrest.

In accordance with procedures prescribed in Police Department instructions,[2] Jenks then began to search respondent. He explained at a subsequent hearing that he was "face to face" with the respondent, and "placed [his] hands on [the respondent], my right hand to his left breast like this (demonstrating) and proceeded to pat him down thus (with the right hand)." During this patdown, Jenks felt an object in the left breast pocket of the heavy coat respondent was wearing, but testified that he "couldn't tell what it was" and also that he "couldn't actually tell the size of it." Jenks then reached into the pocket and pulled out the object, which turned out to be a "crumpled up cigarette package." Jenks testified that at this point he still did not know what was in the package:

> "As I felt the package I could feel objects in the package but I couldn't tell what they were. * * * I knew they weren't cigarettes."

The officer then opened the cigarette pack and found 14 gelatin capsules of white powder which he thought to be, and which later analysis proved to be, heroin. Jenks then continued his search of respondent to completion, feeling around his waist and trouser legs, and examining the remaining pockets. The heroin seized from the respondent was admitted into evidence at the trial which resulted in his conviction in the District Court. * * *

2. The government introduced testimony at the evidentiary hearing upon the original remand by the Court of Appeals as to certain standard operating procedures of the Metropolitan Police Department. Sergeant Dennis C. Donaldson, a Training Division Instructor, testified that when a police officer makes "a full custody arrest" which he defined as where an officer "would arrest a subject and subsequently transport him to a police facility for booking," the officer is trained to make a full "field type search" * * *. Sergeant Donaldson testified that officers are instructed to examine the "contents of all of the pockets" of the arrestee in the course of the field search. * * * Those regulations also provide that in the case of some traffic offenses, including the crime of operating a motor vehicle after revocation of an operator's permit, the officer shall make a summary arrest of the violator and take the violator, in custody, to the stationhouse for booking. D.C. Metropolitan Police Department General Order No. 3, series 1959 (April 24, 1959). Such operating procedures are not, of course, determinative of the constitutional issues presented by this case.

It is well settled that a search incident to a lawful arrest is a traditional exception to the warrant requirement of the Fourth Amendment. This general exception has historically been formulated into two distinct propositions. The first is that a search may be made of the *person* of the arrestee by virtue of the lawful arrest. The second is that a search may be made of the area within the control of the arrestee.

Examination of this Court's decisions in the area show that these two propositions have been treated quite differently. The validity of the search of a person incident to a lawful arrest has been regarded as settled from its first enunciation, and has remained virtually unchallenged until the present case. The validity of the second proposition, while likewise conceded in principle, has been subject to differing interpretations as to the extent of the area which may be searched. * * *

Throughout the series of cases in which the Court has addressed the second proposition relating to a search incident to a lawful arrest—the permissible area beyond the person of the arrestee which such a search may cover—no doubt has been expressed as to the unqualified authority of the arresting authority to search the person of the arrestee. * * *

Thus the broadly stated rule, and the reasons for it, have been repeatedly affirmed in the decisions of this Court since *Weeks v. United States* nearly 60 years ago. Since the statements in the cases speak not simply in terms of an exception to the warrant requirement, but in terms of an affirmative authority to search, they clearly imply that such searches also meet the Fourth Amendment's requirement of reasonableness. * * *

Virtually all of the statements of this Court affirming the existence of an unqualified authority to search incident to a lawful arrest are dicta. We would not therefore be foreclosed by principles of *stare decisis* from further examination into history and practice in order to see whether the sort of qualifications imposed by the Court of Appeals in this case were in fact intended by the Framers of the Fourth Amendment or recognized in cases decided prior to *Weeks*. Unfortunately such authorities as exist are sparse. * * *

While these earlier authorities are sketchy, they tend to support the broad statement of the authority to search incident to arrest found in the successive decisions of this Court, rather than the restrictive one which was applied by the Court of Appeals in this case. * * *

The justification or reason for the authority to search incident to a lawful arrest rests quite as much on the need to disarm the suspect in order to take him into custody as it does on the need to preserve evidence on his person for later use at trial. The standards traditionally governing a search incident to lawful arrest are not, therefore, commuted to the stricter *Terry* standards [a] by the absence of probable fruits or further evidence of the particular crime for which the arrest is made.

Nor are we inclined, on the basis of what seems to us to be a rather speculative judgment, to qualify the breadth of the general authority to search incident to a lawful custodial arrest on an assumption that persons arrested for

---

a. The reference is to *Terry v. Ohio*, § 7 infra, relied upon here by the Court of Appeals, where the Supreme Court held that on reasonable suspicion (that is, individualized suspicion short of the probable cause needed for arrest) the police may stop a person for investigation. The Court also held that incident to such a stop the police may take limited steps for their own protection: a full incident-to-arrest type search of the person is not permitted, but upon reasonable suspicion that the person is "armed and dangerous" the officer may pat him down and then reach into pockets upon feeling an object which might be a weapon.

the offense of driving while their license has been revoked are less likely to be possessed of dangerous weapons than are those arrested for other crimes.[5] It is scarcely open to doubt that the danger to an officer is far greater in the case of the extended exposure which follows the taking of a suspect into custody and transporting him to the police station than in the case of the relatively fleeting contact resulting from the typical *Terry*-type stop. This is an adequate basis for treating all custodial arrests alike for purposes of search justification.

But quite apart from these distinctions, our more fundamental disagreement with the Court of Appeals arises from its suggestion that there must be litigated in each case the issue of whether or not there was present one of the reasons supporting the authority for a search of the person incident to a lawful arrest. We do not think the long line of authorities of this Court dating back to *Weeks,* nor what we can glean from the history of practice in this country and in England, requires such a case by case adjudication. A police officer's determination as to how and where to search the person of a suspect whom he has arrested is necessarily a quick *ad hoc* judgment which the Fourth Amendment does not require to be broken down in each instance into an analysis of each step in the search. The authority to search the person incident to a lawful custodial arrest, while based upon the need to disarm and to discover evidence, does not depend on what a court may later decide was the probability in a particular arrest situation that weapons or evidence would in fact be found upon the person of the suspect. A custodial arrest of a suspect based on probable cause is a reasonable intrusion under the Fourth Amendment; that intrusion being lawful, a search incident to the arrest requires no additional justification. It is the fact of the lawful arrest which establishes the authority to search, and we hold that in the case of a lawful custodial arrest a full search of the person is not only an exception to the warrant requirement of the Fourth Amendment, but is also a "reasonable" search under that Amendment.[b]

---

5. Such an assumption appears at least questionable in light of the available statistical data concerning assaults on police officers who are in the course of making arrests. The danger to the police officer flows from the fact of the arrest, and its attendant proximity, stress and uncertainty, and not from the grounds for arrest. One study concludes that approximately 30% of the shootings of police officers occur when the officer approaches a person seated in a car. Bristow, *Police Officer Shootings—A Tactical Evaluation,* 54 J.Crim.L.C. & P.S. 93 (1963). The Government in its brief notes that the Uniform Crime Reports, prepared by the Federal Bureau of Investigation, indicate that a significant percentage of police officers murders occur when the officers are making traffic stops. Those reports indicate that during January–March, 1973, 35 police officers were murdered; 11 of those officers were killed while engaged in traffic stops.

b. Compare the situation where there is a warrantless search of a person without any contemporaneous arrest, confronted by the Court in the pre-*Robinson* case of *Cupp v. Murphy,* 412 U.S. 291 (1973). The Court, per Stewart, J., held that where Murphy voluntarily appeared at the station for questioning concerning the strangulation of his wife, at which time the police noticed what appeared to be blood on his finger, and the police had probable cause to arrest him but did not formally place him under arrest, the warrantless taking of scrapings from his fingernails "was constitutionally permissible." Noting that Murphy was aware of the police suspicion and tried to wipe his fingers clean, the Court concluded that the rationale underlying the search-incident-to-arrest doctrine "justified the police in subjecting him to the very limited search necessary to preserve the highly evanescent evidence they found under his fingernails." But, because a person not under formal arrest "might well be less hostile to the police and less likely to take conspicuous, immediate steps to destroy incriminating evidence on his person," the Court emphasized it was *not* holding "that a full * * * search would have been justified in this case without a formal arrest and without a warrant." Marshall, J., concurring, noted that the police could not have preserved the evidence by "close surveillance" and that detaining Murphy while a warrant was sought "would have been as much a seizure as detaining him while his fingernails were scraped." Douglas, J., dissenting, argued: "There was time to get a warrant; Murphy could have been detained while one was sought; and that detention would have preserved the perishable evidence the police sought."

The search of respondent's person conducted by Officer Jenks in this case and the seizure from him of the heroin, were permissible under established Fourth Amendment law. * * * Since it is the fact of custodial arrest which gives rise to the authority to search, it is of no moment that Jenks did not indicate any subjective fear of the respondent or that he did not himself suspect that respondent was armed.[7] Having in the course of a lawful search come upon the crumpled package of cigarettes, he was entitled to inspect it; and when his inspection revealed the heroin capsules, he was entitled to seize them as "fruits, instrumentalities, or contraband" probative of criminal conduct. The judgment of the Court of Appeals holding otherwise is reversed.[c]

Reversed.

JUSTICE MARSHALL, with whom JUSTICE DOUGLAS and JUSTICE BRENNAN join, dissenting.

Certain fundamental principles have characterized this Court's Fourth Amendment jurisprudence over the years. Perhaps the most basic of these was expressed by Justice Butler, speaking for a unanimous Court in *Go–Bart Co. v. United States*, 282 U.S. 344 (1931): "There is no formula for the determination of

Murphy was not arrested until over a month later, and thus the case is unlike those in which the arrest followed the search by a matter of minutes. The prevailing view is that a search "incident" to arrest may actually come before the formal making of an arrest if the police had grounds to arrest at the time the search was made. As stated in *Rawlings v. Kentucky*, 448 U.S. 98 (1980): "Where the formal arrest followed quickly on the heels of the challenged search of petitioner's person, we do not believe it particularly important that the search preceded the arrest rather than vice versa."

7. The United States concedes that "in searching respondent, [Officer Jenks] was not motivated by a feeling of imminent danger and was not specifically looking for weapons." Brief for the United States. Officer Jenks testified, "I just searched him [Robinson]. I didn't think about what I was looking for. I just searched him." Officer Jenks also testified that upon removing the cigarette package from the respondent's custody, he was still unsure what was in the package, but that he knew it was not cigarettes.

c. Consider also *Illinois v. Lafayette*, 462 U.S. 640 (1983), concerning the basis for search upon the arrestee's arrival at the place of detention:

"The governmental interests underlying a stationhouse search of the arrestee's person and possessions may in some circumstances be even greater than those supporting a search immediately following arrest. Consequently, the scope of a stationhouse search will often vary from that made at the time of arrest. Police conduct that would be impractical or unreasonable—or embarrassingly intrusive— on the street can more readily—and privately—be performed at the station. For example, the interests supporting a search incident to arrest would hardly justify disrobing an arres-tee on the street, but the practical necessities of routine jail administration may even justify taking a prisoner's clothes before confining him, although that step would be rare. * * *.

"At the stationhouse, it is entirely proper for police to remove and list or inventory property found on the person or in the possession of an arrested person who is to be jailed. A range of governmental interests support an inventory process. It is not unheard of for persons employed in police activities to steal property taken from arrested persons; similarly, arrested persons have been known to make false claims regarding what was taken from their possession at the stationhouse. A standardized procedure for making a list or inventory as soon as reasonable after reaching the stationhouse not only deters false claims but also inhibits theft or careless handling of articles taken from the arrested person. Arrested persons have also been known to injure themselves—or others—with belts, knives, drugs or other items on their person while being detained. Dangerous instrumentali-ties—such as razor blades, bombs, or weap-ons—can be concealed in innocent-looking articles taken from the arrestee's possession. The bare recital of these mundane realities justifies reasonable measures by police to lim-it these risks—either while the items are in the police possession or at the time they are returned to the arrestee upon his release. Examining all the items removed from the ar-restee's person or possession and listing or in-ventorying them is an entirely reasonable ad-ministrative procedure. It is immaterial whether the police actually fear any particular package or container; the need to protect against such risks arises independent of a par-ticular officer's subjective concerns. Finally, inspection of an arrestee's personal property may assist the police in ascertaining or verify-ing his identity."

reasonableness. Each case is to be decided on its own facts and circumstances."
* * *

The majority's attempt to avoid case-by-case adjudication of Fourth Amendment issues is not only misguided as a matter of principle, but is also doomed to fail as a matter of practical application. As the majority itself is well aware, the powers granted the police in this case are strong ones, subject to potential abuse. Although, in this particular case, Officer Jenks was required by Police Department regulation to make an in-custody arrest rather than to issue a citation, in most jurisdictions and for most traffic offenses the determination of whether to issue a citation or effect a full arrest is discretionary with the officer. There is always the possibility that a police officer, lacking probable cause to obtain a search warrant, will use a traffic arrest as a pretext to conduct a search. I suggest this possibility not to impugn the integrity of our police, but merely to point out that case-by-case adjudication will always be necessary to determine whether a full arrest was effected for purely legitimate reasons or, rather, as a pretext for searching the arrestee.

The majority states that "A police officer's determination as to how and where to search the person of a suspect whom he has arrested is necessarily a quick *ad hoc* judgment which the Fourth Amendment does not require to be broken down in each instance into an analysis of each step in the search." No precedent is cited for this broad assertion—not surprisingly, since there is none. Indeed, we only recently rejected such "a rigid all-or-nothing model of justification and regulation under the Amendment, [for] it obscures the utility of limitations upon the scope, as well as the initiation, of police action as a means of constitutional regulation. This Court has held in the past that a search which is reasonable at its inception may violate the Fourth Amendment by virtue of its intolerable intensity and scope." *Terry v. Ohio*. As we there concluded, "in determining whether the seizure and search were 'unreasonable' our inquiry is a dual one—whether the officer's action was justified at its inception, and whether it was reasonably related in scope to the circumstances which justified the interference in the first place."

As I view the matter, the search in this case divides into three distinct phases: the patdown of respondent's coat pocket; the removal of the unknown object from the pocket; and the opening of the crumpled up cigarette package.

No question is raised here concerning the lawfulness of the patdown of respondent's coat pocket. The Court of Appeals unanimously affirmed the right of a police officer to conduct a limited frisk for weapons when making an in-custody arrest, regardless of the nature of the crime for which the arrest was made. As it said,

> "it would seem clearly unreasonable to expect a police officer to place a suspect in his squad car for transportation to the station house without first taking reasonable measures to insure that the suspect is unarmed. We therefore conclude that whenever a police officer, acting within the bounds of his authority, makes an in-custody arrest, he may also conduct a limited *frisk* of the suspect's outer clothing in order to remove any weapons the suspect may have in his possession."

With respect to the removal of the unknown object from the coat pocket, * * * Officer Jenks had no reason to believe and did not in fact believe that the object in respondent's coat pocket was a weapon. He admitted later that the object did not feel like a gun. * * *

Since the removal of the object from the pocket cannot be justified as part of a limited *Terry* weapons frisk, the question arises whether it is reasonable for a police officer, when effecting an in-custody arrest of a traffic offender, to make a fuller search of the person than is permitted pursuant to *Terry.*   * * *

The Government does not now contend that the search of respondent's pocket can be justified by any need to find and seize evidence in order to prevent its concealment or destruction, for as the Court of Appeals found, there are no evidence or fruits of the offense with which respondent was charged. The only rationale for a search in this case, then, is the removal of weapons which the arrestee might use to harm the officer and attempt an escape. This rationale, of course, is identical to the rationale of the search permitted in *Terry.*   * * *

for the arrest

Since the underlying rationale of a *Terry* search and the search of a traffic violator are identical, the Court of Appeals held that the scope of the searches must be the same.   * * *

The problem with this approach, however, is that it ignores several significant differences between the context in which a search incident to arrest for a traffic violation is made, and the situation presented in *Terry.* Some of these differences would appear to suggest permitting a more thorough search in this case than was permitted in *Terry;* other differences suggest a narrower, more limited right to search than was there recognized.

The most obvious difference between the two contexts relates to whether the officer has cause to believe that the individual he is dealing with possesses weapons which might be used against him. *Terry* did not permit an officer to conduct a weapons frisk of anyone he lawfully stopped on the street, but rather, only where "he has reason to believe that he is dealing with an armed and dangerous individual.   * * * " While the policeman who arrests a suspected rapist or robber may well have reason to believe he is dealing with an armed and dangerous person, certainly this does not hold true with equal force with respect to persons arrested for motor vehicle violations of the sort involved in this case.

Nor was there any particular reason in this case to believe that respondent was dangerous. He had not attempted to evade arrest, but had quickly complied with the police both in bringing his car to a stop after being signalled to do so and in producing the documents Officer Jenks requested. In fact, Jenks admitted that he searched respondent face-to-face rather than in spread-eagle fashion because he had no reason to believe respondent would be violent.

While this difference between the situation presented in *Terry* and the context presented in this case would tend to suggest a lesser authority to search here than was permitted in *Terry,* other distinctions between the two contexts suggest just the opposite. As the Court of Appeals noted, a crucial feature distinguishing the in-custody arrest from the *Terry* context "is not the greater likelihood that a person taken into custody is armed, but rather the increased likelihood of danger to the officer *if* in fact the person is armed." A *Terry* stop involves a momentary encounter between officer and suspect, while an in-custody arrest places the two in close proximity for a much longer period of time. If the individual happens to have a weapon on his person, he will certainly have much more opportunity to use it against the officer in the in-custody situation. The prolonged proximity also makes it more likely that the individual will be able to extricate any small hidden weapon which might go undetected in a weapons frisk, such as a safety pin or razor blade. In addition, a suspect taken into custody may feel more threatened by the serious restraint on his liberty than a person who is simply stopped by an officer for questioning, and may therefore be more likely to resort to force.

Thus, in some senses there is less need for a weapons search in the in-custody traffic arrest situation than in a *Terry* context, while in other ways, there is a greater need. Balancing these competing considerations in order to determine what is a reasonable warrantless search in the traffic arrest context is a difficult process, one for which there may be no easy analytical guideposts. We are dealing in factors not easily quantified and, therefore, not easily weighed one against the other. And the competing interests we are protecting—the individual's interest in remaining free from unnecessarily intrusive invasions of privacy and society's interest that police officers not take unnecessary risks in the performance of their duties—are each deserving of our most serious attention and do not themselves tip the balance in any particular direction. * * *

The majority relies on statistics indicating that a significant percentage of police officer murders occur when the officers are making traffic stops. But these statistics only confirm what we recognized in *Terry*—that "American criminals have a long tradition of armed violence, and every year in this country many law enforcement officers are killed in the line of duty, and thousands more are wounded." As the very next sentence in *Terry* recognized, however, "Virtually all of these deaths and a substantial portion of the injuries are inflicted with guns and knives." The statistics relied on by the Government in this case support this observation. Virtually all of the killings are caused by guns and knives, the very type of weapons which will not go undetected in a properly conducted weapons frisk.[5] * * *

The majority opinion fails to recognize that the search conducted by Officer Jenks did not merely involve a search of respondent's person. It also included a separate search of effects found on his person. And even were we to assume, *arguendo,* that it was reasonable for Jenks to remove the object he felt in respondent's pocket, clearly there was no justification consistent with the Fourth Amendment which would authorize his opening the package and looking inside.

To begin with, after Jenks had the cigarette package in his hands, there is no indication that he had reason to believe or did in fact believe that the package contained a weapon. More importantly, even if the crumpled up cigarette package had in fact contained some sort of small weapon, it would have been impossible for respondent to have used it once the package was in the officer's hands. Opening the package therefore did not further the protective purpose of the search. * * *

The Government argues that it is difficult to see what constitutionally protected "expectation of privacy" a prisoner has in the interior of a cigarette pack. One wonders if the result in this case would have been the same were respondent a businessman who was lawfully taken into custody for driving without a license and whose wallet was taken from him by the police. Would it be reasonable for the police officer, because of the possibility that a razor blade was hidden somewhere in the wallet, to open it, remove all the contents, and examine each item carefully? Or suppose a lawyer lawfully arrested for a traffic offense is found to have a sealed envelope on his person. Would it be permissible for the arresting officer to tear open the envelope in order to make sure that it did not contain a clandestine weapon—perhaps a pin or a razor blade? Would it not be more consonant with the purpose of the Fourth Amendment and the legitimate needs of the police to require the officer, if he has any question whatsoever about

---

5. The Uniform Crime Reports prepared by the Federal Bureau of Investigation which are relied on by the majority, see n. 5, indicate that 112 police officers were killed nationwide in 1972. Of these, 108 were killed by firearms. Two of the remaining four were killed with knives, and the last two cases involved a bomb and an automobile.

what the wallet or letter contains, to hold onto it until the arrestee is brought to the precinct station?

I, for one, cannot characterize any of these intrusions into the privacy of an individual's papers and effects as being negligible incidents to the more serious intrusion into the individual's privacy stemming from the arrest itself. Nor can any principled distinction be drawn between the hypothetical searches I have posed and the search of the cigarette package in this case. The only reasoned distinction is between warrantless searches which serve legitimate protective and evidentiary functions and those that do not.[d]

WHREN v. UNITED STATES

517 U.S. 806, 116 S.Ct. 1769, 135 L.Ed.2d 89 (1996).

JUSTICE SCALIA delivered the opinion of the Court. * * *

On the evening of June 10, 1993, plainclothes vice-squad officers of the District of Columbia Metropolitan Police Department were patrolling a "high drug area" of the city in an unmarked car. Their suspicions were aroused when they passed a dark Pathfinder truck with temporary license plates and youthful occupants waiting at a stop sign, the driver looking down into the lap of the passenger at his right. The truck remained stopped at the intersection for what seemed an unusually long time—more than 20 seconds. When the police car executed a U-turn in order to head back toward the truck, the Pathfinder turned suddenly to its right, without signalling, and sped off at an "unreasonable" speed. The policemen followed, and in a short while overtook the Pathfinder when it stopped behind other traffic at a red light. They pulled up alongside, and Officer Ephraim Soto stepped out and approached the driver's door, identifying himself as a police officer and directing the driver, petitioner Brown, to put the vehicle in park. When Soto drew up to the driver's window, he immediately observed two large plastic bags of what appeared to be crack cocaine in petitioner Whren's hands. Petitioners were arrested, and quantities of several types of illegal drugs were retrieved from the vehicle.

Petitioners were charged in a four-count indictment with violating various federal drug laws. At a pretrial suppression hearing, they challenged the legality of the stop and the resulting seizure of the drugs. They argued that the stop had not been justified by probable cause to believe, or even reasonable suspicion, that petitioners were engaged in illegal drug-dealing activity; and that Officer Soto's

---

d. In the companion case of *Gustafson v. Florida*, 414 U.S. 260 (1973), petitioner was arrested for failure to have an operator's license after the car he was driving was observed weaving across the center line several times, and was then searched, resulting in the discovery of a cigarette box within which the arresting officer found marijuana cigarettes. Petitioner contended his case was different from *Robinson* in that (a) he had experienced no previous encounters with the officer; (b) the offense for which he was arrested was "benign or trivial in nature," carrying with it no mandatory minimum sentence; and (c) there were no police regulations which required the officer to take petitioner into custody or which required full scale body searches upon arrest in the field. The Court, per Rehnquist, J., did "not find these differences deter-

minative of the constitutional issue," and thus upheld the search on the basis of *Robinson*.

Marshall, Douglas, and Brennan, JJ., dissented for the reasons stated in *Robinson*. Stewart, J., concurring, noted "that a persuasive claim might have been made in this case that the custodial arrest of the petitioner for a minor traffic offense violated his rights under the Fourth and Fourteenth Amendments," but since petitioner had "fully conceded the constitutional validity of his custodial arrest," the search of his person should be accepted as incidental to that arrest. Powell, J., concurring in both cases, emphasized that for him the "essential premise" of both decisions was "that an individual lawfully subjected to a custodial arrest retains no significant Fourth Amendment interest in the privacy of his person."

asserted ground for approaching the vehicle—to give the driver a warning concerning traffic violations—was pretextual. The District Court denied the suppression motion * * *.

Petitioners were convicted of the counts at issue here. The Court of Appeals affirmed the convictions, holding with respect to the suppression issue that, "regardless of whether a police officer subjectively believes that the occupants of an automobile may be engaging in some other illegal behavior, a traffic stop is permissible as long as a reasonable officer in the same circumstances could have stopped the car for the suspected traffic violation."

The Fourth Amendment guarantees "[t]he right of the people to be secure in their persons, houses, papers, and effects, against unreasonable searches and seizures." Temporary detention of individuals during the stop of an automobile by the police, even if only for a brief period and for a limited purpose, constitutes a "seizure" of "persons" within the meaning of this provision. An automobile stop is thus subject to the constitutional imperative that it not be "unreasonable" under the circumstances. As a general matter, the decision to stop an automobile is reasonable where the police have probable cause to believe that a traffic violation has occurred.

Petitioners accept that Officer Soto had probable cause to believe that various provisions of the District of Columbia traffic code [regarding inattentive driving, speeding, and turning without signalling] had been violated. They argue, however, that "in the unique context of civil traffic regulations" probable cause is not enough. Since, they contend, the use of automobiles is so heavily and minutely regulated that total compliance with traffic and safety rules is nearly impossible, a police officer will almost invariably be able to catch any given motorist in a technical violation. This creates the temptation to use traffic stops as a means of investigating other law violations, as to which no probable cause or even articulable suspicion exists. Petitioners, who are both black, further contend that police officers might decide which motorists to stop based on decidedly impermissible factors, such as the race of the car's occupants. To avoid this danger, they say, the Fourth Amendment test for traffic stops should be, not the normal one (applied by the Court of Appeals) of whether probable cause existed to justify the stop; but rather, whether a police officer, acting reasonably, would have made the stop for the reason given.

Petitioners contend that the standard they propose is consistent with our past cases' disapproval of police attempts to use valid bases of action against citizens as pretexts for pursuing other investigatory agendas. We are reminded that in *Florida v. Wells*, [Ch. 3, § 7], we stated that "an inventory search must not be used as a ruse for a general rummaging in order to discover incriminating evidence"; that in *Colorado v. Bertine*, [Ch. 3, § 7], in approving an inventory search, we apparently thought it significant that there had been "no showing that the police, who were following standard procedures, acted in bad faith or for the sole purpose of investigation"; and that in *New York v. Burger*, 482 U.S. 691 (1987), we observed, in upholding the constitutionality of a warrantless administrative inspection, that the search did not appear to be "a 'pretext' for obtaining evidence of . . . violation of . . . penal laws." But only an undiscerning reader would regard these cases as endorsing the principle that ulterior motives can invalidate police conduct that is justifiable on the basis of probable cause to believe that a violation of law has occurred. In each case we were addressing the validity of a search conducted in the absence of probable cause. Our quoted statements simply explain that the exemption from the need for probable cause (and warrant), which is accorded to searches made for the purpose of inventory or administrative regulation, is not accorded to searches that are not made for those purposes.

* * * Not only have we never held, outside the context of inventory search or administrative inspection (discussed above), that an officer's motive invalidates objectively justifiable behavior under the Fourth Amendment; but we have repeatedly held and asserted the contrary. In *United States v. Villamonte–Marquez*, 462 U.S. 579 (1983), we held that an otherwise valid warrantless boarding of a vessel by customs officials was not rendered invalid "because the customs officers were accompanied by a Louisiana state policeman, and were following an informant's tip that a vessel in the ship channel was thought to be carrying marihuana." We flatly dismissed the idea that an ulterior motive might serve to strip the agents of their legal justification. In *United States v. Robinson*, [Ch. 3, § 5], we held that a traffic-violation arrest (of the sort here) would not be rendered invalid by the fact that it was "a mere pretext for a narcotics search," and that a lawful postarrest search of the person would not be rendered invalid by the fact that it was not motivated by the officer-safety concern that justifies such searches. And in *Scott v. United States*, [Ch. 5, § 1], in rejecting the contention that wiretap evidence was subject to exclusion because the agents conducting the tap had failed to make any effort to comply with the statutory requirement that unauthorized acquisitions be minimized, we said that "[s]ubjective intent alone . . . does not make otherwise lawful conduct illegal or unconstitutional." We described *Robinson* as having established that "the fact that the officer does not have the state of mind which is hypothecated by the reasons which provide the legal justification for the officer's action does not invalidate the action taken as long as the circumstances, viewed objectively, justify that action."

We think these cases foreclose any argument that the constitutional reasonableness of traffic stops depends on the actual motivations of the individual officers involved. We of course agree with petitioners that the Constitution prohibits selective enforcement of the law based on considerations such as race. But the constitutional basis for objecting to intentionally discriminatory application of laws is the Equal Protection Clause, not the Fourth Amendment. Subjective intentions play no role in ordinary, probable-cause Fourth Amendment analysis.

Recognizing that we have been unwilling to entertain Fourth Amendment challenges based on the actual motivations of individual officers, petitioners disavow any intention to make the individual officer's subjective good faith the touchstone of "reasonableness." They insist that the standard they have put forward—whether the officer's conduct deviated materially from usual police practices, so that a reasonable officer in the same circumstances would not have made the stop for the reasons given—is an "objective" one.

But although framed in empirical terms, this approach is plainly and indisputably driven by subjective considerations. Its whole purpose is to prevent the police from doing under the guise of enforcing the traffic code what they would like to do for different reasons. Petitioners' proposed standard may not use the word "pretext," but it is designed to combat nothing other than the perceived "danger" of the pretextual stop, albeit only indirectly and over the run of cases. Instead of asking whether the individual officer had the proper state of mind, the petitioners would have us ask, in effect, whether (based on general police practices) it is plausible to believe that the officer had the proper state of mind.

Why one would frame a test designed to combat pretext in such fashion that the court cannot take into account actual and admitted pretext is a curiosity that can only be explained by the fact that our cases have foreclosed the more sensible option. If those cases were based only upon the evidentiary difficulty of establishing subjective intent, petitioners' attempt to root out subjective vices through objective means might make sense. But they were not based only upon that, or indeed even principally upon that. Their principal basis—which applies equally to attempts to reach subjective intent through ostensibly objective means—is simply that the Fourth Amendment's concern with "reasonableness" allows certain actions to be taken in certain circumstances, whatever the subjective intent. See, e.g., *Robinson*, supra ("Since it is the fact of custodial arrest which gives rise to the authority to search, it is of no moment that [the officer] did not indicate any subjective fear of the [arrestee] or that he did not himself suspect that [the arrestee] was armed"). But even if our concern had been only an evidentiary one, petitioners' proposal would by no means assuage it. Indeed, it seems to us somewhat easier to figure out the intent of an individual officer than to plumb the collective consciousness of law enforcement in order to determine whether a "reasonable officer" would have been moved to act upon the traffic violation. While police manuals and standard procedures may sometimes provide objective assistance, ordinarily one would be reduced to speculating about the hypothetical reaction of a hypothetical constable—an exercise that might be called virtual subjectivity.

Moreover, police enforcement practices, even if they could be practicably assessed by a judge, vary from place to place and from time to time. We cannot accept that the search and seizure protections of the Fourth Amendment are so variable, and can be made to turn upon such trivialities. The difficulty is illustrated by petitioners' arguments in this case. Their claim that a reasonable officer would not have made this stop is based largely on District of Columbia police regulations which permit plainclothes officers in unmarked vehicles to enforce traffic laws "only in the case of a violation that is so grave as to pose an immediate threat to the safety of others." This basis of invalidation would not apply in jurisdictions that had a different practice. And it would not have applied even in the District of Columbia, if Officer Soto had been wearing a uniform or patrolling in a marked police cruiser.

Petitioners argue that our cases support insistence upon police adherence to standard practices as an objective means of rooting out pretext. They cite no holding to that effect, and dicta in only two cases. In *Abel v. United States*, 362 U.S. 217 (1960), the petitioner had been arrested by the Immigration and Naturalization Service (INS), on the basis of an administrative warrant that, he claimed, had been issued on pretextual grounds in order to enable the Federal Bureau of Investigation (FBI) to search his room after his arrest. We regarded this as an allegation of "serious misconduct," but rejected Abel's claims on the ground that "[a] finding of bad faith is ... not open to us on th[e] record" in light of the findings below, including the finding that " 'the proceedings taken by the [INS] differed in no respect from what would have been done in the case of an individual concerning whom [there was no pending FBI investigation].' " But it is a long leap from the proposition that following regular procedures is some evidence of lack of pretext to the proposition that failure to follow regular procedures proves (or is an operational substitute for) pretext. *Abel*, moreover, did not involve the assertion that pretext could invalidate a search or seizure for which there was probable cause—and even what it said about pretext in other contexts is plainly inconsistent with the views we later stated in [the cases summarized above]. In the other case claimed to contain supportive dicta, *United States v. Robinson*, in approving a search incident to an arrest for driving without a license, we noted that the arrest was "not a departure from established police department practice." That was followed, however, by the statement that "[w]e leave for another day questions which would arise on facts different from these." This is not even a dictum that purports to provide an answer, but merely one that leaves the question open.

In what would appear to be an elaboration on the "reasonable officer" test, petitioners argue that the balancing inherent in any Fourth Amendment inquiry requires us to weigh the governmental and individual interests implicated in a traffic stop such as we have here. That balancing, petitioners claim, does not support investigation of minor traffic infractions by plainclothes police in unmarked vehicles; such investigation only minimally advances the government's interest in traffic safety, and may indeed retard it by producing motorist confusion and alarm—a view said to be supported by the Metropolitan Police Department's own regulations generally prohibiting this practice. And as for the Fourth Amendment interests of the individuals concerned, petitioners point out that our cases acknowledge that even ordinary traffic stops entail "a possibly unsettling show of authority"; that they at best "interfere with freedom of movement, are inconvenient, and consume time" and at worst "may create substantial anxiety." That anxiety is likely to be even more pronounced when the stop is conducted by plainclothes officers in unmarked cars.

It is of course true that in principle every Fourth Amendment case, since it turns upon a "reasonableness" determination, involves a balancing of all relevant factors. With rare exceptions not applicable here, however, the result of that balancing is not in doubt where the search or seizure is based upon probable cause. That is why petitioners must rely upon cases like *Prouse* to provide examples of actual "balancing" analysis. There, the police action in question was a random traffic stop for the purpose of checking a motorist's license and vehicle registration, a practice that—like the practices at issue in the inventory search and administrative inspection cases upon which petitioners rely in making their "pretext" claim—involves police intrusion without the probable cause that is its traditional justification. Our opinion in *Prouse* expressly distinguished the case from a stop based on precisely what is at issue here: "probable cause to believe that a driver is violating any one of the multitude of applicable traffic and equipment regulations." It noted approvingly that "[t]he foremost method of enforcing traffic and vehicle safety regulations ... is acting upon observed violations," which afford the " 'quantum of individualized suspicion' " necessary to ensure that police discretion is sufficiently constrained. What is true of *Prouse* is also true of other cases that engaged in detailed "balancing" to decide the constitutionality of automobile stops: the detailed "balancing" analysis was necessary because they involved seizures without probable cause.

Where probable cause has existed, the only cases in which we have found it necessary actually to perform the "balancing" analysis involved searches or seizures conducted in an extraordinary manner, unusually harmful to an individual's privacy or even physical interests—such as, for example, seizure by means of deadly force, see *Tennessee v. Garner*, [Ch. 3, § 5], unannounced entry into a home, see *Wilson v. Arkansas*, Ch. 3, § 4], entry into a home without a warrant, see *Welsh v. Wisconsin*, 466 U.S. 740 (1984), or physical penetration of the body, see *Winston v. Lee*, 470 U.S. 753 (1985). The making of a traffic stop out-of-uniform does not remotely qualify as such an extreme practice, and so is governed by the usual rule that probable cause to believe the law has been broken "outbalances" private interest in avoiding police contact.

Petitioners urge as an extraordinary factor in this case that the "multitude of applicable traffic and equipment regulations" is so large and so difficult to obey perfectly that virtually everyone is guilty of violation, permitting the police to single out almost whomever they wish for a stop. But we are aware of no principle that would allow us to decide at what point a code of law becomes so expansive and so commonly violated that infraction itself can no longer be the ordinary measure of the lawfulness of enforcement. And even if we could identify such exorbitant codes, we do not know by what standard (or what right) we would decide, as petitioners would have us do, which particular provisions are sufficiently important to merit enforcement.

For the run-of-the-mine case, which this surely is, we think there is no realistic alternative to the traditional common-law rule that probable cause justifies a search and seizure.

* * *

Here the District Court found that the officers had probable cause to believe that petitioners had violated the traffic code. That rendered the stop reasonable under the Fourth Amendment, the evidence thereby discovered admissible, and the upholding of the convictions by the Court of Appeals for the District of Columbia Circuit correct.

Judgment affirmed.[a]

ATWATER v. CITY OF LAGO VISTA
___ U.S. ___, 121 S.Ct. 1536, 149 L.Ed.2d 549 (2001).

JUSTICE SOUTER delivered the opinion of the Court.

The question is whether the Fourth Amendment forbids a warrantless arrest for a minor criminal offense, such as a misdemeanor seatbelt violation punishable only by a fine. We hold that it does not.

In Texas, if a car is equipped with safety belts, a front-seat passenger must wear one, and the driver must secure any small child riding in front. Violation of either provision is "a misdemeanor punishable by a fine not less than $25 or more than $50." Texas law expressly authorizes "[a]ny peace officer [to] arrest without warrant a person found committing a violation" of these seatbelt laws, although it permits police to issue citations in lieu of arrest.

In March 1997, Petitioner Gail Atwater was driving her pickup truck in Lago Vista, Texas, with her 3–year-old son and 5–year-old daughter in the front seat. None of them was wearing a seatbelt. Respondent Bart Turek, a Lago Vista police officer at the time, observed the seatbelt violations and pulled Atwater over. According to Atwater's complaint (the allegations of which we assume to be true for present purposes), Turek approached the truck and "yell[ed]" something to the effect of "[w]e've met before" and "[y]ou're going to jail."[1] He then called for backup and asked to see Atwater's driver's license and insurance documentation, which state law required her to carry. When Atwater told Turek that she did not have the papers because her purse had been stolen the day before, Turek said that he had "heard that story two-hundred times."

Atwater asked to take her "frightened, upset, and crying" children to a friend's house nearby, but Turek told her, "[y]ou're not going anywhere." As it turned out, Atwater's friend learned what was going on and soon arrived to take

---

a. Although *Whren* involved a traffic stop, it was assumed to apply to custodial arrests as well, as the Court later confirmed in *Arkansas v. Sullivan*, 121 S.Ct. 1876 (2001).

1. Turek had previously stopped Atwater for what he had thought was a seatbelt viola-tion, but had realized that Atwater's son, although seated on the vehicle's armrest, was in fact belted in. Atwater acknowledged that her son's seating position was unsafe, and Turek issued a verbal warning.

charge of the children. Turek then handcuffed Atwater, placed her in his squad car, and drove her to the local police station, where booking officers had her remove her shoes, jewelry, and eyeglasses, and empty her pockets. Officers took Atwater's "mug shot" and placed her, alone, in a jail cell for about one hour, after which she was taken before a magistrate and released on $310 bond.

Atwater was charged with driving without her seatbelt fastened, failing to secure her children in seatbelts, driving without a license, and failing to provide proof of insurance. She ultimately pleaded no contest to the misdemeanor seatbelt offenses and paid a $50 fine; the other charges were dismissed.

[Atwater filed suit in a Texas state court under 42 U.S.C. § 1983 against Turek, the police chief and the city; the city removed to federal district court, which granted the city's summary judgment motion. A panel of the court of appeals reversed, but the court of appeals sitting en banc vacated the panel's decision and affirmed the district court.]

We granted certiorari to consider whether the Fourth Amendment, either by incorporating common-law restrictions on misdemeanor arrests or otherwise, limits police officers' authority to arrest without warrant for minor criminal offenses. We now affirm.

The Fourth Amendment safeguards "[t]he right of the people to be secure in their persons, houses, papers, and effects, against unreasonable searches and seizures." In reading the Amendment, we are guided by "the traditional protections against unreasonable searches and seizures afforded by the common law at the time of the framing," since "[a]n examination of the common-law understanding of an officer's authority to arrest sheds light on the obviously relevant, if not entirely dispositive, consideration of what the Framers of the Amendment might have thought to be reasonable." Thus, the first step here is to assess Atwater's claim that peace officers' authority to make warrantless arrests for misdemeanors was restricted at common law ("common law" is understood strictly as law judicially derived or, instead, as the whole body of law extant at the time of the framing). Atwater's specific contention is that "founding-era common-law rules" forbade peace officers to make warrantless misdemeanor arrests except in cases of "breach of the peace," a category she claims was then understood narrowly as covering only those nonfelony offenses "involving or tending toward violence." Although her historical argument is by no means insubstantial, it ultimately fails.

(Atwater argues) [margin annotation]

We begin with the state of pre-founding English common law and find that, even after making some allowance for variations in the common-law usage of the term "breach of the peace," the "founding-era common-law" were not nearly as clear as Atwater claims; on the contrary, the common-law commentators (as well as the sparsely reported cases) reached divergent conclusions with respect to officer' warrantless misdemeanor arrest power. Moreover, in the years leading up to American independence, Parliament repeatedly extended express warrantless arrest authority to cover misdemeanor-level offenses not amounting to or involving any violent breach of the peace. * * *

Nor does Atwater's argument from tradition pick up any steam from the historical record as it has unfolded since the framing, there being no indication that her claimed rule has ever become "woven ... into the fabric" of American law. The story, on the contrary, is of two centuries of uninterrupted (and largely unchallenged) state and federal practice permitting warrantless arrests for misdemeanors not amounting to or involving breach of the peace.

* * * Although the Court has not had much to say about warrantless misdemeanor arrest authority, what little we have said tends to cut against

Atwater's argument. In discussing this authority, we have focused on the circumstance that an offense was committed in an officer's presence, to the omission of any reference to a breach-of-the-peace limitation.[11] * * *

While it is true here that history, if not unequivocal, has expressed a decided, majority view that the police need not obtain an arrest warrant merely because a misdemeanor stopped short of violence or a threat of it, Atwater does not wager all on history. Instead, she asks us to mint a new rule of constitutional law on the understanding that when historical practice fails to speak conclusively to a claim grounded on the Fourth Amendment, courts are left to strike a current balance between individual and societal interests by subjecting particular contemporary circumstances to traditional standards of reasonableness. Atwater accordingly argues for a modern arrest rule, one not necessarily requiring violent breach of the peace, but nonetheless forbidding custodial arrest, even upon probable cause, when conviction could not ultimately carry any jail time and when the government shows no compelling need for immediate detention.

If we were to derive a rule exclusively to address the uncontested facts of this case, Atwater might well prevail. She was a known and established resident of Lago Vista with no place to hide and no incentive to flee, and common sense says she would almost certainly have buckled up as a condition of driving off with a citation. In her case, the physical incidents of arrest were merely gratuitous humiliations imposed by a police officer who was (at best) exercising extremely poor judgment. Atwater's claim to live free of pointless indignity and confinement clearly outweighs anything the City can raise against it specific to her case.

But we have traditionally recognized that a responsible Fourth Amendment balance is not well served by standards requiring sensitive, case-by-case determinations of government need, lest every discretionary judgment in the field be converted into an occasion for constitutional review. See, e.g., *United States v. Robinson*, [Ch. 3, § 5]. Often enough, the Fourth Amendment has to be applied on the spur (and in the heat) of the moment, and the object in implementing its command of reasonableness is to draw standards sufficiently clear and simple to be applied with a fair prospect of surviving judicial second-guessing months and years after an arrest or search is made. Courts attempting to strike a reasonable Fourth Amendment balance thus credit the government's side with an essential interest in readily administrable rules.

At first glance, Atwater's argument may seem to respect the values of clarity and simplicity, so far as she claims that the Fourth Amendment generally forbids warrantless arrests for minor crimes not accompanied by violence or some demonstrable threat of it (whether "minor crime" be defined as a fine-only traffic offense, a fine-only offense more generally, or a misdemeanor). But the claim is not ultimately so simple, nor could it be, for complications arise the moment we begin to think about the possible applications of the several criteria Atwater proposes for drawing a line between minor crimes with limited arrest authority and others not so restricted.

One line, she suggests, might be between "jailable" and "fine-only" offenses, between those for which conviction could result in commitment and those for which it could not. The trouble with this distinction, of course, is that an officer on the street might not be able to tell. It is not merely that we cannot expect every

11. We need not, and thus do not, speculate whether the Fourth Amendment entails an "in the presence" requirement for purposes of misdemeanor arrests. Cf. *Welsh v. Wisconsin*, 466 U.S. 740 (1984) (White, J., dissenting) ("[T]he requirement that a misdemeanor must have occurred in the officer's presence to justify a warrantless arrest is not grounded in the Fourth Amendment").

police officer to know the details of frequently complex penalty schemes, but that penalties for ostensibly identical conduct can vary on account of facts difficult (if not impossible) to know at the scene of an arrest. Is this the first offense or is the suspect a repeat offender? Is the weight of the marijuana a gram above or a gram below the fine-only line? Where conduct could implicate more than one criminal prohibition, which one will the district attorney ultimately decide to charge? And so on.

But Atwater's refinements would not end there. She represents that if the line were drawn at nonjailable traffic offenses, her proposed limitation should be qualified by a proviso authorizing warrantless arrests where "necessary for enforcement of the traffic laws or when [an] offense would otherwise continue and pose a danger to others on the road." (Were the line drawn at misdemeanors generally, a comparable qualification would presumably apply.) The proviso only compounds the difficulties. Would, for instance, either exception apply to speeding? * * *

There is no need for more examples to show that Atwater's general rule and *impractical* limiting proviso promise very little in the way of administrability. It is no answer that the police routinely make judgments on grounds like risk of immediate repetition; they surely do and should. But there is a world of difference between making that judgment in choosing between the discretionary leniency of a summons in place of a clearly lawful arrest, and making the same judgment when the question is the lawfulness of the warrantless arrest itself. It is the difference between no basis for legal action challenging the discretionary judgment, on the one hand, and the prospect of evidentiary exclusion or (as here) personal § 1983 liability for the misapplication of a constitutional standard, on the other. Atwater's rule therefore would not only place police in an almost impossible spot but would guarantee increased litigation over many of the arrests that would occur. * * *

One may ask, of course, why these difficulties may not be answered by a simple tie breaker for the police to follow in the field: if in doubt, do not arrest. The first answer is that in practice the tie breaker would boil down to something akin to a least-restrictive-alternative limitation, which is itself one of those "ifs, ands, and buts" rules, generally thought inappropriate in working out Fourth Amendment protection. Beyond that, whatever help the tie breaker might give would come at the price of a systematic disincentive to arrest in situations where even Atwater concedes that arresting would serve an important societal interest. An officer not quite sure that the drugs weighed enough to warrant jail time or not quite certain about a suspect's risk of flight would not arrest, even though it could perfectly well turn out that, in fact, the offense called for incarceration and the defendant was long gone on the day of trial. Multiplied many times over, the costs to society of such underenforcement could easily outweigh the costs to defendants of being needlessly arrested and booked, as Atwater herself acknowledges.

Just how easily the costs could outweigh the benefits may be shown by asking, as one Member of this Court did at oral argument, "how bad the problem is out there" The very fact that the law has never jelled the way Atwater would have it leads one to wonder whether warrantless misdemeanor arrests need constitutional attention, and there is cause to think the answer is no. So far as such arrests might be thought to pose a threat to the probable-cause requirement, anyone arrested for a crime without formal process, whether for felony or misdemeanor, is entitled to a magistrate's review of probable cause within 48 hours, and there is no reason to think the procedure in this case atypical in giving the suspect a prompt opportunity to request release. Many jurisdictions, moreover, have chosen to impose more restrictive safeguards through statutes limiting warrantless arrests for minor offenses. It is of course easier to devise a minor-offense limitation by statute than to derive one through the Constitution, simply because the statute can let the arrest power turn on any sort of practical consideration without having to subsume it under a broader principle. It is, in fact, only natural that States should resort to this sort of legislative regulation, for * * * it is in the interest of the police to limit petty-offense arrests, which carry costs that are simply too great to incur without good reason. Finally, and significantly, under current doctrine the preference for categorical treatment of Fourth Amendment claims gives way to individualized review when a defendant makes a colorable argument that an arrest, with or without a warrant, was "conducted in an extraordinary manner, unusually harmful to [his] privacy or even physical interests." *Whren v. United States*, [Ch. 3, § 5].

The upshot of all these influences, combined with the good sense (and, failing that, the political accountability) of most local lawmakers and law-enforcement officials, is a dearth of horribles demanding redress. Indeed, when Atwater's counsel was asked at oral argument for any indications of comparably foolish, warrantless misdemeanor arrests, he could offer only one. We are sure that there are others, but just as surely the country is not confronting anything like an epidemic of unnecessary minor-offense arrests. That fact caps the reasons for rejecting Atwater's request for the development of a new and distinct body of constitutional law.

Accordingly, we confirm today what our prior cases have intimated: the standard of probable cause "applie[s] to all arrests, without the need to 'balance' the interests and circumstances involved in particular situations." If an officer has probable cause to believe that an individual has committed even a very minor criminal offense in his presence, he may, without violating the Fourth Amendment, arrest the offender.

Atwater's arrest satisfied constitutional requirements. There is no dispute that Officer Turek had probable cause * * *.

Nor was the arrest made in an "extraordinary manner, unusually harmful to [her] privacy or . . . physical interests." As our citations in *Whren* make clear, the question whether a search or seizure is "extraordinary" turns, above all else, on the manner in which the search or seizure is executed. Atwater's arrest was surely "humiliating," as she says in her brief, but it was no more "harmful to . . . privacy or . . . physical interests" than the normal custodial arrest. * * *

JUSTICE O'CONNOR, with whom JUSTICE STEVENS, JUSTICE GINSBURG, and JUSTICE BREYER join, dissenting.

* * * The Court's thorough exegesis makes it abundantly clear that warrantless misdemeanor arrests were not the subject of a clear and consistently applied rule at common law. We therefore must engage in the balancing test required by the Fourth Amendment. While probable cause is surely a necessary condition for warrantless arrests for fine-only offenses, any realistic assessment of the interests implicated by such arrests demonstrates that probable cause alone is not a sufficient condition.

A custodial arrest exacts an obvious toll on an individual's liberty and privacy, even when the period of custody is relatively brief. The arrestee is subject to a full search of her person and confiscation of her possessions. *United States v. Robinson*, supra. If the arrestee is the occupant of a car, the entire passenger compartment of the car, including packages therein, is subject to search as well. See *New*

York v. Belton, [Ch. 3, § 7]. The arrestee may be detained for up to 48 hours without having a magistrate determine whether there in fact was probable cause for the arrest. See *County of Riverside v. McLaughlin*, [Ch. 3, § 5]. Because people arrested for all types of violent and nonviolent offenses may be housed together awaiting such review, this detention period is potentially dangerous. And once the period of custody is over, the fact of the arrest is a permanent part of the public record.

We have said that "the penalty that may attach to any particular offense seems to provide the clearest and most consistent indication of the State's interest in arresting individuals suspected of committing that offense." *Welsh v. Wisconsin*, [supra]. If the State has decided that a fine, and not imprisonment, is the appropriate punishment for an offense, the State's interest in taking a person suspected of committing that offense into custody is surely limited, at best. This is not to say that the State will never have such an interest. A full custodial arrest may on occasion vindicate legitimate state interests, even if the crime is punishable only by fine. Arrest is the surest way to abate criminal conduct. It may also allow the police to verify the offender's identity and, if the offender poses a flight risk, to ensure her appearance at trial. But when such considerations are not present, a citation or summons may serve the State's remaining law enforcement interests every bit as effectively as an arrest.

Because a full custodial arrest is such a severe intrusion on an individual's liberty, its reasonableness hinges on "the degree to which it is needed for the promotion of legitimate governmental interests." In light of the availability of citations to promote a State's interests when a fine-only offense has been committed, I cannot concur in a rule which deems a full custodial arrest to be reasonable in every circumstance. Giving police officers constitutional carte blanche to effect an arrest whenever there is probable cause to believe a fine-only misdemeanor has been committed is irreconcilable with the Fourth Amendment's command that seizures be reasonable. Instead, I would require that when there is probable cause to believe that a fine-only offense has been committed, the police officer should issue a citation unless the officer is "able to point to specific and articulable facts which, taken together with rational inferences from those facts, reasonably warrant [the additional] intrusion" of a full custodial arrest. ⟩ TEST

The majority insists that a bright-line rule focused on probable cause is necessary to vindicate the State's interest in easily administrable law enforcement rules. Probable cause itself, however, is not a model of precision. * * * The rule I propose—which merely requires a legitimate reason for the decision to escalate the seizure into a full custodial arrest—thus does not undermine an otherwise "clear and simple" rule.

While clarity is certainly a value worthy of consideration in our Fourth Amendment jurisprudence, it by no means trumps the values of liberty and privacy at the heart of the Amendment's protections. * * *

The Court's error, however, does not merely affect the disposition of this case. The per se rule that the Court creates has potentially serious consequences for the everyday lives of Americans. A broad range of conduct falls into the category of fine-only misdemeanors. * * * *per se rule*

To be sure, such laws are valid and wise exercises of the States' power to protect the public health and welfare. My concern lies not with the decision to enact or enforce these laws, but rather with the manner in which they may be enforced. Under today's holding, when a police officer has probable cause to believe that a fine-only misdemeanor offense has occurred, that officer may stop the suspect, issue a citation, and let the person continue on her way. Or, if a traffic violation, the officer may stop the car, arrest the driver, search the driver, search the entire passenger compartment of the car including any purse or package inside, and impound the car and inventory all of its contents. Although the Fourth Amendment expressly requires that the latter course be a reasonable and proportional response to the circumstances of the offense, the majority gives officers unfettered discretion to choose that course without articulating a single reason why such action is appropriate.

Such unbounded discretion carries with it grave potential for abuse. The majority takes comfort in the lack of evidence of "an epidemic of unnecessary minor-offense arrests." But the relatively small number of published cases dealing with such arrests proves little and should provide little solace. Indeed, as the recent debate over racial profiling demonstrates all too clearly, a relatively minor traffic infraction may often serve as an excuse for stopping and harassing an individual. After today, the arsenal available to any officer extends to a full arrest and the searches permissible concomitant to that arrest. An officer's subjective motivations for making a traffic stop are not relevant considerations in determining the reasonableness of the stop. See *Whren v. United States*, supra. But it is precisely because these motivations are beyond our purview that we must vigilantly ensure that officers' poststop actions—which are properly within our reach—comport with the Fourth Amendment's guarantee of reasonableness. * * *

TENNESSEE v. GARNER

471 U.S. 1, 105 S.Ct. 1694, 85 L.Ed.2d 1 (1985).

JUSTICE WHITE delivered the opinion of the Court.

* * * At about 10:45 p.m. on October 3, 1974, Memphis Police Officers Elton Hymon and Leslie Wright were dispatched to answer a "prowler inside call." Upon arriving at the scene they saw a woman standing on her porch and gesturing toward the adjacent house. She told them she had heard glass breaking and that "they" or "someone" was breaking in next door. While Wright radioed the dispatcher to say that they were on the scene, Hymon went behind the house. He heard a door slam and saw someone run across the back yard. The fleeing suspect, who was appellee-respondent's decedent, Edward Garner, stopped at a 6–feet-high chain link fence at the edge of the yard. With the aid of a flashlight, Hymon was able to see Garner's face and hands. He saw no sign of a weapon, and, though not certain, was "reasonably sure" and "figured" that Garner was unarmed. He thought Garner was 17 or 18 years old and about 5'5" or 5'7" tall. While Garner was crouched at the base of the fence, Hymon called out "police, halt" and took a few steps toward him. Garner then began to climb over the fence. Convinced that if Garner made it over the fence he would elude capture, Hymon shot him. The bullet hit Garner in the back of the head. Garner was taken by ambulance to a hospital, where he died on the operating table. Ten dollars and a purse taken from the house were found on his body.

In using deadly force to prevent the escape, Hymon was acting under the authority of a Tennessee statute and pursuant to Police Department policy. The statute provides that "[i]f, after notice of the intention to arrest the defendant, he either flee or forcibly resist, the officer may use all the necessary means to effect the arrest." The Department policy was slightly more restrictive than the statute, but still allowed the use of deadly force in cases of burglary. * * *

Garner's father then brought this action in the Federal District Court for the Western District of Tennessee, seeking damages under 42 U.S.C. § 1983 for asserted violations of Garner's constitutional rights. * * * The District Court

* * * found that the statute, and Hymon's actions, were constitutional. * * * The Court of Appeals reversed and remanded. * * *[7] The State of Tennessee, which had intervened to defend the statute, appealed to this Court.

Whenever an officer restrains the freedom of a person to walk away, he has seized that person. While it is not always clear just when minimal police interference becomes a seizure, there can be no question that apprehension by the use of deadly force is a seizure subject to the reasonableness requirement of the Fourth Amendment.[a]

A police officer may arrest a person if he has probable cause to believe that person committed a crime. Petitioners and appellant argue that if this requirement is satisfied the Fourth Amendment has nothing to say about *how* that seizure is made. This submission ignores the many cases in which this Court, by balancing the extent of the intrusion against the need for it, has examined the reasonableness of the manner in which a search or seizure is conducted. * * * Because one of the factors is the extent of the intrusion, it is plain that reasonableness depends on not only when a seizure is made, but also how it is carried out. * * *

The same balancing process applied in the cases cited above demonstrates that, notwithstanding probable cause to seize a suspect, an officer may not always do so by killing him. The intrusiveness of a seizure by means of deadly force is unmatched. The suspect's fundamental interest in his own life need not be elaborated upon. The use of deadly force also frustrates the interest of the individual, and of society, in judicial determination of guilt and punishment.

7. The Court of Appeals concluded that the rule set out in the Model Penal Code "accurately states Fourth Amendment limitations on the use of deadly force against fleeing felons." The relevant portion of the Model Penal Code provides:

"The use of deadly force is not justifiable * * * unless (i) the arrest is for a felony; and (ii) the person effecting the arrest is authorized to act as a peace officer or is assisting a person whom he believes to be authorized to act as a peace officer; and (iii) the actor believes that the force employed creates no substantial risk of injury to innocent persons; and (iv) the actor believes that (1) the crime for which the arrest is made involved conduct including the use or threatened use of deadly force; or (2) there is a substantial risk that the person to be arrested will cause death or serious bodily harm if his apprehension is delayed." American Law Institute, Model Penal Code § 3.07(2)(b) (Proposed Official Draft 1962). * * *

a. On the other hand, that reasonableness requirement does not apply when the police conduct at issue was *not* a search, as was the case (see footnote a, *Florida v. Bostick*, ch. 3, § 8) in *County of Sacramento v. Lewis*, 523 U.S. 833 (1998), where an officer chased a speeding motorcycle at speeds of up to 100 miles an hour, at a distance as short as 100 feet when it would have taken 650 feet to stop, so that when the motorcycle tipped over the police car struck and killed a passenger on the cycle. Rather, in such circumstances the shocks-the-conscience test of the Fourteenth Amendment's due process clause governs. On the question of whether "culpability falling within the middle range," that is, more than negligence but less than intent, would suffice to establish such due process violation, the Court in *Lewis* analogized to its Eight Amendment cases finding deliberate indifference an insufficient showing of constitutional liability in a prison riot context, yet speculating it might suffice as to lack of medical treatment:

"To recognize a substantive due process violation in these circumstances when only mid-level fault has been shown would be to forget that liability for deliberate indifference to inmate welfare rests upon the luxury enjoyed by prison officials of having time to make unhurried judgments, upon the chance for repeated reflection, largely uncomplicated by the pulls of competing obligations. When such extended opportunities to do better are teamed with protracted failure even to care, indifference is truly shocking. But when unforeseen circumstances demand an officer's instant judgment, even precipitate recklessness fails to inch close enough to harmful purpose to spark the shock that implicates 'the large concerns of the governors and the governed.' Just as a purpose to cause harm is needed for Eighth Amendment liability in a riot case, so it ought to be needed for Due Process liability in a pursuit case. Accordingly, we hold that high-speed chases with no intent to harm suspects physically or to worsen their legal plight do not give rise to liability under the Fourteenth Amendment."

Against these interests are ranged governmental interests in effective law enforcement. It is argued that overall violence will be reduced by encouraging the peaceful submission of suspects who know that they may be shot if they flee. Effectiveness in making arrests requires the resort to deadly force, or at least the meaningful threat thereof. "Being able to arrest such individuals is a condition precedent to the state's entire system of law enforcement."

Without in any way disparaging the importance of these goals, we are not convinced that the use of deadly force is a sufficiently productive means of accomplishing them to justify the killing of nonviolent suspects. The use of deadly force is a self-defeating way of apprehending a suspect and so setting the criminal justice mechanism in motion. If successful, it guarantees that that mechanism will not be set in motion. And while the meaningful threat of deadly force might be thought to lead to the arrest of more live suspects by discouraging escape attempts, the presently available evidence does not support this thesis. The fact is that a majority of police departments in this country have forbidden the use of deadly force against nonviolent suspects. If those charged with the enforcement of the criminal law have abjured the use of deadly force in arresting nondangerous felons, there is a substantial basis for doubting that the use of such force is an essential attribute of the arrest power in all felony cases. Petitioners and appellant have not persuaded us that shooting nondangerous fleeing suspects is so vital as to outweigh the suspect's interest in his own life.

The use of deadly force to prevent the escape of all felony suspects, whatever the circumstances, is constitutionally unreasonable. It is not better that all felony suspects die than that they escape. Where the suspect poses no immediate threat to the officer and no threat to others, the harm resulting from failing to apprehend him does not justify the use of deadly force to do so. It is no doubt unfortunate when a suspect who is in sight escapes, but the fact that the police arrive a little late or are a little slower afoot does not always justify killing the suspect. A police officer may not seize an unarmed, nondangerous suspect by shooting him dead. The Tennessee statute is unconstitutional insofar as it authorizes the use of deadly force against such fleeing suspects.

It is not, however, unconstitutional on its face. Where the officer has probable cause to believe that the suspect poses a threat of serious physical harm, either to the officer or to others, it is not constitutionally unreasonable to prevent escape by using deadly force. Thus, if the suspect threatens the officer with a weapon or there is probable cause to believe that he has committed a crime involving the infliction or threatened infliction of serious physical harm, deadly force may be used if necessary to prevent escape, and if, where feasible, some warning has been given. As applied in such circumstances, the Tennessee statute would pass constitutional muster.

It is insisted that the Fourth Amendment must be construed in light of the common-law rule, which allowed the use of whatever force was necessary to effect the arrest of a fleeing felon, though not a misdemeanant. * * *

The State and city argue that because this was the prevailing rule at the time of the adoption of the Fourth Amendment and for some time thereafter, and is still in force in some States, use of deadly force against a fleeing felon must be "reasonable." It is true that this Court has often looked to the common law in evaluating the reasonableness, for Fourth Amendment purposes, of police activity. On the other hand, it "has not simply frozen into constitutional law those law enforcement practices that existed at the time of the Fourth Amendment's passage." Because of sweeping change in the legal and technological context, reliance on the common-law rule in this case would be a mistaken literalism that ignores the purposes of a historical inquiry.

It has been pointed out many times that the common-law rule is best understood in light of the fact that it arose at a time when virtually all felonies were punishable by death. * * * Courts have also justified the common-law rule by emphasizing the relative dangerousness of felons.

Neither of these justifications makes sense today. Almost all crimes formerly punishable by death no longer are or can be. And while in earlier times "the gulf between the felonies and the minor offences was broad and deep," today the distinction is minor and often arbitrary. Many crimes classified as misdemeanors, or nonexistent, at common law are now felonies. These changes have undermined the concept, which was questionable to begin with, that use of deadly force against a fleeing felon is merely a speedier execution of someone who has already forfeited his life. They have also made the assumption that a "felon" is more dangerous than a misdemeanant untenable. Indeed, numerous misdemeanors involve conduct more dangerous than many felonies.

There is an additional reason why the common-law rule cannot be directly translated to the present day. The common-law rule developed at a time when weapons were rudimentary. Deadly force could be inflicted almost solely in a hand-to-hand struggle during which, necessarily, the safety of the arresting officer was at risk. Handguns were not carried by police officers until the latter half of the last century. Only then did it become possible to use deadly force from a distance as a means of apprehension. As a practical matter, the use of deadly force under the standard articulation of the common-law rule has an altogether different meaning—and harsher consequences—now than in past centuries.

One other aspect of the common-law rule bears emphasis. It forbids the use of deadly force to apprehend a misdemeanant, condemning such action as disproportionately severe.

In short, though the common law pedigree of Tennessee's rule is pure on its face, changes in the legal and technological context mean the rule is distorted almost beyond recognition when literally applied.

In evaluating the reasonableness of police procedures under the Fourth Amendment, we have also looked to prevailing rules in individual jurisdictions. The rules in the States are varied. Some 19 States have codified the common-law rule, though in two of these the courts have significantly limited the statute. Four States, though without a relevant statute, apparently retain the common-law rule. Two States have adopted the Model Penal Code's provision [§ 3.07(2)(b)] verbatim. Eighteen others allow, in slightly varying language, the use of deadly force only if the suspect has committed a felony involving the use or threat of physical or deadly force, or is escaping with a deadly weapon, or is likely to endanger life or inflict serious physical injury if not arrested. Louisiana and Vermont, though without statutes or case law on point, do forbid the use of deadly force to prevent any but violent felonies. The remaining States either have no relevant statute or case-law, or have positions that are unclear.

It cannot be said that there is a constant or overwhelming trend away from the common-law rule. In recent years, some States have reviewed their laws and expressly rejected abandonment of the common-law rule. Nonetheless, the long-term movement has been away from the rule that deadly force may be used against any fleeing felon, and that remains the rule in less than half the States.

This trend is more evident and impressive when viewed in light of the policies adopted by the police departments themselves. Overwhelmingly, these are more restrictive than the common-law rule. * * * Overall, only 7.5% of departmental and municipal policies explicitly permit the use of deadly force against any felon; 86.8% explicitly do not. In light of the rules adopted by those who must actually administer them, the older and fading common-law view is a dubious indicium of the constitutionality of the Tennessee statute now before us.

Actual departmental policies are important for an additional reason. We would hesitate to declare a police practice of long standing "unreasonable" if doing so would severely hamper effective law enforcement. But the indications are to the contrary. There has been no suggestion that crime has worsened in any way in jurisdictions that have adopted, by legislation or departmental policy, rules similar to that announced today. * * *

Nor do we agree with petitioners and appellant that the rule we have adopted requires the police to make impossible, split-second evaluations of unknowable facts. We do not deny the practical difficulties of attempting to assess the suspect's dangerousness. However, similarly difficult judgments must be made by the police in equally uncertain circumstances. Nor is there any indication that in States that allow the use of deadly force only against dangerous suspects, the standard has been difficult to apply or has led to a rash of litigation involving inappropriate second-guessing of police officers' split-second decisions. Moreover, the highly technical felony/misdemeanor distinction is equally, if not more, difficult to apply in the field. An officer is in no position to know, for example, the precise value of property stolen, or whether the crime was a first or second offense. Finally, as noted above, this claim must be viewed with suspicion in light of the similar self-imposed limitations of so many police departments.

* * * Officer Hymon could not reasonably have believed that Garner—young, slight, and unarmed—posed any threat. Indeed, Hymon never attempted to justify his actions on any basis other than the need to prevent an escape. * * *

The dissent argues that the shooting was justified by the fact that Officer Hymon had probable cause to believe that Garner had committed a nighttime burglary. While we agree that burglary is a serious crime, we cannot agree that it is so dangerous as automatically to justify the use of deadly force. The FBI classifies burglary as a "property" rather than a "violent" crime. Although the armed burglar would present a different situation, the fact that an unarmed suspect has broken into a dwelling at night does not automatically mean he is physically dangerous. This case demonstrates as much. In fact, the available statistics demonstrate that burglaries only rarely involve physical violence. During the 10–year period from 1973–1982, only 3.8% of all burglaries involved violent crime.[23]

* * * The judgment of the Court of Appeals is affirmed * * *.

JUSTICE O'CONNOR, with whom THE CHIEF JUSTICE and JUSTICE REHNQUIST join, dissenting. * * *

23. The dissent points out that three-fifths of all rapes in the home, three-fifths of all home robberies, and about a third of home assaults are committed by burglars. These figures mean only that if one knows that a suspect committed a rape in the home, there is a good chance that the suspect is also a burglar. That has nothing to do with the question here, which is whether the fact that someone has committed a burglary indicates that he has committed, or might commit, a violent crime.

The dissent also points out that this 3.8% adds up to 2.8 million violent crimes over a 10–year period, as if to imply that today's holding will let loose 2.8 million violent burglars. The relevant universe is, of course, far smaller. At issue is only that tiny fraction of cases where violence has taken place and an officer who has no other means of apprehending the suspect is unaware of its occurrence.

Because burglary is a serious and dangerous felony, the public interest in the prevention and detection of the crime is of compelling importance. Where a police officer has probable cause to arrest a suspected burglar, the use of deadly force as a last resort might well be the only means of apprehending the suspect. With respect to a particular burglary, subsequent investigation simply cannot represent a substitute for immediate apprehension of the criminal suspect at the scene. Indeed, the Captain of the Memphis Police Department testified that in his city, if apprehension is not immediate, it is likely that the suspect will not be caught. Although some law enforcement agencies may choose to assume the risk that a criminal will remain at large, the Tennessee statute reflects a legislative determination that the use of deadly force in prescribed circumstances will serve generally to protect the public. Such statutes assist the police in apprehending suspected perpetrators of serious crimes and provide notice that a lawful police order to stop and submit to arrest may not be ignored with impunity. * * *

Against the strong public interests justifying the conduct at issue here must be weighed the individual interests implicated in the use of deadly force by police officers. The majority declares that "[t]he suspect's fundamental interest in his own life need not be elaborated upon." This blithe assertion hardly provides an adequate substitute for the majority's failure to acknowledge the distinctive manner in which the suspect's interest in his life is even exposed to risk. For purposes of this case, we must recall that the police officer, in the course of investigating a nighttime burglary, had reasonable cause to arrest the suspect and ordered him to halt. The officer's use of force resulted because the suspected burglar refused to heed this command and the officer reasonably believed that there was no means short of firing his weapon to apprehend the suspect. Without questioning the importance of a person's interest in his life, I do not think this interest encompasses a right to flee unimpeded from the scene of a burglary. * * *

A proper balancing of the interests involved suggests that use of deadly force as a last resort to apprehend a criminal suspect fleeing from the scene of a nighttime burglary is not unreasonable within the meaning of the Fourth Amendment. * * *

The Court's silence on critical factors in the decision to use deadly force simply invites second-guessing of difficult police decisions that must be made quickly in the most trying of circumstances. Police are given no guidance for determining which objects, among an array of potentially lethal weapons ranging from guns to knives to baseball bats to rope, will justify the use of deadly force. The Court also declines to outline the additional factors necessary to provide "probable cause" for believing that a suspect "poses a significant threat of death or serious physical injury," when the officer has probable cause to arrest and the suspect refuses to obey an order to halt. But even if it were appropriate in this case to limit the use of deadly force to that ambiguous class of suspects, I believe the class should include nighttime residential burglars who resist arrest by attempting to flee the scene of the crime. We can expect an escalating volume of litigation as the lower courts struggle to determine if a police officer's split-second decision to shoot was justified by the danger posed by a particular object and other facts related to the crime. Thus, the majority opinion portends a burgeoning area of Fourth Amendment doctrine concerning the circumstances in which police officers can reasonably employ deadly force. * * *

SECTION 6. WARRANTLESS SEIZURE AND SEARCH OF PREMISES

The cases in this section reflect the basic notion that in the hierarchy of Fourth Amendment values, the privacy and sanctity of the home rank very high. Thus *Payton v. New York,* in contrast to the *Watson* case in the last section, holds that a warrant usually is required for an in-premises arrest. *Chimel v. California* permits only a limited search of the premises incident to an arrest therein, and *Vale v. Louisiana* holds that a warrant is ordinarily necessary to conduct an in-premises search on probable cause.

PAYTON v. NEW YORK

445 U.S. 573, 100 S.Ct. 1371, 63 L.Ed.2d 639 (1980).

JUSTICE STEVENS delivered the opinion of the Court. * * *

On January 14, 1970, after two days of intensive investigation, New York detectives had assembled evidence sufficient to establish probable cause to believe that Theodore Payton had murdered the manager of a gas station two days earlier. At about 7:30 a.m. on January 15, six officers went to Payton's apartment in the Bronx, intending to arrest him. They had not obtained a warrant. Although light and music emanated from the apartment, there was no response to their knock on the metal door. They summoned emergency assistance and, about 30 minutes later, used crowbars to break open the door and enter the apartment. No one was there. In plain view, however, was a 30-caliber shell casing that was seized and later admitted into evidence at Payton's murder trial. * * *

On March 14, 1974, Obie Riddick was arrested for the commission of two armed robberies that had occurred in 1971. He had been identified by the victims in June of 1973 and in January 1974 the police had learned his address. They did not obtain a warrant for his arrest. At about noon on March 14, a detective, accompanied by three other officers, knocked on the door of the Queens house where Riddick was living. When his young son opened the door, they could see Riddick sitting in bed covered by a sheet. They entered the house and placed him under arrest. Before permitting him to dress, they opened a chest of drawers two feet from the bed in search of weapons and found narcotics and related paraphernalia. Riddick was subsequently indicted on narcotics charges. * * *

The New York Court of Appeals, in a single opinion, affirmed the convictions of both Payton and Riddick. * * *

Before addressing the narrow question presented by these appeals, we put to one side other related problems that are *not* presented today. Although it is arguable that the warrantless entry to effect Payton's arrest might have been justified by exigent circumstances, none of the New York courts relied on any such justification. The Court of Appeals majority treated both *Payton's* and *Riddick's* cases as involving routine arrests in which there was ample time to obtain a warrant, and we will do the same. Accordingly, we have no occasion to consider the sort of emergency or dangerous situation, described in our cases as "exigent circumstances," that would justify a warrantless entry into a home for the purpose of either arrest or search.

Nor do these cases raise any question concerning the authority of the police, without either a search or arrest warrant, to enter a third party's home to arrest a suspect. The police broke into Payton's apartment intending to arrest Payton

had p.c
no consent

and they arrested Riddick in his own dwelling. We also note that in neither case is it argued that the police lacked probable cause to believe that the suspect was at home when they entered. Finally, in both cases we are dealing with entries into homes made without the consent of any occupant. In *Payton*, the police used crowbars to break down the door and in *Riddick,* although his three-year-old son answered the door, the police entered before Riddick had an opportunity either to object or to consent. * * *

It is a "basic principle of Fourth Amendment law" that searches and seizures inside a home without a warrant are presumptively unreasonable. Yet it is also well-settled that objects such as weapons or contraband found in a public place may be seized by the police without a warrant. The seizure of property in plain view involves no invasion of privacy and is presumptively reasonable, assuming that there is probable cause to associate the property with criminal activity. * * *

As the late Judge Leventhal recognized, this distinction has equal force when the seizure of a person is involved. Writing on the constitutional issue now before us for the United States Court of Appeals for the District of Columbia Circuit sitting en banc, *Dorman v. United States,* 435 F.2d 385 (D.C.Cir.1970), Judge Leventhal first noted the settled rule that warrantless arrests in public places are valid. He immediately recognized, however, that

> "[a] greater burden is placed [ ] on officials who enter a home or dwelling without consent. Freedom from intrusion into the home or dwelling is the archetype of the privacy protection secured by the Fourth Amendment."

His analysis of this question then focused on the long-settled premise that, absent exigent circumstances, a warrantless entry to search for weapons or contraband is unconstitutional even when a felony has been committed and there is probable cause to believe that incriminating evidence will be found within. He reasoned that the constitutional protection afforded to the individual's interest in the privacy of his own home is equally applicable to a warrantless entry for the purpose of arresting a resident of the house; for it is inherent in such an entry that a search for the suspect may be required before he can be apprehended. Judge Leventhal concluded that an entry to arrest and an entry to search for and to seize property implicate the same interest in preserving the privacy and the sanctity of the home, and justify the same level of constitutional protection. * * * We find this reasoning to be persuasive and in accord with this Court's Fourth Amendment decisions.

The majority of the New York Court of Appeals, however, suggested that there is a substantial difference in the relative intrusiveness of an entry to search for property and an entry to search for a person. It is true that the area that may legally be searched ·is broader when executing a search warrant than when executing an arrest warrant in the home. This difference may be more theoretical than real, however, because the police may need to check the entire premises for safety reasons, and sometimes they ignore the restrictions on searches incident to arrest.

But the critical point is that any differences in the intrusiveness of entries to search and entries to arrest are merely ones of degree rather than kind. The two intrusions share this fundamental characteristic: the breach of the entrance to an individual's home. * * * In terms that apply equally to seizures of property and to seizures of persons, the Fourth Amendment has drawn a firm line at the entrance to the house. Absent exigent circumstances, that threshold may not reasonably be crossed without a warrant. * * * a

The parties have argued at some length about the practical consequences of a warrant requirement as a precondition to a felony arrest in the home. In the absence of any evidence that effective law enforcement has suffered in those States that already have such a requirement, we are inclined to view such arguments with skepticism. More fundamentally, however, such arguments of policy must give way to a constitutional command that we consider to be unequivocal.

Finally, we note the State's suggestion that only a search warrant based on probable cause to believe the suspect is at home at a given time can adequately protect the privacy interests at stake, and since such a warrant requirement is manifestly impractical, there need be no warrant of any kind. We find this ingenious argument unpersuasive. It is true that an arrest warrant requirement may afford less protection than a search warrant requirement, but it will suffice to interpose the magistrate's determination of probable cause between the zealous officer and the citizen. If there is sufficient evidence of a citizen's participation in a felony to persuade a judicial officer that his arrest is justified, it is constitutionally reasonable to require him to open his doors to the officers of the law. Thus, for Fourth Amendment purposes, an arrest warrant founded on probable cause implicitly carries with it the limited authority to enter a dwelling in which the suspect lives [b] when there is reason to believe the suspect is within.

a. At this point, Stevens, J., observed that New York argued that "the reasons supporting the *Watson* holding require a similar result here. In *Watson* the Court relied on (a) the well-settled common-law rule that a warrantless arrest in a public place is valid if the arresting officer had probable cause to believe the suspect is a felon; (b) the clear consensus among the States adhering to that well-settled common-law rule; and (c) the expression of the judgment of Congress that such an arrest is 'reasonable.' We consider each of these reasons as it applies to a warrantless entry into a home for the purpose of making a routine felony arrest."

In an extended analysis, the *Payton* majority concluded (a) that "the relevant common law does not provide the same guidance that was present in *Watson*," as there is "no direct authority supporting forcible entries into a home to make a routine arrest and the weight of the scholarly opinion is somewhat to the contrary"; (b) that presently 24 states permit such warrantless entries, 15 prohibit them, and 11 have taken no position, with "a significant decline during the last decade in the number of States permitting warrantless entries for arrest"; and (c) that "no congressional determination that warrantless entries into the home are 'reasonable' has been called to our attention." While the majority then concluded from this that "neither history nor this Nation's experience" lent support to the New York position, the *Payton* dissenters read essentially the same data as supporting their position.

b. In *Steagald v. United States,* 451 U.S. 204 (1981), police entered Steagald's home in

an effort to find one Lyons, for whom they had an arrest warrant; they did not find Lyons but did find drugs in plain view, resulting in Steagald's prosecution and conviction. In reversing the conviction, the Court, per Marshall, J., reasoned that "whether the arrest warrant issued in this case adequately safeguarded the interests protected by the Fourth Amendment depends upon what the warrant authorized the agents to do. To be sure, the warrant embodied a judicial finding that there was probable cause to believe that Ricky Lyons had committed a felony, and the warrant therefore authorized the officers to seize Lyons. However, the agents sought to do more than use the warrant to arrest Lyons in a public place or in his home; instead, they relied on the warrant as legal authority to enter the home of a third person based on their belief that Ricky Lyons might be a guest there. Regardless of how reasonable this belief might have been, it was never subjected to the detached scrutiny of a judicial officer. Thus, while the warrant in this case may have protected Lyons from an unreasonable seizure, it did absolutely nothing to protect petitioner's privacy interest in being free from an unreasonable invasion and search of his home. Instead, petitioner's only protection from an illegal entry and search was the agent's personal determination of probable cause. In the absence of exigent circumstances, we have consistently held that such judicially untested determinations are not reliable enough to justify an entry into a person's home to arrest him without a warrant, or a search of a home for objects in the absence of a search warrant. We see no reason to depart from this settled course when the search of a home is for a person rather than an object."

Because no arrest warrant was obtained in either of these cases, the judgments must be reversed * * *.[c]

JUSTICE WHITE, with whom THE CHIEF JUSTICE and JUSTICE REHNQUIST join, dissenting. * * *

Today's decision ignores the carefully crafted restrictions on the common-law power of arrest entry and thereby overestimates the dangers inherent in that practice. At common law, absent exigent circumstances, entries to arrest could be made only for felony. Even in cases of felony, the officers were required to announce their presence, demand admission, and be refused entry before they were entitled to break doors. Further, it seems generally accepted that entries could be made only during daylight hours. And, in my view, the officer entering to arrest must have reasonable grounds to believe, not only that the arrestee has committed a crime, but also that the person suspected is present in the house at the time of the entry.[13]

These four restrictions on home arrests—felony, knock and announce, daytime, and stringent probable cause—constitute powerful and complementary protections for the privacy interests associated with the home. The felony requirement guards against abusive or arbitrary enforcement and ensures that invasions of the home occur only in case of the most serious crimes. The knock and announce and daytime requirement protect individuals against the fear, humiliation and embarrassment of being aroused from the beds in states of partial or complete undress. And these requirements allow the arrestee to surrender at his front door, thereby maintaining his dignity and preventing the officers from entering other rooms of the dwelling. The stringent probable cause requirement would help ensure against the possibility that the police would enter when the suspect was not home, and, in searching for him, frighten members of the family or ransack parts of the house, seizing items in plain view. In short, these requirements, taken together, permit an individual suspected of a serious crime to surrender at the front door of his dwelling and thereby avoid most of the humiliation and indignity that the Court seems to believe necessarily accompany a house arrest entry. Such a front door arrest, in my view, is no more intrusive on personal privacy than the public warrantless arrests which we found to pass constitutional muster in *Watson*.[14]

All of these limitations on warrantless arrest entries are satisfied on the facts of the present cases. The arrests here were for serious felonies—murder and armed robbery—and both occurred during daylight hours. The authorizing statutes required that the police announce their business and demand entry; neither Payton nor Riddick makes any contention that these statutory requirements were not fulfilled. And it is not argued that the police had no probable cause to believe that both Payton and Riddick were in their dwellings at the time of the entries. Today's decision, therefore, sweeps away any possibility that warrantless home entries might be permitted in some limited situations other than those in which exigent circumstances are present. The Court substitutes, in

c. Justice Blackmun's concurring opinion is omitted.

13. I do not necessarily disagree with the Court's discussion of the quantum of probable cause necessary to make a valid home arrest. The Court indicates that only an arrest warrant, and not a search warrant, is required. To obtain the warrant, therefore, the officers need only show probable cause that a crime has been committed and that the suspect committed it. However, under today's decision, the officers apparently need an extra increment of probable cause when executing the arrest warrant, namely grounds to believe that the suspect is within the dwelling.

14. If the suspect flees or hides, of course, the intrusiveness of the entry will be somewhat greater; but the policeman's hands should not be tied merely because of the possibility that the suspect will fail to cooperate with legitimate actions by law enforcement personnel.

one sweeping decision, a rigid constitutional rule in place of the common-law approach, evolved over hundreds of years, which achieved a flexible accommodation between the demands of personal privacy and the legitimate needs of law enforcement.

A rule permitting warrantless arrest entries would not pose a danger that officers would use their entry power as a pretext to justify an otherwise invalid warrantless search. A search pursuant to a warrantless arrest entry will rarely, if ever, be as complete as one under authority of a search warrant. If the suspect surrenders at the door, the officers may not enter other rooms. Of course, the suspect may flee or hide, or may not be at home, but the officers cannot anticipate the first two of these possibilities and the last is unlikely given the requirement of probable cause to believe that the suspect is at home. Even when officers are justified in searching other rooms, they may seize only items within the arrestee's position [sic] or immediate control or items in plain view discovered during the course of a search reasonably directed at discovering a hiding suspect. Hence a warrantless home entry is likely to uncover far less evidence than a search conducted under authority of a search warrant. Furthermore, an arrest entry will inevitably tip off the suspects and likely result in destruction or removal of evidence not uncovered during the arrest. I therefore cannot believe that the police would take the risk of losing valuable evidence through a pretextual arrest entry rather than applying to a magistrate for a search warrant.

While exaggerating the invasion of personal privacy involved in home arrests, the Court fails to account for the danger that its rule will "severely hamper effective law enforcement." The policeman on his beat must now make subtle discriminations that perplex even judges in their chambers. As Justice Powell noted, concurring in *United States v. Watson,* police will sometimes delay making an arrest, even after probable cause is established, in order to be sure that they have enough evidence to convict. Then, if they suddenly have to arrest, they run the risk that the subsequent exigency will not excuse their prior failure to obtain a warrant. This problem cannot effectively be cured by obtaining a warrant as soon as probable cause is established because of the chance that the warrant will go stale before the arrest is made.

Further, police officers will often face the difficult task of deciding whether the circumstances are sufficiently exigent to justify their entry to arrest without a warrant. This is a decision that must be made quickly in the most trying of circumstances. If the officers mistakenly decide that the circumstances are exigent, the arrest will be invalid and any evidence seized incident to the arrest or in plain view will be excluded at trial. On the other hand, if the officers mistakenly determine that exigent circumstances are lacking, they may refrain from making the arrest, thus creating the possibility that a dangerous criminal will escape into the community. The police could reduce the likelihood of escape by staking out all possible exits until the circumstances become clearly exigent or a warrant is obtained. But the costs of such a stakeout seem excessive in an era of rising crime and scarce police resources.

The uncertainty inherent in the exigent circumstances determination burdens the judicial system as well. In the case of searches, exigent circumstances are sufficiently unusual that this Court has determined that the benefits of a warrant outweigh the burdens imposed, including the burdens on the judicial system. In contrast, arrests recurringly involve exigent circumstances, and this Court has heretofore held that a warrant can be dispensed with without undue sacrifice in Fourth Amendment values. The situation should be no different with respect to arrests in the home. Under today's decision, whenever the police have made a warrantless home arrest there will be the possibility of "endless litigation with respect to the existence of exigent circumstances, whether it was practicable to get a warrant, whether the suspect was about to flee, and the like."

* * * It would be far preferable to adopt a clear and simple rule: after knocking and announcing their presence, police may enter the home to make a daytime arrest without a warrant when there is probable cause to believe that the person to be arrested committed a felony and is present in the house. * * *

CHIMEL v. CALIFORNIA

395 U.S. 752, 89 S.Ct. 2034, 23 L.Ed.2d 685 (1969).

JUSTICE STEWART delivered the opinion of the Court. * * *

The relevant facts are essentially undisputed. Late in the afternoon of September 13, 1965, three police officers arrived at the Santa Ana, California, home of the petitioner with a warrant authorizing his arrest for the burglary of a coin shop. The officers knocked on the door, identified themselves to the petitioner's wife, and asked if they might come inside. She ushered them into the house, where they waited 10 or 15 minutes until the petitioner returned home from work. When the petitioner entered the house, one of the officers handed him the arrest warrant and asked for permission to "look around." The petitioner objected, but was advised that "on the basis of the lawful arrest," the officers would nonetheless conduct a search. No search warrant had been issued.

Accompanied by the petitioner's wife, the officers then looked through the entire three-bedroom house, including the attic, the garage, and a small workshop. In some rooms the search was relatively cursory. In the master bedroom and sewing room, however the officers directed the petitioner's wife to open drawers and "to physically move contents of the drawers from side to side so that [they] might view any items that would have come from [the] burglary." After completing the search, they seized numerous items—primarily coins, but also several medals, tokens, and a few other objects. The entire search took between 45 minutes and an hour.

At the petitioner's subsequent state trial on two charges of burglary, the items taken from his house were admitted into evidence against him, over his objection that they had been unconstitutionally seized. He was convicted, and the judgments * * * affirmed * * *.

Without deciding the question, we proceed on the hypothesis that the California courts were correct in holding that the arrest of the petitioner was valid under the Constitution. This brings us directly to the question whether the warrantless search of the petitioner's entire house can be constitutionally justified as incident to that arrest. The decisions of this Court bearing upon that question have been far from consistent, as even the most cursory review makes evident.[a]

a. In an omitted portion of the opinion, the Court described how dictum on search incident to arrest broadened from search of the "person," *Weeks v. United States,* 232 U.S. 383 (1914), to search for what is "upon his person or in his control," *Carroll v. United States,* 267 U.S. 132 (1925), to search of "persons lawfully arrested" and "the place where the arrest is made," *Agnello v. United States,* 269 U.S. 20 (1925). Then, in *Marron v. United States,* 275 U.S. 192 (1927), concerning seizure of evidence at a place where illegal liquor sales were occurring, the Court held that because the police had made an arrest on the premises they "had a right without a warrant contemporaneously to search the place in order to find and seize the things used to carry on the criminal enterprise." But in *Go–Bart Importing Co. v. United States,* 282 U.S. 344 (1931), *Marron* was limited to where the items seized "were visible and accessible and in the offender's immediate custody" and there "was no threat of force or general search or rummaging of the place." This limitation was reiterated in *United States v. Lefkowitz,* 285 U.S. 452 (1932), which, like

In 1950 * * * came *United States v. Rabinowitz,* 339 U.S. 56 (1950), the decision upon which California primarily relies in the case now before us. In *Rabinowitz,* federal authorities had been informed that the defendant was dealing in stamps bearing forged overprints. On the basis of that information they secured a warrant for his arrest, which they executed at his one-room business office. At the time of the arrest, the officers "searched the desk, safe, and file cabinets in the office for about an hour and a half," and seized 573 stamps with forged overprints. The stamps were admitted into evidence at the defendant's trial, and this Court affirmed his conviction, rejecting the contention that the warrantless search had been unlawful. The Court held that the search in its entirety fell within the principle giving law enforcement authorities "[t]he right 'to search the place where the arrest is made in order to find and seize things connected with the crime * * *.'" * * * The test, said the Court, "is not whether it is reasonable to procure a search warrant, but whether the search was reasonable."

Rabinowitz has come to stand for the proposition, inter alia, that a warrantless search "incident to a lawful arrest" may generally extend to the area that is considered to be in the "possession" or under the "control" of the person arrested. And it was on the basis of that proposition that the California courts upheld the search of the petitioner's entire house in this case. That doctrine, however, at least in the broad sense in which it was applied by the California courts in this case, can withstand neither historical nor rational analysis.

Even limited to its own facts, the *Rabinowitz* decision was, as we have seen, hardly founded on an unimpeachable line of authority. * * *

Nor is the rationale by which the State seeks here to sustain the search of the petitioner's house supported by a reasoned view of the background and purpose of the Fourth Amendment. Mr. Justice Frankfurter wisely pointed out in his *Rabinowitz* dissent that the Amendment's proscription of "unreasonable searches and seizures" must be read in light of "the history that gave rise to the words"—a history of "abuses so deeply felt by the Colonies as to be one of the potent causes of the Revolution * * *." The Amendment was in large part a reaction to the general warrants and warrantless searches that had so alienated the colonists and had helped speed the movement for independence. In the scheme of the Amendment, therefore, the requirement that "no Warrants shall issue, but upon probable cause," plays a crucial part. * * * Even in the *Agnello* case the Court relied upon the rule that "[b]elief, however well founded, that an article sought is concealed in a dwelling house furnishes no justification for a search of that place without a warrant. And such searches are held unlawful notwithstanding facts unquestionably showing probable cause." Clearly, the general requirement that a search warrant be obtained is not lightly to be dispensed with, and "the burden is on those seeking [an] exemption [from the requirement] to show the need for it * * *."

* * * When an arrest is made, it is reasonable for the arresting officer to search the person arrested in order to remove any weapons that the latter might seek to use in order to resist arrest or effect his escape. Otherwise, the officer's safety might well be endangered, and the arrest itself frustrated. In addition, it is entirely reasonable for the arresting officer to search for and seize any evidence on the arrestee's person in order to prevent its concealment or destruction. And the

---

Go–Bart, held unlawful a search of a desk despite the fact the search had accompanied a lawful arrest, but was abandoned in *Harris v. United States,* 331 U.S. 145 (1947), upholding the search of a four-room apartment as "incident to arrest." But *Harris* was not followed in *Trupiano v. United States,* 334 U.S. 699 (1948), declaring that "law enforcement agents must secure and use search warrants wherever reasonably practicable."

area into which an arrestee might reach in order to grab a weapon or evidentiary items must, of course, be governed by a like rule. A gun on a table or in a drawer in front of one who is arrested can be as dangerous to the arresting officer as one concealed in the clothing of the person arrested. There is ample justification, therefore, for a search of the arrestee's person and the area "within his immediate control"—construing that phrase to mean the area from within which he might gain possession of a weapon or destructible evidence.

There is no comparable justification, however, for routinely searching rooms other than that in which an arrest occurs—or, for that matter, for searching through all the desk drawers or other closed or concealed areas in that room itself.[b] Such searches, in the absence of well-recognized exceptions, may be made only under the authority of a search warrant. The "adherence to judicial processes" mandated by the Fourth Amendment requires no less. * * *

It is argued in the present case that it is "reasonable" to search a man's house when he is arrested in it. But that argument is founded on little more than a subjective view regarding the acceptability of certain sorts of police conduct, and not on considerations relevant to Fourth Amendment interests. Under such an unconfined analysis, Fourth Amendment protection in this area would approach the evaporation point. It is not easy to explain why, for instance, it is less subjectively "reasonable" to search a man's house when he is arrested on his front lawn—or just down the street—than it is when he happens to be in the house at the time of arrest. * * *

It would be possible, of course, to draw a line between *Rabinowitz* and *Harris* on the one hand, and this case on the other. For *Rabinowitz* involved a single room, and *Harris* a four-room apartment, while in the case before us an entire house was searched. But such a distinction would be highly artificial. The rationale that allowed the searches and seizures in *Rabinowitz* and *Harris* would allow the searches and seizures in this case. No consideration relevant to the Fourth Amendment suggests any point of rational limitation, once the search is allowed to go beyond the area from which the person arrested might obtain weapons or evidentiary items. The only reasoned distinction is one between a search of the person arrested and the area within his reach on the one hand, and more extensive searches on the other.[12]

b. But the Court later held 7–2, in *Maryland v. Buie,* 494 U.S. 325 (1990), that police lawfully inside premises for the purpose of making an arrest may make a "protective sweep" for their own protection:

"We agree with the State, as did the court below, that a warrant was not required. We also hold that as an incident to the arrest the officers could, as a precautionary matter and without probable cause or reasonable suspicion, look in closets and other spaces immediately adjoining the place of arrest from which an attack could be immediately launched. Beyond that, however, we hold that there must be articulable facts which, taken together with the rational inferences from those facts, would warrant a reasonable prudent officer in believing that the area to be swept harbors an individual posing a danger to those on the arrest scene. * * *

"We should emphasize that such a protective sweep, aimed at protecting the arresting officers, if justified by the circumstances, is nevertheless not a full search of the premises, but may extend only to a cursory inspection of those spaces where a person may be found. The sweep lasts no longer than is necessary to dispel the reasonable suspicion of danger and in any event no longer than it takes to complete the arrest and depart the premises."

12. It is argued in dissent that so long as there is probable cause to search the place where an arrest occurs, a search of that place would be permitted even though no search warrant has been obtained. This position seems to be based principally on two premises: first, that once an arrest has been made, the additional invasion of privacy stemming from the accompanying search is "relatively minor"; and second, that the victim of the search may "shortly thereafter" obtain a judicial determination of whether the search was justified by probable cause. With respect to the second premise, one may initially question whether all of the States in fact provide the speedy suppression procedures the dissent assumes. More fundamentally, however, we cannot ac-

The petitioner correctly points out that one result of decisions such as *Rabinowitz* and *Harris* is to give law enforcement officials the opportunity to engage in searches not justified by probable cause, by the simple expedient of arranging to arrest suspects at home rather than elsewhere. We do not suggest that the petitioner is necessarily correct in his assertion that such a strategy was utilized here, but the fact remains that had he been arrested earlier in the day, at his place of employment rather than at home, no search of his house could have been made without a search warrant. In any event, even apart from the possibility of such police tactics, the general point so forcefully made by Judge Learned Hand remains:

> "After arresting a man in his house, to rummage at will among his papers in search of whatever will convict him, appears to us to be indistinguishable from what might be done under a general warrant; indeed, the warrant would give more protection, for presumably it must be issued by a magistrate. True, by hypothesis the power would not exist, if the supposed offender were not found on the premises; but it is small consolation to know that one's papers are safe only so long as one is not at home."

Rabinowitz and *Harris* have been the subject of critical commentary for many years, and have been relied upon less and less in our own decisions. It is time, for the reasons we have stated, to hold that on their own facts, and insofar as the principles they stand for are inconsistent with those that we have endorsed today, they are no longer to be followed.

Application of sound Fourth Amendment principles to the facts of this case produces a clear result. The search here went far beyond the petitioner's person and the area from within which he might have obtained either a weapon or something that could have been used as evidence against him. There was no constitutional justification, in the absence of a search warrant, for extending the search beyond that area. The scope of the search was, therefore, "unreasonable" under the Fourth and Fourteenth Amendments, and the petitioner's conviction cannot stand.

Reversed.

JUSTICE HARLAN, concurring.

* * * The only thing that has given me pause in voting to overrule *Harris* and *Rabinowitz* is that as a result of *Mapp v. Ohio,* every change in Fourth Amendment law must now be obeyed by state officials facing widely different problems of local law enforcement. We simply do not know the extent to which cities and towns across the Nation are prepared to administer the greatly expanded warrant system which will be required by today's decision; nor can we say with assurance that in each and every local situation, the warrant requirement plays an essential role in the protection of those fundamental liberties protected against state infringement by the Fourteenth Amendment. * * *

JUSTICE WHITE, with whom JUSTICE BLACK joins, dissenting.

* * * The Court has always held, and does not today deny, that when there is probable cause to search and it is "impracticable" for one reason or another to get

cept the view that Fourth Amendment interests are vindicated so long as "the rights of the criminal" are "protect[ed] * * * against introduction of evidence seized without probable cause." The Amendment is designed to prevent, not simply to redress, unlawful police action. In any event, we cannot join in characterizing the invasion of privacy that results from a top-to-bottom search of a man's house as "minor." And we can see no reason why, simply because some interference with an individual's privacy and freedom of movement has lawfully taken place, further intrusions should automatically be allowed despite the absence of a warrant that the Fourth Amendment would otherwise require.

a search warrant, then a warrantless search may be reasonable. This is the case whether an arrest was made at the time of the search or not. * * *

This case provides a good illustration of my point that it is unreasonable to require police to leave the scene of an arrest in order to obtain a search warrant when they already have probable cause to search and there is a clear danger that the items for which they may reasonably search will be removed before they return with a warrant. Petitioner was arrested in his home after an arrest whose validity will be explored below, but which I will now assume was valid. There was doubtless probable cause not only to arrest petitioner, but to search his house. He had obliquely admitted both to a neighbor, and to the owner of the burglarized store, that he had committed the burglary. In light of this, and the fact that the neighbor had seen other admittedly stolen property in petitioner's house, there was surely probable cause on which a warrant could have issued to search the house for the stolen coins. Moreover, had the police simply arrested petitioner, taken him off to the station house, and later returned with a warrant,[5] it seems very likely that petitioner's wife, who in view of petitioner's generally garrulous nature must have known of the robbery, would have removed the coins. For the police to search the house while the evidence they had probable cause to search out and seize was still there cannot be considered unreasonable.

This line of analysis, supported by the precedents of this Court, hinges on two assumptions. One is that the arrest of petitioner without a valid warrant [7] was constitutional as the majority assumes; the other is that the police were not required to obtain a search warrant in advance, even though they knew that the effect of the arrest might well be to alert petitioner's wife that the coins had better be removed soon. * * * It must very often be the case that by the time probable cause to arrest a man is accumulated, the man is aware of police interest in him or for other good reasons is on the verge of flight. Moreover, it will likely be very difficult to determine the probability of his flight. Given this situation, it may be best in all cases simply to allow the arrest if there is probable cause, especially since that issue can be determined very shortly after the arrest. * * *

If circumstances so often require the warrantless arrest that the law generally permits it, the typical situation will find the arresting officers lawfully on the premises without arrest or search warrant. * * * [W]here as here the existence of probable cause is independently established and would justify a warrant for a broader search for evidence, I would follow past cases and permit such a search to be carried out without a warrant, since the fact of arrest supplies an exigent circumstance justifying police action before the evidence can be removed, and also alerts the suspect to the fact of the search so that he can immediately seek judicial determination of probable cause in an adversary proceeding, and appropriate redress. * * *

---

5. There were three officers at the scene of the arrest, one from the city where the coin burglary had occurred, and two from the city where the arrest was made. Assuming that one policeman from each city would be needed to bring the petitioner in and obtain a search warrant, one policeman could have been left to guard the house. However, if he not only could have remained in the house against petitioner's wife's will, but followed her about to assure that no evidence was being tampered with, the invasion of her privacy would be almost as great as that accompanying an actual search. Moreover, had the wife summoned an accomplice, one officer could not have watched them both.

7. An arrest warrant was in fact issued, but it was issued on an inadequate supporting affidavit and was therefore invalid, so that the case must be considered as though no warrant had issued.

VALE v. LOUISIANA

399 U.S. 30, 90 S.Ct. 1969, 26 L.Ed.2d 409 (1970).

JUSTICE STEWART delivered the opinion of the Court.

* * * The evidence adduced at the pretrial hearing on a motion to suppress showed that on April 24, 1967, officers possessing two warrants for Vale's arrest and having information that he was residing at a specified address proceeded there in an unmarked car and set up a surveillance of the house. The evidence of what then took place was summarized by the Louisiana Supreme Court as follows:

"After approximately 15 minutes the officers observed a green 1958 Chevrolet drive up and sound the horn and after backing into a parking place, again blew the horn. At this juncture Donald Vale, who was well known to Officer Brady having arrested him twice in the previous month, was seen coming out of the house and walk up to the passenger side of the Chevrolet where he had a close brief conversation with the driver; and after looking up and down the street returned inside of the house. Within a few minutes he reappeared on the porch, and again cautiously looked up and down the street before proceeding to the passenger side of the Chevrolet, leaning through the window. From this the officers were convinced a narcotics sale had taken place. They returned to their car and immediately drove toward Donald Vale, and as they reached within approximately three cars lengths from the accused, (Donald Vale) he looked up and, obviously recognizing the officers, turned around, walking quickly toward the house. At the same time the driver of the Chevrolet started to make his get away when the car was blocked by the police vehicle. The three officers promptly alighted from the car, whereupon Officers Soule and Laumann called to Donald Vale to stop as he reached the front steps of the house, telling him he was under arrest. Officer Brady at the same time, seeing the driver of the Chevrolet, Arizzio Saucier, whom the officers knew to be a narcotic addict, place something hurriedly in his mouth, immediately placed him under arrest and joined his co-officers. Because of the transaction they had just observed they, informed Donald Vale they were going to search the house, and thereupon advised him of his constitutional rights. After they all entered the front room, Officer Laumann made a cursory inspection of the house to ascertain if anyone else was present and within about three minutes Mrs. Vale and James Vale, mother and brother of Donald Vale, returned home carrying groceries and were informed of the arrest and impending search."

The search of a rear bedroom revealed a quantity of narcotics.

The Louisiana Supreme Court held that the search of the house did not violate the Fourth Amendment because it occurred "in the immediate vicinity of the arrest" of Donald Vale and was "substantially contemporaneous therewith * * *." We cannot agree. * * *

A search may be incident to an arrest " 'only if it is substantially contemporaneous with the arrest and is confined to the *immediate* vicinity of the arrest.' " If a search of a house is to be upheld as incident to an arrest, that arrest must take place *inside* the house, not somewhere outside—whether two blocks away, twenty feet away, or on the sidewalk near the front steps. "Belief, however well founded, that an article sought is concealed in a dwelling house furnishes no justification for a search of that place without a warrant." That basic rule "has never been questioned in this Court."

The Louisiana Supreme Court thought the search independently supportable because it involved narcotics, which are easily removed, hidden, or destroyed. It would be unreasonable, the Louisiana court concluded, "to require the officers under the facts of the case to first secure a search warrant before searching the premises, as time is of the essence inasmuch as the officers never know whether there is anyone on the premises to be searched who could very easily destroy the evidence." Such a rationale could not apply to the present case, since by their own account the arresting officers satisfied themselves that no one else was in the house when they first entered the premises. But entirely apart from that point, our past decisions make clear that only in "a few specifically established and well-delineated" situations, may a warrantless search of a dwelling withstand constitutional scrutiny, even though the authorities have probable cause to conduct it. The burden rests on the State to show the existence of such an exceptional situation. And the record before us discloses none.

There is no suggestion that anyone consented to the search. The officers were not responding to an emergency. The goods ultimately seized were not in the process of destruction. Nor were they about to be removed from the jurisdiction.

The officers were able to procure two warrants for Vale's arrest. They also had information that he was residing at the address where they found him. There is thus no reason, so far as anything before us appears, to suppose that it was impracticable for them to obtain a search warrant as well. We decline to hold that an arrest on the street can provide its own "exigent circumstance" so as to justify a warrantless search of the arrestee's house. * * *

Reversed and remanded.

Justice Blackmun took no part in the consideration or decision of this case.

Justice Black, with whom The Chief Justice joins, dissenting.

* * * The police placed both Vale and Saucier under arrest. At this point the police had probable cause to believe that Vale was engaged in a narcotics transfer, and that a supply of narcotics would be found in the house, to which Vale had returned after his first conversation, from which he had emerged furtively bearing what the police could readily deduce was a supply of narcotics, and toward which he hurried after seeing the police. But the police did not know then who else might be in the house. Vale's arrest took place near the house, and anyone observing from inside would surely have been alerted to destroy the stocks of contraband which the police believed Vale had left there. The police had already seen Saucier, the narcotics addict, apparently swallow what Vale had given him. Believing that some evidence had already been destroyed and that other evidence might well be, the police were faced with the choice of risking the immediate destruction of evidence or entering the house and conducting a search. I cannot say that their decision to search was unreasonable. Delay in order to obtain a warrant would have given an accomplice just the time he needed.

That the arresting officers did, in fact, believe that others might be in the house is attested to by their actions upon entering the door left open by Vale. The police at once checked the small house to determine if anyone else was present. Just as they discovered the house was empty, however, Vale's mother and brother arrived. Now what had been a suspicion became a certainty: Vale's relatives were in possession and knew of his arrest. To have abandoned the search at this point, and left the house with Vale, would not have been the action of reasonable police officers. * * * [a]

a. This, of course, raises the question of whether the police could have remained within the premises with Vale's brother and mother while a search warrant was obtained, which necessitates consideration of two Supreme Court decisions addressing similar but not identical situations.

(1) In *Segura v. United States*, 468 U.S. 796 (1984), the police, upon confirming that they had observed a drug sale by Colon and Segura,

Moreover, the circumstances here were sufficiently exceptional to justify a search, even if the search was not strictly "incidental" to an arrest. The Court recognizes that searches to prevent the destruction or removal of evidence have long been held reasonable by this Court. Whether the "exceptional circumstances" justifying such a search exist or not is a question that may be, as it is

went to their apartment building, arrested Segura in the lobby, and then arrested Colon when she answered a knock on the door of their apartment. Police then made a warrantless entry of the apartment and remained there until a search warrant was issued, which occurred some 19 hours later. The Court held "that where officers, having probable cause, enter premises, and with probable cause, arrest the occupants who have legitimate possessory interests in its contents and take them into custody and, for no more than the period here involved, secure the premises from within to preserve the status quo while others, in good faith, are in the process of obtaining a warrant, they do not violate the Fourth Amendment's proscription against unreasonable seizures." That holding was explicated in an opinion by two Justices stating: "Securing of the premises from within * * * was no more an interference with the petitioners' possessory interests in the contents of the apartment than a perimeter 'stakeout.' In other words, the initial entry— legal or not—does not affect the reasonableness of the seizure. Under either method— entry and securing from within or a perimeter stakeout—agents control the apartment pending arrival of the warrant; both an internal securing and a perimeter stakeout interfere to the same extent with the possessory interests of the owners. * * *

" * * * Here, of course, Segura and Colon, whose possessory interests were interfered with by the occupation, were under arrest and in the custody of the police throughout the entire period the agents occupied the apartment. The actual interference with their possessory interests in the apartment and its contents was, thus, virtually nonexistent."

The four dissenters argued that the occupation was an unreasonable search, infringing upon a reasonable expectation of privacy, and an unreasonable seizure, involving exercise of "complete dominion and control over the apartment and its contents"; and that the Fourth Amendment protects possessory interests in a residence even when the occupants are in custody.

(2) In *Illinois v. McArthur*, 531 U.S. 326 (2001), two police officers stood by outside to keep the peace while defendant's wife removed her effects from the family residence, a trailer. Upon exiting, she told the officers her husband had hidden marijuana under the couch, so the officers sought his permission to search the premises. When he refused, one officer left to obtain a search warrant, while another officer remained on the porch with defendant, who was told he could not reenter unless he was accompanied by the officer. A warrant was

obtained an executed two hours later, but in the interim defendant entered the trailer two or three times, and on each occasion the officer stood just inside the door and observe his actions.

By a process of "balanc[ing] the privacy-related and law enforcement-related concerns," the Court concluded "that the restriction at issue was reasonable, and hence lawful, in light of" four enumerated circumstances: (i) "the police had probable cause to believe that McArthur's trailer home contained evidence of a crime and contraband, namely, unlawful drugs"; (ii) "the police had good reason to fear that, unless restrained, McArthur would destroy the drugs before they could return with a warrant," as they reasonably concluded that even before the requested consent to search he realized his angry wife had informed the police about the drugs; (iii) "the police made reasonable efforts to reconcile their law enforcement needs with the demands of personal privacy" by imposing "a significantly less restrictive restraint" than a warrantless search of the premises; and (iv) "the police imposed the restraint for a limited period of time, namely, two hours."

As for defendant's reliance upon *Welsh v. Wisconsin*, 466 U.S. 740 (1984), holding that police could not enter a home without a warrant in order to prevent the loss of evidence (namely, the defendant's blood alcohol level) of the "nonjailable traffic offense" of driving while intoxicated, the *McArthur* majority distinguished *Welsh* because (a) the offense involved here was punishable by up to 30 days in jail, and (b) "the restriction at issue here is less serious." (Only Justice Stevens concluded otherwise as to the *Welsh* doctrine.)

Justice Souter, concurring in *McArthur*, reasoned that had defendant remained inside the trailer then the "probability of destruction" of the marijuana "in anticipation of a warrant * * * would have justified the police in entering McArthur's trailer promptly to make a lawful, warrantless search," that this risk "abated and so did the reasonableness of entry by the police" once he came outside, but that once he came outside it was reasonable for the police to keep him from reentering not because "the law officiously insists on safeguarding a suspect's privacy from search," but rather because of "the law's strong preference for warrants, which underlies the rule that a search with a warrant has a stronger claim to justification on later, judicial review than a search without one. * * * The law can hardly raise incentives to obtain a warrant without giving the police a fair chance to take their probable cause to a magistrate and get one."

here, quite distinct from whether or not the search was incident to a valid arrest. It is thus unnecessary to determine whether the search was valid as incident to the arrest * * *.

The Court, however, finds the search here unreasonable. First, the Court suggests that the contraband was not "in the process of destruction." None of the cases cited by the Court supports the proposition that "exceptional circumstances" exist only when the process of destruction has already begun. On the contrary we implied that those circumstances did exist when "evidence or contraband was *threatened* with removal or destruction."

Second, the Court seems to argue that the search was unreasonable because the police officers had time to obtain a warrant. I agree that the opportunity to obtain a warrant is one of the factors to be weighed in determining reasonableness. But the record conclusively shows that there was no such opportunity here. As I noted above, once the officers had observed Vale's conduct in front of the house they had probable cause to believe that a felony had been committed and that immediate action was necessary. At no time after the events in front of Mrs. Vale's house would it have been prudent for the officers to leave the house in order to secure a warrant.

The Court asserts, however, that because the police obtained two warrants for Vale's arrest there is "no reason * * * to suppose that it was impracticable for them to obtain a search warrant as well." The difficulty is that the two arrest warrants on which the Court seems to rely so heavily were not issued because of any present misconduct of Vale's; they were issued because the bond had been increased for an earlier narcotics charge then pending against Vale. When the police came to arrest Vale, they knew only that his bond had been increased. There is nothing in the record to indicate that, absent the increased bond, there would have been probable cause for an arrest, much less a search. Probable cause for the search arose for the first time when the police observed the activity of Vale and Saucier in and around the house. * * *

SECTION 7. WARRANTLESS SEIZURE AND SEARCH OF VEHICLES AND EFFECTS

Several of the cases in this section clearly illustrate that motor vehicles receive substantially less Fourth Amendment protection than premises. *California v. Carney* (in contradistinction to *Vale*) permits probable cause searches of vehicles without a warrant; *New York v. Belton* (in contradistinction to *Chimel*) allows a broad search of vehicles incident to arrest of an occupant (but, says *Knowles v. Iowa*, not incident to giving an occupant a citation); and *Colorado v. Bertine* authorizes a warrantless inventory of lawfully seized vehicles.

Personal effects, such as luggage, rank somewhere between premises and vehicles in the Fourth Amendment hierarchy of values. Another case in this section, *California v. Acevedo*, explores why this is so and addresses the eventuating issue of what rules should control when personal effects are located inside a vehicle. But when a search is directed at an apparently nonimplicated passengers, as in *Wyoming v. Houghton*, the critical distinction becomes the differing privacy expectations as to a passenger's effects as compared to his or her person.

CALIFORNIA v. CARNEY
471 U.S. 386, 105 S.Ct. 2066, 85 L.Ed.2d 406 (1985).

CHIEF JUSTICE BURGER delivered the opinion of the Court. * * *

On May 31, 1979, Drug Enforcement Agency Agent Robert Williams watched respondent, Charles Carney, approach a youth in downtown San Diego. The youth accompanied Carney to a Dodge Mini Motor Home parked in a nearby lot. Carney and the youth closed the window shades in the motor home, including one across the front window. Agent Williams had previously received uncorroborated information that the same motor home was used by another person who was exchanging marihuana for sex. Williams, with assistance from other agents, kept the motor home under surveillance for the entire one and one-quarter hours that Carney and the youth remained inside. When the youth left the motor home, the agents followed and stopped him. The youth told the agents that he had received marijuana in return for allowing Carney sexual contacts.

At the officers' request, the youth returned to the motor home and knocked on its door; Carney stepped out. The agents identified themselves as law enforcement officers. Without a warrant or consent, one agent entered the motor home and observed marihuana, plastic bags, and a scale of the kind used in weighing drugs on a table. Agent Williams took Carney into custody and took possession of the motor home. A subsequent search of the motor home at the police station revealed additional marihuana in the cupboards and refrigerator.

Respondent was charged with possession of marihuana for sale. At a preliminary hearing, he moved to suppress the evidence discovered in the motor home. The Magistrate denied the motion, [but later the state supreme court reversed the conviction, holding the search was unreasonable because no warrant was obtained.]

* * * There are, of course, exceptions to the general rule that a warrant must be secured before a search is undertaken; one is the so-called "automobile exception" at issue in this case. This exception to the warrant requirement was first set forth by the Court 60 years ago in *Carroll v. United States,* 267 U.S. 132 (1925). There, the Court recognized that the privacy interests in an automobile are constitutionally protected; however, it held that the ready mobility of the automobile justifies a lesser degree of protection of those interests. The Court rested this exception on a long-recognized distinction between stationary structures and vehicles:

> "[T]he guaranty of freedom from unreasonable searches and seizures by the Fourth Amendment has been construed, practically since the beginning of Government, as recognizing a necessary difference between a search of a store, dwelling house or other structure in respect of which a proper official warrant readily may be obtained, and a search of a ship, motor boat, wagon or automobile, for contraband goods, where it is not practicable to secure a warrant because the vehicle can be *quickly moved* out of the locality or jurisdiction in which the warrant must be sought."

The capacity to be "quickly moved" was clearly the basis of the holding in *Carroll,* and our cases have consistently recognized ready mobility as one of the principal bases of the automobile exception. * * *

However, although ready mobility alone was perhaps the original justification for the vehicle exception, our later cases have made clear that ready mobility is not the only basis for the exception. The reasons for the vehicle exception, we have said, are twofold. "Besides the element of mobility, less rigorous warrant requirements govern because the expectation of privacy with respect to one's automobile is significantly less than that relating to one's home or office."

Even in cases where an automobile was not immediately mobile, the lesser expectation of privacy resulting from its use as a readily mobile vehicle justified application of the vehicular exception. In some cases, the configuration of the vehicle contributed to the lower expectations of privacy; for example, we held that, because the passenger compartment of a standard automobile is relatively open to plain view, there are lesser expectations of privacy. But even when enclosed "repository" areas have been involved, we have concluded that the lesser expectations of privacy warrant application of the exception. We have applied the exception in the context of a locked car trunk, a sealed package in a car trunk, a closed compartment under the dashboard, the interior of a vehicle's upholstery, or sealed packages inside a covered pickup truck.

These reduced expectations of privacy derive not from the fact that the area to be searched is in plain view, but from the pervasive regulation of vehicles capable of traveling on the public highways. As we explained in [an earlier] case:

"Automobiles, unlike homes, are subjected to pervasive and continuing governmental regulation and controls, including periodic inspection and licensing requirements. As an everyday occurrence, police stop and examine vehicles when license plates or inspection stickers have expired, or if other violations, such as exhaust fumes or excessive noise, are noted, or if headlights or other safety equipment are not in proper working order."

The public is fully aware that it is accorded less privacy in its automobiles because of this compelling governmental need for regulation. Historically, "individuals always [have] been on notice that movable vessels may be stopped and searched on facts giving rise to probable cause that the vehicle contains contraband, without the protection afforded by a magistrate's prior evaluation of those facts." In short, the pervasive schemes of regulation, which necessarily lead to reduced expectations of privacy, and the exigencies attendant to ready mobility justify searches without prior recourse to the authority of a magistrate so long as the overriding standard of probable cause is met.

When a vehicle is being used on the highways, or if it is readily capable of such use and is found stationary in a place not regularly used for residential purposes—temporary or otherwise—the two justifications for the vehicle exception come into play. First, the vehicle is obviously readily mobile by the turn of a switch key, if not actually moving. Second, there is a reduced expectation of privacy stemming from its use as a licensed motor vehicle subject to a range of police regulation inapplicable to a fixed dwelling. At least in these circumstances, the overriding societal interests in effective law enforcement justify an immediate search before the vehicle and its occupants become unavailable.[a]

a. In *Maryland v. Dyson*, 527 U.S. 465 (1999), the Court, per curiam, summarily reversed a state court decision holding "that in order for the automobile exception to the warrant requirement to apply, there must not only be probable cause to believe that evidence of a crime is contained in the automobile, but also a separate finding of exigency precluding the police from obtaining a warrant." That holding, the Court declared, "rests upon an incorrect interpretation of the automobile exception to the Fourth Amendment's warrant requirement," which "does not have a separate exigency requirement."

In *Florida v. White*, 526 U.S. 559 (1999), upholding the warrantless *seizure* of a car on probable cause that the vehicle was contraband under the state forfeiture law, the Court took note of "the special considerations recognized in the context of movable items" in the *Carroll-Carney* line of cases, and then concluded the need was "equally weighty when the *automobile*, as opposed to its contents, is the contraband that the police seek to secure." The Court also observed that "our Fourth Amendment jurisprudence has consistently accorded law enforcement officials greater latitude in exercising their duties in public places," and deemed the instant case "nearly indistinguishable" from *G.M. Leasing Corp. v. United States*, 429 U.S. 338 (1977), upholding the warrantless seizure from a public area of automobiles in partial satisfaction of income tax assessments. Two dissenters in *White* objected (i) that an exigent circumstances rationale had no application "when the seizure is based upon a belief that the automobile may have been used at some time in the past to assist in illegal activity and the owner is already in custody,"

While it is true that respondent's vehicle possessed some, if not many of the attributes of a home, it is equally clear that the vehicle falls clearly within the scope of the exception laid down in *Carroll* and applied in succeeding cases. Like the automobile in *Carroll,* respondent's motor home was readily mobile. Absent the prompt search and seizure, it could readily have been moved beyond the reach of the police. Furthermore, the vehicle was licensed to "operate on public streets; [was] serviced in public places; * * * and [was] subject to extensive regulation and inspection." And the vehicle was so situated that an objective observer would conclude that it was being used not as a residence, but as a vehicle.

Respondent urges us to distinguish his vehicle from other vehicles within the exception because it was *capable of functioning as a home.* In our increasingly mobile society, many vehicles used for transportation can be and are being used not only for transportation but for shelter, i.e., as a "home" or "residence." To distinguish between respondent's motor home and an ordinary sedan for purposes of the vehicle exception would require that we apply the exception depending upon the size of the vehicle and the quality of its appointments. Moreover, to fail to apply the exception to vehicles such as a motor home ignores the fact that a motor home lends itself easily to use as an instrument of illicit drug traffic and other illegal activity. * * *

Our application of the vehicle exception has never turned on the other uses to which a vehicle might be put. The exception has historically turned on the ready mobility of the vehicle, and on the presence of the vehicle in a setting that objectively indicates that the vehicle is being used for transportation.[3] These two requirements for application of the exception ensure that law enforcement officials are not unnecessarily hamstrung in their efforts to detect and prosecute criminal activity, and that the legitimate privacy interests of the public are protected. Applying the vehicle exception in these circumstances allows the essential purposes served by the exception to be fulfilled, while assuring that the exception will acknowledge legitimate privacy interests. * * *

This search was not unreasonable; it was plainly one that the magistrate could authorize if presented with these facts. * * *

The judgment of the California Supreme Court is reversed * * *.

JUSTICE STEVENS, with whom JUSTICE BRENNAN and JUSTICE MARSHALL join, dissenting. * * *

In this case, the motor home was parked in an off-the-street lot only a few blocks from the courthouse in downtown San Diego where dozens of magistrates were available to entertain a warrant application. The officers clearly had the element of surprise with them, and with curtains covering the windshield, the motor home offered no indication of any imminent departure. The officers plainly had probable cause to arrest the petitioner and search the motor home, and on this record, it is inexplicable why they eschewed the safe harbor of a warrant.

In the absence of any evidence of exigency in the circumstances of this case, the Court relies on the inherent mobility of the motor home to create a conclusive

and (ii) that a warrant requirement "is bolstered by the inherent risks of hindsight at post-seizure hearings and law enforcement agencies' pecuniary interest in the seizure of such property."

3. We need not pass on the application of the vehicle exception to a motor home that is situated in a way or place that objectively indicates that it is being used as a residence.

Among the factors that might be relevant in determining whether a warrant would be required in such a circumstance is its location, whether the vehicle is readily mobile or instead, for instance, elevated on blocks, whether the vehicle is licensed, whether it is connected to utilities, and whether it has convenient access to a public road.

presumption of exigency. This Court, however, has squarely held that mobility of the place to be searched is not a sufficient justification for abandoning the warrant requirement. In *United States v. Chadwick*, 433 U.S. 1 (1977), the Court held that a warrantless search of a footlocker violated the Fourth Amendment even though there was ample probable cause to believe it contained contraband. The Government had argued that the rationale of the automobile exception applied to movable containers in general, and that the warrant requirement should be limited to searches of homes and other "core" areas of privacy. We categorically rejected the Government's argument observing that there are greater privacy interests associated with containers than with automobiles, and that there are less practical problems associated with the temporary detention of a container than with the detention of an automobile.

* * * It is perfectly obvious that the citizen has a much greater expectation of privacy concerning the interior of a mobile home than of a piece of luggage such as a footlocker. If "inherent mobility" does not justify warrantless searches of containers, it cannot rationally provide a sufficient justification for the search of a person's dwelling place.

Unlike a brick bungalow or a frame Victorian, a motor home seldom serves as a permanent lifetime abode. The motor home in this case, however, was designed to accommodate a breadth of ordinary everyday living. Photographs in the record indicate that its height, length and beam provided substantial living space inside: stuffed chairs surround a table; cupboards provide room for storage of personal effects; bunk-beds provide sleeping space; and a refrigerator provides ample space for food and beverages. Moreover, curtains and large opaque walls inhibit viewing the activities inside from the exterior of the vehicle. The interior configuration of the motor home establishes that the vehicle's size, shape, and mode of construction should have indicated to the officers that it was a vehicle containing mobile living quarters.

The State contends that officers in the field will have an impossible task determining whether or not other vehicles contain mobile living quarters. It is not necessary for the Court to resolve every unanswered question in this area in a single case, but common English usage suggests that we already distinguish between a "motor home" which is "equipped as a self-contained traveling home," a "camper" which is only equipped for "casual travel and camping," and an automobile which is "designed for passenger transportation." Surely the exteriors of these vehicles contain clues about their different functions which could alert officers in the field to the necessity of a warrant. * * *

In my opinion, searches of places that regularly accommodate a wide range of private human activity are fundamentally different from searches of automobiles which primarily serve a public transportation function. Although it may not be a castle, a motor home is usually the functional equivalent of a hotel room, a vacation and retirement home, or a hunting and fishing cabin. These places may be as spartan as a humble cottage when compared to the most majestic mansion, but the highest and most legitimate expectations of privacy associated with these temporary abodes should command the respect of this Court. In my opinion, a warrantless search of living quarters in a motor home is "presumptively unreasonable absent exigent circumstances."

I respectfully dissent.

NEW YORK v. BELTON

453 U.S. 454, 101 S.Ct. 2860, 69 L.Ed.2d 768 (1981).

JUSTICE STEWART delivered the opinion of the Court. * * *

On April 9, 1978, Trooper Douglas Nicot, a New York State policeman driving an unmarked car on the New York Thruway, was passed by another automobile travelling at an excessive rate of speed. Nicot gave chase, overtook the speeding vehicle, and ordered its driver to pull it over to the side of the road and stop. There were four men in the car, one of whom was Roger Belton, the respondent in this case. The policeman asked to see the driver's license and automobile registration, and discovered that none of the men owned the vehicle or was related to its owner. Meanwhile, the policeman had smelled burnt marihuana and had seen on the floor of the car an envelope marked "Supergold" that he associated with marihuana. He therefore directed the men to get out of the car, and placed them under arrest for the unlawful possession of marihuana. He patted down each of the men and "split them up into four separate areas of the Thruway at this time so they would not be in physical touching area of each other." He then picked up the envelope marked "Supergold" and found that it contained marihuana. After giving the arrestees the warnings required by *Miranda v. Arizona*, the state policeman searched each one of them. He then searched the passenger compartment of the car. On the back seat he found a black leather jacket belonging to Belton. He unzipped one of the pockets of the jacket and discovered cocaine. Placing the jacket in his automobile, he drove the four arrestees to a nearby police station.

Belton was subsequently indicted for criminal possession of a controlled substance. In the trial court he moved that the cocaine the trooper had seized from the jacket pocket be suppressed. The court denied the motion. Belton then pleaded guilty to a lesser included offense, but preserved his claim that the cocaine had been seized in violation of the Fourth and Fourteenth Amendments. The Appellate Division of the New York Supreme Court upheld the constitutionality of the search and seizure, reasoning that "[o]nce defendant was validly arrested for possession of marihuana, the officer was justified in searching the immediate area for other contraband."

The New York Court of Appeals reversed, holding that "[a] warrantless search of the zippered pockets of an unaccessible jacket may not be upheld as a search incident to a lawful arrest where there is no longer any danger that the arrestee or a confederate might gain access to the article." * * *

It is a first principle of Fourth Amendment jurisprudence that the police may not conduct a search unless they first convince a neutral magistrate that there is probable cause to do so. This Court has recognized, however, that "the exigencies of the situation" may sometimes make exemption from the warrant requirement "imperative." Specifically, the Court held in *Chimel v. California* that a lawful custodial arrest creates a situation which justifies the contemporaneous search without a warrant of the person arrested and of the immediately surrounding area. Such searches have long been considered valid because of the need "to remove any weapons that [the arrestee] might seek to use in order to resist arrest or effect his escape" and the need to prevent the concealment or destruction of evidence.

The Court's opinion in *Chimel* emphasized the principle that, "The scope of [a] search must be 'strictly tied to and justified by' the circumstances which rendered its initiation permissible." Thus while the Court in *Chimel* found "ample justification" for a search of "the area from within which [an arrestee] might gain possession of a weapon or destructible evidence," the Court found "no comparable justification * * * for routinely searching any room other than that in which an arrest occurs—or, for that matter, for searching through all the desk drawers or other closed or concealed areas in that room itself."

Although the principle that limits a search incident to a lawful custodial arrest may be stated clearly enough, courts have discovered the principle difficult to apply in specific cases. Yet, as one commentator has pointed out, the protection of the Fourth and Fourteenth Amendments "can only be realized if the police are acting under a set of rules which, in most instances, makes it possible to reach a correct determination beforehand as to whether an invasion of privacy is justified in the interest of law enforcement." This is because

> "Fourth Amendment doctrine, given force and effect by the exclusionary rule, is primarily intended to regulate the police in their day-to-day activities and thus ought to be expressed in terms that are readily applicable by the police in the context of the law enforcement activities in which they are necessarily engaged. A highly sophisticated set of rules, qualified by all sorts of ifs, ands, and buts and requiring the drawing of subtle nuances and hairline distinctions, may be the sort of heady stuff upon which the facile minds of lawyers and judges eagerly feed, but they may be 'literally impossible of application by the officer in the field.' "

In short, "A single, familiar standard is essential to guide police officers, who have only limited time and expertise to reflect on and balance the social and individual interests involved in the specific circumstances they confront." * * *

But no straightforward rule has emerged from the litigated cases respecting the question involved here—the question of the proper scope of a search of the interior of an automobile incident to a lawful custodial arrest of its occupants. The difficulty courts have had is reflected in the conflicting views of the New York judges who dealt with the problem in the present case, and is confirmed by a look at even a small sample drawn from the narrow class of cases in which courts have decided whether, in the course of a search incident to the lawful custodial arrest of the occupants of an automobile, police may search inside the automobile after the arrestees are no longer in it. * * *

When a person cannot know how a court will apply a settled principle to a recurring factual situation, that person cannot know the scope of his constitutional protection, nor can a policeman know the scope of his authority. While the *Chimel* case established that a search incident to an arrest may not stray beyond the area within the immediate control of the arrestee, courts have found no workable definition of "the area within the immediate control of the arrestee" when that area arguably includes the interior of an automobile and the arrestee is its recent occupant. Our reading of the cases suggests the generalization that articles inside the relatively narrow compass of the passenger compartment of an automobile are in fact generally, even if not inevitably, within "the area into which an arrestee might reach in order to grab a weapon or evidentiary item." In order to establish the workable rule this category of cases requires, we read *Chimel*'s definition of the limits of the area that may be searched in light of that generalization. Accordingly, we hold that when a policeman has made a lawful custodial arrest of the occupant[a] of an automobile, he may, as a contemporaneous

---

a. Lower courts are not in agreement as to what it takes to make a person an "occupant" within the meaning of the *Belton* rule. One view is noted in *Florida v. Thomas*, 121 S.Ct. 1905 (2001), where, while officers were investigating marijuana sales and making arrests at a certain home, Thomas drove up, parked in the driveway and walked toward the back of his car, where one officer then met him and asked for identification. A check revealed an outstanding warrant, so the officer arrested Thomas, handcuffed him, and took him inside the home, and then searched the car and found drugs. The state court's conclusion, that "*Bel-*

incident of that arrest, search the passenger compartment of that automobile.[3]

It follows from this conclusion that the police may also examine the contents of any containers found within the passenger compartment, for if the passenger compartment is within reach of the arrestee, so also will containers in it be within his reach.[4] Such a container may, of course, be searched whether it is open or closed, since the justification for the search is not that the arrestee has no privacy interest in the container, but that the lawful custodial arrest justifies the infringement of any privacy interest the arrestee may have. Thus, while the Court in *Chimel* held that the police could not search all the drawers in an arrestee's house simply because the police had arrested him at home, the Court noted that drawers within an arrestee's reach could be searched because of the danger their contents might pose to the police.

It is true, of course, that these containers will sometimes be such that they could hold neither a weapon nor evidence of the criminal conduct for which the suspect was arrested. However, in *United States v. Robinson,* the Court rejected the argument that such a container—there a "crumpled up cigarette package"—located during a search of Robinson incident to his arrest could not be searched: "The authority to search the person incident to a lawful custodial arrest, while based upon the need to disarm and to discover evidence, does not depend on what a court may later decide was the probability in a particular arrest situation that weapons or evidence would in fact be found upon the person of the suspect. A custodial arrest of a suspect based on probable cause is a reasonable intrusion under the Fourth Amendment; that intrusion being lawful, a search incident to the arrest requires no additional justification." * * *[5]

It is not questioned that the respondent was the subject of a lawful custodial arrest on a charge of possessing marihuana. The search of the respondent's jacket followed immediately upon that arrest. The jacket was located inside the passenger compartment of the car in which the respondent had been a passenger just before he was arrested. The jacket was thus within the area which we have concluded was "within the arrestee's immediate control" within the meaning of the *Chimel* case. The search of the jacket, therefore, was a search incident to a lawful custodial arrest, and it did not violate the Fourth and Fourteenth Amendments. Accordingly, the judgment is reversed.[b]

JUSTICE STEVENS, concurring in the judgment.

ton's bright-line rule is limited to situations where the law enforcement officer initiates contact with the defendant" while defendant remains in the car, was not ruled on by the Supreme Court; the Court decided it lacked jurisdiction because after so holding the state court had remanded for further factfinding and a determination of the outcome under *Chimel.*

3. Our holding today does not more than determine the meaning of *Chimel*'s principles in this particular and problematic content. It in no way alters the fundamental principles established in the *Chimel* case regarding the basic scope of searches incident to lawful custodial arrests.

4. "Container" here denotes any object capable of holding another object. It thus includes closed or open glove compartments, consoles, or other receptacles located anywhere within the passenger compartment, as well as luggage, boxes, bags, clothing, and the like. Our holding encompasses only the interior of the passenger compartment of an automobile and does not encompass the trunk.

5. It seems to have been the theory of the Court of Appeals that the search and seizure in the present case could not have been incident to the respondent's arrest, because Trooper Nicot, by the very act of searching the respondent's jacket and seizing the contents of its pocket, had gained "exclusive control" of them. But under this fallacious theory no search or seizure incident to a lawful custodial arrest would ever be valid; by seizing an article even on the arrestee's person, an officer may be said to have reduced that article to his "exclusive control."

b. Justice Rehnquist's concurring opinion is omitted.

For the reasons stated in my dissenting opinion in *Robbins v. California*, 453 U.S. 420 (1981), I agree [that] this judgment should be reversed. [That opinion follows.—ed.]

The Court's careful and repeated use of the term "lawful custodial arrest" seems to imply that a significant distinction between custodial arrests and ordinary arrests exists. I am familiar with the distinction between a "stop" and an "arrest," but I am not familiar with any difference between custodial arrests and any other kind of arrest. It is, of course, true that persons apprehended for traffic violations are frequently not required to accompany the arresting officer to the police station before they are permitted to leave on their own recognizance or by using their driver's licenses as a form of bond. It is also possible that state law or local regulations may in some cases forbid police officers from taking persons into custody for violation of minor traffic laws. As a matter of constitutional law, however, any person lawfully arrested for the pettiest misdemeanor may be temporarily placed in custody.[11] Indeed, as the Court has repeatedly held, every arrest is a seizure of the person within the meaning of the Fourth Amendment. The rule of constitutional law the Court fashions today therefore potentially applies to every arrest of every occupant of an automobile.[12]

After the vehicle in which respondent was riding was stopped, the officer smelled marihuana and thereby acquired probable cause to believe that the vehicle contained contraband. A thorough search of the car was therefore reasonable. But if there were no reason to believe that anything more than a traffic violation had occurred, I should think it palpably unreasonable to require the driver of a car to open his briefcase or his luggage for inspection by the officer. The driver so compelled, however, could make no constitutional objection to a decision by the officer to take the driver into custody and thereby obtain justification for a search of the entire interior of the vehicle. Indeed, under the Court's new rule, the arresting officer may find reason to follow that procedure whenever he sees an interesting looking briefcase or package in a vehicle that has been stopped for a traffic violation. That decision by a police officer will therefore provide the constitutional predicate for broader vehicle searches than any neutral magistrate could authorize by issuing a warrant.   * * *

JUSTICE BRENNAN, with whom JUSTICE MARSHALL joins, dissenting.   * * *

By approving the constitutionality of the warrantless search in this case, the Court carves out a dangerous precedent that is not justified by the concerns

11. Justice Stewart apparently believes that the Fourth and Fourteenth Amendments might provide some impediment to police taking a defendant into custody for violation of a "minor traffic offense." See *Gustafson v. Florida* (Stewart, J. concurring). Although I agree that a police officer's authority to restrain an individual's liberty should be limited in the context of stops for routine traffic violations, the Court has not directly considered the question whether "there are constitutional limits upon the use of 'custodial arrests' as the means for invoking the criminal process when relatively minor offenses are involved." To the extent that the Court has considered the scope of an officer's authority in making routine traffic stops, the Court has not imposed constitutional restrictions on that authority. Thus the Court may be assuming that its new rule will be limited by a constitutional restriction that does not exist.

12. After today, the driver of a vehicle stopped for a minor traffic violation must look to state law for protection from unreasonable searches. Such protection may come from two sources. Statutory law may provide some protection. Legislatures in some states permit officers to take traffic violators into custody only for certain violations. In some states, however, the police officer has the discretion to make a "custodial arrest" for violation of any motor vehicle law. Additionally, the failure to produce a satisfactory bond will often justify "detention and custodial arrest." Given the incomplete protection afforded by statutory law, drivers in many States will have to persuade state supreme courts to interpret their state constitution's equivalent to the Fourth Amendment to prohibit the unreasonable searches permitted by the Court here.

underlying *Chimel*. Disregarding the principle "that the scope of a warrantless search must be commensurate with the rationale that excepts the search from the warrant requirement," the Court for the first time grants police officers authority to conduct a warrantless "area" search under circumstances where there is no chance that the arrestee "might gain possession of a weapon or destructible evidence." Under the approach taken today, the result would presumably be the same even if Officer Nicot had handcuffed Belton and his companions in the patrol car before placing them under arrest, and even if his search had extended to locked luggage or other inaccessible containers located in the back seat of the car. * * *

The Court seeks to justify its departure from the principles underlying *Chimel* by proclaiming the need for a new bright line rule to guide the officer in the field. * * * [H]owever, "the mere fact that law enforcement may be made more efficient can never by itself justify disregard of the Fourth Amendment." Moreover, the Court's attempt to forge a "bright line" rule fails on its own terms. * * * The Court's new approach leaves open too many questions and, more important, it provides the police and the courts with too few tools with which to find the answers.

Thus, although the Court concludes that a warrantless search of a car may take place even though the suspect was arrested outside the car, it does not indicate how long after the suspect's arrest that search may validly be conducted. Would a warrantless search incident to arrest be valid if conducted five minutes after the suspect left his car? Thirty minutes? Three hours? Does it matter whether the suspect is standing in close proximity to the car when the search is conducted? Does it matter whether the police formed probable cause to arrest before or after the suspect left his car? And *why* is the rule announced today necessarily limited to searches of cars? What if a suspect is seen walking out of a house where the police, peering in from outside, had formed probable cause to believe a crime was being committed? Could the police then arrest that suspect and enter the house to conduct a search incident to arrest? Even assuming today's rule is limited to searches of the "interior" of cars—an assumption not demanded by logic—what is meant by "interior"? Does it include locked glove compartments, the interior of door panels, or the area under the floorboards? Are special rules necessary for station wagons and hatchbacks, where the luggage compartment may be reached through the interior, or taxicabs, where a glass panel might separate the driver's compartment from the rest of the car? Are the only containers that may be searched those that are large enough to be "capable of holding another object"? Or does the new rule apply to any container, even if it "could hold neither a weapon nor evidence of the criminal conduct for which the suspect was arrested"?

The Court does not give the police any "bright line" answers to these questions. More important, because the Court's new rule abandons the justifications underlying *Chimel, it offers no guidance to the police officer seeking to work out these answers for himself.* * * *

The standard announced in *Chimel* is not nearly as difficult to apply as the Court suggests. To the contrary, I continue to believe that *Chimel* provides a sound, workable rule for determining the constitutionality of a warrantless search incident to arrest. Under *Chimel*, searches incident to arrest may be conducted without a warrant only if limited to the person of the arrestee, or to the area within the arrestee's "immediate control." While it may be difficult in some cases to measure the exact scope of the arrestee's immediate control, relevant factors would surely include the relative number of police officers and arrestees, the manner of restraint placed on the arrestee, and the ability of the arrestee to gain access to a particular area or container.[5]   Certainly there will be some close cases, but when in doubt the police can always turn to the rationale underlying *Chimel*—the need to prevent the arrestee from reaching weapons or contraband—before exercising their judgment.   A rule based on that rationale should provide more guidance than the rule announced by the Court today.   Moreover, unlike the Court's rule, it would be faithful to the Fourth Amendment.

JUSTICE WHITE, with whom JUSTICE MARSHALL joins, dissenting.

* * * The Court now holds that as incident to the arrest of the driver or any other person in an automobile, the interior of the car and any container found therein, whether locked or not, may not only be seized but also searched even absent probable cause to believe that contraband or evidence of crime will be found.   As to luggage, briefcases or other containers, this seems to me an extreme extension of *Chimel* and one to which I cannot subscribe.   * * *

KNOWLES v. IOWA

525 U.S. 113, 119 S.Ct. 484, 142 L.Ed.2d 492 (1998).

CHIEF JUSTICE REHNQUIST delivered the opinion of the Court.

An Iowa police officer stopped petitioner Knowles for speeding, but issued him a citation rather than arresting him. The question presented is whether such a procedure authorizes the officer, consistently with the Fourth Amendment, to conduct a full search of the car. We answer this question "no."

Knowles was stopped in Newton, Iowa, after having been clocked driving 43 miles per hour on a road where the speed limit was 25 miles per hour. The police officer issued a citation to Knowles, although under Iowa law he might have arrested him. The officer then conducted a full search of the car, and under the driver's seat he found a bag of marijuana and a "pot pipe." Knowles was then arrested and charged with violation of state laws dealing with controlled substances.

Before trial, Knowles moved to suppress the evidence so obtained. He argued that the search could not be sustained under the "search incident to arrest" exception recognized in *United States v. Robinson*, 414 U.S. 218 (1973), because he had not been placed under arrest. At the hearing on the motion to suppress, the police officer conceded that he had neither Knowles' consent nor probable cause to conduct the search. He relied on Iowa law dealing with such searches.

Iowa Code Ann. § 321.485(1)(a) provides that Iowa peace officers having cause to believe that a person has violated any traffic or motor vehicle equipment law may arrest the person and immediately take the person before a magistrate. Iowa law also authorizes the far more usual practice of issuing a citation in lieu of arrest or in lieu of continued custody after an initial arrest.[1] Section 805.1(4)

5. The Court sets up a straw man when it claims that under the "exclusive control" approach taken by the Court of Appeals, "no search or seizure incident to a lawful custodial arrest would ever be valid; by seizing an article even on the arrestee's person, an officer may be said to have reduced that article to his 'exclusive control.' "

If a police officer could obtain exclusive control of an article by simply holding it in his hand, I would certainly agree with the Court. But as we recognized in *United States v. Chad-*

wick, exclusive control means more than that. It means sufficient control such that there is no significant risk that the arrestee or his confederates "might gain possession of a weapon or destructible evidence." *Chimel v. California.* The issue of exclusive control presents a question of fact to be decided under the circumstances of each case, just as the New York Court of Appeals has decided it here.

1. Iowa law permits the issuance of a citation in lieu of arrest for most offenses for which an accused person would be "eligible for provides that the issuance of a citation in lieu of an arrest "does not affect the officer's authority to conduct an otherwise lawful search." The Iowa Supreme Court has interpreted this provision as providing authority to officers to conduct a full-blown search of an automobile and driver in those cases where police elect not to make a custodial arrest and instead issue a citation—that is, a search incident to citation.

Based on this authority, the trial court denied the motion to suppress and found Knowles guilty. The Supreme Court of Iowa * * * upheld the constitutionality of the search under a bright-line "search incident to citation" exception to the Fourth Amendment's warrant requirement, reasoning that so long as the arresting officer had probable cause to make a custodial arrest, there need not in fact have been a custodial arrest. We granted certiorari, and we now reverse.

* * * Knowles did not argue below, and does not argue here, that the statute could never be lawfully applied. The question we therefore address is whether the search at issue, authorized as it was by state law, nonetheless violates the Fourth Amendment.

In *Robinson*, we noted the two historical rationales for the "search incident to arrest" exception: (1) the need to disarm the suspect in order to take him into custody, and (2) the need to preserve evidence for later use at trial. But neither of these underlying rationales for the search incident to arrest exception is sufficient to justify the search in the present case.

[T]he first rationale—officer safety—is " 'both legitimate and weighty.' " The threat to officer safety from issuing a traffic citation, however, is a good deal less than in the case of a custodial arrest. In *Robinson*, we stated that a custodial arrest involves "danger to an officer" because of "the extended exposure which follows the taking of a suspect into custody and transporting him to the police station." We recognized that "[t]he danger to the police officer flows from the fact of the arrest, and its attendant proximity, stress, and uncertainty, and not from the grounds for arrest." A routine traffic stop, on the other hand, is a relatively brief encounter and "is more analogous to a so-called '*Terry* stop' ... than to a formal arrest."

This is not to say that the concern for officer safety is absent in the case of a routine traffic stop. It plainly is not. But while the concern for officer safety in this context may justify the "minimal" additional intrusion of ordering a driver and passengers out of the car, it does not by itself justify the often considerably greater intrusion attending a full field-type search. Even without the search authority Iowa urges, officers have other, independent bases to search for weapons and protect themselves from danger. For example, they may order out of a vehicle both the driver, [*Pennsylvania v.*] *Mimms*, [434 U.S. 106 (1977)], and any passengers, [*Maryland v.*] *Wilson*, [519 U.S. 408 (1997)]; perform a "patdown" of a driver and any passengers upon reasonable suspicion that they may be armed and dangerous, *Terry v. Ohio*, 392 U.S. 1 (1968); conduct a "*Terry* patdown" of the passenger compartment of a vehicle upon reasonable suspicion that an occupant is dangerous and may gain immediate control of a weapon, *Michigan v. Long*, 463 U.S. 1032 (1983); and even conduct a full search of the passenger compartment, including any containers therein, pursuant to a custodial arrest, *New York v. Belton*, 453 U.S. 454 (1981).

bail." In addition to traffic and motor vehicle equipment violations, this would permit the issuance of a citation in lieu of arrest for such serious felonies as second-degree burglary and first-degree theft, both bailable offenses under Iowa law. The practice in Iowa of permitting citation in lieu of arrest is consistent with law reform efforts. See 3 W. LaFave, Search and Seizure § 5.2(h), p. 99, and n. 151 (3d ed.1996).

Nor has Iowa shown the second justification for the authority to search incident to arrest—the need to discover and preserve evidence. Once Knowles was stopped for speeding and issued a citation, all the evidence necessary to prosecute that offense had been obtained. No further evidence of excessive speed was going to be found either on the person of the offender or in the passenger compartment of the car.

Iowa nevertheless argues that a "search incident to citation" is justified because a suspect who is subject to a routine traffic stop may attempt to hide or destroy evidence related to his identity (e. g., a driver's license or vehicle registration), or destroy evidence of another, as yet undetected crime. As for the destruction of evidence relating to identity, if a police officer is not satisfied with the identification furnished by the driver, this may be a basis for arresting him rather than merely issuing a citation. As for destroying evidence of other crimes, the possibility that an officer would stumble onto evidence wholly unrelated to the speeding offense seems remote.

In *Robinson*, we held that the authority to conduct a full field search as incident to an arrest was a "bright-line rule," which was based on the concern for officer safety and destruction or loss of evidence, but which did not depend in every case upon the existence of either concern. Here we are asked to extend that "bright-line rule" to a situation where the concern for officer safety is not present to the same extent and the concern for destruction or loss of evidence is not present at all. We decline to do so. The judgment of the Supreme Court of Iowa is reversed, and the cause remanded for further proceedings not inconsistent with this opinion. * * *

CALIFORNIA v. ACEVEDO

500 U.S. 565, 111 S.Ct. 1982, 114 L.Ed.2d 619 (1991).

JUSTICE BLACKMUN delivered the opinion of the Court.

[One Daza picked up a package the police knew contained marijuana from a Federal Express office and took it to his apartment. About two hours later, Acevedo entered that apartment and shortly thereafter left carrying a brown paper bag the size of one of the wrapped marijuana packages. He placed the bag in the trunk of his car and drove off; the police then stopped him, opened the trunk and bag, and found marijuana. The California Court of Appeals held the marijuana should have been suppressed, the state supreme court denied review, and the Supreme Court then granted certiorari.]

In *United States v. Ross,* 456 U.S. 798, decided in 1982, we held that a warrantless search of an automobile under the *Carroll* doctrine could include a search of a container or package found inside the car when such a search was supported by probable cause. The warrantless search of Ross' car occurred after an informant told the police that he had seen Ross complete a drug transaction using drugs stored in the trunk of his car. The police stopped the car, searched it, and discovered in the trunk a brown paper bag containing drugs. We decided that the search of Ross' car was not unreasonable under the Fourth Amendment: "The scope of a warrantless search based on probable cause is no narrower—and no broader—than the scope of a search authorized by a warrant supported by probable cause." Thus, "[i]f probable cause justifies the search of a lawfully stopped vehicle, it justifies the search of every part of the vehicle and its contents that may conceal the object of the search." In *Ross*, therefore, we clarified the scope of the *Carroll* doctrine as properly including a "probing search" of compartments and containers within the automobile so long as the search is supported by probable cause.

In addition to this clarification, *Ross* distinguished the *Carroll* doctrine from the separate rule that governed the search of closed containers. The Court had announced this separate rule, unique to luggage and other closed packages, bags, and containers, in *United States v. Chadwick,* 433 U.S. 1 (1977). In *Chadwick,* federal narcotics agents had probable cause to believe that a 200-pound double-locked footlocker contained marijuana. The agents tracked the locker as the defendants removed it from a train and carried it through the station to a waiting car. As soon as the defendants lifted the locker into the trunk of the car, the agents arrested them, seized the locker, and searched it. In this Court, the United States did not contend that the locker's brief contact with the automobile's trunk sufficed to make the *Carroll* doctrine applicable. Rather, the United States urged that the search of movable luggage could be considered analogous to the search of an automobile.

The Court rejected this argument because, it reasoned, a person expects more privacy in his luggage and personal effects than he does in his automobile. Moreover, it concluded that as "may often not be the case when automobiles are seized," secure storage facilities are usually available when the police seize luggage.

In *Arkansas v. Sanders,* 442 U.S. 753 (1979), the Court extended *Chadwick*'s rule to apply to a suitcase actually being transported in the trunk of a car. In *Sanders,* the police had probable cause to believe a suitcase contained marijuana. They watched as the defendant placed the suitcase in the trunk of a taxi and was driven away. The police pursued the taxi for several blocks, stopped it, found the suitcase in the trunk, and searched it. Although the Court had applied the *Carroll* doctrine to searches of integral parts of the automobile itself, (indeed, in *Carroll,* contraband whiskey was in the upholstery of the seats), it did not extend the doctrine to the warrantless search of personal luggage "merely because it was located in an automobile lawfully stopped by the police." Again, the *Sanders* majority stressed the heightened privacy expectation in personal luggage and concluded that the presence of luggage in an automobile did not diminish the owner's expectation of privacy in his personal items.

In *Ross,* the Court endeavored to distinguish between *Carroll,* which governed the *Ross* automobile search, and *Chadwick,* which governed the *Sanders* automobile search. It held that the *Carroll* doctrine covered searches of automobiles when the police had probable cause to search an entire vehicle but that the *Chadwick* doctrine governed searches of luggage when the officers had probable cause to search only a container within the vehicle. Thus, in a *Ross* situation, the police could conduct a reasonable search under the Fourth Amendment without obtaining a warrant, whereas in a *Sanders* situation, the police had to obtain a warrant before they searched.

The dissent is correct, of course, that *Ross* involved the scope of an automobile search. *Ross* held that closed containers encountered by the police during a warrantless search of a car pursuant to the automobile exception could also be searched. Thus, this Court in *Ross* took the critical step of saying that closed containers in cars could be searched without a warrant because of their presence within the automobile. Despite the protection that *Sanders* purported to extend to closed containers, the privacy interest in those closed containers yielded to the broad scope of an automobile search. * * *

This Court in *Ross* rejected *Chadwick*'s distinction between containers and cars. It concluded that the expectation of privacy in one's vehicle is equal to one's expectation of privacy in the container, and noted that "the privacy interests in a car's trunk or glove compartment may be no less than those in a movable container." It also recognized that it was arguable that the same exigent circumstances that permit a warrantless search of an automobile would justify the warrantless search of a movable container. In deference to the rule of *Chadwick* and *Sanders,* however, the Court put that question to one side. It concluded that the time and expense of the warrant process would be misdirected if the police could search every cubic inch of an automobile until they discovered a paper sack, at which point the Fourth Amendment required them to take the sack to a magistrate for permission to look inside. We now must decide the question deferred in *Ross:* whether the Fourth Amendment requires the police to obtain a warrant to open the sack in a movable vehicle simply because they lack probable cause to search the entire car. We conclude that it does not.

Dissenters in *Ross* asked why the suitcase in *Sanders* was "more private, less difficult for police to seize and store, or in any other relevant respect more properly subject to the warrant requirement, than a container that police discover in a probable-cause search of an entire automobile?" We now agree that a container found after a general search of the automobile and a container found in a car after a limited search for the container are equally easy for the police to store and for the suspect to hide or destroy. In fact, we see no principled distinction in terms of either the privacy expectation or the exigent circumstances between the paper bag found by the police in *Ross* and the paper bag found by the police here. Furthermore, by attempting to distinguish between a container for which the police are specifically searching and a container which they come across in a car, we have provided only minimal protection for privacy and have impeded effective law enforcement.

The line between probable cause to search a vehicle and probable cause to search a package in that vehicle is not always clear, and separate rules that govern the two objects to be searched may enable the police to broaden their power to make warrantless searches and disserve privacy interests. * * * At the moment when officers stop an automobile, it may be less than clear whether they suspect with a high degree of certainty that the vehicle contains drugs in a bag or simply contains drugs. If the police know that they may open a bag only if they are actually searching the entire car, they may search more extensively than they otherwise would in order to establish the general probable cause required by *Ross*.

Such a situation is not far fetched. In *United States v. Johns,* 469 U.S. 478 (1985), customs agents saw two trucks drive to a private airstrip and approach two small planes. The agents drew near the trucks, smelled marijuana, and then saw in the backs of the trucks packages wrapped in a manner that marijuana smugglers customarily employed. The agents took the trucks to headquarters and searched the packages without a warrant. Relying on *Chadwick,* the defendants argued that the search was unlawful. The defendants contended that *Ross* was inapplicable because the agents lacked probable cause to search anything but the packages themselves and supported this contention by noting that a search of the entire vehicle never occurred. We rejected that argument and found *Chadwick* and *Sanders* inapposite because the agents had probable cause to search the entire body of each truck, although they had chosen not to do so. We cannot see the benefit of a rule that requires law enforcement officers to conduct a more intrusive search in order to justify a less intrusive one.

To the extent that the *Chadwick-Sanders* rule protects privacy, its protection is minimal. Law enforcement officers may seize a container and hold it until they obtain a search warrant. "Since the police, by hypothesis, have probable cause to seize the property, we can assume that a warrant will be routinely forthcoming in the overwhelming majority of cases." And the police often will be able to search containers without a warrant, despite the *Chadwick-Sanders* rule, as a search incident to a lawful arrest [under] *Belton.* * * *

Finally, the search of a paper bag intrudes far less on individual privacy than does the incursion sanctioned long ago in *Carroll.* In that case, prohibition agents slashed the upholstery of the automobile. This Court nonetheless found their search to be reasonable under the Fourth Amendment. If destroying the interior of an automobile is not unreasonable, we cannot conclude that looking inside a closed container is. In light of the minimal protection to privacy afforded by the *Chadwick-Sanders* rule, and our serious doubt whether that rule substantially serves privacy interests, we now hold that the Fourth Amendment does not compel separate treatment for an automobile search that extends only to a container within the vehicle.

The *Chadwick-Sanders* rule not only has failed to protect privacy but it has also confused courts and police officers and impeded effective law enforcement. * * *

The discrepancy between the two rules has led to confusion for law enforcement officers. For example, when an officer, who has developed probable cause to believe that a vehicle contains drugs, begins to search the vehicle and immediately discovers a closed container, which rule applies? The defendant will argue that the fact that the officer first chose to search the container indicates that his probable cause extended only to the container and that *Chadwick* and *Sanders* therefore require a warrant. On the other hand, the fact that the officer first chose to search in the most obvious location should not restrict the propriety of the search. The *Chadwick* rule, as applied in *Sanders,* has devolved into an anomaly such that the more likely the police are to discover drugs in a container, the less authority they have to search it. * * *

Although we have recognized firmly that the doctrine of *stare decisis* serves profoundly important purposes in our legal system, this Court has overruled a prior case on the comparatively rare occasion when it has bred confusion or been derelict or led to anomalous results. *Sanders* was explicitly undermined in *Ross,* and the existence of the dual regimes for automobile searches that uncover containers has proved as confusing as the *Chadwick* and *Sanders* dissenters predicted. We conclude that it is better to adopt one clear-cut rule to govern automobile searches and eliminate the warrant requirement for closed containers set forth in *Sanders.*

The interpretation of the *Carroll* doctrine set forth in *Ross* now applies to all searches of containers found in an automobile. In other words, the police may search without a warrant if their search is supported by probable cause. The Court in *Ross* put it this way:

> "The scope of a warrantless search of an automobile * * * is not defined by the nature of the container in which the contraband is secreted. Rather, it is defined by the object of the search and the places in which there is probable cause to believe that it may be found."

It went on to note: "Probable cause to believe that a container placed in the trunk of a taxi contains contraband or evidence does not justify a search of the entire cab." We reaffirm that principle. In the case before us, the police had probable cause to believe that the paper bag in the automobile's trunk contained marijuana. That probable cause now allows a warrantless search of the paper bag. The facts in the record reveal that the police did not have probable cause to believe that contraband was hidden in any other part of the automobile and a search of the entire vehicle would have been without probable cause and unreasonable under the Fourth Amendment.

Our holding today neither extends the *Carroll* doctrine nor broadens the scope of the permissible automobile search delineated in *Carroll, Chambers,* and *Ross.* It remains a "cardinal principle that 'searches conducted outside the judicial process, without prior approval by judge or magistrate, are *per se* unreasonable under the Fourth Amendment—subject only to a few specifically established and well-delineated exceptions.' " We held in *Ross:* "The exception recognized in *Carroll* is unquestionably one that is 'specifically established and well delineated.' "

Until today, this Court has drawn a curious line between the search of an automobile that coincidentally turns up a container and the search of a container that coincidentally turns up in an automobile. The protections of the Fourth Amendment must not turn on such coincidences. We therefore interpret *Carroll* as providing one rule to govern all automobile searches. The police may search an automobile and the containers within it where they have probable cause to believe contraband or evidence is contained. * * *

JUSTICE SCALIA, concurring in the judgment.

I agree with the dissent that it is anomalous for a briefcase to be protected by the "general requirement" of a prior warrant when it is being carried along the street, but for that same briefcase to become unprotected as soon as it is carried into an automobile. On the other hand, I agree with the Court that it would be anomalous for a locked compartment in an automobile to be unprotected by the "general requirement" of a prior warrant, but for an unlocked briefcase within the automobile to be protected. I join in the judgment of the Court because I think its holding is more faithful to the text and tradition of the Fourth Amendment, and if these anomalies in our jurisprudence are ever to be eliminated that is the direction in which we should travel. * * *

Although the Fourth Amendment does not explicitly impose the requirement of a warrant, it is of course textually possible to consider that implicit within the requirement of reasonableness. For some years after the (still continuing) explosion in Fourth Amendment litigation that followed our announcement of the exclusionary rule in *Weeks v. United States,* 232 U.S. 383 (1914), our jurisprudence lurched back and forth between imposing a categorical warrant requirement and looking to reasonableness alone. * * *

The victory was illusory. Even before today's decision, the "warrant requirement" had become so riddled with exceptions that it was basically unrecognizable. In 1985, one commentator cataloged nearly 20 such exceptions, including "searches incident to arrest * * * automobile searches * * * border searches * * * administrative searches of regulated businesses * * * exigent circumstances * * * search[es] incident to nonarrest when there is probable cause to arrest * * * boat boarding for document checks * * * welfare searches * * * inventory searches * * * airport searches * * * school search[es] * * *." Bradley, *Two Models of the Fourth Amendment,* 83 Mich.L.Rev. 1468, 1473–1474 (1985) (footnotes omitted). Since then, we have added at least two more. *California v. Carney,* 471 U.S. 386 (1985) (searches of mobile homes); *O'Connor v. Ortega,* 480 U.S. 709 (1987) (searches of offices of government employees). Our intricate body of law regarding "reasonable expectation of privacy" has been developed largely as a means of creating these exceptions, enabling a search to be denominated not a Fourth Amendment "search" and therefore not subject to the general warrant requirement.

Unlike the dissent, therefore, I do not regard today's holding as some momentous departure, but rather as merely the continuation of an inconsistent jurisprudence that has been with us for years. There can be no clarity in this area unless we make up our minds, and unless the principles we express comport with the actions we take.

In my view, the path out of this confusion should be sought by returning to the first principle that the "reasonableness" requirement of the Fourth Amendment affords the protection that the common law afforded. I have no difficulty with the proposition that that includes the requirement of a warrant, where the common law required a warrant; and it may even be that changes in the surrounding legal rules (for example, elimination of the common-law rule that reasonable, good-faith belief was no defense to absolute liability for trespass), may make a warrant indispensable to reasonableness where it once was not. But the supposed "general rule" that a warrant is always required does not appear to have any basis in the common law, and confuses rather than facilitates any attempt to develop rules of reasonableness in light of changed legal circumstances, as the anomaly eliminated and the anomaly created by today's holding both demonstrate.

And there are more anomalies still. Under our precedents (as at common law), a person may be arrested outside the home on the basis of probable cause, without an arrest warrant. *United States v. Watson.* Upon arrest, the person, as well as the area within his grasp, may be searched for evidence related to the crime. *Chimel v. California.* Under these principles, if a known drug dealer is carrying a briefcase reasonably believed to contain marijuana (the unauthorized possession of which is a crime), the police may arrest him and search his person on the basis of probable cause alone. And, under our precedents, upon arrival at the station house, the police may inventory his possessions, including the briefcase, even if there is no reason to suspect that they contain contraband. *Illinois v. Lafayette,* 462 U.S. 640 (1983). According to our current law, however, the police may not, on the basis of the same probable cause, take the less intrusive step of stopping the individual on the street and demanding to see the contents of his briefcase. That makes no sense *a priori,* and in the absence of any common-law tradition supporting such a distinction, I see no reason to continue it.

I would reverse the judgment in the present case, not because a closed container carried inside a car becomes subject to the "automobile" exception to the general warrant requirement, but because the search of a closed container, outside a privately owned building, with probable cause to believe that the container contains contraband, and when it in fact does contain contraband, is not one of those searches whose Fourth Amendment reasonableness depends upon a warrant. For that reason I concur in the judgment of the Court.

Justice White, dissenting.

Agreeing as I do with most of Justice Stevens' opinion and with the result he reaches, I dissent and would affirm the judgment below.

Justice Stevens, with whom Justice Marshall joins, dissenting.

At the end of its opinion, the Court pays lip service to the proposition that should provide the basis for a correct analysis of the legal question presented by this case: It is " 'a cardinal principle that "searches conducted outside the judicial process, without prior approval by judge or magistrate, are *per se* unreasonable under the Fourth Amendment—subject only to a few specifically established and well-delineated exceptions." ' " * * *

The Fourth Amendment is a restraint on Executive power. The Amendment constitutes the Framers' direct constitutional response to the unreasonable law enforcement practices employed by agents of the British Crown. Over the years— particularly in the period immediately after World War II and particularly in opinions authored by Justice Jackson after his service as a special prosecutor at the Nuremburg trials—the Court has recognized the importance of this restraint as a bulwark against police practices that prevail in totalitarian regimes.

This history is, however, only part of the explanation for the warrant requirement. The requirement also reflects the sound policy judgment that, absent exceptional circumstances, the decision to invade the privacy of an individual's personal effects should be made by a neutral magistrate rather than an agent of the Executive. In his opinion for the Court in *Johnson v. United States,* [333 U.S. 10 (1948)], Justice Jackson explained:

> "The point of the Fourth Amendment, which often is not grasped by zealous officers, is not that it denies law enforcement the support of the usual inferences which reasonable men draw from evidence. Its protection consists in requiring that those inferences be drawn by a neutral and detached magistrate instead of being judged by the officer engaged in the often competitive enterprise of ferreting out crime."

Our decisions have always acknowledged that the warrant requirement imposes a burden on law enforcement. And our cases have not questioned that trained professionals normally make reliable assessments of the existence of probable cause to conduct a search. We have repeatedly held, however, that these factors are outweighed by the individual interest in privacy that is protected by advance judicial approval. The Fourth Amendment dictates that the privacy interest is paramount, no matter how marginal the risk of error might be if the legality of warrantless searches were judged only after the fact. * * *

In *Chadwick,* the Department of Justice had mounted a frontal attack on the warrant requirement. The Government's principal contention was that "the Fourth Amendment Warrant Clause protects only interests traditionally identified with the home." We categorically rejected that contention, relying on the history and text of the amendment, the policy underlying the warrant requirement, and a line of cases spanning over a century of our jurisprudence. We also rejected the Government's alternative argument that the rationale of our automobile search cases demonstrated the reasonableness of permitting warrantless searches of luggage.

We concluded that neither of the justifications for the automobile exception could support a similar exception for luggage. We first held that the privacy interest in luggage is "substantially greater than in an automobile." Unlike automobiles and their contents, we reasoned, "[l]uggage contents are not open to public view, except as a condition to a border entry or common carrier travel; nor is luggage subject to regular inspections and official scrutiny on a continuing basis." Indeed, luggage is specifically intended to safeguard the privacy of personal effects, unlike an automobile, "whose primary function is transportation."

We then held that the mobility of luggage did not justify creating an additional exception to the Warrant Clause. Unlike an automobile, luggage can easily be seized and detained pending judicial approval of a search. Once the police have luggage "under their exclusive control, there [i]s not the slightest danger that the [luggage] or its contents could [be] removed before a valid search warrant could be obtained. * * * With the [luggage] safely immobilized, it [i]s unreasonable to undertake the additional and greater intrusion of a search without a warrant" (footnote omitted). * * *

[W]e recognized in *Ross* that *Chadwick* and *Sanders* had not created a special rule for container searches, but rather had merely applied the cardinal principle that warrantless searches are *per se* unreasonable unless justified by an exception to the general rule. *Ross* dealt with the scope of the automobile exception; *Chadwick* and *Sanders* were cases in which the exception simply did not apply.

In its opinion today, the Court recognizes that the police did not have probable cause to search respondent's vehicle and that a search of anything but the paper bag that respondent had carried from Daza's apartment and placed in the trunk of his car would have been unconstitutional. Moreover, as I read the opinion, the Court assumes that the police could not have made a warrantless inspection of the bag before it was placed in the car. Finally, the Court also does not question the fact that, under our prior cases, it would have been lawful for the police to seize the container and detain it (and respondent) until they obtained a search warrant. Thus, all of the relevant facts that governed our decisions in *Chadwick* and *Sanders* are present here whereas the relevant fact that justified the vehicle search in *Ross* is not present.

The Court does not attempt to identify any exigent circumstances that would justify its refusal to apply the general rule against warrantless searches. Instead, it advances these three arguments: First, the rules identified in the foregoing cases are confusing and anomalous. Second, the rules do not protect any significant interest in privacy. And, third, the rules impede effective law enforcement. None of these arguments withstands scrutiny. * * *

The Court summarizes the alleged "anomaly" created by the coexistence of *Ross, Chadwick,* and *Sanders* with the statement that "the more likely the police are to discover drugs in a container, the less authority they have to search it." This juxtaposition is only anomalous, however, if one accepts the flawed premise that the degree to which the police are likely to discover contraband is correlated with their authority to search *without a warrant.* Yet, even proof beyond a reasonable doubt will not justify a warrantless search that is not supported by one of the exceptions to the warrant requirement. And, even when the police have a warrant or an exception applies, once the police possess probable cause, the extent to which they are more or less certain of the contents of a container has no bearing on their authority to search it.

To the extent there was any "anomaly" in our prior jurisprudence, the Court has "cured" it at the expense of creating a more serious paradox. For, surely it is anomalous to prohibit a search of a briefcase while the owner is carrying it exposed on a public street yet to permit a search once the owner has placed the briefcase in the locked trunk of his car. One's privacy interest in one's luggage can certainly not be diminished by one's removing it from a public thoroughfare and placing it—out of sight—in a privately owned vehicle. Nor is the danger that evidence will escape increased if the luggage is in a car rather than on the street. In either location, if the police have probable cause, they are authorized to seize the luggage and to detain it until they obtain judicial approval for a search. Any line demarking an exception to the warrant requirement will appear blurred at the edges, but the Court has certainly erred if it believes that, by erasing one line and drawing another, it has drawn a clearer boundary.

The Court's statement that *Chadwick* and *Sanders* provide only "minimal protection to privacy" is also unpersuasive. Every citizen clearly has an interest in the privacy of the contents of his or her luggage, briefcase, handbag or any other container that conceals private papers and effects from public scrutiny.

That privacy interest has been recognized repeatedly in cases spanning more than a century.

Under the Court's holding today, the privacy interest that protects the contents of a suitcase or a briefcase from a warrantless search when it is in public view simply vanishes when its owner climbs into a taxicab. Unquestionably the rejection of the *Sanders* line of cases by today's decision will result in a significant loss of individual privacy.

To support its argument that today's holding works only a minimal intrusion on privacy, the Court suggests that "[i]f the police know that they may open a bag only if they are actually searching the entire car, they may search more extensively than they otherwise would in order to establish the general probable cause required by *Ross*." As I have already noted, this fear is unexplained and inexplicable. Neither evidence uncovered in the course of a search nor the scope of the search conducted can be used to provide *post hoc* justification for a search unsupported by probable cause at its inception.

The Court also justifies its claim that its holding inflicts only minor damage by suggesting that, under *New York v. Belton,* the police could have arrested respondent and searched his bag if respondent had placed the bag in the passenger compartment of the automobile instead of the trunk. In *Belton,* however, the justification for stopping the car and arresting the driver had nothing to do with the subsequent search, which was based on the potential danger to the arresting officer. The holding in *Belton* was supportable under a straightforward application of the automobile exception. I would not extend *Belton*'s holding to this case, in which the container—which was protected from a warrantless search before it was placed in the car—provided the only justification for the arrest. Even accepting *Belton*'s application to a case like this one, however, the Court's logic extends its holding to a container placed in the *trunk* of a vehicle, rather than in the passenger compartment. And the Court makes this extension without any justification whatsoever other than convenience to law enforcement.

The Court's suggestion that *Chadwick* and *Sanders* have created a significant burden on effective law enforcement is unsupported, inaccurate, and, in any event, an insufficient reason for creating a new exception to the warrant requirement.

Despite repeated claims that *Chadwick* and *Sanders* have "impeded effective law enforcement," the Court cites no authority for its contentions. * * *

Even if the warrant requirement does inconvenience the police to some extent, that fact does not distinguish this constitutional requirement from any other procedural protection secured by the Bill of Rights. It is merely a part of the price that our society must pay in order to preserve its freedom. Thus, in a unanimous opinion that relied on both *Johnson* and *Chadwick,* Justice Stewart wrote:

> "Moreover, the mere fact that law enforcement may be made more efficient can never by itself justify disregard of the Fourth Amendment. The investigation of crime would always be simplified if warrants were unnecessary. But the Fourth Amendment reflects the view of those who wrote the Bill of Rights that the privacy of a person's home and property may not be totally sacrificed in the name of maximum simplicity in enforcement of the criminal law." *Mincey v. Arizona,* 437 U.S. 385, 393 (1978).

It is too early to know how much freedom America has lost today. The magnitude of the loss is, however, not nearly as significant as the Court's willingness to inflict it without even a colorable basis for its rejection of prior law.

I respectfully dissent.

WYOMING v. HOUGHTON

526 U.S. 295, 119 S.Ct. 1297, 143 L.Ed.2d 408 (1999).

JUSTICE SCALIA delivered the opinion of the Court. * * *

In the early morning hours of July 23, 1995, a Wyoming Highway Patrol officer stopped an automobile for speeding and driving with a faulty brake light. There were three passengers in the front seat of the car: David Young (the driver), his girlfriend, and respondent. While questioning Young, the officer noticed a hypodermic syringe in Young's shirt pocket. He left the occupants under the supervision of two backup officers as he went to get gloves from his patrol car. Upon his return, he instructed Young to step out of the car and place the syringe on the hood. The officer then asked Young why he had a syringe; with refreshing candor, Young replied that he used it to take drugs.

At this point, the backup officers ordered the two female passengers out of the car and asked them for identification. Respondent falsely identified herself as "Sandra James" and stated that she did not have any identification. Meanwhile, in light of Young's admission, the officer searched the passenger compartment of the car for contraband. On the back seat, he found a purse, which respondent claimed as hers. He removed from the purse a wallet containing respondent's driver's license, identifying her properly as Sandra K. Houghton. When the officer asked her why she had lied about her name, she replied: "In case things went bad."

Continuing his search of the purse, the officer found a brown pouch and a black wallet-type container. Respondent denied that the former was hers, and claimed ignorance of how it came to be there; it was found to contain drug paraphernalia and a syringe with 60 ccs of methamphetamine. Respondent admitted ownership of the black container, which was also found to contain drug paraphernalia, and a syringe (which respondent acknowledged was hers) with 10 ccs of methamphetamine—an amount insufficient to support the felony conviction at issue in this case. The officer also found fresh needle-track marks on respondent's arms. He placed her under arrest.

The State of Wyoming charged respondent with felony possession of methamphetamine in a liquid amount greater than three-tenths of a gram. After a hearing, the trial court denied her motion to suppress all evidence obtained from the purse as the fruit of a violation of the Fourth and Fourteenth Amendments. The court held that the officer had probable cause to search the car for contraband, and, by extension, any containers therein that could hold such contraband. A jury convicted respondent as charged.

The Wyoming Supreme Court, by divided vote, reversed the conviction and * * * held that the search of respondent's purse violated the Fourth and Fourteenth Amendments because the officer "knew or should have known that the purse did not belong to the driver, but to one of the passengers," and because "here was no probable cause to search the passengers' personal effects and no reason to believe that contraband had been placed within the purse."

The Fourth Amendment protects "[t]he right of the people to be secure in their persons, houses, papers, and effects, against unreasonable searches and seizures." In determining whether a particular governmental action violates this provision, we inquire first whether the action was regarded as an unlawful search or seizure under the common law when the Amendment was framed. Where that inquiry yields no answer, we must evaluate the search or seizure under traditional standards of reasonableness by assessing, on the one hand, the degree to which it intrudes upon an individual's privacy and, on the other, the degree to which it is needed for the promotion of legitimate governmental interests.

It is uncontested in the present case that the police officers had probable cause to believe there were illegal drugs in the car. *Carroll v. United States*, 267 U.S. 132 (1925), similarly involved the warrantless search of a car that law enforcement officials had probable cause to believe contained contraband—in that case, bootleg liquor. The Court concluded that the Framers would have regarded such a search as reasonable in light of legislation enacted by Congress from 1789 through 1799—as well as subsequent legislation from the Founding era and beyond—that empowered customs officials to search any ship or vessel without a warrant if they had probable cause to believe that it contained goods subject to a duty. Thus, the Court held that "contraband goods concealed and illegally transported in an automobile or other vehicle may be searched for without a warrant" where probable cause exists.

We have furthermore read the historical evidence to show that the Framers would have regarded as reasonable (if there was probable cause) the warrantless search of containers within an automobile. In [*United States v.*] *Ross*, [456 U.S. 798 (1982)], we upheld as reasonable the warrantless search of a paper bag and leather pouch found in the trunk of the defendant's car by officers who had probable cause to believe that the trunk contained drugs. JUSTICE STEVENS, writing for the Court, observed:

> "It is noteworthy that the early legislation on which the Court relied in *Carroll* concerned the enforcement of laws imposing duties on imported merchandise. . . . Presumably such merchandise was shipped then in containers of various kinds, just as it is today. Since Congress had authorized warrantless searches of vessels and beasts for imported merchandise, it is inconceivable that it intended a customs officer to obtain a warrant for every package discovered during the search; certainly Congress intended customs officers to open shipping containers when necessary and not merely to examine the exterior of cartons or boxes in which smuggled goods might be concealed. During virtually the entire history of our country—whether contraband was transported in a horse-drawn carriage, a 1921 roadster, or a modern automobile—it has been assumed that a lawful search of a vehicle would include a search of any container that might conceal the object of the search."

Ross summarized its holding as follows: "If probable cause justifies the search of a lawfully stopped vehicle, it justifies the search of *every part of the vehicle and its contents* that may conceal the object of the search" (emphasis added). And our later cases describing *Ross* have characterized it as applying broadly to all containers within a car, without qualification as to ownership. * * *

To be sure, there was no passenger in *Ross*, and it was not claimed that the package in the trunk belonged to anyone other than the driver. Even so, if the rule of law that *Ross* announced were limited to contents belonging to the driver, or contents other than those belonging to passengers, one would have expected that substantial limitation to be expressed. And, more importantly, one would have expected that limitation to be apparent in the historical evidence that formed the basis for *Ross*'s holding. In fact, however, nothing in the statutes *Ross* relied upon, or in the practice under those statutes, would except from authorized warrantless search packages belonging to passengers on the suspect ship, horse-drawn carriage, or automobile.

Finally, we must observe that the analytical principle underlying the rule announced in *Ross* is fully consistent—as respondent's proposal is not—with the balance of our Fourth Amendment jurisprudence. *Ross* concluded from the historical evidence that the permissible scope of a warrantless car search "is defined by the object of the search and the places in which there is probable cause to believe that it may be found." The same principle is reflected in an earlier case involving the constitutionality of a search warrant directed at premises belonging to one who is not suspected of any crime: "The critical element in a reasonable search is not that the owner of the property is suspected of crime but that there is reasonable cause to believe that the specific 'things' to be searched for and seized are located on the property to which entry is sought." *Zurcher v. Stanford Daily*, 436 U.S. 547 (1978). * * *

In sum, neither *Ross* itself nor the historical evidence it relied upon admits of a distinction among packages or containers based on ownership. When there is probable cause to search for contraband in a car, it is reasonable for police officers—like customs officials in the Founding era—to examine packages and containers without a showing of individualized probable cause for each one. A passenger's personal belongings, just like the driver's belongings or containers attached to the car like a glove compartment, are "in" the car, and the officer has probable cause to search for contraband in the car.

Even if the historical evidence, as described by *Ross*, were thought to be equivocal, we would find that the balancing of the relative interests weighs decidedly in favor of allowing searches of a passenger's belongings. Passengers, no less than drivers, possess a reduced expectation of privacy with regard to the property that they transport in cars, which "trave[l] public thoroughfares," "seldom serv[e] as ... the repository of personal effects," are subjected to police stop and examination to enforce "pervasive" governmental controls "[a]s an everyday occurrence," and, finally, are exposed to traffic accidents that may render all their contents open to public scrutiny.

In this regard—the degree of intrusiveness upon personal privacy and indeed even personal dignity—the two cases the Wyoming Supreme Court found dispositive differ substantially from the package search at issue here. *United States v. Di Re*, 332 U.S. 581 (1948), held that probable cause to search a car did not justify a body search of a passenger. And *Ybarra v. Illinois*, 444 U.S. 85 (1979), held that a search warrant for a tavern and its bartender did not permit body searches of all the bar's patrons. These cases turned on the unique, significantly heightened protection afforded against searches of one's person. "Even a limited search of the outer clothing ... constitutes a severe, though brief, intrusion upon cherished personal security, and it must surely be an annoying, frightening, and perhaps humiliating experience." *Terry v. Ohio*, 392 U.S. 1 (1968). Such traumatic consequences are not to be expected when the police examine an item of personal property found in a car.[1]

1. The dissent begins its analysis with an assertion that this case is governed by our decision in *United States v. Di Re*, which held, as the dissent describes it, that the automobile exception to the warrant requirement did not justify "searches of the passenger's pockets and the space between his shirt and underwear." It attributes that holding to "the settled distinction between drivers and passengers," rather than to a distinction between search of the person and search of property, which the dissent claims is "newly minted" by

today's opinion—a "new rule that is based on a distinction between property contained in clothing worn by a passenger and property contained in a passenger's briefcase or purse."

In its peroration, however, the dissent quotes extensively from Justice Jackson's opinion in *Di Re*, which makes it very clear that it is precisely this distinction between search of the person and search of property that the case relied upon: "The Government says it would not contend that, armed "with a search warrant for a residence only, it could search all

Whereas the passenger's privacy expectations are, as we have described, considerably diminished, the governmental interests at stake are substantial. Effective law enforcement would be appreciably impaired without the ability to search a passenger's personal belongings when there is reason to believe contraband or evidence of criminal wrongdoing is hidden in the car. As in all car-search cases, the "ready mobility" of an automobile creates a risk that the evidence or contraband will be permanently lost while a warrant is obtained. In addition, a car passenger—unlike the unwitting tavern patron in Ybarra——will often be engaged in a common enterprise with the driver, and have the same interest in concealing the fruits or the evidence of their wrongdoing. A criminal might be able to hide contraband in a passenger's belongings as readily as in other containers in the car—perhaps even surreptitiously, without the passenger's knowledge or permission. (This last possibility provided the basis for respondent's defense at trial; she testified that most of the seized contraband must have been placed in her purse by her traveling companions at one or another of various times, including the time she was "half asleep" in the car.)

To be sure, these factors favoring a search will not always be present, but the balancing of interests must be conducted with an eye to the generality of cases. To require that the investigating officer have positive reason to believe that the passenger and driver were engaged in a common enterprise, or positive reason to believe that the driver had time and occasion to conceal the item in the passenger's belongings, surreptitiously or with friendly permission, is to impose requirements so seldom met that a "passenger's property" rule would dramatically reduce the ability to find and seize contraband and evidence of crime. Of course these requirements would not attach (under the Wyoming Supreme Court's rule) until the police officer knows or has reason to know that the container belongs to a passenger. But once a "passenger's property" exception to car searches became widely known, one would expect passenger-confederates to claim everything as their own. And one would anticipate a bog of litigation—in the form of both civil lawsuits and motions to suppress in criminal trials—involving such questions as whether the officer should have believed a passenger's claim of ownership, whether he should have inferred ownership from various objective factors, whether he had probable cause to believe that the passenger was a confederate, or to believe that the driver might have introduced the contraband into the package with or without the passenger's knowledge.[2] When balancing the competing

persons found in it. But an occupant of a house could be used to conceal this contraband on his person quite as readily as can an occupant of a car." Does the dissent really believe that Justice Jackson was saying that a house-search could not inspect property belonging to persons found in the house—say a large standing safe or violin case belonging to the owner's visiting godfather? Of course that is not what Justice Jackson meant at all. He was referring precisely to that "distinction between property contained in clothing worn by a passenger and property contained in a passenger's briefcase or purse" that he disparages. This distinction between searches of the person and searches of property is assuredly not "newly minted." And if the dissent thinks "pockets" and "clothing" do not count as part of the person, it must believe that the only searches of the person are strip searches.

2. The dissent is "confident in a police officer's ability to apply a rule requiring a warrant or individualized probable cause to search belongings that are ... obviously owned by and in the custody of a passenger." If this is the dissent's strange criterion for warrant protection ("obviously owned by and in the custody of") its preceding paean to the importance of preserving passengers' privacy rings a little hollow on rehearing. Should it not be enough if the passenger says he owns the briefcase, and the officer has no concrete reason to believe otherwise? Or would the dissent consider that an example of "obvious" ownership? On reflection, it seems not at all obvious precisely what constitutes obviousness—and so even the dissent's on-the-cheap protection of passengers' privacy interest in their property turns out to be unclear, and hence unadministrable. But maybe the dissent does not mean to propose an obviously-owned-by-and-in-the-custody-of test after all, since a few sentences later it endorses, simpliciter, "a rule requiring a warrant or individualized probable cause to search passen-

interests, our determinations of "reasonableness" under the Fourth Amendment must take account of these practical realities. We think they militate in favor of the needs of law enforcement, and against a personal-privacy interest that is ordinarily weak.

Finally, if we were to invent an exception from the historical practice that *Ross* accurately described and summarized, it is perplexing why that exception should protect only property belonging to a passenger, rather than (what seems much more logical) property belonging to anyone other than the driver. Surely Houghton's privacy would have been invaded to the same degree whether she was present or absent when her purse was searched. And surely her presence in the car with the driver provided more, rather than less, reason to believe that the two were in league. It may ordinarily be easier to identify the property as belonging to someone other than the driver when the purported owner is present to identify it—but in the many cases (like *Ross* itself) where the car is seized, that identification may occur later, at the station-house; and even at the site of the stop one can readily imagine a package clearly marked with the owner's name and phone number, by which the officer can confirm the driver's denial of ownership. The sensible rule (and the one supported by history and caselaw) is that such a package may be searched, whether or not its owner is present as a passenger or otherwise, because it may contain the contraband that the officer has reason to believe is in the car.

We hold that police officers with probable cause to search a car may inspect passengers' belongings found in the car that are capable of concealing the object of the search. The judgment of the Wyoming Supreme Court is reversed.

It is so ordered.

Justice Breyer, concurring.

I join the Court's opinion with the understanding that history is meant to inform, but not automatically to determine, the answer to a Fourth Amendment question. I also agree with the Court that when a police officer has probable cause to search a car, say, for drugs, it is reasonable for that officer also to search containers within the car. If the police must establish a container's ownership prior to the search of that container (whenever, for example, a passenger says "that's mine"), the resulting uncertainty will destroy the workability of the bright-line rule set forth in *United States v. Ross*. At the same time, police officers with probable cause to search a car for drugs would often have probable cause to search containers regardless. Hence a bright-line rule will authorize only a limited number of searches that the law would not otherwise justify.

At the same time, I would point out certain limitations upon the scope of the bright-line rule that the Court describes. Obviously, the rule applies only to automobile searches. Equally obviously, the rule applies only to containers found within automobiles. And it does not extend to the search of a person found in that automobile. As the Court notes, and as *United States v. Di Re*, relied on heavily by Justice STEVENS' dissent, makes clear, the search of a person, including even " 'a limited search of the outer clothing,' " is a very different matter in respect to which the law provides "significantly heightened protection."

Less obviously, but in my view also important, is the fact that the container here at issue, a woman's purse, was found at a considerable distance from its owner, who did not claim ownership until the officer discovered her identification while looking through it. Purses are special containers. They are repositories of especially personal items that people generally like to keep with them at all times.

ger belongings." For the reasons described in   text, that will not work.

So I am tempted to say that a search of a purse involves an intrusion so similar to a search of one's person that the same rule should govern both. However, given this Court's prior cases, I cannot argue that the fact that the container was a purse automatically makes a legal difference, for the Court has warned against trying to make that kind of distinction. But I can say that it would matter if a woman's purse, like a man's billfold, were attached to her person. It might then amount to a kind of "outer clothing" which under the Court's cases would properly receive increased protection. In this case, the purse was separate from the person, and no one has claimed that, under those circumstances, the type of container makes a difference. For that reason, I join the Court's opinion.

JUSTICE STEVENS, with whom JUSTICE SOUTER and JUSTICE GINSBURG join, dissenting. * * *

In all of our prior cases applying the automobile exception to the Fourth Amendment's warrant requirement, either the defendant was the operator of the vehicle and in custody of the object of the search, or no question was raised as to the defendant's ownership or custody. In the only automobile case confronting the search of a passenger defendant—United States v. Di Re—the Court held that the exception to the warrant requirement did not apply. In *Di Re*, as here, the information prompting the search directly implicated the driver, not the passenger. Today, instead of adhering to the settled distinction between drivers and passengers, the Court fashions a new rule that is based on a distinction between property contained in clothing worn by a passenger and property contained in a passenger's briefcase or purse. In cases on both sides of the Court's newly minted test, the property is in a "container" (whether a pocket or a pouch) located in the vehicle. Moreover, unlike the Court, I think it quite plain that the search of a passenger's purse or briefcase involves an intrusion on privacy that may be just as serious as was the intrusion in *Di Re*.

Even apart from *Di Re*, the Court's rights-restrictive approach is not dictated by precedent. For example, in *United States v. Ross* we were concerned with the interest of the driver in the integrity of "his automobile," and we categorically rejected the notion that the scope of a warrantless search of a vehicle might be "defined by the nature of the container in which the contraband is secreted." "Rather, it is defined by the object of the search and the places in which there is probable cause to believe that it may be found." We thus disapproved of a possible container-based distinction between a man's pocket and a woman's pocketbook. Ironically, while we concluded in *Ross* that "[p]robable cause to believe that a container placed in the trunk of a taxi contains contraband or evidence does not justify a search of the entire cab," the rule the Court fashions would apparently permit a warrantless search of a passenger's briefcase if there is probable cause to believe the taxidriver had a syringe somewhere in his vehicle.

Nor am I persuaded that the mere spatial association between a passenger and a driver provides an acceptable basis for presuming that they are partners in crime or for ignoring privacy interests in a purse. Whether or not the Fourth Amendment required a warrant to search Houghton's purse, at the very least the trooper in this case had to have probable cause to believe that her purse contained contraband. The Wyoming Supreme Court concluded that he did not.

Finally, in my view, the State's legitimate interest in effective law enforcement does not outweigh the privacy concerns at issue. I am as confident in a police officer's ability to apply a rule requiring a warrant or individualized probable cause to search belongings that are—as in this case—obviously owned by and in the custody of a passenger as is the Court in a "passenger-confederate[']s" ability to circumvent the rule. Certainly the ostensible clarity of the Court's rule is attractive. But that virtue is insufficient justification for its adoption. Moreover, a rule requiring a warrant or individualized probable cause to search passenger belongings is every bit as simple as the Court's rule; it simply protects more privacy.

I would decide this case in accord with what we have said about passengers and privacy, rather than what we might have said in cases where the issue was not squarely presented. What Justice Jackson wrote for the Court fifty years ago is just as sound today:

> "The Government says it would not contend that, armed with a search warrant for a residence only, it could search all persons found in it. But an occupant of a house could be used to conceal this contraband on his person quite as readily as can an occupant of a car. Necessity, an argument advanced in support of this search, would seem as strong a reason for searching guests of a house for which a search warrant had issued as for search of guests in a car for which none had been issued. By a parity of reasoning with that on which the Government disclaims the right to search occupants of a house, we suppose the Government would not contend that if it had a valid search warrant for the car only it could search the occupants as an incident to its execution. How then could we say that the right to search a car without a warrant confers greater latitude to search occupants than a search by warrant would permit?

> "We see no ground for expanding the ruling in the *Carroll* case to justify this arrest and search as incident to the search of a car. We are not convinced that a person, by mere presence in a suspected car, loses immunities from search of his person to which he would otherwise be entitled." *Di Re.*[4]

Instead of applying ordinary Fourth Amendment principles to this case, the majority extends the automobile warrant exception to allow searches of passenger belongings based on the driver's misconduct. Thankfully, the Court's automobile-centered analysis limits the scope of its holding. But it does not justify the outcome in this case.

I respectfully dissent.

COLORADO v. BERTINE

479 U.S. 367, 107 S.Ct. 738, 93 L.Ed.2d 739 (1987).

CHIEF JUSTICE REHNQUIST delivered the opinion of the Court.

[A Boulder, Colorado, police officer arrested respondent for driving his van while under the influence of alcohol. After respondent was taken into custody and before a tow truck arrived to take the van to an impoundment lot, another officer, acting in accordance with local police procedures, inventoried the van's contents, opening a closed backpack in which he found various containers holding controlled substances, cocaine paraphernalia, and a large amount of cash. Prior to his trial on charges including drug offenses, the state trial court granted respondent's motion to suppress the evidence found during the inventory search. Although the court determined that the search did not violate respondent's rights

4. In response to this dissent the Court has crafted an imaginative footnote suggesting that the *Di Re* decision rested, not on Di Re's status as a mere occupant of the vehicle and the importance of individualized suspicion, but rather on the intrusive character of the search. That the search of a safe or violin case would be less intrusive than a strip search does not, however, persuade me that the *Di Re* case would have been decided differently if Di Re had been a woman and the gas coupons had been found in her purse. * * *

under the Fourth Amendment of the Federal Constitution, it held that the search violated the Colorado Constitution. The Colorado Supreme Court affirmed, but premised its ruling on the Federal Constitution.]

We granted certiorari to consider the important and recurring question of federal law decided by the Colorado Supreme Court. As that court recognized, inventory searches are now a well-defined exception to the warrant requirement of the Fourth Amendment. The policies behind the warrant requirement are not implicated in an inventory search, nor is the related concept of probable cause:

> "The standard of probable cause is peculiarly related to criminal investigations, not routine, noncriminal procedures * * *. The probable-cause approach is unhelpful when analysis centers upon the reasonableness of routine administrative caretaking functions, particularly when no claim is made that the protective procedures are a subterfuge for criminal investigations."

For these reasons, the Colorado Supreme Court's reliance on *Arkansas v. Sanders, supra,* and *United States v. Chadwick, supra,* was incorrect. Both of these cases concerned searches solely for the purpose of investigating criminal conduct, with the validity of the searches therefore dependent on the application of the probable cause and warrant requirements of the Fourth Amendment.

By contrast, an inventory search may be "reasonable" under the Fourth Amendment even though it is not conducted pursuant to warrant based upon probable cause. In [*South Dakota v.*] *Opperman* [428 U.S. 364 (1976),] this Court assessed the reasonableness of an inventory search of the glove compartment in an abandoned automobile impounded by the police. We found that inventory procedures serve to protect an owner's property while it is in the custody of the police, to insure against claims of lost, stolen, or vandalized property, and to guard the police from danger. In light of these strong governmental interests and the diminished expectation of privacy in an automobile, we upheld the search. In reaching this decision, we observed that our cases accorded deference to police caretaking procedures designed to secure and protect vehicles and their contents within police custody.

In our more recent decision, [*Illinois v.*] *Lafayette* [462 U.S. 640 (1983),] a police officer conducted an inventory search of the contents of a shoulder bag in the possession of an individual being taken into custody. In deciding whether this search was reasonable, we recognized that the search served legitimate governmental interests similar to those identified in *Opperman.* We determined that those interests outweighed the individual's Fourth Amendment interests and upheld the search.

In the present case, as in *Opperman* and *Lafayette,* there was no showing that the police, who were following standardized procedures, acted in bad faith or for the sole purpose of investigation. In addition, the governmental interests justifying the inventory searches in *Opperman* and *Lafayette* are nearly the same as those which obtain here. In each case, the police were potentially responsible for the property taken into their custody. By securing the property, the police protected the property from unauthorized interference. Knowledge of the precise nature of the property helped guard against claims of theft, vandalism, or negligence. Such knowledge also helped to avert any danger to police or others that may have been posed by the property.[5]

---

5. In arguing that the latter two interests are not implicated here, the dissent overlooks the testimony of the back-up officer who conducted the inventory of Bertine's van. According to the officer, the vehicle inventory procedures of the Boulder Police Department are

The Supreme Court of Colorado opined that *Lafayette* was not controlling here because there was no danger of introducing contraband or weapons into a jail facility. Our opinion in *Lafayette,* however, did not suggest that the station-house setting of the inventory search was critical to our holding in that case. Both in the present case and in *Lafayette,* the common governmental interests described above were served by the inventory searches.

The Supreme Court of Colorado also expressed the view that the search in this case was unreasonable because Bertine's van was towed to a secure, lighted facility and because Bertine himself could have been offered the opportunity to make other arrangements for the safekeeping of his property. But the security of the storage facility does not completely eliminate the need for inventorying; the police may still wish to protect themselves or the owners of the lot against false claims of theft or dangerous instrumentalities. And while giving Bertine an opportunity to make alternate arrangements would undoubtedly have been possible, we said in *Lafayette:*

> "[t]he real question is not what 'could have been achieved,' but whether the Fourth Amendment *requires* such steps * * * The reasonableness of any particular governmental activity does not necessarily or invariably turn on the existence of alternative 'less intrusive' means."

We conclude that here, as in *Lafayette,* reasonable police regulations relating to inventory procedures administered in good faith satisfy the Fourth Amendment, even though courts might as a matter of hindsight be able to devise equally reasonable rules requiring a different procedure.[6]

The Supreme Court of Colorado also thought it necessary to require that police, before inventorying a container, weigh the strength of the individual's privacy interest in the container against the possibility that the container might serve as a repository for dangerous or valuable items. We think that such a requirement is contrary to our decisions in *Opperman* and *Lafayette:*

> "Even if less intrusive means existed of protecting some particular types of property, it would be unreasonable to expect police officers in the everyday course of business to make fine and subtle distinctions in deciding which containers or items may be searched and which must be sealed as a unit." *Lafayette,* supra. * * *

Bertine finally argues that the inventory search of his van was unconstitutional because departmental regulations gave the police officers discretion to choose between impounding his van and parking and locking it in a public parking place. The Supreme Court of Colorado did not rely on this argument in reaching its conclusion, and we reject it. Nothing in *Opperman* or *Lafayette* prohibits the exercise of police discretion so long as that discretion is exercised according to standard criteria and on the basis of something other than suspicion of evidence of criminal activity. Here, the discretion afforded the Boulder police was exercised in light of standardized criteria, related to the feasibility and appropriateness of parking and locking a vehicle rather than impounding it. There was no showing that the police chose to impound Bertine's van in order to investigate suspected

designed for the "[p]rotection of the police department" in the event that an individual later claims that "there was something of value taken from within the vehicle." The officer added that inventories are also conducted in order to check "[f]or any dangerous items such as explosives [or] weapons." The officer testified that he had found such items in vehicles.

6. We emphasize that, in this case, the trial court found that the police department's procedures mandated the opening of closed containers and the listing of their contents. Our decisions have always adhered to the requirement that inventories be conducted according to standardized criteria.

criminal activity.   * * * The judgment of the Supreme Court of Colorado is therefore reversed.

JUSTICE BLACKMUN, with whom JUSTICE POWELL and JUSTICE O'CONNOR join, concurring.

* * * I join the Court's opinion, but write separately to underscore the importance of having such inventories conducted only pursuant to standardized police procedures * * * that mandate the opening of such containers in every impounded vehicle. * * * a

JUSTICE MARSHALL, with whom JUSTICE BRENNAN joins, dissenting.

* * * [T]he record indicates that *no* standardized criteria limit a Boulder police officer's discretion. According to a departmental directive, after placing a driver under arrest, an officer has three options for disposing of the vehicle. First, he can allow a third party to take custody. Second, the officer or the driver (depending on the nature of the arrest) may take the car to the nearest public parking facility, lock it, and take the keys. Finally, the officer can do what was done in this case: impound the vehicle, and search and inventory its contents, including closed containers.

Under the first option, the police have no occasion to search the automobile. Under the "park and lock" option, "[c]losed containers that give no indication of containing either valuables or a weapon *may not be opened and the contents searched* (i.e., inventoried)." (emphasis added). Only if the police choose the third option are they entitled to search closed containers in the vehicle. Where the vehicle is not itself evidence of a crime, as in this case, the police apparently have totally unbridled discretion as to which procedure to use. Consistent with this conclusion, Officer Reichenbach testified that such decisions were left to the discretion of the officer on the scene.

Once a Boulder police officer has made this initial completely discretionary decision to impound a vehicle, he is given little guidance as to which areas to search and what sort of items to inventory. The arresting officer, Officer Toporek, testified at the suppression hearing as to what items would be inventoried: "That would I think be very individualistic as far as what an officer may or may not go into. I think whatever arouses his suspicious [*sic*] as far as what may be contained in any type of article in the car." * * *

Inventory searches are not subject to the warrant requirement because they are conducted by the government as part of "community caretaking" function,

---

a. In *Florida v. Wells,* 495 U.S. 1 (1990), where all members of the Court agreed that the inventory of a locked suitcase found in an impounded vehicle was unlawful under *Bertine* because "the Florida Highway Patrol had no policy whatever with respect to the opening of closed containers encountered during an inventory search," five members of the Court went on to say that the state court erred in saying *Bertine* requires a policy either mandating or barring inventory of all containers: "A police officer may be allowed sufficient latitude to determine whether a particular container should or should not be opened in light of the nature of the search and characteristics of the container itself. Thus, while policies of opening all containers or opening no containers are unquestionably permissible, it would be equally permissible, for example, to allow the opening of closed containers whose contents officers determine they are unable to ascertain from examining the containers' exteriors."

Brennan and Marshall, JJ., concurring, disagreed with that assertion, which they characterized as "pure dictum given the disposition of the case." Blackmun, J. concurring, agreed that the Fourth Amendment did not impose an "all or nothing" requirement, so that a state "probably could adopt a policy which requires the opening of all containers that are not locked, or a policy which requires the opening of all containers over or under a certain size," but objected it was "an entirely different matter * * * to say, as this majority does, that an individual policeman may be afforded discretion in conducting an inventory search." Stevens, J., concurring separately, agreed with Blackmun.

"totally divorced from the detection, investigation, or acquisition of evidence relating to the violation of a criminal statute." Standardized procedures are necessary to ensure that this narrow exception is not improperly used to justify, after the fact, a warrantless investigative foray. Accordingly, to invalidate a search that is conducted without established procedures, it is not necessary to establish that the police actually acted in bad faith, or that the inventory was in fact a "pretext." By allowing the police unfettered discretion, Boulder's discretionary scheme is unreasonable because of the " 'grave danger' of abuse of discretion."

In *South Dakota v. Opperman*, and *Illinois v. Lafayette*, both of which involved inventories conducted pursuant to standardized procedures, we balanced the individual's expectation of privacy against the government's interests to determine whether the search was reasonable. Even if the search in this case did constitute a legitimate inventory, it would nonetheless be unreasonable under this analysis. * * *

Not only are the government's interests weaker here than in *Opperman* and *Lafayette*, but respondent's privacy interest is greater. In upholding the search in *Opperman*, the Court emphasized the fact that the defendant had a diminished expectation of privacy in his automobile, due to "pervasive and continuing governmental regulation and controls, including periodic inspection and licensing requirements" and "the obviously public nature of automobile travel." Similarly, in *Lafayette*, the Court emphasized the fact that the defendant was in custody at the time the inventory took place.

Here the Court completely ignores respondent's expectation of privacy in his backpack. Whatever his expectation of privacy in his automobile generally, our prior decisions clearly establish that he retained a reasonable expectation of privacy in the backpack and its contents. See *Arkansas v. Sanders* ("[L]uggage is a common repository for one's personal effects, and therefore is inevitably associated with the expectation of privacy"); *United States v. Chadwick*, ("[A] person's expectations of privacy in personal luggage are substantially greater than in an automobile"). Indeed, the Boulder police officer who conducted the inventory acknowledged that backpacks commonly serve as repositories for personal effects. Thus, even if the governmental interests in this case were the same as those in *Opperman*, they would nonetheless be outweighed by respondent's comparatively greater expectation of privacy in his luggage. * * *

SECTION 8. LESSER INTRUSIONS: STOP AND FRISK

Under the monolithic approach to the Fourth Amendment which once obtained, the assumption was that every form of activity which constituted either a search or a seizure had to be grounded in the same quantum of evidence suggested by the Amendment's "probable cause" requirement. But this changed when the Supreme Court recognized in *Camara v. Municipal Court,* 387 U.S. 523 (1967), that at least some Fourth Amendment activity should be judged under a balancing test, that is, by "balancing the need to search against the invasion which the search entails." Doubtless the most significant application of this new balancing test came a year later when, in *Terry v. Ohio*, the first case in this section, the Court applied it to the common police practice of detaining suspicious persons briefly on the street for purposes of investigation. The next two cases, *Florida v. J. L.* and *Illinois v. Wardlow*, are two recent efforts by the Court to elaborate what constitutes sufficient grounds for a *Terry* stop.

If there is to be a discrete form of police activity, typically called stop-and-frisk, which is subject to a lesser evidentiary standard, then it is necessary to distinguish such activity from full-fledged arrests requiring probable cause on the one hand and no-seizure police encounters requiring no justification whatsoever on the other. The problems attendant the drawing of such lines are seen in *Florida v. Royer* and *Florida v. Bostick*. The final case, *United States v. Place*, indicates one way in which the *Terry* rule has been expanded: by extension of the authority to seize on reasonable suspicion to personal effects such as luggage.

TERRY v. OHIO

392 U.S. 1, 88 S.Ct. 1868, 20 L.Ed.2d 889 (1968).

Chief Justice Warren delivered the opinion of the court.

[Officer McFadden, a Cleveland plainclothes detective, became suspicious of two men standing on a street corner in the downtown area at about 2:30 in the afternoon. One of the suspects walked up the street, peered into a store, walked on, started back, looked into the same store, and then joined and conferred with his companion. The other suspect repeated this ritual, and between them the two men went through this performance about a dozen times. They also talked with a third man, and then followed him up the street about ten minutes after his departure. The officer, thinking that the suspects were "casing" a stickup and might be armed, followed and confronted the three men as they were again conversing. He identified himself and asked the suspects for their names. The men only mumbled something, and the officer spun Terry around and patted his breast pocket. He felt a pistol, which he removed. A frisk of Terry's companion also uncovered a pistol; a frisk of the third man did not disclose that he was armed, and he was not searched further. Terry was charged with carrying a concealed weapon, and he moved to suppress the weapon as evidence. The motion was denied by the trial judge, who upheld the officer's actions on a stop-and-frisk theory. The Ohio court of appeals affirmed, and the state supreme court dismissed Terry's appeal.]

* * * The question is whether in all the circumstances of this on-the-street encounter, [Terry's] right to personal security was violated by an unreasonable search and seizure.

We would be less than candid if we did not acknowledge that this question thrusts to the fore difficult and troublesome issues regarding a sensitive area of police activity—issues which have never before been squarely presented to this Court. * * *

On the one hand, it is frequently argued that in dealing with the rapidly unfolding and often dangerous situations on city streets the police are in need of an escalating set of flexible responses, graduated in relation to the amount of information they possess. For this purpose it is urged that distinctions should be made between a "stop" and an "arrest" (or a "seizure" of a person), and between a "frisk" and a "search." Thus, it is argued, the police should be allowed to "stop" a person and detain him briefly for questioning upon suspicion that he may be connected with criminal activity. Upon suspicion that the person may be armed, the police should have the power to "frisk" him for weapons. If the "stop" and the "frisk" give rise to probable cause to believe that the suspect has committed a crime, then the police should be empowered to make a formal "arrest," and a full incident "search" of the person. This scheme is justified in part upon the notion that a "stop" and a "frisk" amount to a mere "minor inconvenience and petty indignity," which can properly be imposed upon the citizen in the interest of effective law enforcement on the basis of a police officer's suspicion.

On the other side the argument is made that the authority of the police must be strictly circumscribed by the law of arrest and search as it has developed to date in the traditional jurisprudence of the Fourth Amendment. It is contended with some force that there is not—and cannot be—a variety of police activity which does not depend solely upon the voluntary cooperation of the citizen and yet which stops short of an arrest based upon probable cause to make such an arrest. The heart of the Fourth Amendment, the argument runs, is a severe requirement of specific justification for any intrusion upon protected personal security, coupled with a highly developed system of judicial controls to enforce upon the agents of the State the commands of the Constitution. * * *

* * * The State has characterized the issue here as "the right of a police officer * * * to make an on-the-street stop, interrogate and pat down for weapons (known in the street vernacular as 'stop and frisk')." But this is only partly accurate. For the issue is not the abstract propriety of the police conduct, but the admissibility against petitioner of the evidence uncovered by the search and seizure. * * * [I]n our system evidentiary rulings provide the context in which the judicial process of inclusion and exclusion approves some conduct as comporting with constitutional guarantees and disapproves other actions by state agents. A ruling admitting evidence in a criminal trial, we recognize, has the necessary effect of legitimizing the conduct which produced the evidence, while an application of the exclusionary rule withholds the constitutional imprimatur.

The exclusionary rule has its limitations, however, as a tool of judicial control. It cannot properly be invoked to exclude the products of legitimate police investigative techniques on the ground that much conduct which is closely similar involves unwarranted intrusions upon constitutional protections. Moreover, in some contexts the rule is ineffective as a deterrent. Street encounters between citizens and police officers are incredibly rich in diversity. They range from wholly friendly exchanges of pleasantries or mutually useful information to hostile confrontations of armed men involving arrests, or injuries, or loss of life. Moreover, hostile confrontations are not all of a piece. Some of them begin in a friendly enough manner, only to take a different turn upon the injection of some unexpected element into the conversation. Encounters are initiated by the police for a wide variety of purposes, some of which are wholly unrelated to a desire to prosecute for crime. Doubtless some police "field interrogation" conduct violates the Fourth Amendment. But a stern refusal by this Court to condone such activity does not necessarily render it responsive to the exclusionary rule. Regardless of how effective the rule may be where obtaining convictions is an important objective of the police, it is powerless to deter invasions of constitutionally guaranteed rights where the police either have no interest in prosecuting or are willing to forego successful prosecution in the interest of serving some other goal.

Proper adjudication of cases in which the exclusionary rule is invoked demands a constant awareness of these limitations. The wholesale harassment by certain elements of the police community, of which minority groups, particularly Negroes, frequently complain, will not be stopped by the exclusion of any evidence from any criminal trial. Yet a rigid and unthinking application of the exclusionary rule, in futile protest against practices which it can never be used effectively to control, may exact a high toll in human injury and frustration of efforts to prevent crime. No judicial opinion can comprehend the protean variety of the street encounter, and we can only judge the facts of the case before us. * * *

[W]e turn our attention to the quite narrow question posed by the facts before us: whether it is always unreasonable for a policeman to seize a person and subject him to a limited search for weapons unless there is probable cause for an arrest.

* * * It is quite plain that the Fourth Amendment governs "seizures" of the person which do not eventuate in a trip to the station house and prosecution for crime—"arrests" in traditional terminology. It must be recognized that whenever a police officer accosts an individual and restrains his freedom to walk away, he has "seized" that person. And it is nothing less than sheer torture of the English language to suggest that a careful exploration of the outer surfaces of a person's clothing all over his or her body in an attempt to find weapons is not a "search." Moreover, it is simply fantastic to urge that such a procedure performed in public by a policeman while the citizen stands helpless, perhaps facing a wall with his hands raised, is a "petty indignity." [13] It is a serious intrusion upon the sanctity of the person, which may inflict great indignity and arouse strong resentment, and it is not to be undertaken lightly.

* * * We therefore reject the notions that the Fourth Amendment does not come into play at all as a limitation upon police conduct if the officers stop short of something called a "technical arrest" or a "full-blown search."

In this case there can be no question, then, that Officer McFadden "seized" petitioner and subjected him to a "search" when he took hold of him and patted down the outer surfaces of his clothing. We must decide whether at that point it was reasonable for Officer McFadden to have interfered with petitioner's personal security as he did.[16] And in determining whether the seizure and search were "unreasonable" our inquiry is a dual one—whether the officer's action was justified at its inception, and whether it was reasonably related in scope to the circumstances which justified the interference in the first place.

If this case involved police conduct subject to the Warrant Clause of the Fourth Amendment, we would have to ascertain whether "probable cause" existed to justify the search and seizure which took place. However, that is not the case. We do not retreat from our holdings that the police must, whenever practicable, obtain advance judicial approval of searches and seizures through the warrant procedure, * * * or that in most instances failure to comply with the warrant requirement can only be excused by exigent circumstances. * * * But we deal here with an entire rubric of police conduct—necessarily swift action predicated upon the on-the-spot observations of the officer on the beat—which historically has not been, and as a practical matter could not be, subjected to the warrant procedure. Instead, the conduct involved in this case must be tested by the Fourth Amendment's general proscription against unreasonable searches and seizures.

13. Consider the following apt description:

"[T]he officer must feel with sensitive fingers every portion of the prisoner's body. A thorough search must be made of the prisoner's arms and armpits, waistline and back, the groin and area about the testicles, and entire surface of the legs down to the feet." Priar & Martin, *Searching and Disarming Criminals,* 45 J.Crim.L.C. & P.S. 481 (1954).

16. We thus decide nothing today concerning the constitutional propriety of an investigative "seizure" upon less than probable cause for purposes of "detention" and/or interrogation. Obviously, not all personal intercourse between policemen and citizens involves "seizures" of persons. Only when the officer, by means of physical force or show of authority, has in some way restrained the liberty of a citizen may we conclude that a "seizure" has occurred. We cannot tell with any certainty upon this record whether any such "seizure" took place here prior to Officer McFadden's initiation of physical contact for purposes of searching Terry for weapons, and we thus may assume that up to that point no intrusion upon constitutionally protected rights had occurred.

Nonetheless, the notions which underlie both the warrant procedure and the requirement of probable cause remain fully relevant in this context. In order to assess the reasonableness of Officer McFadden's conduct as a general proposition, it is necessary "first to focus upon the governmental interest which allegedly justifies official intrusion upon the constitutionally protected interests of the private citizen," for there is "no ready test for determining reasonableness other than by balancing the need to search [or seize] against the invasion which the search [or seizure] entails." And in justifying the particular intrusion the police officer must be able to point to specific and articulable facts which, taken together with rational inferences from those facts, reasonably warrant that intrusion. The scheme of the Fourth Amendment becomes meaningful only when it is assured that at some point the conduct of those charged with enforcing the laws can be subjected to the more detached, neutral scrutiny of a judge who must evaluate the reasonableness of a particular search or seizure in light of the particular circumstances. And in making that assessment it is imperative that the facts be judged against an objective standard: would the facts available to the officer at the moment of the seizure or the search "warrant a man of reasonable caution in the belief" that the action taken was appropriate? * * * Anything less would invite intrusions upon constitutionally guaranteed rights based on nothing more substantial than inarticulate hunches, a result this Court has consistently refused to sanction. * * *

Applying these principles to this case, we consider first the nature and extent of the governmental interests involved. One general interest is of course that of effective crime prevention and detection; it is this interest which underlies the recognition that a police officer may in appropriate circumstances and in an appropriate manner approach a person for purposes of investigating possibly criminal behavior even though there is no probable cause to make an arrest. It was this legitimate investigative function Officer McFadden was discharging when he decided to approach petitioner and his companions. He had observed Terry, Chilton, and Katz go through a series of acts, each of them perhaps innocent in itself, but which taken together warranted further investigation. There is nothing unusual in two men standing together on a street corner, perhaps waiting for someone. Nor is there anything suspicious about people in such circumstances strolling up and down the street, singly or in pairs. Store windows, moreover, are made to be looked in. But the story is quite different where, as here, two men hover about a street corner for an extended period of time, at the end of which it becomes apparent that they are not waiting for anyone or anything; where these men pace alternately along an identical route, pausing to stare in the same store window roughly 24 times; where each completion of this route is followed immediately by a conference between the two men on the corner; where they are joined in one of these conferences by a third man who leaves swiftly; and where the two men finally follow the third and rejoin him a couple of blocks away. It would have been poor police work indeed for an officer of 30 years' experience in the detection of thievery from stores in this same neighborhood to have failed to investigate this behavior further.[a]

---

a. This does not mean that a *Terry* stop is never permissible upon suspicion of *past* criminal activity. In *United States v. Hensley,* 469 U.S. 221 (1985), rejecting the lower court's position that *Terry* is limited to ongoing criminal activity, the Court explained:

"The factors in the balance may be somewhat different when a stop to investigate past criminal activity is involved rather than a stop to investigate ongoing criminal conduct. This is because the governmental interest and the nature of the intrusions involved in the two situations may differ. As we noted in *Terry,* one general interest present in the context of ongoing or imminent criminal activity is 'that of effective crime prevention and detection.' A stop to investigate an already completed crime does not necessarily promote the interest of

The crux of this case, however, is not the propriety of Officer McFadden's taking steps to investigate petitioner's suspicious behavior, but rather, whether there was justification for McFadden's invasion of Terry's personal security by searching him for weapons in the course of that investigation. We are now concerned with more than the governmental interest in investigating crime; in addition, there is the more immediate interest of the police officer in taking steps to assure himself that the person with whom he is dealing is not armed with a weapon that could unexpectedly and fatally be used against him. Certainly it would be unreasonable to require that police officers take unnecessary risks in the performance of their duties. American criminals have a long tradition of armed violence, and every year in this country many law enforcement officers are killed in the line of duty, and thousands more are wounded. Virtually all of these deaths and a substantial portion of the injuries are inflicted with guns and knives.

In view of these facts, we cannot blind ourselves to the need for law enforcement officers to protect themselves and other prospective victims of violence in situations where they may lack probable cause for an arrest. When an officer is justified in believing that the individual whose suspicious behavior he is investigating at close range is armed and presently dangerous to the officer or to others, it would appear to be clearly unreasonable to deny the officer the power to take necessary measures to determine whether the person is in fact carrying a weapon and to neutralize the threat of physical harm. * * *

Petitioner * * * does not say that an officer is always unjustified in searching a suspect to discover weapons. Rather, he says it is unreasonable for the policeman to take that step until such time as the situation evolves to a point where there is probable cause to make an arrest. * * *

There are two weaknesses in this line of reasoning however. First, it fails to take account of traditional limitations upon the scope of searches, and thus recognizes no distinction in purpose, character, and extent between a search incident to an arrest and a limited search for weapons. The former, although justified in part by the acknowledged necessity to protect the arresting officer from assault with a concealed weapon, is also justified on other grounds, and can therefore involve a relatively extensive exploration of the person. A search for weapons in the absence of probable cause to arrest, however, must, like any other search, be strictly circumscribed by the exigencies which justify its initiation.

crime prevention as directly as a stop to investigate suspected ongoing criminal activity. Similarly, the exigent circumstances which require a police officer to step in before a crime is committed or completed are not necessarily as pressing long afterwards. Public safety may be less threatened by a suspect in a past crime who now appears to be going about his lawful business than it is by a suspect who is currently in the process of violating the law. Finally, officers making a stop to investigate past crimes may have a wider range of opportunity to choose the time and circumstances of the stop.

"Despite these differences, where police have been unable to locate a person suspected of involvement in a past crime, the ability to briefly stop that person, ask questions, or check identification in the absence of probable cause promotes the strong government interest in solving crimes and bringing offenders to justice. Restraining police action until after probable cause is obtained would not only hinder the investigation, but might also enable the suspect to flee in the interim and to remain at large. Particularly in the context of felonies or crimes involving a threat to public safety, it is in the public interest that the crime be solved and the suspect detained as promptly as possible. The law enforcement interests at stake in these circumstances outweigh the individual's interest to be free of a stop and detention that is no more extensive than permissible in the investigation of imminent or ongoing crimes.

"We need not and do not decide today whether *Terry* stops to investigate all past crimes, however serious, are permitted. It is enough to say that, if police have a reasonable suspicion, grounded in specific and articulable facts, that a person they encounter was involved in or is wanted in connection with a completed felony, then a *Terry* stop may be made to investigate that suspicion."

Thus it must be limited to that which is necessary for the discovery of weapons which might be used to harm the officer or others nearby, and may realistically be characterized as something less than a "full" search, even though it remains a serious intrusion.

A second, and related, objection to petitioner's argument is that it assumes that the law of arrest has already worked out the balance between the particular interests involved here—the neutralization of danger to the policeman in the investigative circumstance and the sanctity of the individual. But this is not so. An arrest is a wholly different kind of intrusion upon individual freedom from a limited search for weapons, and the interests each is designed to serve are likewise quite different. An arrest is the initial stage of a criminal prosecution. It is intended to vindicate society's interest in having its laws obeyed, and it is inevitably accompanied by future interference with the individual's freedom of movement, whether or not trial or conviction ultimately follows. The protective search for weapons, on the other hand, constitutes a brief, though far from inconsiderable intrusion upon the sanctity of the person. It does not follow that because an officer may lawfully arrest a person only when he is apprised of facts sufficient to warrant a belief that the person has committed or is committing a crime, the officer is equally unjustified, absent that kind of evidence, in making any intrusions short of an arrest. Moreover, a perfectly reasonable apprehension of danger may arise long before the officer is possessed of adequate information to justify taking a person into custody for the purpose of prosecuting him for a crime. * * *

Our evaluation of the proper balance that has to be struck in this type of case leads us to conclude that there must be a narrowly drawn authority to permit a reasonable search for weapons for the protection of the police officer, where he has reason to believe that he is dealing with an armed and dangerous individual, regardless of whether he has probable cause to arrest the individual for a crime. The officer need not be absolutely certain that the individual is armed; the issue is whether a reasonably prudent man in the circumstances would be warranted in the belief that his safety or that of others was in danger. * * * And in determining whether the officer acted reasonably in such circumstances, due weight must be given, not to his inchoate and unparticularized suspicion or "hunch", but to the specific reasonable inferences which he is entitled to draw from the facts in light of his experience.

We must now examine the conduct of Officer McFadden in this case to determine whether his search and seizure of petitioner were reasonable, both at their inception and as conducted. He had observed Terry, together with Chilton and another man, acting in a manner he took to be preface to a "stick-up." We think on the facts and circumstances Officer McFadden detailed before the trial judge a reasonably prudent man would have been warranted in believing petitioner was armed and thus presented a threat to the officer's safety while he was investigating his suspicious behavior. The actions of Terry and Chilton were consistent with McFadden's hypothesis that these men were contemplating a daylight robbery—which, it is reasonable to assume, would be likely to involve the use of weapons—and nothing in their conduct from the time he first noticed them until the time he confronted them and identified himself as a police officer gave him sufficient reason to negate that hypothesis. Although the trio had departed the original scene, there was nothing to indicate abandonment of an intent to commit a robbery at some point. Thus, when Officer McFadden approached the three men gathered before the display window at Zucker's store he had observed enough to make it quite reasonable to fear that they were armed; and nothing in their response to his hailing them, identifying himself as a police officer, and asking their names served to dispel that reasonable belief. We cannot say his decision at that point to seize Terry and pat his clothing for weapons was the product of a volatile or inventive imagination, or was undertaken simply as an act of harassment; the record evidences the tempered act of a policeman who in the course of an investigation had to make a quick decision as to how to protect himself and others from possible danger, and took limited steps to do so.

The manner in which the seizure and search were conducted is, of course, as vital a part of the inquiry as whether they were warranted at all. The Fourth Amendment proceeds as much by limitations upon the scope of governmental action as by imposing preconditions upon its initiation. The entire deterrent purpose of the rule excluding evidence seized in violation of the Fourth Amendment rests on the assumption that "limitations upon the fruit to be gathered tend to limit the quest itself." * * * Thus, evidence may not be introduced if it was discovered by means of a seizure and search which were not reasonably related in scope to the justification for their initiation.

[A protective search for weapons,] unlike a search without a warrant incident to a lawful arrest, is not justified by any need to prevent the disappearance or destruction of evidence of crime. The sole justification of the search in the present situation is the protection of the police officer and others nearby, and it must therefore be confined in scope to an intrusion reasonably designed to discover guns, knives, clubs, or other hidden instruments for the assault of the police officer.

The scope of the search in this case presents no serious problem in light of these standards. Officer McFadden patted down the outer clothing of petitioner and his two companions. He did not place his hands in their pockets or under the outer surface of their garments until he had felt weapons, and then he merely reached for and removed the guns. He never did invade Katz's person beyond the outer surfaces of his clothes, since he discovered nothing in his pat down which might have been a weapon. Officer McFadden confined his search strictly to what was minimally necessary to learn whether the men were armed and to disarm them once he discovered the weapons. He did not conduct a general exploratory search for whatever evidence of criminal activity he might find.

We conclude that the revolver seized from Terry was properly admitted in evidence against him. At the time he seized petitioner and searched him for weapons, Officer McFadden had reasonable grounds to believe that petitioner was armed and dangerous, and it was necessary for the protection of himself and others to take swift measures to discover the true facts and neutralize the threat of harm if it materialized. The policeman carefully restricted his search to what was appropriate to the discovery of the particular items which he sought. Each case of this sort will, of course, have to be decided on its own facts. We merely hold today that where a police officer observes unusual conduct which leads him reasonably to conclude in light of his experience that criminal activity may be afoot and that the persons with whom he is dealing may be armed and presently dangerous; where in the course of investigating this behavior he identifies himself as a policeman and makes reasonable inquiries; and where nothing in the initial stages of the encounter serves to dispel his reasonable fear for his own or others' safety, he is entitled for the protection of himself and others in the area to conduct a carefully limited search of the outer clothing of such persons [b] in an attempt to

---

b. *Michigan v. Long,* 463 U.S. 1032 (1983), extended the self-protective search principle of *Terry* to search of a vehicle. Two deputies saw a car swerve into a ditch and stopped to inves-tigate. Long, the only occupant of the car, met the deputies at the rear of the car, supplied his driver's license upon demand, and started back toward the open door when asked for his vehidiscover weapons which might be used to assault him. Such a search is a reasonable search under the Fourth Amendment, and any weapons seized may properly be introduced in evidence against the person from whom they were taken.

Affirmed.

JUSTICE HARLAN, concurring.

* * * The holding has * * * two logical corollaries that I do not think the Court has fully expressed.

In the first place, if the frisk is justified in order to protect the officer during an encounter with a citizen, the officer must first have constitutional grounds to insist on an encounter, to make a *forcible* stop. Any person, including a policeman, is at liberty to avoid a person he considers dangerous. If and when a policeman has a right instead to disarm such a person for his own protection, he must first have a right not to avoid him but to be in his presence. That right

cle registration. The officers saw a large hunting knife on the floorboard, so Long was frisked and one officer then entered the vehicle and found an open pouch of marijuana under an armrest. The Court concluded "that the search of the passenger compartment of an automobile, limited to those areas in which a weapon may be placed or hidden, is permissible if the police officer possesses a reasonable belief based on 'specific and articulable facts which, taken together with the rational inferences from those facts, reasonably warrant' the officers in believing that the suspect is dangerous and the suspect may gain immediate control of weapons." In explaining why this was such a case, the Court stated:

"The Michigan Supreme Court appeared to believe that it was not reasonable for the officers to fear that Long could injure them, because he was effectively under their control during the investigative stop and could not get access to any weapons that might have been located in the automobile. This reasoning is mistaken in several respects. During any investigative detention, the suspect is 'in the control' of the officers in the sense that he 'may be briefly detained against his will * * *.' Just as a *Terry* suspect on the street may, despite being under the brief control of a police officer, reach into his clothing and retrieve a weapon, so might a *Terry* suspect in Long's position break away from police control and retrieve a weapon from his automobile. In addition, if the suspect is not placed under arrest, he will be permitted to reenter his automobile, and he will then have access to any weapons inside. Or, as here, the suspect may be permitted to reenter the vehicle before the *Terry* investigation is over, and again, may have access to weapons. In any event, we stress that a *Terry* investigation, such as the one that occurred here, involves a police investigation 'at close range,' when the officer remains particularly vulnerable in part *because* a full custodial arrest has not been effected, and the officer must make a 'quick decision as to how to protect himself and others from possible danger * * *.' In such circumstances, we

have not required that officers adopt alternative means to ensure their safety in order to avoid the intrusion involved in a *Terry* encounter."

Brennan and Marshall, JJ., dissenting, objected: "Putting aside the fact that the search at issue here involved a far more serious intrusion than that 'involved in a *Terry* encounter,' and as such might suggest the need for resort to 'alternate means,' the Court's reasoning is perverse. The Court's argument in essence is that the *absence* of probable cause to arrest compels the conclusion that a broad search, traditionally associated in scope with a search incident to arrest, must be permitted based on reasonable suspicion. But *United States v. Robinson* stated: 'It is scarcely open to doubt that the danger to an officer is far greater in the case of the extended exposure which follows the taking of a suspect into custody and transporting him to the police station than in the case of the relatively fleeting contact resulting from the typical *Terry*-type stop.' In light of *Robinson*'s observation, today's holding leaves in grave doubt the question of whether the Court's assessment of the relative dangers posed by given confrontations is based on any principled standard."

Even if the *Long* test for a vehicle search cannot be met, the officer may take other steps in the interest of self-protection. In *Pennsylvania v. Mimms*, 434 U.S. 106, 98 S.Ct. 330, 54 L.Ed.2d 331 (1977), the Court held that without any showing the particular suspect may be armed, an officer may require a person lawfully stopped to alight from his car in order to diminish "the possibility, otherwise, substantial, that the driver can make unobserved movements." In *Maryland v. Wilson*, 519 U.S. 408, 117 S.Ct. 882, 137 L.Ed.2d 41 (1997), the *Mimms* rule was held to be equally applicable to passengers; though there has been no reason to detain the passenger, such detention occurs as a practical matter when the vehicle is stopped, and so the minimal added intrusion is justified in the interest of the officer's safety.

must be more than the liberty (again, possessed by every citizen) to address questions to other persons, for ordinarily the person addressed has an equal right to ignore his interrogator and walk away; he certainly need not submit to a frisk for the questioner's protection. I would make it perfectly clear that the right to frisk in this case depends upon the reasonableness of a forcible stop to investigate a suspected crime.

Where such a stop is reasonable, however, the right to frisk must be immediate and automatic if the reason for the stop is, as here, an articulable suspicion of a crime of violence. Just as a full search incident to a lawful arrest requires no additional justification, a limited frisk incident to a lawful stop must often be rapid and routine. There is no reason why an officer, rightfully but forcibly confronting a person suspected of a serious crime, should have to ask one question and take the risk that the answer might be a bullet. * * *

JUSTICE WHITE, concurring.

* * * I think an additional word is in order concerning the matter of interrogation during an investigative stop. There is nothing in the Constitution which prevents a policeman from addressing questions to anyone on the streets. Absent special circumstances, the person approached may not be detained or frisked but may refuse to cooperate and go on his way. However, given the proper circumstances, such as those in this case, it seems to me the person may be briefly detained against his will while pertinent questions are directed to him. Of course, the person stopped is not obliged to answer, answers may not be compelled, and refusal to answer furnishes no basis for an arrest, although it may alert the officer to the need for continued observation. * * *

JUSTICE DOUGLAS, dissenting.

* * * Had a warrant been sought, a magistrate would, therefore, have been unauthorized to issue one, for he can act only if there is a showing of "probable cause." We hold today that the police have greater authority to make a "seizure" and conduct a "search" than a judge has to authorize such action. We have said precisely the opposite over and over again. * * *

The infringement on personal liberty of any "seizure" of a person can only be "reasonable" under the Fourth Amendment if we require the police to possess "probable cause" before they seize him. Only that line draws a meaningful distinction between an officer's mere inkling and the presence of facts within the officer's personal knowledge which would convince a reasonable man that the person seized has committed, is committing, or is about to commit a particular crime. * * *

FLORIDA v. J. L.

529 U.S. 266, 120 S.Ct. 1375, 146 L.Ed.2d 254 (2000).

JUSTICE GINSBURG delivered the opinion of the Court.

The question presented in this case is whether an anonymous tip that a person is carrying a gun is, without more, sufficient to justify a police officer's stop and frisk of that person. We hold that it is not.

On October 13, 1995, an anonymous caller reported to the Miami–Dade Police that a young black male standing at a particular bus stop and wearing a plaid shirt was carrying a gun. So far as the record reveals, there is no audio recording of the tip, and nothing is known about the informant. Sometime after the police received the tip—the record does not say how long—two officers were instructed to respond. They arrived at the bus stop about six minutes later and saw three black males "just hanging out [there]." One of the three, respondent J.L., was wearing a plaid shirt. Apart from the tip, the officers had no reason to suspect any of the three of illegal conduct. The officers did not see a firearm, and J.L. made no threatening or otherwise unusual movements. One of the officers approached J.L., told him to put his hands up on the bus stop, frisked him, and seized a gun from J.L.'s pocket. The second officer frisked the other two individuals, against whom no allegations had been made, and found nothing.

J.L., who was at the time of the frisk "10 days shy of his 16th birth[day]," was charged under state law with carrying a concealed firearm without a license and possessing a firearm while under the age of 18. He moved to suppress the gun as the fruit of an unlawful search, and the trial court granted his motion. The intermediate appellate court reversed, but the Supreme Court of Florida quashed that decision and held the search invalid under the Fourth Amendment. * * *

In the instant case, the officers' suspicion that J.L. was carrying a weapon arose not from any observations of their own but solely from a call made from an unknown location by an unknown caller. Unlike a tip from a known informant whose reputation can be assessed and who can be held responsible if her allegations turn out to be fabricated, "an anonymous tip alone seldom demonstrates the informant's basis of knowledge or veracity," *Alabama v. White*, [496 U.S. 325 (1990)]. As we have recognized, however, there are situations in which an anonymous tip, suitably corroborated, exhibits "sufficient indicia of reliability to provide reasonable suspicion to make the investigatory stop." The question we here confront is whether the tip pointing to J.L. had those indicia of reliability.

In *White*, the police received an anonymous tip asserting that a woman was carrying cocaine and predicting that she would leave an apartment building at a specified time, get into a car matching a particular description, and drive to a named motel. Standing alone, the tip would not have justified a *Terry* stop. Only after police observation showed that the informant had accurately predicted the woman's movements, we explained, did it become reasonable to think the tipster had inside knowledge about the suspect and therefore to credit his assertion about the cocaine. Although the Court held that the suspicion in *White* became reasonable after police surveillance, we regarded the case as borderline. Knowledge about a person's future movements indicates some familiarity with that person's affairs, but having such knowledge does not necessarily imply that the informant knows, in particular, whether that person is carrying hidden contraband. We accordingly classified *White* as a "close case."

The tip in the instant case lacked the moderate indicia of reliability present in *White* and essential to the Court's decision in that case. The anonymous call concerning J.L. provided no predictive information and therefore left the police without means to test the informant's knowledge or credibility. That the allegation about the gun turned out to be correct does not suggest that the officers, prior to the frisks, had a reasonable basis for suspecting J.L. of engaging in unlawful conduct: The reasonableness of official suspicion must be measured by what the officers knew before they conducted their search. All the police had to go on in this case was the bare report of an unknown, unaccountable informant who neither explained how he knew about the gun nor supplied any basis for believing he had inside information about J.L. If *White* was a close case on the reliability of anonymous tips, this one surely falls on the other side of the line. * * *

An accurate description of a subject's readily observable location and appearance is of course reliable in this limited sense: It will help the police correctly identify the person whom the tipster means to accuse. Such a tip, however, does not show that the tipster has knowledge of concealed criminal activity. The reasonable suspicion here at issue requires that a tip be reliable in its assertion of illegality, not just in its tendency to identify a determinate person. * * *

Firearms are dangerous, and extraordinary dangers sometimes justify unusual precautions. Our decisions recognize the serious threat that armed criminals pose to public safety; *Terry*'s rule, which permits protective police searches on the basis of reasonable suspicion rather than demanding that officers meet the higher standard of probable cause, responds to this very concern. But an automatic firearm exception to our established reliability analysis [advanced by Florida and the United States as *amicus*] would rove too far. Such an exception would enable any person seeking to harass another to set in motion an intrusive, embarrassing police search of the targeted person simply by placing an anonymous call falsely reporting the target's unlawful carriage of a gun. Nor could one securely confine such an exception to allegations involving firearms. Several Courts of Appeals have held it per se foreseeable for people carrying significant amounts of illegal drugs to be carrying guns as well. If police officers may properly conduct Terry frisks on the basis of bare-boned tips about guns, it would be reasonable to maintain under the above-cited decisions that the police should similarly have discretion to frisk based on bare-boned tips about narcotics. * * *

The facts of this case do not require us to speculate about the circumstances under which the danger alleged in an anonymous tip might be so great as to justify a search even without a showing of reliability. We do not say, for example, that a report of a person carrying a bomb need bear the indicia of reliability we demand for a report of a person carrying a firearm before the police can constitutionally conduct a frisk. Nor do we hold that public safety officials in quarters where the reasonable expectation of Fourth Amendment privacy is diminished, such as airports and schools, cannot conduct protective searches on the basis of information insufficient to justify searches elsewhere.

Finally, the requirement that an anonymous tip bear standard indicia of reliability in order to justify a stop in no way diminishes a police officer's prerogative, in accord with *Terry*, to conduct a protective search of a person who has already been legitimately stopped. We speak in today's decision only of cases in which the officer's authority to make the initial stop is at issue. In that context, we hold that an anonymous tip lacking indicia of reliability of the kind contemplated in *Adams* and *White* does not justify a stop and frisk whenever and however it alleges the illegal possession of a firearm. * * *

JUSTICE KENNEDY, with whom THE CHIEF JUSTICE joins, concurring. * * *

It seems appropriate to observe that a tip might be anonymous in some sense yet have certain other features, either supporting reliability or narrowing the likely class of informants, so that the tip does provide the lawful basis for some police action. One such feature, as the Court recognizes, is that the tip predicts future conduct of the alleged criminal. There may be others. For example, if an unnamed caller with a voice which sounds the same each time tells police on two successive nights about criminal activity which in fact occurs each night, a similar call on the third night ought not be treated automatically like the tip in the case now before us. In the instance supposed, there would be a plausible argument that experience cures some of the uncertainty surrounding the anonymity, justifying a proportionate police response. In today's case, however, the State provides us with no data about the reliability of anonymous tips. Nor do we know whether the dispatcher or arresting officer had any objective reason to believe that this tip had some particular indicia of reliability.

If an informant places his anonymity at risk, a court can consider this factor in weighing the reliability of the tip. An instance where a tip might be considered anonymous but nevertheless sufficiently reliable to justify a proportionate police response may be when an unnamed person driving a car the police officer later describes stops for a moment and, face to face, informs the police that criminal activity is occurring. This too seems to be different from the tip in the present case.

Instant caller identification is widely available to police, and, if anonymous tips are proving unreliable and distracting to police, squad cars can be sent within seconds to the location of the telephone used by the informant. Voice recording of telephone tips might, in appropriate cases, be used by police to locate the caller. It is unlawful to make false reports to the police, and the ability of the police to trace the identity of anonymous telephone informants may be a factor which lends reliability to what, years earlier, might have been considered unreliable anonymous tips.

These matters, of course, must await discussion in other cases, where the issues are presented by the record.

ILLINOIS v. WARDLOW

528 U.S. 119, 120 S.Ct. 673, 145 L.Ed.2d 570 (2000).

CHIEF JUSTICE REHNQUIST delivered the opinion of the Court.

Respondent Wardlow fled upon seeing police officers patrolling an area known for heavy narcotics trafficking. Two of the officers caught up with him, stopped him and conducted a protective pat-down search for weapons. Discovering a .38-caliber handgun, the officers arrested Wardlow. We hold that the officers' stop did not violate the Fourth Amendment to the United States Constitution.

On September 9, 1995, Officers Nolan and Harvey were working as uniformed officers in the special operations section of the Chicago Police Department. The officers were driving the last car of a four car caravan converging on an area known for heavy narcotics trafficking in order to investigate drug transactions. The officers were traveling together because they expected to find a crowd of people in the area, including lookouts and customers.

As the caravan passed 4035 West Van Buren, Officer Nolan observed respondent Wardlow standing next to the building holding an opaque bag. Respondent looked in the direction of the officers and fled. Nolan and Harvey turned their car southbound, watched him as he ran through the gangway and an alley, and eventually cornered him on the street. Nolan then exited his car and stopped respondent. He immediately conducted a protective pat-down search for weapons because in his experience it was common for there to be weapons in the near vicinity of narcotics transactions. During the frisk, Officer Nolan squeezed the bag respondent was carrying and felt a heavy, hard object similar to the shape of a gun. The officer then opened the bag and discovered a .38-caliber handgun with five live rounds of ammunition. The officers arrested Wardlow. * * *

Nolan and Harvey were among eight officers in a four car caravan that was converging on an area known for heavy narcotics trafficking, and the officers anticipated encountering a large number of people in the area, including drug customers and individuals serving as lookouts. It was in this context that Officer Nolan decided to investigate Wardlow after observing him flee. An individual's presence in an area of expected criminal activity, standing alone, is not enough to support a reasonable, particularized suspicion that the person is committing a crime. But officers are not required to ignore the relevant characteristics of a location in determining whether the circumstances are sufficiently suspicious to warrant further investigation. Accordingly, we have previously noted the fact that the stop occurred in a "high crime area" among the relevant contextual considerations in a *Terry* analysis.

In this case, moreover, it was not merely respondent's presence in an area of heavy narcotics trafficking that aroused the officers' suspicion but his unprovoked flight upon noticing the police. Our cases have also recognized that nervous, evasive behavior is a pertinent factor in determining reasonable suspicion. Headlong flight—wherever it occurs—is the consummate act of evasion: it is not necessarily indicative of wrongdoing, but it is certainly suggestive of such. In reviewing the propriety of an officer's conduct, courts do not have available empirical studies dealing with inferences drawn from suspicious behavior, and we cannot reasonably demand scientific certainty from judges or law enforcement officers where none exists. Thus, the determination of reasonable suspicion must be based on commonsense judgments and inferences about human behavior. We conclude Officer Nolan was justified in suspecting that Wardlow was involved in criminal activity, and, therefore, in investigating further.

Such a holding is entirely consistent with our decision in *Florida v. Royer*, 460 U.S. 491(1983), where we held that when an officer, without reasonable suspicion or probable cause, approaches an individual, the individual has a right to ignore the police and go about his business. And any "refusal to cooperate, without more, does not furnish the minimal level of objective justification needed for a detention or seizure." But unprovoked flight is simply not a mere refusal to cooperate. Flight, by its very nature, is not "going about one's business"; in fact, it is just the opposite. Allowing officers confronted with such flight to stop the fugitive and investigate further is quite consistent with the individual's right to go about his business or to stay put and remain silent in the face of police questioning.

Respondent and amici also argue that there are innocent reasons for flight from police and that, therefore, flight is not necessarily indicative of ongoing criminal activity. This fact is undoubtedly true, but does not establish a violation of the Fourth Amendment. Even in *Terry*, the conduct justifying the stop was ambiguous and susceptible of an innocent explanation. The officer observed two individuals pacing back and forth in front of a store, peering into the window and periodically conferring. All of this conduct was by itself lawful, but it also suggested that the individuals were casing the store for a planned robbery. *Terry* recognized that the officers could detain the individuals to resolve the ambiguity. * * *

JUSTICE STEVENS, with whom JUSTICE SOUTER, JUSTICE GINSBURG, and JUSTICE BREYER join, concurring in part and dissenting in part.

The State of Illinois asks this Court to announce a "bright-line rule" authorizing the temporary detention of anyone who flees at the mere sight of a police officer. Respondent counters by asking us to adopt the opposite per se rule—that the fact that a person flees upon seeing the police can never, by itself, be sufficient to justify a temporary investigative stop of the kind authorized by *Terry v. Ohio*. * * *

Given the diversity and frequency of possible motivations for flight, it would be profoundly unwise to endorse either per se rule. The inference we can reasonably draw about the motivation for a person's flight, rather, will depend on a number of different circumstances. Factors such as the time of day, the number of people in the area, the character of the neighborhood, whether the officer was in uniform, the way the runner was dressed, the direction and speed of the flight, and whether the person's behavior was otherwise unusual might be relevant in specific cases. This number of variables is surely sufficient to preclude either a bright-line rule that always justifies, or that never justifies, an investigative stop based on the sole fact that flight began after a police officer appeared nearby.

Still, Illinois presses for a per se rule regarding "unprovoked flight upon seeing a clearly identifiable police officer." * * *

"Unprovoked flight," in short, describes a category of activity too broad and varied to permit a per se reasonable inference regarding the motivation for the activity. While the innocent explanations surely do not establish that the Fourth Amendment is always violated whenever someone is stopped solely on the basis of an unprovoked flight, neither do the suspicious motivations establish that the Fourth Amendment is never violated when a *Terry* stop is predicated on that fact alone. For these reasons, the Court is surely correct in refusing to embrace either per se rule advocated by the parties. The totality of the circumstances, as always, must dictate the result.

Guided by that totality-of-the-circumstances test, the Court concludes that Officer Nolan had reasonable suspicion to stop respondent. In this respect, my view differs from the Court's. The entire justification for the stop is articulated in the brief testimony of Officer Nolan. Some facts are perfectly clear; others are not. This factual insufficiency leads me to conclude that the Court's judgment is mistaken. [The dissenters here elaborated that they found the record as a whole failed to establish reasonable suspicion, considering that it did not show whether any vehicles in the caravan were marked, whether any other officers were in uniform, where the intended destination of the officers was in relation to where defendant was seen, whether the caravan had passed before defendant ran, etc.]

The State, along with the majority of the Court, relies as well on the assumption that this flight occurred in a high crime area. Even if that assumption is accurate, it is insufficient because even in a high crime neighborhood unprovoked flight does not invariably lead to reasonable suspicion. On the contrary, because many factors providing innocent motivations for unprovoked flight are concentrated in high crime areas, the character of the neighborhood arguably makes an inference of guilt less appropriate, rather than more so.[a] Like unprovoked flight itself, presence in a high crime neighborhood is a fact too generic and susceptible to innocent explanation to satisfy the reasonable suspicion inquiry.

FLORIDA v. ROYER
460 U.S. 491, 103 S.Ct. 1319, 75 L.Ed.2d 229 (1983).

Justice White announced the judgment of the Court and delivered an opinion, in which Justice Marshall, Justice Powell, and Justice Stevens joined.

[After purchasing a one-way airline ticket to New York City at Miami International Airport under an assumed name and checking his two suitcases bearing identification tags with the same assumed name, respondent went to the concourse leading to the airline boarding area, where he was approached by two

---

a. The dissenters elsewhere stated: "Among some citizens, particularly minorities and those residing in high crime areas, there is also the possibility that the fleeing person is entirely innocent, but, with or without justification, believes that contact with the police can itself be dangerous, apart from any criminal activity associated with the officer's sudden presence. For such a person, unprovoked flight is neither 'aberrant' nor 'abnormal.' Moreover, these concerns and fears are known to the police officers themselves, and are validated by law enforcement investigations into their own practices. Accordingly, the evidence supporting the reasonableness of these beliefs is too pervasive to be dismissed as random or rare, and too persuasive to be disparaged as inconclusive or insufficient."

detectives, who previously had observed him and believed that his characteristics fit the so-called "drug courier profile." Upon request, but without oral consent, respondent produced his airline ticket and driver's license, which carried his correct name. When the detectives asked about the discrepancy in names, respondent explained that a friend had made the ticket reservation in the assumed name. The detectives then informed respondent that they were narcotics investigators and that they had reason to suspect him of transporting narcotics, and, without returning his airline ticket or driver's license, asked him to accompany them to a small room adjacent to the concourse. Without respondent's consent, one of the detectives retrieved respondent's luggage from the airline and brought it to the room. While he did not respond to the detectives' request that he consent to a search of the luggage, respondent produced a key and unlocked one of the suitcases in which marihuana was found. When respondent said he did not know the combination to the lock on the second suitcase but did not object to its being opened, the officers pried it open and found more marihuana. Respondent was then told he was under arrest. Following the Florida trial court's denial of his pretrial motion to suppress the evidence obtained in the search of the suitcases, respondent was convicted of felony possession of marihuana. The Florida District Court of Appeal reversed, holding that respondent had been involuntarily confined within the small room without probable cause, that at the time his consent to search was obtained, the involuntary detention had exceeded the limited restraint permitted by *Terry v. Ohio,* and that such consent was therefore invalid because tainted by the unlawful confinement.]

Some preliminary observations are in order. First, it is unquestioned that without a warrant to search Royer's luggage and in the absence of probable cause and exigent circumstances, the validity of the search depended on Royer's purported consent. Neither is it disputed that where the validity of a search rests on consent, the State has the burden of proving that the necessary consent was obtained and that it was freely and voluntarily given, a burden that is not satisfied by showing a mere submission to a claim of lawful authority.

Second, law enforcement officers do not violate the Fourth Amendment by merely approaching an individual on the street or in another public place, by asking him if he is willing to answer some questions, by putting questions to him if the person is willing to listen, or by offering in evidence in a criminal prosecution his voluntary answers to such questions. Nor would the fact that the officer identifies himself as a police officer, without more, convert the encounter into a seizure requiring some level of objective justification. The person approached, however, need not answer any question put to him; indeed, he may decline to listen to the questions at all and may go on his way. He may not be detained even momentarily without reasonable, objective grounds for doing so; and his refusal to listen or answer does not, without more, furnish those grounds. If there is no detention—no seizure within the meaning of the Fourth Amendment—then no constitutional rights have been infringed.

Third, it is also clear that not all seizures of the person must be justified by probable cause to arrest for a crime. * * * *Terry* created a limited exception to this general rule: certain seizures are justifiable under the Fourth Amendment if there is articulable suspicion that a person has committed or is about to commit a crime. * * * Royer does not suggest, nor do we, that a similar rationale would not warrant temporary detention for questioning on less than probable cause where the public interest involved is the suppression of illegal transactions in drugs or of any other serious crime. * * *

Fourth, *Terry* and its progeny nevertheless created only limited exceptions to the general rule that seizures of the person require probable cause to arrest. Detentions may be "investigative" yet violative of the Fourth Amendment absent probable cause. In the name of investigating a person who is no more than suspected of criminal activity, the police may not carry out a full search of the person or of his automobile or other effects. Nor may the police seek to verify their suspicions by means that approach the conditions of arrest. *Dunaway v. New York*, [442 U.S. 200 (1979)], made this clear. There, the suspect was taken to the police station from his home and, without being formally arrested, interrogated for an hour. The resulting incriminating statements were held inadmissible: reasonable suspicion of crime is insufficient to justify custodial interrogation even though the interrogation is investigative.[a]

The Fourth Amendment's prohibition against unreasonable searches and seizures has always been interpreted to prevent a search that is not limited to the particularly described "place to be searched, and the persons or things to be seized," even if the search is made pursuant to a warrant and based upon probable cause. The Amendment's protection is not diluted in those situations where it has been determined that legitimate law enforcement interests justify a warrantless search: the search must be limited in scope to that which is justified by the particular purposes served by the exception. * * * The reasonableness requirement of the Fourth Amendment requires no less when the police action is a seizure permitted on less than probable cause because of legitimate law enforcement interests. The scope of the detention must be carefully tailored to its underlying justification.

The predicate permitting seizures on suspicion short of probable cause is that law enforcement interests warrant a limited intrusion on the personal security of

a. This is not to suggest that all at-the-station investigation must be on full probable cause. In *Davis v. Mississippi*, 394 U.S. 721 (1969), petitioner and 24 other black youths were detained for questioning and fingerprinting in connection with a rape for which the only leads were a general description given by the victim and a set of fingerprints around the window through which the assailant entered. Petitioner's prints were found to match those at the scene of the crime, and this evidence was admitted at his trial. The Court, per Brennan, J., held that the prints should have been excluded as the fruits of a seizure of petitioner in violation of the Fourth Amendment, but intimated that a detention for such a purpose might sometimes be permissible on evidence insufficient for arrest:

"Detentions for the sole purpose of obtaining fingerprints are no less subject to the constraints of the Fourth Amendment. It is arguable, however, that because of the unique nature of the fingerprinting process, such detentions might, under narrowly defined circumstances, be found to comply with the Fourth Amendment even though there is no probable cause in the traditional sense. Detention for fingerprinting may constitute a much less serious intrusion upon personal security than other types of police searches and detentions. Fingerprinting involves none of the probing into an individual's private life and thoughts which marks an interrogation or search. Nor can fingerprint detention be employed repeatedly to harass any individual, since the police need only one set of each person's prints. Furthermore, fingerprinting is an inherently more reliable and effective crime-solving tool than eyewitness identifications or confessions and is not subject to such abuses as the improper line-up and the 'third degree.' Finally, because there is no danger of destruction of fingerprints, the limited detention need not come unexpectedly or at an inconvenient time. For this same reason, the general requirement that the authorization of a judicial officer be obtained in advance of detention would seem not to admit of any exception in the fingerprinting context.

"We have no occasion in this case, however, to determine whether the requirements of the Fourth Amendment could be met by narrowly circumscribed procedures for obtaining, during the course of a criminal investigation, the fingerprints of individuals for whom there is no probable cause to arrest. For it is clear that no attempt was made here to employ procedures which might comply with the requirements of the Fourth Amendment: the detention at police headquarters of petitioner and the other young Negroes was not authorized by a judicial officer; petitioner was unnecessarily required to undergo two fingerprinting sessions; and petitioner was not merely fingerprinted during the December 3 detention but also subjected to interrogation."

the suspect. The scope of the intrusion permitted will vary to some extent with the particular facts and circumstances of each case. This much, however, is clear: an investigative detention must be temporary and last no longer than is necessary to effectuate the purpose of the stop. Similarly, the investigative methods employed should be the least intrusive means reasonably available to verify or dispel the officer's suspicion in a short period of time.[b] It is the State's burden to demonstrate that the seizure it seeks to justify on the basis of a reasonable suspicion was sufficiently limited in scope and duration to satisfy the conditions of an investigative seizure.

Fifth, statements given during a period of illegal detention are inadmissible even though voluntarily given if they are the product of the illegal detention and not the result of an independent act of free will. * * *

Sixth, if the events in this case amounted to no more than a permissible police encounter in a public place or a justifiable *Terry*-type detention, Royer's consent, if voluntary, would have been effective to legalize the search of his two suitcases. * * *

The State proffers three reasons for holding that when Royer consented to the search of his luggage, he was not being illegally detained. First, it is submitted that the entire encounter was consensual and hence Royer was not being held against his will at all. We find this submission untenable. Asking for and examining Royer's ticket and his driver's license were no doubt permissible in themselves, but when the officers identified themselves as narcotics agents, told Royer that he was suspected of transporting narcotics, and asked him to accompany them to the police room, while retaining his ticket and driver's license and without indicating in any way that he was free to depart, Royer was effectively seized for the purposes of the Fourth Amendment. These circumstances surely amount to a show of official authority such that "a reasonable person would have believed that he was not free to leave."

Second, the State submits that if Royer was seized, there existed reasonable, articulable suspicion to justify a temporary detention and that the limits of a *Terry*-type stop were never exceeded. We agree with the State that when the officers discovered that Royer was traveling under an assumed name, this fact, and the facts already known to the officers—paying cash for a one-way ticket, the mode of checking the two bags, and Royer's appearance and conduct in general— were adequate grounds for suspecting Royer of carrying drugs and for temporarily detaining him and his luggage while they attempted to verify or dispel their suspicions in a manner that did not exceed the limits of an investigative detention. We also agree that had Royer voluntarily consented to the search of his luggage while he was justifiably being detained on reasonable suspicion, the products of the search would be admissible against him. We have concluded, however, that at the time Royer produced the key to his suitcase, the detention to which he was

b. But in *United States v. Sharpe*, 470 U.S. 675 (1985), the Court cautioned:

"In assessing whether a detention is too long in duration to be justified as an investigative stop, we consider it appropriate to examine whether the police diligently pursued a means of investigation that was likely to confirm or dispel their suspicions quickly, during which time it was necessary to detain the defendant. A court making this assessment should take care to consider whether the police are acting in a swiftly developing situation, and in such cases the court should not indulge in unrealis-

tic second-guessing. A creative judge engaged in *post hoc* evaluation of police conduct can almost always imagine some alternative means by which the objectives of the police might have been accomplished. But '[t]he fact that the protection of the public might, in the abstract, have been accomplished by "less intrusive" means does not, in itself, render the search unreasonable.' The question is not simply whether some other alternative was available, but whether the police acted unreasonably in failing to recognize or to pursue it."

then subjected was a more serious intrusion on his personal liberty than is allowable on mere suspicion of criminal activity.

By the time Royer was informed that the officers wished to examine his luggage, he had identified himself when approached by the officers and had attempted to explain the discrepancy between the name shown on his identification and the name under which he had purchased his ticket and identified his luggage. The officers were not satisfied, for they informed him they were narcotics agents and had reason to believe that he was carrying illegal drugs. They requested him to accompany them to the police room. Royer went with them. He found himself in a small room—a large closet—equipped with a desk and two chairs. He was alone with two police officers who again told him that they thought he was carrying narcotics. He also found that the officers, without his consent, had retrieved his checked luggage from the airline. What had begun as a consensual inquiry in a public place had escalated into an investigatory procedure in a police interrogation room, where the police, unsatisfied with previous explanations, sought to confirm their suspicions. The officers had Royer's ticket, they had his identification, and they had seized his luggage. Royer was never informed that he was free to board his plane if he so chose, and he reasonably believed that he was being detained. At least as of that moment, any consensual aspects of the encounter had evaporated, and we cannot fault the Florida District Court of Appeal for concluding that *Terry v. Ohio* and the cases following it did not justify the restraint to which Royer was then subjected. As a practical matter, Royer was under arrest. Consistent with this conclusion, the State conceded in the Florida courts that Royer would not have been free to leave the interrogation room had he asked to do so. Furthermore, the State's brief in this Court interprets the testimony of the officers at the suppression hearing as indicating that had Royer refused to consent to a search of his luggage, the officers would have held the luggage and sought a warrant to authorize the search.

We also think that the officers' conduct was more intrusive than necessary to effectuate an investigative detention otherwise authorized by the *Terry* line of cases. First, by returning his ticket and driver's license, and informing him that he was free to go if he so desired, the officers might have obviated any claim that the encounter was anything but a consensual matter from start to finish. Second, there are undoubtedly reasons of safety and security that would justify moving a suspect from one location to another during an investigatory detention, such as from an airport concourse to a more private area. There is no indication in this case that such reasons prompted the officers to transfer the site of the encounter from the concourse to the interrogation room. It appears, rather, that the primary interest of the officers was not in having an extended conversation with Royer but in the contents of his luggage, a matter which the officers did not pursue orally with Royer until after the encounter was relocated to the police room. The record does not reflect any facts which would support a finding that the legitimate law enforcement purposes which justified the detention in the first instance were furthered by removing Royer to the police room prior to the officer's attempt to gain his consent to a search of his luggage. As we have noted, had Royer consented to a search on the spot, the search could have been conducted with Royer present in the area where the bags were retrieved by Detective Johnson and any evidence recovered would have been admissible against him. If the search proved negative, Royer would have been free to go much earlier and with less likelihood of missing his flight, which in itself can be a very serious matter in a variety of circumstances.

Third, the State has not touched on the question whether it would have been feasible to investigate the contents of Royer's bags in a more expeditious way. The courts are not strangers to the use of trained dogs to detect the presence of controlled substances in luggage. There is no indication here that this means was not feasible and available. If it had been used, Royer and his luggage could have been momentarily detained while this investigative procedure was carried out. Indeed, it may be that no detention at all would have been necessary. A negative result would have freed Royer in short order; a positive result would have resulted in his justifiable arrest on probable cause.

We do not suggest that there is a litmus-paper test for distinguishing a consensual encounter from a seizure or for determining when a seizure exceeds the bounds of an investigative stop. Even in the discrete category of airport encounters, there will be endless variations in the facts and circumstances, so much variation that it is unlikely that the courts can reduce to a sentence or a paragraph a rule that will provide unarguable answers to the question whether there has been an unreasonable search or seizure in violation of the Fourth Amendment. Nevertheless, we must render judgment, and we think that the Florida District Court of Appeal cannot be faulted in concluding that the limits of a *Terry* -stop had been exceeded.

The State's third and final argument is that Royer was not being illegally held when he gave his consent because there was probable cause to arrest him at that time. Detective Johnson testified at the suppression hearing and the Florida District Court of Appeal held that there was no probable cause to arrest until Royer's bags were opened, but the fact that the officers did not believe there was probable cause and proceeded on a consensual or *Terry*-stop rationale would not foreclose the State from justifying Royer's custody by proving probable cause and hence removing any barrier to relying on Royer's consent to search. We agree with the Florida District Court of Appeal, however, that probable cause to arrest Royer did not exist at the time he consented to the search of his luggage. The facts are that a nervous young man with two American Tourister bags paid cash for an airline ticket to a "target city". These facts led to inquiry, which in turn revealed that the ticket had been bought under an assumed name. The proffered explanation did not satisfy the officers. We cannot agree with the State, if this is its position, that every nervous young man paying cash for a ticket to New York City under an assumed name and carrying two heavy American Tourister bags may be arrested and held to answer for a serious felony charge.

Because we affirm the Florida District Court of Appeal's conclusion that Royer was being illegally detained when he consented to the search of his luggage, we agree that the consent was tainted by the illegality and was ineffective to justify the search. The judgment of the Florida District Court of Appeal is accordingly affirmed.[c]

JUSTICE BRENNAN, concurring in the result. * * *

To the extent that the plurality endorses the legality of the officers' initial stop of Royer, it was wholly unnecessary to reach that question. For even assuming the legality of the initial stop, the plurality correctly holds, and I agree, that the officers' subsequent actions clearly exceeded the permissible bounds of a *Terry* "investigative" stop. * * *

---

c. Justice Powell's concurring opinion (in which he noted that he "join[ed] the plurality opinion") is omitted.

The scope of a *Terry*-type "investigative" stop and any attendant search must be extremely limited or the *Terry* exception would "swallow the general rule that Fourth Amendment seizures [and searches] are 'reasonable' only if based on probable cause." In my view, any suggestion that the *Terry* reasonable-suspicion standard justifies anything but the briefest of detentions or the most limited of searches finds no support in the *Terry* line of cases.*

In any event, I dissent from the plurality's view that the initial stop of Royer was legal. For plainly Royer was "seized" for purposes of the Fourth Amendment when the officers asked him to produce his driver's license and airline ticket. * * * By identifying themselves and asking for Royer's airline ticket and driver's license the officers, as a practical matter, engaged in a "show of authority" and "restrained [Royer's] liberty." It is simply wrong to suggest that a traveler feels free to walk away when he has been approached by individuals who have identified themselves as police officers and asked for, and received, his airline ticket and driver's license. * * *

JUSTICE BLACKMUN, dissenting.

* * * In my view, the police conduct in this case was minimally intrusive. Given the strength of society's interest in overcoming the extraordinary obstacles to the detection of drug traffickers, such conduct should not be subjected to a requirement of probable cause. Because the Court holds otherwise, I dissent. * * *

At the suppression hearing in this case, Royer agreed that he was not formally arrested until after his suitcases were opened. In my view, it cannot fairly be said that, prior to the formal arrest, the functional equivalent of an arrest had taken place. The encounter had far more in common with automobile stops justifiable on reasonable suspicion, than with the detention deemed the functional equivalent of a formal arrest in *Dunaway v. New York*. In *Dunaway*, the suspect was taken from his neighbor's home and involuntarily transported to the police station in a squad car. At the precinct house, he was placed in an interrogation room and subjected to extended custodial interrogation. Here, Royer was not taken from a private residence, where reasonable expectations of privacy perhaps are at their greatest. Instead, he was approached in a major international airport where, due in part to extensive antihijacking surveillance and equipment, reasonable privacy expectations are of significantly lesser magnitude, certainly no greater than the reasonable privacy expectations of travelers in automobiles. * * *

What followed was within the scope of the lesser intrusions approved on less than probable cause in our prior cases, and was far removed from the circumstances of *Dunaway*. * * * Like Justice Rehnquist, I do not understand the plurality to dispute that Royer consented to go to the police room. Because the detention up to this point was not unlawful, the voluntariness of Royer's consent is to be judged on the totality of the circumstances.

JUSTICE REHNQUIST, with whom THE CHIEF JUSTICE and JUSTICE O'CONNOR join, dissenting. * * *

The point at which I part company with the plurality's opinion is in the assessment of the reasonableness of the officers' conduct following their initial

* I interpret the plurality's requirement that the investigative methods employed pursuant to a *Terry* stop be "the least intrusive means reasonably available to verify or dispel the officer's suspicion in a short period of time," to mean that the availability of a less intrusive means may make an otherwise reasonable stop unreasonable. I do not interpret it to mean that the absence of a less intrusive means can make an otherwise unreasonable stop reasonable. * * *

conversation with Royer. The plurality focuses on the transfer of the place of the interview from the main concourse of the airport to the room off the concourse and observes that Royer "found himself in a small room—a large closet—equipped with a desk and two chairs. He was alone with two police officers who again told him that they thought he was carrying narcotics. He also found that the officers, without his consent, had retrieved his checked luggage from the airlines."

Obviously, this quoted language is intended to convey stern disapproval of the described conduct of the officers. To my mind, it merits no such disapproval and was eminently reasonable. Would it have been preferable for the officers to have detained Royer for further questioning, as they concededly had a right to do, without paying any attention to the fact that his luggage had already been checked on the flight to New York, and might be put aboard the flight even though Royer himself was not on the plane? Would it have been more "reasonable" to interrogate Royer about the contents of his suitcases, and to seek his permission to open the suitcases when they were retrieved, in the busy main concourse of the Miami Airport, rather than to find a room off the concourse where the confrontation would surely be less embarrassing to Royer? If the room had been large and spacious, rather than small, if it had possessed three chairs rather than two, would the officers' conduct have been made reasonable by these facts?

The plurality's answers to these questions, to the extent that it attempts any, are scarcely satisfying. It commences with the observation that "the officers' conduct was more intrusive than necessary to effectuate an investigative detention otherwise authorized by the *Terry* line of cases." * * *

All of this to my mind adds up to little more than saying that if my aunt were a man, she would be my uncle. The officers might have taken different steps than they did to investigate Royer, but the same may be said of virtually every investigative encounter that has more than one step to it. The question we must decide is what was *unreasonable* about the steps which *these officers* took with respect to *this* suspect in the Miami Airport on this particular day. * * *

But since even the plurality concedes that there was articulable suspicion warranting an investigatory detention, the fact that the inquiry had become an "investigatory procedure in a police interrogation room" would seem to have little bearing on the proper disposition of a claim that the officers violated the Fourth Amendment. * * *

The reasonableness of the officers' activity in this case did not depend on Royer's consent to the investigation. Nevertheless, the presence of consent further justifies the action taken. The plurality does not seem to dispute that Royer consented to go to the room in the first instance. Certainly that conclusion is warranted by the totality of the circumstances. * * *

[I]f Royer was legally approached in the first instance and consented to accompany the detectives to the room, it does not follow that his consent went up in smoke and he was "arrested" upon entering the room. As we made clear in *Mendenhall,* logical analysis would focus on whether the environment in the room rendered the subsequent consent to a search of the luggage involuntary. * * *

FLORIDA v. BOSTICK

501 U.S. 429, 111 S.Ct. 2382, 115 L.Ed.2d 389 (1991).

JUSTICE O'CONNOR delivered the opinion of the Court. * * *

Drug interdiction efforts have led to the use of police surveillance at airports, train stations, and bus depots. Law enforcement officers stationed at such locations routinely approach individuals, either randomly or because they suspect in some vague way that the individuals may be engaged in criminal activity, and ask them potentially incriminating questions. Broward County has adopted such a program. County Sheriff's Department officers routinely board buses at scheduled stops and ask passengers for permission to search their luggage.

In this case, two officers discovered cocaine when they searched a suitcase belonging to Terrance Bostick. The underlying facts of the search are in dispute, but the Florida Supreme Court, whose decision we review here, stated explicitly the factual premise for its decision:

> " 'Two officers, complete with badges, insignia and one of them holding a recognizable zipper pouch, containing a pistol, boarded a bus bound from Miami to Atlanta during a stopover in Fort Lauderdale. Eyeing the passengers, the officers admittedly without articulable suspicion, picked out the defendant passenger and asked to inspect his ticket and identification. The ticket, from Miami to Atlanta, matched the defendant's identification and both were immediately returned to him as unremarkable. However, the two police officers persisted and explained their presence as narcotics agents on the lookout for illegal drugs. In pursuit of that aim, they then requested the defendant's consent to search his luggage. Needless to say, there is a conflict in the evidence about whether the defendant consented to the search of the second bag in which the contraband was found and as to whether he was informed of his right to refuse consent. However, any conflict must be resolved in favor of the state, it being a question of fact decided by the trial judge.' "

Two facts are particularly worth noting. First, the police specifically advised Bostick that he had the right to refuse consent. Bostick appears to have disputed the point, but, as the Florida Supreme Court noted explicitly, the trial court resolved this evidentiary conflict in the State's favor. Second, at no time did the officers threaten Bostick with a gun. The Florida Supreme Court indicated that one officer carried a zipper pouch containing a pistol—the equivalent of carrying a gun in a holster—but the court did not suggest that the gun was ever removed from its pouch, pointed at Bostick, or otherwise used in a threatening manner. The dissent's characterization of the officers as "gun-wielding inquisitor[s]" is colorful, but lacks any basis in fact.

Bostick was arrested and charged with trafficking in cocaine. He moved to suppress the cocaine on the grounds that it had been seized in violation of his Fourth Amendment rights. The trial court denied the motion but made no factual findings. Bostick subsequently entered a plea of guilty, but reserved the right to appeal the denial of the motion to suppress.

The Florida District Court of Appeal affirmed, but considered the issue sufficiently important that it certified a question to the Florida Supreme Court. The Supreme Court reasoned that Bostick had been seized because a reasonable passenger in his situation would not have felt free to leave the bus to avoid questioning by the police. It rephrased and answered the certified question so as to make the bus setting dispositive in every case. It ruled categorically that " 'an impermissible seizure result[s] when police mount a drug search on buses during scheduled stops and question boarded passengers without articulable reasons for doing so, thereby obtaining consent to search the passengers' luggage.' " The Florida Supreme Court thus adopted a *per se* rule that the Broward County Sheriff's practice of "working the buses" is unconstitutional.* The result of this

---

* The dissent acknowledges that the Florida   Supreme Court's answer to the certified ques-

decision is that police in Florida, as elsewhere, may approach persons at random in most public places, ask them questions and seek consent to a search, but they may not engage in the same behavior on a bus. We granted certiorari to determine whether the Florida Supreme Court's *per se* rule is consistent with our Fourth Amendment jurisprudence.

The sole issue presented for our review is whether a police encounter on a bus of the type described above necessarily constitutes a "seizure" within the meaning of the Fourth Amendment. The State concedes, and we accept for purposes of this decision, that the officers lacked the reasonable suspicion required to justify a seizure and that, if a seizure took place, the drugs found in Bostick's suitcase must be suppressed as tainted fruit.

Our cases make it clear that a seizure does not occur simply because a police officer approaches an individual and asks a few questions. So long as a reasonable person would feel free "to disregard the police and go about his business," *California v. Hodari D.*, 499 U.S. 621 (1991), the encounter is consensual and no reasonable suspicion is required. The encounter will not trigger Fourth Amendment scrutiny unless it loses its consensual nature. * * *

There is no doubt that if this same encounter had taken place before Bostick boarded the bus or in the lobby of the bus terminal, it would not rise to the level of a seizure. The Court has dealt with similar encounters in airports and has found them to be "the sort of consensual encounter[s] that implicat[e] no Fourth Amendment interest." We have stated that even when officers have no basis for suspecting a particular individual, they may generally ask questions of that individual, ask to examine the individual's identification, and request consent to search his or her luggage—as long as the police do not convey a message that compliance with their requests is required.

Bostick insists that this case is different because it took place in the cramped confines of a bus. A police encounter is much more intimidating in this setting, he argues, because police tower over a seated passenger and there is little room to move around. Bostick claims to find support in cases indicating that a seizure occurs when a reasonable person would believe that he or she is not "free to leave." Bostick maintains that a reasonable bus passenger would not have felt free to leave under the circumstances of this case because there is nowhere to go on a bus. Also, the bus was about to depart. Had Bostick disembarked, he would have risked being stranded and losing whatever baggage he had locked away in the luggage compartment.

The Florida Supreme Court found this argument persuasive, so much so that it adopted a *per se* rule prohibiting the police from randomly boarding buses as a means of drug interdiction. The state court erred, however, in focusing on whether Bostick was "free to leave" rather than on the principle that those words were intended to capture. When police attempt to question a person who is walking down the street or through an airport lobby, it makes sense to inquire whether a reasonable person would feel free to continue walking. But when the person is seated on a bus and has no desire to leave, the degree to which a reasonable person would feel that he or she could leave is not an accurate measure of the coercive effect of the encounter.

tion reads like a *per se* rule, but dismisses as "implausible" the notion that the court would actually apply this rule to "trump" a careful analysis of all the relevant facts. Implausible as it may seem, that is precisely what the Florida Supreme Court does. It routinely grants review in bus search cases and quashes denials of motions to suppress *expressly on the basis of its answer to the certified question in this case.*

Here, for example, the mere fact that Bostick did not feel free to leave the bus does not mean that the police seized him. Bostick was a passenger on a bus that was scheduled to depart. He would not have felt free to leave the bus even if the police had not been present. Bostick's movements were "confined" in a sense, but this was the natural result of his decision to take the bus; it says nothing about whether or not the police conduct at issue was coercive.

In this respect, the Court's decision in *INS v. Delgado*, [466 U.S. 210 (1984)], is dispositive. At issue there was the INS' practice of visiting factories at random and questioning employees to determine whether any were illegal aliens. Several INS agents would stand near the building's exits, while other agents walked through the factory questioning workers. The Court acknowledged that the workers may not have been free to leave their worksite, but explained that this was not the result of police activity: "Ordinarily, when people are at work their freedom to move about has been meaningfully restricted, not by the actions of law enforcement officials, but by the workers' voluntary obligations to their employers." We concluded that there was no seizure because, even though the workers were not free to leave the building without being questioned, the agents' conduct should have given employees "no reason to believe that they would be detained if they gave truthful answers to the questions put to them or if they simply refused to answer."

The present case is analytically indistinguishable from *Delgado*. Like the workers in that case, Bostick's freedom of movement was restricted by a factor independent of police conduct—*i.e.*, by his being a passenger on a bus. Accordingly, the "free to leave" analysis on which Bostick relies is inapplicable. In such a situation, the appropriate inquiry is whether a reasonable person would feel free to decline the officers' requests or otherwise terminate the encounter. This formulation follows logically from prior cases and breaks no new ground. We have said before that the crucial test is whether, taking into account all of the circumstances surrounding the encounter, the police conduct would "have communicated to a reasonable person that he was not at liberty to ignore the police presence and go about his business."[a] Where the encounter takes place is one

a. But, in one of the cases cited by the Court as supporting this "test," *California v. Hodari D.,* 499 U.S. 621 (1991), the Court concluded such communication does not inevitably constitute a seizure. The defendant ran upon seeing a police car, only to be pursued on foot by police, after which the defendant threw away cocaine and the police retrieved it. The state court suppressed the cocaine as the fruit of a seizure made without reasonable suspicion. The Supreme Court, 7–2, stated:

"The narrow question before us is whether, with respect to a show of authority as with respect to application of physical force, a seizure occurs even though the subject does not yield. We hold that it does not.

"The language of the Fourth Amendment, of course, cannot sustain respondent's contention. The word 'seizure' readily bears the meaning of a laying on of hands or application of physical force to restrain movement, even when it is ultimately unsuccessful. ('She seized the purse-snatcher, but he broke out of her grasp.') It does not remotely apply, however, to the prospect of a policeman yelling 'Stop, in the name of the law!' at a fleeing form that continues to flee. That is no seizure.

Nor can the result respondent wishes to achieve be produced—indirectly, as it were—by suggesting that Pertoso's uncomplied-with show of authority was a common-law arrest, and then appealing to the principle that all common-law arrests are seizures. An arrest requires *either* physical force (as described above) *or*, where that is absent, *submission* to the assertion of authority. * * *

"We do not think it desirable, even as a policy matter, to stretch the Fourth Amendment beyond its words and beyond the meaning of arrest, as respondent urges. Street pursuits always place the public at some risk, and compliance with police orders to stop should therefore be encouraged. Only a few of those orders, we must presume, will be without adequate basis, and since the addressee has no ready means of identifying the deficient ones it almost invariably is the responsible course to comply. Unlawful orders will not be deterred, moreover, by sanctioning through the exclusionary rule those of them are *not* obeyed. Since policemen do not command 'Stop!' expecting to be ignored, or give chase hoping to be outrun, it fully suffices to apply the deterrent to their genuine, successful seizures."

factor, but it is not the only one. And, as the Solicitor General correctly observes, an individual may decline an officer's request without fearing prosecution. We have consistently held that a refusal to cooperate, without more, does not furnish the minimal level of objective justification needed for a detention or seizure.

The facts of this case, as described by the Florida Supreme Court, leave some doubt whether a seizure occurred. Two officers walked up to Bostick on the bus, asked him a few questions, and asked if they could search his bags. As we have explained, no seizure occurs when police ask questions of an individual, ask to examine the individual's identification, and request consent to search his or her luggage—so long as the officers do not convey a message that compliance with their requests is required. Here, the facts recited by the Florida Supreme Court indicate that the officers did not point guns at Bostick or otherwise threaten him and that they specifically advised Bostick that he could refuse consent.

Nevertheless, we refrain from deciding whether or not a seizure occurred in this case. The trial court made no express findings of fact, and the Florida Supreme Court rested its decision on a single fact—that the encounter took place on a bus—rather than on the totality of the circumstances. We remand so that the Florida courts may evaluate the seizure question under the correct legal standard. We do reject, however, Bostick's argument that he must have been seized because no reasonable person would freely consent to a search of luggage that he or she knows contains drugs. This argument cannot prevail because the "reasonable person" test presupposes an *innocent* person.

The dissent characterizes our decision as holding that police may board buses and by an "*intimidating* show of authority" demand of passengers their "voluntary" cooperation. That characterization is incorrect. Clearly, a bus passenger's decision to cooperate with law enforcement officers authorizes the police to conduct a search without first obtaining a warrant *only* if the cooperation is voluntary. "Consent" that is the product of official intimidation or harassment is not consent at all. Citizens do not forfeit their constitutional rights when they are coerced to comply with a request that they would prefer to refuse. The question to be decided by the Florida courts on remand is whether Bostick chose to permit the search of his luggage.

The dissent also attempts to characterize our decision as applying a lesser degree of constitutional protection to those individuals who travel by bus, rather than by other forms of transportation. This, too, is an erroneous characterization. Our Fourth Amendment inquiry in this case—whether a reasonable person would have felt free to decline the officers' requests or otherwise terminate the encounter—applies equally to police encounters that take place on trains, planes, and city streets. It is the dissent that would single out this particular mode of travel for differential treatment by adopting a *per se* rule that random bus searches are unconstitutional.

The dissent reserves its strongest criticism for the proposition that police officers can approach individuals as to whom they have no reasonable suspicion and ask them potentially incriminating questions. But this proposition is by no means novel; it has been endorsed by the Court any number of times. As we

---

Citing *Hodari D.* for the proposition "that a police pursuit in attempting to seize a person does not amount to a 'seizure' within the meaning of the Fourth Amendment," the Court in *County of Sacramento v. Lewis,* 523 U.S. 833 (1998), also concluded "that no Fourth Amendment seizure would take place where a 'pursuing police car sought to stop the suspect only by the show of authority represented by flashing lights and continuing pursuit,' but accidentally stopped the suspect by crashing into him." This is because for a seizure there must be "a governmental termination of freedom of movement *through means intentionally applied.*"

have explained, today's decision follows logically from those decisions and breaks no new ground. Unless the dissent advocates overruling a long, unbroken line of decisions dating back more than 20 years, its criticism is not well taken. * * *

JUSTICE MARSHALL, with whom JUSTICE BLACKMUN and JUSTICE STEVENS join, dissenting. * * *

I have no objection to the manner in which the majority frames the test for determining whether a suspicionless bus sweep amounts to a Fourth Amendment "seizure." I agree that the appropriate question is whether a passenger who is approached during such a sweep "would feel free to decline the officers' request or otherwise terminate the encounter." What I cannot understand is how the majority can possibly suggest an affirmative answer to this question.

The majority reverses what it characterizes as the Florida Supreme Court's "*per se* rule" against suspicionless encounters between the police and bus passengers, suggesting only in dictum its "doubt" that a seizure occurred on the facts of this case. However, the notion that the Florida Supreme Court decided this case on the basis of any "*per se* rule" *independent* of the facts of this case is wholly a product of the majority's imagination. As the majority acknowledges, the Florida Supreme Court "stated explicitly the factual premise for its decision." This factual premise contained *all* of the details of the encounter between respondent and the police. The lower court's analysis of whether respondent was seized drew heavily on these facts, and the court repeatedly emphasized that its conclusion was based on "*all the circumstances*" of this case.

The majority's conclusion that the Florida Supreme Court, contrary to all appearances, *ignored* these facts is based solely on the failure of the lower court to expressly incorporate all of the facts into its reformulation of the certified question on which respondent took his appeal. The majority never explains the basis of its implausible assumption that the Florida Supreme Court intended its phrasing of the certified question to trump its opinion's careful treatment of the facts in this case. Certainly, when *this* Court issues an opinion, it does not intend lower courts and parties to treat as irrelevant the analysis of facts that the parties neglected to cram into the question presented in the petition for certiorari. But in any case, because the issue whether a seizure has occurred in any given factual setting is a question of law, nothing prevents this Court from deciding on its own whether a seizure occurred based on *all* of the facts of this case as they appear in the opinion of the Florida Supreme Court.

These facts exhibit all of the elements of coercion associated with a typical bus sweep. Two officers boarded the Greyhound bus on which respondent was a passenger while the bus, en route from Miami to Atlanta, was on a brief stop to pick up passengers in Fort Lauderdale. The officers made a visible display of their badges and wore bright green "raid" jackets bearing the insignia of the Broward County Sheriff's Department; one held a gun in a recognizable weapons pouch. These facts alone constitute an intimidating "show of authority." Once on board, the officers approached respondent, who was sitting in the back of the bus, identified themselves as narcotics officers and began to question him. One officer stood in front of respondent's seat, partially blocking the narrow aisle through which respondent would have been required to pass to reach the exit of the bus.

As far as is revealed by facts on which the Florida Supreme Court premised its decision, the officers did not advise respondent that he was free to break off this "interview." Inexplicably, the majority repeatedly stresses the trial court's implicit finding that the police officers advised respondent that he was free to refuse permission to search his travel bag. This aspect of the exchange between respondent and the police is completely irrelevant to the issue before us. For as the State concedes, and as the majority purports to "accept," *if* respondent was unlawfully seized when the officers approached him and initiated questioning, the resulting search was likewise unlawful no matter how well advised respondent was of his right to refuse it. Consequently, the issue is not whether a passenger in respondent's position would have felt free to deny consent to the search of his bag, but whether such a passenger—without being apprised of his rights—would have felt free to terminate the antecedent encounter with the police.

Unlike the majority, I have no doubt that the answer to this question is no. Apart from trying to accommodate the officers, respondent had only two options. First, he could have remained seated while obstinately refusing to respond to the officers' questioning. But in light of the intimidating show of authority that the officers made upon boarding the bus, respondent reasonably could have believed that such behavior would only arouse the officers' suspicions and intensify their interrogation. Indeed, officers who carry out bus sweeps like the one at issue here frequently admit that this is the effect of a passenger's refusal to cooperate. The majority's observation that a mere refusal to answer questions, "without more," does not give rise to a reasonable basis for seizing a passenger, is utterly beside the point, because a passenger unadvised of his rights and otherwise unversed in constitutional law *has no reason to know* that the police cannot hold his refusal to cooperate against him.

Second, respondent could have tried to escape the officers' presence by leaving the bus altogether. But because doing so would have required respondent to squeeze past the gun-wielding inquisitor who was blocking the aisle of the bus, this hardly seems like a course that respondent reasonably would have viewed as available to him. The majority lamely protests that nothing in the stipulated facts shows that the questioning officer *"point[ed]* [his] gu[n] at [respondent] or otherwise *threatened* him" with the weapon. Our decisions recognize the obvious point, however, that the choice of the police to "display" their weapons during an encounter exerts significant coercive pressure on the confronted citizen. We have never suggested that the police must go so far as to put a citizen in immediate apprehension of *being shot* before a court can take account of the intimidating effect of being questioned by an officer with weapon in hand.

Even if respondent had perceived that the officers would *let* him leave the bus, moreover, he could not reasonably have been expected to resort to this means of evading their intrusive questioning. For so far as respondent knew, the bus' departure from the terminal was imminent. Unlike a person approached by the police on the street or at a bus or airport terminal after reaching his destination, a passenger approached by the police at an intermediate point in a long bus journey cannot simply leave the scene and repair to a safe haven to avoid unwanted probing by law enforcement officials. The vulnerability that an intrastate or interstate traveler experiences when confronted by the police outside of his "own familiar territory" surely aggravates the coercive quality of such an encounter.

The case on which the majority primarily relies, *INS v. Delgado,* is distinguishable in every relevant respect. In *Delgado,* this Court held that workers approached by law-enforcement officials inside of a factory were not "seized" for purposes of the Fourth Amendment. The Court was careful to point out, however, that the presence of the agents did not furnish the workers with a reasonable basis for believing that they were not free to leave the factory, as at least some of them did. Unlike passengers confronted by law-enforcement officials on a bus stopped temporarily at an intermediate point in its journey, workers approached by law-enforcement officials at their workplace need not abandon personal belongings and venture into unfamiliar environs in order to avoid unwanted questioning. Moreover, the workers who did not leave the building in *Delgado* remained free to move about the entire factory, a considerably less confining environment than a bus. Finally, contrary to the officer who confronted respondent, the law-enforcement officials in *Delgado* did not conduct their interviews with guns in hand.

Rather than requiring the police to justify the coercive tactics employed here, the majority blames respondent for his own sensation of constraint. The majority concedes that respondent "did not feel free to leave the bus" as a means of breaking off the interrogation by the Broward County officers. But this experience of confinement, the majority explains, "was the natural result of *his* decision to take the bus." Thus, in the majority's view, because respondent's "freedom of movement was restricted by a factor independent of police conduct—*i.e.,* by his being a passenger on a bus," respondent was not seized for purposes of the Fourth Amendment.

This reasoning borders on sophism and trivializes the values that underlie the Fourth Amendment. Obviously, a person's "voluntary decision" to place himself in a room with only one exit does not authorize the police to force an encounter upon him by placing themselves in front of the exit. It is no more acceptable for the police to force an encounter on a person by exploiting his "voluntary decision" to expose himself to perfectly legitimate personal or social constraints. By consciously deciding to single out persons who have undertaken interstate or intrastate travel, officers who conduct suspicionless, dragnet-style sweeps put passengers to the choice of cooperating or of exiting their buses and possibly being stranded in unfamiliar locations. It is exactly because this "choice" is no "choice" at all that police engage this technique.

In my view, the Fourth Amendment clearly condemns the suspicionless, dragnet-style sweep of intrastate or interstate buses. Withdrawing this particular weapon from the government's drug-war arsenal would hardly leave the police without any means of combatting the use of buses as instrumentalities of the drug trade. The police would remain free, for example, to approach passengers whom they have a reasonable, articulable basis to suspect of criminal wrongdoing. Alternatively, they could continue to confront passengers without suspicion so long as they took simple steps, like advising the passengers confronted of their right to decline to be questioned, to dispel the aura of coercion and intimidation that pervades such encounters. There is no reason to expect that such requirements would render the Nation's buses law-enforcement-free zones. * * *

UNITED STATES v. PLACE

462 U.S. 696, 103 S.Ct. 2637, 77 L.Ed.2d 110 (1983).

Justice O'Connor delivered the opinion of the Court.

Respondent Raymond J. Place's behavior aroused the suspicions of law enforcement officers as he waited in line at the Miami International Airport to purchase a ticket to New York's La Guardia Airport. As Place proceeded to the gate for his flight, the agents approached him and requested his airline ticket and some identification. Place complied with the request and consented to a search of the two suitcases he had checked. Because his flight was about to depart, however, the agents decided not to search the luggage.

Prompted by Place's parting remark that he had recognized that they were police, the agents inspected the address tags on the checked luggage and noted discrepancies in the two street addresses. Further investigation revealed that neither address existed and that the telephone number Place had given the airline belonged to a third address on the same street. On the basis of their encounter with Place and this information, the Miami agents called Drug Enforcement Administration (DEA) authorities in New York to relay their information about Place.

Two DEA agents waited for Place at the arrival gate at La Guardia Airport in New York. There again, his behavior aroused the suspicion of the agents. After he had claimed his two bags and called a limousine, the agents decided to approach him. They identified themselves as federal narcotics agents, to which Place responded that he knew they were "cops" and had spotted them as soon as he had deplaned. One of the agents informed Place that, based on their own observations and information obtained from the Miami authorities, they believed that he might be carrying narcotics. After identifying the bags as belonging to him, Place stated that a number of police at the Miami Airport had surrounded him and searched his baggage. The agents responded that their information was to the contrary. The agents requested and received identification from Place—a New Jersey driver's license, on which the agents later ran a computer check that disclosed no offenses, and his airline ticket receipt. When Place refused to consent to a search of his luggage, one of the agents told him that they were going to take the luggage to a federal judge to try to obtain a search warrant and that Place was free to accompany them. Place declined, but obtained from one of the agents telephone numbers at which the agents could be reached.

The agents then took the bags to Kennedy Airport, where they subjected the bags to a "sniff test" by a trained narcotics detection dog. The dog reacted positively to the smaller of the two bags but ambiguously to the larger bag. Approximately 90 minutes had elapsed since the seizure of respondent's luggage. Because it was late on a Friday afternoon, the agents retained the luggage until Monday morning, when they secured a search warrant from a Magistrate for the smaller bag. Upon opening that bag, the agents discovered 1,125 grams of cocaine.

Place was indicted for possession of cocaine with intent to distribute in violation of 21 U.S.C. § 841(a)(1). In the District Court, Place moved to suppress the contents of the luggage seized from him at La Guardia Airport, claiming that the warrantless seizure of the luggage violated his Fourth Amendment rights. The District Court denied the motion. * * *

On appeal of the conviction, the United States Court of Appeals for the Second Circuit reversed. * * *

In this case, the Government asks us to recognize the reasonableness under the Fourth Amendment of warrantless seizures of personal luggage from the custody of the owner on the basis of less than probable cause, for the purpose of pursuing a limited course of investigation, short of opening the luggage, that would quickly confirm or dispel the authorities' suspicion. Specifically, we are asked to apply the principles of *Terry v. Ohio* to permit such seizures on the basis of reasonable, articulable suspicion, premised on objective facts, that the luggage contains contraband or evidence of a crime. In our view, such application is appropriate. * * *

The exception to the probable-cause requirement for limited seizures of the person recognized in *Terry* and its progeny rests on a balancing of the competing interests to determine the reasonableness of the type of seizure involved within the meaning of "the Fourth Amendment's general proscription against unreasonable searches and seizures." * * *

We examine first the governmental interest offered as a justification for a brief seizure of luggage from the suspect's custody for the purpose of pursuing a limited course of investigation. The Government contends that, where the authorities possess specific and articulable facts warranting a reasonable belief that a traveler's luggage contains narcotics, the governmental interest in seizing the luggage briefly to pursue further investigation is substantial. We agree. * * *

generalized interest in LE is insufficient

Respondent suggests that, absent some special law enforcement interest such as officer safety, a generalized interest in law enforcement cannot justify an intrusion on an individual's Fourth Amendment interests in the absence of probable cause. Our prior cases, however, do not support this proposition. In *Terry*, we described the governmental interests supporting the initial seizure of the person as "effective crime prevention and detection; it is this interest which underlies the recognition that a police officer may in appropriate circumstances and in an appropriate manner approach a person for purposes of investigating possibly criminal behavior even though there is no probable cause to make an arrest." * * *

does Terry notion of "less intrusive apply to property? yes

Against this strong governmental interest, we must weigh the nature and extent of the intrusion upon the individual's Fourth Amendment rights when the police briefly detain luggage for limited investigative purposes. On this point, respondent Place urges that the rationale for a *Terry* stop of the person is wholly inapplicable to investigative detentions of personalty. Specifically, the *Terry* exception to the probable-cause requirement is premised on the notion that a *Terry*-type stop of the person is substantially less intrusive of a person's liberty interests than a formal arrest. In the property context, however, Place urges, there are no degrees of intrusion. Once the owner's property is seized, the dispossession is absolute.

We disagree. The intrusion on possessory interests occasioned by a seizure of one's personal effects can vary both in its nature and extent. The seizure may be made after the owner has relinquished control of the property to a third party or, as here, from the immediate custody and control of the owner. Moreover, the police may confine their investigation to an on-the-spot inquiry—for example, immediate exposure of the luggage to a trained narcotics detection dog—or transport the property to another location. Given the fact that seizures of property can vary in intrusiveness, some brief detentions of personal effects may be so minimally intrusive of Fourth Amendment interests that strong countervailing governmental interests will justify a seizure based only on specific articulable facts that the property contains contraband or evidence of a crime.

In sum, we conclude that when an officer's observations lead him reasonably to believe that a traveler is carrying luggage that contains narcotics, the principles of *Terry* and its progeny would permit the officer to detain the luggage briefly to investigate the circumstances that aroused his suspicion, provided that the investigative detention is properly limited in scope. * * *

* * * We therefore examine whether the agents' conduct in this case was such as to place the seizure within the general rule requiring probable cause for a seizure or within *Terry*'s exception to that rule.

At the outset, we must reject the Government's suggestion that the point at which probable cause for seizure of luggage from the person's presence becomes necessary is more distant than in the case of a *Terry* stop of the person himself. The premise of the Government's argument is that seizures of property are generally less intrusive than seizures of the person. While true in some circumstances, that premise is faulty on the facts we address in this case. The precise type of detention we confront here is seizure of personal luggage from the immediate possession of the suspect for the purpose of arranging exposure to a narcotics detection dog. Particularly in the case of detention of luggage within the traveler's immediate possession, the police conduct intrudes on both the suspect's possessory interest in his luggage as well as his liberty interest in proceeding with his itinerary. The person whose luggage is detained is technically still free to continue his travels or carry out other personal activities pending release of the luggage. Moreover, he is not subjected to the coercive atmosphere of a custodial confinement or to the public indignity of being personally detained. Nevertheless, such a seizure can effectively restrain the person since he is subjected to the possible disruption of his travel plans in order to remain with his luggage or to arrange for its return.[8] Therefore, when the police seize luggage from the suspect's custody, we think the limitations applicable to investigative detentions of the person should define the permissible scope of an investigative detention of the person's luggage on less than probable cause. Under this standard, it is clear that the police conduct here exceeded the permissible limits of a *Terry*-type investigative stop.

The length of the detention of respondent's luggage alone precludes the conclusion that the seizure was reasonable in the absence of probable cause. Although we have recognized the reasonableness of seizures longer than the momentary ones involved in *Terry,* the brevity of the invasion of the individual's Fourth Amendment interests is an important factor in determining whether the seizure is so minimally intrusive as to be justifiable on reasonable suspicion. Moreover, in assessing the effect of the length of the detention, we take into account whether the police diligently pursue their investigation. We note that here the New York agents knew the time of Place's scheduled arrival at La Guardia, had ample time to arrange for their additional investigation at that location, and thereby could have minimized the intrusion on respondent's Fourth Amendment interests. Thus, although we decline to adopt any outside time limitation for a permissible *Terry* stop,[10] we have never approved a seizure of the person for the prolonged 90–minute period involved here and cannot do so on the facts presented by this case.

Although the 90–minute detention of respondent's luggage is sufficient to render the seizure unreasonable, the violation was exacerbated by the failure of the agents to accurately inform respondent of the place to which they were transporting his luggage, of the length of time he might be dispossessed, and of what arrangements would be made for return of the luggage if the investigation dispelled the suspicion. In short, we hold that the detention of respondent's luggage in this case went beyond the narrow authority possessed by police to detain briefly luggage reasonably suspected to contain narcotics. * * *

JUSTICE BRENNAN, with whom JUSTICE MARSHALL joins, concurring in the result. * * *

8. "At least when the authorities do not make it absolutely clear how they plan to reunite the suspect and his possessions at some future time and place, seizure of the object is tantamount to seizure of the person. This is because that person must either remain on the scene or else seemingly surrender his effects permanently to the police."

10. Cf. ALI, Model Code of Pre–Arraignment Procedure § 110.2(1) (1975) (recom-mending a maximum of 20 minutes for a *Terry* stop). We understand the desirability of providing law enforcement authorities with a clear rule to guide their conduct. Nevertheless, we question the wisdom of a rigid time limitation. Such a limit would undermine the equally important need to allow authorities to graduate their responses to the demands of any particular situation.

In this case, the officers' seizure of respondent and their later independent seizure of his luggage implicated separate Fourth Amendment interests. First, respondent had a protected interest in maintaining his personal security and privacy. *Terry* allows this interest to be overcome, and authorizes a limited intrusion, if the officers have reason to suspect that criminal activity is afoot. Second, respondent had a protected interest in retaining possession of his personal effects. While *Terry* may authorize seizures of personal effects incident to a lawful seizure of the person, nothing in the *Terry* line of cases authorizes the police to seize personal property, such as luggage, independent of the seizure of the person. Such seizures significantly expand the scope of a *Terry* stop and may not be effected on less than probable cause. Obviously, they also significantly expand the scope of the intrusion. * * *

In my view, as soon as the officers seized respondent's luggage, independent of their seizure of him, they exceeded the scope of a permissible *Terry* stop and violated respondent's Fourth Amendment rights. In addition, the officers' seizure of respondent's luggage violated the established rule that seizures of personal effects must be based on probable cause. Their actions, therefore, should not be upheld. * * *

JUSTICE BLACKMUN, with whom JUSTICE MARSHALL joins, concurring in the judgment. * * *

In providing guidance to other courts, we often include in our opinions material that, technically, constitutes dictum. I cannot fault the Court's desire to set guidelines for *Terry* seizures of luggage based on reasonable suspicion. I am concerned, however, with what appears to me to be an emerging tendency on the part of the Court to convert the *Terry* decision into a general statement that the Fourth Amendment requires only that any seizure be reasonable.[1] * * *

SECTION 9.   LESSER INTRUSIONS: INSPECTIONS AND REGULATORY SEARCHES

The Supreme Court and the lower courts have upheld a rather broad range of administrative inspections and so-called regulatory searches even when conducted without a warrant and without the traditional quantum of probable cause. These decisions manifest further application of the *Camara* balancing test, previously considered as utilized in *Terry* to assay the discrete police practice of stop-and-frisk. But *Camara* itself was an administrative inspection type of case, involving inspection of dwellings for housing code violations, and thus it is not surprising that this balancing process has since been utilized in various other administrative inspection or regulatory search contexts.

One difficult question presented in such cases is that of what *kind* of departure from the traditional probable cause requirement is permissible. One

---

1. The Court states that the applicability of the *Terry* exception "rests on a balancing of the competing interests to determine the reasonableness of the type of seizure involved within the meaning of 'the Fourth Amendment's general proscription against unreasonable searches and seizures.'" quoting *Terry*. As the context of the quotation from *Terry* makes clear, however, this balancing to determine reasonableness occurs only under the exceptional circumstances that justify the *Terry* exception:

"But we deal here with an entire rubric of police conduct—necessarily swift action predicated upon the on-the-spot observations of the officer on the beat—which historically has not been, and as a practical matter could not be, subjected to the warrant procedure. Instead, the conduct involved in this case must be tested by the Fourth Amendment's general proscription against unreasonable searches and seizures."

kind of departure, which we have already confronted in *Terry* and which is also sometimes used in the present context as well, is to require individualized suspicion (typically referred to as reasonable suspicion) less compelling than is needed for the usual law enforcement search. Illustrative are *O'Connor v. Ortega*, 480 U.S. 709 (1987), authorizing search of a government employee's workplace for work-related reasons on reasonable suspicion; and *New Jersey v. T.L.O.*, 469 U.S. 325 (1985), upholding search of a public school student on reasonable suspicion of a violation of school rules. Another kind of departure is to require no individualized suspicion whatsoever, but instead to require that the inspections or searches be conducted pursuant to some neutral criteria which guard against arbitrary selection of those subjected to such procedures. Illustrative are court decisions upholding airport security checks, driver's license check roadblocks, and sobriety checkpoints. The Court's latest foray into this area, while not a criminal case, provides an excellent vehicle for considering the respective merits of the reasonable suspicion and standardized procedures approaches:

VERNONIA SCHOOL DISTRICT 47J v. ACTON

515 U.S. 646, 115 S.Ct. 2386, 132 L.Ed.2d 564 (1995).

JUSTICE SCALIA delivered the opinion of the Court.

The Student Athlete Drug Policy adopted by School District 47J in the town of Vernonia, Oregon, authorizes random urinalysis drug testing of students who participate in the District's school athletics programs. We granted certiorari to decide whether this violates the Fourth and Fourteenth Amendments to the United States Constitution.

Petitioner Vernonia School District 47J (District) operates one high school and three grade schools in the logging community of Vernonia, Oregon. As elsewhere in small-town America, school sports play a prominent role in the town's life, and student athletes are admired in their schools and in the community.

Drugs had not been a major problem in Vernonia schools. In the mid-to-late 1980's, however, teachers and administrators observed a sharp increase in drug use. Students began to speak out about their attraction to the drug culture, and to boast that there was nothing the school could do about it. Along with more drugs came more disciplinary problems. Between 1988 and 1989 the number of disciplinary referrals in Vernonia schools rose to more than twice the number reported in the early 1980's, and several students were suspended. Students became increasingly rude during class; outbursts of profane language became common.

Not only were student athletes included among the drug users but, as the District Court found, athletes were the leaders of the drug culture. This caused the District's administrators particular concern, since drug use increases the risk of sports-related injury. Expert testimony at the trial confirmed the deleterious effects of drugs on motivation, memory, judgment, reaction, coordination, and performance. The high school football and wrestling coach witnessed a severe sternum injury suffered by a wrestler, and various omissions of safety procedures and misexecutions by football players, all attributable in his belief to the effects of drug use.

Initially, the District responded to the drug problem by offering special classes, speakers, and presentations designed to deter drug use. It even brought in a specially trained dog to detect drugs, but the drug problem persisted. According to the District Court:

"[T]he administration was at its wits end and ... a large segment of the student body, particularly those involved in interscholastic athletics, was in a state of rebellion. Disciplinary problems had reached 'epidemic proportions.' The coincidence of an almost three-fold increase in classroom disruptions and disciplinary reports along with the staff's direct observations of students using drugs or glamorizing drug and alcohol use led the administration to the inescapable conclusion that the rebellion was being fueled by alcohol and drug abuse as well as the student's misperceptions about the drug culture."

At that point, District officials began considering a drug-testing program. They held a parent "input night" to discuss the proposed Student Athlete Drug Policy (Policy), and the parents in attendance gave their unanimous approval. The school board approved the Policy for implementation in the fall of 1989. Its expressed purpose is to prevent student athletes from using drugs, to protect their health and safety, and to provide drug users with assistance programs.

The Policy applies to all students participating in interscholastic athletics. Students wishing to play sports must sign a form consenting to the testing and must obtain the written consent of their parents. Athletes are tested at the beginning of the season for their sport. In addition, once each week of the season the names of the athletes are placed in a "pool" from which a student, with the supervision of two adults, blindly draws the names of 10% of the athletes for random testing. Those selected are notified and tested that same day, if possible.

The student to be tested completes a specimen control form which bears an assigned number. Prescription medications that the student is taking must be identified by providing a copy of the prescription or a doctor's authorization. The student then enters an empty locker room accompanied by an adult monitor of the same sex. Each boy selected produces a sample at a urinal, remaining fully clothed with his back to the monitor, who stands approximately 12 to 15 feet behind the student. Monitors may (though do not always) watch the student while he produces the sample, and they listen for normal sounds of urination. Girls produce samples in an enclosed bathroom stall, so that they can be heard but not observed. After the sample is produced, it is given to the monitor, who checks it for temperature and tampering and then transfers it to a vial.

The samples are sent to an independent laboratory, which routinely tests them for amphetamines, cocaine, and marijuana. Other drugs, such as LSD, may be screened at the request of the District, but the identity of a particular student does not determine which drugs will be tested. The laboratory's procedures are 99.94% accurate. The District follows strict procedures regarding the chain of custody and access to test results. The laboratory does not know the identity of the students whose samples it tests. It is authorized to mail written test reports only to the superintendent and to provide test results to District personnel by telephone only after the requesting official recites a code confirming his authority. Only the superintendent, principals, vice-principals, and athletic directors have access to test results, and the results are not kept for more than one year.

If a sample tests positive, a second test is administered as soon as possible to confirm the result. If the second test is negative, no further action is taken. If the second test is positive, the athlete's parents are notified, and the school principal convenes a meeting with the student and his parents, at which the student is given the option of (1) participating for six weeks in an assistance program that includes weekly urinalysis, or (2) suffering suspension from athletics for the remainder of the current season and the next athletic season. The student is then retested prior to the start of the next athletic season for which he or she is eligible. The Policy states that a second offense results in automatic imposition of option (2); a third offense in suspension for the remainder of the current season and the next two athletic seasons.

In the fall of 1991, respondent James Acton, then a seventh-grader, signed up to play football at one of the District's grade schools. He was denied participation, however, because he and his parents refused to sign the testing consent forms. The Actons filed suit, seeking declaratory and injunctive relief from enforcement of the Policy on the grounds that it violated the Fourth and Fourteenth Amendments * * *. After a bench trial, the District Court entered an order denying the claims on the merits and dismissing the action. The United States Court of Appeals for the Ninth Circuit reversed, holding that the Policy violated both the Fourth and Fourteenth Amendments * * *. We granted certiorari.

The Fourth Amendment to the United States Constitution provides that the Federal Government shall not violate "[t]he right of the people to be secure in their persons, houses, papers, and effects, against unreasonable searches and seizures...." We have held that the Fourteenth Amendment extends this constitutional guarantee to searches and seizures by state officers, including public school officials, *New Jersey v. T.L.O.*, 469 U.S. 325 (1985). In *Skinner v. Railway Labor Executives' Assn.*, 489 U.S. 602 (1989), we held that state-compelled collection and testing of urine, such as that required by the Student Athlete Drug Policy, constitutes a "search" subject to the demands of the Fourth Amendment. See also *National Treasury Employees v. Von Raab*, 489 U.S. 656 (1989).

As the text of the Fourth Amendment indicates, the ultimate measure of the constitutionality of a governmental search is "reasonableness." At least in a case such as this, where there was no clear practice, either approving or disapproving the type of search at issue, at the time the constitutional provision was enacted, whether a particular search meets the reasonableness standard " 'is judged by balancing its intrusion on the individual's Fourth Amendment interests against its promotion of legitimate governmental interests.' " Where a search is undertaken by law enforcement officials to discover evidence of criminal wrongdoing, this Court has said that reasonableness generally requires the obtaining of a judicial warrant. Warrants cannot be issued, of course, without the showing of probable cause required by the Warrant Clause. But a warrant is not required to establish the reasonableness of all government searches; and when a warrant is not required (and the Warrant Clause therefore not applicable), probable cause is not invariably required either. A search unsupported by probable cause can be constitutional, we have said, "when special needs, beyond the normal need for law enforcement, make the warrant and probable-cause requirement impracticable." *Griffin v. Wisconsin*, 483 U.S. 868 (1987).

We have found such "special needs" to exist in the public-school context. There, the warrant requirement "would unduly interfere with the maintenance of the swift and informal disciplinary procedures [that are] needed," and "strict adherence to the requirement that searches be based upon probable cause" would undercut "the substantial need of teachers and administrators for freedom to maintain order in the schools." *T.L.O.* The school search we approved in *T.L.O.*, while not based on probable cause, was based on individualized suspicion of wrongdoing. As we explicitly acknowledged, however, " 'the Fourth Amendment imposes no irreducible requirement of such suspicion.' " We have upheld suspicionless searches and seizures to conduct drug testing of railroad personnel involved in train accidents, see *Skinner;* to conduct random drug testing of federal customs officers who carry arms or are involved in drug interdiction, see

Von Raab; and to maintain automobile checkpoints looking for illegal immigrants and contraband and drunk drivers.

The first factor to be considered is the nature of the privacy interest upon which the search here at issue intrudes. The Fourth Amendment does not protect all subjective expectations of privacy, but only those that society recognizes as "legitimate." What expectations are legitimate varies, of course, with context, depending, for example, upon whether the individual asserting the privacy interest is at home, at work, in a car, or in a public park. In addition, the legitimacy of certain privacy expectations vis-vis the State may depend upon the individual's legal relationship with the State. For example, in *Griffin* we held that, although a "probationer's home, like anyone else's, is protected by the Fourth Amendmen[t]," the supervisory relationship between probationer and State justifies "a degree of impingement upon [a probationer's] privacy that would not be constitutional if applied to the public at large." Central, in our view, to the present case is the fact that the subjects of the Policy are (1) children, who (2) have been committed to the temporary custody of the State as schoolmaster.

Traditionally at common law, and still today, unemancipated minors lack some of the most fundamental rights of self-determination—including even the right of liberty in its narrow sense, i.e., the right to come and go at will. They are subject, even as to their physical freedom, to the control of their parents or guardians. When parents place minor children in private schools for their education, the teachers and administrators of those schools stand in loco parentis over the children entrusted to them. * * *

In *T.L.O.* we rejected the notion that public schools, like private schools, exercise only parental power over their students, which of course is not subject to constitutional constraints. Such a view of things, we said, "is not entirely 'consonant with compulsory education laws,' " * * *. But while denying that the State's power over schoolchildren is formally no more than the delegated power of their parents, *T.L.O.* did not deny, but indeed emphasized, that the nature of that power is custodial and tutelary, permitting a degree of supervision and control that could not be exercised over free adults. "[A] proper educational environment requires close supervision of schoolchildren, as well as the enforcement of rules against conduct that would be perfectly permissible if undertaken by an adult." * * * Thus, while children assuredly do not "shed their constitutional rights … at the schoolhouse gate," the nature of those rights is what is appropriate for children in school. * * *

Fourth Amendment rights * * * are different in public schools than elsewhere; the "reasonableness" inquiry cannot disregard the schools' custodial and tutelary responsibility for children. For their own good and that of their classmates, public school children are routinely required to submit to various physical examinations, and to be vaccinated against various diseases. * * * Particularly with regard to medical examinations and procedures, therefore, "students within the school environment have a lesser expectation of privacy than members of the population generally."

Legitimate privacy expectations are even less with regard to student athletes. School sports are not for the bashful. They require "suiting up" before each practice or event, and showering and changing afterwards. Public school locker rooms, the usual sites for these activities, are not notable for the privacy they afford. The locker rooms in Vernonia are typical: no individual dressing rooms are provided; shower heads are lined up along a wall, unseparated by any sort of partition or curtain; not even all the toilet stalls have doors.

There is an additional respect in which school athletes have a reduced expectation of privacy. By choosing to "go out for the team," they voluntarily subject themselves to a degree of regulation even higher than that imposed on students generally. In Vernonia's public schools, they must submit to a preseason physical exam (James testified that his included the giving of a urine sample), they must acquire adequate insurance coverage or sign an insurance waiver, maintain a minimum grade point average, and comply with any "rules of conduct, dress, training hours and related matters as may be established for each sport by the head coach and athletic director with the principal's approval." Somewhat like adults who choose to participate in a "closely regulated industry," students who voluntarily participate in school athletics have reason to expect intrusions upon normal rights and privileges, including privacy.

Having considered the scope of the legitimate expectation of privacy at issue here, we turn next to the character of the intrusion that is complained of. We recognized in *Skinner* that collecting the samples for urinalysis intrudes upon "an excretory function traditionally shielded by great privacy." We noted, however, that the degree of intrusion depends upon the manner in which production of the urine sample is monitored. Under the District's Policy, male students produce samples at a urinal along a wall. They remain fully clothed and are only observed from behind, if at all. Female students produce samples in an enclosed stall, with a female monitor standing outside listening only for sounds of tampering. These conditions are nearly identical to those typically encountered in public restrooms, which men, women, and especially school children use daily. Under such conditions, the privacy interests compromised by the process of obtaining the urine sample are in our view negligible.

The other privacy-invasive aspect of urinalysis is, of course, the information it discloses concerning the state of the subject's body, and the materials he has ingested. In this regard it is significant that the tests at issue here look only for drugs, and not for whether the student is, for example, epileptic, pregnant, or diabetic. Moreover, the drugs for which the samples are screened are standard, and do not vary according to the identity of the student. And finally, the results of the tests are disclosed only to a limited class of school personnel who have a need to know; and they are not turned over to law enforcement authorities or used for any internal disciplinary function.[a] * * *

---

a. In all cases in which departure from the usual warrant and/or probable cause requirements is claimed to be justified on the basis of some "special need," it is necessary that this need be sufficiently different from and divorced from the state's general law enforcement interest, as is highlighted in two recent cases: *City of Indianapolis v. Edmond*, 531 U.S. 32 (2000); and *Ferguson v. City of Charleston*, 121 S.Ct. 1281 (2001).

Ferguson, because it also involved a drug test, can be most usefully compared with *Acton*. A task force made up of representatives of the Charleston public hospital, police and other public officials developed a policy for identifying and testing pregnant patients suspected of drug use and then turning the results over to law enforcement agents without the knowledge or consent of the patients. This policy, which also contained police procedures for arresting patients and for prosecuting them for drug offenses and/or child neglect, was challenged by a group of obstetrical patients at that hospi-

tal who had been arrested after testing positive for cocaine. The question, as the Supreme Court put it, was "whether the interest in using the threat of criminal sanctions to deter pregnant women from using cocaine can justify a departure from the general rule that an official nonconsensual search is unconstitutional if not authorized by a valid warrant."

The majority in *Ferguson* noted that the instant case was different from *Acton* and the Court's other prior drug testing cases in several material respects: for one, in the previous cases "there was no misunderstanding about the purpose of the test or the potential use of the test results, and there were protections against the dissemination of the results to third parties." But the "critical difference" between the earlier cases and the instant one, the Court emphasized, "lies in the nature of the 'special need' asserted as justification for the warrantless searches," for in all the earlier cases the "special need" advanced was "one

Finally, we turn to consider the nature and immediacy of the governmental concern at issue here, and the efficacy of this means for meeting it. In both *Skinner* and *Von Raab,* we characterized the government interest motivating the search as "compelling." *Skinner* (interest in preventing railway accidents); *Von Raab* (interest in insuring fitness of customs officials to interdict drugs and handle firearms). * * * It is a mistake, however, to think that the phrase "compelling state interest," in the Fourth Amendment context, describes a fixed, minimum quantum of governmental concern, so that one can dispose of a case by answering in isolation the question: Is there a compelling state interest here? Rather, the phrase describes an interest which appears important enough to justify the particular search at hand, in light of other factors which show the search to be relatively intrusive upon a genuine expectation of privacy. Whether that relatively high degree of government concern is necessary in this case or not, we think it is met.

That the nature of the concern is important—indeed, perhaps compelling— can hardly be doubted. Deterring drug use by our Nation's schoolchildren is at least as important as enhancing efficient enforcement of the Nation's laws against the importation of drugs, which was the governmental concern in *Von Raab,* or deterring drug use by engineers and trainmen, which was the governmental concern in *Skinner.* School years are the time when the physical, psychological, and addictive effects of drugs are most severe. * * * And of course the effects of a drug-infested school are visited not just upon the users, but upon the entire student body and faculty, as the educational process is disrupted. In the present

divorced from the State's general interest in law enforcement," which here "the central and indispensable feature of the policy from its inception was the use of law enforcement to coerce the patients into substance abuse treatment." As for the respondents' argument that their ultimate purpose of protecting both the mother and child was "a beneficent one," the majority responded that the policy itself "plainly reveals" that the purpose actually served "is ultimately indistinguishable from the general interest in crime control," for "an initial and continuing focus of the policy was on the arrest and prosecution of drug-abusing mothers," and local "prosecutors and police were extensively involved in the day-to-day administration of the policy." And it made no difference that the "threat of law enforcement" may have been "a means to an end," for if that did make a difference then "virtually any nonconsensual suspicionless search could be immunized under the special needs doctrine by defining the search solely in terms of its ultimate, rather than immediate purpose." (One concurring justice questioned the latter point and would have rested the decision solely on the fact that none of the Court's "special needs precedents has sanctioned the routine inclusion of law enforcement, both in the design of the policy and in using arrests, either threatened or real, to implement the system designed for the special needs objectives." The three dissenters objected that it was not so that "the addition of a law-enforcement related purpose to a legitimate medical purpose destroys applicability of the 'special-needs' doctrine," "since the special-needs doctrine was developed, and is ordinarily employed, precisely to enable searched by law enforcement offi-

cials who, of course, ordinarily have a law enforcement objective," as illustrated by *Griffin v. Wisconsin,* discussed in *Acton.*)

Ferguson relied on *Edmond,* decided just weeks before, where the Court held that city-operated vehicle checkpoints, complete with drug dogs, undertaken to interdict unlawful drugs, contravened the Fourth Amendment. In support of the checkpoints, the city argued that their validity followed from the Court's prior decisions indicating approval of checkpoints conducted to intercept illegal aliens, to remove drunk drivers from the road, or to check driver's licenses and vehicle registrations. But the *Edmond* majority distinguished those cases because in none of them "did we indicate approval of a checkpoint program whose primary purpose was to detect evidence of ordinary criminal wrongdoing." As for the city's response that securing the border and apprehending drunk drivers "are * * * law enforcement activities, and law enforcement officers employ arrests and criminal prosecutions in pursuit of these goals," the Court responded that analysis at that "high level of generality" would mean there "would be little check on the ability of the authorities to construct roadblocks for almost any conceivable law enforcement purpose." The three dissenters in *Edmond,* on the other hand, argued that the checkpoints here at issue shared the critical characteristics of those previously approved by the Court: they "effectively serve the State's legitimate interests; they are executed in a regularized and neutral manner, and they only minimally intrude upon the privacy of the motorists."

case, moreover, the necessity for the State to act is magnified by the fact that this evil is being visited not just upon individuals at large, but upon children for whom it has undertaken a special responsibility of care and direction. Finally, it must not be lost sight of that this program is directed more narrowly to drug use by school athletes, where the risk of immediate physical harm to the drug user or those with whom he is playing his sport is particularly high. Apart from psychological effects, which include impairment of judgment, slow reaction time, and a lessening of the perception of pain, the particular drugs screened by the District's Policy have been demonstrated to pose substantial physical risks to athletes. * * *

As for the immediacy of the District's concerns: We are not inclined to question—indeed, we could not possibly find clearly erroneous—the District Court's conclusion that "a large segment of the student body, particularly those involved in interscholastic athletics, was in a state of rebellion," that "[d]isciplinary actions had reached 'epidemic proportions,'" and that "the rebellion was being fueled by alcohol and drug abuse as well as by the student's misperceptions about the drug culture." That is an immediate crisis of greater proportions than existed in *Skinner,* where we upheld the Government's drug testing program based on findings of drug use by railroad employees nationwide, without proof that a problem existed on the particular railroads whose employees were subject to the test. And of much greater proportions than existed in *Von Raab,* where there was no documented history of drug use by any customs officials.[b]

As to the efficacy of this means for addressing the problem: It seems to us self-evident that a drug problem largely fueled by the "role model" effect of athletes' drug use, and of particular danger to athletes, is effectively addressed by making sure that athletes do not use drugs. Respondents argue that a "less intrusive means to the same end" was available, namely, "drug testing on suspicion of drug use." We have repeatedly refused to declare that only the "least intrusive" search practicable can be reasonable under the Fourth Amendment. Respondents' alternative entails substantial difficulties—if it is indeed practicable at all. It may be impracticable, for one thing, simply because the parents who are willing to accept random drug testing for athletes are not willing to accept accusatory drug testing for all students, which transforms the process into a badge of shame. Respondents' proposal brings the risk that teachers will impose testing arbitrarily upon troublesome but not drug-likely students. It generates the expense of defending lawsuits that charge such arbitrary imposition, or that simply demand greater process before accusatory drug testing is imposed. And not least of all, it adds to the ever-expanding diversionary duties of schoolteachers the new function of spotting and bringing to account drug abuse, a task for which they are ill prepared, and which is not readily compatible with their vocation. In many respects, we think, testing based on "suspicion" of drug use would not be better, but worse.

b. Compare *Chandler v. Miller,* 520 U.S. 305 (1997), invalidating a Georgia statute requiring each candidate for public office to submit to drug testing, where the Court stated: "Georgia asserts no evidence of a drug problem among the State's elected officials, those officials typically do not perform high-risk, safety-sensitive tasks, and the required certification immediately aids no interdiction effort. The need revealed, in short, is symbolic, not 'special,' as that term draws meaning from our case law." As for the state's reliance on *Von Raab,* the Court noted that there the affected employees and their work product were not amenable to "day-to-day scrutiny," and then concluded: "Candidates for public office, in contrast, are subject to relentless scrutiny—by their peers, the public, and the press. Their day-to-day conduct attracts attention notable beyond the norm in ordinary work environments."

Taking into account all the factors we have considered above—the decreased expectation of privacy, the relative unobtrusiveness of the search, and the severity of the need met by the search—we conclude Vernonia's Policy is reasonable and hence constitutional.

We caution against the assumption that suspicionless drug testing will readily pass constitutional muster in other contexts. The most significant element in this case is the first we discussed: that the Policy was undertaken in furtherance of the government's responsibilities, under a public school system, as guardian and tutor of children entrusted to its care. Just as when the government conducts a search in its capacity as employer (a warrantless search of an absent employee's desk to obtain an urgently needed file, for example), the relevant question is whether that intrusion upon privacy is one that a reasonable employer might engage in, so also when the government acts as guardian and tutor the relevant question is whether the search is one that a reasonable guardian and tutor might undertake. Given the findings of need made by the District Court, we conclude that in the present case it is.

We may note that the primary guardians of Vernonia's schoolchildren appear to agree. The record shows no objection to this districtwide program by any parents other than the couple before us here—even though, as we have described, a public meeting was held to obtain parents' views. We find insufficient basis to contradict the judgment of Vernonia's parents, its school board, and the District Court, as to what was reasonably in the interest of these children under the circumstances. * * *

JUSTICE GINSBURG, concurring. * * * I comprehend the Court's opinion as reserving the question whether the District, on no more than the showing made here, constitutionally could impose routine drug testing not only on those seeking to engage with others in team sports, but on all students required to attend school.

JUSTICE O'CONNOR, with whom JUSTICE STEVENS and JUSTICE SOUTER join, dissenting.

The population of our Nation's public schools, grades 7 through 12, numbers around 18 million. By the reasoning of today's decision, the millions of these students who participate in interscholastic sports, an overwhelming majority of whom have given school officials no reason whatsoever to suspect they use drugs at school, are open to an intrusive bodily search.

In justifying this result, the Court dispenses with a requirement of individualized suspicion on considered policy grounds. * * * In making these policy arguments, of course, the Court sidesteps powerful, countervailing privacy concerns. Blanket searches, because they can involve "thousands or millions" of searches, "pos[e] a greater threat to liberty" than do suspicion-based ones, which "affec[t] one person at a time." Searches based on individualized suspicion also afford potential targets considerable control over whether they will, in fact, be searched because a person can avoid such a search by not acting in an objectively suspicious way. And given that the surest way to avoid acting suspiciously is to avoid the underlying wrongdoing, the costs of such a regime, one would think, are minimal.

But whether a blanket search is "better" than a regime based on individualized suspicion is not a debate in which we should engage. In my view, it is not open to judges or government officials to decide on policy grounds which is better and which is worse. For most of our constitutional history, mass, suspicionless searches have been generally considered per se unreasonable within the meaning of the Fourth Amendment. And we have allowed exceptions in recent years only where it has been clear that a suspicion-based regime would be ineffectual. Because that is not the case here, I dissent. * * *

The *Carroll* [*v. United States*, 267 U.S. 132 (1925)] Court's view that blanket searches are "intolerable and unreasonable" is well-grounded in history. As recently confirmed in one of the most exhaustive analyses of the original meaning of the Fourth Amendment ever undertaken, what the Framers of the Fourth Amendment most strongly opposed, with limited exceptions wholly inapplicable here, were general searches—that is, searches by general warrant, by writ of assistance, by broad statute, or by any other similar authority. * * *

More important, there is no indication in the historical materials that the Framers' opposition to general searches stemmed solely from the fact that they allowed officials to single out individuals for arbitrary reasons, and thus that officials could render them reasonable simply by making sure to extend their search to every house in a given area or to every person in a given group. * * *

Perhaps most telling of all, as reflected in the text of the Warrant Clause, the particular way the Framers chose to curb the abuses of general warrants—and by implication, all general searches—was not to impose a novel "evenhandedness" requirement; it was to retain the individualized suspicion requirement contained in the typical general warrant, but to make that requirement meaningful and enforceable, for instance, by raising the required level of individualized suspicion to objective probable cause. * * *

The view that mass, suspicionless searches, however evenhanded, are generally unreasonable remains inviolate in the criminal law enforcement context. * * *

Thus, it remains the law that the police cannot, say, subject to drug testing every person entering or leaving a certain drug-ridden neighborhood in order to find evidence of crime. And this is true even though it is hard to think of a more compelling government interest than the need to fight the scourge of drugs on our streets and in our neighborhoods. Nor could it be otherwise, for if being evenhanded were enough to justify evaluating a search regime under an open-ended balancing test, the Warrant Clause, which presupposes that there is some category of searches for which individualized suspicion is non-negotiable, would be a dead letter.

Outside the criminal context, however, in response to the exigencies of modern life, our cases have upheld several evenhanded blanket searches, including some that are more than minimally intrusive, after balancing the invasion of privacy against the government's strong need. Most of these cases, of course, are distinguishable insofar as they involved searches either not of a personally intrusive nature, such as searches of closely regulated businesses, see, e.g., *New York v. Burger*, 482 U.S. 691 (1987), or arising in unique contexts such as prisons * * *.

In any event, in many of the cases that can be distinguished on the grounds suggested above and, more important, in all of the cases that cannot, see, e.g., *Skinner* (blanket drug testing scheme); *Von Raab* (same); cf. *Camara v. Municipal Court*, 387 U.S. 523 (1967) (area-wide searches of private residences), we upheld the suspicionless search only after first recognizing the Fourth Amendment's longstanding preference for a suspicion-based search regime, and then pointing to sound reasons why such a regime would likely be ineffectual under the unusual circumstances presented. In *Skinner*, for example, we stated outright that " 'some quantum of individualized suspicion' " is "usually required" under the Fourth Amendment, and we built the requirement into the test we an-

Skinner

nounced: "In limited circumstances, where the privacy interests implicated by the search are minimal, and where an important governmental interest furthered by the intrusion would be placed in jeopardy by a requirement of individualized suspicion, a search may be reasonable despite the absence of such suspicion." The obvious negative implication of this reasoning is that, if such an individualized suspicion requirement would not place the government's objectives in jeopardy, the requirement should not be forsaken.

Accordingly, we upheld the suspicionless regime at issue in *Skinner* on the firm understanding that a requirement of individualized suspicion for testing train operators for drug or alcohol impairment following serious train accidents would be unworkable because "the scene of a serious rail accident is chaotic." (Of course, it could be plausibly argued that the fact that testing occurred only after train operators were involved in serious train accidents amounted to an individualized suspicion requirement in all but name, in light of the record evidence of a strong link between serious train accidents and drug and alcohol use.) We have performed a similar inquiry in the other cases as well. * * *

Moreover, an individualized suspicion requirement was often impractical in these cases because they involved situations in which even one undetected instance of wrongdoing could have injurious consequences for a great number of people. See, e.g., *Camara* (even one safety code violation can cause "fires and epidemics [that] ravage large urban areas"); *Skinner,* supra (even one drug- or alcohol-impaired train operator can lead to the "disastrous consequences" of a train wreck, such as "great human loss"); *Von Raab* (even one customs official caught up in drugs can, by virtue of impairment, susceptibility to bribes, or indifference, result in the noninterdiction of a "sizable drug shipmen[t]," which eventually injures the lives of thousands, or to a breach of "national security").

The instant case stands in marked contrast. One searches today's majority opinion in vain for recognition that history and precedent establish that individualized suspicion is "usually required" under the Fourth Amendment (regardless of whether a warrant and probable cause are also required) and that, in the area of intrusive personal searches, the only recognized exception is for situations in which a suspicion-based scheme would be likely ineffectual. * * *

But having misconstrued the fundamental role of the individualized suspicion requirement in Fourth Amendment analysis, the Court never seriously engages the practicality of such a requirement in the instant case. And that failure is crucial because nowhere is it less clear that an individualized suspicion requirement would be ineffectual than in the school context. In most schools, the entire pool of potential search targets—students—is under constant supervision by teachers and administrators and coaches, be it in classrooms, hallways, or locker rooms.

The record here indicates that the Vernonia schools are no exception. The great irony of this case is that most (though not all) of the evidence the District introduced to justify its suspicionless drug-testing program consisted of first- or second-hand stories of particular, identifiable students acting in ways that plainly gave rise to reasonable suspicion of in-school drug use—and thus that would have justified a drug-related search under our *T.L.O.* decision. Small groups of students, for example, were observed by a teacher "passing joints back and forth" across the street at a restaurant before school and during school hours. Another group was caught skipping school and using drugs at one of the students' houses. Several students actually admitted their drug use to school officials (some of them being caught with marijuana pipes). One student presented himself to his teacher as "clearly obviously inebriated" and had to be sent home. Still another was observed dancing and singing at the top of his voice in the back of the classroom; when the teacher asked what was going on, he replied, "Well, I'm just high on life." To take a final example, on a certain road trip, the school wrestling coach smelled marijuana smoke in a hotel room occupied by four wrestlers, an observation that (after some questioning) would probably have given him reasonable suspicion to test one or all of them.

In light of all this evidence of drug use by particular students, there is a substantial basis for concluding that a vigorous regime of suspicion-based testing (for which the District appears already to have rules in place) would have gone a long way toward solving Vernonia's school drug problem while preserving the Fourth Amendment rights of James Acton and others like him. And were there any doubt about such a conclusion, it is removed by indications in the record that suspicion-based testing could have been supplemented by an equally vigorous campaign to have Vernonia's parents encourage their children to submit to the District's voluntary drug testing program. In these circumstances, the Fourth Amendment dictates that a mass, suspicionless search regime is categorically unreasonable. * * *

The principal counterargument to all this, central to the Court's opinion, is that the Fourth Amendment is more lenient with respect to school searches. That is no doubt correct, for, as the Court explains, schools have traditionally had special guardian-like responsibilities for children that necessitate a degree of constitutional leeway. This principle explains the considerable Fourth Amendment leeway we gave school officials in *T.L.O.* In that case, we held that children at school do not enjoy two of the Fourth Amendment's traditional categorical protections against unreasonable searches and seizures: the warrant requirement and the probable cause requirement. * * *

The instant case, however, asks whether the Fourth Amendment is even more lenient than that, i.e., whether it is so lenient that students may be deprived of the Fourth Amendment's only remaining, and most basic, categorical protection: its strong preference for an individualized suspicion requirement, with its accompanying antipathy toward personally intrusive, blanket searches of mostly innocent people. [T]he answer must plainly be no.

I find unpersuasive the Court's reliance on the widespread practice of physical examinations and vaccinations, which are both blanket searches of a sort. [A] suspicion requirement for vaccinations is not merely impractical; it is nonsensical, for vaccinations are not searches for anything in particular and so there is nothing about which to be suspicious. * * * As for physical examinations, the practicability of a suspicion requirement is highly doubtful because the conditions for which these physical exams ordinarily search, such as latent heart conditions, do not manifest themselves in observable behavior the way school drug use does.

I do not believe that suspicionless drug testing is justified on these facts. But even if I agreed that some such testing were reasonable here, I see two other Fourth Amendment flaws in the District's program. First, and most serious, there is virtually no evidence in the record of a drug problem at the Washington Grade School, which includes the 7th and 8th grades, and which Acton attended when this litigation began. * * *

Second, even as to the high school, I find unreasonable the school's choice of student athletes as the class to subject to suspicionless testing—a choice that appears to have been driven more by a belief in what would pass constitutional muster, than by a belief in what was required to meet the District's principal disciplinary concern. Reading the full record in this case, it seems quite obvious that the true driving force behind the District's adoption of its drug testing program was the need to combat the rise in drug-related disorder and disruption in its classrooms and around campus. * * * And the record in this case surely demonstrates there was a drug-related discipline problem in Vernonia of " 'epidemic proportions.' " The evidence of a drug-related sports injury problem at Vernonia, by contrast, was considerably weaker.

On this record, then, it seems to me that the far more reasonable choice would have been to focus on the class of students found to have violated published school rules against severe disruption in class and around campus, disruption that had a strong nexus to drug use, as the District established at trial. Such a choice would share two of the virtues of a suspicion-based regime: testing dramatically fewer students, tens as against hundreds, and giving students control, through their behavior, over the likelihood that they would be tested. Moreover, there would be a reduced concern for the accusatory nature of the search, because the Court's feared "badge of shame," would already exist, due to the antecedent accusation and finding of severe disruption. In a lesser known aspect of *Skinner,* we upheld an analogous testing scheme with little hesitation. See *Skinner* (describing " 'Authorization to Test for Cause' " scheme, according to which train operators would be tested "in the event of certain specific rule violations, including noncompliance with a signal and excessive speeding").

It cannot be too often stated that the greatest threats to our constitutional freedoms come in times of crisis. But we must also stay mindful that not all government responses to such times are hysterical overreactions; some crises are quite real, and when they are, they serve precisely as the compelling state interest that we have said may justify a measured intrusion on constitutional rights. The only way for judges to mediate these conflicting impulses is to do what they should do anyway: stay close to the record in each case that appears before them, and make their judgments based on that alone. Having reviewed the record here, I cannot avoid the conclusion that the District's suspicionless policy of testing all student-athletes sweeps too broadly, and too imprecisely, to be reasonable under the Fourth Amendment.

SECTION 10. CONSENT SEARCHES

So-called consent searches are frequently relied upon by police as a means of investigating suspected criminal conduct. Sometimes probable cause is present but the police feel either that they do not have time to get a warrant or that they would simply like to avoid that time-consuming process, but more often an effort is made to obtain consent where probable cause is lacking and no warrant could be obtained. The exact meaning of "consent" in this context, the question explored in *Schneckloth v. Bustamonte,* is thus a matter of some importance.

In *Schneckloth,* by way of showing that the protections of the Fourth Amendment "are of a wholly different order" than various other constitutional rights, the Court noted that a person's privacy may sometimes be lawfully invaded by virtue of consent obtained by police from a third party. The Supreme Court has experienced some difficulty over the years in identifying just what it takes to give a certain third party this power. The Court's current approach is reflected in *Illinois v. Rodriguez.*

SCHNECKLOTH v. BUSTAMONTE

412 U.S. 218, 93 S.Ct. 2041, 36 L.Ed.2d 854 (1973).

JUSTICE STEWART delivered the opinion of the Court. * * *

[While on routine patrol at 2:40 a.m., a police officer stopped an automobile when he observed that one headlight and its license plate light were burned out. Six men were in the vehicle. When the driver could not produce a driver's license, the officer asked if any of the other five had any evidence of identification. Only Alcala produced a license, and he explained that the car was his brother's. The officer asked Alcala if he could search the car. Alcala replied, "Sure, go ahead," and actually helped in the search of the car, by opening the trunk and glove compartment. Three checks that had previously been stolen from a car wash were found wadded up under the left rear seat. The checks in question were admitted in evidence at Bustamonte's trial. He was convicted, and the California Court of Appeal affirmed the conviction. Thereafter, the respondent sought a writ of habeas corpus in a federal district court. It was denied. On appeal, the Court of Appeals for the Ninth Circuit set aside the District Court's order.]

The precise question in this case is what must the state prove to demonstrate that a consent was "voluntarily" given. * * *

The most extensive judicial exposition of the meaning of "voluntariness" has been developed in those cases in which the Court has had to determine the "voluntariness" of a defendant's confession for purposes of the Fourteenth Amendment. * * * It is to that body of case law to which we turn for initial guidance on the meaning of "voluntariness" in the present context. * * *

The significant fact about all of these decisions is that none of them turned on the presence or absence of a single controlling criterion; each reflected a careful scrutiny of all the surrounding circumstances. In none of them did the Court rule that the Due Process Clause required the prosecution to prove as part of its initial burden that the defendant knew he had a right to refuse to answer the questions that were put. While the state of the accused's mind, and the failure of the police to advise the accused of his rights, were certainly factors to be evaluated in assessing the "voluntariness" of an accused's responses, they were not in and of themselves determinative.

Similar considerations lead us to agree with the courts of California that the question whether a consent to a search was in fact "voluntary" or was the product of duress or coercion, express or implied, is a question of fact to be determined from the totality of all the circumstances. While knowledge of the right to refuse consent is one factor to be taken into account, the government need not establish such knowledge as the *sine qua non* of an effective consent. As with police questioning, two competing concerns must be accommodated in determining the meaning of a "voluntary" consent—the legitimate need for such searches and the equally important requirement of assuring the absence of coercion.

In situations where the police have some evidence of illicit activity, but lack probable cause to arrest or search, a search authorized by a valid consent may be the only means of obtaining important and reliable evidence. In the present case for example, while the police had reason to stop the car for traffic violations, the State does not contend that there was probable cause to search the vehicle or that the search was incident to a valid arrest of any of the occupants. Yet, the search yielded tangible evidence that served as a basis for a prosecution, and provided some assurance that others, wholly innocent of the crime, were not mistakenly brought to trial. And in those cases where there is probable cause to arrest or search, but where the police lack a warrant, a consent search may still be valuable. If the search is conducted and proves fruitless, that in itself may convince the police that an arrest with its possible stigma and embarrassment is unnecessary, or that a far more extensive search pursuant to a warrant is not justified. In short a search pursuant to consent may result in considerably less inconvenience for the subject of the search, and, properly conducted, is a constitutionally permissible and wholly legitimate aspect of effective police activity.

But the Fourth and Fourteenth Amendments require that a consent not be coerced, by explicit or implicit means, by implied threat or covert force. For, no matter how subtly the coercion were applied, the resulting "consent" would be no more than a pretext for the unjustified police intrusion against which the Fourth Amendment is directed. * * *

The problem of reconciling the recognized legitimacy of consent searches with the requirement that they be free from any aspect of official coercion cannot be resolved by an infallible touchstone. To approve such searches without the most careful scrutiny would sanction the possibility of official coercion; to place artificial restrictions upon such searches would jeopardize their basic validity. Just as was true with confessions, the requirement of a "voluntary" consent reflects a fair accommodation of the constitutional requirements involved. In examining all the surrounding circumstances to determine if in fact the consent to search was coerced, account must be taken of subtly coercive police questions, as well as the possibly vulnerable subjective state of the person who consents. Those searches that are the product of police coercion can thus be filtered out without undermining the continuing validity of consent searches. In sum, there is no reason for us to depart in the area of consent searches, from the traditional definition of "voluntariness."

The approach of the Court of Appeals for the Ninth Circuit finds no support in any of our decisions that have attempted to define the meaning of "voluntariness." Its ruling, that the State must affirmatively prove that the subject of the search knew that he had a right to refuse consent, would, in practice, create serious doubt whether consent searches could continue to be conducted. There might be rare cases where it could be proved from the record that a person in fact affirmatively knew of his right to refuse—such as a case where he announced to the police that if he didn't sign the consent form, "you [police] are going to get a search warrant;" or a case where by prior experience and training a person had clearly and convincingly demonstrated such knowledge. But more commonly where there was no evidence of any coercion, explicit or implicit, the prosecution would nevertheless be unable to demonstrate that the subject of the search in fact had known of his right to refuse consent.

The very object of the inquiry—the nature of a person's subjective understanding—underlines the difficulty of the prosecution's burden under the rule applied by the Court of Appeals in this case. Any defendant who was the subject of a search authorized solely by his consent could effectively frustrate the introduction into evidence of the fruits of that search by simply failing to testify that he in fact knew he could refuse to consent. And the near impossibility of meeting this prosecutorial burden suggests why this Court has never accepted any such litmus-paper test of voluntariness. * * *

One alternative that would go far towards proving that the subject of a search did know he had a right to refuse consent would be to advise him of that right before eliciting his consent. That, however, is a suggestion that has been almost universally repudiated by both federal and state courts, and, we think, rightly so. For it would be thoroughly impractical to impose on the normal consent search the detailed requirements of an effective warning. Consent searches are part of the standard investigatory techniques of law enforcement agencies. They normally occur on the highway, or in a person's home or office, and under informal and unstructured conditions. The circumstances that prompt the initial request to search may develop quickly or be a logical extension of investigative police questioning. The police may seek to investigate further suspicious circumstances or to follow up leads developed in questioning persons at the scene of a crime. These situations are a far cry from the structured atmosphere of a trial where, assisted by counsel if he chooses, a defendant is informed of his trial rights. And, while surely a closer question, these situations are still immeasurably far removed from "custodial interrogation" where, in *Miranda v. Arizona* [Ch. 6, § 3] we found that the Constitution required certain now familiar warnings as a prerequisite to police interrogation. * * *

It is said, however, that a "consent" is a "waiver" of a person's rights under the Fourth and Fourteenth Amendments. The argument is that by allowing the police to conduct a search, a person "waives" whatever right he had to prevent the police from searching. It is argued that under the doctrine of *Johnson v. Zerbst*, 304 U.S. 458 (1938), to establish such a "waiver" the state must demonstrate "an intentional relinquishment or abandonment of a known right or privilege." * * *

Almost without exception the requirement of a knowing and intelligent waiver has been applied only to those rights which the Constitution guarantees to a criminal defendant in order to preserve a fair trial. Hence, and hardly surprisingly in view of the facts of *Johnson* itself, the standard of a knowing and intelligent waiver has most often been applied to test the validity of a waiver of counsel, either at trial, or upon a guilty plea. And the Court has also applied the *Johnson* criteria to assess the effectiveness of a waiver of other trial rights such as the right to confrontation, to a jury trial, and to a speedy trial, and the right to be free from twice being placed in jeopardy. Guilty pleas have been carefully scrutinized to determine whether the accused knew and understood all the rights to which he would be entitled at trial, and that he had intentionally chosen to forgo them. And the Court has evaluated the knowing and intelligent nature of the waiver of trial rights in trial-type situations, such as the waiver of the privilege against compulsory self-incrimination before an administrative agency or a congressional committee, or the waiver of counsel in a juvenile proceeding.

The guarantees afforded a criminal defendant at trial also protect him at certain stages before the actual trial, and any alleged waiver must meet the strict standard of an intentional relinquishment of a "known" right. But the "trial" guarantees that have been applied to the "pretrial" stage of the criminal process are similarly designed to protect the fairness of the trial itself. * * *a

The standards of *Johnson* were, therefore, found to be a necessary prerequisite to a finding of a valid waiver.[29] * * *

a. At this point, the Court noted that "the standard of a knowing and intelligent waiver" applies to waiver of counsel at a lineup under *United States v. Wade*, [Ch. 7, § 1], and *Gilbert v. California,* [Ch. 7, § 1] because counsel is provided to protect the right of cross-examination at trial; and that the same standard applies to waiver of counsel at custodial interrogation under *Miranda v. Arizona* because counsel is provided to ensure that the safeguards concerning the giving of testimony at trial do not "become empty formalities."

29. As we have already noted, *Miranda* itself involved interrogation of a suspect detained in custody and did not concern the investigatory procedures of the police in general on-the-scene questioning. By the same token, the present case does not require a determination of the proper standard to be applied in assessing the validity of a search authorized solely by an alleged consent that is obtained from a person after he has been placed in custody. We do note, however, that other courts have been particularly sensitive to the heightened possibilities for coercion when the "consent" to a search was given by a person in custody.

A strict standard of waiver has been applied to those rights guaranteed to a criminal defendant to insure that he will be accorded the greatest possible opportunity to utilize every facet of the constitutional model of a fair criminal trial. Any trial conducted in derogation of that model leaves open the possibility that the trial reached an unfair result precisely because all the protections specified in the Constitution were not provided. A prime example is the right to counsel. For without that right, a wholly innocent accused faces the real and substantial danger that simply because of his lack of legal expertise he may be convicted. * * *

The protections of the Fourth Amendment are of a wholly different order, and have nothing whatever to do with promoting the fair ascertainment of truth at a criminal trial. Rather, as Mr. Justice Frankfurter's opinion for the Court put it in *Wolf v. Colorado* [Ch. 3, § 1] the Fourth Amendment protects the "security of one's privacy against arbitrary intrusion by the police. * * *" * * *

Nor can it even be said that a search, as opposed to an eventual trial, is somehow "unfair" if a person consents to a search. While the Fourth and Fourteenth Amendments limit the circumstances under which the police can conduct a search, there is nothing constitutionally suspect in a person voluntarily allowing a search. The actual conduct of the search may be precisely the same as if the police had obtained a warrant. And, unlike those constitutional guarantees that protect a defendant at trial, it cannot be said every reasonable presumption ought to be indulged against voluntary relinquishment. We have only recently stated: "[I]t is no part of the policy underlying the Fourth and Fourteenth Amendments to discourage citizens from aiding to the utmost of their ability in the apprehension of criminals." Rather the community has a real interest in encouraging consent, for the resulting search may yield necessary evidence for the solution and prosecution of crime, evidence that may insure that a wholly innocent person is not wrongly charged with a criminal offense.

Those cases that have dealt with the application of the *Johnson v. Zerbst* rule make clear that it would be next to impossible to apply to a consent search the standard of "an intentional relinquishment or abandonment of a known right or privilege." To be true to *Johnson* and its progeny, there must be examination into the knowing and understanding nature of the waiver, an examination that was designed for a trial judge in the structured atmosphere of a courtroom. * * * It would be unrealistic to expect that in the informal, unstructured context of a consent search, a policeman, upon pain of tainting the evidence obtained, could make the detailed type of examination demanded by *Johnson*. And, if for this reason a diluted form of "waiver" were found acceptable, that would itself be ample recognition of the fact that there is no universal standard that must be applied in every situation where a person forgoes a constitutional right.[33]

Similarly, a "waiver" approach to consent searches would be thoroughly inconsistent with our decisions that have approved "third party consents." [I]t is inconceivable that the Constitution could countenance the waiver of a defendant's right to counsel by a third party, or that a waiver could be found because a trial

---

33. It seems clear that even a limited view of the demands of "an intentional relinquishment or abandonment of a known right or privilege" standard would inevitably lead to a requirement of detailed warnings before any consent search—a requirement all but universally rejected to date. As the Court stated in *Miranda* with respect to the privilege against compulsory self-incrimination: "[W]e will not pause to inquire in individual cases whether the defendant was aware of his rights without a warning being given. Assessments of the knowledge the defendant possessed, based on information as to his age, education, intelligence, or prior contact with authorities, can never be more than speculation; a warning is a clearcut fact."

judge reasonably though mistakenly believed a defendant had waived his right to plead not guilty. * * *

Much of what has already been said disposes of the argument that the Court's decision in the *Miranda* case requires the conclusion that knowledge of a right to refuse is an indispensable element of a valid consent. The considerations that informed the Court's holding in *Miranda* are simply inapplicable in the present case. In *Miranda* the Court found that the techniques of police questioning and the nature of custodial surroundings produce an inherently coercive situation. The Court concluded that "[u]nless adequate protective devices are employed to dispel the compulsion inherent in custodial surroundings, no statement obtained from the defendant can truly be the product of his free choice." And at another point the Court noted that "without proper safeguards the process of in-custody interrogation of persons suspected or accused of crime contains inherently compelling pressures which work to undermine the individual's will to resist and to compel him to speak where he would not otherwise do so freely."

In this case there is no evidence of any inherently coercive tactics—either from the nature of the police questioning or the environment in which it took place. Indeed, since consent searches will normally occur on a person's own familiar territory, the spectre of incommunicado police interrogation in some remote station house is simply inapposite. There is no reason to believe, under circumstances such as are present here, that the response to a policeman's question is presumptively coerced; and there is, therefore, no reason to reject the traditional test for determining the voluntariness of a person's response. *Miranda,* of course, did not reach investigative questioning of a person not in custody, which is most directly analogous to the situation of a consent search, and it assuredly did not indicate that such questioning ought to be deemed inherently coercive.

It is also argued that the failure to require the Government to establish knowledge as a prerequisite to a valid consent, will relegate the Fourth Amendment to the special province of "the sophisticated, the knowledgeable, and the privileged." We cannot agree. The traditional definition of voluntariness we accept today has always taken into account evidence of minimal schooling, low intelligence, and the lack of any effective warnings to a person of his rights; and the voluntariness of any statement taken under those conditions has been carefully scrutinized to determine whether it was in fact voluntarily given.

Our decision today is a narrow one. We hold only that when the subject of a search is not in custody and the State attempts to justify a search on the basis of his consent, the Fourth and Fourteenth Amendments require that it demonstrate that the consent was in fact voluntarily given, and not the result of duress or coercion, express or implied.[b] Voluntariness is a question of fact to be determined from all the circumstances, and while the subject's knowledge of a right to refuse is a factor to be taken into account, the prosecution is not required to demonstrate such knowledge as a prerequisite to establishing a voluntary consent.[c]

b. The standard for measuring the scope of a suspect's consent, the Court concluded in *Florida v. Jimeno,* 500 U.S. 248 (1991), is neither the suspect's intent nor the officer's perception thereof but rather "that of 'objective' reasonableness—what would the typical reasonable person have understood by the exchange between the officer and the suspect?" Given the officer's statement in *Jimeno* that he would be looking for narcotics, "it was objectively reasonable for the police to conclude that the general consent to search respondent's car included consent to search containers within that car which might bear drugs." But, the nature of the container is also relevant. "It is very likely unreasonable to think that a suspect, by consenting to the search of his trunk, has agreed to the breaking open of a locked briefcase within the trunk, but it is otherwise with respect to a closed paper bag."

c. Powell, J., joined by the Chief Justice and Rehnquist, J., concurred on the ground

18 Oct 01

JUSTICE MARSHALL, dissenting.

* * * The Court assumes that the issue in this case is, what are the standards by which courts are to determine that consent is voluntarily given? It then imports into the law of search and seizure standards developed to decide entirely different questions about coerced confessions.

The Fifth Amendment, in terms, provides that no person "shall be compelled in any criminal case to be a witness against himself." Nor is the interest protected by the Due Process Clause of the Fourteenth Amendment any different. The inquiry in a case where a confession is challenged as having been elicited in an unconstitutional manner is, therefore, whether the behavior of the police amounted to compulsion of the defendant. * * *

In contrast, this case deals not with "coercion," but with "consent," a subtly different concept to which different standards have been applied in the past. Freedom from coercion is a substantive right, guaranteed by the Fifth and Fourteenth Amendments. Consent, however, is a mechanism by which substantive requirements, otherwise applicable, are avoided. * * * Thus, consent searches are permitted not because such an exception to the requirements of probable cause and warrant is essential to proper law enforcement, but because we permit our citizens to choose whether or not they wish to exercise their constitutional rights. Our prior decisions simply do not support the view that a meaningful choice has been made solely because no coercion was brought to bear on the subject. * * *

If consent to search means that a person has chosen to forego his right to exclude the police from the place they seek to search, it follows that his consent cannot be considered a meaningful choice unless he knew that he could in fact exclude the police. * * * I would therefore hold, at a minimum, that the prosecution may not rely on a purported consent to search if the subject of the search did not know that he could refuse to give consent. Where the police claim authority to search yet in fact lack such authority, the subject does not know that he may permissibly refuse them entry, and it is this lack of knowledge that invalidates the consent. * * *

The burden on the prosecutor would disappear, of course, if the police, at the time they requested consent to search, also told the subject that he had a right to refuse consent and thus his decision to refuse would be respected. The Court's assertions to the contrary notwithstanding, there is nothing impractical about this method of satisfying the prosecution's burden of proof. * * *

The Court contends that if an officer paused to inform the subject of his rights, the informality of the exchange would be destroyed. I doubt that a simple statement by an officer of an individual's right to refuse consent would do much to alter the informality of the exchange, except to alert the subject to a fact that he surely is entitled to know. It is not without significance that for many years the agents of the Federal Bureau of Investigation have routinely informed subjects of their right to refuse consent, when they request consent to search. The reported cases in which the police have informed subject of their right to refuse consent show, also, that the information can be given without disrupting the casual flow of

"that federal collateral review of a state prisoner's Fourth Amendment claims—claims which rarely bear on innocence—should be confined solely to the question of whether the petitioner was provided a fair opportunity to raise and have adjudicated the question in state courts." Blackmun, J., concurred to express substantial agreement with the Powell opinion. Douglas, J., dissenting, would have remanded for a determination of whether Alcala knew he had the right to refuse. Brennan, J., dissenting, declared: "It wholly escapes me how our citizens can meaningfully be said to have waived something as precious as a constitutional guarantee without ever being aware of its existence."

events. What evidence there is, then, rather strongly suggests that nothing disastrous would happen if the police, before requesting consent, informed the subject that he had a right to refuse consent and that his refusal would be respected.[12]

I must conclude, with some reluctance, that when the Court speaks of practicality, what it really is talking of is the continued ability of the police to capitalize on the ignorance of citizens so as to accomplish by subterfuge what they could not achieve by relying only on the knowing relinquishment of constitutional rights. Of course it would be "practical" for the police to ignore the commands of the Fourth Amendment, if by practicality we mean that more criminals will be apprehended, even though the constitutional rights of innocent people also go by the boards. But such a practical advantage is achieved only at the cost of permitting the police to disregard the limitations that the Constitution places on their behavior, a cost that a constitutional democracy cannot long absorb. * * *

ILLINOIS v. RODRIGUEZ

497 U.S. 177, 110 S.Ct. 2793, 111 L.Ed.2d 148 (1990).

Justice Scalia delivered the opinion of the Court. * * *

On July 26, 1985, police were summoned to the residence of Dorothy Jackson on South Wolcott in Chicago. They were met by Ms. Jackson's daughter, Gail Fischer, who showed signs of a severe beating. She told the officers that she had been assaulted by respondent Edward Rodriguez earlier that day in an apartment on South California. Fischer stated that Rodriguez was then asleep in the apartment, and she consented to travel there with the police in order to unlock the door with her key so that the officers could enter and arrest him. During this conversation, Fischer several times referred to the apartment on South California as "our" apartment, and said that she had clothes and furniture there. It is unclear whether she indicated that she currently lived at the apartment, or only that she used to live there.

The police officers drove to the apartment on South California, accompanied by Fischer. They did not obtain an arrest warrant for Rodriguez, nor did they seek a search warrant for the apartment. At the apartment, Fischer unlocked the door with her key and gave the officers permission to enter. They moved through the door into the living room, where they observed in plain view drug paraphernalia and containers filled with white powder that they believed (correctly, as later analysis showed) to be cocaine. They proceeded to the bedroom, where they found Rodriguez asleep and discovered additional containers of white powder in two open attaché cases. The officers arrested Rodriguez and seized the drugs and related paraphernalia.

Rodriguez was charged with possession of a controlled substance with intent to deliver. He moved to suppress all evidence seized at the time of his arrest, claiming that Fischer had vacated the apartment several weeks earlier and had no authority to consent to the entry. The Cook County Circuit Court granted the motion, holding that at the time she consented to the entry Fischer did not have

---

12. The Court's suggestion that it would be "unrealistic" to require the officers to make "the detailed type of examination" involved when a court considers whether a defendant has waived a trial right, deserves little comment. The question before us relates to the inquiry to be made in court when the prosecution seeks to establish that consent was given.

I therefore do not address the Court's strained argument that one may waive constitutional rights without making a knowing and intentional choice so long as the rights do not relate to the fairness of a criminal trial. I would suggest, however, that that argument is fundamentally inconsistent with the law of unconstitutional conditions.

common authority over the apartment. The Court concluded that Fischer was not a "usual resident" but rather an "infrequent visitor" at the apartment on South California, based upon its findings that Fischer's name was not on the lease, that she did not contribute to the rent, that she was not allowed to invite others to the apartment on her own, that she did not have access to the apartment when respondent was away, and that she had moved some of her possessions from the apartment. The Circuit Court also rejected the State's contention that, even if Fischer did not possess common authority over the premises, there was no Fourth Amendment violation if the police *reasonably believed* at the time of their entry that Fischer possessed the authority to consent. * * *

The Fourth Amendment generally prohibits the warrantless entry of a person's home, whether to make an arrest or to search for specific objects. The prohibition does not apply, however, to situations in which voluntary consent has been obtained, either from the individual whose property is searched, or from a third party who possesses common authority over the premises, see *United States v. Matlock,* [415 U.S. 164 (1974)]. The State of Illinois contends that that exception applies in the present case.

As we stated in *Matlock,* "[c]ommon authority" rests "on mutual use of the property by persons generally having joint access or control for most purposes. . . ." The burden of establishing that common authority rests upon the State. On the basis of this record, it is clear that burden was not sustained. The evidence showed that although Fischer, with her two small children, had lived with Rodriguez beginning in December 1984, she had moved out on July 1, 1985, almost a month before the search at issue here, and had gone to live with her mother. She took her and her children's clothing with her, though leaving behind some furniture and household effects. During the period after July 1 she sometimes spent the night at Rodriguez's apartment, but never invited her friends there, and never went there herself when he was not home. Her name was not on the lease nor did she contribute to the rent. She had a key to the apartment, which she said at trial she had taken without Rodriguez's knowledge (though she testified at the preliminary hearing that Rodriguez had given her the key). On these facts the State has not established that, with respect to the South California apartment, Fischer had "joint access or control for most purposes." To the contrary, the Appellate Court's determination of no common authority over the apartment was obviously correct.

[R]espondent asserts that permitting a reasonable belief of common authority to validate an entry would cause a defendant's Fourth Amendment rights to be "vicariously waived." We disagree.

We have been unyielding in our insistence that a defendant's waiver of his trial rights cannot be given effect unless it is "knowing" and "intelligent." We would assuredly not permit, therefore, evidence seized in violation of the Fourth Amendment to be introduced on the basis of a trial court's mere "reasonable belief"—derived from statements by unauthorized persons—that the defendant has waived his objection. But one must make a distinction between, on the one hand, trial rights that *derive* from the violation of constitutional guarantees and, on the other hand, the nature of those constitutional guarantees themselves. * * *

What Rodriguez is assured by the trial right of the exclusionary rule, where it applies, is that no evidence seized in violation of the Fourth Amendment will be introduced at his trial unless he consents. What he is assured by the Fourth Amendment itself, however, is not that no government search of his house will occur unless he consents; but that no such search will occur that is "unreasonable." There are various elements, of course, that can make a search of a person's house "reasonable"—one of which is the consent of the person or his cotenant. The essence of respondent's argument is that we should impose upon this element a requirement that we have not imposed upon other elements that regularly compel government officers to exercise judgment regarding the facts: namely, the requirement that their judgment be not only responsible but correct.

[I]n order to satisfy the "reasonableness" requirement of the Fourth Amendment, what is generally demanded of the many factual determinations that must regularly be made by agents of the government—whether the magistrate issuing a warrant, the police officer executing a warrant, or the police officer conducting a search or seizure under one of the exceptions to the warrant requirement—is not that they always be correct, but that they always be reasonable. As we put it in *Brinegar v. United States,* 338 U.S. 160, 176 (1949):

> "Because many situations which confront officers in the course of executing their duties are more or less ambiguous, room must be allowed for some mistakes on their part. But the mistakes must be those of reasonable men, acting on facts leading sensibly to their conclusions of probability."

We see no reason to depart from this general rule with respect to facts bearing upon the authority to consent to a search. Whether the basis for such authority exists is the sort of recurring factual question to which law enforcement officials must be expected to apply their judgment; and all the Fourth Amendment requires is that they answer it reasonably. The Constitution is no more violated when officers enter without a warrant because they reasonably (though erroneously) believe that the person who has consented to their entry is a resident of the premises, than it is violated when they enter without a warrant because they reasonably (though erroneously) believed they are in pursuit of a violent felon who is about to escape.

Stoner v. California, 376 U.S. 483 (1964) is in our view not to the contrary. There, in holding that police had improperly entered the defendant's hotel room based on the consent of a hotel clerk, we stated that "the rights protected by the Fourth Amendment are not to be eroded ... by unrealistic doctrines of 'apparent authority.' " It is ambiguous, of course, whether the word "unrealistic" is descriptive or limiting—that is, whether we were condemning as unrealistic all reliance upon apparent authority, or whether we were condemning only such reliance upon apparent authority as is unrealistic. Similarly ambiguous is the opinion's earlier statement that "there [is no] substance to the claim that the search was reasonable because police, relying upon the night clerk's expressions of consent, had a reasonable basis for the belief that the clerk had authority to consent to the search." Was there no substance to it because it failed as a matter of law, or because the facts could not possibly support it? At one point the opinion does seem to speak clearly:

> "It is important to bear in mind that it was the petitioner's constitutional right which was at stake here, and not the night clerk's nor the hotel's. It was a right, therefore, which only the petitioner could waive by word or deed, either directly or through an agent."

But as we have discussed, what is at issue when a claim of apparent consent is raised is not whether the right to be free of searches has been *waived,* but whether the right to be free of *unreasonable* searches has been *violated.* Even if one does not think the *Stoner* opinion had this subtlety in mind, the supposed clarity of its foregoing statement is immediately compromised, as follows:

"It is true that the night clerk clearly and unambiguously consented to the search. But there is nothing in the record to indicate that *the police had any basis whatsoever to believe that* the night clerk had been authorized by the petitioner to permit the police to search the petitioner's room."

The italicized language should have been deleted, of course, if the statement two sentences earlier meant that an appearance of authority could never validate a search. In the last analysis, one must admit that the rationale of *Stoner* was ambiguous—and perhaps deliberately so. It is at least a reasonable reading of the case, and perhaps a preferable one, that the police could not rely upon the obtained consent because they knew it came from a hotel clerk, knew that the room was rented and exclusively occupied by the defendant, and could not reasonably have believed that the former had general access to or control over the latter. * * *

As *Stoner* demonstrates, what we hold today does not suggest that law enforcement officers may always accept a person's invitation to enter premises. Even when the invitation is accompanied by an explicit assertion that the person lives there, the surrounding circumstances could conceivably be such that a reasonable person would doubt its truth and not act upon it without further inquiry. As with other factual determinations bearing upon search and seizure, determination of consent to enter must "be judged against an objective standard: would the facts available to the officer at the moment . . . 'warrant a man of reasonable caution in the belief' " that the consenting party had authority over the premises? If not, then warrantless entry without further inquiry is unlawful unless authority actually exists. But if so, the search is valid.

In the present case, the Appellate Court found it unnecessary to determine whether the officers reasonably believed that Fischer had the authority to consent, because it ruled as a matter of law that a reasonable belief could not validate the entry. Since we find that ruling to be in error, we remand for consideration of that question. The judgment of the Illinois Appellate Court is reversed and remanded for further proceedings not inconsistent with this opinion.

Justice Marshall, with whom Justice Brennan and Justice Stevens join, dissenting. * * *

Unlike searches conducted pursuant to the recognized exceptions to the warrant requirement, third-party consent searches are not based on an exigency and therefore serve no compelling social goal. Police officers, when faced with the choice of relying on consent by a third party or securing a warrant, should secure a warrant, and must therefore accept the risk of error should they instead choose to rely on consent. * * *

Acknowledging that the third party in this case lacked authority to consent, the majority seeks to rely on cases suggesting that reasonable but mistaken factual judgments by police will not invalidate otherwise reasonable searches. The majority reads these cases as establishing a "general rule" that "what is generally demanded of the many factual determinations that must regularly be made by agents of the government—whether the magistrate issuing a warrant, the police officer executing a warrant, or the police officer conducting a search or seizure under one of the exceptions to the warrant requirement—is not that they always be correct, but that they always be reasonable."

The majority's assertion, however, is premised on the erroneous assumption that third-party consent searches are generally reasonable. The cases the majority cites thus provide no support for its holding. In *Brinegar v. United States,* for example, the Court confirmed the unremarkable proposition that police need only probable cause, not absolute certainty, to justify the arrest of a suspect on a highway. As *Brinegar* makes clear, the possibility of factual error is built into the probable cause standard, and such a standard, by its very definition, will in some cases result in the arrest of a suspect who has not actually committed a crime. Because probable cause defines the reasonableness of searches and seizures outside of the home, a search is reasonable under the Fourth Amendment whenever that standard is met, notwithstanding the possibility of "mistakes" on the part of police. In contrast, our cases have already struck the balance against warrantless home intrusions in the absence of an exigency. Because reasonable factual errors by law enforcement officers will not validate unreasonable searches, the reasonableness of the officer's mistaken belief that the third party had authority to consent is irrelevant. * * *

Chapter 4

POLICE "ENCOURAGEMENT" AND THE DEFENSE OF ENTRAPMENT

"Our national integrity has been on a downhill slide for seven years; we really don't need the FBI to grease the skids with Operation ABSCAM.[a] Where no crime has been contemplated, the FBI has, through entrapment, induced to crime men who were previously involved in no wrongdoing. Aren't there enough naturally encouraging crimes to keep the FBI busy? Must they spend astronomical sums creating crime?"

— Letter to the Editor, Newsweek, Mar. 1, 1980, p. 5.

"House Speaker Thomas P. (Tip) O'Neill may have thundered that '[Operation ABSCAM] was a setup, a goddam setup,' but a crook is a crook is a crook. Whether set up or not, honest people do not take bribes."

— Letter to the Editor, Newsweek, Mar. 1, 1980, p. 5.

As illustrated by the two letters set forth above, the use of undercover police officers or other secret government agents to detect crime or to tempt people into committing crime evokes widely varying responses. Moreover, the label "entrapment" is often affixed to police conduct that is not "entrapment" at all, as the courts have defined that term, but "encouragement"—a police technique whereby an officer or law enforcement agent acts as a willing victim, intends by his action to encourage the suspect (a "target") to commit a crime, communicates this encouragement to the suspect, and thereby influences the commission of a crime.

---

a. "Abscam" is an acronym combining the first two letters of Abdul Enterprises, a fictitious Middle Eastern corporation, and "scam," a slang term for swindle or confidence game. Abscam began as a standard "sting" operation, i.e., an FBI undercover scheme to recover stolen securities and paintings. In 1978, the operation shifted to political corruption in the New Jersey area. A year later, it had turned its attention to the "Asylum Scenario"; unsuspecting "middlemen" (private persons unaware that they were part of a government undercover operation) passed the word to various Congressmen, or to their aides and acquaintants, that wealthy Arabs were willing to bribe members of Congress in order to ensure that they would introduce private immigration bills on the Arabs' behalf if and when

necessary. In early 1980, shortly before shutting down, the operation shifted to political corruption in Philadelphia.

As a result of Abscam, a U.S. Senator, six U.S. Representatives and a number of other public officials and lawyers were convicted of various corrupt acts. Although many of the defendants (and many critics of the operation both in and out of Congress) charged that the FBI's methods constituted entrapment and/or violated the due process rights of the individuals caught in the operation, not a single Abscam defendant prevailed in the courts. See, e.g., *United States v. Kelly,* 707 F.2d 1460 (D.C.Cir.1983), which discusses one phase of the Abscam operation at considerable length.

Such tactics are commonly used to detect "vice crimes" (e.g., prostitution, illicit liquor sales, narcotics and gambling offenses) and, perhaps most spectacularly, to uncover the bribery of public officials. For these offenses are committed privately with a willing victim who will not complain, making normal detection exceedingly difficult.

"Encouragement" as such is not an improper law enforcement technique, but when extended too far—"when the criminal design originates with the officials of the government, and they implant in the mind of an innocent person the disposition to commit the alleged offense and induce its commission in order that they may prosecute"[b]—the government's tactics do constitute "entrapment."

There are currently two major approaches to the defense of entrapment: the majority view, usually called the "subjective approach," and the "objective approach" or "hypothetical person" approach.

Under the "subjective approach," as explained in Justice Rehnquist's opinion for the Court in *United States v. Russell*, infra, "the entrapment defense prohibits law enforcement officers from instigating criminal acts by persons 'otherwise innocent in order to lure them to its commission and to punish them.'" This approach "focus[es] on the intent or predisposition of the defendant to commit the crime" rather than on the government's conduct. Under this approach, to determine whether entrapment has occurred, "a line must be drawn between the trap for the unwary innocent and the trap for the unwary criminal."

The emphasis of the "objective" approach is not on the defendant's propensity to commit the offense, but on the inducements used by the government agents. This approach is based on the premise that an affirmative duty resides in the courts to control police excesses in inducing criminal behavior, and that this duty should not be limited to instances in which the defendant is otherwise "innocent."

Under this approach, as concurring Justice Stewart put it in *United States v. Russell*, the entrapment defense is designed "to prohibit unlawful governmental activity in instigating crime. * * * If that is so, then whether the particular defendant was 'predisposed' or 'otherwise innocent' is irrelevant; and the important question becomes whether the Government's conduct in inducing the crime was beyond judicial toleration."

Although defendants, such as the one in *Russell*, who are forced to concede that the jury could have found them "predisposed" to commit the offense, must urge the court to adopt the objective approach, neither the objective nor the subjective approach is uniformly more favorable to defendants. As explained in the commentary to the American Law Institute's Model Penal Code (which favors the "objective approach"):

"Under the [subjective approach], if A, an informer, makes overreaching appeals to compassion and friendship and thus moves D to sell narcotics, D has no defense if he is predisposed to narcotics peddling. Under the [objective approach] a defense would be established because the police conduct, not D's predisposition, determines the issue. Under the [subjective approach], A's mere offer to purchase narcotics from D may give rise to the defense provided D is not predisposed to sell. A contrary result is reached under the [objective approach]. A mere offer to buy hardly creates a serious risk of offending by the innocent."

b. *Sorrells v. United States,* 287 U.S. 435 (1932), quoted with approval in *Sherman v. United States,* 356 U.S. 369 (1958) (articulat-ing the majority view of entrapment, often called the "subjective" test).

As illustrated by the very recent case of *Jacobson v. United States*, the second case set forth in this chapter, the Court remains sharply divided over what is or ought to be impermissible "entrapment." As *Jacobson* also indicates, it is much easier to keep the "subjective" and "objective" tests separate and distinct in theory than to do so in practice.

In overturning defendant's conviction, the *Jacobson* Court purported to apply the "subjective" test, concluding that the prosecution had failed, as a matter of law, to establish that defendant was predisposed, independent of the government's acts, to receive child pornography through the mail. But the Court also seemed quite offended by the tactics used by the government to induce defendant to order the pornographic material. Thus, the Court observed that defendant did not place his order until he had been "the target of 26 months of repeated mailings and communications from Government agents and fictitious organizations" and that "the strong arguable inference is that [the] Government * * * exerted substantial pressure on [defendant] to obtain and read such material as part of a fight against censorship and the infringement of individual rights."

UNITED STATES v. RUSSELL

411 U.S. 423, 93 S.Ct. 1637, 36 L.Ed.2d 366 (1973).

JUSTICE REHNQUIST delivered the opinion of the Court.

Respondent Richard Russell was charged in three counts of a five-count indictment returned against him and codefendants John and Patrick Connolly. After a jury trial in the District Court, in which his sole defense was entrapment, respondent was convicted on all three counts of having unlawfully manufactured and processed methamphetamine ("speed") and of having unlawfully sold and delivered that drug * * *. On appeal, the United States Court of Appeals for the Ninth Circuit [reversed] the conviction solely for the reason that an undercover agent supplied an essential chemical for manufacturing the methamphetamine which formed the basis of respondent's conviction. * * *

There is little dispute concerning the essential facts in this case. On December 7, 1969, Joe Shapiro, an undercover agent for the Federal Bureau of Narcotics and Dangerous Drugs, went to respondent's home [where] he met with respondent and his two codefendants, John and Patrick Connolly. Shapiro's assignment was to locate a laboratory where it was believed that methamphetamine was being manufactured illicitly. He told the respondent and the Connollys that he represented an organization [that] was interested in controlling the manufacture and distribution of methamphetamine. He then made an offer to supply the defendants with the chemical phenyl–2–propanone, an essential ingredient in the manufacture of methamphetamine, in return for one-half of the drug produced. This offer was made on the condition that Agent Shapiro be shown a sample of the drug which they were making and the laboratory where it was being produced.

During the conversation, Patrick Connolly revealed that he had been making the drug since May 1969 and since then had produced three pounds of it. John Connolly gave the agent a bag containing a quality of methamphetamine that he represented as being from "the last batch that we made." Shortly thereafter, Shapiro and Patrick Connolly left respondent's house to view the laboratory which was located in the Connolly house on Whidbey Island. At the house, Shapiro observed an empty bottle bearing the chemical label phenyl–2–propanone.

By prearrangement, Shapiro returned to the Connolly house on December 9, 1969, to supply 100 grams of propanone and observe the manufacturing process.

When he arrived he observed Patrick Connolly and the respondent cutting up pieces of aluminum foil and placing them in a large flask. There was testimony that some of the foil pieces accidentally fell on the floor and were picked up by the respondent and Shapiro and put into the flask. Thereafter, Patrick Connolly added all of the necessary chemicals, including the propanone brought by Shapiro, to make two batches of methamphetamine. The manufacturing process having been completed the following morning, Shapiro was given one-half of the drug and respondent kept the remainder. Shapiro offered to buy, and the respondent agreed to sell, part of the remainder for $60.

About a month later, Shapiro returned to the Connolly house and met with Patrick Connolly to ask if he was still interested in their "business arrangement." Connolly replied that he was interested but that he had recently obtained two additional bottles of phenyl–2–propanone and would not be finished with them for a couple of days. He provided some additional methamphetamine to Shapiro at that time. Three days later Shapiro returned to the Connolly house with a search warrant and, among other items, seized an empty 500–gram bottle of propanone and a 100–gram bottle, not the one he had provided, that was partially filled with the chemical.

There was testimony at the trial of respondent and Patrick Connolly that phenyl–2–propanone was generally difficult to obtain. At the request of the Bureau of Narcotics and Dangerous Drugs, some chemical supply firms had voluntarily ceased selling the chemical.

At the close of the evidence, and after receiving the District Judge's standard entrapment instruction,[4] the jury found the respondent guilty on all counts charged. On appeal, the respondent conceded that the jury could have found him predisposed to commit the offenses, but argued that on the facts presented there was entrapment as a matter of law. The Court of Appeals agreed, although it did not find the District Court had misconstrued or misapplied the traditional standards governing the entrapment defense. Rather, the court in effect expanded the traditional notion of entrapment, which focuses on the predisposition of the defendant, to mandate dismissal of a criminal prosecution whenever the court determines that there has been "an intolerable degree of governmental participation in the criminal enterprise." In this case the court decided that the conduct of the agent in supplying a scarce ingredient essential for the manufacture of a controlled substance established that defense.

This new defense was held to rest on either of two alternative theories. One theory is based on two lower court decisions which have found entrapment, regardless of predisposition, whenever the government supplies contraband to the defendants. The second theory, a non-entrapment rationale, is based on a recent Ninth Circuit decision that reversed a conviction because a government investigator was so enmeshed in the criminal activity that the prosecution of the defendants was held to be repugnant to the American criminal justice system. The court below held that these two rationales constitute the same defense, and that only the label distinguishes them. In any event, it held that "[b]oth theories are premised on fundamental concepts of due process and evince the reluctance of the judiciary to countenance 'overzealous law enforcement.'"

4. The District Judge stated the governing law on entrapment as follows: "Where a person already has the willingness and the readiness to break the law, the mere fact that the government agent provides what appears to be a favorable opportunity is not entrapment." He then instructed the jury to acquit respondent if it had a "reasonable doubt whether the defendant had the previous intent or purpose to commit the offense * * * and did so only because he was induced or persuaded by some officer or agent of the government." No exception was taken by respondent to this instruction.

This Court first recognized and applied the entrapment defense in *Sorrells v. United States,* 287 U.S. 435 (1932). In *Sorrells,* a federal prohibition agent visited the defendant while posing as a tourist and engaged him in conversation about their common war experiences. After gaining the defendant's confidence, the agent asked for some liquor, was twice refused, but upon asking a third time the defendant finally capitulated, and was subsequently prosecuted for violating the National Prohibition Act.

Mr. Chief Justice Hughes, speaking for the Court, held that as a matter of statutory construction the defense of entrapment should have been available to the defendant. Under the theory propounded by the Chief Justice, the entrapment defense prohibits law enforcement officers from instigating a criminal act by persons "otherwise innocent in order to lure them to its commission and to punish them." Thus, the thrust of the entrapment defense was held to focus on the intent or predisposition of the defendant to commit the crime. "[I]f the defendant seeks acquittal by reason of entrapment he cannot complain of an appropriate and searching inquiry into his own conduct and predisposition as bearing upon that issue."

Mr. Justice Roberts concurred but was of the view "that courts must be closed to the trial of a crime instigated by the government's own agents." The difference in the view of the majority and the concurring opinions is that in the former the inquiry focuses on the predisposition of the defendant, whereas in the latter the inquiry focuses on whether the government "instigated the crime."

In *Sherman v. United States* (1958) the Court again considered the theory underlying the entrapment defense and expressly reaffirmed the view expressed by the *Sorrells* majority. In *Sherman* the defendant was convicted of selling narcotics to a Government informer. As in *Sorrells,* it appears that the Government agent gained the confidence of the defendant and, despite initial reluctance, the defendant finally acceded to the repeated importunings of the agent to commit the criminal act. On the basis of *Sorrells,* this Court reversed the affirmance of the defendant's conviction.

In affirming the theory underlying *Sorrells,* Mr. Chief Justice Warren for the Court, held that "[t]o determine whether entrapment has been established, a line must be drawn between the trap for the unwary innocent and the trap for the unwary criminal." Mr. Justice Frankfurter stated in an opinion concurring in the result that he believed Mr. Justice Roberts had the better view in *Sorrells* and would have framed the question to be asked in an entrapment defense in terms of "whether the police conduct revealed in the particular case falls below standards [for] the proper use of governmental power."

In the instant case, respondent asks us to reconsider the theory of the entrapment defense as it is set forth in the majority opinions in *Sorrells* and *Sherman.* His principal contention is that the defense should rest on constitutional grounds. He argues that the level of Shapiro's involvement in the manufacture of the methamphetamine was so high that a criminal prosecution for the drug's manufacture violates the fundamental principles of due process. The respondent contends that the same factors that led this Court to apply the exclusionary rule to illegal searches and seizures [and] confessions should be considered here. But he would have the Court go further in deterring undesirable official conduct by requiring that any prosecution be barred absolutely because of the police involvement in criminal activity. The analogy is imperfect in any event, for the principal reason behind the adoption of the exclusionary rule was the Government's "failure to observe its own laws." [Here, however, the government's conduct] violated no independent constitutional right of the respondent.

Nor did Shapiro violate any federal statute or rule or commit any crime in infiltrating the respondent's drug enterprise.

Respondent would overcome this basic weakness in his analogy to the exclusionary rule cases by having the Court adopt a rigid constitutional rule that would preclude any prosecution when it is shown that the criminal conduct would not have been possible had not an undercover agent "supplied an indispensable means to the commission of the crime that could not have been obtained otherwise, through legal or illegal channels." Even if we were to surmount the difficulties attending the notion that due process of law can be embodied in fixed rules, and those attending respondent's particular formulation, the rule he proposes would not appear to be of significant benefit to him. For, on the record presented, it appears that he cannot fit within the terms of the very rule he proposes.

The record discloses that although the propanone was difficult to obtain, it was by no means impossible. The defendants admitted making the drug both before and after those batches made with the propanone supplied by Shapiro. [Thus,] the facts in the record amply demonstrate that the propanone used in the illicit manufacture of methamphetamine not only *could* have been obtained without the intervention of Shapiro but was in fact obtained by these defendants.

While we may some day be presented with a situation in which the conduct of law enforcement agents is so outrageous that due process principles would absolutely bar the government from invoking judicial processes to obtain a conviction, the instant case is distinctly not of that breed. Shapiro's contribution of propanone to the criminal enterprise already in process was scarcely objectionable. The chemical is by itself a harmless substance and its possession is legal. While the Government may have been seeking to make it more difficult for drug rings, such as that of which respondent was a member, to obtain the chemical, the evidence described above shows that it nonetheless was obtainable. The law enforcement conduct here stops far short of violating that "fundamental fairness, shocking to the universal sense of justice," mandated by the Due Process Clause of the Fifth Amendment.

The illicit manufacture of drugs is not a sporadic, isolated criminal incident, but a continuing, though illegal, business enterprise. In order to obtain convictions for illegally manufacturing drugs, the gathering of evidence of past unlawful conduct frequently proves to be an all but impossible task. Thus in drug-related offenses law enforcement personnel have turned to one of the only practicable means of detection: the infiltration of drug rings and a limited participation in their unlawful present practices. Such infiltration is a recognized and permissible means of investigation; if that be so, then the supply of some item of value that the drug ring requires must, as a general rule, also be permissible. For an agent will not be taken into the confidence of the illegal entrepreneurs unless he has something of value to offer them. Law enforcement tactics such as this can hardly be said to violate "fundamental fairness" or "shocking to the universal sense of justice."

Respondent also urges, as an alternative to his constitutional argument, that we broaden the nonconstitutional defense of entrapment in order to sustain the judgment of the Court of Appeals. This Court's opinions in *Sorrells* and *Sherman* held that the principal element in the defense of entrapment was the defendant's predisposition to commit the crime. Respondent conceded in the Court of Appeals, as well he might, "that he may have harbored a predisposition to commit the charged offenses." Yet he argues that the jury's refusal to find entrapment under the charge submitted to it by the trial court should be overturned and the views of Justices Roberts and Frankfurter, in *Sorrells* and *Sherman*, respectively, which make the essential element of the defense turn on the type and degree of governmental conduct, be adopted as the law.

We decline to overrule these cases. [Since] the defense is not of a constitutional dimension, Congress may address itself to the question and adopt any substantive definition of the defense that it may find desirable.

Critics of the rule laid down in *Sorrells* and *Sherman* have suggested that its basis in the implied intent of Congress is largely fictitious, and have pointed to what they conceive to be the anomalous difference between the treatment of a defendant who is solicited by a private individual and one who is entrapped by a government agent. Questions have been likewise raised as to whether "predisposition" can be factually established with the requisite degree of certainty. Arguments such as these, while not devoid of appeal, have been twice previously made to this Court, and twice rejected by it, first in *Sorrells* and then in *Sherman.*

We believe that at least equally cogent criticism has been made of the concurring views in these cases. Commenting in *Sherman* on Mr. Justice Roberts' position in *Sorrells* that "although the defendant could claim that the Government had induced him to commit the crime, the Government could not reply by showing that the defendant's criminal conduct was due to his own readiness and not to the persuasion of government agents," Mr. Chief Justice Warren quoted the observation of Judge Learned Hand in an earlier stage of that proceeding:

> " 'Indeed, it would seem probable that, if there were no reply [to the claim of inducement], it would be impossible ever to secure convictions of any offences which consist of transactions that are carried on in secret.' "

Nor does it seem particularly desirable for the law to grant complete immunity from prosecution to one who himself planned to commit a crime, and then committed it, simply because government undercover agents subjected him to inducements which might have seduced a hypothetical individual who was not so predisposed.

[Several lower federal court decisions] have undoubtedly gone beyond this Court's opinions in *Sorrells* and *Sherman* in order to bar prosecutions because of what they thought to be, for want of a better term, "overzealous law enforcement." But the defense of entrapment enunciated in those opinions was not intended to give the federal judiciary a "chancellor's foot" veto over law enforcement practices of which it did not approve. The execution of the federal laws under our Constitution is confided primarily to the Executive Branch of the Government, subject to applicable constitutional and statutory limitations and to judicially fashioned rules to enforce those limitations. We think that the decision of the Court of Appeals in this case quite unnecessarily introduces an unmanageably subjective standard which is contrary to the holdings of this Court in *Sorrells* and *Sherman.*

[In light of *Sorrells* and *Sherman*, respondent's concession] that the jury finding as to predisposition was supported by the evidence [is] therefore, fatal to his claim of entrapment. He was an active participant in an illegal drug manufacturing enterprise which began before the Government agent appeared on the scene, and continued after the Government agent had left the scene. He was, in the words of *Sherman*, not an "unwary innocent" but an "unwary criminal." The Court of Appeals was wrong, we believe, when it sought to broaden the principle laid down in *Sorrells* and *Sherman.* Its judgment is therefore Reversed.

JUSTICE STEWART, with whom JUSTICE BRENNAN and JUSTICE MARSHALL join, dissenting. * * *

In *Sorrells* and *Sherman* the Court took what might be called a "subjective" approach to the defense of entrapment. In that view, the defense is predicated on an unexpressed intent of Congress to exclude from its criminal statutes the prosecution and conviction of persons, "otherwise innocent," who have been lured to the commission of the prohibited act through the Government's instigation. The key phrase in this formulation is "otherwise innocent," for the entrapment defense is available under this approach only to those who would not have committed the crime but for the Government's inducements. Thus, the subjective approach focuses on the conduct and propensities of the particular defendant in each individual case: if he is "otherwise innocent," he may avail himself of the defense; but if he had the "predisposition" to commit the crime, or if the "criminal design" originated with him, then—regardless of the nature and extent of the Government's participation—there has been no entrapment. And, in the absence of a conclusive showing one way or the other, the question of the defendant's "predisposition" to the crime is a question of fact for the jury. The Court today adheres to this approach.

The concurring opinion of Mr. Justice Roberts, joined by Justices Brandeis and Stone, in the *Sorrells* case, and that of Mr. Justice Frankfurter, joined by Justices Douglas, Harlan, and Brennan, in the *Sherman* case, took a different view of the entrapment defense. In their concept, the defense is not grounded on some unexpressed intent of Congress to exclude from punishment under its statutes those otherwise innocent persons tempted into crime by the Government, but rather on the belief that "the methods employed on behalf of the Government to bring about conviction cannot be countenanced." Thus, the focus of this approach is not on the propensities and predisposition of a specific defendant, but on "whether the police conduct revealed in the particular case falls below standards, to which common feelings respond, for the proper use of governmental power." Phrased another way, the question is whether—regardless of the predisposition to crime of the particular defendant involved—the governmental agents have acted in such a way as is likely to instigate or create a criminal offense. Under this approach, the determination of the lawfulness of the Government's conduct must be made—as it is on all questions involving the legality of law enforcement methods—by the trial judge, not the jury.

In my view, this objective approach to entrapment * * * is the only one truly consistent with the underlying rationale of the defense.[1] Indeed, the very basis of the entrapment defense itself demands adherence to an approach that focuses on the conduct of the governmental agents, rather than on whether the defendant was "predisposed" or "otherwise innocent." I find it impossible to believe that the purpose of the defense is to effectuate some unexpressed congressional intent to exclude from its criminal statutes persons who committed a prohibited act, but would not have done so except for the Government's inducements. * * *

Furthermore, to say that such a defendant is "otherwise innocent" or not "predisposed" to commit the crime is misleading, at best. The very fact that he has committed an act that Congress has determined to be illegal demonstrates conclusively that he is not innocent of the offense. He may not have originated the precise plan or the precise details, but he was "predisposed" in the sense that he has proved to be quite capable of committing the crime. That he was induced, provoked, or tempted to do so by government agents does not make him any more innocent or any less predisposed than he would be if he had been induced, provoked, or tempted by a private person—which, of course, would not entitle him

1. Both the Proposed New Federal Criminal Code (1971), Final Report of the National Commission on Reform of Federal Criminal Laws § 702, and the American Law Institute's Model Penal Code § 2.13 (Proposed Official Draft, 1962), adopt this objective approach.

to cry "entrapment." Since the only difference between these situations is the identity of the temptor, it follows that the significant focus must be on the conduct of the government agents, and not on the predisposition of the defendant.

The purpose of the entrapment defense, then, cannot be to protect persons who are "otherwise innocent." Rather, it must be to prohibit unlawful governmental activity in instigating crime. [If] that is so, then whether the particular defendant was "predisposed" or "otherwise innocent" is irrelevant; and the important question becomes whether the Government's conduct in inducing the crime was beyond judicial toleration.

Moreover, a test that makes the entrapment defense depend on whether the defendant had the requisite predisposition permits the introduction into evidence of all kinds of hearsay, suspicion, and rumor—all of which would be inadmissible in any other context—in order to prove the defendant's predisposition. It allows the prosecution, in offering such proof, to rely on the defendant's bad reputation or past criminal activities, including even rumored activities of which the prosecution may have insufficient evidence to obtain an indictment, and to present the agent's suspicions as to why they chose to tempt this defendant. This sort of evidence is not only unreliable, as the hearsay rule recognizes; but it is also highly prejudicial, especially if the matter is submitted to the jury, for, despite instructions to the contrary, the jury may well consider such evidence as probative not simply of the defendant's predisposition, but of his guilt of the offense with which he stands charged.

More fundamentally, focusing on the defendant's innocence or predisposition has the direct effect of making what is permissible or impermissible police conduct depend upon the past record and propensities of the particular defendant involved. Stated another way, this subjective test means that the Government is permitted to entrap a person with a criminal record or bad reputation, and then to prosecute him for the manufactured crime, confident that his record or reputation itself will be enough to show that he was predisposed to commit the offense anyway.   * * *

Since, in my view, it does not matter whether the respondent was predisposed to commit the offense of which he was convicted, the focus must be, rather, on the conduct of the undercover government agent. What the agent did here was to meet with a group of suspected producers of methamphetamine, including the respondent; to request the drug; to offer to supply the chemical phenyl-2-propanone in exchange for one-half of the methamphetamine to be manufactured therewith; and, when that offer was accepted, to provide the needed chemical ingredient, and to purchase some of the drug from the respondent.   * * *

Although the Court of Appeals found that the phenyl-2-propanone could not have been obtained without the agent's intervention—that "there could not have been the manufacture, delivery, or sale of the illicit drug had it not been for the Government's supply of one of the essential ingredients"—the Court today rejects this finding as contradicted by the facts revealed at trial. The record, as the Court states, discloses that one of the respondent's accomplices, though not the respondent himself, had obtained phenyl-2-propanone from independent sources both before and after receiving the agent's supply, and had used it in the production of methamphetamine. This demonstrates, it is said, that the chemical was obtainable other than through the government agent; and hence the agent's furnishing it for the production of the methamphetamine involved in this prosecution did no more than afford an opportunity for its production to one ready and willing to produce it. Thus, the argument seems to be, there was no entrapment here, any more than there would have been if the agent had furnished common table salt, had that been necessary to the drug's production.

It cannot be doubted that if phenyl–2–propanone had been wholly unobtainable from other sources, the agent's undercover offer to supply it to the respondent in return for part of the illicit methamphetamine produced therewith—an offer initiated and carried out by the agent for the purpose of prosecuting the respondent for producing methamphetamine—would be precisely the type of governmental conduct that constitutes entrapment under any definition. For the agent's conduct in that situation would make possible the commission of an otherwise totally impossible crime, and, I should suppose, would thus be a textbook example of instigating the commission of a criminal offense in order to prosecute someone for committing it.[a]

But assuming in this case that the phenyl–2–propanone was obtainable through independent sources, the fact remains that that used for the particular batch of methamphetamine involved in all three counts of the indictment with which the respondent was charged—i.e., that produced on December 10, 1969—was supplied by the Government. This essential ingredient was indisputably difficult to obtain, and yet what was used in committing the offenses of which the respondent was convicted was offered to the respondent by the Government agent, on the agent's own initiative, and was readily supplied to the respondent in needed amounts.

---

a. Consider, however, *Hampton v. United States*, 425 U.S. 484 (1976), where, unlike *Russell*, the material provided by the undercover agents was contraband (heroin). The district court refused to charge the jury that if it found, as petitioner claimed, that the heroin he sold to government agents (posing as narcotics buyers) had been supplied to him by a government informant he must be acquitted regardless of his predisposition to commit the offense charged. On appeal, petitioner conceded he was "predisposed." A majority of the Court rejected petitioner's contention, but there was no opinion of the Court. Justice Rehnquist, who announced the judgment of the Court in an opinion joined by Burger, C.J., and White, J., observed:

"In urging that this [is the case of outrageous police conduct reserved in *Russell*], petitioner misapprehends [the relevant language quoted] in *Russell*. Admittedly petitioner's case is different from Russell's but the difference is one of degree, not of kind. In *Russell* the ingredient supplied by the government agent was a legal drug which the defendants demonstrably could have obtained from other sources besides the Government. Here the drug which the government informant allegedly supplied [was] both illegal and constituted the *corpus delicti* for the sale of which the petitioner was convicted. The Government obviously played a more significant role in enabling petitioner to see contraband in this case than it did in *Russell*.

"But in each case the government agents were acting in concert with the defendant, and in each case either the jury found or the defendant conceded that he was predisposed to commit the crime for which he was convicted. The remedy of the criminal defendant with respect to the act of government agents, which, far from being resisted, are encouraged by him, lies solely in the defense of entrapment. But,

as noted, petitioner's conceded predisposition rendered this defense unavailable to him."

Concurring Justice Powell, joined by Blackmun, J., agreed that "this case is controlled completely by *Russell*," but was unwilling to join the plurality in concluding that, no matter what the circumstances, neither due process principles nor our supervisory power could support a bar to conviction in any case where the Government is able to prove disposition."

Justice Brennan, joined by Stewart and Marshall, JJ., dissented, urging that conviction be "barred as a matter of law where the subject of the criminal charge is the sale of contraband provided to the defendant by a Government agent." The dissenters reiterated support for the "objective" approach to entrapment, but considered reversal compelled even "for those who follow the 'subjective' approach." Continued the dissent:

"Two facts sufficiently distinguish the case from *Russell*. First, the chemical supplied in that case was not contraband. * * * Second, [Russell] 'was an active participant in an illegal drug manufacturing enterprise which began before the Government agent appeared on the scene, and continued after the Government agent had left * * *.' [But] the two sales for which petitioner was convicted were allegedly instigated by Government agents and completed by the Government's purchase.

"[Where] the Government's agent deliberately sets up the accused by supplying him with contraband and then bringing him to another agent as a potential purchaser, the Government's role has passed the point of toleration. The Government is doing nothing less than buying contraband from itself through an intermediary and jailing the intermediary."

[In] this case, the chemical ingredient was available only to licensed persons, and the Government itself had requested suppliers not to sell that ingredient even to people with a license. Yet the Government agent readily offered, and supplied, that ingredient to an unlicensed person and asked him to make a certain illegal drug with it. The Government then prosecuted that person for making the drug produced *with the very ingredient* which its agent had so helpfully supplied. This strikes me as the very pattern of conduct that should be held to constitute entrapment as a matter of law.

It is the Government's duty to prevent crime, not to promote it. Here, the Government's agent asked that the illegal drug be produced for him, solved his quarry's practical problems with the assurance that he could provide the one essential ingredient that was difficult to obtain, furnished that element as he had promised, and bought the finished product from the respondent—all so that the respondent could be prosecuted for producing and selling the very drug for which the agent had asked and for which he had provided the necessary component. Under the objective approach that I would follow, this respondent was entrapped, regardless of his predisposition or "innocence." * * * [b]

JACOBSON v. UNITED STATES

503 U.S. 540, 112 S.Ct. 1535, 118 L.Ed.2d 174 (1992).

JUSTICE WHITE delivered the opinion of the Court.

On September 24, 1987, [petitioner] was indicted for violating a provision of the Child Protection Act of 1984, which criminalizes the knowing receipt through the mails of a "visual depiction [that] involves the use of a minor engaging in sexually explicit conduct...." Petitioner defended on the ground that the Government entrapped him into committing the crime through a series of communications from undercover agents that spanned the 26 months preceding his arrest. Petitioner was found guilty after a jury trial. The Court of Appeals affirmed his conviction, holding that the Government had carried its burden of proving beyond reasonable doubt that petitioner was predisposed to break the law and hence was not entrapped.

Because the Government overstepped the line between setting a trap for the "unwary innocent" and the "unwary criminal," and as a matter of law failed to establish that petitioner was independently predisposed to commit the crime for which he was arrested, we reverse * * *.

I

In February 1984, petitioner, a 56–year–old veteran-turned-farmer who supported his elderly father in Nebraska, ordered two magazines and a brochure from a California adult bookstore. The magazines, entitled *Bare Boys I* and *Bare Boys II* contained photographs of nude preteen and teenage boys. The contents of the magazines startled petitioner, who testified that he had expected to receive photographs of "young men 18 years or older."

[The] young men depicted in the magazines were not engaged in sexual activity, and petitioner's receipt of the magazines was legal under both federal and Nebraska law. Within three months, the law with respect to child pornography

b. In a separate dissent, Justice Douglas, joined by Brennan, J., maintained that "[f]ederal agents play a debased role when they become the instigators of the crime, or partners in its commission, or the creative brain behind the illegal scheme. That is what the federal agent did here when he furnished the accused with one of the chemical ingredients needed to manufacture the unlawful drug."

changed; Congress passed the Act illegalizing the receipt through the mails of sexually explicit depictions of children. In the very month that the new provision became law, postal inspectors found petitioner's name on the mailing list of the California bookstore that had mailed him *Bare Boys I and II.* There followed over the next 2½ years, repeated efforts by two Government agencies, through five fictitious organizations and a bogus pen pal, to explore petitioner's willingness to break the new law by ordering sexually explicit photographs of children through the mail.

The Government began its efforts in January 1985 when a postal inspector sent petitioner a letter supposedly from the American Hedonist Society, which in fact was a fictitious organization. The letter included a membership application and stated the Society's doctrine: that members had the "right to read what we desire, the right to discuss similar interests with those who share our philosophy, and finally that we have the right to seek pleasure without restrictions being placed on us by outdated puritan morality." Petitioner enrolled in the organization and returned a sexual attitude questionnaire that asked him to rank on a scale of one to four his enjoyment of various sexual materials, with one being "really enjoy," two being "enjoy," three being "somewhat enjoy," and four being "do not enjoy." Petitioner ranked the entry "[p]re-teen sex" as a two, but indicated that he was opposed to pedophilia.

For a time, the Government left petitioner alone. But then a new "prohibited mail specialist" in the Postal Service found petitioner's name in a file and in May 1986 petitioner received a solicitation from a second fictitious consumer research company, "Midlands Data Research," seeking a response from those who "believe in the joys of sex and the complete awareness of those lusty and youthful lads and lasses of the neophite [sic] age." The letter never explained whether "neophite" referred to minors or young adults. Petitioner responded: "Please feel free to send me more information, I am interested in teenage sexuality. Please keep my name confidential."

Petitioner then heard from yet another Government creation, "Heartland Institute for a New Tomorrow" (HINT), which proclaimed that it was "an organization founded to protect and promote sexual freedom and freedom of choice. We believe that arbitrarily imposed legislative sanctions restricting *your* sexual freedom should be rescinded through the legislative process." The letter also enclosed a second survey. Petitioner indicated that his interest in "[p]reteen sex-homosexual" material was above average, but not high. In response to another question, petitioner wrote: "Not only sexual expression but freedom of the press is under attack. We must be ever vigilant to counter attack right wing fundamentalists who are determined to curtail our freedoms."

"HINT" replied, portraying itself as a lobbying organization seeking to repeal "all statutes which regulate sexual activities, except those laws which deal with violent behavior, such as rape. HINT is also lobbying to eliminate any legal definition of 'the age of consent'." These lobbying efforts were to be funded by sales from a catalog to be published in the future "offering the sale of various items which we believe you will find to be both interesting and stimulating." HINT also provided computer matching of group members with similar survey responses; and, although petitioner was supplied with a list of potential "pen pals," he did not initiate any correspondence.

Nevertheless, the Government's "prohibited mail specialist" began writing to petitioner, using the pseudonym "Carl Long." The letters employed a tactic known as "mirroring," which the inspector described as "reflect[ing] whatever the interests are of the person we are writing to." Petitioner responded at first, indicating that his interest was primarily in "male-male items." Inspector "Long" wrote back:

> "My interests too are primarily male-male items. Are you satisfied with the type of VCR tapes available? Personally, I like the amateur stuff better if its [sic] well produced as it can get more kinky and also seems more real. I think the actors enjoy it more."

Petitioner responded:

> "As far as my likes are concerned, I like good looking young guys (in their late teens and early 20's) doing their thing together."

Petitioner's letters to "Long" made no reference to child pornography. After writing two letters, petitioner discontinued the correspondence.

By March 1987, 34 months had passed since the Government obtained petitioner's name from the mailing list of the California bookstore, and 26 months had passed since the Postal Service had commenced its mailings to petitioner. Although petitioner had responded to surveys and letters, the Government had no evidence that petitioner had ever intentionally possessed or been exposed to child pornography. The Postal Service had not checked petitioner's mail to determine whether he was receiving questionable mailings from persons—other than the Government—involved in the child pornography industry.

At this point, a second Government agency, the Customs Service, included petitioner in its own child pornography sting, "Operation Borderline," after receiving his name on lists submitted by the Postal Service. Using the name of a fictitious Canadian company called "Produit Outaouais," the Customs Service mailed petitioner a brochure advertising photographs of young boys engaging in sex. Petitioner placed an order that was never filled.

The Postal Service also continued its efforts in the Jacobson case, writing to petitioner as the "Far Eastern Trading Company Ltd." The letter began:

> "As many of you know, much hysterical nonsense has appeared in the American media concerning 'pornography' and what must be done to stop it from coming across your borders. This brief letter does not allow us to give much comments; however, why is your government spending millions of dollars to exercise international censorship while tons of drugs, which makes yours the world's most crime ridden country are passed through easily."

The letter went on to say:

> "[W]e have devised a method of getting these to you without prying eyes of U.S. Customs seizing your mail. . . . After consultations with American solicitors, we have been advised that once we have posted our material through your system, it cannot be opened for any inspection without authorization of a judge."

The letter invited petitioner to send for more information. [He] responded. A catalogue was sent and petitioner ordered *Boys Who Love Boys,* a pornographic magazine depicting young boys engaged in various sexual activities. Petitioner was arrested after a controlled delivery of a photocopy of the magazine.

When petitioner was asked at trial why he placed such an order, he explained that the Government had succeeded in piquing his curiosity:

> "Well, the statement was made of all the trouble and the hysteria over pornography and I wanted to see what the material was. * * * I didn't know for sure what kind of sexual action they were referring to in the Canadian letter . . . ."

In petitioner's home, the Government found the *Bare Boys* magazines and materials that the Government had sent to him in the course of its protracted investigation, but no other materials that would indicate that petitioner collected or was actively interested in child pornography.

Petitioner was indicted for [receiving child pornography through the mails.] The trial court instructed the jury on the petitioner's entrapment defense,[1] petitioner was convicted, and a divided Court of Appeals for the Eighth Circuit, sitting *en banc,* affirmed, concluding that "Jacobson was not entrapped as a matter of law."

II * * *

In [its] zeal to enforce the law [the Government] may not originate a criminal design, implant in an innocent person's mind the disposition to commit a criminal act, and then induce commission of the crime so that the Government may prosecute. Where the Government has induced an individual to break the law and the defense of entrapment is at issue, as it was in this case, the prosecution must prove beyond reasonable doubt that the defendant was disposed to commit the criminal act prior to first being approached by Government agents.[2]

Thus, an agent deployed to stop the traffic in illegal drugs may offer the opportunity to buy or sell drugs, and, if the offer is accepted, make an arrest on the spot or later. In such a typical case, or in a more elaborate "sting" operation involving government-sponsored fencing where the defendant is simply provided with the opportunity to commit a crime, the entrapment defense is of little use because the ready commission of the criminal act amply demonstrates the defendant's predisposition. Had the agents in this case simply offered petitioner the opportunity to order child pornography through the mails, and petitioner—who must be presumed to know the law—had promptly availed himself of this criminal

---

1. The jury was instructed:

"As mentioned, one of the issues in this case is whether the defendant was entrapped. If the defendant was entrapped he must be found not guilty. The government has the burden of proving beyond a reasonable doubt that the defendant was not entrapped.

"If the defendant before contact with law-enforcement officers or their agents did not have any intent or disposition to commit the crime charged and was induced or persuaded by law-enforcement officers o[r] their agents to commit that crime, then he was entrapped. On the other hand, if the defendant before contact with law-enforcement officers or their agents did have an intent or disposition to commit the crime charged, then he was not entrapped even though law-enforcement officers or their agents provided a favorable opportunity to commit the crime or made committing the crime easier or even participated in acts essential to the crime."

2. Inducement is not at issue in this case. The Government does not dispute that it induced petitioner to commit the crime. The sole issue is whether the Government carried its burden of proving that petitioner was predisposed to violate the law *before* the Government intervened. The dissent is mistaken in claiming that this is an innovation in entrapment law and in sug-

gesting that the Government's conduct prior to the moment of solicitation is irrelevant. * * * Indeed, the proposition that the accused must be predisposed prior to contact with law enforcement officers is so firmly established that the Government conceded the point at oral argument, submitting that the evidence it developed during the course of its investigation was probative because it indicated petitioner's state of mind *prior* to the commencement of the Government's investigation.

This long-established standard in no way encroaches upon Government investigatory activities. Indeed, the Government's internal guidelines for undercover operations provide that an inducement to commit a crime should not be offered unless:

"(a) there is a reasonable indication, based on information developed through informants or other means, that the subject is engaging, has engaged, or is likely to engage in illegal activity of a similar type; *or*

"(b) The opportunity for illegal activity has been structured so that there is reason for believing that persons drawn to the opportunity, or brought to it, are predisposed to engage in the contemplated illegal activity." *Attorney General's Guidelines on FBI Undercover Operations* (Dec. 31, 1980).

opportunity, it is unlikely that his entrapment defense would have warranted a jury instruction.

But that is not what happened here. By the time petitioner finally placed his order, he had already been the target of 26 months of repeated mailings and communications from Government agents and fictitious organizations. Therefore, although he had become predisposed to break the law by May 1987, it is our view that the Government did not prove that this predisposition was independent and not the product of the attention that the Government had directed at petitioner since January 1985.

The prosecution's evidence of predisposition falls into two categories: evidence developed prior to the Postal Service's mail campaign, and that developed during the course of the investigation. The sole piece of preinvestigation evidence is petitioner's 1984 order and receipt of the *Bare Boys* magazines. But this is scant if any proof of petitioner's predisposition to commit an illegal act, the criminal character of which a defendant is presumed to know. It may indicate a predisposition to view sexually-oriented photographs that are responsive to his sexual tastes; but evidence that merely indicates a generic inclination to act within a broad range, not all of which is criminal, is of little probative value in establishing predisposition.

Furthermore, petitioner was acting within the law at the time he received these magazines. * * * Evidence of predisposition to do what once was lawful is not, by itself, sufficient to show predisposition to do what is now illegal, for there is a common understanding that most people obey the law even when they disapprove of it. [Hence,] the fact that petitioner legally ordered and received the *Bare Boys* magazines does little to further the Government's burden of proving that petitioner was predisposed to commit a criminal act. This is particularly true given petitioner's unchallenged testimony was that he did not know until they arrived that the magazines would depict minors.

The prosecution's evidence gathered during the investigation also fails to carry the Government's burden. Petitioner's responses to the many communications prior to the ultimate criminal act were at most indicative of certain personal inclinations, including a predisposition to view photographs of preteen sex and a willingness to promote a given agenda by supporting lobbying organizations. Even so, petitioner's responses hardly support an inference that he would commit the crime of receiving child pornography through the mails.[3]

[On] the other hand, the strong arguable inference is that, by waving the banner of individual rights and disparaging the legitimacy and constitutionality of efforts to restrict the availability of sexually explicit materials, the Government not only excited petitioner's interest in sexually explicit materials banned by law but also exerted substantial pressure on petitioner to obtain and read such material as part of a fight against censorship and the infringement of individual rights. * * *

Petitioner's ready response to these solicitations cannot be enough to establish beyond reasonable doubt that he was predisposed, prior to the Government acts intended to create predisposition, to commit the crime of receiving child pornography through the mails. The evidence that petitioner was ready and willing to commit the offense came only after the Government had devoted 2½

---

3. We do not hold, as the dissent suggests, that the Government was required to prove that petitioner knowingly violated the law. We simply conclude that proof that petitioner engaged in legal conduct and possessed certain generalized personal inclinations is not sufficient evidence to prove beyond a reasonable doubt that he would have been predisposed to commit the crime charged independent of the Government's coaxing.

years to convincing him that he had or should have the right to engage in the very behavior proscribed by law. Rational jurors could not say beyond a reasonable doubt that petitioner possessed the requisite predisposition prior to the Government's investigation and that it existed independent of the Government's many and varied approaches to petitioner. As was explained in *Sherman,* where entrapment was found as a matter of law, "the Government [may not] pla[y] on the weaknesses of an innocent party and beguil[e] him into committing crimes which he otherwise would not have attempted."

Law enforcement officials go too far when they "implant in the mind of an innocent person the *disposition* to commit the alleged offense and induce its commission in order that they may prosecute." *Sorrells* (emphasis added). [When] the Government's quest for convictions leads to the apprehension of an otherwise law-abiding citizen who, if left to his own devices, likely would have never run afoul of the law, the courts should intervene. * * *

JUSTICE O'CONNOR, with whom THE CHIEF JUSTICE and JUSTICE KENNEDY join, and with whom JUSTICE SCALIA joins except as to Part II, dissenting.

Keith Jacobson was offered only two opportunities to buy child pornography through the mail. Both times, he ordered. Both times, he asked for opportunities to buy more. He needed no Government agent to coax, threaten, or persuade him; no one played on his sympathies, friendship, or suggested that his committing the crime would further a greater good. In fact, no Government agent even contacted him face-to-face. The Government contends that from the enthusiasm with which Mr. Jacobson responded to the chance to commit a crime, a reasonable jury could permissibly infer beyond a reasonable doubt that he was predisposed to commit the crime. I agree.

[The] first time the Government sent Mr. Jacobson a catalog of illegal materials, he ordered a set of photographs advertised as picturing "young boys in sex action fun." He enclosed the following note with his order: "I received your brochure and decided to place an order. If I like your product, I will order more later." For reasons undisclosed in the record, Mr. Jacobson's order was never delivered.

The second time the Government sent a catalog of illegal materials, Mr. Jacobson ordered a magazine called "Boys Who Love Boys," described as: "11 year old and 14 year old boys get it on in every way possible. Oral, anal sex and heavy masturbation. If you love boys, you will be delighted with this." Along with his order, Mr. Jacobson sent the following note: "Will order other items later. I want to be discreet in order to protect you and me."

Government agents admittedly did not offer Mr. Jacobson the chance to buy child pornography right away. Instead, they first sent questionnaires in order to make sure that he was generally interested in the subject matter. Indeed, a "cold call" in such a business would not only risk rebuff and suspicion, but might also shock and offend the uninitiated, or expose minors to suggestive materials. Mr. Jacobson's responses to the questionnaires gave the investigators reason to think he would be interested in photographs depicting preteen sex.

The Court, however, concludes that a reasonable jury could not have found Mr. Jacobson to be predisposed beyond a reasonable doubt on the basis of his responses to the Government's catalogs, even though it admits that, by that time, he was predisposed to commit the crime. The Government, the Court holds, failed to provide evidence that Mr. Jacobson's obvious predisposition at the time of the crime "was independent and not the product of the attention that the Government had directed at petitioner." In so holding, I believe the Court fails to acknowledge the reasonableness of the jury's inference from the evidence, redefines "predisposition," and introduces a new requirement that Government sting operations have a reasonable suspicion of illegal activity before contacting a suspect.

I

This Court has held previously that a defendant's predisposition is to be assessed as of the time the Government agent first suggested the crime, not when the Government agent first became involved. * * * Even in *Sherman,* in which the Court held that the defendant had been entrapped as a matter of law, the Government agent had repeatedly and unsuccessfully coaxed the defendant to buy drugs, ultimately succeeding only by playing on the defendant's sympathy. The Court found lack of predisposition based on the Government's numerous unsuccessful attempts to induce the crime, not on the basis of preliminary contacts with the defendant.

Today, the Court holds that Government conduct may be considered to create a predisposition to commit a crime, even before any Government action to induce the commission of the crime. In my view, this holding changes entrapment doctrine. Generally, the inquiry is whether a suspect is predisposed before the Government induces the commission of the crime, not before the Government makes initial contact with him. There is no dispute here that the Government's questionnaires and letters were not sufficient to establish inducement; they did not even suggest that Mr. Jacobson should engage in any illegal activity. If all the Government had done was to send these materials, Mr. Jacobson's entrapment defense would fail. Yet the Court holds that the Government must prove not only that a suspect was predisposed to commit the crime before the opportunity to commit it arose, but also before the Government came on the scene.

The rule that preliminary Government contact can create a predisposition has the potential to be misread by lower courts as well as criminal investigators as requiring that the Government must have sufficient evidence of a defendant's predisposition *before it ever seeks to contact him.* Surely the Court cannot intend to impose such a requirement, for it would mean that the Government must have a reasonable suspicion of criminal activity before it begins an investigation, a condition that we have never before imposed. The Court denies that its new rule will affect run-of-the-mill sting operations and one hopes that it means what it says. Nonetheless, after this case, every defendant will claim that something the Government agent did before soliciting the crime "created" a predisposition that was not there before. For example, a bribe taker will claim that the description of the amount of money available was so enticing that it implanted a disposition to accept the bribe later offered. A drug buyer will claim that the description of the drug's purity and effects was so tempting that it created the urge to try it for the first time. In short, the Court's opinion could be read to prohibit the Government from advertising the seductions of criminal activity as part of its sting operation, for fear of creating a predisposition in its suspects. That limitation would be especially likely to hamper sting operations such as this one, which mimic the advertising done by genuine purveyors of pornography. No doubt the Court would protest that its opinion does not stand for so broad a proposition, but the apparent lack of a principled basis for distinguishing these scenarios exposes a flaw in the more limited rule the Court today adopts.

The Court's rule is all the more troubling because it does not distinguish between Government conduct that merely highlights the temptation of the crime itself, and Government conduct that threatens, coerces, or leads a suspect to commit a crime in order to fulfill some other obligation. For example, in *Sorrells,* the Government agent repeatedly asked for illegal liquor, coaxing the defendant to accede on the ground that "one former war buddy would get liquor for another." In *Sherman*, the Government agent played on the defendant's sympathies, pretending to be going through drug withdrawal and begging the defendant to relieve his distress by helping him buy drugs.

The Government conduct in this case is not comparable. While the Court states that the Government "exerted substantial pressure on petitioner to obtain and read such material as part of a fight against censorship and the infringement of individual rights," one looks at the record in vain for evidence of such "substantial pressure." The most one finds is letters advocating legislative action to liberalize obscenity laws, letters which could easily be ignored or thrown away. Much later, the Government sent separate mailings of catalogs of illegal materials. Nowhere did the Government suggest that the proceeds of the sale of the illegal materials would be used to support legislative reforms. * * *

Mr. Jacobson's curiosity to see what " 'all the trouble and the hysteria' " was about is certainly susceptible of more than one interpretation. And it is the jury that is charged with the obligation of interpreting it. In sum, the Court fails to construe the evidence in the light most favorable to the Government, and fails to draw all reasonable inferences in the Government's favor. It was surely reasonable for the jury to infer that Mr. Jacobson was predisposed beyond a reasonable doubt, even if other inferences from the evidence were also possible.

II

The second puzzling thing about the Court's opinion is its redefinition of predisposition. The Court acknowledges that "[p]etitioner's responses to the many communications prior to the ultimate criminal act [were] indicative of certain personal inclinations, including a predisposition to view photographs of preteen sex...." If true, this should have settled the matter; Mr. Jacobson was predisposed to engage in the illegal conduct. Yet, the Court concludes, "petitioner's responses hardly support an inference that he would commit the crime of receiving child pornography through the mails."

The Court seems to add something new to the burden of proving predisposition. Not only must the Government show that a defendant was predisposed to engage in the illegal conduct, here, receiving photographs of minors engaged in sex, but also that the defendant was predisposed to break the law knowingly in order to do so. The statute violated here, however, does not require proof of specific intent to break the law; it requires only knowing receipt of visual depictions produced by using minors engaged in sexually explicit conduct. Under the Court's analysis, however, the Government must prove *more* to show predisposition than it need prove in order to convict.

The Court ignores the judgment of Congress that specific intent is not an element of the crime of receiving sexually explicit photographs of minors. The elements of predisposition should track the elements of the crime. The predisposition requirement is meant to eliminate the entrapment defense for those defendants who would have committed the crime anyway, even absent Government inducement. Because a defendant might very well be convicted of the crime here absent Government inducement even though he did not know his conduct was illegal, a specific intent requirement does little to distinguish between those who would commit the crime without the inducement and those who would not. In sum, although the fact that Mr. Jacobson's purchases of *Bare Boys I* and *Bare Boys II* were legal at the time may have some relevance to the question of predisposition, it is not, as the Court suggests, dispositive.

The crux of the Court's concern in this case is that the Government went too far and "abused" the "processes of detection and enforcement" by luring an innocent person to violate the law. Consequently, the Court holds that the Government failed to prove beyond a reasonable doubt that Mr. Jacobson was predisposed to commit the crime. It was, however, the jury's task, as the conscience of the community, to decide whether or not Mr. Jacobson was a willing participant in the criminal activity here or an innocent dupe. [There] is no dispute that the jury in this case was fully and accurately instructed on the law of entrapment, and nonetheless found Mr. Jacobson guilty. Because I believe there was sufficient evidence to uphold the jury's verdict, I respectfully dissent.

Chapter 5

THE RIGHT TO COUNSEL, TRANSCRIPTS AND OTHER AIDS; POVERTY, EQUALITY AND THE ADVERSARY SYSTEM [a]

SECTION 1. THE RIGHT TO APPOINTED COUNSEL [b]

When the Court, per Sutherland, J., spoke eloquently of the importance of the right to counsel and the essential relationship between "the right to be heard" and "the right to be heard by counsel" in the landmark case of *Powell v. Alabama,* 287 U.S. 45 (1932), which has been called the first "modern" procedural due process case, it was talking about a person's right to be heard by counsel "employed by and appearing for him." Although Justice Black's analysis for the Court thirty years later in *Gideon v. Wainwright* appears to ignore this fact, *Powell* dealt primarily not with the right to appointed counsel, but the historically separate right of the individual to employ her own counsel.

The *Powell* opinion spelled out at some length why the defendants were not afforded "a fair opportunity to secure counsel of [their] own choice" and why, under the circumstances, this constituted a denial of due process. The *Powell* Court went on to say however, and it did this only in the last few pages of a lengthy opinion, that "assuming the inability, even if opportunity had been given, to employ counsel," the failure of the trial court "to make an effective appointment of counsel was likewise a denial of due process." Continued the Court, using very measured language:

> "Whether this would be so in other criminal prosecutions, or under other circumstances, we need not determine. All that is necessary now to decide, as we do decide, is that in a capital case, where the defendant is unable to employ counsel, and is incapable adequately of making his own defense because of ignorance, feeblemindedness, illiteracy, or the like, it is the duty of

a. The right to counsel is treated in Chapter 17 as well as in this chapter. Because the right to appointed counsel and the *Griffin–Douglas* "equality" principle provide important background for the confessions cases (Ch. 6) and the lineup cases (Ch. 7), these aspects of the right to counsel are treated at this point. Because it seemed more appropriate to take up other aspects of the right to counsel, such as

the right to "effective" assistance of counsel, in the context of the role of counsel, these aspects of the right are treated in Chapter 17.

b. *Douglas v. California* also deals with the right to appointed counsel—on the first appeal, granted by the state as a matter of right—but because it is based primarily on the Equal Protection Clause it is set forth in the next section.

the court, whether requested or not, to assign counsel for him as a necessary requisite of due process of law; and that duty is not discharged by an assignment at such a time or under such circumstances as to preclude the giving of effective aid in the preparation and trial of the case."

Despite the *Powell* Court's carefully limited statement about the right to appointed counsel in state criminal cases, when the Court held, six years later, in *Johnson v. Zerbst*, 304 U.S. 458 (1938), that the Sixth Amendment required *federal* courts to provide indigent defendants with appointed counsel in all serious criminal cases (at least all felony cases), many thought the same rule would soon be applied to state prosecutions. For Justice Black, who wrote the opinion for the *Johnson* Court, painted with a broad brush, giving the impression that the Court was prepared to say that the right to counsel, appointed or retained, was a "fundamental" right made obligatory upon the states by the Fourteenth Amendment.

Thus, Justice Black called the right to counsel "one of the safeguards * * * deemed necessary to insure fundamental human rights of life and liberty" and the Sixth Amendment "a constant admonition that if the constitutional safeguards it provides be lost, justice will not 'still be done.'" Relying heavily on *Powell*'s discussion of the general need for, and importance of, the right to counsel, *Johnson* concluded that the Sixth Amendment embodies "the obvious truth that the average defendant does not have the professional legal skill to protect himself when brought before a tribunal" and that the Amendment "withholds from federal courts, in all criminal proceedings, the power and authority to deprive an accused of his life or liberty unless he has or waives the assistance of counsel."

However, in *Betts v. Brady*, the first case set forth in this section, the Court refused to read *Powell* broadly or to apply *Johnson* to the states via the Fourteenth Amendment's due process clause. Instead, the Court formulated a "prejudice" or "special circumstances" rule: an indigent defendant in a non-capital case had to show specifically that he had been "prejudiced" by the absence of a lawyer or that "special circumstances" (e.g., the defendant's lack of education or intelligence or the gravity and complexity of the offense charged) rendered criminal proceedings without the assistance of defense counsel "fundamentally unfair." [d]

One of the troubles with the *Betts v. Brady* doctrine was that its application was inherently speculative and problematic. A record produced by a layperson defending himself often makes the person *look* overwhelmingly guilty and the case *look* exceedingly simple. Such a record does not reflect what defenses or mitigating circumstances a trained advocate would have seen or what lines of inquiry she would have pursued. This point was made very forcefully by Justice Black (joined by Douglas and Murphy, JJ.), dissenting in *Betts*. Twenty-one years later, Justice Black wrote the opinion for the Court in *Gideon v. Wainwright*, overruling *Betts*.

The opinion in *Gideon*, the second case set forth in this section, might have been written differently. It might, to use concurring Justice Harlan's phrase, have accorded *Betts* "a more respectful burial." For example, Justice Black might

c. Soon after *Betts*, the Court indicated that an indigent person had a "flat" or unqualified right to appointed counsel when (but only when) charged with a crime punishable by death.

d. When the Court reviewed Betts' case, he had appellate counsel, but his lawyer was confident—too confident—that the Court would apply the full measure of the Sixth Amendment right to counsel to the states. Thus, he did not make any analysis of the trial and present any specific examples of how Betts was, or might have been, prejudiced by the absence of counsel. Commentators, upon review of the *Betts* record, have maintained that a number of such examples could have been shown.

have pointed out that in the two decades since *Betts* the assumption that a lawyerless defendant would usually be able to defend himself had fared poorly as the Court repeatedly found "special circumstances" requiring the services of counsel and constantly expanded the concept of "special circumstances."[e] Justice Black might also have noted that the assumption that a "special circumstances" test was more consistent with the "obligations of federalism" than an "absolute rule" had collapsed in the face of the proliferation of federal habeas corpus cases produced by the *Betts* rule and the resulting friction between state and federal courts.

But Justice Black made no attempt to show that developments in the two decades since *Betts* militated in favor of its demise. Perhaps he was reluctant to admit even the *original validity* of a decision that exemplified the evils (to him) of the "fundamental rights" interpretation of Fourteenth Amendment Due Process.[f] Perhaps he was determined to vindicate his own dissenting opinion in *Betts*.

Although *Gideon* was one of the most popular cases ever decided by the Supreme Court, it came fairly late in the day. Indeed, it is quite surprising that the Court did not establish the constitutional right to appointed counsel in all serious criminal cases until *two years after* it imposed the Fourth Amendment exclusionary rule on state courts as a matter of due process.

It is helpful to view criminal procedural due process as containing two major values or objectives. The first and the more obvious one is insuring the reliability of the guilt-determining process. The second and more elusive one is insuring respect for the dignity or liberty of the individual without regard to the reliability of the criminal process. The exclusionary rule (Ch. 3, § 1) implements the second goal; the right to counsel (sometimes called "the most pervasive right" of the accused or "the master key" to all rights) effectuates the first—and the most basic goal. Yet the Court moved ahead on the search and seizure front before it overruled the *Betts* rule.

Moreover, a major criticism of *Weeks* and *Mapp* (Ch. 3, § 1) was that because they addressed problems beyond the direct control of the courts these cases could not accomplish their goal—deterring illegal searches and seizures. But this criticism was not applicable to enlargement of the indigent defendant's right to counsel. For the *Betts–Gideon* line of cases dealt with the right to appointed counsel at arraignment, trial and sentencing, matters within the immediate and continuing control of the courts. Assuming arguendo that police officers and sheriffs are insensitive to acquittals and reversals, trial judges and prosecutors are not—and they would be entrusted with the task of carrying out the requirements of an enlarged right to appointed counsel.

Note, too, that when the Court in *Mapp* imposed the exclusionary rule on the states in 1961, the states were evenly split on the question. But when the Court in *Gideon* reconsidered the *Betts* doctrine in 1963, some thirty-seven states—about a three to one margin—provided counsel for all indigent felony defendants regardless of special circumstances. Moreover, as Mr. Gideon's lawyers pointed out to the Supreme Court, of the thirteen states whose laws or rules did not

e. In *Chewning v. Cunningham,* 368 U.S. 443 (1962), the last of the *Betts* rule cases, the Court not only found "special circumstances" requiring the services of counsel, as it had in every case after 1950, but indicated that these circumstances would be made out whenever issues existed that "may well be considered by an *imaginative lawyer*" (emphasis added) without regard to "whether *any would have* merit*" (emphasis added). As concurring Justice Harlan protested on that occasion, "the bare possibility that any of these improbable claims could have been asserted does not amount [to] 'exceptional circumstances' " as the *Betts* rule had long been understood.

f. See also, Black, J., dissenting in *Adamson v. California,* Ch. 2, § 1.

require the appointment of counsel in all felony cases, eight usually did so as a matter of practice. Only five southern states made no regular provision for counsel in noncapital cases.

Of course, three years after *Gideon,* when the Court applied the right to assigned counsel to the proceedings in the police station (see *Miranda*, Ch. 6, § 3), *no* state had chosen to go nearly that far on its own and, unlike *Gideon* (when twenty-two states asked the Court to overrule *Betts*), no state urged the Court to go that far. That is one reason (but hardly the only reason) that *Miranda* had a much colder reception than *Gideon.*

How early in the criminal process the right to counsel should "begin" was not the only question left open by *Gideon.* Another was: At what stage in the criminal process does the right to counsel "end"? The first appeal as of right? Discretionary review in the state supreme court? Discretionary review in the U.S. Supreme Court? (See the next section, infra.) Still another question left open by *Gideon* was: What *kinds* of criminal cases are covered by *Gideon*?

Some thought *Gideon* should be limited to felony cases. Others thought it should include any crime *punishable* by a term of imprisonment. Still others thought a line should be drawn, as it had been in cases dealing with the right to jury, between serious misdemeanors and "petty offenses" (those punishable by six months imprisonment or less). As demonstrated by the last two cases in this section, *Argersinger v. Hamlin* and *Scott v. Illinois,* the Court adopted none of the aforementioned approaches.

BETTS v. BRADY

316 U.S. 455, 62 S.Ct. 1252, 86 L.Ed. 1595 (1942).

Justice Roberts delivered the opinion of the Court.

Petitioner, an indigent, was indicted for robbery. His request for counsel was denied because local practice permitted appointment only in rape and murder prosecutions. Petitioner then pled not guilty and elected to be tried without a jury. At the trial he chose not to take the stand. He was convicted and sentenced to eight years imprisonment.

[The] due process clause of the Fourteenth Amendment does not incorporate, as such, the specific guarantees found in the Sixth Amendment although a denial by a state of rights or privileges specifically embodied in that and others of the first eight amendments may, in certain circumstances, or in connection with other elements, operate, in a given case, to deprive a litigant of due process of law in violation of the Fourteenth. [Due process] formulates a concept less rigid and more fluid than those envisaged in other specific and particular provisions of the Bill of Rights. Its application is less a matter of rule. Asserted denial is to be tested by an appraisal of the totality of facts in a given case.

[Petitioner] says the rule to be deduced from our former decisions is that, in every case, whatever the circumstances, one charged with crime, who is unable to obtain counsel, must be furnished counsel by the state. Expressions in the opinions of this court lend color to the argument, but, as the petitioner admits, none of our decisions squarely adjudicates the question now presented.

In *Powell v. Alabama,* 287 U.S. 45 (1932), ignorant and friendless negro youths, strangers in the community, without friends or means to obtain counsel, were hurried to trial for a capital offense without effective appointment of counsel [and] without adequate opportunity to consult even the counsel casually appointed to represent them. This occurred in a State whose statute law required the appointment of counsel for indigent defendants prosecuted for the offense charged. Thus the trial was conducted in disregard of every principle of fairness and in disregard of that which was declared by the law of the State a requisite of a fair trial. This court [stated] further that "under the circumstances [the] necessity of counsel was so vital and imperative that the failure of the trial court to make an effective appointment of counsel was likewise a denial of due process," but added: "whether this would be so in other criminal prosecutions, or under other circumstances, we need not determine. All that it is necessary now to decide, as we do decide, is that in a capital case, where the defendant is unable to employ counsel, and is incapable adequately of making his own defense because of ignorance, feeble-mindedness, illiteracy, or the like, it is the duty of the court, whether requested or not, to assign counsel for him as a necessary requisite of due process of law * * * "

* * * We have construed the [Sixth Amendment] to require appointment of counsel in all [federal] cases where a defendant is unable to procure the services of an attorney, and where the right has not been intentionally and competently waived. [*Johnson v. Zerbst,* 304 U.S. 458 (1938)]. Though [the] amendment lays down no rule for the conduct of the states, the question recurs whether the constraint laid by the amendment upon the national courts expresses a rule so fundamental and essential to a fair trial, and so, to due process of law, that it is made obligatory upon the states by the Fourteenth Amendment. Relevant data on the subject are afforded by constitutional and statutory provisions subsisting in the colonies and the states prior to the inclusion of the Bill of Rights in the national Constitution, and in the constitutional, legislative, and judicial history of the states to the present date.

[I]n the great majority of the states, it has been the considered judgment of the people, their representatives and their courts that appointment of counsel is not a fundamental right, essential to a fair trial. On the contrary, the matter has generally been deemed one of legislative policy. In the light of this evidence we are unable to say that the concept of due process incorporated in the Fourteenth Amendment obligates the states, whatever may be their own views, to furnish counsel in every such case. Every court has power, if it deems proper, to appoint counsel where that course seems to be required in the interest of fairness.

The practice of the courts of Maryland gives point to the principle that the states should not be straight-jacketed in this respect, by a construction of the Fourteenth Amendment. Judge Bond's opinion states, and counsel at the bar confirmed the fact, that in Maryland the usual practice is for the defendant to waive a trial by jury. This the petitioner did in the present case. Such trials, as Judge Bond remarks, are much more informal than jury trials and it is obvious that the judge can much better control the course of the trial and is in a better position to see impartial justice done than when the formalities of a jury trial are involved.

In this case there was no question of the commission of a robbery. The State's case consisted of evidence identifying the petitioner as the perpetrator. The defense was an alibi. Petitioner called and examined witnesses to prove that he was at another place at the time of the commission of the offense. The simple issue was the veracity of the testimony for the State and that for the defendant. As Judge Bond says, the accused was not helpless, but was a man forty-three years old, of ordinary intelligence and ability to take care of his own interests on the trial of that narrow issue. He had once before been in a criminal court, pleaded guilty to larceny and served a sentence and was not wholly unfamiliar with criminal procedure. It is quite clear that in Maryland, if the situation had been otherwise and it had appeared that the petitioner was, for any reason, at a serious disadvantage by reason of the lack of counsel, a refusal to appoint would have resulted in the reversal of a judgment of conviction.

[To] deduce from the due process clause a rule binding upon the states in this matter would be to impose upon them, as Judge Bond points out, a requirement without distinction between criminal charges of different magnitude or in respect of courts of varying jurisdiction. As he says: "Charges of small crimes tried before justices of the peace and capital charges tried in the higher courts would equally require the appointment of counsel. Presumably it would be argued that trials in the Traffic Court would require it." * * *

As we have said, the Fourteenth Amendment prohibits the conviction and incarceration of one whose trial is offensive to the common and fundamental ideas of fairness and right, and while want of counsel in a particular case may result in a conviction lacking in such fundamental fairness, we cannot say that the amendment embodies an inexorable command that no trial for any offense, or in any court, can be fairly conducted and justice accorded a defendant who is not represented by counsel.

The judgment is affirmed.

JUSTICE BLACK, dissenting, with whom JUSTICE DOUGLAS and JUSTICE MURPHY concur.

To hold that the petitioner had a constitutional right to counsel in this case does not require us to say that "no trial for any offense, or in any court, can be fairly conducted and justice accorded a defendant who is not represented by counsel." This case can be determined by resolution of a narrower question: whether in view of the nature of the offense and the circumstances of his trial and conviction, this petitioner was denied the procedural protection which is his right under the federal constitution. I think he was.

The petitioner [was] a farm hand, out of a job and on relief. [The] court below found that [he] had "at least an ordinary amount of intelligence." It is clear from his examination of witnesses that he was a man of little education.

If this case had come to us from a federal court, it is clear we should have to reverse it, because the Sixth Amendment makes the right to counsel in criminal cases inviolable by the federal government. I believe that the Fourteenth Amendment made the sixth applicable to the states. But this view [has] never been accepted by a majority of this Court and is not accepted today. * * * I believe, however, that under the prevailing view of due process, as reflected in the opinion just announced, a view which gives this Court such vast supervisory powers that I am not prepared to accept it without grave doubts, the judgment below should be reversed.

[The] right to counsel in a criminal proceeding is "fundamental." *Powell v. Alabama.* [A] practice cannot be reconciled with "common and fundamental ideas of fairness and right" which subjects innocent men to increased dangers of conviction merely because of their poverty. Whether a man is innocent cannot be determined from a trial in which as here, denial of counsel has made it impossible to conclude, with any satisfactory degree of certainty, that the defendant's case was adequately presented. * * *

Denial to the poor of the request for counsel in proceedings based on charges of serious crime has long been regarded as shocking to the "universal sense of justice" throughout this country. In 1854, for example, the Supreme Court of Indiana said: "It is not to be thought of, in a civilized community, for a moment, that any citizen put in jeopardy of life or liberty should be debarred of counsel because he was too poor to employ such aid. No Court could be respected, or respect itself, to sit and hear such a trial. The defence of the poor, in such cases, is a duty resting somewhere, which will be at once conceded as essential to the accused, to the Court, and to the public." And most of the other states have shown their agreement by constitutional provisions, statutes, or established practice judicially approved which assure that no man shall be deprived of counsel merely because of his poverty. Any other practice seems to me to defeat the promise of our democratic society to provide equal justice under the law.

GIDEON v. WAINWRIGHT

372 U.S. 335, 83 S.Ct. 792, 9 L.Ed.2d 799 (1963).

JUSTICE BLACK delivered the opinion of the Court.

Petitioner was charged in a Florida state court with having broken and entered a poolroom with intent to commit a misdemeanor. This offense is a felony under Florida law. Appearing in court without funds and without a lawyer, petitioner asked the court to appoint counsel for him, whereupon the following colloquy took place:

> "The Court: Mr. Gideon, I am sorry, but I cannot appoint Counsel to represent you in this case. Under the laws of the State of Florida, the only time the Court can appoint Counsel to represent a Defendant is when that person is charged with a capital offense. * * *

> "The Defendant: The United States Supreme Court says I am entitled to be represented by Counsel."

Put to trial before a jury, Gideon conducted his defense about as well as could be expected from a layman. He made an opening statement to the jury, cross-examined the State's witnesses, presented witnesses in his own defense, declined to testify himself, and made a short argument "emphasizing his innocence to the charge contained in the Information filed in this case." The jury returned a verdict of guilty, and petitioner was sentenced to serve five years in the state prison. Later, petitioner [unsuccessfully attacked his conviction and sentence in the state supreme court on the ground that the trial court's refusal to appoint counsel for him violated his constitutional rights]. Since 1942, when *Betts v. Brady* was decided by a divided Court, the problem of a defendant's federal constitutional right to counsel in a state court has been a continuing source of controversy and litigation in both state and federal courts. To give this problem another review here, we granted certiorari [and] appointed counsel to represent [petitioner].

We accept *Betts*'s assumption, based as it was on our prior cases, that a provision of the Bill of Rights which is "fundamental and essential to a fair trial" is made obligatory upon the States by the Fourteenth Amendment. We think the Court in *Betts* was wrong, however, in concluding that the Sixth Amendment's guarantee of counsel is not one of these fundamental rights. Ten years before *Betts,* this Court, after full consideration of all the historical data examined in *Betts,* had unequivocally declared that "the right to the aid of counsel is of this fundamental character." *Powell.* While the Court at the close of its *Powell* opinion did by its language, as this Court frequently does, limit its holding to the particular facts and circumstances of that case, its conclusions about the fundamental nature of the right to counsel are unmistakable. [The] fact is that in deciding as it did—that "appointment of counsel is not a fundamental right, essential to a fair trial"—the [*Betts* Court] made an abrupt break with its own well-considered precedents. In returning to these old precedents, sounder we believe than the new, we but restore constitutional principles established to achieve a fair system of justice. Not only these precedents but also reason and reflection require us to recognize that in our adversary system of criminal justice, any person haled into court, who is too poor to hire a lawyer, cannot be assured a fair trial unless counsel is provided for him. This seems to us to be an obvious truth. Governments, both state and federal, quite properly spend vast sums of money to establish machinery to try defendants accused of crime. Lawyers to prosecute are everywhere deemed essential to protect the public's interest in an orderly society. Similarly, there are few defendants charged with crime, few indeed, who fail to hire the best lawyers they can get to prepare and present their defenses. That government hires lawyers to prosecute and defendants who have the money hire lawyers to defend are the strongest indications of the widespread belief that lawyers in criminal courts are necessities, not luxuries. The right of one charged with crime to counsel may not be deemed fundamental and essential to fair trials in some countries, but it is in ours. From the very beginning, our state and national constitutions and laws have laid great emphasis on procedural and substantive safeguards designed to assure fair trials before impartial tribunals in which every defendant stands equal before the law. This noble ideal cannot be realized if the poor man charged with crime has to face his accusers without a lawyer to assist him. * * *

The Court in *Betts* departed from the sound wisdom upon which the Court's holding in *Powell* rested. Florida, supported by two other States, has asked that *Betts v. Brady* be left intact. Twenty-two States, as friends of the Court, argue that *Betts* was "an anachronism when handed down" and that it should now be overruled. We agree. * * * Reversed.[a]

Justice Clark, concurring in the result. * * *

[T]he Constitution makes no distinction between capital and noncapital cases. The Fourteenth Amendment requires due process of law for the deprival of "liberty" just as for deprival of "life," and there cannot constitutionally be a difference in the quality of the process based merely upon a supposed difference in the sanction involved. How can the Fourteenth Amendment tolerate a procedure which it condemns in capital cases on the ground that deprival of liberty may be less onerous than deprival of life—a value judgment not universally accepted—or that only the latter deprival is irrevocable? * * *

Justice Harlan, concurring.

I agree that *Betts* should be overruled, but consider it entitled to a more respectful burial than has been accorded, at least on the part of those of us who were not on the Court when that case was decided.

I cannot subscribe to the view that *Betts* represented "an abrupt break with its own well-considered precedents." [In *Powell*] this Court declared that under the particular facts there presented—"the ignorance and illiteracy of the defendants, their youth, the circumstances of public hostility [and] above all that they stood in deadly peril of their lives"—the state court had a duty to assign counsel for the trial as a necessary requisite of due process of law. It is evident that these limiting facts were not added to the opinion as an afterthought; they were repeatedly emphasized [and] were clearly regarded as important to the result.

Thus when this Court, a decade later, decided *Betts,* it did no more than to admit of the possible existence of special circumstances in noncapital as well as

a. Gideon was retried, this time with appointed counsel, and acquitted. See Lewis, *Gideon's Trumpet* 223–38 (1964).

capital trials, while at the same time to insist that such circumstances be shown in order to establish a denial of due process. The right to appointed counsel had been recognized as being considerably broader in federal prosecutions, see *Johnson v. Zerbst,* but to have imposed these requirements on the States would indeed have been "an abrupt break" with the almost immediate past. The declaration that the right to appointed counsel in state prosecutions, as established in *Powell,* was not limited to capital cases was in truth not a departure from, but an extension of, existing precedent.

The principles declared in *Powell* and in *Betts,* however, had a troubled journey throughout the years that have followed first the one case and then the other. Even by the time of the *Betts* decision, dictum in at least one of the Court's opinions had indicated that there was an absolute right to the services of counsel in the trial of state capital cases. * * *

In noncapital cases, the "special circumstances" rule has continued to exist in form while its substance has been substantially and steadily eroded. In the first decade after *Betts,* there were cases in which the Court found special circumstances to be lacking, but usually by a sharply divided vote. However, no such decision has been cited to us, and I have found none, [after] 1950. At the same time, there have been not a few cases in which special circumstances were found in little or nothing more than the "complexity" of the legal questions presented, although those questions were often of only routine difficulty. The Court has come to recognize, in other words, that the mere existence of a serious criminal charge constituted in itself special circumstances requiring the services of counsel at trial. In truth the *Betts* rule is no longer a reality.

This evolution, however, appears not to have been fully recognized by many state courts, in this instance charged with the front-line responsibility for the enforcement of constitutional rights. To continue a rule which is honored by this Court only with lip service is not a healthy thing and in the long run will do disservice to the federal system.

The special circumstances rule has been formally abandoned in capital cases, and the time has now come when it should be similarly abandoned in noncapital cases, at least as to offenses which, as the one involved here, carry the possibility of a substantial prison sentence. (Whether the rule should extend to *all* criminal cases need not now be decided.)

* * * In what is done today I do not understand the Court to depart from the principles laid down in *Palko* [or] to embrace the concept that the Fourteenth Amendment "incorporates" the Sixth Amendment as such. On these premises I join in the judgment of the Court.

ARGERSINGER v. HAMLIN

407 U.S. 25, 92 S.Ct. 2006, 32 L.Ed.2d 530 (1972).

Justice Douglas delivered the opinion of the Court.

Petitioner, an indigent, was charged in Florida with carrying a concealed weapon, an offense punishable by imprisonment up to six months, a $1,000 fine, or both. The trial was to a judge, and petitioner was unrepresented by counsel. [He was convicted and sentenced to 90 days in jail. The Florida Supreme Court affirmed. Following the line marked out in the jury trial cases, the state court] held that the right to court-appointed counsel extends only to trials "for non-petty offenses punishable by more than six months imprisonment." * * *

While there is historical support for limiting the [right] to trial by jury [to] "serious criminal cases," there is no such support for a similar limitation on the right to assistance of counsel. [Thus,] we reject [the] premise that since prosecutions for crimes punishable by imprisonment for less than six months may be tried without a jury, they may always be tried without a lawyer. [The] requirement of counsel may well be necessary for a fair trial even in a petty offense prosecution. We are by no means convinced that legal and constitutional questions involved in a case that actually leads to imprisonment even for a brief period are any less complex than when a person can be sent off for six months or more. * * *

Beyond the problem of trials and appeals is that of the guilty plea, a problem which looms large in misdemeanor as well as in felony cases. Counsel is needed so that the accused may know precisely what he is doing, so that he is fully aware of the prospect of going to jail or prison, and so that he is treated fairly by the prosecution.

In addition, the volume of misdemeanor cases, far greater in number than felony prosecutions, may create an obsession for speedy dispositions, regardless of the fairness of the result. * * *

We must conclude, therefore, that the problems associated with misdemeanor and petty offenses often require the presence of counsel to insure the accused a fair trial. [In his concurring opinion,] Mr. Justice Powell suggests that these problems are raised even in situations where there is no prospect of imprisonment. We need not consider the requirements of the Sixth Amendment as regards the right to counsel where loss of liberty is not involved, however, for here, petitioner was in fact sentenced to jail * * *.

Under the rule we announce today, every judge will know when the trial of a misdemeanor starts that no imprisonment may be imposed, even though local law permits it, unless the accused is represented by counsel. He will have a measure of the seriousness and gravity of the offense and therefore know when to name a lawyer to represent the accused before the trial starts.[a]

Justice Powell, with whom Justice Rehnquist joins, concurring with the result. * * *

I am unable to agree with the Supreme Court of Florida that an indigent defendant, charged with a petty offense, may in every case be afforded a fair trial without the assistance of counsel. Nor can I agree with [the Court's] new rule of due process [that] "absent a [valid] waiver, no person may be imprisoned [unless] he was represented by counsel at his trial." It seems to me that the line should not be drawn with such rigidity.

There is a middle course, between the extremes of Florida's six-month rule and the Court's rule, which comports with the requirements of the Fourteenth Amendment. I would adhere to the principle of due process that requires fundamental fairness in criminal trials, a principle which I believe encompasses the right to counsel in petty cases whenever the assistance of counsel is necessary to assure a fair trial.

Due process, perhaps the most fundamental concept in our law, embodies principles of fairness rather than immutable line-drawing as to every aspect of a criminal trial. While counsel is often essential to a fair trial, this is by no means a universal fact. Some petty offense cases are complex; others are exceedingly simple. [The] government often does not hire lawyers to prosecute petty offenses; instead the arresting police officer presents the case. Nor does every defendant who can afford to do so hire lawyers to defend petty charges. Where the possibility of a jail sentence is remote and the probable fine seems small, or where

---

a. Burger, C.J., concurred in the result. Brennan, J., joined by Douglas and Stewart, JJ., joined the Court's opinion and added a brief concurring opinion.

the evidence of guilt is overwhelming, the costs of assistance of counsel may exceed the benefits. It is anomalous that the Court's opinion today will extend the right of appointed counsel to indigent defendants in cases where the right to counsel would rarely be exercised by nonindigent defendants.

Indeed, one of the effects of this ruling will be to favor defendants classified as indigents over those not so classified yet who are in low income groups where engaging counsel in a minor petty offense case would be a luxury the family could not afford. The line between indigency and assumed capacity to pay for counsel is necessarily somewhat arbitrary, drawn differently from State to State and often resulting in serious inequities to accused persons. The Court's new rule will accent the disadvantage of being barely self-sufficient economically. * * *

The rule adopted today [is] limited to petty offense cases in which the sentence is some imprisonment. The thrust of the Court's position indicates, however, that when the decision must be made, the rule will be extended to all petty offense cases except perhaps the most minor traffic violations. If the Court rejects on constitutional grounds, as it has today, the exercise of any judicial discretion as to need for counsel if a jail sentence is imposed, one must assume a similar rejection of discretion in other petty offense cases. It would be illogical— and without discernible support in the Constitution—to hold that no discretion may ever be exercised where a nominal jail sentence is contemplated and at the same time endorse the legitimacy of discretion in 'non-jail' petty offense cases which may result in far more serious consequences than a few hours or days of incarceration. * * *

[The] Court's opinion foreshadows the adoption of a broad prophylactic rule applicable to all petty offenses [whether or not the defendant is actually incarcerated]. No one can foresee the consequences of such a drastic enlargement of the constitutional right to free counsel. But even today's decision could have a seriously adverse impact upon the day to day functioning of the criminal justice system. * * *

I would hold that the right to counsel in petty offense cases is not absolute but is one to be determined by the trial courts exercising a judicial discretion on a case-by-case basis. * * *

[T]hree general factors should be weighed. First, the court should consider the complexity of the offense charged. For example, charges of traffic law infractions would rarely present complex legal or factual questions, but charges that contain difficult intent elements or which raise collateral legal questions, such as search and seizure problems, would usually be too complex for an unassisted layman. If the offense were one where the State is represented by counsel and where most defendants who can afford to do so obtain counsel, there would be a strong indication that the indigent also needs the assistance of counsel.

Second, the court should consider the probable sentence that will follow if a conviction is obtained. The more serious the likely consequences, the greater is the probability that a lawyer should be appointed. [I]mprisonment is not the only serious consequence the court should consider.

Third, the court should consider the individual factors peculiar to each case. These, of course, would be the most difficult to anticipate. One relevant factor would be the competency of the individual defendant to present his own case. The attitude of the community toward a particular defendant or particular incident would be another consideration. But there might be other reasons why a defendant would have a peculiar need for a lawyer which would compel the appointment of counsel in a case where the court would normally think this unnecessary. * * *

Such a rule is similar in certain respects to the special circumstances rule applied to felony cases in *Betts*, which this Court overruled in *Gideon*. One of the reasons for seeking a more definitive standard in felony cases was the failure of many state courts to live up to their responsibilities in determining on a case-by-case basis whether counsel should be appointed. But this Court should not assume that the past insensitivity of some state courts to the rights of defendants will continue. Certainly if the Court follows the course of reading rigid rules into the Constitution, so that the state courts will be unable to exercise judicial discretion within the limits of fundamental fairness, there is little reason to think that insensitivity will abate.

* * * We are all strongly drawn to the ideal of extending the right to counsel, but I differ as to two fundamentals: (i) what the Constitution *requires,* and (ii) the effect upon the criminal justice system, especially in the smaller cities and the thousands of police, municipal and justice of the peace courts across the country.

SCOTT v. ILLINOIS

440 U.S. 367, 99 S.Ct. 1158, 59 L.Ed.2d 383 (1979).

JUSTICE REHNQUIST delivered the opinion of the Court. * * *

[Petitioner, an indigent, was charged with shoplifting merchandise valued at less than $150, punishable by as much as a $500 fine, or one year in jail, or both. He was not provided counsel. After a bench trial he was convicted of the offense and fined $50. The Supreme Court of Illinois declined to "extend *Argersinger* " to a case where one is charged with an offense for which imprisonment upon conviction is authorized but not actually imposed.]

In *Argersinger* the Court rejected arguments that social cost or a lack of available lawyers militated against its holding, in some part because it thought these arguments were factually incorrect. But they were rejected in much larger part because of the Court's conclusion that incarceration was so severe a sanction that it should not be imposed as a result of a criminal trial unless an indigent defendant has been offered appointed counsel to assist in his defense, regardless of the cost to the States implicit in such a rule. * * *

Although the intentions of the *Argersinger* Court are not unmistakably clear from its opinion, we conclude today that *Argersinger* did indeed delimit the constitutional right to appointed counsel in state criminal proceedings. Even were the matter *res nova*, we believe that the central premise of *Argersinger*—that actual imprisonment is a penalty different in kind from fines or the mere threat of imprisonment—is eminently sound and warrants adoption of actual imprisonment as the line defining the constitutional right to appointment of counsel. *Argersinger* has proved reasonably workable, whereas any extension would create confusion and impose unpredictable, but necessarily substantial, costs on 50 quite diverse States. We therefore hold that the Sixth and Fourteenth Amendments * * * require only that no indigent criminal defendant be sentenced to a term of imprisonment unless the State has afforded him the right to assistance of appointed counsel in his defense. The judgment [below] is accordingly [affirmed.] [a]

a. Concurring Justice Powell noted that "the drawing of a line based on whether there is imprisonment (even for overnight) can have the practical effect of precluding provision of counsel in other types of cases in which conviction can have more serious consequences." He

JUSTICE BRENNAN, with whom JUSTICE MARSHALL and JUSTICE STEVENS join, dissenting. * * *

In my view petitioner could prevail in this case without extending the right to counsel beyond what was assumed to exist in *Argersinger*. Neither party in that case questioned the existence of the right to counsel in trials involving "non-petty" offenses punishable by more than six months in jail. The question the Court addressed was whether the right applied to some "petty" offenses to which the right to jury trial did not extend. The Court's reasoning in applying the right to counsel in the case before it—that the right to counsel is more fundamental to a fair proceeding than the right to jury trial and that the historical limitations on the jury trial right are irrelevant to the right to counsel—certainly cannot support a standard for the right to counsel that is more restrictive than the standard for granting a right to a jury trial. [Argersinger] thus established a "two-dimensional" test for the right to counsel: the right attaches to any "non-petty" offense punishable by more than six months in jail and in addition to any offense where actual incarceration is likely regardless of the maximum authorized penalty.

The offense of "theft" with which Scott was charged is certainly not a "petty" one. It is punishable by a sentence of up to one year in jail. Unlike many traffic or other "regulatory" offenses, it carries the moral stigma associated with common-law crimes traditionally recognized as indicative of moral depravity. The State indicated at oral argument that the services of a professional prosecutor were considered essential to the prosecution of this offense. Likewise, nonindigent defendants charged with this offense would be well advised to hire the "best lawyers they can get." Scott's right to the assistance of appointed counsel is thus plainly mandated by the logic of the Court's prior cases, including *Argersinger* itself.

* * * Not only is the "actual imprisonment" standard unprecedented as the exclusive test, but the problems inherent in its application demonstrate the superiority of an "authorized imprisonment" standard that would require the appointment of counsel for indigents accused of any offense for which imprisonment for any time is authorized. * * *

Perhaps the strongest refutation of respondent's alarmist prophecies that an authorized imprisonment standard would wreak havoc on the States is that the standard has not produced that result in the substantial number of States that already provide counsel in all cases where imprisonment is authorized—States that include a large majority of the country's population and a great diversity of urban and rural environments. Moreover, of those States that do not yet provide counsel in all cases where *any* imprisonment is authorized, many provide counsel when periods of imprisonment longer than 30 days, 3 months, or 6 months are authorized. In fact, Scott would be entitled to appointed counsel under the current laws of at least 33 States.

It may well be that adoption by this Court of an authorized imprisonment standard would lead state and local governments to re-examine their criminal statutes. A state legislature or local government might determine that it no

also thought that an "actual imprisonment" rule "tends to impair the proper functioning of the criminal justice system in that trial judges, in advance of hearing any evidence and before knowing anything about the case except the charge, all too often will be compelled to forego the legislatively granted option to impose a sentence of imprisonment upon conviction." Despite his "continuing reservations about the *Argersinger* rule," however, Justice Powell joined the opinion of the Court because "[i]t is important that this Court provide clear guidance to the hundreds of courts across the country that confront this problem daily." He hoped, however, "that in due time a majority will recognize that a more flexible rule is consistent with due process and will better serve the cause of justice."

longer desired to authorize incarceration for certain minor offenses in light of the expense of meeting the requirements of the Constitution. In my view this re-examination is long overdue. In any event, the Courts actual imprisonment standard must inevitably lead the courts to make this re-examination, which plainly should more properly be a legislative responsibility.

The Court's opinion turns the reasoning of *Argersinger* on its head. It restricts the right to counsel, perhaps the most fundamental Sixth Amendment right, more narrowly than the admittedly less fundamental right to jury trial. * * *b

SECTION 2. THE *GRIFFIN–DOUGLAS* "EQUALITY" PRINCIPLE

Many commentators believe that the Warren Court's "revolution" in criminal procedure got underway when it handed down *Mapp v. Ohio* (Ch. 3, § 1) in 1961. But arguably the revolution began five years earlier, with *Griffin v. Illinois,* 351 U.S. 12 (1956).

In holding that indigent defendants must be furnished trial transcripts at state expense if such transcripts were necessary to effectuate appellate review, *Griffin* departed from then traditional equal protection doctrine. It viewed the "equality" principle as not only prohibiting the creation of inequalities by a state but imposing an "affirmative duty" to eliminate at least some inequalities not of the state's own doing. Illinois had simply ignored private inequalities of wealth and offered trial transcripts to every appellant on "equal terms," i.e., at a price which amounted to the cost of preparing them. But this was not enough.

There was no opinion of the Court in *Griffin.* Justice Black announced the judgment in a forceful and oft-quoted four-Justice opinion. He called the denial of a transcript for those who need but are unable to pay for one "a misfit in a country dedicated to affording equal justice to all and special privileges to none in the administration of its criminal law." Continued Black: "There can be no equal justice where the kind of trial a man gets depends on the amount of money he has. Destitute defendants must be afforded as adequate appellate review as defendants who have money enough to buy transcripts."

Dissenting Justice Harlan voiced sharp disagreement with Justice Black's approach. Harlan maintained that the Court's resolution of the equal protection claim in effect *required state discrimination*—in favor of indigents. It forced Illinois to give free to indigents "what it requires others to pay for."

But for *Douglas v. California,* the first case set forth in this section, *Griffin* and its early progeny,[a] could be narrowly interpreted as not affecting the right to

b. In a separate dissent, Blackmun, J., maintained that the right to appointed counsel "extends at least as far as the right to jury trial" and thus that "an indigent defendant in a state criminal case must be afforded appointed counsel whenever [he] is prosecuted for a nonpetty criminal offense, that is, one punishable by more than six months' imprisonment *or* whenever the defendant is actually subjected to a term of imprisonment."

a. In the decade and a half following *Griffin,* its underlying principle was broadly applied. *Mayer v. Chicago,* 404 U.S. 189 (1971) carried the *Griffin* principle further than the

Court ever carried the *Gideon* principle by holding that an indigent appellant cannot be denied a record of sufficient completeness to permit proper consideration of his claims even though he was convicted of ordinary violations punishable by fine only. More generally, a number of cases seemed to read *Griffin* for the proposition that an indigent defendant must be furnished any valuable or useful "tool" or instrument available for a price to others. See, e.g., *Roberts v. LaVallee,* 389 U.S. 40 (1967) (indigent defendant entitled to free transcript of preliminary hearing for use at trial, even though both defendant and his lawyer attended preliminary hearing and no indication of use to counsel at all. Rather, the *Griffin* principle could be viewed as concerned merely with the *availability* of direct and collateral review, not the *quality* of such review. But for the *Douglas* case, *Griffin* could be read as requiring only that an indigent be allowed *access* to the courts, not that he be furnished with counsel as well. For the presence of counsel is not a *sine qua non* to access to the courts, as was the availability of the transcript in *Griffin* or the payment of filing fees in other cases applying *Griffin*.

Under this analysis, *Griffin* and the pre-*Gideon* doctrine of *Betts v. Brady* were reconcilable: The state need only provide a road, not guarantee that every person have equally as good a car to drive down it. After *Douglas*, however, the "access to the courts" interpretation of *Griffin* seemed untenable. For the *Douglas* Court considered denying counsel to an indigent appellant "a discrimination at least as invidious as that condemned in *Griffin*."

Although it was careful to note that it was "dealing only with the *first appeal* granted as a matter of right to [all]" (emphasis in the original), the *Douglas* opinion contains language suggesting that *whenever* an indigent is permitted access to the courts he is *entitled to counsel* as well—that the state must do more than simply place a defendant "on the road," it must see that he has some vehicle—counsel—to use in travelling that "road." Nor is that all. *Griffin* and *Douglas*, at least if read generously, also suggest that the government must furnish an indigent defendant with *any* and *every* legal tool or legal service that a wealthy defendant is able to purchase.

In short not a few people thought that the *Griffin–Douglas* "equality" principle—the view that the administration of criminal justice cannot turn on the amount of money a defendant has—had no "stopping point," at least no obvious one. But the Court found a stopping point in *Ross v. Moffitt*, the second case set forth in this section.

DOUGLAS v. CALIFORNIA

372 U.S. 353, 83 S.Ct. 814, 9 L.Ed.2d 811 (1963).

JUSTICE DOUGLAS delivered the opinion of the Court. * * *

[The] record shows that petitioners requested, and were denied, the assistance of counsel on appeal, even though it plainly appeared they were indigents. In denying petitioners' requests, the California District Court of Appeal stated that it had "gone through" the record and had come to the conclusion that "no good whatever could be served by appointment of counsel." [The court] was acting in accordance with a California rule of criminal procedure which provides that state appellate courts, upon the request of an indigent for counsel, may make "an independent investigation of the record and determine whether it would be of advantage to the defendant or helpful to the appellate court to have counsel appointed. [After] such investigation, appellate courts should appoint counsel if in their opinion it would be helpful to the defendant or the court, and should deny the appointment of counsel only if in their judgment such appointment would be of no value to either the defendant or the court." * * *

We agree, however, with Justice Traynor of the California Supreme Court, who said that the "[d]enial of counsel on appeal [to an indigent] would seem to be a discrimination at least as invidious as that condemned in [*Griffin*," where] we

which preliminary hearing transcript could be   lan).
put—points stressed by dissenting Justice Har-

held that a State may not grant appellate review in such a way as to discriminate against some convicted defendants on account of their poverty. [Whether the issue is a transcript on appeal or the assistance of counsel on appeal] the evil is the same: discrimination against the indigent. For there can be no equal justice where the kind of an appeal a man enjoys "depends on the amount of money he has." * * *

[Under California's] present practice the type of an appeal [one is afforded] hinges upon whether or not he can pay for the assistance of counsel. If he can the appellate court passes on the merits of his case only after having the full benefit of written briefs and oral argument by counsel. If he cannot the appellate court is forced to prejudge the merits before it can even determine whether counsel should be provided. At this stage in the proceedings only the barren record speaks for the indigent, and, unless the printed pages show that an injustice has been committed, he is forced to go without a champion on appeal. Any real chance he may have had of showing that his appeal has hidden merit is deprived him when the court decides on an *ex parte* examination of the record that the assistance of counsel is not required.

* * * We are dealing only with the first appeal, granted as a matter of right to rich and poor alike, from a criminal conviction. We need not now decide whether California would have to provide counsel for an indigent seeking [discretionary review or] whether counsel must be appointed for an indigent seeking review of an appellate affirmance of his conviction in this Court. [But] it is appropriate to observe that a State can, consistently with the Fourteenth Amendment, provide for differences so long as the result does not amount to a denial of due process or an "invidious discrimination." Absolute equality is not required; lines can be and are drawn and we often sustain them. [But] where the merits of the one and only appeal an indigent has as of right are decided without benefit of counsel, we think an unconstitutional line has been drawn between rich and poor.

When an indigent is forced to run this gantlet of a preliminary showing of merit, the right to appeal does not comport with fair procedure. [T]he discrimination is not between "possibly good and obviously bad cases," but between cases where the rich man can require the court to listen to argument of counsel before deciding on the merits, but a poor man cannot. There is lacking that equality demanded by the Fourteenth Amendment where the rich man, who appeals as of right, enjoys the benefit of counsel's examination into the record, research of the law, and marshalling of arguments on his behalf, while the indigent, already burdened by a preliminary determination that his case is without merit, is forced to shift for himself. The indigent, where the record is unclear or the errors are hidden, has only the right to a meaningless ritual, while the rich man has a meaningful appeal. * * *

Judgment of the District Court of Appeals vacated and case remanded.

Justice Clark, dissenting.

* * * We all know that the overwhelming percentage of *in forma pauperis* appeals are frivolous. Statistics of this Court show that over 96% of the petitions filed here are of this variety. [California's courts] after examining the record certified that [an] appointment [of counsel] would be neither advantageous to the petitioners nor helpful to the court. It, therefore, refused to go through the useless gesture of appointing an attorney. In my view neither the Equal Protection Clause nor the Due Process Clause requires more. I cannot understand why the Court says that this procedure afforded petitioners "a meaningless ritual." To appoint an attorney would not only have been utter extravagance and a waste of the State's funds but as surely "meaningless" to petitioners.

JUSTICE HARLAN, whom JUSTICE STEWART joins, dissenting.

[T]he Court appears to rely both on the Equal Protection Clause and on the guarantees of fair procedure inherent in the Due Process Clause of the Fourteenth Amendment, with obvious emphasis on "equal protection." In my view the Equal Protection Clause is not apposite, and its application to cases like the present one can lead only to mischievous results. This case should be judged solely under the Due Process Clause, and I do not believe that the California procedure violates that provision.

EQUAL PROTECTION

To approach the present problem in terms of the Equal Protection Clause is, I submit, but to substitute resounding phrases for analysis. I dissented from this approach in [*Griffin*] and I am constrained to dissent from the implicit extension of the equal protection approach here—to a case in which the State denies no one an appeal, but seeks only to keep within reasonable bounds the instances in which appellate counsel will be assigned to indigents.

The States, of course, are prohibited by the Equal Protection Clause from discriminating between "rich" and "poor" *as such* in the formulation and application of their laws. But it is a far different thing to suggest that this provision prevents the State from adopting a law of general applicability that may affect the poor more harshly than it does the rich, or, on the other hand, from making some effort to redress economic imbalances while not eliminating them entirely.

Every financial exaction which the State imposes on a uniform basis is more easily satisfied by the well-to-do than by the indigent. Yet I take it that no one would dispute the constitutional power of the State to levy a uniform sales tax, to charge tuition at a state university, to fix rates for the purchase of water from a municipal corporation, to impose a standard fine for criminal violations, or to establish minimum bail for various categories of offenses. Nor could it be contended that the State may not classify as crimes acts which the poor are more likely to commit than are the rich. And surely, there would be no basis for attacking a state law which provided benefits for the needy simply because those benefits fell short of the goods or services that others could purchase for themselves.

Laws such as these do not deny equal protection to the less fortunate for one essential reason: the Equal Protection Clause does not impose on the States "an affirmative duty to lift the handicaps flowing from differences in economic circumstances." To so construe it would be to read into the Constitution a philosophy of leveling that would be foreign to many of our basic concepts of the proper relations between government and society. The State may have a moral obligation to eliminate the evils of poverty, but it is not required by the Equal Protection Clause to give to some whatever others can afford.

* * * [I]t should be noted that if the present problem may be viewed as one of equal protection, so may the question of the right to appointed counsel at trial, and the Court's analysis of that right in *Gideon* [is] wholly unnecessary. The short way to dispose of *Gideon,* in other words, would be simply to say that the State deprives the indigent of equal protection whenever it fails to furnish him with legal services, and perhaps with other services as well, equivalent to those that the affluent defendant can obtain.[a]

---

a. One may ask, too, why the Court failed even to discuss the applicability of the *Griffin–Douglas* "equality" principle to the issue raised in *Scott v. Illinois* (§ 1 supra). Since it is plain that one charged with an offense *punishable* by incarceration may *retain* counsel for

The real question in this case, I submit, and the only one that permits of satisfactory analysis, is whether or not the state rule, as applied in this case, is consistent with the requirements of fair procedure guaranteed by the Due Process Clause. Of course, in considering this question, it must not be lost sight of that the State's responsibility under the Due Process Clause is to provide justice for all. Refusal to furnish criminal indigents with some things that others can afford may fall short of constitutional standards of fairness. The problem before us is whether this is such a case.

Due Process * * *

We have today held that in a case such as the one before us, there is an absolute right to the services of counsel at trial. *Gideon.* [But] the appellate procedures involved here stand on an entirely different constitutional footing. *First,* appellate review is in itself not required by the Fourteenth Amendment, *McKane v. Durston,* 153 U.S. 684 (1894); see *Griffin,* and thus the question presented is the narrow one whether the State's rules with respect to the appointment of counsel are so arbitrary or unreasonable, *in the context of the particular appellate procedure that it has established,* as to require their invalidation. *Second,* the kinds of questions that may arise on appeal are circumscribed by the record of the proceedings that led to the conviction; they do not encompass the large variety of tactical and strategic problems that must be resolved at the trial. *Third,* as California applies its rule, the indigent appellant receives the benefit of expert and conscientious legal appraisal of the merits of his case on the basis of the trial record, and whether or not he is assigned counsel, is guaranteed full consideration of his appeal. It would be painting with too broad a brush to conclude that under these circumstances an appeal is just like a trial.

What the Court finds constitutionally offensive in California's procedure bears a striking resemblance to the rules of this Court and many state courts of last resort on petitions for certiorari or for leave to appeal filed by indigent defendants *pro se.* Under the practice of this Court, only if it appears from the petition for certiorari that a case merits review is leave to proceed *in forma pauperis* granted, the case transferred to the Appellate Docket, and counsel appointed. Since our review is generally discretionary, and since we are often not even given the benefit of a record in the proceedings below, the disadvantages to the indigent petitioner might be regarded as more substantial than in California. But as conscientiously committed as this Court is to the great principle of "Equal Justice Under Law," it has never deemed itself constitutionally required to appoint counsel to assist in the preparation of each of the more than 1,000 *pro se* petitions for certiorari currently being filed each Term. We should know from our own experience that appellate courts generally go out of their way to give fair consideration to those who are unrepresented.

The Court distinguishes our review from the present case on the grounds that the California rule relates to "the first appeal, granted as a matter of right." [But] I fail to see the significance of this difference. Surely, it cannot be contended that the requirements of fair procedure are exhausted once an indigent has been given one appellate review. Nor can it well be suggested that having appointed counsel is more necessary to the fair administration of justice in an initial appeal taken as a matter of right, which the reviewing court on the full record has already determined to be frivolous, than in a petition asking a higher

his defense, does not the "equality" principle—especially in light of its application in *Mayer v. Chicago,* note a supra—suggest that the "actual imprisonment" standard, even if it defensi-bly defines the Sixth Amendment right to appointed counsel, is unsatisfactory under the equal protection clause?

appellate court to exercise its discretion to consider what may be a substantial constitutional claim.

I cannot agree that the Constitution prohibits a State in seeking to redress economic imbalances at its bar of justice and to provide indigents with full review, from taking reasonable steps to guard against needless expense. This is all that California has done. * * *

ROSS v. MOFFITT

417 U.S. 600, 94 S.Ct. 2437, 41 L.Ed.2d 341 (1974).

[Like many other states, the North Carolina appellate system is multitiered, providing for both an intermediate Court of Appeals and a Supreme Court. North Carolina authorizes appointment of counsel for a convicted defendant appealing to the intermediate court of appeals, but not for a defendant who seeks either discretionary review in the state supreme court or a writ of certiorari in the U.S. Supreme Court. In one case, the Mecklenburg County forgery conviction, respondent sought appointed counsel for discretionary review in the state supreme court. In another case, the Guilford County forgery conviction, respondent was represented by the public defender in the state supreme court, but sought court-appointed counsel to prepare a writ of certiorari to the U.S. Supreme Court. On federal habeas corpus, a unanimous panel of the U.S. Court of Appeals for the Fourth Circuit, per Haynsworth, C.J., held that the *Douglas* rationale required appointment of counsel in both instances.]

JUSTICE REHNQUIST delivered the opinion of the Court.

[In *Griffin,* the Court struck down] an Illinois rule allowing a convicted criminal defendant to present claims of trial error to the [state supreme court] only if he procured a transcript of the testimony adduced at his trial. No exception was made for the indigent defendant, and thus one who was unable to pay the cost of obtaining such a transcript was precluded from obtaining appellate review of asserted trial error * * *.

[*Griffin* and succeeding cases] stand for the proposition that a State cannot arbitrarily cut off appeal rights for indigents while leaving open avenues of appeal for more affluent persons. In *Douglas,* however, [the] Court departed somewhat from the limited doctrine of [these] cases and undertook an examination of whether an indigent's access to the appellate system was adequate. [The *Douglas* Court] concluded that a State does not fulfill its responsibility toward indigent defendants merely by waiving its own requirements that a convicted defendant procure a transcript or pay a fee in order to appeal, and held that the State must go further and provide counsel for the indigent on his first appeal as of right. It is this decision we are asked to extend today. * * *

The precise rationale for the *Griffin* and *Douglas* lines of cases has never been explicitly stated, some support being derived from the Equal Protection Clause of the Fourteenth Amendment, and some from the Due Process Clause of that Amendment. Neither clause by itself provides an entirely satisfactory basis for the result reached, each depending on a different inquiry which emphasizes different factors. "Due process" emphasizes fairness between the State and the individual dealing with the State, regardless of how other individuals in the same situation may be treated. "Equal protection," on the other hand, emphasizes disparity in treatment by a State between classes of individuals whose situations are arguably indistinguishable. We will address these issues separately in the succeeding sections.

Recognition of the due process rationale in *Douglas* is found both in the Court's opinion and in the dissenting opinion of Mr. Justice Harlan. The Court in *Douglas* stated that "[w]hen an individual is forced to run this gantlet of a preliminary showing of merit, the right to appeal does not comport with fair procedure." Mr. Justice Harlan thought that the due process issue in *Douglas* was the only one worthy of extended consideration. * * *

We do not believe that the Due Process Clause requires North Carolina to provide respondent with counsel on his discretionary appeal to the State Supreme Court. At the trial stage of a criminal proceeding, the right of an indigent defendant to counsel [is] fundamental and binding upon the States by virtue of the Sixth and Fourteenth Amendments. But there are significant differences between the trial and appellate stages of a criminal proceeding. The purpose of the trial stage from the State's point of view is to convert a criminal defendant from a person presumed innocent to one found guilty beyond a reasonable doubt. To accomplish this purpose, the State employs a prosecuting attorney who presents evidence to the court, challenges any witnesses offered by the defendant, argues rulings of the court, and makes direct arguments to the court or jury seeking to persuade them of the defendant's guilt. Under these circumstances " * * * reason and reflection require us to recognize that in our adversary system of criminal justice, any person haled into court, who is too poor to hire a lawyer, cannot be assured a fair trial unless counsel is provided for him." *Gideon.*

By contrast, it is ordinarily the defendant, rather than the State, who initiates the appellate process, seeking not to fend off the efforts of the State's prosecutor but rather to overturn a finding of guilt made by a judge or jury below. The defendant needs an attorney on appeal not as a shield to protect him against being "haled into court" by the State and stripped of his presumption of innocence, but rather as a sword to upset the prior determination of guilt. This difference is significant for, while no one would agree that the State may simply dispense with the trial stage of proceedings without a criminal defendant's consent, it is clear that the State need not provide any appeal at all. *McKane v. Durston.* The fact that an appeal *has* been provided does not automatically mean that a State then acts unfairly by refusing to provide counsel to indigent defendants at every stage of the way. Unfairness results only if indigents are singled out by the State and denied meaningful access to that system because of their poverty. That question is more profitably considered under an equal protection analysis.

Language invoking equal protection notions is prominent both in *Douglas* and in other cases treating the rights of indigents on appeal. * * * Despite the tendency of all rights "to declare themselves absolute to their logical extreme," there are obviously limits beyond which the equal protection analysis may not be pressed without doing violence to principles recognized in other decisions of this Court. The Fourteenth Amendment "does not require absolute equality or precisely equal advantages," nor does it require the State to "equalize economic conditions." *Griffin* (Frankfurter, J., concurring). It does require [that] indigents have an adequate opportunity to present their claims fairly within the adversarial system. The State cannot adopt procedures which leave an indigent defendant "entirely cut off from any appeal at all," by virtue of his indigency, *Lane,* or extend to such indigent defendants merely a "meaningless ritual" while others in better economic circumstances have a "meaningful appeal." *Douglas.* The question is not one of absolutes, but one of degrees. In this case we do not believe that the Equal Protection Clause when interpreted in the context of these cases, requires North Carolina to provide free counsel for indigent defendants seeking to take discretionary appeals to the North Carolina Supreme Court, or to file petitions for certiorari in this Court.

[The] facts show that respondent, in connection with his Mecklenburg County conviction, received the benefit of counsel in examining the record of his trial and in preparing an appellate brief on his behalf for the state Court of Appeals. Thus, prior to his seeking discretionary review in the State Supreme Court, his claims "had once been presented by a lawyer and passed upon by an appellate court." *Douglas.* We do not believe that it can be said, therefore, that a defendant in respondent's circumstances is denied meaningful access to the North Carolina Supreme Court simply because the State does not appoint counsel to aid him in seeking review in that court. At that stage he will have, at the very least, a transcript or other record of trial proceedings, a brief on his behalf in the Court of Appeals setting forth his claims of error, and in many cases an opinion by the Court of Appeals disposing of his case. These materials, supplemented by whatever submission respondent may make *pro se,* would appear to provide the Supreme Court of North Carolina with an adequate basis on which to base its decision to grant or deny review.

We are fortified in this conclusion by our understanding of the function served by discretionary review in the North Carolina Supreme Court. The critical issue in that court, as we perceive it, is not whether there has been "a correct adjudication of guilt" in every individual case, but rather whether "the subject matter of the appeal has significant public interest," whether "the cause involves legal principles of major significance to the jurisprudence of the state," or whether the decision below is in probable conflict with a decision of the Supreme Court. The Supreme Court may deny certiorari even though it believes that the decision of the Court of Appeals was incorrect, since a decision which appears incorrect may nevertheless fail to satisfy any of the criteria discussed above. Once a defendant's claims of error are organized and presented in a lawyer-like fashion to the Court of Appeals, the justices of the Supreme Court of North Carolina who make the decision to grant or deny discretionary review should be able to ascertain whether his case satisfies the standards established by the legislature for such review.

This is not to say, of course, that a skilled lawyer, particularly one trained in the somewhat arcane art of preparing petitions for discretionary review, would not prove helpful to any litigant able to employ him. An indigent defendant seeking review in the Supreme Court of North Carolina is therefore somewhat handicapped in comparison with a wealthy defendant who has counsel assisting him in every conceivable manner at every stage in the proceeding. But both the opportunity to have counsel prepare an initial brief in the Court of Appeals and the nature of discretionary review in the Supreme Court of North Carolina make this relative handicap far less than the handicap borne by the indigent defendant denied counsel on his initial appeal as of right in *Douglas.* And the fact that a particular service might be of benefit to an indigent defendant does not mean that the service is constitutionally required. The duty of the State under our cases is not to duplicate the legal arsenal that may be privately retained by a criminal defendant in a continuing effort to reverse his conviction, but only to assure the indigent defendant an adequate opportunity to present his claims fairly in the context of the State's appellate process. We think respondent was given that opportunity under the existing North Carolina system.

Much of the discussion in the preceding section is equally relevant to the question of whether a State must provide counsel for a defendant seeking review of his conviction in this Court. North Carolina will have provided counsel for a convicted defendant's only appeal as of right, and the brief prepared by that counsel together with one and perhaps two North Carolina appellate opinions will be available to this Court in order that it may decide whether or not to grant certiorari. This Court's review, much like that of the Supreme Court of North Carolina, is discretionary and depends on numerous factors other than the perceived correctness of the judgment we are asked to review.

There is also a significant difference between the source of the right to seek discretionary review in the Supreme Court of North Carolina and the source of the right to seek discretionary review in this Court. The former is conferred by the statutes of the State of North Carolina, but the latter is granted by statutes enacted by Congress. Thus the argument relied upon in the *Griffin* and *Douglas* cases, that the State having once created a right of appeal must give all persons an equal opportunity to enjoy the right, is by its terms inapplicable. The right to seek certiorari in this Court is not granted by any State, and exists by virtue of federal statute with or without the consent of the State whose judgment is sought to be reviewed.

The suggestion that a State is responsible for providing counsel to one petitioning this Court simply because it initiated the prosecution which led to the judgment sought to be reviewed is unsupported by either reason or authority. It would be quite as logical under the rationale of *Douglas* and *Griffin,* and indeed perhaps more so, to require that the Federal Government or this Court furnish and compensate counsel for petitioners who seek certiorari here to review state judgments of conviction. Yet this Court has followed a consistent policy of denying applications for appointment of counsel by persons seeking to file jurisdictional statements or petitions for certiorari in this Court. In the light of these authorities, it would be odd, indeed, to read the Fourteenth Amendment to impose such a requirement on the States, and we decline to do so.

We do not mean by this opinion to in any way discourage those States which have, as a matter of legislative choice, made counsel available to convicted defendants at all stages of judicial review. Some States which might well choose to do so as a matter of legislative policy may conceivably find that other claims for public funds within or without the criminal justice system preclude the implementation of such a policy at the present time. [T]he Fourteenth Amendment leaves these choices to the State * * *.[a]

JUSTICE DOUGLAS, with whom JUSTICE BRENNAN and JUSTICE MARSHALL concur, dissenting.

[In his opinion below] Chief Judge Haynsworth could find "no logical basis for differentiation between appeals of right and permissive review procedures in the context of the Constitution and the right to counsel." More familiar with the functioning of the North Carolina criminal justice system than are we, he concluded that "in the context of constitutional questions arising in criminal prosecutions, permissive review in the state's highest court may be predictably the most meaningful review the conviction will receive." The North Carolina Court

a. A decade after *Ross v. Moffitt,* the Court broke its many years of silence on the issue of an indigent defendant's right to a psychiatrist and other expert assistance and held that, at least when an indigent defendant has made a preliminary showing that his sanity at the time of the offense is likely to be a significant factor at the trial, the state must provide the assistance of a psychiatrist for his defense. *Ake v. Oklahoma,* 470 U.S. 68 (1985).

Ake confirms the tendency of the post-*Ross* cases to rely on due process rather than equal protection analysis in determining the constitutional rights of indigent criminal defendants.

Thus the *Ake* Court reaffirmed the need for the state to take steps to assure that an indigent defendant had "a fair opportunity" or "an adequate opportunity" to present his defense. The Court also noted that in implementing the *Griffin* "equality" principle it had "focused on identifying the 'basic tools of an adequate defense or appeal' [and] required that such tools be provided to [those] who cannot afford to pay for them." See also *Evitts v. Lucey,* 469 U.S. 387, 403 (1985); *Bearden v. Georgia,* 461 U.S. 660, 665 (1983); *United States v. MacCollom,* 426 U.S. 317, 324 (1976).

of Appeals, for example, will be constrained in diverging from an earlier opinion of the State Supreme Court, even if subsequent developments have rendered the earlier Supreme Court decision suspect. "[T]he state's highest court remains the ultimate arbiter of the rights of its citizens."

Chief Judge Haynsworth also correctly observed that the indigent defendant proceeding without counsel is at a substantial disadvantage relative to wealthy defendants represented by counsel when he is forced to fend for himself in seeking discretionary review from the State Supreme Court or from this Court. It may well not be enough to allege error in the courts below in layman's terms; a more sophisticated approach may be demanded:

"An indigent defendant is as much in need of the assistance of a lawyer in preparing and filing a petition for certiorari as he is in the handling of an appeal as of right. In many appeals, an articulate defendant could file an effective brief by telling his story in simple language without legalisms, but the technical requirement for applications for writs of certiorari are hazards which one untrained in the law could hardly be expected to negotiate.

" 'Certiorari proceedings constitute a highly specialized aspect of appellate work. The factors which [a court] deems important in connection with deciding whether to grant certiorari are certainly not within the normal knowledge of an indigent appellant.' Boskey, *The Right to Counsel in Appellate Proceedings,* 45 Minn.L.Rev. 783, 797 (1961)."

* * * The right to discretionary review is a substantial one, and one where a lawyer can be of significant assistance to an indigent defendant. It was correctly perceived below that the "same concepts of fairness and equality which require counsel in a first appeal of right, require counsel in other and subsequent discretionary appeals."

Chapter 6

POLICE INTERROGATION AND CONFESSIONS

SECTION 1. THE DUE PROCESS "VOLUNTARINESS" TEST FOR ADMITTING CONFESSIONS

Whatever the meaning of the elusive terms "involuntary" and "coerced" confessions in the 1950's and 1960's, for centuries the rule that a confession was admissible so long as it was "voluntary" was more or less an alternative statement of the rule that a confession was admissible so long as it was free of influences which made it "untrustworthy" or "probably untrue." Thus, Wigmore, the leading authority on evidence, reflected the law prevailing at the time when in 1940 he pointed out that a confession was not inadmissible because of "any *illegality* in the method of obtaining it" or "because of any connection with the *privilege against self-incrimination.*" (The Court did not apply the privilege against compulsory self-incrimination to the proceedings in the police station and other "in-custody questioning" until its 1966 decision in *Miranda.*)

The "untrustworthiness" rationale, the view that the rules governing the admissibility of confessions were merely a system of safeguards against false confessions, could explain the exclusion of the confession in *Brown v. Mississippi*, 297 U.S. 278 (1936), the first Fourteenth Amendment Due Process confession case, where the deputy sheriff who had presided over the beatings of the defendants conceded that one had been whipped, "but not too much for a Negro." And the same rationale was also adequate to explain the exclusion of confessions in the cases that immediately followed the *Brown* case, such as *Chambers v. Florida*, 309 U.S. 227 (1940) and *Ward v. Texas*, 316 U.S. 547 (1942), for they too, involved actual or threatened physical violence. But as the crude practices of the early cases grew outmoded and cases involving more subtle pressures began to appear, it became more difficult to assume that the resulting confessions were untrustworthy.

The first case in this section, *Ashcraft v. Tennessee*, illustrates how the rationale for excluding confessions was changing. There was good reason to think that Ashcraft had indeed been involved in his wife's murder. Nevertheless, calling the extended police questioning to which Ashcraft had been subjected "inherently coercive," the Court ruled that the defendant's confession should not have been allowed into evidence. Under the circumstances, *Ashcraft* seems to reflect less concern with the reliability of the confession than disapproval of police methods which the Court considered to be dangerous and subject to abuse.

Although he joined Justice Jackson's dissent in *Ashcraft,* Justice Frankfurter soon became the leading exponent of the "police misconduct" or "police methods" rationale for barring the use of confessions. According to this rationale, in order to condemn, and deter, offensive or otherwise objectionable police interrogation methods, it was necessary to exclude confessions produced by such methods regardless of how trustworthy they might be.

Thus in *Watts v. Indiana,* the second case set forth in this section, and two companion cases, the Court reversed three convictions resting on coerced confessions without disputing the accuracy of Justice Jackson's observation (concurring in *Watts* and dissenting in the other cases) that "checked with external evidence [the confessions in each case] are inherently believable and were not shaken as to truth by anything that occurred at the trial." Justice Frankfurter, who wrote the principal opinion in *Watts,* commented: "In holding that the Due Process Clause *bars police procedure* which violates the basic notions of our accusatorial mode of prosecuting crime and vitiates a conviction based on the fruits of such procedure, we apply the Due Process Clause to its historic function of *assuring appropriate procedure* before liberty is curtailed or life is taken." (Emphasis added.)

Three years later, speaking for the Court in the famous "stomach-pumping" case of *Rochin v. California,* discussed in Chapter Two, Justice Frankfurter viewed the coerced confession cases as "only instances of the general requirement that states in their prosecution respect certain decencies of civilized conduct." Involuntary confessions, he pointed out, "are inadmissible under the Due Process Clause even though statements contained in them may be independently established as true" because they "offend the community's sense of fair play and decency." [a]

---

a. That concern about the unreliability of an involuntary or coerced confession was not the only reason for excluding such confessions is also demonstrated by the so-called "rule of automatic reversal," a rule that governed coerced confession cases at least since *Malinski v. New York,* 324 U.S. 401 (1945). Under this rule, a conviction resting in part on a coerced confession could not be affirmed on the ground that the erroneously admitted confession was "harmless error"; the conviction had to be overturned regardless of how much evidence of guilt remained, aside from the confession, to support the conviction. The "rule of automatic reversal" applied even when another confession (or several other confessions) by the defendant had been properly admitted into evidence.

Chapman v. California, 386 U.S. 18 (1967) (see discussion in Ch. 11, fn. d), held that, as a general proposition, constitutional errors could be deemed "harmless" but, noted that "there are some constitutional rights so basic to a fair trial that their infraction can never be treated as harmless error." One illustration of such an error given by the Court was the admission of a coerced confession.

The Court subsequently applied harmless-error analysis to confessions obtained in violation of the Sixth Amendment right to counsel (see the discussion of the *Massiah* doctrine in § 2). Similarly, the great majority of lower federal courts held that the introduction of incriminating statements obtained in violation

of *Miranda* (see § 3) was subject to treatment as harmless error. Nevertheless, the "rule of automatic reversal" continued to govern coerced confessions until 1991, when a 5–4 majority, per Rehnquist, C.J. held in *Arizona v. Fulminante,* 499 U.S. 279, that the harmless-error rule adopted in *Chapman* applied to the erroneous admission of coerced confessions as well.

"It is evident from a comparison of the constitutional violations which we have held subject to harmless error, and those which we have held not," observed the Chief Justice in *Fulminante,* "that involuntary statements or confessions belong in the former category. The admission of an involuntary confession is a 'trial error,' similar in both degree and kind to the erroneous admission of other types of evidence. [The] inconsistent treatment of statements elicited in violation of the Sixth and Fourteenth Amendments, respectively, can be supported neither by evidentiary or deterrence concerns nor by a belief that there is something more 'fundamental' about involuntary confessions."

The Chief Justice recognized that "an involuntary confession may have a more dramatic effect on the course of a trial than do other trial errors—in particular cases it may be devastating to a defendant." But, he added, "this simply means that a reviewing court will conclude in such a case that its admission was not harmless error; it is not a reason for eschewing the harmless error test entirely."

Perhaps the most emphatic statement of the "police methods" rationale appears in *Rogers v. Richmond,* 365 U.S. 534 (1961), one of Justice Frankfurter's last opinions on confessions. After more conventional methods had failed to produce any incriminating statements, a police chief pretended to order petitioner's ailing wife brought down to headquarters for questioning. Petitioner promptly confessed to the murder for which he was later convicted. The trial judge found that the police chief's pretense had "no tendency to produce a confession that was not in accord with the truth" and in his charge to the jury he indicated that the admissibility of the confession should turn on its probable reliability. But the Court, speaking through Justice Frankfurter, disagreed:

> "[Convictions based on involuntary confessions must fall] not so much because such confessions are unlikely to be true but because the methods used to extract them offend an underlying principle in the enforcement of our criminal law; that ours is an accusatorial and not an inquisitional system. * * * Indeed, in many of the cases [reversing] state convictions involving the use of confessions obtained by impermissible methods, independent corroborating evidence left little doubt of the truth of what the defendant had confessed. * * * The attention of the trial judge should have been focused [on] whether the [police behavior] was such as to overbear petitioner's will to resist and bring about confessions not freely self determined—a question to be answered with complete disregard of whether or not petitioner in fact spoke the truth." [b]

Justice Jackson strongly resisted the expansion of the grounds for excluding confessions. *Ashcraft* is a great case only because Jackson's dissent made it so. No piece of writing better illustrates his famed powers of advocacy and extraordinary directness of approach. The crucial question, maintained Jackson, was not

Dissenting Justice White protested that "permitting a coerced confession to be part of the evidence on which a jury is free to base its verdict of guilty is inconsistent with the thesis that ours is not an inquisitorial system of criminal justice." Justice White recognized that the search for truth is "central to our system of justice," but added: " 'Certain constitutional rights are not, and should not be, subject to harmless-error analysis because these rights protect important values that are unrelated to the truth-seeking function of the trial' " and a defendant's right "not to have his coerced confession used against him is among those rights, for using a coerced confession 'abort[s] the basic trial process' and 'render[s] a trial fundamentally unfair.' "

b. At least in its advanced stage (the early 1960's), some commentators thought that the "due process" or "voluntariness" test had *three* underlying values or goals, barring the use of confessions (a) which were of doubtful reliability because of the police methods used to obtain them; (b) which were produced by offensive police methods even though the reliability of the confession was not in question; and (c) which were obtained from a person whose volitional power was seriously impaired (e.g., a drugged, extremely intoxicated or "insane" person), even though the confession was neither untrustworthy (because impressively corroborated) nor the product of any conscious police wrongdoing. However, in *Colorado v.*

Connelly, 479 U.S. 157 (1986), upholding the confession of a mentally ill person (according to expert testimony, "God's voice" told defendant he had only two options: confess his murder or commit suicide), the Court, per Rehnquist, C.J., rejected the third value or goal:

> "[All the 'involuntary' confession cases] have contained a substantial element of coercive police conduct. Absent police conduct causally related to the confession, there is simply no basis for concluding that any state action has deprived a criminal defendant of due process of law.
>
> " * * * The flaw in respondent's argument is that it would expand our previous line of 'voluntariness' cases into a far-ranging requirement that courts must divine a defendant's motivation for speaking or acting as he did even though there be no claim that governmental conduct coerced his decision.
>
> " * * * We think the Constitution rightly leaves [inquiries into the state of mind of one who has confessed quite apart from any state coercion] to be resolved by state laws governing the admission of evidence and erects no standard of its own in this area. A statement rendered by one in the condition of respondent might be proved to be quite unreliable, but this is a matter to be governed by the evidentiary laws of the forum and not by the Due Process Clause * * *."

whether other suspects might have been overcome by the prolonged questioning, but whether *this particular defendant* had been. Jackson insisted that he had not; Ashcraft "was in possession of his own will and self-control at the time of confession." Ashcraft had decided to match wits with the police and after accusing another who in turn accused him "he knew he had lost the battle of wits." What was wrong with that? If the state is denied the right to apply any pressure to get someone to confess which is "inherently coercive," what pressure *could* it apply? And if it could not apply any "pressure," how could it be expected to get any suspect to confess?

Concurring in *Watts* and dissenting in the two companion cases, Justice Jackson again manifested his resistance to the expansion of the rights of suspects. He articulated concerns that many critics of the Warren Court's "revolution" in criminal procedure would repeat decades later. He underscored the "dilemma" facing a free society: To subject one without counsel to police interrogation "is a real peril to individual freedom," but bringing in a lawyer "means a real peril to solution of the crime."

Jackson voiced strong doubts that prohibiting the police from taking a suspect into custody and questioning him about an unwitnessed murder without advising him of his rights was "a necessary price to pay for the fairness which we know as 'due process of law.'" He recognized that the Bill of Rights, "even if construed as these provisions traditionally have been, * * * contain an aggregate of restrictions which seriously limit the power of society to solve such crimes as confront us in these cases," but he considered that "good reason for indulging in no unnecessary expansion of them."

A majority of the Court, however, was unpersuaded. As perhaps he knew, Jackson was swimming against the tide.

ASHCRAFT v. TENNESSEE

322 U.S. 143, 64 S.Ct. 921, 88 L.Ed. 1192 (1944).

JUSTICE BLACK delivered the opinion of the Court. * * *

[Early in the evening of Saturday, June 14, nine days after Ashcraft's wife had been murdered,] the officers came to Ashcraft's home and "took him into custody." In the words of the Tennessee Supreme Court,

> "They took him to an office or room on the northwest corner of the fifth floor of the Shelby County jail. This office is equipped with all sorts of crime and detective devices such as a fingerprint outfit, cameras, high-powered lights, and such other devices as might be found in a homicide investigating office. * * * It appears that the officers placed Ashcraft at a table in this room on the fifth floor of the county jail with a light over his head and began to quiz him. They questioned him in relays until the following Monday morning, June 16, 1941, around nine-thirty or ten o'clock. It appears that Ashcraft from Saturday evening at seven o'clock until Monday morning at approximately nine-thirty never left this homicide room on the fifth floor."

Testimony of the officers shows that the reason they questioned Ashcraft "in relays" was that they became so tired they were compelled to rest. But from 7:00 Saturday evening until 9:30 Monday morning Ashcraft had no rest. One officer did say that he gave the suspect a single five minutes' respite, but except for this five minutes the procedure consisted of one continuous stream of questions.

As to what happened in the fifth-floor jail room during this thirty-six hour secret examination the testimony follows the usual pattern and is in hopeless conflict. Ashcraft swears that the first thing said to him when he was taken into custody was, "Why in hell did you kill your wife?"; that during the course of the examination he was threatened and abused in various ways; and that as the hours passed his eyes became blinded by a powerful electric light, his body became weary, and the strain on his nerves became unbearable. The officers, on the other hand, swear that throughout the questioning they were kind and considerate. They say that they did not accuse Ashcraft of the murder until four hours after he was brought to the jail building, though they freely admit that from that time on their barrage of questions was constantly directed at him on the assumption that he was the murderer. Together with other persons whom they brought in on Monday morning to witness the culmination of the thirty-six hour ordeal the officers declare that at that time Ashcraft was "cool," "calm," "collected," "normal;" that his vision was unimpaired and his eyes not bloodshot; and that he showed no outward signs of being tired or sleepy.

As to whether Ashcraft actually confessed there is a similar conflict of testimony. Ashcraft maintains that although the officers incessantly attempted by various tactics of intimidation to entrap him into a confession, not once did he admit knowledge concerning or participation in the crime. And he specifically denies the officers' statements that he accused Ware of the crime, insisting that in response to their questions he merely gave them the name of Ware as one of several men who occasionally had ridden with him to work. The officers' version of what happened, however, is that about 11 P.M. on Sunday night, after twenty-eight hours' constant questioning, Ashcraft made a statement that Ware had overpowered him at his home and abducted the deceased, and was probably the killer. About midnight the officers found Ware and took him into custody, and, according to their testimony, Ware made a self-incriminating statement as of early Monday morning, and at 5:40 A.M. signed by mark a written confession in which appeared the statement that Ashcraft had hired him to commit the murder. This alleged confession of Ware was read to Ashcraft about six o'clock Monday morning, whereupon Ashcraft is said substantially to have admitted its truth in a detailed statement taken down by a reporter. About 9:30 Monday morning a transcript of Ashcraft's purported statement was read to him. The State's position is that he affirmed its truth but refused to sign the transcript, saying that he first wanted to consult his lawyer. As to this latter 9:30 episode the officers' testimony is reinforced by testimony of the several persons whom they brought in to witness the end of the examination.

In reaching our conclusion as to the validity of Ashcraft's confession we do not resolve any of the disputed questions of fact relating to the details of what transpired within the confession chamber of the jail or whether Ashcraft actually did confess.[7] Such disputes, we may say, are an inescapable consequence of secret inquisitorial practices. And always evidence concerning the inner details of secret inquisitions [8] is weighted against an accused, particularly where, as here, he is charged with a brutal crime, or where, as in many other cases, his supposed offense bears relation to an unpopular economic, political, or religious cause.

Our conclusion is that if Ashcraft made a confession it was not voluntary but compelled. We reach this conclusion from facts which are not in dispute at all.
* * *

7. The use in evidence of a defendant's coerced confession cannot be justified on the ground that the defendant has denied he ever gave the confession.

8. State and federal courts, textbook writers, legal commentators, and governmental commissions consistently have applied the name of "inquisition" to prolonged examination of suspects conducted as was the examination of Ashcraft. * * *

We think a situation such as that here shown by uncontradicted evidence is so inherently coercive that its very existence is irreconcilable with the possession of mental freedom by a lone suspect against whom its full coercive force is brought to bear. It is inconceivable that any court of justice in the land, conducted as our courts are, open to the public, would permit prosecutors serving in relays to keep a defendant witness under continuous cross examination for thirty-six hours without rest or sleep in an effort to extract a "voluntary" confession. Nor can we, consistently with Constitutional due process of law, hold voluntary a confession where prosecutors do the same thing away from the restraining influences of a public trial in an open court room.

The Constitution of the United States stands as a bar against the conviction of any individual in an American court by means of a coerced confession. There have been, and are now, certain foreign nations with governments dedicated to an opposite policy: governments which convict individuals with testimony obtained by police organizations possessed of an unrestrained power to seize persons suspected of crimes against the state, hold them in secret custody, and wring from them confessions by physical or mental torture. So long as the Constitution remains the basic law of our Republic, America will not have that kind of government. * * *

JUSTICE JACKSON, with whom JUSTICE ROBERTS and JUSTICE FRANKFURTER join, dissenting. * * *

As we read the present decision the Court in effect [departs from] well-established principles. Instead, it: (1) substitutes for determination on conflicting evidence the question whether the confession was actually produced by coercion, a presumption that it was, on a new doctrine that examination in custody of this duration is "inherently coercive;" (2) it makes that presumption irrebuttable—i.e., a rule of law—because, while it goes back of the State decisions to find certain facts, it refuses to resolve conflicts in evidence to determine whether other of the State's proof is sufficient to overcome such presumption; and, in so doing, (3) it sets aside the findings by the courts of Tennessee that on all the facts this confession did not result from coercion, either giving those findings no weight or regarding them as immaterial. * * *

The burden of protecting society from most crimes against persons and property falls upon the state. Different states have different crime problems and some freedom to vary procedures according to their own ideas. Here, a state was forced by an unwitnessed and baffling murder to vindicate its law and protect its society. To nullify its conviction in this particular case upon a consideration of all the facts would be a delicate exercise of federal judicial power. But to go beyond this, as the Court does today, and divine in the due process clause of the Fourteenth Amendment an exclusion of confessions on an irrebuttable presumption that custody and examination are "inherently coercive" if of some unspecified duration within thirty-six hours, requires us to make more than a passing expression of our doubts and disagreements. * * *

This Court never yet has held that the Constitution denies a State the right to use a confession just because the confessor was questioned in custody where it did not also find other circumstances that deprived him of a "free choice to admit, to deny, or to refuse to answer." The Constitution requires that a conviction rest on a fair trial. Forced confessions are ruled out of a fair trial. They are ruled out because they have been wrung from a prisoner by measures which are offensive to concepts of fundamental fairness. Different courts have used different terms to express the test by which to judge the inadmissibility of a confession, such as "forced," "coerced," "involuntary," "extorted," "loss of freedom of will." But always where we have professed to speak with the voice of the due process clause, the test, in whatever words stated, has been applied to the particular confessor at the time of confession.

It is for this reason that American courts hold almost universally and very properly that a confession obtained during or shortly after the confessor has been subjected to brutality, torture, beating, starvation, or physical pain of any kind is prima facie "involuntary." The effect of threats alone may depend more on individual susceptibility to fear. But men are so constituted that many will risk the postponed consequences of yielding to a demand for a confession in order to be rid of present or imminent physical suffering. Actual or threatened violence have no place in eliciting truth and it is fair to assume that no officer of the law will resort to cruelty if truth is what he is seeking. We need not be too exacting about proof of the effects of such violence on the individual involved, for their effect on the human personality is invariably and seriously demoralizing.

When, however, we consider a confession obtained by questioning, even if persistent and prolonged, we are in a different field. Interrogation per se is not, while violence per se is, an outlaw. Questioning is an indispensable instrumentality of justice. It may be abused, of course, as cross-examination in court may be abused, but the principles by which we may adjudge when it passes constitutional limits are quite different from those that condemn police brutality, and are far more difficult to apply. And they call for a more responsible and cautious exercise of our office. For we may err on the side of hostility to violence without doing injury to legitimate prosecution of crime; we cannot read an undiscriminating hostility to mere interrogation into the Constitution without unduly fettering the States in protecting society from the criminal.

It probably is the normal instinct to deny and conceal any shameful or guilty act. Even a "voluntary confession" is not likely to be the product of the same motives with which one may volunteer information that does not incriminate or concern him. The term "voluntary" confession does not mean voluntary in the sense of a confession to a priest merely to rid one's soul of a sense of guilt. "Voluntary confessions" in criminal law are the product of calculations of a different order, and usually proceed from a belief that further denial is useless and perhaps prejudicial. To speak of any confessions of crime made after arrest as being "voluntary" or "uncoerced" is somewhat inaccurate, although traditional.

A confession is wholly and incontestably voluntary only if a guilty person gives himself up to the law and becomes his own accuser. The Court bases its decision on the premise that custody and examination of a prisoner for thirty-six hours is "inherently coercive." Of course it is. And so is custody and examination for one hour. Arrest itself is inherently coercive, and so is detention. When not justified, infliction of such indignities upon the person is actionable as a tort. Of course such acts put pressure upon the prisoner to answer questions, to answer them truthfully, and to confess if guilty.

But does the Constitution prohibit use of all confessions made after arrest because questioning, while one is deprived of freedom, is "inherently coercive?" The Court does not quite say so, but it is moving far and fast in that direction. The step it now takes is to hold this confession inadmissible because of the time taken in getting it.

The duration and intensity of an examination or inquisition always have been regarded as one of the relevant and important considerations in estimating its effect on the will of the individual involved. Thirty-six hours is a long stretch of questioning. That the inquiry was prolonged and persistent is a factor that in any calculation of its effect on Ashcraft would count heavily against the confession.

But some men would withstand for days pressures that would destroy the will of another in hours. Always heretofore the ultimate question has been whether the confessor was in possession of his own will and self-control at the time of confession. For its bearing on this question the Court always has considered the confessor's strength or weakness, whether he was educated or illiterate, intelligent or moronic, well or ill, Negro or white. * * *

If the constitutional admissibility of a confession is no longer to be measured by the mental state of the individual confessor but by a general doctrine dependent on the clock, it should be capable of statement in definite terms. If thirty-six hours is more than is permissible, what about 24? or 12? or 6? or 1? All are "inherently coercive." Of course questions of law like this often turn on matters of degree. But are not the states entitled to know, if this Court is able to state, what the considerations are which make any particular degree decisive? How else may state courts apply our tests? * * *

Apart from Ashcraft's uncorroborated testimony, which the Tennessee courts refused to believe, there is much evidence in this record from persons whom they did believe and were justified in believing. This evidence shows that despite the "inherent coerciveness" of the circumstances of his examination, the confession when made was deliberate, free, and voluntary in the sense in which that term is used in criminal law. This Court could not, in our opinion, hold this confession an involuntary one except by substituting its presumption in place of analysis of the evidence and refusing to weigh the evidence even in rebuttal of its presumption. * * *

[Early Monday morning, a copy of Ware's confession, stating that Ashcraft had hired him to kill the latter's wife,] was given to Ashcraft, and he then admitted that he had hired Ware to kill his wife. He was given breakfast and then in response to questions made a statement which was taken down by the court reporter, Waldauer. It was transcribed, but Ashcraft declined to sign it, saying that he wanted his lawyer to see it before he signed it. No effort was made to compel him to sign the confession. However, two businessmen of Memphis, Mr. Castle, vice president of a bank, and Mr. Pidgeon, president of the Coca–Cola Bottling Company, were called in. Both testified that Ashcraft in their presence asserted that the transcript was correct but that he declined to sign it. The officers also called [Ashcraft's family physician to] the jail to make a physical examination of both Ashcraft and Ware. [In] the presence of this friendly doctor Ashcraft might have complained of his treatment and avowed his innocence. The doctor testified, however, that Ashcraft said he had been treated all right, that he made no complaint about his eyes, and that they were not bloodshot. The doctor made a physical examination, and says Ashcraft appeared normal. He further testified as to Ashcraft, "Well, sir, he said he had not been able to get along with his wife for some time [and] that he offered [Ware] a sum of money to make away with his wife." The doctor says that that statement was entirely voluntary. No matter what pressure had been put on Ashcraft before, the courts below could reasonably believe that he made this statement voluntarily to a man of whom he had no fear and who knew his family relations.

Ashcraft's story of torture could only be accepted by disbelieving such credible and unimpeached contradiction. Ashcraft testified that he was refused food, was not allowed to go to the lavatory, and was denied even a drink of water. Other testimony is that on Saturday night he was brought a sandwich and coffee about midnight; that he drank the coffee but refused the sandwich; that on Sunday morning he was given a breakfast and was fed again about noon a plate lunch consisting of meat and vegetables and coffee. Both Waldauer, the Reporter, and

Dr. McQuiston testified that they saw breakfast served to Ashcraft the next morning, before the statement taken down by Waldauer. Ashcraft claims he was threatened and that a cigarette was slapped out of his mouth. This is all denied.

This Court rejects the testimony of the officers and disinterested witnesses in this case that the confession was voluntary not because it lacked probative value in itself nor because the witnesses were self-contradictory or were impeached. On the contrary, it is impugned only on grounds such as that such disputes "are an inescapable consequence of secret inquisitorial practices." We infer from this that since a prisoner's unsupported word often conflicts with that of the officers, the officer's testimony for constitutional purposes is always prima facie false. We know that police standards often leave much to be desired, but we are not ready to believe that the democratic process brings to office men generally less believable than the average of those accused of crime. * * *

This questioning is characterized as a "secret inquisition," invoking all of the horrendous historical associations of those words. Certainly the inquiry was participated in by a good many persons, and we do not see how it could have been much less "secret" unless the press should have been called in. Of course, any questioning may be characterized as an "inquisition," but the use of such characterizations is no substitute for the detached and judicial consideration that the court below gave to the case.

We conclude that even going behind the state court decisions into the facts, no independent judgment on the whole evidence that Ashcraft's confession was in fact coerced is possible. And against this background of facts the extreme character of the Court's ruling becomes apparent.

I am not sure whether the Court denies the State all right to arrest and question the husband of the slain woman. No investigation worthy of the name could fail to examine him. Of all persons he was most likely to know whether she had enemies or rivals. Would not the State have a constitutional right, whether he was accused or not, to arrest and detain him as a material witness? If it has the right to detain one as a witness, presumably it has the right to examine him.

Could the State not confront Ashcraft with his false statements and ask his explanation? He did not throw himself at any time on his rights, refuse to answer, and demand counsel, even according to his own testimony. The strategy of the officers evidently was to keep him talking, to give him plenty of rope and see if he would not hang himself. He does not claim to have made objection to this. Instead he relied on his wits. The time came when it dawned on him that his own story brought him under suspicion, and that he could not meet it. Must the officers stop at this point because he was coming to appreciate the uselessness of deception?

Then he became desperate and accused [Ware]. Certainly from this point the State was justified in holding and questioning him as a witness, for he claimed to know the killer. That accusation backfired and only turned up a witness against him. He had run out of expedients and inventions; he knew he had lost the battle of wits. After all honesty seemed to be the best, even if the last, policy. He confessed in detail.

At what point in all this investigation does the Court hold that the Constitution commands these officers to send Ashcraft on his way and give up the murder as insoluble? If the state is denied the right to apply any pressure to him which is "inherently coercive" it could hardly deprive him of his freedom at all. I, too, dislike to think of any man, under the disadvantages and indignities of detention being questioned about his personal life for thirty-six hours or for one hour. In fact, there is much in our whole system of penology that seems archaic and vindictive and badly managed. Every person in the community, no matter how inconvenient or embarrassing, no matter what retaliation it exposes him to, may be called upon to take the witness stand and tell all he knows about a crime— except the person who knows most about it. * * *

No conclusion that this confession was actually coerced can be reached on this record except by reliance upon the utterly uncorroborated statements of defendant Ashcraft. His testimony does not carry even ordinary guaranties of truthfulness, and the courts and jury were not bound to accept it. Perjury is a light offense compared to murder and they may well have believed that Ashcraft was ready to resort to a lesser crime to avoid conviction of a greater one. Furthermore, the very grounds on which this Court now upsets his conviction Ashcraft repudiated at the trial. He asserts that he was abused, but he does not testify as this Court holds that it had the effect of forcing an involuntary confession from him. On the contrary, he flatly insists that it had no such effect and that he never did confess at all.

Against Ashcraft's word the state courts and jury accepted the testimony of several apparently disinterested witnesses of high standing in their communities, in addition to that of the accused officers. One of the witnesses to Ashcraft's admission of guilt was his own family physician, two were disinterested business men of substance and standing, another was an experienced court reporter who had long held this position of considerable trust. Another was a member of the bar. Certainly, the state courts were not committing an offense against the Constitution of the United States in refusing to believe that this whole group of apparently reputable citizens entered into a conspiracy to swear a murder onto an innocent man, against whom not one of them is shown to have had a grievance or a grudge.

This is not the case of an ignorant and unrepresented defendant who has been the victim of prejudice. Ashcraft was a white man of good reputation, good position, and substantial property. For a week after this crime was discovered he was not detained, although his stories to the officers did not hang together, but was at large, free to consult his friends and counsel. There was no indecent haste, but on the contrary evident deliberation, in suspecting and accusing him. * * *

The use of the due process clause to disable the states in protection of society from crime is quite as dangerous and delicate a use of federal judicial power as to use it to disable them from social or economic experimentation.

WATTS v. INDIANA

338 U.S. 49, 69 S.Ct. 1347, 93 L.Ed. 1801 (1949).

JUSTICE FRANKFURTER announced the judgment of the Court and a opinion in which JUSTICE MURPHY and JUSTICE RUTLEDGE join.

* * * This case is here because the Supreme Court of Indiana rejected petitioner's claim that confessions elicited from him were procured under circumstances rendering their admission as evidence against him a denial of due process of law.[2]

---

2. In the petitioner's statements there was acknowledgment of the possession of an incriminating gun, the existence of which the police independently established. But a coerced confession is inadmissible under the Due Process Clause even though statements in it may be independently established as true.

In the application of so embracing a constitutional concept as "due process," it would be idle to expect at all times unanimity of views. Nevertheless, in all the cases that have come here during the last decade from the courts of the various States in which it was claimed that the admission of coerced confessions vitiated convictions for murder, there has been complete agreement that any conflict in testimony as to what actually led to a contested confession is not this Court's concern. Such conflict comes here authoritatively resolved by the State's adjudication. Therefore only those elements of the events and circumstances in which a confession was involved that are unquestioned in the State's version of what happened are relevant to the constitutional issue here. But if force has been applied, this Court does not leave to local determination whether or not the confession was voluntary. There is torture of mind as well as body; the will is as much affected by fear as by force. And there comes a point where this Court should not be ignorant as judges of what we know as men. * * *

On November 12, 1947, a Wednesday, petitioner was arrested and held as the suspected perpetrator of an alleged criminal assault earlier in the day. Later the same day, in the vicinity of this occurrence, a woman was found dead under conditions suggesting murder in the course of an attempted criminal assault. Suspicion of murder quickly turned towards petitioner and the police began to question him. They took him from the county jail to State Police Headquarters, where he was questioned by officers in relays from about eleven thirty that night until sometime between 2:30 and 3 o'clock the following morning. The same procedure of persistent interrogation from about 5:30 in the afternoon until about 3 o'clock the following morning, by a relay of six to eight officers, was pursued on Thursday the 13th, Friday the 14th, Saturday the 15th, Monday the 17th. Sunday was a day of rest from interrogation. About 3 o'clock on Tuesday morning, November 18, the petitioner made an incriminating statement after continuous questioning since 6 o'clock of the preceding evening. The statement did not satisfy the prosecutor who had been called in and he then took petitioner in hand. Petitioner, questioned by an interrogator of twenty years' experience as lawyer, judge and prosecutor, yielded a more incriminating document.

Until his inculpatory statements were secured, the petitioner was a prisoner in the exclusive control of the prosecuting authorities. He was kept for the first two days in solitary confinement in a cell aptly enough called "the hole" in view of its physical conditions as described by the State's witnesses. Apart from the five night sessions, the police intermittently interrogated Watts during the day and on three days drove him around town, hours at a time, with a view to eliciting identifications and other disclosures. Although the law of Indiana required that petitioner be given a prompt preliminary hearing before a magistrate, with all the protection a hearing was intended to give him, the petitioner was not only given no hearing during the entire period of interrogation but was without friendly or professional aid and without advice as to his constitutional rights. Disregard of rudimentary needs of life—opportunities for sleep and a decent allowance of food—are also relevant, not as aggravating elements of petitioner's treatment, but as part of the total situation out of which his confessions came and which stamped their character.

A confession by which life becomes forfeit must be the expression of free choice. A statement to be voluntary of course need not be volunteered. But if it is the product of sustained pressure by the police it does not issue from a free choice. When a suspect speaks because he is overborne, it is immaterial whether he has been subjected to a physical or mental ordeal. Eventual yielding to questioning under such circumstances is plainly the product of the suction process of interrogation and therefore the reverse of voluntary. We would have to shut our minds to the plain significance of what here transpired to deny that this was a calculated endeavor to secure a confession through the pressure of unrelenting interrogation. The very relentlessness of such interrogation implies that it is better for the prisoner to answer than to persist in the refusal of disclosure which is his constitutional right. To turn the detention of an accused into a process of wrenching from him evidence which could not be extorted in open court with all its safeguards, is so grave an abuse of the power of arrest as to offend the procedural standards of due process.

This is so because it violates the underlying principle in our enforcement of the criminal law. Ours is the accusatorial as opposed to the inquisitorial system. Such has been the characteristic of Anglo–American criminal justice since it freed itself from practices borrowed by the Star Chamber from the Continent whereby an accused was interrogated in secret for hours on end. Under our system society carries the burden of proving its charge against the accused not out of his own mouth. It must establish its case, not by interrogation of the accused even under judicial safeguards, but by evidence independently secured through skillful investigation. [The] requirement of specific charges, their proof beyond a reasonable doubt, the protection of the accused from confessions extorted through whatever form of police pressures, the right to a prompt hearing before a magistrate, the right to assistance of counsel, to be supplied by government when circumstances make it necessary, the duty to advise an accused of his constitutional rights— these are all characteristics of the accusatorial system and manifestations of its demands. Protracted, systematic and uncontrolled subjection of an accused to interrogation by the police for the purpose of eliciting disclosures or confessions is subversive of the accusatorial system. It is the inquisitial system without its safeguards. For while under that system the accused is subjected to judicial interrogation, he is protected by the disinterestedness of the judge in the presence of counsel.

In holding that the Due Process Clause bars police procedure which violates the basic notions of our accusatorial mode of prosecuting crime and vitiates a conviction based on the fruits of such procedure, we apply the Due Process Clause to its historic function of assuring appropriate procedure before liberty is curtailed or life is taken. We are deeply mindful of the anguishing problems which the incidence of crime presents to the States. But the history of the criminal law proves overwhelmingly that brutal methods of law enforcement are essentially self-defeating, whatever may be their effect in a particular case. Law triumphs when the natural impulses aroused by a shocking crime yield to the safeguards which our civilization has evolved for an administration of criminal justice at once rational and effective. * * * Reversed.

Justice Douglas, concurring * * *.

It would be naive to think that [petitioner] was subject to anything less than the inquisition. The man was held until he broke. Then and only then was he arraigned and given the protection which the law provides all accused. Detention without arraignment is a time-honored method for keeping an accused under the exclusive control of the police. They can then operate at their leisure. The accused is wholly at their mercy. He is without the aid of counsel or friends; and he is denied the protection of the magistrate. We should unequivocally condemn the procedure and stand ready to outlaw [any] confession obtained during the period of unlawful detention. The procedure breeds coerced confessions. It is the root of the evil. It is the procedure without which the inquisition could not flourish in the country.[a]

a. Justice Black's opinion concurring in the   judgment of the Court is omitted.

Justice Jackson, concurring in the result in [*Watts v. Indiana*] and dissenting in [two companion cases, *Harris v. South Carolina* and *Turner v. Pennsylvania*, where the Court also reversed convictions resting on coerced confessions].

These three cases, from widely separated states, present essentially the same problem. Its recurrence suggests that it has roots in some condition fundamental and general to our criminal system.

In each case police were confronted with one or more brutal murders which the authorities were under the highest duty to solve. Each of these murders was unwitnessed, and the only positive knowledge on which a solution could be based was possessed by the killer. In each there was reasonable ground to *suspect* an individual but not enough legal evidence to *charge* him with guilt. In each the police attempted to meet the situation by taking the suspect into custody and interrogating him. This extended over varying periods. In each, confessions were made and received in evidence at the trial. Checked with external evidence, they are inherently believable, and were not shaken as to truth by anything that occurred at the trial. Each confessor was convicted by a jury and state courts affirmed. This Court sets all three convictions aside.

The seriousness of the Court's judgment is that no one suggests that any course held promise of solution of these murders other than to take the suspect into custody for questioning. The alternative was to close the books on the crime and forget it, with the suspect at large. This is a grave choice for a society in which two-thirds of the murders already are closed out as insoluble.

A concurring opinion, however, goes to the very limit and seems to declare for outlawing any confession, however freely given, if obtained during a period of custody between arrest and arraignment—which, in practice, means all of them.

Others would strike down these confessions because of conditions which they say make them "involuntary." In this, on only a printed record, they pit their judgment against that of the trial judge and the jury. Both, with the great advantage of hearing and seeing the confessor and also the officers whose conduct and bearing toward him is in question, have found that the confessions were voluntary. In addition, the majority overrule in each case one or more state appellate courts, which have the same limited opportunity to know the truth that we do.

Amid much that is irrelevant or trivial one serious situation seems to me to stand out in these cases. The suspect neither had nor was advised of his right to get counsel. This presents a real dilemma in a free society. To subject one without counsel to questioning which may and is intended to convict him, is a real peril to individual freedom. To bring in a lawyer means a real peril to solution of the crime because, under our adversary system, he deems that his sole duty is to protect his client—guilty or innocent—and that in such a capacity he owes no duty whatever to help society solve its crime problem. Under this conception of criminal procedure, any lawyer worth his salt will tell the suspect in no uncertain terms to make no statement to police under any circumstances.

If the State may arrest on suspicion and interrogate without counsel, there is no denying the fact that it largely negates the benefits of the constitutional guaranty of the right to assistance of counsel. Any lawyer who has ever been called into a case after his client has "told all" and turned any evidence he has over to the Government, knows how helpless he is to protect his client against the facts thus disclosed.

I suppose the view one takes will turn on what one thinks should be the right of an accused person against the State. Is it his right to have the judgment on the facts? Or is it his right to have a judgment based on only such evidence as he cannot conceal from the authorities, who cannot compel him to testify in court and also cannot question him before? Our system comes close to the latter by any interpretation, for the defendant is shielded by such safeguards as no system of law except the Anglo–American concedes to him.

Of course, no confession that has been obtained by any form of physical violence to the person is reliable and hence no conviction should rest upon one obtained in that manner. Such treatment not only breaks the will to conceal or lie, but may even break the will to stand by the truth. Nor is it questioned that the same result can sometimes be achieved by threats, promises, or inducements, which torture the mind but put no scar on the body. If the opinion of Mr. Justice Frankfurter in *Watts* were based solely on the State's admissions as to the treatment of Watts, I should not disagree. But if ultimate quest in a criminal trial is the truth and if the circumstances indicate no violence or threats of it, should society be deprived of the suspect's help in solving a crime merely because he was confined and questioned when uncounseled?

We must not overlook that in these, as in some previous cases, once a confession is obtained it supplies ways of verifying its trustworthiness. In these cases before us the verification is sufficient to leave me in no doubt that the admissions of guilt were genuine and truthful. Such corroboration consists in one case of finding a weapon where the accused has said he hid it, and in others that conditions which could only have been known to one who was implicated correspond with his story. It is possible, but it is rare, that a confession, if repudiated on the trial, standing alone will convict unless there is external proof of its verity.

In all such cases, along with other conditions criticized, the continuity and duration of the questioning is invoked and it is called an "inquiry," "inquest" or "inquisition," depending mainly on the emotional state of the writer. But as in some of the cases here, if interrogation is permissible at all, there are sound reasons for prolonging it—which the opinions here ignore. The suspect at first perhaps makes an effort to exculpate himself by alibis or other statements. These are verified, found false, and he is then confronted with his falsehood. Sometimes (though such cases do not reach us) verification proves them true or credible and the suspect is released. Sometimes, as here, more than one crime is involved. The duration of an interrogation may well depend on the temperament, shrewdness and cunning of the accused and the competence of the examiner. But assuming a right to examine at all, the right must include what is made reasonably necessary by the facts of the particular case.

If the right of interrogation be admitted, then it seems to me that we must leave it to trial judges and juries and state appellate courts to decide individual cases, unless they show some want of proper standards of decision. I find nothing to indicate that any of the courts below in these cases did not have a correct understanding of the Fourteenth Amendment, unless this Court thinks it means absolute prohibition of interrogation while in custody before arraignment.

I suppose no one would doubt that our Constitution and Bill of Rights, grounded in revolt against the arbitrary measures of George III and in the philosophy of the French Revolution, represent the maximum restrictions upon the power of organized society over the individual that are compatible with the maintenance of organized society itself. They were so intended and should be so interpreted. It cannot be denied that, even if construed as these provisions traditionally have been, they contain an aggregate of restrictions which seriously limit the power of society to solve such crimes as confront us in these cases.

Those restrictions we should not for that reason cast aside, but that is good reason for indulging in no unnecessary expansion of them.

I doubt very much if they require us to hold that the State may not take into custody and question one suspected reasonably of an unwitnessed murder. If it does, the people of this country must discipline themselves to seeing their police stand by helplessly while those suspected of murder prowl about unmolested. Is it a necessary price to pay for the fairness which we know as "due process of law"? And if not a necessary one, should it be demanded by this Court? I do not know the ultimate answer to these questions; but, for the present, I should not increase the handicap on society.[b]

SECTION 2. *MASSIAH* AND *ESCOBEDO*: THE COURT GROWS DISENCHANTED WITH THE "VOLUNTARINESS" TEST AND TURNS TO THE RIGHT TO COUNSEL

As the rationales for the Court's coerced confession cases evolved, it became increasingly doubtful that terms such as "voluntariness," "coercion" and "breaking the will" were very helpful in deciding the admissibility of confessions. It appeared that such terms were not being used as tools of analysis, but as mere conclusions. When a court concluded that the police had resorted to unacceptable interrogation techniques, it called the resulting confession "involuntary." On the other hand, it seemed, when a court decided the methods the police had employed were permissible or tolerable, it called the resulting confession "voluntary." Moreover, such terms as "voluntariness," "coercion" and "overbearing the will" focused directly on neither of the two underlying reasons that led the courts to bar the use of confessions—the offensiveness of police interrogation methods or the risk that these methods had produced an untrue confession. Thus, as the Court, per O'Connor, J., recently noted in *Miller v. Fenton*, 474 U.S. 104 (1985), "[t]he voluntariness rubric has been variously condemned as 'useless,' 'perplexing,' and 'legal "doubletalk." ' "

Almost everything was relevant under the due process "totality of the circumstances"—"voluntariness" test, e.g., the suspect's age, intelligence, education and prior criminal record; whether he was advised of his rights, held incommunicado or given meals at regular intervals. But with a very few exceptions, e.g. the use or threatened use of physical violence, no single factor was decisive. Because there were so many variables in the voluntariness equation that one determination seldom served as a useful precedent for another, the test offered neither the police nor the courts much guidance. Trial courts were almost invited to give weight to their subjective preferences and appellate courts were discouraged from active review.

Understandably, some members of the Court looked for an alternative approach. In the 1959 *Crooker* case, discussed below, the four dissenters turned to the right to counsel. Five years later, as illustrated by the two cases in this section, *Massiah v. United States* and *Escobedo v. Illinois*, the right to counsel approach to confessions had gained ascendancy.

Crooker v. California, 357 U.S. 433 (1958), involved a petitioner who had attended one year of law school, during which time he studied criminal law, and who indicated that he was fully aware of his right to remain silent. On the basis

---

b. Vinson, C.J., and Reed and Burton, JJ. dissented, "on the record before us and in view   of the consideration given to the evidence by the state courts".

of a challenged confession, he was convicted of the murder of his paramour and sentenced to death. A 5–4 majority rejected his argument that by persisting in interrogating him after denying his specific request to contact his lawyer the police had violated his due process right to legal representation and advice and that therefore the use of any confession obtained from him under these circumstances should be barred, even though "voluntarily" made under traditional standards. Such a rule, retorted the Court, per Clark, J., "would have [a] devastating effect on enforcement of criminal law, for it would effectively preclude police questioning—fair as well as unfair—until the accused was afforded opportunity to call his lawyer. Due process * * * demands no such rule." But four dissenting Justices, Douglas, J., joined by Warren, C.J., and Black and Brennan, JJ., maintained that "[t]he demands of our civilization, expressed in the Due Process Clause require that the accused who wants a counsel should have one at any time after the moment of arrest."

The following year, by virtue of *Spano v. New York,* 360 U.S. 315 (1959), it appeared that a majority of the Court may have arrived at the view that once a person is *formally charged* by indictment or information her constitutional right to counsel has "begun"—at least the right to the assistance of counsel she herself has retained. Four concurring Justices took this position in *Spano*: Justices Black, Douglas and Brennan, all of whom had dissented in *Crooker,* and newly appointed Justice Stewart, who had replaced Justice Burton. In two separate opinions, the concurring Justices emphasized that *Spano* was not a case where the police were questioning a suspect in the course of investigating an unsolved crime, but one where the person interrogated was already under indictment for murder when he surrendered to the authorities.

A majority of the *Spano* Court did not decide the case on the grounds suggested by the concurring Justices because it found the confession inadmissible under the traditional due process "voluntariness" test. But Chief Justice Warren, who wrote the majority opinion, had taken the position a year earlier in *Crooker* that the right to counsel should "begin" even earlier than at the point of indictment. Thus, counting heads, it appeared that by 1959 the views of the concurring Justices in *Spano* commanded a majority of the Court. Any doubts were dispelled by *Massiah v. United States,* the first case in this section.

When, a short five weeks after it had decided *Massiah,* the Court threw out the confession in *Escobedo v. Illinois,* the second case in this section, even though Escobedo had been interrogated *before* "judicial" or "adversary" proceedings had commenced against him, many members of the bench and bar grew alarmed. As they saw it, the "right to counsel" approach to the confession problem threatened the admissibility of even *"volunteered"* statements. They feared that the Court might be in the process of shaping a novel right not to confess except knowingly and with the tactical assistance of counsel.

Perhaps the enthusiastic public reaction to the *Gideon* decision a year earlier had led some members of the Court to believe that *Massiah* and *Escobedo* would also be well-received. But many members of the bench and bar, and the general public as well, soon left little doubt that they were much more enthusiastic about a lawyer for a defendant in the courtroom than they were about a lawyer for a suspect in the police station.

MASSIAH v. UNITED STATES

377 U.S. 201, 84 S.Ct. 1199, 12 L.Ed.2d 246 (1964).

JUSTICE STEWART delivered the opinion of the Court. * * *

[After he had been indicted for conspiracy to possess narcotics aboard a United States vessel and other federal narcotics violations, Massiah retained a lawyer, pled not guilty, and was released on bail. Colson, a codefendant, also retained a lawyer, pled not guilty, and was released on bail. Colson then invited Massiah to discuss the pending case in Colson's car, parked on a city street. Unknown to Massiah, Colson had decided to cooperate with federal agents in their continuing investigation of the case. A radio transmitter was installed under the front seat of Colson's car, enabling a nearby federal agent (Murphy), who was equipped with a recording device, to overhear the Massiah–Colson conversation. As expected, Massiah made several damaging admissions. On the basis of these admissions, Massiah was convicted of several narcotics offenses. The convictions were affirmed by the U.S. Court of Appeals for the Second Circuit.]

In *Spano v. New York,* this Court reversed a state criminal conviction because a confession had been wrongly admitted into evidence against the defendant at his trial. In that case the defendant had already been indicted for first-degree murder at the time he confessed. The Court held that the defendant's conviction could not stand under the Fourteenth Amendment. While the Court's opinion relied upon the totality of the circumstances under which the confession had been obtained, four concurring Justices pointed out that the Constitution required reversal of the conviction upon the sole and specific ground that the confession had been deliberately elicited by the police after the defendant had been indicted, and therefore at a time when he was clearly entitled to a lawyer's help. It was pointed out that under our system of justice the most elemental concepts of due process of law contemplate that an indictment be followed by a trial, "in an orderly courtroom, presided over by a judge, open to the public, and protected by all the procedural safeguards of the law." (Stewart, J., concurring). It was said that a Constitution which guarantees a defendant the aid of counsel at such a trial could surely vouchsafe no less to an indicted defendant under interrogation by the police in a completely extrajudicial proceeding. Anything less, it was said, might deny a defendant "effective representation by counsel at the only stage when legal aid and advice would help him." (Douglas, J., concurring).

[The view taken by the *Spano* concurring Justices] no more than reflects a constitutional principle established as long ago as *Powell v. Alabama,* where the Court noted that "during perhaps the most critical period of the proceedings, [that] is to say, from the time of their arraignment until the beginning of their trial, when consultation, thoroughgoing investigation and preparation [are] vitally important, the defendants [are] as much entitled to such aid [of counsel] during that period as at the trial itself." * * *

Here we deal not with a state court conviction, but with a federal case, where the specific guarantee of the Sixth Amendment directly applies. We hold that the petitioner was denied the basic protections of that guarantee when there was used against him at his trial evidence of his own incriminating words, which federal agents had deliberately elicited from him after he had been indicted and in the absence of his counsel. It is true that in the Spano case the defendant was interrogated in a police station, while here the damaging testimony was elicited from the defendant without his knowledge while he was free on bail. But, as Judge Hays pointed out in his dissent in the Court of Appeals, "if such a rule is to have any efficacy it must apply to indirect and surreptitious interrogations as well as those conducted in the jailhouse. In this case, Massiah was more seriously imposed upon * * * because he did not even know that he was under interrogation by a government agent."

The Solicitor General [has] strenuously contended that the federal law enforcement agents had the right, if not indeed the duty, to continue their investigation of the petitioner and his alleged criminal associates even though the petitioner had been indicted. [He] says that the quantity of narcotics involved was such as to suggest that the petitioner was part of a large and well-organized ring, and indeed that the continuing investigation confirmed this suspicion, since it resulted in criminal charges against many defendants. Under these circumstances the Solicitor General concludes that the government agents were completely "justified in making use of Colson's cooperation by having Colson continue his normal associations and by surveilling them."

* * * We do not question that in this case, as in many cases, it was entirely proper to continue an investigation of the suspected criminal activities of the defendant and his alleged confederates, even though the defendant had already been indicted. All that we hold is that the defendant's own incriminating statements, obtained by federal agents under the circumstances here disclosed, could not constitutionally be used by the prosecution as evidence against *him* at his trial. * * *

JUSTICE WHITE, with whom JUSTICE CLARK and JUSTICE HARLAN join, dissenting.

* * * [It is] a rather portentous occasion when a constitutional rule is established barring the use of evidence which is relevant, reliable and highly probative of the issue which the trial court has before it—whether the accused committed the act with which he is charged. Without the evidence, the quest for truth may be seriously impeded and in many cases the trial court, although aware of proof showing defendant's guilt, must nevertheless release him because the crucial evidence is deemed inadmissible. This result is entirely justified in some circumstances because exclusion serves other policies of overriding importance, as where evidence seized in an illegal search is excluded, not because of the quality of the proof, but to secure meaningful enforcement of the Fourth Amendment. But this only emphasizes that the soundest of reasons is necessary to warrant the exclusion of evidence otherwise admissible and the creation of another area of privileged testimony. With all due deference, I am not at all convinced that the additional barriers to the pursuit of truth which the Court today erects rest on anything like the solid foundations which decisions of this gravity should require.

The importance of the matter should not be underestimated, for today's rule promises to have wide application well beyond the facts of this case. The reason given for the result here—the admissions were obtained in the absence of counsel—would seem equally pertinent to statements obtained at any time after the right to counsel attaches, whether there has been an indictment or not; to admissions made prior to arraignment, at least where the defendant has counsel or asks for it; to the fruits of admissions improperly obtained under the new rule; to criminal proceedings in state courts; and to defendants long since convicted upon evidence including such admissions. The new rule will immediately do service in a great many cases.

Whatever the content or scope of the rule may prove to be, I am unable to see how this case presents an unconstitutional interference with Massiah's right to counsel. Massiah was not prevented from consulting with counsel as often as he wished. No meetings with counsel were disturbed or spied upon. Preparation for trial was in no way obstructed. It is only a sterile syllogism—an unsound one, besides—to say that because Massiah had a right to counsel's aid before and during the trial, his out-of-court conversations and admissions must be excluded if obtained without counsel's consent or presence. The right to counsel has never meant as much before and its extension in this case requires some further explanation, so far unarticulated by the Court.

Since the new rule would exclude all admissions made to the police, no matter how voluntary and reliable, the requirement of counsel's presence or approval would seem to rest upon the probability that counsel would foreclose any admissions at all. This is nothing more than a thinly disguised constitutional policy of minimizing or entirely prohibiting the use in evidence of voluntary out-of-court admissions and confessions made by the accused. Carried as far as blind logic may compel some to go, the notion that statements from the mouth of the defendant should not be used in evidence would have a severe and unfortunate impact upon the great bulk of criminal cases.

Viewed in this light, the Court's newly fashioned exclusionary principle goes far beyond the constitutional privilege against self-incrimination, which neither requires nor suggests the barring of voluntary pretrial admissions.

* * * Whether as a matter of self-incrimination or of due process, the proscription is against compulsion—coerced incrimination. Under the prior law, announced in countless cases in this Court, the defendant's pretrial statements were admissible evidence if voluntarily made; inadmissible if not the product of his free will. Hardly any constitutional area has been more carefully patrolled by this Court, and until now the Court has expressly rejected the argument that admissions are to be deemed involuntary if made outside the presence of counsel.

The Court presents no facts, no objective evidence, no reasons to warrant scrapping the voluntary-involuntary test for admissibility in this area. Without such evidence I would retain it in its present form.

This case cannot be analogized to the American Bar Association's rule forbidding an attorney to talk to the opposing party litigant outside the presence of his counsel. Aside from the fact that the Association's canons are not of constitutional dimensions, the specific canon argued is inapposite because it deals with the conduct of lawyers and not with the conduct of investigators. Lawyers are forbidden to interview the opposing party because of the supposed imbalance of legal skill and acumen between the lawyer and the party litigant; the reason for the rule does not apply to nonlawyers and certainly not to Colson, Massiah's codefendant.

Applying the new exclusionary rule is peculiarly inappropriate in this case. At the time of the conversation in question, petitioner was not in custody but free on bail. He was not questioned in what anyone could call an atmosphere of official coercion. What he said was said to his partner in crime who had also been indicted. There was no suggestion or any possibility of coercion. What petitioner did not know was that Colson had decided to report the conversation to the police. Had there been no prior arrangements between Colson and the police, had Colson simply gone to the police after the conversation had occurred, his testimony relating Massiah's statements would be readily admissible at the trial, as would a recording which he might have made of the conversation. In such event, it would simply be said that Massiah risked talking to a friend who decided to disclose what he knew of Massiah's criminal activities. But if, as occurred here, Colson had been cooperating with the police prior to his meeting with Massiah, both his evidence and the recorded conversation are somehow transformed into inadmissible evidence despite the fact that the hazard to Massiah remains precisely the same—the defection of a confederate in crime. * * *

[The question presented] is this: when the police have arrested and released on bail one member of a criminal ring and another member, a confederate, is cooperating with the police, can the confederate be allowed to continue his association with the ring or must he somehow be withdrawn to avoid challenge to trial evidence on the ground that it was acquired after rather than before the arrest, after rather than before the indictment?

Defendants who are out on bail have been known to continue their illicit operations. That an attorney is advising them should not constitutionally immunize their statements made in furtherance of these operations and relevant to the question of their guilt at the pending prosecution. * * * Undoubtedly, the evidence excluded in this case would not have been available but for the conduct of Colson in cooperation with Agent Murphy, but is it this kind of conduct which should be forbidden to those charged with law enforcement? It is one thing to establish safeguards against procedures fraught with the potentiality of coercion and to outlaw "easy but self-defeating ways in which brutality is substituted for brains as an instrument of crime detection." But here there was no substitution of brutality for brains, no inherent danger of police coercion justifying the prophylactic effect of another exclusionary rule. Massiah was not being interrogated in a police station, was not surrounded by numerous officers or questioned in relays, and was not forbidden access to others. Law enforcement may have the elements of a contest about it, but it is not a game. Massiah and those like him receive ample protection from the long line of precedents in this Court holding that confessions may not be introduced unless they are voluntary. In making these determinations the courts must consider the absence of counsel as one of several factors by which voluntariness is to be judged. This is a wiser rule than the automatic rule announced by the Court, which requires courts and juries to disregard voluntary admissions which they might well find to be the best possible evidence in discharging their responsibility for ascertaining truth.

ESCOBEDO v. ILLINOIS

378 U.S. 478, 84 S.Ct. 1758, 12 L.Ed.2d 977 (1964).

JUSTICE GOLDBERG delivered the opinion of the Court.

[On the night of January 19, petitioner's brother-in-law was fatally shot. A few hours later petitioner was taken into custody for questioning, but he made no statement and was released the following afternoon pursuant to a writ of habeas corpus obtained by his retained counsel. On January 30, one DiGerlando, who was then in police custody and who was later indicted for the murder along with petitioner, stated that petitioner had fired the shots which killed his brother-in-law. That evening petitioner was again arrested and taken to police headquarters. En route to the police station he was told that DiGerlando had named him as the one who fired the fatal shots and that he might as well admit it, but petitioner replied (probably because his attorney had obtained his release from police custody only 11 days earlier or because he had consulted with his attorney in the meantime): "I am sorry but I would like to have advice from my lawyer."

[Shortly after petitioner reached police headquarters, his retained lawyer arrived and spent the next three or four hours trying unsuccessfully to speak to his client. He talked to every officer he could find, but was repeatedly told that he could not see his client and that he would have to get a writ of habeas corpus. In the meantime, petitioner repeatedly but unsuccessfully asked to speak to his lawyer. At one point, petitioner and his attorney came into each other's view for a few moments, but the attorney was quickly ushered away. Petitioner testified that he heard a detective tell his attorney that the latter could not see him until the police "were done."

[Instead of allowing petitioner to meet with his lawyer, the police arranged a confrontation between petitioner and DiGerlando. Petitioner denied that he had fired the fatal shots. He maintained that DiGerlando was lying and, in the presence of the police, told him: "I didn't shoot Manuel, you did it." In this way, petitioner admitted to some knowledge of the crime. After that, he made other statements further implicating himself in the murder plot. At this point, an assistant prosecutor arrived "to take" a statement. The statement, made in response to carefully framed questions, was admitted into evidence. Petitioner was convicted of murder. The Supreme Court of Illinois affirmed.]

The critical question in this case is whether, under the circumstances, the refusal by the police to honor petitioner's request to consult with his lawyer during the course of an interrogation constitutes a denial of "the Assistance of Counsel" in violation of the Sixth Amendment to the Constitution as "made obligatory upon the States by the Fourteenth Amendment," *Gideon,* and thereby renders inadmissible in a state criminal trial any incriminating statement elicited by the police during the interrogation. * * *

In *Massiah* this Court observed that "a Constitution which guarantees a defendant the aid of counsel [at] trial could surely vouchsafe no less to an indicted defendant under interrogation by the police in a completely extrajudicial proceeding. Anything less [might] deny a defendant 'effective representation by counsel at the only stage when legal aid and advice would help him.' "

The interrogation here was conducted before petitioner was formally indicted. But in the context of this case, that fact should make no difference. When petitioner requested, and was denied, an opportunity to consult with his lawyer, the investigation had ceased to be a general investigation of "an unsolved crime." Petitioner had become the accused, and the purpose of the interrogation was to "get him" to confess his guilt despite his constitutional right not to do so. At the time of his arrest and throughout the course of the interrogation, the police told petitioner that they had convincing evidence that he had fired the fatal shots. Without informing him of his absolute right to remain silent in the face of this accusation, the police urged him to make a statement.[5] * * *

Petitioner, a layman, was undoubtedly unaware that under Illinois law an admission of "mere" complicity in the murder plot was legally as damaging as an admission of firing of the fatal shots. The "guiding hand of counsel" was essential to advise petitioner of his rights in this delicate situation. This was the "stage when legal aid and advice" were most critical to petitioner. *Massiah.* * * * It would exalt form over substance to make the right to counsel, under these circumstances, depend on whether at the time of the interrogation, the authorities had secured a formal indictment. Petitioner had, for all practical purposes, already been charged with murder. * * *

In *Gideon* we held that every person accused of a crime, whether state or federal, is entitled to a lawyer at trial. The rule sought by the State here, however, would make the trial no more than an appeal from the interrogation; and the "right to use counsel at the formal trial [would be] a very hollow thing [if], for all practical purposes, the conviction is already assured by pretrial examination." *In re Groban,* 352 U.S. 330 (1957) (Black, J., dissenting). "One can imagine a cynical prosecutor saying: 'Let them have the most illustrious

---

5. Although there is testimony in the record that petitioner and his lawyer had previously discussed what petitioner should do in the event of interrogation, there is no evidence that they discussed what petitioner should, or could, do in the face of a false accusation that he had fired the fatal bullets.

counsel, now. They can't escape the noose. There is nothing that counsel can do for them at the trial.' "

It is argued that if the right to counsel is afforded prior to indictment, the number of confessions obtained by the police will diminish significantly, because most confessions are obtained during the period between arrest and indictment, and "any lawyer worth his salt will tell the suspect in no uncertain terms to make no statement to police under any circumstances." This argument, of course, cuts two ways. The fact that many confessions are obtained during this period points up its critical nature as a "stage when legal aid and advice" are surely needed. *Massiah.* The right to counsel would indeed be hollow if it began at a period when few confessions were obtained. There is necessarily a direct relationship between the importance of a stage to the police in their quest for a confession and the criticalness of that stage to the accused in his need for legal advice. Our Constitution, unlike some others, strikes the balance in favor of the right of the accused to be advised by his lawyer of his privilege against self-incrimination.

We have learned the lesson of history, ancient and modern, that a system of criminal law enforcement which comes to depend on the "confession" will, in the long run, be less reliable and more subject to abuses than a system which depends on extrinsic evidence independently secured through skillful investigation. * * *

We have also learned the companion lesson of history that no system of criminal justice can, or should, survive if it comes to depend for its continued effectiveness on the citizens' abdication through unawareness of their constitutional rights. No system worth preserving should have to *fear* that if an accused is permitted to consult with a lawyer, he will become aware of, and exercise, these rights. If the exercise of constitutional rights will thwart the effectiveness of a system of law enforcement, then there is something very wrong with that system.[14]

We hold, therefore, that where, as here, the investigation is no longer a general inquiry into an unsolved crime but has begun to focus on a particular suspect, the suspect has been taken into police custody, the police carry out a process of interrogations that lends itself to eliciting incriminating statements, the suspect has requested and been denied an opportunity to consult with his lawyer, and the police have not effectively warned him of his absolute constitutional right to remain silent, the accused has been denied "the Assistance of Counsel" in violation of the Sixth Amendment to the Constitution as "made obligatory upon the States by the Fourteenth Amendment," *Gideon,* and that no statement elicited by the police during the interrogation may be used against him at a criminal trial. * * *

Nothing we have said today affects the powers of the police to investigate "an unsolved crime" by gathering information from witnesses and by other "proper investigative efforts." We hold only that when the process shifts from investigatory to accusatory—when its focus is on the accused and its purpose is to elicit a confession—our adversary system begins to operate, and, under the circumstances here, the accused must be permitted to consult with his lawyer.

The judgment of the Illinois Supreme Court is reversed and the case remanded for proceedings not inconsistent with this opinion. * * *

JUSTICE HARLAN, dissenting.

---

14. The accused may, of course, intelligently and knowingly waive his privilege against self-incrimination and his right to counsel either at a pretrial stage or at the trial. But no knowing and intelligent waiver of any constitutional right can be said to have occurred under the circumstances of this case.

* * * Like my Brother White, I think the rule announced today is most ill-conceived and that it seriously and unjustifiably fetters perfectly legitimate methods of criminal law enforcement.

JUSTICE STEWART, dissenting. * * *

Massiah is not in point here. * * * Putting to one side the fact that the case now before us is not a federal case, the vital fact remains that this case does not involve the deliberate interrogation of a defendant after the initiation of judicial proceedings against him. The Court disregards this basic difference between the present case and Massiah's, with the bland assertion that "that fact should make no difference."

It is "that fact," I submit, which makes all the difference. Under our system of criminal justice the institution of formal, meaningful judicial proceedings, by way of indictment, information, or arraignment, marks the point at which a criminal investigation has ended and adversary proceedings have commenced. It is at this point that the constitutional guarantees attach which pertain to a criminal trial. Among those guarantees are the right to a speedy trial, the right of confrontation, and the right to trial by jury. Another is the guarantee of the assistance of counsel.

The confession which the Court today holds inadmissible was a voluntary one. It was given during the course of a perfectly legitimate police investigation of an unsolved murder. The Court says that what happened during this investigation "affected" the trial. I had always supposed that the whole purpose of a police investigation of a murder was to "affect" the trial of the murderer, and that it would be only an incompetent, unsuccessful, or corrupt investigation which would not do so. The Court further says that the Illinois police officers did not advise the petitioner of his "constitutional rights" before he confessed to the murder. This Court has never held that the Constitution requires the police to give any "advice" under circumstances such as these.

Supported by no stronger authority than its own rhetoric, the Court today converts a routine police investigation of an unsolved murder into a distorted analogue of a judicial trial. It imports into this investigation constitutional concepts historically applicable only after the onset of formal prosecutorial proceedings. By doing so, I think the Court perverts those precious constitutional guarantees, and frustrates the vital interests of society in preserving the legitimate and proper function of honest and purposeful police investigation. * * *

JUSTICE WHITE, whom JUSTICE CLARK and JUSTICE STEWART join, dissenting.

In *Massiah* the Court held that as of the date of the indictment the prosecution is disentitled to secure admissions from the accused. The Court now moves that date back to the time when the prosecution begins to "focus" on the accused. Although the opinion purports to be limited to the facts of this case, it would be naive to think that the new constitutional right announced will depend upon whether the accused has retained his own counsel, or has asked to consult with counsel in the course of interrogation. At the very least the Court holds that once the accused becomes a suspect and, presumably, is arrested, any admission made to the police thereafter is inadmissible in evidence unless the accused has waived his right to counsel. The decision is thus another major step in the direction of the goal which the Court seemingly has in mind—to bar from evidence all admissions obtained from an individual suspected of crime, whether involuntarily made or not. It does of course put us one step "ahead" of the English judges who have had the good sense to leave the matter a discretionary one with the trial court. I reject this step and the invitation to go farther which the court has now issued.

By abandoning the voluntary-involuntary test for admissibility of confessions, the Court seems driven by the notion that it is uncivilized law enforcement to use an accused's own admissions against him at his trial. It attempts to find a home for this new and nebulous rule of due process by attaching it to the right to counsel guaranteed in the federal system by the Sixth Amendment and binding upon the States by virtue of the due process guarantee of the Fourteenth Amendment. The right to counsel now not only entitles the accused to counsel's advice and aid in preparing for trial but stands as an impenetrable barrier to any interrogation once the accused has become a suspect. From that very moment apparently his right to counsel attaches, a rule wholly unworkable and impossible to administer unless police cars are equipped with public defenders and undercover agents and police informants have defense counsel at their side. I would not abandon the Court's prior cases defining with some care and analysis the circumstances requiring the presence or aid of counsel and substitute the amorphous and wholly unworkable principle that counsel is constitutionally required whenever he would or could be helpful. [Under the Court's] new approach one might just as well argue that a potential defendant is constitutionally entitled to a lawyer before, not after, he commits a crime, since it is then that crucial *extreme* incriminating evidence is put within the reach of the Government by the would-be accused. Until now there simply has been no right guaranteed by the Federal Constitution to be free from the use at trial of a voluntary admission made prior to indictment.

It is incongruous to assume that the provision for counsel in the Sixth Amendment was meant to amend or supersede the self-incrimination provision of the Fifth Amendment, which is now applicable to the States. That amendment addresses itself to the very issue of incriminating admissions of an accused and resolves it by proscribing only compelled statements. Neither the Framers, the constitutional language, a century of decisions of this Court nor Professor Wigmore provides an iota of support for the idea that an accused has an absolute constitutional right not to answer even in the absence of compulsion—the constitutional right not to incriminate himself by making voluntary disclosures.   * * *

The Court chooses [to] rely on the virtues and morality of a system of criminal law enforcement which does not depend on the "confession." No such judgment is to be found in the Constitution. It might be appropriate for a legislature to provide that a suspect should not be consulted during a criminal investigation; that an accused should never be called before a grand jury to answer, even if he wants to, what may well be incriminating questions; and that no person, whether he be a suspect, guilty criminal or innocent bystander, should be put to the ordeal of responding to orderly noncompulsory inquiry by the State. But this is not the system our Constitution requires. The only "inquisitions" the Constitution forbids are those which compel incrimination. Escobedo's statements were not compelled and the Court does not hold that they were.

This new American judges' rule, which is to be applied in both federal and state courts, is perhaps thought to be a necessary safeguard against the possibility of extorted confessions. To this extent it reflects a deep-seated distrust of law enforcement officers everywhere, unsupported by relevant data or current material based upon our own experience. Obviously law enforcement officers can make mistakes and exceed their authority, as today's decision shows that even judges can do, but I have somewhat more faith than the Court evidently has in the ability and desire of prosecutors and of the power of the appellate courts to discern and correct such violations of the law.

The Court may be concerned with a narrower matter: the unknowing defendant who responds to police questioning because he mistakenly believes that he must and that his admissions will not be used against him. But this worry hardly calls for the broadside the Court has now fired. The failure to inform an accused that he need not answer and that his answers may be used against him is very relevant indeed to whether the disclosures are compelled. Cases in this Court, to say the least, have never placed a premium on ignorance of constitutional rights. If an accused is told he must answer and does not know better, it would be very doubtful that the resulting admissions could be used against him. When the accused has not been informed of his rights at all the Court characteristically and properly looks very closely at the surrounding circumstances. I would continue to do so. But in this case Danny Escobedo knew full well that he did not have to answer and knew full well that his lawyer had advised him not to answer.

I do not suggest for a moment that law enforcement will be destroyed by the rule announced today. The need for peace and order is too insistent for that. But it will be crippled and its task made a great deal more difficult, all in my opinion, for unsound, unstated reasons, which can find no home in any of the provisions of the Constitution.

SECTION 3. *MIRANDA*: THE COURT BUILDS A CONFESSION DOCTRINE ON THE PRIVILEGE AGAINST COMPELLED SELF-INCRIMINATION

Recall that dissenting in the 1944 *Ashcraft* case, Justice Jackson agreed that the detention and questioning of a suspect for thirty-six hours is "inherently coercive," but quickly added: "[S]o is custody and examination for one hour. Arrest itself is inherently coercive and so is detention. * * * But does the Constitution prohibit use of all confessions made after arrest because questioning, while one is deprived of freedom, is 'inherently coercive'?" Both Jackson and Justice Black, who wrote the majority opinion in *Ashcraft,* knew that in 1944 the Court was not ready for an affirmative answer to Jackson's question. But by 1966 the Court had grown ready.

Yes, answered a 5–4 majority in *Miranda v. Arizona,* the Constitution does prohibit use of all confessions obtained by "in-custody questioning" unless "adequate protective devices" are used to dispel the coercion inherent in such questioning. The protective devices deemed necessary to neutralize the compulsion inherent in the interrogation environment (unless the government adopts other equally effective means, and what they may be remains unclear) are the now familiar "*Miranda* warnings."

The *Miranda* Court's reasoning, if not its result, surprised the late John J. Flynn, Miranda's lawyer in the U.S. Supreme Court. As Flynn later recalled, he and others working on the case had "agreed that the briefs should be written with the entire focus on the Sixth Amendment [right to counsel] because that is where the Court was headed after *Escobedo,*" but "in the very first paragraph [of the *Miranda* opinion] Chief Justice Warren said [in effect], 'It is the Fifth Amendment [privilege against compulsory self-incrimination] that is at issue today.' That was Miranda's effective use of counsel."

Although not happy with the continued momentum of the Warren Court in favor of the rights of suspects, those alarmed by *Massiah* and *Escobedo* must have found some comfort in the *Miranda* Court's switch in emphasis from the right to counsel to the privilege against compelled self-incrimination. Recall that the *Escobedo* dissenters expressed a preference for a self-incrimination approach, rather than a right to counsel approach, because the self-incrimination clause proscribes only *compelled* statements. Of course, the four *Escobedo* dissenters (all of whom also dissented in *Miranda*) were not pleased with the way the *Miranda* majority defined "compulsion" within the meaning of the privilege.

Why, in the thirty years between *Brown v. Mississippi* (1936), the first Fourteenth Amendment Due Process case, and *Miranda,* had the Fifth Amendment's ban against compelling a person in any criminal case "to be a witness against himself" been so neglected in the confession cases? For one thing, this prohibition had not been deemed applicable to the states until 1964, and by that time a large body of law pertaining to "involuntary" or "coerced" confessions had developed. Moreover, and more important, the prevailing pre-*Miranda* view was that compulsion to testify meant *legal* compulsion.

Since a suspect is threatened neither with perjury for testifying falsely nor contempt for refusing to testify at all, it cannot be said, ran the argument, that a person undergoing police interrogation is being "compelled" to be "a witness against himself" within the meaning of the privilege—even though under such circumstances a person may assume or be led to believe that there *are* legal (or extralegal) sanctions for "refusing to cooperate." Since the police have no *legal right* to make a suspect answer (although, prior to *Miranda,* the police did not have to *tell* a person that), there was no legal obligation to answer, ran the argument, to which a privilege in the technical sense could apply.

Although the right to counsel had dominated the confessions scene in the years immediately preceding *Miranda,* there was some reason to think that, at long last, the self-incrimination clause might move to centerstage. In *Malloy v. Hogan,* 378 U.S. 1 (1964) (which did not involve a confession), the Court, per Brennan, J., performed what some called a "shotgun wedding" of the privilege against self-incrimination to the confession rule. *Malloy* not only held the self-incrimination clause applicable to the states, but declared that whenever a question arises in a state *or* federal court "whether a confession is incompetent because not voluntary, the issue is controlled by [the self-incrimination] portion of the Fifth Amendment."

Whether or not this view made good sense, it constituted very questionable recent history. In none of the dozens of state *or* federal confession cases decided in the 1930's, 40's or 50's had the self-incrimination clause been the basis for judgment (although it had occasionally been mentioned in an opinion). But how the *Malloy* opinion looked back was not as important as how it looked forward. The confession rules and the privilege against self-incrimination had become intertwined in *Malloy*—and they would be fused in *Miranda.*

MIRANDA v. ARIZONA (No. 759) *

384 U.S. 436, 86 S.Ct. 1602, 16 L.Ed.2d 694 (1966).

CHIEF JUSTICE WARREN delivered the opinion of the Court.

The cases before us raise questions which go to the roots of American criminal jurisprudence: the restraints society must observe consistent with the

* Together with No. 760, *Vignera v. New   [and] No. 584,* California v. Stewart * * *.
York [and] No. 761, Westover v. United States

Federal Constitution in prosecuting individuals for crime. More specifically, we deal with the admissibility of statements obtained from an individual who is subjected to custodial police interrogation and the necessity for procedures which assure that the individual is accorded his privilege under the Fifth Amendment to the Constitution not to be compelled to incriminate himself. * * *

We start here, as we did in *Escobedo* with the premise that our holding is not an innovation in our jurisprudence, but is an application of principles long recognized and applied in other settings. We have undertaken a thorough re-examination of the *Escobedo* decision and the principles it announced, and we reaffirm it. That case was but an explication of basic rights that are enshrined in our Constitution—that "No person * * * shall be compelled in any criminal case to be a witness against himself," and that "the accused [shall] have the Assistance of Counsel"—rights which were put in jeopardy in that case through official overbearing. * * *

Our holding will be spelled out with some specificity in the pages which follow but briefly stated it is this: the prosecution may not use statements, whether exculpatory or inculpatory, stemming from custodial interrogation of the defendant unless it demonstrates the use of procedural safeguards effective to secure the privilege against self-incrimination. By custodial interrogation, we mean questioning initiated by law enforcement officers after a person has been taken into custody or otherwise deprived of his freedom of action in any significant way.[4] As for the procedural safeguards to be employed, unless other fully effective means are devised to inform accused persons of their right of silence and to assure a continuous opportunity to exercise it, the following measures are required. Prior to any questioning, the person must be warned that he has a right to remain silent, that any statement he does make may be used as evidence against him, and that he has a right to the presence of an attorney, either retained or appointed. The defendant may waive effectuation of these rights, provided the waiver is made voluntarily, knowingly and intelligently. If, however, he indicates in any manner and at any stage of the process that he wishes to consult with an attorney before speaking there can be no questioning. Likewise, if the individual is alone and indicates in any manner that he does not wish to be interrogated, the police may not question him. The mere fact that he may have answered some questions or volunteered some statements on his own does not deprive him of the right to refrain from answering any further inquiries until he has consulted with an attorney and thereafter consents to be questioned.

The constitutional issue we decide in each of these cases is the admissibility of statements obtained from a defendant questioned while in custody and deprived of his freedom of action in any significant way. In each, the defendant was questioned by police officers, detectives, or a prosecuting attorney in a room in which he was cut off from the outside world. In none of these cases was the defendant given a full and effective warning of his rights at the outset of the interrogation process. In all the cases, the questioning elicited oral admissions, and in three of them, signed statements as well which were admitted at their trials. They all thus share silent features—incommunicado interrogation of individuals in a police-dominated atmosphere, resulting in self-incriminating statements without full warnings of constitutional rights. * * *

Again we stress that the modern practice of in-custody interrogation is psychologically rather than physically oriented. * * * Interrogation still takes

---

4. This is what we meant in *Escobedo* when we spoke of an investigation which had focused on an accused.

place in privacy. Privacy results in secrecy and this in turn results in a gap in our knowledge as to what in fact goes on in the interrogation rooms. A valuable source of information about present police practices, however, may be found in various police manuals and texts which document procedures employed with success in the past, and which recommend various other effective tactics. These texts are used by law enforcement agencies themselves as guides.[9] It should be noted that these texts professedly present the most enlightened and effective means presently used to obtain statements through custodial interrogation. By considering these texts and other data, it is possible to describe procedures observed and noted around the country. * * *

To highlight the isolation and unfamiliar surroundings, the manuals instruct the police to display an air of confidence in the suspect's guilt and from outward appearance to maintain only an interest in confirming certain details. The guilt of the subject is to be posited as a fact. The interrogator should direct his comments toward the reasons why the subject committed the act, rather than court failure by asking the subject whether he did it. Like other men, perhaps the subject has had a bad family life, had an unhappy childhood, had too much to drink, had an unrequited desire for women. The officers are instructed to minimize the moral seriousness of the offense, to cast blame on the victim or on society. These tactics are designed to put the subject in a psychological state where his story is but an elaboration of what the police purport to know already— that he is guilty. Explanations to the contrary are dismissed and discouraged.

The texts thus stress that the major qualities an interrogator should possess are patience and perseverance. * * *

[When other techniques] prove unavailing, the texts recommend they be alternated with a show of some hostility. One ploy often used has been termed the "friendly-unfriendly" or the "Mutt and Jeff" act:

"[In] this technique, two agents are employed. Mutt, the relentless investigator, who knows the subject is guilty and is not going to waste any time. He's sent a dozen men away for this crime and he's going to send the subject away for the full term. Jeff, on the other hand, is obviously a kindhearted man. He has a family himself. He has a brother who was involved in a little scrape like this. He disapproves of Mutt and his tactics and will arrange to get him off the case if the subject will cooperate. He can't hold Mutt off for very long. The subject would be wise to make a quick decision. The technique is applied by having both investigators present while Mutt acts out his role. Jeff may stand by quietly and demur at some of Mutt's tactics. When Jeff makes his plea for cooperation, Mutt is not present in the room."

The interrogators sometimes are instructed to induce a confession out of trickery. The technique here is quite effective in crimes which require identification or which run in series. In the identification situation, the interrogator may

9. The methods described in Inbau and Reid, *Criminal Interrogation and Confessions* (1962), are a revision and enlargement of material presented in three prior editions of a predecessor text, *Lie Detection and Criminal Interrogation* (3d ed. 1953). The authors and their associates are officers of the Chicago Police Scientific Crime–Detection Laboratory and have had extensive experience in writing, lecturing and speaking to law enforcement authorities over a 20–year period. They say that the techniques portrayed in their manuals reflect their experiences and are the most effective psychological strategems to employ during interrogations. Similarly, the techniques described in O'Hara, *Fundamentals of Criminal Investigation* (1959), were gleaned from long service as observer, lecturer in police science, and work as a federal criminal investigator. All these texts have had rather extensive use among law enforcement agencies and among students of police science, with total sales and circulation of over 44,000.

take a break in his questioning to place the subject among a group of men in a line-up. "The witness or complainant (previously coached, if necessary) studies the line-up and confidently points out the subject as the guilty party." Then the questioning resumes "as though there were now no doubt about the guilt of the subject." A variation on this technique is called the "reverse line-up":

> "The accused is placed in a line-up, but this time he is identified by several fictitious witnesses or victims who associated him with different offenses. It is expected that the subject will become desperate and confess to the offense under investigation in order to escape from the false accusations."

The manuals also contain instructions for police on how to handle the individual who refuses to discuss the matter entirely, or who asks for an attorney or relatives. The examiner is to concede him the right to remain silent. "This usually has a very undermining effect. First of all, he is disappointed in his expectation of an unfavorable reaction on the part of the interrogator. Secondly, a concession of this right to remain silent impresses the subject with the apparent fairness of his interrogator." After this psychological conditioning, however, the officer is told to point out the incriminating significance of the suspect's refusal to talk:

> "Joe, you have a right to remain silent. That's your privilege and I'm the last person in the world who'll try to take it away from you. If that's the way you want to leave this, O.K. But let me ask you this. Suppose you were in my shoes and I were in yours and you called me in to ask me about this and I told you, 'I don't want to answer any of your questions.' You'd think I had something to hide, and you'd probably be right in thinking that. That's exactly what I'll have to think about you, and so will everybody else. So let's sit here and talk this whole thing over."

Few will persist in their initial refusal to talk, it is said, if this monologue is employed correctly.

In the event that the subject wishes to speak to a relative or an attorney, the following advice is tendered:

> "[T]he interrogator should respond by suggesting that the subject first tell the truth to the interrogator himself rather than get anyone else involved in the matter. If the request is for an attorney, the interrogator may suggest that the subject save himself or his family the expense of any such professional service, particularly if he is innocent of the offense under investigation. The interrogator may also add, 'Joe, I'm only looking for the truth, and if you're telling the truth, that's it. You can handle this by yourself.'"

From these representative samples of interrogation techniques, the setting prescribed by the manuals and observed in practice becomes clear. In essence, it is this: To be alone with the subject is essential to prevent distraction and to deprive him of any outside support. The aura of confidence in his guilt undermines his will to resist. He merely confirms the preconceived story the police seek to have him describe. Patience and persistence, at times relentless questioning, are employed. To obtain a confession, the interrogator must "patiently maneuver himself or his quarry into a position from which the desired object may be obtained." When normal procedures fail to produce the needed result, the police may resort to deceptive stratagems such as giving false legal advice. It is important to keep the subject off balance, for example, by trading on his insecurity about himself or his surroundings. The police then persuade, trick, or cajole him out of exercising his constitutional rights.

Even without employing brutality, the "third degree" or the specific strategems described above, the very fact of custodial interrogation exacts a heavy toll on individual liberty and trades on the weakness of individuals. * * *

In the cases before us today, given this background, we concern ourselves primarily with this interrogation atmosphere and the evils it can bring. In *Miranda v. Arizona,* the police arrested the defendant and took him to a special interrogation room where they secured a confession. In *Vignera v. New York,* the defendant made oral admissions to the police after interrogation in the afternoon, and then signed an inculpatory statement upon being questioned by an assistant district attorney later the same evening. In *Westover v. United States,* the defendant was handed over to the Federal Bureau of Investigation by local authorities after they had detained and interrogated him for a lengthy period, both at night and the following morning. After some two hours of questioning, the federal officers had obtained signed statements from the defendant. Lastly, in *California v. Stewart,* the local police held the defendant five days in the station and interrogated him on nine separate occasions before they secured his inculpatory statement.

In these cases, we might not find the defendants' statements to have been involuntary in traditional terms. Our concern for adequate safeguards to protect precious Fifth Amendment rights is, of course, not lessened in the slightest. In each of the cases, the defendant was thrust into an unfamiliar atmosphere and run through menacing police interrogation procedures. The potentiality for compulsion is forcefully apparent, for example, in *Miranda,* where the indigent Mexican defendant was a seriously disturbed individual with pronounced sexual fantasies, and in *Stewart,* in which the defendant was an indigent Los Angeles Negro who had dropped out of school in the sixth grade. To be sure, the records do not evince overt physical coercion or patented psychological ploys. The fact remains that in none of these cases did the officers undertake to afford appropriate safeguards at the outset of the interrogation to insure that the statements were truly the product of free choice.

It is obvious that such an interrogation environment is created for no purpose other than to subjugate the individual to the will of his examiner. This atmosphere carries its own badge of intimidation. To be sure, this is not physical intimidation, but it is equally destructive of human dignity. The current practice of incommunicado interrogation is at odds with one of our Nation's most cherished principles—that the individual may not be compelled to incriminate himself. Unless adequate protective devices are employed to dispel the compulsion inherent in custodial surroundings, no statement obtained from the defendant can truly be the product of his free choice.

From the foregoing, we can readily perceive an intimate connection between the privilege against self-incrimination and police custodial questioning. It is fitting to turn to history and precedent underlying the Self–Incrimination Clause to determine its applicability in this situation.

[W]e may view the historical development of the privilege as one which groped for the proper scope of governmental power over the citizen. As a "noble principle often transcends its origins," the privilege has come rightfully to be recognized in part as an individual's substantive right, a "right to a private enclave where he may lead a private life. That right is the hallmark of our democracy." We have recently noted that the privilege against self-incrimination—the essential mainstay of our adversary system—is founded on a complex of values. All these policies point to one overriding thought: the constitutional foundation underlying the privilege is the respect a government—state or federal—must accord to the dignity and integrity of its citizens. To maintain a "fair state-individual balance," to require the government "to shoulder the entire load," 8 Wigmore, *Evidence* (McNaughton rev., 1961), 317, to respect the inviolability of the human personality, our accusatory system of criminal justice demands that the government seeking to punish an individual produce the evidence against him by its own independent labors, rather than by the cruel, simple expedient of compelling it from his own mouth. In sum, the privilege is fulfilled only when the person is guaranteed the right "to remain silent unless he chooses to speak in the unfettered exercise of his own will." *Malloy v. Hogan.*

* * * We are satisfied that all the principles embodied in the privilege apply to informal compulsion exerted by law-enforcement officers during in-custody questioning. An individual swept from familiar surroundings into police custody, surrounded by antagonistic forces, and subjected to the techniques of persuasion described above cannot be otherwise than under compulsion to speak. As a practical matter, the compulsion to speak in the isolated setting of the police station may well be greater than in courts or other official investigations, where there are often impartial observers to guard against intimidation or trickery. * * *

Because of the adoption by Congress of Rule 5(a) of the Federal Rules of Criminal Procedure, and this Court's effectuation of that Rule in *McNabb* and *Malloy*, we have had little occasion in the past quarter century to reach the constitutional issues in dealing with federal interrogations. These supervisory rules, requiring production of an arrested person before a commissioner "without unnecessary delay" and excluding evidence obtained in default of that statutory obligation, were nonetheless responsive to the same considerations of Fifth Amendment policy that unavoidably face us now as to the States. In [the *McNabb* and *Malloy* cases] we recognized both the dangers of interrogation and the appropriateness of prophylaxis stemming from the very fact of interrogation itself.[32]

Our decision in *Malloy v. Hogan* necessitates an examination of the scope of the privilege in state cases as well. In *Malloy*, we squarely held the privilege applicable to the States, and held that the substantive standards underlying the privilege applied with full force to state court proceedings. [T]he reasoning in *Malloy* made clear what had already become apparent—that the substantive and procedural safeguards surrounding admissibility of confessions in state cases had become exceedingly exacting, reflecting all the policies embedded in the privilege. The voluntariness doctrine in the state cases, as *Malloy* indicates, encompasses all interrogation practices which are likely to exert such pressure upon an individual as to disable him from making a free and rational choice. The implications of this proposition were elaborated in our decision in *Escobedo*, decided one week after *Malloy* applied the privilege to the States. * * *

[In *Escobedo*], as in the cases today, we sought a protective device to dispel the compelling atmosphere of the interrogation. In *Escobedo*, however, the police did not relieve the defendant of the anxieties which they had created in the interrogation rooms. Rather, they denied his request for the assistance of counsel.[35] This heightened his dilemma, and made his later statements the

---

32. Our decision today does not indicate in any manner, of course, that these rules can be disregarded. When federal officials arrest an individual, they must as always comply with the dictates of the congressional legislation and cases thereunder. * * *

35. The police also prevented the attorney from consulting with his client. Independent of any other constitutional proscription, this action constitutes a violation of the Sixth Amendment right to the assistance of counsel and excludes any statement obtained in its product of this compulsion. * * * The denial of the defendant's request for his attorney thus undermined his ability to exercise the privilege—to remain silent if he chose or to speak without any intimidation, blatant or subtle. The presence of counsel, in all the cases before us today, would be the adequate protective device necessary to make the process of police interrogation conform to the dictates of the privilege. His presence would insure that statements made in the government-established atmosphere are not the product of compulsion.

It was in this manner that *Escobedo* explicated another facet of the pre-trial privilege, noted in many of the Court's prior decisions: the protection of rights at trial. That counsel is present when statements are taken from an individual during interrogation obviously enhances the integrity of the fact-finding processes in court. The presence of an attorney, and the warnings delivered to the individual, enable the defendant under otherwise compelling circumstances to tell his story without fear, effectively, and in a way that eliminates the evils in the interrogation process. Without the protections flowing from adequate warnings and the rights of counsel, "all the careful safeguards erected around the giving of testimony, whether by an accused or any other witness, would become empty formalities in a procedure where the most compelling possible evidence of guilt, a confession, would have already been obtained at the unsupervised pleasure of the police." *Mapp v. Ohio* (Harlan, J., dissenting).

Today, then, there can be no doubt that the Fifth Amendment privilege is available outside of criminal court proceedings and serves to protect persons in all settings in which their freedom of action is curtailed from being compelled to incriminate themselves. We have concluded that without proper safeguards the process of in-custody interrogation of persons suspected or accused of crime contains inherently compelling pressures which work to undermine the individual's will to resist and to compel him to speak where he would not otherwise do so freely. In order to combat these pressures and to permit a full opportunity to exercise the privilege against self-incrimination, the accused must be adequately and effectively apprised of his rights and the exercise of those rights must be fully honored.

It is impossible for us to foresee the potential alternatives for protecting the privilege which might be devised by Congress or the States in the exercise of their creative rule-making capacities. Therefore we cannot say that the Constitution necessarily requires adherence to any particular solution for the inherent compulsions of the interrogation process as it is presently conducted. Our decision in no way creates a constitutional straitjacket which will handicap sound efforts at reform, nor is it intended to have this effect. We encourage Congress and the States to continue their laudable search for increasingly effective ways of protecting the rights of the individual while promoting efficient enforcement of our criminal laws. However, unless we are shown other procedures which are at least as effective in apprising accused persons of their right of silence and in assuring a continuous opportunity to exercise it, the following safeguards must be observed.

At the outset, if a person in custody is to be subjected to interrogation, he must first be informed in clear and unequivocal terms that he has the right to remain silent. For those unaware of the privilege, the warning is needed simply to make them aware of it—the threshold requirement for an intelligent decision as to its exercise. More important, such a warning is an absolute prerequisite in overcoming the inherent pressures of the interrogation atmosphere. It is not just the subnormal or woefully ignorant who succumb to an interrogator's imprecations, whether implied or expressly stated, that the interrogation will continue

wake. See *People v. Donovan*, 193 N.E.2d 628   (N.Y.1963) (Fuld, J.).

until a confession is obtained or that silence in the face of accusation is itself damning and will bode ill when presented to a jury.[37] Further, the warning will show the individual that his interrogators are prepared to recognize his privilege should he choose to exercise it.

The Fifth Amendment privilege is so fundamental to our system of constitutional rule and the expedient of giving an adequate warning as to the availability of the privilege so simple, we will not pause to inquire in individual cases whether the defendant was aware of his rights without a warning being given. Assessments of the knowledge the defendant possessed, based on information as to his age, education, intelligence, or prior contact with authorities, can never be more than speculation;[38] a warning is a clearcut fact. More important, whatever the background of the person interrogated, a warning at the time of the interrogation is indispensable to overcome its pressures and to insure that the individual knows he is free to exercise the privilege at that point in time.

The warning of the right to remain silent must be accompanied by the explanation that anything said can and will be used against the individual in court. This warning is needed in order to make him aware not only of the privilege, but also of the consequences of forgoing it. It is only through an awareness of these consequences that there can be any assurance of real understanding and intelligent exercise of the privilege. Moreover, this warning may serve to make the individual more acutely aware that he is faced with a phase of the adversary system—that he is not in the presence of persons acting solely in his interest.

The circumstances surrounding in-custody interrogation can operate very quickly to overbear the will of one merely made aware of his privilege by his interrogators. Therefore, the right to have counsel present at the interrogation is indispensable to the protection of the Fifth Amendment privilege under the system we delineate today. Our aim is to assure that the individual's right to choose between silence and speech remains unfettered throughout the interrogation process. A once-stated warning, delivered by those who will conduct the interrogation, cannot itself suffice to that end among those who must require knowledge of their rights. A mere warning given by the interrogators is not alone sufficient to accomplish that end. Prosecutors themselves claim that the admonishment of the right to remain silent without more "will benefit only the recidivist and the professional." Brief for the National District Attorneys Association as *amicus curiae.* Even preliminary advice given to the accused by his own attorney can be swiftly overcome by the secret interrogation process. Thus, the need for counsel to protect the Fifth Amendment privilege comprehends not merely a right to consult with counsel prior to questioning but also to have counsel present during any questioning if the defendant so desires.

The presence of counsel at the interrogation may serve several significant subsidiary functions as well. If the accused decides to talk to his interrogators, the assistance of counsel can mitigate the dangers of untrustworthiness. With a lawyer present the likelihood that the police will practice coercion is reduced, and if coercion is nevertheless exercised the lawyer can testify to it in court. The presence of a lawyer can also help to guarantee that the accused gives a fully

---

37. * * * In accord with this decision, it is impermissible to penalize an individual for exercising his Fifth Amendment privilege when he is under police custodial interrogation. The prosecution may not, therefore, use at trial the fact that he stood mute or claimed his privilege in the face of accusation. Cf. *Griffin v. California* [Ch. 5, § 2].

38. Cf. *Betts v. Brady* [Ch. 5, § 1], and the recurrent inquiry into special circumstances it necessitated. * * *

accurate statement to the police and that the statement is rightly reported by the prosecution at trial. See *Crooker v. California* (Douglas, J., dissenting).

An individual need not make a preinterrogation request for a lawyer. While such request affirmatively secures his right to have one, his failure to ask for a lawyer does not constitute a waiver. No effective waiver of the right to counsel during interrogation can be recognized unless specifically made after the warnings we here delineate have been given. The accused who does not know his rights and therefore does not make a request may be the person who most needs counsel. * * *

Accordingly we hold that an individual held for interrogation must be clearly informed that he has the right to consult with a lawyer and to have the lawyer with him during interrogation under the system for protecting the privilege we delineate today. As with the warnings of the right to remain silent and that anything stated can be used in evidence against him, this warning is an absolute prerequisite to interrogation. No amount of circumstantial evidence that the person may have been aware of this right will suffice to stand in its stead. Only through such a warning is there ascertainable assurance that the accused was aware of this right.

If an individual indicates that he wishes the assistance of counsel before any interrogation occurs, the authorities cannot rationally ignore or deny his request on the basis that the individual does not have or cannot afford a retained attorney. The financial ability of the individual has no relationship to the scope of the rights involved here. The privilege against self-incrimination secured by the Constitution applies to all individuals. The need for counsel in order to protect the privilege exists for the indigent as well as the affluent. In fact, were we to limit these constitutional rights to those who can retain an attorney, our decisions today would be of little significance. The cases before us as well as the vast majority of confession cases with which we have dealt in the past involve those unable to retain counsel. While authorities are not required to relieve the accused of his poverty, they have the obligation not to take advantage of indigence in the administration of justice.[41] Denial of counsel to the indigent at the time of interrogation while allowing an attorney to those who can afford one would be no more supportable by reason or logic than the similar situation at trial and on appeal struck down in *Gideon* and *Douglas v. California.*

In order fully to apprise a person interrogated of the extent of his rights under this system then, it is necessary to warn him not only that he has the right to consult with an attorney, but also that if he is indigent a lawyer will be appointed to represent him. Without this additional warning, the admonition of the right to consult with counsel would often be understood as meaning only that he can consult with a lawyer if he has one or has the funds to obtain one. The warning of a right to counsel would be hollow if not couched in terms that would convey to the indigent—the person most often subjected to interrogation—the knowledge that he too has a right to have counsel present. As with the warnings of the right to remain silent and of the general right to counsel, only by effective and express explanation to the indigent of this right can there be assurance that he was truly in a position to exercise it.[43]

41. See Kamisar, *Equal Justice in the Gatehouses and Mansions of American Criminal Procedure,* in Criminal Justice in Our Time (1965), 64–81; * * * Report of the Attorney General's Committee on *Poverty and the Administration of Federal Criminal Justice* (1963), p. 9 * * *.

43. While a warning that the indigent may have counsel appointed need not be given to the person who is known to have an attorney or is known to have ample funds to secure one, the expedient of giving a warning is too simple and the rights involved too important to en-

Once warnings have been given, the subsequent procedure is clear. If the individual indicates in any manner, at any time prior to or during questioning, that he wishes to remain silent, the interrogation must cease.[44] At this point he has shown that he intends to exercise his Fifth Amendment privilege; any statement taken after the person invokes his privilege cannot be other than the product of compulsion, subtle or otherwise. Without the right to cut off questioning, the setting of in-custody interrogation operates on the individual to overcome free choice in producing a statement after the privilege has been once invoked. If the individual states that he wants an attorney, the interrogation must cease until an attorney is present. At that time, the individual must have an opportunity to confer with the attorney and to have him present during any subsequent questioning. If the individual cannot obtain an attorney and he indicates that he wants one before speaking to police, they must respect his decision to remain silent.

This does not mean, as some have suggested, that each police station must have a "station house lawyer" present at all times to advise prisoners. It does mean, however, that if police propose to interrogate a person they must make known to him that he is entitled to a lawyer and that if he cannot afford one, a lawyer will be provided for him prior to any interrogation. If authorities conclude that they will not provide counsel during a reasonable period of time in which investigation in the field is carried out, they may do so without violating the person's Fifth Amendment privilege so long as they do not question him during that time.

If the interrogation continues without the presence of an attorney and a statement is taken, a heavy burden rests on the Government to demonstrate that the defendant knowingly and intelligently waived his privilege against self-incrimination and his right to retained or appointed counsel. This Court has always set high standards of proof for the waiver of constitutional rights, *Johnson v. Zerbst,* and we reassert these standards as applied to in-custody interrogation. Since the State is responsible for establishing the isolated circumstances under which the interrogation takes place and has the only means of making available corroborated evidence of warnings given during incommunicado interrogation, the burden is rightly on its shoulders.

An express statement that the individual is willing to make a statement and does not want an attorney followed closely by a statement could constitute a waiver. But a valid waiver will not be presumed simply from the silence of the accused after warnings are given or simply from the fact that a confession was in fact eventually obtained. A statement we made in *Carnley v. Cochran,* 369 U.S. 506 (1962), is applicable here:

> "Presuming waiver from a silent record is impermissible. The record must show, or there must be an allegation and evidence which show, that an accused was offered counsel but intelligently and understandably rejected the offer. Anything less is not waiver."

* * * Moreover, where in-custody interrogation is involved, there is no room for the contention that the privilege is waived if the individual answers some

---

gage in *ex post facto* inquiries into financial ability when there is any doubt at all on that score.

44. If an individual indicates his desire to remain silent, but has an attorney present, there may be some circumstances in which further questioning would be permissible. In the absence of evidence of overbearing, statements then made in the presence of counsel might be free of the compelling influence of the interrogation process and might fairly be construed as a waiver of the privilege for purposes of these statements.

questions or gives some information on his own prior to invoking his right to remain silent when interrogated.[45]

Whatever the testimony of the authorities as to waiver of rights by an accused, the fact of lengthy interrogation or incommunicado incarceration before a statement is made is strong evidence that the accused did not validly waive his rights. In these circumstances the fact that the individual eventually made a statement is consistent with the conclusion that the compelling influence of the interrogation finally forced him to do so. It is inconsistent with any notion of a voluntary relinquishment of the privilege. Moreover, any evidence that the accused was threatened, tricked, or cajoled into a waiver will, of course, show that the defendant did not voluntarily waive his privilege. The requirement of warnings and waiver of rights is a fundamental with respect to the Fifth Amendment privilege and not simply a preliminary ritual to existing methods of interrogation.

The warnings required and the waiver necessary in accordance with our opinion today are, in the absence of a fully effective equivalent, prerequisites to the admissibility of any statement made by a defendant. No distinction can be drawn between statements which are direct confessions and statements which amount to "admissions" of part or all of an offense. The privilege against self-incrimination protects the individual from being compelled to incriminate himself in any manner; it does not distinguish degrees of incrimination. Similarly, for precisely the same reason, no distinction may be drawn between inculpatory statements and statements alleged to be merely "exculpatory." If a statement made were in fact truly exculpatory it would, of course, never be used by the prosecution. In fact, statements merely intended to be exculpatory by the defendant are often used to impeach his testimony at trial or to demonstrate untruths in the statement given under interrogation and thus to prove guilt by implication. These statements are incriminating in any meaningful sense of the word and may not be used without the full warnings and effective waiver required for any other statement. In *Escobedo* itself, the defendant fully intended his accusation of another as the slayer to be exculpatory as to himself.

The principles announced today deal with the protection which must be given to the privilege against self-incrimination when the individual is first subjected to police interrogation while in custody at the station or otherwise deprived of his freedom of action in any significant way. It is at this point that our adversary system of criminal proceedings commences, distinguishing itself at the outset from the inquisitorial system recognized in some countries. Under the system of warnings we delineate today or under any other system which may be devised and found effective, the safeguards to be erected about the privilege must come into play at this point.

Our decision is not intended to hamper the traditional function of police officers in investigating crime. When an individual is in custody on probable cause, the police may, of course, seek out evidence in the field to be used at trial against him. Such investigation may include inquiry of persons not under restraint. General on-the-scene questioning as to facts surrounding a crime or other general questioning of citizens in the fact-finding process is not affected by

---

45. Although this Court held in *Rogers v. United States,* 340 U.S. 367 (1951), over strong dissent, that a witness before a grand jury may not in certain circumstances decide to answer some questions and then refuse to answer others that decision has no application to the interrogation situation we deal with today. No legislative or judicial fact-finding authority is involved here, nor is there a possibility that the individual might make self-serving statements of which he could make use at trial while refusing to answer incriminating statements.

our holding. It is an act of responsible citizenship for individuals to give whatever information they may have to aid in law enforcement. In such situations the compelling atmosphere inherent in the process of in-custody interrogation is not necessarily present.[46]

In dealing with statements obtained through interrogation, we do not purport to find all confessions inadmissible. Confessions remain a proper element in law enforcement. Any statement given freely and voluntarily without any compelling influences is, of course, admissible in evidence. The fundamental import of the privilege while an individual is in custody is not whether he is allowed to talk to the police without the benefit of warnings and counsel, but whether he can be interrogated. There is no requirement that police stop a person who enters a police station and states that he wishes to confess to a crime, or a person who calls the police to offer a confession or any other statement he desires to make. Volunteered statements of any kind are not barred by the Fifth Amendment and their admissibility is not affected by our holding today.

To summarize, we hold that when an individual is taken into custody or otherwise deprived of his freedom by the authorities in any significant way and is subjected to questioning, the privilege against self-incrimination is jeopardized. Procedural safeguards must be employed to protect the privilege, and unless other fully effective means are adopted to notify the person of his right of silence and to assure that the exercise of the right will be scrupulously honored, the following measures are required. He must be warned prior to any questioning that he has the right to remain silent, that anything he says can be used against him in a court of law, that he has the right to the presence of an attorney, and that if he cannot afford an attorney one will be appointed for him prior to any questioning if he so desires. Opportunity to exercise these rights must be afforded to him throughout the interrogation. After such warnings have been given, and such opportunity afforded him, the individual may knowingly and intelligently waive these rights and agree to answer questions or make a statement. But unless and until such warnings and waiver are demonstrated by the prosecution at trial, no evidence obtained as a result of interrogation can be used against him. * * *

If the individual desires to exercise his privilege, he has the right to do so. This is not for the authorities to decide. An attorney may advise his client not to talk to police until he has had an opportunity to investigate the case, or he may wish to be present with his client during any police questioning. In doing so an attorney is merely exercising the good professional judgment he has been taught. This is not cause for considering the attorney a menace to law enforcement. He is merely carrying out what he is sworn to do under his oath—to protect to the extent of his ability the rights of his client. In fulfilling this responsibility the attorney plays a vital role in the administration of criminal justice under our Constitution.

In announcing these principles, we are not unmindful of the burdens which law enforcement officials must bear, often under trying circumstances. We also fully recognize the obligation of all citizens to aid in enforcing the criminal law. This Court, while protecting individual rights, has always given ample latitude to law enforcement agencies in the legitimate exercise of their duties. The limits we have placed on the interrogation process should not constitute an undue interfer-

---

46. The distinction and its significance has been aptly described in the opinion of a Scottish court:

"In former times such questioning, if undertaken, would be conducted by police officers visiting the house or place of business of the suspect and there questioning him, probably in the presence of a relation or friend. However convenient the modern practice may be, it must normally create a situation very unfavorable to the suspect." *Chalmers v. H.M. Advocate,* [1954] Sess.Cas. 66, 78 (J.C.).

ence with a proper system of law enforcement. As we have noted, our decision does not in any way preclude police from carrying out their traditional investigatory functions. Although confessions may play an important role in some convictions, the cases before us present graphic examples of the overstatement of the "need" for confessions. In each case authorities conducted interrogations ranging up to five days in duration despite the presence, through standard investigating practices, of considerable evidence against each defendant.[51] Further examples are chronicled in our prior cases.[52]

It is also urged that an unfettered right to detention for interrogation should be allowed because it will often redound to the benefit of the person questioned. When police inquiry determines that there is no reason to believe that the person has committed any crime, it is said, he will be released without need for further formal procedures. The person who has committed no offense, however, will be better able to clear himself after warnings, with counsel present than without. It can be assumed that in such circumstances a lawyer would advise his client to talk freely to police in order to clear himself.

Custodial interrogation, by contrast, does not necessarily afford the innocent an opportunity to clear themselves. A serious consequence of the present practice of the interrogation alleged to be beneficial for the innocent is that many arrests "for investigation" subject large numbers of innocent persons to detention and interrogation. In one of the cases before us, *California v. Stewart,* police held four persons, who were in the defendant's house at the time of the arrest, in jail for five days until defendant confessed. At that time they were finally released. Police stated that there was "no evidence to connect them with any crime." Available statistics on the extent of this practice where it is condoned indicate that these four are far from alone in being subjected to arrest, prolonged detention, and interrogation without the requisite probable cause. * * *

The experience in some other countries * * * suggests that the danger to law enforcement in curbs on interrogation is overplayed. The English procedure since 1912 under the Judge's Rules is significant. As recently strengthened, the Rules require that a cautionary warning be given an accused by a police officer as soon as he has evidence that affords reasonable grounds for suspicion; they also require that any statement made be given by the accused without questioning by police.[57] The right of the individual to consult with an attorney during this period is expressly recognized. * * *

---

51. Miranda, Vignera, and Westover were identified by eyewitnesses. Marked bills from the bank robbed were found in Westover's car. Articles stolen from the victim as well as from several other robbery victims were found in Stewart's home at the outset of the investigation.

52. Dealing as we do here with constitutional standards in relation to statements made, the existence of independent corroborating evidence produced at trial is, of course, irrelevant to our decisions. * * *

57. [1964] Crim.L.Rev. 166–170. These Rules provide in part:

"II. As soon as a police officer has evidence which would afford reasonable grounds for suspecting that a person has committed an offence, he shall caution that person or cause him to be cautioned before putting to him any questions, or further questions, relating to that offence.

"The caution shall be in the following terms:

" 'You are not obliged to say anything unless you wish to do so but what you say may be put into writing and given in evidence.'

"When after being cautioned a person is being questioned, or elects to make a statement, a record shall be kept of the time and place at which any such questioning or statement began and ended and of the persons present.

* * *

"(b) It is only in exceptional cases that questions relating to the offence should be put to the accused person after he has been charged or informed that he may be prosecuted.

* * *

Because of the nature of the problem and because of its recurrent significance in numerous cases, we have to this point discussed the relationship of the Fifth Amendment privilege to police interrogation without specific concentration on the facts of the cases before us. We turn now to these facts to consider the application to these cases of the constitutional principles discussed above. In each instance, we have concluded that statements were obtained from the defendant under circumstances that did not meet constitutional standards for protection of the privilege.

No. 759. *Miranda v. Arizona.*

On March 13, 1963, petitioner, Ernesto Miranda, was arrested at his home and taken in custody to a Phoenix police station. He was there identified by the complaining witness. The police then took him to "Interrogation Room No. 2" of the detective bureau. There he was questioned by two police officers. The officers admitted at trial that Miranda was not advised that he had a right to have an attorney present. Two hours later, the officers emerged from the interrogation room with a written confession signed by Miranda. At the top of the statement was a typed paragraph stating that the confession was made voluntarily, without threats or promises of immunity and "with full knowledge of my legal rights, understanding any statement I make may be used against me." [67]

[Miranda] was found guilty of kidnapping and rape. [On] appeal, the Supreme Court of Arizona held that Miranda's constitutional rights were not violated in obtaining the confession and affirmed the conviction. In reaching its decision, the court emphasized heavily the fact that Miranda did not specifically request counsel.

We reverse. From the testimony of the officers and by the admission of respondent, it is clear that Miranda was not in any way apprised of his right to consult with an attorney and to have one present during the interrogation, nor was his right not to be compelled to incriminate himself effectively protected in any other manner. Without these warnings the statements were inadmissible. The mere fact that he signed a statement which contained a typed-in clause stating that he had "full knowledge" of his legal rights does not approach the knowing and intelligent waiver required to relinquish constitutional rights. * * *

No. 760. *Vignera v. New York.*

"IV. All written statements made after caution shall be taken in the following manner:

"(a) If a person says that he wants to make a statement he shall be told that it is intended to make a written record of what he says.

"He shall always be asked whether he wishes to write down himself what he wants to say; if he says that he cannot write or that he would like someone to write it for him, a police officer may offer to write the statement for him. * * *

"(b) Any person writing his own statement shall be allowed to do so without any prompting as distinct from indicating to him what matters are material.

* * *

"(d) Whenever a police officer writes the statement, he shall take down the exact words spoken by the person making the statement, without putting any questions other than such as may be needed to make the statement co-herent, intelligible and relevant to the material matters: he shall not prompt him." * * *

[Ed. Note—*The Police and Criminal Evidence 1984* grants British police new powers. E.g., the police are permitted to detain a person without charge for questioning for 24 hours and under certain circumstances to detain a person arrested for a "serious arrestable offense" (e.g., treason, terrorism, murder and kidnapping) up to 36 hours when authorized by a police officer of at least superintendent rank. To counterbalance these additional police powers, the Act contains new safeguards. E.g., a person detained in custody has a right to have this fact notified to a friend or relative and a person detained for an offense other than a "serious arrestable offense" has an absolute right to consult a solicitor at any time.]

67. One of the officers testified that he read this paragraph to Miranda. Apparently, however, he did not do so until after Miranda had confessed orally.

Petitioner, Michael Vignera, was picked up by New York police on October 14, 1960, in connection with the robbery three days earlier of a Brooklyn dress shop. They took him to the 17th Detective Squad headquarters in Manhattan. Sometime thereafter he was taken to the 66th Detective Squad. There a detective questioned Vignera with respect to the robbery. Vignera orally admitted the robbery to the detective. [T]he defense was precluded from making any showing that warnings had not been given. While at the 66th Detective Squad, Vignera was identified by the store owner and a saleslady as the man who robbed the dress shop. At about 3:00 p.m. he was formally arrested. The police then transported him to still another station, the 70th Precinct in Brooklyn, "for detention". At 11:00 p.m. Vignera was questioned by an assistant district attorney in the presence of a hearing reporter who transcribed the questions and Vignera's answers. This verbatim account of these proceedings contains no statement of any warnings given by the assistant district attorney. * * *

Vignera was [convicted of first degree robbery]. We reverse. The foregoing indicates that Vignera was not warned of any of his rights before the questioning by the detective and by the assistant district attorney. No other steps were taken to protect these rights. Thus he was not effectively apprised of his Fifth Amendment privilege or of his right to have counsel present and his statements are inadmissible.

No. 761.   *Westover v. United States.*

At approximately 9:45 p.m. on March 20, 1963, petitioner, Carl Calvin Westover, was arrested by local police in Kansas City as a suspect in two Kansas City robberies. A report was also received from the FBI that he was wanted on a felony charge in California. The local authorities took him to a police station and placed him in a line-up on the local charges, and at about 11:45 p.m. he was booked. Kansas City police interrogated Westover on the night of his arrest. He denied any knowledge of criminal activities. The next day local officers interrogated him again throughout the morning. Shortly before noon they informed the FBI that they were through interrogating Westover and that the FBI could proceed to interrogate him. There is nothing in the record to indicate that Westover was ever given any warning as to his rights by local police. At noon, three special agents of the FBI continued the interrogation in a private interview room of the Kansas City Police Department, this time with respect to the robbery of a savings and loan association and a bank in Sacramento, California. After two or two and one-half hours, Westover signed separate confessions to each of these two robberies which had been prepared by one of the agents during the interrogation. At trial one of the agents testified, and a paragraph on each of the statements states, that the agents advised Westover that he did not have to make a statement, that any statement he made could be used against him, and that he had the right to see an attorney.

Westover was tried by a jury in federal court and convicted of the California robberies. * * *

We reverse. On the facts of this case we cannot find that Westover knowingly and intelligently waived his right to remain silent and his right to consult with counsel prior to the time he made the statement. At the time the FBI agents began questioning Westover, he had been in custody for over 14 hours and had been interrogated at length during that period. The FBI interrogation began immediately upon the conclusion of the interrogation by Kansas City police and was conducted in local police headquarters. Although the two law enforcement authorities are legally distinct and the crimes for which they interrogated Westover were different, the impact on him was that of a continuous period of questioning. There is no evidence of any warning given prior to the FBI interrogation nor is there any evidence of an articulated waiver of rights after the FBI commenced their interrogation. The record simply shows that the defendant did in fact confess a short time after being turned over to the FBI following interrogation by local police. Despite the fact that the FBI agents gave warnings at the outset of their interview, from Westover's point of view the warnings came at the end of the interrogation process. In these circumstances an intelligent waiver of constitutional rights cannot be assumed.

We do not suggest that law enforcement authorities are precluded from questioning any individual who has been held for a period of time by other authorities and interrogated by them without appropriate warnings. A different case would be presented if an accused were taken into custody by the second authority, removed both in time and place from his original surroundings, and then adequately advised of his rights and given an opportunity to exercise them. But here the FBI interrogation was conducted immediately following the state interrogation in the same police station—in the same compelling surroundings. Thus, in obtaining a confession from Westover the federal authorities were the beneficiaries of the pressure applied by the local in-custody interrogation. In these circumstances the giving of warnings alone was not sufficient to protect the privilege.

No. 584.   *California v. Stewart.*

In the course of investigating a series of purse-snatch robberies in which one of the victims had died of injuries inflicted by her assailant, respondent, Roy Allen Stewart, was pointed out to Los Angeles police as the endorser of dividend checks taken in one of the robberies. At about 7:15 p.m., January 31, 1963, police officers went to Stewart's house and arrested him. One of the officers asked Stewart if they could search the house, to which he replied, "Go ahead." The search turned up various items taken from the five robbery victims. At the time of Stewart's arrest, police also arrested Stewart's wife and three other persons who were visiting him. These four were jailed along with Stewart and were interrogated. Stewart was taken to the University Station of the Los Angeles Police Department where he was placed in a cell. During the next five days, police interrogated Stewart on nine different occasions. Except during the first interrogation session, when he was confronted with an accusing witness, Stewart was isolated with his interrogators.

During the ninth interrogation session, Stewart admitted that he had robbed the deceased and stated that he had not meant to hurt her. Police then brought Stewart before a magistrate for the first time. Since there was no evidence to connect them with any crime, the police then released the other four persons arrested with him.

Nothing in the record specifically indicates whether Stewart was or was not advised of his right to remain silent or his right to counsel. In a number of instances, however, the interrogating officers were asked to recount everything that was said during the interrogations. None indicated that Stewart was ever advised of his rights.

[The] jury found Stewart guilty of robbery and first degree murder and fixed the penalty as death. On appeal, the Supreme Court of California reversed. It held that under this Court's decision in *Escobedo,* Stewart should have been advised of his right to remain silent and of his right to counsel and that it would not presume in the face of a silent record that the police advised Stewart of his rights.

We affirm. In dealing with custodial interrogation, we will not presume that a defendant has been effectively apprised of his rights and that his privilege against self-incrimination has been adequately safe-guarded on a record that does not show that any warnings have been given or that any effective alternative has been employed. Nor can a knowing and intelligent waiver of these rights be assumed on a silent record. Furthermore, Stewart's steadfast denial of the alleged offenses through eight of the nine interrogations over a period of five days is subject to no other construction than that he was compelled by persistent interrogation to forgo his Fifth Amendment privilege.

Therefore, in accordance with the foregoing, [*Miranda,*[a] *Vignera,* and *Westover* are reversed and *Stewart* is affirmed].[b]

JUSTICE CLARK, dissenting in [*Miranda, Vignera,* and *Westover,* and concurring in the result in *Stewart.*]

[I cannot] agree with the Court's characterization of the present practices of police and investigatory agencies as to custodial interrogation. The materials referred to as "police manuals" are not shown by the record here to be the official manuals of any police department, much less in universal use in crime detection. Moreover, the examples of police brutality mentioned by the Court are rare exceptions to the thousands of cases that appear every year in the law reports. * * *

[The Court's] strict constitutional specific inserted at the nerve center of crime detection may well kill the patient. Since there is at this time a paucity of information and an almost total lack of empirical knowledge on the practical operation of requirements truly comparable to those announced by the majority, I would be more restrained lest we go too far too fast. * * *

Rather than employing the arbitrary Fifth Amendment rule which the Court lays down I would follow the more pliable dictates of Due Process Clauses of the Fifth and Fourteenth Amendments which we are accustomed to administering and which we know from our cases are effective instruments in protecting persons in police custody. In this way we would not be acting in the dark nor in one full sweep changing the traditional rules of custodial interrogation which this Court has for so long recognized as a justifiable and proper tool in balancing individual rights against the rights of society. It will be soon enough to go further when we are able to appraise with somewhat better accuracy the effect of such a holding. * * *

JUSTICE HARLAN, whom JUSTICE STEWART and JUSTICE WHITE join, dissenting. * * *

While the fine points of [the Court's new constitutional code of rules for confessions] are far less clear than the Court admits, the tenor is quite apparent. The new rules are not designed to guard against police brutality or other unmistakably banned forms of coercion. Those who use third-degree tactics and deny them in court are equally able and destined to lie as skillfully about warnings and waivers. Rather, the thrust of the new rules is to negate all pressures, to reinforce the nervous or ignorant suspect, and ultimately to discourage any confession at all. The aim in short is toward "voluntariness" in a utopian sense, or to view it from a different angle, voluntariness with a vengeance.

---

a. On retrial, *Miranda* was again convicted of kidnapping and rape. The conviction was affirmed in *State v. Miranda,* 104 Ariz. 174, 450 P.2d 364 (1969).

b. A week later, the Court ruled that *Escobedo* and *Miranda* applied only to trials begun after the decisions were announced.

To incorporate this notion into the Constitution requires a strained reading of history and precedent and a disregard of the very pragmatic concerns that alone may on occasion justify such strains. I believe that reasoned examination will show that the Due Process Clauses provide an adequate tool for coping with confessions and that, even if the Fifth Amendment privilege against self-incrimination be invoked, its precedents taken as a whole do not sustain the present rules. Viewed as a choice based on pure policy, these new rules prove to be a highly debatable if not one-sided appraisal of the competing interests, imposed over wide-spread objection, at the very time when judicial restraint is most called for by the circumstances. * * *

[The] Court's asserted reliance on the Fifth Amendment [is] an approach which I frankly regard as a *trompe l'oeil*. The Court's opinion in my view reveals no adequate basis for extending the Fifth Amendment's privilege against self-incrimination to the police station. Far more important, it fails to show that the Court's new rules are well supported, let alone compelled, by Fifth Amendment precedents. Instead, the new rules actually derive from quotation and analogy drawn from precedents under the Sixth Amendment, which should properly have no bearing on police interrogation. * * *

Having decided that the Fifth Amendment privilege does apply in the police station, the Court reveals that the privilege imposes more exacting restrictions than does the Fourteenth Amendment's voluntariness test. It then emerges from a discussion of *Escobedo* that the Fifth Amendment requires for an admissible confession that it be given by one distinctly aware of his right not to speak and shielded from "the compelling atmosphere" of interrogation. From these key premises, the Court finally develops the safeguards of warning, counsel, and so forth. I do not believe these premises are sustained by precedents under the Fifth Amendment.[9]

The more important premise is that pressure on the suspect must be eliminated though it be only the subtle influence of the atmosphere and surroundings. The Fifth Amendment, however, has never been thought to forbid *all* pressure to incriminate one's self in the situations covered by it. * * *

A closing word must be said about the Assistance of Counsel Clause of the Sixth Amendment, which is never expressly relied on by the Court but whose judicial precedents turn out to be linchpins of the confession rules announced today. * * *

The only attempt in this Court to carry the right to counsel into the station house occurred in *Escobedo*, the Court repeating several times that that stage was no less "critical" than trial itself. * * * This is hardly persuasive when we consider that a grand jury inquiry, the filing of a certiorari petition, and certainly the purchase of narcotics by an undercover agent from a prospective defendant may all be equally "critical" yet provision of counsel and advice on that score have never been thought compelled by the Constitution in such cases. The sound reason why this right is so freely extended for a criminal trial is the severe injustice risked by confronting an untrained defendant with a range of technical points of law, evidence, and tactics familiar to the prosecutor but not to himself. This danger shrinks markedly in the police station where indeed the lawyer in fulfilling his professional responsibilities of necessity may become an obstacle to truthfinding. See infra, n. 12. * * *

9. I lay aside *Escobedo* itself; it contains no reasoning or even general conclusions addressed to the Fifth Amendment and indeed its citation in this regard seems surprising in view of *Escobedo's* primary reliance on the Sixth Amendment.

The Court's new rules aim to offset [the] minor pressures and disadvantages intrinsic to any kind of police interrogation. The rules do not serve due process interests in preventing blatant coercion since, as I noted earlier, they do nothing to contain the policeman who is prepared to lie from the start. The rules work for reliability in confessions almost only in the Pickwickian sense that they can prevent some from being given at all.[12] * * *

What the Court largely ignores is that its rules impair, if they will not eventually serve wholly to frustrate, an instrument of law enforcement that has long and quite reasonably been thought worth the price paid for it. There can be little doubt that the Court's new code would markedly decrease the number of confessions. To warn the suspect that he may remain silent and remind him that his confession may be used in court are minor obstructions. To require also an express waiver by the suspect and an end to questioning whenever he demurs must heavily handicap questioning. And to suggest or provide counsel for the suspect simply invites the end of the interrogation. See supra, n. 12. * * *

While passing over the costs and risks of its experiment, the Court portrays the evils of normal police questioning in terms which I think are exaggerated. Albeit stringently confined by the due process standards interrogation is no doubt often inconvenient and unpleasant for the suspect. However, it is no less so for a man to be arrested and jailed, to have his house searched, or to stand trial in court, yet all this may properly happen to the most innocent given probable cause, a warrant, or an indictment. Society has always paid a stiff price for law and order, and peaceful interrogation is not one of the dark moments of the law.

This brief statement of the competing considerations seems to me ample proof that the Court's preference is highly debatable at best and therefore not to be read into the Constitution. However, it may make the analysis more graphic to consider the actual facts of one of the four cases reversed by the Court. *Miranda* serves best, being neither the hardest nor easiest of the four under the Court's standards.[15]

On March 3, 1963, an 18–year–old girl was kidnapped and forcibly raped near Phoenix, Arizona. Ten days later, on the morning of March 13, petitioner Miranda was arrested and taken to the police station. At this time Miranda was 23 years old, indigent, and educated to the extent of completing half the ninth grade. He had "an emotional illness" of the schizophrenic type, according to the doctor who eventually examined him; the doctor's report also stated that Miranda was "alert and oriented as to time, place, and person", intelligent within normal limits, competent to stand trial, and sane within the legal definition. At the police station, the victim picked Miranda out of a lineup, and two officers then took him into a separate room to interrogate him, starting about 11:30 a.m. Though at first denying his guilt, within a short time Miranda gave a detailed oral confession and then wrote out in his own hand and signed a brief statement admitting and describing the crime. All this was accomplished in two hours or less without any force, threats or promises and—I will assume this though the record is uncertain * * *—without any effective warnings at all.

---

12. The Court's vision of a lawyer "mitigat[ing] the dangers of untrustworthiness" by witnessing coercion and assisting accuracy in the confession is largely a fancy; for if counsel arrives, there is rarely going to be a police station confession. *Watts v. Indiana* (separate opinion of Jackson, J.): "[A]ny lawyer worth his salt will tell the suspect in no uncertain terms to make no statement to police under any circumstances."

15. In *Westover*, a seasoned criminal was practically given the Court's full complement of warnings and did not heed them. The *Stewart* case, on the other hand, involves long detention and successive questioning. In *Vignera*, the facts are complicated and the record somewhat incomplete.

Miranda's oral and written confessions are now held inadmissible under the Court's new rules. One is entitled to feel astonished that the Constitution can be read to produce this result. These confessions were obtained during brief, daytime questioning conducted by two officers and unmarked by any of the traditional indicia of coercion. They assured a conviction for a brutal and unsettling crime, for which the police had and quite possibly could obtain little evidence other than the victim's identifications, evidence which is frequently unreliable. There was, in sum, a legitimate purpose, no perceptible unfairness, and certainly little risk of injustice in the interrogation. Yet the resulting confessions, and the responsible course of police practice they represent, are to be sacrificed to the Court's own finespun conception of fairness which I seriously doubt is shared by many thinking citizens in this country. * * *

[It is] instructive to compare the attitude in this case of those responsible for law enforcement with the official views that existed when the Court undertook three major revisions of prosecutorial practice prior to this case, *Johnson v. Zerbst, Mapp,* and *Gideon.* In *Johnson,* which established that appointed counsel must be offered the indigent in federal criminal trials, the Federal Government all but conceded the basic issue, which had in fact been recently fixed as Department of Justice policy. In *Mapp,* which imposed the exclusionary rule on the States for Fourth Amendment violations, more than half of the States had themselves already adopted some such rule. In *Gideon,* which extended *Johnson v. Zerbst* to the States, an *amicus* brief was filed by 22 States and Commonwealths urging that course; only two States beside the respondent came forward to protest. By contrast, in this case new restrictions on police questioning have been opposed by the United States and in an *amicus* brief signed by 27 States and Commonwealths, not including the three other States who are parties. No State in the country has urged this Court to impose the newly announced rules, nor has any State chosen to go nearly so far on its own. * * *

The law of the foreign countries described by the Court * * * reflects a more moderate conception of the rights of the accused as against those of society when other data is considered. Concededly, the English experience is most relevant. In that country, a caution as to silence but not counsel has long been mandated by the "Judges' Rules," which also place other somewhat imprecise limits on police cross-examination of suspects. However, in the court's discretion confessions can be and apparently quite frequently are admitted in evidence despite disregard of the Judges' Rules, so long as they are found voluntary under the common-law test. Moreover, the check that exists on the use of pretrial statements is counterbalanced by the evident admissibility of fruits of an illegal confession and by the judge's often-used authority to comment adversely on the defendant's failure to testify. * * *

[S]ome reference must be made to [the] ironic untimeliness [of these confession rules]. There is now in progress in this country a massive re-examination of criminal law enforcement procedures on a scale never before witnessed. Participants in this undertaking include a Special Committee of the American Bar Association, under the chairmanship of Chief Judge Lumbard of the Court of Appeals for the Second Circuit; a distinguished study group of the American Law Institute, headed by Professor Vorenberg of the Harvard Law School; and the President's Commission on Law Enforcement and Administration of Justice, under the leadership of the Attorney General of the United States. Studies are also being conducted by [other groups] equipped to do practical research. * * *

It is no secret that concern has been expressed lest long-range and lasting reforms be frustrated by this Court's too rapid departure from existing constitutional standards. Despite the Court's disclaimer, the practical effect of the decision made today must inevitably be to handicap seriously sound efforts at reform, not least by removing options necessary to a just compromise of competing interests. [T]he legislative reforms when they came would have the vast advantage of empirical data and comprehensive study, they would allow experimentation and use of solutions not open to the courts, and they would restore the initiative in criminal law reform to those forums where it truly belongs. * * *

JUSTICE WHITE, with whom JUSTICE HARLAN and JUSTICE STEWART join, dissenting.

The proposition that the privilege against self-incrimination forbids in-custody interrogation without the warnings specified in the majority opinion and without a clear waiver of counsel has no significant support in the history of the privilege or in the language of the Fifth Amendment. As for the English authorities and the common-law history, the privilege, firmly established in the second half of the seventeenth century, was never applied except to prohibit compelled judicial interrogations. The rule excluding coerced confessions matured about 100 years later, "[b]ut there is nothing in the reports to suggest that the theory has its roots in the privilege against self-incrimination. And so far as the cases reveal, the privilege, as such, seems to have been given effect only in judicial proceedings, including the preliminary examinations by authorized magistrates." Morgan, _The Privilege Against Self–Incrimination,_ 34 Minn.L.Rev. 1, 18 (1949). * * *

That the Court's holding today is neither compelled nor even strongly suggested by the language of the Fifth Amendment, is at odds with American and English legal history, and involves a departure from a long line of precedent does not prove either that the Court has exceeded its powers or that the Court is wrong or unwise in its present reinterpretation of the Fifth Amendment. It does, however, underscore the obvious—that the Court has not discovered or found the law in making today's decision, nor has it derived it from some irrefutable sources; what it has done is to make new law and new public policy in much the same way that it has in the course of interpreting other great clauses of the Constitution. This is what the Court historically has done. Indeed, it is what it must do and will continue to do until and unless there is some fundamental change in the constitutional distribution of governmental powers.

But if the Court is here and now to announce new and fundamental policy to govern certain aspects of our affairs, it is wholly legitimate to examine the mode of this or any other constitutional decision in this Court and to inquire into the advisability of its end product in terms of the long-range interest of the country. At the very least the Court's text and reasoning should withstand analysis and be a fair exposition of the constitutional provision which its opinion interprets. Decisions like these cannot rest alone on syllogism, metaphysics or some ill-defined notions of natural justice, although each will perhaps play its part. * * *

[The Court] extrapolates a picture of what it conceives to be the norm from police investigatorial manuals, published in 1959 and 1962 or earlier, without any attempt to allow for adjustments in police practices that may have occurred in the wake of more recent decisions of state appellate tribunals or this Court. But even if the relentless application of the described procedures could lead to involuntary confessions, it most assuredly does not follow that each and every case will disclose this kind of interrogation or this kind of consequence.[2] Insofar as it

---

2. In fact, the type of sustained interrogation described by the Court appears to be the exception rather than the rule. A survey of 399 cases in one city found that in almost half of the cases the interrogation lasted less than 30 minutes. Barrett, _Police Practices and the Law—From Arrest to Release or Charge,_ 50 Calif.L.Rev. 11, 41–45 (1962). Questioning appears from the Court's opinion, it has not examined a single transcript of any police interrogation, let alone the interrogation that took place in any one of these cases which it decides today. Judged by any of the standards for empirical investigation utilized in the social sciences the factual basis for the Court's premises is patently inadequate.

Although in the Court's view in-custody interrogation is inherently coercive, it says that the spontaneous product of the coercion of arrest and detention is still to be deemed voluntary. An accused, arrested on probable cause, may blurt out a confession which will be admissible despite the fact that he is alone and in custody, without any showing that he had any notion of his right to remain silent or of the consequences of his admission. Yet, under the Court's rule, if the police ask him a single question such as "Do you have anything to say?" or "Did you kill your wife?" his response, if there is one, has somehow been compelled, even if the accused has been clearly warned of his right to remain silent. Common sense informs us to the contrary. While one may say that the response was "involuntary" in the sense the question provoked or was the occasion for the response and thus the defendant was induced to speak out when he might have remained silent if not arrested and not questioned, it is patently unsound to say the response is compelled. * * *

If the rule announced today were truly based on a conclusion that all confessions resulting from custodial interrogation are coerced, then it would simply have no rational foundation. * * * Even if one were to postulate that the Court's concern is not that all confessions induced by police interrogation are coerced but rather that some such confessions are coerced and present judicial procedures are believed to be inadequate to identify the confessions that are coerced and those that are not, it would still not be essential to impose the rule that the Court has now fashioned. Transcripts or observers could be required, specific time limits, tailored to fit the cause, could be imposed, or other devices could be utilized to reduce the chances that otherwise indiscernible coercion will produce an inadmissible confession.

On the other hand, even if one assumed that there was an adequate factual basis for the conclusion that all confessions obtained during in-custody interrogation are the product of compulsion, the rule propounded by the Court would still be irrational, for, apparently, it is only if the accused is also warned of his right to counsel and waives both that right and the right against self-incrimination that the inherent compulsiveness of interrogation disappears. But if the defendant may not answer without a warning a question such as "Where were you last night?" without having his answer be a compelled one, how can the court ever accept his negative answer to the question of whether he wants to consult his retained counsel or counsel whom the court will appoint? And why if counsel is present and the accused nevertheless confesses, or counsel tells the accused to tell the truth, and that is what the accused does, is the situation any less coercive insofar as the accused is concerned? The court apparently realizes its dilemma of foreclosing questioning without the necessary warnings but at the same time permitting the accused, sitting in the same chair in front of the same policemen, to waive his right to consult an attorney. It expects, however, that not too many will waive the right; and if it is claimed that he has, the State faces a severe, if not impossible burden of proof.

tends to be confused and sporadic and is usually concentrated on confrontations with witnesses or new items of evidence, as these are obtained by officers conducting the investigation. See generally LaFave, *Arrest: The Decision to Take a Suspect into Custody 386 (1965); ALI,* Model Pre–Arraignment Procedure Code, *Commentary § 5.01, at 170, n. 4 (Tent.Draft No. 1, 1966).*

All of this makes very little sense in terms of the compulsion which the Fifth Amendment proscribes. That amendment deals with compelling the accused himself. It is his free will that is involved. Confessions and incriminating admissions, as such, are not forbidden evidence; only those which are compelled are banned. I doubt that the Court observes these distinctions today. By considering any answers to any interrogation to be compelled regardless of the content and course of examination and by escalating the requirements to prove waiver, the Court not only prevents the use of compelled confessions but for all practical purposes forbids interrogation except in the presence of counsel. That is, instead of confining itself to protection of the right against compelled self-incrimination the Court has created a limited Fifth Amendment right to counsel— or, as the Court expresses it, a "right to counsel to protect the Fifth Amendment privilege * * *." The focus then is not on the will of the accused but on the will of counsel and how much influence he can have on the accused. Obviously there is no warrant in the Fifth Amendment for thus installing counsel as the arbiter of the privilege.

In sum, for all the Court's expounding on the menacing atmosphere of police interrogation procedures it has failed to supply any foundation for the conclusions it draws or the measures it adopts.

Criticism of the Court's opinion, however, cannot stop at a demonstration that the factual and textual bases for the rule it propounds are, at best, less than compelling. Equally relevant is an assessment of the rule's consequences measured against community values. The Court's duty to assess the consequences of its action is not satisfied by the utterance of the truth that a value of our system of criminal justice is "to respect the inviolability of the human personality" and to require government to produce the evidence against the accused by its own independent labors. More than the human dignity of the accused is involved; the human personality of others in the society must also be preserved. Thus the values reflected by the privilege are not the sole desideratum; society's interest in the general security is of equal weight.

The obvious underpinning of the Court's decision is a deep-seated distrust of all confessions. As the Court declares that the accused may not be interrogated without counsel present, absent a waiver of the right to counsel, and as the Court all but admonishes the lawyer to advise the accused to remain silent, the result adds up to a judicial judgment that evidence from the accused should not be used against him in any way, whether compelled or not. This is the not so subtle overtone of the opinion—that it is inherently wrong for the police to gather evidence from the accused himself. And this is precisely the nub of this dissent. I see nothing wrong or immoral, and certainly nothing unconstitutional, with the police asking a suspect whom they have reasonable cause to arrest whether or not he killed his wife or with confronting him with the evidence on which the arrest was based, at least where he has been plainly advised that he may remain completely silent. * * * Particularly when corroborated, as where the police have confirmed the accused's disclosure of the hiding place of implements or fruits of the crime, such confessions have the highest reliability and significantly contribute to the certitude with which we may believe the accused is guilty. * * *

The rule announced today [is] a deliberate calculus to prevent interrogations, to reduce the incidence of confessions and pleas of guilty and to increase the number of trials. [Under] the present law, the prosecution fails to prove its case in about 30% of the criminal cases actually tried in the federal courts. But it is something else again to remove from the ordinary criminal case all those confessions which heretofore have been held to be free and voluntary acts of the accused and to thus establish a new constitutional barrier to the ascertainment of truth by the judicial process. There is, in my view, every reason to believe that a good many criminal defendants, who otherwise would have been convicted on what this Court has previously thought to be the most satisfactory kind of evidence, will now, under this new version of the Fifth Amendment, either not be tried at all or acquitted if the State's evidence, minus the confession, is put to the test of litigation.

I have no desire whatsoever to share the responsibility for any such impact on the present criminal process. * * *

There is another aspect to the effect of the Court's rule on the person whom the police have arrested on probable cause. The fact is that he may not be guilty at all and may be able to extricate himself quickly and simply if he were told the circumstances of his arrest and were asked to explain. This effort, and his release, must now await the hiring of a lawyer or his appointment by the court, consultation with counsel and then a session with the police or the prosecutor. Similarly, where probable cause exists to arrest several suspects as where the body of the victim is discovered in a house having several residents, it will often be true that a suspect may be cleared only through the results of interrogation of other suspects. Here too the release of the innocent may be delayed by the Court's rule.

Much of the trouble with the Court's new rule is that it will operate indiscriminately in all criminal cases, regardless of the severity of the crime or the circumstances involved. It applies to every defendant whether the professional criminal or one committing a crime of momentary passion who is not part and parcel of organized crime. It will slow down the investigation and the apprehension of confederates in those cases where time is of the essence, such as kidnapping, [those] involving the national security, [and] some organized crime situations. In the latter context the lawyer who arrives may also be the lawyer for the defendants' colleagues and can be relied upon to insure that no breach of the organization's security takes place even though the accused may feel that the best thing he can do is to cooperate.

At the same time, the Court's *per se* approach may not be justified on the ground that it provides a "bright line" permitting the authorities to judge in advance whether interrogation may safely be pursued without jeopardizing the admissibility of any information obtained as a consequence. Nor can it be claimed that judicial time and effort, assuming that is a relevant consideration, will be conserved because of the ease of application of the new rule. Today's decision leaves open such questions as whether the accused was in custody, whether his statements were spontaneous or the product of interrogation, whether the accused has effectively waived his rights, and whether nontestimonial evidence introduced at trial is the fruit of statements made during a prohibited interrogation, all of which are certain to prove productive of uncertainty during investigation and litigation during prosecution. For all these reasons, if further restrictions on police interrogation are desirable at this time, a more flexible approach makes much more sense than the Court's constitutional strait-jacket which forecloses more discriminating treatment by legislative or rule-making pronouncements. * * *

Note: Can Congress "Repeal" Miranda?

Title II of the Crime Control Act of 1968, which purports to repeal *Miranda* in federal prosecutions, amends Chapter 223, title 18, United States Code, by adding the following new sections:

"§ 3501. Admissibility of confessions

"(a) In any criminal prosecution brought by the United States or by the District of Columbia, a confession, as defined in subsection (e) hereof, shall be admissible in evidence if it is voluntarily given. Before such confession is received in evidence, the trial judge shall, out of the presence of the jury, determine any issue as to voluntariness. If the trial judge determines that the confession was voluntarily made it shall be admitted in evidence and the trial judge shall permit the jury to hear relevant evidence on the issue of voluntariness and shall instruct the jury to give such weight to the confession as the jury feels it deserves under all the circumstances.

"(b) The trial judge in determining the issue of voluntariness shall take into consideration all the circumstances surrounding the giving of the confession, including (1) the time elapsing between arrest and arraignment of the defendant making the confession, if it was made after arrest and before arraignment, (2) whether such defendant knew the nature of the offense with which he was charged or of which he was suspected at the time of making the confession, (3) whether or not such defendant was advised or knew that he was not required to make any statement and that any such statement could be used against him, (4) whether or not such defendant had been advised prior to questioning of his right to the assistance of counsel; and (5) whether or not such defendant was without the assistance of counsel when questioned and when giving such confession.

"The presence or absence of any of the above-mentioned factors to be taken into consideration by the judge need not be conclusive on the issue of voluntariness of the confession.

"(c) In any criminal prosecution by the United States or by the District of Columbia, a confession made or given by a person who is a defendant therein, while such person was under arrest or other detention in the custody of any law-enforcement officer or law-enforcement agency, shall not be inadmissible solely because of delay in bringing such person before a commissioner or other officer empowered to commit persons charged with offenses against the laws of the United States or of the District of Columbia if such confession is found by the trial judge to have been made voluntarily and if the weight to be given the confession is left to the jury and if such confession was made or given by such person within six hours immediately following his arrest or other detention: *Provided,* That the time limitation contained in this subsection shall not apply in any case in which the delay in bringing such person before such commissioner or other officer beyond such six-hour period is found by the trial judge to be reasonable considering the means of transportation and the distance to be traveled to the nearest available such commissioner or other officer.

"(d) Nothing contained in this section shall bar the admission in evidence of any confession made or given voluntarily by any person to any other person without interrogation by anyone, or at any time at which the person who made or gave such confession was not under arrest or other detention.

"(e) As used in this section, the term 'confession' means any confession of guilt of any criminal offense or any self-incriminating statement made or given orally or in writing."

Although § 3501 purports to overrule *Miranda,* to date it has not provoked the head-on collision that might have been predicted. The Attorney General in office when the statute was passed instructed his subordinates not to rely on it where it differed from *Miranda,* and, although a later Attorney General changed this as official policy, most U.S. Attorneys appear to have continued to adhere to the restrained position initially taken. According to a 1986 report to the Attorney General by Assistant Attorney General Stephen Markman, head of the Office of Legal Policy (the "Markman report"), at some point the Department of Justice "attempted to establish the validity of [§ 3501] in litigation for several years with inconclusive results," but then "terminated this litigative effort." However, the Markman report urges the Department of Justice "to persuade the Supreme Court to abrogate or overrule the decision in *Miranda* " and views "reliance on [the 1968 statute] designed to achieve that end" as "the most promising line of attack."

When § 3501 was first enacted, most commentators thought it was invalid. Even those who conceded that *Miranda* was subject to congressional revision, i.e., could be displaced by a statute that provides an adequate alternative to the now-familiar warnings, maintained that Title II still fell short because it did little more than "turn the clock back" to the "voluntariness" test espoused by the *Miranda* dissents.

But the case for upholding § 3501 grew stronger with the passage of years. The Supreme Court has repeatedly called the *Miranda* rules "not themselves rights protected by the Constitution" but only "procedural safeguards" or "pro-phylactic rules" designed to "provide practical reinforcement" for the privilege against compelled self-incrimination.

This language first appeared in *Michigan v. Tucker,* 417 U.S. 433 (1974). *Tucker* allowed the testimony of a prosecution witness whose identity had been discovered by questioning defendant in violation of *Miranda.* Although the case involved various factors that arguably limited its implications (e.g., the deviation between the warnings given and the *Miranda* requirements was not substantial and, although the defendant's trial took place after *Miranda,* the police question-ing occurred before that case was decided), the *Tucker* Court, per Rehnquist, J., spoke in general terms of the difference between a *Miranda* violation and a constitutional violation:

> "[T]he Court in *Miranda,* for the first time, expressly declared that the Self–Incrimination Clause was applicable to state interrogations at a police station, and that a defendant's statements might be excluded at trial despite their voluntary character under traditional principles.

> "To supplement this new doctrine, and to help police officers conduct interrogations without facing a continued risk that valuable evidence would be lost, the [*Miranda* Court] established a set of specific guidelines, now commonly known as the *Miranda* rules. * * *

> "The [*Miranda* Court] recognized that these procedural safeguards were not themselves rights protected by the Constitution but were instead mea-sures to insure that the right against compulsory self-incrimination was protected. As [it] remarked: '[W]e cannot say that the Constitution neces-sarily requires adherence to any particular solution for the inherent compul-sions of the interrogation process as it is presently conducted.' The suggested safeguards were not intended to 'create a constitutional straitjacket,' *Mi-randa,* but rather to provide practical reinforcement for the right against compulsory self-incrimination.[d]

d. But as Justice Douglas observed in his *Tucker* dissent, the Court, per Rehnquist, J., overlooked other language in the *Miranda* opinion. For example, in the same paragraph from *Miranda* quoted by Justice Rehnquist in *Tucker,* the *Miranda* Court added: "However,

"A comparison of the facts in this case with the historical circumstances underlying the privilege against compulsory self-incrimination strongly indicates that the police conduct here did not deprive [Tucker] of his privilege against self-incrimination as such, but rather failed to make available to him the full measure of procedural safeguards associated with that right since *Miranda.* Certainly no one could contend that the interrogation faced by [Tucker] bore any resemblance to the historical practices at which the right against compulsory self-incrimination was aimed. [H]is statements could hardly be termed involuntary as that term has been defined in the decisions of this Court. * * *

"Our determination that the interrogation in this case involved no compulsion sufficient to breach the right against compulsory self-incrimination does not mean there was not a disregard, albeit an inadvertent disregard, of the procedural rules later established in *Miranda.* The question for decision is how sweeping the judicially imposed consequences of this disregard shall be."

A decade later, first in *New York v. Quarles* (1984) [§ 4 infra], and then in *Oregon v. Elstad* (1985) [§ 4 infra], the Court reiterated *Tucker*'s way of looking at, and thinking about, *Miranda.* (Both cases are set forth in the next section.) In both *Quarles* and *Elstad* the Court underscored the distinction between incriminating statements that are *actually* "coerced" or "compelled" and those obtained *merely* in violation of *Miranda*'s "procedural safeguards" or "prophylactic rules."

Did the language in *Tucker, Quarles* and *Elstad* imply that the Court would now uphold the validity of § 3501, which purports to "overrule" *Miranda?* Since the Court has no "supervisory power" over *state* criminal justice, if the *Miranda* rules are not constitutional requirements (but only "second-class" prophylactic safeguards) and *Miranda* violations not constitutional violations (but only "second-class" wrongs), where did the Court get the authority to impose *Miranda* on the states in the first place?

Concurring in *Davis v. United States* (1994) (discussed at fn. a of § 4, pt. 3), Justice Scalia sharply criticized the Justice Department's "repeated refusal to invoke § 3501," a refusal that has "caused the federal judiciary to confront a host of '*Miranda*' issues that might be entirely irrelevant under federal law." Justice Scalia also maintained that because § 3501 "is a provision of law directed *to the courts,* reflecting the people's assessment of the proper balance to be struck [in this area], we shirk our duty if we systematically disregard that statutory command simply because the Justice Department declines to remind us of it."

Justice Scalia's comments probably encouraged two conservative legal groups, the Washington Legal Foundation and the Safe Streets Coalition. Led by the indefatigable Paul Cassell, a Utah Law School professor who has become the nation's leading critic of *Miranda*, these groups repeatedly urged the federal courts to inject § 3501 into their cases.

unless we are shown other procedures which are at least as effective in apprising accused persons of their right of silence and in assuring a continuous opportunity to exercise it, the following safeguards [the *Miranda* warnings] must be observed." Moreover, later in the opinion, the *Miranda* Court reiterated: "The warnings required and the waiver necessary in accordance with our opinion today are, in the absence of a fully effective equivalent, prerequisites to the admissibility of any statements made by a defendant. * * * Procedural safeguards must be employed to protect the privilege, and unless other fully effective means are adopted to notify the person of his right of silence and to assure that the exercise of the right will be scrupulously honored, the following measures [the *Miranda* warnings] are required."

In *United States v. Dickerson*, 166 F.3d 667 (4th Cir. 1999), the Washington Legal Foundation and the Safe Streets Coalition finally achieved some success. Although the dissenting judge protested that the ruling was made "without the benefit of any briefing in opposition" and "against the express wishes of the Department of Justice," a 2-1 majority of a panel of the U.S. Court of Appeals ruled that the pre-*Miranda* voluntariness test set forth in § 3501, rather than the famous *Miranda* case, governs the admissibility of confessions in the federal courts. Therefore, the district court had erred when it had suppressed a voluntary confession simply because it was obtained in violation of *Miranda*.

The reasoning of the Fourth Circuit may be summarized quite briefly: Congress has the power to "overrule" rules of evidence and procedure that are not required by the Constitution. The *Miranda* rules are not constitutionally required; they are only "prophylactic" rules designed to implement or reinforce the underlying constitutional right. Therefore, § 3501 is a valid exercise of Congressional authority to override judicially created rules not part of the Constitution. But the Supreme Court was to see matters quite differently:

DICKERSON v. UNITED STATES

530 U.S. 428, 120 S.Ct. 2326, 147 L.Ed.2d 405 (2000).

CHIEF JUSTICE REHNQUIST delivered the opinion of the Court.

In the wake of [*Miranda*], Congress enacted 18 U.S.C. § 3501, which in essence laid down a rule that the admissibility of [a custodial suspect's] statements should turn only on whether or not they were voluntarily made. We hold that *Miranda*, being a constitutional decision of this Court, may not be in effect overruled by an Act of Congress, and we decline to overrule *Miranda* ourselves. We therefore hold that *Miranda* and its progeny in this Court govern the admissibility of statements made during custodial interrogation in both state and federal courts.

* * * Prior to *Miranda*, we evaluated the admissibility of a suspect's confession under a voluntariness test. [Over] time, our cases recognized two constitutional bases for the requirement that a confession be voluntary to be admitted into evidence: the Fifth Amendment right against self-incrimination and the Due Process Clause of the Fourteenth Amendment. See, *e.g.*, Bram v. United States (1897) (stating that the voluntariness test "is controlled by that portion of the Fifth Amendment ... commanding that no person 'shall be compelled in any criminal case to be a witness against himself' "); *Brown v. Mississippi*, (1936) (reversing a criminal conviction under the Due Process Clause because it was based on a confession obtained by physical coercion).

While *Bram* was decided before *Brown* and its progeny, for the middle third of the 20th century our cases based the rule against admitting coerced confessions primarily, if not exclusively, on notions of due process. We applied the due process voluntariness test in "some 30 different cases decided during the era that intervened between *Brown* and *Escobedo v. Illinois*." Those cases refined the test into an inquiry that examines "whether a defendant's will was overborne" by the circumstances surrounding the giving of a confession. The due process test takes into consideration "the totality of all the surrounding circumstances—both the characteristics of the accused and the details of the interrogation." * * *

We have never abandoned this due process jurisprudence, and thus continue to exclude confessions that were obtained involuntarily. But our decisions in *Malloy* and *Miranda* changed the focus of much of the inquiry in determining the admissibility of suspects' incriminating statements. In *Malloy*, we held that the

Fifth Amendment's Self–Incrimination Clause is incorporated in the Due Process Clause of the Fourteenth Amendment and thus applies to the States. We decided _Miranda_ on the heels of _Malloy_.

In _Miranda_, we noted that the advent of modern custodial police interrogation brought with it an increased concern about confessions obtained by coercion. Because custodial police interrogation, by its very nature, isolates and pressures the individual, we stated that "even without employing brutality, the 'third degree' or [other] specific stratagems, . . . custodial interrogation exacts a heavy toll on individual liberty and trades on the weakness of individuals." We concluded that the coercion inherent in custodial interrogation blurs the line between voluntary and involuntary statements, and thus heightens the risk that an individual will not be "accorded his privilege under the Fifth Amendment . . . not to be compelled to incriminate himself." Accordingly, we laid down "concrete constitutional guidelines for law enforcement agencies and courts to follow."

Two years after _Miranda_ was decided, Congress enacted § 3501. * * *

Given § 3501's express designation of voluntariness as the touchstone of admissibility, its omission of any warning requirement, and the instruction for trial courts to consider a nonexclusive list of factors relevant to the circumstances of a confession, we agree with the Court of Appeals that Congress intended by its enactment to overrule _Miranda_. Because of the obvious conflict between our decision in _Miranda_ and § 3501, we must address whether Congress has constitutional authority to thus supersede _Miranda_. If Congress has such authority, § 3501's totality-of-the-circumstances approach must prevail over _Miranda_'s requirement of warnings; if not, that section must yield to _Miranda_'s more specific requirements.

The law in this area is clear. This Court has supervisory authority over the federal courts, and we may use that authority to prescribe rules of evidence and procedure that are binding in those tribunals. However, the power to judicially create and enforce nonconstitutional "rules of procedure and evidence for the federal courts exists only in the absence of a relevant Act of Congress." Congress retains the ultimate authority to modify or set aside any judicially created rules of evidence and procedure that are not required by the Constitution.

But Congress may not legislatively supersede our decisions interpreting and applying the Constitution. See, _e.g._, _Boerne v. Flores_, 521 U.S. 507, 117 S. Ct. 2157, 138 L.Ed.2d 624 (1997). This case therefore turns on whether the _Miranda_ Court announced a constitutional rule or merely exercised its supervisory authority to regulate evidence in the absence of congressional direction. [Relying] on the fact that we have created several exceptions to _Miranda_'s warnings requirement and that we have repeatedly referred to the _Miranda_ warnings as "prophylactic," _Quarles_, and "not themselves rights protected by the Constitution," _Tucker_, the Court of Appeals concluded that the protections announced in _Miranda_ are not constitutionally required.

We disagree * * *, although we concede that there is language in some of our opinions that supports the view taken by that court. But first and foremost of the factors on the other side—that _Miranda_ is a constitutional decision—is that both _Miranda_ and two of its companion cases applied the rule to proceedings in state courts—to wit, Arizona, California, and New York. Since that time, we have consistently applied _Miranda_'s rule to prosecutions arising in state courts. It is beyond dispute that we do not hold a supervisory power over the courts of the several States. With respect to proceedings in state courts, our "authority is limited to enforcing the commands of the United States Constitution."[1]

The *Miranda* opinion itself begins by stating that the Court granted certiorari "to explore some facets of the problems [of] applying the privilege against self-incrimination to in-custody interrogation, *and to give concrete constitutional guidelines for law enforcement agencies and courts to follow.*" (emphasis added). In fact, the majority opinion is replete with statements indicating that the majority thought it was announcing a constitutional rule. Indeed, the Court's ultimate conclusion was that the unwarned confessions obtained in the four cases before the Court in *Miranda* "were obtained from the defendant under circumstances that did not meet constitutional standards for protection of the privilege."

Additional support for our conclusion that *Miranda* is constitutionally based is found in the *Miranda* Court's invitation for legislative action to protect the constitutional right against coerced self-incrimination. [The] Court emphasized that it could not foresee "the potential alternatives for protecting the privilege which might be devised by Congress or the States," and it accordingly opined that the Constitution would not preclude legislative solutions that differed from the prescribed *Miranda* warnings but which were "at least as effective in apprising accused persons of their right of silence and in assuring a continuous opportunity to exercise it."

[Various decisions carving out exceptions to *Miranda*] illustrate the principle—not that *Miranda* is not a constitutional rule—but that no constitutional rule is immutable. No court laying down a general rule can possibly foresee the various circumstances in which counsel will seek to apply it, and the sort of modifications represented by these cases are as much a normal part of constitutional law as the original decision.

The Court of Appeals also noted that in *Elstad*, we stated that " 'the *Miranda* exclusionary rule ... serves the Fifth Amendment and sweeps more broadly than the Fifth Amendment itself.' " Our decision in that case—refusing to apply the traditional "fruits" doctrine developed in Fourth Amendment cases—does not prove that *Miranda* is a nonconstitutional decision, but simply recognizes the fact that unreasonable searches under the Fourth Amendment are different from unwarned interrogation under the Fifth Amendment.

As an alternative argument for sustaining the Court of Appeals' decision, the court-invited *amicus curiae* contends that the section complies with the requirement that a legislative alternative to *Miranda* be equally as effective in preventing coerced confessions. We agree with the *amicus'* contention that there are more remedies available for abusive police conduct than there were at the time *Miranda* was decided. But we do not agree that these additional measures supplement § 3501's protections sufficiently to meet the constitutional minimum. *Miranda* requires procedures that will warn a suspect in custody of his right to remain silent and which will assure the suspect that the exercise of that right will be honored. As discussed above, § 3501 explicitly eschews a requirement of pre-interrogation warnings in favor of an approach that looks to the administration of such warnings as only one factor in determining the voluntariness of a suspect's confession. The additional remedies cited by *amicus* do not, in our view, render

---

1. Our conclusion regarding *Miranda*'s constitutional basis is further buttressed by the fact that we have allowed prisoners to bring alleged *Miranda* violations before the federal courts in habeas corpus proceedings. * * * Habeas corpus proceedings are available only for claims that a person "is in custody in violation of the Constitution or laws or treaties of the United States." 28 U.S.C. § 2254(a). Since the *Miranda* rule is clearly not based on federal laws or treaties, our decision allowing habeas review for *Miranda* claims obviously assumes that *Miranda* is of constitutional origin.

them, together with § 3501 an adequate substitute for the warnings required by *Miranda*.

The dissent argues that it is judicial overreaching for this Court to hold § 3501 unconstitutional unless we hold that the *Miranda* warnings are required by the Constitution, in the sense that nothing else will suffice to satisfy constitutional requirements. But we need not go farther than *Miranda* to decide this case. In *Miranda*, the Court noted that reliance on the traditional totality-of-the-circumstances test raised a risk of overlooking an involuntary custodial confession, a risk that the Court found unacceptably great when the confession is offered in the case in chief to prove guilt. The Court therefore concluded that something more than the totality test was necessary. Section 3501 reinstates the totality test as sufficient. [The statute] therefore cannot be sustained if *Miranda* is to remain the law.

Whether or not we would agree with *Miranda*'s reasoning and its resulting rule, were we addressing the issue in the first instance, the principles of *stare decisis* weigh heavily against overruling it now.

* * * *Miranda* has become embedded in routine police practice to the point where the warnings have become part of our national culture. [While] we have overruled our precedents when subsequent cases have undermined their doctrinal underpinnings, we do not believe that this has happened to the *Miranda* decision. If anything, our subsequent cases have reduced the impact of the *Miranda* rule on legitimate law enforcement while reaffirming the decision's core ruling that unwarned statements may not be used as evidence in the prosecution's case in chief.

The disadvantage of the *Miranda* rule is that statements which may be by no means involuntary, made by a defendant who is aware of his "rights," may nonetheless be excluded and a guilty defendant go free as a result. But experience suggests that the totality-of-the-circumstances test which § 3501 seeks to revive is more difficult than *Miranda* for law enforcement officers to conform to, and for courts to apply in a consistent manner. The requirement that *Miranda* warnings be given does not, of course, dispense with the voluntariness inquiry. [But] "[c]ases in which a defendant can make a colorable argument that a self-incriminating statement was 'compelled' despite the fact that the law enforcement authorities adhered to the dictates of *Miranda* are rare."

In sum, we conclude that *Miranda* announced a constitutional rule that Congress may not supersede legislatively. Following the rule of *stare decisis*, we decline to overrule *Miranda* ourselves. * * *

Justice SCALIA, with whom Justice THOMAS joins, dissenting.

Those to whom judicial decisions are an unconnected series of judgments that produce either favored or disfavored results will doubtless greet today's decision as a paragon of moderation, since it declines to overrule *Miranda*. Those who understand the judicial process will appreciate that today's decision is not a reaffirmation of *Miranda*, but a radical revision of the most significant element of *Miranda* (as of all cases): the rationale that gives it a permanent place in our jurisprudence.

Marbury v. Madison, held that an Act of Congress will not be enforced by the courts if what it prescribes violates the Constitution of the United States. That was the basis on which *Miranda* was decided. One will search today's opinion in vain, however, for a statement (surely simple enough to make) that what § 3501 prescribes—the use at trial of a voluntary confession, even when a *Miranda* warning or its equivalent has failed to be given—violates the Constitution. The reason the statement does not appear is not only (and perhaps not so much) that it would be absurd, inasmuch as § 3501 excludes from trial precisely what the Constitution excludes from trial, viz., compelled confessions; but also that Justices whose votes are needed to compose today's majority are on record as believing that a violation of *Miranda* is *not* a violation of the Constitution. And so, to justify today's agreed-upon result, the Court must adopt a significant *new*, if not entirely comprehensible, principle of constitutional law. As the Court chooses to describe that principle, statutes of Congress can be disregarded, not only when what they prescribe violates the Constitution, but when what they prescribe contradicts a decision of this Court that "announced a constitutional rule." As I shall discuss in some detail, the only thing that can possibly mean in the context of this case is that this Court has the power, not merely to apply the Constitution but to expand it, imposing what it regards as useful "prophylactic" restrictions upon Congress and the States. That is an immense and frightening antidemocratic power, and it does not exist.

It takes only a small step to bring today's opinion out of the realm of power-judging and into the mainstream of legal reasoning: The Court need only go beyond its carefully couched iterations that *"Miranda* is a constitutional decision," that *"Miranda* is constitutionally based," that *Miranda* has "constitutional underpinnings," and come out and say quite clearly: "We reaffirm today that custodial interrogation that is not preceded by *Miranda* warnings or their equivalent violates the Constitution of the United States." It cannot say that, because a majority of the Court does not believe it. The Court therefore acts in plain violation of the Constitution when it denies effect to this Act of Congress.

It was once possible to characterize the so-called *Miranda* rule as resting (however implausibly) upon the proposition that what the statute here before us permits—the admission at trial of un-*Mirandized* confessions—violates the Constitution. That is the fairest reading of the *Miranda* case itself. [Having] extended the privilege into the confines of the station house, the Court liberally sprinkled throughout its sprawling 60–page opinion suggestions that, because of the compulsion inherent in custodial interrogation, the privilege was violated by any statement thus obtained that did not conform to the rules set forth in *Miranda*, or some functional equivalent. * * *

So understood, *Miranda* was objectionable for innumerable reasons, not least the fact that cases spanning more than 70 years had rejected its core premise that, absent the warnings and an effective waiver of the right to remain silent and of the (thitherto unknown) right to have an attorney present, a statement obtained pursuant to custodial interrogation was necessarily the product of compulsion. [Moreover,] history and precedent aside, the decision in *Miranda*, if read as an explication of what the Constitution *requires*, is preposterous. There is, for example, simply no basis in reason for concluding that a response to the very first question asked, by a suspect who already *knows* all of the rights described in the *Miranda* warning, is anything other than a volitional act. And even if one assumes that the elimination of compulsion absolutely requires informing even the most knowledgeable suspect of his right to remain silent, it cannot conceivably require the right to have *counsel* present. There is a world of difference, which the Court recognized under the traditional voluntariness test but ignored in *Miranda*, between compelling a suspect to incriminate himself and preventing him from foolishly doing so of his own accord. Only the latter (which is *not* required by the Constitution) could explain the Court's inclusion of a right to counsel and the requirement that it, too, be knowingly and intelligently waived. Counsel's presence is not required to tell the suspect that he *need* not speak; the interrogators can do that. The only good reason for having counsel there is that he can counted on to advise the suspect that he *should* not speak.

Preventing foolish (rather than compelled) confessions is likewise the only conceivable basis for the rules that courts must exclude any confession elicited by questioning conducted, without interruption, after the suspect has indicated a desire to stand on his right to remain silent or initiated by police after the suspect has expressed a desire to have counsel present. Nonthreatening attempts to persuade the suspect to reconsider that initial decision are not, without more, enough to render a change of heart the product of anything other than the suspect's free will. Thus, what is most remarkable about the *Miranda* decision— and what made it unacceptable as a matter of straightforward constitutional interpretation in the *Marbury* tradition—is its palpable hostility toward the act of confession *per se*, rather than toward what the Constitution abhors, *compelled* confession.

[For] these reasons, and others more than adequately developed in the *Miranda* dissents and in the subsequent works of the decision's many critics, any conclusion that a violation of the *Miranda* rules *necessarily* amounts to a violation of the privilege against compelled self-incrimination can claim no support in history, precedent, or common sense, and as a result would at least presumptively be worth reconsidering even at this late date. But that is unnecessary, since the Court has (thankfully) long since abandoned the notion that failure to comply with *Miranda*'s rules is itself a violation of the Constitution.

As the Court today acknowledges, since *Miranda* we have explicitly, and repeatedly, interpreted that decision as having announced, not the circumstances in which custodial interrogation runs afoul of the Fifth or Fourteenth Amendment, but rather only "prophylactic" rules that go beyond the right against compelled self-incrimination. Of course the seeds of this "prophylactic" interpretation of *Miranda* were present in the decision itself. [In] subsequent cases, the seeds have sprouted and borne fruit: The Court has squarely concluded that it is possible—indeed not uncommon—for the police to violate *Miranda* without also violating the Constitution.

Michigan v. Tucker, an opinion for the Court written by then-Justice Rehnquist, rejected the true-to-*Marbury*, failure-to-warn-as-constitutional-violation interpretation of *Miranda*. It held that exclusion of the "fruits" of a *Miranda* violation—the statement of a witness whose identity the defendant had revealed while in custody—was not required. [The] "procedural safeguards" adopted in *Miranda*, the Court said, "were not themselves rights protected by the Constitution but were instead measures to insure that the right against compulsory self-incrimination was protected," and to "provide practical reinforcement for the right."

[The dissent then discussed *New York v. Quarles, Oregon v. Elstad* and other cases applying and interpreting *Miranda*.]

In light of these cases, and our statements to the same effect in others, it is simply no longer possible for the Court to conclude, even if it wanted to, that a violation of *Miranda*'s rules is a violation of the Constitution. But as I explained at the outset, that is what is required before the Court may disregard a law of Congress governing the admissibility of evidence in federal court. The Court today insists that the *decision* in *Miranda* is a "constitutional" one, that it has "constitutional underpinnings," a "constitutional basis" and a "constitutional origin," that it was "constitutionally based," and that it announced a "constitutional rule." It is fine to play these word games; but what makes a decision "constitutional" in the only sense relevant here—in the sense that renders it impervious to supersession by congressional legislation such as § 3501—is the determination that the Constitution *requires* the result that the decision announces and the statute ignores. By disregarding congressional action that concededly does not violate the Constitution, the Court flagrantly offends fundamental principles of separation of powers, and arrogates to itself prerogatives reserved to the representatives of the people.

The Court seeks to avoid this conclusion in two ways: First, by misdescribing these post-*Miranda* cases as mere dicta. The Court concedes only "that there is language in some of our opinions that supports the view" that *Miranda*'s protections are not "constitutionally required." It is not a matter of *language*; it is a matter of *holdings*. The proposition that failure to comply with *Miranda*'s rules does not establish a constitutional violation was central to the *holdings* of *Tucker*, * * * *Quarles*, and *Elstad*.]

The second way the Court seeks to avoid the impact of these cases is simply to disclaim responsibility for reasoned decisionmaking. It says: "These decisions illustrate the principle—not that *Miranda* is not a constitutional rule—but that no constitutional rule is immutable. * * * " The issue, however, is not whether court rules are "mutable"; they assuredly are. It is not whether, in the light of "various circumstances," they can be "modified"; they assuredly can. The issue is whether, *as mutated and modified*, they must *make sense.* The requirement that they do so is the only thing that prevents this Court from being some sort of nine-headed Caesar, giving thumbs-up or thumbs-down to whatever outcome, case by case, suits or offends its collective fancy. And if confessions procured in violation of *Miranda* are confessions "compelled" in violation of the Constitution, the post-*Miranda* decisions I have discussed do not make sense. The only reasoned basis for their outcome was that a violation of *Miranda* is *not* a violation of the Constitution. * * *

Finally, the Court asserts that *Miranda* must be a "constitutional decision" announcing a "constitutional rule," and thus immune to congressional modification, because we have since its inception applied it to the States. If this argument is meant as an invocation of *stare decisis*, it fails because, though it is true that our cases applying *Miranda* against the States must be reconsidered if *Miranda* is not required by the Constitution, it is likewise true that our cases [based] on the principle that *Miranda* is *not* required by the Constitution will have to be reconsidered if it *is*. So the *stare decisis* argument is a wash.

[There] was available to the Court a means of reconciling the established proposition that a violation of *Miranda* does not itself offend the Fifth Amendment with the Court's assertion of a right to ignore the present statute. That means of reconciliation was argued strenuously by both petitioner and the United States, who were evidently more concerned than the Court is with maintaining the coherence of our jurisprudence. It is not mentioned in the Court's opinion because, I assume, a majority of the Justices intent on reversing believes that incoherence is the lesser evil. They may be right.

Petitioner and the United States contend that there is nothing at all exceptional, much less unconstitutional, about the Court's adopting prophylactic rules to buttress constitutional rights, and enforcing them against Congress and the States. Indeed, the United States argues that "prophylactic rules are now and have been for many years a feature of this Court's constitutional adjudication." That statement is not wholly inaccurate, if by "many years" one means since the mid–1960's. However, in their zeal to validate what is in my view a lawless practice, the United States and petitioner greatly overstate the frequency with which we have engaged in it. * * *

Petitioner and the United States are right on target, [in] characterizing the Court's actions in a case decided within a few years of *Miranda, North Carolina v. Pearce* [discussed in *U.S. v. Goodwin*, Ch. 10, § 2]. There, the Court concluded that due process would be offended were a judge vindictively to resentence with added severity a defendant who had successfully appealed his original conviction. Rather than simply announce that vindictive sentencing violates the Due Process Clause, the Court went on to hold that "in order to assure the absence of such a [vindictive] motivation, [the] reasons for [imposing the increased sentence] must affirmatively appear" and must "be based upon objective information concerning identifiable conduct on the part of the defendant occurring after the time of the original sentencing proceeding." The Court later explicitly acknowledged *Pearce's* prophylactic character. It is true, therefore, that the case exhibits the same fundamental flaw as does *Miranda* when deprived (as it has been) of its original (implausible) pretension to announcement of what the Constitution itself required. That is, although the Due Process Clause may well prohibit punishment based on judicial vindictiveness, the Constitution by no means vests in the courts "any general power to prescribe particular devices 'in order to assure the absence of such a motivation'" (Black, J., dissenting). Justice Black surely had the right idea when he derided the Court's requirement as "pure legislation if there ever was legislation," although in truth *Pearce's* rule pales as a legislative achievement when compared to the detailed code promulgated in *Miranda.*

The foregoing demonstrates that, petitioner's and the United States' suggestions to the contrary notwithstanding, what the Court did in *Miranda* (assuming, as later cases hold, that *Miranda* went beyond what the Constitution actually requires) is in fact extraordinary. That the Court has, on rare and recent occasion, repeated the mistake does not transform error into truth, but illustrates the potential for future mischief that the error entails. [The] power with which the Court would endow itself under a "prophylactic" justification for *Miranda* goes far beyond what it has permitted Congress to do under authority of [U.S. Const., Amdt. 14, § 5].

I applaud [the] refusal of the Justices in the majority to enunciate this boundless doctrine of judicial empowerment as a means of rendering today's decision rational. In nonetheless joining the Court's judgment, however, they overlook two truisms: that actions speak louder than silence, and that (in judge-made law at least) logic will out. Since there is in fact no other principle that can reconcile today's judgment with the post-*Miranda* cases that the Court refuses to abandon, what today's decision will stand for, whether the Justices can bring themselves to say it or not, is the power of the Supreme Court to write a prophylactic, extraconstitutional Constitution, binding on Congress and the States.

[I am not] persuaded by the argument for retaining *Miranda* that touts its supposed workability as compared with the totality-of-the-circumstances test it purported to replace. *Miranda's* proponents cite *ad nauseam* the fact that the Court was called upon to make difficult and subtle distinctions in applying the "voluntariness" test in some 30–odd due process "coerced confessions" cases in the 30 years between *Brown* and *Miranda*. It is not immediately apparent, however, that the judicial burden has been eased by the "bright-line" rules adopted in *Miranda*. In fact, in the 34 years since *Miranda* was decided, this Court has been called upon to decide nearly *60* cases involving a host of *Miranda* issues.

[But] even were I to agree that the old totality-of-the-circumstances test was more cumbersome, it is simply not true that *Miranda* has banished it from the

368 POLICE INTERROGATION & CONFESSIONS Ch. 6

law and replaced it with a new test. Under the current regime, which the Court today retains in its entirety, courts are frequently called upon to undertake *both* inquiries. That is because, as explained earlier, voluntariness remains the *constitutional* standard, and as such continues to govern the admissibility for impeachment purposes of statements taken in violation of *Miranda*, the admissibility of the "fruits" of such statements, and the admissibility of statements challenged as unconstitutionally obtained *despite* the interrogator's compliance with *Miranda*.

Finally, I am not convinced by petitioner's argument that *Miranda* should be preserved because the decision occupies a special place in the "public's consciousness." As far as I am aware, the public is not under the illusion that we are infallible. I see little harm in admitting that we made a mistake in taking away from the people the ability to decide for themselves what protections (beyond those required by the Constitution) are reasonably affordable in the criminal investigatory process. And I see much to be gained by reaffirming for the people the wonderful reality that they govern themselves * * *.

Today's judgment converts *Miranda* from a milestone of judicial overreaching into the very Cheops' Pyramid (or perhaps the Sphinx would be a better analogue) of judicial arrogance. In imposing its Court-made code upon the States, the original opinion at least *asserted* that it was demanded by the Constitution. Today's decision does not pretend that it is—and yet *still* asserts the right to impose it against the will of the people's representatives in Congress. Far from believing that *stare decisis* compels this result, I believe we cannot allow to remain on the books even a celebrated decision—*especially* a celebrated decision—that has come to stand for the proposition that the Supreme Court has power to impose extraconstitutional constraints upon Congress and the States. This is not the system that was established by the Framers, or that would be established by any sane supporter of government by the people.

I dissent from today's decision, and, until § 3501 is repealed, will continue to apply it in all cases where there has been a sustainable finding that the defendant's confession was voluntary.

SECTION 4. APPLYING AND EXPLAINING *MIRANDA*

Because *Miranda* was the centerpiece of the Warren Court's "revolution in American criminal procedure" and the prime target of those who thought the courts were "soft" on criminals, almost everyone expected the so-called Burger Court to treat *Miranda* unkindly. And it did—at first. But it must also be said that the Burger Court interpreted *Miranda* fairly generously in some important respects.

The first blows the Burger Court dealt *Miranda* were the impeachment cases, *Harris v. New York,* 401 U.S. 222 (1971) and *Oregon v. Hass,* 420 U.S. 714 (1975). *Harris* held that statements preceded by defective warnings, and thus inadmissible to establish the prosecution's case-in-chief, could nevertheless be used to impeach the defendant's credibility if he chose to take the stand in his own defense.[a] The Court noted, but seemed unperturbed by the fact, that some language in the *Miranda* opinion could be read as barring the use of statements obtained in violation of *Miranda* for *any* purpose.

a. However, as the Court suggested in *Harris* and subsequently made clear in *Mincey v. Arizona,* 437 U.S. 385 (1978), "involuntary" or "coerced" statements, as opposed to those obtained only in violation of *Miranda,* cannot be used for impeachment purposes.

The Court went a step beyond *Harris* in the *Hass* case. In this case, after being advised of his rights, the defendant *asserted* them. Nevertheless, the police refused to honor the defendant's request for a lawyer and continued to question him. The Court ruled that here, too, the resulting incriminating statements could be used for impeachment purposes. Since many suspects make incriminating statements even after the receipt of complete *Miranda* warnings, *Harris* might have been explained—and contained—on the ground that permitting impeachment use of statements acquired without complete warnings would not greatly encourage the police to violate *Miranda*. But in light of the *Hass* ruling, when a suspect asserts his rights, the police arguably have very little to lose and everything to gain by continuing to question him.[b]

Although language in *Miranda* could be read as establishing a *per se* rule against any further questioning of one who has asserted his "right to silence" (as opposed to his *right to counsel*, discussed below), *Michigan v. Mosley,* 423 U.S. 96 (1975) held that under certain circumstances (and what they are is unclear), if they cease questioning on the spot, the police may "try again," and succeed at a later interrogation session. At the very least, it seems, the police must promptly terminate the original interrogation, resume questioning after the passage of a significant period of time, and give the suspect a fresh set of warnings at the outset of the second session. Whether *Mosley* requires more is a matter of dispute.

Perhaps the most frequently litigated *Miranda* question is what constitutes "custody" or "custodial interrogation"? In the first case in this section, *Berkemer v. McCarty,* the Court, per Marshall, J. one of *Miranda*'s strongest defenders, explains at considerable length why the "roadside questioning" of a motorist detained pursuant to a traffic stop is quite different from stationhouse interrogation and thus should not be deemed "custodial interrogation." The *McCarty* Court reached its conclusion without a dissent. More controversial are *Oregon v. Mathiason,* 429 U.S. 492 (1977) and *California v. Beheler,* 463 U.S. 1121 (1983), which demonstrate that if the suspect goes to the stationhouse on his own or "voluntarily" agrees to accompany the police to that site, even *police station* questioning designed to produce incriminating statements may not be "custodial interrogation." Both cases are discussed in *McCarty*.

Another frequently litigated question is what constitutes "interrogation" or "questioning" within the meaning of *Miranda*? This question is addressed by the next two cases in the section: *Rhode Island v. Innis* (1980) and *Illinois v. Perkins* (1990). Considering the alternatives (e.g., limiting "interrogation" to instances where the police directly address a suspect or to situations where the record establishes that the police *intended* to elicit a response), *Innis* gave the key term "interrogation" a fairly generous reading. *Perkins* holds that the coercive atmosphere calling for the *Miranda* warnings is not present when a suspect is *unaware*

b. The Court subsequently held that a defendant's prior silence could be used to impeach him when he testified in his own defense, *Jenkins v. Anderson,* 447 U.S. 231 (1980), and that even a defendant's *post*arrest silence (so long as he was not given the *Miranda* warnings) could be used for impeachment purposes, *Fletcher v. Weir,* 455 U.S. 603 (1982). Both *Jenkins* and *Weir* distinguished *Doyle v. Ohio,* 426 U.S. 610 (1976), which deemed it a violation of due process to use a defendant's silence for impeachment purposes when the defendant remained silent *after* being given *Miranda* warnings.

But the Court balked at further expansion of the "impeachment exception" to the ban against illegally seized evidence in *James v. Illinois,* 493 U.S. 307 (1990). *James* refused to expand the class of impeachable witnesses from the defendant alone to *all* defense witnesses, maintaining such an expansion "would not promote the truthseeking function to the same extent as did creation of the original exception, and yet it would significantly undermine the deterrent effect of the general exclusionary rule."

that he is speaking to a law enforcement officer (in this instance an undercover agent posing as a fellow-prisoner).

In *Edwards v. Arizona,* 451 U.S. 477 (1981) (whose holding is read broadly in *Minnick v. Mississippi,* the fourth case in this section), the Court gladdened the hearts of *Miranda* supporters by invigorating that case in an important respect. Sharply distinguishing the *Mosley* case, supra, the *Edwards* Court held that when a suspect asserts his right to counsel (as opposed to his right to remain silent), the police *cannot* "try again." Once a suspect "expresse[s] his desire to deal with the police only through counsel," *Edwards* instructs us, the suspect may not be subjected to further interrogation by the authorities "until counsel has been made available to him unless [he] himself initiates further communication, exchanges, or conversations with the police." [c]

But then, as discussed earlier, Justice Rehnquist's way of thinking about *Miranda,* which had first surfaced in *Michigan v. Tucker* [see Note on Congressional Overruling in § 3 supra], reappeared in *New York v. Quarles* and *Oregon v. Elstad,* the next two cases in this section. *Quarles* recognized a "public safety" exception to *Miranda.* *Elstad* held that a second confession, immediately preceded by the *Miranda* warnings, was admissible although an earlier statement from the defendant had been obtained in violation of *Miranda.* More generally, both cases viewed *Miranda* warnings as only second-class prophylactic safeguards and *Miranda* violations as only second-class wrongs.

Some of *Miranda*'s defenders found further cause for concern in *Moran v. Burbine,* next to the last case in this section. That case held that a confession preceded by an otherwise valid waiver of *Miranda* rights should not be excluded either because the police misled an inquiring attorney (asked by defendant's sister to represent him) or because the police failed to inform the defendant that an attorney was trying to reach him. But other commentators noted that the *Burbine* Court had viewed *Miranda* as a serious effort to strike a "proper balance" between, or to "reconcile," law enforcement needs and a suspect's rights and pointed out that this is the way many of *Miranda*'s defenders—not its critics—have talked about the case for the past twenty years.

Miranda fared well in *Withrow v. Williams,* the last case in this section. *Withrow* held that the restriction the Court had placed a decade and a half earlier on the exercise of federal habeas corpus jurisdiction when a state prisoner claims his conviction rests on evidence obtained in violation of the Fourth Amendment does not apply when a state prisoner alleges that his conviction rests on statements obtained in violation of *Miranda.* In the course of his opinion for the Court, Justice Souter compared *Miranda* with (a) the prohibition against the use of involuntary and compelled statements and (b) the Fourth Amendment exclusionary rule. Dissenting Justice O'Connor conducted a similar analysis, but reached different conclusions.

1. What constitutes "custody" or "custodial interrogation?"

BERKEMER v. McCARTY
468 U.S. 420, 104 S.Ct. 3138, 82 L.Ed.2d 317 (1984).

JUSTICE MARSHALL delivered the opinion of the Court.

[After observing McCarty's car weaving in and out of a highway lane, Trooper Williams forced him to stop and asked him to get out of the car. Noticing that

---

c. The *Edwards* rule applies even when the police want to question a suspect about an offense *unrelated* to the subject of their initial interrogation. See *Arizona v. Roberson,* 486 U.S. 675 (1988). Moreover, as the Court recently held in *Minnick,* the fourth case in this section, once a suspect invokes his right to counsel, the police may not reinitiate interrogation in the absence of counsel even if the suspect has consulted with an attorney in the interim.

McCarty had difficulty standing, the officer concluded that he would be charged with a traffic offense and not allowed to leave the scene. But the officer did not tell McCarty this. When asked to perform a field sobriety test, commonly known as a "balancing test," McCarty could not do so without falling. The officer then asked McCarty whether he had been using intoxicants. McCarty replied that he had consumed two beers and smoked marijuana a short time before. Moreover, his speech was slurred. The officer then formally arrested McCarty and drove him to a county jail where questioning resumed and McCarty made more incriminating statements. At no point in this sequence of events did Williams or anyone else give McCarty the *Miranda* warnings. McCarty's statements were admitted into evidence and he was convicted of operating a motor vehicle while under the influence of alcohol and/or drugs, a first-degree misdemeanor under Ohio law.

[The Court rejected the argument that *Miranda* does not apply to misdemeanor traffic offenses and held that one subjected to custodial interrogation is entitled to the *Miranda* warnings "regardless of the nature or severity of the offense of which he is suspected or for which he was arrested." Thus, since "[t]here can be no question that respondent was 'in custody' at least as of the moment he was formally placed under arrest and instructed to get into the police car," and he was not informed of his rights at that juncture, his subsequent admissions should not have been used against him. The Court then addressed the question whether respondent had been in custody at an earlier point, i.e., "whether the roadside questioning of a motorist detained pursuant to a routine traffic stop should be considered 'custodial interrogation.'"]

* * * Fidelity to the doctrine announced in Miranda requires that it be enforced strictly, but only in those types of situations in which the concerns that powered the decision are implicated. Thus, we must decide whether a traffic stop exerts upon a detained person pressures that sufficiently impair his free exercise of his privilege against self-incrimination to require that he be warned of his constitutional rights.

Two features of an ordinary traffic stop mitigate the danger that a person questioned will be induced "to speak where he would not otherwise do so freely," *Miranda*. First, detention of a motorist pursuant to a traffic stop is presumptively temporary and brief. The vast majority of roadside detentions last only a few minutes. A motorist's expectations, when he sees a policeman's light flashing behind him, are that he will be obliged to spend a short period of time answering questions and waiting while the officer checks his license and registration, that he may then be given a citation, but that in the end he most likely will be allowed to continue on his way. In this respect, questioning incident to an ordinary traffic stop is quite different from stationhouse interrogation, which frequently is prolonged, and in which the detainee often is aware that questioning will continue until he provides his interrogators the answers they seek.

Second, circumstances associated with the typical traffic stop are not such that the motorist feels completely at the mercy of the police. To be sure, the aura of authority surrounding an armed, uniformed officer and the knowledge that the officer has some discretion in deciding whether to issue a citation, in combination, exert some pressure on the detainee to respond to questions. But other aspects of the situation substantially offset these forces. Perhaps most importantly, the typical traffic stop is public, at least to some degree. [This] exposure to public view both reduces the ability of an unscrupulous policeman to use illegitimate means to elicit self-incriminating statements and diminishes the motorist's fear that, if he does not cooperate, he will be subjected to abuse. The fact that the detained motorist typically is confronted by only one or at most two policemen further mutes his sense of vulnerability. In short, the atmosphere surrounding an ordinary traffic stop is substantially less "police dominated" than that surrounding the kinds of interrogation at issue in *Miranda* itself and in the subsequent cases in which we have applied *Miranda*.[a]

In both of these respects, the usual traffic stop is more analogous to a so-called "*Terry* stop" than to a formal arrest. Under the Fourth Amendment, we have held, a policeman who lacks probable cause but whose "observations lead him reasonably to suspect" that a particular person has committed, is committing, or is about to commit a crime, may detain that person briefly in order to "investigate the circumstances that provoke suspicion." * * * Typically, this means that the officer may ask the detainee a moderate number of questions to determine his identity and to try to obtain information confirming or dispelling the officer's suspicions. But the detainee is not obliged to respond. And, unless the detainee's answers provide the officer with probable cause to arrest him, he must then be released. The comparatively nonthreatening character of detentions of this sort explains the absence of any suggestion in our opinions that *Terry* stops are subject to the dictates of *Miranda*.

Respondent contends that to "exempt" traffic stops from the coverage of *Miranda* will open the way to widespread abuse. Policemen will simply delay formally arresting detained motorists, and will subject them to sustained and intimidating interrogation at the scene of their initial detention. * * *

We are confident that the state of affairs projected by respondent will not come to pass. It is settled that the safeguards prescribed by *Miranda* become applicable as soon as a suspect's freedom of action is curtailed to a "degree associated with formal arrest." *California v. Beheler,* 463 U.S. 1121 (1983) (per curiam). If a motorist who has been detained pursuant to a traffic stop thereafter is subjected to treatment that renders him "in custody" for practical purposes, he will be entitled to the full panoply of protections prescribed by *Miranda*. See *Oregon v. Mathiason,* 429 U.S. 492 (1977) (per curiam).[b] * * *

a. At this point the Court referred to *Orozco v. Texas,* 394 U.S. 324 (1969) (applying *Miranda* to a situation where defendant was questioned in his bedroom by four police officers at 4:00 a.m., circumstances that produced a "potentiality for compulsion" equivalent to police station interrogation) and *Mathis v. United States,* 391 U.S. 1 (1968) (applying *Miranda* to the questioning of defendant about his tax returns by an internal revenue agent when defendant was incarcerated in jail on another matter.)

b. *Mathiason* makes plain that *Miranda* warnings are not required "simply because the questioning takes place in the station house." *Mathiason,* a suspect in a burglary, agreed over the phone to meet with a police officer at a convenient time and place (the state patrol office, only two blocks from defendant's apartment). *Mathiason* went to the patrol office on his own. When he arrived the officer told him he was not under arrest. The officer then said

he wanted to talk to defendant about a burglary. When Mathiason confessed a few moments later he was not, held the Court, being subjected to "custodial interrogation."

There was some reason to think that *Mathiason* might be limited to situations where suspects go to the station house *unaccompanied* by police officers. But *Beheler* made it clear that *Mathiason* could not be read that narrowly. Some hours after the murder weapon (which defendant claimed others had hidden) was found in his backyard, Beheler, as the Court described it, "voluntarily agreed to accompany police to the station house, although the police specifically told [him] that he was not under arrest." At the station house, Beheler agreed to talk about the murder, but the police did not advise him of his *Miranda* rights. The incriminating statements made at the police station, ruled the Court, were not the product of "custodial interrogation."

Turning to the case before us, we find nothing in the record that indicates that respondent should have been given *Miranda* warnings at any point prior to the time Trooper Williams placed him under arrest. At no point [during the short period of time between the stop and the formal arrest] was respondent informed that his detention would not be temporary. Although Trooper Williams apparently decided as soon as respondent stepped out of his car that respondent would be taken into custody and charged with a traffic offense, Williams never communicated his intention to respondent. A policeman's unarticulated plan has no bearing on the question whether a suspect was "in custody" at a particular time; the only relevant inquiry is how a reasonable man in the suspect's position would have understood his situation.[c] Nor do other aspects of the interaction of Williams and respondent support the contention that respondent was exposed to "custodial interrogation" at the scene of the stop. From aught that appears in the stipulation of facts, a single police officer asked respondent a modest number of questions and requested him to perform a simple balancing test at a location visible to passing motorists. Treatment of this sort cannot fairly be characterized as the functional equivalent of formal arrest.

We conclude, in short, that respondent was not taken into custody for the purposes of *Miranda* until Williams arrested him. Consequently, the statements respondent made prior to that point were admissible against him. * * *

2. What constitutes "interrogation" within the meaning of Miranda?

RHODE ISLAND v. INNIS

446 U.S. 291, 100 S.Ct. 1682, 64 L.Ed.2d 297 (1980).

JUSTICE STEWART delivered the opinion of the Court.

[*Miranda*] held that, once a defendant in custody asks to speak with a lawyer, all interrogation must cease until a lawyer is present. The issue in this case is whether the respondent was "interrogated" in violation [of *Miranda*].

[At approximately 4:30 a.m., a patrolman arrested respondent, suspected of robbing a taxicab driver and murdering him with a shotgun blast to the back of the head. Respondent was unarmed. He was advised of his rights. Within minutes a sergeant (who advised respondent of his rights) and then a captain arrived at the scene of the arrest. The captain also gave respondent the *Miranda* warnings, whereupon respondent asked to speak with a lawyer. The captain then directed that respondent be placed in a police vehicle with a wire screen mesh between the front and rear seats and be driven to the police station. Three officers were assigned to accompany the arrestee. Although the record is somewhat unclear, it appears that Patrolman Williams was in the back seat with respondent and that Patrolmen Gleckman and McKenna were in front.]

While enroute to the central station, Patrolman Gleckman initiated a conver-

---

c. Prior to *Berkemer v. McCarty*, it was unclear what test should apply in determining when questioning becomes "custodial": (a) the *subjective intention* of the questioning officer to take the suspect into custody; (b) the *subjective belief* of the suspect that he was in custody; or (c) whether *a reasonable person* in the suspect's situation would believe he was in custody. The objective standard adopted by the *McCarty* Court reflects the approach taken by most of the lower courts. They regarded this test as the most sensible and the most consistent with *Miranda*'s underlying concerns. For it avoided reliance on self-serving statements by the police or the suspect, also avoided the need to determine the officer's state of mind, and freed the police of responsibility for the idiosyncracies of various suspects.

sation with Patrolman McKenna concerning the missing shotgun.[1] As Patrolman Gleckman later testified:

> "A. At this point, I was talking back and forth with Patrolman McKenna stating that I frequent this area while on patrol and [that because a school for handicapped children is located nearby,] there's a lot of handicapped children running around in this area, and God forbid one of them might find a weapon with shells and they might hurt themselves."

Patrolman McKenna apparently shared his fellow officer's concern:

> "A. I more or less concurred with him [Gleckman] that it was a safety factor and that we should, you know, continue to search for the weapon and try to find it."
>
>   * * *

[Respondent then interrupted the conversation, stating that he would show the officers where the gun was located. The police vehicle then returned to the scene of the arrest where a search for the shotgun was in progress. There, the captain again advised respondent of his rights. He replied that he understood his rights, but "wanted to get the gun out of the way because of the kids in the area in the school." He then led the police to a nearby field, where he pointed out the shotgun under some rocks.

[Respondent was convicted of murder. The trial judge admitted the shotgun and testimony related to its discovery. On appeal, the Rhode Island Supreme Court concluded that the police had "interrogated" respondent without a valid waiver of his right to counsel; the conversation in the police vehicle had constituted "subtle coercion" that was the equivalent of *Miranda* "interrogation."]

[Since the parties agree that respondent was fully informed of his *Miranda* rights, that he asserted his right to counsel, and that he was "in custody" while being driven to the police station, the issue is whether he was "interrogated" in violation of *Miranda*.] In resolving this issue, we first define the term "interrogation" under *Miranda* before turning to a consideration of the facts of this case.

[Various references throughout the *Miranda* opinion] to "questioning" might suggest that the *Miranda* rules were to apply only to those police interrogation practices that involve express questioning of a defendant while in custody.

We do not, however, construe the *Miranda* opinion so narrowly. The concern of the Court in *Miranda* was that the "interrogation environment" created by the interplay of interrogation and custody would "subjugate the individual to the will of his examiner" and thereby undermine the privilege against compulsory self-incrimination. The police practices that evoked this concern included several that did not involve express questioning [such as] the so-called "reverse lineup" in which a defendant would be identified by coached witnesses as the perpetrator of a fictitious crime, [to induce] him to confess to the actual crime of which he was suspected in order to escape the false prosecution. * * * It is clear that these techniques of persuasion, no less than express questioning, were thought, in a custodial setting, to amount to interrogation.

This is not to say, however, that all statements obtained by the police after a person has been taken into custody are to be considered the product of interrogation. * * * It is clear [that the *Miranda* warnings] are required not where a suspect is simply taken into custody, but rather where a suspect in custody is subjected to interrogation. "Interrogation," as conceptualized [in *Miranda*],

---

1. Although there was conflicting testimony about the exact seating arrangements, it is clear that everyone in the vehicle heard the conversation.

must reflect a measure of compulsion above and beyond that inherent in custody itself.[4]

We conclude that the *Miranda* safeguards come into play whenever a person in custody is subjected to either express questioning or its functional equivalent. That is to say, the term "interrogation" under *Miranda* refers not only to express questioning, but also to any words or actions on the part of the police (other than those normally attendant to arrest and custody) that the police should know are reasonably likely to elicit an incriminating response from the suspect. The latter portion of this definition focuses primarily upon the perceptions of the suspect, rather than the intent of the police. This focus reflects the fact that the *Miranda* safeguards were designed to vest a suspect in custody with an added measure of protection against coercive police practices, without regard to objective proof of the underlying intent of the police. A practice that the police should know is reasonably likely to evoke an incriminating response from a suspect thus amounts to interrogation.[7] But, since the police surely cannot be held accountable for the unforeseeable results of their words or actions, the definition of interrogation can extend only to words or actions on the part of police officers that they *should have known* were reasonably likely to elicit an incriminating response.[8]

Turning to the facts of the present case, we conclude that the respondent was not "interrogated" within the meaning of *Miranda*. It is undisputed that the first prong of the definition of "interrogation" was not satisfied, for the [Gleckman–McKenna conversation] included no express questioning of the respondent. Rather, that conversation was, at least in form, nothing more than a dialogue between the two officers to which no response from the respondent was invited.

Moreover, it cannot be fairly concluded that the respondent was subjected to the "functional equivalent" of questioning. It cannot be said, in short, that [the officers should have known that their conversation was reasonably likely to elicit an incriminating response from the respondent. There is nothing in the record to suggest that the officers were aware that the respondent was peculiarly susceptible to an appeal to his conscience concerning the safety of handicapped children [or that] the police knew that the respondent was unusually disoriented or upset at the time of his arrest.[9]

4. There is language in the opinion of the Rhode Island Supreme Court in this case suggesting that the definition of "interrogation" under *Miranda* is informed by this Court's decision in *Brewer v. Williams,* [Sec. 5 infra, reaffirming and expansively interpreting the *Massiah* doctrine]. This suggestion is erroneous. Our decision in *Brewer* rested solely on the Sixth and Fourteenth Amendment right to counsel. That right, as we held in *Massiah,* prohibits law enforcement officers from "deliberately elicit[ing]" incriminating information from a defendant in the absence of counsel after a formal charge against the defendant has been filed. Custody in such a case is not controlling; indeed, the petitioner in *Massiah* was not in custody. By contrast, the right to counsel at issue in the present case is based not on the Sixth and Fourteenth Amendments, but rather on the Fifth and Fourteenth Amendments as interpreted in the *Miranda* opinion. The definitions of "interrogation" under the Fifth and Sixth Amendments, if indeed the term "interrogation" is even apt in the Sixth Amendment context, are not necessarily interchangeable, since the policies under-

lying the two constitutional protections are quite distinct.

7. This is not to say that the intent of the police is irrelevant, for it may well have a bearing on whether the police should have known that their words or actions were reasonably likely to evoke an incriminating response. In particular, where a police practice is designed to elicit an incriminating response from the accused, it is unlikely that the practice will not also be one which the police should have known was reasonably likely to have that effect.

8. Any knowledge the police may have had concerning the unusual susceptibility of a defendant to a particular form of persuasion might be an important factor in determining whether the police should have known that their words or actions were reasonably likely to elicit an incriminating response from the suspect.

9. The record in no way suggests that the officers' remarks were *designed* to elicit a response. It is significant that the trial judge,

The case thus boils down to whether, in the context of a brief conversation, the officers should have known that the respondent would suddenly be moved to make a self-incriminating response. Given the fact that the entire conversation appears to have consisted of no more than a few off-hand remarks, we cannot say that the officers should have known that it was reasonably likely that Innis would so respond. This is not a case where the police carried on a lengthy harangue in the presence of the suspect. Nor does the record support the respondent's contention that, under the circumstances, the officers' comments were particularly "evocative." * * *

The Rhode Island Supreme Court erred, in short, in equating "subtle compulsion" with interrogation. That the officers' comments struck a responsive cord is readily apparent. Thus, it may be said, as the Rhode Island Supreme Court did say, that one respondent was subjected to "subtle compulsion." But that is not the end of the inquiry. It must also be established that a suspect's incriminating response was the product of words or actions on the part of the police that they should have known were reasonably likely to elicit an incriminating response.[10] This was not established in the present case. * * *[a]

CHIEF JUSTICE BURGER, concurring in the judgment. * * *

The meaning of *Miranda* has become reasonably clear and law enforcement practices have adjusted to its strictures; I would neither overrule *Miranda,* disparage it, nor extend it at this late date. I fear, however, that [the Court's opinion] may introduce new elements of uncertainty; under the Court's test, a police officer, in the brief time available, apparently must evaluate the suggestibility and susceptibility of an accused. Few, if any, police officers are competent to make the kind of evaluation seemingly contemplated; even a psychiatrist asked to express an expert opinion on these aspects of a suspect in custody would very

after hearing the officers' testimony, concluded that it was "entirely understandable that [the officers] would voice their concern [for the safety of the handicapped children] to each other."

10. By way of example, if the police had done no more than to drive past the site of the concealed weapon while taking the most direct route to the police station, and if the respondent, upon noticing for the first time the proximity of the school for handicapped children, had blurted out that he would show the officers where the gun was located, it could not seriously be argued that this "subtle compulsion" would have constituted "interrogation" within the meaning of the *Miranda* opinion.

a. Notwithstanding language in *Innis,* as *Arizona v. Mauro,* 481 U.S. 520 (1987) illustrates, it is not inevitably "interrogation" within the meaning of *Miranda* for the police to allow a scenario to occur which they know may prompt the defendant to incriminate himself. In *Mauro,* a 5–4 majority, per Powell, J., held that it was not interrogation for the police to accede to the request of defendant's wife, also a suspect in the murder of their son, to speak with defendant (who had been given the *Miranda* warnings and had asserted his right to counsel) in the presence of a police officer, who placed a tape recorder in plain sight on a desk. Observed the Court:

"The tape recording of the conversation between Mauro and his wife shows that [the detective who attended their meeting] asked Mauro no questions about the crime or his conduct. Nor is it suggested [that the police decision] to allow Mauro's wife to see him was the kind of psychological ploy that properly could be treated as the functional equivalent of interrogation.

" * * * Mauro was not subjected to compelling influences, psychological ploys, or direct questioning. Thus, his volunteered statements cannot properly be considered the result of police interrogation.

"In deciding whether particular police conduct is interrogation, we must remember the purpose behind [*Miranda*]: preventing government officials from using the coercive nature of confinement to extract confessions that would not be given in an unrestrained environment. The government actions in this case do not implicate this purpose in any way. Police departments need not adopt inflexible rules barring suspects from speaking with their spouses, nor must they ignore legitimate security concerns by allowing spouses to meet in private. In short, the officers in this case acted reasonably and lawfully by allowing Mrs. Mauro to speak with her husband."

likely employ extensive questioning and observation to make the judgment now charged to police officers. * * *

JUSTICE MARSHALL, with whom JUSTICE BRENNAN joins, dissenting.

I am substantially in agreement with the Court's definition of "interrogation" within the meaning of *Miranda*. In my view, the *Miranda* safeguards apply whenever police conduct is intended or likely to produce a response from a suspect in custody. As I read the Court's opinion, its definition of "interrogation" for *Miranda* purposes is equivalent, for practical purposes, to my formulation, since it contemplates that "where a police practice is designed to elicit an incriminating response from the accused, it is unlikely that the practice will not also be one which the police should have known was reasonably likely to have that effect" [fn. 7]. Thus, the Court requires an objective inquiry into the likely effect of police conduct on a typical individual, taking into account any special susceptibility of the suspect to certain kinds of pressure of which the police know or have reason to know.

I am utterly at a loss, however, to understand how this objective standard as applied to the facts before us can rationally lead to the conclusion that there was no interrogation. * * *

One can scarcely imagine a stronger appeal to the conscience of a suspect— *any* suspect—than the assertion that if the weapon is not found an innocent person will be hurt or killed. And not just any innocent person, but an innocent child—a little girl—a helpless, handicapped little girl on her way to school. The notion that such an appeal could not be expected to have any effect unless the suspect were known to have some special interest in handicapped children verges on the ludicrous. As a matter of fact, the appeal to a suspect to confess for the sake of others, to "display some evidence of decency and honor," is a classic interrogation technique.

Gleckman's remarks would obviously have constituted interrogation if they had been explicitly directed to petitioner, and the result should not be different because they were nominally addressed to McKenna. This is not a case where police officers speaking among themselves are accidentally overheard by a suspect. These officers were "talking back and forth" in close quarters with the hand-cuffed suspect, traveling past the very place where they believed the weapon was located. They knew petitioner would hear and attend to their conversation, and they are chargeable with knowledge of and responsibility for the pressures to speak which they created.

I firmly believe that this case is simply an aberration, and that in future cases the Court will apply the standard adopted today in accordance with its plain meaning.

JUSTICE STEVENS, dissenting.

* * * In my view any statement that would normally be understood by the average listener as calling for a response is the functional equivalent of a direct question, whether or not it is punctuated by a question mark. The Court, however, takes a much narrower view. It holds that police conduct is not the "functional equivalent" of direct questioning unless the police should have known that what they were saying or doing was likely to elicit an incriminating response from the suspect. This holding represents a plain departure from the principles set forth in *Miranda*. * * *

From the suspect's point of view, the effectiveness of the warnings depends on whether it appears that the police are scrupulously honoring his rights. Apparent attempts to elicit information from a suspect after he has invoked his right to cut off questioning necessarily demean that right and tend to reinstate the imbalance between police and suspect that the *Miranda* warnings are designed to correct. Thus, if the rationale for requiring those warnings in the first place is to be respected, any police conduct or statements that would appear to a reasonable person in the suspect's position to call for a response must be considered "interrogation."

In short, in order to give full protection to a suspect's right to be free from any interrogation at all, the definition of "interrogation" must include any police statement or conduct that has the same purpose or effect as a direct question. Statements that appear to call for a response from the suspect, as well as those that are designed to do so, should be considered interrogation. By prohibiting only those relatively few statements or actions that a police officer should know are likely to elicit an incriminating response, the Court today accords a suspect considerably less protection. Indeed, since I suppose most suspects are unlikely to incriminate themselves even when questioned directly, this new definition will almost certainly exclude every statement that is not punctuated with a question mark from the concept of "interrogation."

The difference between the approach required by a faithful adherence to *Miranda* and the stinted test applied by the Court today can be illustrated by comparing three different ways in which Officer Gleckman could have communicated his fears about the possible dangers posed by the shotgun to handicapped children. He could have:

(1) directly asked Innis:

Will you please tell me where the shotgun is so we can protect handicapped schoolchildren from danger?

(2) announced to the other officers in the wagon:

If the man sitting in the back seat with me should decide to tell us where the gun is, we can protect handicapped children from danger.

or (3) stated to the other officers:

It would be too bad if a little handicapped girl would pick up the gun that this man left in the area and maybe kill herself.

In my opinion, all three of these statements should be considered interrogation because all three appear to be designed to elicit a response from anyone who in fact knew where the gun was located. Under the Court's test, on the other hand, the form of the statements would be critical. Statement # 3 would not be interrogation because in the Court's view there was no reason for Officer Gleckman to believe that Innis was susceptible to this type of an implied appeal; therefore, the statement would not be reasonably likely to elicit an incriminating response. Assuming that this is true, then it seems to me that the first two statements, which would be just as unlikely to elicit such a response, should also not be considered interrogation. But, because the first statement is clearly an express question, it *would* be considered interrogation under the Court's test. The second statement, although just as clearly a deliberate appeal to Innis to reveal the location of the gun, would presumably not be interrogation because (a) it was not in form a direct question and (b) it does not fit within the "reasonably likely to elicit an incriminating response" category that applies to indirect interrogation.

As this example illustrates, the Court's test creates an incentive for police to ignore a suspect's invocation of his rights in order to make continued attempts to extract information from him. If a suspect does not appear to be susceptible to a particular type of psychological pressure, the police are apparently free to exert that pressure on him despite his request for counsel, so long as they are careful not to punctuate their statements with question marks. And if, contrary to all reasonable expectations, the suspect makes an incriminating statement, that statement can be used against him at trial. The Court thus turns *Miranda's* unequivocal rule against any interrogation at all into a trap in which unwary suspects may be caught by police deception.

* * * I think the Court is clearly wrong in holding, as a matter of law, that Officer Gleckman should not have realized that his statement was likely to elicit an incriminating response. Moreover, there is evidence in the record to support the view that Officer Gleckman's statement was intended to elicit a response from Innis. Officer Gleckman, who was not regularly assigned to the caged wagon, was directed by a police captain to ride with respondent to the police station. [The] record does not explain why, notwithstanding the fact that respondent was handcuffed, unarmed, and had offered no resistance when arrested by an officer acting alone, the captain ordered Officer Gleckman to ride with respondent. It is not inconceivable that two professionally trained police officers concluded that a few well-chosen remarks might induce respondent to disclose the whereabouts of the shotgun.[18] This conclusion becomes even more plausible in light of the emotionally charged words chosen by Officer Gleckman ("God forbid" that a "little girl" should find the gun and hurt herself).* * *

ILLINOIS v. PERKINS

496 U.S. 292, 110 S.Ct. 2394, 110 L.Ed.2d 243 (1990).

JUSTICE KENNEDY delivered the opinion of the Court.

* * * We hold [that] *Miranda* warnings are not required when the suspect is unaware that he is speaking to a law enforcement officer and gives a voluntary statement.

[When Charlton, who had been a fellow inmate of respondent Perkins in another prison, told police that Perkins had implicated himself in the Stephenson murder, the police placed Charlton and Parisi, an undercover agent, in the same cellblock with Perkins, who was incarcerated on charges unrelated to the Stephenson murder. Parisi and Charlton posed as escapees from a work release program who had been arrested in the course of a burglary. They were instructed to engage Perkins in casual conversation and to report anything he said about the Stephenson murder.

[The cellblock consisted of 12 separate cells that opened onto a common room. Perkins greeted Charlton, who introduced Parisi by his alias. Parisi suggested that the three of them escape. There was further conversation. After telling Charlton that he would be responsible for any killing that might occur during a prison break, Parisi asked Perkins if he had ever "done" anybody. Perkins replied that he had, and proceeded to describe the Stephenson murder in detail.

[The trial court suppressed the statements made to Parisi in the jail. The Appellate Court of Illinois affirmed, reading *Miranda* as prohibiting all undercover contacts with incarcerated suspects which are reasonably likely to elicit an incriminating response.]

18. Although Officer Gleckman testified that the captain told him not to interrogate, intimidate or coerce respondent on the way back, this does not rule out the possibility that either or both of them thought an indirect psychological ploy would be permissible.

Conversations between suspects and undercover agents do not implicate the concerns underlying *Miranda*. The essential ingredients of a "police-dominated atmosphere" and compulsion are not present when an incarcerated person speaks freely to someone that he believes to be a fellow inmate. Coercion is determined from the perspective of the suspect. When a suspect considers himself in the company of cellmates and not officers, the coercive atmosphere is lacking. * * * There is no empirical basis for the assumption that a suspect speaking to those whom he assumes are not officers will feel compelled to speak by the fear of reprisal for remaining silent or in the hope of more lenient treatment should he confess.

It is the premise of *Miranda* that the danger of coercion results from the interaction of custody and official interrogation. We reject the argument that *Miranda* warnings are required whenever a suspect is in custody in a technical sense and converses with someone who happens to be a government agent. Questioning by captors, who appear to control the suspect's fate, may create mutually reinforcing pressures that the Court has assumed will weaken the suspect's will, but where a suspect does not know that he is conversing with a government agent, these pressures do not exist. The State Court here mistakenly assumed that because the suspect was in custody, no undercover questioning could take place. When the suspect has no reason to think that the listeners have official power over him, it should not be assumed that his words are motivated by the reaction he expects from his listeners. "[W]hen the agent carries neither badge nor gun and wears not 'police blue,' but the same prison gray" as the suspect, there is no "*interplay* between police interrogation and police custody." Kamisar, *Brewer v. Williams, Massiah and Miranda: What is "Interrogation"? When Does it Matter?*, 67 Geo.L.J. 1, 67, 63 (1978). * * *

The tactic employed here to elicit a voluntary confession from a suspect does not violate the Self–Incrimination Clause. We held in *Hoffa v. United States*, 385 U.S. 293 (1966), that placing an undercover agent near a suspect in order to gather incriminating information was permissible under the Fifth Amendment. In *Hoffa*, while petitioner Hoffa was on trial, he met often with one Partin, who, unbeknownst to Hoffa, was cooperating with law enforcement officials. Partin reported to officials that Hoffa had divulged his attempts to bribe jury members. We approved using Hoffa's statements at his subsequent trial for jury tampering, on the rationale that "no claim ha[d] been or could [have been] made that [Hoffa's] incriminating statements were the product of any sort of coercion, legal or factual." [The] only difference between this case and *Hoffa* is that the suspect here was incarcerated, but detention, whether or not for the crime in question, does not warrant a presumption that the use of an undercover agent to speak with an incarcerated suspect makes any confession thus obtained involuntary. * * *

This Court's Sixth Amendment decisions in *Massiah v. United States, United States v. Henry, and Maine v. Moulton* [all discussed in Section 5 of this Chapter], also do not avail respondent. We held in those cases that the government may not use an undercover agent to circumvent the Sixth Amendment right to counsel once a suspect has been charged with the crime. After charges have been filed, the Sixth Amendment prevents the government from interfering with the accused's right to counsel. In the instant case no charges had been filed on the subject of the interrogation, and our Sixth Amendment precedents are not applicable. * * *

JUSTICE BRENNAN, concurring in the judgment.

Although I do not subscribe to the majority's characterization of *Miranda* in its entirety, I do agree that when a suspect does not know that his questioner is a police agent, such questioning does not amount to "interrogation" in an "inherently coercive" environment so as to require application of *Miranda*. Since the only issue raised at this stage of the litigation is the applicability of *Miranda*, I concur in the judgment of the Court.

This is not to say that I believe the Constitution condones the method by which the police extracted the confession in this case. To the contrary, the deception and manipulation practiced on respondent raise a substantial claim that the confession was obtained in violation of the Due Process Clause.

[The] method used to elicit the confession in this case deserves close scrutiny. [As] Justice Marshall points out, the pressures of custody make a suspect more likely to confide in others and to engage in "jailhouse bravado." The State is in a unique position to exploit this vulnerability because it has virtually complete control over the suspect's environment. Thus, the State can ensure that a suspect is barraged with questions from an undercover agent until the suspect confesses. The testimony in this case suggests the State did just that.

The deliberate use of deception and manipulation by the police appears to be incompatible "with a system that presumes innocence and assures that a conviction will not be secured by inquisitorial means," *Miller,* and raises serious concerns that respondent's will was overborne. It is open to the lower court on remand to determine whether, under the totality of the circumstances, respondent's confession was elicited in a manner that violated the Due Process Clause. * * *

JUSTICE MARSHALL, dissenting.

The conditions that require the police to apprise a defendant of his constitutional rights—custodial interrogation conducted by an agent of the police—were present in this case. [Because] Perkins received no *Miranda* warnings before he was subjected to custodial interrogation, his confession was not admissible. * * *

Because Perkins was interrogated by police while he was in custody, *Miranda* required that the officer inform him of his rights. In rejecting that conclusion, the Court finds that "conversations" between undercover agents and suspects are devoid of the coercion inherent in stationhouse interrogations conducted by law enforcement officials who openly represent the State. *Miranda* was not, however, concerned solely with police *coercion*. It dealt with any police tactics that may operate to compel a suspect in custody to make incriminating statements without full awareness of his constitutional rights. [Thus,] when a law enforcement agent structures a custodial interrogation so that a suspect feels compelled to reveal incriminating information, he must inform the suspect of his constitutional rights and give him an opportunity to decide whether or not to talk. * * *

Custody works to the State's advantage in obtaining incriminating information. The psychological pressures inherent in confinement increase the suspect's anxiety, making him likely to seek relief by talking with others. Dix, *Undercover Investigations and Police Rulemaking*, 53 Texas L.Rev. 203, 230 (1975). The inmate is thus more susceptible to efforts by undercover agents to elicit information from him. Similarly, where the suspect is incarcerated, the constant threat of physical danger peculiar to the prison environment may make him demonstrate his toughness to other inmates by recounting or inventing past violent acts. [In] this case, the police deceptively took advantage of Perkins' psychological vulnerability by including him in a sham escape plot, a situation in which he would feel compelled to demonstrate his willingness to shoot a prison guard by revealing his past involvement in a murder. ([The] agent stressed that a killing might be necessary in the escape and then asked Perkins if he had ever murdered some-one).

Thus, the pressures unique to custody allow the police to use deceptive interrogation tactics to compel a suspect to make an incriminating statement. The compulsion is not eliminated by the suspect's ignorance of his interrogator's true identity. The Court therefore need not inquire past the bare facts of custody and interrogation to determine whether *Miranda* warnings are required. * * *

3. If a suspect asserts his right to counsel, may the police "try again"? If a suspect who has asserted his right to counsel is allowed to consult with an attorney, may the police reinitiate interrogation in the absence of counsel?

MINNICK v. MISSISSIPPI

498 U.S. 146, 111 S.Ct. 486, 112 L.Ed.2d 489 (1990).

JUSTICE KENNEDY delivered the opinion of the Court.

To protect the privilege against self-incrimination guaranteed by the Fifth Amendment, we have held that the police must terminate interrogation of an accused in custody if the accused requests the assistance of counsel. *Miranda.* We reinforced the protections of *Miranda* in *Edwards v. Arizona,* 451 U.S. 477 (1981), which held that once the accused requests counsel, officials may not reinitiate questioning "until counsel has been made available" to him.[a] The issue

a. But what constitutes a request for counsel within the meaning of the *Edwards* rule? For example, how should the police respond if a suspect makes an ambiguous or equivocal reference to an attorney? Consider *Davis v. United States,* 512 U.S. 452 (1994), which arose as follows:

Defendant, a member of the U.S. Navy, initially waived his rights when interviewed by naval investigative agents in connection with a murder. About an hour and a half into the interview, he said, "Maybe I should talk to a lawyer." However, when asked whether he was requesting a lawyer, defendant replied: "No, I'm not asking for a lawyer." And then he continued on, and said: "No, I don't want a lawyer." After a short break, the interview continued for another hour, until defendant asked to have a lawyer present before saying anything more. The military judge admitted the statements made during the interview and defendant was convicted of murder.

The Supreme Court, per O'Connor, J., upheld the admissibility of the statements, declining to adopt a rule requiring law enforcement officers to cease questioning immediately or to ask clarifying questions when a suspect makes an ambiguous or equivocal reference to an attorney:

"[A] suspect must unambiguously request counsel. [He] must articulate his desire to have counsel present sufficiently clearly that a reasonable police officer in the circumstances would understand the statement to be a request for an attorney. If the statement fails to meet the requisite level of

clarity, *Edwards* does not require that the officer stop questioning the suspect. * * *

"The *Edwards* rule—questioning must cease if the suspect asks for a lawyer—provides a bright line that can be applied by officers in the real world of investigation and interrogation without unduly hampering the gathering of information. But if we were to require questioning to cease if a suspect makes a statement that *might* be a request for an attorney, this clarity and ease of application would be lost. Police officers would be forced to make difficult judgment calls about whether the suspect in fact wants a lawyer even though he hasn't said so, with the threat of suppression if they guess wrong. We therefore hold that, after a knowing and voluntary waiver of the *Miranda* rights, law enforcement officers may continue questioning until and unless the suspect clearly requests an attorney.

"Of course, when a suspect makes an ambiguous or equivocal statement it will often be good police practice to clarify whether or not he actually wants an attorney. That was the procedure followed [in] this case. [But] we decline to adopt a rule requiring officers to ask clarifying questions. If the suspect's statement is not an unambiguous or unequivocal request for counsel, the officer have no obligation to stop questioning him."

Souter, J., joined by Blackmun, Stevens and Ginsburg, JJ., concurred in the judgment, but could not join in the majority's "further con-in the case before us is whether *Edwards'* protection ceases once the suspect has consulted with an attorney.

[Petitioner Minnick and fellow prisoner Dykes escaped from a Mississippi jail and broke into a trailer in search of weapons. In the course of the burglary, they killed two people. Minnick and Dykes fled to Mexico, where they fought, and Minnick then proceeded alone to California where, some four months after the murders, he was arrested by local police and placed in a San Diego jail. The day following his arrest, Saturday, two FBI agents came to the jail to interview him. After being advised of his rights and acknowledging that he understood them, Minnick refused to sign a rights waiver form, but agreed to answer some questions. He maintained that Dykes had killed one victim and forced him to shoot the other, but otherwise he hesitated to discuss what happened at the trailer.]

[At this point] the [FBI] agents reminded him he did not have to answer questions without a lawyer present. According to the [FBI] report, "Minnick stated that he would make a more complete statement then with his lawyer present." The FBI interview ended.

After the FBI interview, an appointed attorney met with petitioner. [He] spoke with the lawyer on two or three occasions, though it is not clear from the record whether all of these conferences were in person.

On Monday [Denham, a Mississippi deputy sheriff,] came to the San Diego jail to question Minnick. Minnick testified that his jailers * * * told him he would "have to talk" to Denham and that he "could not refuse." Denham advised petitioner of his rights, and petitioner again declined to sign a rights waiver form. [However, Minnick agreed to answer some questions and made a number of incriminating statements].

Minnick was tried for murder in Mississippi. He moved to suppress all statements given to the FBI or other police officers, including Denham. The trial court denied the motion with respect to petitioner's statements to Denham, but suppressed his other statements. Petitioner was convicted on two counts of capital murder and sentenced to death. [The state supreme court affirmed.]

Edwards is "designed to prevent police from badgering a defendant into waiving his previously asserted *Miranda* rights." *Michigan v. Harvey,* 110 S.Ct. 1176 (1990). The rule ensures that any statement made in subsequent interrogation is not the result of coercive pressures. *Edwards* conserves judicial resources which would otherwise be expended in making difficult determinations of voluntariness, and implements the protections of *Miranda* in practical and straightforward terms.

The merit of the *Edwards* decision lies in the clarity of its command and the certainty of its application. We have confirmed that the *Edwards* rule provides " 'clear and unequivocal' guidelines to the law enforcement profession." * * *

Our cases following *Edwards* have interpreted the decision to mean that the authorities may not initiate questioning of the accused in counsel's absence. Writing for a plurality of the Court, for instance, then Justice Rehnquist described the holding of *Edwards* to be "that subsequent incriminating statements made *without [Edwards']* attorney present violated the rights secured to the defendant by the Fifth and Fourteenth Amendments to the United States Constitution."

clusion that if the investigators here had been so inclined, they were at liberty to disregard Davis's reference to a lawyer entirely, in accordance with a general rule that interrogators have no legal obligation to discover what a custodial subject meant by an ambiguous statement that could reasonably be understood to express a desire to consult a lawyer."

Oregon v. Bradshaw, 462 U.S. 1039 (1983) [b] (emphasis added). [In] our view, a fair reading of *Edwards* and subsequent cases demonstrates that we have interpreted the rule to bar police-initiated interrogation unless the accused has counsel with him at the time of questioning. Whatever the ambiguities of our earlier cases on this point, we now hold that when counsel is requested, interrogation must cease, and officials may not reinitiate interrogation without counsel present, whether or not the accused has consulted with his attorney.

We consider our ruling to be an appropriate and necessary application of the *Edwards* rule. A single consultation with an attorney does not remove the suspect from persistent attempts by officials to persuade him to waive his rights, or from the coercive pressures that accompany custody and that may increase as custody is prolonged. The case before us well illustrates the pressures, and abuses, that may be concomitants of custody. Petitioner testified that though he resisted, he was required to submit to both the FBI and the Denham interviews. In the latter instance, the compulsion to submit to interrogation followed petitioner's unequivocal request during the FBI interview that questioning cease until counsel was present. The case illustrates also that consultation is not always effective in instructing the suspect of his rights. One plausible interpretation of the record is that petitioner thought he could keep his admissions out of evidence by refusing to sign a formal waiver of rights. If the authorities had complied with Minnick's request to have counsel present during interrogation, the attorney could have corrected Minnick's misunderstanding, or indeed counseled him that he need not make a statement at all. We decline to remove protection from police-initiated questioning based on isolated consultations with counsel who is absent when the interrogation resumes.

The exception to *Edwards* here proposed is inconsistent with *Edwards'* purpose to protect the suspect's right to have counsel present at custodial interrogation. It is inconsistent as well with *Miranda,* where we specifically rejected respondent's theory that the opportunity to consult with one's attorney would substantially counteract the compulsion created by custodial interrogation. We noted in *Miranda* that "[e]ven preliminary advice given to the accused by his own attorney can be swiftly overcome by the secret interrogation process. Thus the need for counsel to protect the Fifth Amendment privilege comprehends not

b. The *Bradshaw* case indicates that it may not be too difficult to establish that a suspect "initiated" further communication with the police. In *Bradshaw,* defendant asserted his right to counsel but a few moments later, either while still at the police station or enroute to jail, asked the officer: "Well, what is going to happen to me now?" The officer responded: "You do not have to talk to me. * * * I don't want you talking to me unless you so desire * * *." Defendant said he understood and general conversation followed. A 5–4 majority held that the incriminating statements obtained as a result of the general conversation were admissible.

The plurality opinion, written by Justice Rehnquist, joined by Burger, C.J., and White and O'Connor, JJ., observed:

"There are some inquiries such as a request for a drink of water or a request to use a telephone that are so routine that they cannot be fairly said to represent a desire on the part of an accused to open up a more generalized discussion relating directly or in-

directly to the investigation. Such [statements] relating to routine incidents of the custodial relationship, will not generally 'initiate' a conversation in the sense in which that word was used in *Edwards.* [But Bradshaw's question] as to what was going to happen to him evinced a willingness and a desire for a generalized discussion about the investigation; it was not merely a necessary inquiry arising out of the incidents of the custodial relationship. It could reasonably have been interpreted by the officer as relating generally to the investigation."

Dissenting Justice Marshall, joined by Brennan, Blackmun and Stevens, JJ., "agree[d] with the plurality that in order to constitute 'initiation' under *Edwards,* an accused's inquiry must demonstrate a desire to discuss the subject matter of the criminal investigation," but was "baffled [at] the plurality's application of that standard to the facts of this case. * * * [It] is plain that [Bradshaw's] only 'desire' was to find out where the police were going to take him."

merely a right to consult with counsel prior to questioning, but also to have counsel present during any questioning if the defendant so desires."

The exception proposed, furthermore, would undermine the advantages flowing from *Edwards'* "clear and unequivocal" character. Respondent concedes that even after consultation with counsel, a second request for counsel should reinstate the *Edwards* protection. We are invited by this formulation to adopt a regime in which *Edwards'* protection could pass in and out of existence multiple times prior to arraignment, at which point the same protection might reattach by virtue of our Sixth Amendment jurisprudence, see *Michigan v. Jackson,* 475 U.S. 625 (1986). Vagaries of this sort spread confusion through the justice system and lead to a consequent loss of respect for the underlying constitutional principle.

In addition, adopting the rule proposed would leave far from certain the sort of consultation required to displace *Edwards.* Consultation is not a precise concept, for it may encompass variations from a telephone call to say that the attorney is in route, to a hurried interchange between the attorney and client in a detention facility corridor, to a lengthy in-person conference in which the attorney gives full and adequate advice respecting all matters that might be covered in further interrogations. And even with the necessary scope of consultation settled, the officials in charge of the case would have to confirm the occurrence and, possibly, the extent of consultation to determine whether further interrogation is permissible. The necessary inquiries could interfere with the attorney-client privilege.

Added to these difficulties in definition and application of the proposed rule is our concern over its consequence that the suspect whose counsel is prompt would lose the protection of *Edwards,* while the one whose counsel is dilatory would not. There is more than irony to this result. There is a strong possibility that it would distort the proper conception of the attorney's duty to the client and set us on a course at odds with what ought to be effective representation.

Both waiver of rights and admission of guilt are consistent with the affirmation of individual responsibility that is a principle of the criminal justice system. It does not detract from this principle, however, to insist that neither admissions nor waivers are effective unless there are both particular and systemic assurances that the coercive pressures of custody were not the inducing cause. The *Edwards* rule sets forth a specific standard to fulfill these purposes, and we have declined to confine it in other instances. See *Arizona v. Roberson,* 486 U.S. 675 (1988). [*Edwards* applies even when the police want to question a suspect about an offense unrelated to the subject of their initial interrogation]. It would detract from the efficacy of the rule to remove its protections based on consultation with counsel.

Edwards does not foreclose finding a waiver of Fifth Amendment protections after counsel has been requested, provided the accused has initiated the conversation or discussions with the authorities; but that is not the case before us. There can be no doubt that the interrogation in question was initiated by the police; it was a formal interview which petitioner was compelled to attend. Since petitioner made a specific request for counsel before the interview, the police-initiated interrogation was impermissible. Petitioner's statement to Denham was not admissible at trial. * * * c

JUSTICE SCALIA, with whom THE CHIEF JUSTICE joins, dissenting.

The Court today establishes an irrebuttable presumption that a criminal suspect, after invoking his *Miranda* right to counsel, can *never* validly waive that

c. Justice Souter took no part in the con-   sideration or decision of this case.

right during any police-initiated encounter, even after the suspect has been provided multiple *Miranda* warnings and has actually consulted his attorney. This holding builds on foundations already established in *Edwards,* but "the rule of *Edwards* is our rule, not a constitutional command; and it is our obligation to justify its expansion." *Arizona v. Roberson* (Kennedy, J., dissenting). Because I see no justification for applying the *Edwards* irrebuttable presumption when a criminal suspect has actually consulted with his attorney, I respectfully dissent.
* * *

The Court [holds that,] because Minnick had asked for counsel during the interview with the FBI agents, he could not—as a matter of law—validly waive the right to have counsel present during the conversation initiated by Denham. That Minnick's original request to see an attorney had been honored, that Minnick had consulted with his attorney on several occasions, and that the attorney had specifically warned Minnick not to speak to the authorities, are irrelevant. That Minnick was familiar with the criminal justice system in general or *Miranda* warnings in particular (he had previously been convicted of robbery in Mississippi and assault with a deadly weapon in California) is also beside the point. The confession must be suppressed, not because it was "compelled," nor even because it was obtained from an individual who could realistically be assumed to be unaware of his rights, but simply because this Court sees fit to prescribe as a "systemic assuranc[e]" that a person in custody who has once asked for counsel cannot thereafter be approached by the police unless counsel is present. Of course the Constitution's proscription of compelled testimony does not remotely authorize this incursion upon state practices; and even our recent precedents are not a valid excuse.

[The *Miranda* Court] expressly adopted the "high standar[d] of proof for the waiver of constitutional rights" set forth in *Johnson v. Zerbst* (1938) [Ch. 5, § 1].

Notwithstanding our acknowledgment that *Miranda* rights are "not themselves rights protected by the Constitution but * * * instead measures to insure that the right against compulsory self-incrimination [is] protected," *Michigan v. Tucker,* we have adhered to the principle that nothing less than the *Zerbst* standard for the waiver of constitutional rights applies to the waiver of *Miranda* rights. Until *Edwards,* however, we refrained from imposing on the States a *higher* standard for the waiver of *Miranda* rights. For example, in *Michigan v. Mosley,* 423 U.S. 96 (1975), we rejected a proposed irrebuttable presumption that a criminal suspect, after invoking the *Miranda* right to remain silent, could not validly waive the right during any subsequent questioning by the police.[d] In

d. In *Mosley* the Court, per Stewart, rejected the argument that *Miranda* created "a *per se* proscription of indefinite duration upon any further questioning by any police officer on any subject, once the person in custody has indicated a desire to remain silent." Rather, "the admissibility of statements obtained after [a suspect] has decided to remain silent depends under *Miranda* on whether his right to cut off questioning was 'scrupulously honored.'"

After receiving the *Miranda* warnings, Mosley declined to discuss the robberies for which he was arrested. But two hours later, after again being advised of his *Miranda* rights by another officer, Mosley agreed to talk about an unrelated holdup murder. In holding his incriminating statements admissible, the Court emphasized:

"This is not a case [where] the police failed to honor a decision of a person in custody to cut off questioning, either by refusing to discontinue the interrogation upon request or by persisting in repeated efforts to wear down his resistance and make him change his mind. [Instead,] the police here immediately ceased the interrogation, resumed questioning only after the passage of a significant period of time and the provision of a fresh set of warnings, and restricted the second interrogation to a crime that had not been a subject of the earlier interrogation."

Concurring Justice White added that when the *Miranda* Court "wanted to create a *per se* rule against further interrogation after assertion of a right, it knew how to do so. The Court [said that] 'if the individual states that

North Carolina v. Butler, 441 U.S. 369 (1979), we rejected a proposed rule that waivers of *Miranda* rights must be deemed involuntary absent an explicit assertion of waiver by the suspect.[e] And in *Fare v. Michael C.* we declined to hold that waivers of *Miranda* rights by juveniles are *per se* involuntary.

Edwards, however, broke with this approach * * *. The case stands as a solitary exception to our waiver jurisprudence. It does, to be sure, have the desirable consequences described in today's opinion. In the narrow context in which it applies, it provides 100% assurance against confessions that are "the result of coercive pressures"; it " 'prevent[s] police from badgering a defendant' "; it "conserves judicial resources which would otherwise be expended in making difficult determinations of voluntariness"; and it provides " 'clear and unequivocal" guidelines to the law enforcement profession.' " But so would a rule that simply excludes all confessions by all persons in police custody. The value of any prophylactic rule (assuming the authority to adopt a prophylactic rule) must be assessed not only on the basis of what is gained, but also on the basis of what is lost. In all other contexts we have thought the above-described consequences of abandoning *Zerbst* outweighed by " 'the need for police questioning as a tool for effective enforcement of criminal laws,' " *Moran v. Burbine,* [the last case set forth in this section].

In this case, of course, we have not been called upon to reconsider *Edwards,* but simply to determine whether its irrebuttable presumption should continue after a suspect has actually consulted with his attorney. Whatever justifications might support *Edwards* are even less convincing in this context.

Most of the Court's discussion of *Edwards*—which stresses repeatedly, in various formulations, the case's emphasis upon "the 'right to have counsel *present* during custodial interrogation' " (emphasis added by the Court)—is beside the point. The existence and the importance of the *Miranda*-created right "to have counsel *present*" are unquestioned here. What *is* questioned is why a State should not be given the opportunity to prove (under *Zerbst*) that the right was *voluntarily waived* by a suspect who, after having been read his *Miranda* rights twice and having consulted with counsel at least twice, chose to speak to a police officer (and to admit his involvement in two murders) without counsel present.

[The *Edwards* Rule] should not, in my view, extend beyond the circumstances present in *Edwards* itself—where the suspect in custody asked to consult an attorney, and was interrogated before that attorney had ever been provided. In those circumstances, the *Edwards* rule rests upon an assumption similar to that of *Miranda* itself: that when a suspect in police custody is first questioned he is likely to be ignorant of his rights and to feel isolated in a hostile environment. This likelihood is thought to justify special protection against unknowing or coerced waiver of rights. After a suspect has seen his request for an attorney honored, however, and has actually spoken with that attorney, the probabilities change. The suspect then knows that he has an advocate on his side, and that the

he wants an attorney, the interrogation must cease *until an attorney is present.*' However, when the individual indicates that *he* will decide unaided by counsel whether or not to assert his 'right to silence' the situation is different."

e. The *Butler* Court pointed out that a waiver of *Miranda* rights may be recognized even though not "specifically made" after the warnings are given. Although "mere silence" in the face of the warnings is not enough, "the defendant's silence, coupled with an understanding of his rights and a course of conduct indicating waiver," may support a conclusion that a defendant has waived his rights. Not only may an "implied" waiver suffice, but as *Butler* also indicates, so may a "qualified" waiver. A suspect may refuse to sign a waiver form, but nonetheless indicate that he is willing to talk. Or he may object to any notetaking by an officer but agree to discuss the case or indicate that he will talk only if a tape recorder is turned off.

police will permit him to consult that advocate. He almost certainly also has a heightened awareness (above what the *Miranda* warning itself will provide) of his right to remain silent—since at the earliest opportunity "any lawyer worth his salt will tell the suspect in no uncertain terms to make no statement to the police under any circumstances." * * *

One should not underestimate the extent to which the Court's expansion of *Edwards* constricts law enforcement. Today's ruling, that the invocation of a right to counsel permanently prevents a police-initiated waiver, makes it largely impossible for the police to urge a prisoner who has initially declined to confess to change his mind—or indeed, even to ask whether he has changed his mind. Many persons in custody will invoke the *Miranda* right to counsel during the first interrogation, so that the permanent prohibition will attach at once. Those who do not do so will almost certainly request or obtain counsel at arraignment. We have held that a general request for counsel, after the Sixth Amendment right has attached, also triggers the *Edwards* prohibition of police-solicited confessions, see *Michigan v. Jackson,* 475 U.S. 625 (1986), and I presume that the perpetuality of prohibition announced in today's opinion applies in that context as well. "Perpetuality" is not too strong a term, since although the Court rejects one logical moment at which the *Edwards* presumption might end, it suggests no alternative. In this case Minnick was reapproached by the police three days after he requested counsel, but the result would presumably be the same if it had been three months, or three years, or even three decades. This perpetual irrebuttable presumption will apply, I might add, not merely to interrogations involving the original crime but to those involving other subjects as well. See *Arizona v. Roberson.*

* * * Clear and simple rules are desirable, but only in pursuance of authority that we possess. We are authorized by the Fifth Amendment to exclude confessions that are "compelled," which we have interpreted to include confessions that the police obtain from a suspect in custody without a knowing and voluntary waiver of his right to remain silent. Undoubtedly some bright-line rules can be adopted to implement that principle, marking out the situations in which knowledge or voluntariness cannot possibly be established—for example, a rule excluding confessions obtained after five hours of continuous interrogation. But a rule excluding all confessions that follow upon even the slightest police inquiry cannot conceivably be justified on this basis. It does not rest upon a reasonable prediction that all such confessions, or even most such confessions, will be unaccompanied by a knowing and voluntary waiver.

It can be argued that the same is true of the category of confessions excluded by the *Edwards* rule itself. I think that is so, but, as I have discussed above, the presumption of involuntariness is at least more plausible for that category. There is, in any event, a clear and rational line between that category and the present one, and I see nothing to be said for expanding upon a past mistake. Drawing a distinction between police-initiated inquiry before consultation with counsel and police-initiated inquiry after consultation with counsel is assuredly more reasonable than other distinctions *Edwards* has already led us into—such as the distinction between police-initiated inquiry after assertion of the *Miranda* right to remain silent, and police-initiated inquiry after assertion of the *Miranda* right to counsel or the distinction between what is needed to prove waiver of the *Miranda* right to have counsel present and what is needed to prove waiver of rights found in the Constitution.

[As] for the "irony" that "the suspect whose counsel is prompt would lose the protection of *Edwards,* while the one whose counsel is dilatory would not": There seems to me no irony in applying a special protection only when it is needed. The

Edwards rule is premised on an (already tenuous) assumption about the suspect's psychological state, and when the event of consultation renders that assumption invalid the rule should no longer apply. One searching for ironies in the state of our law should consider, first, the irony created by *Edwards* itself: The suspect in custody who says categorically "I do not wish to discuss this matter" can be asked to change his mind; but if he should say, more tentatively, "I do not think I should discuss this matter without my attorney present" he can no longer be approached. To that there is added, by today's decision, the irony that it will be far harder for the state to establish a knowing and voluntary waiver of Fifth Amendment rights by a prisoner who has already consulted with counsel than by a newly arrested suspect. * * *

Today's extension of the *Edwards* prohibition is the latest stage of prophylax- is built upon prophylaxis, producing a veritable fairyland castle of imagined constitutional restriction upon law enforcement. This newest tower, according to the Court, is needed to avoid "inconsisten[cy] with [the] purpose" of *Edwards'* prophylactic rule, which was needed to protect *Miranda*'s prophylactic right to have counsel present, which was needed to protect the right against *compelled self-incrimination* found (at last!) in the Constitution.

It seems obvious to me that, even in *Edwards* itself but surely in today's decision, we have gone far beyond any genuine concern about suspects who do not *know* their right to remain silent, or who have been *coerced* to abandon it. Both holdings are explicable, in my view, only as an effort to protect suspects against what is regarded as their own folly. The sharp-witted criminal would know better than to confess; why should the dull-witted suffer for his lack of mental endow- ment? Providing him an attorney at every stage where he might be induced or persuaded (though not coerced) to incriminate himself will even the odds. Apart from the fact that this protective enterprise is beyond our authority under the Fifth Amendment or any other provision of the Constitution, it is unwise. The procedural protections of the Constitution protect the guilty as well as the innocent, but it is not their objective to set the guilty free. That some clever criminals may employ those protections to their advantage is poor reason to allow criminals who have not done so to escape justice.

Thus, even if I were to concede that an honest confession is a foolish mistake, I would welcome rather than reject it; a rule that foolish mistakes do not count would leave most offenders not only unconvicted but undetected. More funda- mentally, however, it is wrong, and subtly corrosive of our criminal justice system, to regard an honest confession as a "mistake." While every person is entitled to stand silent, it is more virtuous for the wrongdoer to admit his offense and accept the punishment he deserves. [A] confession is rightly regarded by the sentencing guidelines as warranting a reduction of sentence, because it "demonstrates a recognition and affirmative acceptance of personal responsibility [for] criminal conduct," U.S. Sentencing Commission, Guidelines Manual § 3E1.1 (1988), which is the beginning of reform. We should, then, rejoice at an honest confession, rather than pity the "poor fool" who has made it; and we should regret the attempted retraction of that good act, rather than seek to facilitate and encourage it. To design our laws on premises contrary to these is to abandon belief in either personal responsibility or the moral claim of just government to obedience. Cf. Caplan, Questioning *Miranda*, 38 Vand.L.Rev. 1417, 1471–1473 (1985). Today's decision is misguided, it seems to me, in so readily exchanging, for marginal, *super-Zerbst* protection against genuinely compelled testimony, investigators' abil- ity to urge, or even ask, a person in custody to do what is right.[f]

---

f. Under *Michigan v. Jackson*, 475 U.S. 625 (1986), a defendant's appearance with counsel

4. *Questioning prompted by concern for "public safety"*

NEW YORK v. QUARLES

467 U.S. 649, 104 S.Ct. 2626, 81 L.Ed.2d 550 (1984).

JUSTICE REHNQUIST delivered the opinion of the Court.

[At approximately 12:30 a.m., police apprehended respondent in the rear of a supermarket. He matched the description of the man who had just raped a woman. The woman had told the police that the rapist had just entered the supermarket and that he was carrying a gun. Apparently upon seeing Officer Kraft enter the store, respondent turned and ran toward the rear. Officer Kraft pursued him with a drawn gun and, upon regaining sight of him, ordered him to stop and put his hands over his head. Although several other officers had arrived at the scene by then, Kraft was the first to reach respondent. He frisked him and discovered he was wearing an empty shoulder holster. After handcuffing him, the officer asked where the gun was. Respondent nodded in the direction of some empty cartons and responded, "the gun is over there." At that time, emphasized the New York Court of Appeals, respondent was surrounded by four officers whose guns had been returned to their holsters because, as one testified, the situation was under control.

[The gun was not visible, but Officer Kraft reached into one of the cartons and retrieved a loaded revolver. Respondent was then formally placed under arrest and advised of his *Miranda* rights. Respondent waived his rights. In response to questions, he then stated that he owned the revolver and had purchased it in Miami.

[In the subsequent prosecution of respondent for criminal possession of a weapon (the record does not reveal why the state failed to pursue the rape charge), the New York courts suppressed the statement "the gun is over there" as well as the gun itself because they had been obtained in violation of respondent's *Miranda* rights. Respondent's statements about his ownership of the gun and the place of purchase were also excluded as having been fatally tainted by the seizure of the gun and the prewarning response as to its location.]

at a bail hearing or other pretrial judicial proceeding invokes his Sixth Amendment right to counsel and prevents the police from approaching him for uncounseled questioning about the *charged* offense. But assertion of this right does not serve as an invocation of the Fifth Amendment-based *Miranda-Edwards-Roberson* right to counsel and thus does not prevent the police from initiating counselless interrogation about *uncharged* crimes. *McNeil v. Wisconsin*, 501 U.S. 171 (1991). The Sixth Amendment right to counsel is "offense specific" and the rule of *Michigan v. Jackson*—unlike the *Edwards-Roberson* rule—is similarly limited. Id.

In *Texas v. Cobb*, 121 S.Ct. 1335 (2001), a 5-4 majority, per Rehnquist, C.J., emphasized that because the Sixth Amendment right to counsel is "offense specific"—it cannot be invoked once for all future prosecutions—it does not necessarily extend to offenses that are "factually related" to those that have actually been charged. However, when it attaches the Sixth Amendment right to counsel "does encompass offenses that, even if not formally charged, would be considered the same offense under *the Blockburger* test," discussed in *United States v. Dixon*, Ch. 19, § 1, a test that delineates the scope of the prohibition against double jeopardy which prevents multiple or successive prosecutions for the "same offence".

Defendant was indicted for the burglary of a home and counsel was appointed to represent him. While in police custody, defendant waived his *Miranda* rights and confessed to the murders of a woman and child who had disappeared from the home. He was convicted of capital murder and sentenced to death. In upholding the admissibility of defendant's confession to the murders, the Court pointed out that "[a]s defined by Texas law, burglary and capital murder are not the same offense under *Blockburger*. [Thus,] the Sixth Amendment right to counsel did not bar police from interrogating [defendant] regarding the murders."

* * * We conclude that under the circumstances involved in this case, overriding considerations of public safety justify the officer's failure to provide *Miranda* warnings before he asked questions devoted to locating the abandoned weapon. * * *

The Fifth Amendment itself does not prohibit all incriminating admissions; "[a]bsent some officially *coerced* self-accusation, the Fifth Amendment privilege is not violated by even the most damning admissions." *United States v. Washington,* 431 U.S. 181 (1977) (emphasis added).[a]

The *Miranda* Court, however, presumed that interrogation in certain custodial circumstances is inherently coercive and held that statements made under those circumstances are inadmissible unless the suspect is specifically informed of his *Miranda* rights and freely decides to forgo those rights. The prophylactic *Miranda* warnings therefore are "not themselves rights protected by the Constitution but [are] instead measures to insure that the right against compulsory self-incrimination [is] protected." *Michigan v. Tucker.* * * *

In this case we have before us no claim that respondent's statements were actually compelled by police conduct which overcame his will to resist. Thus the only issue before us is whether Officer Kraft was justified in failing to make available to respondent the procedural safeguards associated with the privilege against compulsory self-incrimination since *Miranda*.

The New York Court of Appeals was undoubtedly correct in deciding that the facts of this case come within the ambit of the *Miranda* decision as we have subsequently interpreted it. [As] the New York Court of Appeals observed, [when the questioning at issue took place] there was nothing to suggest that any of the officers were any longer concerned for their own physical safety. The New York Court of Appeals' majority declined to express an opinion as to whether there might be an exception to the *Miranda* rule if the police had been acting to protect the public, because the lower courts in New York had made no factual determination that the police had acted with that motive.

We hold that on these facts there is a "public safety" exception to the requirement that *Miranda* warnings be given before a suspect's answers may be admitted into evidence, and that the availability of that exception does not depend upon the motivation of the individual officers involved. In a kaleidoscopic situation such as the one confronting these officers, where spontaneity rather than adherence to a police manual is necessarily the order of the day, the application of the exception which we recognize today should not be made to depend on *post hoc* findings at a suppression hearing concerning the subjective motivation of the arresting officer. Undoubtedly most police officers, if placed in Officer Kraft's position, would act out of a host of different, instinctive, and largely unverifiable motives—their own safety, the safety of others, and perhaps as well the desire to obtain incriminating evidence from the suspect.

Whatever the motivation of individual officers in such a situation, we do not believe that the doctrinal underpinnings of *Miranda* require that it be applied in

---

a. *Washington* held that a person appearing before a grand jury need not be warned that he is a target of the grand jury investigation. Defendant had been given *Miranda* warnings prior to any questioning. He replied that he understood these rights and was prepared to answer questions relating to the crime being investigated. He contended, however that his grand jury testimony should be suppressed on the ground that his privilege against self-incrimination had been violated by the prosecutor's failure to advise him that he was a potential defendant. In rejecting this argument the Court noted that because a witness' target status "neither enlarges nor diminishes the constitutional protection against compelled self-incrimination, potential defendant warnings add nothing of value to protection of Fifth Amendment rights." See also note c to *Mandujano*, Ch. 8, § 2.

all its rigor to a situation in which police officers ask questions reasonably prompted by a concern for the public safety.

[The] police in this case, in the very act of apprehending a suspect, were confronted with the immediate necessity of ascertaining the whereabouts of a gun which they had every reason to believe the suspect had just removed from his empty holster and discarded in the supermarket. So long as the gun was concealed somewhere in the supermarket, with its actual whereabouts unknown, it obviously posed more than one danger to the public safety: an accomplice might make use of it, a customer or employee might later come upon it.

In such a situation, if the police are required to recite the familiar *Miranda* warnings before asking the whereabouts of the gun, suspects in Quarles' position might well be deterred from responding. Procedural safeguards which deter a suspect from responding were deemed acceptable in *Miranda* in order to protect the Fifth Amendment privilege; when the primary social cost of those added protections is the possibility of fewer convictions, the *Miranda* majority was willing to bear that cost. Here, had *Miranda* warnings deterred Quarles from responding to Officer Kraft's question about the whereabouts of the gun, the cost would have been something more than merely the failure to obtain evidence useful in convicting Quarles. Officer Kraft needed an answer to his question not simply to make his case against Quarles but to insure that further danger to the public did not result from the concealment of the gun in a public area.

We conclude that the need for answers to questions in a situation posing a threat to the public safety outweighs the need for the prophylactic rule protecting the Fifth Amendment's privilege against self-incrimination. We decline to place officers such as Officer Kraft in the untenable position of having to consider, often in a matter of seconds, whether it best serves society for them to ask the necessary questions without the *Miranda* warnings and render whatever probative evidence they uncover inadmissible, or for them to give the warnings in order to preserve the admissibility of evidence they might uncover but possibly damage or destroy their ability to obtain that evidence and neutralize the volatile situation confronting them.[7]

* * * [W]e recognize [the] importance of a workable rule "to guide police officers, who have only limited time and expertise to reflect on and balance the social and individual interests involved in the specific circumstances they confront." *Dunaway*. [But] we believe that the exception which we recognize today lessens the necessity of that on-the-scene balancing process. The exception will not be difficult for police officers to apply because in each case it will be circumscribed by the exigency which justifies it. We think police officers can and will distinguish almost instinctively between questions necessary to secure their own safety or the safety of the public and questions designed solely to elicit testimonial evidence from a suspect.

The facts of this case clearly demonstrate that distinction and an officer's ability to recognize it. Officer Kraft asked only the question necessary to locate the missing gun before advising respondent of his rights. It was only after securing the loaded revolver and giving the warnings that he continued with

---

7. The dissent argues that a public safety exception to *Miranda* is unnecessary because in every case an officer can simply ask the necessary questions to protect himself or the public, and then the prosecution can decline to introduce any incriminating responses at a subsequent trial. But absent actual coercion by the officer, there is no constitutional imper- ative requiring the exclusion of the evidence that results from police inquiry of this kind; and we do not believe that the doctrinal under- pinnings of *Miranda* require us to exclude the evidence, thus penalizing officers for asking the very questions which are the most crucial to their efforts to protect themselves and the public.

investigatory questions about the ownership and place of purchase of the gun. The exception which we recognize today, far from complicating the thought processes and the on-the-scene judgments of police officers, will simply free them to follow their legitimate instincts when confronting situations presenting a danger to the public safety.[8]

We hold that the Court of Appeals in this case erred in excluding the statement, "the gun is over there," and the gun because of the officer's failure to read respondent his *Miranda* rights before attempting to locate the weapon. Accordingly we hold that it also erred in excluding the subsequent statements as illegal fruits of a *Miranda* violation.[9] * * *

JUSTICE O'CONNOR, concurring in part in the judgment and dissenting in part. * * *

In my view, a "public safety" exception unnecessarily blurs the edges of the clear line heretofore established and makes *Miranda's* requirements more difficult to understand. In some cases, police will benefit because a reviewing court will find that an exigency excused their failure to administer the required warnings. But in other cases, police will suffer because, though they thought an exigency excused their noncompliance, a reviewing court will view the "objective" circumstances differently and require exclusion of admissions thereby obtained. The end result will be a finespun new doctrine on public safety exigencies incident to custodial interrogation, complete with the hair-splitting distinctions that currently plague our Fourth Amendment jurisprudence. * * *

The justification the Court provides for upsetting the equilibrium that has finally been achieved—that police cannot and should not balance considerations of public safety against the individual's interest in avoiding compulsory testimonial self-incrimination—really misses the critical question to be decided. *Miranda* has never been read to prohibit the police from asking questions to secure the public safety. Rather, the critical question *Miranda* addresses is who shall bear the cost of securing the public safety when such questions are asked and answered: the defendant or the State. *Miranda,* for better or worse, found the resolution of that question implicit in the prohibition against compulsory self-incrimination and placed the burden on the State. When police ask custodial questions without administering the required warnings, *Miranda* quite clearly requires that the answers received be presumed compelled and that they be excluded from evidence

---

8. Although it involves police questions in part relating to the whereabouts of a gun, Orozco v. Texas, 394 U.S. 324 (1969) [where the police entered a sleeping defendant's room in the early hours of the morning and questioned him about a gun used in a murder several hours earlier] is in no sense inconsistent with our disposition of this case. [In *Orozco,*] the questions about the gun were clearly investigatory; they did not in any way relate to an objectively reasonable need to protect the police or the public from any immediate danger associated with the weapon. In short there was no exigency requiring immediate action by the officers beyond the normal need expeditiously to solve a serious crime.

Innis also involved the whereabouts of a missing weapon, but our holding in that case depended entirely on our conclusion that no police interrogation took place so as to require

consideration of the applicability of the *Miranda* prophylactic.

9. Because we hold that there is no violation of *Miranda* in this case, we have no occasion to [decide whether] the gun is admissible either because it is nontestimonial or because the police would inevitably have discovered it absent their questioning.

[A year earlier, in *Nix v. Williams* (Williams II), 467 U.S. 431 (1984), the Court ruled that the "fruit of the poisonous tree" doctrine did not bar the use of evidence derived from a constitutional violation if such evidence would "ultimately" or "inevitably" have been discovered as a result of lawful police investigatory work without regard to that violation. The "fruits" doctrine, formulated initially in applying the Fourth Amendment exclusionary rule, bars the use of evidence derived from, and thus "tainted" by, a constitutional violation.]

at trial.   * * * c

JUSTICE MARSHALL, with whom JUSTICE BRENNAN and JUSTICE STEVENS join, dissenting * * *.

The majority's entire analysis rests on the factual assumption that the public was at risk during Quarles' interrogation.   This assumption is completely in conflict with the facts as found by New York's highest court.   Before the interrogation began, Quarles had been "reduced to a condition of physical power-lessness."   Contrary to the majority's speculations, Quarles was not believed to have, nor did he in fact have, an accomplice to come to his rescue.   When the questioning began, the arresting officers were sufficiently confident of their safety to put away their guns.

[The] New York court's conclusion that neither Quarles nor his missing gun posed a threat to the public's safety is amply supported by the evidence presented at the suppression hearing.   * * * Although the supermarket was open to the public, Quarles' arrest took place during the middle of the night when the store was apparently deserted except for the clerks at the checkout counter.   The police could easily have cordoned off the store and searched for the missing gun.   Had they done so, they would have found the gun forthwith.   [As] the State acknowl-edged before the New York Court of Appeals: "After Officer Kraft had handcuffed and frisked the defendant in the supermarket, *he knew with a high degree of certainty that the defendant's gun was within the immediate vicinity of the encounter.*   He undoubtedly would have searched for it in the carton a few feet away without the defendant having looked in that direction and saying that it was there."   (Emphasis added.)   * * *

This case is illustrative of the chaos the "public-safety" exception will unleash.   The circumstances of Quarles' arrest have never been in dispute.   [T]he New York Court of Appeals concluded that there was "no evidence in the record before us that there were exigent circumstances posing a risk to the public safety."   Upon reviewing the same facts and hearing the same arguments, a majority of this Court has come to precisely the opposite conclusion * * *.

If after plenary review two appellate courts so fundamentally differ over the threat to public safety presented by the simple and uncontested facts of this case, one must seriously question how law enforcement officers will respond to the majority's new rule in the confusion and haste of the real world.   * * * Not only will police officers have to decide whether the objective facts of an arrest justify an unconsented custodial interrogation; they will also have to remember to interrupt the interrogation and read the suspect his *Miranda* warnings once the focus of the inquiry shifts from protecting the public's safety to ascertaining the suspect's guilt.   Disagreements of the scope of the "public-safety" exception and mistakes in its application are inevitable.[4]   * * *

c.   Although Justice O'Connor would sup-press Quarles' initial statement, "the gun is over there," she would not exclude the gun itself because "nothing in *Miranda* or the privilege [against compelled self-incrimination] itself requires exclusion of nontestimonial evidence derived from informal custodial interro-gation."   "Only the introduction of a defen-dant's own *testimony*," maintained Justice O'Connor, "is proscribed by the Fifth Amend-ment's mandate that no person 'shall be com-pelled in any criminal case to be a witness against himself.'   That mandate does not pro-tect an accused from being compelled to sur-render *nontestimonial* evidence against him-self."

For further discussion of the application (or nonapplication) of the "fruit of the poisonous tree" doctrine to *Miranda* violations, see *Ore-gon v. Elstad*, the next case set forth in this section.

4.   One of the peculiarities of the majori-ty's decision is its suggestion that police offi-cers can "distinguish almost instinctively" questions tied to public safety and questions designed to elicit testimonial evidence.   Obvi-ously, these distinctions are extraordinarily

Though unfortunate, the difficulty of administering the "public-safety" exception is not the most profound flaw in the majority's decision. The majority has lost sight of the fact that *Miranda* and our earlier custodial-interrogation cases all implemented a constitutional privilege against self-incrimination. The rules established in these cases were designed to protect criminal defendants against prosecutions based on coerced self-incriminating statements. The majority today turns its back on these constitutional considerations, and invites the government to prosecute through the use of what necessarily are coerced statements.

The majority's error stems from a serious misunderstanding of *Miranda* and of the Fifth Amendment upon which that decision was based. The majority implies that *Miranda* consisted of no more than a judicial balancing act in which the benefits of "enlarged protection for the Fifth Amendment privilege" were weighed against "the cost to society in terms of fewer convictions of guilty suspects." Supposedly because the scales tipped in favor of the privilege against self-incrimination, the *Miranda* Court erected a prophylactic barrier around statements made during custodial interrogations. The majority now proposes to return to the scales of social utility to calculate whether *Miranda's* prophylactic rule remains cost-effective when threats to the public's safety are added to the balance.

[The] majority misreads *Miranda*. Though the *Miranda* dissent prophesized dire consequences, the *Miranda* Court refused to allow such concerns to weaken the protections of the Constitution * * *.

Whether society would be better off if the police warned suspects of their rights before beginning an interrogation or whether the advantages of giving such warnings would outweigh their costs did not inform the *Miranda* decision. On the contrary, the *Miranda* Court was concerned with the proscriptions of the Fifth Amendment, and, in particular, whether the Self–Incrimination Clause permits the government to prosecute individuals based on statements made in the course of custodial interrogations.

[In] fashioning its "public-safety" exception to *Miranda,* the majority makes no attempt to deal with the constitutional presumption established by that case. The majority does not argue that police questioning about issues of public safety is any less coercive than custodial interrogations into other matters. The majority's only contention is that police officers could more easily protect the public if *Miranda* did not apply to custodial interrogations concerning the public's safety. But *Miranda* was not a decision about public safety; it was a decision about coerced confessions. Without establishing that interrogations concerning the public's safety are less likely to be coercive than other interrogations, the majority cannot endorse the "public-safety" exception and remain faithful to the logic of *Miranda*.

[That] the application of the "public-safety" exception in this case entailed coercion is no happenstance. The majority's *ratio decidendi* is that interrogating suspects about matters of public safety *will* be coercive. In its cost-benefit analysis, the Court's strongest argument in favor of a public-safety exception to *Miranda* is that the police would be better able to protect the public's safety if they were not always required to give suspects their *Miranda* warnings. The crux of this argument is that, by deliberately withholding *Miranda* warnings, the police can get information out of suspects who would refuse to respond to police questioning were they advised of their constitutional rights. The "public-safety"

difficult to draw. In many cases—like this one—custodial questioning may serve both purposes. It is therefore wishful thinking for the majority to suggest that the intuitions of police officers will render its decision self-executing.

exception is efficacious precisely because it permits police officers to coerce criminal defendants into making involuntary statements. * * *

[The] irony of the majority's decision is that the public's safety can be perfectly well protected without abridging the Fifth Amendment. If a bomb is about to explode or the public is otherwise imminently imperiled, the police are free to interrogate suspects without advising them of their constitutional rights. * * * If trickery is necessary to protect the public, then the police may trick a suspect into confessing. While the Fourteenth Amendment sets limits on such behavior, nothing in the Fifth Amendment or our decision in *Miranda* proscribes this sort of emergency questioning. All the Fifth Amendment forbids is the introduction of coerced statements at trial.

* * * [The] policies underlying the Fifth Amendment's privilege against self-incrimination are not diminished simply because testimony is compelled to protect the public's safety. The majority should not be permitted to elude the Amendment's absolute prohibition simply by calculating special costs that arise when the public's safety is at issue. Indeed, were constitutional adjudication always conducted in such an *ad hoc* manner, the Bill of Rights would be a most unreliable protector of individual liberties.

5. Does an initial failure to inform a suspect of his rights bar subsequent admissions by the suspect after he has been fully advised of his rights?

OREGON v. ELSTAD

470 U.S. 298, 105 S.Ct. 1285, 84 L.Ed.2d 222 (1985).

JUSTICE O'CONNOR delivered the opinion of the Court.

This case requires us to decide whether an initial failure of law enforcement officers to administer the warnings required by *Miranda,* without more, "taints" subsequent admissions made after a suspect has been fully advised of and has waived his *Miranda* rights. [Respondent was convicted of burglary.] The Oregon Court of Appeals reversed, holding that respondent's signed confession, although voluntary, was rendered inadmissible by a prior remark made in response to questioning without benefit of *Miranda* warnings. [We] reverse.

[When the Gross home was burglarized, a witness contacted the sheriff's office, implicating respondent Elstad, an 18–year–old neighbor and friend of the Grosses' teenage son. Officers Burke and McAllister went to Elstad's home, with a warrant for his arrest for the aforementioned burglary. Elstad's mother led the officers to his room. The officers asked Elstad to get dressed and to accompany them to the living room. Officer Burke sat down with Elstad in the living room and, without telling him that the police had a warrant for his arrest, stated that he "felt" Elstad was involved in the Gross burglary. Elstad replied, "Yes, I was there."

[Elstad was then transported to sheriff headquarters and, approximately an hour later, Officer McAllister, in the presence of Officer Burke, advised Elstad of his *Miranda* rights for the first time. Elstad agreed to talk to the police and made a statement detailing his involvement in the burglary. The statement was typed, reviewed by Elstad, read back to him for correction and signed by him.

[The trial judge excluded the incriminating remark Elstad made in his living room, but admitted the statement made at the sheriff's office. Following his conviction of burglary, Elstad appealed. The state conceded that Elstad had been in custody when he replied, "Yes, I was there," and thus that this statement was obtained in violation of *Miranda,* but maintained that any conceivable "taint" had been dissipated prior to Elstad's written confession by Officer McAllister's careful administration of the *Miranda* warnings. The Oregon Court of Appeals disagreed.

[In reversing Elstad's conviction, the Oregon court identified the crucial constitutional inquiry as whether there was "a sufficient break in the stream of events" between the inadmissible statement in respondent's living room and the written confession in the sheriff's office "to insulate the latter statement from the effect of what went before." It concluded that, because of the brief period separating the two incidents, the "cat was sufficiently out of the bag to exert a coercive impact on [respondent's later admissions."]

[The] Oregon court assumed and respondent here contends that a failure to administer *Miranda* warnings necessarily breeds the same consequences as police infringement of a constitutional right, so that evidence uncovered following an unwarned statement must be suppressed as "fruit of the poisonous tree." We believe this view misconstrues the nature of the protections afforded by *Miranda* warnings and therefore misreads the consequences of police failure to supply them.

[A]s we explained in *Quarles* and *Tucker,* a procedural *Miranda* violation differs in significant respects from violations of the Fourth Amendment, which have traditionally mandated a broad application of the "fruits" doctrine. The purpose of the Fourth Amendment exclusionary rule is to deter unreasonable searches, no matter how probative their fruits. * * *

The *Miranda* exclusionary rule, however, serves the Fifth Amendment and sweeps more broadly than the Fifth Amendment itself. It may be triggered even in the absence of a Fifth Amendment violation.[1] The Fifth Amendment prohibits use by the prosecution in its case in chief only of *compelled* testimony. Failure to administer *Miranda* warnings creates a presumption of compulsion. * * *

But the *Miranda* presumption, though irrebuttable for purposes of the prosecution's case in chief, does not require that the statements and their fruits be discarded as inherently tainted. * * * [a]

Where an unwarned statement is preserved for use in situations that fall outside the sweep of the *Miranda* presumption, "the primary criterion of admissi-

---

1. Justice Stevens expresses puzzlement at our statement that a simple failure to administer *Miranda* warnings is not in itself a violation of the Fifth Amendment. Yet the Court so held in *Quarles* and *Tucker.* The *Miranda* Court itself recognized this point when it disclaimed any intent to create a "constitutional straight-jacket" and invited Congress and the States to suggest "potential alternatives for protecting the privilege." A *Miranda* violation does not *constitute* coercion but rather affords a bright-line, legal presumption of coercion, requiring suppression of all unwarned statements. It has never been remotely suggested that any statement taken from Mr. Elstad without benefit of *Miranda* warnings would be admissible.

a. At this point, the Court discusses *Harris v. New York,* 401 U.S. 222 (1971) and *Michigan v. Tucker,* 417 U.S. 433 (1974). *Harris* held that incriminating statements preceded by defective *Miranda* warnings, and thus inadmissible for the purposes of establishing the prosecution's case-in-chief, could nevertheless be used to impeach the defendant's credibility if he chose to take the stand in his own defense. *Tucker* declined to apply the "fruit of the poisonous tree" doctrine to the testimony of a witness whose identity had been discovered by questioning the defendant without giving him a complete set of *Miranda* warnings. Although the *Tucker* case involved various factors that arguably limited its implications, the *Tucker* Court, per Rehnquist, J., spoke in general terms of the difference between a *Miranda* violation and a constitutional violation. See the Note on Congressional Overruling in § 3 supra.

bility [remains] the 'old' due process voluntariness test." Schulholfer, *Confessions and the Court,* 79 Mich.L.Rev. 865, 877 (1981).

[In] deciding "how sweeping the judicially imposed consequences" of a failure to administer *Miranda* warnings should be, the *Tucker* Court noted that neither the general goal of deterring improper police conduct nor the Fifth Amendment goal of assuring trustworthy evidence would be served by suppression of the witness' testimony. The unwarned confession must, of course, be suppressed, but the Court ruled that introduction of the third-party witness' testimony did not violate Tucker's Fifth Amendment rights.

We believe that this reasoning applies with equal force when the alleged "fruit" of a noncoercive *Miranda* violation is neither a witness nor an article of evidence but the accused's own voluntary testimony. As in *Tucker,* the absence of any coercion or improper tactics undercuts the twin rationales—trustworthiness and deterrence—for a broader rule. Once warned, the suspect is free to exercise his own volition in deciding whether or not to make a statement to the authorities.

* * * If errors are made by law enforcement officers in administering the prophylactic *Miranda* procedures, they should not breed the same irremediable consequences as police infringement of the Fifth Amendment itself. It is an unwarranted extension of *Miranda* to hold that a simple failure to administer the warnings, unaccompanied by any actual coercion or other circumstances calculated to undermine the suspect's ability to exercise his free will so taints the investigatory process that a subsequent voluntary and informed waiver is ineffective for some indeterminate period. Though *Miranda* requires that the unwarned admission must be suppressed, the admissibility of any subsequent statement should turn in these circumstances solely on whether it is knowingly and voluntarily made. * * *

There is a vast difference between the direct consequences flowing from coercion of a confession by physical violence or other deliberate means calculated to break the suspect's will and the uncertain consequences of disclosure of a "guilty secret" freely given in response to an unwarned but noncoercive question, as in this case. Justice Brennan's contention that it is impossible to perceive any causal distinction between this case and one involving a confession that is coerced by torture is wholly unpersuasive.[3] Certainly, in respondent's case, the causal connection between any psychological disadvantage created by his admission and his ultimate decision to cooperate is speculative and attenuated at best. It is difficult to tell with certainty what motivates a suspect to speak. * * * We must conclude that, absent deliberately coercive or improper tactics in obtaining the initial statement, the mere fact that a suspect has made an unwarned admission does not warrant a presumption of compulsion. A subsequent administration of *Miranda* warnings to a suspect who has given a voluntary but unwarned statement ordinarily should suffice to remove the conditions that precluded admission of the earlier statement. In such circumstances, the finder of fact may reasonably conclude that the suspect made a rational and intelligent choice whether to waive or invoke his rights.

3. Most of the 50 cases cited by Justice Brennan in his discussion of consecutive confessions concern an initial unwarned statement obtained through overtly or inherently coercive methods which raise serious Fifth Amendment and Due Process concerns [discussing many cases].

Justice Brennan cannot seriously mean to equate such situations with the case at bar. Likewise inapposite are the cases the dissent cites concerning suspects whose invocation of their rights to remain silent and to have counsel present were flatly ignored while police subjected them to continued interrogation. * * *

Though belated, the reading of respondent's rights was undeniably complete. [There] is no question that respondent knowingly and voluntarily waived his right to remain silent before he described his participation in the burglary. It is also beyond dispute that respondent's earlier remark was voluntary, within the meaning of the Fifth Amendment. Neither the environment nor the manner of either "interrogation" was coercive. The initial conversation took place at midday, in the living room area of respondent's own home, with his mother in the kitchen area, a few steps away. Although in retrospect the officers testified that respondent was then in custody, at the time he made his statement he had not been informed that he was under arrest. The arresting officers' testimony indicates that the brief stop in the living room before proceeding to the station house was not to interrogate the suspect but to notify his mother of the reason for his arrest.

The state has conceded the issue of custody and thus we must assume that Burke breached *Miranda* procedures in failing to administer *Miranda* warnings before initiating the discussion in the living room. [But] the incident had none of the earmarks of coercion. Nor did the officers exploit the unwarned admission to pressure respondent into waiving his right to remain silent.

Respondent, however, has argued that he was unable to give a fully *informed* waiver of his rights because he was unaware that his prior statement could not be used against him. Respondent suggests that Deputy McAllister, to cure this deficiency, should have added an additional warning to those given him at the Sheriff's office. Such a requirement is neither practicable nor constitutionally necessary. In many cases, a breach of *Miranda* procedures may not be identified as such until long after full *Miranda* warnings are administered and a valid confession obtained. The standard *Miranda* warnings explicitly inform the suspect of his right to consult a lawyer before speaking. Police officers are ill equipped to pinch-hit for counsel, construing the murky and difficult questions of when "custody" begins or whether a given unwarned statement will ultimately be held admissible.

[Where] the suspect's initial inculpatory statement, though technically in violation of *Miranda,* was voluntary, [the] relevant inquiry is whether, in fact, the second statement was also voluntarily made. As in any such inquiry, the finder of fact must examine the surrounding circumstances and the entire course of police conduct with respect to the suspect in evaluating the voluntariness of his statements. The fact that a suspect chooses to speak after being informed of his rights is, of course, highly probative. We find that the dictates of *Miranda* and the goals of the Fifth Amendment proscription against use of compelled testimony are fully satisfied in the circumstances of this case by barring use of the unwarned statement in the case in chief. No further purpose is served by imputing "taint" to subsequent statements obtained pursuant to a voluntary and knowing waiver. We hold today that a suspect who has once responded to unwarned yet uncoercive questioning is not thereby disabled from waiving his rights and confessing after he has been given the requisite *Miranda* warnings. * * *

JUSTICE BRENNAN, with whom JUSTICE MARSHALL joins, dissenting.

* * * [Today's decision] delivers a potentially crippling blow to *Miranda* and the ability of courts to safeguard the rights of persons accused of crime. For at least with respect to successive confessions, the Court today appears to strip remedies for *Miranda* violations of the "fruit of the poisonous tree" doctrine prohibiting the use of evidence presumptively derived from official illegality.[2]

2. The Court repeatedly casts its analysis in terms of the "fruits" of a *Miranda* violation, but its dicta nevertheless surely should not be read as necessarily foreclosing application of

[The] threshold question is this: What effect should an admission or confession of guilt obtained in violation of an accused's *Miranda* rights be presumed to have upon the voluntariness of subsequent confessions that are preceded by*Miranda* warnings? * * *

This Court has had long experience with the problem of confessions obtained after an earlier confession has been illegally secured. Subsequent confessions in these circumstances are not *per se* inadmissible, but the prosecution must demonstrate facts "sufficient to insulate the [subsequent] statement from the effect of all that went before." *Clewis v. Texas,* 386 U.S. 707 (1967). [The] question in each case is whether the accused's will was "overborne at the time he confessed," and the prosecution must demonstrate that the second confession "was an act independent of the [earlier] confession." *Reck v. Pate,* 367 U.S. 433 (1961).

* * * Although we have thus rejected a *per se* rule forbidding the introduction of subsequent statements in these circumstances, we have emphasized that the psychological impact of admissions and confessions of criminal guilt nevertheless can have a decisive impact in undermining the voluntariness of a suspect's responses to continued police interrogation and must be accounted for in determining their admissibility. * * *

Our precedents did not develop in a vacuum. They reflect an understanding of the realities of police interrogation * * *. Standard interrogation manuals advise that "[t]he securing of the first admission is the biggest stumbling block." A. Aubry & R. Caputo, *Criminal Interrogation* 290 (3d ed. 1980). If this first admission can be obtained, "there is every reason to expect that the first admission will lead to others and eventually to the full confession." * * *

* * * Expert interrogators and experienced lower-court judges will be startled, to say the least, to learn that the connection between multiple confessions is "speculative" and that a subsequent rendition of *Miranda* warnings "ordinarily" enables the accused in these circumstances to exercise his "free will" and to make "a rational and intelligent choice whether to waive or invoke his rights." * * *

* * * Where an accused believes that it is futile to resist because the authorities already have elicited an admission of guilt, the mere rendition of *Miranda* warnings does not convey the information most critical at that point to ensuring his informed and voluntary decision to speak again: that the earlier confession may not be admissible and thus that he need not speak out of any feeling that he already has sealed his fate. The Court therefore is flatly wrong in arguing, as it does repeatedly, that the mere provision of *Miranda* warnings prior to subsequent interrogation supplies the accused with "the relevant information" and ensures that a subsequent confession "ordinarily" will be the product of "a rational and intelligent choice" and "an act of free will."

[The] foundation of the derivative-evidence doctrine has always been that, where the authorities have acted illegally, *they* must bear the "ultimate burden" of proving that their misconduct did not "taint" subsequently obtained evidence. That is precisely the point of the derivative-evidence presumption. By rejecting this presumption in *Miranda* cases, the Court today appears to adopt a "go ahead and try to prove it" posture toward citizens whose Fifth Amendment *Miranda* rights have been violated, an attitude that marks a sharp break from the Court's traditional approach to official lawlessness. * * *

Not content merely to ignore the practical realities of police interrogation and the likely effects of its abolition of the derivative-evidence presumption, the Court

---

derivative-evidence rules where the *Miranda* violation produces evidence other than a subse-quent confession by the accused. See n. 29, infra.

goes on to assert that nothing in the Fifth Amendment or the general judicial policy of deterring illegal police conduct "ordinarily" requires the suppression of evidence derived proximately from a confession obtained in violation of *Miranda*. The Court does not limit its analysis to successive confessions, but recurrently refers generally to the "fruits" of the illegal confession. Thus the potential impact of the Court's reasoning might extend far beyond the "cat out of the bag" context to include the discovery of physical evidence and other derivative fruits of *Miranda* violations as well.[29] * * *

[The] Court today refuses to apply the derivative-evidence rule even to the extent necessary to deter objectively unreasonable failures by the authorities to honor a suspect's *Miranda* rights. Incredibly, faced with an obvious violation of *Miranda,* the Court asserts that it will not countenance suppression of a subsequent confession in such circumstances where the authorities have acted "legitimate[ly]" and have not used "improper tactics." One can only respond: whither went *Miranda?*

* * * How can the Court possibly expect the authorities to obey *Miranda* when they have every incentive now to interrogate suspects without warnings or an effective waiver, knowing that the fruits of such interrogations "ordinarily" will be admitted, that an admissible subsequent confession "ordinarily" can be obtained simply by reciting the *Miranda* warnings shortly after the first has been procured and asking the accused to repeat himself, and that unless the accused can demonstrate otherwise his confession will be viewed as an "act of free will" in response to "legitimate law enforcement activity"? By condoning such a result, the Court today encourages practices that threaten to reduce *Miranda* to a mere "form of words," and it is shocking that the Court nevertheless disingenuously purports that it "in no way retreats" from the *Miranda* safeguards. * * *

JUSTICE STEVENS, dissenting. * * *

In my opinion, the Court's attempt to fashion a distinction between actual coercion "by physical violence or other deliberate means calculated to break the suspect's will" and irrebuttably presumed coercion cannot succeed. The presumption is only legitimate if it is assumed that there is always a coercive aspect to custodial interrogation that is not preceded by adequate advice of the constitutional right to remain silent. Although I would not support it, I could understand a rule that refused to apply the presumption unless the interrogation took place in an especially coercive setting—perhaps only in the police station itself—but if the presumption arises whenever the accused has been taken into custody or his freedom has been restrained in any significant way, it will surely be futile to try to develop subcategories of custodial interrogation. Indeed, a major purpose of treating the presumption of coercion as irrebuttable is to avoid the kind of fact-bound inquiry that today's decision will surely engender.

* * * [S]urely the fact that an earlier confession was obtained by unlawful methods should add force to the presumption of coercion that attaches to subsequent custodial interrogation and should require the prosecutor to shoulder a heavier burden of rebuttal than in a routine case. Simple logic, as well as the interest in not providing an affirmative incentive to police misconduct, requires

---

29. Notwithstanding the sweep of the Court's language, today's opinion surely ought not be read as also foreclosing application of the traditional derivative-evidence presumption to physical evidence obtained as a proximate result of a *Miranda* violation. The Court relies heavily on individual "volition" as an insulating factor in successive-confession cases.

Although the Court's reliance on this factor is clearly misplaced, the factor is altogether missing in the context of inanimate evidence.

As they have in successive-confession cases, most courts considering the issue have recognized that physical evidence proximately derived from a *Miranda* violation is presumptively inadmissible. * * *

that result. I see no reason why the violation of a rule that is as well recognized and easily administered as the duty to give *Miranda* warnings should not also impose an additional burden on the prosecutor.[13] If we are faithful to the holding in *Miranda* itself, when we are considering the admissibility of evidence in the prosecutor's case-in-chief, we should not try to fashion a distinction between police misconduct that warrants a finding of actual coercion and police misconduct that establishes an irrebuttable presumption of coercion.

For me, the most disturbing aspect of the Court's opinion is its somewhat opaque characterization of the police misconduct in this case. The Court appears ambivalent on the question whether there was any constitutional violation.[14] This ambivalence is either disingenuous or completely lawless. This Court's power to require state courts to exclude probative self-incriminatory statements rests entirely on the premise that the use of such evidence violates the Federal Constitution.[15] The same constitutional analysis applies whether the custodial interrogation is actually coercive or irrebuttably presumed to be coercive. If the Court does not accept that premise, it must regard the holding in the *Miranda* case itself, as well as all of the Federal jurisprudence that has evolved from that decision, as nothing more than an illegitimate exercise of raw judicial power.
* * *

6.   If a suspect does not request a lawyer but, unbeknownst to him, a relative or friend retains a lawyer for him, does the failure of the police to allow the lawyer to see the suspect or the failure to inform the suspect that an attorney is trying to reach him vitiate an otherwise valid waiver of Miranda rights?

MORAN v. BURBINE

475 U.S. 412, 106 S.Ct. 1135, 89 L.Ed.2d 410 (1986).

Justice O'Connor delivered the opinion of the Court.

After being informed of his rights pursuant to *Miranda* and after executing a series of written waivers, respondent confessed to the murder of a young woman. At no point during the course of the interrogation, which occurred prior to arraignment, did he request an attorney. While he was in police custody, his sister attempted to retain a lawyer to represent him. The attorney telephoned the police station and received assurances that respondent would not be questioned further until the next day. In fact, the interrogation session that yielded the inculpatory statements began later that evening. The question presented is whether either the conduct of the police or respondent's ignorance of the attor-

---

13. In view of the Court's holding, it is not necessary to consider how that additional burden should be discharged in all cases. In general, however, I should think that before the second session of custodial interrogation begins, the prisoner should be advised that his earlier statement is, or may be, inadmissible. I am not persuaded that the *Miranda* rule is so "murky" that the law-enforcement profession would be unable to identify the cases in which a supplementary warning would be appropriate. *Miranda* was written, in part, "to give concrete constitutional guidelines for law enforcement agencies and courts to follow." * * * Nearly two decades after that disposition, it is undisputed that the *Miranda* rule—

now so deeply embedded in our culture that most schoolchildren know not only the warnings, but also when they are required—has given that clarity. * * *

14. * * * Indeed, the Court's holding rests on its view that there were no "improper tactics in obtaining the initial statement."

15. At least that is my view. In response to this dissent, however, the Court has added a fn. 1, implying that whenever the Court commands exclusion of a presumptively coerced confession, it is standing—not on a constitutional predicate—but merely on its own shoulders.

ney's efforts to reach him taints the validity of the waivers and therefore requires exclusion of the confessions.

On the morning of March 3, 1977, Mary Jo Hickey was found unconscious in a factory parking lot in Providence, Rhode Island. Suffering from injuries to her skull apparently inflicted by a metal pipe found at the scene, she was rushed to a nearby hospital. Three weeks later she died from her wounds.

Several months after her death, the Cranston, Rhode Island police arrested respondent and two others in connection with a local burglary. Shortly before the arrest, Detective Ferranti of the Cranston police force had learned from a confidential informant that the man responsible for Ms. Hickey's death lived at a certain address and went by the name of "Butch." Upon discovering that respondent lived at that address and was known by that name, Detective Ferranti informed respondent of his *Miranda* rights. When respondent refused to execute a written waiver, Detective Ferranti spoke separately with the two other suspects arrested on the breaking and entering charge and obtained statements further implicating respondent in Ms. Hickey's murder. At approximately 6:00 p.m., Detective Ferranti telephoned the police in Providence to convey the information he had uncovered. An hour later, three officers from that department arrived at the Cranston headquarters for the purpose of questioning respondent about the murder.

That same evening, at about 7:45 p.m., respondent's sister telephoned the Public Defender's Office to obtain legal assistance for her brother. Her sole concern was the breaking and entering charge, as she was unaware that respondent was then under suspicion for murder. She asked for Richard Casparian, who had been scheduled to meet with respondent earlier that afternoon to discuss another charge unrelated to either the break-in or the murder. As soon as the conversation ended, the attorney who took the call attempted to reach Mr. Casparian. When those efforts were unsuccessful, she telephoned Allegra Munson, another Assistant Public Defender, and told her about respondent's arrest and his sister's subsequent request that the office represent him.

At 8:15 p.m., Ms. Munson telephoned the Cranston police station and asked that her call be transferred to the detective division. In the words of the Supreme Court of Rhode Island, whose factual findings we treat as presumptively correct, 28 U.S.C. § 2254(d), the conversation proceeded as follows:

> "A male voice responded with the word 'Detectives.' Ms. Munson identified herself and asked if Brian Burbine was being held; the person responded affirmatively. Ms. Munson explained to the person that Burbine was represented by attorney Casparian who was not available; she further stated that she would act as Burbine's legal counsel in the event that the police intended to place him in a lineup or question him. The unidentified person told Ms. Munson that the police would not be questioning Burbine or putting him in a lineup and that they were through with him for the night. Ms. Munson was not informed that the Providence Police were at the Cranston police station or that Burbine was a suspect in Mary's murder."

At all relevant times, respondent was unaware of his sister's efforts to retain counsel and of the fact and contents of Ms. Munson's telephone conversation.

Less than an hour later, the police brought respondent to an interrogation room and conducted the first of a series of interviews concerning the murder. Prior to each session, respondent was informed of his *Miranda* rights, and on three separate occasions he signed a written form acknowledging that he understood his right to the presence of an attorney and explicitly indicating that he "[did] not want an attorney called or appointed for [him]" before he gave a statement. Uncontradicted evidence at the suppression hearing indicated that at least twice during the course of the evening, respondent was left in a room where he had access to a telephone, which he apparently declined to use. Eventually, respondent signed three written statements fully admitting to the murder.

Prior to trial, respondent moved to suppress the statements. The court denied the motion, finding that respondent had received the *Miranda* warnings and had "knowingly, intelligently, and voluntarily waived his privilege against self-incrimination [and] his right to counsel." Rejecting the contrary testimony of the police, the court found that Ms. Munson did telephone the detective bureau on the evening in question, but concluded that "there was no * * * conspiracy or collusion on the part of the Cranston Police Department to secrete this defendant from his attorney." In any event, the court held, the constitutional right to request the presence of an attorney belongs solely to the defendant and may not be asserted by his lawyer. Because the evidence was clear that respondent never asked for the services of an attorney, the telephone call had no relevance to the validity of the waiver or the admissibility of the statements.

The jury found respondent guilty of murder in the first degree, and he appealed to the Supreme Court of Rhode Island. A divided court rejected his contention that the Fifth and Fourteenth Amendments to the Constitution required the suppression of the inculpatory statements and affirmed the conviction. Failure to inform respondent of Ms. Munson's efforts to represent him, the court held, did not undermine the validity of the waivers. "It hardly seems conceivable that the additional information that an attorney whom he did not know had called the police station would have added significantly to the quantum of information necessary for the accused to make an informed decision as to waiver." Nor, the court concluded, did *Miranda* or any other decision of this Court independently require the police to honor Ms. Munson's request that interrogation not proceed in her absence. In reaching that conclusion, the court noted that because two different police departments were operating in the Cranston station house on the evening in question, the record supported the trial court's finding that there was no "conspiracy or collusion" to prevent Ms. Munson from seeing respondent. In any case, the court held, the right to the presence of counsel belongs solely to the accused and may not be asserted by "benign third parties, whether or not they happen to be attorneys."

[On federal habeas corpus, the U.S. Court of Appeals for the First Circuit] held that the police's conduct had fatally tainted respondent's "otherwise valid" waiver of his Fifth Amendment privilege against self incrimination and right to counsel. The court reasoned that by failing to inform respondent that an attorney had called and that she had been assured that no questioning would take place until the next day, the police had deprived respondent of information crucial to his ability to waive his rights knowingly and intelligently. The court also found that the record would support "no other explanation for the refusal to tell Burbine of Attorney Munson's call [than] deliberate or reckless irresponsibility." This kind of "blameworthy action by the police," the court concluded, together with respondent's ignorance of the telephone call, "vitiate[d] any claim that [the] waiver of counsel was knowing and voluntary."

We granted certiorari to decide whether a pre-arraignment confession preceded by an otherwise valid waiver must be suppressed either because the police misinformed an inquiring attorney about their plans concerning the suspect or because they failed to inform the suspect of the attorney's efforts to reach him. We now reverse. * * *

Respondent does not dispute that the Providence police followed [the *Miranda* procedures] with precision. [Nor does he contest the state] courts' determination that he at no point requested the presence of a lawyer. He contends instead that the confessions must be suppressed because the police's failure to inform him of the attorney's telephone call deprived him of information essential to his ability to knowingly waive his Fifth Amendment rights. In the alternative, he suggests that to fully protect the Fifth Amendment values served by *Miranda,* we should extend that decision to condemn the conduct of the Providence police. We address each contention in turn.

Echoing the standard first articulated in *Johnson v. Zerbst, Miranda* holds that "[t]he defendant may waive effectuation" of the rights conveyed in the warnings "provided the waiver is made voluntarily, knowingly and intelligently." The inquiry has two distinct dimensions. First the relinquishment of the right must have been voluntary in the sense that it was the product of a free and deliberate choice rather than intimidation, coercion or deception. Second, the waiver must have been made with a full awareness both of the nature of the right being abandoned and the consequences of the decision to abandon it. Only if the "totality of the circumstances surrounding the interrogation" reveal both an uncoerced choice and the requisite level of comprehension may a court properly conclude that the *Miranda* rights have been waived.

Under this standard, we have no doubt that respondent validly waived his right to remain silent and to the presence of counsel. The voluntariness of the waiver is not at issue. [Nor] is there any question about respondent's comprehension of the full panoply of rights set out in the *Miranda* warnings and of the potential consequences of a decision to relinquish them. Nonetheless, the Court of Appeals believed that the "[d]eliberate or reckless" conduct of the police, in particular their failure to inform respondent of the telephone call, fatally undermined the validity of the otherwise proper waiver. We find this conclusion untenable as a matter of both logic and precedent.

Events occurring outside of the presence of the suspect and entirely unknown to him surely can have no bearing on the capacity to comprehend and knowingly relinquish a constitutional right. Under the analysis of the Court of Appeals, the same defendant, armed with the same information and confronted with precisely the same police conduct, would have knowingly waived his *Miranda* rights had a lawyer not telephoned the police station to inquire about his status. Nothing in any of our waiver decisions or in our understanding of the essential components of a valid waiver requires so incongruous a result. No doubt the additional information would have been useful to respondent; perhaps even it might have affected his decision to confess. But we have never read the Constitution to require that the police supply a suspect with a flow of information to help him calibrate his self interest in deciding whether to speak or stand by his rights.[a] Once it is determined that a suspect's decision not to rely on his rights was uncoerced, that he at all times knew he could stand mute and request a lawyer, and that he was aware of the state's intention to use his statements to secure a conviction, the analysis is complete and the waiver is valid as a matter of law.[1] The Court of Appeals' conclusion to the contrary was in error.

a. A year later, this language was quoted with approval in *Colorado v. Spring,* 479 U.S. 564 (1987), holding that the police need not advise a suspect of the crimes they wish to question him about even though the subject matter of the interrogation is likely to be quite different from what the suspect expects.

1. The dissent incorrectly reads our analysis of the components of a valid waiver to be inconsistent [with] *Edwards.* [But] the dissent never comes to grips with the crucial distinguishing feature of this case—that Burbine at no point requested the presence of counsel, as was his right under *Miranda* to do.

Nor do we believe that the level of the police's culpability in failing to inform respondent of the telephone call has any bearing on the validity of the waiver. In light of the state-court findings that there was no "conspiracy or collusion" on the part of the police, we have serious doubts about whether the Court of Appeals was free to conclude that their conduct constituted "deliberate or reckless irresponsibility." But whether intentional or inadvertent, the state of mind of the police is irrelevant to the question of the intelligence and voluntariness of respondent's election to abandon his rights. Although highly inappropriate, even deliberate deception of an attorney could not possibly affect a suspect's decision to waive his *Miranda* rights unless he were at least aware of the incident. Compare *Escobedo* (excluding confession where police incorrectly told the *suspect* that his lawyer " 'didn't want to see' him"). Nor was the failure to inform respondent of the telephone call the kind of "trick[ery]" that can vitiate the validity of a waiver. *Miranda*. Granting that the "deliberate or reckless" withholding of information is objectionable as a matter of ethics, such conduct is only relevant to the constitutional validity of a waiver if it deprives a defendant of knowledge essential to his ability to understand the nature of his rights and the consequences of abandoning them. Because respondent's voluntary decision to speak was made with full awareness and comprehension of all the information *Miranda* requires the police to convey, the waivers were valid.

At oral argument respondent acknowledged that a constitutional rule requiring the police to inform a suspect of an attorney's efforts to reach him would represent a significant extension of our precedents. He contends, however, that the conduct of the Providence police was so inimical to the Fifth Amendment values *Miranda* seeks to protect that we should read that decision to condemn their behavior. Regardless of any issue of waiver, he urges, the Fifth Amendment requires the reversal of a conviction if the police are less than forthright in their dealings with an attorney or if they fail to tell a suspect of a lawyer's unilateral efforts to contact him. Because the proposed modification ignores the underlying purposes of the *Miranda* rules and because we think that the decision as written strikes the proper balance between society's legitimate law enforcement interests and the protection of the defendant's Fifth Amendment rights, we decline the invitation to further extend *Miranda's* reach.

At the outset, while we share respondent's distaste for the deliberate misleading of an officer of the court, reading *Miranda* to forbid police deception of an *attorney* "would cut [the decision] completely loose from its own explicitly stated rationale." As is now well established, "[the] *Miranda* warnings are 'not themselves rights protected by the Constitution but [are] instead measures to insure that the [suspect's] right against compulsory self-incrimination [is] protected.' " *Quarles*. Their objective is not to mold police conduct for its own sake. Nothing in the Constitution vests in us the authority to mandate a code of behavior for state officials wholly unconnected to any federal right or privilege. The purpose of the *Miranda* warnings instead is to dissipate the compulsion inherent in custodial interrogation and, in so doing, guard against abridgement of the suspect's Fifth Amendment rights. Clearly, a rule that focuses on how the police treat an attorney—conduct that has no relevance at all to the degree of compulsion experienced by the defendant during interrogation—would ignore both *Miranda's* mission and its only source of legitimacy.

Nor are we prepared to adopt a rule requiring that the police inform a suspect of an attorney's efforts to reach him. While such a rule might add marginally to

[We reject] the dissent's entirely undefended suggestion that the Fifth Amendment "right to counsel" requires anything more than that the police inform the suspect of his right to representation and honor his request that the interrogation cease until his attorney is present.

Miranda's goal of dispelling the compulsion inherent in custodial interrogation, overriding practical considerations counsel against its adoption. As we have stressed on numerous occasions, "[o]ne of the principal advantages" of *Miranda* is the ease and clarity of its application. *Berkemer v. McCarty.* We have little doubt that the approach urged by respondent and endorsed by the Court of Appeals would have the inevitable consequence of muddying *Miranda's* otherwise relatively clear waters. The legal questions it would spawn are legion: To what extent should the police be held accountable for knowing that the accused has counsel? Is it enough that someone in the station house knows, or must the interrogating officer himself know of counsel's efforts to contact the suspect? Do counsel's efforts to talk to the suspect concerning one criminal investigation trigger the obligation to inform the defendant before interrogation may proceed on a wholly separate matter? We are unwilling to modify *Miranda* in a manner that would so clearly undermine the decision's central "virtue of informing police and prosecutors with specificity [what] they may do in conducting [a] custodial interrogation, and of informing courts under what circumstances statements obtained during such interrogation are not admissible."

Moreover, problems of clarity to one side, reading *Miranda* to require the police in each instance to inform a suspect of an attorney's efforts to reach him would work a substantial and, we think, inappropriate shift in the subtle balance struck in that decision. Custodial interrogations implicate two competing concerns. On the one hand, "the need for police questioning as a tool for effective enforcement of criminal laws" cannot be doubted. Admissions of guilt [are] essential to society's compelling interest in finding, convicting and punishing those who violate the law. On the other hand, the Court has recognized that the interrogation process is "inherently coercive" and that, as a consequence, there exists a substantial risk that the police will inadvertently traverse the fine line between legitimate efforts to elicit admissions and constitutionally impermissible compulsion. *Miranda* attempted to reconcile these opposing concerns by giving the *defendant* the power to exert some control over the course of the interrogation. Declining to adopt the more extreme position that the actual presence of a lawyer was necessary to dispel the coercion inherent in custodial interrogation, the Court found that the suspect's Fifth Amendment rights could be adequately protected by less intrusive means. Police questioning, often an essential part of the investigatory process, could continue in its traditional form, the Court held, but only if the suspect clearly understood that, at any time, he could bring the proceeding to a halt or, short of that, call in an attorney to give advice and monitor the conduct of his interrogators.

The position urged by respondent would upset this carefully drawn approach in a manner that is both unnecessary for the protection of the Fifth Amendment privilege and injurious to legitimate law enforcement. Because, as *Miranda* holds, full comprehension of the rights to remain silent and request an attorney are sufficient to dispel whatever coercion is inherent in the interrogation process, a rule requiring the police to inform the suspect of an attorney's efforts to contact him would contribute to the protection of the Fifth Amendment privilege only incidentally, if at all. This minimal benefit, however, would come at a substantial cost to society's legitimate and substantial interest in securing admissions of guilt. Indeed, the very premise of the Court of Appeals was not that awareness of Ms. Munson's phone call would have dissipated the coercion of the interrogation room, but that it might have convinced respondent not to speak at all. Because neither the letter nor purposes of *Miranda* require this additional handicap on otherwise permissible investigatory efforts, we are unwilling to expand the *Miranda* rules to require the police to keep the suspect abreast of the status of his legal representation.

We acknowledge that a number of state courts have reached a contrary conclusion. We recognize also that our interpretation of the Federal Constitution, if given the dissent's expansive gloss, is at odds with the police recommendations embodied in the American Bar Association Standards of Criminal Justice. [§ 5–7.1.] Notwithstanding the dissent's protestations, however, our interpretive duties go well beyond deferring to the numerical preponderance of lower court decisions or to the subconstitutional recommendations of even so esteemed a body as the American Bar Association. Nothing we say today disables the States from adopting different requirements for the conduct of its employees and officials as a matter of state law. We hold only that the Court of Appeals erred in construing the Fifth Amendment to the Federal Constitution to require the exclusion of respondent's three confessions.

Respondent also contends that the Sixth Amendment requires exclusion of his three confessions. It is clear, of course, that, absent a valid waiver, the defendant has the right to the presence of an attorney during any interrogation occurring after the first formal charging proceeding, the point at which the Sixth Amendment right to counsel initially attaches. And we readily agree that once the right *has* attached, it follows that the police may not interfere with the efforts of a defendant's attorney to act as a " 'medium' between [the suspect] and the State" during the interrogation. The difficulty for respondent is that the interrogation sessions that yielded the inculpatory statements took place *before* the initiation of "adversary judicial proceedings." He contends, however, that this circumstance is not fatal to his Sixth Amendment claim. At least in some situations, he argues, the Sixth Amendment protects the integrity of the attorney-client relationship regardless of whether the prosecution has in fact commenced "by way of formal charge, preliminary hearing, indictment, information or arraignment." Placing principal reliance on a footnote in *Miranda* [n. 35] and on *Escobedo*, he maintains that [the] right to non-interference with an attorney's dealings with a [suspect] arises the moment that the relationship is formed, or, at the very least, once the defendant is placed in custodial interrogation.

We are not persuaded. At the outset, subsequent decisions foreclose any reliance on *Escobedo* and *Miranda* for the proposition that the Sixth Amendment right, in any of its manifestations, applies prior to the initiation of adversary judicial proceedings. Although *Escobedo* was originally decided as a Sixth Amendment case, "the Court in retrospect perceived that the 'prime purpose' of *Escobedo* was not to vindicate the constitutional right to counsel as such, but, like *Miranda*, 'to guarantee full effectuation of the privilege against self-incrimination. * * * ' " *Kirby v. Illinois* [Ch. 7, § 2, holding that the right to counsel at pretrial identifications attaches "only at or after the time that adversary judicial proceedings have been initiated."] Clearly then, *Escobedo* provides no support for respondent's argument. Nor, of course, does *Miranda*, the holding of which rested exclusively on the Fifth Amendment. * * *

Questions of precedent to one side, we find respondent's understanding of the Sixth Amendment both practically and theoretically unsound. As a practical matter, it makes little sense to say that the Sixth Amendment right to counsel attaches at different times depending on the fortuity of whether the suspect or his family happens to have retained counsel prior to interrogation. More importantly, the suggestion that the existence of an attorney-client relationship itself triggers the protections of the Sixth Amendment misconceives the underlying purposes of the right to counsel. The Sixth Amendment's intended function is not to wrap a protective cloak around the attorney-client relationship for its own sake any more than it is to protect a suspect from the consequences of his own candor. [By] its very terms, [the Sixth Amendment] becomes applicable only when the government's role shifts from investigation to accusation. * * *

Finally, respondent contends that the conduct of the police was so offensive as to deprive him of the fundamental fairness guaranteed by the Due Process Clause of the Fourteenth Amendment. Focusing primarily on the impropriety of conveying false information to an attorney, he invites us to declare that such behavior should be condemned as violative of canons fundamental to the " 'traditions and conscience of our people.' " *Rochin.* We do not question that on facts more egregious than those presented here police deception might rise to a level of a due process violation. Accordingly, Justice Stevens' apocalyptic suggestion that we have approved any and all forms of police misconduct is demonstrably incorrect.[4] We hold only that, on these facts, the challenged conduct falls short of the kind of misbehavior that so shocks the sensibilities of civilized society as to warrant a federal intrusion into the criminal processes of the States. * * *

JUSTICE STEVENS, with whom JUSTICE BRENNAN and JUSTICE MARSHALL join, dissenting.

This case poses fundamental questions about our system of justice. As this Court has long recognized, * * * "ours is an accusatorial and not an inquisitorial system." The Court's opinion today represents a startling departure from that basic insight.

[The] Court's holding focuses on the period after a suspect has been taken into custody and before he has been charged with an offense. The core of the Court's holding is that police interference with an attorney's access to her client during that period is not unconstitutional. The Court reasons that a State has a compelling interest, not simply in custodial interrogation, but in lawyer-free, incommunicado custodial interrogation. Such incommunicado interrogation is so important that a lawyer may be given false information that prevents her presence and representation; it is so important that police may refuse to inform a

---

4. Among its other failings, the dissent declines to follow *Oregon v. Elstad,* a decision that categorically forecloses Justice Stevens' major premise—that *Miranda* requires the police to inform a suspect of any and all information that would be useful to a decision whether to remain silent or speak with the police. The dissent also launches a novel "agency" theory of the Fifth Amendment under which any perceived deception of a lawyer is automatically treated as deception of his or her client. This argument entirely disregards the elemental and established proposition that the privilege against compulsory self-incrimination is, by hypothesis, a personal one that can only be invoked by the individual whose testimony is being compelled.

Most importantly, the dissent's misreading of *Miranda* itself is breathtaking in its scope. For example, it reads *Miranda* as creating an undifferentiated right to the presence of an attorney that is triggered automatically by the initiation of the interrogation itself. Yet, as both *Miranda* and subsequent decisions construing *Miranda* make clear beyond refute, " 'the interrogation must cease until an attorney is present' *only* '[i]f the individual states

that he wants an attorney.' " *Michigan v. Mosley* (emphasis added). The dissent condemns us for embracing "incommunicado questioning [as] a societal goal of the highest order that justifies police deception of the shabbiest kind." We, of course, do nothing of the kind. As any reading of *Miranda* reveals, the decision, rather than proceeding from the premise that the rights and needs of the defendant are paramount to all others, embodies a carefully crafted balance designed to fully protect *both* the defendant's and society's interests. The dissent may not share our view that the Fifth Amendment rights of the defendant are amply protected by application of *Miranda as written.* But the dissent is "simply wrong" in suggesting that exclusion of Burbine's three confessions follows perfunctorily from *Miranda's* mandate. Y. Kamisar, *Police Interrogation and Confessions* 217–218, n. 94 (1980).

Quite understandably, the dissent is outraged by the very idea of police deception of a lawyer. Significantly less understandable is its willingness to misconstrue this Court's constitutional holdings in order to implement its subjective notions of sound policy.

suspect of his attorney's communications and immediate availability.[8] This conclusion flies in the face of this Court's repeated expressions of deep concern about incommunicado questioning.[a] Until today, incommunicado questioning has been viewed with the strictest scrutiny by this Court; today, incommunicado questioning is embraced as a societal goal of the highest order that justifies police deception of the shabbiest kind. * * *

Police interference with communications between an attorney and his client is a recurrent problem. The factual variations in the many state court opinions condemning this interference as a violation of the federal Constitution suggest the variety of contexts in which the problem emerges. In Oklahoma, police led a lawyer to several different locations while they interrogated the suspect; in Oregon, police moved a suspect to a new location when they learned that his lawyer was on his way; in Illinois, authorities failed to tell a suspect that his lawyer had arrived at the jail and asked to see him; in Massachusetts, police did not tell suspects that their lawyers were at or near the police station. In all these cases, the police not only failed to inform the suspect, but also misled the attorneys. The scenarios vary, but the core problem of police interference remains.

[The] near-consensus of state courts and the legal profession's Standards about this recurrent problem lends powerful support to the conclusion that police may not interfere with communications between an attorney and the client whom they are questioning. Indeed, at least two opinions from this Court seemed to express precisely that view.[20] The Court today flatly rejects that widely held view and responds to this recurrent problem by adopting the most restrictive interpretation of the federal constitutional restraints on police deception, misinformation, and interference in attorney-client communications. * * *

Well-settled principles of law lead inexorably to the conclusion that the failure to inform Burbine of the call from his attorney makes the subsequent waiver of his constitutional rights invalid. Analysis should begin with an acknowledgment that the burden of proving the validity of a waiver of constitutional rights is always on the *government*. When such a waiver occurs in a custodial setting, that burden is an especially heavy one because custodial interrogation is inherently

---

8. This kind of police-maintained incommunicado questioning becomes, in the Court's rendition, "an essential part of the investigatory process." Police interference in communications between a lawyer and her client are justified because "[a]dmissions of guilt [are] essential to society's compelling interest in finding, convicting, and punishing those who violate the law." It is this overriding interest in obtaining self-incriminatory statements in the lawyer-free privacy of the police interrogation room that motivates the Court's willingness to swallow its admitted "distaste for the deliberate misleading of an officer of the court."

a. [Justice Stevens refers to, and quotes from, numerous cases and then adds:]

To be sure, in many of these cases, the evidence showed that the suspect had requested, and was denied access to, a lawyer. Until today, however, the Court has never viewed "incommunicado" as applying only to the denial of the suspect's efforts to reach the attorney, and not to the attorney's efforts to reach the suspect. * * * It is also true that many of these cases involved incommunicado interrogations for very long periods of time; not one of those cases suggested that incommunicado interrogations for shorter periods, maintained by misinforming attorney and client of each other's actions, was supported by a compelling societal interest that justified police deception and misinformation about attorney communications.

20. See *Miranda* n. 35 (in *Escobedo*, "[t]he police also prevented the attorney from consulting with his client. Independent of any other constitutional proscription, this action constitutes a violation of the Sixth Amendment right to the assistance of counsel and excludes any statement obtained in its wake"); *Escobedo* ("[I]t 'would be highly incongruous if our system of justice permitted the district attorney, the lawyer representing the State, to extract a confession from the accused while his own lawyer, seeking to speak with him, was kept from him by the police' ").

coercive, because disinterested witnesses are seldom available to describe what actually happened, and because history has taught us that the danger of over-reaching during incommunicado interrogation is so real.

In applying this heavy presumption against the validity of waivers, this Court has sometimes relied on a case-by-case totality of the circumstances analysis. We have found, however, that some custodial interrogation situations require strict presumptions against the validity of a waiver. *Miranda* established that a waiver is not valid in the absence of certain warnings. *Edwards* similarly established that a waiver is not valid if police initiate questioning after the defendant has invoked his right to counsel. In these circumstances, the waiver is invalid as a matter of law even if the evidence overwhelmingly establishes, as a matter of fact, that "a suspect's decision not to rely on his rights was uncoerced, that he at all times knew that he could stand mute and request a lawyer, and that he was aware of the state's intention to use his statement to secure a conviction." In light of our decision in *Edwards,* the Court is simply wrong in stating that "the analysis is complete and the waiver is valid as a matter of law" when these facts have been established. Like the failure to give warnings and like police initiation of interrogation after a request for counsel, police deception of a suspect through omission of information regarding attorney communications greatly exacerbates the inherent problems of incommunicado interrogation and requires a clear principle to safeguard the presumption against the waiver of constitutional rights. As in those situations, the police deception should render a subsequent waiver invalid.

Indeed, as *Miranda* itself makes clear, proof that the required warnings have been given is a necessary, but by no means sufficient, condition for establishing a valid waiver. As the Court plainly stated in *Miranda,* "any evidence that the accused was threatened, tricked, or cajoled into a waiver will, of course, show that the defendant did not voluntarily waive his privilege. The requirement of warnings and waiver of rights is a fundamental with respect to the Fifth Amendment privilege and not simply a preliminary ritual to existing methods of interrogation."

In this case it would be perfectly clear that Burbine's waiver was invalid if, for example, Detective Ferranti had "threatened, tricked, or cajoled" Burbine in their private pre-confession meeting—perhaps by misdescribing the statements obtained from DiOrio and Sparks—even though, under the Court's truncated analysis of the issue, Burbine fully understood his rights. For *Miranda* clearly condemns threats or trickery that cause a suspect to make an unwise waiver of his rights even though he fully understands those rights. In my opinion there can be no constitutional distinction—as the Court appears to draw—between a deceptive misstatement and the concealment by the police of the critical fact that an attorney retained by the accused or his family has offered assistance, either by telephone or in person.[38]

Thus, the Court's truncated analysis, which relies in part on a distinction between deception accomplished by means of an omission of a critically important fact and deception by means of a misleading statement, is simply untenable. If, as the Court asserts, "the analysis is at an end" as soon as the suspect is provided

---

38. The Court cites *Johnson v. Zerbst*, a case involving a claim that a defendant had waived his right to trial counsel. I find it inconceivable that, in such a situation, an otherwise sufficient series of questions and answers can support a valid waiver if the government misinforms an attorney about the defendant's trial date, and if the government fails to tell the defendant of the attorney's communications. Yet that would be the consequence of the Court's "what the suspect doesn't know can't hurt him" approach to this case.

with enough information to have the *capacity* to understand and exercise his rights, I see no reason why the police should not be permitted to make the same kind of misstatements to the suspect that they are apparently allowed to make to his lawyer. *Miranda,* however, clearly establishes that both kinds of deception vitiate the suspect's waiver of his right to counsel. * * *[42]

[In] short, settled principles about construing waivers of constitutional rights and about the need for strict presumptions in custodial interrogations, as well as a plain reading of the *Miranda* opinion itself, overwhelmingly support the conclusion reached by almost every state court that has considered the matter—a suspect's waiver of his right to counsel is invalid if police refuse to inform the suspect of his counsel's communications.

The Court makes the alternative argument that requiring police to inform a suspect of his attorney's communications to and about him is not required because it would upset the careful "balance" of *Miranda.* Despite its earlier notion that the attorney's call is an "outside event" that has "no bearing" on a knowing and intelligent waiver, the majority does acknowledge that information of attorney Munson's call "would have been useful to respondent" and "might have affected his decision to confess." Thus, a rule requiring the police to inform a suspect of an attorney's call would have two predictable effects. It would serve "*Miranda's* goal of dispelling the compulsion inherent in custodial interrogation" and it would disserve the goal of custodial interrogation because it would result in fewer confessions. By a process of balancing these two concerns, the Court finds the benefit to the individual outweighed by the "substantial cost to society's legitimate and substantial interest in securing admissions of guilt."

The Court's balancing approach is profoundly misguided. The cost of suppressing evidence of guilt will always make the value of a procedural safeguard appear "minimal," "marginal," or "incremental." Indeed, the value of any trial at all seems like a "procedural technicality" when balanced against the interest in administering prompt justice to a murderer or a rapist caught redhanded. The individual interest in procedural safeguards that minimize the risk of error is easily discounted when the fact of guilt appears certain beyond doubt.

What is the cost of requiring the police to inform a suspect of his attorney's call? It would decrease the likelihood that custodial interrogation will enable the police to obtain a confession. This is certainly a real cost, but it is the same cost that this Court has repeatedly found necessary to preserve the character of our free society and our rejection of an inquisitorial system. * * *

[The] Court also argues that a rule requiring the police to inform a suspect of an attorney's efforts to reach him would have an additional cost: it would undermine the "clarity" of the rule of the *Miranda* case. This argument is not supported by any reference to the experience in the States that have adopted such a rule. The Court merely professes concern about its ability to answer three quite simple questions.[46]

---

42. * * * The majority mischaracterizes this dissent by stating that its "major premise" is that "*Miranda* requires the police to inform a suspect of any and all information that would be useful to a decision whether to remain silent or speak with police." The majority's response ignores the fact that the police action here is not simply a failure to provide "useful" information; rather, it is affirmative police interference in a communication between an attorney and a suspect.

Moreover, the "information" intercepted by the police bears directly on the right to counsel that police are asking the suspect to waive. The "information" at issue is thus far different from information about "the nature and quality of the evidence," or about a grand jury witness's possible target status.

46. Thus, the Court asks itself:

(1) "To what extent should the police be held accountable for knowing that the accused has counsel?" The simple answer is

Moreover, the Court's evaluation of the interest in "clarity" is rather one-sided. For a police officer with a printed card containing the exact text he is supposed to recite, perhaps the rule is clear. But the interest in clarity that the *Miranda* decision was intended to serve is not merely for the benefit of the police. Rather, the decision was also, and primarily, intended to provide adequate guidance to the person in custody who is being asked to waive the protections afforded by the Constitution. Inevitably, the *Miranda* decision also serves the judicial interest in clarifying the inquiry into what actually transpired during a custodial interrogation.[48] Under the Court's conception of the interest in clarity, however, the police would presumably prevail whenever they could convince the trier of fact that a required ritual was performed before the confession was obtained.

At the time attorney Munson made her call to the Cranston Police Station, she was acting as Burbine's attorney. Under ordinary principles of agency law the deliberate deception of Munson was tantamount to deliberate deception of her client. If an attorney makes a mistake in the course of her representation of her client, the client must accept the consequences of that mistake. It is equally clear that when an attorney makes an inquiry on behalf of her client, the client is entitled to a truthful answer. Surely the client must have the same remedy for a false representation to his lawyer that he would have if he were acting *pro se* and had propounded the question himself.

The majority brushes aside the police deception involved in the misinformation of attorney Munson. It is irrelevant to the Fifth Amendment analysis, concludes the majority, because that right is personal; it is irrelevant to the Sixth Amendment analysis, continues the majority, because the Sixth Amendment does not apply until formal adversary proceedings have begun.

In my view, as a matter of law, the police deception of Munson was tantamount to deception of Burbine himself. It constituted a violation of Burbine's right to have an attorney present during the questioning that began shortly thereafter. The existence of that right is undisputed. Whether the source of that right is the Sixth Amendment, the Fifth Amendment, or a combination of the two is of no special importance, for I do not understand the Court to deny the existence of the right.

The pertinent question is whether police deception of the attorney is utterly irrelevant to that right. In my judgment, it blinks at reality to suggest that misinformation which prevented the presence of an attorney has no bearing on the protection and effectuation of the right to counsel in custodial interrogation. The majority parses the role of attorney and suspect so narrowly that the deception of the attorney is of no constitutional significance. [The] character of the attorney-client relationship requires rejection of the Court's notion that the

that police should be held accountable to the extent that the attorney or the suspect informs the police of the representation.

(2) "Is it enough that someone in the station house knows, or must the interrogating officer himself know of counsel's efforts to contact the suspect?" Obviously, police should be held responsible for getting a message of this importance from one officer to another.

(3) "Do counsel's efforts to talk to the suspect concerning one criminal investigation trigger the obligation to inform the defendant before interrogation may proceed on a wholly separate matter?" As the facts of

this case forcefully demonstrate, the answer is "yes."

48. Indeed, in contrast to the majority's remarks about clarity, the operation of the principle expressed by almost all the state courts would be far clearer than the operation of the Court's contrary principle. For it is surely easier to administer a rule that applies to an external event, such as an attorney's telephone call or a visit to the police station, than a rule that requires an evaluation of the state of mind of a person undergoing custodial interrogation.

attorney is some entirely distinct, completely severable entity and that deception of the attorney is irrelevant to the right of counsel in custodial interrogation.[53]

The possible reach of the Court's opinion is stunning. For the majority seems to suggest that police may deny counsel all access to a client who is being held. At least since *Escobedo,* it has been widely accepted that police may not simply deny attorneys access to their clients who are in custody. This view has survived the recasting of *Escobedo* from a Sixth Amendment to a Fifth Amendment case that the majority finds so critically important. That this prevailing view is shared *by the police* can be seen in the state court opinions detailing various forms of police deception of attorneys. For, if there were no obligation to give attorneys access, there would be no need to take elaborate steps to avoid access, such as shuttling the suspect to a different location, or taking the lawyer to different locations; police could simply refuse to allow the attorneys to see the suspects. But the law enforcement profession has apparently believed, quite rightly in my view, that denying lawyers access to their clients is impermissible. The Court today seems to assume that this view was error—that, from the federal constitutional perspective, the lawyer's access is, as a question from the Court put it in oral argument, merely "a matter of prosecutorial grace." Certainly, nothing in the Court's Fifth and Sixth Amendments analysis acknowledges that there is *any* federal constitutional bar to an absolute denial of lawyer access to a suspect who is in police custody.

[In] my judgment, police interference in the attorney-client relationship is the type of governmental misconduct on a matter of central importance to the administration of justice that the Due Process Clause prohibits. Just as the police cannot impliedly promise a suspect that his silence will not be used against him and then proceed to break that promise, so too police cannot tell a suspect's attorney that they will not question the suspect and then proceed to question him. Just as the government cannot conceal from a suspect material and exculpatory evidence, so too the government cannot conceal from a suspect the material fact of his attorney's communication.

[This] case turns on a proper appraisal of the role of the lawyer in our society. If a lawyer is seen as a nettlesome obstacle to the pursuit of wrongdoers—as in an inquisitorial society—then the Court's decision today makes a good deal of sense. If a lawyer is seen as an aid to the understanding and protection of constitutional rights—as in an accusatorial society—then today's decision makes no sense at all. * * *

7. *Comparing and contrasting Miranda with (a) the prohibition against the use of involuntary and compelled statements and (b) the Fourth Amendment exclusionary rule*

WITHROW v. WILLIAMS
507 U.S. 680, 113 S.Ct. 1745, 123 L.Ed.2d 407 (1993).

JUSTICE SOUTER delivered the opinion of the Court.

In *Stone v. Powell,* 428 U.S. 465 (1976), we held that when a State has given a full and fair choice to litigate a Fourth Amendment claim, federal habeas corpus

53. Prevailing norms of legal practice prevent a lawyer from communicating with a party, rather than a lawyer. See Disciplinary Rule 7–104(A)(1), ABA Code of Professional Responsibility ("During the course of his representation of a client a lawyer shall not: Communicate or cause another to communicate on the subject of the representation with a party he knows to be represented by a lawyer in that matter unless he has the prior consent of the lawyer representing such other party or is authorized by law to do so"). * * *

review is not available to a state prisoner alleging that his conviction rests on evidence obtained through an unconstitutional search or seizure. Today we hold [that *Stone*] does not extend to a state prisoner's claim that his conviction rests on statements obtained in violation [of] *Miranda.*

[Although respondent Williams, a murder suspect, was not advised of his *Miranda* rights until the police had taken him into custody and questioned him for some 40 minutes, during which time he made several incriminating statements, a Michigan court declined to suppress any of these statements. He was subsequently convicted on two counts of murder. A federal district court found that his *Miranda* rights had been violated and granted habeas corpus relief. The U.S. Court of Appeals for the Sixth Circuit affirmed.]

II

We have made it clear that *Stone's* limitations on federal habeas relief was not jurisdictional in nature, but rested on prudential concerns counselling against the application of the Fourth Amendment exclusionary rule on collateral review. * * * We simply concluded in *Stone* that the costs of applying the exclusionary rule on collateral review outweighed any potential advantage to be gained by applying it there. * * *

[Petitioner] argues that *Miranda*'s safeguards are not constitutional in character, but merely "prophylactic," and that in consequence habeas review should not extend to a claim that a state conviction rests on statements obtained in the absence of those safeguards. We accept petitioner's premise for purposes of this case, but not her conclusion.

[The *Miranda* Court] indeed acknowledged that, in barring introduction of a statement obtained without the required warnings, *Miranda* might exclude a confession that we would not condemn as "involuntary in traditional terms," and for this reason we have sometimes called the *Miranda* safeguards "prophylactic" in nature. * * * Calling the *Miranda* safeguards "prophylactic," however, is a far cry from putting *Miranda* on all fours with *Mapp* or from rendering *Miranda* subject to *Stone.*

As we explained in *Stone,* the *Mapp* rule "is not a personal constitutional right," but serves to deter future constitutional violations; although it mitigates the juridical consequences of invading the defendant's privacy, the exclusion of evidence at trial can do nothing to remedy the completed and wholly extrajudicial Fourth Amendment violation. Nor can the *Mapp* rule be thought to enhance the soundness of the criminal process by improving the reliability of evidence introduced at trial. Quite the contrary, as we explained in *Stone,* the evidence excluded under *Mapp* "is typically reliable and often the most probative information bearing on the guilt or innocence of the defendant."

Miranda differs from *Mapp* in both respects. "Prophylactic" though it may be, in protecting a defendant's Fifth Amendment privilege against self-incrimination *Miranda* safeguards "a fundamental *trial* right." The privilege embodies "principles of humanity and civil liberty, which had been secured in the mother country only after years of struggle" and reflects

> "many of our fundamental values and most noble aspirations: * * * our preference for an accusatorial rather than an inquisitorial system of criminal justice; * * * our sense of fair play which dictates 'a fair state-individual balance by requiring the government to leave the individual alone until good cause is shown for disturbing him and by requiring the government in its contest with the individual to shoulder the entire load;' [and] our realization

that the privilege, while sometimes 'a shelter to the guilty,' is often 'a protection to the innocent.' " *Murphy v. Waterfront Comm'n* [Ch. 8, § 2].

Nor does the Fifth Amendment "trial right" protected by *Miranda* serve some value necessarily divorced from the correct ascertainment of guilt. " '[A] system of criminal law enforcement which comes to depend on the "confession" will, in the long run, be less reliable and more subject to abuses' than a system relying on independent investigation." *Michigan v. Tucker* (quoting *Escobedo*). By bracing against "the possibility of unreliable statements in every instance of in-custody interrogation," *Miranda* serves to guard against "the use of unreliable statements at trial." * * *

Finally, and most importantly, eliminating review of *Miranda* claims would not significantly benefit the federal courts in their exercise of habeas jurisdiction, or advance the cause of federalism in any substantial way. As one *amicus* [the United States] concedes, eliminating habeas review of *Miranda* issues would not prevent a state prisoner from simply converting his barred *Miranda* claim into a due process claim that his conviction rested on an involuntary confession. Indeed, although counsel could provide us with no empirical basis for projecting the consequence of adopting petitioner's position, it seems reasonable to suppose that virtually all *Miranda* claims would simply be recast in this way.[5]

If that is so, the federal courts would certainly not have heard the last of *Miranda* on collateral review. Under the due process approach, [courts] look to the totality of circumstances to determine whether a confession was voluntary. Those potential circumstances include not only the crucial element of police coercion [and such factors as the location and the length of the interrogation and the suspect's maturity, education and mental health, but] the failure of police to advise the defendant of his rights to remain silent and to have counsel present during custodial interrogation. We could lock the front door against *Miranda,* but not the back.

We thus fail to see how abdicating *Miranda*'s bright-line (or, at least, brighter-line) rules in favor of an exhaustive totality-of-circumstances approach on habeas would do much of anything to lighten the burdens placed on busy federal courts. * * * We likewise fail to see how purporting to eliminate *Miranda* issues from federal habeas would go very far to relieve such tensions as *Miranda* may now raise between the two judicial systems. Relegation of habeas petitioners to straight involuntariness claims would not likely reduce the amount of litigation, and each such claim would in any event present a legal question requiring an "independent federal determination" on habeas.

One might argue that tension results between the two judicial systems whenever a federal habeas court overturns a state conviction on finding that the state court let in a voluntary confession obtained by the police without the *Miranda* safeguards. And one would have to concede that this has occurred in the past, and doubtless will occur again. It is not reasonable, however, to expect such occurrences to be frequent enough to amount to a substantial cost of reviewing *Miranda* claims on habeas or to raise federal-state tensions to an appreciable degree. We must remember in this regard that *Miranda* came down some 27 years ago. In that time, law enforcement has grown in constitutional as well as technological sophistication, and there is little reason to believe that the police today are unable, or even generally unwilling, to satisfy *Miranda*'s requirements. [And] if, finally, one should question the need for federal collateral review

---

5. Justice O'Connor is confident that many such claims would be unjustified, but that is beside the point. Justifiability is not much of a gatekeeper on habeas.

of requirements that merit such respect, the answer simply is that the respect is sustained in no small part by the existence of such review. * * *

JUSTICE O'CONNOR, with whom THE CHIEF JUSTICE joins, [dissenting from Part II of the Court's opinion].

Today the Court permits the federal courts to overturn on habeas the conviction of a double-murderer, not on the basis of an inexorable constitutional or statutory command, but because it believes the result desirable from the standpoint of equity and judicial administration. Because the principles that inform our habeas jurisprudence—finality, federalism, and fairness—counsel decisively against the result the Court reaches, I respectfully dissent from this holding. * * *

Today we face the question whether alleged violations of the prophylactic rule of *Miranda* should be cognizable on habeas. [In] my view, the "prudential concerns" that inform our habeas jurisprudence counsel the exclusion of *Miranda* claims just as strongly as they did the exclusionary rule claims at issue in *Stone* itself. * * *

* * * Like the suppression of the fruits of an illegal search or seizure, the exclusion of statements obtained in violation of *Miranda* is not constitutionally required. This Court repeatedly has held that *Miranda*'s warning requirement is not a dictate of the Fifth Amendment itself, but a prophylactic rule. * * * Because *Miranda* "sweeps more broadly than the Fifth Amendment itself," it excludes some confessions even though the Constitution would not. Indeed, "in the individual case, *Miranda*'s preventive medicine [often] provides a remedy even to the defendant who has suffered no identifiable constitutional harm."

Miranda's overbreadth, of course, is not without justification. The exclusion of unwarned statements provides a strong incentive for the police to adopt "procedural safeguards" against the exaction of compelled or involuntary statements. It also promotes institutional respect for constitutional values. But, like the exclusionary rule for illegally seized evidence, *Miranda*'s prophylactic rule does so at a substantial cost. Unlike involuntary or compelled statements—which are of dubious reliability and are therefore inadmissible for any purpose— confessions obtained in violation of *Miranda* are not necessarily untrustworthy. In fact, because *voluntary* statements are "trustworthy" even when obtained without proper warnings, their suppression actually *impairs* the pursuit of truth by concealing probative information from the trier of fact.

[When] the case is on direct review, that damage to the truth-seeking function is deemed an acceptable sacrifice for the deterrence and respect for constitutional values that the *Miranda* rule brings. But once a case is on collateral review, the balance between the costs and benefits shifts; the interests of federalism, finality, and fairness compel *Miranda*'s exclusion from habeas. The benefit of enforcing *Miranda* through habeas is marginal at best. To the extent *Miranda* ensures the exclusion of involuntary statements, that task can be performed more accurately by adjudicating the voluntariness question directly. * * *

Despite its meager benefits, the relitigation of *Miranda* claims on habeas imposes substantial costs. Just like the application of the exclusionary rule, application of *Miranda*'s prophylactic rule on habeas consumes scarce judicial resources on an issue unrelated to guilt or innocence. No less than the exclusionary rule, it undercuts finality. It creates tension between the state and federal courts. And it upsets the division of responsibilities that underlies our federal system. But most troubling of all, *Miranda*'s application on habeas sometimes precludes the just application of law altogether. The order excluding the statement will often be issued "years after trial, when a new trial may be a practical impossibility." Whether the Court admits it or not, the grim result of applying *Miranda* on habeas will be, time and time again, "the release of an admittedly guilty individual who may pose a continuing threat to society."

Any rule that so demonstrably renders truth and society "the loser" " 'bear[s] a heavy burden of justification, and must be carefully limited to the circumstances in which it will pay its way by deterring official lawlessness.' " That burden is heavier still on collateral review. In light of the meager deterrent benefit it brings and the tremendous costs it imposes, in my view application of *Miranda*'s prophylactic rule on habeas "falls short" of justification.

The Court identifies a number of differences that, in its view, distinguish this case from *Stone*. I am sympathetic to the Court's concerns but find them misplaced nonetheless.

The first difference the Court identifies concerns the nature of the right protected. *Miranda,* the Court correctly points out, fosters Fifth Amendment rather than Fourth Amendment values. [The] Court's spirited defense of the Fifth Amendment is, of course, entirely beside the point. The question is not whether *true* Fifth Amendment claims—the extraction and use of *compelled* testimony—should be cognizable on habeas. It is whether violations of *Miranda*'s prophylactic rule, which excludes from trial voluntary confessions obtained without the benefit of *Miranda*'s now-familiar warnings, should be. The questions are not the same; nor are their answers.

To say that the Fifth Amendment is a " 'fundamental *trial* right' " is thus both correct and irrelevant. *Miranda*'s warning requirement may bear many labels, but "fundamental trial right" is not among them. * * *

Excluding *Miranda* claims from habeas * * * denies collateral relief only in those cases in which the prisoner's statement was neither compelled nor involuntary but merely obtained without the benefit of *Miranda*'s prophylactic warnings. The availability of a suppression remedy in such cases cannot be labeled a "fundamental trial right," for there is no constitutional right to the suppression of *voluntary* statements. Quite the opposite: The Fifth Amendment, by its terms, prohibits only *compelled* self-incrimination; it makes no mention of "unwarned" statements. * * *

Similarly unpersuasive is the Court's related argument [that] the Fifth Amendment trial right is not "necessarily divorced" from the interest of reliability. Whatever the Fifth Amendment's relationship to reliability, *Miranda*'s prophylactic rule is not merely "divorced" from the quest for truth but at war with it as well. The absence of *Miranda* warnings does not by some mysterious alchemy convert a voluntary and trustworthy statement into an involuntary and unreliable one. To suggest otherwise is both unrealistic and contrary to precedent.

[The] consideration the Court identifies as being "most importan[t]" of all, is an entirely pragmatic one. Specifically, the Court "project[s]" that excluding *Miranda* questions from habeas will not significantly promote efficiency or federalism because some *Miranda* issues are relevant to a statement's voluntariness. It is true that barring *Miranda* claims from habeas poses no barrier to the adjudication of voluntariness questions. But that does not make it "reasonable to suppose that virtually all *Miranda* claims [will] simply be recast" and litigated as voluntariness claims. Involuntariness requires coercive state action, such as trickery, psychological pressure, or mistreatment. [A] *Miranda* claim, by contrast, requires no evidence of police overreaching whatsoever; it is enough that law enforcement officers commit a technical error.

[The] published decisions of the lower federal courts show that what the Court assumes to be true demonstrably is not. In case after case, the courts are asked on habeas to decide purely technical *Miranda* questions that contain not even a hint of police overreaching. And in case after case, no voluntariness issue is raised, primarily because none exists.

[Even] assuming that many *Miranda* claims could "simply be recast" as voluntariness claims, it does not follow that barring *Miranda*'s prophylactic rule from habeas would unduly complicate their resolution. The Court labels *Miranda* a "bright-line (or, at least, brighter-line) rul[e]" and involuntariness an "exhaustive totality-of-circumstances approach," but surely those labels overstate the differences. *Miranda,* for all its alleged brightness, is not without its difficulties [as Justice White pointed out in his *Miranda* dissent]; and voluntariness is not without its strengths.

* * * *Miranda* creates as many close questions as it resolves. The task of determining whether a defendant is in "custody" has proved to be "a slippery one." And the supposedly "bright" lines that separate interrogation from spontaneous declaration, the exercise of a right from waiver, and the adequate warning from the inadequate, likewise have turned out to be rather dim and ill-defined. [Yet] *Miranda* requires those lines to be drawn with precision in each case.

The totality-of-the-circumstances approach, on the other hand, permits each fact to be taken into account without resort to formal and dispositive labels. By dispensing with the difficulty of producing a yes-or-no answer to questions that are often better answered in shades and degrees, the voluntariness inquiry often can make judicial decisionmaking easier rather than more onerous. Thus, it is true that the existence of warnings is still a consideration under the totality-of-the-circumstances approach, but it is unnecessary to determine conclusively whether "custody" existed and triggered the warning requirement, or whether the warnings given were sufficient. It is enough that the habeas court look to the warnings or their absence, along with all other factors, and consider them in deciding what is, after all, the ultimate question: whether the confession was compelled and involuntary or the product of a free and unimpaired will.

[The] Court's final rationale is that, because the federal courts rarely issue writs for *Miranda* violations, eliminating *Miranda* claims from *habeas* will not decrease state-federal tensions to an appreciable degree. The relative infrequency of relief, however, does not diminish the intrusion on state sovereignty; it diminishes only our justification for intruding in the first place. After all, even if relief is denied at the end of the day, the State still must divert its scarce prosecutorial resources to defend an otherwise final conviction. If relief is truly rare, efficiency counsels in favor of dispensing with the search for the prophylactic rule violation in a haystack; instead, the federal courts should concentrate on the search for true Fifth Amendment violations by adjudicating the questions of voluntariness and compulsion directly.

[As] the Court emphasizes today, *Miranda* 's prophylactic rule is now 26 years old; the police and the state courts have indeed grown accustomed to it. But it is precisely because the rule is well accepted that there is little further benefit to enforcing it on habeas. We can depend on law enforcement officials to administer warnings in the first instance and the state courts to provide a remedy when law enforcement officers err. * * *a

a. In a separate dissent from Part II of the Court's opinion, Justice Scalia, joined by Thomas, J., maintained: "[T]he question before us is not whether a holding unique to Fourth Amendment claims (and resting upon nothing more principled than our estimation that Fourth Amendment exclusion claims are not very important) should be expanded to

SECTION 5. *MASSIAH* REVISITED: *MASSIAH* AND *MIRANDA* COMPARED AND CONTRASTED

Until the Court handed down the first case in this section, *Brewer v. Williams,* often called the "Christian burial speech" case, lasting fame had eluded *Massiah v. United States* [§ 2 supra]. Many thought that *Massiah* had been only a steppingstone to *Escobedo,* decided a scant five weeks later, and that both cases had been largely displaced by *Miranda.* But *Williams* made plain that despite the Court's shift from a "right to counsel" base in *Escobedo* to a "compelled self-incrimination base" in *Miranda,* the *Massiah* doctrine was still alive and well. Indeed, although few, if any, would have predicted it in the early 1970's, the *Massiah* doctrine has emerged as a much more potent force than it had ever been in the Warren Court era.

In the process of revivifying *Massiah,* however, the *Williams* Court blurred the *Massiah* and *Miranda* rationales. Although this is not clear from the *Williams* opinion, application of *Massiah* turns on neither "custody" nor "interrogation," the key *Miranda* concepts. Rather, the *Massiah* doctrine represents a pure right to counsel approach.

Once adversary proceedings have commenced against an individual (e.g., he has been indicted or arraigned) he is entitled to the assistance of counsel and the government may not "deliberately elicit" incriminating statements from him, neither openly by uniformed police officers nor surreptitiously by "secret agents." This prohibition applies regardless of whether the individual is in "custody" or being subjected to "interrogation" in the *Miranda* sense. There need not be any compelling influences at work, inherent, informal or otherwise. (There certainly were not any in the *Massiah* case itself.)

Nevertheless, perhaps because the lower courts had treated *Williams* as a *Miranda* case, a majority of the *Williams* Court thought it important, if not crucial, to establish that the "Christian burial speech" delivered by Captain Leaming did constitute "interrogation"—and all four dissenters insisted it was not. Considering the Court's subsequent discussion of "interrogation" in *Rhode Island v. Innis* [§ 4 supra], the captain's "speech" does appear to have been a form of "*Miranda* interrogation," but *it did not have to be,* in order for the *Massiah* doctrine to have protected Williams.

United States v. Henry, 447 U.S. 264 (1980), not only reaffirmed the *Massiah–Williams* doctrine, but expanded it by applying it to a situation where the FBI had instructed its paid government informant, ostensibly defendant's "cellmate," not to question defendant about the crime, and there was no showing that he had. Nevertheless, the Court, per Burger, C.J., rejected the government's argument that the incriminating statements were not the result of any "affirmative conduct" on the part of government agents to elicit evidence. The informant "was not a passive listener; rather he had 'some conversations with Mr. Henry' while he was in jail and Henry's incriminatory statements were 'the product of this conversation.' "

Moreover, and more generally, observed the Court: Even if the FBI agent's statement is accepted that "he did not intend that [the informant] would take

some other arbitrary category beyond that; but rather, whether the general principle that is the only valid justification for *Stone v. Powell* should for some reason *not* be applied to *Miranda* claims. I think the answer to that question is clear: Prior opportunity to litigate an issue should be an important equitable consideration in *any* habeas case, and should ordinarily preclude the court from reaching the merits of a claim, unless it goes to the fairness of the trial process or to the accuracy of the ultimate result."

affirmative steps to secure incriminating information, he must have known that such propinquity likely would lead to that result. * * * By intentionally creating a situation likely to induce Henry to make incriminating statements without the assistance of counsel [after Henry had been indicted and counsel had been appointed for him], the government violated Henry's Sixth Amendment right to counsel."

This broad—some would say, loose—language would seem to prohibit the government from "planting" even a completely "passive" secret agent in a person's cell once adversary proceedings have commenced against him. But the *Henry* Court cautioned that it was not "called upon to pass on the situation where an informant is placed in [close] proximity [to a prisoner] but makes no effort to stimulate conversations about the crime charged." Moreover, concurring Justice Powell made it plain that he could not join the majority opinion if it held that "the mere presence or incidental conversation of an informant in a jail cell would violate *Massiah*." The *Massiah* doctrine, emphasized Powell, "does not prohibit the introduction of spontaneous conversations that are not elicited by governmental action."

May the government employ a "passive informant" without violating the *Massiah* doctrine? Must the informant be—is it possible for him to be—completely "passive"? These questions are addressed in the second case in this section, *Kuhlmann v. Wilson*, the most recent "jail plant" case. As is graphically illustrated by *Kuhlmann*, the line between "active" and "passive" secret agents— between "*stimulating*" conversations with a defendant in order to "elicit" incriminating statements from him and taking no action "beyond *merely listening*"—is an exceedingly difficult one to draw.

BREWER v. WILLIAMS (WILLIAMS I)

430 U.S. 387, 97 S.Ct. 1232, 51 L.Ed.2d 424 (1977).

JUSTICE STEWART delivered the opinion of the Court. * * *

On the afternoon of December 24, 1968, a 10–year–old girl named Pamela Powers went with her family to the YMCA in Des Moines, Iowa. [When] she failed to return from a trip to the washroom, a search for her began. The search was unsuccessful.

Robert Williams, who had recently escaped from a mental hospital, was a resident of the YMCA. Soon after the girl's disappearance Williams was seen in the YMCA lobby carrying some clothing and a large bundle wrapped in a blanket. He obtained help from a 14–year–old boy in opening the street door of the YMCA and the door to his automobile parked outside. When Williams placed the bundle in the front seat of his car the boy "saw two legs in it and they were skinny and white." Before anyone could see what was in the bundle Williams drove away. His abandoned car was found the following day in Davenport, Iowa, roughly 160 miles east of Des Moines. A warrant was then issued in Des Moines for his arrest on a charge of abduction.

On the morning of December 26, a Des Moines lawyer named Henry McKnight went to the Des Moines police station and informed the officers present that he had just received a long distance call from Williams, and that he had advised Williams to turn himself in to the Davenport police. Williams did surrender that morning to the police in Davenport, and they booked him on the charge specified in the arrest warrant and gave him the [*Miranda* warnings]. The Davenport police then telephoned their counterparts in Des Moines to inform them that Williams had surrendered. McKnight, the lawyer, was still at the Des

Moines police headquarters, and Williams conversed with McKnight on the telephone. In the presence of the Des Moines Chief of Police and a Police Detective named Leaming [a captain and 20–year veteran of the Des Moines police department], McKnight advised Williams that Des Moines police officers would be driving to Davenport to pick him up, that the officers would not interrogate him or mistreat him, and that Williams was not to talk to the officers about Pamela Powers until after consulting with McKnight upon his return to Des Moines. As a result of these conversations, it was agreed between McKnight and the Des Moines police officials that Detective Leaming and a fellow officer would drive to Davenport to pick up Williams, that they would bring him directly back to Des Moines, and that they would not question him during the trip.

In the meantime Williams was arraigned before a judge in Davenport on the outstanding arrest warrant. The judge advised him of his *Miranda* rights and committed him to jail. Before leaving the courtroom, Williams conferred with a lawyer named Kelly, who advised him not to make any statements until consulting with McKnight back in Des Moines.

Detective Leaming and his fellow officer arrived in Davenport about noon to pick up Williams and return him to Des Moines. Soon after their arrival they met with Williams and Kelly, who, they understood, was acting as Williams' lawyer. Detective Leaming repeated the *Miranda* warnings, and told Williams:

> "* * * we both know that you're being represented here by Mr. Kelly and you're being represented by Mr. McKnight in Des Moines, and * * * I want you to remember this because we'll be visiting between here and Des Moines."

Williams then conferred again with Kelly alone, and after this conference Kelly reiterated to Detective Leaming that Williams was not to be questioned about the disappearance of Pamela Powers until after he had consulted with McKnight back in Des Moines. When Leaming expressed some reservations, Kelly firmly stated that the agreement with McKnight was to be carried out—that there was to be no interrogation of Williams during the automobile journey to Des Moines. Kelly was denied permission to ride in the police car back to Des Moines with Williams and the two officers.

The two Detectives, with Williams in their charge, then set out on the 160–mile drive. At no time during the trip did Williams express a willingness to be interrogated in the absence of an attorney. Instead, he stated several times that "[w]hen I get to Des Moines and see Mr. McKnight, I am going to tell you the whole story." Detective Leaming knew that Williams was a former mental patient, and knew also that he was deeply religious.

The Detective and his prisoner soon embarked on a wide-ranging conversation covering a variety of topics, including the subject of religion. Then, not long after leaving Davenport and reaching the interstate highway, Detective Leaming delivered what has been referred to [as] the "Christian burial speech." Addressing Williams as "Reverend," the Detective said:

> "I want to give you something to think about while we're traveling down the road. * * * Number one, I want you to observe the weather conditions, it's raining, it's sleeting, it's freezing, driving is very treacherous, visibility is poor, it's going to be dark early this evening. They are predicting several inches of snow for tonight, and I feel that you yourself are the only person that knows where this little girl's body is, that you yourself have only been there once, and if you get a snow on top of it you yourself may be unable to find it. And, since we will be going right past the area on the way into Des

Moines, I feel that we could stop and locate the body, that the parents of this little girl should be entitled to a Christian burial for the little girl who was snatched away from them on Christmas Eve and murdered. And I feel we should stop and locate it on the way in rather than waiting until morning and trying to come back out after a snow storm and possibly not being able to find it at all.''

Williams asked Detective Leaming why he thought their route to Des Moines would be taking them past the girl's body, and Leaming responded that he knew the body was in the area of Mitchellville—a town they would be passing on the way to Des Moines.[1] Leaming then stated: "I do not want you to answer me. I don't want to discuss it further. Just think about it as we're riding down the road."

As the car approached Grinell, a town approximately 100 miles west of Davenport, Williams asked whether the police had found the victim's shoes. When Detective Leaming replied that he was unsure, Williams directed the officers to a service station where he said he had left the shoes; a search for them proved unsuccessful. As they continued towards Des Moines, Williams asked whether the police had found the blanket, and directed the officers to a rest area where he said he had disposed of the blanket. Nothing was found. The car continued towards Des Moines, and as it approached Mitchellville, Williams said that he would show the officers where the body was. He then directed the police to the body of Pamela Powers.

[The trial judge admitted all evidence relating to or resulting from statements Williams made in the car ride. He found that "an agreement" had been made between defense counsel and the police that Williams would not be questioned on the return trip to Des Moines, but ruled that Williams had waived his rights before giving such information.]

[On federal habeas corpus, the] District Court made findings of fact as summarized above, and concluded as a matter of law that the evidence in question had been wrongly admitted at Williams' trial. This conclusion was based on three alternative and independent grounds: (1) that Williams had been denied his constitutional right to the assistance of counsel; (2) that he had been denied [his *Miranda* rights]; and (3) that in any event, [his] statements [had] been involuntarily made.

[The] Court of Appeals appears to have affirmed the judgment on [the first two] grounds. We have concluded that only one of them need be considered here.

Specifically, there is no need to review the [*Miranda* doctrine] [or the] the ruling of the District Court that Williams' self-incriminating statements were, indeed, involuntarily made. For it is clear that the judgment before us must in any event be affirmed upon the ground that Williams was deprived of a different constitutional right—the right to the assistance of counsel.

* * * Whatever else it may mean, the right to counsel * * * means at least that a person is entitled to the help of a lawyer at or after the time that judicial proceedings have been initiated against him—"whether by way of formal charge, preliminary hearing, indictment, information, or arraignment." *Kirby v. Illinois* [Ch. 7, § 2].

There can be no doubt in the present case that judicial proceedings had been initiated against Williams before the start of the automobile ride from Davenport

---

1. The fact of the matter, of course, was   knowledge.
that Detective Leaming possessed no such

to Des Moines. A warrant had been issued for his arrest, he had been arraigned on that warrant before a judge in a Davenport courtroom, and he had been committed by the court to confinement in jail. The State does not contend otherwise.

There can be no serious doubt, either, that Detective Leaming deliberately and designedly set out to elicit information from Williams just as surely as—and perhaps more effectively than—if he had formally interrogated him. Detective Leaming was fully aware before departing for Des Moines that Williams was being represented in Davenport by Kelly and in Des Moines by McKnight. Yet he purposely sought during Williams' isolation from his lawyers to obtain as much incriminating information as possible. Indeed, Detective Leaming conceded as much when he testified at Williams' trial:

> "Q. In fact, Captain, whether he was a mental patient or not, you were trying to get all the information you could before he got to his lawyer, weren't you?
>
> "A. I was sure hoping to find out where that little girl was, yes, sir.
>
> * * *
>
> "Q. Well, I'll put it this way: You [were] hoping to get all the information you could before Williams got back to McKnight, weren't you?
>
> "A. Yes, sir." [6]

The state courts clearly proceeded upon the hypothesis that Detective Leaming's "Christian burial speech" had been tantamount to interrogation. Both courts recognized that Williams had been entitled to the assistance of counsel at the time he made the incriminating statements. Yet no such constitutional protection would have come into play if there had been no interrogation.

The circumstances of this case are thus constitutionally indistinguishable from those presented in *Massiah*. [That] the incriminating statements were elicited surreptitiously in [*Massiah*], and otherwise here, is constitutionally irrelevant. Rather, the clear rule of *Massiah* is that once adversary proceedings have commenced against an individual, he has a right to legal representation when the government interrogates him. It thus requires no wooden or technical application of the *Massiah* doctrine to conclude that Williams was entitled to the assistance of counsel guaranteed to him by the Sixth and Fourteenth Amendments.

The Iowa courts recognized that Williams had been denied the constitutional right to the assistance of counsel. They held, however, that he had waived that right during the course of the automobile trip from Davenport to Des Moines. The state trial court explained its determination of waiver as follows:

> "The time element involved on the trip, the general circumstances of it, and more importantly the absence on the Defendant's part of any assertion of his right or desire not to give information absent the presence of his attorney, are the main foundations for the Court's conclusion that he voluntarily waived such right."

[The] District Court and the Court of Appeals were correct in the view that the question of waiver was not a question of historical fact, but one [that], requires "application of constitutional principles to the facts as found."

The [lower federal courts] were also correct in their understanding of the proper standard to be applied in determining the question of waiver as a matter of

---

6. Counsel for the State, in the course of oral argument in this Court, acknowledged that the "Christian burial speech" was tantamount to interrogation * * *.

federal constitutional law—that it was incumbent upon the State to prove "an intentional relinquishment or abandonment of a known right or privilege." *Johnson v. Zerbst.* [That] strict standard applies equally to an alleged waiver of the right to counsel whether at trial or at a critical stage of pretrial proceedings.

We conclude, finally that the Court of Appeals was correct in holding that, judged by these standards, the record in this case falls far short of sustaining the State's burden. It is true that Williams had been informed of and appeared to understand his right to counsel. But waiver requires not merely comprehension but relinquishment, and Williams' consistent reliance upon the advice of counsel in dealing with the authorities refutes any suggestion that he waived that right. * * * His statements while in the car that he would tell the whole story *after* seeing McKnight in Des Moines were the clearest expressions by Williams himself that he desired the presence of an attorney before any interrogation took place. But even before making these statements, Williams had effectively asserted his right to counsel by having secured attorneys at both ends of the automobile trip, both of whom, acting as his agents, had made clear to the police that no interrogation was to occur during the journey. Williams knew of that agreement and, particularly in view of his consistent reliance on counsel, there is no basis for concluding that he disavowed it.

Despite Williams' express and implicit assertions of his right to counsel, Detective Leaming proceeded to elicit incriminating statements from Williams. Leaming did not preface this effort by telling Williams that he had a right to the presence of a lawyer, and made no effort at all to ascertain whether Williams wished to relinquish that right. The circumstances of record in this case thus provide no reasonable basis for finding that Williams waived his right to the assistance of counsel.

The Court of Appeals did not hold, nor do we, that under the circumstances of this case Williams *could not,* without notice to counsel, have waived his rights under the Sixth and Fourteenth Amendments. It only held, as do we, that he did not.

* * * Although we do not lightly affirm the issuance of a writ of habeas corpus in this case, so clear a violation of the Sixth and Fourteenth Amendments as here occurred cannot be condoned. * * * The judgment of the Court of Appeals is affirmed.[12]

12. The District Court stated that its decision "does not touch upon the issue of what evidence, if any, beyond the incriminating statements themselves must be excluded as 'fruit of the poisonous tree.'" We too have no occasion to address this issue, and in the present posture of the case there is no basis for the view of our dissenting Brethren [that] any attempt to retry the respondent would probably be futile. While neither Williams' incriminating statements themselves nor any testimony describing his having led the police to the victim's body can constitutionally be admitted into evidence, evidence of where the body was found and of its condition might well be admissible on the theory that the body would have been discovered in any event, even had incriminating statements not been elicited from Williams. In the event that a retrial is instituted, it will be for the state courts in the first instance to determine whether particular items of evidence may be admitted.

[On retrial, the state court admitted evidence of the condition of the body of Pamela Powers and the results of post mortem tests on the body because the body "would have been found in any event"—if Williams had not led the police to the victim the search would have been taken up again where it left off and the body would have been discovered within a short time in essentially the same condition as it was actually found. Williams was again convicted of murder. The case came to the U.S. Supreme Court a second time, *Nix v. Williams (Williams II),* 467 U.S. 431 (1984). The Court, per Burger, C.J., upheld the state court's use of the "inevitable discovery" exception, observing:

["Exclusion of physical evidence that would inevitably have been discovered adds nothing to either the integrity or fairness of a criminal trial. * * * [I]f the government can prove that the evidence would have been obtained inevitably and, therefore, would have been admitted

JUSTICE MARSHALL, concurring.

I concur wholeheartedly in my Brother Stewart's opinion for the Court, but add these words in light of the dissenting opinions filed today. The dissenters have, I believe, lost sight of the fundamental constitutional backbone of our criminal law. They seem to think that Detective Leaming's actions were perfectly proper, indeed laudable, examples of "good police work." In my view, good police work is something far different from catching the criminal at any price. It is equally important that the police, as guardians of the law, fulfill their responsibility to obey its commands scrupulously.

[In] this case, there can be no doubt that Detective Leaming consciously and knowingly set out to violate Williams' Sixth Amendment right to counsel and his Fifth Amendment privilege against self-incrimination, as Leaming himself understood those rights. * * * Leaming surely understood, because he had overheard McKnight tell Williams as much, that the location of the body would be revealed to police. Undoubtedly Leaming realized the way in which that information would be conveyed to the police: McKnight would learn it from his client and then he would lead police to the body. Williams would thereby be protected by the attorney-client privilege from incriminating himself by directly demonstrating his knowledge of the body's location, and the unfortunate Powers child could be given a "Christian burial."

Of course, this scenario would accomplish all that Leaming sought from his investigation except that it would not produce incriminating statements or actions from Williams. Accordingly, Leaming undertook his charade to pry such evidence from Williams. After invoking the no-passengers rule to prevent attorney Kelly from accompanying the prisoner, Leaming had Williams at his mercy: during the three- or four-hour trip he could do anything he wished to elicit a confession.

* * * If Williams is to go free—and given the ingenuity of Iowa prosecutors on retrial or in a civil commitment proceeding, I doubt very much that there is any chance a dangerous criminal will be loosed on the streets, the blood-curdling cries of the dissents notwithstanding—it will hardly be because he deserves it. It will be because Detective Leaming, knowing full well that he risked reversal of Williams' conviction, intentionally denied Williams the right of *every* American under the Sixth Amendment to have the protective shield of a lawyer between himself and the awesome power of the State.

     * * *

JUSTICE POWELL, concurring. * * *

The critical factual issue is whether there had been a voluntary waiver, and this turns in large part upon whether there was interrogation. * * *

Prior to the automobile trip from Davenport to Des Moines, Williams had been arrested, booked, and carefully given *Miranda* warnings. It is settled constitutional doctrine that he then had the right to the assistance of counsel. His exercise of this right was evidenced uniquely in this case. * * * Significantly, the recognition by the police of the status of counsel was evidenced by the *express agreement* between McKnight and the appropriate police officials that the officers

regardless of any over-reaching by the police, there is no rational basis to keep that evidence from the jury in order to ensure the fairness of the trial proceedings. In that situation, the State has gained no advantage at trial and the defendant has suffered no prejudice. Indeed, suppression of the evidence would operate to undermine the adversary system by putting the State in a *worse* position than it would have occupied without any police misconduct."]

who would drive Williams to Des Moines would not interrogate him in the absence of counsel.

The incriminating statements were made by Williams during the long ride while in the custody of two police officers, and in the absence of his retained counsel. The dissent of the Chief Justice concludes that prior to these statements, Williams had "made a valid waiver" of his right to have counsel present. This view disregards the record evidence clearly indicating that the police engaged in interrogation of Williams.

[The] dissenting opinion of the Chief Justice states that the Court's holding today "conclusively presumes a suspect is legally incompetent to change his mind and tell the truth until an attorney is present." I find no justification for this view. On the contrary, the opinion of the Court is explicitly clear that the right to assistance of counsel may be waived, after it has attached, without notice to or consultation with counsel. We would have such a case here if [the State] had proved that the police officers refrained from coercion and interrogation, as they had agreed, and that Williams freely on his own initiative had confessed the crime. * * *a

CHIEF JUSTICE BURGER, dissenting.

The result in this case ought to be intolerable in any society which purports to call itself an organized society. It continues the Court—by the narrowest margin—on the much-criticized course of punishing the public for the mistakes and misdeeds of law enforcement officers, instead of punishing the officer directly, if in fact he is guilty of wrongdoing. It mechanically and blindly keeps reliable evidence from juries whether the claimed constitutional violation involves gross police misconduct or honest human error.

Williams is guilty of the savage murder of a small child; no member of the Court contends he is not. While in custody, and after no fewer than _five_ warnings of his rights to silence and to counsel, he led police to the concealed body of his victim. The Court concedes Williams was not threatened or coerced and that he spoke and acted voluntarily and with full awareness of his constitutional rights. In the face of all this, the Court now holds that because Williams was prompted by the detective's statement—not interrogation but a statement—the jury must not be told how the police found the body. * * *

Under well-settled precedents which the Court freely acknowledges, it is very clear that Williams had made a valid waiver of his Fifth Amendment right to silence and his Sixth Amendment right to counsel when he led police to the child's body. Indeed, even under the Court's analysis I do not understand how a contrary conclusion is possible. * * *

The evidence is uncontradicted that Williams had abundant knowledge of his right to have counsel present and of his right to silence. Since the Court does not question his mental competence, it boggles the mind to suggest that Williams could not understand that leading police to the child's body would have other than the most serious consequences. * * *

One plausible but unarticulated basis for the result reached is that once a suspect has asserted his right not to talk without the presence of an attorney, it becomes legally impossible for him to waive that right until he has seen an attorney. But constitutional rights are _personal,_ and an otherwise valid waiver

---

a. Stevens, J., joined the opinion of the Court, but also added a brief comment concluding: "If, in the long run, we are seriously concerned about the individual's effective representation by counsel, the State cannot be permitted to dishonor its promise to this lawyer."

should not be brushed aside by judges simply because an attorney was not present. * * *[2]

* * * Mr. Justice Powell suggests that the result in this case turns on whether Detective Leaming's remarks constituted "interrogation," as he views them, or whether they were "statements" intended to prick the conscience of the accused. I find it most remarkable that a murder case should turn on judicial interpretation that a statement becomes a question simply because it is followed by an incriminating disclosure from the suspect. The Court seems to be saying that since Williams said he would "tell the whole story" at Des Moines, the police should have been content and waited; of course, that would have been the wiser course, especially in light of the nuances of constitutional jurisprudence applied by the Court, but a murder case ought not turn on such tenuous strands.

In any case, the Court assures us, this is not at all what it intends, and that a valid waiver was *possible* in these circumstances, but was not quite made. Here of course Williams did not confess to the murder in so many words; it was his conduct in guiding police to the body, not his words, which incriminated him. And the record is replete with evidence that Williams knew precisely what he was doing when he guided police to the body. The human urge to confess wrongdoing is, of course, normal in all save hardened, professional criminals, as psychiatrists and analysts have demonstrated.

Even if there was no waiver, and assuming a technical violation occurred, the Court errs gravely in mechanically applying the exclusionary rule without considering whether that draconian judicial doctrine should be invoked in these circumstances, or indeed whether any of its conceivable goals will be furthered by its application here.

* * * Today's holding interrupts what has been a more rational perception of the constitutional and social utility of excluding reliable evidence from the truthseeking process. In its Fourth Amendment context, we have now recognized that the exclusionary rule is in no sense a *personal* constitutional right, but a judicially conceived remedial device designed to safeguard and effectuate guaranteed legal rights generally [referring to *Stone v. Powell,* 428 U.S. 465 (1976), holding the exclusionary rule inapplicable to habeas review, *United States v. Janis,* 428 U.S. 433 (1976), holding the exclusionary rule inapplicable in a civil tax proceeding, *United States v. Calandra,* holding the exclusionary rule inapplicable in a grand jury proceeding]. We have repeatedly emphasized that deterrence of unconstitutional or otherwise unlawful police conduct is the only valid justification for excluding reliable and probative evidence from the criminal factfinding process.

Accordingly, unlawfully obtained evidence is not automatically excluded from the factfinding process in all circumstances. In a variety of contexts we inquire whether application of the rule will promote its objectives sufficiently to justify the enormous cost it imposes on society. * * *

Against this background, it is striking that the Court fails even to consider whether the benefits secured by application of the exclusionary rule in this case outweigh its obvious social costs. Perhaps the failure is due to the fact that this case arises not under the Fourth Amendment, but under *Miranda,* and the Sixth Amendment right to counsel. The Court apparently perceives the function of the exclusionary rule to be so different in these varying contexts that it must be

---

2. [A] paternalistic rule is particularly anomalous in the Sixth Amendment context, where this Court has only recently discovered an independent constitutional right of self-representation, allowing an accused the absolute right to proceed without a lawyer at trial, once he is aware of the consequences. *Faretta* [Ch. 17 infra].

mechanically and uncritically applied in all cases arising outside the Fourth Amendment. * * *

JUSTICE WHITE, with whom JUSTICE BLACKMUN and JUSTICE REHNQUIST join, dissenting.

* * * The issue in this case is whether respondent—who was entitled not to make any statements to the police without consultation with and/or presence of counsel[1]—validly waived those rights. * * *

[I disagree with the majority's finding that no waiver was proved in this case.] That respondent knew of his right not to say anything to the officers without advice and presence of counsel is established on this record to a moral certainty. He was advised of the right by three officials of the State—telling at least one that he understood the right—and by two lawyers.[4] Finally, he further demonstrated his knowledge of the right by informing the police that he would tell them the story in the presence of McKnight when they arrived in Des Moines. The issue in this case, then, is whether respondent relinquished that right intentionally.

Respondent relinquished his right not to talk to the police about his crime when the car approached the place where he had hidden the victim's clothes. Men usually intend to do what they do and there is nothing in the record to support the proposition that respondent's decision to talk was anything but an exercise of his own free will. Apparently, without any prodding from the officers, respondent—who had earlier said that he would tell the whole story when he arrived in Des Moines—spontaneously changed his mind about the timing of his disclosures when the car approached the places where he had hidden the evidence. However, even if his statements were influenced by Detective Leaming's above-quoted statement, respondent's decision to talk in the absence of counsel can hardly be viewed as the product of an overborn will. The statement by Leaming was not coercive; it was accompanied by a request that respondent not respond to it; and it was delivered hours before respondent decided to make any statement. Respondent's waiver was thus knowing and intentional.

The majority's contrary conclusion seems to rest on the fact that respondent "asserted" his right to counsel by retaining and consulting with one lawyer and by consulting with another. How this supports the conclusion that respondent's later relinquishment of his right not to talk in the absence of counsel was unintentional is a mystery. The fact that respondent consulted with counsel on the question whether he should talk to the police in counsel's absence makes his later decision to talk in counsel's absence *better* informed and, if anything, more intelligent.

The majority recognizes that even after this "assertion" of his right to counsel, it would have found that respondent waived his right not to talk in counsel's absence if his waiver had been express—i.e., if the officers had asked him in the car whether he would be willing to answer questions in counsel's absence and if he had answered "yes." But waiver is not a formalistic concept. Waiver is shown whenever the facts establish that an accused knew of a right and intended to relinquish it. Such waiver, even if not express, was plainly shown here. The only other conceivable basis for the majority's holding is the implicit

1. It does not matter whether the right not to make statements in the absence of counsel stems from *Massiah* or *Miranda*. In either case the question is one of waiver. Waiver was not addressed in *Massiah* because there the statements were being made to an informant and the defendant had no way of knowing that he had a right not to talk to him without counsel.

4. Moreover, he in fact received advice of counsel on at least two occasions on the question whether he should talk to the police on the trip to Des Moines.

suggestion that the right involved in *Massiah,* as distinguished from the right involved in *Miranda,* is a right not to be *asked* any questions in counsel's absence rather than a right not to *answer* any questions in counsel's absence, and that the right not to be *asked* questions must be waived *before* the questions are asked. Such wafer thin distinctions cannot determine whether a guilty murderer should go free. The only conceivable purpose for the presence of counsel during questioning is to protect an accused from making incriminating *answers.* Questions, unanswered, have no significance at all. Absent coercion—no matter how the right involved is defined—an accused is amply protected by a rule requiring waiver before or simultaneously with the giving by him of an answer or the making by him of a statement.

* * *

MR. JUSTICE BLACKMUN, with whom MR. JUSTICE WHITE and MR. JUSTICE REHNQUIST join, dissenting. * * *

What the Court chooses to do here, and with which I disagree, is to hold that respondent Williams' situation was in the mold of *Massiah,* that is, that it was dominated by a denial to Williams of his Sixth Amendment right to counsel after criminal proceedings had been instituted against him. The Court rules that the Sixth Amendment was violated because Detective Leaming "purposely sought during Williams' isolation from his lawyers to obtain as much incriminating information as possible." I cannot regard that as unconstitutional *per se.*

First, the police did not deliberately seek to isolate Williams from his lawyers so as to deprive him of the assistance of counsel. Cf. *Escobedo.* The isolation in this case was a necessary incident of transporting Williams to the county where the crime was committed.

Second, Leaming's purpose was not solely to obtain incriminating evidence. The victim had been missing for only two days, and the police could not be certain that she was dead. Leaming, of course, and in accord with his duty, was "hoping to find out where that little girl was," but such motivation does not equate with an intention to evade the Sixth Amendment. * * *

Third, not every attempt to elicit information should be regarded as "tantamount to interrogation." I am not persuaded that Leaming's observations and comments, made as the police car traversed the snowy and slippery miles between Davenport and Des Moines that winter afternoon, were an interrogation, direct or subtle, of Williams. Williams, after all, was counseled by lawyers, and warned by the arraigning judge in Davenport and by the police, and yet it was he who started the travel conversations and brought up the subject of the criminal investigation.

[In] summary, it seems to me that the Court is holding that *Massiah* is violated whenever police engage in any conduct, in the absence of counsel, with the subjective desire to obtain information from a suspect after arraignment. Such a rule is far too broad. Persons in custody frequently volunteer statements in response to stimuli other than interrogation. * * *

KUHLMANN v. WILSON
477 U.S. 436, 106 S.Ct. 2616, 91 L.Ed.2d 364 (1986).

JUSTICE POWELL delivered the opinion of the Court.

[Respondent Wilson and two confederates robbed a garage and fatally shot the night dispatcher. Four days later, respondent turned himself in. He admitted that he had witnessed the robbery and murder, but denied any involvement in them, claiming that he had fled because he was afraid of being blamed for the crimes. He gave the police a description of the robbers, but denied knowing them.

[After his arraignment, Wilson was placed in a cell with a prisoner named Benny Lee. Unknown to Wilson, Lee had agreed to act as a police informant. Since the police had positive evidence of Wilson's involvement, the purpose of placing Lee in the cell was to determine the identities of the other perpetrators. According to his arrangement with Detective Cullen, Lee was not to ask Wilson any questions, but simply to "keep his ears open" for the names of Wilson's confederates. Wilson first spoke to Lee about the crimes after looking out the cellblock window at the garage, where the crime had occurred. He told Lee the same story he had given the police. Lee advised Wilson that his story "didn't sound too good" and that "things didn't look too good for him," but Wilson did not alter his story at that time. However, several days later, after a visit from his brother, who mentioned that members of the family were upset because they believed he had killed the dispatcher, Wilson changed his story. He admitted to Lee that he and two other men had planned and carried out the robbery and killed the dispatcher. Lee reported these incriminating statements to Detective Cullen.

[The trial court denied Wilson's motion to suppress the incriminating statements, finding that Lee had obeyed police instructions only to listen to Wilson for the purpose of identifying his confederates, but not to question him about the crime. The trial court also found that Wilson's statements were "spontaneous" and "unsolicited." After he was convicted of murder and the conviction was affirmed, Wilson sought federal habeas corpus relief. After considering *Massiah*, the district court denied relief, finding "no interrogation whatsoever" by Lee and "only spontaneous statements" from Wilson. A divided U.S. Court of Appeals affirmed.

[Following the decision in *Henry*, Wilson decided to relitigate his Sixth Amendment claim. After his motion to vacate his conviction was denied, Wilson again sought federal habeas corpus relief. The district court concluded that the trial court's findings were "fatal" to Wilson's claim under *Henry* since they showed that the informant made "no affirmative effort" of any kind to elicit information from him. A divided Court of Appeals reversed, finding the circumstances indistinguishable from the facts of *Henry*.]

      *   *   *

In *United States v. Henry,* the Court applied the *Massiah* test to incriminating statements made to a jailhouse informant. The Court of Appeals in that case found a violation of *Massiah* because the informant had engaged the defendant in conversations and "had developed a relationship of trust and confidence with [the defendant] such that [the defendant] revealed incriminating information." This Court affirmed, holding that the Court of Appeals reasonably concluded that the government informant "deliberately used his position to secure incriminating information from [the defendant] when counsel was not present." Although the informant had not questioned the defendant, the informant had "stimulated" conversations with the defendant in order to "elicit" incriminating information. The Court emphasized that those facts, like the facts of *Massiah*, amounted to " 'indirect and surreptitious interrogatio[n]' " of the defendant. * * *

[As] *Maine v. Moulton,* 474 U.S. 159 (1985),[a] makes clear, the primary concern of the *Massiah* line of decisions is secret interrogation by investigatory

---

a. *Moulton* holds that the *Massiah* doctrine applies to a crime for which the defendant has already been indicted even though the government had other, legitimate reasons for intercepting defendant's conversations—to insure the safety of its secret agent and to gather information concerning a report that defendant was planning to kill a witness. The Court, per Brennan, J., agreed that it was "entirely proper" for the government to conduct an investigation of defendant's activities, even though he had already been indicted, and techniques that are the equivalent of direct police interrogation. Since "the Sixth Amendment is not violated whenever—by luck or happenstance—the State obtains incriminating statements from the accused after the right to counsel has attached," a defendant does not make out a violation of that right simply by showing that an informant, either through prior arrangement or voluntarily, reported his incriminating statements to the police. Rather, the defendant must demonstrate that the police and their informant took some action, beyond merely listening, that was designed deliberately to elicit incriminating remarks.

It is thus apparent that the Court of Appeals erred in concluding that respondent's right to counsel was violated under the circumstances of this case. [It failed] to accord to the state trial court's factual findings the presumption of correctness expressly required by 28 U.S.C. § 2254(d).

The state court found that Officer Cullen had instructed Lee only to listen to respondent for the purpose of determining the identities of the other participants in the robbery and murder. The police already had solid evidence of respondent's participation. The court further found that Lee followed those instructions, that he "at no time asked any questions" of respondent concerning the pending charges, and that he "only listened" to respondent's "spontaneous" and "unsolicited" statements. The only remark made by Lee that has any support in this record was his comment that respondent's initial version of his participation in the crimes "didn't sound too good." Without holding that any of the state court's findings were not entitled to the presumption of correctness under § 2254(d), the Court of Appeals focused on that one remark and gave a description of Lee's interaction with respondent that is completely at odds with the facts found by the trial court. In the Court of Appeals' view, "Subtly and slowly, but surely, Lee's ongoing verbal intercourse with [respondent] served to exacerbate [respondent's] already troubled state of mind." [24] After thus revising some of the trial court's findings, and ignoring other more relevant findings, the Court of Appeals concluded that the police "deliberately elicited" respondent's incriminating statements. This conclusion conflicts with the decision of every other state and federal judge who reviewed this record, and is clear error in light of the provisions and intent of § 2254(d).[b]

JUSTICE BRENNAN, with whom JUSTICE MARSHALL joins, dissenting.   * * *

[The] Court concludes [that] the Court of Appeals failed to recognize that this case presents the question, reserved in *Henry,* whether the Sixth Amendment forbids the admission into evidence of an accused's statements to a jailhouse informant who was "placed in close proximity but [made] no effort to stimulate conversations about the crime charged." I disagree with the Court's characterization of the Court of Appeals' treatment of the state court's findings and, conse-

---

statements obtained from him would be admissible at a subsequent trial for crimes *apart* from those for which defendant had already been indicted. But statement pertaining to *pending charges* had to be excluded at the trial of those charges despite the fact the government was also investigating other crimes. For to allow incriminating statements pertaining to pending charges to be used "whenever the police assert an alternative, legitimate reason for their surveillance invites abuse by law enforcement personnel in the form of fabricated investigations and risks the evisceration of the Sixth Amendment right recognized in *Massiah.*"

24. Curiously, the Court of Appeals expressed concern that respondent was placed in a cell that overlooked the scene of his crimes. For all the record shows, however, that fact was sheer coincidence. Nor do we perceive any reason to require police to isolate one charged with crime so that he cannot view the scene, whatever it may be, from his cell window.

b. Chief Justice Burger, the author of *Henry,* joined the opinion of the Court, but also wrote a brief concurring opinion noting "a vast difference between placing an 'ear' in the suspect's cell and placing a voice in the cell to encourage conversation for the 'ear' to record."

quently, I disagree with the Court that the instant case presents the "listening post" question.

The state trial court simply found that Lee did not ask respondent any direct questions about the crime for which respondent was incarcerated. The trial court considered the significance of this fact only under State precedents, which the court interpreted to require affirmative "interrogation" by the informant as a prerequisite to a constitutional violation. The court did not indicate whether it referred to a Fifth Amendment or to a Sixth Amendment violation in identifying "interrogation" as a precondition to a violation. * * *

The Court of Appeals did not disregard the state court's finding that Lee asked respondent no direct questions regarding the crime. Rather, the Court of Appeals *expressly accepted* that finding, but concluded that, as a matter of law, the deliberate elicitation standard of *Henry* and *Massiah*, encompasses other, more subtle forms of stimulating incriminating admissions than overt questioning. The court suggested that the police deliberately placed respondent in a cell that overlooked the scene of the crime, hoping that the view would trigger an inculpatory comment to respondent's cellmate.[8] The court also observed that, while Lee asked respondent no questions, Lee nonetheless stimulated conversation concerning respondents' role in [the] robbery and murder by remarking that respondent's exculpatory story did not " 'sound too good' " and that he had better come up with a better one. Thus, the Court of Appeals concluded that the respondent's case did not present the situation reserved in *Henry*, [but was] virtually indistinguishable from *Henry*. * * *

In *Henry*, [we] rejected the Government's argument that because Henry initiated the discussion of his crime, no Sixth Amendment violation had occurred. We pointed out that under *Massiah*, it is irrelevant whether the informant asks pointed questions about the crime or "merely engage[s] in general conversation about it." * * *

In the instant case, as in *Henry*, the accused was incarcerated and therefore was "susceptible to the ploys of undercover Government agents." Like Nichols, Lee was a secret informant, usually received consideration for the services he rendered the police, and therefore had an incentive to produce the information which he knew the police hoped to obtain. Just as Nichols had done, Lee obeyed instructions not to question respondent and to report to the police any statements made by the respondent in Lee's presence about the crime in question. And, like Nichols, Lee encouraged respondent to talk about his crime by conversing with him on the subject over the course of several days and by telling respondent that his exculpatory story would not convince anyone without more work. However, unlike the situation in *Henry*, a disturbing visit from respondent's brother, rather than a conversation with the informant, seems to have been the immediate catalyst for respondent's confession to Lee. While it might appear from this sequence of events that Lee's comment regarding respondent's story and his general willingness to converse with respondent about the crime were not the *immediate* causes of respondent's admission, I think that the deliberate elicitation standard requires consideration of the entire course of government behavior.

The State intentionally created a situation in which it was foreseeable that respondent would make incriminating statements without the assistance of counsel, *Henry*, it assigned respondent to a cell overlooking the scene of the crime and designated a secret informant to be respondent's cellmate. The informant, while avoiding direct questions, nonetheless developed a relationship of cellmate cama-

---

8. The Court of Appeals noted that "[a]s soon as Wilson arrived and viewed the garage, he became upset and stated that 'someone's messing with me.' "

raderie with respondent and encouraged him to talk about his crime. While the *coup de grace* was delivered by respondent's brother, the groundwork for respondent's confession was laid by the State. Clearly the State's actions had a sufficient nexus with respondent's admission of guilt to constitute deliberate elicitation within the meaning of *Henry*.[c]

c. Stevens, J., filed a separate dissent, agreeing with Justice Brennan's analysis of the   merits of respondent's habeas petition.

Chapter 7

LINEUPS, SHOWUPS AND OTHER PRE–TRIAL IDENTIFICATION PROCEDURES

Although mistaken identification has probably been the single greatest cause of conviction of the innocent, the Supreme Court did not come to grips with this problem until surprisingly late in the day. When it finally did, in 1967, the Court seemed bent on making up for lost time. Although it might have undertaken a case-by-case analysis of various identification situations, as had been done in the confession area in the thirty years prior to *Escobedo* and *Miranda,* only throwing out convictions based on unreliable identifications, the Court leapfrogged the fairness stage and applied the right to counsel to pretrial identifications in one swoop.

As explained in *United States v. Wade,* the first case set forth in this chapter, the right to counsel in the lineup context is supportive of another right—in this instance, the right to confrontation—in much the same manner that the *Miranda* counsel requirement rests upon the privilege against self-incrimination. (But see *Kirby v. Illinois,* the second case in this chapter.) For various reasons spelled out in the *Wade* opinion, under past lineup practices the defense was often unable "meaningfully to attack the credibility of the witness' courtroom identification." Moreover, pointed out the Court, the need to learn what occurred at the lineup is great, the risk of improper suggestion is substantial, and once the witness has picked out the accused in a pretrial identification proceeding, she is unlikely to go back on her word in court.[a]

Absent circumstances that presented "substantial countervailing policy considerations * * * against the requirement of the presence of counsel" (the Court may have had in mind "alley confrontations," i.e., prompt confrontations with the

---

a. *Wade* and *Gilbert* also raised a self-incrimination issue. Relying on *Schmerber v. California,* 384 U.S. 757 (1966), a 5–4 majority ruled that requiring a person to appear in a lineup and to speak for identification (*Wade*) or to provide handwriting exemplars (*Gilbert*) did not violate the privilege. In *Schmerber,* which involved the taking of a blood sample, over his objection, from a person arrested for drunken driving, the Court rejected the contention that the defendant had been "compelled [to] be a witness against himself" in violation of the Fifth Amendment. The self-incrimination clause, observed the Court, "protects an accused only from * * * provid[ing] the State with evidence of a testimonial or communicative nature." See also *Pennsylvania v. Muniz,* 496 U.S. 582 (1990) (evidence of slurred speech and lack of muscular coordination exhibited by drunk-driving arrestee during administration of sobriety tests amounts to non-testimonial information that falls outside scope of self-incrimination clause).

victim or an eyewitness at the scene of the crime),[b] the 1967 cases seemed to require the presence of counsel at *all* pretrial identifications. The pretrial identifications in *Wade* and *Gilbert* did take place after the defendants had been indicted, and the Court did mention this fact. But such references seemed—and most lower courts considered them to be—merely descriptive of the facts before the Court in those cases, not meant to restrict the operation of the new rule. For nothing in the *Wade* Court's reasoning suggested that a lineup or showup held before formal judicial proceedings begin—which is usually the case—is less riddled with dangers or less difficult for a suspect to reconstruct then one occurring after that point.

Nevertheless, in *Kirby v. Illinois* (1972), the second case in this chapter, the Court did announce a "post-indictment" rule—over the dissent of Justice Brennan, author of the *Wade* and *Gilbert* opinions. Following *Kirby* it became the common practice of law enforcement agencies to avoid the applicability of the right to counsel by conducting identification proceedings before the filing of formal charges.

A year after *Kirby,* the Burger Court struck the *Wade–Gilbert* rule another blow. This time, however, the Court's ruling confirmed the great weight of lower court authority. Unmoved by the argument that the availability of the photographs at trial provides no protection against the suggestive manner in which they may have been originally displayed to the witness or the comments or gestures that may have accompanied the display, the Court ruled in *United States v. Ash* (1973) (discussed infra, in a footnote to *Kirby*) that photographic identification may take place without defense counsel's participation, whether conducted before or after the filing of formal charges, and even though the suspect could have appeared in person at a lineup. Throughout the expansion of the constitutional right to counsel to certain pretrial proceedings, observed the Court, "the function of the lawyer has remained essentially the same as his function at trial"—to assist the accused "in meeting his adversary." But at a photo-identification, unlike a lineup, there is no "trial-like confrontation" involving the "presence of the accused." Again the author of *Wade* and *Gilbert,* Justice Brennan, was among those who dissented.[c]

Although *Kirby* and *Ash* severely restricted the potential reach of the original lineup decisions, abuses in photographic displays and in preindictment lineups are not, in theory at least, thereby placed beyond the reach of the Constitution: a defendant may still convince a court that the circumstances surrounding his identification present so "substantial" a "likelihood of misidentification" as to violate due process. But as illustrated by the last case in the chapter, *Manson v. Brathwaite*, this is a difficult task. An "unnecessarily suggestive" identification is

---

b. Even prior to *Kirby v. Illinois,* which limited the 1967 cases to post-indictment identifications, the great majority of lower courts had exempted alley confrontations from the right to counsel requirement.

c. The Warren Court had carved out an exception to the *Wade–Gilbert* rule for pretrial photographic identifications, but apparently a narrow one. In concluding that there was no right to have counsel present at the photo-identification in *Simmons v. United States,* 390 U.S. 377 (1968) and, alternatively, that the procedures utilized in that case were not "impermissively suggestive," the Court stressed, first, that at the time the witnesses viewed the photographs for identification purposes "the

perpetrators were still at large" and "it was essential for the FBI agents swiftly to determine whether they were on the right track"; and second, that the witnesses were shown the photographs "only a day [after the bank robbery] while their memories were still fresh."

In *Ash,* although the defendant had been indicted, had been appointed counsel, and had been in detention for more than two years prior to trial, a photo-identification was conducted in the absence of counsel a day before the trial began. It was a photo display that seemed designed more to prompt the witness than to secure an identification.

not enough—the "totality of the circumstances" may still allow identification evidence if, despite the unnecessary "suggestiveness," the out-of-court identification "possesses certain features of reliability."

SECTION 1. *WADE* AND *GILBERT*: CONSTITUTIONAL CONCERN ABOUT THE DANGERS INVOLVED IN EYEWITNESS IDENTIFICATIONS

UNITED STATES v. WADE

388 U.S. 218, 87 S.Ct. 1926, 18 L.Ed.2d 1149 (1967).

JUSTICE BRENNAN delivered the opinion of the Court.

The question here is whether courtroom identifications of an accused at trial are to be excluded from evidence because the accused was exhibited to the witnesses before trial at a post-indictment lineup conducted for identification purposes without notice to and in the absence of the accused's appointed counsel.

The federally insured bank in Eustace, Texas, was robbed on September 21, 1964. A man with a small strip of tape on each side of his face entered the bank, pointed a pistol at the female cashier and the vice president, the only persons in the bank at the time, and forced them to fill a pillowcase with the bank's money. The man then drove away with an accomplice who had been waiting in a stolen car outside the bank. On March 23, 1965, an indictment was returned against respondent, Wade, and two others for conspiring to rob the bank, and against Wade and the accomplice for the robbery itself. Wade was arrested on April 2, and counsel was appointed to represent him on April 26. Fifteen days later [after counsel was appointed] an FBI agent, without notice to Wade's lawyer, arranged to have the two bank employees observe a lineup made up of Wade and five or six other prisoners and conducted in a courtroom of the local county courthouse. Each person in the line wore strips of tape such as allegedly worn by the robber and upon direction each said something like "put the money in the bag," the words allegedly uttered by the robber. Both bank employees identified Wade in the lineup as the bank robber.

At trial the two employees, when asked on direct examination if the robber was in the courtroom, pointed to Wade. The prior lineup identification was then elicited from both employees on cross-examination. At the close of testimony, Wade's counsel moved [to] strike the bank officials' courtroom identifications on [self-incrimination and right to counsel grounds]. The motion was denied, and Wade was convicted. The Court of Appeals for the Fifth Circuit reversed the conviction and ordered a new trial at which the in-court identification evidence was to be excluded, holding that [conducting the lineup in the absence of Wade's appointed counsel violated his Sixth Amendment rights]. * * *

[T]he principle of *Powell v. Alabama* and succeeding cases requires that we scrutinize *any* pretrial confrontation of the accused to determine whether the presence of his counsel is necessary to preserve the defendant's basic right to a fair trial as affected by his right meaningfully to cross-examine the witnesses against him and to have effective assistance of counsel at the trial itself. It calls upon us to analyze whether potential substantial prejudice to defendant's rights inheres in the particular confrontation and the ability of counsel to help avoid that prejudice.

cross exam
sufficient

The Government characterizes the lineup as a mere preparatory step in the gathering of the prosecution's evidence, not different—for Sixth Amendment purposes—from various other preparatory steps, such as systematized or scientific analyzing of the accused's fingerprints, blood sample, clothing, hair, and the like. We think there are differences which preclude such stages being characterized as critical stages at which the accused has the right to the presence of his counsel. Knowledge of the techniques of science and technology is sufficiently available, and the variables in techniques few enough, that the accused has the opportunity for a meaningful confrontation of the Government's case at trial through the ordinary processes of cross-examination of the Government's expert witnesses and the presentation of the evidence of his own experts. The denial of a right to have his counsel present at such analyses does not therefore violate the Sixth Amendment; they are not critical stages since there is minimal risk that his counsel's absence at such stages might derogate from his right to a fair trial.[a]

But the confrontation compelled by the State between the accused and the victim or witnesses to a crime to elicit identification evidence is peculiarly riddled with innumerable dangers and variable factors which might seriously, even crucially, derogate from a fair trial. The vagaries of eyewitness identification are well-known; the annals of criminal law are rife with instances of mistaken identification. * * * A major factor contributing to the high incidence of miscarriage of justice from mistaken identification has been the degree of suggestion inherent in the manner in which the prosecution presents the suspect to witnesses for pretrial identification. A commentator has observed that "[t]he influence of improper suggestion upon identifying witnesses probably accounts for more miscarriages of justice than any other single factor—perhaps it is responsible for more such errors than all other factors combined." Wall, *Eye–Witness Identification in Criminal Cases* 26 [1965]. Suggestion can be created intentionally or unintentionally in many subtle ways. And the dangers for the suspect are particularly grave when the witness' opportunity for observation was insubstantial, and thus his susceptibility to suggestion the greatest.

Moreover, "[i]t is a matter of common experience that, once a witness has picked out the accused at the line-up, he is not likely to go back on his word later on, so that in practice the issue of identity may (in the absence of other relevant evidence) for all practical purposes be determined there and then, before the trial."

The pretrial confrontation for purpose of identification may take the form of a lineup, also known as an "identification parade" or "showup," as in the present case, or presentation of the suspect alone to the witness, as in *Stovall v. Denno*.[b] It is obvious that risks of suggestion attend either form of confrontation and increase the dangers inhering in eyewitness identification. But as is the case with secret interrogations, there is serious difficulty in depicting what transpires at lineups and other forms of identification confrontations. [For] the same reasons,

---

a. Consider, too, the companion case of *Gilbert v. California,* where the Court held, 5–4 on this issue, that the taking of handwriting exemplars from petitioner "was not a 'critical' stage of the criminal proceedings entitling petitioner to the assistance of counsel" for "there is minimal risk that the absence of counsel might derogate from his right to a fair trial. [If,] for some reason, an unrepresentative exemplar is taken, this can be brought out and corrected through the adversary process at trial since the accused can make an unlimited number of additional exemplars for analysis and comparison by government and defense handwriting experts."

b. In *Stovall,* discussed in § 3 infra, the Court noted the practice of showing suspects singly to potential witnesses "has been widely condemned," but held that under the extraordinary circumstances of the case ("an immediate hospital confrontation was imperative" because it appeared that the sole eye witness was near death) the one-person showing was justified.

the defense can seldom reconstruct the manner and mode of lineup identification for judge or jury at trial. [The] impediments to an objective observation are increased when the victim is the witness. Lineups are prevalent in rape and robbery prosecutions and present a particular hazard that a victim's understandable outrage may excite vengeful or spiteful motives. In any event, neither witnesses nor lineup participants are apt to be alert for conditions prejudicial to the suspect. And if they were, it would likely be of scant benefit to the suspect since neither witnesses nor lineup participants are likely to be schooled in the detection of suggestive influences.[13] Improper influences may go undetected by a suspect, guilty or not, who experiences the emotional tension which we might expect in one being confronted with potential accusers. Even when he does observe abuse, if he has a criminal record he may be reluctant to take the stand and open up the admission of prior convictions. Moreover any protestations by the suspect of the fairness of the lineup made at trial are likely to be in vain; the jury's choice is between the accused's unsupported version and that of the police officers present. In short, the accused's inability effectively to reconstruct at trial any unfairness that occurred at the lineup may deprive him of his only opportunity meaningfully to attack the credibility of the witness' courtroom identification. * * *

The potential for improper influence is illustrated by the circumstances, insofar as they appear, surrounding the prior identifications in the three cases we decide today. In the present case, the testimony of the identifying witnesses elicited on cross-examination revealed that those witnesses were taken to the courthouse and seated in the courtroom to await assembly of the lineup. The courtroom faced on a hallway observable to the witnesses through an open door. The cashier testified that she saw Wade "standing in the hall" within sight of an FBI agent. Five or six other prisoners later appeared in the hall. The vice president testified that he saw a person in the hall in the custody of the agent who "resembled the person that we identified as the one that had entered the bank."

The lineup in *Gilbert* was conducted in an auditorium in which some 100 witnesses to several alleged state and federal robberies charged to Gilbert made wholesale identifications of Gilbert as the robber in each other's presence, a procedure said to be fraught with dangers of suggestion. And the vice of suggestion created by the identification in *Stovall* was the presentation to the witness of the suspect alone handcuffed to police officers. It is hard to imagine a situation more clearly conveying the suggestion to the witness that the one presented is believed guilty by the police.

The few cases that have surfaced therefore reveal the existence of a process attended with hazards of serious unfairness to the criminal accused and strongly suggest the plight of the more numerous defendants who are unable to ferret out suggestive influences in the secrecy of the confrontation. We do not assume that these risks are the result of police procedures intentionally designed to prejudice an accused. Rather we assume they derive from the dangers inherent in eyewitness identification and the suggestibility inherent in the context of the pretrial identification. * * *

Insofar as the accused's conviction may rest on a courtroom identification in fact the fruit of a suspect pretrial identification which the accused is helpless to subject to effective scrutiny at trial, the accused is deprived of that right of cross-

13. An additional impediment to the detection of such influences by participants, including the suspect, is the physical conditions often surrounding the conduct of the lineup. In many, lights shine on the stage in such a way that the suspect cannot see the witness. [In] some a one-way mirror is used and what is said on the witness' side cannot be heard. * * *

examination which is an essential safeguard to his right to confront the witnesses against him. And even though cross-examination is a precious safeguard to a fair trial, it cannot be viewed as an absolute assurance of accuracy and reliability. Thus in the present context, where so many variables and pitfalls exist, the first line of defense must be the prevention of unfairness and the lessening of the hazards of eyewitness identification at the lineup itself. The trial which might determine the accused's fate may well not be that in the courtroom but that at the pretrial confrontation, with the State aligned against the accused, the witness the sole jury, and the accused unprotected against the overreaching, intentional or unintentional, and with little or no effective appeal from the judgment there rendered by the witness—"that's the man."

Since it appears that there is grave potential for prejudice, intentional or not, in the pretrial lineup, which may not be capable of reconstruction at trial, and since presence of counsel itself can often avert prejudice and assure a meaningful confrontation at trial, there can be little doubt that for Wade the post-indictment lineup was a critical stage of the prosecution at which he was "as much entitled to such aid [of counsel as] at the trial itself." *Powell v. Alabama.* Thus both Wade and his counsel should have been notified of the impending lineup, and counsel's presence should have been a requisite to conduct of the lineup, absent an "intelligent waiver." No substantial countervailing policy considerations have been advanced against the requirement of the presence of counsel. Concern is expressed that the requirement will forestall prompt identifications and result in obstruction of the confrontations. As for the first, we note that in the two cases in which the right to counsel is today held to apply, counsel had already been appointed and no argument is made in either case that notice to counsel would have prejudicially delayed the confrontations. Moreover, we leave open the question whether the presence of substitute counsel might not suffice where notification and presence of the suspect's own counsel would result in prejudicial delay. And to refuse to recognize the right to counsel for fear that counsel will obstruct the course of justice is contrary to the basic assumptions upon which this Court has operated in Sixth Amendment cases. [In] our view counsel can hardly impede legitimate law enforcement; on the contrary, for the reasons expressed, law enforcement may be assisted by preventing the infiltration of taint in the prosecution's identification evidence. That result cannot help the guilty avoid conviction but can only help assure that the right many has been brought to justice.

Legislative or other regulations, such as those of local police departments, which eliminate the risks of abuse and unintentional suggestion at lineup proceedings and the impediments to meaningful confrontation at trial may also remove the basis for regarding the stage as "critical." But neither Congress nor the federal authorities have seen fit to provide a solution.[c]

We come now to the question whether the denial of Wade's motion to strike the courtroom identification by the bank witnesses at trial because of the absence of his counsel at the lineup required, as the Court of Appeals held, the grant of a new trial at which such evidence is to be excluded. We do not think this disposition can be justified without first giving the Government the opportunity to establish by clear and convincing evidence that the in-court identifications were

---

c. Nor, it seems, is a solution provided by 18 U.S.C. § 3502, a part of the Omnibus Crime Control and Safe Streets Act of 1968, which states that "the testimony of a witness that he saw the accused commit [the] crime" is admissible in a federal court. This appears to be an unconstitutional attempt to "repeal" *Wade.* According to several commentators, the lower federal courts have ignored this statute and it exists on the books more as an expression of legislative hope than as a binding rule.

based upon observations of the suspect other than the lineup identification. * * * Where, as here, the admissibility of evidence of the lineup identification itself is not involved, a *per se* rule of exclusion of courtroom identification would be unjustified.[d] [A] rule limited solely to the exclusion of testimony concerning identification at the lineup itself, without regard to admissibility of the courtroom identification, would render the right to counsel an empty one. The lineup is most often used, as in the present case, to crystallize the witnesses' identification of the defendant for future reference. We have already noted that the lineup identification will have that effect. The State may then rest upon the witnesses' unequivocal courtroom identification, and not mention the pretrial identification as part of the State's case at trial. Counsel is then in the predicament in which Wade's counsel found himself—realizing that possible unfairness at the lineup may be the sole means of attack upon the unequivocal courtroom identification, and having to probe in the dark in an attempt to discover and reveal unfairness, while bolstering the government witness' courtroom identification by bringing out and dwelling upon his prior identification. Since counsel's presence at the lineup would equip him to attack not only the lineup identification but the courtroom identification as well, limiting the impact of violation of the right to counsel to exclusion of evidence only of identification at the lineup itself disregards a critical element of that right.

We think it follows that the proper test to be applied in these situations is that quoted in *Wong Sun v. United States,* 371 U.S. 471 (1963), " '[W]hether, granting establishment of the primary illegality the evidence to which instant objection is made has been come at by exploitation of that illegality or instead by means sufficiently distinguishable to be purged of the primary taint.' " Application of this test in the present context requires consideration of various factors; for example, the prior opportunity to observe the alleged criminal act, the existence of any discrepancy between any pre-lineup description and the defendant's actual description, any identification prior to lineup of another person, the identification by picture of the defendant prior to the lineup, failure to identify the defendant on a prior occasion, and the lapse of time between the alleged act and the lineup identification. It is also relevant to consider those facts which, despite the absence of counsel, are disclosed concerning the conduct of the lineup. * * *

On the record now before us we cannot make the determination whether the in-court identifications had an independent origin. [T]he appropriate procedure to be followed is to vacate the conviction pending a hearing to determine whether the in-court identifications had an independent source, or whether, in any event, the introduction of the evidence was harmless error, *Chapman v. California,* 386 U.S. 18 (1967), and for the District Court to reinstate the conviction or order a new trial, as may be proper.[e] * * *

d. In *Gilbert,* however, the Court did apply a *per se* exclusionary rule to the testimony of various prosecution witnesses that they had also identified petitioner at a pretrial lineup. See note e infra.

e. Compare *Gilbert,* where various witnesses who identified petitioner in the courtroom also testified, on direct examination by the prosecution, that they had identified petitioner at a prior lineup. "That [pretrial lineup] testimony," ruled the Court, "is the direct result of the illegal lineup 'come at by exploitation of [the primary] illegality.' *Wong Sun.* The State is therefore not entitled to an opportunity to show that that testimony had an independent source. Only a *per se* exclusionary rule as to such testimony can be an effective sanction to assure that law enforcement authorities will respect the accused's constitutional right to the presence of his counsel at the critical lineup. [That] conclusion is buttressed by the consideration that the witness' testimony of his lineup identification will enhance the impact of his in-court identification on the jury and seriously aggravate whatever derogation exists of the accused's right to a fair trial. Therefore, unless the [state supreme court] is 'able to declare a belief that it was harmless beyond a reasonable doubt,' *Chap-*

Judgment of Court of Appeals vacated and case remanded with direction.[f]

Justice White whom Justice Harlan and Justice Stewart join, dissenting in part and concurring in part.

The Court has again propounded a broad constitutional rule barring the use of a wide spectrum of relevant and probative evidence, solely because a step in its ascertainment or discovery occurs outside the presence of defense counsel.

[The] Court's opinion is far-reaching. It proceeds first by creating a new *per se* rule of constitutional law: a criminal suspect cannot be subjected to a pretrial identification process in the absence of his counsel without violating the Sixth Amendment. If he is, the State may not buttress a later courtroom identification of the witness by any reference to the previous identification. Furthermore, the courtroom identification is not admissible at all unless the State can establish by clear and convincing proof that the testimony is not the fruit of the earlier identification made in the absence of defendant's counsel—admittedly a heavy burden for the State and probably an impossible one. To all intents and purposes, courtroom identifications are barred if pretrial identifications have occurred without counsel being present.

The rule applies to any lineup, to any other techniques employed to produce an identification and *a fortiori* to a face-to-face encounter between the witness and the suspect alone, regardless of when the identification occurs, in time or place, and whether before or after indictment or information.[g]

[The] premise for the Court's rule is not the general unreliability of eyewitness identifications nor the difficulties inherent in observation, recall, and recognition. The Court assumes a narrower evil as the basis for its rule—improper police suggestion which contributes to erroneous identifications. The Court apparently believes that improper police procedures are so widespread that a broad prophylactic rule must be laid down, requiring the presence of counsel at all pretrial identifications, in order to detect recurring instances of police misconduct. I do not share this pervasive distrust of all official investigations. None of the materials the Court relies upon supports it. Certainly, I would bow to solid fact, but the Court quite obviously does not have before it any reliable, comprehensive survey of current police practices on which to base its new rule. Until it does, the Court should avoid excluding relevant evidence from state criminal trials. * * *

There are several striking aspects to the Court's holding. First, the rule does not bar courtroom identifications where there have been no previous identifications in the presence of the police, although when identified in the courtroom, the defendant is known to be in custody and charged with the commission of a crime.[h] Second, the Court seems to say that if suitable legislative standards were adopted for the conduct of pretrial identifications, thereby lessening the hazards in such confrontations, it would not insist on the presence of counsel. But if this is true, why does not the Court simply fashion what it deems to be constitutionally

man, Gilbert will be entitled on remand to a new trial * * *."

f. Justice Black's opinion, dissenting in part and concurring in part, is omitted.

g. But see *Kirby v. Illinois,* infra § 2.

h. These identifications are, in effect, one-person showups, albeit in the courtroom. They probably give the witness even a stronger impression that the authorities are convinced they have the right person than do pretrial one-person showups.

In *Moore v. Illinois,* 434 U.S. 220 (1977), where "a one-on-one confrontation" occurred at a preliminary hearing, the Court stated that if defendant had been represented by counsel at this hearing, counsel might have avoided the suggestive identification by asking that the defendant be seated in the audience before the identifying witness was called or by seeking to have the hearing postponed until a lineup was conducted. Although such requests are occasionally granted, trial judges, in their discretion, often deny them.

acceptable procedures for the authorities to follow? Certainly the Court is correct in suggesting that the new rule will be wholly inapplicable where police departments themselves have established suitable safeguards.

Third, courtroom identification may be barred, absent counsel at a prior identification, regardless of the extent of counsel's information concerning the circumstances of the previous confrontation between witness and defendant— apparently even if there were recordings or sound-movies of the events as they occurred. But if the rule is premised on the defendant's right to have his counsel know, there seems little basis for not accepting other means to inform. A disinterested observer, recordings, photographs—any one of them would seem adequate to furnish the basis for a meaningful cross-examination of the eyewitness who identifies the defendant in the courtroom. * * *

Finally, I think the Court's new rule is vulnerable in terms of its own unimpeachable purpose of increasing the reliability of identification testimony.

Law enforcement officers have the obligation to convict the guilty and to make sure they do not convict the innocent. They must be dedicated to making the criminal trial a procedure for the ascertainment of the true facts surrounding the commission of the crime. To this extent, our so-called adversary system is not adversary at all; nor should it be. But defense counsel has no comparable obligation to ascertain or present the truth. Our system assigns him a different mission. He must be and is interested in preventing the conviction of the innocent, but, absent a voluntary plea of guilty, we also insist that he defend his client whether he is innocent or guilty. The State has the obligation to present the evidence. Defense counsel need present nothing, even if he knows what the truth is. [If] he can confuse a witness, even a truthful one, or make him appear at a disadvantage, unsure or indecisive, that will be his normal course. * * *

I would not extend this system, at least as it presently operates, to police investigations and would not require counsel's presence at pretrial identification procedures. Counsel's interest is in not having his client placed at the scene of the crime, regardless of his whereabouts. Some counsel may advise their clients to refuse to make any movements or to speak any words in a lineup or even to appear in one.[j] [Others] will hover over witnesses and begin their cross-examination then, menacing truthful factfinding as thoroughly as the Court fears the police now do. Certainly there is an implicit invitation to counsel to suggest rules for the lineup and to manage and produce it as best he can.[k] I therefore doubt that the Court's new rule, at least absent some clearly defined limits on counsel's role, will measurably contribute to more reliable pretrial identifications. My fears are that it will have precisely the opposite result. [In] my view, the State is entitled to investigate and develop its case outside the presence of defense counsel. This includes the right to have private conversations with identification witnesses,

j. Since requiring a person to appear in a lineup or to use his voice as an identifying physical characteristic or to provide handwriting exemplars is not prohibited by the privilege against self-incrimination, the prosecution may comment on the suspect's refusal to cooperate. On occasion, courts have utilized civil or criminal contempt to coerce or punish the suspect who refuses to comply with a court order to participate in some identification proceeding.

k. The cases and commentaries indicate that the prevailing practice has been for counsel to attend the lineup merely as an observer to assure against abuse and bad faith by law enforcement officers, and to provide the basis for any attack she might wish to make on the identification at trial. Any attempt to give counsel at identification a more active role is fraught with difficulties not only for the police but for counsel herself. If she is entitled to make objections at the lineup procedure, she would be held to have waived these objections if she does not make them at the procedure. If such a possibility of waiver exists, will counsel be under an obligation to raise every conceivable objection?

just as defense counsel may have his own consultations with these and other witnesses without having the prosecutor present. * * *

SECTION 2. THE COURT RETREATS: *KIRBY* AND *ASH*

KIRBY v. ILLINOIS

406 U.S. 682, 92 S.Ct. 1877, 32 L.Ed.2d 411 (1972).

JUSTICE STEWART announced the judgment of the Court in an opinion in which THE CHIEF JUSTICE, JUSTICE BLACKMUN, and JUSTICE REHNQUIST join.

* * * In the present case we are asked to extend the *Wade–Gilbert* per se exclusionary rule to identification testimony based upon a police station show-up that took place *before* the defendant had been indicted or otherwise formally charged with any criminal offense.

On February 21, 1968, [one] Willie Shard reported to the Chicago police that the previous day two men had robbed him on a Chicago street of a wallet containing, among other things, travellers checks and a Social Security card. On February 22, two police officers [investigating an unrelated crime] stopped petitioner and a companion, [Bean], [on a Chicago street]. When asked for identification, the petitioner produced a wallet that contained three travellers checks and a Social Security card, all bearing the name of Willie Shard. * * *

Only after arriving at the police station, and checking the records there, did the arresting officers learn of the Shard robbery. [A police car] picked up Shard and brought him to the police station. Immediately upon entering the room [where petitioner and Bean were seated], Shard positively identified them as [his robbers].[a] No lawyer was present [and neither suspect had asked for] or been advised of any right to the presence of counsel. [At the trial Shard] described his identification of the two men at the police station [and] identified them again in the courtroom as the men who had robbed him.

[In] a line of constitutional cases in this Court stemming back to the Court's landmark opinion in *Powell v. Alabama,* it has been firmly established that a person's Sixth and Fourteenth Amendment right to counsel attaches only at or after the time that adversary judicial proceedings have been initiated against him.

This is not to say that a defendant in a criminal case has a constitutional right to counsel only at the trial itself. [But] the point is [that] *all* of [the right to counsel cases] have involved points of time at or after the initiation of adversary judicial criminal proceedings—whether by way of formal charge, preliminary hearing, indictment, information, or arraignment.

The only seeming deviation from this long line of constitutional decisions was *Escobedo* [which] is not apposite here for two distinct reasons. First, the Court in retrospect perceived that the "prime purpose" of *Escobedo* was not to vindicate the constitutional right to counsel as such, but, like *Miranda,* "to guarantee full effectuation of the privilege against self-incrimination. * * * " *Johnson v. New Jersey,* 384 U.S. 719 (1966). Secondly, and perhaps even more important for purely practical purposes, the Court has limited the holding of *Escobedo* to its own facts, and those facts are not remotely akin to the facts of the case before us.

---

a. According to dissenting Justice Brennan, Shard testified that he identified petitioner and Bean only after the officers who brought him to the room asked him if they were the robbers.

The initiation of judicial criminal proceedings is far from a mere formalism. It is the starting point of our whole system of adversary criminal justice. For it is only then that the Government has committed itself to prosecute, and only then that the adverse positions of Government and defendant have solidified. It is then that a defendant finds himself faced with the prosecutorial forces of organized society, and immersed in the intricacies of substantive and procedural criminal law. It is this point, therefore, that marks the commencement of the "criminal prosecutions" to which alone the explicit guarantees of the Sixth Amendment are applicable.[b]

In this case we are asked to import into a routine police investigation an absolute constitutional guarantee historically and rationally applicable only after the onset of formal prosecutorial proceedings. We decline to do so. * * * We decline to [impose] a *per se* exclusionary rule upon testimony concerning an identification that took place long before the commencement of any prosecution whatever.

What has been said is not to suggest that there may not be occasions during the course of a criminal investigation when the police do abuse identification procedures. Such abuses are not beyond the reach of the Constitution. [The] Due Process Clause of the Fifth and Fourteenth Amendments forbids a lineup that is unnecessarily suggestive and conducive to irreparable mistaken identification.[8] When a person has not been formally charged with a criminal offense, *Stovall* strikes the appropriate constitutional balance between the right of a suspect to be protected from prejudicial procedures and the interest of society in the prompt and purposeful investigation of an unsolved crime.

The judgment is affirmed.[c]

JUSTICE BRENNAN, with whom JUSTICE DOUGLAS and JUSTICE MARSHALL join, dissenting. * * *

While it should go without saying, it appears necessary, in view of the plurality opinion today, to re-emphasize that *Wade* did not require the presence of counsel at pretrial confrontations for identification purposes simply on the basis of an abstract consideration of the words "criminal prosecutions" in the Sixth Amendment, [but] in order to safeguard the accused's constitutional rights to confrontation and the effective assistance of counsel at his trial.

In view of *Wade*, it is plain, and the plurality today does not attempt to dispute it, that there inhere in a confrontation for identification conducted after arrest the identical hazards to a fair trial that inhere in such a confrontation conducted "after the onset of formal prosecutorial proceedings." The plurality apparently considers an arrest, which for present purposes we must assume to be based upon probable cause, to be nothing more than part of "a routine police

b. Except for the language in this paragraph, *Kirby* does not explore what constitutes the "initiation" of adversary judicial criminal proceedings. But this language was subsequently relied upon in holding it sufficed that defendant appeared at a preliminary hearing to determine whether he should be bound over to the grand jury and to set bail. *Moore v. Illinois*, 434 U.S. 220 (1977). It is generally agreed that a warrantless arrest is not sufficient, but courts differ as to whether adversary proceedings are initiated by the issuance of an arrest warrant upon information and oath.

8. In view of our limited grant of certiorari, we do not consider whether there might have

been a deprivation of due process in the particularized circumstances of this case. That question remains open for inquiry in a federal habeas corpus proceeding.

[Following the U.S. Supreme Court's decision, the denial of Kirby's petition for federal habeas corpus relief was affirmed by the Seventh Circuit in *United States ex rel. Kirby v. Sturges*, 510 F.2d 397 (1975).]

c. As he "would not extend the *Wade–Gilbert* exclusionary rule," Powell, J., concurred in the result.

investigation," and thus not "the starting point of our whole system of adversary criminal justice." [The] plurality offers no reason, and I can think of none, for concluding that a post-arrest confrontation for identification, unlike a post-charge confrontation, is not among those "critical confrontations of the accused by the prosecution at pretrial proceedings where the results might well settle the accused's fate and reduce the trial itself to a mere formality."

The highly suggestive form of confrontation employed in this case underscores the point. This showup was particularly fraught with the peril of mistaken identification. In the setting of a police station squad room where all present except petitioner and Bean were police officers, the danger was quite real that Shard's understandable resentment might lead him too readily to agree with the police that the pair under arrest, and the only persons exhibited to him, were indeed the robbers. [On] direct examination, Shard identified petitioner and Bean not as the alleged robbers on trial in the courtroom, but as the pair he saw at the police station. * * *

Wade and *Gilbert,* of course, happened to involve post-indictment confrontations. Yet even a cursory perusal of the opinions in those cases reveals that nothing at all turned upon that particular circumstance. In short, it is fair to conclude that rather than "declin[ing] to depart from [the] rationale" of *Wade* and *Gilbert,* the plurality today, albeit purporting to be engaged in "principled constitutional adjudication," refuses even to recognize that "rationale." * * * Because Shard testified at trial about his identification of petitioner at the police station showup, the exclusionary rule of *Gilbert* requires reversal.

JUSTICE WHITE, dissenting.

Wade and *Gilbert* govern this case and compel reversal of the judgment below.[d]

d. A year later, in a decision the dissenters there maintained "mark[ed] simply another step towards the complete evisceration of the fundamental constitutional principles" established in the 1967 lineup cases, the Court held that a defendant has no right to have his counsel present while witnesses view pictures of him for identification purposes at a post-indictment photographic display. *United States v. Ash,* 413 U.S. 300 (1973). Shortly before trial, almost three years after the crime, and long after defendant had been incarcerated and appointed counsel, the prosecutor showed five color photographs to a number of witnesses who previously had tentatively identified the black-and-white photograph of defendant. Three witnesses selected defendant's photo. In holding that the right to counsel did not extend to post-indictment photo-identifications, the Court, per Blackmun, J., observed:

"[Although the right to counsel guarantee has been expanded beyond the formal trial itself], the function of the lawyer has remained essentially the same as his function at trial. In all cases considered by the Court, counsel has continued to act as a spokesman for, or advisor to, the accused. * * *

"The function of counsel in rendering 'assistance' continued at the lineup under consideration in *Wade* and its companion cases. Although the accused was not confronted there with legal questions, the lineup offered oppor-

tunities for prosecuting authorities to take advantage of the accused. * * *

"Even if we were willing to view the counsel guarantee in broad terms as a generalized protection of the adversary process, we would be unwilling to go so far as to extend the right to a portion of the prosecutor's trial-preparation interviews with witnesses. [The] traditional counterbalance in the American adversary system for these interviews arises from the equal ability of defense counsel to seek and interview witnesses himself.

"That adversary mechanism remains as effective for a photographic display as for other parts of pretrial interviews. No greater limitations are placed on defense counsel in constructing displays, seeking witnesses, and conducting photographic identifications than those applicable to the prosecution. * * *

"Pretrial [photo-identifications] are hardly unique in offering possibilities for the actions of the prosecutor unfairly to prejudice the accused. [In] many ways the prosecutor, by accident or by design, may improperly subvert the trial. The primary safeguard against abuses of this kind is the ethical responsibility of the prosecutor. * * * If that safeguard fails, review remains available under due process standards. These same safeguards apply to misuse of photographs.

"We are not persuaded that the risks inherent in the use of photographic displays are so

Stovall 1967
Biggers 1972
Manson 1977

SECTION 3.   DUE PROCESS AND OTHER LIMITATIONS

As pointed out in *Stovall v. Denno,* 388 U.S. 293 (1967), one unable to make a *Wade–Gilbert* right to counsel argument may still establish that the identification procedure conducted in his case "was so unnecessarily suggestive and conducive to irreparable mistaken identification that he was denied due process of law."   In *Stovall,* the stabbing victim (Mrs. Behrendt), was hospitalized for major surgery. Without affording petitioner time to retain counsel (an arraignment had been promptly held but then postponed until petitioner could retain counsel), the police, with the cooperation of the victim's surgeon, arranged a confrontation between petitioner and the victim in her hospital room.   Petitioner was hand-cuffed to one of the seven law enforcement officials who brought him to the hospital room.   He was the only black person in the room.   After being asked by an officer whether petitioner "was the man," the victim identified him from her hospital bed.   Both Mrs. Behrendt and the police then testified at the trial to her identification in the hospital.   Despite the suggestiveness of the confrontation, the Court, per Brennan, J., affirmed the Second Circuit's denial of federal habeas corpus relief, observing that "a claimed violation of due process of law in the conduct of a confrontation depends on the totality of the circumstances surrounding it, and the record in the present case reveals that the showing of Stovall to Mrs. Behrendt in an immediate hospital confrontation was imperative."   The Court then quoted with approval from the court below: "Here was the only person in the world who could possibly exonerate Stovall.   * * * No one knew how long Mrs. Behrendt might live.   [Under the circumstances] and with the

pernicious that an extraordinary system of safeguards is required."

Dissenting Justice Brennan, joined by Douglas and Marshall, JJ., observed:

"[A]lthough retention of the photographs may mitigate the dangers of misidentification due to the suggestiveness of the photographs themselves, it cannot in any sense reveal to defense counsel the more subtle, and therefore more dangerous, suggestiveness that might derive from the manner in which the photographs were displayed or any accompanying comments or gestures.

"[Moreover] and unlike the lineup situation, the accused himself is not even present at the photographic identification, thereby reducing the likelihood that irregularities in the procedures will ever come to light.   * * *

"[A]lthough apparently conceding that the right to counsel attached, not only at the trial itself, but at all 'critical stages' of the prosecution, the Court holds today that, in order to be deemed 'critical,' the particular 'stage of the prosecution' under consideration must, at the very least, involve the physical 'presence of the accused,' at a 'trial-like confrontation' with the Government, at which the accused requires the 'guiding hand of counsel.'   A pretrial photographic identification does not, of course, meet these criteria.   * * *

"[But the] fundamental premise underlying *all* of this Court's decisions holding the right to

counsel applicable at 'critical' pretrial proceedings, is that a 'stage' of the prosecution must be deemed 'critical' for the purposes of the Sixth Amendment if it is one at which the presence of counsel is necessary 'to protect the fairness of *trial itself.*'

"[This] established conception of the Sixth Amendment guarantee is, of course, in no sense dependent upon the physical 'presence of the accused,' at a 'trial-like confrontation' with the Government, at which the accused requires the 'guiding hand of counsel.'   * * *

"[C]ontrary to the suggestion of the Court, the conclusion in *Wade* that a pretrial lineup is a 'critical stage' of the prosecution did not in any sense turn on the fact that a lineup involves the physical 'presence of the accused' at a 'trial-like confrontation' with the Government.   And that conclusion most certainly did not turn on the notion that presence of counsel was necessary so that counsel could offer legal advice or 'guidance' to the accused at the lineup.   On the contrary, *Wade* envisioned counsel's function at the lineup to be primarily that of a trained observer, able to detect the existence of any suggestive influences and capable of understanding the legal implications of the events that transpire.   Having witnessed the proceedings, counsel would then be in a position effectively to reconstruct at trial any unfairness that occurred at the lineup, thereby preserving the accused's fundamental right to a fair trial on the issue of identification."

knowledge that Mrs. Behrendt could not visit the jail, the police followed the only feasible procedure and took Stovall to the hospital."

Stovall may not be as easy a case as it appears to be at first blush.[a] But it is a good deal easier than *Manson v. Brathwaite,* below.

MANSON v. BRATHWAITE

432 U.S. 98, 97 S.Ct. 2243, 53 L.Ed.2d 140 (1977).

JUSTICE BLACKMUN delivered the opinion of the Court. * * *

[Several minutes before sunset, Glover, a black undercover police officer, purchased heroin from a seller through the open doorway of an apartment while standing for two or three minutes within two feet of the seller in a hallway illuminated by natural light. A few minutes later, Glover described the seller to a back-up officer, D'Onofrio, as being "a colored man, approximately five feet eleven inches tall, dark complexion, black hair, short Afro style, and having high cheekbones, and of heavy build. He was wearing at the time blue pants and a plaid shirt."

[On the basis of the description, D'Onofrio thought that respondent might be the heroin seller. He obtained a single photograph of respondent from police files and left it at Glover's office. Two days later, while alone, Glover viewed the photograph and identified it as that of the seller. At respondent's trial, Glover testified that there was "no doubt whatsoever" that the person shown in the photograph was respondent. Glover also made a positive in-court identification. No explanation was offered by the prosecution for the failure to utilize a photographic array or to conduct a lineup.

[After the Connecticut Supreme Court affirmed respondent's conviction, he sought federal habeas corpus relief. The Second Circuit, per Friendly, J., held that because the showing of the single photograph was "suggestive" and concededly "unnecessarily so," evidence pertaining to it was subject to a *per se* rule of exclusion.]

Neil v. Biggers, 409 U.S. 188 (1972), concerned a respondent who had been convicted [of] rape, on evidence consisting in part of the victim's visual and voice identification of Biggers at a [one-person] station-house showup seven months after the crime. * * * The Court expressed concern about the lapse of seven months between the crime and the confrontation, [but pointed out that the] "central question" [was] "whether under the 'totality of the circumstances' the identification was reliable even though the confrontation procedure was suggestive." Applying that test, the Court found "no substantial likelihood of misidentification. The evidence was properly allowed to go to the jury." [a]

---

a. According to the two judges who dissented below, Friendly, J., joined by Waterman, J., the argument that law enforcement officers were confronted with an emergency "ignores the huge amount of circumstantial identification the excellent police investigation had produced." Moreover, if law enforcement officials were really motivated by solicitude for defendant "the natural course would have been to ask [him] whether he wanted to go. The emergency argument fails both on the facts and on the law." The question was also raised as to whether, if a lineup were out of the question, a photographic display might not have been preferable to a one-person showup.

a. The *Biggers* Court, per Powell, J., observed:

"The victim spent a considerable period of time with her assailant, up to half an hour. She was with him under adequate artificial light in her house and under a full moon outdoors, and at least twice, once in the house and later in the woods, faced him directly and intimately. [Her] description to the police, which included the assailant's approximate age, height, weight, complexion, skin texture, build, and voice [was] more than ordinarily thorough. She had 'no doubt' that respondent was the person who raped her. [The] victim here, a practical

Biggers well might be seen to provide an unambiguous answer to the question before us: The admission of testimony concerning a suggestive and unnecessary identification procedure does not violate due process so long as the identification possesses sufficient aspects of reliability. In one passage, however, the Court observed that the challenged procedure occurred pre-*Stovall* and that a strict rule would make little sense with regard to a confrontation that preceded the Court's first indication that a suggestive procedure might lead to the exclusion of evidence. One perhaps might argue that, by implication, the Court suggested that a different rule could apply post-*Stovall*. The question before us, then, is simply whether the *Biggers* analysis applies to post-*Stovall* confrontations as well to those pre-*Stovall*. * * *

Petitioner at the outset acknowledges that "the procedure in the instant case was suggestive [because only one photograph was used] and unnecessary" [because there was no emergency or exigent circumstance]. The respondent, in agreement with the Court of Appeals, proposes a *per se* rule of exclusion that he claims is dictated by the demands of the Fourteenth Amendment's guarantee of due process. He rightly observes that this is the first case in which this Court has had occasion to rule upon strictly post-*Stovall* out-of-court identification evidence of the challenged kind.

Since the decision in *Biggers,* the Courts of Appeals appear to have developed at least two approaches to such evidence. The first, or *per se* approach, employed by the Second Circuit in the present case, focuses on the procedures employed and requires exclusion of the out-of-court identification evidence, without regard to reliability, whenever it has been obtained through unnecessarily suggested confrontation procedures.[10] The justifications advanced are the elimination of evidence of uncertain reliability, deterrence of the police and prosecutors, and the stated "fair assurance against the awful risks of misidentification."

The second, or more lenient, approach is one that continues to rely on the totality of the circumstances. It permits the admission of the confrontation evidence if, despite the suggestive aspect, the out-of-court identification possesses certain features of reliability. This second approach, in contrast to the other, is ad hoc and serves to limit the societal costs imposed by a sanction that excludes relevant evidence from consideration and evaluation by the trier of fact. * * *

There are, of course, several interests to be considered and taken into account. The driving force behind [*Wade, Gilbert* and *Stovall*] was the Court's concern with the problems of eyewitness identification. Usually the witness must testify about an encounter with a total stranger under circumstances of emergency or emotional stress. The witness' recollection of the stranger can be distorted easily by the circumstances or by later actions of the police. Thus, *Wade* and its companion cases reflect the concern that the jury not hear eyewitness testimony

---

nurse by profession, had an unusual opportunity to observe and identify her assailant. She testified at the habeas corpus hearing that there was something about his face 'I don't think I could ever forget.'

"There was, to be sure, a lapse of seven months between the rape and the confrontation. This would be a seriously negative factor in most cases. Here, however, the testimony is undisputed that the victim made no previous identification at any of the showups, lineups, or photographic showings. Her record for reliability was thus a good one, as she had previously resisted whatever suggestiveness inheres in a showup. Weigh-

ing all the factors, we find no substantial likelihood of misidentification."

10. Although the *per se* approach demands the exclusion of testimony concerning unnecessarily suggestive identifications, it does permit the admission of testimony concerning a subsequent identification, including an in-court identification, if the subsequent identification is determined to be reliable. The totality approach, in contrast, is simpler: if the challenged identification is reliable, then testimony as to it and any identification in its wake is admissible.

unless that evidence has aspects of reliability. It must be observed that both approaches before us are responsive to this concern. The *per se* rule, however, goes too far since its application automatically and peremptorily, and without consideration of alleviating factors, keeps evidence from the jury that is reliable and relevant.

The second factor is deterrence. Although the *per se* approach has the more significant deterrent effect, the totality approach also has an influence on police behavior. The police will guard against unnecessarily suggestive procedures under the totality rule, as well as the *per se* one, for fear that their actions will lead to the exclusion of identifications as unreliable.

The third factor is the effect on the administration of justice. Here the *per se* approach suffers serious drawbacks. Since it denies the trier reliable evidence, it may result, on occasion, in the guilty going free. Also, because of its rigidity, the *per se* approach may make error by the trial judge more likely than the totality approach. And in those cases in which the admission of identification evidence is error under the *per se* approach but not under the totality approach—cases in which the identification is reliable despite an unnecessarily suggestive identification procedure—reversal is a Draconian sanction. Certainly, inflexible rules of exclusion that may frustrate rather than promote justice have not been viewed recently by this Court with unlimited enthusiasm. * * *

We therefore conclude that reliability is the linchpin in determining the admissibility of identification testimony for both pre- and post-*Stovall* confrontations. The factors to be considered are set out in *Biggers.* These include the opportunity of the witness to view the criminal at the time of the crime, the witness' degree of attention, the accuracy of his prior description of the criminal, the level of certainty demonstrated at the confrontation, and the time between the crime and the confrontation. Against these factors is to be weighed the corrupting effect of the suggestive identification itself.

We turn, then, to the facts of this case and apply the analysis:

1. The opportunity to view. Glover testified that for two to three minutes he stood at the apartment door, within two feet of the respondent. The door opened twice, and each time the man stood at the door. * * * Natural light from outside entered the hallway through a window. There was natural light, as well, from inside the apartment.

2. The degree of attention. Glover was not a casual or passing observer, [but] a trained police officer on duty—and specialized and dangerous duty—when he [made the heroin purchase]. Glover himself was a Negro and unlikely to perceive only general features of [black males].

3. The accuracy of the description. Glover's description was given to D'Onofrio within minutes after the transaction. It included the vendor's race, his height, his build, the color and style of his hair, and the high cheekbone facial feature. It also included clothing the vendor wore. No claim has been made that respondent did not possess the physical characteristics so described. * * *

4. The witness' level of certainty. There is no dispute that the photograph in question was that of respondent. Glover, in response to a question whether the photograph was that of the person from whom he made the purchase, testified: "There is no question whatsoever." This positive assurance was repeated.

5. The time between the crime and the confrontation. Glover's description of his vendor was given to D'Onofrio within minutes of the crime. The photographic identification took place only two days later. We do not have here the passage of weeks or months between the crime and the viewing of the photograph.

These indicators of Glover's ability to make an accurate identification are hardly outweighed by the corrupting effect of the challenged identification itself. Although identifications arising from single-photograph displays may be viewed in general with suspicion, we find in the instant case little pressure on the witness to acquiesce in the suggestion that such a display entails. D'Onofrio had left the photograph at Glover's office and was not present when Glover first viewed it two days after the event. There thus was little urgency and Glover could view the photograph at his leisure. And since Glover examined the photograph alone, there was no coercive pressure to make an identification arising from the presence of another. The identification was made in circumstances allowing care and reflection. * * *

Surely, we cannot say that under all the circumstances of this case there is "a very substantial likelihood of irreparable misidentification." Short of that point, such evidence is for the jury to weigh. * * *

We conclude that the criteria laid down in *Biggers* are to be applied in determining the admissibility of evidence offered by the prosecution concerning a post-*Stovall* identification, and that those criteria are satisfactorily met and complied with here.

[Reversed][b]

JUSTICE MARSHALL, with whom JUSTICE BRENNAN joins, dissenting.

Today's decision can come as no surprise to those who have been watching the Court dismantle the protections against mistaken eyewitness testimony erected a decade ago in [*Wade, Gilbert* and *Stovall*]. But it is still distressing to see the Court virtually ignore the teaching of experience embodied in those decisions and blindly uphold the conviction of a defendant who may well be innocent.

[In] determining the admissibility of the post-*Stovall* identification in this case, the Court considers two alternatives, a *per se* exclusionary rule and a totality-of-the circumstances approach. The Court weighs three factors in deciding that the totality approach, which is essentially the test used in *Biggers,* should be applied. In my view, the Court wrongly evaluates the impact of these factors.

First, the Court acknowledges that one of the factors, deterrence of police use of unnecessarily suggestive identification procedures, favors the *per se* rule. Indeed, it does so heavily, for such a rule would make it unquestionably clear to the police they must never use a suggestive procedure when a fairer alternative is available. I have no doubt that conduct would quickly conform to the rule.

Second, the Court gives passing consideration to the dangers of eyewitness identification recognized in the *Wade* trilogy. It concludes, however, that the grave risk of error does not justify adoption of the *per se* approach because that would too often result in exclusion of relevant evidence. In my view, this conclusion totally ignores the lessons of *Wade.* The dangers of mistaken identification are, as *Stovall* held, simply too great to permit unnecessarily suggestive identifications. Neither *Biggers* nor the Court's opinion today points to any contrary empirical evidence. * * *

Finally, the Court errs in its assessment of the relative impact of the two approaches on the administration of justice. * * * Relying on little more than a

b. Stevens, J., concurring, joined the Court's opinion, but emphasized that although "the arguments in favor of fashioning new rules to minimize the danger of convicting the innocent on the basis of unreliable eyewitness testimony carry substantial force [this] rule-making function can be performed 'more effectively by the legislative process than by somewhat clumsy judicial fiat,' and that the Federal Constitution does not foreclose experimentation by the States in the development of such rules."

strong distaste for "inflexible rules of exclusion," the Court rejects the *per se* test. In so doing, the Court disregards two significant distinctions between the *per se* rule advocated in this case and the exclusionary remedies for certain other constitutional violations.

First, the *per se* rule here is not "inflexible." Where evidence is suppressed, for example, as the fruit of an unlawful search, it may well be forever lost to the prosecution. Identification evidence, however, can by its very nature be readily and effectively reproduced. The in-court identification, permitted under *Wade* and *Simmons* if it has a source independent of an uncounseled or suggestive procedure, is one example. Similarly, when a prosecuting attorney learns that there has been a suggestive confrontation, he can easily arrange another lineup conducted under scrupulously fair conditions. * * *

Second, other exclusionary rules have been criticized for preventing jury consideration of relevant and usually reliable evidence in order to serve interest unrelated to guilt or innocence, such as discouraging illegal searches or denial of counsel. Suggestively obtained eyewitness testimony is excluded, in contrast, precisely because of its unreliability and concomitant irrelevance. Its exclusion both protects the integrity of the truth-seeking function of the trial and discourages police use of needlessly inaccurate and ineffective investigatory methods.

[For] these reasons, I conclude that adoption of the *per se* rule would enhance, rather than detract from, the effective administration of justice. In my view, the Court's totality test will allow seriously unreliable and misleading evidence to be put before juries. * * *

Even more disturbing than the Court's reliance on the totality test, however, is the analysis it uses, which suggests a reinterpretation of the concept of due process of law in criminal cases. The decision suggests that due process violations in identification procedures may not be measured by whether the government employed procedures violating standards of fundamental fairness. By relying on the probable accuracy of a challenged identification, instead of the necessity for its use, the Court seems to be ascertaining whether the defendant was probably guilty. * * *

Despite my strong disagreement with the Court over the proper standards to be applied in this case, I am pleased that its application of the totality test does recognize the continuing vitality of *Stovall*. In assessing the reliability of the identification, the Court mandates weighing "the corrupting effect of the suggestive identification itself" against the "indicators of [a witness'] ability to make an accurate identification." The Court holds, as *Biggers* failed to, that a due process identification inquiry must take account of the suggestiveness of a confrontation and the likelihood that it led to mis-identification, as recognized in *Stovall* and *Wade*. Thus, even if a witness did have an otherwise adequate opportunity to view a criminal, the later use of a highly suggestive identification procedure can render his testimony inadmissible. Indeed, it is my view that, assuming applicability of the totality test enunciated by the Court, the facts of the present case require that result.

I consider first the opportunity that Officer Glover had to view the suspect. Careful review of the record shows that he could see the heroin seller only for the time it took to speak three sentences of four or five short words, to hand over some money, and later after the door reopened, to receive the drugs in return. The entire face-to-face transaction could have taken as little as 15 or 20 seconds. But during this time, Glover's attention was not focused exclusively on the seller's face. He observed that the door was opened 12 to 18 inches, that there was a window in the room behind the door, and, most importantly, that there was a woman standing behind the man. Glover was, of course, also concentrating on the details of the transaction—he must have looked away from the seller's face to hand him the money and receive the drugs. The observation during the conversation thus may have been as brief as 5 or 10 seconds.

As the Court notes, Glover was a police officer trained in and attentive to the need for making accurate identifications. [But] the mere fact that he has been so trained is no guarantee that he is correct in a specific case. * * * Moreover, "identifications made by policemen in highly competitive activities, such as undercover narcotic [work], should be scrutinized with special care." P. Wall, *Eye–Witness Identification in Criminal Cases* 14 (1965). Yet it is just such a searching inquiry that the Court fails to make here.

Another factor on which the Court relies—the witness' degree of certainty in making the identification—is worthless as an indicator that he is correct. Even if Glover had been unsure initially about his identification of respondent's picture, by the time he was called at trial to present a key piece of evidence for the State that paid his salary, it is impossible to imagine his responding negatively to such questions as "is there any doubt in your mind whatsoever" that the identification was correct. * * *

Next, the Court finds that because the identification procedure took place two days after the crime, its reliability is enhanced. While such temporal proximity makes the identification more reliable than one occurring months later, the fact is that the greatest memory loss occurs within hours after an event. After that, the drop-off continues much more slowly. * * *

Finally, the Court makes much of the fact that Glover gave a description of the seller to D'Onofrio shortly after the incident. [But the description] was actually no more than a general summary of the seller's appearance. * * * Conspicuously absent is any indication that the seller was a native of the West Indies, certainly something which a member of the black community could immediately recognize from both appearance and accent.[12]

From all of this, I must conclude that the evidence of Glover's ability to make an accurate identification is far weaker than the Court finds it. In contrast, the procedure used to identify respondent was both extraordinarily suggestive and strongly conducive to error. [By] displaying a single photograph of respondent to the witness Glover under the circumstances in this record almost everything that could have been done wrong was done wrong.

[The] use of a single picture (or the display of a single live suspect, for that matter) is a grave error, of course, because it dramatically suggests to the witness that the person shown must be the culprit. Why else would the police choose the person? And it is deeply ingrained in human nature to agree with the expressed opinions of others—particularly others who should be more knowledgeable—when making a difficult decision. In this case, moreover, the pressure was not limited to that inherent in the display of a single photograph. Glover, the identifying witness, was a state police officer on special assignment. He knew that D'Onofrio, an [experienced] narcotics detective, presumably familiar with local drug operations, believed respondent to be the seller. There was at work, then, both loyalty to another police officer and deference to a better-informed colleague.

---

12. Brathwaite had come to the United States from his native Barbados as an adult. It is also noteworthy that the informant who witnessed the transaction and was described by Glover as "trustworthy," disagreed with Glo-   ver's recollection of the event. The informant testified that it was a woman in the apartment who took the money from Glover and gave him the drugs in return.

Finally, of course, there was Glover's knowledge that without an identification and arrest, government funds used to buy heroin had been wasted. * * *

I must conclude that this record presents compelling evidence that there was "a very substantial likelihood of misidentification" of respondent Brathwaite. The suggestive display of respondent's photograph to the witness Glover likely erased any independent memory that Glover had retained of the seller from his barely adequate opportunity to observe the criminal. * * *

Chapter 8

INVESTIGATION BY SUBPOENA

455 - 486

INTRODUCTION

To understand the criminal investigation conducted by subpoena, one must understand the grand jury.[a] For the grand jury historically was the primary agency conducting investigations through the use of subpoenas, and the vast majority of investigations by subpoena today, though directed by prosecutors, continue to be conducted through the grand jury.

Few elements of our criminal justice process have more ancient roots than the grand jury, which was introduced into the English criminal process in the twelfth century. By the time the United States Constitution was adopted, the grand jury was well established in this country as both a screening and investigatory body. The grand jury performed its screening function in determining whether the government had developed sufficient evidence to bring criminal charges through an indictment. Under the federal constitution's Fifth Amendment and similar provisions in state constitutions, felony charges could be brought only on a grand jury's decision to indict. The grand jury performed its investigatory function through its own resources and its capacity to require potential witnesses to come before it and testify as to suspected crimes. As a result of its dual functions, the grand jury came to be known as the "shield and sword" of the criminal justice process. In its role as a screening agency, the grand jury provided a shield against mistaken or vindictive prosecution of the innocent by refusing to indict. In its role as an investigative agency, it provided the state with a sword to combat crime that could not be reached through other investigative processes.

The shielding or screening function of the grand jury will be discussed in Chapter Eleven. In this Chapter, we will look only at the investigative authority of the grand jury. While the grand jury remains an important investigative agency, its significance in this regard is less than it once was. With the development of professional police departments, the major share of the responsibility for investigation today falls on the police. Compared to police investigations, grand jury investigations are expensive, time-consuming, and logistically cumbersome. The grand jury is a group of lay persons (as large as 23, its traditional size, in some jurisdictions), who commonly are selected in much the same manner as the trial jury. The jurors meet as a body, hearing witnesses and examining physical evidence. While early grand juries, operating in small communities, often could bring to an investigation relevant information gathered through the jurors' own efforts, the grand jury today must rely primarily on the lead of the

a. The organization and operation of the grand jury are briefly described in Chapter 1, particularly in the description of step 11 (grand jury review).

455

prosecutor, who serves as its legal advisor and sets the direction, scope, and pace of its investigation. It is the prosecutor who determines which witnesses will be presented before the grand jury, and the prosecutor who examines those witnesses, although the grand jury has the power to ask its own questions and to insist that the prosecutor present such additional witnesses as it specifies. Those rare grand juries that have made extensive use of such powers and have taken investigations in new directions (commonly assisted by special prosecutors, appointed by the court at the grand jury's request) have come to be known as "runaway grand juries."

The extra burdens of the grand jury investigation lead prosecutors today to turn to the grand jury process only where it offers a distinct investigative advantage over the police. That advantage is most likely to be present where investigators must unravel a complex criminal structure, deal with victims reluctant to cooperate, obtain information contained in extensive business records, or keep a continuing investigative effort from the public gaze. Criminal activities presenting such investigative problems include public corruption (e.g., bribery), misuse of economic power (e.g., price-fixing), and widespread distribution of illegal services and goods (e.g., gambling or narcotics distribution), and most grand jury investigations are directed at such activities. The grand jury's advantages in investigating this type of criminal activity stem primarily from its use of subpoena authority to compel the production of testimony and physical evidence, although certain other aspects of the grand jury investigation—most notably secrecy requirements [b] and lay participation [c]—may also contribute to its effectiveness.

The subpoena authority utilized in a grand jury investigation comes from the courts. Although described as an independent body, the grand jury exists as an arm of the court. The court calls the grand jury into being and grants to it the power of the court to compel persons to appear and testify or produce physical evidence. A subpoena is a court order directing a person to appear to testify (the subpoena "ad testificandum") or to present to it physical evidence (the subpoena "duces tecum"). Both forms of subpoena may present significant investigative advantages over procedures available to the police.

The subpoena duces tecum offers various advantages over the primary device available to the police for obtaining physical evidence—the search pursuant to a warrant. Initially, as will be seen, the subpoena duces tecum can issue without

b. Grand jury secrecy requirements vary in scope from one jurisdiction to another, but all jurisdictions prohibit the prosecution's staff, the grand jurors, and court personnel from disclosing what occurred before the grand jury (absent a court order allowing such disclosure). In several jurisdictions the witness himself is also subject to a secrecy requirement (being allowed to discuss his testimony only with his lawyer), but most do not restrict disclosure by the witness. The end result is that the witness who wants his testimony to be kept secret knows that those who have heard his testimony have been sworn to secrecy; disclosure lies in his own hands—at least until charges are brought (when the witness' testimony will most likely be made public if he is to testify at trial).

c. Lay participation is said to add primarily two elements to the effectiveness of grand jury investigations. First, witnesses are said to feel a "moral compulsion to be honest and forth-right" in their testimony before a group of peers, who have themselves accepted the inconvenience of becoming involved. Second, particularly where the subject under investigation has political overtones that might produce claims of prosecutorial political partisanship, the participation of the lay jurors is said to help maintain public confidence in the integrity of the investigatory process. Critics discount both of these contentions. They suggest that the psychological pressures felt by the witness are more likely to come from the fact that the witness knows that he "stands alone"—that he must "appear before an often hostile prosecutor and a group of strangers, with no judge present to guard his rights, no counsel present to counsel him, and sometimes no indication of why he is being questioned." As for public confidence, critics suggest that the public recognizes that the key figure in a grand jury investigation is an elected official, the prosecutor, not the grand jury.

the showing of probable cause required for a search warrant. In the grand jury setting the subpoena duces tecum usually seeks documents, and it also has the advantage of requiring the party subpoenaed to sort through what may be a vast quantity of records in order to find the document subpoenaed (a sorting task that might often be so burdensome for police to undertake that a search would be impracticable). Finally, where records are to be obtained from an uninvolved third party (e.g., a bank), a subpoena may be preferred because it will be far less disruptive than a police search of the files of that party.[d]

The subpoena to testify similarly offers several advantages over police questioning. Initially, as will be seen in section one, there is no need for a showing of probable cause or even reasonable suspicion to require a person to come before the grand jury and testify. Second, whereas a person may simply refuse to answer police questions (having no duty to cooperate), a subpoenaed person must give testimony as requested (absent the exercise of some valid privilege)—or be held in contempt by the court. Moreover, when that person does testify, a failure to tell the truth will subject him to criminal liability for perjury, for the testimony is given under oath. Lying to police officers generally is not a crime under state law (although the federal system makes it criminal as to federal officers).

The power of the subpoena to compel testimony commonly is supplemented by legislation authorizing the prosecutor to obtain a court order granting a form of "immunity" to the grand jury witness. The primary limit upon the witness' legal duty to testify, as well as be seen, is the privilege against self-incrimination. The witness' self-incrimination privilege may be supplanted, however, through the grant of immunity, as discussed in the *Kastigar* case (see § 2). The immunity grant gives the prosecution an opportunity to "break" a case by forcing critical testimony from a lower-level participant in a criminal enterprise who otherwise would rely on his self-incrimination privilege. Of course, the price for such testimony ordinarily will be foregoing the prosecution of that person, but that may be a worthwhile cost for gaining from the immunized witness evidence that will permit prosecution of the high-level participants. Also, immunity may be used for prospective witnesses who have only an incidental relationship to the enterprise which probably would not justify their prosecution but would allow them to refuse to testify on the basis of the privilege if not given immunity.

Desiring to keep the advantages of investigation by subpoena, but to eliminate the element of lay participation in the investigation, a small group of states have created investigative alternatives to the grand jury that can make similar use of the court's subpoena authority and the grant of immunity. Several of these states allow the prosecutor to seek a judicial inquiry into possible criminal activity. The judge so designated may then conduct an investigation (commonly assisted by the local prosecutor or a specially appointed prosecutor) through the use of the subpoena power. Such judicial investigations are known in different parts of the country as "one-man grand juries" or "John Doe" proceedings. Still other states authorize the prosecutor, acting alone, to conduct investigations upon application to the court for use of its subpoena power. This authority is commonly used for investigations less extensive than those submitted to the grand jury. The witnesses in these prosecutorial "investigatory deposition" proceedings are subpoenaed to appear at the prosecutor's office (with counsel, if they so choose), where they will be required to testify under oath or to present documents as specified in a subpoena duces tecum. Finally, most jurisdictions have allowed the subpoena authority to be used by administrative agencies or other bodies that have the responsibility for investigating possible infractions of civil laws, including those

---

d. But consider *Zurcher v. Stanford Daily*,   Ch. 3, § 2.

that may overlap with criminal offenses. Thus, one of the main cases in section two, *Fisher v. United States,* involves an Internal Revenue Service summons that is basically a subpoena duces tecum.

The investigation by subpoena, whether conducted through a grand jury or an alternative agency, is not without constitutional limitations. The cases presented in this chapter deal with the most significant of those limitations.

SECTION 1. FOURTH AMENDMENT LIMITATIONS

The first case in this section, *Boyd v. United States,* is a widely celebrated case, once described by Justice Brandeis as a case "that will be remembered as long as civil liberty lives in the United States." *Olmstead v. United States,* 277 U.S. 438 (1928) (dissent). Although *Boyd* involved an order to produce documents at trial, its reasoning clearly encompassed as well a subpoena issued in the course of an investigatory setting. While one could contend that *Boyd* today constitutes no more than a "historic relic," a false start in the application to subpoenas of both the Fourth Amendment and the Fifth Amendment's self-incrimination clause, the *Boyd* opinion continues to be cited by the Supreme Court and its analysis continues to be treated as at least demanding reexamination, if not application. The *Fisher* and *Doe* cases, contained in the next section, reexamine the self-incrimination aspects of the *Boyd* analysis. The *Dionisio* opinion in this section considers the scope of the Fourth Amendment's application to subpoenas in light of post-*Boyd* precedent.[a]

BOYD v. UNITED STATES
116 U.S. 616, 6 S.Ct. 524, 29 L.Ed. 746 (1886).

[Customs officials seized 35 cases of glass, imported by the partnership of Boyd and Sons, and instituted a forfeiture proceeding. That proceeding was brought under a statute providing that any importer who defrauded the government and thereby avoided payment of customs revenue was subject to fine, incarceration, and forfeiture of the imported merchandise. Utilizing an 1874 statute, the government's attorney obtained a court "notice" directing Boyd to produce an invoice covering 29 of the cases of glass. That statute authorized the trial judge, on motion of the prosecutor describing a particular document and indicating what it might prove, to issue a notice directing the importer to produce the document. The importer could refuse to produce without being held in contempt (which distinguished the notice from a subpoena) but the consequence of a failure to produce was that the allegation of the prosecution as to what the document stated was "taken as confessed."]

a. *Boyd, Dionisio,* and cases discussed therein deal only with constitutional limits upon the scope of an investigation conducted by subpoena. It should be kept in mind, however, that both state and federal courts recognize certain additional limitations that are not constitutionally based. Those limitations vary with the particular jurisdiction and are commonly tied to the use of subpoena authority by investigative grand juries. Among the limitations commonly recognized in this context are the prohibitions against the use of the grand jury subpoena to obtain evidence primarily for the purpose of developing civil suits or preparing criminal cases that have already resulted in an indictment. Several courts have also recognized witness objections to the alleged use of grand jury subpoenas to assist police investigations (as opposed to the grand jury's own investigation), and a few courts also permit objections challenging the prosecution's good faith by alleging that it is seeking information not relevant to the subject of the grand jury's investigation. Since all of these objections are based on the misuse of the grand jury for purposes other than its traditional investigatory role, and since jurisdictions generally recognize a "presumption of regularity" in the prosecution's use of the grand jury, courts traditionally impose a heavy burden on the subpoenaed party raising such objections, and the objections are not readily sustained.

[The defendants produced the invoice in compliance with the notice, but objected to the validity of the court's action, and objected again when the invoice was offered as evidence. The jury subsequently found for the United States, and a judgment of forfeiture against the 35 cases was granted.]

JUSTICE BRADLEY delivered the opinion of the Court.

* * * [I]n regard to Fourth Amendment, it is contended that * * * [the Act of 1874], under which the order in the present case was made, is free from constitutional objection, because it does not authorize the search and seizure of books and papers, but only requires the defendant or claimant to produce them. That is so; but it declares that if he does not produce them, the allegations which it is affirmed they will prove shall be taken as confessed. This is tantamount to compelling their production; for the prosecuting attorney will always be sure to state the evidence expected to be derived from them as strongly as the case will admit of. It is true that certain aggravating incidents of actual search and seizure, such as forcible entry into a man's house and searching amongst his papers, are wanting, and to this extent the proceeding under the act of 1874 is a mitigation of that which was authorized by the former acts; but it accomplishes the substantial object of those acts in forcing from a party evidence against himself. It is our opinion, therefore, that a compulsory production of a man's private papers to establish a criminal charge against him, or to forfeit his property, is within the scope of the Fourth Amendment to the Constitution, in all cases in which a search and seizure would be; because it is a material ingredient, and effects the sole object and purpose of search and seizure.

[handwritten margin note: order to produce was search + seizure]

The principal question, however, remains to be considered. Is a search and seizure, or, what is equivalent thereto, a compulsory production of a man's private papers, to be used in evidence against him in a proceeding to forfeit his property for alleged fraud against the revenue laws—is such a proceeding for such a purpose an *"unreasonable* search and seizure" within the meaning of the Fourth Amendment of the Constitution? or, is it a legitimate proceeding? * * *

[handwritten margin note: was it reasonable?]

In order to ascertain the nature of the proceedings intended by the Fourth Amendment to the Constitution under the terms "unreasonable searches and seizures," it is only necessary to recall the contemporary or then recent history of the controversies on the subject, both in this country and in England. * * * Prominent and principal among these was the practice of issuing general warrants by the Secretary of State, for searching private houses for the discovery and seizure of books and papers that might be used to convict their owner of the charge of libel. * * * The case, * * * which will always be celebrated as being the occasion of Lord Camden's memorable discussion of the subject, was that of *Entick v. Carrington and Three Other King's Messengers* * * *. The action was trespass for entering the plaintiff's dwelling-house in November, 1762, and breaking open his desks, boxes, &c., and searching and examining his papers. The jury rendered a special verdict, and the case was twice solemnly argued at the bar. Lord Camden pronounced the judgment of the court in Michaelmas Term, 1765, and the law as expounded by him has been regarded as settled from that time to this, and his great judgment on that occasion is considered as one of the landmarks of English liberty. It was welcomed and applauded by the lovers of liberty in the colonies as well as in the mother country. It is regarded as one of the permanent monuments of the British Constitution, and is quoted as such by the English authorities on that subject down to the present time. As every American statesmen, during our revolutionary and formative period as a nation, was undoubtedly familiar with this monument of English freedom, and considered it as the true and ultimate expression of constitutional law, it may be confidently asserted that its propositions were in the minds of those who framed the Fourth Amendment to the Constitution, and were considered as sufficiently explanatory of what was meant by unreasonable searches and seizures. * * *

After describing the power claimed by the Secretary of State for issuing general search warrants, and the manner in which they were executed, Lord Camden says [in *Entick*]:

> * * * Papers are the owner's goods and chattels; they are his dearest property; and are so far from enduring a seizure, that they will hardly bear an inspection; and though the eye cannot by the laws of England be guilty of a trespass, yet where private papers are removed and carried away the secret nature of those goods will be an aggravation of the trespass, and demand more considerable damages in that respect. Where is the written law that gives any magistrate such a power? I can safely answer, there is none; and therefore, it is too much for us, without such authority, to pronounce a practice legal which would be subversive of all the comforts of society. * * *

> Lastly, it is urged as an argument of utility, that such a search is a means of detecting offenders by discovering evidence. I wish some cases had been shown, where the law forceth evidence out of the owner's custody by process. There is no process against papers in civil causes. It has been often tried, but never prevailed. Nay, where the adversary has by force or fraud got possession of your own proper evidence, there is no way to get it back but by action. In the criminal law such a proceeding was never heard of; and yet there are some crimes, such, for instance, as murder, rape, robbery, and house-breaking, to say nothing of forgery and perjury, that are more atrocious than libelling. But our law has provided no paper-search in these cases to help forward the conviction. Whether this proceedeth from the gentleness of the law towards criminals, or from a consideration that such a power would be more pernicious to the innocent than useful to the public, I will not say. It is very certain that the law obligeth no man to accuse himself; because the necessary means of compelling self-accusation, falling upon the innocent as well as the guilty, would be both cruel and unjust; and it would seem, that search for evidence is disallowed upon the same principle. Then, too, the innocent would be confounded with the guilty.

* * * The principles laid down in this opinion affect the very essence of constitutional liberty and security. They reach farther than the concrete form of the case then before the court, with its adventitious circumstances; they apply to all invasions on the part of the government and its employees of the sanctity of a man's home and the privacies of life. It is not the breaking of his doors, and the rummaging of his drawers, that constitutes the essence of the offence; but it is the invasion of his indefeasible right of personal security, personal liberty and private property, where that right has never been forfeited by his conviction of some public offence,—it is the invasion of this sacred right which underlies and constitutes the essence of Lord Camden's judgment. Breaking into a house and opening boxes and drawers are circumstances of aggravation; but any forcible and compulsory extortion of a man's own testimony or of his private papers to be used as evidence to convict him of crime or to forfeit his goods, is within the condemnation of that judgment. In this regard the Fourth and Fifth Amendments run almost into each other. * * *

We have already noticed the intimate relation between the two amendments. They throw great light on each other. For the "unreasonable searches and seizures" condemned in the Fourth Amendment are almost always made for the purpose of compelling a man to give evidence against himself, which in criminal cases is condemned in the Fifth Amendment; and compelling a man "in a criminal case to be a witness against himself," which is condemned in the Fifth Amendment, throws light on the question as to what is an "unreasonable search and seizure" within the meaning of the Fourth Amendment. And we have been unable to perceive that the seizure of a man's private books and papers to be used in evidence against him is substantially different from compelling him to be a witness against himself. * * * We are also clearly of opinion that proceedings instituted for the purpose of declaring the forfeiture of a man's property by reason of offences committed by him, though they may be civil in form, are in their nature criminal. In this very case, the ground of forfeiture * * * consists of certain acts of fraud committed against the public revenue in relation to imported merchandise, which are made criminal by the statute * * *. As, therefore, suits for penalties and forfeitures incurred by the commission of offences against the law, are of this quasi-criminal nature, we think that they are within the reason of criminal proceedings for all the purposes of the Fourth Amendment of the Constitution, and of that portion of the Fifth Amendment which declares that no person shall be compelled in any criminal case to be a witness against himself; and we are further of opinion that a compulsory production of the private books and papers of the owner of goods sought to be forfeited in such a suit is compelling him to be a witness against himself, within the meaning of the Fifth Amendment to the Constitution, and is the equivalent of a search and seizure—and an unreasonable search and seizure—within the meaning of the Fourth Amendment.

Though the proceeding in question is divested of many of the aggravating incidents of actual search and seizure, yet, as before said, it contains their substance and essence, and effects their substantial purpose. It may be that it is the obnoxious thing in its mildest and least repulsive form; but illegitimate and unconstitutional practices get their first footing in that way, namely, by silent approaches and slight deviations from legal modes of procedure. This can only be obviated by adhering to the rule that constitutional provisions for the security of person and property should be liberally construed. A close and literal construction deprives them of half their efficacy, and leads to gradual depreciation of the right, as if it consisted more in sound than in substance. It is the duty of courts to be watchful for the constitutional rights of the citizen, and against any stealthy encroachments thereon. Their motto should be *obsta principiis*. * * *

JUSTICE MILLER, with whom was THE CHIEF JUSTICE concurring:

I concur in the judgment of the court * * * and in so much of the opinion of this court as holds the 5th section of the act of 1874 void as applicable to the present case. * * * The order of the court under the statute is in effect a subpoena duces tecum, and, though the penalty for the witness's failure to appear in court with the criminating papers is not fine and imprisonment, it is one which may be made more severe, namely, to have charges against him of a criminal nature, taken for confessed, and made the foundation of the judgment of the court. That this is within the protection which the Constitution intended against compelling a person to be a witness against himself, is, I think, quite clear.

But this being so, there is no reason why this court should assume that the action of the court below, in requiring a party to produce certain papers as evidence on the trial, authorizes an unreasonable search or seizure of the house, papers, or effects of that party. There is in fact no search and no seizure authorized by the statute. No order can be made by the court under it which requires or permits anything more than service of notice on a party to the suit. * * *

Nothing in the nature of a search is here hinted at. Nor is there any seizure, because the party is not required at any time to part with the custody of the papers. They are to be produced in court, and, when produced, the United States attorney is permitted, under the direction of the court, to make examination in presence of the claimant, and may offer in evidence such entries in the books, invoices, or papers as relate to the issue. The act is careful to say that "the owner of said books and papers, his agent or attorney, shall have, subject to the order of the court, the custody of them, except pending their examination in court as aforesaid." * * *

The things * * * forbidden [by the Fourth Amendment] are two—search and seizure. * * * But what search does this statute authorize? If the mere service of a notice to produce a paper to be used as evidence, which the party can obey or not as he chooses is a search, then a change has taken place in the meaning of words, which has not come within my reading, and which I think was unknown at the time the Constitution was made. The searches meant by the Constitution were such as led to seizure when the search was successful. But the statute in this case uses language carefully framed to forbid any seizure under it, as I have already pointed out. * * * a

UNITED STATES v. DIONISIO

410 U.S. 1, 93 S.Ct. 764, 35 L.Ed.2d 67 (1973).

JUSTICE STEWART delivered the opinion of the Court.

A special grand jury was convened * * * to investigate possible violations of federal criminal statutes relating to gambling. In the course of its investigation the grand jury received in evidence certain voice recordings that had been obtained pursuant to court orders. The grand jury subpoenaed approximately 20 persons, including the respondent Dionisio, seeking to obtain from them voice exemplars for comparison with the recorded conversations that had been received in evidence. Each witness was advised that he was a potential defendant in a criminal prosecution. Each was asked to examine a transcript of an intercepted

---

a. Insofar as *Boyd* suggested that the Fourth Amendment prohibited searches for property the defendant was entitled to possess (i.e., property other than the fruits or instrumentalities of crime), that aspect of *Boyd* was flatly rejected in *Warden v. Hayden,* 387 U.S. 294 (1967). Insofar as *Boyd* read the Fourth Amendment as prohibiting a search for documents, that interpretation was overturned in *Andresen v. Maryland,* 427 U.S. 463 (1976) (see Ch. 3, § 2). But long before these rulings, the Court restructured *Boyd*'s view of the bearing of the Fourth Amendment upon a subpoena duces tecum. In *Hale v. Henkel,* 201 U.S. 43 (1906), the Court had before it a challenge to a subpoena directing the petitioner to produce before a grand jury (which was conducting an investigation into possible violations of the antitrust laws) various corporate documents. Petitioner's challenge was based on the combined impact of the Fourth and Fifth Amendments, but the Court initially separated those claims. Cases subsequent to *Boyd,* it noted, had "treated the Fourth and Fifth Amendments as quite distinct, having different histories, and performing separate

functions." Turning first to the petitioner's self-incrimination claim, the Court found that claim clearly failed since the statute authorizing the subpoena granted petitioner immunity from prosecution and the corporation itself had no self-incrimination privilege (see § 2 infra). The petitioner's Fourth Amendment claim did have merit, but for reasons other than what might have been assumed from *Boyd.* A subpoena compelling the production of documents violated the Fourth Amendment only where it was "far too sweeping in its terms to be regarded as reasonable." That was true here as the subpoena required production of a vast range of documents, covering a lengthy period, making it even questionable how the corporation could continue to carry on its business "after it had been denuded of this mass of material." In *See v. City of Seattle,* 387 U.S. 541 (1967), the Fourth Amendment limitation set forth in *Hale* was described as "requir[ing] that the subpoena be sufficiently limited in scope, relevant in purpose, and specific in directive so that compliance will not be unreasonably burdened."

conversation, and to go to a nearby office of the United States Attorney to read the transcript into a recording device. The witnesses were advised that they would be allowed to have their attorneys present when they read the transcripts. Dionisio and other witnesses refused to furnish the voice exemplars, asserting that these disclosures would violate their rights under the Fourth and Fifth Amendments. The Government then filed separate petitions in the District Court to compel Dionisio and the other witnesses to furnish the voice exemplars to the grand jury. * * * Following a hearing, the district judge rejected the witnesses' constitutional arguments and ordered them to comply with the grand jury's request. * * * When Dionisio persisted in his refusal to respond to the grand jury's directive, the District Court adjudged him in civil contempt and ordered him committed to custody. * * *

The Court of Appeals for the Seventh Circuit reversed. * * * The court found that the Fourth Amendment applied to the grand jury process * * *. Equating the procedures followed by the grand jury in the present case to the fingerprint detentions in *Davis v. Mississippi* [Ch. 3, § 7], the Court of Appeals reasoned that "[t]he dragnet effect here, where approximately 30 persons were subpoenaed for purposes of identification, has the same invidious effect on fourth amendment rights as the practice condemned in *Davis*." The Court of Appeals held that the Fourth Amendment required a preliminary showing of reasonableness before a grand jury witness could be compelled to furnish a voice exemplar, and that in this case the proposed "seizures" of the voice exemplars would be unreasonable because of the large number of witnesses summoned by the grand jury and directed to produce such exemplars. We disagree. * * *

[T]he obtaining of physical evidence from a person involves a potential Fourth Amendment violation at two different levels—the "seizure" of the "person" necessary to bring him into contact with government agents, see *Davis v. Mississippi,* and the subsequent search for and seizure of the evidence. * * * The constitutionality of the compulsory production of exemplars from a grand jury witness necessarily turns on the same dual inquiry—whether either the initial compulsion of the person to appear before the grand jury, or the subsequent directive to make a voice recording is an unreasonable "seizure" within the meaning of the Fourth Amendment.

It is clear that a subpoena to appear before a grand jury is not a "seizure" in the Fourth Amendment sense, even though that summons may be inconvenient or burdensome. Last Term we again acknowledged what has long been recognized, that "[c]itizens generally are not constitutionally immune from grand jury subpoenas. * * *" *Branzburg v. Hayes* [408 U.S. 665 (1972)].[a] * * * [*Branzburg* and other decisions] are recent reaffirmations of the historically grounded obligations of every person to appear and give his evidence before the grand jury. "The personal sacrifice involved is a part of the necessary contribution of the individual to the welfare of the public." *Blair v. United States,* 250 U.S. 273 (1919).

The compulsion exerted by a grand jury subpoena differs from the seizure effected by an arrest or even an investigative "stop" in more than civic obligation. For, as Judge Friendly wrote for the Court of Appeals for the Second Circuit:

---

a. The Court in *Branzburg* rejected a First Amendment claim raised by reporters who had been subpoenaed to testify before grand juries. The reporters had argued that they should not be compelled to reveal the identity of confidential sources or relevant facts obtained from those sources, at least absent an initial showing by the grand jury of a "compelling need" to obtain such information. The Court majority responded that it was "unclear" whether requiring the reporters to testify before the grand jury might have a negative impact on their future newsgathering capacity, but, in any event, that impact did not outweigh the interest of the public in the grand jury's unencumbered investigation of crime.

"The latter is abrupt, is effected with force or the threat of it and often in demeaning circumstances, and, in the case of arrest, results in a record involving social stigma. A subpoena is served in the same manner as other legal process; it involves no stigma whatever; if the time for appearance is inconvenient, this can generally be altered; and it remains at all times under the control and supervision of a court."

Thus, the Court of Appeals for the Seventh Circuit correctly recognized in a case subsequent to the one now before us, that a "grand jury subpoena to testify is not that kind of governmental intrusion on privacy against which the Fourth Amendment affords protection, once the Fifth Amendment is satisfied."

This case is thus quite different from *Davis v. Mississippi,* on which the Court of Appeals primarily relied. For in *Davis* it was the initial seizure—the lawless dragnet detention—that violated the Fourth and Fourteenth Amendments—not the taking of the fingerprints. * * * *Davis* is plainly inapposite to a case where the initial restraint does not itself infringe the Fourth Amendment.

This is not to say that a grand jury subpoena is some talisman that dissolves all constitutional protections. The grand jury cannot require a witness to testify against himself. It cannot require the production by a person of private books and records that would incriminate him. See *Boyd v. United States.* The Fourth Amendment provides protection against a grand jury subpoena *duces tecum* too sweeping in its terms "to be regarded as reasonable." *Hale v. Henkel.* And last Term, in the context of a First Amendment claim, we indicated that the Constitution could not tolerate the transformation of the grand jury into an instrument of oppression: "Official harassment of the press undertaken not for purposes of law enforcement but to disrupt a reporter's relationship with his news sources would have no justification. Grand juries are subject to judicial control and subpoenas to motions to quash. We do not expect courts will forget that grand juries must operate within the limits of the First Amendment as well as the Fifth." *Branzburg v. Hayes.*

But we are here faced with no such constitutional infirmities in the subpoena to appear before the grand jury or in the order to make the voice recordings. There is * * * no valid Fifth Amendment claim. There was no order to produce private books and papers, and no sweeping subpoena *duces tecum.* And even if *Branzburg* be extended beyond its First Amendment moorings and tied to a more generalized due process concept, there is still no indication in this case of the kind of harassment that was of concern there.

The Court of Appeals found critical significance in the fact that the grand jury had summoned approximately 20 witnesses to furnish voice exemplars. We think that fact is basically irrelevant to the constitutional issues here. The grand jury may have been attempting to identify a number of voices on the tapes in evidence, or it might have summoned the 20 witnesses in an effort to identify one voice. But whatever the case, "[a] grand jury's investigation is not fully carried out until every available clue has been run down and all witnesses examined in every proper way to find if a crime has been committed." * * * The grand jury may well find it desirable to call numerous witnesses in the course of an investigation. It does not follow that each witness may resist a subpoena on the ground that too many witnesses have been called. Neither the order to Dionisio to appear, nor the order to make a voice recording was rendered unreasonable by the fact that many others were subjected to the same compulsion.

But the conclusion that Dionisio's compulsory appearance before the grand jury was not an unreasonable "seizure" is the answer to only the first part of the Fourth Amendment inquiry here. Dionisio argues that the grand jury's subsequent directive to make the voice recording was itself an infringement of his rights under the Fourth Amendment. We cannot accept that argument. In *Katz v. United States* [Ch. 3, § 1], we said that the Fourth Amendment provides no protection for what "a person knowingly exposes to the public, even in his home or office * * *." The physical characteristics of a person's voice, its tone and manner, as opposed to the content of a specific conversation, are constantly exposed to the public. Like a man's facial characteristics, or handwriting, his voice is repeatedly produced for others to hear. No person can have a reasonable expectation that others will not know the sound of his voice, any more than he can reasonably expect that his face will be a mystery to the world.   * * *

Since neither the summons to appear before the grand jury, nor its directive to make a voice recording infringed upon any interest protected by the Fourth Amendment, there was no justification for requiring the grand jury to satisfy even the minimal requirement of "reasonableness" imposed by the Court of Appeals. A grand jury has broad investigative powers to determine whether a crime has been committed and who has committed it. The jurors may act on tips, rumors, evidence offered by the prosecutor, or their own personal knowledge. *Branzburg v. Hayes.* No grand jury witness is "entitled to set limits to the investigation that the grand jury may conduct." And a sufficient basis for an indictment may only emerge at the end of the investigation when all the evidence has been received. * * * Since Dionisio raised no valid Fourth Amendment claim, there is no more reason to require a preliminary showing of reasonableness here than there would be in the case of any witness who, despite the lack of any constitutional or statutory privilege, declined to answer a question or comply with a grand jury request. Neither the Constitution nor our prior cases justify any such interference with grand jury proceedings.[14]

The Fifth Amendment guarantees that no civilian may be brought to trial for an infamous crime "unless on a presentment or indictment of a Grand Jury." This constitutional guarantee presupposes an investigative body "acting independently of either prosecuting attorney or judge," whose mission is to clear the innocent, no less than to bring to trial those who may be guilty. Any holding that would saddle a grand jury with minitrials and preliminary showing would assuredly impede its investigation and frustrate the public's interest in the fair and expeditious administration of the criminal laws. The grand jury may not always serve its historic role as a protective bulwark standing solidly between the ordinary citizen and an overzealous prosecutor, but if it is even to approach the proper performance of its constitutional mission, it must be free to pursue its investigations unhindered by external influence or supervision so long as it does not trench upon the legitimate rights of any witness called before it.   * * *

JUSTICE MARSHALL, dissenting.[b]

* * * There can be no question that investigatory seizures effected by the police are subject to the constraints of the Fourth and Fourteenth Amendments. *Davis v. Mississippi.* * * * Like *Davis,* the present cases involve official investigatory seizures which interfere with personal liberty. The Court considers

---

14. Mr. Justice Marshall in dissent suggests that a preliminary showing of "reasonableness" is required where the grand jury subpoenas a witness to appear and produce handwriting or voice exemplars, but not when it subpoenas him to appear and testify. Such a distinction finds no support in the Constitution. The dissent argues that there is a potential Fourth Amendment violation in the case of a subpoenaed grand jury witness because of the asserted intrusiveness of the initial subpoena to appear—the possible stigma from a grand jury appearance and the inconvenience of the official restraint. But the initial directive to appear is as intrusive if the witness is called simply to testify as it is if he is summoned to produce physical evidence.

b. The separate dissents of Justices Douglas and Brennan are omitted.

dispositive, however, the fact that the seizures were effected by the grand jury, rather than the police. I cannot agree. * * * [I]n *Hale v. Henkel,* the Court held that a subpoena *duces tecum* ordering "the production of books and papers [before a grand jury] may constitute an unreasonable search and seizure within the Fourth Amendment," and on the particular facts of the case, it concluded that the subpoena was "far too sweeping in its terms to be regarded as reasonable." Considered alone, *Hale* would certainly seem to carry a strong implication that a subpoena compelling an individual's personal appearance before a grand jury, like a subpoena ordering the production of private papers, is subject to the Fourth Amendment standard of reasonableness. The protection of the Fourth Amendment is not, after all, limited to personal "papers," but extends also to "persons," "houses," and "effects." It would seem a strange hierarchy of constitutional values that would afford papers more protection from arbitrary governmental intrusion than people.

The Court, however, offers two interrelated justifications for excepting grand jury subpoenas directed at "persons," rather than "papers," from the constraints of the Fourth Amendment. These are an "historically grounded obligation of every person to appear and give his evidence before the grand jury," and the relative unintrusiveness of the grand jury subpoena on an individual's liberty.

In my view, the Court makes more of history than is justified. The Court treats the "historically grounded obligation" which it now discerns as extending to all "evidence," whatever its character. Yet, so far as I am aware, the obligation "to appear and give evidence" has heretofore been applied by this Court only in the context of testimonial evidence, either oral or documentary. * * * In the present case, * * * it was not testimony that the grand jury sought from respondents, but physical evidence. * * *

The Court seems to reason that the exception to the Fourth Amendment for grand jury subpoenas directed at persons is justified by the relative unintrusiveness of the grand jury process on an individual's liberty. * * * It may be that service of a grand jury subpoena does not involve the same potential for momentary embarrassment as does an arrest or investigatory "stop." But this difference seems inconsequential in comparison to the substantial stigma which—contrary to the Court's assertion—may result from a grand jury appearance as well as from an arrest or investigatory seizure. Public knowledge that a man has been summoned by a federal grand jury investigating, for instance, organized criminal activity can mean loss of friends, irreparable injury to business, and tremendous pressures on one's family life. Whatever nice legal distinctions may be drawn between police and prosecutor, on the one hand, and the grand jury, on the other, the public often treats an appearance before a grand jury as tantamount to a visit to the station house. Indeed, the former is frequently more damaging than the latter, for a grand jury appearance has an air of far greater gravity than a brief visit "downtown" for a "talk." The Fourth Amendment was placed in our Bill of Rights to protect the individual citizen from such potentially disruptive governmental intrusion into his private life unless conducted reasonably and with sufficient cause.

Nor do I believe that the constitutional problems inherent in such governmental interference with an individual's person are substantially alleviated because one may seek to appear at a "convenient time." In *Davis v. Mississippi,* it was recognized that an investigatory detention effected by the police "need not come unexpectedly or at an inconvenient time." But this fact did not suggest to the Court that the Fourth Amendment was inapplicable * * *. No matter how considerate a grand jury may be in arranging for an individual's appearance, the basic fact remains that his liberty has been officially restrained for some period of time. In terms of its effect on the individual, this restraint does not differ meaningfully from the restraint imposed on a suspect compelled to visit the police station house. Thus, the nature of the intrusion on personal liberty caused by a grand jury subpoena cannot, without more, be considered sufficient basis for denying respondents the protection of the Fourth Amendment.

Of course, the Fourth Amendment does not bar all official seizures of the person, but only those that are unreasonable and are without sufficient cause. With this in mind, it is possible at least to explain, if not justify, the failure to apply the protection of the Fourth Amendment to grand jury subpoenas requiring individuals to appear and *testify*. Thus, while it is true that we have traditionally given the grand jury broad investigatory powers, particularly in terms of compelling the appearance of persons before it, it must be understood that we have done so in heavy reliance on certain essential assumptions.

Certainly the most celebrated function of the grand jury is to stand between the Government and the citizen and thus to protect the latter from harassment and unfounded prosecution. The grand jury does not shed those characteristics which give it insulating qualities when it acts in its investigative capacity. Properly functioning, the grand jury is to be the servant of neither the Government nor the courts, but of the people. As such, we assume that it comes to its task without bias or self-interest. Unlike the prosecutor or policeman, it has no election to win or executive appointment to keep. The anticipated neutrality of the grand jury, even when acting in its investigative capacity, may perhaps be relied upon to prevent unwarranted interference with the lives of private citizens and to ensure that the grand jury's subpoena powers over the person are exercised in only a reasonable fashion. Under such circumstances, it may be justifiable to give the grand jury broad personal subpoena powers that are outside the purview of the Fourth Amendment, for—in contrast to the police—it is not likely that it will abuse those powers.

Whatever the present day validity of the historical assumption of neutrality which underlies the grand jury process, it must at least be recognized that if a grand jury is deprived of the independence essential to the assumption of neutrality—if it effectively surrenders that independence to a prosecutor—the dangers of excessive and unreasonable official interference with personal liberty are exactly those which the Fourth Amendment was intended to prevent. So long as the grand jury carries on its investigatory activities only through the mechanism of testimonial inquiries, the danger of such official usurpation of the grand jury process may not be unreasonably great. Individuals called to testify before the grand jury will have available their Fifth Amendment privilege against self-incrimination. Thus, at least insofar as incriminating information is sought directly from a particular criminal suspect, the grand jury process would not appear to offer law enforcement officials a substantial advantage over ordinary investigative techniques.

But when we move beyond the realm of grand jury investigations limited to testimonial inquiries, as the Court does today, the danger increases that law enforcement officials may seek to usurp the grand jury process for the purpose of securing incriminating evidence from a particular suspect through the simple expedient of a subpoena. * * * Thus, if the grand jury may summon criminal suspects [to obtain handwriting and voice exemplars] without complying with the Fourth Amendment, it will obviously present an attractive investigative tool to prosecutor and police. For what law enforcement officers could not accomplish directly themselves after our decision in *Davis v. Mississippi*, they may now accomplish indirectly through the grand jury process.

Thus, the Court's decisions today can serve only to encourage prosecutorial exploitation of the grand jury process, at the expense of both individual liberty and the traditional neutrality of the grand jury. * * * [B]y holding that the grand jury's power to subpoena these respondents for the purpose of obtaining exemplars is completely outside the purview of the Fourth Amendment, the Court fails to appreciate the essential difference between real and testimonial evidence in the context of these cases, and thereby hastens the reduction of the grand jury into simply another investigative device of law enforcement officials. By contrast, the Court of Appeals, in proper recognition of these dangers, imposed narrow limitations on the subpoena power of the grand jury which are necessary to guard against unreasonable official interference with individual liberty but which would not impair significantly the traditional investigatory powers of that body. * * *

SECTION 2. THE PRIVILEGE AGAINST SELF–INCRIMINATION

A person subpoenaed in connection with a grand jury or any other criminal investigation has available all of the evidentiary privileges available to witnesses in general (i.e., the right, at the witness' option, to refuse to provide information where the law designates that information as "privileged" and therefore free from compelled disclosure). In this context, clearly the most significant privilege is that guaranteed by the Fifth Amendment of the Constitution—the privilege against compulsory self-incrimination.[a] The Fifth Amendment states that no person "shall be compelled in any criminal case to be a witness against himself." The self-incrimination clause has an extensive common law background, and it was with respect to the interpretation of this clause that Justice Frankfurter once noted that "a page of history is worth a volume of logic." *Ullmann v. United States,* 350 U.S. 422 (1956) (concurring). Yet the Court also has frequently cited the important and diverse values underlying the privilege [b] and noted the need to give the privilege a construction "as broad as the mischief against which it seeks to guard." *Counselman v. Hitchcock,* 142 U.S. 547 (1892).[c]

a. The other privileges that witnesses may raise as a grounding for refusing to disclose information ordinarily flow from the law of the particular jurisdiction, and therefore will vary in scope from one state to another. These include such privileges as the marital privilege (protecting at least the confidential communications between spouses), the doctor/patient privilege (protecting information passed between doctor and patient that is germane to treatment or consultation), and the lawyer/client privilege (protecting, with some exceptions, communications of clients to lawyers for the purpose of legal consultation). While all of these may arise in the grand jury context, none rivals the self-incrimination privilege either as to the frequency with which it arises or its practical significance.

b. The most frequently cited statement of those values comes from Justice Goldberg's opinion for the Court in *Murphy v. Waterfront Commission,* 378 U.S. 52 (1964), a case discussed infra in the *Kastigar* opinion. That opinion stated: "The privilege against self-incrimination * * * reflects many of our fun-

damental values and most noble aspirations: our unwillingness to subject those suspected of crime to the cruel trilemma of self-accusation, perjury or contempt; our preference for an accusatorial rather than an inquisitorial system of criminal justice; our fear that self-incriminating statements will be elicited by inhumane treatment and abuses; our sense of fair play which dictates 'a fair state-individual balance by requiring the government to leave the individual alone until good cause is shown for disturbing him and by requiring the government in its contest with the individual to shoulder the entire load'; our respect for the inviolability of the human personality and the right of each individual 'to a private enclave where he may lead a private life'; our distrust of self-deprecatory statements; and our realization that the privilege, while sometimes 'a shelter to the guilty,' is often 'a protection to the innocent.'"

c. *Counselman* accordingly concluded that the privilege went beyond granting a defendant the right not to testify in his own criminal

The first two cases in this section deal with the relinquishment of the privilege against self-incrimination by a grand jury witness. The *Rogers* case treats the issue of waiver through partial disclosure. *Mandujano* raises, but does not resolve by a majority decision, the question of whether there can be a waiver without first advising the grand jury witness of his rights and offering access to counsel, where the witness is one who may be viewed as a "target" of the investigation. Following the *Mandujano* decision, the Justice Department issued an internal guideline on federal grand jury practice which requires prosecutors to give the following notification to all grand jury witnesses: (1) "that the witness may refuse to answer any question if a truthful answer to the question would tend to incriminate him," (2) "that anything that the witness does say may be used against him," and (3) "that the grand jury will permit the witness the reasonable opportunity to step outside the grand jury room to consult with counsel if he desires." Warnings relating to the self-incrimination privilege are commonly used in state grand jury proceedings as well. As to consulting with counsel, most states follow the federal practice, but a small number of states allow the witness to be assisted by counsel located within the grand jury room and several of these provide for appointment of counsel at the state's expense where the witness is indigent.

The *Kastigar* case treats the important practice of providing to the witness a grant of immunity that precludes reliance upon the privilege. Following that decision, many states moved from transactional immunity grants to the use/derivative-use grant upheld in *Kastigar*, but a fair number of states still provide transactional immunity.

The last two cases in this section, *Fisher* and *Braswell*, return to the issue first raised in *Boyd*—the availability of the privilege in responding to a subpoena duces tecum requiring the production of documents. As noted in these cases, the Court had earlier held that the privilege was not available to a corporation or similar entity, such as a partnership. Thus, as the Court notes in *Fisher*, A.E. Boyd and Sons, a partnership, would not have the privilege available to it today to contest a subpoena requiring production of its records. The question presented in *Fisher* is the extent to which the privilege applies (and *Boyd* survives) as to a subpoena directing production of the papers of an individual. *Braswell* considers whether, in light of *Fisher*'s analysis, an agent of an entity may assert his personal privilege in response to a subpoena directing him personally to produce entity records.

ROGERS v. UNITED STATES

340 U.S. 367, 71 S.Ct. 438, 95 L.Ed. 344 (1951).

CHIEF JUSTICE VINSON delivered the opinion of the Court.

This case arises out of an investigation by the regularly convened grand jury of the United States District Court for the District of Colorado. The books and records of the Communist Party of Denver were sought as necessary to that inquiry and were the subject of questioning by the grand jury. In September, 1948, petitioner, in response to a subpoena, appeared before the grand jury. She testified that she held the position of Treasurer of the Communist Party of Denver

case. The Fifth Amendment prohibition against compelling testimony "in a criminal case," the Court noted, referred to the eventual use of the compelled testimony in a criminal case, not to the type of proceeding in which the testimony was first compelled. The Fifth Amendment privilege therefore was available to a witness in "any proceeding" who is being compelled to give testimony that might be used as incriminating evidence in a subsequent criminal case. *Counselman* itself involved a witness before a grand jury.

until January, 1948, and that, by virtue of her office, she had been in possession of membership lists and dues records of the Party. Petitioner denied having possession of the records and testified that she had turned them over to another. But she refused to identify the person to whom she had given the Party's books, stating to the court as her only reason: "I don't feel that I should subject a person or persons to the same thing that I'm going through." The court thereupon committed petitioner to the custody of the marshal until ten o'clock the next morning, expressly advising petitioner of her right to consult with counsel.

The next day, counsel for petitioner informed the court that he had read the transcript of the prior day's proceedings and that, upon his advice, petitioner would answer the questions to purge herself of contempt. However, upon reappearing before the grand jury, petitioner again refused to answer the question. The following day she was again brought into court. Called before the district judge immediately after he had heard oral argument concerning the privilege against self-incrimination in another case, petitioner repeated her refusal to answer the question, asserting this time the privilege against self-incrimination. After ruling that her refusal was not privileged, the district judge imposed a sentence of four months for contempt. The Court of Appeals for the Tenth Circuit affirmed, and we granted certiorari.

* * * [T]he decisions of this Court are explicit in holding that the privilege against self-incrimination "is solely for the benefit of the witness," and "is purely a personal privilege of the witness." Petitioner expressly placed her original declination to answer on an untenable ground, since a refusal to answer cannot be justified by a desire to protect others from punishment, much less to protect another from interrogation by a grand jury. Petitioner's claim of the privilege against self-incrimination was pure afterthought. Although the claim was made at the time of her second refusal to answer in the presence of the court, it came only after she had voluntarily testified to her status as an officer of the Communist Party of Denver. To uphold a claim of privilege in this case would open the way to distortion of facts by permitting a witness to select any stopping place in the testimony. * * *

In *Patricia Blau v. United States*, 340 U.S. 159 (1950), we held that questions as to connections with the Communist Party are subject to the privilege against self-incrimination as calling for disclosure of facts tending to criminate under the Smith Act.[a] But petitioner's conviction stands on an entirely different footing, for she had freely described her membership, activities and office in the Party. Since the privilege against self-incrimination presupposes a real danger of legal detriment arising from the disclosure, petitioner cannot invoke the privilege where response to the specific question in issue here would not further incriminate her. Disclosure of a fact waives the privilege as to details. As this Court stated in *Brown v. Walker*, 161 U.S. 591 (1896):

> "Thus, if the witness himself elects to waive his privilege, as he may doubtless do, since the privilege is for his protection and not for that of other parties, and discloses his criminal connections, he is not permitted to stop, but must go on and make a full disclosure."

a. The Smith Act made it a crime to advocate the overthrow of the government by force or violence or to become a member of a group which advocates such overthrow with knowledge of that purpose. The Court in *Blau* noted that it was "immaterial" whether a witness' admission of "employment by the Communist Party or intimate knowledge of its workings" would in itself support a criminal conviction; such admissions surely "would have furnished a link in the chain of evidence needed in a prosecution of petitioner for violation of (or conspiracy to violate) the Smith Act" and that was sufficient, under longstanding Fifth Amendment precedent, to "give a witness the privilege of remaining silent."

* * * Requiring full disclosure of details after a witness freely testifies as to a criminating fact does not rest upon a further "waiver" of the privilege against self-incrimination. Admittedly, petitioner had already "waived" her privilege of silence when she freely answered criminating questions relating to her connection with the Communist Party. But when petitioner was asked to furnish the name of the person to whom she turned over Party records, the court was required to determine, as it must whenever the privilege is claimed, whether the question presented a reasonable danger of further crimination in light of all the circumstances, including any previous disclosures. As to each question to which a claim of privilege is directed, the court must determine whether the answer to that particular question would subject the witness to a "real danger" of further crimination. After petitioner's admission that she held the office of Treasurer of the Communist Party of Denver, disclosure of acquaintance with her successor presents no more than a "mere imaginary possibility" of increasing the danger of prosecution. * * *

JUSTICE CLARK took no part in the consideration or decision of this case.

JUSTICE BLACK, with whom JUSTICE FRANKFURTER and JUSTICE DOUGLAS concur, dissenting.

Some people are hostile to the Fifth Amendment's provision unequivocally commanding that no United States official shall compel a person to be a witness against himself. They consider the provision as an outmoded relic of past fears generated by ancient inquisitorial practices that could not possibly happen here. For this reason the privilege to be silent is sometimes accepted as being more or less of a constitutional nuisance which the courts should abate whenever and however possible. Such an end could be achieved by two obvious judicial techniques: (1) narrow construction of the scope of the privilege; (2) broad construction of the doctrine of "waiver." Any attempt to use the first of these methods, however, runs afoul of approximately 150 years of precedent. This Court has almost always construed the Amendment broadly on the view that compelling a person to convict himself of crime is "contrary to the principles of a free government" and "abhorrent to the instincts of an American"; that while such a coercive practice "may suit the purposes of despotic power * * * it cannot abide the pure atmosphere of political liberty and personal freedom." *Boyd v. United States*.

The doctrine of waiver seems to be a more palatable but equally effective device for whittling away the protection afforded by the privilege, although I think today's application of that doctrine cannot be supported by our past decisions. * * * In the case of this petitioner, there is no evidence that she intended to give up her privilege of silence concerning the persons in possession of the Communist Party records. To the contrary, the record—as set out in the Court's opinion— shows she intended to avoid answering the question on whatever ground might be available and asserted the privilege against self-incrimination at the first moment she became aware of its existence. This fact and the cases which make it crucial are ignored in the decision today.

Apparently, the Court's holding is that at some uncertain point in petitioner's testimony, regardless of her intention, admission of associations with the Communist Party automatically effected a "waiver" of her constitutional protection as to all related questions. To adopt such a rule for the privilege against self-incrimination, when other constitutional safeguards must be knowingly waived, relegates the Fifth Amendment's privilege to a second-rate position. Moreover, today's holding creates this dilemma for witnesses: On the one hand, they risk imprisonment for contempt by asserting the privilege prematurely; on the other, they might lose the privilege if they answer a single question. The Court's view makes the protection depend on timing so refined that lawyers, let alone laymen, will have difficulty in knowing when to claim it. In this very case, it never occurred to the trial judge that petitioner waived anything. And even if voluntary testimony can under some circumstances work a waiver, it did not do so here because what petitioner stated to the grand jury "standing alone did not amount to an admission of guilt or furnish clear proof of crime * * *." *Arndstein v. McCarthy,* 254 U.S. 71 (1920).

Furthermore, unlike the Court, I believe that the question which petitioner refused to answer did call for additional incriminating information. She was asked the names of the persons to whom she had turned over the Communist Party books and records. Her answer would not only have been relevant in any future prosecution of petitioner for violation of the Smith Act but also her conviction might depend on testimony of the witnesses she was thus asked to identify. For these reasons the question sought a disclosure which would have been incriminating to the highest degree. Certainly no one can say that the answer "[could not] possibly be used as a basis for, or in aid of, a criminal prosecution against the witness * * *." *Brown v. Walker,* 161 U.S. 591 (1896).
* * *

UNITED STATES v. MANDUJANO

425 U.S. 564, 96 S.Ct. 1768, 48 L.Ed.2d 212 (1976).

CHIEF JUSTICE BURGER announced the judgment of the Court in an opinion in which JUSTICE WHITE, JUSTICE POWELL, and JUSTICE REHNQUIST join.

This case presents the question whether the warnings called for by *Miranda v. Arizona* [Ch. 6, § 3], must be given to a grand jury witness who is called to testify about criminal activities in which he may have been personally involved; and, whether absent such warnings, false statements made to the grand jury must be suppressed in a prosecution for perjury based on those statements.

[In March 1973, an undercover agent received information that Mandujano was dealing in narcotics. Keeping his identity secret, the agent met Mandujano and arranged for the purchase of heroin. Mandujano received $650.00 for the purchase, but returned the same night without the heroin and refunded the money. After Mandujano failed to keep a subsequent appointment, the agent closed the investigative file and reported his contact with Mandujano to federal prosecutors. Six weeks later Mandujano was subpoenaed to testify before a special grand jury investigating the drug traffic in the local area. Before testifying, the prosecutor informed Mandujano of his general duty to answer, his right not to answer incriminatory questions, and of possible perjury liability for false answers. Mandujano was also told that he could have a lawyer outside the room with whom he could consult. When asked if he had a lawyer, Mandujano responded: "I don't have one. I don't have the money to get one."]

[During the grand jury questioning, Mandujano admitted that he had purchased heroin as recently as five months ago, but denied knowledge of the identity of any dealers, except for one street-corner source. He maintained this position notwithstanding the prosecutor's suggestion that "our information is that you can tell us more * * * than you have today." Mandujano "steadfastly denied either selling or attempting to sell heroin since the time of his conviction 15 years before." He "specifically disclaimed having discussed the sale of heroin with anyone during the preceding year and stated that he would not even try to purchase an ounce of heroin for $650.00."]

[Mandujano subsequently was indicted for attempting to distribute heroin and for willfully and knowingly making a false material declaration to the grand jury. The prosecution sought to introduce the grand jury testimony as the basis for the false declaration charge. Mandujano argued that his grand jury testimony should be suppressed since he was not given full *Miranda* warnings prior to his testimony. The District Court sustained the motion on the ground that a "putative" or "virtual" defendant was entitled to *Miranda* warnings. The Court of Appeals affirmed.]

* * * The very availability of the Fifth Amendment privilege to grand jury witnesses suggests that occasions will often arise when potentially incriminating questions will be asked in the ordinary course of the jury's investigation. * * * It is in keeping with the grand jury's historic function as a shield against arbitrary accusations to call before it persons suspected of criminal activity, so that the investigation can be complete. This is true whether the grand jury embarks upon an inquiry focused upon individuals suspected of wrongdoing, or is directed at persons suspected of no misconduct but who may be able to provide links in a chain of evidence relating to criminal conduct of others, or is centered upon broader problems of concern to society. It is entirely appropriate—indeed imperative—to summon individuals who may be able to illuminate the shadowy precincts of corruption and crime. Since the subject matter of the inquiry is crime, and often organized, systematic crime—as is true with drug traffic—it is unrealistic to assume that all of the witnesses capable of providing useful information will be pristine pillars of the community untainted by criminality. * * *

Accordingly, the witness, though possibly engaged in some criminal enterprise, can be required to answer before a grand jury, so long as there is no compulsion to answer questions that are self-incriminating * * *. The witness must invoke the privilege, however, as the "Constitution does not forbid the asking of criminative questions." *United States v. Monia,* 317 U.S., at 433 (1943) (Frankfurter, J., dissenting).

> "The [Fifth] Amendment speaks of compulsion. It does not preclude a witness from testifying voluntarily in matters which may incriminate him. If, therefore, he desires the protection of the privilege, he must claim it or he will not be considered to have been 'compelled' within the meaning of the Amendment." Id.

Absent a claim of the privilege, the duty to give testimony remains absolute.

The stage is therefore set when the question is asked. If the witness interposes his privilege, the grand jury has two choices. If the desired testimony is of marginal value, the grand jury can pursue other avenues of inquiry; if the testimony is thought sufficiently important, the grand jury can seek a judicial determination as to the bona fides of the witness' Fifth Amendment claim, in which case the witness must satisfy the presiding judge that the claim of privilege is not a subterfuge. If in fact "there is reasonable ground to apprehend danger to the witness from his being compelled to answer," the prosecutor must then determine whether the answer is of such overriding importance as to justify a grant of immunity to the witness. If immunity is sought by the prosecutor and granted by the presiding judge, the witness can then be compelled to answer, on pain of contempt, even though the testimony would implicate the witness in criminal activity. * * *

In this constitutional process of securing a witness' testimony, perjury simply has no place whatever. Perjured testimony is an obvious and flagrant affront to the basic concepts of judicial proceedings. Effective restraints against this type of egregious offense are therefore imperative. The power of subpoena, broad as it is, and the power of contempt for refusing to answer, drastic as that is—and even the solemnity of the oath—cannot insure truthful answers. Hence, Congress has made the giving of false answers a criminal act punishable by severe penalties; in no other way can criminal conduct be flushed into the open where the law can deal with it.

Similarly, our cases have consistently—indeed without exception—allowed sanctions for false statements or perjury; they have done so even in instances where the perjurer complained that the Government exceeded its constitutional powers in making the inquiry. See, e.g., *Bryson v. United States,* 396 U.S. 64 (1969). In *Bryson,* a union officer was required by federal labor law to file an affidavit averring that he was not a Communist. The affidavit was false in material statements. In a collateral attack on his conviction, Bryson argued that since the statute required him either to incriminate himself or lie, he could not lawfully be imprisoned for failure to comply. This Court rejected the contention:

> "[I]t cannot be thought that as a general principle of our law a citizen has a privilege to answer fraudulently a question that the Government should not have asked. Our legal system provides methods for challenging the Government's right to ask questions—lying is not one of them."

* * * In this case, the Court of Appeals required the suppression of perjured testimony given by respondent, as a witness under oath, lawfully summoned before an investigative grand jury and questioned about matters directly related to the grand jury's inquiry. The court reached this result because the prosecutor failed to give *Miranda* warnings at the outset of Mandujano's interrogation. Those warnings were required, in the Court of Appeals' view, because Mandujano was a "virtual" or "putative" defendant—that is, the prosecutor had specific information concerning Mandujano's participation in an attempted sale of heroin and the focus of the grand jury interrogation, as evidenced by the prosecutor's questions, centered on Mandujano's involvement in narcotics traffic. * * *

The court's analysis, premised upon the prosecutor's failure to give *Miranda* warnings, erroneously applied the standards fashioned by this Court in *Miranda.* Those warnings were aimed at the evils seen by the Court as endemic to police interrogation of a person in custody. *Miranda* addressed extra-judicial confessions or admissions procured in a hostile, unfamiliar environment which lacked procedural safeguards. The decision expressly rested on the privilege against compulsory self-incrimination; the prescribed warnings sought to negate the "compulsion" thought to be inherent in police station interrogation. But the *Miranda* Court simply did not perceive judicial inquiries and custodial interrogation as equivalents: " * * * the compulsion to speak in the isolated setting of the police station may well be greater than in courts or other official investigations, where there are often impartial observers to guard against intimidation or trickery."

The Court thus recognized that many official investigations, such as grand jury questioning, take place in a setting wholly different from custodial police interrogation. Indeed, the Court's opinion in *Miranda* reveals a focus on what was seen by the Court as police "coercion" derived from "factual studies [relating to] police violence and the 'third degree' * * * physical brutality—beating, hanging, whipping—and to sustained and protracted questioning incommunicado in order to extort confessions. * * *" To extend these concepts to questioning before a grand jury inquiring into criminal activity under the guidance of a judge is an extravagant expansion never remotely contemplated by this Court in *Miranda* ; the dynamics of constitutional interpretation do not compel constant extension of every doctrine announced by the Court. * * *

The warnings volunteered by the prosecutor to respondent in this case were more than sufficient to inform him of his rights—and his responsibilities—and particularly of the consequences of perjury.[a] To extend the concepts of *Miranda*, as contemplated by the Court of Appeals, would require that the witness be told that there was an absolute right to silence, and obviously any such warning would be incorrect, for there is no such right before a grand jury. Under *Miranda*, a person in police custody has, of course, an absolute right to decline to answer any question, incriminating or innocuous, whereas a grand jury witness, on the contrary, has an absolute duty to answer all questions, subject only to a valid Fifth Amendment claim. And even when the grand jury witness asserts the privilege, questioning need not cease, except as to the particular subject to which the privilege has been addressed. Other lines of inquiry may properly be pursued.

Respondent was also informed that if he desired he could have the assistance of counsel, but that counsel could not be inside the grand jury room. That statement was plainly a correct recital of the law. No criminal proceedings had been instituted against respondent, hence the Sixth Amendment right to counsel had not come into play. *Kirby v. Illinois* [Ch. 7, § 2].[6] A witness "before a grand jury cannot insist, as a matter of constitutional right, on being represented by his counsel * * *." *In re Groban*, 352 U.S. 330 (1957).[b] Under settled principles the witness may not insist upon the presence of his attorney in the grand jury room. Fed.Rule Crim.Proc. 6(d).

* * * Respondent was free at every stage to interpose his constitutional privilege against self-incrimination, but perjury was not a permissible option. * * * The judgment of the Court of Appeals is therefore reversed.

JUSTICE STEVENS took no part in the consideration or decision of this case.

JUSTICE BRENNAN, with whom JUSTICE MARSHALL joins, concurring in the judgment.

I concur in the result reached by the Court, for "even when the privilege against self-incrimination permits an individual to refuse to answer questions asked by the Government, if false answers are given the individual may be prosecuted for making false statements." *Mackey v. United States*, 401 U.S. 667 (1971) (Brennan, J., concurring). * * * "Our legal system provides methods for challenging the Government's right to ask questions—lying is not one of them."

a. At a subsequent point in the opinion, Chief Justice Burger added in a footnote [note 7] the following: "The fact that warnings were provided in this case to advise respondent of his Fifth Amendment privilege makes it unnecessary to consider whether any warning is required, as the Government asks us to determine. In addition to the warning implicit in the oath, federal prosecutors apparently make it a practice to inform a witness of the privilege before questioning begins."

6. The right to counsel mandated by *Miranda* was fashioned to secure the suspect's Fifth Amendment privilege in a setting thought inherently coercive. The Sixth Amendment was not implicated.

b. In *Groban*, a witness was not allowed to have counsel present during his examination by a state fire marshall in a proceeding designed to determine the cause of a fire. In finding that the denial of counsel did not violate due process, the majority cited as analogous the grand jury proceeding, where "a witness [also] * * * cannot insist as a matter of constitutional right, on being represented by his counsel." The dissent, by Justice Black, argued that the fire marshall's investigation was not analogous, but agreed as to the lack of a constitutional right to counsel before the grand jury. The dissent noted: "They [the grand jurors] bring into the grand jury room the experience, knowledge and viewpoint of all sections of the community. They have no axes to grind and are not charged personally with the administration of the law. No one of them is a prosecuting attorney or law-enforcement officer ferreting out crime. It would be very difficult for officers of the state seriously to abuse or deceive a witness in the presence of the grand jury. Similarly the presence of the jurors offers a substantial safeguard against the officers' misrepresentation, unintentional or otherwise, of the witness' statements and conduct before the grand jury."

Bryson v. United States. Further, the record satisfies me that the respondent's false answers were not induced by governmental tactics or procedures so inherently unfair under all the circumstances as to constitute a prosecution for perjury a violation of the Due Process Clause of the Fifth Amendment.

However, two aspects of the plurality opinion for the Court suggests a denigration of the privilege against self-incrimination and the right to the assistance of counsel with which I do not agree.

The plurality opinion mechanically quotes *United States v. Monia,* for the proposition that

"[t]he [Fifth] Amendment speaks of compulsion. It does not preclude a witness from testifying voluntarily in matters which may incriminate him. If, therefore, he desires the protection of the privilege, he must claim it or he will not be considered to have been 'compelled' within the meaning of the Amendment." * * *

In my view, the conception of the Fifth Amendment privilege expressed in the *Monia* dictum is explainable only by reference to the facts and circumstances of the only case cited in support by *Monia*—[a case, Justice Brennan explained, in which the potential for incrimination could not be evaluated without a claim by the witness because that potential was not readily apparent from the context of the question]. * * * It is only in a context where this "lack of notice on the part of the government" rationale has significance that we can possibly justify the *Monia* dictum that a witness testifying under judicial compulsion—that classic form of compulsion to which the Fifth Amendment is centrally addressed—must claim the privilege or else, without any further analysis, "he will not be considered to have been 'compelled' within the meaning of the Amendment." * * *

* * * [T]he use by prosecutors of the tactic of calling a putative defendant before a grand jury and interrogating him regarding the transactions and events for which he is about to be indicted is, in the absence of an "intentional relinquishment or abandonment" of his "known" privilege against compulsory self-incrimination, a blatant subversion of the fundamental adversary principle— that the State "establish its case, not by interrogation of the accused even under judicial safeguards, but by evidence independently secured through skillful investigation." * * * Such tactics by prosecutors are exemplars of the very evils sought to be prevented by the enshrinement of the Fifth Amendment privilege in the Constitution. * * *

Thus, I would hold that, in the absence of an intentional and intelligent waiver by the individual of his known right to be free from compulsory self-incrimination, the Government may not call before a grand jury one whom it has probable cause—as measured by an objective standard—to suspect committed a crime, and by use of judicial compulsion compel him to testify with regard to that crime. In the absence of such a waiver, the Fifth Amendment requires that any testimony obtained in this fashion be unavailable to the Government for use at trial. Such a waiver could readily be demonstrated by proof that the individual was warned prior to questioning that he is currently subject to possible criminal prosecution for the commission of a stated crime,[c] that he has a constitutional

c. In *United States v. Washington,* 431 U.S. 181 (1977), the Court held that a witness need not be warned that he is a target of a grand jury investigation. The Court majority, per Burger, C.J., noted that "even in the presumed psychologically coercive atmosphere of police custodial interrogation, *Miranda* does not re- quire that any additional warnings be given simply because the suspect is a potential defendant." Justice Brennan, joined by Justice Marshall, dissented, relying on Justice Brennan's opinion in *Mandujano.* See also note a to *New York v. Quarles,* Ch. 6, § 4.

right to refuse to answer any and all questions that may tend to incriminate him, and by record evidence that the individual understood the nature of his situation and privilege prior to giving testimony. * * *

A second and also disturbing facet of the plurality opinion today is its statement that "[n]o criminal proceedings had been instituted against respondent, hence, the Sixth Amendment right to counsel had not come into play." It will not do simply to cite, as does the plurality opinion, *Kirby v. Illinois*, for this proposition. *Kirby's* premise, so fundamental that it was "note[d] at the outset," was that "the constitutional privilege against compulsory self-incrimination is in no way implicated here." In sharp contrast, the privilege against compulsory self-incrimination is inextricably involved in this case since a putative defendant is called and interrogated before a grand jury. Clearly in such a case a defendant is "faced with the prosecutorial forces of organized society, and immersed in the intricacies of substantive and procedural criminal law."

It is true that dictum in *In re Groban* [fn. b supra] denied there is any constitutional right of a witness to be represented by counsel when testifying before a grand jury. But neither *Groban* nor any other case in this Court has squarely presented the question. Moreover, more recent decisions, e.g., *Miranda v. Arizona*, and *Escobedo v. Illinois*, recognizing the "substantive affinity" and therefore the "coextensive[ness]" in certain circumstances of the right to counsel and the privilege against compulsory self-incrimination, have led many to question the continuing vitality of such older dicta.

* * * Given the inherent danger of subversion of the adversary system in the case of a putative defendant called to testify before a grand jury, and the peculiarly critical role of the Fifth Amendment privilege as the bulwark against such abuse, it is plainly obvious that some guidance by counsel is required. * * * It may be that a putative defendant's Fifth Amendment privilege will be adequately preserved by a procedure whereby, in addition to warnings, he is told that he has a right to consult with an attorney prior to questioning, that if he cannot afford an attorney one will be appointed for him, that during the questioning he may have that attorney wait outside the grand jury room, and that he may at any and all times during questioning consult with the attorney prior to answering any question posed.[22] At least if such minimal protections were present, a putative defendant would be able to consult with counsel prior to answering any question that he might in any way suspect may incriminate him. * * *

It is of course unnecessary in this case to define the exact dimensions of the right to counsel since the testimony obtained by the grand jury interrogation was not introduced as evidence at respondent's trial on the charge concerning which he was questioned. I write only to make plain my disagreement with the implication in the plurality opinion that constitutional rights to counsel are not involved in a grand jury proceeding, and my disagreement with the further implication that there is a right to have counsel present for consultation outside the grand jury room but that it is not constitutionally derived and therefore may be enjoyed only by those wealthy enough to hire a lawyer. I cannot accede to a return to the regime of "squalid discrimination," where the justice "a man gets depends on the amount of money he has." *Griffin v. Illinois* [Ch. 5, § 2]. * * * If indeed there is, as the plurality opinion says, a right to have counsel present

22. [Justice Brennan here noted that several commentators had argued that more was needed, "that the presence of counsel inside the grand jury room is required." He then added: "Certainly there is no viable argument that allowing counsel to be present in the grand jury room for purposes of consultation regarding testimonial privileges would subvert the nature or functioning of the grand jury proceeding. Such a procedure is sanctioned by statute in several states."]

outside the door to the grand jury room, it is most assuredly in my view everyone's right, regardless of economic circumstance. * * *

Justice Stewart, with whom Justice Blackmun joins, concurring in the judgment.

The Fifth Amendment privilege against compulsory self-incrimination provides no protection for the commission of perjury. * * * *Bryson v. United States*. The respondent's grand jury testimony is relevant only to his prosecution for perjury and was not introduced in the prosecution for attempting to distribute heroin. Since this is not a case where it could plausibly be argued that the perjury prosecution must be barred because of prosecutorial conduct amounting to a denial of due process, I would reverse the judgment without reaching the other issues explored in The Chief Justice's opinion and by Mr. Justice Brennan in his separate opinion.

KASTIGAR v. UNITED STATES

406 U.S. 441, 92 S.Ct. 1653, 32 L.Ed.2d 212 (1972).

Justice Powell delivered the opinion of the Court.

This case presents the question whether the United States Government may compel testimony from an unwilling witness, who invokes the Fifth Amendment privilege against compulsory self-incrimination, by conferring on the witness immunity from use of the compelled testimony in subsequent criminal proceedings, as well as immunity from use of evidence derived from the testimony.

Petitioners were subpoenaed to appear before a United States grand jury * * *. The Government believed that petitioners were likely to assert their Fifth Amendment privilege. Prior to the scheduled appearances, the Government applied to the District Court for an order directing petitioners to answer questions and produce evidence before the grand jury under a grant of immunity conferred pursuant to 18 U.S.C. §§ 6002–6003. Petitioners opposed issuance of the order, contending primarily that the scope of the immunity provided by the statute was not coextensive with the scope of the privilege against self-incrimination, and therefore was not sufficient to supplant the privilege and compel their testimony. The District Court rejected this contention, and ordered petitioners to appear before the grand jury and answer its questions under the grant of immunity. * * *

The power of government to compel persons to testify in court or before grand juries and other governmental agencies is firmly established in Anglo–American jurisprudence. * * * While it is not clear when grand juries first resorted to compulsory process to secure the attendance and testimony of witnesses, the general common-law principle that "the public has a right to every man's evidence" was considered an "indubitable certainty" that "cannot be denied" by 1742. * * * Mr. Justice White noted the importance of this essential power of government in his concurring opinion in *Murphy v. Waterfront Comm'n*, 378 U.S. 52 (1964):

> "Among the necessary and most important of the powers of the States as well as the Federal Government to assure the effective functioning of government in an ordered society is the broad power to compel residents to testify in court or before grand juries or agencies. * * * Such testimony constitutes one of the Government's primary sources of information."

But the power to compel testimony is not absolute. There are a number of exemptions from the testimonial duty, the most important of which is the Fifth

Amendment privilege against compulsory self-incrimination. The privilege reflects a complex of our fundamental values and aspirations, *Murphy*, supra, and marks an important advance in the development of our liberty. * * * This Court has been zealous to safeguard the values that underlie the privilege.

Immunity statutes, which have historical roots deep in Anglo–American jurisprudence, are not incompatible with these values. Rather, they seek a rational accommodation between the imperatives of the privilege and the legitimate demands of government to compel citizens to testify. The existence of these statutes reflects the importance of testimony, and the fact that many offenses are of such a character that the only persons capable of giving useful testimony are those implicated in the crime. Indeed, their origins were in the context of such offenses, and their primary use has been to investigate such offenses. Congress included immunity statutes in many of the regulatory measures adopted in the first half of this century. Indeed, prior to the enactment of the statute under consideration in this case, there were in force over 50 federal immunity statutes. In addition, every State in the Union, as well as the District of Columbia and Puerto Rico, has one or more such statutes. The commentators, and this Court on several occasions, have characterized immunity statutes as essential to the effective enforcement of various criminal statutes. As Mr. Justice Frankfurter observed, speaking for the Court in *Ullmann v. United States*, 350 U.S. 422 (1956), such statutes have "become part of our constitutional fabric."

Petitioners contend, first, that the Fifth Amendment's privilege against compulsory self-incrimination, which is that "[n]o person * * * shall be compelled in any criminal case to be a witness against himself," deprives Congress of power to enact laws that compel self-incrimination, even if complete immunity from prosecution is granted prior to the compulsion of the incriminatory testimony. In other words, petitioners assert that no immunity statute, however drawn, can afford a lawful basis for compelling incriminatory testimony. They ask us to reconsider and overrule *Brown v. Walker*, 161 U.S. 591 (1896), and *Ullmann v. United States*, decisions that uphold the constitutionality of immunity statutes. We find no merit to this contention and reaffirm the decisions in *Brown* and *Ullmann*.[a]

Petitioners' second contention is that the scope of immunity provided by the federal witness immunity statute, 18 U.S.C. § 6002, is not coextensive with the scope of the Fifth Amendment privilege against compulsory self-incrimination, and therefore is not sufficient to supplant the privilege and compel testimony over a claim of the privilege. The statute provides that when a witness is compelled by district court order to testify over a claim of the privilege:

> "the witness may not refuse to comply with the order on the basis of his privilege against self-incrimination; but no testimony or other information

---

a. In *Brown*, the Court reasoned that the Fifth Amendment could not be "construed literally as authorizing the witness to refuse to disclose any fact which might tend to incriminate, disgrace, or expose him to unfavorable comments." The history of the privilege clearly indicated that its objective was solely to "secure the witness against criminal prosecution." Thus the privilege had been held inapplicable where the witness' compelled testimony would relate only to an offense for which he had received a pardon or would tend to "disgrace him or bring him into disrepute" but would furnish no information relating to a criminal offense. In *Ullmann*, a witness who had received complete immunity from prosecution argued that the rationale of *Brown* should not apply where the compelled testimony (relating to alleged spying activities by certain members of the Communist Party) could subject him to a wide range of disabilities, such as "loss of job, expulsion from labor union, state registration and investigation statutes, passport eligibility, and general public opprobrium." Rejecting that contention, the Court majority concluded that *Brown* had correctly defined the total purpose of the privilege, and that purpose was fully met by granting the witness immunity from prosecution.

compelled under the order (or any information directly or indirectly derived from such testimony or other information) may be used against the witness in any criminal case, except a prosecution for perjury, giving a false statement, or otherwise failing to comply with the order." 18 U.S.C. § 6002.

The constitutional inquiry, rooted in logic and history, as well as in the decisions of this Court, is whether the immunity granted under this statute is coextensive with the scope of the privilege. If so, petitioners' refusals to answer based on the privilege were unjustified, and the judgments of contempt were proper, for the grant of immunity has removed the dangers against which the privilege protects. *Brown v. Walker.* If, on the other hand, the immunity granted is not as comprehensive as the protection afforded by the privilege, petitioners were justified in refusing to answer, and the judgments of contempt must be vacated. *McCarthy v. Arndstein*, 266 U.S. 34 (1924).

Petitioners draw a distinction between statutes that provide transactional immunity and those that provide, as does the statute before us, immunity from use and derivative use. They contend that a statute must at a minimum grant full transactional immunity in order to be coextensive with the scope of the privilege. In support of this contention, they rely on *Counselman v. Hitchcock,* 142 U.S. 547 (1892), the first case in which this Court considered a constitutional challenge to an immunity statute. The statute, [there] * * * provided that no "evidence obtained from a party or witness by means of a judicial proceeding . . . shall be given in evidence, or in any manner used against him . . . in any court of the United States . . . ." * * * [T]his Court construed the statute as affording a witness protection only against the use of the specific testimony compelled from him under the grant of immunity. This construction meant that the statute "could not, and would not, prevent the use of his testimony to search out other testimony to be used in evidence against him." Since the [statute] * * * would permit the use against the immunized witness of evidence derived from his compelled testimony, it did not protect the witness to the same extent that a claim of the privilege would protect him. Accordingly, under the principle that a grant of immunity cannot supplant the privilege, and is not sufficient to compel testimony over a claim of the privilege, unless the scope of the grant of immunity is coextensive with the scope of the privilege, the witness' refusal to testify was held proper. In the course of its opinion, the Court made the following statement, on which petitioners heavily rely:

"We are clearly of opinion that no statute which leaves the party or witness subject to prosecution after he answers the criminating question put to him, can have the effect of supplanting the privilege conferred by the Constitution of the United States. [The immunity statute under consideration] does not supply a complete protection from all the perils against which the constitutional prohibition was designed to guard, and is not a full substitute for that prohibition. In view of the constitutional provision, a statutory enactment, to be valid, must afford absolute immunity against future prosecution for the offence to which the question relates."

Sixteen days after the *Counselman* decision, a new immunity bill * * * was drafted specifically to meet the broad language in *Counselman* set forth above. The new Act removed the privilege against self-incrimination in [specified] hearings * * * and provided that:

"no person shall be prosecuted or subjected to any penalty or forfeiture for or on account of any transaction, matter or thing, concerning which he may testify, or produce evidence, documentary or otherwise * * *." Act of Feb. 11, 1893.

This transactional immunity statute became the basic form for the numerous federal immunity statutes until 1970, when, after re-examining applicable constitutional principles and the adequacy of existing law, Congress enacted the statute here under consideration. The new statute, which does not "afford [the] absolute immunity against future prosecution" referred to in *Counselman*, was drafted to meet what Congress judged to be the conceptual basis of *Counselman*, as elaborated in subsequent decisions of the Court, namely, that immunity from the use of compelled testimony and evidence derived therefrom is coextensive with the scope of the privilege.

The statute's explicit proscription of the use in any criminal case of "testimony or other information compelled under the order (or any information directly or indirectly derived from such testimony or other information)" is consonant with Fifth Amendment standards. We hold that such immunity from use and derivative use is coextensive with the scope of the privilege against self-incrimination, and therefore is sufficient to compel testimony over a claim of the privilege. While a grant of immunity must afford protection commensurate with that afforded by the privilege, it need not be broader. Transactional immunity, which accords full immunity from prosecution for the offense to which the compelled testimony relates, affords the witness considerably broader protection than does the Fifth Amendment privilege. The privilege has never been construed to mean that one who invokes it cannot subsequently be prosecuted. Its sole concern is to afford protection against being "forced to give testimony leading to the infliction of 'penalties affixed to * * * criminal acts.'" Immunity from the use of compelled testimony, as well as evidence derived directly and indirectly therefrom, affords this protection. It prohibits the prosecutorial authorities from using the compelled testimony in *any* respect, and it therefore insures that the testimony cannot lead to the infliction of criminal penalties on the witness.

Our holding is consistent with the conceptual basis of *Counselman*. The *Counselman* statute, as construed by the Court, was plainly deficient in its failure to prohibit the use against the immunized witness of evidence derived from his compelled testimony. The Court repeatedly emphasized this deficiency * * *. The broad language in *Counselman* relied upon by petitioners was unnecessary to the Court's decision, and cannot be considered binding authority.

In *Murphy v. Waterfront Comm'n*, 378 U.S. 52 (1964), the Court carefully considered immunity from use of compelled testimony and evidence derived therefrom. The *Murphy* petitioners were subpoenaed to testify at a hearing conducted by the Waterfront Commission of New York Harbor. After refusing to answer certain questions on the ground that the answers might tend to incriminate them, petitioners were granted immunity from prosecution under the laws of New Jersey and New York. They continued to refuse to testify, however, on the ground that their answers might tend to incriminate them under federal law, to which the immunity did not purport to extend. * * *

The issue before the Court in *Murphy* was whether New Jersey and New York could compel the witnesses, whom these States had immunized from prosecution under their laws, to give testimony that might then be used to convict them of a federal crime. Since New Jersey and New York had not purported to confer immunity from federal prosecution, the Court was faced with the question what limitations the Fifth Amendment privilege imposed on the prosecutorial powers of the Federal Government, a nonimmunizing sovereign. After undertaking an examination of the policies and purposes of the privilege, the Court overturned the rule that one jurisdiction within our federal structure may compel a witness to give testimony which could be used to convict him of a crime in another jurisdiction. The Court held that the privilege protects state witnesses against incrimination under federal as well as state law, and federal witnesses against incrimination under state as well as federal law.[b] Applying this principle to the state immunity legislation before it, the Court held the constitutional rule to be that:

> "[A] state witness may not be compelled to give testimony which may be incriminating under federal law unless the compelled testimony and its fruits cannot be used in any manner by federal officials in connection with a criminal prosecution against him. We conclude, moreover, that in order to implement this constitutional rule and accommodate the interests of the State and Federal Governments in investigating and prosecuting crime, the Federal Government must be prohibited from making any such use of compelled testimony and its fruits."

The Court emphasized that this rule left the state witness and the Federal Government, against which the witness had immunity only from the *use* of the compelled testimony and evidence derived therefrom, "in substantially the same position as if the witness had claimed his privilege in the absence of a state grant of immunity."

It is true that in *Murphy* the Court was not presented with the precise question presented by this case, whether a jurisdiction seeking to compel testimony may do so by granting only use and derivative-use immunity, for New Jersey and New York had granted petitioners transactional immunity. * * * But both the reasoning of the Court in *Murphy* and the result reached compel the conclusion that use and derivative-use immunity is constitutionally sufficient to compel testimony over a claim of the privilege. Since the privilege is fully applicable and its scope is the same whether invoked in a state or in a federal jurisdiction, the *Murphy* conclusion that a prohibition on use and derivative use secures a witness' Fifth Amendment privilege against infringement by the Federal Government demonstrates that immunity from use and derivative use is coextensive with the scope of the privilege. As the *Murphy* Court noted, immunity from use and derivative use "leaves the witness and the Federal Government in substantially the same position as if the witness had claimed his privilege" in the absence of a grant of immunity. * * *

Although an analysis of prior decisions and the purpose of the Fifth Amendment privilege indicates that use and derivative-use immunity is coextensive with the privilege, we must consider additional arguments advanced by petitioners against the sufficiency of such immunity. * * * Petitioners argue that use and derivative-use immunity will not adequately protect a witness from various possible incriminating uses of the compelled testimony: for example, the prosecutor or other law enforcement officials may obtain leads, names of witnesses, or other information not otherwise available that might result in a prosecution. It will be difficult and perhaps impossible, the argument goes, to identify, by testimony or cross-examination, the subtle ways in which the compelled testimony may disadvantage a witness, especially in the jurisdiction granting the immunity.

b. *United States v. Balsys,* 524 U.S. 666 (1998), held that the privilege does not protect against incrimination under the laws of a foreign government, as the Fifth Amendment applies only to "action of the government it binds." *Murphy* was grounded on the dual applicability of the self-incrimination clause to the federal government and to the states (via the due process clause of the Fourteenth Amendment) and the need to ensure that the witness not be "whipsawed into incriminating himself under both state and federal law even though the constitutional privilege against self-incrimination is applicable to each."

This argument presupposes that the statute's prohibition will prove impossible to enforce. The statute provides a sweeping proscription of any use, direct or indirect, of the compelled testimony and any information derived therefrom:

> "[N]o testimony or other information compelled under the order (or any information directly or indirectly derived from such testimony or other information) may be used against the witness in any criminal case * * *." 18 U.S.C. § 6002.

This total prohibition on use provides a comprehensive safeguard, barring the use of compelled testimony as an "investigatory lead," and also barring the use of any evidence obtained by focusing investigation on a witness as a result of his compelled disclosures.

A person accorded this immunity under 18 U.S.C. § 6002, and subsequently prosecuted, is not dependent for the preservation of his rights upon the integrity and good faith of the prosecuting authorities. As stated in *Murphy*:

> "Once a defendant demonstrates that he has testified, under a state grant of immunity, to matters related to the federal prosecution, the federal authorities have the burden of showing that their evidence is not tainted by establishing that they had an independent, legitimate source for the disputed evidence."

This burden of proof, which we reaffirm as appropriate, is not limited to a negation of taint; rather, it imposes on the prosecution the affirmative duty to prove that the evidence it proposes to use is derived from a legitimate source wholly independent of the compelled testimony.

This is very substantial protection, commensurate with that resulting from invoking the privilege itself. The privilege assures that a citizen is not compelled to incriminate himself by his own testimony. It usually operates to allow a citizen to remain silent when asked a question requiring an incriminatory answer. This statute, which operates after a witness has given incriminatory testimony, affords the same protection by assuring that the compelled testimony can in no way lead to the infliction of criminal penalties. The statute, like the Fifth Amendment, grants neither pardon nor amnesty. Both the statute and the Fifth Amendment allow the government to prosecute using evidence from legitimate independent sources.

The statutory proscription is analogous to the Fifth Amendment requirement in cases of coerced confessions. A coerced confession, as revealing of leads as testimony given in exchange for immunity, is inadmissible in a criminal trial, but it does not bar prosecution. Moreover, a defendant against whom incriminating evidence has been obtained through a grant of immunity may be in a stronger position at trial than a defendant who asserts a Fifth Amendment coerced-confession claim. One raising a claim under this statute need only show that he testified under a grant of immunity in order to shift to the government the heavy burden of proving that all of the evidence it proposes to use was derived from legitimate independent sources. On the other hand, a defendant raising a coerced-confession claim under the Fifth Amendment must first prevail in a voluntariness hearing before his confession and evidence derived from it become inadmissible.

There can be no justification in reason or policy for holding that the Constitution requires an amnesty grant where, acting pursuant to statute and accompanying safeguards, testimony is compelled in exchange for immunity from use and derivative use when no such amnesty is required where the government, acting without colorable right, coerces a defendant into incriminating himself.

JUSTICE BRENNAN and JUSTICE REHNQUIST took no part in the consideration or decision of this case.

JUSTICE DOUGLAS, dissenting.

* * * In *Counselman v. Hitchcock*, the Court adopted the transactional immunity test. * * * This Court, however, apparently believes that *Counselman* and its progeny were overruled *sub silentio* in *Murphy v. Waterfront Com'n*. *Murphy* involved state witnesses, granted transactional immunity under state law, who refused to testify for fear of subsequent federal prosecution. We held that the testimony in question could be compelled, but that the Federal Government would be barred from using any of the testimony, or its fruits, in a subsequent federal prosecution. * * *

* * * *Counselman*, as the *Murphy* Court recognized, "said nothing about the problem of incrimination under the law of another sovereign." That problem is one of federalism, as to require transactional immunity between jurisdictions might

> "deprive a state of the right to prosecute a violation of its criminal law on the basis of another state's grant of immunity [a result which] would be gravely in derogation of its sovereignty and obstructive of its administration of justice." *United States ex rel. Catena v. Elias*, 449 F.2d 40, 44 (C.A.3 1971).

* * * If, as some have thought, the Bill of Rights contained only "counsels of moderation" from which courts and legislatures could deviate according to their conscience or discretion, then today's contraction of the Self–Incrimination Clause of the Fifth Amendment would be understandable. But that has not been true, starting with Chief Justice Marshall's opinion in *United States v. Burr*, 25 F.Cas. 30 (C.C.D.Va. 1807) where he ruled that the reach of the Fifth Amendment was so broad as to make the privilege applicable when there was a mere possibility of a criminal charge being made. * * *

The Court said in *Hale v. Henkel*, 201 U.S. 43 (1906), that "if the criminality has already been taken away, the Amendment ceases to apply." In other words, the immunity granted is adequate if it operates as a complete pardon for the offense. *Brown v. Walker*. That is the true measure of the Self–Incrimination Clause. * * *

JUSTICE MARSHALL, dissenting.

* * * The Court recognizes that an immunity statute must be tested by * * * whether it "leaves the witness and the prosecutorial authorities in substantially the same position as if the witness had claimed the Fifth Amendment privilege." I assume, moreover, that in theory that test would be met by a complete ban on the use of the compelled testimony, including all derivative use, however remote and indirect. But I cannot agree that a ban on use will in practice be total, if it remains open for the government to convict the witness on the basis of evidence derived from a legitimate independent source. The Court asserts that the witness is adequately protected by a rule imposing on the government a heavy burden of proof if it would establish the independent character of evidence to be used against the witness. But in light of the inevitable uncertainties of the factfinding process, a greater margin of protection is required in order to provide a reliable guarantee that the witness is in exactly the same position as if he had not testified. That margin can be provided only by immunity from prosecution for the offenses to which the testimony relates, i.e., transactional immunity.

I do not see how it can suffice merely to put the burden of proof on the government. First, contrary to the Court's assertion, the Court's rule does leave the witness "dependent for the preservation of his rights upon the integrity and good faith of the prosecuting authorities." For the information relevant to the question of taint is uniquely within the knowledge of the prosecuting authorities. They alone are in a position to trace the chains of information and investigation that lead to the evidence to be used in a criminal prosecution. A witness who suspects that his compelled testimony was used to develop a lead will be hard pressed indeed to ferret out the evidence necessary to prove it. And of course it is no answer to say he need not prove it, for though the Court puts the burden of proof on the government, the government will have no difficulty in meeting its burden by mere assertion if the witness produces no contrary evidence. The good faith of the prosecuting authorities is thus the sole safeguard of the witness' rights. Second, even their good faith is not a sufficient safeguard. For the paths of information through the investigative bureaucracy may well be long and winding, and even a prosecutor acting in the best of faith cannot be certain that somewhere in the depths of his investigative apparatus, often including hundreds of employees, there was not some prohibited use of the compelled testimony. * * * The Court today sets out a loose net to trap tainted evidence and prevent its use against the witness, but it accepts an intolerably great risk that tainted evidence will in fact slip through that net.

In my view the Court turns reason on its head when it compares a statutory grant of immunity to the "immunity" that is inadvertently conferred by an unconstitutional interrogation. The exclusionary rule of evidence that applies in that situation has nothing whatever to do with this case. Evidence obtained through a coercive interrogation, like evidence obtained through an illegal search, is excluded at trial because the Constitution prohibits such methods of gathering evidence. The exclusionary rules provide a partial and inadequate remedy to some victims of illegal police conduct, and a similarly partial and inadequate deterrent to police officers. An immunity statute, on the other hand, is much more ambitious than any exclusionary rule. It does not merely attempt to provide a remedy for past police misconduct, which never should have occurred. An immunity statute operates in advance of the event, and it authorizes—even encourages—interrogation that would otherwise be prohibited by the Fifth Amendment. An immunity statute thus differs from an exclusionary rule of evidence in at least two critical respects.

First, because an immunity statute gives constitutional approval to the resulting interrogation, the government is under an obligation here to remove the danger of incrimination completely and absolutely, whereas in the case of the exclusionary rules it may be sufficient to shield the witness from the fruits of the illegal search or interrogation in a partial and reasonably adequate manner. * * * The Constitution does not authorize police officers to coerce confessions or to invade privacy without cause, so long as no use is made of the evidence they obtain. But this Court has held that the Constitution does authorize the government to compel a witness to give potentially incriminating testimony, so long as no incriminating use is made of the resulting evidence. Before the government puts its seal of approval on such an interrogation, it must provide an absolutely reliable guarantee that it will not use the testimony in any way at all in aid of prosecution of the witness. The only way to provide that guarantee is to give the witness immunity from prosecution for crimes to which his testimony relates.

Second, because an immunity statute operates in advance of the interrogation, there is room to require a broad grant of transactional immunity without imperiling large numbers of otherwise valid convictions. An exclusionary rule comes into play after the interrogation or search has occurred; and the decision to question or to search is often made in haste, under pressure, by an officer who is not a lawyer. If an unconstitutional interrogation or search were held to create transactional immunity, that might well be regarded as an excessively high price to pay for the "constable's blunder." An immunity statute, on the other hand, creates a framework in which the prosecuting attorney can make a calm and reasoned decision whether to compel testimony and suffer the resulting ban on prosecution, or to forgo the testimony.

For both these reasons it is clear to me that an immunity statute must be tested by a standard far more demanding than that appropriate for an exclusionary rule fashioned to deal with past constitutional violations. Measured by that standard, the statute approved today by the Court fails miserably. I respectfully dissent.

FISHER v. UNITED STATES

425 U.S. 391, 96 S.Ct. 1569, 48 L.Ed.2d 39 (1976).

JUSTICE WHITE delivered the opinion of the Court.

In these two cases we are called upon to decide whether a summons directing an attorney to produce documents delivered to him by his client in connection with the attorney-client relationship is enforceable over claims that the documents were constitutionally immune from summons in the hands of the client and retained that immunity in the hands of the attorney. In each case, an Internal Revenue agent visited the taxpayer or taxpayers and interviewed them in connection with an investigation of possible civil or criminal liability under the federal income tax laws. Shortly after the interviews * * *, the taxpayers obtained from their respective accountants certain documents relating to the preparation by the accountant of their tax returns. Shortly after obtaining the documents * * *, the taxpayers transferred the documents to their lawyers—each of whom was retained to assist the taxpayer in connection with the investigation. Upon learning of the whereabouts of the documents, the Internal Revenue Service served summonses on the attorneys directing them to produce documents listed therein. [Those documents were accountants' work sheets, retained copies of income tax returns, and the accountants' copies of correspondence between the accounting firm and the taxpayer]. * * * In each case, the lawyer declined to comply with the summons directing production of the documents, and enforcement actions were commenced by the Government. * * *

All of the parties in these cases and the Court of Appeals have concurred in the proposition that if the Fifth Amendment would have excused a *taxpayer* from turning over the accountant's papers had he possessed them, the *attorney* to whom they are delivered for the purpose of obtaining legal advice should also be immune from subpoena. Although we agree with this proposition for the reasons set forth infra, we are convinced that, under our decision in *Couch v. United States,* 409 U.S. 322 (1973), it is not the taxpayer's Fifth Amendment privilege that would excuse the *attorney* from production.

The relevant part of that Amendment provides:

"No person * * * shall be *compelled* in any criminal case to be a *witness against himself.*" (Emphasis added.)

The taxpayer's privilege under this Amendment is not violated by enforcement of the summonses involved in these cases because enforcement against a taxpayer's lawyer would not "compel" the taxpayer to do anything—and certainly would not compel him to be a "witness" against himself. The Court has held repeatedly that the Fifth Amendment is limited to prohibiting the use of "physical or moral compulsion" exerted on the person asserting the privilege. In *Couch v. United States,* we recently ruled that the Fifth Amendment rights of a taxpayer were not violated by the enforcement of a documentary summons directed to her accountant and requiring production of the taxpayer's own records in the possession of the accountant. We did so on the ground that in such a case "the ingredient of personal compulsion against an accused is lacking." Here, the taxpayers are compelled to do no more than was the taxpayer in *Couch.* The taxpayers' Fifth Amendment privilege is therefore not violated by enforcement of the summonses directed toward their attorneys. This is true whether or not the Amendment would have barred a subpoena directing the taxpayer to produce the documents while they were in his hands.

The fact that the attorneys are agents of the taxpayers does not change this result. *Couch* held as much, since the accountant there was also the taxpayer's agent, and in this respect reflected a longstanding view. * * * "It is extortion of information from the accused which offends our sense of justice." *Couch v. United States.* Agent or no, the lawyer is not the taxpayer. The taxpayer is the "accused," and nothing is being extorted from him. Nor is this one of those situations, which *Couch* suggested might exist, where constructive possession is so clear or relinquishment of possession so temporary and insignificant as to leave the personal compulsion upon the taxpayer substantially intact. * * *

The Court of Appeals suggested that because legally and ethically the attorney was required to respect the confidences of his client, the latter had a reasonable expectation of privacy for the records in the hands of the attorney and therefore did not forfeit his Fifth Amendment privilege with respect to the records by transferring them in order to obtain legal advice. It is true that the Court has often stated that one of the several purposes served by the constitutional privilege against compelled testimonial self-incrimination is that of protecting personal privacy. See, e.g., *Murphy v. Waterfront Comm'n.* But the Court has never suggested that every invasion of privacy violates the privilege. Within the limits imposed by the language of the Fifth Amendment, which we necessarily observe, the privilege truly serves privacy interests; but the Court has never on any ground, personal privacy included, applied the Fifth Amendment to prevent the otherwise proper acquisition or use of evidence which, in the Court's view, did not involve compelled testimonial self-incrimination of some sort.

The proposition that the Fifth Amendment protects private information obtained without compelling self-incriminating testimony is contrary to the clear statements of this Court that under appropriate safeguards private incriminating statements of an accused may be overheard and used in evidence, if they are not compelled at the time they were uttered, *Katz v. United States* [Ch. 3, § 2], and that disclosure of private information may be compelled if immunity removes the risk of incrimination. *Kastigar v. United States.* If the Fifth Amendment protected generally against the obtaining of private information from a man's mouth or pen or house, its protections would presumably not be lifted by probable cause and a warrant or by immunity. * * * We cannot cut the Fifth Amendment completely loose from the moorings of its language, and make it serve as a general protector of privacy—a word not mentioned in its text and a concept directly addressed in the Fourth Amendment. We adhere to the view that the Fifth Amendment protects against "compelled self-incrimination, not [the disclosure of] private information." *United States v. Nobles,* 422 U.S. 225 (1975). * * *

* * * [While the] taxpayers have erroneously relied on the Fifth Amendment without urging the attorney-client privilege in so many words, they have nevertheless invoked the relevant body of law and policies that govern the attorney-client

privilege.   * * * This Court and the lower courts have * * * uniformly held that pre-existing documents which could have been obtained by court process from the client when he was in possession may also be obtained from the attorney by similar process following transfer by the client in order to obtain more informed legal advice.   * * * It is otherwise if the documents are not obtainable by subpoena duces tecum or summons while in the exclusive possession of the client, for the client will then be reluctant to transfer possession to the lawyer unless the documents are also privileged in the latter's hands.   Where the transfer is made for the purpose of obtaining legal advice, the purposes of the attorney-client privilege would be defeated unless the privilege is applicable.   * * *

Since each taxpayer [here] transferred possession of the documents in question from himself to his attorney in order to obtain legal assistance in the tax investigations in question, the papers, if unobtainable by summons from the client, are unobtainable by summons directed to the attorney by reason of the attorney-client privilege.   We accordingly proceed to the question whether the documents could have been obtained by summons addressed to the taxpayer while the documents were in his possession.   The only bar to enforcement of such summons asserted by the parties or the courts below is the Fifth Amendment's privilege against self-incrimination.   * * *

The proposition that the Fifth Amendment prevents compelled production of documents over objection that such production might incriminate stems from *Boyd v. United States* * * *.

Several of *Boyd's* express or implicit declarations have not stood the test of time.   The application of the Fourth Amendment to subpoenas was limited by *Hale v. Henkel,* and more recent cases.   Purely evidentiary (but "nontestimonial") materials, as well as contraband and fruits and instrumentalities of crime, may now be searched for and seized under proper circumstances, *Warden v. Hayden* [see fn. a following *Boyd*, § 1 supra].   Also, any notion that "testimonial" evidence may never be seized and used in evidence is inconsistent with [various cases] approving the seizure under appropriate circumstances of conversations of a person suspected of crime.   It is also clear that the Fifth Amendment does not independently proscribe the compelled production of every sort of incriminating evidence but applies only when the accused is compelled to make a *testimonial* communication that is incriminating.   * * * Furthermore, despite *Boyd*, neither a partnership nor the individual partners are shielded from compelled production of partnership records on self-incrimination grounds.   *Bellis v. United States*, 417 U.S. 85 (1974).   It would appear that under that case the precise claim sustained in *Boyd* would now be rejected for reasons not there considered.

The pronouncement in *Boyd* that a person may not be forced to produce his private papers has nonetheless often appeared as dictum in later opinions of this Court.   * * * To the extent, however, that the rule against compelling production of private papers rested on the proposition that seizures of or subpoenas for "mere evidence," including documents, violated the Fourth Amendment and therefore also transgressed the Fifth, the foundations for the rule have been washed away. In consequence, the prohibition against forcing the production of private papers has long been a rule searching for a rationale consistent with the proscriptions of the Fifth Amendment against compelling a person to give "testimony" that incriminates him.   Accordingly, we turn to the question of what, if any, incriminating testimony within the Fifth Amendment's protection, is compelled by a documentary summons.

A subpoena served on a taxpayer requiring him to produce an accountant's workpapers in his possession without doubt involves substantial compulsion.   But it does not compel oral testimony; nor would it ordinarily compel the taxpayer to restate, repeat, or affirm the truth of the contents of the documents sought. Therefore, the Fifth Amendment would not be violated by the fact alone that the papers on their face might incriminate the taxpayer, for the privilege protects a person only against being incriminated by his own compelled testimonial communications. The accountant's workpapers are not the taxpayer's. They were not prepared by the taxpayer, and they contain no testimonial declarations by him. Furthermore, as far as this record demonstrates, the preparation of all of the papers sought in these cases was wholly voluntary, and they cannot be said to contain compelled testimonial evidence, either of the taxpayers or of anyone else. The taxpayer cannot avoid compliance with the subpoena merely by asserting that the item of evidence which he is required to produce contains incriminating writing, whether his own or that of someone else.

The act of producing evidence in response to a subpoena nevertheless has communicative aspects of its own, wholly aside from the contents of the papers produced. Compliance with the subpoena tacitly concedes the existence of the papers demanded and their possession or control by the taxpayer. It also would indicate the taxpayer's belief that the papers are those described in the subpoena. The elements of compulsion are clearly present, but the more difficult issues are whether the tacit averments of the taxpayer are both "testimonial" and "incriminating" for purposes of applying the Fifth Amendment. These questions perhaps do not lend themselves to categorical answers; their resolution may instead depend on the facts and circumstances of particular cases or classes thereof. In light of the records now before us, we are confident that however incriminating the contents of the accountant's workpapers might be, the act of producing them—the only thing which the taxpayer is compelled to do—would not itself involve testimonial self-incrimination.

It is doubtful that implicitly admitting the existence and possession of the papers rises to the level of testimony within the protection of the Fifth Amendment. The papers belong to the accountant, were prepared by him, and are the kind usually prepared by an accountant working on the tax returns of his client. Surely the Government is in no way relying on the "truthtelling" of the taxpayer to prove the existence of or his access to the documents. The existence and location of the papers are a foregone conclusion and the taxpayer adds little or nothing to the sum total of the Government's information by conceding that he in fact has the papers. Under these circumstances by enforcement of the summons "no constitutional rights are touched. The question is not one of testimony but of surrender."

When an accused is required to submit a handwriting exemplar he admits his ability to write and impliedly asserts that the exemplar is his writing. But in common experience, the first would be a near truism and the latter self-evident. In any event, although the exemplar may be incriminating to the accused and although he is compelled to furnish it, his Fifth Amendment privilege is not violated because nothing he has said or done is deemed to be sufficiently testimonial for purposes of the privilege. This Court has also time and again allowed subpoenas against the custodian of corporate documents or those belonging to other collective entities such as unions and partnerships and those of bankrupt businesses over claims that the documents will incriminate the custodian despite the fact that producing the documents tacitly admits their existence and their location in the hands of their possessor. The existence and possession or control of the subpoenaed documents being no more in issue here than in the above cases, the summons is equally enforceable.

Moreover, assuming that these aspects of producing the accountant's papers have some minimal testimonial significance, surely it is not illegal to seek accounting help in connection with one's tax returns or for the accountant to prepare workpapers and deliver them to the taxpayer. At this juncture, we are quite unprepared to hold that either the fact of existence of the papers or of their possession by the taxpayer poses any realistic threat of incrimination to the taxpayer.

As for the possibility that responding to the subpoena would authenticate the workpapers, production would express nothing more than the taxpayer's belief that the papers are those described in the subpoena. The taxpayer would be no more competent to authenticate the accountant's workpapers or reports by producing them than he would be to authenticate them if testifying orally. The taxpayer did not prepare the papers and could not vouch for their accuracy. The documents would not be admissible in evidence against the taxpayer without authenticating testimony. Without more, responding to the subpoena in the circumstances before us would not appear to represent a substantial threat of self-incrimination. * * *

Whether the Fifth Amendment would shield the taxpayer from producing his own tax records in his possession is a question not involved here; for the papers demanded here are not his "private papers," see *Boyd v. United States*, supra. We do hold that compliance with a summons directing the taxpayer to produce the accountant's documents involved in this case would involve no incriminating testimony within the protection of the Fifth Amendment.[d]

JUSTICE STEVENS took no part in the consideration or disposition of these cases.

JUSTICE BRENNAN, concurring in the judgment.

Given the prior access by accountants retained by the taxpayers to the papers involved in these cases and the wholly business rather than personal nature of the

---

d. In two subsequent cases the Supreme Court applied *Fisher's* act-of-production doctrine and held the self-incrimination privilege applicable to subpoenas compelling production of documents relating to the business activities of individuals. The first of these cases, *United States v. Doe*, is described in footnote a to the next reprinted opinion, *Braswell v. United States*. In *United States v. Hubbell*, 530 U.S. 27 (2000), the subpoena required production of 11 categories of documents. The Court reasoned that, "given the breadth of the 11 categories [as illustrated by a category calling for "any and all materials * * * relating to any direct or indirect sources of money or other things of value received"] ..., the collection and production of the materials demanded was tantamount to answering a series of interrogatories asking a witness to disclose the existence and location of particular documents fitting certain broad descriptions." The Court rejected the contention that this "communicative aspect of respondent's act" was "insufficiently testimonial" because the existence and possession of such records were "forgone conclusions": "While in *Fisher* the Government already knew that the documents were in the attorney's possession and could independently confirm their existence through the accountants who created them, here the Government has not shown it had any prior knowledge of either the existence or whereabouts of the 13,120

pages of documents ultimately produced * * * [and it] cannot cure this deficiency through the overbroad argument that a businessman such as respondent will always possess general business and tax records that fall within the broad categories described in this subpoena."

The government in *Hubbell* had compelled production of the documents through a grant of act-of-production immunity under § 6002 (See *Kastigar* supra), and it argued that since this immunity extended only to the testimonial content of the act-of-production, it could use the content of the documents produced to lead it to still other documents, provided it did not "advert to the respondent's act of production in order to prove the existence, authenticity, or custody of * * * [its documentary] evidence." Rejecting that position, the Court noted that the government must also show that it had not made "derivative use" of the "testimonial aspects" of respondent's act of production, and it obviously could not do so since that act conveyed information as to the documents produced constituting the "first step in the chain of evidence." It "was only through the respondent's truthful reply to the subpoena that the Government received the incriminating documents of which it made 'substantial use ... in the investigation.'"

papers, I agree that the privilege against compelled self-incrimination did not in either of these cases protect the papers from production in response to the summonses. I do not join the Court's opinion, however, because of the portent of much of what is said of a serious crippling of the protection secured by the privilege against compelled production of one's private books and papers. * * * [I]t is but another step in the denigration of privacy principles settled nearly 100 years ago in *Boyd v. United States*. * * *

Expressions are legion in opinions of this Court that the protection of personal privacy is a central purpose of the privilege against compelled self-incrimination. * * * The Court pays lip-service to this bedrock premise of privacy in the statement that "[w]ithin the limits imposed by the language of the Fifth Amendment, which we necessarily observe, the privilege truly serves privacy interests." But this only makes explicit what elsewhere highlights the opinion, namely, the view that protection of personal privacy is merely a byproduct and not, as our precedents and history teach, a factor controlling in part the determination of the scope of the privilege. This cart-before-the-horse approach is fundamentally at odds with the settled principle that the scope of the privilege is not constrained by the limits of the wording of the Fifth Amendment but has the reach necessary to protect the cherished value of privacy which it safeguards. * * * History and principle, not the mechanical application of its wording, have been the life of the amendment. * * *

History and principle teach that the privacy protected by the Fifth Amendment extends not just to the individual's immediate declarations, oral or written, but also to his testimonial materials in the form of books and papers. * * * An individual's books and papers are generally little more than an extension of his person. They reveal no less than he could reveal upon being questioned directly. Many of the matters within an individual's knowledge may as easily be retained within his head as set down on a scrap of paper. I perceive no principle which does not permit compelling one to disclose the contents of one's mind but does permit compelling the disclosure of the contents of that scrap of paper by compelling its production. Under a contrary view, the constitutional protection would turn on fortuity, and persons would, at their peril, record their thoughts and the events of their lives. The ability to think private thoughts, facilitated as it is by pen and paper, and the ability to preserve intimate memories would be curtailed through fear that those thoughts or the events of those memories would become the subjects of criminal sanctions however invalidly imposed. Indeed, it was the very reality of those fears that helped provide the historical impetus for the privilege. * * *

The Court's treatment of the privilege falls far short of giving it the scope required by history and our precedents. * * * [The Court's] analysis is patently incomplete: the threshold inquiry is whether the taxpayer is compelled to produce incriminating papers. That inquiry is not answered in favor of production merely because the subpoena requires neither oral testimony from nor affirmation of the papers' contents by the taxpayer. To be sure, the Court correctly observes that "[t]he taxpayer cannot avoid compliance with the subpoena *merely* by asserting that the item of evidence which he is required to produce contains incriminating writing, whether his own or that of someone else." For it is not enough that the production of a writing, or books and papers, is compelled. Unless those materials are such as to come within the zone of privacy recognized by the Amendment, the privilege against compulsory self-incrimination does not protect against their production.

We are not without guideposts for determining what books, papers, and writings come within the zone of privacy recognized by the Amendment. * * * *Couch v. United States* expressly held that the Fifth Amendment protected against the compelled production of testimonial evidence only if the individual resisting production had a reasonable expectation of privacy with respect to the evidence. * * * Under *Couch,* therefore, one criterion is whether or not the information sought to be produced has been disclosed to or was within the knowledge of a third party. That is to say, one relevant consideration is the degree to which the paper holder has sought to keep private the contents of the papers he desires not to produce. * * *

A precise cataloguing of private papers within the ambit of the privacy protected by the privilege is probably impossible. Some papers, however, do lend themselves to classification. Production of documentary materials created or authenticated by a State or the Federal Government, such as automobile registrations or property deeds, would seem ordinarily to fall outside the protection of the privilege. They hardly reflect an extension of the person. Economic and business records may present difficulty in particular cases. The records of business entities generally fall without the scope of the privilege. But, as noted, the Court has recognized that the privilege extends to the business records of the sole proprietor or practitioner. Such records are at least an extension of an aspect of a person's activities, though concededly not the more intimate aspects of one's life. Where the privilege would have protected one's mental notes of his business affairs in a less complicated day and age, it would seem that that protection should not fall away because the complexities of another time compel one to keep business records.

Nonbusiness economic records in the possession of an individual, such as canceled checks or tax records, would also seem to be protected. They may provide clear insights into a person's total lifestyle. They are, however, like business records and the papers involved in these cases, frequently, though not always, disclosed to other parties; and disclosure, in proper cases, may foreclose reliance upon the privilege. Personal letters constitute an integral aspect of a person's private enclave. And while letters, being necessarily interpersonal, are not wholly private, their peculiarly private nature and the generally narrow extent of their disclosure would seem to render them within the scope of the privilege. Papers in the nature of a personal diary are *a fortiori* protected under the privilege.

The Court's treatment in the instant cases of the question whether the evidence involved here is within the protection of the privilege is, with all respect, most inadequate. The gaping hole is in the omission of any reference to the taxpayer's privacy interests and to whether the subpoenas impermissibly invade those interests. * * * For the reasons I have stated at the outset, however, I do not believe that the evidence involved in these cases falls within the scope of privacy protected by the Fifth Amendment. * * *

Justice Marshall, concurring in the judgment.

* * * I would have preferred it had the Court found some room in its theory for recognition of the import of the contents of the documents themselves. * * * Nonetheless, I am hopeful that the Court's new theory, properly understood and applied, will provide substantially the same protection as our prior focus on the contents of the documents. * * * Indeed, there would appear to be a precise inverse relationship between the private nature of the document and the permissibility of assuming its existence. Therefore, under the Court's theory, the admission through production that one's diary, letters, prior tax returns, personally

maintained financial records, or canceled checks exist would ordinarily provide substantial testimony. The incriminating nature of such an admission is clear, for while it may not be criminal to keep a diary, or write letters or checks, the admission that one does and that those documents are still available may quickly—or simultaneously—lead to incriminating evidence. If there is a "real danger" of such a result, that is enough under our cases to make such testimony subject to the claim of privilege. Thus, in practice, the Court's approach should still focus upon the private nature of the papers subpoenaed and protect those about which *Boyd* and its progeny were most concerned. * * * For the reasons stated by Mr. Justice Brennan, I concur in the judgment of the Court.e

BRASWELL v. UNITED STATES

487 U.S. 99, 108 S.Ct. 2284, 101 L.Ed.2d 98 (1988).

CHIEF JUSTICE REHNQUIST delivered the opinion of the Court.

This case presents the question whether the custodian of corporate records may resist a subpoena for such records on the ground that the act of production would incriminate him in violation of the Fifth Amendment. We conclude that he may not. * * *

[A federal grand jury issued a subpoena to petitioner Braswell, as the president of two corporations, requiring him to produce the books and records of the two corporations. Worldwide Machinery, Inc. and Worldwide Purchasing, Inc. Petitioner had funded Worldwide Purchasing with his 100 percent interest in Worldwide Machinery and was the sole shareholder of Worldwide Purchasing. While both corporations had three directors, petitioner, his wife, and his mother, only petitioner had authority over the business affairs of the corporations. The grand jury subpoena provided that petitioner could deliver the records to the grand jury agent serving the subpoena and did not require petitioner to testify. Petitioner moved to quash the subpoena, arguing that the act or producing the records would continue a violation of his Fifth Amendment privilege against self-

---

e. In *United States v. Doe*, 465 U.S. 605 (1984), the lower court had concluded that, notwithstanding *Fisher*, the reasoning of *Boyd* continued to hold privileged under the self-incrimination clause a sole proprietor's business records, so long as the content of those records was potentially incriminatory. Rejecting that ruling, the Supreme Court in *Doe* held that the rationale of *Fisher had* established that, where "the preparation of business records is voluntary," the "contents of those records are not privileged." A self-incrimination claim could be based only on the act of production, not the contents of the subpoenaed records. Justice O'Connor, wrote separately "to make explicit what is implicit in the analysis of [the Court's] opinion: that the Fifth Amendment provides absolutely no protection for the contents of private papers of any kind. The notion that the Fifth Amendment protects the privacy of papers originated in *Boyd v. United States*, but our decision in *Fisher v. United States*, sounded the death-knell for *Boyd*." Justice Marshall, joined by Justice Brennan, responded to Justice O'Connor, noting: "Contrary to what Justice O'Connor contends, I do not view the Court's opinion in this case as having reconsidered whether the Fifth Amend-

ment provides protection for the contents of 'private papers of any kind.' * * * [T]he documents at stake here are business records which implicate a lesser degree of concern for privacy interests than, for example, personal diaries. * * * I continue to believe that under the Fifth Amendment 'there are certain documents no person ought to be compelled to produce at the Government's request.' "

In *United States v. Hubbell*, described at footnote d supra, Justice Thomas, in a concurring opinion jointed by Justice Scalia, suggested that the Court should reexamine its rulings limiting the self-incrimination privilege to the testimonial aspects of the act-of-production. He noted that "[a] substantial body of evidence suggests that the Fifth Amendment privilege [was intended to] protect against the compelled production not just of incriminating testimony, but of any incriminating evidence." Justice Thomas noted that such a reading would restore *Boyd* in full force and would render irrelevant "the difficult parsing of the act of responding to a subpoena duces tecum" required by *Fisher*.

incrimination. The district court denied the motion and the Fifth Circuit affirmed.]

There is no question but that the contents of the subpoenaed business records are not privileged. See *United States v. Doe,* 465 U.S. 605 (1984); *Fisher v. United States.* Similarly, petitioner asserts no self-incrimination claim on behalf of the corporations; it is well established that such artificial entities are not protected by the Fifth Amendment. *Bellis v. United States,* 417 U.S. 85 (1974). Petitioner instead relies solely upon the argument that his act of producing the documents has independent testimonial significance, which would incriminate him individually, and that the Fifth Amendment prohibits government compulsion of that act. The bases for this argument are extrapolated from the decisions of this Court in *Fisher* and *Doe.*

In *Fisher,* the Court was presented with the question whether an attorney may resist a subpoena demanding that he produce tax records which had been entrusted to him by his client. * * * In analyzing the Fifth Amendment claim forwarded by the attorney, the Court considered whether the client-taxpayer would have had a valid Fifth Amendment claim had he retained the records and the subpoena been issued to him. After explaining that the Fifth Amendment prohibits "compelling a person to give 'testimony' that incriminates him," the Court rejected the argument that the contents of the records were protected. The Court, however, went on to observe [that] "the act of producing evidence in response to a subpoena nevertheless has communicative aspects of its own, wholly aside from the contents of the papers produced. * * *" The Court concluded that under the "facts and circumstances" there presented, the act of producing the accountants' papers would not "involve testimonial self-incrimination."

Eight years later, in *United States v. Doe,* the Court revisited the question, this time in the context of a claim by a sole proprietor that the compelled production of business records would run afoul of the Fifth Amendment. After rejecting the contention that the contents of the records were themselves protected, the Court proceeded to address whether respondent's act of producing the records would constitute protected testimonial incrimination. The Court concluded that respondent had established a valid Fifth Amendment claim. It deferred to the lower courts, which had found that enforcing the subpoenas at issue would provide the Government valuable information: By producing the records, respondent would admit that the records existed, were in his possession, and were authentic. *Doe* at n. 11.[a]

Had petitioner conducted his business as a sole proprietorship, *Doe* would require that he be provided the opportunity to show that his act of production

---

a. Setting forth the reasoning of the two lower courts, the Supreme Court in *Doe* noted that the District Court had concluded that " 'enforcement of the subpoenas would compel [respondent] to admit that the records exist, that they are in his possession, and that they are authentic.' " The District Court had taken note of the government's contention that the " 'existence, possession, and authenticity of the documents can be proved without [respondent's] testimonial communication,' " but had responded that it was not satisfied " 'as to how that representation can be implemented.' " *Doe* at n. 11. The Court of Appeals had stated that the record failed to indicate that the government knew that "each of the myriad documents demanded * * * in fact is in the appellee's possession," and that the " 'most plausible inference to be drawn from the broad-sweeping subpoenas is that the Government, unable to prove that the subpoenaed documents exist—or that the appellee even is somehow connected to the business entities under investigation—is attempting to compensate for its lack of knowledge by requiring the appellant to become in effect the primary informant against himself.' " *Doe* at n. 12. The Supreme Court later noted that the Government was not foreclosed "from rebutting respondent's claim by producing evidence that possession, existence, and authentication were a 'foregone conclusion' [citing *Fisher*]," but "in this case * * * the Government failed to make such a showing."

would entail testimonial self-incrimination. But petitioner has operated his business through the corporate form, and we have long recognized that for purposes of the Fifth Amendment, corporations and other collective entities are treated differently from individuals. This doctrine—known as the collective entity rule—has a lengthy and distinguished pedigree.

The rule was first articulated by the Court in the case of *Hale v. Henkel*, 201 U.S. 43 (1906). Hale, a corporate officer, had been served with a subpoena ordering him to produce corporate records and to testify concerning certain corporate transactions. Although Hale was protected by personal immunity, he sought to resist the demand for the records by interposing a Fifth Amendment privilege on behalf of the corporation. The Court rejected that argument: "[W]e are of the opinion that there is a clear distinction * * * between an individual and a corporation, and * * * the latter has no right to refuse to submit its books and papers for an examination at the suit of the State." The Court explained that the corporation "is a creature of the State," with powers limited by the State. As such, the State may, in the exercise of its right to oversee the corporation, demand the production of corporate records. * * *

Although *Hale* settled that a corporation has no Fifth Amendment privilege, the Court did not address whether a corporate officer could resist a subpoena for corporate records by invoking his personal privilege—Hale had been protected by immunity. In *Wilson v. United States*, 221 U.S. 361 (1911), the Court answered that question in the negative. There, a grand jury investigating Wilson had issued a subpoena to a corporation demanding the production of corporate letter press copy books, which Wilson, the corporation's president, possessed. Wilson refused to produce the books, arguing that the Fifth Amendment prohibited compulsory production of personally incriminating books that be held and controlled. The Court rejected this argument, observing first that the records sought were not private or personal, but rather belonged to the corporation. The Court continued:

> "[Wilson] held the corporate books subject to the corporate duty. If the corporation were guilty of misconduct, he could not withhold its books to save it; and if he were implicated in the violations of law, he could not withhold the books to protect himself from the effect of their disclosures. The [State's] reserved power of visitation would seriously be embarrassed, if not wholly defeated in its effective exercise, if guilty officers could refuse inspection of the records and papers of the corporation. No personal privilege to which they are entitled requires such a conclusion. * * *"

In a companion case, *Dreier v. United States*, 221 U.S. 394 (1911), the Court applied the holding in *Wilson* to a Fifth Amendment attack on a subpoena addressed to the corporate custodian. Although the subpoena in *Wilson* had been addressed to the corporation, the Court found the distinction irrelevant: "Dreier was not entitled to refuse the production of the corporate records. By virtue of the fact that they were the documents of the corporation in his custody, and not his private papers, he was under the obligation to produce them when called for by proper process."

The next significant step in the development of the collective entity rule occurred in *United States v. White*, 322 U.S. 694 (1944), in which the Court held that a labor union is a collective entity unprotected by the Fifth Amendment. * * * We [reasoned] * * * that the Fifth Amendment privilege applies only to natural individuals and protects only private papers. Representatives of a "collective group" act as agents "[a]nd the official records and documents of the organization that are held by them in a representative rather than in a personal capacity cannot be the subject of the personal privilege against self-incrimination, even though production of the papers might tend to incriminate them personally." With this principle in mind, the Court turned to whether a union is a collective group:

> "The test * * * is whether one can fairly say under all the circumstances that a particular type of organization has a character so impersonal in the scope of its membership and activities that it cannot be said to embody or represent the purely private or personal interests of its constituents, but rather to embody their common or group interests only. If so, the privilege cannot be invoked on behalf of the organization or its representatives in their official capacity. Labor unions—national or local, incorporated or unincorporated—clearly meet that test."

In applying the collective entity rule to unincorporated associations such as unions, the Court jettisoned reliance on the visitatorial powers of the State over corporations owing their existence to the State—one of the bases for earlier decisions.

The frontiers of the collective entity rule were expanded even further in *Bellis v. United States*, 417 U.S. 85 (1974), in which the Court ruled that a partner in a small partnership could not properly refuse to produce partnership records. * * * After rehearsing prior precedent involving corporations and unincorporated associations, the Court examined the partnership form and observed that is had many of the incidents found relevant in prior collective entity decisions. The Court suggested that the test articulated in *White* for determining the applicability of the Fifth Amendment to organizations was "not particularly helpful in the broad range of cases." The Court rejected the notion that the "formulation in *White* can be reduced to a simple proposition based solely upon the size of the organization. It is well settled that no privilege can be claimed by the custodian of corporate records, regardless of how small the corporation may be." * * *

The plain mandate of these decisions is that without regard to whether the subpoena is addressed to the corporation, or as here, to the individual in his capacity as a custodian, see *Dreier*; *Bellis*, a corporate custodian such as petitioner may not resist a subpoena for corporate records on Fifth Amendment grounds. Petitioner argues, however, that this rule falls in the wake of *Fisher* and *Doe*. In essence, petitioner's argument is as follows: In response to *Boyd v. United States*, with its privacy rationale shielding personal books and records, the Court developed the collective entity rule, which declares simply that corporate records are not private and therefore are not protected by the Fifth Amendment. The collective entity decisions were concerned with the contents of the documents subpoenaed, however, and not with the act of production. In *Fisher* and *Doe*, the Court moved away from the privacy based collective entity rule, replacing it with a compelled testimony standard under which the contents of business documents are never privileged but the act of producing the documents may be. Under this new regime, the act of production privilege is available without regard to the entity whose records are being sought. * * *

To be sure, the holding in *Fisher*—later reaffirmed in *Doe*—embarked upon a new course of Fifth Amendment analysis. We cannot agree, however, that it rendered the collective entity rule obsolete. The agency rationale undergirding the collective entity decisions, in which custodians asserted that production of entity records would incriminate them personally, survives. From *Wilson* forward, the Court has consistently recognized that the custodian of corporate or entity records holds those documents in a representative rather than a personal capacity. Artificial entities such as corporations may act only through their agents, and, a custodian's assumption of his representative capacity leads to certain obligations, including the duty to produce corporate records on proper demand by the Government. Under those circumstances, the custodian's act of production is not deemed a personal act, but rather an act of the corporation. Any claim of Fifth Amendment privilege asserted by the agent would be tantamount to a claim of privilege by the corporation—which of course possesses no such privilege. * * *

Indeed, the opinion in *Fisher*—upon which petitioner places primary reliance—indicates that the custodian of corporate records may not interpose a Fifth Amendment objection to the compelled production of corporate records, even though the act of production may prove personally incriminating. The *Fisher* court cited the collective entity decisions with approval and offered those decisions to support the conclusion that the production of the accountant's workpapers would "not * * * involve testimonial self-incrimination." * * * In a footnote, the Court explained: "In these cases compliance with the subpoena is required even though the books have been kept by the person subpoenaed and his producing them would itself be sufficient authentication to permit their introduction against him." n. 14. The Court thus reaffirmed the obligation of a corporate custodian to comply with a subpoena addressed to him.

That point was reiterated by Justice Brennan in his concurrence in *Fisher*. Although Justice Brennan disagreed with the majority as to its use of the collective entity cases to support the proposition that the act of production is not testimonial, he nonetheless acknowledged that a custodian may not resist a subpoena on the ground that the act of production would be incriminating. * * * [For] "one in control of the records of an artificial organization undertakes an obligation with respect to those records foreclosing any exercise of his privilege." Thus, whether one concludes—as did the Court—that a custodian's production of corporate records is deemed not to constitute testimonial self-incrimination, or instead that a custodian waives the right to exercise the privilege, the lesson of *Fisher* is clear: A custodian may not resist a subpoena for corporate records on Fifth Amendment grounds. * * *

We note further that recognizing a Fifth Amendment privilege on behalf of the records custodians of collective entities would have a detrimental impact on the Government's efforts to prosecute "white-collar crime," one of the most serious problems confronting law enforcement authorities. "The greater portion of evidence of wrongdoing by an organization or its representatives is usually found in the official records and documents of that organization. Were the cloak of the privilege to be thrown around these impersonal records and documents, effective enforcement of many federal and state laws would be impossible." *White.* If custodians could assert a privilege, authorities would by stymied not only in their enforcement efforts against those individuals but also in their prosecutions of organizations. In *Bellis,* the Court observed: "In view of the inescapable fact that an artificial entity can only act to produce its records through its individual offices or agents, recognition of the individual's claim of privilege with respect to the financial records of the organization would substantially undermine the unchallenged rule that the organization itself is not entitled to claim any Fifth Amendment privilege, and largely frustrate legitimate governmental regulation of such organizations."

Petitioner suggests, however, that these concerns can be minimized by the simple expedient of either granting the custodian statutory immunity as to the act of production, 18 U.S.C. §§ 6002–6003, or addressing the subpoena to the corporation and allowing it to chose an agent to produce the records who can do so without incriminating himself. We think neither proposal satisfactorily addresses these concerns. Taking the last first, it is no doubt true that if a subpoena is addressed to a corporation, the corporation "must find some means by which to comply because no Fifth Amendment defense is available to it." The means most commonly used to comply is the appointment of an alternate custodian. But petitioner insists he cannot be required to aid the appointed custodian in his search for the demanded records, for any statement to the surrogate would itself be testimonial and incriminating. If this is correct, then petitioner's "solution" is a chimera. In situations such as this—where the corporate custodian is likely the only person with knowledge about the demanded documents—the appointment of a surrogate will simply not ensure that the documents sought will ever reach the grand jury room; the appointed custodian will essentially be sent on an unguided search.

This problem is eliminated if the Government grants the subpoenaed custodian statutory immunity for the testimonial aspects of his act of production. But that "solution" also entails a significant drawback. All of the evidence obtained under a grant of immunity to the custodian may of course be used freely against the corporation, but if the Government has any thought of prosecuting the custodian, a grant of act of production immunity can have serious consequences. Testimony obtained pursuant to a grant of statutory use immunity may be used neither directly nor derivatively. 18 U.S.C. § 6002. And "[o]ne raising a claim under [the federal immunity] statute need only show that he testified under a grant of immunity in order to shift to the government the heavy burden of proving that all of the evidence it proposes to use was derived from legitimate independent sources." *Kastigar.* Even in cases where the Government does not employ the immunized testimony for any purpose—direct or derivative—against the witness, the Government's inability to meet the "heavy burden" it bears may result in the preclusion of crucial evidence that was obtained legitimately.[10]

Although a corporate custodian is not entitled to resist a subpoena on the ground that his act of production will be personally incriminating, we do think certain consequences flow from the fact that the custodian's act of production is one in his representative rather than personal capacity. Because the custodian acts as a representative, the act is deemed one of the corporation and not the individual. Therefore, the Government concedes, as it must, that it may make no evidentiary use of the "individual act" against the individual. For example, in a criminal prosecution against the custodian, the Government may not introduce into evidence before the jury the fact that the subpoena was served upon and the corporation's documents were delivered by one particular individual, the custodian. The Government has the right, however, to use the corporation's act of production against the custodian. The Government may offer testimony—for example, from the process server who delivered the subpoena and from the individual who received the records—establishing that the corporation produced the records subpoenaed. The jury may draw from the corporation's act of production the conclusion that the records in question are authentic corporate records, which the corporation possessed, and which it produced in response to the subpoena. And if the defendant held a prominent position within the corporation that produced the records, the jury may, just as it would had someone else produced the documents, reasonably infer that he had possession of the docu-

10. The dissent asserts that recognition of an act of production privilege on behalf of corporate custodians will not seriously undermine law enforcement efforts directed against those custodians because only the custodian's act of production need be immunized. But the burden of proving an independent source that a grant of immunity places on the Government could, in our view, have just such a deleterious effect on law enforcement efforts.

ments or knowledge of their contents. Because the jury is not told that the defendant produced the records, any nexus between the defendant and the documents results solely from the corporation's act of production and other evidence in the case.[11]

Consistent with our precedent, the United States Court of Appeals for the Fifth Circuit ruled that petitioner could not resist the subpoena for corporate documents on the ground that the act of production might tend to incriminate him. The judgment is therefore affirmed.

JUSTICE KENNEDY, with whom JUSTICE BRENNAN, JUSTICE MARSHALL, and JUSTICE SCALIA join, dissenting.

* * * The majority's apparent reasoning is that collective entities have no privilege and so their employees must have none either. The Court holds that a corporate agent must incriminate himself even when he is named in the subpoena and is a target of the investigation, and even when it is conceded that compliance requires compelled, personal, testimonial, incriminating assertions. I disagree with that conclusion; find no precedent for it; maintain that if there is a likelihood of personal self-incrimination the narrow use immunity permitted by statute can be granted without frustrating the investigation of collective entities; and submit that basic Fifth Amendment principles should not be avoided and manipulated, which is the necessary effect of this decision.

* * * The majority does not challenge the assumption that compliance with the subpoena here would require acts of testimonial self-incrimination from Braswell; indeed, the Government itself made this assumption in submitted its argument. The question presented, therefore, is whether an individual may be compelled, simply by virtue of his status as a corporate custodian, to perform a testimonial act which will incriminate him personally. The majority relies entirely on the collective entity rule in holding that such compulsion is constitutional.

The collective entity rule provides no support for the majority's holding. * * * In none of the collective entity cases cited by the majority, and in none that I have found, were we presented with a claim that the custodian would be incriminated by the act of production, in contrast to the contents of the documents.

The distinction is central. * * * Our decision in *Wilson*, and in later collective entity cases reflected, I believe, the Court's understandable unease with drawing too close a connection between an individual and an artificial entity. On a more practical level, the Court was also unwilling to draw too close a connection between the custodian and the contents of business documents over which he had temporary control but which belonged to his employer, often were prepared by others, and in all events were prepared voluntarily. This last factor became the focus of our analysis in *Fisher*, where we made clear that the applicability of the Fifth Amendment privilege depends on compulsion. *Fisher* put to rest the notion that a privilege may be claimed with respect to the contents of business records that were voluntarily prepared.

The act of producing documents stands on an altogether different footing. While a custodian has no necessary relation to the contents of documents within his control, the act of production is inescapably his own. Production is the precise act compelled by the subpoena, and obedience, in some cases, will require the

---

11. * * * We leave open the question whether the agency rationale supports compelling a custodian to produce corporate records when the custodian is able to establish, by showing for example that he is the sole employee and officer of the corporation, that the jury would inevitably conclude that he produced the records.

custodian's own testimonial assertions. That was the basis of our recognition of the privilege in *United States v. Doe.*

The entity processing the documents in *Doe* was, as the majority points out, a sole proprietorship, not a corporation, partnership, or labor union. But the potential for self-incrimination inheres in the act demanded of the individual, and as a consequence the nature of the entity is irrelevant to determining whether there is ground for the privilege. * * *

Recognition of the privilege here would * * * avoid adoption of the majority's metaphysical progression, which, I respectfully submit, is flawed. Beginning from ordinary principles of agency, the majority proceeds to the conclusion that when a corporate employee, or an employee of a labor union or partnership, complies with a subpoena for production of documents, his act is necessarily and solely the act of the entity. * * * [However,] [t]he heart of the matter, as everyone knows, is that the Government does not see Braswell as a mere agent at all; and the majority's theory is difficult to square with what will often be the Government's actual practice. The subpoena in this case was not directed to Worldwide Machinery Sales, Inc., or Worldwide Purchasing, Inc. It was directed to "Randy Braswell, President, Worldwide Machinery Sales, Inc., Worldwide Purchasing, Inc." and informed him that "[y]ou are hereby commanded" to provide the specified documents. The Government explained at oral argument that it often chooses to designate an individual recipient, rather than the corporation generally, when it serves a subpoena because "[we] want the right to make that individual comply with the subpoena." This is not the language of agency. By issuing a subpoena which the Government insists is "directed to petitioner personally," it has forfeited any claim that it is simply making a demand on a corporation that, in turn, will have to find a physical agent to perform its duty. What the Government seeks instead is the right to choose any corporate agent as a target of its subpoena and compel that individual to disclose certain information by his own actions.

The majority gives the corporate agent fiction a weight it simply cannot bear. In a peculiar attempt to mitigate the force of its own holdings, it impinges upon its own analysis by concluding that, while the Government may compel a named individual to produce records, in any later proceeding against the person it cannot divulge that he performed the act. But if that is so, it is because the Fifth Amendment protects the person without regard to his status as a corporate employee; and once this be admitted, the necessary support for the majority's case has collapsed. * * *

The majority's abiding concern is that if a corporate officer who is the target of a subpoena is allowed to assert the privilege, it will impede the Government's power to investigate corporations, unions, and partnerships, to uncover and prosecute white collar crimes, and otherwise to enforce its visitatorial powers. There are at least two answers to this. The first, and most fundamental, is that the text of the Fifth Amendment does not authorize exceptions premised on such rationales. Second, even if it were proper to invent such exceptions, the dangers prophesied by the majority are overstated.

Recognition of the right to assert a privilege does not mean it will exist in many cases. In many instances, the production of documents may implicate no testimonial assertions at all. In *Fisher,* for example, we held that the specific acts required by the subpoena before us "would not itself involve testimonial self-incrimination" because, in that case, "the existence and location of the papers [were] a foregone conclusion and the taxpayer adds little or nothing to the sum total of the Government's information by conceding that he in fact has the papers." Whether a particular act is testimonial and self-incriminating is largely a factual issue to be decided in each case. In the case before us, the Government has made its submission on the assumption that the subpoena would result in incriminating testimony. The existence of a privilege in future cases, however, is not an automatic result.

Further, to the extent testimonial assertions are being compelled, use immunity can be granted without impeding the investigation. Where the privilege is applicable, immunity will be needed for only one individual, and solely with respect to evidence derived from the act of production itself. The Government would not be denied access to the records it seeks, it would be free to use the contents of the records against everyone, and it would be free to use any testimonial act implicit in production against all but the custodian it selects. In appropriate cases the Government will be able to establish authenticity, possession, and control by means other than compelling assertions about them from a suspect.

In one sense the case before use may not be a particularly sympathetic one. Braswell was the sole stockholder of the corporation and ran it himself. Perhaps that is why the Court suggests he waived his Fifth Amendment self-incrimination rights by using the corporate form. One does not always, however, have the choice of his or her employer, much less the choice of the business enterprise through which the employer conducts its business. Though the Court here hints at a waiver, nothing in Fifth Amendment jurisprudence indicates that the acceptance of employment should be deemed a waiver of a specific protection that is as basic a part of our constitutional heritage as is the privilege against self-incrimination.

The law is not captive to its own fictions. Yet, in the matter before us the Court employs the fiction that personal incrimination of the employee is neither sought by the Government nor cognizable by the law. That is a regrettable holding, for the conclusion is factually unsound, unnecessary for legitimate regulation, and a violation of the Self-Incrimination Clause of the Fifth Amendment of the Constitution. For these reasons, I dissent.[b]

b. The implications of the several doctrines discussed in this section were brought together in an unusual setting in *Baltimore City Department of Social Services v. Bouknight,* 493 U.S. 549 (1990). The Supreme Court there rejected a self-incrimination objection to a subpoena directing respondent Bouknight to produce her infant son, an abused child who had previously been declared a ward of the Court. The Court noted that the respondent could not claim the privilege based upon "anything an examination of the [child] might reveal," as that would be a claim based upon "the contents or nature of the thing demanded." However, the mother could conceivably claim the privilege because "the act of production would amount to testimony regarding her control over and possession of [the child]." While the state could "readily introduce [other] evidence of Bouknight's continuing control over the child" (including the Court order giving her limited custody and her previous statements reflecting control), her "implicit communication of control over [the child] at the moment of production might aid the state in prosecuting Bouknight [for child abuse]." The Court had no need to decide, however, whether "this limited testimonial assertion is sufficiently incriminating and sufficiently testimonial for purposes of the privilege." In receiving conditional custody from the juvenile court, the mother had "assumed custodial duties related to production" (analogous to that of an entity agent) and had done so as part of noncriminal regulatory scheme which included a production component. The Court added that it had no need in the case before it "to define the precise limitations that may exist upon the State's ability to use the testimonial aspects of Bouknight's act of production in subsequent criminal proceedings," but the "imposition of such limitations," as done in *Braswell,* was not "foreclosed."

Chapter 9

PRETRIAL RELEASE

Persons apprehended by the police in the expectation that they will be prosecuted are usually provided an opportunity for pretrial release by one of a variety of means, depending upon the circumstances. If the offense is a very minor one, then release will occur in the field or at the stationhouse upon acceptance of a citation from the officer. In the case of more serious misdemeanors, the arrestee can obtain his release once at the police station by posting cash as a security payment in an amount set in a bail schedule, which simply lists bail amounts for various offenses. Other arrestees must await their first appearance before a judicial officer, when the magistrate will determine the conditions under which the defendant can obtain his release from custody pending the final disposition of the case.

Though bail was once limited almost entirely to the posting of cash or a secured bond, purchased from a professional bondsman, many jurisdictions now permit the defendant to obtain his release by depositing cash amounting to 10% of the amount of bond set by the magistrate. Sometimes the judge will instead release the defendant on his unsecured promise to appear, or in addition impose such nonfinancial conditions as a curfew or reporting periodically to a designated agency. In the many cases in which the magistrate sets financial conditions upon release, he is subject to the Eighth Amendment command: "Excessive bail shall not be required." Just what this means is considered in the first case in this chapter, *Stack v. Boyle.*

The term "preventive detention" is usually used to describe the pretrial detention of a defendant to protect society from the risk of criminal conduct by him pending disposition of the outstanding charges. For many years this was accomplished sub rosa; the magistrate would set money bail purportedly for the purpose of ensuring defendant's appearance at trial, but the amount would be high enough to prevent defendant's release. But because of reform in bail laws contemporaneous with more direct attention to the question of whether such pretrial detention is justified, the process of preventive detention is today a much more open one. This is especially true in the federal criminal justice system; the Bail Reform Act of 1984 on the one hand provides that a judicial officer "may not impose a financial condition that results in the pretrial detention of the person," but on the other expressly authorizes judicially-ordered pretrial detention of defendants in some circumstances to ensure "the safety of any other person or the community." Whether such preventive detention can be squared with the Eighth Amendment provision quoted above is the issue addressed in the other case in this chapter, *United States v. Salerno.*

STACK v. BOYLE

342 U.S. 1, 72 S.Ct. 1, 96 L.Ed. 3 (1951).

CHIEF JUSTICE VINSON delivered the opinion of the Court.

Indictments have been returned in the Southern District of California charging the twelve petitioners with conspiring to violate the Smith Act, [proscribing advocacy of the overthrow of the government by force or violence]. Upon their arrest, bail was fixed for each petitioner in the widely varying amounts of $2,500, $7,500, $75,000 and $100,000. On motion of petitioner Schneiderman following arrest in the Southern District of New York, his bail was reduced to $50,000 before his removal to California. On motion of the Government to increase bail in the case of other petitioners, and after several intermediate procedural steps not material to the issues presented here, bail was fixed in the District Court for the Southern District of California in the uniform amount of $50,000 for each petitioner.

Petitioners moved to reduce bail on the ground that bail as fixed was excessive under the Eighth Amendment. In support of their motion, petitioners submitted statements as to their financial resources, family relationships, health, prior criminal records, and other information. The only evidence offered by the Government was a certified record showing that four persons previously convicted under the Smith Act in the Southern District of New York had forfeited bail. No evidence was produced relating those four persons to the petitioners in this case. At a hearing on the motion, petitioners were examined by the District Judge and cross-examined by an attorney for the Government. Petitioners' factual statements stand uncontroverted.

After their motion to reduce bail was denied, petitioners filed applications for habeas corpus in the same District Court. Upon consideration of the record on the motion to reduce bail, the writs were denied. The Court of Appeals for the Ninth Circuit affirmed.

* * * From the passage of the Judiciary Act of 1789 to the present Federal Rules of Criminal Procedure, Rule 46(a)(1), federal law has unequivocally provided that a person arrested for a non-capital offense *shall* be admitted to bail. This traditional right to freedom before conviction permits the unhampered preparation of a defense, and serves to prevent the infliction of punishment prior to conviction. Unless this right to bail before trial is preserved, the presumption of innocence, secured only after centuries of struggle, would lose its meaning.

The right to release before trial is conditioned upon the accused's giving adequate assurance that he will stand trial and submit to sentence if found guilty. Like the ancient practice of securing the oaths of responsible persons to stand as sureties for the accused, the modern practice of requiring a bail bond or the deposit of a sum of money subject to forfeiture serves as additional assurance of the presence of an accused. Bail set at a figure higher than an amount reasonably calculated to fulfill this purpose is "excessive" under the Eighth Amendment.

Since the function of bail is limited, the fixing of bail for any individual defendant must be based upon standards relevant to the purpose of assuring the presence of that defendant. The traditional standards as expressed in the Federal Rules of Criminal Procedure [3] are to be applied in each case to each defendant.

---

3. Rule 46(c). "AMOUNT. If the defendant is admitted to bail, the amount thereof shall be such as in the judgment of the commissioner or court or judge or justice will insure the presence of the defendant, having regard to the nature and circumstances of the offense

* * * Upon final judgment of conviction, petitioners face imprisonment of not more than five years and a fine of not more than $10,000. It is not denied that bail for each petitioner has been fixed in a sum much higher than that usually imposed for offenses with like penalties and yet there has been no factual showing to justify such action in this case. The Government asks the courts to depart from the norm by assuming, without the introduction of evidence, that each petitioner is a pawn in a conspiracy and will, in obedience to a superior, flee the jurisdiction. To infer from the fact of indictment alone a need for bail in an unusually high amount is an arbitrary act. Such conduct would inject into our own system of government the very principles of totalitarianism which Congress was seeking to guard against in passing the statute under which petitioners have been indicted.

If bail in an amount greater than that usually fixed for serious charges of crimes is required in the case of any of the petitioners, that is a matter to which evidence should be directed in a hearing so that the constitutional rights of each petitioner may be preserved. In the absence of such a showing, we are of the opinion that the fixing of bail before trial in these cases cannot be squared with the statutory and constitutional standards for admission to bail.

* * * Accordingly, [p]etitioners may move for reduction of bail in the criminal proceeding so that a hearing may be held for the purpose of fixing reasonable bail for each petitioner. * * * [a]

UNITED STATES v. SALERNO

481 U.S. 739, 107 S.Ct. 2095, 95 L.Ed.2d 697 (1987).

CHIEF JUSTICE REHNQUIST delivered the opinion of the Court. * * *

I

Responding to "the alarming problem of crimes committed by persons on release," Congress formulated the Bail Reform Act of 1984, 18 U.S.C. § 3141 et seq., as the solution to a bail crisis in the federal courts. The Act represents the National Legislature's considered response to numerous perceived deficiencies in the federal bail process. By providing for sweeping changes in both the way federal courts consider bail applications and the circumstances under which bail is granted, Congress hoped to "give the courts adequate authority to make release decisions that give appropriate recognition to the danger a person may pose to others if released."

To this end, § 3141(a) of the Act requires a judicial officer to determine whether an arrestee shall be detained. Section 3142(e) provides that "[i]f, after a hearing pursuant to the provisions of subsection (f), the judicial officer finds that no condition or combination of conditions will reasonably assure the appearance of the person as required and the safety of any other person and the community, he shall order the detention of the person prior to trial." Section 3142(f) provides the arrestee with a number of procedural safeguards. He may request the presence of counsel at the detention hearing, he may testify and present witnesses in his behalf, as well as proffer evidence, and he may cross-examine other witnesses appearing at the hearing. If the judicial officer finds that no conditions of pretrial release can reasonably assure the safety of other persons and the

charged, the weight of the evidence against him, the financial ability of the defendant to give bail and the character of the defendant."

a. The separate opinion of Justice Jackson, joined by Justice Frankfurter, is omitted. Justice Minton did not participate.

community, he must state his findings of fact in writing, and support his conclusion with "clear and convincing evidence."

The judicial officer is not given unbridled discretion in making the detention determination. Congress has specified the considerations relevant to that decision. These factors include the nature and seriousness of the charges, the substantiality of the government's evidence against the arrestee, the arrestee's background and characteristics, and the nature and seriousness of the danger posed by the suspect's release. Should a judicial officer order detention, the detainee is entitled to expedited appellate review of the detention order.

Respondents Anthony Salerno and Vincent Cafaro were arrested on March 21, 1986, after being charged in a 29–count indictment alleging various Racketeer Influenced and Corrupt Organizations Act (RICO) violations, mail and wire fraud offenses, extortion, and various criminal gambling violations. The RICO counts alleged 35 acts of racketeering activity, including fraud, extortion, gambling, and conspiracy to commit murder. At respondents' arraignment, the Government moved to have Salerno and Cafaro detained pursuant to § 3142(e), on the ground that no condition of release would assure the safety of the community or any person. The District Court held a hearing at which the Government made a detailed proffer of evidence. The Government's case showed that Salerno was the "boss" of the Genovese Crime Family of La Cosa Nostra and that Cafaro was a "captain" in the Genovese Family. According to the Government's proffer, based in large part on conversations intercepted by a court-ordered wiretap, the two respondents had participated in wide-ranging conspiracies to aid their illegitimate enterprises through violent means. The Government also offered the testimony of two of its trial witnesses, who would assert that Salerno personally participated in two murder conspiracies. Salerno opposed the motion for detention, challenging the credibility of the Government's witnesses. He offered the testimony of several character witnesses as well as a letter from his doctor stating that he was suffering from a serious medical condition. Cafaro presented no evidence at the hearing, but instead characterized the wiretap conversations as merely "tough talk."

The District Court granted the Government's detention motion, concluding that the Government had established by clear and convincing evidence that no condition or combination of conditions of release would ensure the safety of the community or any person. * * *

Respondents appealed, contending that to the extent that the Bail Reform Act permits pretrial detention on the ground that the arrestee is likely to commit future crimes, it is unconstitutional on its face. Over a dissent, the United States Court of Appeals for the Second Circuit agreed. Although the court agreed that pretrial detention could be imposed if the defendants were likely to intimidate witnesses or otherwise jeopardize the trial process, it found "§ 3142(e)'s authorization of pretrial detention [on the ground of future dangerousness] repugnant to the concept of substantive due process, which we believe prohibits the total deprivation of liberty simply as a means of preventing future crimes." The court concluded that the Government could not, consistent with due process, detain persons who had not been accused of any crime merely because they were thought to present a danger to the community. It reasoned that our criminal law system holds persons accountable for past actions, not anticipated future actions. Although a court could detain an arrestee who threatened to flee before trial, such detention would be permissible because it would serve the basic objective of a criminal system—bringing the accused to trial. The court distinguished our decision in *Gerstein v. Pugh* [fn. a, ch. 3, § 5], in which we upheld police detention pursuant to arrest. The court construed *Gerstein* as limiting such detention to the " 'administrative steps incident to arrest.' " The Court of Appeals also found our decision in *Schall v. Martin,* 467 U.S. 253 (1984), upholding postarrest pretrial detention of juveniles, inapposite because juveniles have a lesser interest in liberty than do adults. * * *

II

A facial challenge to a legislative Act is, of course, the most difficult challenge to mount successfully, since the challenger must establish that no set of circumstances exists under which the Act would be valid. The fact that the Bail Reform Act might operate unconstitutionally under some conceivable set of circumstances is insufficient to render it wholly invalid, since we have not recognized an "overbreadth" doctrine outside the limited context of the First Amendment. We think respondents have failed to shoulder their heavy burden to demonstrate that the Act is "facially" unconstitutional.[3]

Respondents present two grounds for invalidating the Bail Reform Act's provisions permitting pretrial detention on the basis of future dangerousness. First, they rely upon the Court of Appeals' conclusion that the Act exceeds the limitations placed upon the Federal Government by the Due Process Clause of the Fifth Amendment. Second, they contend that the Act contravenes the Eighth Amendment's proscription against excessive bail. We treat these contentions in turn.

A

The Due Process Clause of the Fifth Amendment provides that "No person shall * * * be deprived of life, liberty, or property, without due process of law * * *." This Court has held that the Due Process Clause protects individuals against two types of government action. So-called "substantive due process" prevents the government from engaging in conduct that "shocks the conscience," or interferes with rights "implicit in the concept of ordered liberty." When government action depriving a person of life, liberty, or property survives substantive due process scrutiny, it must still be implemented in a fair manner. This requirement has traditionally been referred to as "procedural" due process.

Respondents first argue that the Act violates substantive due process because the pretrial detention it authorizes constitutes impermissible punishment before trial. The Government, however, has never argued that pretrial detention could be upheld if it were "punishment." The Court of Appeals assumed that pretrial detention under the Bail Reform Act is regulatory, not penal, and we agree that it is.

As an initial matter, the mere fact that a person is detained does not inexorably lead to the conclusion that the government has imposed punishment. To determine whether a restriction on liberty constitutes impermissible punishment or permissible regulation, we first look to legislative intent. Unless Congress expressly intended to impose punitive restrictions, the punitive/regulatory distinction turns on " 'whether an alternative purpose to which [the restriction] may rationally be connected is assignable for it, and whether it appears excessive in relation to the alternative purpose assigned [to it].' "

We conclude that the detention imposed by the Act falls on the regulatory side of the dichotomy. The legislative history of the Bail Reform Act clearly

3. We intimate no view on the validity of any aspects of the Act that are not relevant to respondents' case. Nor have respondents claimed that the Act is unconstitutional because of the way it was applied to the particular facts of their case.

indicates that Congress did not formulate the pretrial detention provisions as punishment for dangerous individuals. Congress instead perceived pretrial detention as a potential solution to a pressing societal problem. There is no doubt that preventing danger to the community is a legitimate regulatory goal.

Nor are the incidents of pretrial detention excessive in relation to the regulatory goal Congress sought to achieve. The Bail Reform Act carefully limits the circumstances under which detention may be sought to the most serious of crimes. See 18 U.S.C. § 3142(f) (detention hearings available if case involves crimes of violence, offenses for which the sentence is life imprisonment or death, serious drug offenses, or certain repeat offenders). The arrestee is entitled to a prompt detention hearing, and the maximum length of pretrial detention is limited by the stringent time limitations of the Speedy Trial Act.[4] Moreover, as in *Schall v. Martin,* the conditions of confinement envisioned by the Act "appear to reflect the regulatory purposes relied upon by the" government. As in *Schall,* the statute at issue here requires that detainees be housed in a "facility separate, to the extent practicable, from persons awaiting or serving sentences or being held in custody pending appeal." We conclude, therefore, that the pretrial detention contemplated by the Bail Reform Act is regulatory in nature, and does not constitute punishment before trial in violation of the Due Process Clause.

The Court of Appeals nevertheless concluded that "the Due Process Clause prohibits pretrial detention on the ground of danger to the community as a regulatory measure, without regard to the duration of the detention." Respondents characterize the Due Process Clause as erecting an impenetrable "wall" in this area that "no governmental interest—rational, important, compelling or otherwise—may surmount."

We do not think the Clause lays down any such categorical imperative. We have repeatedly held that the government's regulatory interest in community safety can, in appropriate circumstances, outweigh an individual's liberty interest. For example, in times of war or insurrection, when society's interest is at its peak, the government may detain individuals whom the government believes to be dangerous. Even outside the exigencies of war, we have found that sufficiently compelling governmental interests can justify detention of dangerous persons. Thus, we have found no absolute constitutional barrier to detention of potentially dangerous resident aliens pending deportation proceedings. We have also held that the government may detain mentally unstable individuals who present a danger to the public, and dangerous defendants who become incompetent to stand trial. We have approved of postarrest regulatory detention of juveniles when they present a continuing danger to the community. *Schall v. Martin.* Even competent adults may face substantial liberty restrictions as a result of the operation of our criminal justice system. If the police suspect an individual of a crime, they may arrest and hold him until a neutral magistrate determines whether probable cause exists. *Gerstein v. Pugh.* Finally, respondents concede and the Court of Appeals noted that an arrestee may be incarcerated until trial if he presents a risk of flight or a danger to witnesses.

Respondents characterize all of these cases as exceptions to the "general rule" of substantive due process that the government may not detain a person prior to a judgment of guilt in a criminal trial. Such a "general rule" may freely be conceded, but we think that these cases show a sufficient number of exceptions to the rule that the congressional action challenged here can hardly be character-

4. We intimate no view as to the point at which detention in a particular case might become excessively prolonged, and therefore punitive, in relation to Congress' regulatory goal.

ized as totally novel. Given the well-established authority of the government, in special circumstances, to restrain individuals' liberty prior to or even without criminal trial and conviction, we think that the present statute providing for pretrial detention on the basis of dangerousness must be evaluated in precisely the same manner that we evaluated the laws in the cases discussed above.

The government's interest in preventing crime by arrestees is both legitimate and compelling. In *Schall,* we recognized the strength of the State's interest in preventing juvenile crime. This general concern with crime prevention is no less compelling when the suspects are adults. Indeed, "[t]he harm suffered by the victim of a crime is not dependent upon the age of the perpetrator." The Bail Reform Act of 1984 responds to an even more particularized governmental interest than the interest we sustained in *Schall.* The statute we upheld in *Schall* permitted pretrial detention of any juvenile arrested on any charge after a showing that the individual might commit some undefined further crimes. The Bail Reform Act, in contrast, narrowly focuses on a particularly acute problem in which the government interests are overwhelming. The Act operates only on individuals who have been arrested for a specific category of extremely serious offenses. Congress specifically found that these individuals are far more likely to be responsible for dangerous acts in the community after arrest. Nor is the Act by any means a scattershot attempt to incapacitate those who are merely suspected of these serious crimes. The government must first of all demonstrate probable cause to believe that the charged crime has been committed by the arrestee, but that is not enough. In a full-blown adversary hearing, the government must convince a neutral decisionmaker by clear and convincing evidence that no conditions of release can reasonably assure the safety of the community or any person. While the government's general interest in preventing crime is compelling, even this interest is heightened when the government musters convincing proof that the arrestee, already indicted or held to answer for a serious crime, presents a demonstrable danger to the community. Under these narrow circumstances, society's interest in crime prevention is at its greatest.

On the other side of the scale, of course, is the individual's strong interest in liberty. We do not minimize the importance and fundamental nature of this right. But, as our cases hold, this right may, in circumstances where the government's interest is sufficiently weighty, be subordinated to the greater needs of society. We think that Congress' careful delineation of the circumstances under which detention will be permitted satisfies this standard. When the government proves by clear and convincing evidence that an arrestee presents an identified and articulable threat to an individual or the community, we believe that, consistent with the Due Process Clause, a court may disable the arrestee from executing that threat. Under these circumstances, we cannot categorically state that pretrial detention "offends some principle of justice so rooted in the traditions and conscience of our people as to be ranked as fundamental."

Finally, we may dispose briefly of respondents' facial challenge to the procedures of the Bail Reform Act. To sustain them against such a challenge, we need only find them "adequate to authorize the pretrial detention of at least some [persons] charged with crimes," whether or not they might be insufficient in some particular circumstances. We think they pass that test. As we stated in *Schall,* "there is nothing inherently unattainable about a prediction of future criminal conduct."

Under the Bail Reform Act, the procedures by which a judicial officer evaluates the likelihood of future dangerousness are specifically designed to further the accuracy of that determination. Detainees have a right to counsel at the detention hearing. They may testify in their own behalf, present information by proffer or otherwise, and cross-examine witnesses who appear at the hearing. Ibid. The judicial officer charged with the responsibility of determining the appropriateness of detention is guided by statutorily enumerated factors, which include the nature and the circumstances of the charges, the weight of the evidence, the history and characteristics of the putative offender, and the danger to the community. The government must prove its case by clear and convincing evidence. Finally, the judicial officer must include written findings of fact and a written statement of reasons for a decision to detain. The Act's review provisions provide for immediate appellate review of the detention decision.

We think these extensive safeguards suffice to repel a facial challenge. The protections are more exacting than those we found sufficient in the juvenile context, see *Schall,* and they far exceed what we found necessary to effect limited postarrest detention in *Gerstein v. Pugh.* Given the legitimate and compelling regulatory purpose of the Act and the procedural protections it offers, we conclude that the Act is not facially invalid under the Due Process Clause of the Fifth Amendment.

B

Respondents also contend that the Bail Reform Act violates the Excessive Bail Clause of the Eighth Amendment. * * *

The Eighth Amendment addresses pretrial release by providing merely that "Excessive bail shall not be required." This Clause, of course, says nothing about whether bail shall be available at all. Respondents nevertheless contend that this Clause grants them a right to bail calculated solely upon considerations of flight. They rely on *Stack v. Boyle* in which the Court stated that "Bail set at a figure higher than an amount reasonably calculated [to ensure the defendant's presence at trial] is 'excessive' under the Eighth Amendment." In respondents' view, since the Bail Reform Act allows a court essentially to set bail at an infinite amount for reasons not related to the risk of flight, it violates the Excessive Bail Clause. Respondents concede that the right to bail they have discovered in the Eighth Amendment is not absolute. A court may, for example, refuse bail in capital cases. And, as the Court of Appeals noted and respondents admit, a court may refuse bail when the defendant presents a threat to the judicial process by intimidating witnesses. Respondents characterize these exceptions as consistent with what they claim to be the sole purpose of bail—to ensure integrity of the judicial process.

While we agree that a primary function of bail is to safeguard the courts' role in adjudicating the guilt or innocence of defendants, we reject the proposition that the Eighth Amendment categorically prohibits the government from pursuing other admittedly compelling interests through regulation of pretrial release. The above-quoted *dicta* in *Stack v. Boyle* is far too slender a reed on which to rest this argument. The Court in *Stack* had no occasion to consider whether the Excessive Bail Clause requires courts to admit all defendants to bail, because the statute before the Court in that case in fact allowed the defendants to be bailed. * * *

The holding of *Stack* is illuminated by the Court's holding just four months later in *Carlson v. Landon,* 342 U.S. 524 (1952). In that case, remarkably similar to the present action, the detainees had been arrested and held without bail pending a determination of deportability. The Attorney General refused to release the individuals, "on the ground that there was reasonable cause to believe that [their] release would be prejudicial to the public interest and *would endanger the welfare and safety of the United States.*" (emphasis added). The detainees brought the same challenge that respondents bring to us today: the Eighth Amendment required them to be admitted to bail. The Court squarely rejected this proposition:

> "The bail clause was lifted with slight changes from the English Bill of Rights Act. In England that clause has never been thought to accord a right to bail in all cases, but merely to provide that bail shall not be excessive in those cases where it is proper to grant bail. When this clause was carried over into our Bill of Rights, nothing was said that indicated any different concept. The Eighth Amendment has not prevented Congress from defining the classes of cases in which bail shall be allowed in this country. Thus, in criminal cases bail is not compulsory where the punishment may be death. Indeed, the very language of the Amendment fails to say all arrests must be bailable."

Carlson v. Landon was a civil case, and we need not decide today whether the Excessive Bail Clause speaks at all to Congress' power to define the classes of criminal arrestees who shall be admitted to bail. For even if we were to conclude that the Eighth Amendment imposes some substantive limitations on the National Legislature's powers in this area, we would still hold that the Bail Reform Act is valid. Nothing in the text of the Bail Clause limits permissible government considerations solely to questions of flight. The only arguable substantive limitation of the Bail Clause is that the government's proposed conditions of release or detention not be "excessive" in light of the perceived evil. Of course, to determine whether the government's response is excessive, we must compare that response against the interest the government seeks to protect by means of that response. Thus, when the government has admitted that its only interest is in preventing flight, bail must be set by a court at a sum designed to ensure that goal, and no more. We believe that when Congress has mandated detention on the basis of a compelling interest other than prevention of flight, as it has here, the Eighth Amendment does not require release on bail.

III

In our society liberty is the norm, and detention prior to trial or without trial is the carefully limited exception. We hold that the provisions for pretrial detention in the Bail Reform Act of 1984 fall within that carefully limited exception. * * * We are unwilling to say that this congressional determination, based as it is upon that primary concern of every government—a concern for the safety and indeed the lives of its citizens—on its face violates either the Due Process Clause of the Fifth Amendment or the Excessive Bail Clause of the Eighth Amendment.

JUSTICE MARSHALL, with whom JUSTICE BRENNAN joins, dissenting. * * *

II

The majority approaches respondents' challenge to the Act by dividing the discussion into two sections, one concerned with the substantive guarantees implicit in the Due Process Clause, and the other concerned with the protection afforded by the Excessive Bail Clause of the Eighth Amendment. This is a sterile formalism, which divides a unitary argument into two independent parts and then professes to demonstrate that the parts are individually inadequate.

On the due process side of this false dichotomy appears an argument concerning the distinction between regulatory and punitive legislation. The majority concludes that the Act is a regulatory rather than a punitive measure. The ease with which the conclusion is reached suggests the worthlessness of the achievement. The major premise is that "[u]nless Congress expressly intended to impose punitive restrictions, the punitive/regulatory distinction turns on ' "whether an alternative purpose to which [the restriction] may rationally be connected is assignable for it, and whether it appears excessive in relation to the alternative purpose assigned [to it]." ' " The majority finds that "Congress did not formulate the pretrial detention provisions as punishment for dangerous individuals," but instead was pursuing the "legitimate regulatory goal" of "preventing danger to the community." Concluding that pretrial detention is not an excessive solution to the problem of preventing danger to the community, the majority thus finds that no substantive element of the guarantee of due process invalidates the statute.

This argument does not demonstrate the conclusion it purports to justify. Let us apply the majority's reasoning to a similar, hypothetical case. After investigation, Congress determines (not unrealistically) that a large proportion of violent crime is perpetrated by persons who are unemployed. It also determines, equally reasonably, that much violent crime is committed at night. From amongst the panoply of "potential solutions," Congress chooses a statute which permits, after judicial proceedings, the imposition of a dusk-to-dawn curfew on anyone who is unemployed. Since this is not a measure enacted for the purpose of punishing the unemployed, and since the majority finds that preventing danger to the community is a legitimate regulatory goal, the curfew statute would, according to the majority's analysis, be a mere "regulatory" detention statute, entirely compatible with the substantive components of the Due Process Clause.

The absurdity of this conclusion arises, of course, from the majority's cramped concept of substantive due process. The majority proceeds as though the only substantive right protected by the Due Process Clause is a right to be free from punishment before conviction. The majority's technique for infringing this right is simple: merely redefine any measure which is claimed to be punishment as "regulation," and, magically, the Constitution no longer prohibits its imposition. Because, as I discuss in Part III, infra, the Due Process Clause protects other substantive rights which are infringed by this legislation, the majority's argument is merely an exercise in obfuscation.

The logic of the majority's Eighth Amendment analysis is equally unsatisfactory. The Eighth Amendment, as the majority notes, states that "[e]xcessive bail shall not be required." The majority then declares, as if it were undeniable, that: "[t]his Clause, of course, says nothing about whether bail shall be available at all." If excessive bail is imposed the defendant stays in jail. The same result is achieved if bail is denied altogether. Whether the magistrate sets bail at $1 billion or refuses to set bail at all, the consequences are indistinguishable. It would be mere sophistry to suggest that the Eighth Amendment protects against the former decision, and not the latter. Indeed, such a result would lead to the conclusion that there was no need for Congress to pass a preventive detention measure of any kind; every federal magistrate and district judge could simply refuse, despite the absence of any evidence of risk of flight or danger to the community, to set bail. This would be entirely constitutional, since, according to the majority, the Eighth Amendment "says nothing about whether bail shall be available at all."

But perhaps, the majority says, this manifest absurdity can be avoided. Perhaps the Bail Clause is addressed only to the judiciary. "[W]e need not decide today," the majority says, "whether the Excessive Bail Clause speaks at all to Congress' power to define the classes of criminal arrestees who shall be admitted to bail." The majority is correct that this question need not be decided today; it was decided long ago. Federal and state statutes which purport to accomplish what the Eighth Amendment forbids, such as imposing cruel and unusual punishments, may not stand. The text of the Amendment, which provides simply that "[e]xcessive bail shall not be required, nor excessive fines imposed, nor cruel and unusual punishments inflicted," provides absolutely no support for the majority's speculation that both courts and Congress are forbidden to inflict cruel and unusual punishments, while only the courts are forbidden to require excessive bail.[5]

* * * The majority concedes, as it must, that "when the government has admitted that its only interest is in preventing flight, bail must be set by a court at a sum designed to ensure that goal, and no more." But, the majority says, "when Congress has mandated detention on the basis of a compelling interest other than prevention of flight, as it has here, the Eighth Amendment does not require release on bail." This conclusion follows only if the "compelling" interest upon which Congress acted is an interest which the Constitution permits Congress to further through the denial of bail. The majority does not ask, as a result of its disingenuous division of the analysis, if there are any substantive limits contained in both the Eighth Amendment and the Due Process Clause which render this system of preventive detention unconstitutional. The majority does not ask because the answer is apparent and, to the majority, inconvenient.

III

The essence of this case may be found, ironically enough, in a provision of the Act to which the majority does not refer. Title 18 U.S.C. § 3142(j) provides that "[n]othing in this section shall be construed as modifying or limiting the presumption of innocence." But the very pith and purpose of this statute is an abhorrent limitation of the presumption of innocence. The majority's untenable conclusion that the present Act is constitutional arises from a specious denial of the role of the Bail Clause and the Due Process Clause in protecting the invaluable guarantee afforded by the presumption of innocence.

"The principle that there is a presumption of innocence in favor of the accused is the undoubted law, axiomatic and elementary, and its enforcement lies at the foundation of the administration of our criminal law." Our society's belief, reinforced over the centuries, that all are innocent until the state has proven them to be guilty, like the companion principle that guilt must be proved beyond a reasonable doubt, is "implicit in the concept of ordered liberty," and is established beyond legislative contravention in the Due Process Clause.

The statute now before us declares that persons who have been indicted may be detained if a judicial officer finds clear and convincing evidence that they pose a danger to individuals or to the community. The statute does not authorize the government to imprison anyone it has evidence is dangerous; indictment is necessary. But let us suppose that a defendant is indicted and the government shows by clear and convincing evidence that he is dangerous and should be detained pending a trial, at which trial the defendant is acquitted. May the

---

5. The majority refers to the statement in *Carlson v. Landon* that the Bail Clause was adopted by Congress from the English Bill of Rights Act of 1689, and that "[i]n England that clause has never been thought to accord a right to bail in all cases, but merely to provide that bail shall not be excessive in those cases where it is proper to grant bail." A sufficient answer to this meagre argument was made at the time by Justice Black:

"The Eighth Amendment is in the American Bill of Rights of 1789, not the English Bill of Rights of 1689." *Carlson v. Landon* (dissenting opinion). Our Bill of Rights is contained in a written Constitution one of whose purposes is to protect the rights of the people against infringement by the Legislature, and its provisions, whatever their origins, are interpreted in relation to those purposes.

government continue to hold the defendant in detention based upon its showing that he is dangerous? The answer cannot be yes, for that would allow the government to imprison someone for uncommitted crimes based upon "proof" not beyond a reasonable doubt. The result must therefore be that once the indictment has failed, detention cannot continue. But our fundamental principles of justice declare that the defendant is as innocent on the day before his trial as he is on the morning after his acquittal. Under this statute an untried indictment somehow acts to permit a detention, based on other charges, which after an acquittal would be unconstitutional. The conclusion is inescapable that the indictment has been turned into evidence, if not that the defendant is guilty of the crime charged, then that left to his own devices he will soon be guilty of something else.

To be sure, an indictment is not without legal consequences. It establishes that there is probable cause to believe that an offense was committed, and that the defendant committed it. Upon probable cause a warrant for the defendant's arrest may issue; a period of administrative detention may occur before the evidence of probable cause is presented to a neutral magistrate. See *Gerstein v. Pugh.* Once a defendant has been committed for trial he may be detained in custody if the magistrate finds that no conditions of release will prevent him from becoming a fugitive. But in this connection the charging instrument is evidence of nothing more than the fact that there will be a trial, and

> "release before trial is conditioned upon the accused's giving adequate assurance that he will stand trial and submit to sentence if found guilty. Like the ancient practice of securing the oaths of responsible persons to stand as sureties for the accused, the modern practice of requiring a bail bond or the deposit of a sum of money subject to forfeiture serves as additional assurance of the presence of an accused." *Stack v. Boyle.*[6]

The finding of probable cause conveys power to try, and the power to try imports of necessity the power to assure that the processes of justice will not be evaded or obstructed. "Pretrial detention to prevent future crimes against society at large, however, is not justified by any concern for holding a trial on the charges for which a defendant has been arrested." The detention purportedly authorized by this statute bears no relation to the government's power to try charges supported by a finding of probable cause, and thus the interests it serves are outside the scope of interests which may be considered in weighing the excessiveness of bail under the Eighth Amendment. * * *

IV

* * * Honoring the presumption of innocence is often difficult; sometimes we must pay substantial social costs as a result of our commitment to the values we espouse. But at the end of the day the presumption of innocence protects the innocent; the shortcuts we take with those whom we believe to be guilty injure only those wrongfully accused and, ultimately, ourselves. * * *

I dissent.

JUSTICE STEVENS, dissenting.

6. The majority states that denial of bail in capital cases has traditionally been the rule rather than the exception. And this of course is so, for it has been the considered presumption of generations of judges that a defendant in danger of execution has an extremely strong incentive to flee. If in any particular case the presumed likelihood of flight should be made irrebuttable, it would in all probability violate the Due Process Clause. Thus what the majority perceives as an exception is nothing more than an example of the traditional operation of our system of bail.

There may be times when the government's interest in protecting the safety of the community will justify the brief detention of a person who has not committed any crime.   * * * [But] it is clear to me that a pending indictment may not be given any weight in evaluating an individual's risk to the community or the need for immediate detention.

If the evidence of imminent danger is strong enough to warrant emergency detention, it should support that preventive measure regardless of whether the person has been charged, convicted, or acquitted of some other offense.   In this case, for example, it is unrealistic to assume that the danger to the community that was present when respondents were at large did not justify their detention before they were indicted, but did require that measure the moment that the grand jury found probable cause to believe they had committed crimes in the past. It is equally unrealistic to assume that the danger will vanish if a jury happens to acquit them.   Justice Marshall has demonstrated that the fact of indictment cannot, consistent with the presumption of innocence and the Eighth Amendment's Excessive Bail Clause, be used to create a special class the members of which are, alone, eligible for detention because of future dangerousness.

* * *

Chapter 10

THE DECISION WHETHER TO PROSECUTE

SECTION 1. THE DECISION TO PROSECUTE

The charging decision, made by the prosecutor except in minor cases, involves a determination of whether a person should be formally accused of a crime and thus subjected to trial if he does not first plead guilty. Although the charging decision is not inevitably so complex, it often involves these determinations: (i) whether there is sufficient evidence to support a prosecution (which, as a practical matter, the prosecutor will determine by assessing whether the likelihood of conviction is sufficiently strong to justify use of his resources to that end); (ii) if so, whether there are nonetheless reasons for not subjecting the defendant to the criminal process; and (iii) if so, whether nonprosecution should be conditioned upon the defendant's participation in a pretrial diversion program (much like probation, but without an antecedent conviction).

The American prosecutor has traditionally exercised considerable discretion in deciding whether or not to prosecute, that is, in determining whether prosecution is called for in a given case as a matter of enforcement policy. The explanations for this phenomenon most often given are (a) because of legislative "overcriminalization," (b) because of limitations in available enforcement resources; and (c) because of a need to individualize justice beyond that possible under existing crime definitions and sentencing options. This discretion is largely uncontrolled; especially when the prosecutor elects in a particular case *not* to proceed with prosecution, there is seldom available any mechanism by which any dissatisfied person may challenge that decision. When the prosecutor instead decides *in favor* of prosecution, the defendant is obviously motivated to challenge this exercise of discretion and at least sometimes may have a potential legal basis for doing so—such as that his selection for prosecution is a denial of equal protection of the laws or constitutes an impermissible "chilling" of some constitutional right (e.g., freedom of speech). But, as *United States v. Armstrong* teaches, it is very difficult for a defendant to prevail in such a challenge.

UNITED STATES v. ARMSTRONG

517 U.S. 456, 116 S.Ct. 1480, 134 L.Ed.2d 687 (1996).

CHIEF JUSTICE REHNQUIST delivered the opinion of the Court. * * *

In April 1992, respondents were indicted in the United States District Court for the Central District of California on charges of conspiring to possess with

515

intent to distribute more than 50 grams of cocaine base (crack) and conspiring to distribute the same, in violation of 21 U.S.C. §§ 841 and 846, and federal firearms offenses. For three months prior to the indictment, agents of the Federal Bureau of Alcohol, Tobacco, and Firearms and the Narcotics Division of the Inglewood, California, Police Department had infiltrated a suspected crack distribution ring by using three confidential informants. On seven separate occasions during this period, the informants had bought a total of 124.3 grams of crack from respondents and witnessed respondents carrying firearms during the sales. The agents searched the hotel room in which the sales were transacted, arrested respondents Armstrong and Hampton in the room, and found more crack and a loaded gun. The agents later arrested the other respondents as part of the ring.

In response to the indictment, respondents filed a motion for discovery or for dismissal of the indictment, alleging that they were selected for federal prosecution because they are black. In support of their motion, they offered only an affidavit by a "Paralegal Specialist," employed by the Office of the Federal Public Defender representing one of the respondents. The only allegation in the affidavit was that, in every one of the 24 §§ 841 or 846 cases closed by the office during 1991, the defendant was black. Accompanying the affidavit was a "study" listing the 24 defendants, their race, whether they were prosecuted for dealing cocaine as well as crack, and the status of each case.

The Government opposed the discovery motion, arguing, among other things, that there was no evidence or allegation "that the Government has acted unfairly or has prosecuted non-black defendants or failed to prosecute them." The District Court granted the motion. It ordered the Government (1) to provide a list of all cases from the last three years in which the Government charged both cocaine and firearms offenses, (2) to identify the race of the defendants in those cases, (3) to identify what levels of law enforcement were involved in the investigations of those cases, and (4) to explain its criteria for deciding to prosecute those defendants for federal cocaine offenses.

The Government moved for reconsideration of the District Court's discovery order. With this motion it submitted affidavits and other evidence to explain why it had chosen to prosecute respondents and why respondents' study did not support the inference that the Government was singling out blacks for cocaine prosecution. The federal and local agents participating in the case alleged in affidavits that race played no role in their investigation. An Assistant United States Attorney explained in an affidavit that the decision to prosecute met the general criteria for prosecution, because "there was over 100 grams of cocaine base involved, over twice the threshold necessary for a ten year mandatory minimum sentence; there were multiple sales involving multiple defendants, thereby indicating a fairly substantial crack cocaine ring; ... there were multiple federal firearms violations intertwined with the narcotics trafficking; the overall evidence in the case was extremely strong, including audio and videotapes of defendants; ... and several of the defendants had criminal histories including narcotics and firearms violations." The Government also submitted sections of a published 1989 Drug Enforcement Administration report which concluded that "[l]arge-scale, interstate trafficking networks controlled by Jamaicans, Haitians and Black street gangs dominate the manufacture and distribution of crack."

In response, one of respondents' attorneys submitted an affidavit alleging that an intake coordinator at a drug treatment center had told her that there are "an equal number of caucasian users and dealers to minority users and dealers." Respondents also submitted an affidavit from a criminal defense attorney alleging that in his experience many nonblacks are prosecuted in state court for crack offenses, and a newspaper article reporting that Federal "crack criminals ... are being punished far more severely than if they had been caught with powder cocaine, and almost every single one of them is black."

The District Court denied the motion for reconsideration. When the Government indicated it would not comply with the court's discovery order, the court dismissed the case.[2]

A divided three-judge panel of the Court of Appeals for the Ninth Circuit reversed, holding that, because of the proof requirements for a selective-prosecution claim, defendants must "provide a colorable basis for believing that 'others similarly situated have not been prosecuted'" to obtain discovery. The Court of Appeals voted to rehear the case en banc, and the en banc panel affirmed the District Court's order of dismissal, holding that "a defendant is not required to demonstrate that the government has failed to prosecute others who are similarly situated." We granted certiorari to determine the appropriate standard for discovery for a selective-prosecution claim.

Neither the District Court nor the Court of Appeals mentioned Federal Rule of Criminal Procedure 16, which by its terms governs discovery in criminal cases. Both parties now discuss the Rule in their briefs, and respondents contend that it supports the result reached by the Court of Appeals. Rule 16 provides, in pertinent part: "Upon request of the defendant the government shall permit the defendant to inspect and copy or photograph books, papers, documents, photographs, tangible objects, buildings or places, or copies or portions thereof, which are within the possession, custody or control of the government, and which are material to the preparation of the defendant's defense or are intended for use by the government as evidence in chief at the trial, or were obtained from or belong to the defendant." Fed.R.Crim.P. 16(a)(1)(C). Respondents argue that documents "within the possession ... of the government" that discuss the government's prosecution strategy for cocaine cases are "material" to respondents' selective-prosecution claim. Respondents argue that the Rule applies because any claim that "results in nonconviction" if successful is a "defense" for the Rule's purposes, and a successful selective-prosecution claim has that effect.

We reject this argument, because we conclude that in the context of Rule 16 "the defendant's defense" means the defendant's response to the Government's case-in-chief. While it might be argued that as a general matter, the concept of a "defense" includes any claim that is a "sword," challenging the prosecution's conduct of the case, the term may encompass only the narrower class of "shield" claims, which refute the Government's arguments that the defendant committed the crime charged. Rule 16(a)(1)(C) tends to support the "shield-only" reading. If "defense" means an argument in response to the prosecution's case-in-chief, there is a perceptible symmetry between documents "material to the preparation of the defendant's defense," and, in the very next phrase, documents "intended for use by the government as evidence in chief at the trial."

If this symmetry were not persuasive enough, paragraph (a)(2) of Rule 16 establishes beyond peradventure that "defense" in section (a)(1)(C) can refer only to defenses in response to the Government's case-in-chief. Rule 16(a)(2), as relevant here, exempts from defense inspection "reports, memoranda, or other internal government documents made by the attorney for the government or other

---

2. We have never determined whether dismissal of the indictment, or some other sanction, is the proper remedy if a court determines that a defendant has been the victim of prose- cution on the basis of his race. Here, "it was the government itself that suggested dismissal of the indictments to the district court so that an appeal might lie."

government agents in connection with the investigation or prosecution of the case."

Under Rule 16(a)(1)(C), a defendant may examine documents material to his defense, but, under Rule 16(a)(2), he may not examine Government work product in connection with his case. If a selective-prosecution claim is a "defense," Rule 16(a)(1)(C) gives the defendant the right to examine Government work product in every prosecution except his own. Because respondents' construction of "defense" creates the anomaly of a defendant's being able to examine all Government work product except the most pertinent, we find their construction implausible. We hold that Rule 16(a)(1)(C) authorizes defendants to examine Government documents material to the preparation of their defense against the Government's case-in-chief, but not to the preparation of selective-prosecution claims. * * *

A selective-prosecution claim is not a defense on the merits to the criminal charge itself, but an independent assertion that the prosecutor has brought the charge for reasons forbidden by the Constitution. Our cases delineating the necessary elements to prove a claim of selective prosecution have taken great pains to explain that the standard is a demanding one. These cases afford a "background presumption" that the showing necessary to obtain discovery should itself be a significant barrier to the litigation of insubstantial claims.

A selective-prosecution claim asks a court to exercise judicial power over a "special province" of the Executive. The Attorney General and United States Attorneys retain " 'broad discretion' " to enforce the Nation's criminal laws. They have this latitude because they are designated by statute as the President's delegates to help him discharge his constitutional responsibility to "take Care that the Laws be faithfully executed." U.S. Const., Art. II, § 3. As a result, "[t]he presumption of regularity supports" their prosecutorial decisions and "in the absence of clear evidence to the contrary, courts presume that they have properly discharged their official duties." In the ordinary case, "so long as the prosecutor has probable cause to believe that the accused committed an offense defined by statute, the decision whether or not to prosecute, and what charge to file or bring before a grand jury, generally rests entirely in his discretion."

Of course, a prosecutor's discretion is "subject to constitutional constraints." One of these constraints, imposed by the equal protection component of the Due Process Clause of the Fifth Amendment, is that the decision whether to prosecute may not be based on "an unjustifiable standard such as race, religion, or other arbitrary classification," *Oyler v. Boles*, 368 U.S. 448, 82 S.Ct. 501, 7 L.Ed.2d 446 (1962). A defendant may demonstrate that the administration of a criminal law is "directed so exclusively against a particular class of persons . . . with a mind so unequal and oppressive" that the system of prosecution amounts to "a practical denial" of equal protection of the law. *Yick Wo v. Hopkins*, 118 U.S. 356 (1886).

In order to dispel the presumption that a prosecutor has not violated equal protection, a criminal defendant must present "clear evidence to the contrary." We explained in *Wayte* [*v. United States*, 470 U.S. 598 (1985)], why courts are "properly hesitant to examine the decision whether to prosecute." Judicial deference to the decisions of these executive officers rests in part on an assessment of the relative competence of prosecutors and courts. "Such factors as the strength of the case, the prosecution's general deterrence value, the Government's enforcement priorities, and the case's relationship to the Government's overall enforcement plan are not readily susceptible to the kind of analysis the courts are competent to undertake." It also stems from a concern not to unnecessarily impair the performance of a core executive constitutional function. "Examining the basis of a prosecution delays the criminal proceeding, threatens to chill law enforcement by subjecting the prosecutor's motives and decisionmaking to outside inquiry, and may undermine prosecutorial effectiveness by revealing the Government's enforcement policy."

The requirements for a selective-prosecution claim draw on "ordinary equal protection standards." The claimant must demonstrate that the federal prosecutorial policy "had a discriminatory effect and that it was motivated by a discriminatory purpose." To establish a discriminatory effect in a race case, the claimant must show that similarly situated individuals of a different race were not prosecuted. This requirement has been established in our case law since *Ah Sin v. Wittman*, 198 U.S. 500 (1905). Ah Sin, a subject of China, petitioned a California state court for a writ of habeas corpus, seeking discharge from imprisonment under a San Francisco county ordinance prohibiting persons from setting up gambling tables in rooms barricaded to stop police from entering. He alleged in his habeas petition "that the ordinance is enforced 'solely and exclusively against persons of the Chinese race and not otherwise.' " We rejected his contention that this averment made out a claim under the Equal Protection Clause, because it did not allege "that the conditions and practices to which the ordinance was directed did not exist exclusively among the Chinese, or that there were other offenders against the ordinance than the Chinese as to whom it was not enforced."

The similarly situated requirement does not make a selective-prosecution claim impossible to prove. Twenty years before *Ah Sin*, we invalidated an ordinance, also adopted by San Francisco, that prohibited the operation of laundries in wooden buildings. *Yick Wo*, supra. The plaintiff in error successfully demonstrated that the ordinance was applied against Chinese nationals but not against other laundry-shop operators. The authorities had denied the applications of 200 Chinese subjects for permits to operate shops in wooden build ings, but granted the applications of 80 individuals who were not Chinese subjects to operate laundries in wooden buildings "under similar conditions." We explained in *Ah Sin* why the similarly situated requirement is necessary: "No latitude of intention should be indulged in a case like this. There should be certainty to every intent. Plaintiff in error seeks to set aside a criminal law of the State, not on the ground that it is unconstitutional on its face, not that it is discriminatory in tendency and ultimate actual operation as the ordinance was which was passed on in the *Yick Wo* case, but that it was made so by the manner of its administration. This is a matter of proof, and no fact should be omitted to make it out completely, when the power of a Federal court is invoked to interfere with the course of criminal justice of a State." Although *Ah Sin* involved federal review of a state conviction, we think a similar rule applies where the power of a federal court is invoked to challenge an exercise of one of the core powers of the Executive Branch of the Federal Government, the power to prosecute.[a] * * *

Having reviewed the requirements to prove a selective-prosecution claim, we turn to the showing necessary to obtain discovery in support of such a claim. If discovery is ordered, the Government must assemble from its own files documents

a. At this juncture, respondents urged that *Batson* [Ch. 15, § 2] "cut against any absolute requirement that there be a showing of failure to prosecute similarly situated individuals", but the Court responded that *Batson* was different: "During jury selection, the entire res gestae take place in front of the trial judge. Because the judge has before him the entire venire, he is well situated to detect whether a challenge to the seating of one juror is part of a 'pattern' of singling out members of a single race for peremptory challenges. He is in a position to discern whether a challenge to a black juror has evidentiary significance; the significance may differ if the venire consists mostly of blacks or of whites. Similarly, if the defendant makes out a prima facie case, the prosecutor is called upon to justify only decisions made in the very case then before the court. The trial judge need not review prosecutorial conduct in relation to other venires in other cases."

which might corroborate or refute the defendant's claim. Discovery thus imposes many of the costs present when the Government must respond to a prima facie case of selective prosecution. It will divert prosecutors' resources and may disclose the Government's prosecutorial strategy. The justifications for a rigorous standard for the elements of a selective-prosecution claim thus require a correspondingly rigorous standard for discovery in aid of such a claim.

The parties, and the Courts of Appeals which have considered the requisite showing to establish entitlement to discovery, describe this showing with a variety of phrases, like "colorable basis," "substantial threshold showing," "substantial and concrete basis," or "reasonable likelihood." However, the many labels for this showing conceal the degree of consensus about the evidence necessary to meet it. The Courts of Appeals "require some evidence tending to show the existence of the essential elements of the defense," discriminatory effect and discriminatory intent.

In this case we consider what evidence constitutes "some evidence tending to show the existence" of the discriminatory effect element. The Court of Appeals held that a defendant may establish a colorable basis for discriminatory effect without evidence that the Government has failed to prosecute others who are similarly situated to the defendant. We think it was mistaken in this view. The vast majority of the Courts of Appeals require the defendant to produce some evidence that similarly situated defendants of other races could have been prosecuted, but were not, and this requirement is consistent with our equal protection case law. * * *[b]

The Court of Appeals reached its decision in part because it started "with the presumption that people of all races commit all types of crimes—not with the premise that any type of crime is the exclusive province of any particular racial or ethnic group." It cited no authority for this proposition, which seems contradicted by the most recent statistics of the United States Sentencing Commission. Those statistics show that: More than 90% of the persons sentenced in 1994 for crack cocaine trafficking were black; 93.4% of convicted LSD dealers were white; and 91% of those convicted for pornography or prostitution were white. Presumptions at war with presumably reliable statistics have no proper place in the analysis of this issue.

The Court of Appeals also expressed concern about the "evidentiary obstacles defendants face." But all of its sister Circuits that have confronted the issue have required that defendants produce some evidence of differential treatment of similarly situated members of other races or protected classes. In the present case, if the claim of selective prosecution were well founded, it should not have been an insuperable task to prove that persons of other races were being treated differently than respondents. For instance, respondents could have investigated whether similarly situated persons of other races were prosecuted by the State of California, were known to federal law enforcement officers, but were not prosecuted in federal court. We think the required threshold—a credible showing of different treatment of similarly situated persons—adequately balances the Government's interest in vigorous prosecution and the defendant's interest in avoiding selective prosecution.

In the case before us, respondents' "study" did not constitute "some evidence tending to show the existence of the essential elements of" a selective-prosecution claim. The study failed to identify individuals who were not black, could have

b. We reserve the question whether a defendant must satisfy the similarly situated requirement in a case "involving direct admissions by [prosecutors] of discriminatory purpose."

been prosecuted for the offenses for which respondents were charged, but were not so prosecuted. This omission was not remedied by respondents' evidence in opposition to the Government's motion for reconsideration. The newspaper article, which discussed the discriminatory effect of federal drug sentencing laws, was not relevant to an allegation of discrimination in decisions to prosecute. Respondents' affidavits, which recounted one attorney's conversation with a drug treatment center employee and the experience of another attorney defending drug prosecutions in state court, recounted hearsay and reported personal conclusions based on anecdotal evidence. The judgment of the Court of Appeals is therefore reversed, and the case is remanded for proceedings consistent with this opinion.

It is so ordered.[b]

JUSTICE STEVENS, dissenting. * * *

The Court correctly concludes that in this case the facts presented to the District Court in support of respondents' claim that they had been singled out for prosecution because of their race were not sufficient to prove that defense. Moreover, I agree with the Court that their showing was not strong enough to give them a right to discovery, either under Rule 16 or under the District Court's inherent power to order discovery in appropriate circumstances. Like Chief Judge Wallace of the Court of Appeals, however, I am persuaded that the District Judge did not abuse her discretion when she concluded that the factual showing was sufficiently disturbing to require some response from the United States Attorney's Office. Perhaps the discovery order was broader than necessary, but I cannot agree with the Court's apparent conclusion that no inquiry was permissible.

The District Judge's order should be evaluated in light of three circumstances that underscore the need for judicial vigilance over certain types of drug prosecutions. First, the Anti–Drug Abuse Act of 1986 and subsequent legislation established a regime of extremely high penalties for the possession and distribution of so-called "crack" cocaine. Those provisions treat one gram of crack as the equivalent of 100 grams of powder cocaine. The distribution of 50 grams of crack is thus punishable by the same mandatory minimum sentence of 10 years in prison that applies to the distribution of 5,000 grams of powder cocaine. The Sentencing Guidelines extend this ratio to penalty levels above the mandatory minimums: for any given quantity of crack, the guideline range is the same as if the offense had involved 100 times that amount in powder cocaine. These penalties result in sentences for crack offenders that average three to eight times longer than sentences for comparable powder offenders.

Second, the disparity between the treatment of crack cocaine and powder cocaine is matched by the disparity between the severity of the punishment imposed by federal law and that imposed by state law for the same conduct. For a variety of reasons, often including the absence of mandatory minimums, the existence of parole, and lower baseline penalties, terms of imprisonment for drug offenses tend to be substantially lower in state systems than in the federal system. The difference is especially marked in the case of crack offenses. The majority of

---

b. Justice Souter, concurring, joined the Court's discussion of Rule 16 "only to the extent of its application to the issue in this case." Justice Ginsburg, concurring, emphasized that the "Court was not called upon to decide here whether Rule 16(a)(1)(C) applies in any other context, for example, to affirmative defenses unrelated to the merits." Justice Breyer, concurring in part and concurring in the judgment, though concluding that "neither the alleged 'symmetry' in the structure of Rule 16(a)(1)(C), nor the work product exception of Rule 16(a)(2), supports the majority's limitation of discovery under Rule 16(a)(1)(C) to documents related to the government's 'case-in-chief,'" concluded that the defendants' discovery request failed to satisfy the Rule's requirement that the discovery be "material to the preparation of the defendant's defense."

States draw no distinction between types of cocaine in their penalty schemes; of those that do, none has established as stark a differential as the Federal Government. For example, if respondent Hampton is found guilty, his federal sentence might be as long as a mandatory life term. Had he been tried in state court, his sentence could have been as short as 12 years, less worktime credits of half that amount.

Finally, it is undisputed that the brunt of the elevated federal penalties falls heavily on blacks. While 65% of the persons who have used crack are white, in 1993 they represented only 4% of the federal offenders convicted of trafficking in crack. Eighty-eight percent of such defendants were black. During the first 18 months of full guideline implementation, the sentencing disparity between black and white defendants grew from preguideline levels: blacks on average received sentences over 40% longer than whites. Those figures represent a major threat to the integrity of federal sentencing reform, whose main purpose was the elimination of disparity (especially racial) in sentencing. The Sentencing Commission acknowledges that the heightened crack penalties are a "primary cause of the growing disparity between sentences for Black and White federal defendants."

The extraordinary severity of the imposed penalties and the troubling racial patterns of enforcement give rise to a special concern about the fairness of charging practices for crack offenses. Evidence tending to prove that black defendants charged with distribution of crack in the Central District of California are prosecuted in federal court, whereas members of other races charged with similar offenses are prosecuted in state court, warrants close scrutiny by the federal judges in that District. In my view, the District Judge, who has sat on both the federal and the state benches in Los Angeles, acted well within her discretion to call for the development of facts that would demonstrate what standards, if any, governed the choice of forum where similarly situated offenders are prosecuted.

Respondents submitted a study showing that of all cases involving crack offenses that were closed by the Federal Public Defender's Office in 1991, 24 out of 24 involved black defendants. To supplement this evidence, they submitted affidavits from two of the attorneys in the defense team. The first reported a statement from an intake coordinator at a local drug treatment center that, in his experience, an equal number of crack users and dealers were caucasian as belonged to minorities. The second was from David R. Reed, counsel for respondent Armstrong. Reed was both an active court- appointed attorney in the Central District of California and one of the directors of the leading association of criminal defense lawyers who practice before the Los Angeles County courts. Reed stated that he did not recall "ever handling a [crack] cocaine case involving non-black defendants" in federal court, nor had he even heard of one. He further stated that "[t]here are many crack cocaine sales cases prosecuted in state court that do involve racial groups other than blacks."

The majority discounts the probative value of the affidavits, claiming that they recounted "hearsay" and reported "personal conclusions based on anecdotal evidence." But the Reed affidavit plainly contained more than mere hearsay; Reed offered information based on his own extensive experience in both federal and state courts. Given the breadth of his background, he was well qualified to compare the practices of federal and state prosecutors. In any event, the Government never objected to the admission of either affidavit on hearsay or any other grounds. It was certainly within the District Court's discretion to credit the affidavits of two members of the bar of that Court, at least one of whom had presumably acquired a reputation by his frequent appearances there, and both of whose statements were made on pains of perjury.

The criticism that the affidavits were based on "anecdotal evidence" is also unpersuasive. I thought it was agreed that defendants do not need to prepare sophisticated statistical studies in order to receive mere discovery in cases like this one. Certainly evidence based on a drug counselor's personal observations or on an attorney's practice in two sets of courts, state and federal, can "ten[d] to show the existence" of a selective prosecution.

Even if respondents failed to carry their burden of showing that there were individuals who were not black but who could have been prosecuted in federal court for the same offenses, it does not follow that the District Court abused its discretion in ordering discovery. There can be no doubt that such individuals exist, and indeed the Government has never denied the same. In those circumstances, I fail to see why the District Court was unable to take judicial notice of this obvious fact and demand information from the Government's files to support or refute respondents' evidence. The presumption that some whites are prosecuted in state court is not "contradicted" by the statistics the majority cites, which show only that high percentages of blacks are convicted of certain federal crimes, while high percentages of whites are convicted of other federal crimes. Those figures are entirely consistent with the allegation of selective prosecution. The relevant comparison, rather, would be with the percentages of blacks and whites who commit those crimes. But, as discussed above, in the case of crack far greater numbers of whites are believed guilty of using the substance. The District Court, therefore, was entitled to find the evidence before her significant and to require some explanation from the Government.[6]

In sum, I agree with the Sentencing Commission that "[w]hile the exercise of discretion by prosecutors and investigators has an impact on sentences in almost all cases to some extent, because of the 100–to–1 quantity ratio and federal mandatory minimum penalties, discretionary decisions in cocaine cases often have dramatic effects."[7] The severity of the penalty heightens both the danger of arbitrary enforcement and the need for careful scrutiny of any colorable claim of discriminatory enforcement. In this case, the evidence was sufficiently disturbing to persuade the District Judge to order discovery that might help explain the conspicuous racial pattern of cases before her Court. I cannot accept the majority's conclusion that the District Judge either exceeded her power or abused her discretion when she did so. I therefore respectfully dissent.

---

6. Also telling was the Government's response to respondents' evidentiary showing. It submitted a list of more than 3,500 defendants who had been charged with federal narcotics violations over the previous 3 years. It also offered the names of 11 nonblack defendants whom it had prosecuted for crack offenses. All 11, however, were members of other racial or ethnic minorities. The District Court was authorized to draw adverse inferences from the Government's inability to produce a single example of a white defendant, especially when the very purpose of its exercise was to allay the Court's concerns about the evidence of racially selective prosecutions. As another court has said: "Statistics are not, of course, the whole answer, but nothing is as emphatic as zero...."

7. For this and other reasons, the Sentencing Commission in its Special Report to Congress "strongly recommend[ed] against a 100–to–1 quantity ratio." The Commission shortly thereafter, by a 4–to–3 vote, amended the guidelines so as to equalize the treatment of crack and other forms of cocaine, and proposed modification of the statutory mandatory minimum penalties for crack offenses. In October 1995, Congress overrode the Sentencing Commission's guideline amendments. Nevertheless, Congress at the same time directed the Commission to submit recommendations regarding changes to the statutory and guideline penalties for cocaine distribution, including specifically "revision of the drug quantity ratio of crack cocaine to powder cocaine."

SECTION 2.   SELECTION OF THE CHARGE

If the prosecutor has decided upon prosecution, there often remains the question of what the charge should be. Sometimes this is simply a matter of whether the charge should be of a greater or lesser crime—for example, felony burglary versus misdemeanor breaking and entering. On other occasions, the prosecutor must determine whether to charge the defendant with more than one offense, either because the defendant has committed a series of offenses (e.g., a number of burglaries) over time or because the defendant violated more than one statute during a single course of conduct. In this third situation, the defendant's challenge, as in *United States v. Batchelder,* may be grounded primarily in the contention that the applicable statutes improperly overlap. More generally, as in the second case in this section, *United States v. Goodwin,* a defendant might challenge the prosecutor's charge selection decision on the ground of actual or apparent vindictiveness.

UNITED STATES v. BATCHELDER

442 U.S. 114, 99 S.Ct. 2198, 60 L.Ed.2d 755 (1979).

JUSTICE MARSHALL delivered the opinion of the Court.

At issue in this case are two overlapping provisions of the Omnibus Crime Control and Safe Streets Act of 1968 (the Omnibus Act). Both prohibit convicted felons from receiving firearms, but each authorizes different maximum penalties. We must determine whether a defendant convicted of the offense carrying the greater penalty may be sentenced only under the more lenient provision when his conduct violates both statutes.

Respondent, a previously convicted felon, was found guilty of receiving a firearm that had traveled in interstate commerce, in violation of 18 U.S.C. § 922(h).[2] The District Court sentenced him under 18 U.S.C. § 924(a) to five years' imprisonment, the maximum term authorized for violation of § 922(h).

The Court of Appeals affirmed the conviction but, by a divided vote, remanded for resentencing. The majority recognized that respondent had been indicted and convicted under § 922(h) and that § 924(a) permits five years' imprisonment for such violations. However, noting that the substantive elements of § 922(h) and 18 U.S.C.App. § 1202(a) are identical as applied to a convicted felon who unlawfully receives a firearm, the court interpreted the Omnibus Act to allow no more than the two-year maximum sentence provided by § 1202(a).[4] * * *

This Court has previously noted the partial redundancy of §§ 922(h) and 1202(a), both as to the conduct they proscribe and the individuals they reach.

2. In pertinent part, 18 U.S.C. § 922(h) provides:

"It shall be unlawful for any person—

"(1) who is under indictment for, or who has been convicted in any court of, a crime punishable by imprisonment for a term exceeding one year;

"(2) who is a fugitive from justice;

"(3) who is an unlawful user of or addicted to marihuana or any depressant or stimulant drug * * * or narcotic drug * * *; or

"(4) who has been adjudicated as a mental defective or who has been committed to any mental institution;

"to receive any firearm or ammunition which has been shipped or transported in interstate or foreign commerce."

4. Section 1202(a) states:

"Any person who—

"(1) has been convicted by a court of the United States or of a State or any political subdivision thereof of a felony, or

"(2) has been discharged from the Armed Forces under dishonorable conditions, or

"(3) has been adjudged by a court of the United States or of a State or any political subdivision thereof of being mentally incompetent, or

However, we find nothing in the language structure or legislative history of the Omnibus Act to suggest that because of this overlap, a defendant convicted under § 922(h) may be imprisoned for no more than the maximum term specified in § 1202(a). As we read the Act, each substantive statute, in conjunction with its own sentencing provision, operates independently of the other. * * *

In resolving the statutory question, the majority below expressed "serious doubts about the constitutionality of two statutes that provide different penalties for identical conduct." Specifically, the court suggested that the statutes might (1) be void for vagueness, (2) implicate "due process and equal protection interest[s] in avoiding excessive prosecutorial discretion and in obtaining equal justice," and (3) constitute an impermissible delegation of congressional authority. We find no constitutional infirmities.

[margin note: Lower Ct: ambiguous due to conflict]

It is a fundamental tenet of due process that "[n]o one may be required at peril of life, liberty or property to speculate as to the meaning of penal statutes." A criminal statute is therefore invalid if it "fails to give a person of ordinary intelligence fair notice that his contemplated conduct is forbidden." So too, vague sentencing provisions may pose constitutional questions if they do not state with sufficient clarity the consequences of violating a given criminal statute.

The provisions in issue here, however, unambiguously specify the activity proscribed and the penalties available upon conviction. That this particular conduct may violate both Titles does not detract from the notice afforded by each. Although the statutes create uncertainty as to which crime may be charged and therefore what penalties may be imposed, they do so to no greater extent than would a single statute authorizing various alternative punishments. So long as overlapping criminal provisions clearly define the conduct prohibited and the punishment authorized, the notice requirements of the Due Process Clause are satisfied.

[margin note: S. Ct: each is NOT ambiguous same as single statute w/ alternative punishments]

This Court has long recognized that when an act violates more than one criminal statute, the Government may prosecute under either so long as it does not discriminate against any class of defendants. Whether to prosecute and what charge to file or bring before a grand jury are decisions that generally rest in the prosecutor's discretion.

[margin note: Pros. Discretion]

The Court of Appeals acknowledged this "settled rule" allowing prosecutorial choice. Nevertheless, the court distinguished overlapping statutes with identical standards of proof from provisions that vary in some particular. In the court's view, when two statutes prohibit "exactly the same conduct," the prosecutor's "selection of which of two penalties to apply" would be "unfettered." Because such prosecutorial discretion could produce "unequal justice," the court expressed doubt that this form of legislative redundancy was constitutional. We find this analysis factually and legally unsound.

Contrary to the Court of Appeals' assertions, a prosecutor's discretion to choose between §§ 922(h) and 1202(a) is not "unfettered." Selectivity in the enforcement of criminal laws is, of course, subject to constitutional constraints.[9] And a decision to proceed under § 922(h) does not empower the Government to

---

"(4) having been a citizen of the United States has renounced his citizenship, or

"(5) being an alien is illegally or unlawfully in the United States,

"and who receives, possesses, or transports in commerce or affecting commerce, after the date of enactment of this Act, any firearm shall be fined not more than $10,000 or imprisoned for not more than two years, or both." 18 U.S.C.App. § 1202(a).

9. The Equal Protection Clause prohibits selective enforcement "based upon an unjustifiable standard such as race, religion, or other arbitrary classification." Respondent does not allege that his prosecution was motivated by improper considerations.

predetermine ultimate criminal sanctions. Rather, it merely enables the sentencing judge to impose a longer prison sentence than § 1202(a) would permit and precludes him from imposing the greater fine authorized by § 1202(a). More importantly, there is no appreciable difference between the discretion a prosecutor exercises when deciding whether to charge under one of two statutes with different elements and the discretion he exercises when choosing one of two statutes with identical elements. In the former situation, once he determines that the proof will support conviction under either statute, his decision is indistinguishable from the one he faces in the latter context. The prosecutor may be influenced by the penalties available upon conviction, but this fact standing alone does not give rise to a violation of the Equal Protection or Due Process Clauses. Just as a defendant has no constitutional right to elect which of two applicable federal statutes shall be the basis of his indictment and prosecution neither is he entitled to choose the penalty scheme under which he will be sentenced.

Approaching the problem of prosecutorial discretion from a slightly different perspective, the Court of Appeals postulated that the statutes might impermissibly delegate to the Executive Branch the legislature's responsibility to fix criminal penalties. We do not agree. The provisions at issue plainly demarcate the range of penalties that prosecutors and judges may seek and impose. In light of that specificity, the power that Congress has delegated to those officials is no broader than the authority they routinely exercise in enforcing the criminal laws. Having informed the courts, prosecutors and defendants of the permissible punishment alternatives available under each Title, Congress has fulfilled its duty.

Accordingly, the judgment of the Court of Appeals is reversed.

UNITED STATES v. GOODWIN
457 U.S. 368, 102 S.Ct. 2485, 73 L.Ed.2d 74 (1982).

JUSTICE STEVENS delivered the opinion of the Court. * * *

Respondent Goodwin was stopped for speeding by a United States Park Policeman on the Baltimore–Washington Parkway. Goodwin emerged from his car to talk to the policeman. After a brief discussion, the officer noticed a clear plastic bag underneath the armrest next to the driver's seat of Goodwin's car. The officer asked Goodwin to return to his car and to raise the armrest. Respondent did so, but as he raised the armrest he placed the car into gear and accelerated rapidly. The car struck the officer, knocking him first onto the back of the car and then onto the highway. The policeman returned to his car, but Goodwin eluded him in a highspeed chase.

The following day, the officer filed a complaint in the District Court charging respondent with several misdemeanor and petty offenses, including assault. Goodwin was arrested and arraigned before a United States Magistrate. The Magistrate set a date for trial, but respondent fled the jurisdiction. Three years later Goodwin was found in custody in Virginia and was returned to Maryland.

Upon his return, respondent's case was assigned to an attorney from the Department of Justice, who was detailed temporarily to try petty crime and misdemeanor cases before the Magistrate. The attorney did not have authority to try felony cases or to seek indictments from the grand jury. Respondent initiated plea negotiations with the prosecutor, but later advised the Government that he did not wish to plead guilty and desired a trial by jury in the District Court.[1]

1. At that time, there was no statutory provision allowing a trial by jury before a mag- istrate.

The case was transferred to the District Court and responsibility for the prosecution was assumed by an Assistant United States Attorney. Approximately six weeks later, after reviewing the case and discussing it with several parties, the prosecutor obtained a four-count indictment charging respondent with one felony count of forcibly assaulting a federal officer and three related counts arising from the same incident.[2] A jury convicted respondent on the felony count and on one misdemeanor count.

Respondent moved to set aside the verdict on the ground of prosecutorial vindictiveness, contending that the indictment on the felony charge gave rise to an impermissible appearance of retaliation. The District Court denied the motion, finding that "the prosecutor in this case has adequately dispelled any appearance of retaliatory intent."

Although the Court of Appeals readily concluded that "the prosecutor did not act with actual vindictiveness in seeking a felony indictment," it nevertheless reversed. Relying on our decisions in *North Carolina v. Pearce,* [395 U.S. 711 (1969)], and *Blackledge v. Perry,* [417 U.S. 21 (1974)], the court held that the Due Process Clause of the Fifth Amendment prohibits the Government from bringing more serious charges against a defendant after he has invoked his right to a jury trial, unless the prosecutor comes forward with objective evidence to show that the increased charges could not have been brought before the defendant exercised his rights. Because the court believed that the circumstances surrounding the felony indictment gave rise to a genuine risk of retaliation, it adopted a legal presumption designed to spare courts the "unseemly task" of probing the actual motives of the prosecutor. * * *

In *North Carolina v. Pearce,* the Court held that neither the Double Jeopardy Clause nor the Equal Protection Clause prohibits a trial judge from imposing a harsher sentence on retrial after a criminal defendant successfully attacks an initial conviction on appeal. The Court stated, however, that "[i]t can hardly be doubted that it would be a flagrant violation [of the Due Process Clause] of the Fourteenth Amendment for a state trial court to follow an announced practice of imposing a heavier sentence upon every reconvicted defendant for the explicit purpose of punishing the defendant for his having succeeded in getting his original conviction set aside." The Court continued:

> "Due process of law, then, requires that vindictiveness against a defendant for having successfully attacked his first conviction must play no part in the sentence he receives after a new trial. And since the fear of such vindictiveness may unconstitutionally deter a defendant's exercise of the right to appeal or collaterally attack his first conviction, due process also requires that a defendant be freed of apprehension of such a retaliatory motivation on the part of the sentencing judge."

In order to assure the absence of such a motivation, the Court concluded:

> "[W]henever a judge imposes a more severe sentence upon a defendant after a new trial, the reasons for his doing so must affirmatively appear. Those reasons must be based upon objective information concerning identifiable

---

2. By affidavit, the Assistant United States Attorney later set forth his reasons for this action:

(1) he considered respondent's conduct on the date in question to be a serious violation of law, (2) respondent had a lengthy history of violent crime, (3) the prosecutor considered respondent's conduct to be related to major narcotics transactions, (4) the prosecu-

tor believed that respondent had committed perjury at his preliminary hearing, and (5) respondent had failed to appear for trial as originally scheduled. The Government attorney stated that his decision to seek a felony indictment was not motivated in any way by Goodwin's request for a jury trial in District Court.

conduct on the part of the defendant occurring after the time of the original sentencing proceeding. And the factual data upon which the increased sentence is based must be made part of the record, so that the constitutional legitimacy of the increased sentence may be fully reviewed on appeal."

In sum, the Court applied a presumption of vindictiveness, which may be overcome only by objective information in the record justifying the increased sentence.[a]

In *Blackledge v. Perry,* the Court confronted the problem of increased punishment upon retrial after appeal in a setting different from that considered in *Pearce.* Perry was convicted of assault in an inferior court having exclusive jurisdiction for the trial of misdemeanors. The court imposed a 6-month sentence. Under North Carolina law, Perry had an absolute right to a trial *de novo* in the Superior Court, which possessed felony jurisdiction. After Perry filed his notice of appeal, the prosecutor obtained a felony indictment charging him with assault with a deadly weapon. Perry pleaded guilty to the felony and was sentenced to a term of five to seven years in prison.

In reviewing Perry's felony conviction and increased sentence, this Court first stated the essence of the holdings in *Pearce* and the cases that had followed it:

"The lesson that emerges from *Pearce* is that the Due Process Clause is not offended by all possibilities of increased punishment upon retrial after appeal, but only by those that pose a realistic likelihood of 'vindictiveness.'"

The Court held that the opportunities for vindictiveness in the situation before it were such "as to impel the conclusion that due process of law requires a rule analogous to that of the *Pearce* case." It explained:

"A prosecutor clearly has a considerable stake in discouraging convicted misdemeanants from appealing and thus obtaining a trial *de novo* in the Superior Court, since such an appeal will clearly require increased expenditures of prosecutorial resources before the defendant's conviction becomes final, and may even result in a formerly convicted defendant's going free. And, if the prosecutor has the means readily at hand to discourage such appeals—by 'upping the ante' through a felony indictment whenever a convicted misdemeanant pursues his statutory appellate remedy—the State can

a. Stating that "the reach of *Pearce* is best captured" by this sentence, the Court in *Texas v. McCullough,* 475 U.S. 134 (1986), said of the above quotation from *Pearce:* "This language, however, was never intended to describe exhaustively all of the possible circumstances in which a sentence increase could be justified. Restricting justifications for a sentence increase to *only* 'events that occurred subsequent to the original sentencing proceedings' could in some circumstances lead to absurd results. The Solicitor General provides the following hypothetical example:

'Suppose * * * that a defendant is convicted of burglary, a non-violent, and apparently first, offense. He is sentenced to a short prison term or perhaps placed on probation. Following a successful appeal and a conviction on retrial, it is learned that the defendant has been using an alias and in fact has a long criminal record that includes other burglaries, several armed robbery convictions, and a conviction for murder committed in the course of a burglary. None of the reasons underlying *Pearce* in any way justi-

fies the perverse result that the defendant receive no greater sentence in light of this information than he originally received when he was thought to be a first offender.'

We agree with the Solicitor General and find nothing in *Pearce* that would require such a bizarre conclusion."

Marshall, J., joined by Blackmun and Stevens, JJ., dissenting, objected: "There is neither any reason nor any need for us to believe that dishonest and unconstitutionally vindictive judges actually hold sway in American courtrooms * * *. The message of *Pearce* is that the fear of such vindictiveness is real enough. And a defendant plagued by such an apprehension is likely to take small comfort in any presumption of vindictiveness established for his benefit if the means of rebutting that presumption will always be within the easy reach of the judge who will sentence him should the challenge to his conviction prove unsuccessful."

insure that only the most hardy defendants will brave the hazards of a *de novo* trial."

The Court emphasized in *Blackledge* that it did not matter that no evidence was present that the prosecutor had acted in bad faith or with malice in seeking the felony indictment. As in *Pearce,* the Court held that the likelihood of vindictiveness justified a presumption that would free defendants of apprehension of such a retaliatory motivation on the part of the prosecutor.[8] * * *

In *Bordenkircher v. Hayes* [Ch. 14, § 1], the Court for the first time considered an allegation of vindictiveness that arose in a pretrial setting. In that case the Court held that the Due Process Clause of the Fourteenth Amendment did not prohibit a prosecutor from carrying out a threat, made during plea negotiations, to bring additional charges against an accused who refused to plead guilty to the offense with which he was originally charged. * * *

The outcome in *Bordenkircher* was mandated by this Court's acceptance of plea negotiation as a legitimate process. In declining to apply a presumption of vindictiveness, the Court recognized that "additional" charges obtained by a prosecutor could not necessarily be characterized as an impermissible "penalty." Since charges brought in an original indictment may be abandoned by the prosecutor in the course of plea negotiation—in often what is clearly a "benefit" to the defendant—changes in the charging decision that occur in the context of plea negotiation are an inaccurate measure of improper prosecutorial "vindictiveness." An initial indictment—from which the prosecutor embarks on a course of plea negotiation—does not necessarily define the extent of the legitimate interest in prosecution. For just as a prosecutor may forgo legitimate charges already brought in an effort to save the time and expense of trial, a prosecutor may file additional charges if an initial expectation that a defendant would plead guilty to lesser charges proves unfounded.

This case, like *Bordenkircher,* arises from a pretrial decision to modify the charges against the defendant. Unlike *Bordenkircher,* however, there is no evidence in this case that could give rise to a claim of *actual* vindictiveness; the prosecutor never suggested that the charge was brought to influence the respondent's conduct. The conviction in this case may be reversed only if a *presumption* of vindictiveness—applicable in all cases—is warranted.

There is good reason to be cautious before adopting an inflexible presumption of prosecutorial vindictiveness in a pretrial setting. In the course of preparing a case for trial, the prosecutor may uncover additional information that suggests a basis for further prosecution or he simply may come to realize that information possessed by the State has a broader significance. At this stage of the proceedings, the prosecutor's assessment of the proper extent of prosecution may not have crystallized. In contrast, once a trial begins—and certainly by the time a conviction has been obtained—it is much more likely that the State has discovered and assessed all of the information against an accused and has made a determination, on the basis of that information, of the extent to which he should be prosecuted. Thus, a change in the charging decision made after an initial trial is completed is much more likely to be improperly motivated than is a pretrial decision.

In addition, a defendant before trial is expected to invoke procedural rights that inevitably impose some "burden" on the prosecutor. Defense counsel routinely file pretrial motions to suppress evidence; to challenge the sufficiency

---

8. The presumption again could be overcome by objective evidence justifying the prosecutor's action. The Court noted: "This would clearly be a different case if the State had shown that it was impossible to proceed on the more serious charge at the outset."

and form of an indictment; to plead an affirmative defense; to request psychiatric services; to obtain access to government files; to be tried by jury. It is unrealistic to assume that a prosecutor's probable response to such motions is to seek to penalize and to deter. The invocation of procedural rights is an integral part of the adversary process in which our criminal justice system operates.

Thus, the timing of the prosecutor's action in this case suggests that a presumption of vindictiveness is not warranted. A prosecutor should remain free before trial to exercise the broad discretion entrusted to him to determine the extent of the societal interest in prosecution. An initial decision should not freeze future conduct. As we made clear in *Bordenkircher,* the initial charges filed by a prosecutor may not reflect the extent to which an individual is legitimately subject to prosecution.

The nature of the right asserted by the respondent confirms that a presumption of vindictiveness is not warranted in this case. After initially expressing an interest in plea negotiation, respondent decided not to plead guilty and requested a trial by jury in District Court. In doing so, he forced the Government to bear the burdens and uncertainty of a trial. This Court in *Bordenkircher* made clear that the mere fact that a defendant refuses to plead guilty and forces the government to prove its case is insufficient to warrant a presumption that subsequent changes in the charging decision are unjustified. Respondent argues that such a presumption is warranted in this case, however, because he not only requested a trial—he requested a trial by jury.

We cannot agree. The distinction between a bench trial and a jury trial does not compel a special presumption of prosecutorial vindictiveness whenever additional charges are brought after a jury is demanded. To be sure, a jury trial is more burdensome than a bench trial. The defendant may challenge the selection of the venire; the jury itself must be impaneled; witnesses and arguments must be prepared more carefully to avoid the danger of a mistrial. These matters are much less significant, however, than the facts that before either a jury or a judge the State must present its full case against the accused and the defendant is entitled to offer a full defense. As compared to the complete trial *de novo* at issue in *Blackledge,* a jury trial—as opposed to a bench trial—does not require duplicative expenditures of prosecutorial resources before a final judgment may be obtained. Moreover, unlike the trial judge in *Pearce,* no party is asked "to do over what it thought it had already done correctly." A prosecutor has no "personal stake" in a bench trial and thus no reason to engage in "self-vindication" upon a defendant's request for a jury trial. Perhaps most importantly, the institutional bias against the retrial of a decided question that supported the decisions in *Pearce* and *Blackledge* simply has no counterpart in this case.

There is an opportunity for vindictiveness, [but] a mere opportunity for vindictiveness is insufficient to justify the imposition of a prophylactic rule. As *Blackledge* makes clear, "the Due Process Clause is not offended by all possibilities of increased punishment * * * but only by those that pose a realistic likelihood of 'vindictiveness.' " The possibility that a prosecutor would respond to a defendant's pretrial demand for a jury trial by bringing charges not in the public interest that could be explained only as a penalty imposed on the defendant is so *unlikely* that a presumption of vindictiveness certainly is not warranted.

In declining to apply a presumption of vindictiveness, we of course do not foreclose the possibility that a defendant in an appropriate case might prove objectively that the prosecutor's charging decision was motivated by a desire to punish him for doing something that the law plainly allowed him to do. * * *

JUSTICE BLACKMUN, concurring in the judgment.

* * * I find no support in our prior cases for any distinction between pretrial and post-trial vindictiveness. * * *

[T]he Due Process Clause does not deprive a prosecutor of the flexibility to add charges after a defendant has decided not to plead guilty and has elected a jury trial in District Court—so long as the adjustment is based on "objective information concerning identifiable conduct on the part of the defendant occurring after the time of the original" charging decision. In addition, I believe that the prosecutor adequately explains an increased charge by pointing to objective information that he could not reasonably have been aware of at the time charges were initially filed.

Because I find that the Assistant United States Attorney's explanation for seeking a felony indictment satisfies these standards, I conclude that the Government has dispelled the appearance of vindictiveness and, therefore, that the imposition of additional charges did not violate respondent's due process rights. Accordingly, I concur in the judgment.

JUSTICE BRENNAN, with whom JUSTICE MARSHALL joins, dissenting. * * *

The Court suggests that the distinction between a bench trial and a jury trial is unimportant in this context. Such a suggestion is demonstrably fallacious. Experienced criminal practitioners, for both prosecution and defense, know that a jury trial entails far more prosecutorial work than a bench trial. Defense challenges to the potential-juror array, *voir dire* examination of potential jurors, and suppression hearings all take up a prosecutor's time before a jury trial, adding to his scheduling difficulties and caseload. More care in the preparation of his requested instructions, of his witnesses, and of his own remarks is necessary in order to avoid mistrial or reversible error. And there is always the specter of the "irrational" acquittal by a jury that is unreviewable on appeal. Thus it is simply inconceivable that a criminal defendant's election to be tried by jury would be a matter of indifference to his prosecutor. On the contrary, the prosecutor would almost always prefer that the defendant waive such a "troublesome" right. And if the defendant refuses to do so, the prosecutor's subsequent elevation of the charges against the defendant manifestly poses a realistic likelihood of vindictiveness. * * *

Chapter 11

SCREENING THE PROSECUTOR'S DECISION TO CHARGE

An innocent individual subjected to a trial pays a substantial price even though acquitted. Being accused of a serious crime creates a blot on one's reputation that may not be fully erased by an acquittal. Even where the acquittal does provide full vindication, it does not remedy other burdens borne in the course of gaining that vindication. Once accused, a defendant must await trial, a process that brings with it a degree of anxiety and insecurity that often disrupts the flow of daily life. The trial itself is even more of an ordeal and carries with it a significant expense. In light of these burdens, it is not surprising that a criminal justice process concerned with the protection of the innocent will incorporate safeguards that go beyond ensuring against erroneous convictions and seek also to ensure that unfounded charges are not brought against the innocent. A major element of such protection comes from the requirement that the prosecution's decision to charge be reviewed by some neutral agency. That agency generally is either the grand jury that "screens" the prosecution's case in deciding whether to indict or the magistrate who must determine at a preliminary hearing whether a charge has sufficient support to be sent forward to the next step in the process.[a]

The Fifth Amendment provides that, except in certain military cases, "no person shall be held to answer for a capital, or otherwise infamous offense, unless on presentment or indictment of a Grand Jury." It thus guarantees to any potential defendant in a federal criminal case involving an "infamous offense" (held to encompass all felony offenses) that no charge will be brought against him without the concurrence of a group of his peers, as expressed in the decision of the grand jury to issue an indictment. (The alternative form of accusation, the presentment, which was issued at the grand jury's own initiative, is no longer used). In requiring prosecution by indictment, the Fifth Amendment interposes the grand jury between the prosecutor and the prospective defendant and casts upon it a "shielding" function. The classic description of that function is found in *Wood v. Georgia*, 370 U.S. 375 (1962):

> "Historically, this body [the grand jury] has been regarded as a primary security to the innocent against hasty, malicious and oppressive prosecution; it serves the invaluable function in our society of standing between the accuser and the accused, whether the latter be an individual, minority group,

---

a. These screening procedures are briefly described in Ch. 1, § 1 at steps 10 and 11. As noted there, they are utilized in most jurisdic- tions only for felony charges. Neither is re- quired for misdemeanors.

or other, to determine whether a charge is founded upon reason or was dictated by an intimidating power or by malice and personal ill will."

At the time of the adoption of the Fifth Amendment, all of the states also required that felony prosecutions be brought by indictment. In the mid-1800's, however, several of the newer states shifted from prosecution by grand jury indictment to prosecution by an information (an accusation issued by the prosecutor, rather than the grand jury). To ensure independent screening, those states restricted use of the information to cases in which the magistrate made a finding of probable cause in support of the information at a preliminary hearing. In *Hurtado v. California*, 110 U.S. 516 (1884), that procedure was sustained against constitutional challenge. The Supreme Court there held that the guarantee of prosecution by grand jury indictment, though found in the Fifth Amendment, did not reflect a "fundamental principle of liberty and justice" and therefore was not applicable to the states under the due process clause of the Fourteenth Amendment. Although the Supreme Court, with the adoption in the 1960's of a different view of the Fourteenth Amendment generally overruled its earlier decisions that had refused to find in due process a right specified in the Bill of Rights (see Ch. 2, § 1), the *Hurtado* ruling provided the one major exception to that pattern. The Court has continued to hold that the states need not prosecute by indictment, and today only about twenty states still require grand jury review.[b] In the remaining states, the prosecution may proceed by indictment or information, and most prosecutors in those states proceed by information in most cases.

In the vast majority of the states allowing prosecution by information at the prosecutor's discretion, the information can be filed only if there has been a determination of probable cause by a magistrate at a preliminary hearing.[c] Defense counsel generally view this requirement as providing a more favorable screening process than the grand jury because the preliminary hearing is an adversary proceeding at which the defense may cross-examine the prosecution's witnesses and present its own evidence. This stands in contrast to the secret and non-adversary grand jury proceeding, in which only the prosecution participates, presenting its side of the case and serving as the legal advisor to the lay jurors. The preliminary hearing also may provide the defense with other procedural advantages, as noted in *Coleman v. Alabama*, infra.

In a few of the states allowing prosecution by information, the prosecution has available the option of direct filing of the information without a preliminary hearing. Because the practice upheld in *Hurtado* required a preliminary hearing, it was not clear from that case whether due process permitted a state to utilize an accusatory process in a felony case that dispensed with any form of screening procedure by a neutral agency. That issue was presented in *Lem Woon v. Oregon*, 229 U.S. 586 (1913), which presented a challenge to the direct filing of an

b. These jurisdictions commonly allow for defense waiver of the indictment, so a felony prosecution can be brought by information in such states when the defendant makes a proper waiver of his right to grand jury review.

c. These jurisdictions also allow for defense waiver of the preliminary hearing, so a felony information can be filed without a magistrate's probable cause determination when there has been a waiver.

Jurisdictions requiring prosecution by indictment also provide for a preliminary hearing in felony cases within a specified period after arrest, but that hearing will not be held if an indictment is obtained prior to the scheduled date of hearing. The indictment establishes probable cause as found by the grand jury, and since the grand jury finding prevails over any determination to the contrary that the magistrate might make, there is no need for the preliminary hearing. In some indictment jurisdictions, it is common for prosecutors to "bypass" the preliminary hearing by first obtaining an indictment, while the practice in other indictment jurisdictions is to have a prompt preliminary hearing followed by the taking of the case to the grand jury. The latter practice was followed in *Coleman v. Alabama*, infra.

information without "any examination, or commitment by a magistrate * * * or any verification other than [the prosecutor's] official oath." Relying on the fundamental fairness analysis of *Hurtado,* the Court in *Lem Woon* sustained the state's direct filing procedure. It noted:

> "[T]his court has * * * held [that] the 'due process of law' clause does not require the State to adopt the institution and procedure of a grand jury, [and] we are unable to see upon what theory it can be held that an examination or the opportunity for one, prior to the formal accusation by the district attorney, is obligatory upon the States."

Although the Supreme Court subsequently held in *Gerstein v. Pugh,* 420 U.S. 103 (1975), that the Fourth Amendment requires a magistrate's ex parte determination of probable cause (as in the issuance of an arrest warrant) where there is "extended restraint of liberty following arrest" (see fn. a to *Watson* in Ch. 3, § 5), the opinion there reaffirmed the holding in *Lem Woon* "that a judicial hearing is not a prerequisite to prosecution by information." The Constitution does not require the state to provide "judicial oversight or review [as in a preliminary hearing] of the decision to prosecute." *Gerstein.*

While states are not constitutionally required to provide for screening by either the grand jury or the preliminary hearing, once they do afford such screening, constitutional limitations may apply. The first two cases in this chapter, *Coleman v. Alabama* and *Vasquez v. Hillery,* treat the two major constitutional limitations applicable to the preliminary hearing (*Coleman*) and the grand jury (*Hillery*). Those cases also raise the question of whether a conviction should be reversed where there was constitutional error in the screening process but the defendant was then found guilty after a trial that complied in all respects with constitutional requirements.[d]

In federal prosecutions, of course, the Fifth Amendment requires prosecution by grand jury indictment. The third case in the chapter, *Costello v. United States,* raises the question of whether the Fifth Amendment requires that the grand jury's decision to indict be based on evidence that would be admissible at trial. Following *Costello,* the Supreme Court indicated in a series of cases that the rationale of *Costello* was also applicable to grand jury consideration of evidence that would be inadmissible at trial because obtained in violation of the federal constitution. In the latest of those Supreme Court rulings, *United States v. Calandra,* 414 U.S. 338 (1974), holding that a grand jury witness could not refuse to answer questions based on information obtained through an unconstitutional search, the Court noted:

---

d. The issue posed in this regard relates to applicability of the constitutional "harmless error" doctrine set forth in *Chapman v. California,* 386 U.S. 18 (1967). Prior to *Chapman,* it frequently had been assumed that all constitutional errors automatically required reversal of a conviction on appeal because such errors were "per se injurious." *Chapman* held, however, that constitutional errors were not exempted from the usual rule of appellate review that requires affirmance where the error in prior proceedings is deemed "harmless" (see Ch. 1, § 1, at step 17). The Court reasoned that this "harmless error" principle served a "very useful purpose insofar as * * * [it] block[s] setting aside convictions for small errors or defects that have little, if any likelihood of having changed the result of the trial." Accordingly, as to most constitutional errors, reversal of a conviction would not be required where the state could establish that that error was in fact harmless. This required the state to "prove beyond a reasonable doubt that the error * * * did not contribute to the verdict obtained." The Court added, however, that "there are some constitutional rights so basic to a fair trial that their infraction can never be treated as harmless error." Cited as illustrations of such errors (calling for automatic reversal) were a state's failure to provide appointed counsel at trial as required under the Sixth Amendment (see Ch. 5, § 1), and a due process violation resulting from the possible bias of a trial judge whose fees were derived from the fines he imposed (see *Tumey v. Ohio,* described in the *Hillery* opinion). See also fn. a, Ch. 6.

"The grand jury's sources of information are widely drawn and the validity of an indictment is not affected by the character of the evidence considered. Thus, an indictment valid on its face is not subject to challenge on the ground that the grand jury acted on the basis of inadequate or incompetent evidence, *Costello v. United States;* or even on the basis of information obtained in violation of a defendant's Fifth Amendment privilege against self-incrimination."

COLEMAN v. ALABAMA

399 U.S. 1, 90 S.Ct. 1999, 26 L.Ed.2d 387 (1970).

JUSTICE BRENNAN announced the judgment of the Court and delivered the following opinion.

Petitioners were convicted in an Alabama Circuit Court of assault with intent to murder in the shooting of one Reynolds after he and his wife parked their car on an Alabama highway to change a flat tire. The Alabama Court of Appeals affirmed, and the Alabama Supreme Court denied review. We vacate and remand.

Petitioners * * * argue that the preliminary hearing prior to their indictment was a "critical stage" of the prosecution and that Alabama's failure to provide them with appointed counsel at the hearing therefore unconstitutionally denied them the assistance of counsel. * * *

II [2]

This Court has held that a person accused of crime "requires the guiding hand of counsel at every step in the proceedings against him," *Powell v. Alabama* [Ch. 5, § 1], and that that constitutional principle is not limited to the presence of counsel at trial. "It is central to that principle that in addition to counsel's presence at trial, the accused is guaranteed that he need not stand alone against the State at any stage of the prosecution, formal or informal, in court or out, where counsel's absence might derogate from the accused's right to a fair trial." *United States v. Wade* [Ch. 7, § 1]. Accordingly, "the principle of *Powell v. Alabama* and succeeding cases requires that we scrutinize *any* pretrial confrontation of the accused to determine whether the presence of his counsel is necessary to preserve the defendant's basic right to a fair trial as affected by his right meaningfully to cross-examine the witnesses against him and to have effective assistance of counsel at the trial itself. It calls upon us to analyze whether potential substantial prejudice to defendant's rights inheres in the particular confrontation and the ability of counsel to help avoid that prejudice."

Applying this test, the Court has held that "critical stages" include the pretrial type of arraignment where certain rights may be sacrificed or lost, *Hamilton v. Alabama,* 368 U.S. 52 (1961), and the pretrial lineup, *United States v. Wade.* Cf. *Miranda v. Arizona,* where the Court held that the privilege against compulsory self-incrimination includes a right to counsel at a pretrial custodial interrogation.

The preliminary hearing is not a required step in an Alabama prosecution. The prosecutor may seek an indictment directly from the grand jury without a preliminary hearing. The opinion of the Alabama Court of Appeals in this case instructs us that under Alabama law the sole purposes of a preliminary hearing are to determine whether there is sufficient evidence against the accused to

---

2. Justice Douglas, Justice White, and Jus-   tice Marshall join this Part II.

warrant presenting his case to the grand jury, and if so to fix bail if the offense is bailable. See Code of Alabama, Tit. 15, §§ 139, 140, 151. The court continued:

> "At the preliminary hearing * * * the accused is not required to advance any defenses, and failure to do so does not preclude him from availing himself of every defense he may have upon the trial of the case. Also *Pointer v. Texas,* 380 U.S. 400 (1965), bars the admission of testimony given at a pretrial proceeding where the accused did not have the benefit of cross-examination by and through counsel. Thus, nothing occurring at the preliminary hearing in the absence of counsel can substantially prejudice the rights of the accused on trial."

This Court is of course bound by this construction of the governing Alabama law. However, from the fact that in cases where the accused has no lawyer at the hearing the Alabama courts prohibit the State's use at trial of anything that occurred at the hearing, it does not follow that the Alabama preliminary hearing is not a "critical stage" of the State's criminal process. The determination whether the hearing is a "critical stage" requiring the provision of counsel depends, as noted, upon an analysis "whether potential substantial prejudice to defendant's rights inheres in the * * * confrontation and the ability of counsel to help avoid that prejudice." *United States v. Wade.* Plainly the guiding hand of counsel at the preliminary hearing is essential to protect the indigent accused against an erroneous or improper prosecution. First, the lawyer's skilled examination and cross-examination of witnesses may expose fatal weaknesses in the State's case, that may lead the magistrate to refuse to bind the accused over. Second, in any event, the skilled interrogation of witnesses by an experienced lawyer can fashion a vital impeachment tool for use in cross-examination of the State's witnesses at the trial, or preserve testimony favorable to the accused of a witness who does not appear at the trial. Third, trained counsel can more effectively discover the case the State has against his client and make possible the preparation of a proper defense to meet that case at the trial. Fourth, counsel can also be influential at the preliminary hearing in making effective arguments for the accused on such matters as the necessity for an early psychiatric examination or bail. The inability of the indigent accused on his own to realize these advantages of a lawyer's assistance compels the conclusion that the Alabama preliminary hearing is a "critical stage" of the State's criminal process at which the accused is "as much entitled to such aid [of counsel] * * * as at the trial itself." *Powell v. Alabama.*

III [4]

There remains, then, the question of the relief to which petitioners are entitled. The trial transcript indicates that the prohibition against use by the State at trial of anything that occurred at the preliminary hearing was scrupulously observed. But on the record it cannot be said whether or not petitioners were otherwise prejudiced by the absence of counsel at the preliminary hearing. That inquiry in the first instance should more properly be made by the Alabama courts. The test to be applied is whether the denial of counsel at the preliminary hearing was harmless error under *Chapman v. California* [fn. d of introduction]. We accordingly vacate the petitioners' convictions and remand the case to the Alabama courts for such proceedings not inconsistent with this opinion as they may deem appropriate to determine whether such denial of counsel was harmless error, and therefore whether the convictions should be reinstated or a new trial ordered.

4. Justice Black, Justice Douglas, Justice   White, and Justice Marshall join this Part III.

JUSTICE BLACK, concurring.

I wholeheartedly agree with the Court's holding in Part II of its opinion that an accused has a constitutional right to the assistance of counsel at the preliminary hearing which Alabama grants criminal defendants. * * * The preliminary hearing is * * * a definite part or stage of a criminal prosecution in Alabama, and the plain language of the Sixth Amendment requires that "[i]n all criminal prosecutions, the accused shall enjoy the right * * * to have the Assistance of Counsel for his defence." * * * I fear that the Court's opinion seems at times to proceed on the premise that the constitutional principle ultimately at stake here is not the defendant's right to counsel as guaranteed by the Sixth and Fourteenth Amendments but rather a right to a "fair trial" as conceived by judges. While that phrase is an appealing one, neither the Bill of Rights nor any other part of the Constitution contains it. * * *

JUSTICE DOUGLAS.

While I have joined Mr. Justice Brennan's opinion, I add a word as to why I think that a strict construction of the Constitution requires the result reached.

The critical words are "In all criminal prosecutions, the accused shall enjoy the right * * * to have the assistance of Counsel for his defence." As Mr. Justice Black states, a preliminary hearing is "a definite part or stage of a criminal prosecution in Alabama." A "criminal prosecution" certainly does not start only when the trial starts. If the commencement of the trial were the start of the "criminal prosecution" in the constitutional sense, then indigents would likely go to trial without effective representation by counsel. Lawyers for the defense need time to prepare a defense. The prosecution needs time for investigations and procedures to make that investigation timely and telling. As a shorthand expression we have used the words "critical stage" to describe whether the preliminary phase of a criminal trial was part of the "criminal prosecution" as used in the Sixth Amendment. But it is the Sixth Amendment that controls, not our own ideas as to what an efficient criminal code should provide. It did not take nearly 200 years of doubt to decide whether Alabama's preliminary hearing is a part of the "criminal prosecution" within the meaning of the Sixth Amendment. The question has never been reached prior to this case. * * * If we are to adhere to the mandate of the Constitution and not give it merely that meaning which appeals to the personal tastes of those who from time to time sit here, we should read its terms in light of the realities of what "criminal prosecutions" truly mean. * * *

JUSTICE WHITE, concurring.

I agree with Mr. Justice Harlan that recent cases furnish ample ground for holding the preliminary hearing a critical event in the progress of a criminal case. I therefore join the opinion of the Court, but with some hesitation since requiring the appointment of counsel may result in fewer preliminary hearings in jurisdictions where the prosecutor is free to avoid them by taking a case directly to a grand jury. Our ruling may also invite eliminating the preliminary hearing system entirely.

I would expect the application of the harmless-error standard on remand to produce results approximating those contemplated by Mr. Justice Harlan's separately stated views. Whether denying petitioner counsel at the preliminary hearing was harmless beyond a reasonable doubt depends upon an assessment of those factors which made the denial error. But that assessment cannot ignore the fact that petitioner has been tried and found guilty by a jury.

The possibility that counsel would have detected preclusive flaws in the State's probable cause showing is for all practical purposes mooted by the trial where the State produced evidence satisfying the jury of the petitioner's guilt beyond a reasonable doubt. Also, it would be wholly speculative in this case to assume either (1) that the State's witnesses at the trial testified inconsistently with what their testimony would have been if petitioner had had counsel to cross-examine them at the preliminary hearing, or (2) that counsel, had he been present at the hearing, would have known so much more about the State's case than he actually did when he went to trial that the result of the trial might have been different. So too it seems extremely unlikely that matters related to bail or early psychiatric examination would ever raise reasonable doubts about the integrity of the trial. There remains the possibility, as Mr. Justice Harlan suggests, that important testimony of witnesses unavailable at the trial could have been preserved had counsel been present to cross-examine opposing witnesses or to examine witnesses for the defense. If such was the case, petitioner would be entitled to a new trial.

JUSTICE HARLAN, concurring in part and dissenting in part.

If I felt free to consider this case upon a clean slate I would have voted to affirm these convictions. But in light of the lengths to which the right to appointed counsel has been carried in recent decisions of this Court, see *Miranda v. Arizona, United States v. Wade,* * * * —I consider that course is not open to me with due regard for the way in which the adjudicatory process of this Court, as I conceive it, should work. * * *

While, given the cases referred to, I cannot escape the conclusion that petitioners' constitutional rights must be held to have been violated by denying them appointed counsel at the preliminary hearing, I consider the scope of the Court's remand too broad and amorphous. I do not think that reversal of these convictions, for lack of counsel at the preliminary hearing, should follow unless petitioners are able to show on remand that they have been prejudiced in their defense at trial, in that favorable testimony that might otherwise have been preserved was irretrievably lost by virtue of not having counsel to help present an affirmative case at the preliminary hearing. * * * In my opinion mere speculation that defense counsel might have been able to do better at trial had he been present at the preliminary hearing should not suffice to vitiate a conviction. The Court's remand under the *Chapman* harmless-error rule seems to me to leave the way open for that sort of speculation. * * *

JUSTICE STEWART, with whom THE CHIEF JUSTICE joins, dissenting.

* * * If at the trial the prosecution had used any incriminating statements made by the petitioners at the preliminary hearing, the convictions before us would quite properly have to be set aside. But that did not happen in this case. Or if the prosecution had used the statement of any other witness at the preliminary hearing against the petitioners at their trial, we would likewise quite properly have to set aside these convictions. But that did not happen in this case either. For as the Court today perforce concedes, "the prohibition against use by the State at trial of anything that occurred at the preliminary hearing was scrupulously observed." * * *

But the Court holds today that the Constitution required Alabama to provide a lawyer for the petitioners at their preliminary hearing, not so much, it seems, to assure a fair trial as to assure a fair preliminary hearing. A lawyer at the preliminary hearing, the Court says, might have led the magistrate to "refuse to bind the accused over." Or a lawyer might have made "effective arguments for the accused on such matters as bail or the necessity for an early psychiatric examination." If *those* are the reasons a lawyer must be provided, then the most elementary logic requires that a new preliminary hearing must now be held, with counsel made available to the petitioners. In order to provide such relief, it would, of course, be necessary not only to set aside these convictions, but also to set aside the grand jury indictments, and the magistrate's orders fixing bail and binding over the petitioners. Since the petitioners have now been found by a jury in a constitutional trial to be guilty beyond a reasonable doubt, the Court understandably boggles at these logical consequences of its own reasoning. It refrains, in short, from now turning back the clock by ordering a new preliminary hearing to determine all over again whether there is sufficient evidence against the accused to present their case to a grand jury. Instead, the Court sets aside these convictions and remands the case for determination "whether the convictions should be reinstated or a new trial ordered," and this action seems to me even more quixotic. * * *

No record or transcript of any kind was made of the preliminary hearing. Therefore, if the burden on remand is on the petitioners to show that they were prejudiced, it is clear that that burden cannot be met, and the remand is a futile gesture. If, on the other hand, the burden is on the State to disprove beyond a reasonable doubt any and all speculative advantages that the petitioners might conceivably have enjoyed if counsel had been present at their preliminary hearing, then obviously that burden cannot be met either, and the Court should simply reverse these convictions. All I can say is that if the Alabama courts can figure out what they are supposed to do with this case now that it has been remanded to them, their perceptiveness will far exceed mine.

The record before us makes clear that no evidence of what occurred at the preliminary hearing was used against the petitioners at their now completed trial. I would hold, therefore, that the absence of counsel at the preliminary hearing deprived the petitioners of no constitutional rights. Accordingly, I would affirm these convictions.

CHIEF JUSTICE BURGER, [dissenting].

I agree that as a matter of *sound policy* counsel should be made available to all persons subjected to a preliminary hearing and that this should be provided either by statute or by the rulemaking process. However, I cannot accept the notion that the Constitution commands it because it is a "criminal prosecution." * * * Certainly, as Mr. Justice Harlan and Mr. Justice White suggest, not a word in the Constitution itself either requires or contemplates the result reached; unlike them, however, I do not acquiesce in prior holdings which purportedly, but nonetheless erroneously, are based on the Constitution. That approach simply is an acknowledgment that the Court having previously amended the Sixth Amendment now feels bound by its action. While I do not rely solely on 183 years of contrary constitutional interpretation, it is indeed an odd business that it has taken this Court nearly two centuries to "discover" a constitutional mandate to have counsel at a preliminary hearing. Here there is not even the excuse that conditions have changed; the preliminary hearing is an ancient institution.

* * * If the Constitution provided that counsel be furnished for every "critical event in the progress of a criminal case," that would be another story, but it does not. In contrast to the variety of verbal combinations employed by the majority to justify today's disposition, the Sixth Amendment states with laudable precision that "In all *criminal prosecutions,* the accused shall * * * have the Assistance of Counsel." (Emphasis added.) The only relevant determination is whether a preliminary hearing is a "criminal prosecution," *not* whether it is a "*critical event* in the progress of a criminal case." By inventing its own verbal formula the Court simply seeks to reshape the Constitution in accordance with its own predilections of what is desirable. Constitutional interpretation is not an easy matter, but we should be especially cautious of substituting our own notions for those of the Framers. * * *

Under today's holding we * * * have something of an anomaly under the new "discovery" of the Court that counsel is *constitutionally* required at the preliminary hearing since counsel cannot attend a subsequent grand jury inquiry, even though witnesses, including the person eventually charged, may be interrogated in secret session. If the current mode of constitutional analysis subscribed to by this Court in recent cases requires that counsel be present at preliminary hearings, how can this be reconciled with the fact that the Constitution itself does not permit the assistance of counsel at the decidedly more "critical" grand jury inquiry.

Finally, as pointed out, the Court has already protected an accused from absence of counsel at the preliminary hearing by providing that statements of an uncounseled person are inadmissible at trial. The Court fails to explain why that salutary—indeed drastic—remedy is no longer sufficient protection for the preliminary hearing stage, unless what the Court is doing—surreptitiously—is to convert the preliminary hearing into a discovery device. * * *

VASQUEZ v. HILLERY

474 U.S. 254, 106 S.Ct. 617, 88 L.Ed.2d 598 (1986).

JUSTICE MARSHALL delivered the opinion of the Court.

The Warden of San Quentin State Prison asks this Court to retire a doctrine of equal protection jurisprudence first announced in 1880. The time has come, he urges, for us to abandon the rule requiring reversal of the conviction of any defendant indicted by a grand jury from which members of his own race were systematically excluded.

In 1962, the grand jury of Kings County, California, indicted respondent, Booker T. Hillery, for a brutal murder. Before trial in Superior Court, respondent moved to quash the indictment on the ground that it had been issued by a grand jury from which blacks had been systematically excluded. A hearing on respondent's motion was held by Judge Meredith Wingrove, who was the sole Superior Court Judge in the county and had personally selected all grand juries, including the one that indicted respondent, for the previous seven years. Absolving himself of any discriminatory intent, Judge Wingrove refused to quash the indictment. Respondent was subsequently convicted of first-degree murder.

For the next 16 years, respondent pursued appeals and collateral relief in the state courts, raising at every opportunity his equal protection challenge to the grand jury that indicted him. Less than one month after the California Supreme Court foreclosed his final avenue of state relief in 1978, respondent filed a petition for a writ of habeas corpus in federal court, raising that same challenge. The District Court concluded that respondent had established discrimination in the grand jury, and granted the writ.[a] The Court of Appeals affirmed, and we granted certiorari.

a. In a portion of its opinion that has been deleted, the Court sustained the district court's consideration of a computer analysis that had not been submitted before the state courts. That analysis assessed the "mathematical probability that chance or accident could have accounted for the exclusion of blacks from the Kings County grand jury over the years at issue." The district court "accepted the experts conclusion that had the grand jurors been selected by chance, the probability that no black would have been selected over the 17

* * * [P]etitioner urges this Court to find that discrimination in the grand jury amounted to harmless error in this case, claiming that the evidence against respondent was overwhelming and that discrimination no longer infects the selection of grand juries in Kings County. Respondent's conviction after a fair trial, we are told, purged any taint attributable to the indictment process. Our acceptance of this theory would require abandonment of more than a century of consistent precedent.

In 1880, this Court reversed a state conviction on the ground that the indictment charging the offense had been issued by a grand jury from which blacks had been excluded. We reasoned that deliberate exclusion of blacks "is practically a brand upon them, affixed by the law, an assertion of their inferiority, and a stimulant to that race prejudice which is an impediment to securing to individuals of the race that equal justice which the law aims to secure to all others." *Strauder v. West Virginia,* 100 U.S. 303 (1880).

Thereafter, the Court has repeatedly rejected all arguments that a conviction may stand despite racial discrimination in the selection of the grand jury.[b] Only six years ago, the Court explicitly addressed the question whether this unbroken line of case law should be reconsidered in favor of a harmless-error standard, and determined that it should not. *Rose v. Mitchell,* 443 U.S. 545 (1979). We reaffirmed our conviction that discrimination on the basis of race in the selection of grand jurors "strikes at the fundamental values of our judicial system and our society as a whole," and that the criminal defendant's right to equal protection of the laws has been denied when he is indicted by a grand jury from which members of a racial group purposefully have been excluded.

Petitioner argues here that requiring a State to retry a defendant, sometimes years later, imposes on it an unduly harsh penalty for a constitutional defect bearing no relation to the fundamental fairness of the trial. Yet intentional discrimination in the selection of grand jurors is a grave constitutional trespass, possible only under color of state authority, and wholly within the power of the State to prevent. Thus, the remedy we have embraced for over a century—the only effective remedy for this violation [5]—is not disproportionate to the evil that it seeks to deter. If grand jury discrimination becomes a thing of the past, no conviction will ever again be lost on account of it.

Nor are we persuaded that discrimination in the grand jury has no effect on the fairness of the criminal trials that result from that grand jury's actions. The grand jury does not determine only that probable cause exists to believe that a defendant committed a crime, or that it does not. In the hands of the grand jury lies the power to charge a greater offense or a lesser offense; numerous counts or a single count; and perhaps most significant of all, a capital offense or a noncapital offense—all on the basis of the same facts. Moreover, "[t]he grand

year period of Judge Wingrove's tenure was 2 in 1,000.

b. The Court here cited 13 Supreme Court opinion, decided between 1881 and 1972, in which convictions had been reversed on direct appeal based on racial discrimination in the selection of the grand jury.

5. As we pointed out in *Rose v. Mitchell,* alternative remedies are ineffectual. Federal law provides a criminal prohibition against discrimination in the selection of grand jurors, 18 U.S.C. § 243, but according to statistics compiled by the Administrative Office of the United States Courts, that section has not been the basis for a single prosecution in the past nine

years. With respect to prior years, for which precise information is not available, we have been unable to find evidence of any prosecution or conviction under the statute in the last century. The other putative remedy for grand jury discrimination is 42 U.S.C. § 1983, which, in theory, allows redress for blacks who have been excluded from grand jury service. These suits are also extremely rare, undoubtedly because the potential plaintiffs, eligible blacks not called for grand jury service, are often without knowledge of the discriminatory practices and without incentive to launch costly legal battles to stop them.

jury is not bound to indict in every case where a conviction can be obtained."
United States v. Ciambrone, 601 F.2d 616, 629 (C.A.2 1979) (Friendly, J., dissenting). Thus, even if a grand jury's determination of probable cause is confirmed in
hindsight by a conviction on the indicted offense, that confirmation in no way
suggests that the discrimination did not impermissibly infect the framing of the
indictment and, consequently, the nature or very existence of the proceedings to
come.

When constitutional error calls into question the objectivity of those charged
with bringing a defendant to judgment, a reviewing court can neither indulge a
presumption of regularity nor evaluate the resulting harm. Accordingly, when
the trial judge is discovered to have had some basis for rendering a biased
judgment, his actual motivations are hidden from review, and we must presume
that the process was impaired. See *Tumey v. Ohio,* 273 U.S. 510, 535 (1927)
(reversal required when judge has financial interest in conviction, despite lack of
indication that bias influenced decisions). Similarly, when a petit jury has been
selected upon improper criteria or has been exposed to prejudicial publicity, we
have required reversal of the conviction because the effect of the violation cannot
be ascertained. Like these fundamental flaws, which never have been thought
harmless, discrimination in the grand jury undermines the structural integrity of
the criminal tribunal itself, and is not amenable to harmless-error review.[6]

Just as a conviction is void under the Equal Protection Clause if the
prosecutor deliberately charged the defendant on account of his race, see *United
States v. Batchelder* [see Ch. 10, § 2], a conviction cannot be understood to cure
the taint attributable to a charging body selected on the basis of race. Once
having found discrimination in the selection of a grand jury, we simply cannot
know that the need to indict would have been assessed in the same way by a
grand jury properly constituted. The overriding imperative to eliminate this
systemic flaw in the charging process, as well as the difficulty of assessing its
effect on any given defendant, requires our continued adherence to a rule of
mandatory reversal.

The opinion of the Court in *Mitchell* ably presented other justifications, based
on the necessity for vindicating Fourteenth Amendment rights, supporting a
policy of automatic reversal in cases of grand jury discrimination. That analysis
persuasively demonstrated that the justifications retain their validity in modern
times, for "114 years after the close of the War Between the States and nearly 100
years after *Strauder,* racial and other forms of discrimination still remain a fact of
life, in the administration of justice as in our society as a whole." The six years
since *Mitchell* have given us no reason to doubt the continuing truth of that
observation.

The dissent propounds a theory, not advanced by any party, which would
condition the grant of relief upon the passage of time between a conviction and
the filing of a petition for federal habeas corpus, depending upon the ability of a
State to obtain a second conviction. Sound jurisprudence counsels against our
adoption of that approach to habeas corpus claims.

The Habeas Corpus Rules permit a State to move for dismissal of a habeas
petition when it "has been prejudiced in its ability to respond to the petition by
delay in its filing." Indeed, petitioner filed such a motion in this case, and it was
denied because the District Court found that no prejudicial delay had been caused
by respondent. Congress has not seen fit, however, to provide the State with an

6. Justice White does not join in the forego-   ing paragraph.

additional defense to habeas corpus petitions based on the difficulties that it will face if forced to retry the defendant.   * * *

Today's decision is supported, though not compelled, by the important doctrine of *stare decisis*, the means by which we ensure that the law will not merely change erratically, but will develop in a principled and intelligible fashion. That doctrine permits society to presume that bedrock principles are founded in the law rather than in the proclivities of individuals, and thereby contributes to the integrity of our constitutional system of government, both in appearance and in fact. While *stare decisis* is not an inexorable command, the careful observer will discern that any detours from the straight path of *stare decisis* in our past have occurred for articulable reasons, and only when the Court has felt obliged "to bring its opinions into agreement with experience and with facts newly ascertained." *Burnet v. Coronado Oil & Gas Co.*, 285 U.S. 393 (1932) (Brandeis, J., dissenting). * * * [E]very successful proponent of overruling precedent has borne the heavy burden of persuading the Court that changes in society or in the law dictate that the values served by *stare decisis* yield in favor of a greater objective. In the case of grand jury discrimination, we have been offered no reason to believe that any such metamorphosis has rendered the Court's long commitment to a rule of reversal outdated, ill-founded, unworkable, or otherwise legitimately vulnerable to serious reconsideration. On the contrary, the need for such a rule is as compelling today as it was at its inception.[c]

JUSTICE POWELL, with whom THE CHIEF JUSTICE and JUSTICE REHNQUIST join, dissenting.

Respondent, a black man, was indicted by a grand jury having no black members for the stabbing murder of a 15–year–old girl. A petit jury found respondent guilty of that charge beyond a reasonable doubt, in a trial the fairness of which is unchallenged here. Twenty-three years later, we are asked to grant respondent's petition for a writ of habeas corpus—and thereby require a new trial if that is still feasible—on the ground that blacks were purposefully excluded from the grand jury that indicted him. It is undisputed that race discrimination has long since disappeared from the grand jury selection process in Kings County, California. It is undisputed that a grand jury that perfectly represented Kings County's population at the time of respondent's indictment would have contained only one black member. Yet the Court holds that respondent's petition must be granted, and that respondent must be freed unless the State is able to reconvict, more than two decades after the murder that led to his incarceration.

It is difficult to reconcile this result with a rational system of justice. The Court nevertheless finds its decision compelled by a century of precedent and by the interests of respondent and of society in ending race discrimination in the selection of grand juries. I dissent for two reasons. First, in my view, any error in the selection of the grand jury that indicted respondent is constitutionally harmless. Second, even assuming that the harmless-error rule does not apply, reversal of respondent's conviction is an inappropriate remedy for the wrong that prompts this case.

c. Justice O'Connor's opinion, concurring in the judgment, is omitted. Justice O'Connor noted that she shared the "view expressed by Justice Powell in *Rose* [that] a petitioner who has been afforded by the state courts a full and fair opportunity to litigate the claims that blacks were discriminatorily excluded from the grand jury * * * should be foreclosed from relitigating that claim on federal habeas." The district court here, however, had held that respondent Hillery "was not given a full and fair hearing on his discrimination claim in state court." Nor had a "sufficiently compelling case been made for reversing this Court's precedents with respect to the remedy applicable to properly cognizable claims of discriminatory exclusion of grand jurors."

The Court concludes that the harmless-error rule does not apply to claims of grand jury discrimination. This conclusion is said to follow from a line of cases going back over 100 years. In my view, it follows from a misapplication of the doctrine of *stare decisis*. Adhering to precedent "is usually the wise policy, because in most matters it is more important that the applicable rule of law be settled than that it be settled right." *Burnet v. Coronado Oil & Gas Co.,* 285 U.S. 393 (1932) (Brandeis, J., dissenting). Accordingly, "any departure from the doctrine of *stare decisis* demands special justification." Nevertheless, when governing decisions are badly reasoned, or conflict with other, more recent authority, the Court "has never felt constrained to follow precedent." Instead, particularly where constitutional issues are involved, "[t]his Court has shown a readiness to correct its errors even though of long standing." In this case, the Court misapplies *stare decisis* because it relies only on decisions concerning grand jury discrimination. There is other precedent, including important cases of more recent vintage than those cited by the Court, that should control this case. Those cases hold, or clearly imply, that a conviction should not be reversed for constitutional error where the error did not affect the outcome of the prosecution.

In *Chapman v. California,* 386 U.S. 18 (1967), the Court held that a trial judge's improper comment on the defendant's failure to testify—a clear violation of the Fifth and Fourteenth Amendments—was not a proper basis for reversal if harmless. Since *Chapman,* "the Court has consistently made clear that it is the duty of a reviewing court to consider the trial record as a whole and to ignore errors that are harmless, including most constitutional violations." This rule has been applied to a variety of constitutional violations. See *Harrington v. California,* 395 U.S. 250 (1969) (use of co-conspirator confession in violation of Confrontation Clause); *Coleman v. Alabama,* 399 U.S. 1 (1970) (denial of counsel at preliminary hearing); *Milton v. Wainwright,* 407 U.S. 371 (1972) (use of confession obtained in violation of right to counsel); *Gerstein v. Pugh,* 420 U.S. 103 (1975) (illegal arrest). * * *

In *Rose v. Mitchell,* 443 U.S. 545 (1979), the Court contended that the principle of these cases is inapplicable to grand jury discrimination claims, because grand jury discrimination "destroys the appearance of justice and thereby casts doubt on the integrity of the judicial process." But *every* constitutional error may be said to raise questions as to the "appearance of justice" and the "integrity of the judicial process." Nevertheless, as the cases cited above show, the Court has required some showing of actual prejudice to the defendant as a prerequisite to reversal, even when the constitutional error directly affects the fairness of the defendant's trial. Compare *Strickland v. Washington* [Ch. 17, § 2] (requiring prejudice in ineffective assistance of counsel claims), with *Gideon v. Wainwright* [Ch. 5, § 1] (emphasizing importance of right to counsel to ensure fair trial). Grand jury discrimination is a serious violation of our constitutional order, but so also are the deprivations of rights guaranteed by the Fourth, Fifth, Sixth, and Fourteenth Amendments to which we have applied harmless-error analysis or an analogous prejudice requirement. Moreover, grand jury discrimination occurs *prior* to trial, while the asserted constitutional violations in most of the above-cited cases occurred *during* trial. The Court does not adequately explain why grand jury discrimination affects the "integrity of the judicial process" to a greater extent than the deprivation of equally vital constitutional rights, nor why it is exempt from a prejudice requirement while other constitutional errors are not. * * *

Even assuming that now-established harmless-error principles are inapplicable, this case unjustifiably extends the "century of precedent" on which the Court relies. * * * No one questions that race discrimination in grand jury selection violates the Equal Protection Clause of the Fourteenth Amendment. The issue in this case is not whether the State erred, but what should be done about it. The question is whether reversal of respondent's conviction either is compelled by the Constitution or is an appropriate, but not constitutionally required, remedy for racial discrimination in the selection of grand jurors.

The Constitution does not compel the rule of automatic reversal that the Court applies today. In *Hobby v. United States,* 468 U.S. 339 (1984), we acknowledged that discriminatory selection of grand jury foremen violated the Constitution, but we concluded that reversing the petitioner's conviction was an inappropriate remedy for the violation since grand jury foremen play a minor part in federal prosecutions. See also *Oregon v. Elstad* [Ch. 6, § 4] (suppression of evidence obtained in violation of *Miranda v. Arizona,* is not constitutionally compelled); *United States v. Leon* [Ch. 3, § 1] (suppression of evidence obtained in violation of the Fourth Amendment is not constitutionally compelled). * * * The rationale of *Hobby* cannot be squared with the claim that discriminatory selection of the body that charged the defendant *compels* reversal of the defendant's conviction. Rather, it is necessary to determine whether reversal of respondent's conviction is an "appropriate remedy" for the exclusion of blacks from grand juries in Kings County, California, in 1962. * * * That determination depends on (i) the utility of the remedy in either correcting any injustice to respondent or deterring unconstitutional conduct by state officials, and (ii) the remedy's costs to society. *United States v. Leon.*

The scope of the remedy depends in part on the nature and degree of the harm caused by the wrong. The Court perceives two kinds of harm flowing from grand jury discrimination: harm to the respondent's interest in not being charged and convicted because of his race, and harm to society's interest in deterring racial discrimination. I consider in turn these asserted interests and the degree to which they are served in this case by the Court's automatic reversal rule.

The Court does not contend that the discriminatory selection of the grand jury that indicted respondent calls into question the correctness of the decision to indict. Such a contention could not withstand analysis. Following his indictment for murder, respondent was convicted of that charge in a trial and by a jury whose fairness is not now challenged. The conviction, affirmed on direct appeal in 1965, establishes that the grand jury's decision to indict was indisputably correct. * * *

The Court nevertheless decides that discrimination in the selection of the grand jury potentially harmed respondent, because the grand jury is vested with broad discretion in deciding whether to indict and in framing the charges, and because it is impossible to know whether this discretion would have been exercised differently by a properly selected grand jury. The point appears to be that an all-white grand jury from which blacks are systematically excluded might be influenced by race in determining whether to indict and for what charge. Since the State may not imprison respondent for a crime if one of its elements is his race, the argument goes, his conviction must be set aside.

This reasoning ignores established principles of equal protection jurisprudence. We have consistently declined to find a violation of the Equal Protection Clause absent a finding of intentional discrimination. There has been no showing in this case—indeed, respondent does not even allege—that the Kings County grand jury indicted respondent because of his race, or that the grand jury declined to indict white suspects in the face of similarly strong evidence. Nor is it sensible to assume that impermissible discrimination might have occurred simply because the grand jury had no black members. This Court has never suggested that the racial composition of a grand jury gives rise to the inference that indictments are racially motivated, any more than it has suggested that a suspect arrested by a policeman of a different race may challenge his subsequent conviction on that basis. * * *

Once the inference of racial bias in the decision to indict is placed to one side, as it must be under our precedents, it is impossible to conclude that the discriminatory selection of Kings County's grand jurors caused respondent to suffer any cognizable injury. There may be a theoretical possibility that a different grand jury might have decided not to indict or to indict for a less serious charge. The fact remains, however, that the grand jury's decision to indict was *correct as a matter of law*, given respondent's subsequent, unchallenged conviction. A defendant has no right to a grand jury that errs in his favor. * * *

As respondent suffered no prejudice from the grand jury discrimination that prompted his claim, the Court's remedy must stand or fall on its utility as a deterrent to government officials who seek to exclude particular groups from grand juries, weighed against the cost that the remedy imposes on society. The Court properly emphasizes that grand jury discrimination is "a grave constitutional trespass," but it leaps from that observation to the conclusion that *no matter when the claim is raised* the appropriate response is to reverse the conviction of one indicted by a discriminatorily selected body. That conclusion is not, as the Court erroneously suggests, compelled by precedent; equally important, it seriously disserves the public interest.

The cases on which the Court relies involved relatively brief lapses of time between the defendant's trial and the granting of relief. This fact is unsurprising, since the Court only recently determined that claims of grand jury discrimination may be raised in federal habeas corpus proceedings. See *Rose v. Mitchell.* * * * In all of * * * [prior] cases, the time between the defendant's indictment and this Court's decision was six years or less. * * * This case raises the open question whether relief should be denied where the discrimination claim is pressed many years after conviction, and where the State can show that the delay prejudiced its ability to retry the defendant. * * * It is now almost a quarter-century since respondent was tried for murder and since the discrimination occurred. The Court finds this time lapse irrelevant. In my view, it is critically important, because it both increases the societal cost of the Court's chosen remedy and lessens any deterrent force the remedy may otherwise have.

In *Rose v. Mitchell,* supra, the Court reasoned that the rule of automatic reversal imposes limited costs on society, since the State is able to retry successful petitioners, and since "the State remains free to use all the proof it introduced to obtain the conviction in the first trial." This is not the case when relief is granted many years after the original conviction. In those circumstances, the State may find itself severely handicapped in its ability to carry its heavy burden of proving guilt beyond a reasonable doubt. * * * Witnesses die or move away; physical evidence is lost; memories fade. * * *

Long delays also dilute the effectiveness of the reversal rule as a deterrent. This case is illustrative. The architect of the discriminatory selection system that led to respondent's claim, Judge Wingrove, died 19 years ago. Respondent does not allege that the discriminatory practices survived Judge Wingrove, nor is there any evidence in the record to support such an allegation. It is hard to believe that Judge Wingrove might have behaved differently had he known that a convicted defendant might be freed 19 years after his death. Yet that is exactly the proposition that must justify the remedy imposed in this case: that people in positions similar to Judge Wingrove's will change their behavior out of the fear of successful habeas petitions long after they have left office or otherwise passed from the scene. * * *

Twenty-three years ago, respondent was fairly convicted of the most serious of crimes. Respondent's grand jury discrimination claim casts no doubt on the adequacy of the procedures used to convict him or on the sufficiency of the evidence of his guilt. For that reason alone, the Court should reverse the Court of Appeals' decision.[16] Even assuming the harmlessness of the error is irrelevant, however, reversal is still required. The Court inappropriately applies a deterrence rule in a context where it is unlikely to deter, and where its costs to society are likely to be especially high. These considerations should at least lead the Court to remand for a determination of whether the long lapse of time since respondent's conviction would prejudice the State's ability to retry respondent.

COSTELLO v. UNITED STATES

350 U.S. 359, 76 S.Ct. 406, 100 L.Ed. 397 (1956).

JUSTICE BLACK delivered the opinion of the Court.

We granted certiorari in this case to consider a single question: "May a defendant be required to stand trial and a conviction be sustained where only hearsay evidence was presented to the grand jury which indicted him?"

Petitioner, Frank Costello, was indicted for wilfully attempting to evade payment of income taxes due the United States for the years 1947, 1948 and 1949. The charge was that petitioner falsely and fraudulently reported less income than he and his wife actually received during the taxable years in question. Petitioner promptly filed a motion for inspection of the minutes of the grand jury and for a dismissal of the indictment. His motion was based on an affidavit stating that he was firmly convinced there could have been no legal or competent evidence before the grand jury which indicted him since he had reported all his income and paid all taxes due. The motion was denied. At the trial which followed the Government offered evidence designed to show increases in Costello's net worth in an attempt to prove that he had received more income during the years in question than he had reported. To establish its case the Government called and examined 144 witnesses and introduced 368 exhibits. All of the testimony and documents related to business transactions and expenditures by petitioner and his wife. The prosecution concluded its case by calling three government agents. Their investigations had produced the evidence used against petitioner at the trial. They were allowed to summarize the vast amount of evidence already heard and to introduce computations showing, if correct, that petitioner and his wife had received far greater income than they had reported. We have held such summarizations admissible in a "net worth" case like this.

Counsel for petitioner asked each government witness at the trial whether he had appeared before the grand jury which returned the indictment. This cross-examination developed the fact that the three investigating officers had been the only witnesses before the grand jury. After the Government concluded its case, petitioner again moved to dismiss the indictment on the ground that the only evidence before the grand jury was "hearsay," since the three officers had no first-hand knowledge of the transactions upon which their computations were based.

---

16. Confidence in our system of justice is eroded when one found guilty of murder, in a trial conceded to be fair, is set free. It is important to remember that the criminal law's aim is twofold: "that guilt shall not escape or innocence suffer." The Court's decision in this case plainly undermines the State's interest in punishing the guilty, without either protecting the innocent or ensuring the fundamental fairness of the procedures pursuant to which one such as respondent is tried and convicted.

Nevertheless the trial court again refused to dismiss the indictment, and petitioner was convicted. The Court of Appeals affirmed. * * * Petitioner here urges: (1) that an indictment based solely on hearsay evidence violates that part of the Fifth Amendment providing that "No person shall be held to answer for a capital, or otherwise infamous crime, unless on a presentment or indictment of a Grand Jury * * *." and (2) that if the Fifth Amendment does not invalidate an indictment based solely on hearsay we should now lay down such a rule for the guidance of federal courts. * * * [N]either the Fifth Amendment nor any other constitutional provision prescribes the kind of evidence upon which grand juries must act. The grand jury is an English institution, brought to this country by the early colonists and incorporated in the Constitution by the Founders. There is every reason to believe that our constitutional grand jury was intended to operate substantially like its English progenitor. The basic purpose of the English grand jury was to provide a fair method for instituting criminal proceedings against persons believed to have committed crimes. Grand jurors were selected from the body of the people and their work was not hampered by rigid procedural or evidential rules. In fact, grand jurors could act on their own knowledge and were free to make their presentments or indictments on such information as they deemed satisfactory. Despite its broad power to institute criminal proceedings the grand jury grew in popular favor with the years. It acquired an independence in England free from control by the Crown or judges. Its adoption in our Constitution as the sole method for preferring charges in serious criminal cases shows the high place it held as an instrument of justice. And in this country as in England of old the grand jury has convened as a body of laymen, free from technical rules, acting in secret, pledged to indict no one because of prejudice and to free no one because of special favor. As late as 1927 an English historian could say that English grand juries were still free to act on their own knowledge if they pleased to do so. And in 1852 Mr. Justice Nelson on circuit could say "No case has been cited, nor have we been able to find any, furnishing an authority for looking into and revising the judgment of the grand jury upon the evidence, for the purpose of determining whether or not the finding was founded upon sufficient proof * * *." *United States v. Reed,* 27 Fed.Cas. 727, 738 (1852).

In *Holt v. United States,* 218 U.S. 245 (1910), this Court had to decide whether an indictment should be quashed because supported in part by incompetent evidence. Aside from the incompetent evidence "there was very little evidence against the accused." The Court refused to hold that such an indictment should be quashed, pointing out that "The abuses of criminal practice would be enhanced if indictments could be upset on such a ground." The same thing is true where as here all the evidence before the grand jury was in the nature of "hearsay." If indictments were to be held open to challenge on the ground that there was inadequate or incompetent evidence before the grand jury, the resulting delay would be great indeed. The result of such a rule would be that before trial on the merits a defendant could always insist on a kind of preliminary trial to determine the competency and adequacy of the evidence before the grand jury. This is not required by the Fifth Amendment. An indictment returned by a legally constituted and unbiased grand jury, like an information drawn by the prosecutor, if valid on its face, is enough to call for trial of the charge on the merits. The Fifth Amendment requires nothing more.

Petitioner urges that this Court should exercise its power to supervise the administration of justice in federal courts and establish a rule permitting defendants to challenge indictments on the ground that they are not supported by adequate or competent evidence. No persuasive reasons are advanced for establishing such a rule. It would run counter to the whole history of the grand jury institution, in which laymen conduct their inquiries unfettered by technical rules. Neither justice nor the concept of a fair trial requires such a change. In a trial on the merits, defendants are entitled to a strict observance of all the rules designed to bring about a fair verdict. Defendants are not entitled, however, to a rule which would result in interminable delay but add nothing to the assurance of a fair trial. Affirmed.[a]

JUSTICE CLARK and JUSTICE HARLAN took no part in the consideration or decision of this case.

JUSTICE BURTON, concurring.

I agree with the denial of the motion to quash the indictment. In my view, however, this case does not justify the breadth of the declarations made by the Court. I assume that this Court would not preclude an examination of grand jury action to ascertain the existence of bias or prejudice in an indictment. Likewise, it seems to me that if it is shown that the grand jury had before it no substantial or rationally persuasive evidence upon which to base its indictment, that indictment should be quashed. To hold a person to answer to such an empty indictment for a capital or otherwise infamous federal crime robs the Fifth Amendment of much of its protective value to the private citizen. * * *

---

a. Relying in part on *Costello, United States v. Williams*, 504 U.S. 36 (1992), held that a federal court lacked supervisory power to dismiss an indictment based upon the prosecutor's failure to inform the grand jury of material exculpatory evidence known to the government. Stressing the grand jury's "functional independence from the judicial branch," the Court concluded that, "as a general matter at least," federal courts lacked the authority to create "common law" rules of grand jury practice, as the lower court had done here with respect to exculpatory evidence. The supervisory power of the federal courts was limited basically to responding to prosecutorial actions before the grand jury that violated either the constitution or "one of those 'few clear rules' which were carefully drafted and approved by this Court and by Congress to ensure the integrity of the grand jury's functions." Moreover, in *United States v. Mechanik*, 475 U.S. 66 (1986), the Court held that violation of one such rule, set forth in the Federal Rules of Criminal Procedure, could not be remedied on review following a conviction. The function of the rule (which prohibited grand jury witnesses from testifying in the presence of other witnesses) was to ensure against an erroneous charging decision, but "the petit jury verdict [establishing guilt beyond a reasonable doubt] rendered harmless any conceivable error in the charging decision that might have flowed from the violation." The application of an automatic reversal standard in *Vasquez v. Hillery* was distinguished as that ruling was grounded on "considerations that have little force outside the context of racial discrimination in the composition of the grand jury."

Chapter 12

SPEEDY TRIAL AND OTHER
SPEEDY DISPOSITION

The matter of the time within which a trial must be commenced is often treated in statutes and court rules. Some of these provisions are rather general in nature, meaning courts have considerable discretion in determining how long a delay is excessive and what intervals in the pretrial stages are to be discounted in ascertaining what the period of delay has actually been. Some other provisions, as illustrated by the federal Speedy Trial Act of 1974, go into considerable detail by setting specific time limits and enumerating what events toll the running of the specified time.

But speedy trial is not simply a matter of local law. The Sixth Amendment declares: "In all criminal prosecutions, the accused shall enjoy the right to a speedy * * * trial." Just what this means is explored in the first case, *Barker v. Wingo*. Certain periods of delay (e.g., prior to arrest or charge) are not encompassed by the Sixth Amendment, so that a defendant's constitutional challenge to them will likely be grounded in the due process clause, as in *United States v. Lovasco*.

BARKER v. WINGO

407 U.S. 514, 92 S.Ct. 2182, 33 L.Ed.2d 101 (1972).

JUSTICE POWELL delivered the opinion of the Court.

[A] speedy trial is guaranteed the accused by the Sixth Amendment to the Constitution. [T]he right to speedy trial is "fundamental" and is imposed by the Due Process Clause of the Fourteenth Amendment on the States. [I]n none of [our prior] cases have we attempted to set out the criteria by which the speedy trial right is to be judged. This case compels us to make such an attempt.

On July 20, 1958, in Christian County, Kentucky, an elderly couple was beaten to death by intruders wielding an iron tire tool. Two suspects, Silas Manning and Willie Barker, the petitioner, were arrested shortly thereafter. The grand jury indicted them on September 15. Counsel was appointed on September 17, and Barker's trial was set for October 21. The Commonwealth had a stronger case against Manning, and it believed that Barker could not be convicted unless Manning testified against him. Manning was naturally unwilling to incriminate himself. Accordingly, on October 23, the day Silas Manning was brought to trial, the Commonwealth sought and obtained the first of what was to be a series of 16 continuances of Barker's trial. Barker made no objection. By first convicting

550

Manning, the Commonwealth would remove possible problems of self-incrimination and would be able to assure his testimony against Barker.

The Commonwealth encountered more than a few difficulties in its prosecution of Manning. The first trial ended in a hung jury. A second trial resulted in a conviction, but the Kentucky Court of Appeals reversed because of the admission of evidence obtained by an illegal search. At his third trial, Manning was again convicted, and the Court of Appeals again reversed because the trial court had not granted a change of venue. A fourth trial resulted in a hung jury. Finally, after five trials, Manning was convicted, in March 1962, of murdering one victim, and after a sixth trial, in December 1962, he was convicted of murdering the other.

The Christian County Circuit Court holds three terms each year—in February, June, and September. Barker's initial trial was to take place in the September term of 1958. The first continuance postponed it until the February 1959 term. The second continuance was granted for one month only. Every term thereafter for as long as the Manning prosecutions were in process, the Commonwealth routinely moved to continue Barker's case to the next term. When the case was continued from the June 1959 term until the following September, Barker, having spent 10 months in jail, obtained his release by posting a $5,000 bond. He thereafter remained free in the community until his trial. Barker made no objection, through his counsel, to the first 11 continuances.

When on February 12, 1962, the Commonwealth moved for the twelfth time to continue the case until the following term, Barker's counsel filed a motion to dismiss the indictment. The motion to dismiss was denied two weeks later, and the State's motion for a continuance was granted. The State was granted further continuances in June 1962 and September 1962, to which Barker did not object.

In February 1963, the first term of court following Manning's final conviction, the Commonwealth moved to set Barker's trial for March 19. But on the day scheduled for trial, it again moved for a continuance until the June term. It gave as its reason the illness of the ex-sheriff who was the chief investigating officer in the case. To this continuance, Barker objected unsuccessfully.

The witness was still unable to testify in June, and the trial, which had been set for June 19, was continued again until the September term over Barker's objection. This time the court announced that the case would be dismissed for lack of prosecution if it were not tried during the next term. The final trial date was set for October 9, 1963. On that date, Barker again moved to dismiss the indictment, and this time specified that his right to a speedy trial had been violated. The motion was denied; the trial commenced with Manning as the chief prosecution witness; Barker was convicted and given a life sentence. * * *

The right to a speedy trial is generically different from any of the other rights enshrined in the Constitution for the protection of the accused. In addition to the general concern that all accused persons be treated according to decent and fair procedures, there is a societal interest in providing a speedy trial which exists separate from and at times in opposition to the interests of the accused. The inability of courts to provide a prompt trial has contributed to a large backlog of cases in urban courts which, among other things, enables defendants to negotiate more effectively for pleas of guilty to lesser offenses and otherwise manipulate the system. In addition, persons released on bond for lengthy periods awaiting trial have an opportunity to commit other crimes. It must be of little comfort to the residents of Christian County, Kentucky, to know that Barker was at large on bail for over four years while accused of a vicious and brutal murder of which he was ultimately convicted. Moreover, the longer an accused is free awaiting trial, the more tempting becomes his opportunity to jump bail and escape. Finally, delay between arrest and punishment may have a detrimental effect on rehabilitation.

If an accused cannot make bail, he is generally confined, as was Barker for 10 months, in a local jail. This contributes to the overcrowding and generally deplorable state of those institutions. Lengthy exposure to these conditions "has a destructive effect on human character and makes the rehabilitation of the individual offender much more difficult." At times the result may even be violent rioting. Finally, lengthy pretrial detention is costly. The cost of maintaining a prisoner in jail varies from $3 to $9 per day, and this amounts to millions across the Nation. In addition, society loses wages which might have been earned, and it must often support families of incarcerated breadwinners.

A second difference between the right to speedy trial and the accused's other constitutional rights is that deprivation of the right may work to the accused's advantage. Delay is not an uncommon defense tactic. As the time between the commission of the crime and trial lengthens, witnesses may become unavailable or their memories may fade. If the witnesses support the prosecution, its case will be weakened, sometimes seriously so. And it is the prosecution which carries the burden of proof. Thus, unlike the right to counsel or the right to be free from compelled self-incrimination, deprivation of the right to speedy trial does not *per se* prejudice the accused's ability to defend himself.

Finally, and perhaps most importantly, the right to speedy trial is a more vague concept than other procedural rights. It is, for example, impossible to determine with precision when the right has been denied. * * * There is nothing comparable to the point in the process when a defendant exercises or waives his right to counsel or his right to a jury trial. * * *

The amorphous quality of the right also leads to the unsatisfactorily severe remedy of dismissal of the indictment when the right has been deprived. This is indeed a serious consequence because it means that a defendant who may be guilty of a serious crime will go free, without having been tried. Such a remedy is more serious than an exclusionary rule or a reversal for a new trial, but it is the only possible remedy.

Proposed Alternative Solutions ①

Perhaps because the speedy trial right is so slippery, two rigid approaches are urged upon us as ways of eliminating some of the uncertainty which courts experience in protecting the right. The first suggestion is that we hold that the Constitution requires a criminal defendant to be offered a trial within a specified time period. The result of such a ruling would have the virtue of clarifying when the right is infringed and of simplifying courts' application of it. Recognizing this, some legislatures have enacted laws, and some courts have adopted procedural rules which more narrowly define the right. * * *

But such a result would require this Court to engage in legislative or rulemaking activity, rather than in the adjudicative process to which we should confine our efforts. We do not establish procedural rules for the States, except when mandated by the Constitution. We find no constitutional basis for holding that the speedy trial right can be quantified into a specified number of days or months. The States, of course, are free to prescribe a reasonable period consistent with constitutional standards, but our approach must be less precise.

②

The second suggested alternative would restrict consideration of the right to those cases in which the accused has demanded a speedy trial. * * * Under this rigid approach, a prior demand is a necessary condition to the consideration of the speedy trial right. This essentially was the approach the Sixth Circuit took below.

Such an approach, by presuming waiver of a fundamental right from inaction, is inconsistent with this Court's pronouncements on waiver of constitutional rights. The Court has defined waiver as "an intentional relinquishment or abandonment of a known right or privilege." Courts should "indulge every reasonable presumption against waiver," and they should "not presume acquiescence in the loss of fundamental rights." * * *

In excepting the right to speedy trial from the rule of waiver we have applied to other fundamental rights, courts * * * have relied on the assumption that delay usually works for the benefit of the accused and on the absence of any readily ascertainable time in the criminal process for a defendant to be given the choice of exercising or waiving his right. But it is not necessarily true that delay benefits the defendant. There are cases in which delay appreciably harms the defendant's ability to defend himself. Moreover, a defendant confined to jail prior to trial is obviously disadvantaged by delay as is a defendant released on bail but unable to lead a normal life because of community suspicion and his own anxiety.

The nature of the speedy-trial right does make it impossible to pinpoint a precise time in the process when the right must be asserted or waived, but that fact does not argue for placing the burden of protecting the right solely on defendants. A defendant has no duty to bring himself to trial; the State has that duty as well as the duty of insuring that the trial is consistent with due process. Moreover, for the reasons earlier expressed, society has a particular interest in bringing swift prosecutions, and society's representatives are the ones who should protect that interest.

It is also noteworthy that such a rigid view of the demand rule places defense counsel in an awkward position. Unless he demands a trial early and often, he is in danger of frustrating his client's right. If counsel is willing to tolerate some delay because he finds it reasonable and helpful in preparing his own case, he may be unable to obtain a speedy trial for his client at the end of that time. * * *

We reject, therefore, the rule that a defendant who fails to demand a speedy trial forever waives his right. This does not mean, however, that the defendant has no responsibility to assert his right. We think the better rule is that the defendant's assertion of or failure to assert his right to a speedy trial is one of the factors to be considered in an inquiry into the deprivation of the right. Such a formulation * * * allows the trial court to exercise a judicial discretion based on the circumstances, including due consideration of any applicable formal procedural rule. It would permit, for example, a court to attach a different weight to a situation in which the defendant knowingly fails to object from a situation in which his attorney acquiesces in long delay without adequately informing his client or from a situation in which no counsel is appointed. It would also allow a court to weigh the frequency and force of the objections as opposed to attaching significant weight to a purely *pro forma* objection.

In ruling that a defendant has some responsibility to assert a speedy-trial claim, we do not depart from our holdings in other cases concerning the waiver of fundamental rights, in which we have placed the entire responsibility on the prosecution to show that the claimed waiver was knowingly and voluntarily made. Such cases have involved rights which must be exercised or waived at a specific time or under clearly identifiable circumstances, such as the rights to plead not guilty, to demand a jury trial, to exercise the privilege against self incrimination, and to have the assistance of counsel. We have shown above that the right to a speedy trial is unique in its uncertainty as to when and under what circumstances it must be asserted or may be deemed waived. But the rule we announce today, which comports with constitutional principles, places the primary burden on the courts and the prosecutors to assure that cases are brought to trial. We hardly need add that if delay is attributable to the defendant, then his waiver may be given effect under standard waiver doctrine, the demand rule aside.

* * * The approach we accept is a balancing test, in which the conduct of both the prosecution and the defendant are weighed.

A balancing test necessarily compels courts to approach speedy-trial cases on an *ad hoc* basis. We can do little more than identify some of the factors which courts should assess in determining whether a particular defendant has been deprived of his right. Though some might express them in different ways, we identify four such factors: Length of delay, the reason for the delay, the defendant's assertion of his right, and prejudice to the defendant.

The length of the delay is to some extent a triggering mechanism. Until there is some delay which is presumptively prejudicial, there is no necessity for inquiry into the other factors that go into the balance. Nevertheless, because of the imprecision of the right to speedy trial, the length of delay that will provoke such an inquiry is necessarily dependent upon the peculiar circumstances of the case. To take but one example, the delay that can be tolerated for an ordinary street crime is considerably less than for a serious, complex conspiracy charge.

Closely related to length of delay is the reason the government assigns to justify the delay. Here, too, different weights should be assigned to different reasons. A deliberate attempt to delay the trial in order to hamper the defense should be weighed heavily against the government. A more neutral reason such as negligence or overcrowded courts should be weighed less heavily but nevertheless should be considered since the ultimate responsibility for such circumstances must rest with the government rather than with the defendant. Finally, a valid reason, such as a missing witness, should serve to justify appropriate delay.

We have already discussed the third factor, the defendant's responsibility to assert his right. Whether and how a defendant asserts his right is closely related to the other factors we have mentioned. The strength of his efforts will be affected by the length of the delay, to some extent by the reason for the delay, and most particularly by the personal prejudice, which is not always readily identifiable, that he experiences. The more serious the deprivation, the more likely a defendant is to complain. The defendant's assertion of his speedy trial right, then, is entitled to strong evidentiary weight in determining whether the right is being deprived. We emphasize that failure to assert the right will make it difficult for a defendant to prove that he was denied a speedy trial.

A fourth factor is prejudice to the defendant. Prejudice, of course, should be assessed in the light of the interests of defendants which the speedy trial right was designed to protect. This Court has identified three such interests: (i) to prevent oppressive pretrial incarceration; (ii) to minimize anxiety and concern of the accused; and (iii) to limit the possibility that the defense will be impaired. Of these, the most serious is the last, because the inability of a defendant adequately to prepare his case skews the fairness of the entire system. If witnesses die or disappear during a delay, the prejudice is obvious. There is also prejudice if defense witnesses are unable to recall accurately events of the distant past. Loss of memory, however, is not always reflected in the record because what has been forgotten can rarely be shown.

We have discussed previously the societal disadvantages of lengthy pretrial incarceration, but obviously the disadvantages for the accused who cannot obtain his release are even more serious. The time spent in jail awaiting trial has a detrimental impact on the individual. It often means loss of a job; it disrupts family life; and it enforces idleness. Most jails offer little or no recreational or rehabilitative programs. The time spent in jail is simply dead time. Moreover, if a defendant is locked up, he is hindered in his ability to gather evidence, contact witnesses, or otherwise prepare his defense. Imposing those consequences on anyone who has not yet been convicted is serious. It is especially unfortunate to impose them on those persons who are ultimately found to be innocent. Finally, even if an accused is not incarcerated prior to trial, he is still disadvantaged by restraints on his liberty and by living under a cloud of anxiety, suspicion, and often hostility.

We regard none of the four factors identified above as either a necessary or sufficient condition to the finding of a deprivation of the right of speedy trial. Rather, they are related factors and must be considered together with such other circumstances as may be relevant. In sum, these factors have no talismanic qualities; courts must still engage in a difficult and sensitive balancing process. But, because we are dealing with a fundamental right of the accused, this process must be carried out with full recognition that the accused's interest in a speedy trial is specifically affirmed in the Constitution.

The difficulty of the task of balancing these factors is illustrated by this case, which we consider to be close. It is clear that the length of delay between arrest and trial—well over five years—was extraordinary. Only seven months of that period can be attributed to a strong excuse, the illness of the ex-sheriff who was in charge of the investigation. Perhaps some delay would have been permissible under ordinary circumstances, so that Manning could be utilized as a witness in Barker's trial, but more than four years was too long a period, particularly since a good part of that period was attributable to the Commonwealth's failure or inability to try Manning under circumstances that comported with due process.

Two counter-balancing factors, however, outweigh these deficiencies. The first is that prejudice was minimal. Of course, Barker was prejudiced to some extent by living for over four years under a cloud of suspicion and anxiety. Moreover, although he was released on bond for most of the period, he did spend 10 months in jail before trial. But there is no claim that any of Barker's witnesses died or otherwise became unavailable owing to the delay. The trial transcript indicates only two very minor lapses of memory—one on the part of a prosecution witness—which were in no way significant to the outcome.

More important than the absence of serious prejudice, is the fact that Barker did not want a speedy trial. Counsel was appointed for Barker immediately after his indictment and represented him throughout the period. No question is raised as to the competency of such counsel. Despite the fact that counsel had notice of the motions for continuances, the record shows no action whatever taken between October 21, 1958, and February 12, 1962, that could be construed as the assertion of the speedy-trial right. On the latter date, in response to another motion for continuance, Barker moved to dismiss the indictment. The record does not show on what ground this motion was based, although it is clear that no alternative motion was made for an immediate trial. Instead the record strongly suggests that while he hoped to take advantage of the delay in which he had acquiesced, and thereby obtain a dismissal of the charges, he definitely did not want to be tried. Counsel conceded as much at oral argument:

> "Your honor, I would concede that Willie Mae Barker—probably—I don't know this for a fact—probably did not want to be tried. I don't think any man wants to be tried. And I don't consider this a liability on his behalf. I don't blame him."

The probable reason for Barker's attitude was that he was gambling on Manning's acquittal. The evidence was not terribly strong against Manning, as the reversals and hung juries suggest, and Barker undoubtedly thought that if Manning were acquitted, he would never be tried. Counsel also conceded this:

> "Now, it's true that the reason for this delay was the Commonwealth of Kentucky's desire to secure the testimony of the accomplice, Silas Manning. And it's true that if Silas Manning were never convicted, Willie Mae Barker would never have been convicted. We concede this."

That Barker was gambling on Manning's acquittal is also suggested by his failure, following the *pro forma* motion to dismiss filed in February 1962, to object to the Commonwealth's next two motions for continuances. Indeed, it was not until March 1963, after Manning's convictions were final, that Barker, having lost his gamble, began to object to further continuances. At that time, the Commonwealth's excuse was the illness of the ex-sheriff, which Barker has conceded justified the further delay.

We do not hold that there may never be a situation in which an indictment may be dismissed on speedy-trial grounds where the defendant has failed to object to continuances. There may be a situation in which the defendant was represented by incompetent counsel, was severely prejudiced, or even cases in which the continuances were granted *ex parte*. But barring extraordinary circumstances, we would be reluctant indeed to rule that a defendant was denied this constitutional right on a record that strongly indicates, as does this one, that the defendant did not want a speedy trial. We hold, therefore, that Barker was not deprived of his due process right to a speedy trial. * * * [a]

DOGGETT v. UNITED STATES

505 U.S. 647, 112 S.Ct. 2686, 120 L.Ed.2d 520 (1992).

JUSTICE SOUTER delivered the opinion of the Court. * * *

On February 22, 1980, petitioner Marc Doggett was indicted for conspiring with several others to import and distribute cocaine. Douglas Driver, the Drug Enforcement Administration's principal agent investigating the conspiracy, told the United States Marshal's Service that the DEA would oversee the apprehension of Doggett and his confederates. On March 18, 1980, two police officers set out under Driver's orders to arrest Doggett at his parents' house in Raleigh, North Carolina, only to find that he was not there. His mother told the officers that he had left for Colombia four days earlier.

To catch Doggett on his return to the United States, Driver sent word of his outstanding arrest warrant to all United States Customs stations and to a number of law enforcement organizations. He also placed Doggett's name in the Treasury Enforcement Communication System (TECS), a computer network that helps Customs agents screen people entering the country, and in the National Crime Information Center computer system, which serves similar ends. The TECS entry expired that September, however, and Doggett's name vanished from the system.

In September 1981, Driver found out that Doggett was under arrest on drug charges in Panama and, thinking that a formal extradition request would be futile, simply asked Panama to "expel" Doggett to the United States. Although the Panamanian authorities promised to comply when their own proceedings had run their course, they freed Doggett the following July and let him go to

---

a. The concurring opinion of Justice White, joined by Justice Brennan, is omitted.

Colombia, where he stayed with an aunt for several months. On September 25, 1982, he passed unhindered through Customs in New York City and settled down in Virginia. Since his return to the United States, he has married, earned a college degree, found a steady job as a computer operations manager, lived openly under his own name, and stayed within the law.

Doggett's travels abroad had not wholly escaped the Government's notice, however. In 1982, the American Embassy in Panama told the State Department of his departure to Colombia, but that information, for whatever reason, eluded the DEA, and Agent Driver assumed for several years that his quarry was still serving time in a Panamanian prison. Driver never asked DEA officials in Panama to check into Doggett's status, and only after his own fortuitous assignment to that country in 1985 did he discover Doggett's departure for Colombia. Driver then simply assumed Doggett had settled there, and he made no effort to find out for sure or to track Doggett down, either abroad or in the United States. Thus Doggett remained lost to the American criminal justice system until September 1988, when the Marshal's Service ran a simple credit check on several thousand people subject to outstanding arrest warrants and, within minutes, found out where Doggett lived and worked. On September 5, 1988, nearly 6 years after his return to the United States and 8½ years after his indictment Doggett was arrested.

He naturally moved to dismiss the indictment, arguing that the Government's failure to prosecute him earlier violated his Sixth Amendment right to a speedy trial. The Federal Magistrate hearing his motion * * * found, however, that Doggett had made no affirmative showing that the delay had impaired his ability to mount a successful defense or had otherwise prejudiced him. In his recommendation to the District Court, the Magistrate contended that this failure to demonstrate particular prejudice sufficed to defeat Doggett's speedy trial claim.

The District Court took the recommendation and denied Doggett's motion. * * *

A split panel of the Court of Appeals affirmed. * * *

The Sixth Amendment guarantees that, "[i]n all criminal prosecutions, the accused shall enjoy the right to a speedy * * * trial * * *." On its face, the Speedy Trial Clause is written with such breadth that, taken literally, it would forbid the government to delay the trial of an "accused" for any reason at all. Our cases, however, have qualified the literal sweep of the provision by specifically recognizing the relevance of four separate enquiries: whether delay before trial was uncommonly long, whether the government or the criminal defendant is more to blame for that delay, whether, in due course, the defendant asserted his right to a speedy trial, and whether he suffered prejudice as the delay's result.

The first of these is actually a double enquiry. Simply to trigger a speedy trial analysis, an accused must allege that the interval between accusation and trial has crossed the threshold dividing ordinary from "presumptively prejudicial" delay, since, by definition, he cannot complain that the government has denied him a "speedy" trial if it has, in fact, prosecuted his case with customary promptness. If the accused makes this showing, the court must then consider, as one factor among several, the extent to which the delay stretches beyond the bare minimum needed to trigger judicial examination of the claim. This latter enquiry is significant to the speedy trial analysis because, as we discuss below, the presumption that pretrial delay has prejudiced the accused intensifies over time. In this case, the extraordinary 8½ year lag between Doggett's indictment and arrest clearly suffices to trigger the speedy trial enquiry; its further significance within that enquiry will be dealt with later.

As for *Barker's* second criterion, the Government claims to have sought Doggett with diligence. The findings of the courts below are to the contrary, however, and we review trial court determinations of negligence with considerable deference. The Government gives us nothing to gainsay the findings that have come up to us, and we see nothing fatal to them in the record. For six years, the Government's investigators made no serious effort to test their progressively more questionable assumption that Doggett was living abroad, and, had they done so, they could have found him within minutes. While the Government's lethargy may have reflected no more than Doggett's relative unimportance in the world of drug trafficking, it was still findable negligence, and the finding stands.

The Government goes against the record again in suggesting that Doggett knew of his indictment years before he was arrested. Were this true, *Barker's* third factor, concerning invocation of the right to a speedy trial, would be weighed heavily against him. But here again, the Government is trying to revisit the facts. At the hearing on Doggett's speedy trial motion, it introduced no evidence challenging the testimony of Doggett's wife, who said that she did not know of the charges until his arrest, and of his mother, who claimed not to have told him or anyone else that the police had come looking for him. * * *

The Government is left, then, with its principal contention: that Doggett fails to make out a successful speedy trial claim because he has not shown precisely how he was prejudiced by the delay between his indictment and trial.

We have observed in prior cases that unreasonable delay between formal accusation and trial threatens to produce more than one sort of harm, including "oppressive pretrial incarceration," "anxiety and concern of the accused," and "the possibility that the [accused's] defense will be impaired" by dimming memories and loss of exculpatory evidence. Of these forms of prejudice, "the most serious is the last, because the inability of a defendant adequately to prepare his case skews the fairness of the entire system." Doggett claims this kind of prejudice, and there is probably no other kind that he can claim, since he was subjected neither to pretrial detention nor, he has successfully contended, to awareness of unresolved charges against him.

The Government answers Doggett's claim by citing language in three cases, *United States v. Marion,* 404 U.S. 307 (1971), *United States v. MacDonald,* 456 U.S. 1 (1982), and *United States v. Loud Hawk,* 474 U.S. 302 (1986), for the proposition that the Speedy Trial Clause does not significantly protect a criminal defendant's interest in fair adjudication. In so arguing, the Government asks us, in effect, to read part of *Barker* right out of the law, and that we will not do. In context, the cited passages support nothing beyond the principle, which we have independently based on textual and historical grounds, that the Sixth Amendment right of the accused to a speedy trial has no application beyond the confines of a formal criminal prosecution. Once triggered by arrest, indictment, or other official accusation, however, the speedy trial enquiry must weigh the effect of delay on the accused's defense just as it has to weigh any other form of prejudice that *Barker* recognized.

As an alternative to limiting *Barker,* the Government claims Doggett has failed to make any affirmative showing that the delay weakened his ability to raise specific defenses, elicit specific testimony, or produce specific items of evidence. Though Doggett did indeed come up short in this respect, the Government's argument takes it only so far: consideration of prejudice is not limited to the specifically demonstrable, and, as it concedes, affirmative proof of particularized prejudice is not essential to every speedy trial claim. *Barker* explicitly recognized that impairment of one's defense is the most difficult form of speedy trial prejudice to prove because time's erosion of exculpatory evidence and testimony "can rarely be shown." And though time can tilt the case against either side, one cannot generally be sure which of them it has prejudiced more severely. Thus, we generally have to recognize that excessive delay presumptively compromises the reliability of a trial in ways that neither party can prove or, for that matter, identify. While such presumptive prejudice cannot alone carry a Sixth Amendment claim without regard to the other *Barker* criteria, it is part of the mix of relevant facts, and its importance increases with the length of delay.

This brings us to an enquiry into the role that presumptive prejudice should play in the disposition of Doggett's speedy trial claim. We begin with hypothetical and somewhat easier cases and work our way to this one.

Our speedy trial standards recognize that pretrial delay is often both inevitable and wholly justifiable. The government may need time to collect witnesses against the accused, oppose his pretrial motions, or, if he goes into hiding, track him down. We attach great weight to such considerations when balancing them against the costs of going forward with a trial whose probative accuracy the passage of time has begun by degrees to throw into question. Thus, in this case, if the Government had pursued Doggett with reasonable diligence from his indictment to his arrest, his speedy trial claim would fail. Indeed, that conclusion would generally follow as a matter of course however great the delay, so long as Doggett could not show specific prejudice to his defense.

The Government concedes, on the other hand that Doggett would prevail if he could show that the Government had intentionally held back in its prosecution of him to gain some impermissible advantage at trial. That we cannot doubt. *Barker* stressed that official bad faith in causing delay will be weighed heavily against the government, and a bad-faith delay the length of this negligent one would present an overwhelming case for dismissal.

Between diligent prosecution and bad-faith delay, official negligence in bringing an accused to trial occupies the middle ground. While not compelling relief in every case where bad-faith delay would make relief virtually automatic, neither is negligence automatically tolerable simply because the accused cannot demonstrate exactly how it has prejudiced him. It was on this point that the Court of Appeals erred, and on the facts before us, it was reversible error.

Barker made it clear that "different weights [are to be] assigned to different reasons" for delay. Although negligence is obviously to be weighed more lightly than a deliberate intent to harm the accused's defense, it still falls on the wrong side of the divide between acceptable and unacceptable reasons for delaying a criminal prosecution once it has begun. And such is the nature of the prejudice presumed that the weight we assign to official negligence compounds over time as the presumption of evidentiary prejudice grows. Thus, our toleration of such negligence varies inversely with its protractedness, and its consequent threat to the fairness of the accused's trial. Condoning prolonged and unjustifiable delays in prosecution would both penalize many defendants for the state's fault and simply encourage the government to gamble with the interests of criminal suspects assigned a low prosecutorial priority. The Government, indeed, can hardly complain too loudly, for persistent neglect in concluding a criminal prosecution indicates an uncommonly feeble interest in bringing an accused to justice; the more weight the Government attaches to securing a conviction, the harder it will try to get it.

To be sure, to warrant granting relief, negligence unaccompanied by particularized trial prejudice must have lasted longer than negligence demonstrably causing such prejudice. But even so, the Government's egregious persistence in failing to prosecute Doggett is clearly sufficient. The lag between Doggett's indictment and arrest was 8½ years, and he would have faced trial 6 years earlier than he did but for the Government's inexcusable oversights. The portion of the delay attributable to the Government's negligence far exceeds the threshold needed to state a speedy trial claim; indeed, we have called shorter delays "extraordinary." When the Government's negligence thus causes delay six times as long as that generally sufficient to trigger judicial review, and when the presumption of prejudice, albeit unspecified, is neither extenuated, as by the defendant's acquiescence, nor persuasively rebutted, the defendant is entitled to relief.

JUSTICE THOMAS, with whom THE CHIEF JUSTICE and JUSTICE SCALIA join, dissenting. * * * a

We have long identified the "major evils" against which the Speedy Trial Clause is directed as "undue and oppressive incarceration" and the "anxiety and concern accompanying public accusation." * * *

Thus, this unusual case presents the question whether, independent of these core concerns, the Speedy Trial Clause protects an accused from two additional harms: (1) prejudice to his ability to defend himself caused by the passage of time; and (2) disruption of his life years after the alleged commission of his crime. The Court today proclaims that the first of these additional harms is indeed an independent concern of the Clause, and on that basis compels reversal of Doggett's conviction and outright dismissal of the indictment against him. As to the second of these harms, the Court remains mum—despite the fact that we requested supplemental briefing on this very point.

I disagree with the Court's analysis. In my view, the Sixth Amendment's speedy trial guarantee does not provide independent protection against either prejudice to an accused's defense or the disruption of his life. I shall consider each in turn. * * *

We are * * * confronted with two conflicting lines of authority, the one declaring that "limit[ing] the possibility that the defense will be impaired" is an independent and fundamental objective of the Speedy Trial Clause, e.g., *Barker*, supra, and the other declaring that it is not, e.g., *Marion*, supra; *MacDonald*, supra; *Loud Hawk*, supra. The Court refuses to acknowledge this conflict. Instead, it simply reiterates the relevant language from *Barker* and asserts that *Marion, MacDonald*, and *Loud Hawk* "support nothing beyond the principle . . . that the Sixth Amendment right of the accused to a speedy trial has no application beyond the confines of a formal criminal prosecution." That attempt at reconciliation is eminently unpersuasive.

It is true, of course, that the Speedy Trial Clause by its terms applies only to an "accused"; the right does not attach before indictment or arrest. But that limitation on the Clause's protection only confirms that preventing prejudice to the defense is not one of its independent and fundamental objectives. For prejudice to the defense stems from the interval between crime and trial, which is quite distinct from the interval between accusation and trial. If the Clause were indeed aimed at safeguarding against prejudice to the defense, then it would presumably limit all prosecutions that occur long after the criminal events at issue. A defendant prosecuted 10 years after a crime is just as hampered in his ability to defend himself whether he was indicted the week after the crime or the

---

a. O'Connor, J., dissented separately on the ground that "a showing of actual prejudice   to the defense" is required.

week before the trial—but no one would suggest that the Clause protects him in the latter situation, where the delay did not substantially impair his liberty, either through oppressive incarceration or the anxiety of known criminal charges. * * *

It is misleading, then, for the Court to accuse the Government of "ask[ing] us, in effect, to read part of *Barker* right out of the law," a course the Court resolutely rejects. For the issue here is not simply whether the relevant language from *Barker* should be read out of the law, but whether that language trumps the contrary logic of *Marion, MacDonald*, and *Loud Hawk*. The Court's protestations notwithstanding, the two lines of authority cannot be reconciled; to reaffirm the one is to undercut the other.

In my view, the choice presented is not a hard one. *Barker*'s suggestion that preventing prejudice to the defense is a fundamental and independent objective of the Clause is plainly dictum. Never, until today, have we confronted a case where a defendant subjected to a lengthy delay after indictment nonetheless failed to suffer any substantial impairment of his liberty. I think it fair to say that *Barker* simply did not contemplate such an unusual situation. Moreover, to the extent that the *Barker* dictum purports to elevate considerations of prejudice to the defense to fundamental and independent status under the Clause, it cannot be deemed to have survived our subsequent decisions in *MacDonald* and *Loud Hawk*. * * *

Therefore, I see no basis for the Court's conclusion that Doggett is entitled to relief under the Speedy Trial Clause simply because the Government was negligent in prosecuting him and because the resulting delay may have prejudiced his defense.

It remains to be considered, however, whether Doggett is entitled to relief under the Speedy Trial Clause because of the disruption of his life years after the criminal events at issue. In other words, does the Clause protect a right to repose, free from secret or unknown indictments? In my view, it does not, for much the same reasons set forth above.

The common law recognized no right of criminals to repose. * * *

That is not to deny that our legal system has long recognized the value of repose, both to the individual and to society. But that recognition finds expression not in the sweeping commands of the Constitution, or in the common law, but in any number of specific statutes of limitations enacted by the federal and state legislatures. * * *

Doggett, however, asks us to hold that a defendant's interest in repose is a value independently protected by the Speedy Trial Clause. He emphasizes that at the time of his arrest he was "leading a normal, productive and law-abiding life," and that his "arrest and prosecution at this late date interrupted his life as a productive member of society and forced him to answer for actions taken in the distant past." However uplifting this tale of personal redemption, our task is to illuminate the protections of the Speedy Trial Clause, not to take the measure of one man's life.

There is no basis for concluding that the disruption of an accused's life years after the commission of his alleged crime is an evil independently protected by the Speedy Trial Clause. Such disruption occurs regardless of whether the individual is under indictment during the period of delay. Thus, had Doggett been indicted shortly before his 1988 arrest rather than shortly after his 1980 crime, his repose would have been equally shattered—but he would not have even a colorable speedy-trial claim. To recognize a constitutional right to repose is to recognize a right to be tried speedily after the offense. That would, of course, convert the

Speedy Trial Clause into a constitutional statute of limitations—a result with no basis in the text or history of the Clause or in our precedents. * * *

Today's opinion, I fear, will transform the courts of the land into boards of law-enforcement supervision. For the Court compels dismissal of the charges against Doggett not because he was harmed in any way by the delay between his indictment and arrest,[6] but simply because the Government's efforts to catch him are found wanting. * * * Our Constitution neither contemplates nor tolerates such a role. I respectfully dissent.

UNITED STATES v. LOVASCO

431 U.S. 783, 97 S.Ct. 2044, 52 L.Ed.2d 752 (1977).

JUSTICE MARSHALL delivered the opinion of the Court. * * *

On March 6, 1975, respondent was indicted for possessing eight firearms stolen from the United States mail, and for dealing in firearms without a license. The offenses were alleged to have occurred between July 25 and August 31, 1973, more than 18 months before the indictment was filed. Respondent moved to dismiss the indictment due to the delay.

The District Court conducted a hearing on respondent's motion at which the respondent sought to prove that the delay was unnecessary and that it had prejudiced his defense. In an effort to establish the former proposition, respondent presented a Postal Inspector's report on his investigation that was prepared one month after the crimes were committed, and a stipulation concerning the post-report progress of the probe. The report stated, in brief, that within the first month of the investigation respondent had admitted to Government agents that he had possessed and then sold five of the stolen guns, and that the agents had developed strong evidence linking respondent to the remaining three weapons. The report also stated, however, that the agents had been unable to confirm or refute respondent's claim that he had found the guns in his car when he returned to it after visiting his son, a mail handler, at work. The stipulation into which the Assistant United States Attorney entered indicated that little additional information concerning the crimes was uncovered in the 17 months following the preparation of the Inspector's report.

To establish prejudice to the defense, respondent testified that he had lost the testimony of two material witnesses due to the delay. The first witness, Tom Stewart, died more than a year after the alleged crimes occurred. At the hearing respondent claimed that Stewart had been his source for two or three of the guns. The second witness, respondent's brother, died in April 1974, nine months after the crimes were completed. Respondent testified that his brother was present when respondent called Stewart to secure the guns, and witnessed all of respondent's sales. Respondent did not state how the witnesses would have aided the defense had they been willing to testify.

The Government made no systematic effort in the District Court to explain its long delay. The Assistant United States Attorney did expressly disagree, however, with defense counsel's suggestion that the investigation had ended after the

6. It is quite likely, in fact, that the delay benefitted Doggett. At the time of his arrest, he had been living an apparently normal, law-abiding life for some five years—a point not lost on the District Court Judge, who, instead of imposing a prison term, sentenced him to three years' probation and a $1000 fine. Thus, the delay gave Doggett the opportunity to prove what most defendants can only promise: that he no longer posed a threat to society. There can be little doubt that, had he been tried immediately after his cocaine-importation activities, he would have received a harsher sentence.

Postal Inspector's Report was prepared. The prosecutor also stated that it was the Government's theory that respondent's son, who had access to the mail at the railroad terminal from which the guns were "possibly stolen," was responsible for the thefts. Finally, the prosecutor elicited somewhat cryptic testimony from the Postal Inspector indicating that the case "as to these particular weapons involves other individuals"; that information had been presented to a grand jury "in regard to this case other than * * * [on] the day of the indictment itself"; and that he had spoken to the prosecutors about the case on four or five occasions.

Following the hearing, the District Court filed a brief opinion and order. The court found that by October 2, 1973, the date of the postal inspector's report, "The Government had all the information relating to defendant's alleged commission of the offense charged against him," and that the 17-month delay before the case was presented to the grand jury "had not been explained or justified" and was "unnecessary and unreasonable." The Court also found that "[a]s a result of the delay defendant has been prejudiced by reason of the death of Tom Stewart, a material witness on his behalf." Accordingly, the court dismissed the indictment.

The Government appealed to the United States Court of Appeals for the Eighth Circuit. In its brief the Government explained the months of inaction by stating:

> "[T]here was a legitimate Government interest in keeping the investigation open in the instant case. The defendant's son worked for the Terminal Railroad and had access to mail. It was the Government's position that the son was responsible for the theft and therefore further investigation to establish this fact was important.

> " * * * Although the investigation did not continue on a full time basis, there was contact between the United States Attorney's office and the Postal Inspector's office throughout * * * and certain matters were brought before a Federal Grand Jury prior to the determination that the case should be presented for indictment * * *."

The Court of Appeals accepted the Government's representation as to the motivation for the delay, but a majority of the court nevertheless affirmed the District Court's finding that the Government's actions were "unjustified, unnecessary, and unreasonable." The majority also found that respondent had established that his defense had been impaired by the loss of Stewart's testimony because it understood respondent to contend that "were Stewart's testimony available it would support [respondent's] claim that he did not know that the guns were stolen from the United States mails." * * *

We granted certiorari, and now reverse.

In *United States v. Marion*, 404 U.S. 307 (1971), this Court considered the significance, for constitutional purposes, of a lengthy preindictment delay. We held that as far as the Speedy Trial Clause of the Sixth Amendment is concerned, such delay is wholly irrelevant, since our analysis of the language, history, and purposes of the Clause persuaded us that only "a formal indictment or information or else the actual restraints imposed by arrest and holding to answer a criminal charge * * * engage the particular protections" of that provision. We went on to note that statutes of limitations, which provide predictable, legislatively enacted limits on prosecutorial delay, provide "the primary guarantee, against bringing overly stale criminal charges." [a] But we did acknowledge that the

---

a. The statute of limitations, in contrast to the speedy trial time limitations, runs from the date the offense is committed (or, in a few states, from the date the offense is discovered) to the date prosecution is commenced (in some states this means the date an indictment or "statute of limitations does not fully define [defendants'] rights with respect to the events occurring prior to indictment," and that the Due Process Clause has a limited role to play in protecting against oppressive delay.

Respondent seems to argue that due process bars prosecution whenever a defendant suffers prejudice as a result of preindictment delay. To support that proposition respondent relies on the concluding sentence of the Court's opinion in *Marion* where, in remanding the case, we stated that "[e]vents of the trial may demonstrate actual prejudice, but at the present time appellees' due process claims are speculative and premature." But the quoted sentence establishes only that proof of actual prejudice makes a due process claim concrete and ripe for adjudication, not that it makes the claim automatically valid. Indeed, two pages earlier in the opinion we expressly rejected the argument respondent advances here:

> "[W]e need not * * * determine when and in what circumstances actual prejudice resulting from preaccusation delay requires the dismissal of the prosecution. Actual prejudice to the defense of a criminal case may result from the shortest and most necessary delay; and no one suggests that every delay-caused detriment to a defendant's case should abort a criminal prosecution."

Thus *Marion* makes clear that proof of prejudice is generally a necessary but not sufficient element of a due process claim, and that the due process inquiry must consider the reasons for the delay as well as the prejudice to the accused.

The Court of Appeals found that the sole reason for the delay here was "a hope on the part of the Government that others might be discovered who may have participated in the theft * * *." It concluded that this hope did not justify the delay, and therefore affirmed the dismissal of the indictment. But the Due Process Clause does not permit courts to abort criminal prosecutions simply because they disagree with a prosecutor's judgment as to when to seek an indictment. Judges are not free, in defining "due process," to impose on law enforcement officials our "personal and private notions" of fairness and to "disregard the limits that bind judges in their judicial function." Our task is more circumscribed. We are to determine only whether the actions complained of—here, compelling respondent to stand trial after the Government delayed indictment to investigate further—violates those "fundamental conceptions of justice which lie at the base of our civil and political institutions," and which define "the community's sense of fair play and decency."

information is filed, in others the date a warrant of arrest is issued). The typical statute specifies situations in which time is not counted against the period of limitation, such as when the defendant is out of the state or is away from his usual residence for the purpose of avoiding prosecution. "There are several reasons for the imposition of time limitations: First, and foremost, is the desirability that prosecutions be based upon reasonably fresh evidence. With the passage of time memories fade, witnesses die or leave the area, and physical evidence becomes more difficult to obtain, identify, or preserve. In short, possibility of erroneous conviction is minimized when prosecution is prompt. Second, if the actor long refrains from further criminal activity, the likelihood increases that he has reformed, diminishing the necessity for imposition of the criminal sanction. If he has repeated his criminal behavior, he can be prosecuted for recent offenses committed within the period of limitation. Hence, the need for protecting society against the perpetrator of a particular offense becomes less compelling as the years pass. Third, after a protracted period the retributive impulse which may have existed in the community is likely to yield to a sense of compassion aroused by the prosecution for an offense long forgotten. Fourth, it is desirable to reduce the possibility of blackmail based on a threat to prosecute or to disclose evidence to enforcement officials. Finally, statutes of limitations 'promote repose by giving security and stability to human affairs.'" *Model Penal Code* § 1.06, Comment (1985).

It requires no extended argument to establish that prosecutors do not deviate from "fundamental conceptions of justice" when they defer seeking indictments until they have probable cause to believe an accused is guilty; indeed it is unprofessional conduct for a prosecutor to recommend an indictment on less than probable cause. It should be equally obvious that prosecutors are under no duty to file charges as soon as probable cause exists but before they are satisfied they will be able to establish the suspect's guilt beyond a reasonable doubt. To impose such a duty "would have a deleterious effect both upon the rights of the accused and upon the ability of society to protect itself." From the perspective of potential defendants, requiring prosecutions to commence when probable cause is established is undesirable because it would increase the likelihood of unwarranted charges being filed, and would add to the time during which defendants stand accused but untried. * * * From the perspective of law enforcement officials, a requirement of immediate prosecution upon probable cause is equally unacceptable because it could make obtaining proof of guilt beyond a reasonable doubt impossible by causing potentially fruitful sources of information to evaporate before they are fully exploited. And from the standpoint of the courts, such a requirement is unwise because it would cause scarce resources to be consumed on cases that prove to be insubstantial, or that involve only some of the responsible parties or some of the criminal acts.[12] Thus, no one's interests would be well served by compelling prosecutors to initiate prosecutions as soon as they are legally entitled to do so.

It might be argued that once the Government has assembled sufficient evidence to prove guilt beyond a reasonable doubt, it should be constitutionally required to file charges promptly, even if its investigation of the entire criminal transaction is not complete. Adopting such a rule, however, would have many of the same consequences as adopting a rule requiring immediate prosecution upon probable cause.

First, compelling a prosecutor to file public charges as soon as the requisite proof has been developed against one participant on one charge would cause numerous problems in those cases in which a criminal transaction involves more than one person or more than one illegal act. In some instances, an immediate arrest or indictment would impair the prosecutor's ability to continue his investigation, thereby preventing society from bringing lawbreakers to justice. In other cases, the prosecutor would be able to obtain additional indictments despite an early prosecution, but the necessary result would be multiple trials involving a single set of facts. Such trials place needless burdens on defendants, law enforcement officials, and courts.

Second, insisting on immediate prosecution once sufficient evidence is developed to obtain a conviction would pressure prosecutors into resolving doubtful cases in favor of early—and possibly unwarranted—prosecutions. The determination of when the evidence available to the prosecution is sufficient to obtain a conviction is seldom clear-cut, and reasonable persons often will reach conflicting conclusions. In the instant case, for example, since respondent admitted possessing at least five of the firearms, the primary factual issue in dispute was whether respondent knew the guns were stolen as required by 18 U.S.C. § 1708. Not surprisingly, the Postal Inspector's report contained no direct evidence bearing on this issue. The decision whether to prosecute, therefore, required a necessarily subjective evaluation of the strength of the circumstantial evidence available and the credibility of respondent's denial. Even if a prosecutor concluded that the

---

12. Defendants also would be adversely affected by trials involving less than all of the criminal acts for which they are responsible, since they likely would be subjected to multiple trials growing out of the same transaction or occurrence.

case was weak and further investigation appropriate, he would have no assurance that a reviewing court would agree. To avoid the risk that a subsequent indictment would be dismissed for preindictment delay, the prosecutor might feel constrained to file premature charges with all the disadvantages that entails.[14]

Finally, requiring the Government to make charging decisions immediately upon assembling evidence sufficient to establish guilt would preclude the Government from giving full consideration to the desirability of not prosecuting in particular cases. The decision to file criminal charges, with the awesome consequences it entails, requires consideration of a wide range of factors in addition to the strength of the Government's case, in order to determine whether prosecution would be in the public interest. Prosecutors often need more information than proof of a suspect's guilt, therefore, before deciding whether to seek an indictment. Again the instant case provides a useful illustration. Although proof of the identity of the mail thieves was not necessary to convict respondent of the possessory crimes with which he was charged, it might have been crucial in assessing respondent's culpability, as distinguished from his legal guilt. If, for example, further investigation were to show that respondent had no role in or advance knowledge of the theft and simply agreed, out of paternal loyalty, to help his son dispose of the guns once respondent discovered his son had stolen them, the United States Attorney might have decided not to prosecute, especially since at the time of the crime respondent was over 60 years old and had no prior criminal record. Requiring prosecution once the evidence of guilt is clear, however, could prevent a prosecutor from awaiting the information necessary for such a decision.

We would be most reluctant to adopt a rule which would have these consequences absent a clear constitutional command to do so. We can find no such command in the Due Process Clause of the Fifth Amendment. In our view, investigative delay is fundamentally unlike delay undertaken by the Government solely "to gain tactical advantage over the accused," precisely because investigative delay is not so one-sided.[17] Rather than deviating from elementary standards of "fair play and decency," a prosecutor abides by them if he refuses to seek indictments until he is completely satisfied that he should prosecute and will be able promptly to establish guilt beyond a reasonable doubt. Penalizing prosecutors who defer action for these reasons would subordinate the goal of "orderly expedition" to that of "mere speed." This the Due Process Clause does not require. We therefore hold that to prosecute a defendant following investigative delay does not deprive him of due process, even if his defense might have been somewhat prejudiced by the lapse of time.

In the present case, the Court of Appeals stated that the only reason the Government postponed action was to await the results of additional investigation. Although there is, unfortunately, no evidence concerning the reasons for the delay in the record, the court's "finding" is supported by the prosecutor's implicit representation to the District Court, and explicit representation to the Court of

14. In addition, if courts were required to decide in every case when the prosecution should have commenced, it would be necessary for them to trace the day-by-day progress of each investigation. Maintaining daily records would impose an administrative burden on prosecutors, and reviewing them would place an even greater burden on the courts.

17. In *Marion* we noted with approval that the Government conceded that a "tactical" delay would violate the Due Process Clause. The

Government renews that concession here, and expands it somewhat by stating that "A due process violation might also be made out upon a showing of prosecutorial delay incurred in reckless disregard of circumstances, known to the prosecution, suggesting that there existed an appreciable risk that delay would impair the ability to mount an effective defense." As the Government notes, however, there is no evidence of recklessness here.

Appeals, that the investigation continued during the time that the Government deferred taking action against respondent. The finding is, moreover, buttressed by the Government's repeated assertions in their Petition for Certiorari, their Brief, and their oral argument in this Court, "that the delay was caused by the Government's efforts to identify persons in addition to respondent who may have participated in the offenses." We must assume that these statements by counsel have been made in good faith. In light of this explanation, it follows that compelling respondent to stand trial would not be fundamentally unfair. The Court of Appeals therefore erred in affirming the District Court's decision dismissing the indictment.[b]

b. Stevens, J., dissenting, agreed with the foregoing principles, but concluded the majority had erred in not deciding the case on the record made in the district court, wherein the government's delay was unexplained.

Chapter 13

THE DUTY TO DISCLOSE

In order to make the criminal trial "less a game of blindman's bluff and more a fair contest with the basic issues and facts disclosed to the fullest practical extent," *United States v. Procter & Gamble Co.*, 356 U.S. 677 (1958), the state and federal criminal justice systems, over the last few decades, have expanded dramatically the obligations of both prosecution and defense to disclose to the other side before trial the evidence that each intends to use at trial. This movement toward liberal pretrial "discovery" initially emphasized prosecution disclosure to the defense. The permissible scope of defense discovery varied,[a] but one constant objection to expanding such discovery was the absence of "reciprocity" in disclosure obligations—the failure to make discovery a "two-way street." This, in turn, led to expansion of the defense obligation to disclose its evidence to the prosecution. Most jurisdictions, however, concerned about possible constitutional objections to imposing such an obligation on the defense, initially provided the prosecution with very limited discovery. One of the earliest measures providing for prosecution discovery was the reciprocal alibi-notice statute. The first case in this chapter, *Williams v. Florida*, treats the constitutionality of such a statute. The ruling in *Williams* was seen by many as giving the states leeway constitutionally to grant the prosecution a fairly expansive right of discovery. It led to a variety of broadened reciprocal discovery requirements (e.g., requiring defense disclosure of the names of all of its intended witnesses), none of which have subsequently reached the Court.

While pretrial discovery requirements are designed primarily to avoid surprise and thereby allow a party ample time to build a case responsive to its opponent, the due process doctrine explored in *United States v. Bagley* actually requires the prosecution to assist the defense in building its case. In *Brady v. Maryland,* 373 U.S. 83 (1963), the Supreme Court established a constitutional duty of the prosecution to disclose to the defense exculpatory evidence that is material to the

---

a. Some jurisdictions basically give the defense access to all of the evidence that the prosecution intends to use at trial, including not only a list of the prosecution's intended witnesses, but also any written summaries of statements those witnesses have made to the police or prosecutor. In other jurisdictions, discovery requirements are more limited out of concern that the defendant, if he knew who would be testifying for the prosecution and what they would say, would either develop perjured testimony to rebut their testimony or seek to intimidate those witnesses. Here disclosure is likely to be limited to documents, the reports of experts, and any recorded statements of defendant himself (usually given in response to police interrogation) that the prosecution intends to use at trial. What the states provide in the way of defense discovery is basically a matter of state choice. The Supreme Court had noted on several occasions that "there is no general constitutional right to discovery in a criminal case." *Weatherford v. Bursey*, 429 U.S. 545 (1977).

issues of either guilt or punishment. *Bagley* explores the scope of this *"Brady rule."* *Pennsylvania v. Ritchie* raises the question of whether the prosecution's obligation to assist the defense in preparing its case goes beyond the *Brady* rule as a result of the defendant's Sixth Amendment rights to confront opposing witnesses and to present witnesses in his favor. Other aspects of those rights are considered in Chapter Eighteen.

WILLIAMS v. FLORIDA

399 U.S. 78, 90 S.Ct. 1893, 26 L.Ed.2d 446 (1970).

JUSTICE WHITE delivered the opinion of the Court.

Prior to his trial for robbery in the State of Florida, petitioner filed a "Motion for a Protective Order," seeking to be excused from the requirements of Rule 1.200 [now Rule 3.200] of the Florida Rules of Criminal Procedure. That rule requires a defendant, on written demand of the prosecuting attorney, to give notice in advance of trial if the defendant intends to claim an alibi, and to furnish the prosecuting attorney with information as to the place he claims to have been and with the names and addresses of the alibi witnesses he intends to use. In his motion petitioner openly declared his intent to claim an alibi, but objected to the further disclosure requirements on the ground that the Rule "compels the defendant in a criminal case to be a witness against himself" in violation of his Fifth and Fourteenth Amendment rights. The motion was denied. * * *

Florida's notice-of-alibi rule is in essence a requirement that a defendant submit to a limited form of pretrial discovery by the State whenever he intends to rely at trial on the defense of alibi. In exchange for the defendant's disclosure of the witnesses he proposes to use to establish that defense, the State in turn is required to notify the defendant of any witnesses it proposes to offer in rebuttal to that defense. Both sides are under a continuing duty promptly to disclose the names and addresses of additional witnesses bearing on the alibi as they become available. The threatened sanction for failure to comply is the exclusion at trial of the defendant's alibi evidence—except for his own testimony—or, in the case of the State, the exclusion of the State's evidence offered in rebuttal to the alibi.

In this case, following the denial of his Motion for a Protective Order, petitioner complied with the alibi rule and gave the State the name and address of one Mary Scotty. Mrs. Scotty was summoned to the office of the State Attorney on the morning of the trial, where she gave pretrial testimony. At the trial itself, Mrs. Scotty, petitioner and petitioner's wife all testified that the three of them had been in Mrs. Scotty's apartment during the time of the robbery. On two occasions during cross-examination of Mrs. Scotty, the prosecuting attorney confronted her with her earlier deposition in which she had given dates and times which in some respects did not correspond with the dates and times given at trial. Mrs. Scotty adhered to her trial story, insisting that she had been mistaken in her earlier testimony. The State also offered in rebuttal the testimony of one of the officers investigating the robbery who claimed that Mrs. Scotty had asked him for directions on the afternoon in question during the time when she claimed to have been in her apartment with petitioner and his wife.

We need not linger over the suggestion that the discovery permitted the State against petitioner in this case deprived him of "due process" or a "fair trial." Florida law provides for liberal discovery by the defendant against the State, and the notice-of-alibi rule is itself carefully hedged with reciprocal duties requiring state disclosure to the defendant.[a] Given the ease with which an alibi can be fabricated, the State's interest in protecting itself against an eleventh hour defense is both obvious and legitimate. Reflecting this interest, notice-of-alibi provisions, dating at least from 1927, are now in existence in a substantial number of States. The adversary system of trial is hardly an end to itself; it is not yet a poker game in which players enjoy an absolute right always to conceal their cards until played. We find ample room in that system, at least as far as "due process" is concerned, for the instant Florida rule, which is designed to enhance the search for truth in the criminal trial by insuring both the defendant and the State ample opportunity to investigate certain facts crucial to the determination of guilt or innocence.

Petitioner's major contention is that he was "compelled to be a witness against himself" contrary to the commands of the Fifth and Fourteenth Amendments because the notice-of-alibi rule required him to give the State the name and address of Mrs. Scotty in advance of trial and thus to furnish the State with information useful in convicting him. No pretrial statement of petitioner was introduced at trial; but armed with Mrs. Scotty's name and address and the knowledge that she was to be petitioner's alibi witness, the State was able to take her deposition in advance of trial and to find rebuttal testimony. Also, requiring him to reveal the elements of his defense is claimed to have interfered with his right to wait until after the State had presented its case to decide how to defend against it. We conclude, however, as has apparently every other court which has considered the issue, that the privilege against self-incrimination is not violated by a requirement that the defendant give notice of an alibi defense and disclose his alibi witnesses.

The defendant in a criminal trial is frequently forced to testify himself and to call other witnesses in an effort to reduce the risk of conviction. When he presents his witnesses, he must reveal their identity and submit them to cross-examination which in itself may prove incriminating or which may furnish the State with leads to incriminating rebuttal evidence. That the defendant faces such a dilemma demanding a choice between complete silence and presenting a defense has never been thought an invasion of the privilege against compelled self-incrimination. The pressures generated by the State's evidence may be severe but they do not vitiate the defendant's choice to present an alibi defense and witnesses to prove it, even though the attempted defense ends in catastrophe for the defendant. However "testimonial" and "incriminating" the alibi defense proves to be, it cannot be considered "compelled" within the meaning of the Fifth and Fourteenth Amendments.

Very similar constraints operate on the defendant when the State requires pretrial notice of alibi and the naming of alibi witnesses. Nothing in such a rule requires the defendant to rely on an alibi or prevents him from abandoning the defense; these matters are left to his unfettered choice. That choice must be made, but the pressures which bear on his pretrial decision are of the same nature as those which would induce him to call alibi witnesses at the trial: the force of historical fact beyond both his and the State's control and the strength of the State's case built on these facts. Response to that kind of pressure by offering

---

a. The critical nature of this feature of the Florida alibi-discovery rule was later brought home in *Wardius v. Oregon,* 412 U.S. 470 (1973). Distinguishing *Williams,* the Court there held that an alibi-discovery rule which failed to provide reciprocal defense discovery violated due process. *Wardius* noted: "The State may not insist that trials be run as a 'search for the truth' so far as defense witnesses are concerned, while maintaining 'poker game secrecy' for its own witnesses."

evidence or testimony is not compelled self-incrimination transgressing the Fifth and Fourteenth Amendments.

In the case before us, the notice-of-alibi rule by itself in no way affected petitioner's crucial decision to call alibi witnesses or added to the legitimate pressures leading to that course of action. At most, the rule only compelled petitioner to accelerate the timing of his disclosure, forcing him to divulge at an earlier date information which the petitioner from the beginning planned to divulge at trial. Nothing in the Fifth Amendment privilege entitles a defendant as a matter of constitutional right to await the end of the State's case before announcing the nature of his defense, any more than it entitles him to await the jury's verdict on the State's case-in-chief before deciding whether or not to take the stand himself.

Petitioner concedes that absent the notice-of-alibi rule the Constitution would raise no bar to the court's granting the State a continuance at trial on the grounds of surprise as soon as the alibi witness is called. Nor would there be self-incrimination problems if, during that continuance, the State was permitted to do precisely what it did here prior to trial: to depose the witness and find rebuttal evidence. But if so utilizing a continuance is permissible under the Fifth and Fourteenth Amendments, then surely the same result may be accomplished through pretrial discovery, as it was here, avoiding the necessity of a disrupted trial.[17] We decline to hold that the privilege against compulsory self-incrimination guarantees the defendant the right to surprise the state with an alibi defense.

CHIEF JUSTICE BURGER, concurring.

I join fully in Mr. Justice White's opinion for the Court. I see an added benefit to the alibi notice rule in that it will serve important functions by way of disposing of cases without trial in appropriate circumstances—a matter of considerable importance when courts, prosecution offices and legal aid and defender agencies are vastly overworked. [The Chief Justice noted that a prosecutor receiving the names of alibi witnesses in advance of trial often would be able to determine whether an alibi defense was "reliable and unimpeachable" or "contrived and fabricated." The former determination "would very likely lead to dismissal of the charges," while the latter could lead to a defense decision to plead guilty. In either instance, the Chief Justice noted, "the ends of justice will have been served and the processes expedited."] * * *

JUSTICE BLACK, with whom JUSTICE DOUGLAS joins, dissenting.

* * * Although this case itself involves only a notice-of-alibi provision, it is clear that the decision means that a State can require a defendant to disclose in advance of trial any and all information he might possibly use to defend himself at trial. This decision, in my view, is a radical and dangerous departure from the historical and constitutionally guaranteed right of a defendant in a criminal case to remain completely silent, requiring the State to prove its case without any assistance of any kind from the defendant himself.

The core of the majority's decision is an assumption that compelling a defendant to give notice of an alibi defense before a trial is no different from requiring a defendant, after the State has produced the evidence against him at trial, to plead alibi before the jury retires to consider the case. * * * [But] when a defendant is required to indicate whether he might plead alibi in advance of trial, he faces a vastly different decision than that faced by one who can wait until

---

17. It might also be argued that the "testimonial" disclosures protected by the Fifth Amendment include only statements relating to the historical facts of the crime, not statements relating solely to what a defendant proposes to do at trial.

the State has presented the case against him before making up his mind. Before trial the defendant knows only what the State's case *might* be. Before trial there is no such thing as the "strength of the State's case," there is only a range of possible cases. At that time there is no certainty as to what kind of case the State will ultimately be able to prove at trial. Therefore any appraisal of the desirability of pleading alibi will be beset with guesswork and gambling far greater than that accompanying the decision at the trial itself. * * * Clearly the pressures on defendants to plead an alibi created by this procedure are not only quite different than the pressures operating at the trial itself, but are in fact significantly greater. Contrary to the majority's assertion, the pretrial decision cannot be analyzed as simply a matter of "timing," influenced by the same factors operating at the trial itself.

The Court apparently also assumes that a defendant who has given the required notice can abandon his alibi without hurting himself. Such an assumption is implicit in and necessary for the majority's argument that the pretrial decision is no different than that at the trial itself. I, however, cannot so lightly assume that pretrial notice will have no adverse effects on a defendant who later decides to forego such a defense. Necessarily the defendant will have given the prosecutor the names of persons who may have some knowledge about the defendant himself or his activities. Necessarily the prosecutor will have every incentive to question these persons fully, and in doing so he may discover new leads or evidence. Undoubtedly there will be situations in which the State will seek to use such information—information it would probably never have obtained but for the defendant's coerced cooperation.

It is unnecessary for me, however, to engage in any such intellectual gymnastics concerning the practical effects of the notice-of-alibi procedure, because the Fifth Amendment itself clearly provides that "[n]o person * * * shall be compelled in any criminal case to be a witness against himself." If words are to be given their plain and obvious meaning, that provision, in my opinion, states that a criminal defendant cannot be required to give evidence, testimony, or any other assistance to the State to aid it in convicting him of crime. The Florida notice-of-alibi rule in my opinion is a patent violation of that constitutional provision because it requires a defendant to disclose information to the State so that the State can use that information to destroy him. * * *

It is no answer to this argument to suggest that the Fifth Amendment as so interpreted would give the defendant an unfair element of surprise, turning a trial into a "poker game" or "sporting contest," for that tactical advantage to the defendant is inherent in the type of trial required by our Bill of Rights. The Framers were well aware of the awesome investigative and prosecutorial powers of government and it was in order to limit those powers that they spelled out in detail in the Constitution the procedure to be followed in criminal trials. * * * The defendant, under our Constitution, need not do anything at all to defend himself, and certainly he cannot be required to help convict himself. Rather he has an absolute, unqualified right to compel the State to investigate its own case, find its own witnesses, prove its own facts, and convince the jury through its own resources. Throughout the process the defendant has a fundamental right to remain silent, in effect challenging the State at every point to "Prove it!" * * *

This constitutional right to remain absolutely silent cannot be avoided by superficially attractive analogies to any so-called "compulsion" inherent in the trial itself which may lead a defendant to put on evidence in his own defense. Obviously the Constitution contemplates that a defendant can be "compelled" to stand trial, and obviously there will be times when the trial process itself will require the defendant to do something in order to try to avoid a conviction. But nothing in the Constitution permits the State to add to the natural consequences of a trial and compel the defendant in advance of trial to participate in any way in the State's attempt to condemn him. * * *

On the surface this case involves only a notice-of-alibi provision, but in effect the decision opens the way for a profound change in one of the most important traditional safeguards of a criminal defendant. The rationale of today's decision is in no way limited to alibi defenses, or any other type or classification of evidence. The theory advanced goes at least so far as to permit the State to obtain under threat of sanction complete disclosure by the defendant in advance of trial of all evidence, testimony and tactics he plans to use at that trial. In each case the justification will be that the rule affects only the "timing" of the disclosure, and not the substantive decision itself. * * * b

UNITED STATES v. BAGLEY

473 U.S. 667, 105 S.Ct. 3375, 87 L.Ed.2d 481 (1985).

JUSTICE BLACKMUN announced the judgment of the Court and delivered an opinion of the Court except as to Part III.

In *Brady v. Maryland,* 373 U.S. 83 (1963), this Court held that "the suppression by the prosecution of evidence favorable to an accused upon request violates due process where the evidence is material either to guilt or punishment." The issue in the present case concerns the standard of materiality to be applied in

---

b. A footnote in the *Williams* opinion noted that the case there before the Court did not present the question of the "validity of the threatened sanction" (the exclusion of the testimony of unlisted witnesses) as "no such penalty was exacted here." In a later case, *Taylor v. Illinois,* 108 S.Ct. 646 (1988), the Court upheld the exclusion of the testimony of defense witness who had not been listed at discovery. In that case, as authorized by state law, the prosecution requested a pretrial listing of all defense witnesses after it had provided defense with a list of its witnesses. Defense counsel listed four witnesses, but during the midst of the trial, sought to add two additional witnesses. Counsel initially stated that he had just been informed about these persons and that they had probably seen the incident in question (a shooting). In response to the trial judge's inquiry, counsel then acknowledged that the defendant had previously told him about one of the witnesses, but counsel stated that he had been unable until now to locate that witness. The trial court then questioned that witness and learned both that the witness had not actually seen the incident (although he claimed to have information that would be relevant to defendant's explanation of the shooting) and that counsel had met with the witness a week before trial. The trial court concluded that counsel's failure to give earlier notice of his intent to call the witness constituted a "blatant" and "willful" violation of the discovery rules that would require precluding the witness from testifying.

Sustaining the application of the preclusion sanction, the Supreme Court majority initially rejected the contention that the Sixth Amendment's compulsory process clause creates an absolute bar to the preclusion of the testimony of a surprise witness. It noted that the "adversary process could not function effectively without rules of procedure that govern the orderly presentation of facts and arguments to provide each party with a fair opportunity to assemble and submit evidence to contradict or explain the opponent's case," and that those rules served "the same high purpose" in "full and truthful disclosure of critical facts" as the compulsory process clause and other rights protected by the Sixth Amendment. Defendant argued that alternative and more appropriate sanctions than preclusion were available, (e.g., allowing the state a continuance or disciplining the defense counsel), but the Court responded that, while "it may well be true that alternative sanctions are adequate and appropriate in most cases," a preclusion sanction could not be absolutely barred as it is "equally clear that [those alternative sanctions] would be less effective than the preclusion sanction and that there are instances in which they would perpetuate rather than limit the prejudice to the State and harm to the adversary process." As for the case before it, the Court concluded that circumstances clearly indicated that defense counsel was "deliberately seeking a tactical advantage," and "regardless of whether the prejudice to the prosecution could have been avoided," the case fit into "the category of willful misconduct in which the severest sanction is appropriate."

determining whether a conviction should be reversed because the prosecutor failed to disclose requested evidence that could have been used to impeach Government witnesses.

I

[Respondent Bagley was indicted on 15 counts of violating federal narcotics and firearms statutes. The Government's two principal witnesses were O'Connor and Mitchell, private security guards who had assisted the Bureau of Alcohol, Tobacco and Firearms (ATF) in conducting an undercover investigation of respondent. Several weeks before trial, respondent filed a discovery motion that requested disclosure of a variety of matters, including "any deals, promises or inducements made to witnesses in exchange for their testimony." The Government's response to the discovery motion did not disclose that any "deals, promises or inducements" had been made to O'Connor or Mitchell. In apparent reply to another part of the discovery request, the Government produced a series of affidavits that O'Connor and Mitchell had signed while the undercover investigation was in progress. Those affidavits recounted in detail their undercover dealings with respondent. Each affidavit concluded with the statement, "I made this statement freely and voluntarily without any threats or rewards, or promises of reward having been made to me in return for it."]

[Respondent waived his right to a jury trial and was tried before the district court. At the trial, O'Connor and Mitchell testified about both the firearms and the narcotics charges. The court found respondent guilty on the narcotics charges, but not guilty on the firearms charges. Sometime later, respondent filed requests for information pursuant to the Freedom of Information Act. He received in response copies of ATF form contracts between ATF and O'Connor and Mitchell. The printed portion of the form stated that the informant would provide information to ATF and that "upon receipt of such information * * * and upon the accomplishment of the objective sought to be obtained by the use of such information to the satisfaction of (the ATF), the United States will pay to said vendor a sum commensurate with services and information rendered." The figure "$300.00" was handwritten in each form on a line entitled "Sum to Be Paid to Vendor." Because these contracts had not been disclosed in response to his pretrial discovery motion, respondent moved the district court to vacate his sentence. The Assistant United States Attorney who prosecuted respondent stated that he had not known that the contracts existed, and that he would have furnished them to respondent had he known of them, but the government also argued that there had been no constitutional error.]

[The motion came before the same district judge who had presided at respondent's bench trial. The district judge accepted the findings of a magistrate that the printed form contracts were blank when O'Connor and Mitchell signed them, that they were not signed by an ATF representative until after the trial, and that ATF made payments of $300 to both O'Connor and Mitchell at that time. Although the ATF case agent who dealt with O'Connor and Mitchell testified that the $300 payments simply reimbursed expenses, the district judge found that it was "probable" that O'Connor and Mitchell expected to receive compensation, in addition to their expenses. The judge concluded that "the United States did * * * withhold, during pretrial discovery, information as to any 'deals, promises or inducements' to these witnesses," but also found, beyond a reasonable doubt, that had the existence of the agreements been disclosed during trial, the disclosure would have had no effect upon his finding that the Government had proved its case on the narcotics charges. The United States Court of Appeals for the

Ninth Circuit reversed, reasoning that the failure to disclose automatically required reversal of the conviction.]

II

The holding in *Brady v. Maryland,* 373 U.S. 83 (1963), requires disclosure only of evidence that is both favorable to the accused and "material either to guilt or punishment." The Court explained in *United States v. Agurs,* 427 U.S. 97 (1976): "A fair analysis of the holding in *Brady* indicates that implicit in the requirement of materiality is a concern that the suppressed evidence might have affected the outcome of the trial." The evidence suppressed in *Brady* would have been admissible only on the issue of punishment and not on the issue of guilt, and therefore could have affected only Brady's sentence and not his conviction. Accordingly, the Court affirmed the lower court's restriction of Brady's new trial to the issue of punishment.[a]

The *Brady* rule is based on the requirement of due process. Its purpose is not to displace the adversary system as the primary means by which truth is uncovered, but to ensure that a miscarriage of justice does not occur.[6] Thus, the prosecutor is not required to deliver his entire file to defense counsel,[7] but only to disclose evidence favorable to the accused that, if suppressed, would deprive the defendant of a fair trial. * * * As *Agurs* noted: "For unless the omission deprived the defendant of a fair trial, there was no constitutional violation requiring that the verdict be set aside; and absent a constitutional violation, there was no breach of the prosecutor's constitutional duty to disclose. * * * " *United States v. Agurs.*

In *Brady* * * *, the prosecutor failed to disclose exculpatory evidence. In the present case, the prosecutor failed to disclose evidence that the defense might have used to impeach the Government's witnesses by showing bias or interest. Impeachment evidence, however, as well as exculpatory evidence, falls within the *Brady* rule. Such evidence is "evidence favorable to an accused," *Brady,* so that, if disclosed and used effectively, it may make the difference between conviction and acquittal. Cf. *Napue v. Illinois* [fn. 8 infra] ("The jury's estimate of the

---

a. The defendant Brady and a companion, Boblit, had been found guilty of felony murder and sentenced to death. Prior to Brady's separate trial, his counsel had asked the prosecutor to allow him to examine all of the statements that Boblit had given to the police. Counsel was shown several of Boblit's statements, but for some unexplained reason failed to receive one statement in which Boblit admitted that he had done the actual killing. At trial, defendant admitted his participation in the crime, but claimed that he had not himself killed the victim. Defense counsel stressed this claim in his closing argument, asking the jury to show leniency and not impose the death penalty. Following defendant's conviction, defense counsel learned of the undisclosed statement and sought a new trial based on this newly discovered evidence. The Supreme Court affirmed a state court ruling granting a new trial as to the issue of punishment alone. Whether or not defendant himself killed the victim had no bearing on his liability for the homicide, and Boblit's statement therefore would not have been admissible in evidence on that issue. On the other hand, the statement could have been used to support defendant's plea for le-

niency as to punishment, and the prosecution's failure to disclose the statement had deprived Brady of a fair hearing on that issue.

6. By requiring the prosecutor to assist the defense in making its case, the *Brady* rule represents a limited departure from a pure adversary model. The Court has recognized, however, that the prosecutor's role transcends that of an adversary: he "is the representative not of an ordinary party to a controversy, but of a sovereignty * * * whose interest * * * in a criminal prosecution is not that it shall win a case, but that justice shall be done." *Berger v. United States,* 295 U.S. 78 (1935).

7. * * * An interpretation of *Brady* to create a broad, constitutionally required right of discovery "would entirely alter the character and balance of our present systems of criminal justice." *Giles v. Maryland,* 386 U.S. 66 (1967) (dissenting opinion). Furthermore, a rule that the prosecutor commits error by any failure to disclose evidence favorable to the accused, no matter how insignificant, would impose an impossible burden on the prosecutor and would undermine the interest in the finality of judgments.

truthfulness and reliability of a given witness may well be determinative of guilt or innocence, and it is upon such subtle factors as the possible interest of the witness in testifying falsely that a defendant's life or liberty may depend"). * * *

III

It remains to determine the standard of materiality applicable to the nondisclosed evidence at issue in this case. Our starting point is the framework for evaluating the materiality of *Brady* evidence established in *United States v. Agurs.* The Court in *Agurs* distinguished three situations involving the discovery, after trial, of information favorable to the accused that had been known to the prosecution but unknown to the defense. The first situation was the prosecutor's knowing use of perjured testimony or, equivalently, the prosecutor's knowing failure to disclose that testimony used to convict the defendant was false. The Court noted the well-established rule that "a conviction obtained by the knowing use of perjured testimony is fundamentally unfair, and must be set aside if there is any reasonable likelihood that the false testimony could have affected the judgment of the jury." 427 U.S., at 103.[8] Although this rule is stated in terms that treat the knowing use of perjured testimony as error subject to harmless-error review, it may as easily be stated as a materiality standard under which the fact that testimony is perjured is considered material unless failure to disclose it would be harmless beyond a reasonable doubt. The Court in *Agurs* justified this standard of materiality on the ground that the knowing use of perjured testimony involves prosecutorial misconduct and, more importantly, involves "a corruption of the truth-seeking function of the trial process."

At the other extreme is the situation in *Agurs* itself, where the defendant does not make a *Brady* request and the prosecutor fails to disclose certain evidence favorable to the accused. The Court rejected a harmless-error rule in that situation, because under that rule every nondisclosure is treated as error, thus imposing on the prosecutor a constitutional duty to deliver his entire file to defense counsel. At the same time, the Court rejected a standard that would require the defendant to demonstrate that the evidence if disclosed probably would have resulted in acquittal.[b] The Court reasoned: "If the standard applied to the usual motion for a new trial based on newly discovered evidence were the

---

8. In fact, the *Brady* rule has its roots in a series of cases dealing with convictions based on the prosecution's knowing use of perjured testimony. In *Mooney v. Holohan,* 294 U.S. 103 (1935), the Court established the rule that the knowing use by a state prosecutor of perjured testimony to obtain a conviction and the deliberate suppression of evidence that would have impeached and refuted the testimony constitutes a denial of due process. The Court reasoned that "a deliberate deception of court and jury by the presentation of testimony known to be perjured" is inconsistent with "the rudimentary demands of justice." The Court reaffirmed this principle in broader terms in *Napue v. Illinois,* 360 U.S. 264 (1959). In *Napue,* the principal witness for the prosecution falsely testified that he had been promised no consideration for his testimony. The Court held that the knowing use of false testimony to obtain a conviction violates due process regardless of whether the prosecutor solicited the false testimony or merely allowed it to go uncorrected when it appeared. The Court explained that the principle that a State may

not knowingly use false testimony to obtain a conviction—even false testimony that goes only to the credibility of the witness—is "implicit in any concept of ordered liberty." Finally, the Court held that it was not bound by the state court's determination that the false testimony "could not in any reasonable likelihood have affected the judgment of the jury." The Court conducted its own independent examination of the record and concluded that the false testimony "may have had an effect on the outcome of the trial." Accordingly, the Court reversed the judgment of conviction.

b. The reference here was to what *Agurs* described as the "Rule 33 Standard"—the test applied to a motion for a new trial based on evidence newly discovered by the defense. That standard typically requires that the defense establish (1) that its failure to learn of the evidence previously was due to no lack of diligence, (2) that the evidence is material, not merely "cumulative or impeaching," and (3) that the evidence "will probably produce an acquittal."

same when the evidence was in the State's possession as when it was found in a neutral source, there would be no special significance to the prosecutor's obligation to serve the cause of justice." The standard of materiality applicable in the absence of a specific *Brady* request is therefore stricter than the harmless-error standard but more lenient to the defense than the newly discovered evidence standard.

The third situation identified by the Court in *Agurs* is where the defense makes a specific request and the prosecutor fails to disclose responsive evidence. The Court did not define the standard of materiality applicable in this situation, but suggested that the standard might be more lenient to the defense than in the situation in which the defense makes no request or only a general request. The Court also noted: "When the prosecutor receives a specific and relevant request, the failure to make any response is seldom, if ever, excusable."

The Court has relied on and reformulated the *Agurs* standard for the materiality of undisclosed evidence in two subsequent cases arising outside the *Brady* context. In neither case did the Court's discussion of the *Agurs* standard distinguish among the three situations described in *Agurs*. In *United States v. Valenzuela–Bernal,* 458 U.S. 858 (1982), the Court held that due process is violated when testimony is made unavailable to the defense by Government deportation of witnesses "only if there is a reasonable likelihood that the testimony could have affected the judgment of the trier of fact." And in *Strickland v. Washington,* [Ch. 17, § 2], the Court held that a new trial must be granted when evidence is not introduced because of the incompetence of counsel only if "there is a reasonable probability that, but for counsel's unprofessional errors, the result of the proceeding would have been different." The *Strickland* Court defined a "reasonable probability" as "a probability sufficient to undermine confidence in the outcome."

We find the *Strickland* formulation of the *Agurs* test for materiality sufficiently flexible to cover the "no request," "general request," and "specific request" cases of prosecutorial failure to disclose evidence favorable to the accused: The evidence is material only if there is a reasonable probability that, had the evidence been disclosed to the defense, the result of the proceeding would have been different. A "reasonable probability" is a probability sufficient to undermine confidence in the outcome.[c]

c. In *Kyles v. Whitley,* 115 S.Ct. 1555 (1995), the Supreme Court further explored this standard. The Court noted that "four aspects of materiality under *Bagley* bear emphasis." First, "a showing of materiality does not require demonstration by a preponderance that disclosure of the suppressed evidence would have resulted ultimately in the defendant's acquittal * * *. *Bagley*'s touchstone of materiality is a 'reasonable probability' of a different result, and the adjective is important. The question is not whether the defendant would more likely than not have received a different verdict with the evidence, but whether in its absence he received a fair trial, understood as a trial resulting in a verdict worthy of confidence." Second, the "*Bagley* materiality [test] * * * is not a sufficiency of evidence test." A defendant need not demonstrate that after discounting the inculpatory evidence in light of the undisclosed evidence, there would not have been enough left to convict." Third, "once a reviewing court applying *Bagley* has found con-

stitutional error there is no need for further harmless-error review." For if "a harmless error enquiry were to * * * [be undertaken], a *Bagley* error could not be treated as harmless, since 'a reasonable probability that had the evidence been disclosed to the defense, the result would have been different,' *Bagley,* necessarily entails the conclusion that the suppression must have had 'substantial and injurious effect or influence in determining the jury verdict,' *Brecht v. Abrahamson* [holding that an error having that impact is not harmless]." Fourth, "*Bagley* materiality" is to be judged by reference to the "suppressed evidence considered collectively, not item-by-item," with the focus on the "cumulative effect of suppression."

The Court in *Kyles* also refused to adopt "an even more lenient rule" where the "favorable evidence in issue * * * [was] known only to police investigators and not to the prosecutor." It noted: "To accommodate the State in this

The Government suggests that a materiality standard more favorable to the defendant reasonably might be adopted in specific request cases. The Government notes that an incomplete response to a specific request not only deprives the defense of certain evidence, but has the effect of representing to the defense that the evidence does not exist. In reliance on this misleading representation, the defense might abandon lines of independent investigation, defenses, or trial strategies that it otherwise would have pursued.

We agree that the prosecutor's failure to respond fully to a *Brady* request may impair the adversary process in this manner. And the more specifically the defense requests certain evidence, thus putting the prosecutor on notice of its value, the more reasonable it is for the defense to assume from the nondisclosure that the evidence does not exist, and to make pretrial and trial decisions on the basis of this assumption. This possibility of impairment does not necessitate a different standard of materiality, however, for under the *Strickland* formulation the reviewing court may consider directly any adverse effect that the prosecutor's failure to respond might have had on the preparation or presentation of the defendant's case. The reviewing court should assess the possibility that such effect might have occurred in light of the totality of the circumstances and with an awareness of the difficulty of reconstructing in a post-trial proceeding the course that the defense and the trial would have taken had the defense not been misled by the prosecutor's incomplete response.

In the present case, we think that there is a significant likelihood that the prosecutor's response to respondent's discovery motion misleadingly induced defense counsel to believe that O'Connor and Mitchell could not be impeached on the basis of bias or interest arising from inducements offered by the Government. Defense counsel asked the prosecutor to disclose any inducements that had been made to witnesses, and the prosecutor failed to disclose that the possibility of a reward had been held out to O'Connor and Mitchell if the information they supplied led to "the accomplishment of the objective sought to be obtained * * * to the satisfaction of [the Government]." This possibility of a reward gave O'Connor and Mitchell a direct, personal stake in respondent's conviction. The fact that the stake was not guaranteed through a promise or binding contract, but was expressly contingent on the Government's satisfaction with the end result, served only to strengthen any incentive to testify falsely in order to secure a conviction. Moreover, the prosecutor disclosed affidavits that stated that O'Connor and Mitchell received no promises of reward in return for providing information in the affidavits implicating respondent in criminal activity. In fact, O'Connor and Mitchell signed the last of these affidavits the very day after they signed the ATF contracts. While petitioner is technically correct that the blank contracts did not constitute a "promise of reward," the natural effect of these affidavits would be misleadingly to induce defense counsel to believe that O'Connor and Mitchell provided the information in the affidavits, and ultimately their testimony at trial recounting the same information, without any "inducements."

manner would * * * amount to a serious change of course from the *Brady* line of cases. In the State's favor it may be said that no one doubts that police investigators sometimes fail to inform a prosecutor of all they know. But neither is there any serious doubt that 'procedures and regulations can be established to carry [the prosecutor's] burden and to insure communication of all relevant information on each case to every lawyer who deals with it.'

* * * Since, then, the prosecutor has the means to discharge the government's *Brady* responsibility if he will, any argument for excusing a prosecutor from disclosing what he does not happen to know about boils down to a plea to substitute the police for the prosecutor, and even for the courts themselves, as the final arbiters of the government's obligation to ensure fair trials."

The District Court, nonetheless, found beyond a reasonable doubt that, had the information that the Government held out the possibility of reward to its witnesses been disclosed, the result of the criminal prosecution would not have been different.   If this finding were sustained by the Court of Appeals, the information would be immaterial even under the standard of materiality applicable to the prosecutor's knowing use of perjured testimony.   Although the express holding of the Court of Appeals was that the nondisclosure in this case required automatic reversal, the Court of Appeals also stated that it "disagreed" with the District Court's finding of harmless error.   * * * Accordingly, we reverse the judgment of the Court of Appeals and remand the case to that court for a determination whether there is a reasonable probability that, had the inducement offered by the Government to O'Connor and Mitchell been disclosed to the defense, the result of the trial would have been different.

JUSTICE POWELL took no part in the decision of this case.

JUSTICE WHITE, with whom THE CHIEF JUSTICE and JUSTICE REHNQUIST join, concurring in part and concurring in the judgment.

I agree with the Court that respondent is not entitled to have his conviction overturned unless he can show that the evidence withheld by the Government was "material," and I therefore join Parts I and II of the Court's opinion.   I also agree with Justice Blackmun that for purposes of this inquiry, "evidence is material only if there is a reasonable probability that, had the evidence been disclosed to the defense, the result of the proceeding would have been different."   As the Justice correctly observes, this standard is "sufficiently flexible" to cover all instances of prosecutorial failure to disclose evidence favorable to the accused. Given the flexibility of the standard and the inherently fact-bound nature of the cases to which it will be applied, however, I see no reason to attempt to elaborate on the relevance to the inquiry of the specificity of the defense's request for disclosure, either generally or with respect to this case.   I would hold simply that the proper standard is one of reasonable probability and that the Court of Appeals' failure to apply this standard necessitates reversal.   I therefore concur in the judgment.

JUSTICE MARSHALL, with whom JUSTICE BRENNAN joins, dissenting.

The Court today chooses to reverse and remand the case for application of its newly stated standard to the facts of this case.   While I believe that the evidence at issue here, which remained undisclosed despite a particular request, undoubtedly was material under the Court's standard, I also have serious doubts whether the Court's definition of the constitutional right at issue adequately takes account of the interests this Court sought to protect in its decision in *Brady v. Maryland*.

I begin from the fundamental premise, which hardly bears repeating, that "[t]he purpose of a trial is as much the acquittal of an innocent person as it is the conviction of a guilty one."   When evidence favorable to the defendant is known to exist, disclosure only enhances the quest for truth;   it takes no direct toll on that inquiry.   Moreover, the existence of any small piece of evidence favorable to the defense may, in a particular case, create just the doubt that prevents the jury from returning a verdict of guilty.   The private whys and wherefores of jury deliberations pose an impenetrable barrier to our ability to know just which piece of information might make, or might have made, a difference.

* * * We have long recognized that, within the limit of the State's ability to identify so-called exculpatory information, the State's concern for a fair verdict precludes it from withholding from the defense evidence favorable to the defendant's case in the prosecutor's files.   * * * This recognition no doubt stems in

part from the frequently considerable imbalance in resources between most criminal defendants and most prosecutors' offices. Many, perhaps most, criminal defendants in the United States are represented by appointed counsel, who often are paid minimal wages and operate on shoestring budgets. In addition, unlike police, defense counsel generally is not present at the scene of the crime, or at the time of arrest, but instead comes into the case late. Moreover, unlike the Government, defense counsel is not in the position to make deals with witnesses to gain evidence. Thus, an inexperienced, unskilled, or unaggressive attorney often is unable to amass the factual support necessary to a reasonable defense. When favorable evidence is in the hands of the prosecutor but not disclosed, the result may well be that the defendant is deprived of a fair chance before the trier of fact, and the trier of fact is deprived of the ingredients necessary to a fair decision. This grim reality, of course, poses a direct challenge to the traditional model of the adversary criminal process, and perhaps because this reality so directly questions the fairness of our longstanding processes, change has been cautious and halting. Thus, the Court has not gone the full road and expressly required that the State provide to the defendant access to the prosecutor's complete files, or investigators who will assure that the defendant has an opportunity to discover every existing piece of helpful evidence. Instead, in acknowledgment of the fact that important interests are served when potentially favorable evidence is disclosed, the Court has fashioned a compromise, requiring that the prosecution identify and disclose to the defendant favorable material that it possesses. This requirement is but a small, albeit important; step toward equality of justice.

Brady v. Maryland, of course, established this requirement of disclosure as a fundamental element of a fair trial by holding that a defendant was denied due process if he was not given access to favorable evidence that is material either to guilt or punishment. Since *Brady* was decided, this Court has struggled, in a series of decisions, to define how best to effectuate the right recognized. To my mind, the *Brady* decision, the reasoning that underlay it, and the fundamental interest in a fair trial, combine to give the criminal defendant the right to receive from the prosecutor, and the prosecutor the affirmative duty to turn over to the defendant, *all* information known to the government that might reasonably be considered favorable to the defendant's case. Formulation of this right, and imposition of this duty, are "the essence of due process of law. It is the State that tries a man, and it is the State that must insure that the trial is fair." * * * If that right is denied, or if that duty is shirked, however, I believe a reviewing court should not automatically reverse but instead should apply the harmless error test the Court has developed for instances of error affecting constitutional rights. See *Chapman v. California,* 386 U.S. 18 (1967).[d]

My view is based in significant part on the reality of criminal practice and on the consequently inadequate protection to the defendant that a different rule would offer. * * * At the trial level, the duty of the state to effectuate *Brady* devolves into the duty of the prosecutor; the dual role that the prosecutor must play poses a serious obstacle to implementing *Brady*. The prosecutor is by trade, if not necessity, a zealous advocate. He is a trained attorney who must aggressively seek convictions in court on behalf of a victimized public. At the same time, as a representative of the State, he must place foremost in his hierarchy of interests the determination of truth. Thus, for purposes of *Brady*, the prosecutor must abandon his role as an advocate and pore through his files, as objectively as

d. *Chapman* is discussed at footnote d of the introduction to Chapter 11 and in the   *Coleman* and *Hillery* cases in Chapter 11.

possible, to identify the material that could undermine his case. Given this obviously unharmonious role, it is not surprising that these advocates oftentimes overlook or downplay potentially favorable evidence, often in cases in which there is no doubt that the failure to disclose was a result of absolute good faith. Indeed, one need only think of the Fourth Amendment's requirement of a neutral intermediary, who tests the strength of the policeman-advocate's facts, to recognize the curious status *Brady* imposes on a prosecutor. * * *

The prosecutor surely greets the moment at which he must turn over *Brady* material with little enthusiasm. In perusing his files, he must make the often difficult decision as to whether evidence is favorable, and must decide on which side to err when faced with doubt. In his role as advocate, the answers are clear. In his role as representative of the State, the answers should be equally clear, and often to the contrary. Evidence that is of doubtful worth in the eyes of the prosecutor could be of inestimable value to the defense, and might make the difference to the trier of fact.

Once the prosecutor suspects that certain information might have favorable implications for the defense, either because it is potentially exculpatory or relevant to credibility, I see no reason why he should not be required to disclose it. After all, favorable evidence indisputably enhances the truth-seeking process at trial. And it is the job of the defense, not the prosecution, to decide whether and in what way to use arguably favorable evidence. In addition, to require disclosure of all evidence that might reasonably be considered favorable to the defendant would have the precautionary effect of assuring that no information of potential consequence is mistakenly overlooked. By requiring full disclosure of favorable evidence in this way, courts could begin to assure that a possibly dispositive piece of information is not withheld from the trier of fact by a prosecutor who is torn between the two roles he must play. A clear rule of this kind, coupled with a presumption in favor of disclosure, also would facilitate the prosecutor's admittedly difficult task by removing a substantial amount of unguided discretion. * * *

* * * The State's interest in nondisclosure at trial is minimal, and should therefore yield to the readily apparent benefit that full disclosure would convey to the search for truth. After trial, however, the benefits of disclosure may at times be tempered by the State's legitimate desire to avoid retrial when error has been harmless. However, in making the determination of harmlessness, I would apply our normal constitutional error test and reverse unless it is clear beyond a reasonable doubt that the withheld evidence would not have affected the outcome of the trial. See *Chapman v. California.*[6]

Any rule other than automatic reversal, of course, dilutes the *Brady* right to some extent and offers the prosecutor an incentive not to turn over all information. In practical effect, it might be argued, there is little difference between the rule I propose—that a prosecutor must disclose all favorable evidence in his files, subject to harmless error review—and the rule the Court adopts—that the prosecutor must disclose only the favorable information that might affect the outcome of the trial. According to this argument, if a constitutional right to all favorable evidence leads to reversal only when the withheld evidence might have affected the outcome of the trial, the result will be the same as with a constitutional right only to evidence that will affect the trial outcome. For several reasons, however, I disagree. First, I have faith that a prosecutor would treat a

6. In a case of deliberate prosecutorial misconduct, automatic reversal might well be proper. Certain kinds of constitutional error so infect the system of justice as to require reversal in all cases, such as discrimination in jury selection. A deliberate effort of the prosecutor to undermine the search for truth clearly is in the category of offenses anathema to our most basic vision of the role of the State in the criminal process.

rule requiring disclosure of all information of a certain kind differently from a rule requiring disclosure only of some of that information. Second, persistent or egregious failure to comply with the constitutional duty could lead to disciplinary actions by the courts. Third, the standard of harmlessness I adopt is more protective of the defendant than that chosen by the Court, placing the burden on the prosecutor, rather than the defendant, to prove the harmlessness of his actions. It would be a foolish prosecutor who gambled too glibly with that standard of review. * * * e

PENNSYLVANIA v. RITCHIE

480 U.S. 39, 107 S.Ct. 989, 94 L.Ed.2d 40 (1987).

JUSTICE POWELL, announced the judgment of the Court and delivered the opinion of the Court with respect to Parts I, II, III–B, III–C, and IV, and an opinion with respect to Part III–A in which THE CHIEF JUSTICE, JUSTICE WHITE, and JUSTICE O'CONNOR join.

I

[Respondent Ritchie's 13 year-old daughter reported to the police that she had been sexually assaulted by Ritchie two or three times per week over the previous four years. The matter was referred to Children and Youth Services (CYS), a state protective service agency charged with investigating the suspected mistreatment or neglect of children. Ritchie subsequently was charged with rape, involuntary deviate sexual intercourse, incest, and corruption of a minor. During pretrial discovery, Ritchie served CYS with a subpoena, seeking access to all of its records relating to the immediate charges, as well as to certain earlier records compiled when CYS investigated a separate report that Ritchie's children were being abused. CYS refused to comply with the subpoena. It cited a Pennsylvania statute providing that all CYS records must be kept confidential, subject to specified exceptions, including one authorizing disclosure to a "court of competent jurisdiction pursuant to a court order." At an in-chambers hearing, respondent Ritchie argued that he was entitled to the CYS file because it might contain the names of favorable witnesses, as well as other, unspecified exculpatory evidence. Ritchie also claimed that the file contained a medical report prepared in conjunction with the earlier investigation, but CYS asserted that there was no such report in the record. The trial judge, without examining the entire file, refused to order disclosure. At the subsequent trial, which resulted in respondent's conviction, the main witness against him was his daughter. She was cross-examined at length by defense counsel, who questioned her on all aspects of the reported incidents, including her reasons for not reporting them sooner.]

[On appeal, the Pennsylvania Superior Court held that the failure to disclose the CYS file resulted in a constitutional violation insofar as it denied defendant the opportunity to cross-examine his daughter with respect to recorded statements she made to the CYS counselor. It ordered that a new trial be held unless the trial judge determined that the failure to disclose those statements had constitut-

e. Justice Stevens' dissent is omitted. Justice Stevens argued that where there was a specific request for the disclosure of relevant evidence that was exculpatory, the standard applied in the perjured testimony cases should control in determining whether the failure to disclose required a reversal of a conviction. A standard more lenient to the prosecution had been established for non-request cases in *Agurs* because, "where there had been no specific defense request for the later-discovered evidence, there was no notice to the prosecution that the defense did not already have that evidence or that it considered the evidence to be of particular value." As *Agurs* had noted, "where the prosecutor receives a specific and relevant request, the failure to make any response is seldom, if ever, excusable."

ed harmless error. On appeal by the prosecution, the Pennsylvania Supreme Court agreed that the conviction should be vacated and the case remanded to determine if a new trial was necessary. However, it issued a broader ruling then the Superior Court. It directed that Ritchie, through his lawyer, be entitled to review the entire file to search for any useful evidence. This ruling was based on both the Confrontation and Compulsory Process clauses of the Sixth Amendment.]

II

[In part II of his opinion, Justice Powell concluded that the decision below constituted a "final judgment or decree," as required for United States Supreme Court review.[a]]

III

The Pennsylvania Supreme Court held that Ritchie, through his lawyer, has the right to examine the full contents of the CYS records. The court found that this right of access is required by both the Confrontation Clause and the Compulsory Process Clause. We discuss these constitutional provisions in turn.

A

* * * Ritchie claims that by denying him access to the information necessary to prepare his defense, the trial court interfered with his right of cross-examination. Ritchie argues that he could not effectively question his daughter because, without the CYS material, he did not know which types of questions would best expose the weaknesses in her testimony. Had the files been disclosed, Ritchie argues that he might have been able to show that the daughter made statements to the CYS counselor that were inconsistent with her trial statements, or perhaps to reveal that the girl acted with an improper motive. * * * [R]itchie argues that the failure to disclose [such] information that might have made cross-examination more effective undermines the Confrontation Clause's purpose of increasing the accuracy of the truth-finding process at trial. The Pennsylvania Supreme Court accepted this argument, relying in part on our decision in *Davis v. Alaska* [Ch. 18, § 2]. * * * The Pennsylvania Supreme Court apparently interpreted our decision in *Davis* to mean that a statutory privilege cannot be maintained when a defendant asserts a need, prior to trial, for the protected information that might be used at trial to impeach or otherwise undermine a witness' testimony.

If we were to accept this broad interpretation of *Davis,* the effect would be to transform the Confrontation Clause into a constitutionally-compelled rule of pretrial discovery. Nothing in the case law supports such a view. The opinions of this Court show that the right of confrontation is a *trial* right, designed to prevent improper restrictions on the types of questions that defense counsel may ask during cross-examination. * * * The ability to question adverse witnesses, however, does not include the power to require the pretrial disclosure of any and all information that might be useful in contradicting unfavorable testimony.[9] Normally the right to confront one's accusers is satisfied if defense counsel receives wide latitude at trial to question witnesses. *Delaware v. Fensterer*, 474 U.S. 15 (1985). In short, the Confrontation Clause only guarantees "an *opportu-*

---

a. Justice Stevens' separate dissent on this point is omitted.

9. This is not to suggest, of course, that there are no protections for pretrial discovery in criminal cases. See discussion in Part III(B), infra. We simply hold that with respect to this issue, the Confrontation Clause only protects a defendant's trial rights, and does not compel the pretrial production of information that might be useful in preparing for trial. * * *

nity for effective cross-examination, not cross-examination that is effective in whatever way, and to whatever extent, the defense might wish." Id. * * *

The lower court's reliance on *Davis v. Alaska* therefore is misplaced. There the state court had prohibited defense counsel from questioning the witness about his criminal record, even though that evidence might have affected the witness' credibility. The constitutional error in that case was *not* that Alaska made this information confidential; it was that the defendant was denied the right "to expose to the jury the facts from which jurors * * * could appropriately draw inferences relating to the reliability of the witness." Similarly, in this case the Confrontation Clause was not violated by the withholding of the CYS file; it only would have been impermissible for the judge to have prevented Ritchie's lawyer from cross-examining the daughter. Because defense counsel was able to cross-examine all of the trial witnesses fully, we find that the Pennsylvania Supreme Court erred in holding that the failure to disclose the CYS file violated the Confrontation Clause.

B

The Pennsylvania Supreme Court also suggested that the failure to disclose the CYS file violated the Sixth Amendment's guarantee of compulsory process. Ritchie asserts that the trial court's ruling prevented him from learning the names of the "witnesses in his favor," as well as other evidence that might be contained in the file. Although the basis for the Pennsylvania Supreme Court's ruling on this point is unclear, it apparently concluded that the right of compulsory process includes the right to have the State's assistance in uncovering arguably useful information, without regard to the existence of a state-created restriction—here, the confidentiality of the files. * * *

This Court has never squarely held that the Compulsory Process Clause guarantees the right to discover the *identity* of witnesses, or to require the Government to produce exculpatory evidence. * * * Instead, the Court traditionally has evaluated claims such as those raised by Ritchie under the broader protections of the Due Process Clause of the Fourteenth Amendment. See *United States v. Bagley.* Because the applicability of the Sixth Amendment to this type of case is unsettled, and because our Fourteenth Amendment precedents addressing the fundamental fairness of trials establish a clear framework for review, we adopt a due process analysis for purposes of this case. Although we conclude that compulsory process provides no *greater* protections in this area than those afforded by due process, we need not decide today whether and how the guarantees of the Compulsory Process Clause differ from those of the Fourteenth Amendment. It is enough to conclude that on these facts, Ritchie's claims more properly are considered by reference to due process.

It is well-settled that the Government has the obligation to turn over evidence in its possession that is both favorable to the accused and material to guilt or punishment. *Brady v. Maryland.* Although courts have used different terminologies to define "materiality," a majority of this Court has agreed, "[e]vidence is material only if there is a reasonable probability, that, had the evidence been disclosed to the defense, the result of the proceeding would have been different. A 'reasonable probability' is a probability sufficient to undermine confidence in the outcome." *United States v. Bagley,* supra (opinion of Blackmun, J.); see Id. (opinion of White, J.).

At this stage, of course, it is impossible to say whether any information in the CYS records may be relevant to Ritchie's claim of innocence, because neither the prosecution nor defense counsel has seen the information, and the trial judge acknowledged that he had not reviewed the full file. The Commonwealth, however, argues that no materiality inquiry is required, because a statute renders the contents of the file privileged. Requiring disclosure here, it is argued, would override the Commonwealth's compelling interest in confidentiality on the mere speculation that the file "might" have been useful to the defense.

Although we recognize that the public interest in protecting this type of sensitive information is strong, we do not agree that this interest necessarily prevents disclosure in all circumstances. This is not a case where a state statute grants CYS the absolute authority to shield its files from all eyes. Cf. 42 Pa.Cons.Stat. § 5945.1(b) (unqualified statutory privilege for communications between sexual assault counselors and victims).[14] Rather, the Pennsylvania law provides that the information shall be disclosed in certain circumstances, including when CYS is directed to do so by court order. Given that the Pennsylvania Legislature contemplated *some* use of CYS records in judicial proceedings, we cannot conclude that the statute prevents all disclosure in criminal prosecutions. In the absence of any apparent state policy to the contrary, we therefore have no reason to believe that relevant information would not be disclosed when a court of competent jurisdiction determines that the information is "material" to the defense of the accused. * * * Ritchie is entitled to have the CYS file reviewed by the trial court to determine whether it contains information that probably would have changed the outcome of his trial. * * *

C

This ruling does not end our analysis because the Pennsylvania Supreme Court did more than simply remand. It also held that defense counsel must be allowed to examine all of the confidential information, both relevant and irrelevant, and present arguments in favor of disclosure. The court apparently concluded that whenever a defendant alleges that protected evidence might be material, the appropriate method of assessing this claim is to grant full access to the disputed information, regardless of the State's interest in confidentiality. We cannot agree.

A defendant's right to discover exculpatory evidence does not include the unsupervised authority to search through the Commonwealth's files. Although the eye of an advocate may be helpful to a defendant in ferreting out information, this Court has never held—even in the absence of a statute restricting disclosure—that a defendant alone may make the determination as to the materiality of the information. Settled practice is to the contrary. * * *

We find that Ritchie's interest (as well as that of the Commonwealth) in ensuring a fair trial can be protected fully by requiring that the CYS files be submitted only to the trial court for *in camera* review. Although this rule denies Ritchie the benefits of an "advocate's eye," we note that the trial court's discretion is not unbounded. If a defendant is aware of specific information contained in the file (e.g., the medical report), he is free to request it directly from the court, and argue in favor of its materiality. * * *

To allow full disclosure to defense counsel in this type of case would sacrifice unnecessarily the Commonwealth's compelling interest in protecting its child abuse information. If the CYS records were made available to defendants, even through counsel, it could have a seriously adverse effect on Pennsylvania's efforts to uncover and treat abuse. Child abuse is one of the most difficult crimes to

14. We express no opinion on whether the result in this case would have been different if the statute had protected the CYS files from disclosure to *anyone*, including law-enforcement and judicial personnel.

detect and prosecute, in large part because there often are no witnesses except the victim. A child's feelings of vulnerability and guilt, and his or her unwillingness to come forward are particularly acute when the abuser is a parent. It therefore is essential that the child have a state-designated person to whom he may turn, and to do so with the assurance of confidentiality. Relatives and neighbors who suspect abuse also will be more willing to come forward if they know that their identities will be protected. Recognizing this, the Commonwealth—like all other States—has made a commendable effort to assure victims and witnesses that they may speak to the CYS counselors without fear of general disclosure. The Commonwealth's purpose would be frustrated if this confidential material had to be disclosed upon demand to a defendant charged with criminal child abuse, simply because a trial court may not recognize exculpatory evidence. Neither precedent nor common sense requires such a result.

IV

We agree that Ritchie is entitled to know whether the CYS file contains information that may have changed the outcome of his trial had it been disclosed. Thus we agree that a remand is necessary. We disagree with the decision of the Pennsylvania Supreme Court to the extent that it allows defense counsel access to the CYS file. An *in camera* review by the trial court will serve Ritchie's interest without destroying the Commonwealth's need to protect the confidentiality of those involved in child-abuse investigations. The decision of the Pennsylvania Supreme Court is affirmed in part, reversed in part, and remanded for further proceedings not inconsistent with this opinion.

JUSTICE BLACKMUN, concurring in part and concurring in the judgment.

I join Parts I, II, III–B, III–C, and IV of the Court's opinion. I write separately, however, because I do not accept the plurality's conclusion, as expressed in Part III–A of Justice Powell's opinion, that the Confrontation Clause protects only a defendant's trial rights and has no relevance to pretrial discovery. * * * The plurality believes that [the Confrontation Clause] is satisfied so long as defense counsel can *question* a witness on any proper subject of cross-examination. For the plurality, the existence of a confrontation violation turns on whether counsel has the opportunity to conduct such questioning; the Court in effect dismisses—or, at best, downplays—any inquiry into the effectiveness of the cross-examination. * * * If I were to accept the plurality's effort to divorce confrontation analysis from any examination into the effectiveness of cross-examination, I believe that in some situations the confrontation right would become an empty formality. * * *

The similarities between *Davis* and this case are much greater than are any differences that may exist. * * * It is true that, in a technical sense, the situations of Davis and Ritchie are different. Davis' counsel had access to the juvenile record of the witness and could have used it but for the Alaska prohibition. Thus, the infringement upon Davis' confrontation right occurred at the trial stage when his counsel was unable to pursue an available line of inquiry. Respondent's attorney could not cross-examine his client's daughter with the help of the possible evidence in the CYS file because of the Pennsylvania prohibition that affected his pretrial preparations. I do not believe, however, that a State can avoid Confrontation Clause problems simply by deciding to hinder the defendant's right to effective cross-examination, on the basis of a desire to protect the confidentiality interests of a particular class of individuals, at the pretrial, rather than at the trial, stage.

Despite my disagreement with the plurality's reading of the Confrontation Clause, I am able to concur in the Court's judgment because, in my view, the procedure the Court has set out for the lower court to follow on remand is adequate to address any confrontation problem. * * *

JUSTICE BRENNAN, with whom JUSTICE MARSHALL joins, dissenting.

* * * In this case, the trial court properly viewed Ritchie's vague speculations that the agency file might contain something useful as an insufficient basis for permitting general access to the file. However, in denying access to the prior statements of the victim the court deprived Ritchie of material crucial to any effort to impeach the victim at trial. I view this deprivation as a violation of the Confrontation Clause.

One way in which cross-examination may be restricted is through preclusion at trial itself of a line of inquiry that counsel seeks to pursue. The logic of our concern for restriction on the ability to engage in cross-examination does not suggest, however, that the Confrontation Clause prohibits *only* such limitation. A crucial avenue of cross-examination also may be foreclosed by the denial of access to material that would serve as the basis for this examination. Where denial of access is complete, counsel is in no position to formulate a line of inquiry potentially grounded on the material sought. Thus, he or she cannot point to a specific subject of inquiry that has been foreclosed, as can a counsel whose interrogation at trial has been limited by the trial judge. Nonetheless, there occurs as effective preclusion of a topic of cross-examination as if the judge at trial had ruled an entire area of questioning off limits.

* * * *Jencks v. United States*, 353 U.S. 657 (1957), held that the defendant was entitled to obtain the prior statements of persons to government agents when those persons testified against him at trial. * * * As I later noted in *Palermo v. United States,* 360 U.S. 343 (1959), *Jencks* was based on our supervisory authority rather than the Constitution, "but it would be idle to say that the commands of the Constitution were not close to the surface of the decision." * * *

The ability to obtain material information through reliance on a Due Process claim will not in all cases nullify the damage of the Court's overly restrictive reading of the Confrontation Clause. As the Court notes, evidence is regarded as material only if there is a reasonable probability that it might affect the outcome of the proceeding. Prior statements on their face may not appear to have such force, since their utility may lie in their more subtle potential for diminishing the credibility of a witness. The prospect that these statements will not be regarded as material is enhanced by the fact that due process analysis requires that information be evaluated by the trial judge, not defense counsel. By contrast, *Jencks,* informed by confrontation and cross-examination concerns, insisted that defense counsel, not the court, perform such an evaluation, "[b]ecause only the defense is adequately equipped to determine the effective use for the purpose of discrediting the Government's witness and thereby furthering the accused's defense." Therefore, while Confrontation Clause and due process analysis may in some cases be congruent, the Confrontation Clause has independent significance in protecting against infringements on the right to cross-examination.[b]

b. In *Arizona v. Youngblood*, 488 U.S. 51 (1988), the Court adopted a different due process standard for cases involving governmental loss or destruction of evidence of potential use to the defendant. The defendant there had been convicted of child molestation, sexual assault, and kidnapping. Prior to his arrest, state agents had collected semen samples from the 10-year-old victim's body and clothing, but they had then inadvertently failed to preserve those samples in a condition that would permit blood substance testing that could be matched against the accused's blood group. The state court held that since defendant had claimed mistaken identity, the state's loss of the possibly useful evidence precluded a conviction consistent with due process. Rejecting that ruling, the Supreme Court majority reasoned: "The Due Process Clause of the Fourteenth Amendment, as interpreted in *Brady v. Maryland*, makes the good or bad faith of the State irrelevant when the State fails to disclose to the defendant material exculpatory evidence. But we think the Due Process Clause requires a different result when we deal with the failure of the State to preserve evidentiary material of which no more can be said than that it could have been subjected to tests, the results of which might have exonerated the defendant. Part of the reason for the difference in treatment is found in the observation made by the Court in [an earlier case] that '[w]henever potentially exculpatory evidence is permanently lost, courts face the treacherous task of divining the import of materials whose contents are unknown and, very often, disputed.' Part of it stems from our unwillingness to read the 'fundamental fairness' requirement of the Due Process Clause as imposing on the police an undifferentiated and absolute duty to retain and to preserve all material that might be of conceivable evidentiary significance in a particular prosecution. We think that requiring a defendant to show bad faith on the part of the police both limits the extent of the police's obligation to preserve evidence to reasonable bounds and confines it to that class of cases where the interests of justice most clearly require it, i.e., those cases in which the police themselves by their conduct indicate that the evidence could form a basis for exonerating the defendant. We therefore hold that unless a criminal defendant can show bad faith on the part of the police, failure to preserve potentially useful evidence does not constitute a denial of due process of law."

Chapter 14

GUILTY PLEAS

SECTION 1. PLEA BARGAINING

The great majority of criminal cases in the United States are disposed of by plea of guilty rather than by trial. The guilty plea is very often a negotiated plea, that is, a defendant's agreement to plead guilty to a criminal charge with the reasonable expectation of receiving some consideration from the government. Sometimes this plea is the result of nothing more than implicit plea bargaining; there is no actual bargaining between the defendant or his attorney and the prosecutor or judge, and the defendant enters his plea merely because it is generally known that this is the route to a lesser sentence. But more common is explicit bargaining in which the defendant enters a plea of guilty only after a commitment has been made that concessions will be granted (or at least sought) in his particular case.

One common form of plea negotiation consists of an arrangement whereby the defendant and prosecutor agree that the defendant should be permitted to plead guilty to a charge less serious than is supported by the evidence. A second form involves an agreement whereby the defendant pleads "on the nose," that is, to the original charge, in exchange for some kind of promise from the prosecutor concerning the sentence to be imposed (that he will recommend or not oppose a certain sentence, or even that he will ensure that the sentence will not exceed a certain amount). Still another kind of plea bargain—the one most likely to be illusory—is where the defendant pleads "on the nose" in exchange for the prosecutor's promise to drop or not file other charges.

Plea bargaining is a long time (though only recently highly visible) practice in the United States. There is considerable disagreement as to what caused this practice to develop and continue, though it seems likely a combination of factors is involved. One explanation is that plea bargaining is a response to crowded court dockets, but this is not inevitably the case, for negotiation practices have developed at times and places where there was no serious court congestion. Some have attributed plea bargaining to inadequate public defenders, the financial incentives of private attorneys, and the laziness of prosecutors, but this is hardly an entirely accurate or complete explanation either. Certainly there are at least some more favorable explanations, such as that there are today fewer genuine disputes of fact to be resolved by trials because of the increased professionalism of police and prosecutors and the enhanced role of defense attorneys at the pretrial stages.

But whether the institution of plea bargaining is viewed favorably or unfavorably, there is no denying that this process of negotiation for and granting of concessions can give rise to difficult and important legal issues. Just how much pressure may the prosecutor put on the defendant in an effort to induce him to go the guilty plea route? What are the defendant's rights if notwithstanding his plea he does not receive the contemplated concessions? How hard must the prosecutor try to obtain the concessions he promised to seek? If defendant has not yet entered his plea, may the prosecutor renege on the agreement? Those issues are explored in the four Supreme Court decisions in this section.

BORDENKIRCHER v. HAYES

434 U.S. 357, 98 S.Ct. 663, 54 L.Ed.2d 604 (1978).

Justice Stewart delivered the opinion of the Court. * * *

[Paul Hayes was indicted in Fayette County, Ky., on a charge of uttering a forged instrument in the amount of $88.30, punishable by two to 10 years in prison. Hayes and his retained counsel met with the prosecutor who offered to recommend a sentence of five years if Hayes would plead guilty and added that if Hayes did not plead guilty he would seek an indictment under the Kentucky Habitual Criminal Act, which would subject Hayes to a mandatory sentence of life imprisonment by reason of his two prior felony convictions. Hayes chose not to plead guilty, and the prosecutor did obtain such an indictment. A jury found Hayes guilty on the principal charge of uttering a forged instrument and, in a separate proceeding, further found that he had twice before been convicted of felonies. As required by the habitual offender statute, he was sentenced to a life term in the penitentiary. The Kentucky Court of Appeals rejected Hayes' constitutional objections to the enhanced sentence, and on Hayes' petition for a federal writ of habeas corpus the district court agreed that there had been no constitutional violation in the sentence or the indictment procedure. The Court of Appeals for the Sixth Circuit reversed on the ground that the prosecutor's conduct had violated the principles of *Blackledge v. Perry,* 417 U.S. 21 (1974), which "protect defendants from the vindictive exercise of a prosecutor's discretion."]

It may be helpful to clarify at the outset the nature of the issue in this case. While the prosecutor did not actually obtain the recidivist indictment until after the plea conferences had ended, his intention to do so was clearly put forth at the outset of the plea negotiations. Hayes was thus fully informed of the true terms of the offer when he made his decision to plead not guilty. This is not a situation, therefore, where the prosecutor without notice brought an additional and more serious charge after plea negotiations relating only to the original indictment had ended with the defendant's insistence on pleading not guilty. As a practical matter, in short, this case would be no different if the grand jury had indicted Hayes as a recidivist from the outset, and the prosecutor had offered to drop that charge as part of the plea bargain.

The Court of Appeals nonetheless drew a distinction between "concessions relating to prosecution under an existing indictment," and threats to bring more severe charges not contained in the original indictment—a line it thought necessary in order to establish a prophylactic rule to guard against the evil of prosecutorial vindictiveness. Quite apart from this chronological distinction, however, the Court of Appeals found that the prosecutor had acted vindictively in the present case since he had conceded that the indictment was influenced by his desire to induce a guilty plea. The ultimate conclusion of the Court of Appeals thus seems to have been that a prosecutor acts vindictively and in violation of due process of law whenever his charging decision is influenced by what he hopes to gain in the course of plea bargaining negotiations.

We have recently had occasion to observe that "[w]hatever might be the situation in an ideal world, the fact is that the guilty plea and the often concomitant plea bargain are important components of this country's criminal justice system. Properly administered, they can benefit all concerned." The open acknowledgment of this previously clandestine practice has led this Court to recognize the importance of counsel during plea negotiations, the need for a public record indicating that a plea was knowingly and voluntarily made, and the requirement that a prosecutor's plea bargaining promise must be kept. The decision of the Court of Appeals in the present case, however, did not deal with considerations such as these, but held that the substance of the plea offer itself violated the limitations imposed by the Due Process Clause of the Fourteenth Amendment. For the reasons that follow, we have concluded that the Court of Appeals was mistaken in so ruling.

This Court held in *North Carolina v. Pearce*, 395 U.S. 711 (1969), that the Due Process Clause of the Fourteenth Amendment "requires that vindictiveness against a defendant for having successfully attacked his first conviction must play no part in the sentence he receives after a new trial." The same principle was later applied to prohibit a prosecutor from reindicting a convicted misdemeanant on a felony charge after the defendant had invoked an appellate remedy, since in this situation there was also a "realistic likelihood of 'vindictiveness.' " *Blackledge v. Perry.*

In those cases the Court was dealing with the State's unilateral imposition of a penalty upon a defendant who had chosen to exercise a legal right to attack his original conviction—a situation "very different from the give-and-take negotiation common in plea bargaining between the prosecution and the defense, which arguably possess relatively equal bargaining power." The Court has emphasized that the due process violation in cases such as *Pearce* and *Perry* lay not in the possibility that a defendant might be deterred from the exercise of a legal right, but rather in the danger that the State might be retaliating against the accused for lawfully attacking his conviction.

To punish a person because he has done what the law plainly allows him to do is a due process violation of the most basic sort, and for an agent of the State to pursue a course of action whose objective is to penalize a person's reliance on his legal rights is "patently unconstitutional." But in the "give-and-take" of plea bargaining, there is no such element of punishment or retaliation so long as the accused is free to accept or reject the prosecution's offer.

Plea bargaining flows from "the mutuality of advantage" to defendants and prosecutors, each with his own reasons for wanting to avoid trial. *Brady v. United States*, 397 U.S. 742 (1970).[a] Defendants advised by competent counsel

---

a. Although *Brady* did not involve a plea bargaining situation, the Court analogized the plea involved there to a plea obtained through plea bargaining, and then commented generally on the validity of a plea produced by the "mutuality of advantage" that flows from a negotiated plea: "We decline to hold * * * that a guilty plea is compelled and invalid under the Fifth Amendment whenever motivated by the defendant's desire to accept the certainty or probability of a lesser penalty rather than face a wider range of possibilities extending from acquittal to conviction and a higher penalty authorized by law for the crime charged. * * * [B]oth the state and the defendant often find it advantageous to preclude the possibility of the maximum penalty authorized by law. For a defendant who sees slight possibility of acquittal, the advantages of pleading guilty and limiting the probable penalty are obvious—his exposure is reduced, the correctional processes can begin immediately, and the practical burdens of a trial are eliminated. For the State there are also advantages—the more promptly imposed punishment after an admission of guilty may more effectively attain the objectives of punishment; and with the avoidance of trial, scarce judicial and prosecutorial resources are conserved for those cases in which there is a substantial issue of the defendant's guilt or in which there is substan-

and protected by other procedural safeguards are presumptively capable of intelligent choice in response to prosecutorial persuasion, and unlikely to be driven to false self-condemnation. Indeed, acceptance of the basic legitimacy of plea bargaining necessarily implies rejection of any notion that a guilty plea is involuntary in a constitutional sense simply because it is the end result of the bargaining process. By hypothesis, the plea may have been induced by promises of a recommendation of a lenient sentence or a reduction of charges, and thus by fear of the possibility of a greater penalty upon conviction after a trial.

While confronting a defendant with the risk of more severe punishment clearly may have a "discouraging effect on the defendant's assertion of his trial rights, the imposition of these difficult choices [is] an inevitable"—and permissible—"attribute of any legitimate system which tolerates and encourages the negotiation of pleas." It follows that, by tolerating and encouraging the negotiation of pleas, this Court has necessarily accepted as constitutionally legitimate the simple reality that the prosecutor's interest at the bargaining table is to persuade the defendant to forego his right to plead not guilty.

It is not disputed here that Hayes was properly chargeable under the recidivist statute, since he had in fact been convicted of two previous felonies. In our system, so long as the prosecutor has probable cause to believe that the accused committed an offense defined by statute, the decision whether or not to prosecute, and what charge to file or bring before a grand jury, generally rests entirely in his discretion.[8] Within the limits set by the legislature's constitutionally valid definition of chargeable offenses, "the conscious exercise of some selectivity in enforcement is not in itself a federal constitutional violation" so long as "the selection was [not] deliberately based upon an unjustifiable standard such as race, religion, or other arbitrary classification." To hold that the prosecutor's desire to induce a guilty plea is an "unjustifiable standard," which, like race or religion, may play no part in his charging decision, would contradict the very premises that underlie the concept of plea bargaining itself. Moreover, a rigid constitutional rule that would prohibit a prosecutor from acting forthrightly in his dealings with the defense could only invite unhealthy subterfuge that would drive the practice of plea bargaining back into the shadows from which it has so recently emerged.

There is no doubt that the breadth of discretion that our country's legal system vests in prosecuting attorneys carries with it the potential for both individual and institutional abuse. And broad though that discretion may be, there are undoubtedly constitutional limits upon its exercise. We hold only that the course of conduct engaged in by the prosecutor in this case, which no more than openly presented the defendant with the unpleasant alternatives of foregoing trial or facing charges on which he was plainly subject to prosecution, did not violate the Due Process Clause of the Fourteenth Amendment.

Accordingly, the judgment of the Court of Appeals is reversed.

tial doubt that the State can sustain its burden of proof. It is this mutuality of advantage which perhaps explains the fact that at present well over three-fourths of the criminal convictions in this country rest on pleas of guilty, a great many of them no doubt motivated at least in part by the hope or assurance of a lesser penalty than might be imposed if there were a guilty verdict after a trial to judge or jury."

8. This case does not involve the constitutional implications of a prosecutor's offer during plea bargaining of adverse or lenient treatment for some person *other* than the accused, which might pose a greater danger of inducing a false guilty plea by skewing the assessment of the risks a defendant must consider.

JUSTICE BLACKMUN, with whom JUSTICE BRENNAN and JUSTICE MARSHALL, join dissenting.

I feel that the Court, although purporting to rule narrowly (that is, on "the course of conduct engaged in by the prosecutor in this case"), is departing from, or at least restricting, the principles established in *North Carolina v. Pearce,* and in *Blackledge v. Perry.*   * * *

In *Pearce,* as indeed the Court notes, it was held that "vindictiveness against a defendant for having successfully attacked his first conviction must play no part in the sentence he receives after a new trial."   * * *

Then later, in *Perry,* the Court applied the same principle to prosecutorial conduct where there was a "realistic likelihood of 'vindictiveness.'"   * * *

The Court now says, however, that this concern with vindictiveness is of no import in the present case, despite the difference between five years in prison and a life sentence, because we are here concerned with plea bargaining where there is give-and-take negotiation, and where, it is said, "there is no such element of punishment or retaliation so long as the accused is free to accept or reject the prosecution's offer." Yet in this case vindictiveness is present to the same extent as it was thought to be in *Pearce* and in *Perry:* the prosecutor here admitted that the sole reason for the new indictment was to discourage the respondent from exercising his right to a trial. Even had such an admission not been made, when plea negotiations, conducted in the face of the less serious charge under the first indictment, fail, charging by a second indictment a more serious crime for the same conduct creates "a strong inference" of vindictiveness. As then Judge McCree aptly observed, in writing for a unanimous panel of the Sixth Circuit, the prosecutor initially "makes a discretionary determination that the interests of the state are served by not seeking more serious charges." I therefore do not understand why, as in *Pearce,* due process does not require that the prosecution justify its action on some basis other than discouraging respondent from the exercise of his right to a trial.

Prosecutorial vindictiveness, it seems to me, in the present narrow context, is the fact against which the Due Process Clause ought to protect. I perceive little difference between vindictiveness after what the Court describes as the exercise of a "legal right to attack his original conviction," and vindictiveness in the "give-and-take negotiation common in plea bargaining." Prosecutorial vindictiveness in any context is still prosecutorial vindictiveness. The Due Process Clause should protect an accused against it, however it asserts itself. The Court of Appeals rightly so held, and I would affirm the judgment.

It might be argued that it really makes little difference how this case, now that it is here, is decided. The Court's holding gives plea bargaining full sway despite vindictiveness. A contrary result, however, merely would prompt the aggressive prosecutor to bring the greater charge initially in every case, and only thereafter to bargain. The consequences to the accused would still be adverse, for then he would bargain against a greater charge, face the likelihood of increased bail, and run the risk that the court would be less inclined to accept a bargain plea. Nonetheless, it is far preferable to hold the prosecution to the charge it was originally content to bring and to justify in the eyes of its public.[2]

2. That prosecutors, without saying so, may sometimes bring charges more serious than they think appropriate for the ultimate disposition of a case, in order to gain bargaining leverage with a defendant, does not add support to today's decision, for this Court, in its approval of the advantages to be gained from plea negotiations, has never openly sanctioned such deliberate overcharging or taken such a cynical view of the bargaining process. Normally, of course, it is impossible to show that this is what the prosecutor is doing, and

JUSTICE POWELL, dissenting.

Although I agree with much of the Court's opinion, I am not satisfied that the result in this case is just or that the conduct of the plea bargaining met the requirements of due process. * * *

The prosecutor's initial assessment of respondent's case led him to forego an indictment under the habitual criminal statute. The circumstances of respondent's prior convictions are relevant to this assessment and to my view of the case. Respondent was 17 years old when he committed his first offense. He was charged with rape but pled guilty to the lesser included offense of "detaining a female." One of the other participants in the incident was sentenced to life imprisonment. Respondent was sent not to prison but to a reformatory where he served five years. Respondent's second offense was robbery. This time he was found guilty by a jury and was sentenced to five years in prison, but he was placed on probation and served no time. Although respondent's prior convictions brought him within the terms of the Habitual Criminal Act, the offenses themselves did not result in imprisonment; yet the addition of a conviction on a charge involving $88.30 subjected respondent to a mandatory sentence of imprisonment for life. Persons convicted of rape and murder often are not punished so severely. * * *

It seems to me that the question to be asked under the circumstances is whether the prosecutor reasonably might have charged respondent under the Habitual Criminal Act in the first place. The deference that courts properly accord the exercise of a prosecutor's discretion perhaps would foreclose judicial criticism if the prosecutor originally had sought an indictment under that act, as unreasonable as it would have seemed.[2] But here the prosecutor evidently made a reasonable, responsible judgment not to subject an individual to a mandatory life

the courts necessarily have deferred to the prosecutor's exercise of discretion in initial charging decisions.

Even if overcharging is to be sanctioned, there are strong reasons of fairness why the charges should be presented at the beginning of the bargaining process, rather than as a filliped threat at the end. First, it means that a prosecutor is required to reach a charging decision without any knowledge of the particular defendant's willingness to plead guilty; hence the defendant who truly believes himself to be innocent, and wishes for that reason to go to trial, is not likely to be subject to quite such a devastating gamble since the prosecutor has fixed the incentives for the average case.

Second, it is healthful to keep charging practices visible to the general public, so that political bodies can judge whether the policy being followed is a fair one. Visibility is enhanced if the prosecutor is required to lay his cards on the table with an indictment of public record at the beginning of the bargaining process, rather than making use of unrecorded verbal warnings of more serious indictments yet to come.

Finally, I would question whether it is fair to pressure defendants to plead guilty by threat of reindictment on an enhanced charge for the same conduct when the defendant has no way of knowing whether the prosecutor would indeed be entitled to bring him to trial on the enhanced charge. Here, though there is no

dispute that respondent met the then current definition of a habitual offender under Kentucky law, it is conceivable that a properly instructed Kentucky grand jury, in response to the same considerations that ultimately moved the Kentucky Legislature to amend the habitual offender statute, would have refused to subject respondent to such an onerous penalty for his forgery charge. There is no indication in the record that, once the new indictment was obtained, respondent was given another chance to plead guilty to the forged check charge in exchange for a five year sentence.

2. The majority suggests that this case cannot be distinguished from the case where the prosecutor initially obtains an indictment under an enhancement statute and later agrees to drop the enhancement charge in exchange for a guilty plea. I would agree that these two situations would be alike *only if* it were assumed that the hypothetical prosecutor's decision to charge under the enhancement statute was occasioned not by consideration of the public interest but by a strategy to discourage the defendant from exercising his constitutional rights. In theory, I would condemn both practices. In practice, the hypothetical situation is largely unreviewable. The majority's view confuses the propriety of a particular exercise of prosecutorial discretion with its unreviewability. In the instant case, however, we have no problem of proof.

sentence when his only new offense had societal implications as limited as those accompanying the uttering of a single $88 forged check and when the circumstances of his prior convictions confirmed the inappropriateness of applying the habitual criminal statute. I think it may be inferred that the prosecutor himself deemed it unreasonable and not in the public interest to put this defendant in jeopardy of a sentence of life imprisonment.

There may be situations in which a prosecutor would be fully justified in seeking a fresh indictment for a more serious offense. The most plausible justification might be that it would have been reasonable and in the public interest initially to have charged the defendant with the greater offense. In most cases a court could not know why the harsher indictment was sought, and an inquiry into the prosecutor's motive would neither be indicated nor likely to be fruitful. In those cases, I would agree with the majority that the situation would not differ materially from one in which the higher charge was brought at the outset.

But this is not such a case. Here, any inquiry into the prosecutor's purpose is made unnecessary by his candid acknowledgement that he threatened to procure and in fact procured the habitual criminal indictment because of respondent's insistence on exercising his constitutional rights. [I]n *Brady v. United States,* we drew a distinction between the situation there approved and the "situation where the prosecutor or judge, or both, deliberately employ their charging and sentencing powers to induce a particular defendant to tender a plea of guilty."

The plea-bargaining process, as recognized by this Court, is essential to the functioning of the criminal-justice system. It normally affords genuine benefits to defendants as well as to society. And if the system is to work effectively, prosecutors must be accorded the widest discretion, within constitutional limits, in conducting bargaining. This is especially true when a defendant is represented by counsel and presumably is fully advised of his rights. Only in the most exceptional case should a court conclude that the scales of the bargaining are so unevenly balanced as to arouse suspicion. In this case, the prosecutor's actions denied respondent due process because their admitted purpose was to discourage and then to penalize with unique severity his exercise of constitutional rights. Implementation of a strategy calculated solely to deter the exercise of constitutional rights is not a constitutionally permissible exercise of discretion. I would affirm the opinion of the Court of Appeals on the facts of this case.

SANTOBELLO v. NEW YORK
404 U.S. 257, 92 S.Ct. 495, 30 L.Ed.2d 427 (1971).

CHIEF JUSTICE BURGER delivered the opinion of the Court.

[After negotiations with the prosecutor, petitioner withdrew his previous not-guilty plea to two felony counts and pleaded guilty to a lesser-included offense, the prosecutor having agreed to make no recommendation as to sentence. At petitioner's appearance for sentencing many months later a new prosecutor recommended the maximum sentence, which the judge (who stated that he was uninfluenced by that recommendation) imposed. Petitioner attempted unsuccessfully to withdraw his guilty plea, and his conviction was affirmed on appeal.]

* * * The disposition of criminal charges by agreement between the prosecutor and the accused, sometimes loosely called "plea bargaining," is an essential component of the administration of justice. Properly administered, it is to be encouraged. If every criminal charge were subjected to a full-scale trial, the

States and the Federal Government would need to multiply by many times the number of judges and court facilities.

Disposition of charges after plea discussions is not only an essential part of the process but a highly desirable part for many reasons. It leads to prompt and largely final disposition of most criminal cases; it avoids much of the corrosive impact of enforced idleness during pretrial confinement for those who are denied release pending trial; it protects the public from those accused persons who are prone to continue criminal conduct even while on pretrial release; and, by shortening the time between charge and disposition, it enhances whatever may be the rehabilitative prospects of the guilty when they are ultimately imprisoned. * * *

This phase of the process of criminal justice, and the adjudicative element inherent in accepting a plea of guilty, must be attended by safeguards to insure the defendant what is reasonably due in the circumstances. Those circumstances will vary, but a constant factor is that when a plea rests in any significant degree on a promise or agreement of the prosecutor, so that it can be said to be part of the inducement or consideration, such promise must be fulfilled. * * *

We need not reach the question whether the sentencing judge would or would not have been influenced had he known all the details of the negotiations for the plea. He stated that the prosecutor's recommendation did not influence him and we have no reason to doubt that. Nevertheless, we conclude that the interests of justice and appropriate recognition of the duties of the prosecution in relation to promises made in the negotiation of pleas of guilty will be best served by remanding the case to the state courts for further consideration. The ultimate relief to which petitioner is entitled we leave to the discretion of the state court, which is in a better position to decide whether the circumstances of this case require only that there be specific performance of the agreement on the plea, in which case petitioner should be resentenced by a different judge, or whether, in the view of the state court, the circumstances require granting the relief sought by petitioner, i.e., the opportunity to withdraw his plea of guilty.[2] * * *

JUSTICE DOUGLAS, concurring. * * *

I join the opinion of the Court and favor a constitutional rule for this as well as for other pending or oncoming cases. Where the "plea bargain" is not kept by the prosecutor, the sentence must be vacated and the state court will decide in light of the circumstances of each case whether due process requires (a) that there be specific performance of the plea bargain or (b) that the defendant be given the option to go to trial on the original charges. One alternative may do justice in one case, and the other in a different case. In choosing a remedy, however, a court ought to accord a defendant's preference considerable, if not controlling, weight inasmuch as the fundamental rights flouted by a prosecutor's breach of a plea bargain are those of the defendant, not of the State.

JUSTICE MARSHALL, with whom JUSTICE BRENNAN and JUSTICE STEWART join, concurring in part and dissenting in part.

* * * When a prosecutor breaks the bargain, he undercuts the basis for the waiver of constitutional rights implicit in the plea. This, it seems to me, provides the defendant ample justification for rescinding the plea. Where a promise is "unfulfilled," *Brady v. United States* specifically denies that the plea "must stand." Of course, where the prosecutor has broken the plea agreement, it may be appropriate to permit the defendant to enforce the plea bargain. But that is

---

2. If the state court decides to allow withdrawal of the plea, the petitioner will, of course, plead anew to the original charge on two felony counts.

not the remedy sought here.* Rather, it seems to me that a breach of the plea bargain provides ample reason to permit the plea to be vacated.

It is worth noting that in the ordinary case where a motion to vacate is made prior to sentencing, the government has taken no action in reliance on the previously entered guilty plea and would suffer no harm from the plea's withdrawal. More pointedly, here the State claims no such harm beyond disappointed expectations about the plea itself. At least where the government itself has broken the plea bargain, this disappointment cannot bar petitioner from withdrawing his guilty plea and reclaiming his right to a trial.

I would remand the case with instructions that the plea be vacated and petitioner given an opportunity to replead to the original charges in the indictment.

MABRY v. JOHNSON

467 U.S. 504, 104 S.Ct. 2543, 81 L.Ed.2d 437 (1984).

JUSTICE STEVENS delivered the opinion of the Court.

The question presented is whether a defendant's acceptance of a prosecutor's proposed plea bargain creates a constitutional right to have the bargain specifically enforced.

In the late evening of May 22, 1970, three members of a family returned home to find a burglary in progress. Shots were exchanged resulting in the daughter's death and the wounding of the father and respondent—one of the burglars. Respondent was tried and convicted on three charges: burglary, assault, and murder. The murder conviction was set aside by the Arkansas Supreme Court. Thereafter, plea negotiations ensued.

At the time of the negotiations respondent was serving his concurrent 21– and 12–year sentences on the burglary and assault convictions. On Friday, October 27, 1972, a deputy prosecutor proposed to respondent's attorney that in exchange for a plea of guilty to the charge of accessory after a felony murder, the prosecutor would recommend a sentence of 21 years to be served concurrently with the burglary and assault sentences. On the following day, counsel communicated the offer to respondent who agreed to accept it. On the next Monday the lawyer called the prosecutor "and communicated [respondent's] acceptance of the offer." The prosecutor then told counsel that a mistake had been made and withdrew the offer. He proposed instead that in exchange for a guilty plea he would recommend a sentence of 21 years to be served consecutively to respondent's other sentences.

Respondent rejected the new offer and elected to stand trial. On the second day of trial, the judge declared a mistrial and plea negotiations resumed, ultimately resulting in respondent's acceptance of the prosecutor's second offer. In accordance with the plea bargain, the state trial judge imposed a 21–year sentence to be served consecutively to the previous sentences.

* * * The [federal] Court of Appeals reversed [on habeas review]. The majority concluded that "fairness" precluded the prosecution's withdrawal of a

---

* Justice Douglas, although joining the Court's opinion (apparently because he thinks the remedy should be chosen by the state court), concludes that the state court "ought to accord a defendant's preference considerable, if not controlling, weight." Thus, a majority of the Court appears to believe that in cases like these, when the defendant seeks to vacate the plea, that relief should generally be granted. [Ed. note: there were two vacancies on the Court at the time.]

plea proposal once accepted by respondent. We now reverse [that judgment]. * * *

It is well-settled that a voluntary and intelligent plea of guilty made by an accused person, who has been advised by competent counsel, may not be collaterally attacked. It is also well-settled that plea agreements are consistent with the requirements of voluntariness and intelligence—because each side may obtain advantages when a guilty plea is exchanged for sentencing concessions, the agreement is no less voluntary than any other bargained-for exchange. It is only when the consensual character of the plea is called into question that the validity of a guilty plea may be impaired. In *Brady v. United States,* we stated the applicable standard:

> "[A] plea of guilty entered by one fully aware of the direct consequences, including the actual value of any commitments made to him by the court, prosecutor, or his own counsel, must stand unless induced by threats (or promises to discontinue improper harassment), misrepresentation (including unfulfilled or unfulfillable promises), or perhaps by promises that are by their nature improper as having no proper relationship to the prosecutor's business (e.g., bribes)."

Thus, only when it develops that the defendant was not fairly apprised of its consequences can his plea be challenged under the Due Process Clause. *Santobello v. New York* illustrates the point.

Santobello demonstrates why respondent may not successfully attack his plea of guilty. Respondent's plea was in no sense induced by the prosecutor's withdrawn offer; unlike Santobello, who pleaded guilty thinking he had bargained for a specific prosecutorial sentencing recommendation which was not ultimately made, at the time respondent pleaded guilty he knew the prosecution would recommend a 21–year consecutive sentence. Respondent * * * pleaded guilty with the advice of competent counsel and with full awareness of the consequences—he knew that the prosecutor would recommend and that the judge could impose the sentence now under attack. Respondent's plea was thus in no sense the product of governmental deception; it rested on no "unfulfilled promise" and fully satisfied the test for voluntariness and intelligence.

Thus, because it did not impair the voluntariness or intelligence of his guilty plea, respondent's inability to enforce the prosecutor's offer is without constitutional significance.[11] Neither is the question whether the prosecutor was negligent or otherwise culpable in first making and then withdrawing his offer relevant. The Due Process Clause is not a code of ethics for prosecutors; its concern is with the manner in which persons are deprived of their liberty. Here respondent was not deprived of his liberty in any fundamentally unfair way. Respondent was fully aware of the likely consequences when he pleaded guilty; it is not unfair to expect him to live with those consequences now. * * *

11. Indeed, even if respondent's plea were invalid, *Santobello* expressly declined to hold that the Constitution compels specific performance of a broken prosecutorial promise as the remedy for such a plea; the Court made it clear that permitting Santobello to replead was within the range of constitutionally appropriate remedies. It follows that respondent's constitutional rights could not have been violated. Because he pleaded after the prosecution had breached its "promise" to him; he was in no worse position than Santobello would have been had he been permitted to replead.

UNITED STATES v. BENCHIMOL

471 U.S. 453, 105 S.Ct. 2103, 85 L.Ed.2d 462 (1985).

PER CURIAM.

[Respondent pleaded guilty to an information charging him with one count of mail fraud pursuant to a plea bargain whereby the Government agreed to recommend probation on condition that restitution be made. The District Court disregarded the recommendation and sentenced respondent to six years of treatment and supervision under the Youth Corrections Act. He filed a motion to withdraw his guilty plea or, in the alternative, to have his sentence vacated and be resentenced to the time already served, claiming that the Government had failed to comply with its part of the plea bargain.]

The District Court that had received the guilty plea also heard respondent's application for collateral relief, and denied it. The Court of Appeals by a divided vote reversed that judgment. * * * The Court of Appeals had this view of the facts:

> "Benchimol agreed to plead guilty. The government concedes that in exchange for the guilty plea it promised to recommend probation with restitution. However, at the sentencing hearing, the presentence report incorrectly stated that the government would stand silent. Benchimol's counsel informed the court that the government instead recommended probation with restitution. The Assistant United States Attorney then stated: 'That is an accurate representation.' "

The Court of Appeals concluded that the Government had breached its plea bargain because, although the Assistant United States Attorney concurred with defense counsel's statement that the Government recommended probation with restitution, it "made no effort to explain its reasons for agreeing to recommend a lenient sentence but rather left an impression with the court of less-than-enthusiastic support for leniency."

We think this holding misconceives the effect of the relevant rules and of the applicable case law. Federal Rule of Criminal Procedure 11(e) provides an elaborate formula for the negotiation of plea bargains, which allows the attorney for the Government to agree to move for dismissal of other charges and to agree that a specific sentence is the appropriate disposition of the case. It also authorizes the Government attorney to make a recommendation for a particular sentence, or agree not to oppose the defendant's request for such a sentence, with the understanding that such recommendation or request shall not be binding upon the court.

It may well be that the Government in a particular case might commit itself to "enthusiastically" make a particular recommendation to the Court, and it may be that the Government in a particular case might agree to explain to the Court the reasons for the Government's making a particular recommendation. But respondent does not contend, nor did the Court of Appeals find, that the Government had in fact undertaken to do either of these things here. The Court of Appeals simply held that as a matter of law such an undertaking was to be implied from the Government's agreement to recommend a particular sentence. But our view of Rule 11(e) is that it speaks in terms of what the parties in fact agree to, and does not suggest that such implied-in-law terms as were read into this agreement by the Court of Appeals have any place under the Rule.

The Court of Appeals relied on [certain] cases for the conclusion it reached with respect to the requirement of "enthusiasm," but it appears to us that in each of these cases the Government attorney appearing personally in court at the time of the plea bargain expressed personal reservations about the agreement to which the Government had committed itself. This is quite a different proposition than an appellate determination from a transcript of the record made many years earlier that the Government attorney had "left an impression with the court of less-than-enthusiastic support for leniency." When the Government agrees pursuant to Rule 11(e) to make a recommendation with respect to sentence, it must carry out its part of the bargain by making the promised recommendation; but even if Rule 11(e) allows bargaining about degrees of enthusiasm, there appears to have been none here.

Rule 11(e) may well contemplate agreement by the Government in a particular case to state to the court its reasons for making the recommendation which it agrees to make. The Government suggests that spreading on the record its reasons for agreement to a plea bargain in a particular case—for example, that it did not wish to devote scarce resources to a trial of this particular defendant, or that it wished to avoid calling the victim as a witness—would frequently harm, rather than help, the defendant's quest for leniency. These may well be reasons why the defendant would not wish to exact such a commitment from the Government, but for purposes of this case it is enough that no such agreement was made in fact. Since Rule 11(e) speaks generally of the plea bargains that the parties make, it was error for the Court of Appeals to imply as a matter of law a term which the parties themselves did not agree upon.

For these reasons, we conclude that there was simply no default on the part of the Government in this case * * *.

Reversed.

JUSTICE STEVENS, concurring in the judgment.

* * * If the Government erred in failing to recommend affirmatively the proper sentence, the time to object was at the sentencing hearing or on direct appeal. * * *

JUSTICE BRENNAN, with whom JUSTICE MARSHALL joins, dissenting.

The Court today continues its unsettling practice of summarily reversing decisions rendered in favor of criminal defendants, based not on broad principle but on idiosyncratic facts and without full briefing or oral argument. * * * Because I find this one-sided practice of summary error correction inappropriate, I would vote merely to deny this petition for certiorari. Accordingly, I respectfully dissent.

SECTION 2. REQUISITES OF A VALID PLEA

At an earlier time, when the validity of plea bargaining was in doubt, the general practice was not to reveal in court at the time the guilty plea was received that a bargain had been struck. This is no longer the case. Moreover, there has been increased acceptance of the notion that the plea receiving process should be more cautious in other respects as well, so that today in most jurisdictions a court rule or statute imposes several responsibilities upon the judge in connection with receipt of defendant's guilty plea. Typical is Federal Rule of Criminal Procedure 11, which requires the judge to (i) inform the defendant and determine that he understands the nature of the charge and the possible penalty and various rights he is surrendering by pleading guilty; (ii) determine that the plea is voluntary; (iii) require disclosure of any plea agreement and accept or reject that agreement; and (iv) make sufficient inquiry to ensure there is a factual basis for the plea.

As the cases in this section illustrate, constitutional considerations lie close to the surface of such provisions. *Boykin v. Alabama* deals with the waiver-of-rights aspect of a guilty plea, *Henderson v. Morgan* with the necessity that defendant understand the charge against him, and *North Carolina v. Alford* with the special circumstances in which a factual basis for the plea is constitutionally mandated. The final case, *Blackledge v. Allison,* considers the important question of whether full compliance with procedures such as those in rule 11 forecloses subsequent efforts by a defendant to have his guilty plea invalidated.

BOYKIN v. ALABAMA

395 U.S. 238, 89 S.Ct. 1709, 23 L.Ed.2d 274 (1969).

JUSTICE DOUGLAS delivered the opinion of the Court.

In the spring of 1966, within the period of a fortnight, a series of armed robberies occurred in Mobile, Alabama. The victims, in each case, were local shopkeepers open at night who were forced by a gunman to hand over money. While robbing one grocery store, the assailant fired his gun once, sending a bullet through a door into the ceiling. A few days earlier in a drugstore, the robber had allowed his gun to discharge in such a way that the bullet, on ricochet from the floor, struck a customer in the leg. Shortly thereafter, a local grand jury returned five indictments against petitioner, a 27–year–old Negro, for common-law robbery—an offense punishable in Alabama by death.

Before the matter came to trial, the court determined that petitioner was indigent and appointed counsel to represent him. Three days later, at his arraignment, petitioner pleaded guilty to all five indictments. So far as the record shows, the judge asked no questions of petitioner concerning his plea, and petitioner did not address the court.

Trial strategy may of course make a plea of guilty seem the desirable course. But the record is wholly silent on that point and throws no light on it.

Alabama provides that when a defendant pleads guilty, "the court must cause the punishment to be determined by a jury" (except where it is required to be fixed by the court) and may "cause witnesses to be examined, to ascertain the character of the offense." In the present case a trial of that dimension was held, the prosecution presenting its case largely through eyewitness testimony. Although counsel for petitioner engaged in cursory cross-examination, petitioner neither testified himself nor presented testimony concerning his character and background. There was nothing to indicate that he had a prior criminal record.

In instructing the jury, the judge stressed that petitioner had pleaded guilty in five cases of robbery, defined as "the felonious taking of money * * * from another against his will * * * by violence or by putting him in fear * * * [carrying] from ten years minimum in the penitentiary to the supreme penalty of death by electrocution." The jury, upon deliberation, found petitioner guilty and sentenced him severally to die on each of the five indictments. * * *

A plea of guilty is more than a confession which admits that the accused did various acts; it is itself a conviction; nothing remains but to give judgment and determine punishment. Admissibility of a confession must be based on a "reliable determination on the voluntariness issue which satisfies the constitutional rights of the defendant." The requirement that the prosecution spread on the record the prerequisites of a valid waiver is no constitutional innovation. In [dealing with a problem of waiver of the right to counsel we] held: "Presuming waiver from a silent record is impermissible. The record must show, or there must be an allegation and evidence which show, that an accused was offered counsel but intelligently and understandingly rejected the offer. Anything less is not waiver."

We think that the same standard must be applied to determining whether a guilty plea is voluntarily made. For, as we have said, a plea of guilty is more than an admission of conduct; it is a conviction. Ignorance, incomprehension, coercion, terror, inducements, subtle or blatant threats might be a perfect cover-up of unconstitutionality. The question of an effective waiver of a federal constitutional right in a proceeding is of course governed by federal standards.

Several federal constitutional rights are involved in a waiver that takes place when a plea of guilty is entered in a state criminal trial. First, is the privilege against compulsory self-incrimination guaranteed by the Fifth Amendment and applicable to the States by reason of the Fourteenth.[a] Second, is the right to trial by jury. Third, is the right to confront one's accusers. We cannot presume a waiver of these three important federal rights from a silent record.

What is at stake for an accused facing death or imprisonment demands the utmost solicitude of which courts are capable in canvassing the matter with the accused to make sure he has a full understanding of what the plea connotes and of its consequence. When the judge discharges that function, he leaves a record adequate for any review that may be later sought and forestalls the spin-off of collateral proceedings that seek to probe murky memories.

The three dissenting justices in the Alabama Supreme Court stated the law accurately when they concluded that there was reversible error "because the record does not disclose that the defendant voluntarily and understandingly entered his pleas of guilty."[b]

Reversed.

JUSTICE HARLAN, whom JUSTICE BLACK joins, dissenting. * * *

[T]he Court's disposition is plainly out of keeping with * * * *Halliday v. United States*, 394 U.S. 831 (1969), [where the Court] affirmed the conviction even though Halliday's guilty plea was accepted in 1954 without any explicit inquiry into whether it was knowingly and understandingly made * * * In justification, the Court noted that two lower courts had found in collateral proceedings that the plea was voluntary. * * *

It seems elementary that the Fifth Amendment due process to which petitioner Halliday was entitled must be at least as demanding as the Fourteenth Amendment process due petitioner Boykin. Yet petitioner Halliday's federal conviction has been affirmed as "constitutionally valid," despite the omission of any judicial inquiry of record at the time of his plea, because he initiated collateral proceedings which revealed that the plea was actually voluntary. Petitioner Boykin, on the other hand, today has his Alabama conviction reversed because of exactly the same omission, even though he too "may * * * resort to appropriate

---

a. As the Court later explained, the guilty plea is actually a waiver of a trial at which the privilege against self-incrimination would apply, and thus a guilty plea defendant may remain silent at the time of sentencing without an adverse inference being drawn from such silence. See *Mitchell v. United States*, Ch. 20.

b. Inquiry into a criminal defendant's competency is required whenever the trial court has a "reasonable doubt" on that matter. *Pate v. Robinson*, 383 U.S. 375 (1966). For a defendant standing trial, the test is whether "he has sufficient present ability to consult with his lawyer with a reasonable degree of rational understanding" and "a rational as

well as factual understanding of the proceedings against him." *Dusky v. United States*, 362 U.S. 402 (1960). In *Godinez v. Moran*, 509 U.S. 389 (1993), the Supreme Court rejected a lower court's holding that "a higher level of mental functioning," i.e., "the capacity for 'reasoned choice' among the alternatives available to him," is required with respect to a defendant pleading guilty. The Court explained that "while the decision to plead guilty is undeniably a profound one, it is no more complicated than the sum total of decisions that a defendant may be called upon to make during the course of a trial." See also fn. b to *Faretta* [Ch. 17].

post-conviction remedies to attack his plea's voluntariness" and thus "is not without a remedy to correct constitutional defects in his conviction." In short, I find it utterly impossible to square today's holding with what the Court has so recently done. * * *

HENDERSON v. MORGAN

426 U.S. 637, 96 S.Ct. 2253, 49 L.Ed.2d 108 (1976).

[Respondent was indicted for first-degree murder, but by agreement with the prosecution and on counsel's advice respondent pleaded guilty to second-degree murder and was sentenced. Subsequently, after exhausting his state remedies in an unsuccessful attempt to have his conviction vacated on the ground that his guilty plea was involuntary, respondent filed a habeas corpus petition in Federal District Court, alleging that his guilty plea was involuntary because, *inter alia,* he was not aware that intent to cause death was an element of second-degree murder. The District Court ultimately heard the testimony of several witnesses, including respondent and his defense counsel in the original prosecution; and the transcript of the relevant state-court proceedings and certain psychological evaluations of respondent, who was substantially below average intelligence, were made part of the record. On the basis of the evidence thus developed the District Court found that respondent had not been advised by counsel or the state court that an intent to cause death was an essential element of second-degree murder, and, based on this finding, held that the guilty plea was involuntary and had to be set aside. The Court of Appeals affirmed.]

JUSTICE STEVENS delivered the opinion of the Court. * * *

Petitioner contends that the District Court applied an unrealistically rigid rule of law. Instead of testing the voluntariness of a plea by determining whether a ritualistic litany of the formal legal elements of an offense was read to the defendant, petitioner argues that the court should examine the totality of the circumstances and determine whether the substance of the charge, as opposed to its technical elements, was conveyed to the accused. We do not disagree with the thrust of petitioner's argument, but we are persuaded that even under the test which he espouses, this judgment finding respondent guilty of second-degree murder was defective.

We assume, as petitioner argues, that the prosecutor had overwhelming evidence of guilt available. We also accept petitioner's characterization of the competence of respondent's counsel and of the wisdom of their advice to plead guilty to a charge of second-degree murder. Nevertheless, such a plea cannot support a judgment of guilt unless it was voluntary in a constitutional sense.[13] And clearly the plea could not be voluntary in the sense that it constituted an intelligent admission that he committed the offense unless the defendant received "real notice of the true nature of the charge against him, the first and most universally recognized requirement of due process."

The charge of second-degree murder was never formally made. Had it been made, it necessarily would have included a charge that respondent's assault was "committed with a design to effect the death of the person killed." That element of the offense might have been proved by the objective evidence even if respon-

13. A plea may be involuntary either because the accused does not understand the nature of the constitutional protections that he is waiving, or because he has such an incomplete understanding of the charge that his plea cannot stand as an intelligent admission of guilt. Without adequate notice of the nature of the charge against him, or proof that he in fact understood the charge, the plea cannot be voluntary in this latter sense.

dent's actual state of mind was consistent with innocence or manslaughter. But even if such a design to effect death would almost inevitably have been inferred from evidence that respondent repeatedly stabbed Mrs. Francisco, it is nevertheless also true that a jury would not have been required to draw that inference. The jury would have been entitled to accept defense counsel's appraisal of the incident as involving only manslaughter in the first degree. Therefore, an admission by respondent that he killed Mrs. Francisco does not necessarily also admit that he was guilty of second-degree murder.

There is nothing in this record that can serve as a substitute for either a finding after trial, or a voluntary admission, that respondent had the requisite intent. Defense counsel did not purport to stipulate to that fact; they did not explain to him that his plea would be an admission of that fact; and he made no factual statement or admission necessarily implying that he had such intent. In these circumstances it is impossible to conclude that his plea to the unexplained charge of second-degree murder was voluntary.

Petitioner argues that affirmance of the Court of Appeals will invite countless collateral attacks on judgments entered on pleas of guilty, since frequently the record will not contain a complete enumeration of the elements of the offense to which an accused person pleads guilty.[18] We think petitioner's fears are exaggerated.

Normally the record contains either an explanation of the charge by the trial judge, or at least a representation by defense counsel that the nature of the offense has been explained to the accused. Moreover, even without such an express representation, it may be appropriate to presume that in most cases defense counsel routinely explain the nature of the offense in sufficient detail to give the accused notice of what he is being asked to admit. This case is unique because the trial judge found as a fact that the element of intent was not explained to respondent. Moreover, respondent's unusually low mental capacity provides a reasonable explanation for counsel's oversight; it also forecloses the conclusion that the error was harmless beyond a reasonable doubt, for it lends at least a modicum of credibility to defense counsel's appraisal of the homicide as a manslaughter rather than a murder.

Since respondent did not receive adequate notice of the offense to which he pleaded guilty, his plea was involuntary and the judgment of conviction was entered without due process of law.

Affirmed.

JUSTICE WHITE, with whom JUSTICE STEWART, JUSTICE BLACKMUN, and JUSTICE POWELL join, concurring. * * *

The problem in this case is that the defendant's guilt has been established neither by a finding of guilt beyond a reasonable doubt after trial nor by the defendant's own admission that he is in fact guilty. The defendant did not expressly admit that he intended the victim's death (such intent being an element of the crime for which he stands convicted); and his plea of guilty cannot be construed as an implied admission that he intended her death because the District Court has found that he was not told and did not know that intent to kill was an element of the offense with which he was charged.[2] * * *

18. There is no need in this case to decide whether notice of the true nature, or substance, of a charge always requires a description of every element of the offense; we assume it does not. Nevertheless, intent is such a critical element of the offense of second-degree murder that notice of that element is required.

2. This case is unusual in that the offense to which the defendant pleaded was not charged in the indictment. The indictment

The dissent concedes that the conviction in this case was entered in violation of the United States Constitution. The dissent argues, however, that to set this defendant's conviction aside is to apply a new constitutional rule retroactively. The argument was not made by the petitioner in this case and is, in any event, untenable. * * * Either a new constitutional rule is being established in *this* case—in which event we will have to address at some future time the question whether this rule is retroactive—or, as I believe to be true, this case rests on the long-accepted principle that a guilty plea must provide a trustworthy basis for believing that the defendant is in fact guilty. If so, then the principle will and should govern all similar cases presented to us in the future. In any event, the judgment of the court below should be affirmed, and I join the opinion of the Court.

JUSTICE REHNQUIST, with whom THE CHIEF JUSTICE joins, dissenting.

Since it seems clear * * * that respondent's plea was "voluntarily made," and since it is undisputed that it was made with full understanding of its consequences, the only remaining issue is whether he was "properly advised." This inquiry, in turn, depends upon the sort of advice reasonably competent counsel would have been expected to give him. * * *

Respondent was originally indicted for the crime of first-degree murder, and that indictment charged that in April 1965, he had "willfully, feloniously and of malice aforethought, stabbed and cut Ada Francisco with a dangerous knife * * * and that thereafter * * * the said Ada Francisco died of said wounds and injuries, said killing being inexcusable and unjustifiable." Respondent's attorney at the habeas hearing testified that respondent had stabbed his victim "many times" which suggests that experienced counsel would not consider the "design to effect death" issue to be in serious dispute. * * *

I do not see how this Court, or any court, could conclude on this state of the record that respondent was not "properly advised" at the time he entered his plea of guilty to the charge of second-degree murder.

His attorneys were motivated by the eminently reasonable tactical judgment on their part that he should plead guilty to second-degree murder in order to avoid the possibility of conviction for first-degree murder with its more serious attendant penalties. Since the Court concedes both the competence of respondent's counsel and the wisdom of their advice, that should be the end of the matter.

There are intimations in the Court's opinion that the vice which it finds in the guilty plea is not that respondent was not *informed* of all the elements of the offense, but that instead he did not *admit* to all of those elements. But it is quite clear under our decision in *North Carolina v. Alford* that the latter fact, standing alone, is not sufficient to invalidate a guilty plea. * * *

NORTH CAROLINA v. ALFORD
400 U.S. 25, 91 S.Ct. 160, 27 L.Ed.2d 162 (1970).

JUSTICE WHITE delivered the opinion of the Court.

[Appellee was indicted for the capital crime of first-degree murder. At that time North Carolina law provided for the penalty of life imprisonment when a plea charged first-degree murder. The defendant pleaded guilty to the included offense of second-degree murder, the elements of which were not set forth in any document which had been read to the defendant or to which he had access. In those cases in which the indictment is read to the defendant by the court at arraignment or at the time of his plea, his plea of guilty may well be deemed a factual admission that he did what he is charged with doing so that a judgment of conviction may validly be entered against him.

of guilty was accepted to a first-degree murder charge; for the death penalty following a jury verdict of guilty, unless the jury recommended life imprisonment; and for a penalty of from two to 30 years' imprisonment for second-degree murder. Appellee's attorney, in the face of strong evidence of guilt, recommended a guilty plea, but left the decision to appellee. The prosecutor agreed to accept a plea of guilty to second-degree murder. The trial court heard damaging evidence from certain witnesses before accepting a plea. Appellee pleaded guilty, although disclaiming guilt, because of the threat of the death penalty, and was sentenced to 30 years' imprisonment. The Court of Appeals, on an appeal from a denial of a writ of habeas corpus, found that appellee's guilty plea was involuntary because it was motivated principally by fear of the death penalty.]

We held in *Brady v. United States,* 397 U.S. 742 (1970), that a plea of guilty which would not have been entered except for the defendant's desire to avoid a possible death penalty and to limit the maximum penalty to life imprisonment or a term of years was not for that reason compelled within the meaning of the Fifth Amendment. * * * The standard was and remains whether the plea represents a voluntary and intelligent choice among the alternative courses of action open to the defendant. * * * That he would not have pleaded except for the opportunity to limit the possible penalty does not necessarily demonstrate that the plea of guilty was not the product of a free and rational choice, especially where the defendant was represented by competent counsel whose advice was that the plea would be to the defendant's advantage. The standard fashioned and applied by the Court of Appeals was therefore erroneous and we would, without more, vacate and remand the case for further proceedings with respect to any other claims of Alford which are properly before that court, if it were not for other circumstances appearing in the record which might seem to warrant an affirmance of the Court of Appeals.

As previously recounted after Alford's plea of guilty was offered and the State's case was placed before the judge, Alford denied that he had committed the murder but reaffirmed his desire to plead guilty to avoid a possible death sentence and to limit the penalty to the 30–year maximum provided for second-degree murder. Ordinarily, a judgment of conviction resting on a plea of guilty is justified by the defendant's admission that he committed the crime charged against him and his consent that judgment be entered without a trial of any kind. The plea usually subsumes both elements, and justifiably so, even though there is no separate, express admission by the defendant that he committed the particular acts claimed to constitute the crime charged in the indictment. Here Alford entered his plea but accompanied it with the statement that he had not shot the victim.

If Alford's statements were to be credited as sincere assertions of his innocence, there obviously existed a factual and legal dispute between him and the State. Without more, it might be argued that the conviction entered on his guilty plea was invalid, since his assertion of innocence negatived any admission of guilt, which, as we observed last Term in *Brady,* is normally "[c]entral to the plea and the foundation for entering judgment against the defendant * * *."

In addition to Alford's statement, however, the court had heard an account of the events on the night of the murder, including information from Alford's acquaintances that he had departed from his home with his gun stating his intention to kill and that he had later declared that he had carried out his intention. Nor had Alford wavered in his desire to have trial court determine his guilt without a jury trial. Although denying the charge against him, he neverthe-less preferred the dispute between him and the State to be settled by the judge in the context of a guilty plea proceeding rather than by a formal trial. Thereupon, with the State's telling evidence and Alford's denial before it, the trial court proceeded to convict and sentence Alford for second-degree murder.

State and lower federal courts are divided upon whether a guilty plea can be accepted when it is accompanied by protestations of innocence and hence contains only a waiver of trial but no admission of guilt. Some courts, giving expression to the principle that "[o]ur law only authorizes a conviction where guilt is shown," require that trial judges reject such pleas. But others have concluded that they should not "force any defense on a defendant in a criminal case," particularly when advancement of the defense might "end in disaster * * *." They have argued that, since "guilt, or the degree of guilt, is at times uncertain and elusive," "[a]n accused, though believing in or entertaining doubts respecting his innocence, might reasonably conclude a jury would be convinced of his guilt and that he would fare better in the sentence by pleading guilty * * *."[7]

This Court has not confronted this precise issue, but prior decisions do yield relevant principles. In *Lynch v. Overholser,* 369 U.S. 705 (1962), Lynch, who had been charged in the Municipal Court of the District of Columbia with drawing and negotiating bad checks, a misdemeanor punishable by a maximum of one year in jail, sought to enter a plea of guilty, but the trial judge refused to accept the plea since a psychiatric report in the judge's possession indicated that Lynch had been suffering from "a manic depressive psychosis, at the time of the crime charged," and hence might have been not guilty by reason of insanity. Although at the subsequent trial Lynch did not rely on the insanity defense, he was found not guilty by reason of insanity and committed for an indeterminate period to a mental institution. On habeas corpus, the Court ordered his release, construing the congressional legislation seemingly authorizing the commitment as not reaching a case where the accused preferred a guilty plea to a plea of insanity. The Court expressly refused to rule that Lynch had an absolute right to have his guilty plea accepted, but implied that there would have been no constitutional error had his plea been accepted even though evidence before the judge indicated that there was a valid defense.

The issue in *Hudson v. United States,* 272 U.S. 451 (1926), was whether a federal court has power to impose a prison sentence after accepting a plea of *nolo contendere,* a plea by which a defendant does not expressly admit his guilt, but nonetheless waives his right to a trial and authorizes the court for purposes of the case to treat him as if he were guilty.[8] The Court held that a trial court does have such power, and except for the cases which were rejected in *Hudson,* the federal courts have uniformly followed this rule, even in cases involving moral turpitude. Implicit in the *nolo contendere* cases is a recognition that the Constitution does not bar imposition of a prison sentence upon an accused who is unwilling

---

7. A third approach has been to decline to rule definitively that a trial judge must either accept or reject an otherwise valid plea containing a protestation of innocence, but to leave that decision to his sound discretion.

8. Courts have defined the plea of *nolo contendere* in a variety of different ways, describing it, on the one hand, as "in effect, a plea of guilty," and on the other, as a query directed to the court to determine the defendant's guilt. As a result, it is impossible to state precisely what a defendant does admit when he enters a *nolo* plea in a way that will consistently fit all the cases. * * *

Throughout its history, that is, the plea of *nolo contendere* has been viewed not as an express admission of guilt but as a consent by the defendant that he may be punished as if he were guilty and a prayer for leniency. Fed. Rule Crim.Proc. 11 preserves this distinction in its requirement that a court cannot accept a guilty plea "unless it is satisfied that there is a factual basis for the plea"; there is no similar requirement for pleas of *nolo contendere,* since it was thought desirable to permit defendants to plead *nolo* without making any inquiry into their actual guilt.

expressly to admit his guilt but who, faced with grim alternatives, is willing to waive his trial and accept the sentence.

These cases would be directly in point if Alford had simply insisted on his plea but refused to admit the crime. The fact that his plea was denominated a plea of guilty rather than a plea of *nolo contendere* is of no constitutional significance with respect to the issue now before us, for the Constitution is concerned with the practical consequences, not the formal categorizations, of state law. Thus, while most pleas of guilty consist of both a waiver of trial and an express admission of guilt, the latter element is not a constitutional requisite to the imposition of criminal penalty. An individual accused of crime may voluntarily, knowingly, and understandingly consent to the imposition of a prison sentence even if he is unwilling or unable to admit his participation in the acts constituting the crime.

Nor can we perceive any material difference between a plea that refuses to admit commission of the criminal act and a plea containing a protestation of innocence when, as in the instant case, a defendant intelligently concludes that his interests require entry of a guilty plea and the record before the judge contains strong evidence of actual guilt. Here the State had a strong case of first-degree murder against Alford. Whether he realized or disbelieved his guilt, he insisted on his plea because in his view he had absolutely nothing to gain by a trial and much to gain by pleading. Because of the overwhelming evidence against him, a trial was precisely what neither Alford nor his attorney desired. Confronted with the choice between a trial for first-degree murder, on the one hand, and a plea of guilty to second-degree murder, on the other, Alford quite reasonably chose the latter and thereby limited the maximum penalty to a 30–year term. When his plea is viewed in light of the evidence against him, which substantially negated his claim of innocence and which further provided a means by which the judge could test whether the plea was being intelligently entered, its validity cannot be seriously questioned. In view of the strong factual basis for the plea demonstrated by the State and Alford's clearly expressed desire to enter it despite his professed belief in his innocence, we hold that the trial judge did not commit constitutional error in accepting it.[11] * * *

Justice Black, * * * concurs in the judgment and in substantially all of the opinion in this case.

Justice Brennan, with whom Justice Douglas and Justice Marshall join, dissenting.

* * * [I]t is sufficient in my view to state that the facts set out in the majority opinion demonstrate that Alford was "so gripped by fear of the death penalty" that his decision to plead guilty was not voluntary but was "the product of duress as much so as choice reflecting physical constraint."

BLACKLEDGE v. ALLISON
431 U.S. 63, 97 S.Ct. 1621, 52 L.Ed.2d 136 (1977).

Justice Stewart delivered the opinion of the Court.

[At the arraignment of respondent, who had been indicted in North Carolina for various state criminal offenses, he entered a guilty plea to a single count of

---

11. Our holding does not mean that a trial judge must accept every constitutionally valid guilty plea merely because a defendant wishes so to plead. A criminal defendant does not have an absolute right under the Constitution to have his guilty plea accepted by the court, although the States may by statute or other- wise confer such a right. Likewise, the States may bar their courts from accepting guilty pleas from any defendants who assert their innocence. Cf. Fed.Rule Crim.Proc. 11, which gives a trial judge discretion to "refuse to accept a plea of guilty * * *." We need not now delineate the scope of that discretion.

attempted safe robbery. In response to two of various form questions that under then-applicable procedures were put by the trial judge to those entering guilty pleas, respondent acknowledged that he understood that he could be imprisoned for a minimum of 10 years to a maximum of life and that no one had made promises or threats to influence him to plead guilty. Without further questioning, the judge accepted the plea on an "Adjudication" form, which recited that respondent had pleaded guilty to attempted safe robbery "freely, understandingly and voluntarily," with full awareness of the consequences, and "without undue * * * compulsion * * * duress, [or] promise of leniency." At a sentencing hearing three days later respondent was sentenced to 17–21 years. Respondent sought a writ of habeas corpus in a Federal District Court, claiming that his guilty plea had been induced by the promise of his attorney, who presumably had consulted with the judge and Solicitor, that he would get only a 10–year sentence. He also stated that he was aware that he had been questioned by the judge before sentencing but thought that he was going to get only 10 years and had been instructed to answer the questions so that the court would accept the guilty plea. The District Court granted a motion to dismiss the petition, on the ground that the form conclusively showed that respondent had chosen to plead guilty knowingly, voluntarily, and with full awareness of the consequences. The Court of Appeals reversed, holding that respondent's allegation of a broken promise, as amplified by the explanation that his lawyer instructed him to deny the existence of any promises, was not foreclosed by his responses to the form questions and that he was entitled to an evidentiary hearing, at least in the absence of counter-affidavits conclusively proving the falsity of respondent's allegations.]

Whatever might be the situation in an ideal world, the fact is that the guilty plea and the often concomitant plea bargain are important components of this country's criminal justice system. Properly administered, they can benefit all concerned. The defendant avoids extended pretrial incarceration and the anxieties and uncertainties of a trial; he gains a speedy disposition of his case, the chance to acknowledge his guilt, and a prompt start in realizing whatever potential there may be for rehabilitation. Judges and prosecutors conserve vital and scarce resources. The public is protected from the risks posed by those charged with criminal offenses who are at large on bail while awaiting completion of criminal proceedings.

These advantages can be secured, however, only if dispositions by guilty plea are accorded a great measure of finality. To allow indiscriminate hearings in federal postconviction proceedings would eliminate the chief virtues of the plea system—speed, economy, and finality. And there is reason for concern about that prospect. More often than not a prisoner has everything to gain and nothing to lose from filing a collateral attack upon his guilty plea. If he succeeds in vacating the judgment of conviction, retrial may be difficult. If he convinces a court that his plea was induced by an advantageous plea agreement that was violated, he may obtain the benefit of its terms. A collateral attack may also be inspired by "a mere desire to be freed temporarily from the confines of the prison."

Yet arrayed against the interest in finality is the very purpose of the writ of habeas corpus—to safeguard a person's freedom from detention in violation of constitutional guarantees. * * * And a prisoner in custody after pleading guilty, no less than one tried and convicted by a jury, is entitled to avail himself of the writ in challenging the constitutionality of his custody.

In *Machibroda v. United States,* 368 U.S. 487 (1962), the defendant had pleaded guilty in federal court to bank robbery charges and been sentenced to 40 years in prison. He later filed a § 2255 motion alleging that his plea had been induced by an Assistant United States Attorney's promises that his sentence would not exceed 20 years, that the prosecutor had admonished him not to tell his lawyer about the agreement, and that the trial judge had wholly failed to inquire whether the guilty plea was made voluntarily before accepting it. This Court noted that the allegations, if proved, would entitle the defendant to relief, and that they raised an issue of fact that could not be resolved simply on the basis of an affidavit from the prosecutor denying the allegations. Because those allegations "related primarily to purported occurrences outside the courtroom and upon which the record could, therefore, cast no real light," and were not so "vague [or] conclusory," as to permit summary disposition, the Court ruled that the defendant was entitled to the opportunity to substantiate them at an evidentiary hearing.

The later case of *Fontaine v. United States,* 411 U.S. 213 (1973), followed the same approach. The defendant there, having waived counsel, had also pleaded guilty to federal bank robbery charges. Before accepting the plea, the District Judge addressed the defendant personally, and the defendant stated in substance "that his plea was given voluntarily and knowingly, that he understood the nature of the charge and the consequences of the plea, and that he was in fact guilty." The defendant later filed a § 2255 motion to vacate his sentence on the ground that his plea had been coerced "by a combination of fear, coercive police tactics, and illness, including mental illness." The motion included supporting factual allegations, as well as hospital records documenting some of the contentions.

Although noting that in collaterally attacking a plea of guilty a prisoner "may not ordinarily repudiate" statements made to the sentencing judge when the plea was entered, the Court observed that no procedural device for the taking of guilty pleas is so perfect in design and exercise as to warrant a *per se* rule rendering it "uniformly invulnerable to subsequent challenge." Because the record of the plea hearing did not, in view of the allegations made, " 'conclusively show that the prisoner [was] entitled to no relief,' " the Court ruled that the prisoner should be given an evidentiary hearing.

These cases do not in the least reduce the force of the original plea hearing. For the representations of the defendant, his lawyer, and the prosecutor at such a hearing, as well as any findings made by the judge accepting the plea, constitute a formidable barrier in any subsequent collateral proceedings. Solemn declarations in open court carry a strong presumption of verity. The subsequent presentation of conclusory allegations unsupported by specifics is subject to summary dismissal, as are contentions that in the face of the record are wholly incredible.

What *Machibroda* and *Fontaine* indisputably teach, however, is that the barrier of the plea or sentencing proceeding record, although imposing, is not invariably insurmountable. In administering the writ of habeas corpus and its § 2255 counterpart, the federal courts cannot fairly adopt a *per se* rule excluding all possibility that a defendant's representations at the time his guilty plea was accepted were so much the product of such factors as misunderstanding, duress, or misrepresentation by others as to make the guilty plea a constitutionally inadequate basis for imprisonment.

The allegations in this case were not in themselves so "vague [or] conclusory" as to warrant dismissal for that reason alone. Allison alleged as a ground for relief that his plea was induced by an unkept promise. But he did not stop there. He proceeded to elaborate upon this claim with specific factual allegations. The petition indicated exactly what the terms of the promise were; when, where, and by whom the promise had been made; and the identity of one witness to its communication. The critical question is whether these allegations, when viewed against the record of the plea hearing, were so "palpably incredible," so "patently frivolous or false" as to warrant summary dismissal. In the light of the nature of the record of the proceeding at which the guilty plea was accepted, and of the ambiguous status of the process of plea bargaining at the time the guilty plea was made, we conclude that Allison's petition should not have been summarily dismissed.

Only recently has plea bargaining become a visible practice accepted as a legitimate component in the administration of criminal justice. For decades it was a *sub rosa* process shrouded in secrecy and deliberately concealed by participating defendants, defense lawyers, prosecutors, and even judges. Indeed, it was not until our decision in *Santobello v. New York* that lingering doubts about the legitimacy of the practice were finally dispelled.

Allison was arraigned a mere 37 days after the *Santobello* decision was announced, under a North Carolina procedure that had not been modified in light of *Santobello* or earlier decisions of this Court recognizing the process of plea bargaining. That procedure itself reflected the atmosphere of secrecy which then characterized plea bargaining generally. No transcript of the proceeding was made. The only record was a standard printed form. There is no way of knowing whether the trial judge in any way deviated from or supplemented the text of the form. The record is silent as to what statements Allison, his lawyer, or the prosecutor might have made regarding promised sentencing concessions. And there is no record at all of the sentencing hearing three days later, at which one of the participants might well have made a statement shedding light upon the veracity of the allegations Allison later advanced.

The litany of form questions followed by the trial judge at arraignment nowhere indicated to Allison (or indeed to the lawyers involved) that plea bargaining was a legitimate practice that could be freely disclosed in open court. Neither lawyer was asked to disclose any agreement that had been reached, or sentencing recommendation that had been promised. The process thus did nothing to dispel a defendant's relief that any bargain struck must remain concealed—a belief here allegedly reinforced by the admonition of Allison's lawyer himself that disclosure could jeopardize the agreement. Rather than challenging respondent's counsel's contention at oral argument in this Court that "at that time in North Carolina plea bargains were never disclosed in response to such a question on such a form," counsel for the petitioners conceded at oral argument that "[t]hat form was a minimum inquiry."

Although "[l]ogically the general inquiry should elicit information about plea bargaining, * * * it seldom has in the past." Particularly if, as Allison alleged, he was advised by counsel to conceal any plea bargain, his denial that any promises had been made might have been a courtroom ritual more sham than real. We thus cannot conclude that the allegations in Allison's habeas corpus petition, when measured against the "record" of the arraignment, were so "patently false or frivolous" as to warrant summary dismissal.

North Carolina has recently undertaken major revisions of its plea-bargaining procedures in part to prevent the very kind of problem now before us. Plea bargaining is expressly legitimate. The judge is directed to advise the defendant that courts have approved plea bargaining and he may thus admit to any promises without fear of jeopardizing an advantageous agreement or prejudicing himself in the judge's eyes. Specific inquiry about whether a plea bargain has been struck is then made not only of the defendant, but also of his counsel and the prosecutor. Finally, the entire proceeding is to be transcribed verbatim.

Had these commendable procedures been followed in the present case, Allison's petition would have been cast in a very different light. The careful explication of the legitimacy of plea bargaining, the questioning of both lawyers, and the verbatim record of their answers at the guilty-plea proceedings would almost surely have shown whether any bargain did exist and, if so, insured that it was not ignored. But the salutary reforms recently implemented by North Carolina highlight even more sharply the deficiencies in the record before the District Court in the present case.

This is not to say that every set of allegations not on its face without merit entitles a habeas corpus petitioner to an evidentiary hearing. As in civil cases generally, there exists a procedure whose purpose is to test whether facially adequate allegations have sufficient basis in fact to warrant plenary presentation of evidence. That procedure is, of course, the motion for summary judgment. Upon remand the warden will be free to make such a notion, supporting it with whatever proof he wishes to attach. If he chooses to do so, Allison will then be required either to produce some contrary proof indicating that there is a genuine issue of fact to be resolved by the District Court or to explain his inability to provide such proof. * * *

THE CHIEF JUSTICE concurs in the judgment.

JUSTICE REHNQUIST took no part in the consideration or decision of this case.

JUSTICE POWELL, concurring.

I join the opinion of the Court, and write briefly only to emphasize the importance of finality to a system of justice. * * *

As the Court's opinion indicates, there is every reason to believe that if a procedure similar to that prescribed by the new North Carolina statute is followed, a contention such as that made by respondent will justify an evidentiary hearing "only in the most extraordinary circumstances." If all participants in the process at the plea stage are mindful of the importance of adhering carefully to prescribed procedures and of preserving a full record thereof, the causes of justice and finality both will be served.

Chapter 15

TRIAL BY JURY

613–652

SECTION 1. RIGHT TO JURY TRIAL

The Sixth Amendment declares that in "all criminal prosecutions, the accused shall enjoy the right to a * * * trial, by an impartial jury of the State and district wherein the crime shall have been committed." *Duncan v. Louisiana* discusses why jury trial is so important in the American system of criminal justice and why, consequently, this Sixth Amendment right is also applicable to the states. *Blanton v. City of North Las Vegas* examines when an offense is "petty" and thus is not covered by the jury trial right. Though the traditional criminal jury is one made up of 12 persons who must unanimously agree to the verdict, *Burch v. Louisiana* teaches that something less will suffice under the Sixth Amendment. The final case in this section, *Singer v. United States,* considers whether a defendant should have an unrestrained right to have his case tried by the judge alone.

DUNCAN v. LOUISIANA

[*set forth in Ch. 2, § 2*]

BLANTON v. CITY OF NORTH LAS VEGAS

489 U.S. 538, 109 S.Ct. 1289, 103 L.Ed.2d 550 (1989).

JUSTICE MARSHALL delivered the opinion of the Court.

The issue in this case is whether there is a constitutional right to a trial by jury for persons charged under Nevada law with driving under the influence of alcohol (DUI). We hold that there is not. * * *

It has long been settled "that there is a category of petty crimes or offenses which is not subject to the Sixth Amendment jury trial provision." *Duncan v. Louisiana.* In determining whether a particular offense should be categorized as "petty," our early decisions focused on the nature of the offense and on whether it was triable by a jury at common law. In recent years, however, we have sought more "objective indications of the seriousness with which society regards the offense." "[W]e have found the most relevant such criteria in the severity of the maximum authorized penalty." *Baldwin v. New York*, 399 U.S. 66, 68, 90 S.Ct. 1886, 1887, 26 L.Ed.2d 437 (1970). In fixing the maximum penalty for a crime, a legislature "include[s] within the definition of the crime itself a judgment about the seriousness of the offense." The judiciary should not substitute its judgment as to seriousness for that of a legislature, which is "far better equipped to perform the task, and [is] likewise more responsive to changes in attitude and more

613

amenable to the recognition and correction of their misperceptions in this respect."

In using the word "penalty," we do not refer solely to the maximum prison term authorized for a particular offense. A legislature's view of the seriousness of an offense also is reflected in the other penalties that it attaches to the offense. * * * [*6] Primary emphasis, however, must be placed on the maximum authorized period of incarceration. Penalties such as probation or a fine may engender "a significant infringement of personal freedom," but they cannot approximate in severity the loss of liberty that a prison term entails. Indeed, because incarceration is an "intrinsically different" form of punishment, it is the most powerful indication of whether an offense is "serious."

Following this approach, our decision in *Baldwin* established that a defendant is entitled to a jury trial whenever the offense for which he is charged carries a maximum authorized prison term of greater than six months. * * * As for a prison term of six months or less, we recognized that it will seldom be viewed by the defendant as "trivial or 'petty.'" But we found that the disadvantages of such a sentence, "onerous though they may be, may be outweighed by the benefits that result from speedy and inexpensive nonjury adjudications."

Although we did not hold in *Baldwin* that an offense carrying a maximum prison term of six months or less automatically qualifies as a "petty" offense, and decline to do so today, we do find it appropriate to presume for purposes of the Sixth Amendment that society views such an offense as "petty." A defendant is entitled to jury trial in such circumstances only if he can demonstrate that any additional statutory penalties, viewed in conjunction with the maximum authorized period of incarceration, are so severe that they clearly reflect a legislative determination that the offense in question is a "serious" one. This standard, albeit somewhat imprecise, should ensure the availability of a jury trial in the rare situation where a legislature packs an offense it deems "serious" with onerous penalties that nonetheless "do not puncture the 6-month incarceration line." [*8]

Applying these principles here, it is apparent that petitioners are not entitled to a jury trial. The maximum authorized prison sentence for first-time DUI offenders does not exceed six months. A presumption therefore exists that the Nevada legislature views DUI as a "petty" offense for purposes of the Sixth Amendment. [a] Considering the additional statutory penalties as well, we do not

---

6. In criminal contempt prosecutions, "where no maximum penalty is authorized, the severity of the penalty actually imposed is the best indication of the seriousness of the particular offense."

8. In performing this analysis, only penalties resulting from state action, *e.g.,* those mandated by statute or regulation, should be considered. * * *

a. In *Lewis v. United States,* 518 U.S. 322 (1996), petitioner argued "that, where a defendant is charged with multiple petty offenses in a single prosecution, the Sixth Amendment requires that the aggregate potential penalty be the basis for determining whether a jury trial is required." The Court, per O'Connor, J., disagreed, noting that per *Blanton* "we determine whether an offense is serious by looking to the judgment of the legislature, primarily as expressed in the maximum authorized term of imprisonment. Here, by setting the maximum authorized prison term at six months, the legislature categorized the offense of obstructing the mail as petty. The fact that the petitioner was charged with two counts of a petty offense does not revise the legislative judgment as to the gravity of that particular offense, nor does it transform the petty offense into a serious one, to which the jury-trial right would apply." As for petitioner's reliance on *Codispoti v. Pennsylvania,* 418 U.S. 506 (1974), where the defendant was deemed entitled to jury trial because the aggregate penalties actually imposed exceeded six months, the Court distinguished that case on two grounds: (1) there "the legislature had not set a specific penalty for criminal contempt," in which case "courts use the severity of the penalty actually imposed as the measure of the character of the particular offense," and (2) the "benefit of a jury trial, 'as a protection against the arbitrary exercise of official power,'" was deemed particularly important in [the criminal contempt] context."

believe that the Nevada Legislature has clearly indicated that DUI is a "serious" offense.

In the first place, it is immaterial that a first-time DUI offender may face a minimum term of imprisonment. In settling on six months' imprisonment as the constitutional demarcation point, we have assumed that a defendant convicted of the offense in question would receive the *maximum* authorized prison sentence. It is not constitutionally determinative, therefore, that a particular defendant may be required to serve some amount of jail time *less* than six months. Likewise, it is of little moment that a defendant may receive the maximum prison term because of the prohibitions on plea bargaining and probation. As for the 90-day license suspension, it, too, will be irrelevant if it runs concurrently with the prison sentence, which we assume for present purposes to be the maximum of six months.[9]

We are also unpersuaded by the fact that, instead of a prison sentence, a DUI offender may be ordered to perform 48 hours of community service dressed in clothing identifying him as a DUI offender. Even assuming the outfit is the source of some embarrassment during the 48-hour period, such a penalty will be less embarrassing and less onerous than six months in jail. As for the possible $1,000 fine, it is well below the $5,000 level set by Congress in its most recent definition of a "petty" offense, 18 U.S.C. § 1, and petitioners do not suggest that this congressional figure is out of step with state practice for offenses carrying prison sentences of six months or less.[11] * * *

BURCH v. LOUISIANA

441 U.S. 130, 99 S.Ct. 1623, 60 L.Ed.2d 96 (1979).

JUSTICE REHNQUIST delivered the opinion of the Court.

The Louisiana Constitution and Code of Criminal Procedure provide that criminal cases in which the punishment imposed may be confinement for a period in excess of six months "shall be tried before a jury of six persons, five of whom must concur to render a verdict." We granted certiorari to decide whether

Kennedy, J., joined by Breyer, J., concurring, concluded that the "right to jury trial extends as well to a defendant who is sentenced in one proceeding to more than six months' imprisonment." He reasoned that while a defendant has a right to jury trial as to a nonpetty offense, without regard to what sentence is actually imposed, because of the stigma which attaches because of the legislature's judgment that the offense is serious, "the Sixth Amendment also serves the different and more practical purpose of preventing a court from effecting a most serious deprivation of liberty—ordering a defendant to prison for a substantial period of time—without the Government's persuading a jury he belongs there. * * * If[, as in the instant case,] the trial court rules at the outset that no more than six months' imprisonment will be imposed for the combined petty offenses, however, the liberty the jury serves to protect will not be endangered, and there is no corresponding right to jury trial." Stevens, J., joined by Ginsburg, J., dissenting, agreed with Justice Kennedy except for that last point: "I see no basis for assuming that the dishonor associated with multiple convictions for petty offenses is less than the dishonor associated with conviction of a single serious crime. Because the right attaches at the moment of prosecution, a judge may not deprive a defendant of a jury trial by making a pretrial determination that the crimes charged will not warrant a sentence exceeding six months."

9. It is unclear whether the license suspension and prison sentence in fact run concurrently. But even if they do not, we cannot say that a 90-day license suspension is that significant as a Sixth Amendment matter, particularly when a restricted license may be obtained after only 45 days. Furthermore, the requirement that an offender attend an alcohol abuse education course can only be described as *de minimis.*

11. * * * We decline petitioners' invitation to survey the statutory penalties for drunken driving in other States. The question is not whether other States consider drunken driving a "serious" offense, but whether Nevada does.

conviction by a nonunanimous six-person jury in a state criminal trial for a nonpetty offense as contemplated by these provisions of Louisiana law violates the rights of an accused to trial by jury guaranteed by the Sixth and Fourteenth Amendments.

Petitioners, an individual and a Louisiana corporation, were jointly charged in two counts with the exhibition of two obscene motion pictures. Pursuant to Louisiana law, they were tried before a six-person jury, which found both petitioners guilty as charged. A poll of the jury after verdict indicated that the jury had voted unanimously to convict petitioner Wrestle, Inc., and had voted 5–1 to convict petitioner Burch. Burch was sentenced to two consecutive 7–month prison terms, which were suspended, and fined $1,000; Wrestle, Inc., was fined $600 on each count.

Petitioners appealed their convictions to the Supreme Court of Louisiana, where they argued that the provisions of Louisiana law permitting conviction by a nonunanimous six-member jury violated the rights of persons accused of nonpetty criminal offenses to trial by jury guaranteed by the Sixth and Fourteenth Amendments. Though acknowledging that the issue was "close," the court held that conviction by a nonunanimous six-person jury did not offend the Constitution. The court concluded that none of this Court's decisions precluded use of a nonunanimous six-person jury. " 'If 75 percent concurrence ($\%_{12}$) was enough for a verdict as determined in *Johnson v. Louisiana,* 406 U.S. 356 (1972), then requiring 83 percent concurrence ($\%$) ought to be within the permissible limits of *Johnson.*'" And our recent decision in *Ballew v. Georgia,* 435 U.S. 223 (1978), striking down a Georgia law allowing conviction by a unanimous five-person jury in nonpetty criminal cases, was distinguishable in the Louisiana Supreme Court's view:

> "[I]n *Williams*[*v. Florida,* 399 U.S. 78 (1970)] the court held that a six-person jury was of sufficient size to promote adequate group deliberation, to insulate members from outside intimidation, and to provide a representative cross-section of the community. These values, which *Ballew* held a five-person jury is inadequate to serve, are not necessarily defeated because the six-person jury's verdict may be rendered by five instead of by six persons."

Since the Louisiana Supreme Court believed that conviction by a nonunanimous six-person jury was not necessarily foreclosed by this Court's decisions, it stated that it preferred to "indulg[e] in the presumption of federal constitutionality which must be afforded to provisions of our state constitution."

We agree with the Louisiana Supreme Court that the question presented is a "close" one. Nonetheless, we believe that conviction by a nonunanimous six-member jury in a state criminal trial for a nonpetty offense deprives an accused of his constitutional right to trial by jury.

Only in relatively recent years has this Court had to consider the practices of the several States relating to jury size and unanimity. *Duncan v. Louisiana* marked the beginning of our involvement with such questions. * * *

Two Terms later in *Williams v. Florida,* the Court held that this constitutional guarantee of trial by jury did not require a State to provide an accused with a jury of 12 members and that Florida did not violate the jury trial rights of criminal defendants charged with nonpetty offenses by affording them jury panels comprised of only 6 persons. After canvassing the common-law development of the jury and the constitutional history of the jury trial right, the Court concluded that the 12–person requirement was "a historical accident" and that there was no indication that the Framers intended to preserve in the Constitution the features of the jury system as it existed at common law. Thus freed from strictly historical considerations, the Court turned to examine the function that this particular feature performs and its relation to the purposes of jury trial. The purpose of trial by jury, as noted in *Duncan,* is to prevent government oppression by providing a "safeguard against the corrupt or overzealous prosecutor and against the compliant, biased, or eccentric judge." Given this purpose, the *Williams* Court observed that the jury's essential feature lies in the "interposition between the accused and his accuser of the commonsense judgment of a group of laymen, and in the community participation and shared responsibility that results from that group's determination of guilt or innocence." These purposes could be fulfilled, the Court believed, so long as the jury was of a sufficient size to promote group deliberation, free from outside intimidation, and to provide a fair possibility that a cross section of the community would be represented on it. The Court concluded, however, that there is "little reason to think that these goals are in any meaningful sense less likely to be achieved when the jury numbers six, than when it numbers 12—*particularly if the requirement of unanimity is retained.*" (emphasis added).[7]

A similar analysis led us to conclude in 1972 that a jury's verdict need not be unanimous to satisfy constitutional requirements, even though unanimity had been the rule at common law. Thus, in *Apodaca v. Oregon,* 406 U.S. 404 (1972), we upheld a state statute providing that only 10 members of a 12–person jury need concur to render a verdict in certain noncapital cases. In terms of the role of the jury as a safeguard against oppression, the plurality opinion perceived no difference between those juries required to act unanimously and those permitted to act by votes of 10 to 2. Nor was unanimity viewed by the plurality as contributing materially to the exercise of the jury's common-sense judgment or as a necessary precondition to effective application of the requirement that jury panels represent a fair cross section of the community.

Last Term, in *Ballew v. Georgia,* we considered whether a jury of less than six members passes constitutional scrutiny, a question that was explicitly reserved in *Williams v. Florida.* The Court, in separate opinions, held that conviction by a unanimous five-person jury in a trial for a nonpetty offense deprives an accused of his right to trial by jury. While readily admitting that the line between six members and five was not altogether easy to justify, at least five Members of the Court believed that reducing a jury to five persons in nonpetty cases raised sufficiently substantial doubts as to the fairness of the proceeding and proper functioning of the jury to warrant drawing the line at six.

We thus have held that the Constitution permits juries of less than 12 members, but that it requires at least 6. And we have approved the use of certain nonunanimous verdicts in cases involving 12–person juries. These principles are not questioned here. Rather, this case lies at the intersection of our decisions concerning jury size and unanimity. As in *Ballew,* we do not pretend the ability to discern *a priori* a bright line below which the number of jurors participating in the trial or in the verdict would not permit the jury to function in the manner required by our prior cases. But having already departed from the strictly historical requirements of jury trial, it is inevitable that lines must be drawn somewhere if the substance of the jury trial right is to be preserved. Even the State concedes as much.

7. The Court also believed that a jury of 12 was neither more reliable as a factfinder, more advantageous to the defendant, nor more representative of the variety of viewpoints in the community than a jury of 6.

This line-drawing process, "although essential, cannot be wholly satisfactory, for it requires attaching different consequences to events which, when they lie near the line, actually differ very little." However, much the same reasons that led us in *Ballew* to decide that use of a five-member jury threatened the fairness of the proceeding and the proper role of the jury, lead us to conclude now that conviction for a nonpetty offense by only five members of a six-person jury presents a similar threat to preservation of the substance of the jury trial guarantee and justifies our requiring verdicts rendered by six-person juries to be unanimous. We are buttressed in this view by the current jury practices of the several States. It appears that of those States that utilize six-member juries in trials of nonpetty offenses, only two, including Louisiana, also allow nonunanimous verdicts. We think that this near-uniform judgment of the Nation provides a useful guide in delimiting the line between those jury practices that are constitutionally permissible and those that are not.

The State seeks to justify its use of nonunanimous six-person juries on the basis of the "considerable time" savings that it claims results from trying cases in this manner. It asserts that under its system, juror deliberation time is shortened and the number of hung juries is reduced. Undoubtedly, the State has a substantial interest in reducing the time and expense associated with the administration of its system of criminal justice. But that interest cannot prevail here. First, on this record, any benefits that might accrue by allowing five members of a six-person jury to render a verdict, as compared with requiring unanimity of a six-member jury, are speculative, at best. More importantly, we think that when a State has reduced the size of its juries to the minimum number of jurors permitted by the Constitution, the additional authorization of nonunanimous verdicts by such juries sufficiently threatens the constitutional principles that led to the establishment of the size threshold that any countervailing interest of the State should yield. * * * a

SINGER v. UNITED STATES

380 U.S. 24, 85 S.Ct. 783, 13 L.Ed.2d 630 (1965).

CHIEF JUSTICE WARREN delivered the opinion of the Court.

Rule 23(a) of the Federal Rules of Criminal Procedure provides:

"Cases required to be tried by jury shall be so tried unless the defendant waives a jury trial in writing with the approval of the court and the consent of the government."

Petitioner challenges the permissibility of this rule, arguing that the Constitution gives a defendant in a federal criminal case the right to waive a jury trial whenever he believes such action to be in his best interest, regardless of whether the prosecution and the court are willing to acquiesce in the waiver.

Petitioner was charged in a federal district court with 30 infractions of the mail fraud statute. * * * On the opening day of trial petitioner offered in writing to waive a trial by jury "[f]or the purpose of shortening the trial." The trial court was willing to approve the waiver, but the Government refused to give its consent. Petitioner was subsequently convicted by a jury on 29 of the 30 counts.

Petitioner's argument is that a defendant in a federal criminal case has not only an unconditional constitutional right, guaranteed by Art. III, § 2, and the

a. The concurring opinion of Justice Stevens, and the opinion of Justice Brennan (joined by Stewart and Marshall, JJ.), concurring as to the jury trial issue, but dissenting as to the constitutionality of the obscenity statute, are omitted.

Sixth Amendment, to a trial by jury, but also a correlative right to have his case decided by a judge alone if he considers such a trial to be to his advantage. * * *

We have examined petitioner's arguments and find them to be without merit. We can find no evidence that the common law recognized that defendants had the right to choose between court and jury trial. Although instances of waiver of jury trial can be found in certain of the colonies prior to the adoption of the Constitution, they were isolated instances occurring pursuant to colonial "constitutions" or statutes and were clear departures from the common law. There is no indication that the colonists considered the ability to waive a jury trial to be of equal importance to the right to demand one. Having found that the Constitution neither confers nor recognizes a right of criminal defendants to have their cases tried before a judge alone, we also conclude that Rule 23(a) sets forth a reasonable procedure governing attempted waivers of jury trials.

English Common Law. * * * Not until 1827, long after the adoption of our Constitution, did England provide by statute for the trial of those who stood mute. Even this statute did not give the defendant the right to plead his case before a judge alone, but merely provided that he would be subject to jury trial without his formal consent.

Thus, as late as 1827 the English common law gave criminal defendants no option as to the mode of trial. * * *

The Colonial Experience. * * * The most that can be said for these examples [of jury waiver] is that they are evidence that the colonists believed it was possible to try criminal defendants without a jury. They in no way show that there was any general recognition of a defendant's right to be tried by the court instead of by a jury. Indeed, if there had been recognition of such a right, it would be difficult to understand why Article III and the Sixth Amendment were not drafted in terms which recognized an option.

The Constitution and Its Judicial Interpretation. The proceedings at the Constitutional Convention give little insight into what was meant by the direction in Art. III, § 2, that the "Trial of all Crimes * * * shall be by Jury." The clause was clearly intended to protect the accused from oppression by the Government, but, since the practice of permitting defendants a choice as to the mode of trial was not widespread, it is not surprising that some of the framers apparently believed that the Constitution designated trial by jury as the exclusive method of determining guilt. * * *

The issue whether a defendant could waive a jury trial in federal criminal cases was finally presented to this Court in *Patton v. United States,* 281 U.S. 276 (1930). * * * The Court examined Art. III, § 2, and the Sixth Amendment and concluded that a jury trial was a right which the accused might "forego at his election." The Court also spoke of jury trial as a "privilege," not an "imperative requirement," and remarked that jury trial was principally for the benefit of the accused. Nevertheless, the Court * * * concluded its opinion, with carefully chosen language that dispelled any notion that the defendant had an absolute right to demand trial before a judge sitting alone:

> "Not only must the right of the accused to a trial by a constitutional jury be jealously preserved, but the maintenance of the jury as a factfinding body in criminal cases is of such importance and has such a place in our traditions, that, before any waiver can become effective, the consent of government counsel and the sanction of the court must be had, in addition to the express and intelligent consent of the defendant. And the duty of the trial court in that regard is not to be discharged as a mere matter of rote, but with sound

and advised discretion, with an eye to avoid unreasonable or undue departures from that mode of trial or from any of the essential elements thereof, and with a caution increasing in degree as the offenses dealt with increase in gravity."

* * *

Thus, there is no federally recognized right to a criminal trial before a judge sitting alone, but a defendant can, as was held in *Patton,* in some instances waive his right to a trial by jury. The question remains whether the effectiveness of this waiver can be conditioned upon the consent of the prosecuting attorney and the trial judge.

The ability to waive a constitutional right does not ordinarily carry with it the right to insist upon the opposite of that right. For example, although a defendant can, under some circumstances, waive his constitutional right to a public trial, he has no absolute right to compel a private trial; although he can waive his right to be tried in the State and district where the crime was committed, he cannot in all cases compel transfer of the case to another district; and although he can waive his right to be confronted by the witnesses against him, it has never been seriously suggested that he can thereby compel the Government to try the case by stipulation. Moreover, it has long been accepted that the waiver of constitutional rights can be subjected to reasonable procedural regulations. * * *

Trial by jury has been established by the Constitution as the "normal and * * * preferable mode of disposing of issues of fact in criminal cases." As with any mode that might be devised to determine guilt, trial by jury has its weaknesses and the potential for misuse. However, the mode itself has been surrounded with safeguards to make it as fair as possible—for example, venue can be changed when there is a well-grounded fear of jury prejudice, and prospective jurors are subject to *voir dire* examination, to challenge for cause, and to peremptory challenge.

In light of the Constitution's emphasis on jury trial, we find it difficult to understand how the petitioner can submit the bald proposition that to compel a defendant in a criminal case to undergo a jury trial against his will is contrary to his right to a fair trial or to due process. A defendant's only constitutional right concerning the method of trial is to an impartial trial by jury. We find no constitutional impediment to conditioning a waiver of this right on the consent of the prosecuting attorney and the trial judge when, if either refuses to consent, the result is simply that the defendant is subject to an impartial trial by jury—the very thing that the Constitution guarantees him. The Constitution recognizes an adversary system as the proper method of determining guilt, and the Government, as a litigant, has a legitimate interest in seeing that cases in which it believes a conviction is warranted are tried before the tribunal which the Constitution regards as most likely to produce a fair result. * * *

We are aware that the States have adopted a variety of procedures relating to the waiver of jury trials in state criminal cases. Some have made waiver contingent on approval by the prosecutor. Others, while not giving the prosecutor a voice, have made court approval a prerequisite for waiver. Still others have provided that the question of waiver is a matter solely for the defendant's informed decision, however, the framers of the federal rules were aware of possible alternatives when they recommended the present rule to this Court; this Court promulgated the rule as recommended; and Congress can be deemed to have adopted it.

In upholding the validity of Rule 23(a), we reiterate that the government attorney in a criminal prosecution is not an ordinary party to a controversy, but a "servant of the law" with a "twofold aim * * * that guilt shall not escape or innocence suffer." It was in light of this concept of the role of prosecutor that Rule 23(a) was framed, and we are confident that it is in this light that it will continue to be invoked by government attorneys. Because of this confidence in the integrity of the federal prosecutor, Rule 23(a) does not require that the Government articulate its reasons for demanding a jury trial at the time it refuses to consent to a defendant's proffered waiver. Nor should we assume that federal prosecutors would demand a jury trial for an ignoble purpose. We need not determine in this case whether there might be some circumstances where a defendant's reasons for wanting to be tried by a judge alone are so compelling that the Government's insistence on trial by jury would result in the denial to a defendant of an impartial trial. Petitioner argues that there might arise situations where "passion, prejudice * * * public feeling" or some other factor may render impossible or unlikely an impartial trial by jury. However, since petitioner gave no reason for wanting to forgo jury trial other than to save time, this is not such a case, and petitioner does not claim that it is. * * *

SECTION 2. JURY SELECTION

Although the procedures for selecting juries to serve in criminal cases are governed by statute in all jurisdictions, the operation of those procedures sometimes produces serious and difficult constitutional questions. In most states, lists of prospective jurors are prepared by random selection from those registered to vote. Certain other lists (e.g., city directories) are sometimes used in addition or instead, and in some jurisdictions "key men" (political and civic leaders) supply names of prospective jurors. Some of those initially selected are thereafter stricken from the list because they are deemed lacking in the intellectual or other qualifications for jury service. Others are excused on the assumption that they would find jury service especially burdensome. It is apparent that the manner in which these lists of prospective jurors are initially prepared and then reduced can have a significant effect upon the makeup of particular jury panels available for jury selection in particular cases. It is not surprising, therefore, that defendants sometimes challenge the above described procedures on constitutional grounds. The first two cases in this section, *Carter v. Jury Commission* and *Taylor v. Louisiana,* discuss two types of challenges: respectively, the objection that the selection constitutes a denial of defendant's Fourteenth Amendment right to equal protection; and the objection that the selection does not accord with the Sixth Amendment right to a jury drawn from a cross-section of the community.

A process called voir dire is used to select from the panel of prospective jurors those who will serve as jurors in a particular case. The prospective jurors are questioned by the attorneys or the judge in order to reveal facts relevant to the exercise of challenges for cause and peremptory challenges. Each side may challenge for cause any prospective juror for lack of impartiality, and in addition each side has a specified number of peremptory challenges, for which no reason ordinarily need be given. The last three cases in this section illustrate the kinds of problems of constitutional dimension which can arise from this voir dire process. *Turner v. Murray* concerns how far it is necessary to go to protect the defendant against biased jurors; *Lockhart v. McCree* involves, on the other hand, how much can be done to ensure against anti-prosecution bias without violating the defendant's rights; and *Batson v. Kentucky* teaches that even the prosecution's manner of using peremptory challenges can run afoul of the Constitution.

CARTER v. JURY COMMISSION

396 U.S. 320, 90 S.Ct. 518, 24 L.Ed.2d 549 (1970).

Justice Stewart delivered the opinion of the Court.

The appellants, Negro citizens of Greene County, Alabama, commenced this class action against officials charged with the administration of the State's jury-selection laws: the county jury commissioners and their clerk, the local circuit court judge, and the Governor of Alabama. The complaint alleged that the appellants were fully qualified to serve as jurors and desired to serve, but had never been summoned for jury service. It charged that the appellees had effected a discriminatory exclusion of Negroes from grand and petit juries in Greene County—the Governor in his selection of the county jury commission, and the commissioners and judge in their arbitrary exclusion of Negroes. The complaint sought (1) a declaration that qualified Negroes were systematically excluded from Greene County grand and petit juries, that the Alabama statutes governing jury selection were unconstitutional on their face and as applied, and that the jury commission was a deliberately segregated governmental agency; (2) a permanent injunction forbidding the systematic exclusion of Negroes from Greene County juries pursuant to the challenged statutes and requiring that all eligible Negroes be placed on the jury roll; and (3) an order vacating the appointments of the jury commissioners and compelling the Governor to select new members without racial discrimination.

Alabama's jury-selection procedure is governed by statute. The Governor appoints a three-member jury commission for each county. The commission employs a clerk, who is charged with the duty of obtaining the name of every citizen of the county over 21 and under 65 years of age, together with his occupation and places of residence and business. The clerk must "scan the registration lists, the lists returned to the tax assessor, any city directories, telephone directories and any and every other source of information from which he may obtain information * * *." He must also "visit every precinct at least once a year to enable the jury commission to properly perform the duties required of it * * *." Once the clerk submits his list of names, the commission is under a duty to prepare a jury roll and jury box containing the names of all qualified, nonexempt citizens in the county, who are "generally reputed to be honest and intelligent and are esteemed in the community for their integrity, good character and sound judgment * * *."

A three-judge District Court * * * conducted an extensive evidentiary hearing on the appellants' complaint. The record fully supports the trial court's conclusion, set out in its detailed opinion, that the jury-selection process as it actually operated in Greene County at the outset of this litigation departed from the statutory mandate in several respects:

"The clerk does not obtain the names of all potentially eligible jurors as provided by § 18, in fact was not aware that the statute directed that this be done and knew of no way in which she could do it. The starting point each year is last year's roll. Everyone thereon is considered to be qualified and remains on the roll unless he dies or moves away (or, presumably, is convicted of a felony). New names are added to the old roll. Almost all of the work of the commission is devoted to securing names of persons suggested for consideration as new jurors. The clerk performs some duties directed toward securing such names. This is a part-time task, done without compensation, in spare time available from performance of her duties as clerk of the Circuit

Court. She uses voter lists but not the tax assessor's lists. Telephone directories for some of the communities are referred to, city directories not at all since Greene County is largely rural.

"The clerk goes into each of the eleven beats or precincts annually, usually one time. Her trips out into the county for this purpose never consume a full day. At various places in the county she talks with persons she knows and secures suggested names. She is acquainted with a good many Negroes, but very few 'out in the county.' She does not know the reputation of most of the Negroes in the county. Because of her duties as clerk of the Circuit Court the names and reputations of Negroes most familiar to her are those who have been convicted of crime or have been 'in trouble.' She does not know any Negro ministers, does not seek names from any Negro or white churches or fraternal organizations. She obtains some names from the county's Negro deputy sheriff. * * *

"At the August, 1966 meeting one commissioner was new and submitted no names, white or Negro, and merely did clerical work at the meeting. Another had been ill and able to seek names little if at all. The third could remember one Negro name that he suggested. This commissioner brought the name, or names, he proposed on a trade bill he had received, and after so using it threw it away. All lists of suggested names were destroyed. As a result of that meeting the number of Negro names on the jury roll increased by 37. * * * Approximately 32 of those names came from lists given the clerk or commissioners by others. The testimony is that at the one-day August meeting the entire voter list was scanned. It contained the names of around 2,000 Negroes.

"Thus in practice, through the August, 1966 meeting the system operated exactly in reverse from what the state statutes contemplate. It produced a small group of individually selected or recommended names for consideration. Those potentially qualified but whose names were never focused upon were given no consideration. Those who prepared the roll and administered the system were white and with limited means of contact with the Negro community. Though they recognized that the most pertinent information as to which Negroes do, and which do not, meet the statutory qualifications comes from Negroes there was no meaningful procedure by which Negro names were fed into the machinery for consideration or effectual means of communication by which the knowledge possessed by the Negro community was utilized. In practice most of the work of the commission has been devoted to the function of securing names to be considered. Once a name has come up for consideration it usually has been added to the rolls unless that person has been convicted of a felony. The function of applying the statutory criteria has been carried out only in part, or by accepting as conclusive the judgment of others, and for some criteria not at all."

The District Court's further findings demonstrated the impact of the selection process on the racial composition of Greene County juries. According to the 1960 census, Negroes composed three-fourths of the county's population. Yet from 1961 to 1963 the largest number of Negroes ever to appear on the jury list was about 7% of the total. The court noted that in 1964 a single-judge federal district court had entered a declaratory judgment setting forth the duties of the jury commissioners and their clerk under Alabama law, instructing them not to pursue a course of conduct operating to discriminate against Negroes, forbidding them to employ numerical or proportional limitations with respect to race, and directing an examination of the jury roll for compliance with the judgment. Thereafter, the situation had improved only marginally. In 1966 only 82 Negroes appeared among the 471 citizens listed on the jury roll; 50% of the white male population of the county found its way to the jury roll in that year, but only 4% of the Negro. In 1967, following a statutory amendment, the commission added women to the jury roll. Upon the expansion of the list, Negroes composed 388 of the 1,198 potential jurors—still only 32% of the total, even though the 1967 population of the county was estimated to be about 65% Negro.

The District Court found that "there is invalid exclusion of Negroes on a racially discriminatory basis." It enjoined the jury commissioners and their clerk from systematically excluding Negroes from the jury roll, and directed them "to take prompt action to compile a jury list * * * in accordance with the laws of Alabama and * * * constitutional principles"; to file a jury list so compiled within 60 days, showing the information required by Alabama law for each potential juror, together with his race and, if available, his age; and to submit a report setting forth the procedure by which the commission had compiled the list and applied the statutory qualifications and exclusions.

The court declined, however, * * * to enjoin the enforcement of the challenged Alabama statutory provisions[, so] the appellants took a direct appeal to this Court.

This is the first case to reach the Court in which an attack upon alleged racial discrimination in choosing juries has been made by plaintiffs seeking affirmative relief, rather than by defendants challenging judgments of criminal conviction on the ground of systematic exclusion of Negroes from the grand juries that indicted them, the trial juries that found them guilty, or both. The District Court found no barrier to such a suit, and neither do we. Defendants in criminal proceedings do not have the only cognizable legal interest in nondiscriminatory jury selection. People excluded from juries because of their race are as much aggrieved as those indicted and tried by juries chosen under a system of racial exclusion. * * *

On the merits, the appellants argue that the District Court erred in refusing to invalidate the Alabama statute requiring the jury commissioners to select for jury service those persons who are "generally reputed to be honest and intelligent and * * * esteemed in the community for their integrity, good character and sound judgment * * *." The appellants say § 21 is unconstitutional on its face because, by leaving Alabama's jury officials at large in their selection of potential jurors, it provides them an opportunity to discriminate on the basis of race—an opportunity of which they have in fact taken advantage. * * *

While there is force in what the appellants say, we cannot agree that § 21 is irredeemably invalid on its face. It has long been accepted that the Constitution does not forbid the States to prescribe relevant qualifications for their jurors. The States remain free to confine the selection to citizens, to persons meeting specified qualifications of age and educational attainment, and to those possessing good intelligence, sound judgment, and fair character. "Our duty to protect the federal constitutional rights of all does not mean we must or should impose on states our conception of the proper source of jury lists, so long as the source reasonably reflects a cross-section of the population suitable in character and intelligence for that civic duty."

Statutory provisions such as those found in § 21 are not peculiar to Alabama, or to any particular region of the country. Nearly every State requires that its jurors be citizens of the United States, residents of the locality, of a specified minimum age, and able to understand English. Many of the States require that jurors be of "good character" or the like; some, that they be "intelligent" or "well informed."

* * * Despite the overwhelming proof the appellants have adduced in support of their claim that the jury clerk and commissioners have abused the discretion that Alabama law confers on them in the preparation of the jury roll, we cannot say that § 21 is necessarily and under all circumstances invalid. The provision is devoid of any mention of race. Its antecedents are of ancient vintage, and there is no suggestion that the law was originally adopted or subsequently carried forward for the purpose of fostering racial discrimination. The federal courts are not incompetent to fashion detailed and stringent injunctive relief that will remedy any discriminatory application of the statute at the hands of the officials empowered to administer it. In sum, we cannot conclude, even on so compelling a record as that before us, that the guarantees of the Constitution can be secured only by the total invalidation of the challenged provisions of § 21. * * *

TAYLOR v. LOUISIANA

419 U.S. 522, 95 S.Ct. 692, 42 L.Ed.2d 690 (1975).

JUSTICE WHITE delivered the opinion of the Court.

When this case was tried, Art. VII, § 41, of the Louisiana Constitution, and Art. 402 of the Louisiana Code of Criminal Procedure provided that a woman should not be selected for jury service unless she had previously filed a written declaration of her desire to be subject to jury service. The constitutionality of these provisions is the issue in this case. * * *

The Louisiana jury selection system does not disqualify women from jury service, but in operation its conceded systematic impact is that only a very few women, grossly disproportionate to the number of eligible women in the community, are called for jury service.[a] In this case, no women were on the venire from which the petit jury was drawn. The issue we have, therefore, is whether a jury selection system which operates to exclude from jury service an identifiable class of citizens constituting 53% of eligible jurors in the community comports with the Sixth and Fourteenth Amendments.

The State first insists that Taylor, a male, has no standing to object to the exclusion of women from his jury. But Taylor's claim is that he was constitutionally entitled to a jury drawn from a venire constituting a fair cross section of the community and that the jury that tried him was not such a jury by reason of the exclusion of women. Taylor was not a member of the excluded class; but there is no rule that claims such as Taylor presents may be made only by those defendants who are members of the group excluded from jury service. * * * Taylor, in the case before us, was * * * entitled to tender and have adjudicated the claim that the exclusion of women from jury service deprived him of the kind of fact finder to which he was constitutionally entitled.

* * * Our inquiry is whether the presence of a fair cross section of the community on venires, panels or lists from which petit juries are drawn is essential to the fulfillment of the Sixth Amendment's guarantee of an impartial jury trial in criminal prosecutions. * * *

The unmistakable import of this Court's opinions, at least since 1941, and not repudiated by intervening decisions, is that the selection of a petit jury from a representative cross section of the community is an essential component of the Sixth Amendment right to a jury trial. * * *

a. It was stipulated that no more than 10% of the persons on the jury wheel were women, that only 12 females were among the 1,800 persons drawn to fill petit jury venires, and that this discrepancy was the result of the operation of the challenged provisions.

We accept the fair cross section requirement as fundamental to the jury trial guaranteed by the Sixth Amendment and are convinced that the requirement has solid foundation. The purpose of a jury is to guard against the exercise of arbitrary power—to make available the common-sense judgment of the community as a hedge against the overzealous or mistaken prosecutor and in preference to the professional or perhaps overconditioned or biased response of a judge. This prophylactic vehicle is not provided if the jury pool is made up of only special segments of the populace or if large, distinctive groups are excluded from the pool. Community participation in the administration of the criminal law, moreover, is not only consistent with our democratic heritage but is also critical to public confidence in the fairness of the criminal justice system. Restricting jury service to only special groups or excluding identifiable segments playing major roles in the community cannot be squared with the constitutional concept of jury trial. * * *

We are also persuaded that the fair cross section requirement is violated by the systematic exclusion of women, who in the judicial district involved here amounted to 53% of the citizens eligible for jury service. This conclusion necessarily entails the judgment that women are sufficiently numerous and distinct from men that if they are systematically eliminated from jury panels, the Sixth Amendment's fair cross section requirement cannot be satisfied. This very matter was debated in *Ballard v. United States,* 329 U.S. 187 (1946). Positing the fair cross-section rule—there said to be a statutory one—the Court concluded that the systematic exclusion of women was unacceptable. The dissenting view that an all-male panel drawn from various groups in the community would be as truly representative as if women were included, was firmly rejected:

> "The thought is that the factors which tend to influence the action of women are the same as those which influence the action of men—personality, background, economic status—and not sex. Yet it is not enough to say that women when sitting as jurors neither act nor tend to act as a class. Men likewise do not act as a class. But, if the shoe were on the other foot, who would claim that a jury was truly representative of the community if all men were intentionally and systematically excluded from the panel? The truth is that the two sexes are not fungible; a community made up exclusively of one is different from a community composed of both; the subtle interplay of influence one on the other is among the imponderables. To insulate the courtroom from either may not in a given case make an iota of difference. Yet a flavor, a distinct quality is lost if either sex is excluded. The exclusion of one may indeed make the jury less representative of the community than would be true if an economic or racial group were excluded."

In this respect, we agree with the Court in *Ballard:* If the fair cross-section rule is to govern the selection of juries, as we have concluded it must, women cannot be systematically excluded from jury panels from which petit juries are drawn. This conclusion is consistent with the current judgment of the country, now evidenced by legislative or constitutional provisions in every State and at the federal level qualifying women for jury service.

There remains the argument that women as a class serve a distinctive role in society and that jury service would so substantially interfere with that function that the State has ample justification for excluding women from service unless they volunteer, even though the result is that almost all jurors are men. It is true that *Hoyt v. Florida,* 368 U.S. 57 (1961), held that such a system did not deny due process of law or equal protection of the laws because there was a sufficiently rational basis for such an exemption. But *Hoyt* did not involve a defendant's Sixth Amendment right to a jury drawn from a fair cross section of the community and the prospect of depriving him of that right if women as a class are systematically excluded. The right to a proper jury cannot be overcome on merely rational grounds. There must be weightier reasons if a distinctive class representing 53% of the eligible jurors is for all practical purposes to be excluded from jury service. No such basis has been tendered here.

The States are free to grant exemptions from jury service to individuals in case of special hardship or incapacity and to those engaged in particular occupations the uninterrupted performance of which is critical to the community's welfare. It would not appear that such exemptions would pose substantial threats that the remaining pool of jurors would not be representative of the community. A system excluding all women, however, is a wholly different matter. It is untenable to suggest these days that it would be a special hardship for each and every woman to perform jury service or that society cannot spare *any* women from their present duties. This may be the case with many, and it may be burdensome to sort out those who should serve. But that task is performed in the case of men, and the administrative convenience in dealing with women as a class is insufficient justification for diluting the quality of community judgment represented by the jury in criminal trials. * * *

Our holding does not augur or authorize the fashioning of detailed jury selection codes by federal courts. The fair cross section principle must have much leeway in application. The States remain free to prescribe relevant qualifications for their jurors and to provide reasonable exemptions so long as it may be fairly said that the jury lists or panels are representative of the community. * * *

It should also be emphasized that in holding that petit juries must be drawn from a source fairly representative of the community we impose no requirement that petit juries actually chosen must mirror the community and reflect the various distinctive groups in the population. Defendants are not entitled to a jury of any particular composition; but the jury wheels, pools of names, panels or venires from which juries are drawn must not systematically exclude distinctive groups in the community and thereby fail to be reasonably representative thereof. * * *

Reversed and remanded.

Chief Justice Burger concurred in the result.

Justice Rehnquist, dissenting. * * *

I cannot conceive that today's decision is necessary to guard against oppressive or arbitrary law enforcement, or to prevent miscarriages of justice and to assure fair trials. Especially is this so when the criminal defendant involved makes no claims of prejudice or bias. The Court does accord some slight attention to justifying its ruling in terms of the basis on which the right to jury trial was read into the Fourteenth Amendment. It concludes that the jury is not effective, as a prophylaxis against arbitrary prosecutorial and judicial power, if the "jury pool is made up of only special segments of the populace or if large, distinctive groups are excluded from the pool." It fails, however, to provide any satisfactory explanation of the mechanism by which the Louisiana system undermines the prophylactic role of the jury, either in general or in this case. The best it can do is to posit "a flavor, a distinct quality," which allegedly is lost if either sex is excluded. However, this "flavor" is not of such importance that the Constitution is offended if any given petit jury is not so enriched. This smacks more of mysticism than of law. The Court does not even purport to practice its mysticism in a consistent fashion—presumably doctors, lawyers, and other groups, whose frequent exemption from jury service is endorsed by the majority, also offer qualities as distinct and important as those at issue here. * * *

TURNER v. MURRAY

476 U.S. 28, 106 S.Ct. 1683, 90 L.Ed.2d 27 (1986).

JUSTICE WHITE announced the judgment of the Court and delivered the opinion of the Court with respect to Parts I and III, and an opinion with respect to Parts II and IV, in which JUSTICE BLACKMUN, JUSTICE STEVENS, and JUSTICE O'CONNOR join.

[Petitioner, a black man, was indicted in Virginia on charges of capital murder for fatally shooting the white proprietor of a jewelry store in the course of a robbery. During *voir dire*, the state trial judge refused petitioner's request to question the prospective jurors on racial prejudice. The jury convicted petitioner, and, after a separate sentencing hearing, recommended that he be sentenced to death, a recommendation the trial judge accepted. The Virginia Supreme Court upheld the death sentence, rejecting petitioner's argument that the trial judge deprived him of a fair trial by refusing to question the prospective jurors on racial prejudice. Petitioner then sought habeas corpus relief in Federal District Court, which rejected the same argument and denied relief, and the Court of Appeals affirmed.]

II

The Fourth Circuit's opinion correctly states the analytical framework for evaluating petitioner's argument: "The broad inquiry in each case must be whether under all of the circumstances presented there was a constitutionally significant likelihood that, absent questioning about racial prejudice, the jurors would not be indifferent as they stand unsworn." The Fourth Circuit was correct, too, in holding that under *Ristaino* the mere fact that petitioner is black and his victim white does not constitute a "special circumstance" of constitutional proportions.[a] What sets this case apart from *Ristaino,* however, is that in addition to petitioner's being accused of a crime against a white victim, the crime charged was a capital offense.

In a capital sentencing proceeding before a jury, the jury is called upon to make a "highly subjective, 'unique, individualized judgment regarding the punishment that a particular person deserves.'" The Virginia statute under which petitioner was sentenced is instructive of the kinds of judgments a capital sentencing jury must make. First, in order to consider the death penalty, a Virginia jury must find either that the defendant is likely to commit future violent crimes or that his crime was "outrageously or wantonly vile, horrible or inhuman in that it involved torture, depravity of mind or an aggravated battery to the

a. The reference is to *Ristaino v. Ross,* 424 U.S. 589 (1976), where the Court elaborated upon *Ham v. South Carolina,* 409 U.S. 524 (1973). As the Court explained in fn. 3 of the instant case:

"In *Ham,* a young black man known in his small South Carolina hometown as a civil rights activist was arrested and charged with possession of marihuana. We held that the trial judge committed reversible error in refusing to honor Ham's request to question prospective jurors on racial prejudice. In *Ristaino,* supra, we specified the factors which mandated an inquiry into racial prejudice in *Ham:*

" 'Ham's defense was that he had been framed because of his civil rights activities. His prominence in the community as a civil rights activist, if not already known to veniremen, inevitably would have been revealed to the members of the jury in the course of his presentation of that defense. Racial issues therefore were inextricably bound up with the conduct of the trial. Further, Ham's reputation as a civil rights activist and the defense he interposed were likely to intensify any prejudice that individual members of the jury might harbor.' "

victim." Second, the jury must consider any mitigating evidence offered by the defendant. Mitigating evidence may include, but is not limited to, facts tending to show that the defendant acted under the influence of extreme emotional or mental disturbance, or that at the time of the crime the defendant's capacity "to appreciate the criminality of his conduct or to conform his conduct to the requirements of law was significantly impaired." Finally, even if the jury has found an aggravating factor, and irrespective of whether mitigating evidence has been offered, the jury has discretion not to recommend the death sentence, in which case it may not be imposed.

Virginia's death-penalty statute gives the jury greater discretion than other systems which we have upheld against constitutional challenge. However, our cases establish that every capital sentencer must be free to weigh relevant mitigating evidence before deciding whether to impose the death penalty, and that in the end it is the jury that must make the difficult, individualized judgment as to whether the defendant deserves the sentence of death.

Because of the range of discretion entrusted to a jury in a capital sentencing hearing, there is a unique opportunity for racial prejudice to operate but remain undetected. On the facts of this case, a juror who believes that blacks are violence-prone or morally inferior might well be influenced by that belief in deciding whether petitioner's crime involved the aggravating factors specified under Virginia law. Such a juror might also be less favorably inclined toward petitioner's evidence of mental disturbance as a mitigating circumstance. More subtle, less consciously held racial attitudes could also influence a juror's decision in this case. Fear of blacks, which could easily be stirred up by the violent facts of petitioner's crime, might incline a juror to favor the death penalty.[7]

The risk of racial prejudice infecting a capital sentencing proceeding is especially serious in light of the complete finality of the death sentence. "The Court, as well as the separate opinions of a majority of the individual Justices, has recognized that the qualitative difference of death from all other punishments requires a correspondingly greater degree of scrutiny of the capital sentencing determination." In the present case, we find the risk that racial prejudice may have infected petitioner's capital sentencing unacceptable in light of the ease with which that risk could have been minimized. By refusing to question prospective jurors on racial prejudice, the trial judge failed to adequately protect petitioner's constitutional right to an impartial jury.

III

We hold that a capital defendant accused of an interracial crime is entitled to have prospective jurors informed of the race of the victim and questioned on the issue of racial bias. The rule we propose is minimally intrusive; as in other cases involving "special circumstances," the trial judge retains discretion as to the form and number of questions on the subject, including the decision whether to question the venire individually or collectively. Also, a defendant cannot complain of a judge's failure to question the venire on racial prejudice unless the defendant has specifically requested such an inquiry.

7. In referring to the facts of petitioner's crime, we do not retreat from our holding in *Ristaino*. The fact of interracial violence alone is not a "special circumstance" entitling the defendant to have prospective jurors questioned about racial prejudice. It should be clear, though, that our holding in *Ristaino* was not based on a blind belief that the facts presented in that case could not evoke racial prejudice. * * * *Ristaino* * * * simply leaves it to the trial judge's discretion to decide what measures to take in screening out racial prejudice, absent a showing of "significant likelihood that racial prejudice might infect [the] trial."

IV

The inadequacy of *voir dire* in this case requires that petitioner's death sentence be vacated. It is not necessary, however, that he be retried on the issue of guilt. Our judgment in this case is that there was an unacceptable risk of racial prejudice infecting the *capital sentencing proceeding*. This judgment is based on a conjunction of three factors: the fact that the crime charged involved interracial violence, the broad discretion given the jury at the death-penalty hearing, and the special seriousness of the risk of improper sentencing in a capital case." At the guilt phase of petitioner's trial, the jury had no greater discretion than it would have had if the crime charged had been noncapital murder. Thus, with respect to the guilt phase of petitioner's trial, we find this case to be indistinguishable from *Ristaino,* to which we continue to adhere.

THE CHIEF JUSTICE concurs in the judgment.

JUSTICE BRENNAN, concurring in part and dissenting in part. * * *

To sentence an individual to death on the basis of a proceeding tainted by racial bias would violate the most basic values of our criminal justice system. This the Court understands. But what it seems not to comprehend is that to permit an individual to be *convicted* by a prejudiced jury violates those same values in precisely the same way. The incongruity of the Court's split judgment is made apparent after it is appreciated that the opportunity for bias to poison decisionmaking operates at a guilt trial in the same way as it does at a sentencing hearing and after one returns to the context of the case before us. Implicit in the Court's judgment is the acknowledgment that there was a likelihood that the jury that pronounced the death sentence acted, in part, on the basis of racial prejudice. But the exact same jury convicted Turner. Does the Court really mean to suggest that the constitutional entitlement to an impartial jury attaches only at the sentencing phase? Does the Court really believe that racial biases are turned on and off in the course of one criminal prosecution? * * *

JUSTICE MARSHALL, with whom JUSTICE BRENNAN joins, concurring in the judgment in part and dissenting in part.

* * * I believe that a criminal defendant is entitled to inquire on *voir dire* about the potential racial bias of jurors whenever the case involves a violent interracial crime. As the Court concedes, "it is plain that there is some risk of racial prejudice influencing a jury whenever there is a crime involving interracial violence." To my mind that risk plainly outweighs the slight cost of allowing the defendant to choose whether to make an inquiry concerning such possible prejudice. This Court did not identify in *Ristaino v. Ross,* nor does it identify today, any additional burdens that would accompany such a rule. I therefore cannot agree with the Court's continuing rejection of the simple prophylactic rule proposed in *Ristaino.* * * *

JUSTICE POWELL, with whom JUSTICE REHNQUIST joins, dissenting.

* * * In *Ristaino,* the Court expressly declined to adopt a *per se* rule requiring *voir dire* inquiry into racial bias in every trial for an interracial crime. Neither the Constitution nor sound policy considerations supported such a *per se* approach. But today the Court decides that the Constitution does require a *per se* rule in capital cases because the capital jury exercises discretion at the sentencing phase. The Court's reasoning ignores the many procedural and substantive safeguards, similar to those governing the jury's decision on guilt or innocence, that circumscribe the capital jury's sentencing decision.

Under Virginia law, murder is a capital offense only if it is "willful, deliberate and premeditated" and is committed while the perpetrator is engaged in another crime or under specified aggravating circumstances. As in any criminal prosecution, of course, the State carries the burden of proving all elements of the capital offense beyond a reasonable doubt. Following a sentencing hearing, the death sentence may not be imposed unless the State proves beyond a reasonable doubt statutorily defined aggravating factors. Virginia law recognizes only two aggravating factors: whether, based on the defendant's criminal record, there is a probability that he would commit future crimes of violence, and whether the defendant's crime was "outrageously or wantonly vile, horrible or inhuman, in that it involved torture, depravity of mind or aggravated battery to the victim." The jury also is required to consider any relevant mitigating evidence offered by the defendant.

The existence of these significant limitations on the jury's exercise of sentencing discretion illustrates why the Court's *per se* rule is wholly unfounded. Just as the trial judge's charge at the guilt phase instructs the jurors that they may consider only the evidence in the case and that they must determine if the prosecution has established each element of the crime beyond a reasonable doubt, the charge at the penalty phase directs the jurors to focus solely on considerations relevant to determination of appropriate punishment and to decide if the prosecution has established beyond a reasonable doubt factors warranting imposition of death. Accordingly, just as there is no reason to presume racial bias on the part of jurors who determine the guilt of a defendant who has committed a violent crime against a person of another race, there is no reason to constitutionalize such a presumption with respect to the jurors who sit to recommend the penalty in a capital case. * * *

LOCKHART v. McCREE

476 U.S. 162, 106 S.Ct. 1758, 90 L.Ed.2d 137 (1986).

JUSTICE REHNQUIST delivered the opinion of the Court.

In this case we address the question left open by our decision nearly 18 years ago in *Witherspoon v. Illinois,* 391 U.S. 510 (1968)[a.] Does the Constitution

---

a. In *Witherspoon* the Court held "that a sentence of death cannot be carried out if the jury that imposed or recommended it was chosen by excluding veniremen for cause simply because they voiced general objections to the death penalty or expressed conscientious or religious scruples against its infliction."

In *Gray v. Mississippi,* 481 U.S. 648 (1987), the Court declined to abandon the ruling in *Davis v. Georgia,* 429 U.S. 122 (1976), that even a single misapplication of *Witherspoon* invalidates a death sentence. One way of looking at the trial judge's granting of an invalid *Witherspoon* motion in the instant case was that it was intended to remedy an earlier erroneous denial of a *Witherspoon* motion regarding another prospective juror. As to this, the Court declined to "condone the 'correction' of one error by the commitment of another," especially where, as here, the first error was a violation of the prosecutor's statutory right and the second a violation of defendant's constitutional right. The Court next rejected the state court's reasoning "that a *Witherspoon* violation constitutes harmless error when the prosecutor has an unexercised peremptory challenge that he states he would have used to excuse the juror," stating:

"The practical result of adoption of this unexercised peremptory argument would be to insulate jury-selection error from meaningful appellate review. By simply stating during *voir dire* that the State is prepared to exercise a peremptory challenge if the court denies its motion for cause, a prosecutor would ensure that a reviewing court would consider any erroneous exclusion harmless. A prosecutor, as a routine matter, would likely append a statement to this effect to his motion for cause."

Finally, as to the state's argument that a single *Witherspoon* error should be deemed harmless because it did not have any prejudicial effect, the Court found it "equally unavailing." Because courts do not generally review a prosecutor's exercise of peremptory challenges, which are often used (and in this case were used) to remove prospective jurors who express hesitation against the death penalty, "a court cannot say with confidence that an erroneous exclusion for cause of a scrupled, yet eligible, venire member is an isolated incident in that particular case."

prohibit the removal for cause, prior to the guilt phase of a bifurcated capital trial, of prospective jurors whose opposition to the death penalty is so strong that it would prevent or substantially impair the performance of their duties as jurors at the sentencing phase of the trial? * * *

McCree was charged with capital felony murder. In accordance with Arkansas law, the trial judge at *voir dire* removed for cause, over McCree's objections, those prospective jurors who stated that they could not under any circumstances vote for the imposition of the death penalty. Eight prospective jurors were excluded for this reason. The jury convicted McCree of capital felony murder, but rejected the State's request for the death penalty, instead setting McCree's punishment at life imprisonment without parole. McCree's conviction was affirmed on direct appeal, and his petition for state post-conviction relief was denied.

McCree then filed a federal habeas corpus petition raising *inter alia* the claim that "death qualification," or the removal for cause of the so-called "*Witherspoon*-excludable" prospective jurors,[1] violated his right under the Sixth and Fourteenth Amendments to have his guilt or innocence determined by an impartial jury selected from a representative cross-section of the community. * * *

The District Court held a hearing on the "death qualification" issue in July 1981, receiving in evidence numerous social science studies concerning the attitudes and beliefs of "*Witherspoon*-excludables," along with the potential effects of excluding them from the jury prior to the guilt phase of a bifurcated capital trial. In August 1983, the court concluded, based on the social science evidence, that "death qualification" produced juries that "were more prone to convict" capital defendants than "non-death-qualified" juries. The court ruled that "death qualification" thus violated both the fair cross-section and impartiality requirements of the Sixth and Fourteenth Amendments, and granted McCree habeas relief.

The Eighth Circuit found "substantial evidentiary support" for the District Court's conclusion that the removal for cause of "*Witherspoon*-excludables" resulted in "conviction-prone" juries, and affirmed the grant of habeas relief on the ground that such removal for cause violated McCree's constitutional right to a jury selected from a fair cross-section of the community. * * *

Before turning to the legal issues in the case, we are constrained to point out what we believe to be several serious flaws in the evidence upon which the courts

In *Morgan v. Illinois*, 112 S.Ct. 2222 (1992), the Court rejected the state court's conclusion that a trial judge need not, on defendant's request, ask a "reverse-*Witherspoon*" question on voir dire so as to identify and exclude any prospective juror who would vote for the death penalty in every capital case. "A juror who will automatically vote for the death penalty in every case will fail in good faith to consider the evidence of aggravating and mitigating circumstances as the instructions require him to do. Indeed, because such a juror has already formed an opinion on the merits, the presence or absence of either aggravating or mitigating circumstances is entirely irrelevant to such a juror. Therefore, based on the requirement of impartiality embodied in the Due Process Clause of the Fourteenth Amendment, a capital defendant may challenge for cause any prospective juror who maintains such views. If even one such juror is empaneled and the death sentence is imposed, the State is disentitled to execute the sentence." As for the state's claim that the trial judge's "general fairness and 'follow the law' questions" sufficed, the Court answered that the state's "own request for questioning under *Witherspoon* * * * belies this argument."

1. [T]he proper constitutional standard is simply whether a prospective juror's views would " 'prevent or substantially impair the performance of his duties as a juror in accordance with his instructions and his oath.' " Thus, the term "*Witherspoon*-excludable" is something of a misnomer. Nevertheless, because the parties and the courts below have used the term "*Witherspoon*-excludables" to identify the group of prospective jurors at issue in this case, we will use the same term in this opinion.

below reached the conclusion that "death qualification" produces "conviction-prone" juries. * * *

Of the six studies introduced by McCree that at least purported to deal with the central issue in this case, namely, the potential effects on the determination of guilt or innocence of excluding "*Witherspoon*-excludables" from the jury, three were also before this Court when it decided *Witherspoon.* * * * It goes almost without saying that if these studies were "too tentative and fragmentary" to make out a claim of constitutional error in 1968, the same studies, unchanged but for having aged some eighteen years, are still insufficient to make out such a claim in this case.

Nor do the three post-*Witherspoon* studies introduced by McCree on the "death qualification" issue provide substantial support for the "*per se* constitutional rule" McCree asks this Court to adopt. All three of the "new" studies were based on the responses of individuals randomly selected from some segment of the population, but who were not actual jurors sworn under oath to apply the law to the facts of an actual case involving the fate of an actual capital defendant. We have serious doubts about the value of these studies in predicting the behavior of actual jurors. * * *

Having identified some of the more serious problems with McCree's studies, however, we will assume for purposes of this opinion that the studies are both methodologically valid and adequate to establish that "death qualification" in fact produces juries somewhat more "conviction-prone" than "non-death-qualified" juries. We hold, nonetheless, that the Constitution does not prohibit the States from "death qualifying" juries in capital cases.

The Eighth Circuit ruled that "death qualification" violated McCree's right under the Sixth Amendment, as applied to the States via incorporation through the Fourteenth Amendment, to a jury selected from a representative cross-section of the community. But we do not believe that the fair cross-section requirement can, or should, be applied as broadly as that court attempted to apply it. We have never invoked the fair cross-section principle to invalidate the use of either for-cause or peremptory challenges to prospective jurors, or to require petit juries, as opposed to jury panels or venires, to reflect the composition of the community at large. * * * The limited scope of the fair cross-section requirement is a direct and inevitable consequence of the practical impossibility of providing each criminal defendant with a truly "representative" petit jury. * * * We remain convinced that an extension of the fair cross-section requirement to petit juries would be unworkable and unsound, and we decline McCree's invitation to adopt such an extension.

But even if we were willing to extend the fair cross-section requirement to petit juries, we would still reject the Eighth Circuit's conclusion that "death qualification" violates that requirement. The essence of a "fair cross-section" claim is the systematic exclusion of "a 'distinctive' group in the community." In our view, groups defined solely in terms of shared attitudes that would prevent or substantially impair members of the group from performing one of their duties as jurors, such as the "*Witherspoon*-excludables" at issue here, are not "distinctive groups" for fair cross-section purposes.

We have never attempted to precisely define the term "distinctive group," and we do not undertake to do so today. But we think it obvious that the concept of "distinctiveness" must be linked to the purposes of the fair cross-section requirement. In *Taylor,* we identified those purposes as (1) "guard[ing] against the exercise of arbitrary power" and ensuring that the "commonsense judgment of the community" will act as "a hedge against the overzealous or mistaken prosecutor," (2) preserving "public confidence in the fairness of the criminal justice system," and (3) implementing our belief that "sharing in the administration of justice is a phase of civic responsibility."

Our prior jury-representativeness cases, whether based on the fair cross-section component of the Sixth Amendment or the Equal Protection Clause of the Fourteenth Amendment, have involved such groups as blacks, women, and Mexican-Americans. The wholesale exclusion of these large groups from jury service clearly contravened all three of the aforementioned purposes of the fair cross-section requirement. Because these groups were excluded for reasons completely unrelated to the ability of members of the group to serve as jurors in a particular case, the exclusion raised at least the possibility that the composition of juries would be arbitrarily skewed in such a way as to deny criminal defendants the benefit of the common-sense judgment of the community. In addition, the exclusion from jury service of large groups of individuals not on the basis of their inability to serve as jurors, but on the basis of some immutable characteristic such as race, gender, or ethnic background, undeniably gave rise to an "appearance of unfairness." Finally, such exclusion improperly deprived members of these often historically disadvantaged groups of their right as citizens to serve on juries in criminal cases.

The group of "*Witherspoon*-excludables" involved in the case at bar differs significantly from the groups we have previously recognized as "distinctive." "Death qualification," unlike the wholesale exclusion of blacks, women, or Mexican-Americans from jury service, is carefully designed to serve the State's concededly legitimate interest in obtaining a single jury that can properly and impartially apply the law to the facts of the case at both the guilt and sentencing phases of a capital trial. There is very little danger, therefore, and McCree does not even argue, that "death qualification" was instituted as a means for the State to arbitrarily skew the composition of capital-case juries.

Furthermore, unlike blacks, women, and Mexican-Americans, "*Witherspoon*-excludables" are singled out for exclusion in capital cases on the basis of an attribute that is within the individual's control. It is important to remember that not all who oppose the death penalty are subject to removal for cause in capital cases; those who firmly believe that the death penalty is unjust may nevertheless serve as jurors in capital cases so long as they state clearly that they are willing to temporarily set aside their own beliefs in deference to the rule of law. Because the group of "*Witherspoon*-excludables" includes only those who cannot and will not conscientiously obey the law with respect to one of the issues in a capital case, "death qualification" hardly can be said to create an "appearance of unfairness."

Finally, the removal for cause of "*Witherspoon*-excludables" in capital cases does not prevent them from serving as jurors in other criminal cases, and thus leads to no substantial deprivation of their basic rights of citizenship. They are treated no differently than any juror who expresses the view that he would be unable to follow the law in a particular case. * * *

McCree argues that, even if we reject the Eighth Circuit's fair cross-section holding, we should affirm the judgment below on the alternative ground, adopted by the District Court, that "death qualification" violated his constitutional right to an impartial jury. * * * McCree argues that his jury lacked impartiality because the absence of "*Witherspoon* -excludables" "slanted" the jury in favor of conviction.

We do not agree. McCree's "impartiality" argument apparently is based on the theory that, because all individual jurors are to some extent predisposed towards one result or another, a constitutionally impartial *jury* can be constructed only by "balancing" the various predispositions of the individual *jurors*. Thus, according to McCree, when the State "tips the scales" by excluding prospective jurors with a particular viewpoint, an impermissibly partial jury results. We have consistently rejected this view of jury impartiality, including as recently as last Term when we squarely held that an impartial *jury* consists of nothing more than "*jurors* who will conscientiously apply the law and find the facts."

McCree argues, however, that this Court's decisions in *Witherspoon, supra,* and *Adams v. Texas,* 448 U.S. 38 (1980), [applying *Witherspoon,*] stand for the proposition that a State violates the Constitution whenever it "slants" the jury by excluding a group of individuals more likely than the population at large to favor the criminal defendant. We think McCree overlooks two fundamental differences between *Witherspoon* and *Adams* and the instant case, and therefore misconceives the import and scope of those two decisions.

First, the Court in *Witherspoon* viewed the Illinois system as having been deliberately slanted for the purpose of making the imposition of the death penalty more likely.   * * *

Here, on the other hand, the removal for cause of "*Witherspoon*-excludables" serves the State's entirely proper interest in obtaining a single jury that could impartially decide all of the issues in McCree's case. Arkansas by legislative enactment and judicial decision provides for the use of a unitary jury in capital cases.   * * *

The Arkansas Supreme Court recently explained the State's legislative choice to require unitary juries in capital cases:

> "It has always been the law in Arkansas, except when the punishment is mandatory, that the same jurors who have the responsibility for determining guilt or innocence must also shoulder the burden of fixing the punishment. That is as it should be, for the two questions are necessarily interwoven."

Another interest identified by the State in support of its system of unitary juries is the possibility that, in at least some capital cases, the defendant might benefit at the sentencing phase of the trial from the jury's "residual doubts" about the evidence presented at the guilt phase.   * * * Finally, it seems obvious to us that in most, if not all, capital cases much of the evidence adduced at the guilt phase of the trial will also have a bearing on the penalty phase; if two different juries were to be required, such testimony would have to be presented twice, once to each jury.   * * *

Second, and more importantly, both *Witherspoon* and *Adams* dealt with the special context of capital sentencing, where the range of jury discretion necessarily gave rise to far greater concern over the possible effects of an "imbalanced" jury. * * *

In the case at bar, by contrast, we deal not with capital sentencing, but with the jury's more traditional role of finding the facts and determining the guilt or innocence of a criminal defendant, where jury discretion is more channeled. We reject McCree's suggestion that *Witherspoon* and *Adams* have broad applicability outside the special context of capital sentencing, and conclude that those two decisions do not support the result reached by the Eighth Circuit here.   * * *

JUSTICE BLACKMUN concurs in the result.

JUSTICE MARSHALL, with whom JUSTICE BRENNAN and JUSTICE STEVENS join, dissenting.

* * * The data strongly suggest that death qualification excludes a significantly large subset—at least 11% to 17%—of potential jurors who could be

impartial during the guilt phase of trial. Among the members of this excludable class are a disproportionate number of blacks and women.

The perspectives on the criminal justice system of jurors who survive death qualification are systematically different from those of the excluded jurors. Death-qualified jurors are, for example, more likely to believe that a defendant's failure to testify is indicative of his guilt, more hostile to the insanity defense, more mistrustful of defense attorneys, and less concerned about the danger of erroneous convictions. This pro-prosecution bias is reflected in the greater readiness of death-qualified jurors to convict or to convict on more serious charges. And, finally, the very process of death qualification—which focuses attention on the death penalty before the trial has even begun—has been found to predispose the jurors that survive it to believe that the defendant is guilty.

The evidence thus confirms, and is itself corroborated by, the more intuitive judgments of scholars and of so many of the participants in capital trials—judges, defense attorneys, and prosecutors. * * *

Faced with the near unanimity of authority supporting respondent's claim that death qualification gives the prosecution a particular advantage in the guilt phase of capital trials, the majority here makes but a weak effort to contest that proposition. Instead, it merely assumes for the purposes of this opinion "that 'death-qualification' in fact produces juries somewhat more 'conviction-prone' than 'non-death-qualified' juries," and then holds that this result does not offend the Constitution. This disregard for the clear import of the evidence tragically misconstrues the settled constitutional principles that guarantee a defendant the right to a fair trial and an impartial jury whose composition is not biased toward the prosecution. * * *

As the *Witherspoon* Court recognized, "the State's interest in submitting the penalty issue to a jury capable of imposing capital punishment" may be accommodated without infringing a capital defendant's interest in a fair determination of his guilt if the State uses "one jury to decide guilt and another to fix punishment." Any exclusion of death-penalty opponents, the Court reasoned, could await the penalty phase of a trial. The question here is thus whether the State has *other* interests that require the use of a single jury and demand the subordination of a capital defendant's Sixth and Fourteenth Amendment rights.

The only two reasons that the Court invokes to justify the State's use of a single jury are efficient trial management and concern that a defendant at his sentencing proceedings may be able to profit from "residual doubts" troubling jurors who have sat through the guilt phase of his trial. The first of these purported justifications is merely unconvincing. The second is offensive. * * *

In a system using separate juries for guilt and penalty phases, time and resources would be saved every time a capital case did not require a penalty phase. The *voir dire* needed to identify nullifiers before the guilt phase is less extensive than the questioning that under the current scheme conducted before *every* capital trial. The State could, of course, choose to empanel a death-qualified jury at the start of every trial, to be used only if a penalty stage is required. However, if it opted for the cheaper alternative of empanelling a death-qualified jury only in the event that a defendant were convicted of capital charges, the State frequently would be able to avoid retrying the entire guilt phase for the benefit of the penalty jury. Stipulated summaries of prior evidence might, for example, save considerable time. Thus, it cannot fairly be said that the costs of accommodating a defendant's constitutional rights under these circumstances are prohibitive, or even significant.

Even less convincing is the Court's concern that a defendant be able to appeal at sentencing to the "residual doubts" of the jurors who found him guilty. Any suggestion that the current system of death qualification "may be in the defendant's best interests, seems specious unless the state is willing to grant the defendant the option to waive this paternalistic protection in exchange for better odds against conviction." Furthermore, this case will stand as one of the few times in which any legitimacy has been given to the power of a convicted capital defendant facing the possibility of a death sentence to argue as a mitigating factor the chance that he might be innocent. Where a defendant's sentence but not his conviction has been set aside on appeal, States have routinely empanelled juries whose only duty is to assess punishment, thereby depriving defendants of the chance to profit from the "residual doubts" that jurors who had already sat through a guilt phase might bring to the sentencing proceeding. * * *

But most importantly, it ill-behooves the majority to allude to a defendant's power to appeal to "residual doubts" at his sentencing when this Court has consistently refused to grant certiorari in state cases holding that these doubts cannot properly be considered during capital sentencing proceedings. * * *

BATSON v. KENTUCKY

476 U.S. 79, 106 S.Ct. 1712, 90 L.Ed.2d 69 (1986).

JUSTICE POWELL delivered the opinion of the Court.

This case requires us to reexamine that portion of *Swain v. Alabama,* 380 U.S. 202 (1965), concerning the evidentiary burden placed on a criminal defendant who claims that he has been denied equal protection through the State's use of peremptory challenges to exclude members of his race from the petit jury.[1]

Petitioner, a black man, was indicted in Kentucky on charges of second-degree burglary and receipt of stolen goods. On the first day of trial in Jefferson Circuit Court, the judge conducted *voir dire* examination of the venire, excused certain jurors for cause, and permitted the parties to exercise peremptory challenges. The prosecutor used his peremptory challenges to strike all four black persons on the venire, and a jury composed only of white persons was selected. Defense counsel moved to discharge the jury before it was sworn on the ground that the prosecutor's removal of the black veniremen violated petitioner's rights under the Sixth and Fourteenth Amendments to a jury drawn from a cross-section of the community, and under the Fourteenth Amendment to equal protection of the laws. Counsel requested a hearing on his motion. Without expressly ruling on the request for a hearing, the trial judge observed that the parties were entitled to use their peremptory challenges to "strike anybody they want to." The judge then denied petitioner's motion, reasoning that the cross-section requirement applies only to selection of the venire and not to selection of the petit jury itself.

The jury convicted petitioner on both counts. On appeal to the Supreme Court of Kentucky, petitioner pressed, among other claims, the argument concerning the prosecutor's use of peremptory challenges. Conceding that *Swain v. Alabama* apparently foreclosed an equal protection claim based solely on the prosecutor's conduct in this case, petitioner urged the court to follow decisions of other states, and to hold that such conduct violated his rights under the Sixth

1. Following the lead of a number of state courts construing their state's constitution, two federal Courts of Appeals recently have accepted the view that peremptory challenges used to strike black jurors in a particular case may violate the Sixth Amendment. Other Courts of Appeals have rejected that position * * *.

Amendment and Section 11 of the Kentucky Constitution to a jury drawn from a cross-section of the community. Petitioner also contended that the facts showed that the prosecutor had engaged in a "pattern" of discriminatory challenges in this case and established an equal protection violation under *Swain.*

The Supreme Court of Kentucky affirmed. * * * We granted certiorari, and now reverse.

In *Swain v. Alabama,* this Court recognized that a "State's purposeful or deliberate denial to Negroes on account of race of participation as jurors in the administration of justice violates the Equal Protection Clause." This principle has been "consistently and repeatedly" reaffirmed, in numerous decisions of this Court both preceding and following *Swain.* We reaffirm the principle today.[4]
* * *

Accordingly, the component of the jury selection process at issue here, the State's privilege to strike individual jurors through peremptory challenges, is subject to the commands of the Equal Protection Clause.[12] Although a prosecutor ordinarily is entitled to exercise permitted peremptory challenges "for any reason at all, as long as that reason is related to his view concerning the outcome" of the case to be tried, the Equal Protection Clause forbids the prosecutor to challenge potential jurors solely on account of their race or on the assumption that black jurors as a group will be unable impartially to consider the State's case against a black defendant. * * *

Swain required the Court to decide, among other issues, whether a black defendant was denied equal protection by the State's exercise of peremptory challenges to exclude members of his race from the petit jury. The record in

---

4. In this Court, petitioner has argued that the prosecutor's conduct violated his rights under the Sixth and Fourteenth Amendments to an impartial jury and to a jury drawn from a cross-section of the community. Petitioner has framed his argument in these terms in an apparent effort to avoid inviting the Court directly to reconsider one of its own precedents. On the other hand, the State has insisted that petitioner is claiming a denial of equal protection and that we must reconsider *Swain* to find a constitutional violation on this record. We agree with the State that resolution of petitioner's claim properly turns on application of equal protection principles and express no view on the merits of any of petitioner's Sixth Amendment arguments.

[**Editors' note:** Later in *Holland v. Illinois,* 493 U.S. 474 (1990), the Court rejected, 5–4, "the thesis that a prosecutor's use of peremptory challenges to eliminate a distinctive group in the community deprives the defendant of a Sixth Amendment right to the 'fair possibility' of a representative jury. While statements in our prior cases have alluded to such a 'fair possibility' requirement, satisfying it has not been held to require anything beyond the inclusion of all cognizable groups in the venire, and the use of a jury numbering at least six persons."]

12. We express no views on whether the Constitution imposes any limit on the exercise of peremptory challenges by defense counsel.
* * *

[**Editor's note:** Later in *Georgia v. McCollum,* 502 U.S. 1056 (1992), the Court held *Batson* was applicable where the prosecutor sought to prevent white defendants, charged with assaulting blacks, from striking black prospective jurors because of their race. The Court reasoned that (i) "a criminal defendant's exercise of peremptory challenges in a racially discriminatory manner inflicts the harms addressed by *Batson,*" denial of prospective jurors' right to serve as jurors and loss of public confidence in the fairness of jury verdicts; (ii) such exercise of peremptories "constitutes state action," as a defendant in exercising peremptories "is performing a traditional governmental function"; (iii) "the State has standing to challenge a defendant's discriminatory use of peremptory challenges," as "its own judicial process is undermined" thereby and there are significant barriers to the excluded jurors themselves obtaining relief; and (iv) the interests served by *Batson* need not "give way to the rights of a criminal defendant," as a defendant's rights to a fair trial, counsel and an impartial jury do not include "the right to discriminate against a group of citizens based upon their race." Thomas, J., concurring, found "difficult" a statement in the NAACP's brief stating that "whether white defendants can use peremptory challenges to purge minority jurors presents quite different issues from whether a minority defendant can strike majority group jurors."]

Swain showed that the prosecutor had used the State's peremptory challenges to strike the six black persons included on the petit jury venire. While rejecting the defendant's claim for failure to prove purposeful discrimination, the Court nonetheless indicated that the Equal Protection Clause placed some limits on the State's exercise of peremptory challenges.

The Court sought to accommodate the prosecutor's historical privilege of peremptory challenge free of judicial control, and the constitutional prohibition on exclusion of persons from jury service on account of race. While the Constitution does not confer a right to peremptory challenges, those challenges traditionally have been viewed as one means of assuring the selection of a qualified and unbiased jury.[15] To preserve the peremptory nature of the prosecutor's challenge, the Court in *Swain* declined to scrutinize his actions in a particular case by relying on a presumption that he properly exercised the State's challenges.

The Court went on to observe, however, that a state may not exercise its challenges in contravention of the Equal Protection Clause. It was impermissible for a prosecutor to use his challenges to exclude blacks from the jury "for reasons wholly unrelated to the outcome of the particular case on trial" or to deny to blacks "the same right and opportunity to participate in the administration of justice enjoyed by the white population." Accordingly, a black defendant could make out a prima facie case of purposeful discrimination on proof that the peremptory challenge system was "being perverted" in that manner. For example, an inference of purposeful discrimination would be raised on evidence that a prosecutor, "in case after case, whatever the circumstances, whatever the crime and whoever the defendant or the victim may be, is responsible for the removal of Negroes who have been selected as qualified jurors by the jury commissioners and who have survived challenges for cause, with the result that no Negroes ever serve on petit juries." Evidence offered by the defendant in *Swain* did not meet that standard. While the defendant showed that prosecutors in the jurisdiction had exercised their strikes to exclude blacks from the jury, he offered no proof of the circumstances under which prosecutors were responsible for striking black jurors beyond the facts of his own case.

A number of lower courts following the teaching of *Swain* reasoned that proof of repeated striking of blacks over a number of cases was necessary to establish a violation of the Equal Protection Clause. Since this interpretation of *Swain* has placed on defendants a crippling burden of proof,[17] prosecutors' peremptory challenges are now largely immune from constitutional scrutiny. For reasons that follow, we reject this evidentiary formulation as inconsistent with standards that have been developed since *Swain* for assessing a prima facie case under the Equal Protection Clause.

[S]ince the decision in *Swain*, this Court has recognized that a defendant may make a prima facie showing of purposeful racial discrimination in selection of the venire by relying solely on the facts concerning its selection *in his case*. These decisions are in accordance with the proposition that "a consistent pattern of

[handwritten margin note: wrong interpretation of Swain]

---

15. In *Swain*, the Court reviewed the "very old credentials" of the peremptory challenge system and noted the "long and widely held belief that peremptory challenge is a necessary part of trial by jury."

17. The lower courts have noted the practical difficulties of proving that the State systematically has exercised peremptory challenges to exclude blacks from the jury on account of race. [T]he defendant would have to investigate, over a number of cases, the race of persons tried in the particular jurisdiction, the racial composition of the venire and petit jury, and the manner in which both parties exercised their peremptory challenges. * * * In jurisdictions where court records do not reflect the jurors' race and where *voir dire* proceedings are not transcribed, the burden would be insurmountable.

official racial discrimination" is not "a necessary predicate to a violation of the Equal Protection Clause. A single invidiously discriminatory governmental act" is not "immunized by the absence of such discrimination in the making of other comparable decisions." For evidentiary requirements to dictate that "several must suffer discrimination" before one could object, would be inconsistent with the promise of equal protection to all.

The standards for assessing a prima facie case in the context of discriminatory selection of the venire have been fully articulated since *Swain*. These principles support our conclusion that a defendant may establish a prima facie case of purposeful discrimination in selection of the petit jury solely on evidence concerning the prosecutor's exercise of peremptory challenges at the defendant's trial. To establish such a case, the defendant first must show that he is a member of a cognizable racial group, and that the prosecutor has exercised peremptory challenges to remove from the venire members of the defendant's race.[a] Second, the defendant is entitled to rely on the fact, as to which there can be no dispute, that peremptory challenges constitute a jury selection practice that permits "those to discriminate who are of a mind to discriminate." Finally, the defendant must show that these facts and any other relevant circumstances raise an inference that the prosecutor used that practice to exclude the veniremen from the petit jury on account of their race. This combination of factors in the empanelling of the petit jury, as in the selection of the venire, raises the necessary inference of purposeful discrimination.

In deciding whether the defendant has made the requisite showing, the trial court should consider all relevant circumstances. For example, a "pattern" of strikes against black jurors included in the particular venire might give rise to an inference of discrimination. Similarly, the prosecutor's questions and statements during *voir dire* examination and in exercising his challenges may support or refute an inference of discriminatory purpose. These examples are merely illustrative. We have confidence that trial judges, experienced in supervising *voir dire,* will be able to decide if the circumstances concerning the prosecutor's use of peremptory challenges creates a prima facie case of discrimination against black jurors.

Once the defendant makes a prima facie showing, the burden shifts to the State to come forward with a neutral explanation for challenging black jurors.[b]

a. But in *Powers v. Ohio,* 499 U.S. 400 (1991), the Court held, 7–2, that "a white defendant may object to the prosecution's peremptory challenges of black venirepersons." The majority reasoned that such challenges, if based upon race, violate the venirepersons' right to equal protection under the Fourteenth Amendment, as to which "a criminal defendant has standing" to object because the three criteria for recognizing third-party standing are present: (1) The defendant has "suffered an 'injury-in-fact'" by such peremptory challenges adequate to give "him or her a 'sufficiently concrete interest' in the outcome of the issue in dispute," for the "overt wrong, often apparent to the entire jury panel, casts doubt over the obligation of the parties, the jury, and indeed the court to adhere to the law throughout the trial of the cause." (2) The defendant has "a close relation to the third party" excluded venirepersons, as he or she "will be a motivated, effective advocate for the excluded venirepersons' rights" given "that discrimina-

tion in the jury selection process may lead to the reversal of a conviction." (3) There exists "some hindrance to the third party's ability to protect his or her own interests," for potential jurors "have no opportunity to be heard at the time of their exclusion," cannot "easily obtain declaratory or injunctive relief" later given the need to show a likely reoccurrence of their own exclusion based on race, and are unlikely to undertake an action for damages "because of the small financial stake involved and the economic burdens of litigation."

b. As the Court later explained in *Purkett v. Elem,* 514 U.S. 765 (1995), at this second stage it is not necessary that the prosecutor's explanation also be "at least minimally persuasive," for such a requirement would violate "the principle that the ultimate burden of persuasion regarding racial motivation rests with, and never shifts from, the opponent of the strike." But at the third stage, when the trial court must decide if that opponent did carry

Though this requirement imposes a limitation in some cases on the full peremptory character of the historic challenge, we emphasize that the prosecutor's explanation need not rise to the level justifying exercise of a challenge for cause. But the prosecutor may not rebut the defendant's prima facie case of discrimination by stating merely that he challenged jurors of the defendant's race on the assumption—or his intuitive judgment—that they would be partial to the defendant because of their shared race. Just as the Equal Protection Clause forbids the States to exclude black persons from the venire on the assumption that blacks as a group are unqualified to serve as jurors, so it forbids the States to strike black veniremen on the assumption that they will be biased in a particular case simply because the defendant is black. The core guarantee of equal protection, ensuring citizens that their State will not discriminate on account of race, would be meaningless were we to approve the exclusion of jurors on the basis of such assumptions, which arise solely from the jurors' race. Nor may the prosecutor rebut the defendant's case merely by denying that he had a discriminatory motive or "affirming his good faith in individual selections." If these general assertions were accepted as rebutting a defendant's prima facie case, the Equal Protection Clause "would be but a vain and illusory requirement." The prosecutor therefore must articulate a neutral explanation related to the particular case to be tried. The trial court then will have the duty to determine if the defendant has established purposeful discrimination.[c]

The State contends that our holding will eviscerate the fair trial values served by the peremptory challenge. Conceding that the Constitution does not guarantee a right to peremptory challenges and that *Swain* did state that their use ultimately is subject to the strictures of equal protection, the State argues that the privilege of unfettered exercise of the challenge is of vital importance to the criminal justice system.

this burden, "implausible or fantastic justifications may (and probably will) be found to be pretexts for purposeful discrimination." See also the *Hernandez* case in note c infra.

c. In *Hernandez v. New York,* 500 U.S. 352 (1991), Kennedy, J., for four members of the Court, concluded: "The prosecutor here offered a race-neutral basis for these peremptory strikes. As explained by the prosecutor, the challenges rested neither on the intention to exclude Latino or bilingual jurors, nor on stereotypical assumptions about Latinos or bilinguals. The prosecutor's articulated basis for these challenges divided potential jurors into two classes: those whose conduct during *voir dire* would persuade him they might have difficulty in accepting the translator's rendition of Spanish-language testimony and those potential jurors who gave no such reason for doubt. Each category would include both Latinos and non-Latinos. While the prosecutor's criterion might well result in the disproportionate removal of prospective Latino jurors, that disproportionate impact does not turn the prosecutor's actions into a *per se* violation of the Equal Protection Clause. [However, if] a prosecutor articulates a basis for a peremptory challenge that results in the disproportionate exclusion of members of a certain race, the trial judge may consider that fact as evidence that the prosecutor's stated reason constitutes a pretext for racial discrimination." The Court then

concluded the state court's finding of no discriminatory intent should stand because not clearly erroneous.

Two concurring members of the Court emphasized that if "the trial court believes the prosecutor's nonracial justification, and that finding is not clearly erroneous, that is the end of the matter," meaning disproportionate effect is then irrelevant. The three dissenters concluded the prosecutor's explanation "was insufficient for three reasons. First, the justification would inevitably result in a disproportionate disqualification of Spanish-speaking venirepersons. An explanation that is 'race-neutral' on its face is nonetheless unacceptable if it is merely a proxy for a discriminatory practice. Second, the prosecutor's concern could easily have been accommodated by less drastic means. As is the practice in many jurisdictions, the jury could have been instructed that the official translation alone is evidence; bilingual jurors could have been instructed to bring to the attention of the judge any disagreements they might have with the translation so that any disputes could be resolved by the court. Third, if the prosecutor's concern was valid and substantiated by the record, it would have supported a challenge for cause. The fact that the prosecutor did not make any such challenge should disqualify him from advancing the concern as a justification for a peremptory challenge."

While we recognize, of course, that the peremptory challenge occupies an important position in our trial procedures, we do not agree that our decision today will undermine the contribution the challenge generally makes to the administration of justice. The reality of practice, amply reflected in many state and federal court opinions, shows that the challenge may be, and unfortunately at times has been, used to discriminate against black jurors. By requiring trial courts to be sensitive to the racially discriminatory use of peremptory challenges, our decision enforces the mandate of equal protection and furthers the ends of justice.[22] In view of the heterogeneous population of our nation, public respect for our criminal justice system and the rule of law will be strengthened if we ensure that no citizen is disqualified from jury service because of his race.

Nor are we persuaded by the State's suggestion that our holding will create serious administrative difficulties. In those states applying a version of the evidentiary standard we recognize today, courts have not experienced serious administrative burdens, and the peremptory challenge system has survived. We decline, however, to formulate particular procedures to be followed upon a defendant's timely objection to a prosecutor's challenges.[24]

In this case, petitioner made a timely objection to the prosecutor's removal of all black persons on the venire. Because the trial court flatly rejected the objection without requiring the prosecutor to give an explanation for his action, we remand this case for further proceedings. If the trial court decides that the facts establish, prima facie, purposeful discrimination and the prosecutor does not come forward with a neutral explanation for his action, our precedents require that petitioner's conviction be reversed.

JUSTICE MARSHALL, concurring. * * *

I wholeheartedly concur in the Court's conclusion that use of the peremptory challenge to remove blacks from juries, on the basis of their race, violates the Equal Protection Clause. I would go further, however, in fashioning a remedy adequate to eliminate that discrimination. Merely allowing defendants the opportunity to challenge the racially discriminatory use of peremptory challenges in individual cases will not end the illegitimate use of the peremptory challenge.

Evidentiary analysis similar to that set out by the Court has been adopted as a matter of state law in States including Massachusetts and California. Cases from those jurisdictions illustrate the limitations of the approach. First, defendants cannot attack the discriminatory use of peremptory challenges at all unless the challenges are so flagrant as to establish a prima facie case. This means, in those States, that where only one or two black jurors survive the challenges for

22. While we respect the views expressed in Justice Marshall's concurring opinion, concerning prosecutorial and judicial enforcement of our holding today, we do not share them. The standard we adopt under the federal Constitution is designed to ensure that a State does not use peremptory challenges to strike any black juror because of his race. We have no reason to believe that prosecutors will not fulfill their duty to exercise their challenges only for legitimate purposes. Certainly, this Court may assume that trial judges, in supervising *voir dire* in light of our decision today, will be alert to identify a prima facie case of purposeful discrimination. Nor do we think that this historic trial practice, which long has served the selection of an impartial jury, should be abolished because of an apprehen-

sion that prosecutors and trial judges will not perform conscientiously their respective duties under the Constitution.

24. In light of the variety of jury selection practices followed in our state and federal trial courts, we make no attempt to instruct these courts how best to implement our holding today. For the same reason, we express no view on whether it is more appropriate in a particular case, upon a finding of discrimination against black jurors, for the trial court to discharge the venire and select a new jury from a panel not previously associated with the case, or to disallow the discriminatory challenges and resume selection with the improperly challenged jurors reinstated on the venire.

cause, the prosecutor need have no compunction about striking them from the jury because of their race. Prosecutors are left free to discriminate against blacks in jury selection provided that they hold that discrimination to an "acceptable" level.

Second, when a defendant can establish a prima facie case, trial courts face the difficult burden of assessing prosecutors' motives. Any prosecutor can easily assert facially neutral reasons for striking a juror, and trial courts are ill-equipped to second-guess those reasons. How is the court to treat a prosecutor's statement that he struck a juror because the juror had a son about the same age as defendant, or seemed "uncommunicative," or "never cracked a smile" and, therefore "did not possess the sensitivities necessary to realistically look at the issues and decide the facts in this case." If such easily generated explanations are sufficient to discharge the prosecutor's obligation to justify his strikes on nonracial grounds, then the protection erected by the Court today may be illusory.

Nor is outright prevarication by prosecutors the only danger here. "[I]t is even possible that an attorney may lie to himself in an effort to convince himself that his motives are legal." A prosecutor's own conscious or unconscious racism may lead him easily to the conclusion that a prospective black juror is "sullen," or "distant," a characterization that would not have come to his mind if a white juror had acted identically. A judge's own conscious or unconscious racism may lead him to accept such an explanation as well supported. * * *

The inherent potential of peremptory challenges to distort the jury process by permitting the exclusion of jurors on racial grounds should ideally lead the Court to ban them entirely from the criminal justice system. * * *

Some authors have suggested that the courts should ban prosecutors' peremptories entirely, but should zealously guard the defendant's peremptory as "essential to the fairness of trial by jury" and "one of the most important of the rights secured to the accused." I would not find that an acceptable solution. Our criminal justice system "requires not only freedom from any bias against the accused, but also from any prejudice against his prosecution. Between him and the state the scales are to be evenly held." We can maintain that balance, not by permitting both prosecutor and defendant to engage in racial discrimination in jury selection, but by banning the use of peremptory challenges by prosecutors and by allowing the States to eliminate the defendant's peremptory as well. * * *

Chief Justice Burger, joined by Justice Rehnquist, dissenting.

* * * The Court acknowledges, albeit in a footnote, the " 'very old credentials' " of the peremptory challenge and " 'the widely held belief that peremptory challenge is a necessary part of trial by jury.' " But proper resolution of this case requires more than a nodding reference to the purpose of the challenge. * * *

The Court's opinion, in addition to ignoring the teachings of history, also contrasts with *Swain* in its failure to even discuss the rationale of the peremptory challenge. *Swain* observed:

> "The function of the challenge is not only to eliminate extremes of partiality on both sides, but to assure the parties that the jurors before whom they try the case will decide on the basis of the evidence placed for them, and not otherwise. In this way the peremptory satisfies the rule that 'to perform its high function in the best way, justice must satisfy the appearance of justice.' "

Permitting unexplained peremptories has long been regarded as a means to strengthen our jury system in other ways as well. One commentator has recognized:

"The peremptory, made without giving any reason, avoids trafficking in the core of truth in most common stereotypes. * * * Common human experience, common sense, psychosociological studies, and public opinion polls tell us that it is likely that certain classes of people statistically have predispositions that would make them inappropriate jurors for particular kinds of cases. But to allow this knowledge to be expressed in the evaluative terms necessary for challenges for cause would undercut our desire for a society in which all people are judged as individuals and in which each is held reasonable and open to compromise. * * * [For example,] [a]lthough experience reveals that black males as a class can be biased against young alienated blacks who have not tried to join the middle class, to enunciate this in the concrete expression required of a challenge for cause is societally divisive. Instead we have evolved in the peremptory challenge a system that allows the covert expression of what we dare not say but know is true more often than not."

For reasons such as these, this Court concluded in *Swain* that "the [peremptory] challenge is 'one of the most important of the rights' " in our justice system. For close to a century, then, it has been settled that "[t]he denial or impairment of the right is reversible error without a showing of prejudice."

[T]he Court also invokes general equal protection principles in support of its holding. But peremptory challenges are often lodged, of necessity, for reasons "normally thought irrelevant to legal proceedings or official action, namely, the race, religion, nationality, occupation or affiliations of people summoned for jury duty." *Swain.* Moreover, in making peremptory challenges, both the prosecutor and defense attorney necessarily act on only limited information or hunch. The process can not be indicted on the sole basis that such decisions are made on the basis of "assumption" or "intuitive judgment." As a result, unadulterated equal protection analysis is simply inapplicable to peremptory challenges exercised in any particular case. A clause that requires a minimum "rationality" in government actions has no application to " 'an arbitrary and capricious right' "; a constitutional principle that may invalidate state action on the basis of "stereotypic notions" does not explain the breadth of a procedure exercised on the " 'sudden impressions and unaccountable prejudices we are apt to conceive upon the bare looks and gestures of another.' "

That the Court is not applying conventional equal protection analysis is shown by its limitation of its new rule to allegations of impermissible challenge *on the basis of race;* the Court's opinion clearly contains such a limitation. * * * But if conventional equal protection principles apply, then presumably defendants could object to exclusions on the basis of not only race, but also sex, age, religious or political affiliation, mental capacity, number of children, living arrangements, and employment in a particular industry or profession.[4]

In short, it is quite probable that every peremptory challenge could be objected to on the basis that, because it excluded a venireman who had some characteristic not shared by the remaining members of the venire, it constituted a "classification" subject to equal protection scrutiny. Compounding the difficulties, under conventional equal protection principles some uses of peremptories would be reviewed under "strict scrutiny and * * * sustained only if * * * suitably tailored to serve a compelling state interest," others would be reviewed to determine if they were "substantially related to a sufficiently important govern-

---

4. While all these distinctions might support a claim under conventional equal protection principles, a defendant would also have to establish standing to raise them before obtaining any relief.

ment interest," and still others would be reviewed to determine whether they were "a rational means to serve a legitimate end."

The Court never applies this conventional equal protection framework to the claims at hand, perhaps to avoid acknowledging that the state interest involved here has historically been regarded by this Court as substantial, if not compelling. * * *

The Court also purports to express "no views on whether the Constitution imposes any limit on the exercise of peremptory challenges by *defense* counsel." But the clear and inescapable import of this novel holding will inevitably be to limit the use of this valuable tool to both prosecutors and defense attorneys alike. Once the Court has held that *prosecutors* are limited in their use of peremptory challenges, could we rationally hold that defendants are not?[6] * * *

Confronted with the dilemma it created, the Court today attempts to decree a middle ground. To rebut a prima facie case, the Court requires a "neutral explanation" for the challenge, but is at pains to "emphasize" that the "explanation need not rise to the level justifying exercise of a challenge for cause." I am at a loss to discern the governing principles here. A "clear and reasonably specific" explanation of "legitimate reasons" for exercising the challenge will be difficult to distinguish from a challenge for cause. Anything short of a challenge for cause may well be seen as an "arbitrary and capricious" challenge, to use Blackstone's characterization of the peremptory. Apparently the Court envisions permissible challenges short of a challenge for cause that are just a little bit arbitrary—but not too much. While our trial judges are "experienced in supervising *voir dire*," they have no experience in administering rules like this.

An example will quickly demonstrate how today's holding, while purporting to "further the ends of justice," will not have that effect. Assume an Asian defendant, on trial for the capital murder of a white victim, asks prospective jury members, most of whom are white, whether they harbor racial prejudice against Asians. The basis for such a question is to flush out any "juror who believes that [Asians] are violence-prone or morally inferior. * * * Assume further that all white jurors deny harboring racial prejudice but that the defendant, on trial for his life, remains unconvinced by these protestations. Instead, he continues to harbor a hunch, an "assumption" or "intuitive judgment," that these white jurors will be prejudiced against him, presumably based in part on race. The time honored rule before today was that peremptory challenges could be exercised on such a basis. * * * The effect of the Court's decision, however, will be to force the defendant to come forward and "articulate a neutral explanation," for his peremptory challenge, a burden he probably cannot meet. This example demonstrates that today's holding will produce juries that the parties do not believe are truly impartial. This will surely do more than "disconcert" litigants; it will diminish confidence in the jury system. * * *

Today we mark the return of racial differentiation as the Court accepts a positive evil for a perceived one. Prosecutors and defense attorneys alike will build records in support of their claims that peremptory challenges have been exercised in a racially discriminatory fashion by asking jurors to state their racial background and national origin for the record, despite the fact that "such questions may be offensive to some jurors and thus are not ordinarily asked on voir dire." This process is sure to tax even the most capable counsel and judges since determining whether a prima facie case has been established will "require a

6. "[E]very jurisdiction which has spoken to the matter, and prohibited prosecution case-specific peremptory challenges on the basis of cognizable group affiliation, has held that the defense must likewise be so prohibited."

continued monitoring and recording of the 'group' composition of the panel present and prospective. * * * " * * *

JUSTICE REHNQUIST with whom THE CHIEF JUSTICE joins, dissenting. * * *

I cannot subscribe to the Court's unprecedented use of the Equal Protection Clause to restrict the historic scope of the peremptory challenge, which has been described as "a necessary part of trial by jury." In my view, there is simply nothing "unequal" about the State using its peremptory challenges to strike blacks from the jury in cases involving black defendants, so long as such challenges are also used to exclude whites in cases involving white defendants, Hispanics in cases involving Hispanic defendants, Asians in cases involving Asian defendants, and so on. This case-specific use of peremptory challenges by the State does not single out blacks, or members of any other race for that matter, for discriminatory treatment. Such use of peremptories is at best based upon seat-of-the-pants instincts, which are undoubtedly crudely stereotypical and may in many cases be hopelessly mistaken. But as long as they are applied across the board to jurors of all races and nationalities, I do not see—and the Court most certainly has not explained—how their use violates the Equal Protection Clause.

Nor does such use of peremptory challenges by the State infringe upon any other constitutional interests. The Court does not suggest that exclusion of blacks from the jury through the State's use of peremptory challenges results in a violation of either the fair cross-section or impartiality component of the Sixth Amendment. And because the case-specific use of peremptory challenges by the State does not deny blacks the right to serve as jurors in cases involving non-black defendants, it harms neither the excluded jurors nor the remainder of the community.

The use of group affiliations, such as age, race, or occupation, as a "proxy" for potential juror partiality, based on the assumption or belief that members of one group are more likely to favor defendants who belong to the same group, has long been accepted as a legitimate basis for the State's exercise of peremptory challenges. Indeed, given the need for reasonable limitations on the time devoted to *voir dire,* the use of such "proxies" by both the State and the defendant may be extremely useful in eliminating from the jury persons who might be biased in one way or another. * * *

J.E.B. v. ALABAMA EX REL. T.B.

511 U.S. 127, 114 S.Ct. 1419, 128 L.Ed.2d 89 (1994).

JUSTICE BLACKMUN delivered the opinion of the Court. * * *

On behalf of relator T.B., the mother of a minor child, respondent State of Alabama filed a complaint for paternity and child support against petitioner J.E.B. in the District Court of Jackson County, Alabama. On October 21, 1991, the matter was called for trial and jury selection began. The trial court assembled a panel of 36 potential jurors, 12 males and 24 females. After the court excused three jurors for cause, only 10 of the remaining 33 jurors were male. The State then used 9 of its 10 peremptory strikes to remove male jurors; petitioner used all but one of his strikes to remove female jurors. As a result, all the selected jurors were female.

Before the jury was empaneled, petitioner objected to the State's peremptory challenges on the ground that they were exercised against male jurors solely on the basis of gender, in violation of the Equal Protection Clause of the Fourteenth Amendment. * * * The court rejected petitioner's claim and empaneled the all-female jury. The jury found petitioner to be the father of the child and the court entered an order directing him to pay child support. On post-judgment motion, the court reaffirmed its ruling that *Batson* does not extend to gender-based peremptory challenges.

We granted certiorari to resolve a question that has created a conflict of authority—whether the Equal Protection Clause forbids peremptory challenges on the basis of gender as well as on the basis of race. Today we reaffirm what, by now, should be axiomatic: Intentional discrimination on the basis of gender by state actors violates the Equal Protection Clause, particularly where, as here, the discrimination serves to ratify and perpetuate invidious, archaic, and overbroad stereotypes about the relative abilities of men and women.

Discrimination on the basis of gender in the exercise of peremptory challenges is a relatively recent phenomenon. Gender-based peremptory strikes were hardly practicable for most of our country's existence, since, until the 19th century, women were completely excluded from jury service. So well-entrenched was this exclusion of women that in 1880 this Court, while finding that the exclusion of African–American men from juries violated the Fourteenth Amendment, expressed no doubt that a State "may confine the selection [of jurors] to males." *Strauder v. West Virginia,* 100 U.S. 303.

Many States continued to exclude women from jury service well into the present century, despite the fact that women attained suffrage upon ratification of the Nineteenth Amendment in 1920. States that did permit women to serve on juries often erected other barriers, such as registration requirements and automatic exemptions, designed to deter women from exercising their right to jury service.

The prohibition of women on juries was derived from the English common law which, according to Blackstone, rightfully excluded women from juries under "the doctrine of *propter defectum sexus,* literally, the 'defect of sex.'" In this country, supporters of the exclusion of women from juries tended to couch their objections in terms of the ostensible need to protect women from the ugliness and depravity of trials. Women were thought to be too fragile and virginal to withstand the polluted courtroom atmosphere. * * *

Taylor [*v. Louisiana,* supra] relied on Sixth Amendment principles, but the opinion's approach is consistent with the heightened equal protection scrutiny afforded gender-based classifications. Since *Reed v. Reed,* 404 U.S. 71 (1971), this Court consistently has subjected gender-based classifications to heightened scrutiny in recognition of the real danger that government policies that professedly are based on reasonable considerations in fact may be reflective of "archaic and overbroad" generalizations about gender, or based on "outdated misconceptions concerning the role of females in the home rather than in the 'marketplace and world of ideas.'"

Despite the heightened scrutiny afforded distinctions based on gender, respondent argues that gender discrimination in the selection of the petit jury should be permitted, though discrimination on the basis of race is not. Respondent suggests that "gender discrimination in this country ... has never reached the level of discrimination" against African–Americans, and therefore gender discrimination, unlike racial discrimination, is tolerable in the courtroom. While the prejudicial attitudes toward women in this country have not been identical to those held toward racial minorities, the similarities between the experiences of racial minorities and women, in some contexts, "overpower those differences." As a plurality of this Court observed in *Frontiero v. Richardson,* 411 U.S. 677 (1973):

"[T]hroughout much of the 19th century the position of women in our society was, in many respects, comparable to that of blacks under the pre-Civil War slave codes. Neither slaves nor women could hold office, serve on juries, or bring suit in their own names, and married women traditionally were denied the legal capacity to hold or convey property or to serve as legal guardians of their own children. . . . And although blacks were guaranteed the right to vote in 1870, women were denied even that right—which is itself 'preservative of other basic civil and political rights'—until adoption of the Nineteenth Amendment half a century later."

Certainly, with respect to jury service, African–Americans and women share a history of total exclusion, a history which came to an end for women many years after the embarrassing chapter in our history came to an end for African–Americans.

We need not determine, however, whether women or racial minorities have suffered more at the hands of discriminatory state actors during the decades of our Nation's history. It is necessary only to acknowledge that "our Nation has had a long and unfortunate history of sex discrimination," a history which warrants the heightened scrutiny we afford all gender-based classifications today. Under our equal protection jurisprudence, gender-based classifications require "an exceedingly persuasive justification" in order to survive constitutional scrutiny. Thus, the only question is whether discrimination on the basis of gender in jury selection substantially furthers the State's legitimate interest in achieving a fair and impartial trial. In making this assessment, we do not weigh the value of peremptory challenges as an institution against our asserted commitment to eradicate invidious discrimination from the courtroom. Instead, we consider whether peremptory challenges based on gender stereotypes provide substantial aid to a litigant's effort to secure a fair and impartial jury.

Far from proffering an exceptionally persuasive justification for its gender-based peremptory challenges, respondent maintains that its decision to strike virtually all the males from the jury in this case "may reasonably have been based upon the perception, supported by history, that men otherwise totally qualified to serve upon a jury might be more sympathetic and receptive to the arguments of a man alleged in a paternity action to be the father of an out-of-wedlock child, while women equally qualified to serve upon a jury might be more sympathetic and receptive to the arguments of the complaining witness who bore the child." [9]

We shall not accept as a defense to gender-based peremptory challenges "the very stereotype the law condemns." Respondent's rationale, not unlike those regularly expressed for gender-based strikes, is reminiscent of the arguments advanced to justify the total exclusion of women from juries. Respondent offers

9. Respondent cites one study in support of its quasi-empirical claim that women and men may have different attitudes about certain issues justifying the use of gender as a proxy for bias. See R. Hastie, S. Penrod & N. Pennington, Inside the Jury 140 (1983). The authors conclude: "Neither student nor citizen judgments for typical criminal case material have revealed differences between male and female verdict preferences. * * * The picture differs [only] for rape cases, where female jurors appear to be somewhat more conviction-prone than male jurors". The majority of studies suggest that gender plays no identifiable role in jurors' attitudes. See, e.g., V. Hans & N. Vidmar, Judging the Jury 76 (1986) ("[I]n the majority of studies there are no significant differences in the way men and women perceive and react to trials; yet a few studies find women more defense-oriented, while still others show women more favorable to the prosecutor"). Even in 1956, before women had a constitutional right to serve on juries, some commentators warned against using gender as a proxy for bias. See 1 F. Busch, Law and Tactics in Jury Trials § 143, p. 207 (1949) ("In this age of general and specialized education, availed of generally by both men and women, it would appear unsound to base a peremptory challenge in any case upon the sole ground of sex. . . .").

virtually no support for the conclusion that gender alone is an accurate predictor of juror's attitudes; yet it urges this Court to condone the same stereotypes that justified the wholesale exclusion of women from juries and the ballot box.[11] Respondent seems to assume that gross generalizations that would be deemed impermissible if made on the basis of race are somehow permissible when made on the basis of gender.

Discrimination in jury selection, whether based on race or on gender, causes harm to the litigants, the community, and the individual jurors who are wrongfully excluded from participation in the judicial process. The litigants are harmed by the risk that the prejudice which motivated the discriminatory selection of the jury will infect the entire proceedings. The community is harmed by the State's participation in the perpetuation of invidious group stereotypes and the inevitable loss of confidence in our judicial system that state-sanctioned discrimination in the courtroom engenders. When state actors exercise peremptory challenges in reliance on gender stereotypes, they ratify and reinforce prejudicial views of the relative abilities of men and women. Because these stereotypes have wreaked injustice in so many other spheres of our country's public life, active discrimination by litigants on the basis of gender during jury selection "invites cynicism respecting the jury's neutrality and its obligation to adhere to the law." The potential for cynicism is particularly acute in cases where gender-related issues are prominent, such as cases involving rape, sexual harassment, or paternity. Discriminatory use of peremptory challenges may create the impression that the judicial system has acquiesced in suppressing full participation by one gender or that the "deck has been stacked" in favor of one side.

In recent cases we have emphasized that individual jurors themselves have a right to nondiscriminatory jury selection procedures. Contrary to respondent's suggestion, this right extends to both men and women. All persons, when granted the opportunity to serve on a jury, have the right not to be excluded summarily because of discriminatory and stereotypical presumptions that reflect and reinforce patterns of historical discrimination.[13] Striking individual jurors on the assumption that they hold particular views simply because of their gender is "practically a brand upon them, affixed by law, an assertion of their inferiority." It denigrates the dignity of the excluded juror, and, for a woman, reinvokes a history of exclusion from political participation.[14] The message it sends to all those in the courtroom, and all those who may later learn of the discriminatory act, is that certain individuals, for no reason other than gender, are presumed unqualified by state actors to decide important questions upon which reasonable persons could disagree.

---

11. Even if a measure of truth can be found in some of the gender stereotypes used to justify gender-based peremptory challenges, that fact alone cannot support discrimination on the basis of gender in jury selection. We have made abundantly clear in past cases that gender classifications that rest on impermissible stereotypes violate the Equal Protection Clause, even when some statistical support can be conjured up for the generalization. * * *

13. It is irrelevant that women, unlike African–Americans, are not a numerical minority and therefore are likely to remain on the jury if each side uses its peremptory challenges in an equally discriminatory fashion. Because the right to nondiscriminatory jury selection procedures belongs to the potential jurors, as well as to the litigants, the possibility that members of both genders will get on the jury despite the intentional discrimination is beside the point. The exclusion of even one juror for impermissible reasons harms that juror and undermines public confidence in the fairness of the system.

14. The popular refrain is that all peremptory challenges are based on stereotypes of some kind, expressing various intuitive and frequently erroneous biases. But where peremptory challenges are made on the basis of group characteristics other than race or gender (like occupation, for example), they do not reinforce the same stereotypes about the group's competence or predispositions that have been used to prevent them from voting, participating on juries, pursuing their chosen professions, or otherwise contributing to civic life.

Our conclusion that litigants may not strike potential jurors solely on the basis of gender does not imply the elimination of all peremptory challenges. Neither does it conflict with a State's legitimate interest in using such challenges in its effort to secure a fair and impartial jury. Parties still may remove jurors whom they feel might be less acceptable than others on the panel; gender simply may not serve as a proxy for bias. Parties may also exercise their peremptory challenges to remove from the venire any group or class of individuals normally subject to "rational basis" review. Even strikes based on characteristics that are disproportionately associated with one gender could be appropriate, absent a showing of pretext.[16] * * *

Failing to provide jurors the same protection against gender discrimination as race discrimination could frustrate the purpose of *Batson* itself. Because gender and race are overlapping categories, gender can be used as a pretext for racial discrimination. Allowing parties to remove racial minorities from the jury not because of their race, but because of their gender, contravenes well-established equal protection principles and could insulate effectively racial discrimination from judicial scrutiny.

JUSTICE O'CONNOR, concurring.

I agree with the Court that the Equal Protection Clause prohibits the government from excluding a person from jury service on account of that person's gender. * * *. I therefore join the Court's opinion in this case. But today's important blow against gender discrimination is not costless. I write separately to discuss some of these costs, and to express my belief that today's holding should be limited to the government's use of gender-based peremptory strikes.

Batson v. Kentucky itself was a significant intrusion into the jury selection process. *Batson* mini-hearings are now routine in state and federal trial courts, and *Batson* appeals have proliferated as well. Demographics indicate that today's holding may have an even greater impact than did *Batson* itself. In further constitutionalizing jury selection procedures, the Court increases the number of cases in which jury selection—once a sideshow—will become part of the main event.

For this same reason, today's decision further erodes the role of the peremptory challenge. * * *

* * * Our belief that experienced lawyers will often correctly intuit which jurors are likely to be the least sympathetic, and our understanding that the lawyer will often be unable to explain the intuition, are the very reason we cherish the peremptory challenge. But, as we add, layer by layer, additional constitutional restraints on the use of the peremptory, we force lawyers to articulate what we know is often inarticulable.

In so doing we make the peremptory challenge less discretionary and more like a challenge for cause. We also increase the possibility that biased jurors will be allowed onto the jury, because sometimes a lawyer will be unable to provide an acceptable gender-neutral explanation even though the lawyer is in fact correct that the juror is unsympathetic. Similarly, in jurisdictions where lawyers exercise their strikes in open court, lawyers may be deterred from using their peremptories, out of the fear that if they are unable to justify the strike the court will seat a juror who knows that the striking party thought him unfit. Because I believe the

16. For example, challenging all persons who have had military experience would disproportionately affect men at this time, while challenging all persons employed as nurses would disproportionately affect women. Without a showing of pretext, however, these challenges may well not be unconstitutional, since they are not gender- or race-based.

peremptory remains an important litigator's tool and a fundamental part of the process of selecting impartial juries, our increasing limitation of it gives me pause.

Nor is the value of the peremptory challenge to the litigant diminished when the peremptory is exercised in a gender-based manner. We know that like race, gender matters. A plethora of studies make clear that in rape cases, for example, female jurors are somewhat more likely to vote to convict than male jurors. Moreover, though there have been no similarly definitive studies regarding, for example, sexual harassment, child custody, or spousal or child abuse, one need not be a sexist to share the intuition that in certain cases a person's gender and resulting life experience will be relevant to his or her view of the case.

Today's decision severely limits a litigant's ability to act on this intuition, for the import of our holding is that any correlation between a juror's gender and attitudes is irrelevant as a matter of constitutional law. But to say that gender makes no difference as a matter of law is not to say that gender makes no difference as a matter of fact. * * * In extending *Batson* to gender we have added an additional burden to the state and federal trial process, taken a step closer to eliminating the peremptory challenge, and diminished the ability of litigants to act on sometimes accurate gender-based assumptions about juror attitudes. * * *

Accordingly, I adhere to my position that the Equal Protection Clause does not limit the exercise of peremptory challenges by private civil litigants and criminal defendants. This case itself presents no state action dilemma, for here the State of Alabama itself filed the paternity suit on behalf of petitioner. But what of the next case? Will we, in the name of fighting gender discrimination, hold that the battered wife—on trial for wounding her abusive husband—is a state actor? Will we preclude her from using her peremptory challenges to ensure that the jury of her peers contains as many women members as possible? I assume we will, but I hope we will not.

CHIEF JUSTICE REHNQUIST, dissenting.

* * * Unlike the Court, I think the State has shown that jury strikes on the basis of gender "substantially further" the State's legitimate interest in achieving a fair and impartial trial through the venerable practice of peremptory challenges. The two sexes differ, both biologically and, to a diminishing extent, in experience. It is not merely "stereotyping" to say that these differences may produce a difference in outlook which is brought to the jury room. Accordingly, use of peremptory challenges on the basis of sex is generally not the sort of derogatory and invidious act which peremptory challenges directed at black jurors may be. * * *

JUSTICE SCALIA, with whom THE CHIEF JUSTICE and JUSTICE THOMAS join, dissenting. * * *

The core of the Court's reasoning is that peremptory challenges on the basis of any group characteristic subject to heightened scrutiny are inconsistent with the guarantee of the Equal Protection Clause. That conclusion can be reached only by focusing unrealistically upon individual exercises of the peremptory challenge, and ignoring the totality of the practice. Since all groups are subject to the peremptory challenge (and will be made the object of it, depending upon the nature of the particular case) it is hard to see how any group is denied equal protection. That explains why peremptory challenges coexisted with the Equal Protection Clause for 120 years. This case is a perfect example of how the system as a whole is even-handed. While the only claim before the Court is petitioner's complaint that the prosecutor struck male jurors, for every man struck by the government petitioner's own lawyer struck a woman. To say that men were singled out for discriminatory treatment in this process is preposterous. The situation would be different if both sides systematically struck individuals of one group, so that the strikes evinced group-based animus and served as a proxy for segregated venire lists. The pattern here, however, displays not a systemic sex-based animus but each side's desire to get a jury favorably disposed to its case. That is why the Court's characterization of respondent's argument as "reminiscent of the arguments advanced to justify the total exclusion of women from juries" is patently false. Women were categorically excluded from juries because of doubt that they were competent; women are stricken from juries by peremptory challenge because of doubt that they were well disposed to the striking party's case.   * * *

Even if the line of our later cases guaranteed by today's decision limits the theoretically boundless *Batson* principle to race, sex, and perhaps other classifications subject to heightened scrutiny (which presumably would include religious belief), much damage has been done. It has been done, first and foremost, to the peremptory challenge system, which loses its whole character when (in order to defend against "impermissible stereotyping" claims) "reasons" for strikes must be given.   * * * And make no mistake about it: there really is no substitute for the peremptory. Voir dire (though it can be expected to expand as a consequence of today's decision) cannot fill the gap. The biases that go along with group characteristics tend to be biases that the juror himself does not perceive, so that it is no use asking about them. It is fruitless to inquire of a male juror whether he harbors any subliminal prejudice in favor of unwed fathers.   * * *

SKIP TO
788

Chapter 16

FAIR TRIAL/FREE PRESS

This chapter introduces a new participant in the criminal justice process—the media (or, if one prefers, the public that is the audience of the media). In many situations the interests of the media and the accused coincide; indeed, the accused's Sixth Amendment right to insist upon a public trial is premised on the significant value of public disclosure in ensuring that the trial is a fair one. *In re Oliver,* 333 U.S. 257 (1948).[a] But there are instances when potential conflicts arise between the media's right to report and the accused's right to a fair trial. In *Nebraska Press Association v. Stuart,* 427 U.S. 539 (1976), the Supreme Court reviewed what had long been its basic approach in responding to such conflicts.

The Court in *Nebraska Press* noted that "the authors of the Bill of Rights did not undertake to assign priorities as between First Amendment and Sixth Amendment rights [although] fully aware of the potential conflicts between them." This placed the Supreme Court in a similar position. It could not "rewrite the Constitution by undertaking what they [the framers] declined to do." Rather, it had sought to develop constitutional standards, responsive to the particular situation, that accommodated both the freedom of the press under the First Amendment and the constitutional rights of the accused. The cases in this chapter reflect several different aspects of the Court's efforts in this process of accommodation or "balancing."

Perhaps the most significant source of conflict between the media and the accused arises from the impact upon the jury selection process of extensive media coverage of a case prior to trial. That coverage often starts with the reporting on the commission of the crime and carries through to the eve of the trial, reporting not only matters of public record but also information developed by the media itself. It produces what the Court commonly describes as "pretrial publicity." Such publicity, often adverse to the accused and sometimes highly inflammatory, has the potential for influencing the attitudes of a large segment of the potential pool of jurors—both those who themselves read, saw, or listened to the coverage and others who have heard about it second-hand.

Fortunately, as the Court noted in *Nebraska Press,* in "the overwhelming majority of criminal trials, pretrial publicity presents few unmanageable threats"

---

a. *Oliver* noted that the public trial serves the defendant's interest in a fair trial in several ways: (i) the knowledge that the trial is "subject to contemporaneous review in the form of public opinion" serves as "an effective restraint on possible abuse of judicial power"; (ii) the presence of interested spectators assures testimonial trustworthiness by inducing a fear in witnesses that false testimony will be detected; and (iii) public disclosure may call the proceedings to the attention of key witnesses who might be unknown to the defense and who might respond by coming forward with critical testimony.

to the selection of an impartial jury. "But when the case is a 'sensational' one," the defendant's right to an impartial jury may be severely threatened. *Nebraska Press* held that the first line of response to that threat, under a Constitution that also recognizes the value to society of press coverage of matters of public concern, is to look to remedies that preserve the accused's right to an impartial jury without restricting the press.

Thus, in holding invalid a "gag order" which sought to bar the pretrial publication of certain information about the defendant (in particular, that he had confessed), *Nebraska Press* stressed the lack of any showing there that the defendant's right to an impartial jury could not have been preserved through the alternative measures traditionally used by the courts.[b] These included: "(a) change of trial venue to a place less exposed to the intense publicity * * *; (b) postponement of the trial to allow public attention to subside; [and] (c) searching questioning of prospective jurors [to] screen out those with fixed opinions as to guilt or innocence."

Of these three measures, the most significant is the juror screening process. A postponement raises a potential for conflict with the defendant's right to a speedy trial, and a change of venue will be of little value where the publicity extends throughout the state. Moreover, notwithstanding the *Rideau* case (discussed in *Murphy* infra), many courts will not grant a change of venue unless the screening process is tried and fails to produce a satisfactory jury. *Murphy,* the first case in this chapter, explores the question of when that process requires the exclusion of a prospective juror based upon the possible impact of pretrial publicity.

Nebraska Press dealt only with a prohibition against pretrial publication by the press. Should the same approach, stressing reliance on the traditional protections available in jury selection, produce a similar First Amendment bar against restrictions upon pretrial public statements of the attorneys in the case that could pose a threat to the selection of an unbiased jury? That is the general issue posed in the second case in this chapter, *Gentile v. State Bar of Nevada.* Note that the division of votes in this case is such that the initial opinion, by Justice Kennedy, does not set forth the position of the majority on the basic First Amendment standard that defines the limits of a state's authority in prohibiting extrajudicial statements by the attorneys. This is provided by Parts I and II of Chief Justice Rehnquist's opinion.

b. The Court in *Nebraska Press* noted that orders restraining publication had always been viewed as the "most serious and least tolerable infringements on First Amendment rights" and would be allowed only upon an extraordinary showing of justification. In the context of protecting the defendant's right to an impartial jury, this would require consideration of: "(a) the nature and extent of pretrial news coverage; (b) whether other measures would be likely to mitigate the effects of the unrestrained pretrial publicity; and (c) how effectively a restraining order would operate to prevent a threatened danger." Upon consideration of these factors, an order restraining publication would only be justified where " 'the gravity of the evil [to be avoided], discounted by its improbability, justifies such invasion of free speech as is necessary to avoid the danger.' " A concurring opinion for three Justices argued that this burden of justification could never be met, considering the "broad spectrum of [alternative] devices" judges have available for "ensuring that fundamental fairness is accorded the accused." Another concurring Justice agreed generally with that conclusion, leaving aside special situations (e.g., where the information to be published was obtained by illegal means or was patently false). Still another Justice expressed "grave doubt" that a restraining order could ever be justified, and yet another stressed the "unique burden" that would rest on a party who sought to establish the "necessity for a prior restraint on pretrial publicity." Thus, while the opinion for the Court noted that it was not "ruling out the possibility of [a defendant] showing the kind of threat to fair trial rights that would possess the requisite degree of certainty to justify restraint," the combination of opinions signaled, as a practical matter, a death knell for such restraining orders.

The fair trial right of the accused also can be threatened by media coverage at the trial itself. Here, the concern is that the jurors (and perhaps other participants, such as witnesses) will be influenced in carrying out their responsibilities by the actions of media representatives in covering the trial. Thus, in finding a denial of defendant's right to a fair trial, the *Sheppard* case (discussed in *Murphy*) dwelt on two factors exerting such an influence: (i) the disruptive activities of media representatives (both in the noise and confusion they created within the courtroom and in their behavior in photographing the witnesses and jurors as they left the courtroom), and (ii) the trial court's failure to insulate the jurors from the media coverage during the trial (that coverage having included considerable material never introduced at trial). The *Sheppard* Court also stressed, however, that these difficulties were not the inevitable consequences of substantial media coverage, but could have been avoided through various precautions that would not have interfered with the media's capacity to cover the trial (e.g., controlling the location and number of newspersons in the courtroom, and directing the jurors not to read papers or watch television, or even sequestering the jury during the trial).

Will such administrative controls suffice when criminal trials are televised? The third case in this chapter, *Chandler v. Florida,* speaks to this question. In an earlier case discussed in *Chandler, Estes v. Texas,* four Justices had suggested that the televising of trials was "inherently prejudicial" and therefore constitutionally precluded under whatever form it might take.

While *Nebraska Press* held that the press could not be banned from reporting on judicial proceedings open to the public, it left open the question of whether the First Amendment was implicated in the closing of a proceeding to the public (and thereby to the press). *Richmond Newspapers, Inc. v. Virginia*, 448 U.S. 555 (1980), marked the first time the Court was asked to decide "whether *a criminal trial itself* may be closed upon the unopposed request of a defendant, without any demonstration that closure is required to protect the defendant's superior right to a fair trial [or] some other overriding consideration." (Emphasis added.) No, answered the Court, holding that the right of the public and the press to attend criminal trials is implicit in the guarantees of the First Amendment. There was no opinion of the Court. In the lead opinion, Burger, C.J., joined by White and Stevens, JJ., observed that "the Bill of Rights was enacted against the backdrop of the long history of trials being presumptively open" and that "the First Amendment can be read as protecting the right of everyone to attend trials" "so as to give meaning" to the explicit guarantees of freedom of speech and press. Concurring Justice Brennan, joined by Marshall, J., emphasized that public access to trials is essential "to achieve the objective of maintaining public confidence in the administration of justice."

Richmond Newspapers left open the question whether the right of access to the criminal trial itself extended to *pretrial* proceedings. The Court suggested this possibility in *Press-Enterprise Co. v. Superior Court*, 464 U.S. 501 (1984) (*Press-Enterprise I*), when it held, without a dissent, that the First Amendment right of access applied to the *voir dire* examination of potential jurors. The Court emphasized the historical tradition of openness and the functional value of openness for the particular proceeding rather than any characterization of the jury selection process as a part of the trial itself. Two years later, in *Press-Enterprise II*, the last case in this chapter, the Court applied the public right of access to a proceeding that was clearly not part of the trial—the preliminary hearing.

MURPHY v. FLORIDA

421 U.S. 794, 95 S.Ct. 2031, 44 L.Ed.2d 589 (1975).

JUSTICE MARSHALL delivered the opinion of the Court.

The question presented by this case is whether the petitioner was denied a fair trial because members of the jury had learned from news accounts about a prior felony conviction or certain facts about the crime with which he was charged. Under the circumstances of this case, we find that petitioner has not been denied due process, and we therefore affirm the judgment below.

Petitioner was convicted in the Dade County, Fla., Criminal Court in 1970 of breaking and entering a home, while armed, with intent to commit robbery, and of assault with intent to commit robbery. The charges stemmed from the January 1968 robbery of a Miami Beach home and petitioner's apprehension, with three others, while fleeing from the scene. The robbery and petitioner's arrest received extensive press coverage because petitioner had been much in the news before. He had first made himself notorious for his part in the 1964 theft of the Star of India sapphire from a museum in New York. His flamboyant lifestyle made him a continuing subject of press interest; he was generally referred to—at least in the media—as "Murph the Surf."

Before the date set for petitioner's trial on the instant charges, he was indicted on two counts of murder in [adjoining] Broward County * * * [and] for conspiring to transport stolen securities in interstate commerce [in the federal courts], * * * and was convicted on one count of murder in Broward County (March 1969) and pleaded guilty to one count of the federal indictment * * * (December 1969). * * *

The events of 1968 and 1969 drew extensive press coverage. Each new case against petitioner was considered newsworthy, not only in Dade County but elsewhere as well. The record in this case contains scores of articles reporting on petitioner's trials and tribulations during this period; many purportedly relate statements that petitioner or his attorney made to reporters.

Jury selection in the present case began in August 1970. Seventy-eight jurors were questioned. Of these, 30 were excused for miscellaneous personal reasons; 20 were excused peremptorily by the defense or prosecution; 20 were excused by the court as having prejudged petitioner; and the remaining eight served as the jury and two alternates. Petitioner's motions to dismiss the chosen jurors, on the ground that they were aware that he had previously been convicted of either the 1964 Star of India theft or the Broward County murder, were denied, as was his renewed motion for a change of venue based on allegedly prejudicial pretrial publicity.

At trial, petitioner did not testify or put in any evidence; assertedly in protest of the selected jury, he did not cross-examine any of the State's witnesses. He was convicted on both counts, and after an unsuccessful appeal he sought habeas corpus relief in the [federal district court]. * * *

Petitioner relies principally upon *Irvin v. Dowd,* 366 U.S. 717 (1961), *Rideau v. Louisiana,* 373 U.S. 723 (1963), *Estes v. Texas,* 381 U.S. 532 (1965), and *Sheppard v. Maxwell,* 384 U.S. 333 (1966). In each of these cases, this Court overturned a state-court conviction obtained in a trial atmosphere that had been utterly corrupted by press coverage.

In *Irvin v. Dowd* the rural community in which the trial was held had been subjected to a barrage of inflammatory publicity immediately prior to trial, including information on the defendant's prior convictions, his confession to 24 burglaries and six murders including the one for which he was tried, and his unaccepted offer to plead guilty in order to avoid the death sentence. As a result, eight of the 12 jurors had formed an opinion that the defendant was guilty before the trial began; some went "so far as to say that it would take evidence to overcome their belief" in his guilt. In these circumstances, the Court readily found actual prejudice against the petitioner to a degree that rendered a fair trial impossible.

Prejudice was presumed in the circumstances under which the trials in *Rideau, Estes,* and *Sheppard* were held. In those cases the influence of the news media, either in the community at large or in the courtroom itself, pervaded the proceedings. In *Rideau* the defendant had "confessed" under police interrogation to the murder of which he stood convicted. A 20–minute film of his confession was broadcast three times by a television station in the community where the crime and the trial took place. In reversing, the Court did not examine the *voir dire* for evidence of actual prejudice because it considered the trial under review "but a hollow formality"—the real trial had occurred when tens of thousands of people, in a community of 150,000, had seen and heard the defendant admit his guilt before the cameras.

The trial in *Estes* had been conducted in a circus atmosphere, due in large part to the intrusions of the press, which was allowed to sit within the bar of the court and to overrun it with television equipment. Similarly, *Sheppard* arose from a trial infected not only by a background of extremely inflammatory publicity but also by a courthouse given over to accommodate the public appetite for carnival. The proceedings in these cases were entirely lacking in the solemnity and sobriety to which a defendant is entitled in a system that subscribes to any notion of fairness and rejects the verdict of a mob. They cannot be made to stand for the proposition that juror exposure to information about a state defendant's prior convictions or to news accounts of the crime with which he is charged alone presumptively deprives the defendant of due process. To resolve this case, we must turn, therefore, to any indications in the totality of circumstances that petitioner's trial was not fundamentally fair.

The constitutional standard of fairness requires that a defendant have "a panel of impartial, 'indifferent' jurors." *Irvin v. Dowd.* Qualified jurors need not, however, be totally ignorant of the facts and issues involved.

> "To hold that the mere existence of any preconceived notion as to the guilt or innocence of an accused, without more, is sufficient to rebut the presumption of a prospective juror's impartiality would be to establish an impossible standard. It is sufficient if the juror can lay aside his impression or opinion and render a verdict based on the evidence presented in court." *Irvin v. Dowd.*

At the same time, the juror's assurances that he is equal to this task cannot be dispositive of the accused's rights, and it remains open to the defendant to demonstrate "the actual existence of such an opinion in the mind of the juror as will raise the presumption of partiality." Ibid.

The *voir dire* in this case indicates no such hostility to petitioner by the jurors who served in his trial as to suggest a partiality that could not be laid aside. Some of the jurors had a vague recollection of the robbery with which petitioner was charged and each had some knowledge of petitioner's past crimes,[3] but none

---

3. One juror who did not know that petitioner had been previously convicted for the theft of the Star of India sapphire, one who did not know of the murder conviction, and one betrayed any belief in the relevance of petitioner's past to the present case. Indeed, four of the six jurors volunteered their views of its irrelevance, and one suggested that people who have been in trouble before are too often singled out for suspicion of each new crime—a predisposition that could only operate in petitioner's favor.

In the entire *voir dire* transcript furnished to us, there is only one colloquy on which petitioner can base even a colorable claim of partiality by a juror. In response to a leading and hypothetical question, presupposing a two- or three-week presentation of evidence against petitioner and his failure to put on any defense, one juror conceded that his prior impression of petitioner would dispose him to convict.[5] We cannot attach great significance to this statement, however, in light of the leading nature of counsel's questions and the juror's other testimony indicating that he had no deep impression of petitioner at all.

The juror testified that he did not keep up with current events and, in fact, had never heard of petitioner until he arrived in the room for prospective jurors where some veniremen were discussing him. He did not know that petitioner was "a convicted jewel thief" even then; it was petitioner's counsel who informed him of this fact. And he volunteered that petitioner's murder conviction, of which he had just heard, would not be relevant to his guilt or innocence in the present case, since "[w]e are not trying him for murder."

Even these indicia of impartiality might be disregarded in a case where the general atmosphere in the community or courtroom is sufficiently inflammatory, but the circumstances surrounding petitioner's trial are not at all of that variety. Petitioner attempts to portray them as inflammatory by reference to the publicity to which the community was exposed. The District Court found, however, that the news articles concerning petitioner had appeared almost entirely during the period between December 1967 and January 1969, the latter date being seven months before the jury in this case was selected. They were, moreover, largely factual in nature.

who had never heard about the securities case were informed about them by petitioner's counsel, who then asked whether that knowledge would not prejudice them against petitioner. We will not readily discount the assurances of a juror insofar as his exposure to a defendant's past crimes comes from the defendant or counsel. We note also, and disapprove, counsel's habitual references to his client, at *voir dire*, as "Murph the Surf" rather than by his name.

5. The entire exchange appears at App. 139:

"Q. Now, when you go into that jury room and you decide upon Murphy's guilt or innocence, you are going to take into account that fact that he is a convicted murderer; aren't you?

"A. Not if we are listening to the case, I wouldn't.

"Q. But you know about it?

"A. How can you not know about it?

"Q. Fine, thank you.

"When you go into the jury room, the fact that he is a convicted murderer, that is going to influence your verdict; is it not?

"A. We are not trying him for murder.

"Q. The fact that he is a convicted murderer and jewel thief, that would influence your verdict?

"A. I didn't know he was a convicted jewel thief.

"Q. Oh, I see.

"I am sorry I put words in your mouth.

"Now, sir, after two or three weeks of being locked up in a downtown hotel, as the Court determines, and after hearing the State's case, and after hearing no case on behalf of Murphy, and hearing no testimony from Murphy saying, 'I am innocent, Mr. [juror's name],'—when you go into the jury room, sir, all these facts are going to influence your verdict?

"A. I imagine it would be.

"Q. And in fact, you are saying if Murphy didn't testify, and if he doesn't offer evidence, 'My experience of him is such that right now I would find him guilty.'

"A. I believe so."

The length to which the trial court must go in order to select jurors who appear to be impartial is another factor relevant in evaluating those jurors' assurances of impartiality. In a community where most veniremen will admit to a disqualifying prejudice, the reliability of the others' protestations may be drawn into question; for it is then more probable that they are part of a community deeply hostile to the accused, and more likely that they may unwittingly have been influenced by it. In *Irvin v. Dowd,* for example, the Court noted that 90% of those examined on the point were inclined to believe in the accused's guilt, and the court had excused for this cause 268 of the 430 veniremen. In the present case, by contrast, 20 of the 78 persons questioned were excused because they indicated an opinion as to petitioner's guilt. This may indeed be 20 more than would occur in the trial of a totally obscure person, but it by no means suggests a community with sentiment so poisoned against petitioner as to impeach the indifference of jurors who displayed no animus of their own.

In sum, we are unable to conclude, in the circumstances presented in this case, that petitioner did not receive a fair trial. Petitioner has failed to show that the setting of the trial was inherently prejudicial or that the jury-selection process of which he complains permits an inference of actual prejudice. * * *

CHIEF JUSTICE BURGER, concurring in the judgment.

I agree with Mr. Justice Brennan that the trial judge was woefully remiss in failing to insulate prospective jurors from the bizarre media coverage of this case and in not taking steps to prevent pretrial discussion of the case among them. Although I would not hesitate to reverse petitioner's conviction in the exercise of our supervisory powers, were this a federal case, I agree with the Court that the circumstances of petitioner's trial did not rise to the level of a violation of the Due Process Clause of the Fourteenth Amendment.

JUSTICE BRENNAN, dissenting.

I dissent. *Irvin v. Dowd,* requires reversal of this conviction. As in that case, petitioner here was denied a fair trial. The risk that taint of widespread publicity regarding his criminal background, known to all members of the jury, infected the jury's deliberations is apparent, the trial court made no attempt to prevent discussion of the case or petitioner's previous criminal exploits among the prospective jurors, and one juror freely admitted that he was predisposed to convict petitioner.

During *voir dire,* petitioner's counsel had the following colloquy with that juror [Justice Brennan here set forth the latter part of the *voir dire* exchange quoted in note 5 of the Court's opinion].

I cannot agree with the Court that the obvious bias of this juror may be overlooked simply because the juror's response was occasioned by a "leading and hypothetical question." Indeed, the hypothetical became reality when petitioner chose not to take the stand and offered no evidence. Thus petitioner was tried by a juror predisposed, because of his knowledge of petitioner's previous crimes, to find him guilty of this one.

Others who ultimately served as jurors revealed similar prejudice toward petitioner on *voir dire.* One juror conceded that it would be difficult, during deliberations, to put out of his mind that petitioner was a convicted criminal. He also admitted that he did not "hold a convicted felon in the same regard as another person who has never been convicted of a felony," and admitted further that he had termed petitioner a "menace."

A third juror testified that she knew from several sources that petitioner was a convicted murderer, and was aware that the community regarded petitioner as a criminal who "should be put away." She disclaimed having a fixed opinion about the result she would reach, but acknowledged that the fact that petitioner was a convicted criminal would probably influence her verdict. * * * Still another juror testified that the comments of venire members in discussing the case had made him "sick to [his] stomach." He testified that one venireman had said that petitioner was "thoroughly rotten," and that another had said: "Hang him, he's guilty."

Moreover, the Court ignores the crucial significance of the fact that at no time before or during this daily buildup of prejudice against Murphy did the trial judge instruct the prospective jurors not to discuss the case among themselves. Indeed the trial judge took no steps to insulate the jurors from media coverage of the case or from the many news articles that discussed petitioner's last criminal exploits.

It is of no moment that several jurors ultimately testified that they would try to exclude from their deliberations their knowledge of petitioner's past misdeeds and of his community reputation. *Irvin* held in like circumstances that little weight could be attached to such self-serving protestations. * * *

On the record of this *voir dire,* therefore, the conclusion is to me inescapable that the attitude of the entire venire toward Murphy reflected the "then current community pattern of thought as indicated by the popular news media," and was infected with the taint of the view that he was a "criminal" guilty of notorious offenses, including that for which he was on trial. It is a plain case, from a review of the entire *voir dire,* where "the extent and nature of the publicity has caused such a build up of prejudice that excluding the preconception of guilt from the deliberations would be too difficult for the jury to be honestly found impartial." In my view, the denial of a change of venue was therefore prejudicial error, and I would reverse the conviction.[a]

GENTILE v. STATE BAR OF NEVADA

501 U.S. 1030, 111 S.Ct. 2720, 115 L.Ed.2d 888 (1991).

JUSTICE KENNEDY announced the judgment of the Court and delivered the opinion of the Court with respect to Parts III and VI, and an opinion with respect to Parts I, II, IV, and V in which JUSTICE MARSHALL, JUSTICE BLACKMUN and JUSTICE STEVENS joined.

[The Las Vegas Metropolitan Police Department (Metro) stored in a safety deposit box at Western Vault drugs and money used in an undercover operation.

---

a. While a criminal defendant may properly ask on *voir dire* whether a prospective juror has previously acquired any information about the case, she does not have a constitutional right to explore the *content* of the acquired information. Thus, ruled a 5–4 majority, per Rehnquist, C.J., in *Mu'Min v. Virginia,* 500 U.S. 415 (1991), a trial judge's refusal to question prospective jurors specifically about the content of the news reports to which each had been exposed violated neither the defendant's Sixth Amendment right to an impartial jury nor his Fourteenth Amendment right to due process. The Court emphasized that trial judges have wide discretion in conducting *voir dire* in the area of pretrial publicity and stressed that the critical issue is not whether jurors know about the case but whether they can judge it impartially. Justice O'Connor, who supplied the critical fifth vote, wrote a separate concurring opinion. She emphasized that the trial judge was aware of the full range of publicity about the case (which was characterized by the Chief Justice as not nearly as extensive or prejudicial as the publicity in *Irvin v. Dowd*) and could appropriately conclude that even if the jurors were aware of all of that publicity, their assurances of impartiality were acceptable. Three dissenters, in an opinion by Marshall, J., characterized the publicity as exceptionally prejudicial and contended that "a trial judge cannot realistically assess the jurors impartiality without first establishing that the juror already has learned about the case." Justice Kennedy, in a separate dissent, argued that "findings of impartiality must be based on something more than the mere silence of the individual [juror] in response to questions asked *en masse.*"

On February 2nd, 1987, the Las Vegas Sheriff announced in a press conference that large amounts of cocaine and travelers' checks were missing from that box. Announced as possible suspects were the police and Western Vault employees. Initial reports suggested that the primary suspects were two detectives (Schaub and Scholl) who had free access to the deposit box, but later reports suggested that the attention of investigators had turned to Grady Sanders, the owner of Western Vault. Media coverage continued over the next year with reports that: (1) others with deposit boxes at Western Vault had subsequently reported that items were missing from their boxes, and the police had opened still other deposit boxes in search of the missing items; (2) $264,900 had been found in a box listed as unrented, and that money had apparently been stored there by Tammy Markham, a person who had reported missing items, and who was facing drug charges in another jurisdiction; (3) another person who had reported missing items (Connick) was a "Columbian national" who was "not facing any drug related charges" and who had passed a lie detector test to substantiate her claim; (4) the initial police theory was that the theft from the Metro box was part of an effort to discredit the undercover police operation, and business records indicated a relationship between Sanders and the targets of that operation; (5) the subsequent police theory was that the thief had unwittingly stolen from the police; (6) the sheriff had expressed "complete faith and trust" in his officers, but the F.B.I. suspected that the officers were responsible for the theft and that had severely damaged relations between the F.B.I. and Metro; (7) the detectives Scholl and Schaub had been cleared by police investigators after passing lie detector tests; and (8) Sanders had refused to take a lie detector test.

[On February 4, 1988, Sanders was indicted on theft charges, and on February 5th, he was arraigned, with trial set for August 1988. The petitioner Gentile, the attorney representing Sanders, had advance notice of the indictment, and on the day of the arraignment held a press conference (his first in a long career as a defense attorney). At the press conference, Gentile issued a prepared statement in which he stated that: (1) the case was similar to those in other cities, but there the authorities had been "honest enough to indict the people who did it"—"the police department, crooked cops"; (2) when the case is tried the evidence will prove "not only [that] Sanders is an innocent person," but that Detective Scholl "was in the most direct position to have stolen the drugs and money"; (3) there is "far more evidence [that] Detective Scholl took the drugs [and] travelers' checks than any other living human being"; (4) "I feel [that] Sanders is being used as a scapegoat to cover up for what has to be obvious to [law enforcement authorities]"; and (5) with respect to the claimed thefts from other boxes, "the so-called victims" "are known drug dealers and convicted money launderers and drug dealers" and had accused Sanders in response to police pressure. In response to a question from a reporter, Gentile strongly implied that Detective Scholl could be observed in a videotape suffering from symptoms of cocaine use. In several instances, he refused to answer reporters' questions on specific details, noting that he could not elaborate "because ethics prohibit me from doing so." The two newspaper stories and two TV news broadcast that mentioned Gentile's press conference also mentioned a prosecution response and a police press conference in response. The prosecution characterized the indictment as legitimate, and the police stated that they remained satisfied that the two detectives were "above reproach."

[Some six months later, Sanders' criminal case was tried by a jury and he was acquitted on all counts. A state disciplinary board then brought proceedings against Gentile and concluded that he had violated Nevada Supreme Court Rule

177, set forth below.[a]   That Rule was based on Rule 3.6 of the ABA Model Rules of Professional Conduct, and is an almost verbatim duplicate of ABA Rule 3.6.   The disciplinary board recommended issuance of a private reprimand for violation of Rule 177.   The state supreme court then affirmed that decision.]

I

* * * At issue here is the constitutionality of a ban on political speech critical of the government and its officials.   Unlike other First Amendment cases * * * in which speech is not the direct target of the regulation or statute in question, this case involves punishment of pure speech in the political forum.   Petitioner engaged not in solicitation of clients or advertising for his practice, as in our precedents from which some of our colleagues would discern a standard of diminished First Amendment protection.   His words were directed at public officials and their conduct in office.   * * *

The judicial system, and in particular our criminal justice courts, play a vital part in a democratic state, and the public has a legitimate interest in their operations.   See, e.g., *Landmark Communications, Inc. v. Virginia,* 435 U.S. 829 (1978).   "[I]t would be difficult to single out any aspect of government of higher

a. *Nevada Supreme Court Rule 177, "Trial Publicity*

"1.   A lawyer shall not make an extrajudicial statement that a reasonable person would expect to be disseminated by means of public communication if the lawyer knows or reasonably should know that it will have a substantial likelihood of materially prejudicing an adjudicative proceeding.

"2.   A statement referred to in subsection 1 ordinarily is likely to have such an effect when it refers to a civil matter triable to a jury, a criminal matter, or any other proceeding that could result in incarceration, and the statement relates to:

"(a) the character, credibility, reputation or criminal record of a party, suspect in a criminal investigation or witness, or the identity of a witness, or the expected testimony of a party or witness;

"(b) in a criminal case or proceeding that could result in incarceration, the possibility of a plea of guilty to the offense or the existence or contents of any confession, admission, or statement given by a defendant or suspect or that person's refusal or failure to make a statement;

"(c) the performance or results of any examination or test or the refusal or failure of a person to submit to an examination or test, or the identity or nature of physical evidence expected to be presented;

"(d) any opinion as to the guilt or innocence of a defendant or suspect in a criminal case or proceeding that could result in incarceration;

"(e) information the lawyer knows or reasonably should know is likely to be inadmissible as evidence in a trial and would if disclosed create a substantial risk of prejudicing an impartial trial; or

"(f) the fact that a defendant has been charged with a crime, unless there is included therein a statement explaining that the charge is merely an accusation and that the defendant is presumed innocent until and unless proven guilty.

"3.   Notwithstanding subsection 1 and 2(a–f), a lawyer involved in the investigation or litigation of a matter may state without elaboration:

"(a) the general nature of the claim or defense;

"(b) the information contained in a public record;

"(c) that an investigation of the matter is in progress, including the general scope of the investigation, the offense or claim or defense involved and, except when prohibited by law, the identity of the persons involved;

"(d) the scheduling or result of any step in litigation;

"(e) a request for assistance in obtaining evidence and information necessary thereto;

"(f) a warning of danger concerning the behavior of a person involved, when there is reason to believe that there exists the likelihood of substantial harm to an individual or to the public interest; and

"(g) in a criminal case:

"(i) the identity, residence, occupation and family status of the accused;

"(ii) if the accused has not been apprehended, information necessary to aid in apprehension of that person;

"(iii) the fact, time and place of arrest; and

"(iv) the identity of investigating and arresting officers or agencies and the length of the investigation."

concern and importance to the people than the manner in which criminal trials are conducted." *Richmond Newspapers, Inc. v. Virginia,* 448 U.S. 555 (1980). Public vigilance serves us well, for "[t]he knowledge that every criminal trial is subject to contemporaneous review in the forum of public opinion is an effective restraint on possible abuse of judicial power. . . . Without publicity, all other checks are insufficient; in comparison of publicity, all other checks are of small account." *In re Oliver,* 333 U.S. 257 (1948).   * * *

Public awareness and criticism have even greater importance where, as here, they concern allegations of police corruption, see *Nebraska Press Assn. v. Stuart,* 427 U.S. 539 (1976) (Brennan, J., concurring in judgment) ("commentary on the fact that there is strong evidence implicating a government official in criminal activity goes to the very core of matters of public concern"), or where, as is also the present circumstance, the criticism questions the judgment of an elected public prosecutor. Our system grants prosecutors vast discretion at all stages of the criminal process. The public has an interest in its responsible exercise. * * *

We are not called upon to determine the constitutionality of the ABA Model Rule of Professional Conduct 3.6 (1981), but only Rule 177 as it has been interpreted and applied by the State of Nevada. Model Rule 3.6's requirement of substantial likelihood of material prejudice [duplicated in Rule 177(1)] is not necessarily flawed. Interpreted in a proper and narrow manner, for instance, to prevent an attorney of record from releasing information of grave prejudice on the eve of jury selection, the phrase substantial likelihood of material prejudice might punish only speech that creates a danger of imminent and substantial harm. A rule governing speech, even speech entitled to full constitutional protection, need not use the words "clear and present danger" in order to pass constitutional muster.   * * * The drafters of Model Rule 3.6 apparently thought the substantial likelihood of material prejudice formulation approximated the clear and present danger test. See ABA Annotated Model Rules of Professional Conduct 243 (1984). * * *

The difference between the requirement of serious and imminent threat found in the disciplinary rules of some States and the more common formulation of substantial likelihood of material prejudice could prove mere semantics. Each standard requires an assessment of proximity and degree of harm. Each may be capable of valid application. Under those principles, nothing inherent in Nevada's formulation fails First Amendment review; but as this case demonstrates, Rule 177 has not been interpreted in conformance with those principles by the Nevada Supreme Court.

II

Even if one were to accept respondent's argument that lawyers participating in judicial proceedings may be subjected, consistent with the First Amendment, to speech restrictions that could not be imposed on the press or general public, the judgment should not be upheld. The record does not support the conclusion that petitioner knew or reasonably should have known his remarks created a substantial likelihood of material prejudice, if the Rule's terms are given any meaningful content.

We have held that "in cases raising First Amendment issues . . . an appellate court has an obligation to 'make an independent examination of the whole record' in order to make sure that 'the judgment does not constitute a forbidden intrusion on the field of free expression.'" *Bose Corp. v. Consumers Union of United States, Inc.,* 466 U.S. 485 (1984). Rather, this Court is "compelled to examine for [itself] the statements in issue and the circumstances under which they were made to see whether or not they do carry a threat of clear and present danger to the impartiality and good order of the courts or whether they are of a character which the principles of the First Amendment, as adopted by the Due Process Clause of the Fourteenth Amendment, protect." * * * *Landmark Communications, Inc. v. Virginia,* supra.

Whether one applies the standard set out in *Landmark Communications* or the lower standard our colleagues find permissible, an examination of the record reveals no basis for the Nevada court's conclusion that the speech presented a substantial likelihood of material prejudice. * * *

   1. *Petitioner's Motivation.* As petitioner explained to the disciplinary board, his primary motivation was the concern that, unless some of the weaknesses in the State's case were made public, a potential jury venire would be poisoned by repetition in the press of information being released by the police and prosecutors, in particular the repeated press reports about polygraph tests and the fact that the two police officers were no longer suspects. Respondent distorts Rule 177 when it suggests this explanation admits a purpose to prejudice the venire and so proves a violation of the Rule. Rule 177 only prohibits the dissemination of information that one knows or reasonably should know has a "substantial likelihood of materially prejudicing an adjudicative proceeding." Petitioner did not indicate he thought he could sway the pool of potential jurors to form an opinion in advance of the trial, nor did he seek to discuss evidence that would be inadmissible at trial. He sought only to counter publicity already deemed prejudicial. The Southern Nevada Disciplinary Board so found. It said petitioner attempted

> "(i) to counter public opinion which he perceived as adverse to Mr. Sanders, (ii) . . . to refute certain matters regarding his client which had appeared in the media, (iii) to fight back against the perceived efforts of the prosecution to poison the prospective juror pool, and (iv) to publicly present Sanders' side of the case."

Far from an admission that he sought to "materially prejudic[e] an adjudicative proceeding," petitioner sought only to stop a wave of publicity he perceived as prejudicing potential jurors against his client and injuring his client's reputation in the community.

   Petitioner gave a second reason for holding the press conference, which demonstrates the additional value of his speech. Petitioner acted in part because the investigation had taken a serious toll on his client. Sanders was "not a man in good health," having suffered multiple open-heart surgeries prior to these events. And prior to indictment, the mere suspicion of wrongdoing had caused the closure of Western Vault and the loss of Sanders' ground lease on an Atlantic City, New Jersey property.

   An attorney's duties do not begin inside the courtroom door. He or she cannot ignore the practical implications of a legal proceeding for the client. Just as an attorney may recommend a plea bargain or civil settlement to avoid the adverse consequences of a possible loss after trial, so too an attorney may take reasonable steps to defend a client's reputation and reduce the adverse consequences of indictment, especially in the face of a prosecution deemed unjust or commenced with improper motives. A defense attorney may pursue lawful strategies to obtain dismissal of an indictment or reduction of charges, including an attempt to demonstrate in the court of public opinion that the client does not deserve to be tried.

2. Petitioner's Investigation of Rule 177. Rule 177 is phrased in terms of what an attorney "knows or reasonably should know." On the evening before the press conference, petitioner and two colleagues spent several hours researching the extent of an attorney's obligations under Rule 177. He decided, as we have held, see *Patton v. Yount,* 467 U.S. 1025 (1984), that the timing of a statement was crucial in the assessment of possible prejudice and the Rule's application, accord. * * * Petitioner knew, at the time of his statement, that a jury would not be empaneled for six months at the earliest, if ever. He recalled reported cases finding no prejudice resulting from juror exposure to "far worse" information two and four months before trial, and concluded that his proposed statement was not substantially likely to result in material prejudice.

A statement which reaches the attention of the venire on the eve of *voir dire* might require a continuance or cause difficulties in securing an impartial jury, and at the very least could complicate the jury selection process. * * * As turned out to be the case here, exposure to the same statement six months prior to trial would not result in prejudice, the content fading from memory long before the trial date.

In 1988, Clark County, Nevada had population in excess of 600,000 persons. Given the size of the community from which any potential jury venire would be drawn and the length of time before trial, only the most damaging of information could give rise to any likelihood of prejudice. The innocuous content of petitioner's statement reinforces my conclusion.

3. The Content of Petitioner's Statement. * * * Much of the information provided by petitioner had been published in one form or another, obviating any potential for prejudice. See ABA Annotated Model Rules of Professional Conduct 243 (1984) (extent to which information already circulated significant factor in determining likelihood of prejudice). The remainder, and details petitioner refused to provide, were available to any journalist willing to do a little bit of investigative work.

Petitioner's statement lacks any of the more obvious bases for a finding of prejudice. Unlike the police, he refused to comment on polygraph tests except to confirm earlier reports that Sanders had not submitted to the police polygraph; he mentioned no confessions, and no evidence from searches or test results; he refused to elaborate upon his charge that the other so-called victims were not credible, except to explain his general theory that they were pressured to testify in an attempt to avoid drug-related legal trouble, and that some of them may have asserted claims in an attempt to collect insurance money.

[4.] *Events following the Press Conference.* Petitioner's judgment that no likelihood of material prejudice would result from his comments was vindicated by events at trial. While it is true that Rule 177's standard for controlling pretrial publicity must be judged at the time a statement is made, *ex post* evidence can have probative value in some cases. Here, where the Rule purports to demand, and the Constitution requires, consideration of the character of the harm and its heightened likelihood of occurrence, the record is altogether devoid of facts one would expect to follow upon any statement that created a real likelihood of material prejudice to a criminal jury trial.

The trial took place on schedule in August, 1988, with no request by either party for a venue change or continuance. The jury was empaneled with no apparent difficulty. The trial judge questioned the jury venire about publicity. Although many had vague recollections of reports that cocaine stored at Western Vault had been stolen from a police undercover operation, and, as petitioner had feared, one remembered that the police had been cleared of suspicion, not a single juror indicated any recollection of petitioner or his press conference.

At trial, all material information disseminated during petitioner's press conference was admitted in evidence before the jury, including information questioning the motives and credibility of supposed victims who testified against Sanders, and Detective Scholl's ingestion of drugs in the course of undercover operations (in order, he testified, to gain the confidence of suspects). The jury acquitted petitioner's client, and, as petitioner explained before the disciplinary board,

> "when the trial was over with and the man was acquitted the next week the foreman of the jury phoned me and said to me that if they would have had a verdict form before them with respect to the guilt of Steve Scholl they would have found the man proven guilty beyond a reasonable doubt."

There is no support for the conclusion that petitioner's statement created a likelihood of material prejudice, or indeed of any harm of sufficient magnitude or imminence to support a punishment for speech.

III

As interpreted by the Nevada Supreme Court, the Rule is void for vagueness, in any event, for its safe harbor provision, Rule 177(3), misled petitioner into thinking that he could give his press conference without fear of discipline. Rule 177(3)(a) provides that a lawyer "may state without elaboration . . . the general nature of the . . . defense." Statements under this provision are protected "[n]otwithstanding subsection 1 and 2(a–f)." By necessary operation of the word "notwithstanding," the Rule contemplates that a lawyer describing the "general nature of the . . . defense" "without elaboration" need fear no discipline, even if he comments on "[t]he character, credibility, reputation or criminal record of a . . . witness," and even if he "knows or reasonably should know that [the statement] will have a substantial likelihood of materially prejudicing an adjudicative proceeding."

Given this grammatical structure, and absent any clarifying interpretation by the state court, the Rule fails to provide " 'fair notice to those to whom [it] is directed.' " *Grayned v. City of Rockford,* 408 U.S. 104 (1972). A lawyer seeking to avail himself of Rule 177(3)'s protection must guess at its contours. The right to explain the "general" nature of the defense without "elaboration" provides insufficient guidance because "general" and "elaboration" are both classic terms of degree. In the context before us, these terms have no settled usage or tradition of interpretation in law. The lawyer has no principle for determining when his remarks pass from the safe harbor of the general to the forbidden sea of the elaborated.

Petitioner testified he thought his statements were protected by Rule 177(3), App. 59. A review of the press conference supports that claim. He gave only a brief opening statement, and on numerous occasions declined to answer reporters' questions seeking more detailed comments. * * * Nevertheless, the disciplinary board said only that petitioner's comments "went beyond the scope of the statements permitted by SCR 177(3)," and the Nevada Supreme Court's rejection of petitioner's defense based on Rule 177(3) was just as terse. The fact Gentile was found in violation of the Rules after studying them and making a conscious effort at compliance demonstrates that Rule 177 creates a trap for the wary as well as the unwary.

The prohibition against vague regulations of speech is based in part on the need to eliminate the impermissible risk of discriminatory enforcement, for history shows that speech is suppressed when either the speaker or the message is critical of those who enforce the law. The question is not whether discriminatory enforcement occurred here, and we assume it did not, but whether the Rule is so imprecise that discriminatory enforcement is a real possibility. The inquiry is of particular relevance when one of the classes most affected by the regulation is the criminal defense bar, which has the professional mission to challenge actions of the State. Petitioner, for instance, succeeded in preventing the conviction of his client, and the speech in issue involved criticism of the government.

IV

The analysis to this point resolves the case, and in the usual order of things the discussion should end here. Five members of the Court, however, endorse an extended discussion which concludes that Nevada may interpret its requirement of substantial likelihood of material prejudice under a standard more deferential than is the usual rule where speech is concerned. It appears necessary, therefore, to set forth my objections to that conclusion and to the reasoning which underlies it. * * *

Respondent would justify a substantial limitation on speech by attorneys because "lawyers have special access to information, including confidential statements from clients and information obtained through pretrial discovery or plea negotiations" and so lawyers' statements "are likely to be received as especially authoritative." Rule 177, however, does not reflect concern for the attorney's special access to client confidences, material gained through discovery, or other proprietary or confidential information. We have upheld restrictions upon the release of information gained "only by virtue of the trial court's discovery processes." *Seattle Times Co. v. Rhinehart,* 467 U.S. 20 (1984). And *Seattle Times* would prohibit release of discovery information by the attorney as well as the client. Similar rules require an attorney to maintain client confidences. See, *e.g.,* ABA Model Rule of Professional Conduct 1.6 (1981).

This case involves no speech subject to a restriction under the rationale of *Seattle Times.* Much of the information in petitioner's remarks was included by explicit reference or fair inference in earlier press reports. Petitioner could not have learned what he revealed at the press conference through the discovery process or other special access afforded to attorneys, for he spoke to the press on the day of indictment, at the outset of his formal participation in the criminal proceeding. We have before us no complaint from the prosecutors, police or presiding judge that petitioner misused information to which he had special access. And there is no claim that petitioner revealed client confidences, which may be waived in any event. Rule 177, on its face and as applied here, is neither limited to nor even directed at preventing release of information received through court proceedings or special access afforded attorneys.

Respondent [also] relies upon *obiter dicta* from *In re Sawyer,* 360 U.S. 622 (1959), *Sheppard v. Maxwell,* 384 U.S. 333 (1966), and *Nebraska Press Assn. v. Stuart,* 427 U.S. 539 (1976), for the proposition that an attorney's speech about ongoing proceedings must be subject to pervasive regulation in order to ensure the impartial adjudication of criminal proceedings. * * * Each case suggests restrictions upon information release, but none confronted their permitted scope. At the very least, our cases recognize that disciplinary rules governing the legal profession cannot punish activity protected by the First Amendment, and that First Amendment protection survives even when the attorney violates a disciplinary rule he swore to obey when admitted to the practice of law. * * * We have not in recent years accepted our colleagues' apparent theory that the practice of law brings with it comprehensive restrictions, or that we will defer to professional bodies when those restrictions impinge upon First Amendment freedoms. And none of the justifications put forward by respondent suffice to sanction abandonment of our normal First Amendment principles in the case of speech by an attorney regarding pending cases.

Even if respondent is correct, and as in *Seattle Times* we must balance "whether the 'practice in question [furthers] an important or substantial governmental interest unrelated to the suppression of expression' and whether 'the limitation of First Amendment freedoms [is] no greater than is necessary or essential to the protection of the particular governmental interest involved,'" *Seattle Times,* supra, the Rule as interpreted by Nevada fails the searching inquiry required by those precedents.

Only the occasional case presents a danger of prejudice from pretrial publicity. Empirical research suggests that in the few instances when jurors have been exposed to extensive and prejudicial publicity, they are able to disregard it and base their verdict upon the evidence presented in court. * * * *Voir dire* can play an important role in reminding jurors to set aside out-of-court information, and to decide the case upon the evidence presented at trial. All of these factors weigh in favor of affording an attorney's speech about ongoing proceedings our traditional First Amendment protections. Our colleagues' historical survey notwithstanding, respondent has not demonstrated any sufficient state interest in restricting the speech of attorneys to justify a lower standard of First Amendment scrutiny.

Still less justification exists for a lower standard of scrutiny here, as this speech involved not the prosecutor or police, but a criminal defense attorney. Respondent and its *amici* present not a single example where a defense attorney has managed by public statements to prejudice the prosecution of the state's case. Even discounting the obvious reason for a lack of appellate decisions on the topic—the difficulty of appealing a verdict of acquittal—the absence of anecdotal or survey evidence in a much-studied area of the law is remarkable.

The various bar association and advisory commission reports which resulted in promulgation of ABA Model Rule of Professional Conduct 3.6 (1981), and other regulations of attorney speech, and sources they cite, present no convincing case for restrictions upon the speech of defense attorneys. * * * The police, the prosecution, other government officials, and the community at large hold innumerable avenues for the dissemination of information adverse to a criminal defendant, many of which are not within the scope of Rule 177 or any other regulation. By contrast, a defendant cannot speak without fear of incriminating himself and prejudicing his defense, and most criminal defendants have insufficient means to retain a public relations team apart from defense counsel for the sole purpose of countering prosecution statements. These factors underscore my conclusion that blanket rules restricting speech of defense attorneys should not be accepted without careful First Amendment scrutiny.

Respondent uses the "officer of the court" label to imply that attorney contact with the press somehow is inimical to the attorney's proper role. Rule 177 posits no such inconsistency between an attorney's role and discussions with the press. It permits all comment to the press absent "a substantial likelihood of materially prejudicing an adjudicative proceeding." Respondent does not articulate the principle that contact with the press cannot be reconciled with the attorney's role or explain how this might be so.

Because attorneys participate in the criminal justice system and are trained in its complexities, they hold unique qualifications as a source of information about pending cases. "Since lawyers are considered credible in regard to pending litigation in which they are engaged and are in one of the most knowledgeable positions, they are a crucial source of information and opinion." *Chicago Council of Lawyers v. Bauer,* 522 F.2d 242, 250 (7th Cir.1975). To the extent the press and public rely upon attorneys for information because attorneys are well-informed, this may prove the value to the public of speech by members of the bar. If the dangers of their speech arise from its persuasiveness, from their ability to explain judicial proceedings, or from the likelihood the speech will be believed, these are not the sort of dangers that can validate restrictions. The First Amendment does not permit suppression of speech because of its power to command assent.

One may concede the proposition that an attorney's speech about pending cases may present dangers that could not arise from statements by a nonpartici-pant, and that an attorney's duty to cooperate in the judicial process may prevent him or her from taking actions with an intent to frustrate that process. The role of attorneys in the criminal justice system subjects them to fiduciary obligations to the court and the parties. An attorney's position may result in some added ability to obstruct the proceedings through well-timed statements to the press, though one can debate the extent of an attorney's ability to do so without violating other established duties. A court can require an attorney's cooperation to an extent not possible of nonparticipants. A proper weighing of dangers might consider the harm that occurs when speech about ongoing proceedings forces the court to take burdensome steps such as sequestration, continuance, or change of venue.

If as a regular matter speech by an attorney about pending cases raised real dangers of this kind then a substantial governmental interest might support additional regulation of speech. But this case involves the sanction of speech so innocuous, and an application of Rule 177(3)'s safe harbor provision so begrudg-ing, that it is difficult to determine the force these arguments would carry in a different setting. The instant case is a poor vehicle for defining with precision the outer limits under the Constitution of a court's ability to regulate an attorney's statements about ongoing adjudicative proceedings. At the very least, however, we can say that the Rule which punished petitioner's statement represents a limitation of First Amendment freedoms greater than is necessary or essential to the protection of the particular governmental interest, and does not protect against a danger of the necessary gravity, imminence, or likelihood.

The vigorous advocacy we demand of the legal profession is accepted because it takes place under the neutral, dispassionate control of the judicial system. Though cost and delays undermine it in all too many cases, the American judicial trial remains one of the purest, most rational forums for the lawful determination of disputes. A profession which takes just pride in these traditions may consider them disserved if lawyers use their skills and insight to make untested allegations in the press instead of in the courtroom. But constraints of professional responsi-bility and societal disapproval will act as sufficient safeguards in most cases. And in some circumstances press comment is necessary to protect the rights of the client and prevent abuse of the courts. It cannot be said that petitioner's conduct demonstrated any real or specific threat to the legal process, and his statements have the full protection of the First Amendment. * * *

CHIEF JUSTICE REHNQUIST delivered the opinion of the Court with respect to parts I and II, and delivered a dissenting opinion with respect to part III in which JUSTICE WHITE, JUSTICE SCALIA, and JUSTICE SOUTER have joined. * * *

I

Petitioner's client was the subject of a highly publicized case, and in response to adverse publicity about his client, Gentile held a press conference on the day after Sanders was indicted. At the press conference, petitioner made, among others the following statements: * * * [that] "there is far more evidence that will establish that Detective Scholl took these drugs and American Express Travelers' checks than any other living being"; * * * [that] "the so-called other victims * * * are known drug dealers and convicted money launderers, three of whom didn't say a word about anything until after they were approached by Metro and after they were already in trouble and * * * trying to work themselves out of something"; * * * [that] "I know I represent an innocent man"; [and that] "we've got some video tapes that if you took a look at them, I'll tell you that [Scholl] either had a cold or he should have seen a better doctor."

The Southern Nevada Disciplinary Board found that petitioner knew the detective he accused of perpetrating the crime and abusing drugs would be a witness for the prosecution. It also found that petitioner believed others whom he characterized as money launderers and drug dealers would be called as prosecution witnesses. Petitioner's admitted purpose for calling the press conference was to counter public opinion which he perceived as adverse to his client, to fight back against the perceived efforts of the prosecution to poison the prospective juror pool, and to publicly present his client's side of the case. The Board found that in light of the statements, their timing, and petitioner's purpose, petitioner knew or should have known that there was a substantial likelihood that the statements would materially prejudice the Sanders trial.

The Nevada Supreme Court affirmed the Board's decision, finding by clear and convincing evidence that petitioner "knew or reasonably should have known that his comments had a substantial likelihood of materially prejudicing the adjudication of his client's case." The court noted that the case was "highly publicized"; that the press conference, held the day after the indictment and the same day as the arraignment, was "timed to have maximum impact"; and that petitioner's comments "related to the character, credibility, reputation or criminal record of the police detective and other potential witnesses." The court concluded that the "absence of actual prejudice does not establish that there was no substantial likelihood of material prejudice."

II

Gentile asserts that the same stringent standard applied in *Nebraska Press Assn. v. Stuart,* 427 U.S. 539 (1976), to restraints on press publication during the pendency of a criminal trial should be applied to speech by a lawyer whose client is a defendant in a criminal proceeding. * * * Respondent, on the other hand, relies on statements in cases such as *Sheppard v. Maxwell,* 384 U.S. 333 (1966), which sharply distinguished between restraints on the press and restraints on lawyers whose clients are parties to the proceeding:

"Collaboration between counsel and the press as to information affecting the fairness of a criminal trial is not only subject to regulation, but is highly censurable and worthy of disciplinary measures."

To evaluate these opposing contentions, some references must be made to the history of the regulation of the practice of law by the courts.

In the United States, the courts have historically regulated admission to the practice of law before them, and exercised the authority to discipline and ultimately to disbar lawyers whose conduct departed from prescribed standards. * * * More than a century ago, the first official code of legal ethics promulgated in this country, the Alabama Code of 1887, warned attorneys to "Avoid Newspaper Discussion of Legal Matters," and stated that "[n]ewspaper publications by an attorney as to the merits of pending or anticipated litigation ... tend to prevent a fair trial in the courts, and otherwise prejudice the due administration of justice." In 1908, the American Bar Association promulgated its own code, entitled "Canons of Professional Ethics," [which noted that]: "Newspaper publications by a lawyer as to pending or anticipated litigation may interfere with a fair trial * * * [G]enerally they are to be condemned. * * * "

In the last-quarter-century, the legal profession has reviewed its ethical limitations on extrajudicial statements by lawyers in the context of this Court's cases interpreting the First Amendment. ABA Model Rule of Professional Responsibility 3.6 resulted from the recommendations of the Advisory Committee on Fair Trial and Free Press (Advisory Committee), created in 1964 upon the recommendation of the Warren Commission. The Warren Commission's report on the assassination of President Kennedy included the recommendation that

> "representatives of the bar, law enforcement associations, and the news media work together to establish ethical standards concerning the collection and presentation of information to the public so that there will be no interference with pending criminal investigations, court proceedings, or the right of individuals to a fair trial."

The Advisory Committee developed the ABA Standards Relating to Fair Trial and Free Press, comprehensive guidelines relating to disclosure of information concerning criminal proceedings, which were relied upon by the ABA in 1968 in formulating [the predecessor to] Rule 3.6. The need for and appropriateness of such a rule had been identified by this Court two years earlier in *Sheppard v. Maxwell*. * * * [Courts] proceeded to enact local rules incorporating these standards, and thus the "reasonable likelihood of prejudicing a fair trial" test was used by a majority of courts, state and federal, in the years following *Sheppard*. Ten years later, the ABA amended its guidelines, and the "reasonable likelihood" test was changed to a "clear and present danger" test.

When the Model Rules of Professional Conduct were drafted in the early 1980's, the drafters did not go as far as the revised Fair Trial–Free Press Standards in giving precedence to the lawyer's right to make extrajudicial statements when fair trial rights are implicated, and instead adopted the "substantial likelihood of material prejudice" test. Currently, 31 States in addition to Nevada have adopted—either verbatim or with insignificant variations—Rule 3.6 of the ABA's Model Rules. Eleven States have adopted Disciplinary Rule 7–107 of the ABA's Code of Professional Responsibility, which is less protective of lawyer speech than Model Rule 3.6, in that it applies a "reasonable likelihood of prejudice" standard. Only one State, Virginia, has explicitly adopted a clear and present danger standard, while four States and the District of Columbia have adopted standards that arguably approximate "clear and present danger."

Petitioner maintains, however, that the First Amendment to the United States Constitution requires a State, such as Nevada in this case, to demonstrate a "clear and present danger" of "actual prejudice or an imminent threat" before any discipline may be imposed on a lawyer who initiates a press conference such as occurred here. He relies on [cases in which] * * * we held that trial courts might not constitutionally punish, through use of the contempt power, newspapers and others for publishing editorials, cartoons, and other items critical of judges in particular cases. We held that such punishments could be imposed only if there were a clear and present danger of "some serious substantive evil which they are designed to avert." *Bridges v. California,* 314 U.S. 252 (1941). Petitioner also relies on *Wood v. Georgia,* 370 U.S. 375 (1962), which held that a court might not punish a sheriff for publicly criticizing a judge's charges to a grand jury. * * *

The question we must answer in this case is whether a lawyer who represents a defendant involved with the criminal justice system may insist on the same standard before he is disciplined for public pronouncements about the case, or whether the State instead may penalize that sort of speech upon a lesser showing. It is unquestionable that in the courtroom itself, during a judicial proceeding, whatever right to "free speech" an attorney has is extremely circumscribed. * * * Even outside the courtroom, a majority of the Court in two separate opinions in the case of *In re Sawyer*, 360 U.S. 622 (1959), observed that lawyers in pending cases were subject to ethical restrictions on speech to which an ordinary citizen would not be. * * * Likewise, in *Sheppard v. Maxwell*, where the defendant's conviction was overturned because extensive prejudicial pretrial publicity had denied the defendant a fair trial, we held that a new trial was a remedy for such publicity, but [we also] * * * expressly contemplated that the speech of *those participating before the courts* could be limited.[5] This distinction between participants in the litigation and strangers to it is brought into sharp relief by our holding in *Seattle Times Co. v. Rhinehart*, 467 U.S. 20 (1984). There, we unanimously held that a newspaper, which was itself a defendant in a libel action, could be restrained from publishing material about the plaintiffs and their supporters to which it had gained access through court-ordered discovery. In that case we said that "[a]lthough litigants do not 'surrender their First Amendment rights at the courthouse door,' those rights may be subordinated to other interests that arise in this setting," and noted that "on several occasions [we have] approved restriction on the communications of trial participants where necessary to ensure a fair trial for a criminal defendant." * * *

We think that the * * * statements from our opinions in *In re Sawyer* and *Sheppard v. Maxwell* rather plainly indicate that the speech of lawyers representing clients in pending cases may be regulated under a less demanding standard than that established for regulation of the press in *Nebraska Press Assn. v. Stuart*. Lawyers representing clients in pending cases are key participants in the criminal justice system, and the State may demand some adherence to the precepts of that system in regulating their speech as well as their conduct. As noted by Justice Brennan in his concurring opinion in *Nebraska Press*, which was joined by Justices Stewart and Marshall, "[a]s officers of the court, court personnel and attorneys have a fiduciary responsibility not to engage in public debate that will rebound to the detriment of the accused or that will obstruct the fair administration of justice." Because lawyers have special access to information through discovery and client communications, their extrajudicial statements pose a threat to the fairness of a pending proceeding since lawyers' statements are likely to be received as especially authoritative. See, *e.g., In re Hinds*, 90 N.J. 604, 627, 449 A.2d 483, 496 (1982) (statements by attorneys of record relating to the case "are likely to be considered knowledgeable, reliable and true" because of attorneys' unique access to information); *In re Rachmiel*, 90 N.J. 646, 656, 449 A.2d 505, 511 (N.J.1982) (attorneys' role as advocates gives them "extraordinary power to

---

5. The Nevada Supreme Court has consistently read all parts of Rule 177 as applying only to lawyers in pending cases, and not to other lawyers or nonlawyers. We express no opinion on the constitutionality of a rule regulating the statements of a lawyer who is not participating in the pending case about which the statements are made. We note that of all the cases petitioner cites as supporting the use of the clear and present danger standard, the only one that even arguably involved a non-third party was *Wood v. Georgia*, supra, where a county sheriff was held in contempt for publicly criticizing instructions given by a judge to a grand jury. Although the sheriff was technically an "officer of the court" by virtue of his position, the Court determined that his statements were made in his capacity as a private citizen, with no connection to his official duties. The same cannot be said about petitioner, whose statements were made in the course of and in furtherance of his role as defense counsel.

undermine or destroy the efficacy of the criminal justice system"). We agree with the majority of the States that the "substantial likelihood of material prejudice" standard constitutes a constitutionally permissible balance between the First Amendment rights of attorneys in pending cases and the state's interest in fair trials.

When a state regulation implicates First Amendment rights, the Court must balance those interests against the State's legitimate interest in regulating the activity in question. The "substantial likelihood" test embodied in Rule 177 is constitutional under this analysis, for it is designed to protect the integrity and fairness of a state's judicial system, and it imposes only narrow and necessary limitations on lawyers' speech. The limitations are aimed at two principal evils: (1) comments that are likely to influence the actual outcome of the trial, and (2) comments that are likely to prejudice the jury venire, even if an untainted panel can ultimately be found. Few, if any, interests under the Constitution are more fundamental than the right to a fair trial by "impartial" jurors, and an outcome affected by extrajudicial statements would violate that fundamental right. * * * Even if a fair trial can ultimately be ensured through *voir dire*, change of venue, or some other device, these measures entail serious costs to the system. Extensive *voir dire* may not be able to filter out all of the effects of pretrial publicity, and with increasingly widespread media coverage of criminal trials, a change of venue may not suffice to undo the effects of statements such as those made by petitioner. The State has a substantial interest in preventing officers of the court, such as lawyers, from imposing such costs on the judicial system and on the litigants.

The restraint on speech is narrowly tailored to achieve those objectives. The regulation of attorneys' speech is limited—it applies only to speech that is substantially likely to have a materially prejudicial effect; it is neutral as to points of view, applying equally to all attorneys participating in a pending case; and it merely postpones the attorneys' comments until after the trial. While supported by the substantial state interest in preventing prejudice to an adjudicative proceeding by those who have a duty to protect its integrity, the rule is limited on its face to preventing only speech having a substantial likelihood of materially prejudicing that proceeding.

III

To assist a lawyer in deciding whether an extrajudicial statement is problematic, Rule 177 sets out statements that are likely to cause material prejudice. Contrary to petitioner's contention, these are not improper evidentiary presumptions. Model Rule 3.6, from which Rule 177 was derived, was specifically designed to avoid the categorical prohibitions of attorney speech contained in ABA Model Code of Professional Responsibility Disciplinary Rule 7–107 (1981). * * * The statements listed as likely to cause material prejudice closely track a similar list outlined by this Court in *Sheppard*. * * * [However,] Gentile claims that Rule 177 is overbroad, and thus unconstitutional on its face, because it applies to more speech than is necessary to serve the State's goals. The "overbreadth" doctrine applies if an enactment "prohibits constitutionally protected conduct." To be unconstitutional, overbreadth must be "substantial." Rule 177 is no broader than necessary to protect the State's interests. It applies only to lawyers involved in the pending case at issue, and even those lawyers involved in pending cases can make extrajudicial statements as long as such statements do not present a substantial risk of material prejudice to an adjudicative proceeding. The fact that Rule 177 applies to bench trials does not make it overbroad, for a substantial likelihood of prejudice is still required before the Rule is violated. That test will rarely be met where the judge is the trier of fact, since trial judges often have access to inadmissible and highly prejudicial information and are presumed to be able to discount or disregard it. For these reasons Rule 177 is constitutional on its face.

Gentile also argues that Rule 177 is void for vagueness because it did not provide adequate notice that his comments were subject to discipline. The void-for-vagueness doctrine is concerned with a defendant's right to fair notice and adequate warning that his conduct runs afoul of the law. Rule 177 was drafted with the intent to provide "an illustrative compilation that gives fair notice of conduct ordinarily posing unacceptable dangers to the fair administration of justice." Proposed Final Draft 143. The Rule provides sufficient notice of the nature of the prohibited conduct. Under the circumstances of his case, petitioner cannot complain about lack of notice, as he has admitted that his primary objective in holding the press conference was the violation of Rule 177's core prohibition—to prejudice the upcoming trial by influencing potential jurors. Petitioner was clearly given notice that such conduct was forbidden, and the list of conduct likely to cause prejudice, while only advisory, certainly gave notice that the statements made would violate the rule if they had the intended effect.

The majority agrees with petitioner that he was the victim of unconstitutional vagueness in the regulations because of the relationship between subsection 3 and subsections 1 and 2 of rule 177. Subsection 3 allows an attorney to state "the general nature of the claim or defense" notwithstanding the prohibition contained in subsection 1 and the examples contained in subsection 2. It is of course true, as the majority points out, that the word "general" and the word "elaboration" are both terms of degree. But combined as they are in the first sentence of subsection 3, they convey the very definite proposition that the authorized statements must not contain the sort of detailed allegations that petitioner made at his press conference. No sensible person could think that the following were "general" statements of a claim or defense made "without elaboration": "the person that was in the most direct position to have stolen the drugs and the money ... is Detective Steve Scholl"; "there is far more evidence that will establish that Detective Scholl took these drugs and took these American Express travelers' checks than any other living human being"; "[Detective Scholl] either had a hell of a cold, or he should have seen a better doctor"; and "the so-called other victims ... one, two—four of them are known drug dealers and convicted money launderers." Subsection 3, as an exception to the provisions of subsections 1 and 2, must be read in the light of the prohibitions and examples contained in the first two sections. It was obviously not intended to negate the prohibitions or the examples wholesale, but simply intended to provide a "safe harbor" where there might be doubt as to whether one of the examples covered proposed conduct. These provisions were not vague as to the conduct for which petitioner was disciplined; "[i]n determining the sufficiency of the notice a statute must of necessity be examined in the light of the conduct with which a defendant is charged." *United States v. National Dairy Products Corp.*, 372 U.S. 29, 33 (1963).

Petitioner's strongest arguments are that the statement was made well in advance of trial, and that the statements did not in fact taint the jury panel. But the Supreme Court of Nevada pointed out that petitioner's statements were not only highly inflammatory—they portrayed prospective government witnesses as drug users and dealers, and as money launderers—but the statements were timed to have maximum impact, when public interest in the case was at its height immediately after Sanders was indicted. Reviewing independently the entire record, we are convinced that petitioner's statements were "substantially likely to cause material prejudice" to the proceedings. While there is evidence pro and con on that point, we find it persuasive that, by his own admission, petitioner called the press conference for the express purpose of influencing the venire. It is difficult to believe that he went to such trouble, and took such a risk, if there was no substantial likelihood that he would succeed.

While in a case such as this we must review the record for ourselves, when the highest court of a state has reached a determination "we give most respectful attention to its reasoning and conclusion." The State Bar of Nevada, which made its own factual findings, and the Supreme Court of Nevada, which upheld those findings, were in a far better position than we are to appreciate the likely effect of petitioner's statements on potential members of a jury panel in a highly publicized case such as this. The Board and Nevada Supreme Court did not apply the list of statements likely to cause material prejudice as presumptions, but specifically found that petitioner had intended to prejudice the trial,[6] and that based upon the nature of the statements and their timing, they were in fact substantially likely to cause material prejudice. We cannot, upon our review of the record, conclude that they were mistaken.

Several amici argue that the First Amendment requires the state to show actual prejudice to a judicial proceeding before an attorney may be disciplined for extrajudicial statements, and since the Board and Nevada Supreme Court found no actual prejudice, petitioner should not have been disciplined. But this is simply another way of stating that the stringent standard of Nebraska Press should be applied to the speech of a lawyer in a pending case, and for the reasons heretofore given we decline to adopt it. An added objection to the stricter standard when applied to lawyer participants is that if it were adopted, even comments more flagrant than those made by petitioner could not serve as the basis for disciplinary action if, for wholly independent reasons, they had no effect on the proceedings. An attorney who made prejudicial comments would be insulated from discipline if the government, for reasons unrelated to the comments, decided to dismiss the charges, or if a plea bargain were reached. An equally culpable attorney whose client's case went to trial would be subject to discipline. The United States Constitution does not mandate such a fortuitous difference.

When petitioner was admitted to practice law before the Nevada courts, the oath which he took recited that "I will support, abide by and follow the Rules of Professional Conduct as are now or may hereafter be adopted by the Supreme Court . . ." Rule 73, Nevada Supreme Court Rules (1991). The First Amendment does not excuse him from that obligation, nor should it forbid the discipline imposed upon him by the Supreme Court of Nevada. I would affirm the decision of the Supreme Court of Nevada.

---

6. Justice Kennedy appears to contend that there can be no material prejudice when the lawyer's publicity is in response to publicity favorable to the other side. Justice Kennedy would find that publicity designed to counter prejudicial publicity cannot be itself prejudicial, despite its likelihood of influencing potential jurors, unless it actually would go so far as to cause jurors to be affirmatively biased in favor of the lawyer's client. In the first place, such a test would be difficult, if not impossible, to apply. But more fundamentally, it misconceives the constitutional test for an impartial juror—whether the "juror can lay aside his impression or opinion and render a verdict on the evidence presented in Court." *Murphy v.* *Florida,* 421 U.S. 794 (1975). A juror who may have been initially swayed from openmindedness by publicity favorable to the prosecution is not rendered fit for service by being bombarded by publicity favorable to the defendant. The basic premise of our legal system is that law suits should be tried in court, not in the media. A defendant may be protected from publicity by, or in favor of, the police and prosecution through voir dire, change of venue, jury instructions and, in extreme cases, reversal on due process grounds. The remedy for prosecutorial abuses that violate the rule lies not in self-help in the form of similarly prejudicial comments by defense counsel, but in disciplining the prosecutor.

JUSTICE O'CONNOR, concurring.

I agree with much of The Chief Justice's opinion. In particular, I agree that a State may regulate speech by lawyers representing clients in pending cases more readily than it may regulate the press. Lawyers are officers of the court and, as such, may legitimately be subject to ethical precepts that keep them from engaging in what otherwise might be constitutionally protected speech. This does not mean, of course, that lawyers forfeit their First Amendment rights, only that a less demanding standard applies. I agree with The Chief Justice that the "substantial likelihood of material prejudice" standard articulated in Rule 177 passes constitutional muster. Accordingly, I join Parts I and II of The Chief Justice's opinion.

CHANDLER v. FLORIDA

449 U.S. 560, 101 S.Ct. 802, 66 L.Ed.2d 740 (1981).

CHIEF JUSTICE BURGER delivered the opinion of the Court.

The question presented on this appeal is whether, consistent with constitutional guarantees, a state may provide for radio, television, and still photographic coverage of a criminal trial for public broadcast, notwithstanding the objection of the accused.

Background. Over the past 50 years, some criminal cases characterized as "sensational" have been subjected to extensive coverage by news media, sometimes seriously interfering with the conduct of the proceedings and creating a setting wholly inappropriate for the administration of justice. Judges, lawyers, and others soon became concerned, and in 1937, after study, the American Bar Association House of Delegates adopted Judicial Canon 35, declaring that all photographic and broadcast coverage of courtroom proceedings should be prohibited. In 1952, the House of Delegates amended Canon 35 to proscribe television coverage as well. [A] majority of the states, including Florida, adopted the substance of the ABA provision and its amendments. In Florida, the rule was embodied in Canon 3A(7) of the Florida Code of Judicial Conduct.

In February 1978, the American Bar Association Committee on Fair Trial–Free Press proposed revised standards. These included a provision permitting courtroom coverage by the electronic media under conditions to be established by local rule and under the control of the trial judge, but only if such coverage was carried out unobtrusively and without affecting the conduct of the trial. The revision was endorsed by the ABA's Standing Committee on Standards for Criminal Justice, [but] rejected by the House of Delegates on February 12, 1979.

[In] January 1975, while these developments were unfolding, the Post–Newsweek Stations of Florida petitioned the Supreme Court of Florida urging a change in Florida's Canon 3A(7). [The] Florida Supreme Court [eventually established a] 1–year pilot program during which the electronic media were permitted to cover all judicial proceedings in Florida without reference to the consent of participants, subject to detailed standards with respect to technology and the conduct of operators. * * * When the pilot program ended, the Florida Supreme Court received and reviewed briefs, reports, letters of comment, and studies. It conducted its own survey of attorneys, witnesses, jurors, and court personnel through the Office of the State Court Coordinator. A separate survey was taken of judges by the Florida Conference of Circuit Judges. The court also studied the experience of 6 States that had, by 1979, adopted rules relating to electronic coverage of trials, as well as that of the 10 other States that, like Florida, were experimenting with such coverage.

Following its review of this material, the Florida Supreme Court concluded "that on balance there [was] more to be gained than lost by permitting electronic media coverage of judicial proceedings subject to standards for such coverage." The Florida court was of the view that because of the significant effect of the courts on the day-to-day lives of the citizenry, it was essential that the people have confidence in the process. It felt that broadcast coverage of trials would contribute to wider public acceptance and understanding of decisions. Consequently, after revising the 1977 guidelines to reflect its evaluation of the pilot program, the Florida Supreme Court promulgated a revised Canon 3A(7). The Canon provides:

> "Subject at all times to the authority of the presiding judge to (i) control the conduct of proceedings before the court, (ii) ensure decorum and prevent distractions, and (iii) ensure the fair administration of justice in the pending cause, electronic media and still photography coverage of public judicial proceedings in the appellate and trial courts of this state shall be allowed in accordance with standards of conduct and technology promulgated by the Supreme Court of Florida." Ibid.

The implementing guidelines specify in detail the kind of electronic equipment to be used and the manner of its use. For example, no more than one television camera and only one camera technician are allowed. Existing recording systems used by court reporters are used by broadcasters for audio pickup. Where more than one broadcast news organization seeks to cover a trial, the media must pool coverage. No artificial lighting is allowed. The equipment is positioned in a fixed location, and it may not be moved during trial. Videotaping equipment must be remote from the courtroom. Film, videotape, and lenses may not be changed while the court is in session. No audio recording of conferences between lawyers, between parties and counsel, or at the bench is permitted. The judge has sole and plenary discretion to exclude coverage of certain witnesses, and the jury may not be filmed. The judge has discretionary power to forbid coverage whenever satisfied that coverage may have a deleterious effect on the paramount right of the defendant to a fair trial. * * *

In July 1977, appellants were charged with conspiracy to commit burglary, grand larceny, and possession of burglary tools. The counts covered breaking and entering a well-known Miami Beach restaurant.

The details of the alleged criminal conduct are not relevant to the issue before us, but several aspects of the case distinguish it from a routine burglary. At the time of their arrest, appellants were Miami Beach policemen. The State's principal witness was John Sion, an amateur radio operator who, by sheer chance, had overheard and recorded conversations between the appellants over their police walkie-talkie radios during the burglary. Not surprisingly, these novel factors attracted the attention of the media.

By pretrial motion, counsel for the appellants sought to have experimental Canon 3A(7) declared unconstitutional on its face and as applied. The trial court denied relief * * *. After several additional fruitless attempts by the appellants to prevent electronic coverage of the trial, the jury was selected. At *voir dire,* the appellants' counsel asked each prospective juror whether he or she would be able to be "fair and impartial" despite the presence of a television camera during some, or all, of the trial. Each juror selected responded that such coverage would not affect his or her consideration in any way. A television camera recorded the *voir dire.*

A defense motion to sequester the jury because of the television coverage was denied by the trial judge. However, the court instructed the jury not to watch or read anything about the case in the media and suggested that jurors "avoid the local news and watch only the national news on television." Subsequently, defense counsel requested that the witnesses be instructed not to watch any television accounts of testimony presented at trial. The trial court declined to give such an instruction, for "no witness' testimony was [being] reported or televised [on the evening news] in any way."

A television camera was in place for one entire afternoon, during which the State presented the testimony of Sion, its chief witness. No camera was present for the presentation of any part of the case for the defense. The camera returned to cover closing arguments. Only 2 minutes and 55 seconds of the trial below were broadcast—and those depicted only the prosecution's side of the case.

The jury returned a guilty verdict on all counts. Appellants moved for a new trial, claiming that because of the television coverage, they had been denied a fair and impartial trial. No evidence of specific prejudice was tendered.

[At] the outset, it is important to note that in promulgating the revised Canon 3A(7), the Florida Supreme Court pointedly rejected any state or federal constitutional right of access on the part of photographers or the broadcast media to televise or electronically record and thereafter disseminate court proceedings. [The] Florida court relied on our holding in *Nixon v. Warner Communications, Inc.,* 435 U.S. 589 (1978), where we said:

> "In the first place, [there] is no constitutional right to have [live witness] testimony recorded and broadcast. Second, while the guarantee of a public trial, in the words of Mr. Justice Black, is 'a safeguard against any attempt to employ our courts as instruments of persecution,' it confers no special benefit on the press. Nor does the Sixth Amendment require that the trial—or any part of it—be broadcast live or on tape to the public. The requirement of a public trial is satisfied by the opportunity of members of the public and the press to attend the trial and to report what they have observed."

The Florida Supreme Court predicated the revised Canon 3A(7) upon its supervisory authority over the Florida courts, and not upon any constitutional imperative. Hence, we have before us only the limited question of the Florida Supreme Court's authority to promulgate the Canon for the trial of cases in Florida courts. * * *

Appellants rely chiefly on *Estes v. Texas,* 381 U.S. 532 (1965), and Chief Justice Warren's separate concurring opinion in that case. They argue that the televising of criminal trials is inherently a denial of due process, and they read *Estes* as announcing a *per se* constitutional rule to that effect. Chief Justice Warren's concurring opinion, in which he was joined by Justices Douglas and Goldberg, indeed provides some support for the appellants' position. * * * [However], [t]he six separate opinions in *Estes* must be examined carefully to evaluate the claim that it represents a *per se* constitutional rule forbidding all electronic coverage.[a] Chief Justice Warren and Justices Douglas and Goldberg

---

a. Justice Clark delivered an opinion in *Estes* that was described as the "opinion for the Court," although (as the *Chandler* opinion notes infra) Justice Harlan was listed as concurring only to the extent indicated in his separate opinion. Justice Clark's opinion reasoned: "The State * * * says that the use of television in the instant case was 'without injustice to the person immediately concerned;' basing its position on the fact that the petitioner has established no isolatable prejudice and that this must be shown in order to invalidate a conviction * * *. The State paints too

broadly * * *, for this Court itself has found instances in which a showing of actual prejudice is not a prerequisite to reversal. This is such a case. [In *Rideau* and certain other cases, e.g., one in which two sheriffs deputies who were principle prosecution witnesses also had custody of the jurors], the Court did not stop to consider the actual effect of the practice, but struck down the conviction on the ground that prejudice was inherent. [T]he circumstances were held to be inherently suspect and therefore, such a showing [of actual joined Justice Clark's opinion announcing the judgment, thereby creating only a plurality. Justice Harlan provided the fifth vote necessary in support of the judgment. In a separate opinion, he pointedly limited his concurrence:

> "I concur in the opinion of the Court, subject, however, to the reservations and only to the extent indicated in this opinion."

A careful analysis of Justice Harlan's opinion is therefore fundamental to an understanding of the ultimate holding of *Estes*.

Justice Harlan began by observing that the question of the constitutional permissibility of televised trials was one fraught with unusual difficulty:

> "Permitting television in the courtroom undeniably has mischievous potentialities for intruding upon the detached atmosphere which should always surround the judicial process. Forbidding this innovation, however, would doubtless impinge upon one of the valued attributes of our federalism by preventing the states from pursing a novel course of procedural experimentation. My conclusion is that there is no constitutional requirement that television be allowed in the courtroom, *and, at least as to a notorious criminal trial such as this one, the considerations against allowing television in the courtroom so far outweigh the countervailing factors advanced in its support as to require a holding that what was done in this case infringed the fundamental right to a fair trial* assured by the Due Process Clause of the Fourteenth Amendment." (emphasis added).

He then proceeded to catalog what he perceived as the inherent dangers of televised trials.

> "In the context of a trial of intense public interest, there is certainly a strong possibility that the timid or reluctant witness, for whom a court appearance even at its traditional best is a harrowing affair, will become more timid or reluctant when he finds he will also be appearing before a 'hidden audience' of unknown but large dimensions. There is certainly a strong possibility that the 'cocky' witness having a thirst for the limelight will become more 'cocky' under the influence of television. And who can say that the juror who is gratified by having been chosen for a front-line case, an ambitious prosecutor, a publicity-minded defense attorney, and even a conscientious judge will not stray, albeit unconsciously, from doing what 'comes naturally' into pluming themselves for a satisfactory television 'performance'?"

Justice Harlan faced squarely the reality that these possibilities carry "grave potentialities for distorting the integrity of the judicial process," and that, although such distortions may produce no telltale signs, "their effects may be far more pervasive and deleterious than the physical disruptions which all would

prejudice] was not held to be a requisite to reversal. Likewise in this case the application of this principle is especially appropriate. Television in its present state and by its very nature, reaches into a variety of areas in which it may cause prejudice to an accused. Still one cannot put his finger on its specific mischief and prove with particularity wherein he was prejudiced. * * * Forty-eight of our states and the Federal Rules have deemed the use of television improper in the courtroom. This fact is most telling in buttressing our conclusion that any change in procedure which would permit its use would be inconsistent with our concepts of due process in this field."

Three members of the majority, speaking through Chief Justice Warren's concurring opinion stated that they "join[ed] the Court's opinion and agree[d] that televising of criminal trials is inherently a denial of due process," but wished to offer "additional views on why this is so." The concurring opinion of the fifth member of the majority, Justice Harlan, is discussed infra. In addition, there were three dissents (reflecting the views of four dissenters). The dissents argued against the adoption of a "per se rule" rendering the televising of trials constitutionally unacceptable without a showing that the risks of disruption, distraction, and juror viewing of the broadcasts actually had materialized in the particular case.

concede would vitiate a conviction." The "countervailing factors" alluded to by Justice Harlan were, as here, the educational and informational value to the public.

[I]t is fair to say that Justice Harlan viewed the holding as limited to the proposition that "*what was done in this case* infringed the fundamental right to a fair trial assured by the Due Process Clause of the Fourteenth Amendment" (emphasis added). * * * Justice Harlan's opinion, upon which analysis of the constitutional holding of *Estes* turns, must be read as defining the scope of that holding; we conclude that *Estes* is not to be read as announcing a constitutional rule barring still photographic, radio, and television coverage in all cases and under all circumstances. [Since] we are satisfied that *Estes* did not announce a constitutional rule that all photographic or broadcast coverage of criminal trials is inherently a denial of due process, we turn to consideration, as a matter of first impression, of the appellants' suggestion that we now promulgate such a *per se* rule.

Any criminal case that generates a great deal of publicity presents some risks that the publicity may compromise the right of the defendant to a fair trial. Trial courts must be especially vigilant to guard against any impairment of the defendant's right to a verdict based solely upon the evidence and the relevant law. Over the years, courts have developed a range of curative devices to prevent publicity about a trial from infecting jury deliberations. See, e.g., *Nebraska Press Assn. v. Stuart.*

An absolute constitutional ban on broadcast coverage of trials cannot be justified simply because there is a danger that, in some cases, prejudicial broadcast accounts of pretrial and trial events may impair the ability of jurors to decide the issue of guilt or innocence uninfluenced by extraneous matter. The risk of juror prejudice in some cases does not justify an absolute ban on news coverage of trials by the printed media; so also the risk of such prejudice does not warrant an absolute constitutional ban on all broadcast coverage. A case attracts a high level of public attention because of its intrinsic interest to the public and the manner of reporting the event. The risk of juror prejudice is present in any publication of a trial, but the appropriate safeguard against such prejudice is the defendant's right to demonstrate that the media's coverage of his case—be it printed or broadcast—compromised the ability of the particular jury that heard the case to adjudicate fairly.

[T]he concurring opinions in *Estes* expressed concern that the very presence of media cameras and recording devices at a trial inescapably gives rise to an adverse psychological impact on the participants in the trial. This kind of general psychological prejudice, allegedly present whenever there is broadcast coverage of a trial, is different from the more particularized problem of prejudicial impact discussed earlier. If it could be demonstrated that the mere presence of photographic and recording equipment and the knowledge that the event would be broadcast invariably and uniformly affected the conduct of participants so as to impair fundamental fairness, our task would be simple; prohibition of broadcast coverage of trials would be required.

In confronting the difficult and sensitive question of the potential psychological prejudice associated with broadcast coverage of trials, we have been aided by *amici* briefs submitted by various state officers involved in law enforcement, the Conference of Chief Justices, and the Attorneys General of 17 States in support of continuing experimentation such as that embarked upon by Florida, and by the American College of Trial Lawyers, and various members of the defense bar representing essentially the views expressed by the concurring Justices in *Estes.*

Not unimportant to the position asserted by Florida and other states is the change in television technology since 1962, when Estes was tried. It is urged, and some empirical data are presented, that many of the negative factors found in *Estes* —cumbersome equipment, cables, distracting lighting, numerous camera technicians—are less substantial factors today than they were at that time.

It is also significant that safeguards have been built into the experimental programs in state courts, and into the Florida program, to avoid some of the most egregious problems envisioned by the six opinions in the *Estes* case. Florida admonishes its courts to take special pains to protect certain witnesses—for example, children, victims of sex crimes, some informants, and even the very timid witness or party—from the glare of publicity and the tensions of being "on camera."

The Florida guidelines place on trial judges positive obligations to be on guard to protect the fundamental right of the accused to a fair trial. The Florida Canon, being one of the few permitting broadcast coverage of criminal trials over the objection of the accused, raises problems not present in the rules of other states. Inherent in electronic coverage of a trial is the risk that the very awareness by the accused of the coverage and the contemplated broadcast may adversely affect the conduct of the participants and the fairness of the trial, yet leave no evidence of how the conduct or the trial's fairness was affected. Given this danger, it is significant that Florida requires that objections of the accused to coverage be heard and considered on the record by the trial court. In addition to providing a record for appellate review, a pre-trial hearing enables a defendant to advance the basis of his objection to broadcast coverage and allows the trial court to define the steps necessary to minimize or eliminate the risks of prejudice to the accused. Experiments such as the one presented here may well increase the number of appeals by adding a new basis for claims to reverse, but this is a risk Florida has chosen to take after preliminary experimentation. Here, the record does not indicate that appellants requested an evidentiary hearing to show adverse impact or injury. Nor does the record reveal anything more than generalized allegations of prejudice.

Nonetheless, it is clear that the general issue of the psychological impact of broadcast coverage upon the participants in a trial, and particularly upon the defendant, is still a subject of sharp debate—as the *amici* briefs of the American College of Trial Lawyers and others of the trial bar in opposition to Florida's experiment demonstrate. These *amici* state the view that the concerns expressed by the concurring opinions in *Estes,* have been borne out by actual experience. [Yet], [c]omprehensive empirical data are still not available—at least on some aspects of the problem. * * * Whatever may be the "mischievous potentialities [of broadcast coverage] for intruding upon the detached atmosphere which should always surround the judicial process," *Estes v. Texas,* at present no one has been able to present empirical data sufficient to establish that the mere presence of the broadcast media inherently has an adverse effect on that process. * * *

Where, as here, we cannot say that a denial of due process automatically results from activity authorized by a state, the admonition of Justice Brandeis, dissenting in *New State Ice Co. v. Liebmann,* 285 U.S. 262 (1932), is relevant:

> "To stay experimentation in things social and economic is a grave responsibility. Denial of the right to experiment may be fraught with serious consequences to the Nation. It is one of the happy incidents of the federal system that a single courageous State may, if its citizens choose, serve as a laboratory; and try novel social and economic experiments without risk to the rest of the country. This Court has the power to prevent an experiment. We

may strike down the statute which embodies it on the ground that, in our opinion, the measure is arbitrary, capricious, or unreasonable. [But] in the exercise of this high power, we must be ever on our guard, lest we erect our prejudices into legal principles. If we would guide by the light of reason, we must let our minds be bold." (Footnote omitted.)

This concept of federalism, echoed by the states favoring Florida's experiment, must guide our decision.

Amici members of the defense bar vigorously contend that displaying the accused on television is in itself a denial of due process. This was a source of concern to Chief Justice Warren and Justice Harlan in *Estes:* that coverage of select cases "singles out certain defendants and subjects them to trials under prejudicial conditions not experienced by others." Selection of which trials, or parts of trials, to broadcast will inevitably be made not by judges but by the media, and will be governed by such factors as the nature of the crime and the status and position of the accused—or of the victim; the effect may be to titillate rather than to educate and inform. The unanswered question is whether electronic coverage will bring public humiliation upon the accused with such randomness that it will evoke due process concerns by being "unusual in the same way that being struck by lightning" is "unusual." *Furman v. Georgia,* 408 U.S. 238 (1972) (Stewart, J., concurring). Societies and political systems, that, from time to time, have put on "Yankee Stadium" "show trials" tell more about the power of the state than about its concern for the decent administration of justice—with every citizen receiving the same kind of justice.

The concurring opinion of Chief Justice Warren joined by Justices Douglas and Goldberg in *Estes* can fairly be read as viewing the very broadcast of some trials as potentially a form of punishment in itself—a punishment before guilt. This concern is far from trivial. But, whether coverage of a few trials will, in practice, be the equivalent of a "Yankee Stadium" setting—which Justice Harlan likened to the public pillory long abandoned as a barbaric perversion of decent justice—must also await the continuing experimentation.

To say that the appellants have not demonstrated that broadcast coverage is inherently a denial of due process is not to say that the appellants were in fact accorded all of the protections of due process in their trial. As noted earlier, a defendant has the right on review to show that the media's coverage of his case—printed or broadcast—compromised the ability of the jury to judge him fairly. Alternatively, a defendant might show that broadcast coverage of his particular case had an adverse impact on the trial participants sufficient to constitute a denial of due process. Neither showing was made in this case.

To demonstrate prejudice in a specific case a defendant must show something more than juror awareness that the trial is such as to attract the attention of broadcasters. *Murphy v. Florida.* No doubt the very presence of a camera in the courtroom made the jurors aware that the trial was thought to be of sufficient interest to the public to warrant coverage. Jurors, forbidden to watch all broadcasts, would have had no way of knowing that only fleeting seconds of the proceeding would be reproduced. But the appellants have not attempted to show with any specificity that the presence of cameras impaired the ability of the jurors to decide the case on only the evidence before them or that their trial was affected adversely by the impact on any of the participants of the presence of cameras and the prospect of broadcast.

Although not essential to our holding, we note that at *voir dire,* the jurors were asked if the presence of the camera would in any way compromise their ability to consider the case. Each answered that the camera would not prevent him or her from considering the case solely on the merits. The trial court instructed the jurors not to watch television accounts of the trial, and the appellants do not contend that any juror violated this instruction. The appellants have offered no evidence that any participant in this case was affected by the presence of cameras. In short, there is no showing that the trial was compromised by television coverage, as was the case in *Estes*.

[In] this setting, because this Court has no supervisory authority over state courts, our review is confined to whether there is a constitutional violation. We hold that the Constitution does not prohibit a state from experimenting with the program authorized by revised Canon 3A(7).

JUSTICE STEVENS took no part in the decision of this case.

JUSTICE STEWART, concurring in the result.

Although concurring in the judgment, I cannot join the opinion of the Court because I do not think the convictions in this case can be affirmed without overruling *Estes v. Texas*. I believe now, as I believed in dissent then, that *Estes* announced a *per se* rule that the Fourteenth Amendment "prohibits all television cameras from a state courtroom whenever a criminal trial is in progress." Accordingly, rather than join what seems to me a wholly unsuccessful effort to distinguish that decision, I would now flatly overrule it. * * *

JUSTICE WHITE, concurring in the judgment.

* * * Whether the decision in *Estes* is read broadly or narrowly, I agree with Justice Stewart that it should be overruled. I was in dissent in that case, and I remain unwilling to assume or conclude without more proof than has been marshaled to date that televising criminal trials is inherently prejudicial even when carried out under properly controlled conditions. * * * Although the Court's opinion today contends that it is consistent with *Estes,* I believe that it effectively eviscerates *Estes*. The Florida rule has no exception for the sensational or widely publicized case. Absent a showing of specific prejudice, *any* kind of case may be televised as long as the rule is otherwise complied with. Thus, even if the present case is precisely the kind of case referred to in Justice Harlan's concurrence in *Estes,* the Florida rule overrides the defendant's objections. The majority opinion does not find it necessary to deal with appellants' contention that because their case attracted substantial publicity, specific prejudice need not be shown. By affirming the judgment below, which sustained the rule, the majority indicates that not even the narrower reading of *Estes* will any longer be authoritative. * * *

PRESS–ENTERPRISE CO. v. SUPERIOR COURT [PRESS–ENTERPRISE II]

478 U.S. 1, 106 S.Ct. 2735, 92 L.Ed.2d 1 (1986).

CHIEF JUSTICE BURGER delivered the opinion of the Court.

We granted certiorari to decide whether petitioner has a First Amendment right of access to transcripts of a preliminary hearing growing out of a criminal prosecution.

On December 23, 1981, the State of California filed a complaint in the Riverside County Municipal Court, charging Robert Diaz with 12 counts of murder and seeking the death penalty. The complaint alleged that Diaz, a nurse, murdered 12 patients by administering massive doses of the heart drug lidocaine.

The preliminary hearing on the complaint commenced on July 6, 1982. Diaz moved to exclude the public from the proceedings under California Penal Code § 868, which requires such proceedings to be open unless "exclusion of the public is necessary in order to protect the defendant's right to a fair and impartial trial." The Magistrate granted the unopposed motion, finding that closure was necessary because the case had attracted national publicity and "only one side may get reported in the media."

The preliminary hearing continued for 41 days. Most of the testimony and the evidence presented by the State was medical and scientific; the remainder consisted of testimony by personnel who worked with Diaz on the shifts when the 12 patients died. Diaz did not introduce any evidence, but his counsel subjected most of the witnesses to vigorous cross-examination. Diaz was held to answer on all charges. At the conclusion of the hearing, petitioner Press–Enterprise Company asked that the transcript of the proceedings be released. The Magistrate refused and sealed the record.

On January 21, 1983, the State moved in Superior Court to have the transcripts of the preliminary hearing released to the public; petitioner later joined in support of the motion. Diaz opposed the motion, contending that release of the transcripts would result in prejudicial pretrial publicity. The Superior Court found that the information in the transcript was "as factual as it could be," and that the facts were neither "inflammatory" nor "exciting" but there was, nonetheless, "a reasonable likelihood that release of all or any part of the transcript might prejudice defendant's right to a fair and impartial trial."

Petitioner then filed a peremptory writ of mandate [seeking appellate review]. Meanwhile, Diaz waived his right to a jury trial and the Superior Court released the transcript. [The] California Supreme Court thereafter denied petitioner's peremptory writ of mandate, holding that there is no general First Amendment right of access to preliminary hearings. * * *

It is important to identify precisely what the California Supreme Court decided:

> "[W]e conclude that the magistrate shall close the preliminary hearing upon finding a reasonable likelihood of substantial prejudice which would impinge upon the right to a fair trial. Penal code section 868 makes clear that the primary right is the right to a fair trial and that the public's right of access must give way when there is conflict."

It is difficult to disagree in the abstract with that court's analysis balancing the defendant's right to a fair trial against the public right of access. It is also important to remember that these interests are not necessarily inconsistent. Plainly the defendant has a right to a fair trial but, as we have repeatedly recognized, one of the important means of assuring a fair trial is that the process be open to neutral observers.

The right to an open public trial is a shared right of the accused and the public, the common concern being the assurance of fairness. Only recently, in *Waller v. Georgia,* 467 U.S. 39 (1984), for example, we considered whether the defendant's Sixth Amendment right to an open trial prevented the closure of a suppression hearing over the defendant's objection. We noted that the First Amendment right of access would in most instances attach to such proceedings and that "the explicit Sixth Amendment right of the accused is no less protective of a public trial than the implicit First Amendment right of the press and public." When the defendant objects to the closure of a suppression hearing, therefore, the hearing must be open unless the party seeking to close the hearing advances an overriding interest that is likely to be prejudiced.

Here, unlike *Waller,* the right asserted is not the defendant's Sixth Amendment right to a public trial since the defendant requested a *closed* preliminary hearing. Instead, the right asserted here is that of the public under the First Amendment. The California Supreme Court concluded that the First Amendment was not implicated because the proceeding was not a criminal trial, but a preliminary hearing. However, the First Amendment question cannot be resolved solely on the label we give the event, i.e., "trial" or otherwise, particularly where the preliminary hearing functions much like a full scale trial.

In cases dealing with the claim of a First Amendment right of access to criminal proceedings, our decisions have emphasized two complementary considerations. First, because a " 'tradition of accessibility implies the favorable judgment of experience,' " we have considered whether the place and process has historically been open to the press and general public. * * * Second, [the] Court has traditionally considered whether public access plays a significant positive role in the functioning of the particular process in question. Although many governmental processes operate best under public scrutiny, it takes little imagination to recognize that there are some kinds of government operations that would be totally frustrated if conducted openly. A classic example is that "the proper functioning of our grand jury system depends upon the secrecy of grand jury proceedings." Other proceedings plainly require public access. In *Press–Enterprise I,* we summarized the holdings of prior cases, noting that openness in criminal trials, including the selection of jurors, "enhances both the basic fairness of the criminal trial and the appearance of fairness so essential to public confidence in the system."

These considerations of experience and logic are, of course, related, for history and experience shape the functioning of governmental processes. If the particular proceeding in question passes these tests of experience and logic, a qualified First Amendment right of public access attaches. But even when a right of access attaches, it is not absolute. *Globe Newspapers Co. v. Superior Court* [infra note 2]. While open criminal proceedings give assurances of fairness to both the public and the accused, there are some limited circumstances in which the right of the accused to a fair trial might be undermined by publicity.[2] In such cases, the trial court must determine whether the situation is such that the rights of the accused override the qualified First Amendment right of access. In *Press-Enterprise I* we stated:

> "the presumption may be overcome only by an overriding interest based on findings that closure is essential to preserve higher values and is narrowly tailored to serve that interest. The interest is to be articulated along with findings specific enough that a reviewing court can determine whether the closure order was properly entered."

2. Similarly, the interests of those other than the accused may be implicated. The protection of victims of sex crimes from the trauma and embarrassment of public scrutiny may justify closing certain aspects of a criminal proceeding. See *Globe Newspaper Co. v. Superior Court,* 457 U.S. 596 (1982). [In *Globe Newspaper,* the Court struck down as overbroad a state statute that required the trial court, at rape and sex offense trials involving complainants under age 18, to exclude the press and general public. The Court agreed that a state interest in "safeguarding the physical and psychological well-being of a minor" was a "compelling" interest, but found that it "does not justify a *mandatory*-closure rule, for it is clear that the circumstances of the particular case may affect the significance of the interest."]

The considerations that led the Court to apply the First Amendment right of access to criminal trials in *Richmond Newspapers* [and] the selection of jurors in *Press-Enterprise I* lead us to conclude that the right of access applies to preliminary hearings as conducted in California.

First, there has been a tradition of accessibility to preliminary hearings of the type conducted in California. Although grand jury proceedings have traditionally been closed to the public and the accused, preliminary hearings conducted before neutral and detached magistrates have been open to the public. Long ago in the celebrated trial of Aaron Burr for treason, for example, with Chief Justice Marshall sitting as trial judge, the probable cause hearing was held in the Hall of the House of Delegates in Virginia, the court room being too small to accommodate the crush of interested citizens. From *Burr* until the present day, the near uniform practice of state and federal courts has been to conduct preliminary hearings in open court. * * * Open preliminary hearings, therefore, have been accorded " 'the favorable judgment of experience.' "

The second question is whether public access to preliminary hearings as they are conducted in California plays a particularly significant positive role in the actual functioning of the process. We have already determined [that] public access to criminal trials and the selection of jurors is essential to the proper functioning of the criminal justice system. California preliminary hearings are sufficiently like a trial to justify the same conclusion. [The] accused has the right to personally appear at the hearing, to be represented by counsel, to cross-examine hostile witnesses, to present exculpatory evidence, and to exclude illegally obtained evidence. If the magistrate determines that probable cause exists, the accused is bound over for trial; such a finding leads to a guilty plea in the majority of cases.

It is true that unlike a criminal trial, the California preliminary hearing cannot result in the conviction of the accused and the adjudication is before a magistrate or other judicial officer without a jury. But these features, standing alone, do not make public access any less essential to the proper functioning of the proceedings in the overall criminal justice process. Because of its extensive scope, the preliminary hearing is often the final and most important step in the criminal proceeding. As the California Supreme Court stated, the preliminary hearing in many cases provides "the sole occasion for public observation of the criminal justice system."

Similarly, the absence of a jury, long recognized as "an inestimable safeguard against the corrupt or overzealous prosecutor and against the complaint, biased, or eccentric judge," makes the importance of public access to a preliminary hearing even more significant. "People in an open society do not demand infallibility from their institutions, but it is difficult for them to accept what they are prohibited from observing." *Richmond Newspapers.*

Denying the transcripts of a 41-day preliminary hearing would frustrate what we have characterized as the "community therapeutic value" of openness. Criminal acts, especially certain violent crimes, provoke public concern, outrage, and hostility. "When the public is aware that the law is being enforced and the criminal justice system is functioning, an outlet is provided for these understandable reactions and emotions." *Press–Enterprise I.* * * *

We therefore conclude that the qualified First Amendment right of access to criminal proceedings applies to preliminary hearings as they are conducted in California. Since [that right] attaches to preliminary hearings in California [the] proceedings cannot be closed unless specific, on the record findings are made demonstrating that "closure is essential to preserve higher values and is narrowly tailored to serve that interest." *Press-Enterprise I.* If the interest asserted is the right of the accused to a fair trial, the preliminary hearing shall be closed only if specific findings are made demonstrating that first, there is a substantial probability that the defendant's right to a fair trial will be prejudiced by publicity that closure would prevent and, second, reasonable alternatives to closure cannot adequately protect the defendant's free trial rights.

The California Supreme Court, interpreting its access statute, concluded "that the magistrate shall close the preliminary hearing upon finding a reasonable likelihood of substantial prejudice." As the court itself acknowledged, the "reasonable likelihood" test places a lesser burden on the defendant than the "substantial probability" test which we hold is called for by the First Amendment. Moreover, the court failed to consider whether alternatives short of complete closure would have protected the interests of the accused.

In *Gannett Co., Inc. v. DePasquale,* 443 U.S. 368 (1979) [involving the closure of a pretrial suppression hearing in which evidence was taken to determine the voluntariness of defendant's confession], we observed that:

"Publicity concerning pretrial suppression hearings such as the one involved in the present case poses special risks of unfairness. The whole purpose of such hearings is to screen out unreliable or illegally obtained evidence and insure that this evidence does not become known to the jury. Publicity concerning the proceedings at a pretrial hearing, however, could influence public opinion against a defendant and inform potential jurors of inculpatory information wholly inadmissible at the actual trial."

But this risk of prejudice does not automatically justify refusing public access to hearings on every motion to suppress. Through *voir dire,* cumbersome as it is in some circumstances, a court can identify those jurors whose prior knowledge of the case would disable them from rendering an impartial verdict. And even if closure were justified for the hearings on a motion to suppress, closure of an entire 41-day proceeding would rarely be warranted. The First Amendment right of access cannot be overcome by the conclusory assertion that publicity might deprive the defendant of that right. And any limitation " 'must be narrowly tailored to serve that interest.' " *Press-Enterprise I.* * * *

Justice Stevens, with whom Justice Rehnquist joins as to Part II, dissenting.

The constitutional question presented by this case is whether members of the public have a First Amendment right to insist upon access to the transcript of a preliminary hearing during the period before the public trial, even though the accused, the prosecutor, and the trial judge have all agreed to the sealing of the transcript in order to assure a fair trial. * * *

I

Although perhaps obvious, it bears emphasis that the First Amendment right asserted by petitioner is not a right to publish or otherwise communicate information lawfully or unlawfully acquired. That right, which lies at the core of the First Amendment and which erased the legacy of restraints on publication against which the drafters of that Amendment rebelled, may be overcome only by a governmental objective of the highest order attainable in no less intrusive way. The First Amendment right asserted by petitioner in this case, in contrast, is not the right to publicize information in its possession, but the right to acquire access thereto.

I have long believed that a proper construction of the First Amendment embraces a right of access to information about the conduct of public affairs.

* * * Neither our elected nor our appointed representatives may abridge the free flow of information simply to protect their own activities from public scrutiny. An official policy of secrecy must be supported by some legitimate justification that serves the interest of the public office. * * *

But it has always been apparent that the freedom to obtain information that the Government has a legitimate interest in not disclosing, is far narrower than the freedom to disseminate information, which is "virtually absolute" in most contexts, *Richmond Newspapers, Inc. v. Virginia* (Stevens, J., concurring). In this case, the risk of prejudice to the defendant's right to a fair trial is perfectly obvious. For me, that risk is far more significant than the countervailing interest in publishing the transcript of the preliminary hearing sooner rather than later. [The] interest in prompt publication—in my view—is no greater than the interest in prompt publication of grand jury transcripts. [W]e have always recognized the legitimacy of the governmental interest in the secrecy of grand jury proceedings, and I am unpersuaded that the difference between such proceedings and the rather elaborate procedure for determining probable cause that California has adopted strengthens the First Amendment claim to access asserted in this case.

II

[The Court] reaches the opposite conclusion by applying the "two complementary considerations," of "experience and logic." In my view neither the Court's reasoning nor the result it reaches is supported by our precedents.

The historical evidence proffered in this case is far less probative than the evidence adduced in prior cases granting public access to criminal proceedings. In those cases, a common law tradition of openness at the time the First Amendment was ratified suggested an intention and expectation on the part of the Framers and ratifiers that those proceedings would remain presumptively open. [In] this case, however, it is uncontroverted that a common law right of access did not inhere in preliminary proceedings at the time the First Amendment was adopted, and that the Framers and ratifiers of that provision could not have intended such proceedings to remain open.

[In] the final analysis, the Court's lengthy historical disquisition demonstrates only that in many States preliminary proceedings are generally open to the public. In other States, numbering California * * * among them, such proceedings have been closed. [That California's] particular approach has been adopted in few other States does not render [its] choice unconstitutional." * * *

If the Court's historical evidence proves too little, the "value of openness," on which it relies proves too much, for this measure would open to public scrutiny far more than preliminary hearings "as they are conducted in California" (a comforting phrase invoked by the Court in one form or another more than 8 times in its opinion). In brief, the Court's rationale for opening the "California preliminary hearing" is that it "is often the final and most important step in the criminal proceeding"; that it provides " 'the sole occasion for public observation of the criminal justice system' "; that it lacks the protective presence of a jury; and that closure denies an outlet for community catharsis. The obvious defect in the Court's approach is that its reasoning applies to the traditionally secret grand jury with as much force as it applies to California preliminary hearings. A grand jury indictment is just as likely to be the "final step" in a criminal proceeding and the "sole occasion" for public scrutiny as is a preliminary hearing. Moreover, many critics of the grand jury maintain that the grand jury protects the accused less well than does a legally-knowledgeable judge who personally presides over a preliminary hearing. * * * Finally, closure of grand juries denies an outlet for community rage. When the Court's explanatory veneer is stripped away, what emerges is the reality that the California preliminary hearing is functionally identical to the traditional grand jury. [Yet] [t]his Court has previously described grand jury secrecy as "indispensable," and has remarked that "the proper functioning of our grand jury system depends upon the secrecy of grand jury proceedings."

In fact, the logic of the Court's access right extends even beyond the confines of the criminal justice system to encompass proceedings held on the civil side of the docket as well. * * * Despite the Court's valiant attempt to limit the logic of its holding, the *ratio decidendi* of today's decision knows no bounds. [The] presence of a legitimate reason for closure in this case requires an affirmance. The constitutionally-grounded fair trial interests of the accused if he is bound over for trial, and the reputational interests of the accused if he is not, provide a substantial reason for delaying access to the transcript for at least the short time before trial. * * *

Chapter 17

THE ROLE OF COUNSEL

Chapter Five looked at where and when the defendant has a constitutional right to the assistance of counsel. This chapter looks at the level and range of the assistance that counsel must provide to fulfill that constitutional right of defendant. The first case, *Strickland v. Washington,* is the seminal ruling on the standards to be applied in determining whether defendant did in fact receive the "effective assistance" of counsel guaranteed by the Sixth Amendment. Although the *Strickland* standards are announced in a case challenging the performance of trial counsel, they also apply to the performance of appellate counsel on a first appeal of right, where defendant also has a constitutional right to the assistance of counsel. They do not apply, however, to later stages, since the defendant there has no constitutional right to counsel. The right to the effective assistance of counsel is an aspect of a constitutional right to counsel, and does not extend to ineffective assistance where such a right does not exist. See e.g., *Wainright v. Torna*, 455 U.S. 586 (1982) (ineffective assistance claim not available where retained counsel failed to file a timely application for discretionary review, a stage at which defendant has no constitutional right to counsel, see *Ross v. Moffitt*, ch. 5, § 2). This limitation is especially significant for legal claims that typically can be raised only in postconviction proceedings either because (1) the factual predicate ordinarily is not discover until after trial (e.g., the prosecution's failure to disclose exculpatory evidence, see United States v. Bagley, ch. 13) or (2) the trial attorney is placed in a position where that attorney cannot reasonably be expected to raise the claim (as in the case of ineffective assistance, where the attorney cannot be expected, and will not be allowed, to challenge his own performance). If the defendant is represented by counsel in the postconviction proceeding at which such claims should be raised, and that counsel's incompetence leads to the claims not being raised in a timely fashion, the defendant cannot gain relief through an ineffective assistance claim, and as discussed below, the claim not raised is likely to be treated as procedurally defaulted and not cognizable in later postconviction proceedings.

The competency standard set forth in *Strickland* hardly requires perfection and situations arise in which trial counsel has met the *Strickland* standard but nonetheless failed to raise a legal issue or discover evidence that might have made a difference in the outcome of the case. The question then presented is whether counsel's failure will be binding on the client and foreclose later relief. As for evidence that is later discovered, a motion for new trial based on newly discovered evidence typically must meet the "Rule 33" standard, described in footnote b to the *Bagley* opinion in ch. 13. This standard bars use of evidence that counsel could have discovered prior to trial with "due diligence." In addition, as dis-

690

cussed in *Herrera v. Collins,* ch. 18, § 4, the state also is likely to impose a strict time limitation on such motions.

As to legal objections that defense counsel failed to raise, the usual rule is that the defendant is bound by that failure, assuming no ineffective assistance. However, certain avenues for relief may be available for particular types of objections. The usual rule applied on appeal—commonly described as the raise-or-waive rule—precludes review of a legal objection that counsel failed to advance at trial in a timely fashion. This rule is based on a variety of considerations, including the need for orderly procedure, the desirability of binding parties to their tactical decisions, the inappropriateness of considering issues not developed factually at the trial level, and the desirability of avoiding unnecessary retrials (by requiring the defense to raise its objections as early as possible in the process, so curative action can be taken before the trial starts, or at least before it comes to an end). Nonetheless, appellate courts do make an exception for "plain error," that is, an error that is both apparent on the face of the trial record and that clearly had an adverse impact upon the substantial rights of the defendant.

If the objection that counsel failed to raise had a constitutional grounding, relief also may be available through a state collateral remedy or the federal writ of habeas corpus.[a] (See ch. 1, § 2, step 18). Here again, the raise-or-waive rule is likely to prevail. If the claim was reasonably available to trial counsel (e.g., the factual predicate was discoverable with due diligence and the legal theory was not so clearly foreclosed by precedent as to be only "remotely plausible"), and counsel's failure to raise the claim did not constitute ineffective assistance under *Strickland,* the claim ordinarily will be treated as procedurally defaulted by the failure to present it in a timely fashion in accord with state rules, and postconviction relief therefore will be unavailable. Certain narrow exceptions may apply, however. Constitutional claims that go to the very power of the state to prosecute (e.g., the unconstitutionality of the criminal offense or a double jeopardy bar) traditionally have been available on collateral attack even though not presented at trial or on appeal.[b] Also, as discussed in *Herrera* and the note following *Herrera,* the federal writ may permit consideration of a constitutional claim, notwithstanding the procedural default by failing to raise that claim in the state proceedings, if

a. The federal writ ordinarily is available to state prisoners to collaterally attack a conviction on most, but not all, federal constitutional grounds. See Ch. 1 at § 2, at step 18. Most notably, even where properly raised at trial, a claim that a conviction is based on the admission of evidence in violation of the Fourth Amendment (see Ch. 3) is not cognizable on federal habeas corpus if the "State has provided for full and fair litigation of * * * [that] Fourth Amendment claim." *Stone v. Powell,* 428 U.S. 465 (1976).

b. This exception commonly applies to convictions following a guilty plea as well as convictions following a trial. In general, "a voluntary and intelligent plea of guilty made by an accused person, who has been advised by competent counsel, may not be collaterally attacked" by reference to procedural errors that occurred prior to the entry of the plea. *Mabry v. Johnson,* 467 U.S. 504 (1984). This is true even though such errors were constitutional violations. See e.g., *McMann v. Richardson,* 397 U.S. 759 (1970) (plea could not be challenged on the basis of an underlying coerced confession). Where a defendant chooses to take "the benefit, if any, of a guilty plea," he or she "accepts the inherent risk that good-faith evaluations of a reasonably competent attorney will turn out to be mistaken either as to the facts or as to what a court's judgment might be on given facts." However, a constitutional claim will be open to review, notwithstanding the guilty plea, where it rests on a "right not to be hailed into court at all" as to the offense to which defendant pleaded. *Blackledge v. Perry,* 417 U.S. 21 (1974) (plea did not bar collateral challenge where the prosecution acted vindictively in bringing the charge, see Ch. 10, § 2). While a voluntary guilty plea admits "factual guilt" and thereby "renders irrelevant those constitutional violations not logically inconsistent with the valid establishment of factual guilt," that is not the case for a claim that argues "that the State may not convict petitioner no matter how validly his factual guilt is established." *Menna v. New York,* 423 U.S. 61 (1975) (guilty plea did not preclude collateral challenge based on double jeopardy bar to the prosecution).

the habeas petitioner can make a proper showing of "actual innocence" related to that claim.

Because of the narrowness of the exceptions to the raise-or-waive concept on both direct appeal and postconviction review, the first line of attack where trial counsel failed to present a particular objection will be an ineffective assistance of counsel claim. That claim also is the primary vehicle for dealing with newly discovered evidence where the motion to present such evidence is not available because the evidence in question could have been discovered prior to trial with due diligence. The second case in this chapter, *Nix v. Whiteside*, deals with counsel's failure to present particular evidence, but not because counsel failed to uncover the evidence. It applies the *Strickland* standards in the context of an age-old problem facing defense counsel, the client who desires to present perjured testimony.

As the Court also noted in *Strickland*, the possibility that counsel acted under the burden of a "conflict of interest" complicates a post-trial determination as to whether counsel rendered effective representation. This naturally leads to the question as to whether a trial court, upon determining prior to trial that such a conflict may or does exist, can insist that defendant proceed with another counsel who clearly will not be so burdened. The next case, *Wheat v. United States*, considers that issue in its most troublesome context, where the conflict is "potential," rather than currently operating (i.e., "actual"), and the defendant is willing to waive his right to conflict-free counsel in order to be represented by counsel of his choice.

The last case in the chapter, *Faretta v. California* raises the question of whether the defendant has a constitutional right to refuse the assistance of counsel and proceed *pro se* at trial (i.e., represent himself). Defendants not infrequently will waive counsel when they wish to enter a guilty plea, but requests to proceed *pro se* at trial are fairly rare. These requests tend to arise in two somewhat different situations. First, there are the requests of defendants who decide at the outset that they would prefer to represent themselves. That choice may be based on a variety of reasons, including a general distrust of attorneys, a belief that an attorney's assistance will not be worth the expense (where defendant is not indigent), or a belief that self-representation will provide a tactical advantage (as where a codefendant in a joint trial will be represented by counsel and defendant believes that self-representation will permit him to present himself in a more sympathetic light, while still gaining the advantage of the challenge to the prosecution's case presented by codefendant's counsel). Second, there are the requests of defendants who would prefer representation by counsel but are dissatisfied with their current counsel. Very often these defendants are not in a position where they can obtain alternative counsel and they would prefer continuing *pro se* to continuing with their current counsel.[c]

---

c. Defendants with court appointed counsel will find it difficult to obtain alternative counsel because courts commonly will not replace appointed counsel unless defendant can establish a complete breakdown in communications with counsel or a failure of counsel to provide effective representation. The Supreme Court has noted in this regard that the Sixth Amendment guarantees only competent representation, not a relationship with counsel that defendant views as personally satisfactory. *Morris v. Slappy*, 461 U.S. 1 (1983) (where original public defender was hospitalized, substitute announced that he was prepared to go to trial, and state trial court then refused to grant a continuance until the original defender could return, federal habeas court erred in reversing defendant's conviction; it could not be maintained that defendant was entitled to "a meaningful attorney-client relationship" rather than simply the effective assistance of counsel).

Where counsel is retained, defendant has more leeway in replacing current counsel with another attorney more to his liking, but he may face difficulties where such action would require a delay in the trial. The trial court in

STRICKLAND v. WASHINGTON

466 U.S. 668, 104 S.Ct. 2052, 80 L.Ed.2d 674 (1984).

JUSTICE O'CONNOR delivered the opinion of the Court.

This case requires us to consider the proper standards for judging a criminal defendant's contention that the Constitution requires a conviction or death sentence to be set aside because counsel's assistance at the trial or sentencing was ineffective.

During a 10-day period in September 1976, respondent planned and committed three groups of crimes, which included three brutal stabbing murders, torture, kidnaping, severe assaults, attempted murders, attempted extortion, and theft. After his two accomplices were arrested, respondent surrendered to police and voluntarily gave a lengthy statement confessing to the third of the criminal episodes. The State of Florida indicted respondent for kidnaping and murder and appointed an experienced criminal lawyer to represent him.

Counsel actively pursued pretrial motions and discovery. He cut his efforts short, however, and he experienced a sense of hopelessness about the case, when he learned that, against his specific advice, respondent had also confessed to the first two murders. By the date set for trial, respondent was subject to indictment for three counts of first-degree murder and multiple counts of robbery, kidnaping for ransom, breaking and entering and assault, attempted murder, and conspiracy to commit robbery. Respondent waived his right to a jury trial, again acting against counsel's advice, and pleaded guilty to all charges, including the three capital murder charges.

In the plea colloquy, respondent told the trial judge that, although he had committed a string of burglaries, he had no significant prior criminal record and that at the time of his criminal spree he was under extreme stress caused by his inability to support his family. He also stated, however, that he accepted responsibility for the crimes. The trial judge told respondent that he had "a great deal of respect for people who are willing to step forward and admit their responsibility" but that he was making no statement at all about his likely sentencing decision.

Counsel advised respondent to invoke his right under Florida law to an advisory jury at his capital sentencing hearing. Respondent rejected the advice and waived the right. He chose instead to be sentenced by the trial judge without a jury recommendation.

In preparing for the sentencing hearing, counsel spoke with respondent about his background. He also spoke on the telephone with respondent's wife and mother, though he did not follow up on the one unsuccessful effort to meet with them. He did not otherwise seek out character witnesses for respondent. Nor did he request a psychiatric examination, since his conversations with his client gave no indication that respondent had psychological problems.

such a situation must balance the defendant's interest in having counsel of his choice against the public's interest in prompt and efficient administration of justice. As the Supreme Court has noted: "There are no mechanical tests for deciding when a denial of a continuance is so arbitrary as to violate * * * [defendant's constitutional right to counsel]. The answer must be found in the circumstances present in every case." *Ungar v. Sarafite*, 376 U.S. 575 (1964) (rejecting a constitutional challenge to a continuance denial that resulted in the withdrawal of defense counsel and self-representation by defendant, who was a lawyer, and citing such factors as defendant's delay in seeking the continuance, ample time for counsel's preparation in light of the evidence and clearly identified issues, and the need to give deference to the trial judge's judgment). Consider also *Wheat v. United States*, infra.

Counsel decided not to present and hence not to look further for evidence concerning respondent's character and emotional state. That decision reflected trial counsel's sense of hopelessness about overcoming the evidentiary effect of respondent's confessions to the gruesome crimes. It also reflected the judgment that it was advisable to rely on the plea colloquy for evidence about respondent's background and about his claim of emotional stress: the plea colloquy communicated sufficient information about these subjects, and by forgoing the opportunity to present new evidence on these subjects, counsel prevented the State from cross-examining respondent on his claim and from putting on psychiatric evidence of its own.

Counsel also excluded from the sentencing hearing other evidence he thought was potentially damaging. He successfully moved to exclude respondent's "rap sheet." Because he judged that a presentence report might prove more detrimental than helpful, as it would have included respondent's criminal history and thereby would have undermined the claim of no significant history of criminal activity, he did not request that one be prepared.

At the sentencing hearing, counsel's strategy was based primarily on the trial judge's remarks at the plea colloquy as well as on his reputation as a sentencing judge who thought it important for a convicted defendant to own up to his crime. Counsel argued that respondent's remorse and acceptance of responsibility justified sparing him from the death penalty. Counsel also argued that respondent had no history of criminal activity and that respondent committed the crimes under extreme mental or emotional disturbance, thus coming within the statutory list of mitigating circumstances. He further argued that respondent should be spared death because he had surrendered, confessed, and offered to testify against a codefendant and because respondent was fundamentally a good person who had briefly gone badly wrong in extremely stressful circumstances. The State put on evidence and witnesses largely for the purpose of describing the details of the crimes. Counsel did not cross-examine the medical experts who testified about the manner of death of respondent's victims. * * *

[T]he trial judge found numerous aggravating circumstances and no (or a single comparatively insignificant) mitigating circumstance. With respect to each of the three convictions for capital murder, the trial judge concluded: "A careful consideration of all matters presented to the court impels the conclusion that there are insufficient mitigating circumstances * * * to outweigh the aggravating circumstances." He therefore sentenced respondent to death on each of the three counts of murder and to prison terms for the other crimes. The Florida Supreme Court upheld the convictions and sentences on direct appeal.

Respondent subsequently sought collateral relief in state court on numerous grounds, among them that counsel had rendered ineffective assistance at the sentencing proceeding. Respondent challenged counsel's assistance in six respects. He asserted that counsel was ineffective because he failed to move for a continuance to prepare for sentencing, to request a psychiatric report, to investigate and present character witnesses, to seek a presentence investigation report, to present meaningful arguments to the sentencing judge, and to investigate the medical examiner's reports or cross-examine the medical experts. In support of the claim, respondent submitted 14 affidavits from friends, neighbors, and relatives stating that they would have testified if asked to do so. He also submitted one psychiatric report and one psychological report stating that respondent, though not under the influence of extreme mental or emotional disturbance, was "chronically frustrated and depressed because of his economic dilemma" at the time of his crimes.

The trial court denied relief without an evidentiary hearing, finding that the record evidence conclusively showed that the ineffectiveness claim was meritless. * * * Applying the standard for ineffectiveness claims articulated by the Florida Supreme Court * * *, the trial court concluded that respondent had not shown that counsel's assistance reflected any substantial and serious deficiency measurably below that of competent counsel that was likely to have affected the outcome of the sentencing proceeding. * * *

Respondent next filed a petition for a writ of habeas corpus in the United States District Court * * *. [After an evidentiary hearing,] the District Court disputed none of the state court factual findings concerning trial counsel's assistance and made findings of its own that are consistent with the state court findings. * * * [T]he District Court concluded that, although trial counsel made errors in judgment in failing to investigate nonstatutory mitigating evidence further than he did, no prejudice to respondent's sentence resulted from any such error in judgment. On appeal, * * * the Court of Appeals developed its own framework for analyzing ineffective assistance claims and reversed the judgment of the District Court and remanded the case for new factfinding under the newly announced standard. * * *

[P]utting guilty-plea cases to one side, [the Court of Appeals] attempted to classify cases presenting issues concerning the scope of the duty to investigate before proceeding to trial. If there is only one plausible line of defense, the court concluded, counsel must conduct a "reasonably substantial investigation" into that line of defense, since there can be no strategic choice that renders such an investigation unnecessary. * * * If there is more than one plausible line of defense, the court held, counsel should ideally investigate each line substantially before making a strategic choice about which lines to rely on at trial. * * * If counsel does not conduct a substantial investigation into each of several plausible lines of defense, assistance may nonetheless be effective. Counsel may not exclude certain lines of defense for other than strategic reasons. Limitations of time and money, however, may force early strategic choices, often based solely on conversations with the defendant and a review of the prosecution's evidence. * * * Among the factors relevant to deciding whether particular strategic choices are reasonable are the experience of the attorney, the inconsistency of unpursued and pursued lines of defense, and the potential for prejudice from taking an unpursued line of defense. * * * Petitioners, who are officials of the State of Florida, filed a petition for a writ of certiorari seeking review of the decision of the Court of Appeals. * * *

Because of the vital importance of counsel's assistance, this Court has held that, with certain exceptions, a person accused of a federal or state crime has the right to have counsel appointed if retained counsel cannot be obtained. See *Argersinger v. Hamlin* [Ch. 5, § 1]; *Gideon v. Wainwright* [Ch. 5, § 1]. That a person who happens to be a lawyer is present at trial alongside the accused, however, is not enough to satisfy the constitutional command. The Sixth Amendment recognizes the right to the assistance of counsel because it envisions counsel's playing a role that is critical to the ability of the adversarial system to produce just results. An accused is entitled to be assisted by an attorney, whether retained or appointed, who plays the role necessary to ensure that the trial is fair.

For that reason, the Court has recognized that "the right to counsel is the right to the effective assistance of counsel." *McMann v. Richardson*, 397 U.S. 759 (1970). Government violates the right to effective assistance when it interferes in certain ways with the ability of counsel to make independent decisions about how to conduct the defense. See, e.g., *Geders v. United States*, 425 U.S. 80 (1976) (bar on attorney-client consultation during overnight recess); *Herring v. New York,* 422 U.S. 853 (1975) (bar on summation at bench trial); *Brooks v. Tennessee,* 406 U.S. 605 (1972) (requirement that defendant be first defense witness); *Ferguson v. Georgia,* 365 U.S. 570 (1961) (bar on direct examination of defendant). Counsel, however, can also deprive a defendant of the right to effective assistance, simply by failing to render "adequate legal assistance," *Cuyler v. Sullivan,* 446 U.S. 335 (1980) (actual conflict of interest adversely affecting lawyer's performance renders assistance ineffective).

The Court has not elaborated on the meaning of the constitutional requirement of effective assistance in the latter class of cases—that is, those presenting claims of "actual ineffectiveness." In giving meaning to the requirement, however, we must take its purpose—to ensure a fair trial—as the guide. The benchmark for judging any claim of ineffectiveness must be whether counsel's conduct so undermined the proper functioning of the adversarial process that the trial cannot be relied on as having produced a just result.

The same principle applies to a capital sentencing proceeding such as that provided by Florida law. We need not consider the role of counsel in an ordinary sentencing, which may involve informal proceedings and standardless discretion in the sentencer, and hence may require a different approach to the definition of constitutionally effective assistance. A capital sentencing proceeding like the one involved in this case, however, is sufficiently like a trial in its adversarial format and in the existence of standards for decision, that counsel's role in the proceeding is comparable to counsel's role at trial—to ensure that the adversarial testing process works to produce a just result under the standards governing decision. For purposes of describing counsel's duties, therefore, Florida's capital sentencing proceeding need not be distinguished from an ordinary trial.

A convicted defendant's claim that counsel's assistance was so defective as to require reversal of a conviction or death sentence has two components. First, the defendant must show that counsel's performance was deficient. This requires showing that counsel made errors so serious that counsel was not functioning as the "counsel" guaranteed the defendant by the Sixth Amendment. Second, the defendant must show that the deficient performance prejudiced the defense. This requires showing that counsel's errors were so serious as to deprive the defendant of a fair trial, a trial whose result is reliable. Unless a defendant makes both showings, it cannot be said that the conviction or death sentence resulted from a breakdown in the adversary process that renders the result unreliable.

As all the Federal Courts of Appeals have now held, the proper standard for attorney performance is that of reasonably effective assistance. The Court indirectly recognized as much when it stated in *McMann v. Richardson* that a guilty plea cannot be attacked as based on inadequate legal advice unless counsel was not "a reasonably competent attorney" and the advice was not "within the range of competence demanded of attorneys in criminal cases." When a convicted defendant complains of the ineffectiveness of counsel's assistance, the defendant must show that counsel's representation fell below an objective standard of reasonableness.

More specific guidelines are not appropriate. The Sixth Amendment refers simply to "counsel," not specifying particular requirements of effective assistance. It relies instead on the legal profession's maintenance of standards sufficient to justify the law's presumption that counsel will fulfill the role in the adversary process that the Amendment envisions. The proper measure of attorney performance remains simply reasonableness under prevailing professional norms.

Representation of a criminal defendant entails certain basic duties. Counsel's function is to assist the defendant, and hence counsel owes the client a duty of loyalty, a duty to avoid conflicts of interest. From counsel's function as assistant to the defendant derive the overarching duty to advocate the defendant's cause and the more particular duties to consult with the defendant on important decisions and to keep the defendant informed of important developments in the course of the prosecution. Counsel also has a duty to bring to bear such skill and knowledge as will render the trial a reliable adversarial testing process.

These basic duties neither exhaustively define the obligations of counsel nor form a checklist for judicial evaluation of attorney performance. In any case presenting an ineffectiveness claim, the performance inquiry must be whether counsel's assistance was reasonable considering all the circumstances. Prevailing norms of practice as reflected in American Bar Association standards and the like are guides to determining what is reasonable, but they are only guides. No particular set of detailed rules for counsel's conduct can satisfactorily take account of the variety of circumstances faced by defense counsel or the range of legitimate decisions regarding how best to represent a criminal defendant. Any such set of rules would interfere with the constitutionally protected independence of counsel and restrict the wide latitude counsel must have in making tactical decisions. Indeed, the existence of detailed guidelines for representation could distract counsel from the overriding mission of vigorous advocacy of the defendant's cause. Moreover, the purpose of the effective assistance guarantee of the Sixth Amendment is not to improve the quality of legal representation, although that is a goal of considerable importance to the legal system. The purpose is simply to ensure that criminal defendants receive a fair trial.

Judicial scrutiny of counsel's performance must be highly deferential. It is all too tempting for a defendant to second-guess counsel's assistance after conviction or adverse sentence, and it is all too easy for a court, examining counsel's defense after it has proved unsuccessful, to conclude that a particular act or omission of counsel was unreasonable. A fair assessment of attorney performance requires that every effort be made to eliminate the distorting effects of hindsight, to reconstruct the circumstances of counsel's challenged conduct, and to evaluate the conduct from counsel's perspective at the time. Because of the difficulties inherent in making the evaluation, a court must indulge a strong presumption that counsel's conduct falls within the wide range of reasonable professional assistance; that is, the defendant must overcome the presumption that, under the circumstances, the challenged action "might be considered sound trial strategy." There are countless ways to provide effective assistance in any given case. Even the best criminal defense attorneys would not defend a particular client in the same way.

The availability of intrusive post-trial inquiry into attorney performance or of detailed guidelines for its evaluation would encourage the proliferation of ineffectiveness challenges. Criminal trials resolved unfavorably to the defendant would increasingly come to be followed by a second trial, this one of counsel's unsuccessful defense. Counsel's performance and even willingness to serve could be adversely affected. Intensive scrutiny of counsel and rigid requirements for acceptable assistance could dampen the ardor and impair the independence of defense counsel, discourage the acceptance of assigned cases, and undermine the trust between attorney and client.

Thus, a court deciding an actual ineffectiveness claim must judge the reasonableness of counsel's challenged conduct on the facts of the particular case, viewed as of the time of counsel's conduct. A convicted defendant making a claim of ineffective assistance must identify the acts or omissions of counsel that are alleged not to have been the result of reasonable professional judgment. The court must then determine whether, in light of all the circumstances, the identified acts or omissions were outside the wide range of professionally competent assistance. In making that determination, the court should keep in mind that counsel's function, as elaborated in prevailing professional norms, is to make the adversarial testing process work in the particular case. At the same time, the court should recognize that counsel is strongly presumed to have rendered adequate assistance and made all significant decisions in the exercise of reasonable professional judgment.

These standards require no special amplification in order to define counsel's duty to investigate, the duty at issue in this case. As the Court of Appeals concluded, strategic choices made after thorough investigation of law and facts relevant to plausible options are virtually unchallengeable; and strategic choices made after less than complete investigation are reasonable precisely to the extent that reasonable professional judgments support the limitations on investigation. In other words, counsel has a duty to make reasonable investigations or to make a reasonable decision that makes particular investigations unnecessary. In any ineffectiveness case, a particular decision not to investigate must be directly assessed for reasonableness in all the circumstances, applying a heavy measure of deference to counsel's judgments.

The reasonableness of counsel's actions may be determined or substantially influenced by the defendant's own statements or actions. Counsel's actions are usually based, quite properly, on informed strategic choices made by the defendant and on information supplied by the defendant. In particular, what investigation decisions are reasonable depends critically on such information. For example, when the facts that support a certain potential line of defense are generally known to counsel because of what the defendant has said, the need for further investigation may be considerably diminished or eliminated altogether. And when a defendant has given counsel reason to believe that pursuing certain investigations would be fruitless or even harmful, counsel's failure to pursue those investigations may not later be challenged as unreasonable. In short, inquiry into counsel's conversations with the defendant may be critical to a proper assessment of counsel's investigation decisions, just as it may be critical to a proper assessment of counsel's other litigation decisions.

An error by counsel, even if professionally unreasonable, does not warrant setting aside the judgment of a criminal proceeding if the error had no effect on the judgment. The purpose of the Sixth Amendment guarantee of counsel is to ensure that a defendant has the assistance necessary to justify reliance on the outcome of the proceeding. Accordingly, any deficiencies in counsel's performance must be prejudicial to the defense in order to constitute ineffective assistance under the Constitution.

In certain Sixth Amendment contexts, prejudice is presumed. Actual or constructive denial of the assistance of counsel altogether is legally presumed to result in prejudice. So are various kinds of state interference with counsel's assistance. See *United States v. Cronic,* 466 U.S. 648 (1984).[a] Prejudice in these

a. The reference here is to a discussion in *Cronic* of the *Geders, Herring, Brooks,* and *Ferguson* cases, also described previously in Justice O'Connor's opinion. *Cronic* characterized these cases as involving situations in which counsel was "prevented from assisting the accused during a critical stage of the proceeding" and therefore "no specific showing of prejudice was required." *Cronic* rejected a defense contention that a similar approach should be taken in an alleged "defective" appointment of counsel case. The lower court in *Cronic,* without referring to any specific error or inadequacy in counsel's performance, had circumstances is so likely that case-by-case inquiry into prejudice is not worth the cost. Moreover, such circumstances involve impairments of the Sixth Amendment right that are easy to identify and, for that reason and because the prosecution is directly responsible, easy for the government to prevent.

One type of actual ineffectiveness claim warrants a similar, though more limited, presumption of prejudice. In *Cuyler v. Sullivan,* 446 U.S. 335 (1980), the Court held that prejudice is presumed when counsel is burdened by an actual conflict of interest. In those circumstances, counsel breaches the duty of loyalty, perhaps the most basic of counsel's duties. Moreover, it is difficult to measure the precise effect on the defense of representation corrupted by conflicting interests. Given the obligation of counsel to avoid conflicts of interest and the ability of trial courts to make early inquiry in certain situations likely to give rise to conflicts, see, e.g., Fed.Rule Crim.Proc. 44(c), it is reasonable for the criminal justice system to maintain a fairly rigid rule of presumed prejudice for conflicts of interest. Even so, the rule is not quite the *per se* rule of prejudice that exists for the Sixth Amendment claims mentioned above. Prejudice is presumed only if the defendant demonstrates that counsel "actively represented conflicting interests" and that "an actual conflict of interest adversely affected his lawyer's performance." *Cuyler v. Sullivan.*[b]

Conflict of interest claims aside, actual ineffectiveness claims alleging a deficiency in attorney performance are subject to a general requirement that the defendant affirmatively prove prejudice. The government is not responsible for, and hence not able to prevent, attorney errors that will result in reversal of a conviction or sentence. Attorney errors come in an infinite variety and are as likely to be utterly harmless in a particular case as they are to be prejudicial. They cannot be classified according to likelihood of causing prejudice. Nor can they be defined with sufficient precision to inform defense attorneys correctly just what conduct to avoid. Representation is an art, and an act or omission that is unprofessional in one case may be sound or even brilliant in another. Even if a defendant shows that particular errors of counsel were unreasonable, therefore, the defendant must show that they actually had an adverse effect on the defense.
* * *

[T]he appropriate test for prejudice finds its roots in the test for materiality of exculpatory information not disclosed to the defense by the prosecution, *United*

found that counsel could not have been able to "discharge his duties" in light of five factors: "(1) [T]he [limited] time afforded for investigation and preparation; (2) the [in]experience of counsel; (3) the gravity of the charge; (4) the complexity of possible defenses; and (5) the [limited] accessibility of witnesses to counsel." The *Cronic* majority acknowledged that these five factors were "relevant to an evaluation of a lawyer's ineffectiveness in a particular case," but concluded that "neither separately nor in combination [did] they provide a basis for concluding that competent counsel was not able to provide * * * the guiding hand that the Constitution guarantees." The Court held that a determination of competency in this case must rest on an examination of the actual performance of counsel in light of the circumstances of the case.

The *Cronic* Court did note, however, that there could be extreme circumstances in which the appointment process was so deficient as to

be treated as an automatic violation of the Sixth Amendment in much the same fashion as a denial of counsel or a state interference at a critical stage. There may be "occasions when, although counsel is available to assist the accused during trial, the likelihood that any lawyer, even a fully competent one, could provide effective assistance is so small that a presumption of prejudice is appropriate without inquiry into the actual conduct of the trial." Offered as an illustration of such a case was *Powell v. Alabama,* 287 U.S. 45 (1932) [see Ch. 5, § 1]. The trial court there had utilized such a haphazard process of appointment—ordering admittedly unprepared outstate counsel to proceed with whatever help the local bar, appointed en masse, might provide—that there was no need to look at the actual performance of counsel in determining that defendant's constitutional rights had been violated.

b. See also fn. a to *Wheat v. United States,* infra this Chapter.

States v. Agurs, 427 U.S. 97 (1976) and in the test for materiality of testimony made unavailable to the defense by Government deportation of a witness, *United States v. Valenzuela–Bernal,* 458 U.S. 858 (1982).[c] The defendant must show that there is a reasonable probability that, but for counsel's unprofessional errors, the result of the proceeding would have been different. A reasonable probability is a probability sufficient to undermine confidence in the outcome.

In making the determination whether the specified errors resulted in the required prejudice, a court should presume, absent challenge to the judgment on grounds of evidentiary insufficiency, that the judge or jury acted according to law. An assessment of the likelihood of a result more favorable to the defendant must exclude the possibility of arbitrariness, whimsy, caprice, "nullification," and the like. A defendant has no entitlement to the luck of a lawless decisionmaker, even if a lawless decision cannot be reviewed. The assessment of prejudice should proceed on the assumption that the decisionmaker is reasonably, conscientiously, and impartially applying the standards that govern the decision. It should not depend on the idiosyncracies of the particular decisionmaker, such as unusual propensities toward harshness or leniency. Although these factors may actually have entered into counsel's selection of strategies and, to that limited extent, may thus affect the performance inquiry, they are irrelevant to the prejudice inquiry. Thus, evidence about the actual process of decision, if not part of the record of the proceeding under review, and evidence about, for example, a particular judge's sentencing practices, should not be considered in the prejudice determination.

The governing legal standard plays a critical role in defining the question to be asked in assessing the prejudice from counsel's errors. When a defendant challenges a conviction, the question is whether there is a reasonable probability that, absent the errors, the factfinder would have had a reasonable doubt respecting guilt. When a defendant challenges a death sentence such as the one at issue in this case, the question is whether there is a reasonable probability that, absent the errors, the sentencer—including an appellate court, to the extent it independently reweighs the evidence—would have concluded that the balance of aggravating and mitigating circumstances did not warrant death.

In making this determination, a court hearing an ineffectiveness claim must consider the totality of the evidence before the judge or jury. Some of the factual findings will have been unaffected by the errors, and factual findings that were affected will have been affected in different ways. Some errors will have had a pervasive effect on the inferences to be drawn from the evidence, altering the entire evidentiary picture, and some will have had an isolated, trivial effect. Moreover, a verdict or conclusion only weakly supported by the record is more likely to have been affected by errors than one with overwhelming record support. Taking the unaffected findings as a given, and taking due account of the effect of the errors on the remaining findings, a court making the prejudice inquiry must ask if the defendant has met the burden of showing that the decision reached would reasonably likely have been different absent the errors.

A number of practical considerations are important for the application of the standards we have outlined. Most important, in adjudicating a claim of actual ineffectiveness of counsel, a court should keep in mind that the principles we have stated do not establish mechanical rules. Although those principles should guide the process of decision, the ultimate focus of inquiry must be on the fundamental fairness of the proceeding whose result is being challenged. In every case the

c. The materiality standard applicable in   Ch. 13 supra.
these situations is further discussed in *Bagley,*

court should be concerned with whether, despite the strong presumption of reliability, the result of the particular proceeding is unreliable because of a breakdown in the adversarial process that our system counts on to produce just results.   * * *

Although we have discussed the performance component of an ineffectiveness claim prior to the prejudice component, there is no reason for a court deciding an ineffective assistance claim to approach the inquiry in the same order or even to address both components of the inquiry if the defendant makes an insufficient showing on one.   In particular, a court need not determine whether counsel's performance was deficient before examining the prejudice suffered by the defendant as a result of the alleged deficiencies.   The object of an ineffectiveness claim is not to grade counsel's performance.   If it is easier to dispose of an ineffectiveness claim on the ground of lack of sufficient prejudice, which we expect will often be so, that course should be followed.   Courts should strive to ensure that ineffectiveness claims not become so burdensome to defense counsel that the entire criminal justice system suffers as a result.   * * *

Having articulated general standards for judging ineffectiveness claims, we think it useful to apply those standards to the facts of this case in order to illustrate the meaning of the general principles.   * * *   The facts as described above make clear that the conduct of respondent's counsel at and before respondent's sentencing proceeding cannot be found unreasonable.   They also make clear that, even assuming the challenged conduct of counsel was unreasonable, respondent suffered insufficient prejudice to warrant setting aside his death sentence.

With respect to the performance component, the record shows that respondent's counsel made a strategic choice to argue for the extreme emotional distress mitigating circumstance and to rely as fully as possible on respondent's acceptance of responsibility for his crimes.   Although counsel understandably felt hopeless about respondent's prospects, nothing in the record indicates * * * that counsel's sense of hopelessness distorted his professional judgment.   Counsel's strategy choice was well within the range of professionally reasonable judgments, and the decision not to seek more character or psychological evidence than was already in hand was likewise reasonable.

The trial judge's views on the importance of owning up to one's crimes were well known to counsel.   The aggravating circumstances were utterly overwhelming.   Trial counsel could reasonably surmise from his conversations with respondent that character and psychological evidence would be of little help.   Respondent had already been able to mention at the plea colloquy the substance of what there was to know about his financial and emotional troubles.   Restricting testimony on respondent's character to what had come in at the plea colloquy ensured that contrary character and psychological evidence and respondent's criminal history, which counsel had successfully moved to exclude, would not come in.   On these facts, there can be little question, even without application of the presumption of adequate performance, that trial counsel's defense, though unsuccessful, was the result of reasonable professional judgment.

With respect to the prejudice component, the lack of merit of respondent's claim is even more stark.   The evidence that respondent says his trial counsel should have offered at the sentencing hearing would barely have altered the sentencing profile presented to the sentencing judge.   As the state courts and District Court found, at most this evidence shows that numerous people who knew respondent thought he was generally a good person and that a psychiatrist and a psychologist believed he was under considerable emotional stress that did not rise to the level of extreme disturbance. Given the overwhelming aggravating factors, there is no reasonable probability that the omitted evidence would have changed the conclusion that the aggravating circumstances outweighed the mitigating circumstances and, hence, the sentence imposed. Indeed, admission of the evidence respondent now offers might even have been harmful to his case: his "rap sheet" would probably have been admitted into evidence, and the psychological reports would have directly contradicted respondent's claim that the mitigating circumstance of extreme emotional disturbance applied to his case. * * *

Failure to make the required showing of either deficient performance or sufficient prejudice defeats the ineffectiveness claim. Here there is a double failure. More generally, respondent has made no showing that the justice of his sentence was rendered unreliable by a breakdown in the adversary process caused by deficiencies in counsel's assistance. Respondent's sentencing proceeding was not fundamentally unfair. We conclude, therefore, that the District Court properly declined to issue a writ of habeas corpus. The judgment of the Court of Appeals is accordingly reversed.[d]

JUSTICE BRENNAN, concurring in part and dissenting in part.

I join the Court's opinion but dissent from its judgment.[e] * * *

I join the Court's opinion because I believe that the standards it sets out today will both provide helpful guidance to courts considering claims of actual ineffectiveness of counsel and also permit those courts to continue their efforts to achieve progressive development of this area of the law. * * *

[T]he standards announced today can and should be applied with concern for the special considerations that must attend review of counsel's performance in a capital sentencing proceeding. In contrast to a case in which a finding of ineffective assistance requires a new trial, a conclusion that counsel was ineffective with respect to only the penalty phase of a capital trial imposes on the state the far lesser burden of reconsideration of the sentence alone. On the other hand, the consequences to the defendant of incompetent assistance at a capital sentencing could not, of course, be greater. * * *

JUSTICE MARSHALL, dissenting. * * *

The opinion of the Court revolves around two holdings. First, the majority ties the constitutional minima of attorney performance to a simple "standard of reasonableness." Second, the majority holds that only an error of counsel that has sufficient impact on a trial to "undermine confidence in the outcome" is grounds for overturning a conviction. I disagree with both of these rulings.

My objection to the performance standard adopted by the Court is that it is so malleable that, in practice, it will either have no grip at all or will yield excessive variation in the manner in which the Sixth Amendment is interpreted and applied by different courts. To tell lawyers and the lower courts that counsel for a

d. In a later case, *Hill v. Lockhart*, 474 U.S. 52 (1985), the Court held "that the two-part *Strickland v. Washington* test" also applies to "challenges to guilty pleas based on ineffective assistance of counsel." The Court noted: "In the context of guilty pleas, the first half of the *Strickland v. Washington* test is nothing more than a restatement of the standard of attorney competence already set forth in * * * *McMann v. Richardson* [discussed supra in *Strickland*]. The second, or 'prejudice,' requirement, on the other hand, focuses on whether counsel's constitutionally ineffective performance affected the outcome of the plea process. In other words, in order to satisfy the 'prejudice' requirement, the defendant must show that there is a reasonable probability that, but for counsel's errors, he would not have pleaded guilty and would have insisted on going to trial."

e. Adhering to his view that the death penalty is in all circumstances forbidden cruel and unusual punishment, Justice Brennan noted that he would vacate respondent's death sentence on that ground.

criminal defendant must behave "reasonably" and must act like "a reasonably competent attorney" is to tell them almost nothing. In essence, the majority has instructed judges called upon to assess claims of ineffective assistance of counsel to advert to their own intuitions regarding what constitutes "professional" representation, and has discouraged them from trying to develop more detailed standards governing the performance of defense counsel. In my view, the Court has thereby not only abdicated its own responsibility to interpret the Constitution, but also impaired the ability of the lower courts to exercise theirs.

The debilitating ambiguity of an "objective standard of reasonableness" in this context is illustrated by the majority's failure to address important issues concerning the quality of representation mandated by the Constitution. It is an unfortunate but undeniable fact that a person of means, by selecting a lawyer and paying him enough to ensure he prepares thoroughly, usually can obtain better representation than that available to an indigent defendant, who must rely on appointed counsel, who, in turn, has limited time and resources to devote to a given case. Is a "reasonably competent attorney" a reasonably competent adequately paid retained lawyer or a reasonably competent appointed attorney? It is also a fact that the quality of representation available to ordinary defendants in different parts of the country varies significantly. Should the standard of performance mandated by the Sixth Amendment vary by locale? The majority offers no clues as to the proper responses to these questions.

* * * I agree that counsel must be afforded "wide latitude" when making "tactical decisions" regarding trial strategy, but many aspects of the job of a criminal defense attorney are more amenable to judicial oversight [than the majority indicates]. For example, much of the work involved in preparing for a trial, applying for bail, conferring with one's client, making timely objections to significant, arguably erroneous rulings of the trial judge, and filing a notice of appeal if there are colorable grounds therefor could profitably be made the subject of uniform standards. * * *

I object to the prejudice standard adopted by the Court for two independent reasons. First, it is often very difficult to tell whether a defendant convicted after a trial in which he was ineffectively represented would have fared better if his lawyer had been competent. Seemingly impregnable cases can sometimes be dismantled by good defense counsel. On the basis of a cold record, it may be impossible for a reviewing court confidently to ascertain how the government's evidence and arguments would have stood up against rebuttal and cross-examination by a shrewd, well prepared lawyer. The difficulties of estimating prejudice after the fact are exacerbated by the possibility that evidence of injury to the defendant may be missing from the record precisely because of the incompetence of defense counsel. In view of all these impediments to a fair evaluation of the probability that the outcome of a trial was affected by ineffectiveness of counsel, it seems to me senseless to impose on a defendant whose lawyer has been shown to have been incompetent the burden of demonstrating prejudice.

Second and more fundamentally, the assumption on which the Court's holding rests is that the only purpose of the constitutional guarantee of effective assistance of counsel is to reduce the chance that innocent persons will be convicted. In my view, the guarantee also functions to ensure that convictions are obtained only through fundamentally fair procedures. The majority contends that the Sixth Amendment is not violated when a manifestly guilty defendant is convicted after a trial in which he was represented by a manifestly ineffective attorney. I cannot agree. Every defendant is entitled to a trial in which his interests are vigorously and conscientiously advocated by an able lawyer. A proceeding in which the defendant does not receive meaningful assistance in meeting the forces of the state does not, in my opinion, constitute due process. * * * I would thus hold that a showing that the performance of a defendant's lawyer departed from constitutionally prescribed standards requires a new trial regardless of whether the defendant suffered demonstrable prejudice thereby.

Even if I were inclined to join the majority's two central holdings, I could not abide the manner in which the majority elaborates upon its rulings.   * * *

Experienced members of the death-penalty bar have long recognized the crucial importance of adducing evidence at a sentencing proceeding that establishes the defendant's social and familial connections.   The State makes a colorable—though in my view not compelling—argument that defense counsel in this case might have made a reasonable "strategic" decision not to present such evidence at the sentencing hearing on the assumption that an unadorned acknowledgment of respondent's responsibility for his crimes would be more likely to appeal to the trial judge, who was reputed to respect persons who accepted responsibility for their actions.   But however justifiable such a choice might have been after counsel had fairly assessed the potential strength of the mitigating evidence available to him, counsel's failure to make any significant effort to find out what evidence might be garnered from respondent's relatives and acquaintances surely cannot be described as "reasonable."   Counsel's failure to investigate is particularly suspicious in light of his candid admission that respondent's confession and conduct in the course of the trial gave him a feeling of "hopelessness" regarding the possibility of saving respondent's life.

If counsel had investigated the availability of mitigating evidence, he might well have decided to present some such material at the hearing.   If he had done so, there is a significant chance that respondent would have been given a life sentence.   In my view, those possibilities, conjoined with the unreasonableness of counsel's failure to investigate, are more than sufficient to establish a violation of the Sixth Amendment and to entitle respondent to a new sentencing proceeding. * * *

NIX v. WHITESIDE

475 U.S. 157, 106 S.Ct. 988, 89 L.Ed.2d 123 (1986).

[In preparing for his Iowa state-court trial for murder, respondent Whiteside consistently told his appointed counsel, Robinson, that, although he had not actually seen a gun in the hand of the person he had stabbed to death, he was convinced that the victim had a gun.   When Robinson interviewed those who were present during the stabbing, they told him that they had not seen a gun during the incident.   And no gun was found on the premises.   Robinson told his client that the actual existence of a weapon was not necessary to establish a claim of self-defense, and that only a reasonable belief that the victim had a gun nearby would suffice.

[Shortly before trial, during preparation for direct examination, Whiteside for the first time told his lawyer that he had seen "something metallic" in the victim's hand.   When asked about this, Whiteside responded: "If I don't say I saw a gun, I'm dead."   Robinson told Whiteside that such testimony would be lying and repeated that it was unnecessary to prove that the victim actually had a gun. On Whiteside's insisting that he would testify that he saw "something metallic," Robinson told him, according to Robinson's testimony, that if Whiteside testified falsely, "it would be my duty to advise the Court of what he was doing and that I felt he was committing perjury; also, that I probably would be allowed to impeach that particular testimony." Robinson also indicated that he would seek to withdraw from the case if his client insisted on committing perjury.

[Whiteside ultimately testified as originally contemplated, stating that he believed that the victim was reaching for a gun, but admitting on cross-examination that he had not actually seen a weapon in the victim's hand. The jury found Whiteside guilty of second-degree murder.

[Whiteside then moved for a new trial, claiming he had been denied a fair trial by his lawyer's admonitions not to state that he saw a gun or "something metallic." The trial court denied the motion and the state supreme court affirmed. Whiteside then sought federal habeas corpus relief, maintaining that he had been denied effective assistance of counsel by his attorney's refusal to allow him to testify as he proposed. The district court denied relief, but the Court of Appeals for the Eighth Circuit reversed, concluding that counsel's threatened violation of his client's confidences violated the "effective representation" standards set forth in *Strickland.*]

CHIEF JUSTICE BURGER delivered the opinion of the Court.

In *Strickland v. Washington,* we held that to obtain relief by way of federal habeas corpus on a claim of a deprivation of effective assistance of counsel under the Sixth Amendment, the movant must establish both serious attorney error and prejudice. To show such error, it must be established that the assistance rendered by counsel was constitutionally deficient in that "counsel made errors so serious that counsel was not functioning as 'counsel' guaranteed the defendant by the Sixth Amendment." To show prejudice, it must be established that the claimed lapses in counsel's performance rendered the trial unfair so as to "undermine confidence in the outcome" of the trial. * * *

Under the *Strickland* standard, breach of an ethical standard does not necessarily make out a denial of the Sixth Amendment guarantee of assistance of counsel. When examining attorney conduct, a court must be careful not to narrow the wide range of conduct acceptable under the Sixth Amendment so restrictively as to constitutionalize particular standards of professional conduct and thereby intrude into the State's proper authority to define and apply the standards of professional conduct applicable to those it admits to practice in its courts. In some future case challenging attorney conduct in the course of a state court trial, we may need to define with greater precision the weight to be given to recognized canons of ethics, the standards established by the State in statutes or professional codes, and the Sixth Amendment, in defining the proper scope and limits on that conduct. Here we need not face that question, since virtually all of the sources speak with one voice.

We turn next to the question presented: the definition of the range of "reasonable professional" responses to a criminal defendant client who informs counsel that he will perjure himself on the stand. We must determine whether, in this setting, Robinson's conduct fell within the wide range of professional responses to threatened client perjury acceptable under the Sixth Amendment.

In *Strickland,* we recognized counsel's duty of loyalty and his "overarching duty to advocate the defendant's cause." Plainly, that duty is limited to legitimate, lawful conduct compatible with the very nature of a trial as a search for truth. Although counsel must take all reasonable lawful means to attain the objectives of the client, counsel is precluded from taking steps or in any way assisting the client in presenting false evidence or otherwise violating the law. This principle has consistently been recognized in most unequivocal terms by expositors of the norms of professional conduct since the first Canons of Professional Ethics were adopted by the American Bar Association in 1908. * * *

"No client, corporate or individual, however powerful, nor any cause, civil or political, however important, is entitled to receive nor should any lawyer render any service or advice involving disloyalty to the law whose ministers we are, or disrespect of the judicial office, which we are bound to uphold, or corruption of any person or persons exercising a public office or private trust, or deception or betrayal of the public. ... He must ... observe and advise his client to observe the statute law. ..." Canons of Professional Ethics, Canon 32.

[This principle has] been carried through to contemporary codifications [4] of an attorney's professional responsibility. Disciplinary Rule 7–102 of the Model Code of Professional Responsibility (1980), entitled "Representing a Client Within the Bounds of the Law," provides that

"(A) In his representation of a client, a lawyer shall not: ... (4) Knowingly use perjured testimony or false evidence; ... (7) Counsel or assist his client in conduct that the lawyer knows to be illegal or fraudulent."

This provision has been adopted by Iowa, and is binding on all lawyers who appear in its courts. The more recent Model Rules of Professional Conduct (1983) similarly admonish attorneys to obey all laws in the course of representing a client:

"*RULE 1.2* Scope of Representation ...

"(d) A lawyer shall not counsel a client to engage, or assist a client, in conduct that the lawyer knows is criminal or fraudulent ...."

Both the Model Code of Professional Conduct and the Model Rules of Professional Conduct also adopt the specific exception from the attorney-client privilege for disclosure of perjury that his client intends to commit or has committed. Indeed, both the Model Code and the Model Rules do not merely *authorize* disclosure by counsel of client perjury; they *require* such disclosure. * * *

These standards confirm that the legal profession has accepted that an attorney's ethical duty to advance the interests of his client is limited by an equally solemn duty to comply with the law and standards of professional conduct; it specifically ensures that the client may not use false evidence. This special duty of an attorney to prevent and disclose frauds upon the court derives from the recognition that perjury is as much a crime as tampering with witnesses or jurors by way of promises and threats, and undermines the administration of justice. * * * The suggestion sometimes made that "a lawyer must believe his client not judge him" in no sense means a lawyer can honorably be a party to or in any way give aid to presenting known perjury.

Considering Robinson's representation of respondent in light of these accepted norms of professional conduct, we discern no failure to adhere to reasonable professional standards that would in any sense make out a deprivation of the Sixth Amendment right to counsel. Whether Robinson's conduct is seen as a successful attempt to dissuade his client from committing the crime of perjury, or

---

4. There currently exist two different codifications of uniform standards of professional conduct. The Model Code of Professional Responsibility was originally adopted by the American Bar Association in 1969, and was subsequently adopted (in many cases with modification) by nearly every state. The more recent Model Rules of Professional Conduct were adopted by the American Bar Association in 1983. Since their promulgation by the American Bar Association, the Model Rules have been adopted by 11 States * * *. Iowa is one of the States that adopted a form of the Model Code of Professional Responsibility, but has yet to adopt the Model Rules.

whether seen as a "threat" to withdraw from representation and disclose the illegal scheme, Robinson's representation of Whiteside falls well within accepted standards of professional conduct and the range of reasonable professional conduct acceptable under *Strickland.* * * *

While purporting to follow the Iowa's highest court "on all questions of state law," the Court of Appeals reached its conclusions on the basis of federal constitutional due process and right to counsel. * * * [While accepting the conclusion of the Iowa trial court that Whiteside's proposed testimony would have been a criminal act, the Court of Appeals held that Robinson's efforts to persuade Whiteside not to commit that crime were improper, *first,* as forcing an impermissible choice between the right to counsel and the right to testify; and *second,* as compromising client confidences because of Robinson's threat to disclose the contemplated perjury.[7] * * *

Whatever the scope of a constitutional right to testify, it is elementary that such a right does not extend to testifying *falsely.* * * * Robinson's admonitions to his client can in no sense be said to have forced respondent into an *impermissible* choice between his right to counsel and his right to testify as he proposed for there was no *permissible* choice to testify falsely. For defense counsel to take steps to persuade a criminal defendant to testify truthfully, or to withdraw, deprives the defendant of neither his right to counsel nor the right to testify truthfully. * * *

On this record, the accused enjoyed continued representation within the bounds of reasonable professional conduct and did in fact exercise his right to testify; at most he was denied the right to have the assistance of counsel in the presentation of false testimony. Similarly, we can discern no breach of professional duty in Robinson's admonition to respondent that he would disclose respondent's perjury to the court. The crime of perjury in this setting is indistinguishable in substance from the crime of threatening or tampering with a witness or a juror. A defendant who informed his counsel that he was arranging to bribe or threaten witnesses or members of the jury would have no "right" to insist on counsel's assistance or silence. Counsel would not be limited to advising against that conduct. An attorney's duty of confidentiality, which totally covers the client's admission of guilt, does not extend to a client's announced plans to engage in future criminal conduct. In short, the responsibility of an ethical lawyer, as an officer of the court and a key component of a system of justice, dedicated to a search for truth, is essentially the same whether the client announces an intention to bribe or threaten witnesses or jurors or to commit or procure perjury. No system of justice worthy of the name can tolerate a lesser standard.

The rule adopted by the Court of Appeals, which seemingly would require an attorney to remain silent while his client committed perjury, is wholly incompatible with the established standards of ethical conduct and the laws of Iowa and contrary to professional standards promulgated by that State. The position advocated by petitioner, on the contrary, is wholly consistent with the Iowa standards of professional conduct and law, with the overwhelming majority of courts, and with codes of professional ethics. Since there has been no breach of any recognized professional duty, it follows that there can be no deprivation of the right to assistance of counsel under the *Strickland* standard.

7. The Court of Appeals also determined that Robinson's efforts to persuade Whiteside to testify truthfully constituted an impermissible threat to testify against his own client. We find no support for a threat to testify against Whiteside while he was acting as counsel. The record reflects testimony by Robinson that he had admonished Whiteside that if he withdrew he "probably would be allowed to attempt to impeach that particular testimony," if Whiteside testified falsely. The trial court accepted this version of the conversation as true.

We hold that, as a matter of law, counsel's conduct complained of here cannot establish the prejudice required for relief under the second strand of the *Strickland* inquiry. Although a defendant need not establish that the attorney's deficient performance more likely than not altered the outcome in order to establish prejudice under *Strickland,* a defendant must show "that there is a reasonable probability that, but for counsel's unprofessional errors, the result of the proceeding would have been different." According to *Strickland,* "[a] reasonable probability is a probability sufficient to undermine confidence in the outcome." The *Strickland* Court noted that the "benchmark" of an ineffective assistance claim is the fairness of the adversary proceeding, and that in judging prejudice and the likelihood of a different outcome, "[a] defendant has no entitlement to the luck of a lawless decisionmaker."

Whether he was persuaded or compelled to desist from perjury, Whiteside has no valid claim that confidence in the result of his trial has been diminished by his desisting from the contemplated perjury. Even if we were to assume that the jury might have believed his perjury, it does not follow that Whiteside was prejudiced.
* * *

Whiteside's attorney treated Whiteside's proposed perjury in accord with professional standards, and since Whiteside's truthful testimony could not have prejudiced the result of his trial, the Court of Appeals * * * must be reversed.[a]

a. Although some language in *Strickland* and *Whiteside* suggests otherwise, a defendant claiming that she has been denied the effective assistance of counsel may not prevail even though she establishes that (a) her lawyer's performance was seriously deficient and (b) there is a reasonable probability that but for that deficiency the result of the proceeding would have been different. As the Court, per Rehnquist, C.J., emphasized in *Lockhart v. Fretwell,* 506 U.S. 364 (1993), the "prejudice" component of the *Strickland* test involves more than a determination that the outcome would have been different. "It focuses on the question whether a counsel's deficient performance renders the result of the trial unreliable or the proceeding fundamentally unfair." And "unreliability or unfairness does not result if the ineffectiveness of counsel does not deprive the defendant of any substantive or procedural right to which the law entitles him."

The *Fretwell* case grew out of an unusual set of facts. An Arkansas jury convicted respondent of capital felony murder. During the death penalty phase of the case, the jury found an aggravating factor—that the murder, which occurred during a robbery, had been committed for pecuniary gain. But under *Collins v. Lockhart,* 754 F.2d 258 (1985) a then-existing (but subsequently overruled) Eighth Circuit precedent, an aggravating factor could not duplicate an element of the underlying felony—murder in the course of a robbery. However, respondent's lawyer failed to make any objection.

By the time the Eighth Circuit considered respondent's case on federal habeas corpus, it had already overruled *Collins.* Nevertheless, it held that respondent was entitled to relief, reasoning that had his lawyer objected to the use of the aggravating factor at the sentencing phase the trial judge would have sustained it and respondent would not have been sentenced to death. The Supreme Court disagreed. Observed Chief Justice Rehnquist:

"To set aside a conviction or sentence solely because the outcome would have been different but for counsel's error may grant the defendant a windfall to which the law does not entitle him.

"Our decision in *Nix v. Whiteside* makes this very point. * * * Obviously, had [Whiteside] presented false testimony to the jury, there would have been a reasonable probability that the jury would not have returned a verdict of guilty. Sheer outcome determination, however, was not sufficient to make out a claim under the Sixth Amendment. [The] touchstone of an ineffective assistance claim is the fairness of the adversary proceeding and [in determining that] 'a defendant has no entitlement to the luck of a lawless decisionmaker.'

"[The] result of the sentencing proceeding in the present case was neither unfair nor unreliable. The Court of Appeals, which had decided *Collins* in 1985, overruled [it] four years later. Had the trial court chosen to follow *Collins,* counsel's error would have 'deprived respondent of the chance to have the state court make an error in his favor.' "

In a concurring opinion, the author of *Strickland,* Justice O'Connor, wrote separately "only to point out that today's decision will, in the vast majority of cases, have no effect on the prejudice inquiry under *Strickland*":

"Since *Strickland,* we have recognized that neither the likely effect of perjured testimony

JUSTICE BLACKMUN, with whom JUSTICE BRENNAN, JUSTICE MARSHALL, and JUSTICE STEVENS join, concurring in the judgment.[b]

How a defense attorney ought to act when faced with a client who intends to commit perjury at trial has long been a controversial issue. But I do not believe that a federal habeas corpus case challenging a state criminal conviction is an appropriate vehicle for attempting to resolve this thorny problem. When a defendant argues that he was denied effective assistance of counsel because his lawyer dissuaded him from committing perjury, the only question properly presented to this Court is whether the lawyer's actions deprived the defendant of the fair trial which the Sixth Amendment is meant to guarantee. Since I believe that the respondent in this case suffered no injury justifying federal habeas relief, I concur in the Court's judgment. * * *

The touchstone of a claim of prejudice is an allegation that counsel's behavior did something "to deprive the defendant of a fair trial, a trial whose result is reliable." *Strickland.* The only effect Robinson's threat had on Whiteside's trial is that Whiteside did not testify, falsely, that he saw a gun in Love's hand.[4] Thus, this Court must ask whether its confidence in the outcome of Whiteside's trial is in any way undermined by the knowledge that he refrained from presenting false testimony.

* * * To the extent that Whiteside's claim rests on the assertion that he would have been acquitted had he been able to testify falsely, Whiteside claims a right the law simply does not recognize. * * * Since Whiteside was deprived of neither a fair trial nor any of the specific constitutional rights designed to guarantee a fair trial, he has suffered no prejudice. * * *

In light of respondent's failure to show any cognizable prejudice, I see no need to "grade counsel's performance." *Strickland.* The only federal issue in this case is whether Robinson's behavior deprived Whiteside of the effective assistance of counsel; it is not whether Robinson's behavior conformed to any particular code of legal ethics.

Whether an attorney's response to what he sees as a client's plan to commit perjury violates a defendant's Sixth Amendment rights may depend on many factors: how certain the attorney is that the proposed testimony is false, the stage of the proceedings at which the attorney discovers the plan, or the ways in which the attorney may be able to dissuade his client, to name just three. The complex interaction of factors, which is likely to vary from case to case, makes inappropriate a blanket rule that defense attorneys must reveal, or threaten to reveal, a client's anticipated perjury to the court. Except in the rarest of cases, attorneys who adopt "the role of the judge or jury to determine the facts," *Wilcox,* pose a

nor the impact of a meritless Fourth Amendment objection is an appropriate consideration in the prejudice inquiry. * * * Today the Court identifies another factor that ought not inform the prejudice inquiry. [W]e hold that the court making the prejudice determination may not consider the effect of an objection it knows to be wholly meritless under current governing law, even if the objection might have been considered meritorious at the time of its omission."

b. Justice Brennan also wrote a separate opinion concurring in the judgment. He agreed that "respondent has failed to prove the kind of prejudice necessary to make out a claim under *Strickland,*" and wrote separately to emphasize that the "Court's essay regarding what constitutes the correct response to a criminal client's suggestion that he will perjure himself is pure discourse without force of law."

4. This is not to say that a lawyer's threat to reveal his client's confidences may never have other effects on a defendant's trial. Cf. *United States ex rel. Wilcox v. Johnson,* 555 F.2d 115 (3d Cir.1977) (finding a violation of Sixth Amendment when an attorney's threat to reveal client's purported perjury caused defendant not to take the stand at all).

danger of depriving their clients of the zealous and loyal advocacy required by the Sixth Amendment.[8]

I therefore am troubled by the Court's implicit adoption of a set of standards of professional responsibility for attorneys in state criminal proceedings. The States, of course, do have a compelling interest in the integrity of their criminal trials that can justify regulating the length to which an attorney may go in seeking his client's acquittal. But the American Bar Association's implicit suggestion in its brief *amicus curiae* that the Court find that the Association's Model Rules of Professional Conduct should govern an attorney's responsibilities is addressed to the wrong audience. It is for the States to decide how attorneys should conduct themselves in state criminal proceedings, and this Court's responsibility extends only to ensuring that the restrictions a State enacts do not infringe a defendant's federal constitutional rights. Thus, I would follow the suggestion made in the joint brief *amici curiae* filed by 37 States at the certiorari stage that we allow the States to maintain their "differing approaches" to a complex ethical question. The signal merit of asking first whether a defendant has shown any adverse prejudicial effect before inquiring into his attorney's performance is that it avoids unnecessary federal interference in a State's regulation of its bar. Because I conclude that the respondent in this case failed to show such an effect, I join the Court's judgment that he is not entitled to federal habeas relief.

JUSTICE STEVENS, concurring in the judgment. * * *

As we view this case, it appears perfectly clear that respondent intended to commit perjury, that his lawyer knew it, and that the lawyer had a duty—both to the court and to his client, for perjured testimony can ruin an otherwise meritorious case—to take extreme measures to prevent the perjury from occurring. The lawyer was successful and, from our unanimous and remote perspective, it is now pellucidly clear that the client suffered no "legally cognizable prejudice."

Nevertheless, beneath the surface of this case there are areas of uncertainty that cannot be resolved today. A lawyer's certainty that a change in his client's recollection is a harbinger of intended perjury—as well as judicial review of such apparent certainty—should be tempered by the realization that, after reflection, the most honest witness may recall (or sincerely believe he recalls) details that he previously overlooked. Similarly, the post-trial review of a lawyer's pre-trial threat to expose perjury that had not yet been committed—and, indeed, may have been prevented by the threat—is by no means the same as review of the way in which such a threat may actually have been carried out. Thus, one can be convinced—as I am—that this lawyer's actions were a proper way to provide his client with effective representation without confronting the much more difficult questions of what a lawyer must, should, or may do after his client has given testimony that the lawyer does not believe. The answer to such questions may well be colored by the particular circumstances attending the actual event and its aftermath.

---

8. A comparison of this case with *Wilcox* [note 4 supra] is illustrative. Here, Robinson testified in detail to the factors that led him to conclude that respondent's assertion he had seen a gun was false. The Iowa Supreme Court found "good cause" and "strong support" for Robinson's conclusion. Moreover, Robinson gave credence to those parts of Whiteside's account which, although he found them implausible and unsubstantiated, were not clearly false. By contrast, in *Wilcox,* where defense counsel actually informed the judge that she believed her client intended to lie and where her threat to withdraw in the middle of the trial led the defendant not to take the stand at all, the Court of Appeals found "no evidence on the record of this case indicating that Mr. Wilcox intended to perjure himself," and characterized counsel's beliefs as "private conjectures about the guilt or innocence of [her] client."

Because Justice Blackmun has preserved such questions for another day, and because I do not understand him to imply any adverse criticism of this lawyer's representation of his client, I join his opinion concurring in the judgment.

WHEAT v. UNITED STATES

486 U.S. 153, 108 S.Ct. 1692, 100 L.Ed.2d 140 (1988).

[Petitioner, along with numerous codefendants, including Gomez-Barajas and Bravo, was charged with participating in a far-flung drug conspiracy. Both Gomez-Barajas and Bravo were represented by attorney Iredale. Gomez-Barajas was tried first and was acquitted on drug charges overlapping with those against petitioner. To avoid a second trial on still further charges, Gomez-Barajas offered to plead guilty to tax-evasion and illegal-importation offenses stemming from the conspiracy. However, at the commencement of petitioner's trial, that plea had not yet been accepted by the district court, so there remained the possibility that it could be rejected by the district court or withdrawn by Gomez-Barajas. Bravo pleaded guilty in a proceeding that occurred two days before defendant's scheduled trial.

[At the conclusion of Bravo's guilty plea proceeding, petitioner moved for the substitution of Iredale as his counsel. The government objected on the ground that Iredale's representation of the defendant as well as the two other codefendants created a multiple conflict of interest: (1) In the event that Gomez-Barajas's plea and negotiated sentencing arrangement were rejected by the court, or Gomez-Barajas withdrew his plea, petitioner was likely to be called as a witness for the prosecution at Gomez-Barajas's second trial, and Iredale would face a conflict in cross-examining him; (2) In the likely event that Bravo was called as a witness for the prosecution against petitioner, Iredale would face a conflict of interest in cross-examining Bravo. Iredale, in either situation, the government argued, would not be able to fully cross-examine the prosecution witness because of confidences received from previously representing him, and could not effectively represent the particular criminal defendant, petitioner or Gomez-Barajas, without having the capacity to fully cross-examine the witness.

[In response, to the government, petitioner emphasized his right to have counsel of his own choosing and his willingness, and the willingness of the other codefendants, to waive the right to conflict-free counsel. Moreover, maintained petitioner, the circumstances posited by the government that would create a conflict of interest were highly speculative and bore no connection to the true relationship among the co-conspirators. If called to testify against petitioner, Bravo would simply say that he did not know petitioner and had had no dealings with him. In the unlikely event that Gomez-Barajas went to trial, petitioner's lack of involvement in his alleged crimes made his appearance as a witness highly improbable. According to petitioner, the government was "manufacturing implausible conflicts" in an attempt to disqualify Iredale, who had already proved extremely effective in representing the other codefendants.

[The district court denied petitioner's request to substitute Iredale as his attorney, concluding, on the basis of the representation of the government, that it "really has no choice at this point other than to find that an irreconcilable conflict of interest exists." Petitioner proceeded to trial with his original counsel and was convicted of various drug offenses. The Court of Appeals for the Ninth Circuit affirmed.]

Chief Justice Rehnquist delivered the opinion of the Court.

* * * [W]hile the right to select and be represented by one's preferred attorney is comprehended by the Sixth Amendment, the essential aim of the Amendment is to guarantee an effective advocate for each criminal defendant rather than to ensure that a defendant will inexorably be represented by the lawyer whom he prefers.

The Sixth Amendment right to choose one's own counsel is circumscribed in several important respects. Regardless of his persuasive powers, an advocate who is not a member of the bar may not represent clients (other than himself) in court. Similarly, a defendant may not insist on representation by an attorney he cannot afford or who for other reasons declines to represent the defendant. Nor may a defendant insist on the counsel of an attorney who has a previous or ongoing relationship with an opposing party, even when the opposing party is the Government. The question raised in this case is the extent to which a criminal defendant's right under the Sixth Amendment to his chosen attorney is qualified by the fact that the attorney has represented other defendants charged in the same criminal conspiracy. * * *

Petitioner insists that the provision of waivers by all affected defendants cures any problems created by the multiple representation. But no such flat rule can be deduced from the Sixth Amendment presumption in favor of counsel of choice. Federal courts have an independent interest in ensuring that criminal trials are conducted within the ethical standards of the profession and that legal proceedings appear fair to all who observe them. Both the American Bar Association's Model Code of Professional Responsibility and its Model Rules of Professional Conduct, as well as the rules of the California Bar Association (which governed the attorneys in this case), impose limitations on multiple representation of clients. Not only the interest of a criminal defendant but the institutional interest in the rendition of just verdicts in criminal cases may be jeopardized by unregulated multiple representation.

For this reason, the Federal Rules of Criminal Procedure direct trial judges to investigate specially cases involving joint representation. In pertinent part, Rule 44(c) provides:

> "[T]he court shall promptly inquire with respect to such joint representation and shall personally advise each defendant of his right to the effective assistance of counsel, including separate representation. Unless it appears that there is good cause to believe no conflict of interest is likely to arise, the court shall take such measures as may be appropriate to protect each defendant's right to counsel."

Although Rule 44(c) does not specify what particular measures may be taken by a district court, one option suggested by the Notes of the Advisory Committee is an order by the court that the defendants be separately represented in subsequent proceedings in the case. This suggestion comports with our instructions in *Holloway* and in *Glasser v. United States* that the trial courts, when alerted by objection from one of the parties, have an independent duty to ensure that criminal defendants receive a trial that is fair and does not contravene the Sixth Amendment.[a]

a. In *Glasser v. United States*, 315 U.S. 60 (1942), the Court held that the defendant was denied the effective assistance of counsel when the trial court placed his retained counsel in an actual conflict situation by appointing the attorney to also represent a codefendant whose strategic position differed from defendant. In *Holloway v. Arkansas*, 435 U.S. 475 (1978), the Court found constitutional error in a trial court's failure to make an inquiry, such as that prescribed under Rule 44(c), into counsel's multiple representation of defendants. *Holloway* involved a situation in which previously appointed counsel had asked the trial court to

To be sure, this need to investigate potential conflicts arises in part from the legitimate wish of District Courts that their judgments remain intact on appeal. As the Court of Appeals accurately pointed out, trial courts confronted with multiple representations face the prospect of being "whip-sawed" by assertions of error no matter which way they rule. If a district court agrees to the multiple representation, and the advocacy of counsel is thereafter impaired as a result, the defendant may well claim that he did not receive effective assistance. On the other hand, a district court's refusal to accede to the multiple representation may result in a challenge such as petitioner's in this case. Nor does a waiver by the defendant necessarily solve the problem, for we note, without passing judgment on, the apparent willingness of Courts of Appeals to entertain ineffective assistance claims from defendants who have specifically waived the right to conflict-free counsel.

Thus, where a court justifiably finds an actual conflict of interest, there can be no doubt that it may decline a proffer of waiver, and insist that defendants be separately represented.

Unfortunately for all concerned, a district court must pass on the issue of whether or not to allow a waiver of a conflict of interest by a criminal defendant not with the wisdom of hindsight after the trial has taken place, but the murkier pretrial context when relationships between parties are seen through a glass, darkly. The likelihood and dimensions of nascent conflicts of interest are notoriously hard to predict, even for those thoroughly familiar with criminal trials. It is a rare attorney who will be fortunate enough to learn the entire truth from his own client, much less be fully apprised before trial of what each of the Government's witnesses will say on the stand. A few bits of unforeseen testimony or a single previously unknown or unnoticed document may significantly shift the relationship between multiple defendants. These imponderables are difficult enough for a lawyer to assess, and even more difficult to convey by way of explanation to a criminal defendant untutored in the niceties of legal ethics. Nor is it amiss to observe that the willingness of an attorney to obtain such waivers from his clients may bear an inverse relation to the care with which he conveys all the necessary information to them.

relieve him of the obligation of jointly representing three codefendants. Counsel had explained that he would not be able to cross-examine a testifying codefendant on behalf of the other codefendants because of "confidential information" he had received from each of the codefendants. The trial court, however, refused to relieve counsel without even exploring the possibility that such a conflict existed. That failure, in light of the warning from counsel, constituted a violation of the Sixth Amendment in itself; there was no need to determine after the fact whether an actual conflict had indeed existed (as it had in *Glasser*).

The *Holloway* opinion specifically left open the question of what the trial court's constitutional responsibilities were "where the trial counsel did nothing to advise the trial court as to the actuality or possibility of a conflict." *Cuyler v. Sullivan*, 446 U.S. 335 (1980), subsequently held that a considerably different standard applied to that situation. The Court there rejected the contention that a trial court had a constitutional duty to make some inquiry

as to a possible conflict in all cases of multiple representation (as Federal Rule 44(c) requires of federal courts). Ordinarily, the Court noted, the trial judge could rely upon the absence of any objection by counsel, since counsel has "an ethical obligation to avoid conflicting representations and to advise the court promptly when a conflict arises during the course of the trial." Thus, as a matter of constitutional law, "absent special circumstances" indicating that the court "reasonably should know" that a particular conflict exists, where counsel has raised no objection, the trial court "may assume either that multiple representation entails no conflict or that the lawyer and his clients knowingly accept such a risk of conflict as may exist." In such cases, to establish incompetency, defendant must show not merely a failure of the court to conduct an inquiry (as in *Holloway*), but "an actual conflict of interest [that] adversely affected his lawyer's performance." See also *Strickland*, supra, in the paragraph ending with note b.

For these reasons we think the District Court must be allowed substantial latitude in refusing waivers of conflicts of interest not only in those rare cases where an actual conflict may be demonstrated before trial, but in the more common cases where a potential for conflict exists which may or may not burgeon into an actual conflict as the trial progresses. In the circumstances of this case, with the motion for substitution of counsel made so close to the time of trial, the District Court relied on instinct and judgment based on experience in making its decision. We do not think it can be said that the court exceeded the broad latitude which must be accorded it in making this decision. Petitioner of course rightly points out that the government may seek to "manufacture" a conflict in order to prevent a defendant from having a particularly able defense counsel at his side; but trial courts are undoubtedly aware of this possibility, and must take it into consideration along with all of the other factors which inform this sort of a decision.

Here the District Court was confronted not simply with an attorney who wished to represent two coequal defendants in a straightforward criminal prosecution; rather, Iredale proposed to defend three conspirators of varying stature in a complex drug distribution scheme. The Government intended to call Bravo as a witness for the prosecution at petitioner's trial.[4] The Government might readily have tied certain deliveries of marijuana by Bravo to petitioner, necessitating vigorous cross-examination of Bravo by petitioner's counsel. Iredale, because of his prior representation of Bravo, would have been unable ethically to provide that cross-examination.

Iredale had also represented Gomez-Barajas, one of the alleged kingpins of the distribution ring, and had succeeded in obtaining a verdict of acquittal for him. Gomez-Barajas had agreed with the Government to plead guilty to other charges, but the District Court had not yet accepted the plea arrangement. If the agreement were rejected, petitioner's probable testimony at the resulting trial of Gomez-Barajas would create an ethical dilemma for Iredale from which one or the other of his clients would likely suffer.

Viewing the situation as it did before trial, we hold that the District Court's refusal to permit the substitution of counsel in this case was within its discretion and did not violate petitioner's Sixth Amendment rights. Other district courts might have reached differing or opposite conclusions with equal justification, but that does not mean that one conclusion was "right" and the other "wrong." The District Court must recognize a presumption in favor of petitioner's counsel of choice, but that presumption may be overcome not only by a demonstration of actual conflict but by a showing of a serious potential for conflict. The evaluation of the facts and circumstances of each case under this standard must be left primarily to the informed judgment of the trial court. * * *

JUSTICE MARSHALL, with whom JUSTICE BRENNAN joins, dissenting.

* * * The right to counsel of choice, as the Court notes, is not absolute. When a defendant's selection of counsel, under the particular facts and circumstances of a case, gravely imperils the prospect of a fair trial, a trial court may justifiably refuse to accede to the choice. Thus, a trial court may in certain situations reject a defendant's choice of counsel on the ground of a potential conflict of interest, because a serious conflict may indeed destroy the integrity of the trial process. As the Court states, however, the trial court must recognize a presumption in favor of a defendant's counsel of choice. This presumption means that a trial court may not reject a defendant's chosen counsel on the ground of a

---

4. Bravo was in fact called as a witness at petitioner's trial. His testimony was elicited to demonstrate the transportation of drugs that the prosecution hoped to link to petitioner.

potential conflict of interest absent a showing that both the likelihood and the dimensions of the feared conflict are substantial.[1] Unsupported or dubious speculation as to a conflict will not suffice. The Government must show a substantial potential for the kind of conflict that would undermine the fairness of the trial process. In these respects, I do not believe my position differs significantly, if at all, from that expressed in the opinion of the Court.

I do disagree, however, with the Court's suggestion that the trial court's decision as to whether a potential conflict justifies rejection of a defendant's chosen counsel is entitled to some kind of special deference on appeal. The Court grants trial courts "broad latitude" over the decision to accept or reject a defendant's choice of counsel; although never explicitly endorsing a standard of appellate review, the Court appears to limit such review to determining whether an abuse of discretion has occurred. This approach, which the Court supports solely by noting the difficulty of evaluating the likelihood and magnitude of a conflict, accords neither with the nature of the trial court's decision nor with the importance of the interest at stake.

The trial court's decision as to whether the circumstances of a given case constitute grounds for rejecting a defendant's chosen counsel—that is, as to whether these circumstances present a substantial potential for a serious conflict of interest—is a mixed determination of law and fact. The decision is properly described in this way because it requires and results from the application of a legal standard to the established facts of a case. Appellate courts traditionally do not defer to such determinations. * * *

The inappropriateness of deferring to this determination becomes even more apparent when its constitutional significance is taken into account. * * * [The] interest at stake in this kind of decision is nothing less than a criminal defendant's Sixth Amendment right to counsel of his choice. The trial court simply does not have "broad latitude" to vitiate this right. In my view, a trial court that rejects a criminal defendant's chosen counsel on the ground of a potential conflict should make findings on the record to facilitate review, and an appellate court should scrutinize closely the basis for the trial court's decision. Only in this way can a criminal defendant's right to counsel of his choice be appropriately protected.

The Court's resolution of the instant case flows from its deferential approach to the District Court's denial of petitioner's motion to add or substitute counsel; absent deference, a decision upholding the District Court's ruling would be inconceivable. * * * At the time of petitioner's trial, Iredale's representation of Gomez-Barajas was effectively completed. * * * The only possible conflict this Court can divine from Iredale's representation of both petitioner and Gomez-Barajas rests on the premise that the trial court would reject the negotiated plea agreement and that Gomez-Barajas then would decide to go to trial. In this event, the Court tells us, "petitioner's probable testimony at the resulting trial of Gomez-Barajas would create an ethical dilemma for Iredale."

This argument rests on speculation of the most dubious kind. The Court offers no reason to think that the trial court would have rejected Gomez-Barajas's plea agreement; neither did the Government posit any such reason in its argument or brief before this Court. The most likely occurrence at the time petitioner moved to retain Iredale as his defense counsel was that the trial court

1. In stating this principle, I mean to address only cases in which all parties to the potential conflict have made a fully informed waiver of their right to conflict-free representa-tion. It is undisputed in this case that petitioner, as well as Juvenal Gomez-Barajas and Javier Bravo, had agreed to waive this right.

would accept Gomez-Barajas's plea agreement, as the court in fact later did. Moreover, even if Gomez-Barajas had gone to trial, petitioner probably would not have testified. * * * The only alleged connection between petitioner and Gomez-Barajas sprang from the conspiracy to distribute marijuana, and a jury already had acquitted Gomez-Barajas of that charge. It is therefore disingenuous to say that representation of both petitioner and Gomez-Barajas posed a serious potential for a conflict of interest.

Similarly, Iredale's prior representation of Bravo was not a cause for concern. * * * [The facts] belie the claim that Bravo's anticipated testimony created a serious potential for conflict. Contrary to the Court's inference, Bravo could not have testified about petitioner's involvement in the alleged marijuana distribution scheme. As all parties were aware at the time, Bravo did not know and could not identify petitioner; indeed, prior to the commencement of legal proceedings, the two men never had heard of each other. Bravo's eventual testimony at petitioner's trial related to a shipment of marijuana in which petitioner was not involved; the testimony contained not a single reference to petitioner. Petitioner's counsel did not cross-examine Bravo, and neither petitioner's counsel nor the prosecutor mentioned Bravo's testimony in closing argument. All of these developments were predictable when the District Court ruled on petitioner's request that Iredale serve as trial counsel. * * * The District Court therefore had no authority to deny petitioner's Sixth Amendment right to retain counsel of his choice. * * *[b]

FARETTA v. CALIFORNIA
422 U.S. 806, 95 S.Ct. 2525, 45 L.Ed.2d 562 (1975).

JUSTICE STEWART delivered the opinion of the Court.

The Sixth and Fourteenth Amendments of our Constitution guarantee that a person brought to trial in any state or federal court must be afforded the right to the assistance of counsel before he can be validly convicted and punished by imprisonment. This clear constitutional rule has emerged from a series of cases decided here over the last 50 years. The question before us now is whether a defendant in a state criminal trial has a constitutional right to proceed *without* counsel when he voluntarily and intelligently elects to do so. Stated another way, the question is whether a State may constitutionally hale a person into its criminal courts and there force a lawyer upon him, even when he insists that he wants to conduct his own defense. It is not an easy question, but we have concluded that a State may not constitutionally do so.

Anthony Faretta was charged with grand theft in * * * the Superior Court of Los Angeles County, Cal. At the arraignment, the Superior Court Judge assigned to preside at the trial appointed the public defender to represent Faretta. Well before the date of trial, however, Faretta requested that he be permitted to represent himself. Questioning by the judge revealed that Faretta had once represented himself in a criminal prosecution, that he had a high school education, and that he did not want to be represented by the public defender because he believed that that office was "very loaded down with * * * a heavy case load." The judge responded that he believed Faretta was "making a mistake" and emphasized that in further proceedings Faretta would receive no special favors. Nevertheless, * * * the judge, in a "preliminary ruling," accepted Faretta's

---

b. In a separate dissent, Stevens, J., joined by Blackmun, J., noted agreement with "the Court's premise that district judges must be afforded wide latitude in passing on motions of this kind," but found it "abundantly clear" that the district judge here "abused his discretion."

waiver of the assistance of counsel. The judge indicated, however, that he might reverse this ruling if it later appeared that Faretta was unable adequately to represent himself.

Several weeks thereafter, but still prior to trial, the judge *sua sponte* held a hearing to inquire into Faretta's ability to conduct his own defense, and questioned him specifically about both the hearsay rule and the state law governing the challenge of potential jurors. After consideration of Faretta's answers, and observation of his demeanor, the judge ruled that Faretta had not made an intelligent and knowing waiver of his right to the assistance of counsel, and also ruled that Faretta had no constitutional right to conduct his own defense. The judge, accordingly, reversed his earlier ruling permitting self-representation and again appointed the public defender to represent Faretta. Faretta's subsequent request for leave to act as cocounsel was rejected, as were his efforts to make certain motions on his own behalf. Throughout the subsequent trial, the judge required that Faretta's defense be conducted only through the appointed lawyer from the public defender's office. At the conclusion of the trial, the jury found Faretta guilty as charged, and the judge sentenced him to prison.

The California Court of Appeal * * * affirmed the trial judge's ruling that Faretta had no federal or state constitutional right to represent himself, * * * and the California Supreme Court denied review.

In the federal courts, the right of self-representation has been protected by statute since the beginnings of our Nation. Section 35 of the Judiciary Act of 1789, 1 Stat. 73, 92, enacted by the First Congress and signed by President Washington one day before the Sixth Amendment was proposed, provided that "in all the courts of the United States, the parties may plead and manage their own causes personally or by the assistance of * * * counsel * * *." * * * With few exceptions, each of the several States also accords a defendant the right to represent himself in any criminal case. The Constitutions of 36 States explicitly confer that right. Moreover, many state courts have expressed the view that the right is also supported by the Constitution of the United States. This Court has more than once indicated the same view. * * * [And] the United States Courts of Appeals have repeatedly held that the right of self-representation is protected by the Bill of Rights.

This Court's past recognition of the right of self-representation, the federal-court authority holding the right to be of constitutional dimension, and the state constitutions pointing to the right's fundamental nature form a consensus not easily ignored. "[T]he mere fact that a path is a beaten one," Mr. Justice Jackson once observed, "is a persuasive reason for following it." We confront here a nearly universal conviction, on the part of our people as well as our courts, that forcing a lawyer upon an unwilling defendant is contrary to his basic right to defend himself if he truly wants to do so. This consensus is soundly premised. The right of self-representation finds support in the structure of the Sixth Amendment, as well as in the English and colonial jurisprudence from which the Amendment emerged.

The Sixth Amendment includes a compact statement of the rights necessary to a full defense. * * * The rights to notice, confrontation, and compulsory process, when taken together, guarantee that a criminal charge may be answered in a manner now considered fundamental to the fair administration of American justice—through the calling and interrogation of favorable witnesses, the cross-examination of adverse witnesses, and the orderly introduction of evidence. In short, the Amendment constitutionalizes the right in an adversary criminal trial to make a defense as we know it.

The Sixth Amendment does not provide merely that a defense shall be made for the accused; it grants to the accused personally the right to make his defense. It is the accused, not counsel, who must be "informed of the nature and cause of the accusation," who must be "confronted with the witnesses against him," and who must be accorded "compulsory process for obtaining witnesses in his favor." Although not stated in the Amendment in so many words, the right to self-representation—to make one's own defense personally—is thus necessarily implied by the structure of the Amendment.[15] The right to defend is given directly to the accused; for it is he who suffers the consequences if the defense fails.

The counsel provision supplements this design. It speaks of the "assistance" of counsel, and an assistant, however expert, is still an assistant. The language and spirit of the Sixth Amendment contemplate that counsel, like the other defense tools guaranteed by the Amendment, shall be an aid to a willing defendant—not an organ of the State interposed between an unwilling defendant and his right to defend himself personally. To thrust counsel upon the accused, against his considered wish, thus violates the logic of the Amendment. In such a case, counsel is not an assistant, but a master; and the right to make a defense is stripped of the personal character upon which the Amendment insists. It is true that when a defendant chooses to have a lawyer manage and present his case, law and tradition may allocate to the counsel the power to make binding decisions of trial strategy in many areas.[a] This allocation can only be justified, however, by the defendant's consent, at the outset, to accept counsel as his representative. An unwanted counsel "represents" the defendant only through a tenuous and unacceptable legal fiction. Unless the accused has acquiesced in such representation,

15. This Court has often recognized the constitutional stature of rights that, though not literally expressed in the document, are essential to due process of law in a fair adversary process. It is now accepted, for example, that an accused has a right to be present at all stages of the trial where his absence might frustrate the fairness of the proceedings, to testify on his own behalf, and to be convicted only if his guilt is proved beyond a reasonable doubt. * * *

The inference of rights is not, of course, a mechanical exercise. In *Singer v. United States,* 380 U.S. 24 (1965), the Court held that an accused has no right to a bench trial, despite his capacity to waive his right to a jury trial. In so holding, the Court stated that "[t]he ability to waive a constitutional right does not ordinarily carry with it the right to insist upon the opposite of that right." But that statement was made only *after* the Court had concluded that the Constitution does not affirmatively protect any right to be tried by a judge. * * * We follow the approach of *Singer* here. Our concern is with an *independent* right of self-representation. We do not suggest that this right arises mechanically from a defendant's power to waive the right to the assistance of counsel. * * *

a. Prior to *Faretta,* a long line of lower court cases had held that defense counsel had the authority to make various defense decisions on his own initiative. Those decisions, commonly characterized as relating to matters of "strategy" or "tactics," were said to be within the "exclusive province" of the lawyer.

To provide effective assistance as required under the Sixth Amendment, counsel did not have to consult with the defendant on such strategic decisions, and if there was consultation, did not have to follow the defendant's wishes. A post-*Faretta* ruling, *Jones v. Barnes,* 463 U.S. 745 (1983), reaffirmed this traditional viewpoint. The Court there held that appellate counsel did not have to present a nonfrivolous claim that his client wished to press if counsel believed that the better strategy was to limit the appellate argument to other issues. Counsel was free to follow the time tested advice of countless advocates that inclusion of "every colorable claim" will "dilute and weaken a good case and will not save a bad one." It was for counsel to decide which claims were strong enough to be presented consistent with this strategy.

As Chief Justice Burger noted in a concurring opinion in *Jones,* there are certain decisions that fall outside the range of control given to counsel in determining strategy. These decisions, because of their special significance or their involvement with the personal actions of defendant, are matters as to which defendant's choice prevails over a strategic preference of counsel. The Supreme Court has stated in dictum or holding that the following five decisions fall in this category: (1) pleading guilty or taking action tantamount to entering a guilty plea; (2) waiving the right to jury trial; (3) waiving the right to be present at the trial (4) defendant testifying on his own behalf; and (5) foregoing an appeal.

the defense presented is not the defense guaranteed him by the Constitution, for, in a very real sense, it is not *his* defense.

The Sixth Amendment, when naturally read, thus implies a right of self-representation. This reading is reinforced by the Amendment's roots in English legal history. In the long history of British criminal jurisprudence, there was only one tribunal that ever adopted a practice of forcing counsel upon an unwilling defendant in a criminal proceeding. The tribunal was the Star Chamber. That curious institution, which flourished in the late 16th and early 17th centuries, was of mixed executive and judicial character, and characteristically departed from common-law traditions. For those reasons, and because it specialized in trying "political" offenses, the Star Chamber has for centuries symbolized disregard of basic individual rights. * * *

In the American Colonies the insistence upon a right of self-representation was, if anything, more fervent than in England. The colonists brought with them an appreciation of the virtues of self-reliance and a traditional distrust of lawyers. When the Colonies were first settled, "the lawyer was synonymous with the cringing Attorneys–General and Solicitors–General of the Crown and the arbitrary Justices of the King's Court, all bent on the conviction of those who opposed the King's prerogatives, and twisting the law to secure convictions." This prejudice gained strength in the Colonies where "distrust of lawyers became an institution." * * *

This is not to say that the Colonies were slow to recognize the value of counsel in criminal cases. Colonial judges soon departed from ancient English practice and allowed accused felons the aid of counsel for their defense. At the same time, however, the basic right of self-representation was never questioned. We have found no instance where a colonial court required a defendant in a criminal case to accept as his representative an unwanted lawyer. Indeed, even where counsel was permitted, the general practice continued to be self-representation. * * * After the Declaration of Independence, the right of self-representation, along with other rights basic to the making of a defense, entered the new state constitutions in wholesale fashion. The right to counsel was clearly thought to supplement the primary right of the accused to defend himself, utilizing his personal rights to notice, confrontation, and compulsory process. * * * At the time James Madison drafted the Sixth Amendment, some state constitutions guaranteed an accused the right to be heard "by himself" and by counsel; others provided that an accused was to be "allowed" counsel. The various state proposals for the Bill of Rights had similar variations in terminology. In each case, however, the counsel provision was embedded in a package of defense rights granted personally to the accused. There is no indication that the differences in phrasing about "counsel" reflected any differences of principle about self-representation. * * *

There can be no blinking the fact that the right of an accused to conduct his own defense seems to cut against the grain of this Court's decisions holding that the Constitution requires that no accused can be convicted and imprisoned unless he has been accorded the right to the assistance of counsel. See *Powell v. Alabama*; *Johnson v. Zerbst*; *Gideon v. Wainwright*; *Argersinger v. Hamlin* [all discussed in Ch. 5, § 1]. For it is surely true that the basic thesis of those decisions is that the help of a lawyer is essential to assure the defendant a fair trial. And a strong argument can surely be made that the whole thrust of those decisions must inevitably lead to the conclusion that a State may constitutionally impose a lawyer upon even an unwilling defendant.

But it is one thing to hold that every defendant, rich or poor, has the right to the assistance of counsel, and quite another to say that a State may compel a defendant to accept a lawyer he does not want. The value of state-appointed counsel was not unappreciated by the Founders, yet the notion of compulsory counsel was utterly foreign to them. And whatever else may be said of those who wrote the Bill of Rights, surely there can be no doubt that they understood the inestimable worth of free choice.

It is undeniable that in most criminal prosecutions defendants could better defend with counsel's guidance than by their own unskilled efforts. But where the defendant will not voluntarily accept representation by counsel, the potential advantage of a lawyer's training and experience can be realized, if at all, only imperfectly. To force a lawyer on a defendant can only lead him to believe that the law contrives against him. Moreover, it is not inconceivable that in some rare instances, the defendant might in fact present his case more effectively by conducting his own defense. Personal liberties are not rooted in the law of averages. The right to defend is personal. The defendant, and not his lawyer or the State, will bear the personal consequences of a conviction. It is the defendant, therefore, who must be free personally to decide whether in his particular case counsel is to his advantage. And although he may conduct his own defense ultimately to his own detriment, his choice must be honored out of "that respect for the individual which is the lifeblood of the law." [46]

When an accused manages his own defense, he relinquishes, as a purely factual matter, many of the traditional benefits associated with the right to counsel. For this reason, in order to represent himself, the accused must "knowingly and intelligently" forgo those relinquished benefits. Although a defendant need not himself have the skill and experience of a lawyer in order competently and intelligently to choose self-representation, he should be made aware of the dangers and disadvantages of self-representation, so that the record will establish that "he knows what he is doing and his choice is made with eyes open."[b]

46. We are told that many criminal defendants representing themselves may use the courtroom for deliberate disruption of their trials. But the right of self-representation has been recognized from our beginnings by federal law and by most of the States, and no such result has thereby occurred. Moreover, the trial judge may terminate self-representation by a defendant who deliberately engages in serious and obstructionist misconduct. See *Illinois v. Allen* [Ch. 18, § 1]. Of course, a State may—even over objection by the accused—appoint a "standby counsel" to aid the accused if and when the accused requests help, and to be available to represent the accused in the event that termination of the defendant's self-representation is necessary.

The right of self-representation is not a license to abuse the dignity of the courtroom. Neither is it a license not to comply with relevant rules of procedural and substantive law. Thus, whatever else may or may not be open to him on appeal, a defendant who elects to represent himself cannot thereafter complain that the quality of his own defense amounted to a denial of "effective assistance of counsel."

b. Is the competency standard for pleading guilty or waiving the right to counsel higher than the competency standard for standing trial? No, answered a 7–2 majority, per Thomas, J., in *Godinez v. Moran*, 509 U.S. 389 (1993), also discussed in fn. a to *Boykin* [Ch. 14, § 2].

The standard for competency to stand trial is whether the defendant has "sufficient present ability to consult with his lawyer with a reasonable degree of rational understanding" and has "a rational as well as factual understanding of the proceedings against him." The *Godinez* majority rejected the notion that competence to plead guilty or to waive the right to counsel must be measured by a higher or different standard. The argument that a "defendant who represents himself must have greater powers to comprehension, judgment, and reason than would be necessary to stand trial with the aid of an attorney" rested "on a flawed premise: the competence that is required of a defendant seeking to waive his right to counsel is the competence to waive the right, not the competence to represent himself." As *Faretta* clearly indicated, a "criminal defendant's ability to represent himself has no bearing upon his competence to choose self-representation."

Here, weeks before trial, Faretta clearly and unequivocally declared to the trial judge that he wanted to represent himself and did not want counsel. The record affirmatively shows that Faretta was literate, competent, and understanding, and that he was voluntarily exercising his informed free will. The trial judge had warned Faretta that he thought it was a mistake not to accept the assistance of counsel, and that Faretta would be required to follow all the "ground rules" of trial procedure. We need make no assessment of how well or poorly Faretta had mastered the intricacies of the hearsay rule and the California code provisions that govern challenges of potential jurors on *voir dire*. For his technical legal knowledge, as such, was not relevant to an assessment of his knowing exercise of the right to defend himself.

In forcing Faretta, under these circumstances, to accept against his will a state-appointed public defender, the California courts deprived him of his constitutional right to conduct his own defense. * * *

CHIEF JUSTICE BURGER, with whom JUSTICE BLACKMUN and JUSTICE REHNQUIST join, dissenting. * * *

The most striking feature of the Court's opinion is that it devotes so little discussion to the matter which it concedes is the core of the decision, that is, discerning an independent basis in the Constitution for the supposed right to represent oneself in a criminal trial. Its ultimate assertion that such a right is tucked between the lines of the Sixth Amendment is contradicted by the Amendment's language and its consistent judicial interpretation.

[T]he conclusion that the rights guaranteed by the Sixth Amendment are "personal" to an accused reflects nothing more than the obvious fact that it is he who is on trial and therefore has need of a defense.[3] But neither that nearly trivial proposition nor the language of the Amendment, which speaks in uniformly mandatory terms, leads to the further conclusion that the right to counsel is merely supplementary and may be dispensed with at the whim of the accused. Rather, this Court's decisions have consistently included the right to counsel as an integral part of the bundle making up the larger "right to a defense as we know it." [The] reason for this hardly requires explanation. The fact of the matter is that in all but an extraordinarily small number of cases an accused will lose whatever defense he may have if he undertakes to conduct the trial himself.

[Nor] is it accurate to suggest, as the Court seems to later in its opinion, that the quality of his representation at trial is a matter with which only the accused is legitimately concerned. Although we have adopted an adversary system of criminal justice, the prosecution is more than an ordinary litigant, and the trial judge is not simply an automaton who insures that technical rules are adhered to. Both are charged with the duty of insuring that justice, in the broadest sense of

But a determination that a defendant is competent to stand trial is not enough when she seeks to plead guilty or waive her right to counsel: "[A] trial court must satisfy itself that the waiver of [one's] constitutional rights is knowing and voluntary. In this sense, there is a 'heightened' standard for pleading guilty and for waiving the right to counsel, but it is not a heightened standard of competence." The purpose of a competency inquiry, explained the Court, is to determine whether a defendant has the ability to understand the proceedings, but "the purpose of the 'knowing and voluntary' inquiry * * * is to determine whether the defendant actually does understand the significance and consequences of a particular decision and whether the decision is uncoerced."

3. The Court's attempt to derive support for its position from the fact that the Sixth Amendment speaks in terms of the "Assistance of Counsel" requires little comment. It is most curious to suggest that an accused who exercises his right to "assistance" has thereby impliedly consented to subject himself to a "master." And counsel's responsibility to his client and role in the litigation do not vary depending upon whether the accused would have preferred to represent himself.

that term, is achieved in every criminal trial. That goal is ill-served, and the integrity of and public confidence in the system are undermined, when an easy conviction is obtained due to the defendant's ill-advised decision to waive counsel. The damage thus inflicted is not mitigated by the lame explanation that the defendant simply availed himself of the "freedom" "to go to jail under his own banner * * *." The system of criminal justice should not be available as an instrument of self-destruction.

* * * True freedom of choice and society's interest in seeing that justice is achieved can be vindicated only if the trial court retains discretion to reject any attempted waiver of counsel and insist that the accused be tried according to the Constitution. This discretion is as critical an element of basic fairness as a trial judge's discretion to decline to accept a plea of guilty. See *Santobello v. New York* [Ch. 14, § 1].

[The Court] attempts to use history to take it where legal analysis cannot. Piecing together shreds of English legal history and early state constitutional and statutory provisions, without a full elaboration of the context in which they occurred or any evidence that they were relied upon by the drafters of our Federal Constitution, creates more questions than it answers and hardly provides the firm foundation upon which the creation of new constitutional rights should rest.* * * In this case, * * * history ought to lead judges to conclude that the Constitution leaves to the judgment of legislatures, and the flexible process of statutory amendment, the question whether criminal defendants should be permitted to conduct their trials *pro se.* See *Betts v. Brady.* And the fact that we have not hinted at a contrary view for 185 years is surely entitled to some weight in the scales. * * *

Society has the right to expect that, when courts find new rights implied in the Constitution, their potential effect upon the resources of our criminal justice system will be considered. However, such considerations are conspicuously absent from the Court's opinion in this case. [The] Court blandly assumes that once an accused has elected to defend himself he will be bound by his choice and not be heard to complain of it later. n. 46. This assumption ignores the role of appellate review, for the reported cases are replete with instances of a convicted defendant being relieved of a deliberate decision even when made *with the advice of counsel.* It is totally unrealistic, therefore, to suggest that an accused will always be held to the consequences of a decision to conduct his own defense. Unless, as may be the case, most persons accused of crime have more wit than to insist upon the dubious benefit that the Court confers today, we can expect that many expensive and good-faith prosecutions will be nullified on appeal for reasons that trial courts are now deprived of the power to prevent.[c]

---

c. *In Martinez v. Court Appeal of California*, 528 U.S. 152 (2000), the Court unanimously refused to extend *Faretta* to self-representation on appeal. *Faretta*, the Court noted, relied on the structure of the Sixth Amendment, but since the Sixth Amendment does not apply once the case has gone beyond the trial stage, a right to self-representation on appeal would have to be based on due process. From the perspective afforded by due process, the Court was "entirely unpersuaded," in light of the "practices that prevail in the nation today," that the "risk of either disloyalty or suspicion of disloyalty [in representation] is of sufficient concern to conclude that a constitutional right of self-representation is a neces-

sary component of a fair appellate proceeding." Also, with defendant's position having shifted from that of an "accused" to a convicted defendant, the "autonomy interests" presented at this point are "less compelling" than in *Faretta.*

The Court also examined the history relied upon in *Faretta* and found it less than convincing and inapplicable to the appellate process. The historical practice cited by *Faretta*, as to self-representation at trial in the colonial and post-revolutionary periods, suffered from the limitation of its context; it "pertained to times when lawyers were scarce, often mistrusted, and not readily available to the average person accused of crime." In any event, it did not

Justice Blackmun, with whom The Chief Justice and Justice Rehnquist join, dissenting.

* * * I fear that the right to self-representation constitutionalized today frequently will cause procedural confusion without advancing any significant strategic interest of the defendant. [Although] the Court indicates that a *pro se* defendant necessarily waives any claim he might otherwise make of ineffective assistance of counsel, n. 46, the opinion leaves open a host of other procedural questions. Must every defendant be advised of his right to proceed *pro se?* If so, when must that notice be given? Since the right to assistance of counsel and the right to self-representation are mutually exclusive, how is the waiver of each right to be measured? If a defendant has elected to exercise his right to proceed *pro se,* does he still have a constitutional right to assistance of standby counsel? How soon in the criminal proceeding must a defendant decide between proceeding by counsel or *pro se?* Must he be allowed to switch in midtrial? May a violation of the right to self-representation ever be harmless error? Must the trial court treat the *pro se* defendant differently than it would professional counsel? I assume that many of these questions will be answered with finality in due course. Many of them, however, such as the standards of waiver and the treatment of the *pro se* defendant, will haunt the trial of every defendant who elects to exercise his right to self-representation. The procedural problems spawned by an absolute right to self-representation will far outweigh whatever tactical advantage the defendant may feel he has gained by electing to represent himself.

If there is any truth to the old proverb that "one who is his own lawyer has a fool for a client," the Court by its opinion today now bestows a *constitutional* right on one to make a fool of himself.[d]

carry over to the appellate process at that time, as "appellate review of any sort was 'limited' and 'rarely allowed'." Justice Kennedy, concurring, observed that he believed it "unnecessary to cast doubt upon the rationale of *Faretta*" to agree with the Court's ruling. Justice Breyer, also concurring, noted that "judges closer to the firing line has sometimes expressed dismay about the practical consequences of *Faretta*." However, he added, empirical research on whether the *Faretta* right "furthers or inhibits the Constitution's basic guarantee of fairness" was lacking, and "without some strong factual basis for believing *Faretta's* holding has proved counterproductive in practice, we are not in a position to reconsider the constitutional assumptions that underlie that case." Concurring in the judgment, Justice Scalia noted that he did not "share the apparent skepticism of today's opinion concerning *Faretta*," although he might have "rested the decision [there] upon the Due Process Clause rather than the Sixth Amendment." "I have no doubt," he noted, "that the Framers of our Constitution, who were suspicious enough of governmental power–including judicial power–that they insisted upon a citizen's right to be judged by an independent jury of private citizens, would not have found acceptable the compulsory assignment of counsel by the Government to plead a criminal defendant's case."

d. *McKaskle v. Wiggins,* 465 U.S. 168 (1984), the leading post-*Faretta* ruling of the Supreme Court, spoke to some of the issues

raised by Justice Blackmun, but most have been left to lower court rulings. *McKaskle* involved a defense challenge to the actions of a standby counsel appointed to assist the *pro se* defendant. The Court initially held that "a defendant's Sixth Amendment rights are not violated when a trial judge appoints standby counsel—even over the defendant's objection—to relieve the judge of the need to explain and enforce basic rules of courtroom protocol or to assist the defendant in overcoming routine obstacles that stand in way of defendant's achievement of his own clearly indicated goals." The counsel in *McKaskle,* however, had gone beyond "steer[ing] the defendant through the basic procedures of the trial"; he had engaged in arguably unsolicited participation on various substantive matters (although defendant conducted the major portion of the trial). The Court held that, under the circumstances of the case, the unsolicited participation that went beyond "routine clerical or procedural matters" would not be deemed to violate defendant's pro se right because (i) it did not interfere with defendant's own actions in such a way as to deprive him of "actual control over the case he chose to present to the jury" and (ii) it did not "destroy the jury's perception that the defendant [was] representing himself."

Commenting generally on the *pro se* right, *McKaskle* added that denial of the right could not be treated as a harmless error even though counsel subsequently gave defendant far better representation than he could have given himself. The Court noted: "Since the right of representation is a right that when exercised usually increases the likelihood of a trial outcome unfavorable to the defendant, its denial is not amenable to 'harmless error' analysis." Lower courts speaking to other issues cited by Justice Blackmun have generally held that (1) the defendant need not be advised of a right to proceed *pro se* unless he or she expresses an interest in doing so; (2) the trial court has broad discretion to deny a request to proceed *pro se* on administrative grounds if the request is first presented after the trial has started; (3) *Faretta* does not demand that the defendant be given a standby counsel and does not require the court to allow a "hybrid representation"; and (4) *pro se* defendants will be treated on appeal no differently than defendants with counsel as to objections that were not properly raised at trial, as the trial court has no special obligation to bend rules relating to the presentation of evidence or the raising of objections (and, in the usual instance, defendant could have relied upon the assistance of standby counsel on those matters).

Chapter 18

THE TRIAL

As was noted in Chapter One, the trial has traditionally been viewed as the capstone of the criminal justice, the "crown jewel" that reflects most of the basic elements of the process. It is not surprising, therefore, that many of the Bill of Rights guarantees relating to the criminal justice process refer specifically to the trial. Materials in previous chapters explore the Supreme Court's interpretation of several of those guarantees—the rights to a speedy trial (Ch. 12), to a trial by an impartial jury (Ch. 15), to a public trial (discussed at various points in Ch. 16 in comparing the public's right of access), and to the assistance of counsel (Chs. 5 and 17). The cases in this chapter deal with still other trial guarantees.

SECTION 1: PRESENCE OF THE DEFENDANT

Cases defining the defendant's constitutional "right of presence" tend to focus on two different issues. First, the constitutional right of presence, although "rooted to large extent in the confrontation clause of the Sixth Amendment," also has due process component. *United States v. Gagnon,* 470 U.S. 522 (1985). Accordingly, the right is not restricted to those parts of the trial in which the defendant is "actually confronting witnesses or evidence against him," and the issue is presented as to what other aspects of the trial itself, or proceedings related to the trial, fall within the scope of the defendant's right. The critical question here is whether defendant's presence at the particular proceeding "has a relation, reasonably substantial to the fullness of his opportunity to defend against the charge." *Gagnon.* As to proceedings not directly a part of the trial, the Court tends to focus on the context of the particular case in answering that question. See e.g., *Kentucky v. Stincer,* 482 U.S. 730 (1987) (judge's in-chambers examination of two young victims of alleged sex offense, to determine solely whether they were competent to testify, did not constitutionally require defendant's presence where defense counsel participated and further questions concerning competency could be raised at trial with defendant present).

A second major issue presented in defining the defendant's right of presence is what conditions permissibly can be attached to that right, so that a defense failure to comply with those conditions results in a loss of the right. *Illinois v. Allen,* the single case in section one, deals with this issue. Prior to *Allen,* in *Taylor v. United States,* 414 U.S. 17 (1973), the Court had held that a defendant cannot complain if he voluntarily absents himself during trial and the court continues the trial through to verdict. The Court has not had occasion to rule on the state's authority to proceed to trial in defendant's absence where the defendant was not even present at the commencement of the trial.

SECTION 2: THE RIGHTS OF CONFRONTATION AND COMPULSORY PROCESS

The Supreme Court has characterized its cases dealing with the Sixth Amendment's confrontation clause as "fall[ing] into two broad, albeit not exclusive categories: 'cases involving the admission of out-of-court statements and cases involving restrictions imposed by law or by the trial court on the scope of cross-examination.'" *Kentucky v. Stincer,* 482 U.S. 730 (1987). The first two cases in this section fall within the first grouping while the third case falls within the second grouping.

The cases in the first grouping generally have involved the constitutionality of admitting into evidence "hearsay"—that is, a statement that was made out of court and is being offered in evidence to prove the truth of the facts asserted in that statement. Under the rules of evidence currently applied in the different states, as at common law, most hearsay testimony is not admissible in evidence, but there are exceptions. Certain types of out-of-court statements are classified as not truly hearsay (as measured by the primary functions of the hearsay ban) and others are viewed as within special exceptions to the ban that support their admissibility. Confrontation clause concerns obviously arise when a state, under one rationale or another, allows a prosecution witness to testify to a hearsay statement made by a third party; here only the witness is before the defendant and subject to cross-examination, not the third party (the hearsay declarant) whose statement is being used to prove the truth of its contents. However, the confrontation clause has never been read literally to exclude from evidence all out-of-court statements of non-witnesses. The clause has been interpreted, in light of its common law background and the functions served by confrontation, to allow the admission of certain types of out-of-court statements that local evidentiary rules also accept.

The first case in this section, *Lilly v. Virginia,* raises some fundamental issues regarding the scope of the confrontation clause as it relates to hearsay. *Richardson v. Marsh,* the second case in this section, considers the related issue of the bearing of the confrontation clause on a joint trial in which the prosecution seeks to use a confession of one of the jointly tried codefendants. The issue presented in *Richardson* is of great practical significance. Few jurisdictions grant a defendant the right to trial separate from his codefendants. A jointly tried codefendant may request a severance based upon potential prejudice (e.g., a conflicting defense or strategy, or a risk of guilt by association), but such requests are only infrequently granted.

Davis v. Alaska, the third case, falls in the second grouping of confrontation clause cases—those cases concerned with the restriction of cross-examination opportunity by law or by trial court ruling. *Davis* should be read in light of *Pennsylvania v. Ritchie,* previously included in Chapter Thirteen on the duty to disclose. *Ritchie* not only discusses the scope of *Davis* but also speaks to the scope of the Sixth Amendment's guarantee of compulsory process. The Supreme Court has had very little to say about the Sixth Amendment's compulsory process clause. The leading case applying the clause, *Washington v. Texas,* 388 U.S. 14 (1967), struck down a state rule that the Court characterized as an "absurdity"—one that prohibited the defendant from introducing the testimony of an accomplice on his behalf but allowed the prosecution to put on the stand accomplices who would testify in its favor.

SECTION 3: THE DEFENDANT'S RIGHT TO REMAIN SILENT—OR TO TESTIFY

The Fifth Amendment privilege against self-incrimination has been examined previously in the context of the investigatory process (see Chs. 6, 7, and 8) and pretrial disclosure (see Ch. 13). In its application to the defendant at trial, the privilege has special meaning, for it confers on defendant a right not simply to refuse to respond to questioning, but to refuse to be placed on the stand where he can be subjected to such questioning. This right not to be called to testify—commonly described as the defendant's "right of silence"—is a basic element of an accusatorial system of justice that requires the government to make its case through its own evidence and allows the accused "to remain inactive and secure, until the prosecution has taken up its burden and produced evidence and effected persuasion." *Taylor v. Kentucky,* 436 U.S. 478 (1978). *Griffin v. California,* the first case in this section, is the leading case on the reach of this right of silence. The Court there considers whether the Fifth Amendment requires that there be no adverse comment, by trial judge or prosecutor, on the defendant's exercise of that right.

The second case in this section, *Rock v. Arkansas,* marks the Court's recognition of a constitutional right of the defendant to take the stand and testify, a practice that was not allowed at the time of the adoption of the Constitution. *Rock* also considers the appropriate scope of state authority to impose evidentiary limitations that restrict the defendant's exercise of this right to testify.

SECTION 4: DUE PROCESS REQUIREMENTS

The Supreme Court has long held that due process can be the source of trial rights not found in the more specific guarantees of the Sixth and Fifth Amendments. Due process, for example, imposes upon the state the obligation to establish guilt beyond a reasonable doubt. *In re Winship,* 397 U.S. 358 (1970). From that requirement flows a series of related constitutional prerequisites. *Taylor v. Kentucky* considers whether one of these is a jury instruction on the "presumption of innocence."

Constitutional challenges to alleged prosecutorial misconduct at trial also are raised under the "fundamental fairness" standard of due process. Building upon the prosecutor's role as a representative of the state "whose interest in criminal prosecution is not that it shall win the case, but that justice shall be done," *Berger v. United States,* 295 U.S. 78 (1935), the Court has recognized prosecutorial obligations to correct the material testimony of its witnesses known to be false and to disclose material exculpatory evidence within its control. See *United States v. Bagley,* Ch. 13. The second case in this section, *Darden v. Wainwright,* considers the application of the due process clause to the misconduct of the prosecutor in presenting the state's closing argument.

The last case in this section, *Herrera v. Collins,* raises the question as to whether the constitution requires anything more than a fair adjudication of guilt. Once the defendant has been found guilty in a trial that accords with all constitutional guarantees, can the State grant finality to that determination and impose criminal punishment, notwithstanding a postverdict showing of actual innocence based on newly discovered evidence? While *Herrara* does not provide a definitive answer to this question, and presents the question in the special context of capital punishment, the several opinions there are helpful in bringing to the forefront the various concerns beyond protection against erroneous convictions that enter into the constitutional regulation of the criminal justice process.

SECTION 1. PRESENCE OF THE DEFENDANT
ILLINOIS v. ALLEN
397 U.S. 337, 90 S.Ct. 1057, 25 L.Ed.2d 353 (1970).

JUSTICE BLACK delivered the opinion of the Court.

[Allen was convicted by an Illinois jury of armed robbery and was sentenced to a term of 10 to 30 years. Before trial, the judge acceded to Allen's wish to conduct his own defense, although court-appointed counsel would "sit in and protect the record." During the *voir dire* examination, Allen "started to argue with the judge in a most abusive and disrespectful manner" when the judge directed him to confine his questioning to matters relating to the prospective juror's qualifications. The judge then asked appointed counsel to proceed with the examination, upon which Allen continued to talk and concluded his remarks by saying to the judge, "When I go out for lunchtime, you're going to be a corpse here." The judge then warned Allen that he would be removed from the courtroom if there was another outbreak of that sort. Allen continued to talk back, saying, "There's not going to be no trial, either. I'm going to sit here and you're going to talk and you can bring your shackles out and straight jacket and put them on me and tape my mouth, but it will do no good because there's not going to be no trial." After more abusive remarks, the judge ordered the trial to proceed in Allen's absence. After a noon recess, the judge permitted Allen to return to the courtroom with the warning that he could remain only so long as he behaved himself. Shortly thereafter, Allen spoke out again, saying, "There is going to be no proceeding. I'm going to start talking all through the trial. There's not going to be no trial like this." The judge again ordered Allen removed, and he remained out of the courtroom during the presentation of the State's case-in-chief except when brought in for purposes of identification. Thereafter, Allen was permitted to return to the courtroom upon his promise to conduct himself properly, and he remained for the rest of the trial, principally his defense, which was conducted by his appointed counsel. Allen's conviction was affirmed by the Supreme Court of Illinois, and on federal habeas corpus the district court found no constitutional violation and declined to issue the writ. The court of appeals reversed.]

The Court of Appeals felt that the defendant's Sixth Amendment right to be present at his own trial was so "absolute" that, no matter how unruly or disruptive the defendant's conduct might be, he could never be held to have lost that right so long as he continued to insist upon it, as Allen clearly did. * * * We cannot agree that the Sixth Amendment, the cases upon which the Court of Appeals relied, or any other cases of this Court so handicap a trial judge in conducting a criminal trial. * * * We accept instead the statement of Justice Cardozo who, speaking for the Court in *Snyder v. Massachusetts,* 291 U.S. 97, 106 (1934), said: "No doubt the privilege [of personally confronting witnesses] may be lost by consent or at times even by misconduct." Although mindful that courts must indulge every reasonable presumption against the loss of constitutional rights, we explicitly hold today that a defendant can lose his right to be present at trial if, after he has been warned by the judge that he will be removed if he continues his disruptive behavior, he nevertheless insists on conducting himself in a manner so disorderly, disruptive, and disrespectful of the court that his trial cannot be carried on with him in the courtroom. Once lost, the right to be present can, of course, be reclaimed as soon as the defendant is willing to conduct himself consistently with the decorum and respect inherent in the concept of courts and judicial proceedings.

It is essential to the proper administration of criminal justice that dignity, order, and decorum be the hallmarks of all court proceedings in our country. The flagrant disregard in the courtroom of elementary standards of proper conduct should not and cannot be tolerated. We believe trial judges confronted with disruptive, contumacious, stubbornly defiant defendants must be given sufficient discretion to meet the circumstances of each case. No one formula for maintaining the appropriate courtroom atmosphere will be best in all situations. We think there are at least three constitutionally permissible ways for a trial judge to handle an obstreperous defendant like Allen: (1) bind and gag him, thereby keeping him present; (2) cite him for contempt; (3) take him out of the courtroom until he promises to conduct himself properly.

Trying a defendant for a crime while he sits bound and gagged before the judge and jury would to an extent comply with that part of the Sixth Amendment's purposes that accords the defendant an opportunity to confront the witnesses at the trial. But even to contemplate such a technique, much less see it, arouses a feeling that no person should be tried while shackled and gagged except as a last resort. Not only is it possible that the sight of shackles and gags might have a significant effect on the jury's feelings about the defendant, but the use of this technique is itself something of an affront to the very dignity and decorum of judicial proceedings that the judge is seeking to uphold. Moreover, one of the defendant's primary advantages of being present at the trial, his ability to communicate with his counsel, is greatly reduced when the defendant is in a condition of total physical restraint. It is in part because of these inherent disadvantages and limitations in this method of dealing with disorderly defendants that we decline to hold with the Court of Appeals that a defendant cannot under any possible circumstances be deprived of his right to be present at trial. However, in some situations which we need not attempt to foresee, binding and gagging might possibly be the fairest and most reasonable way to handle a defendant who acts as Allen did here.

In a footnote the Court of Appeals suggested the possible availability of contempt of court as a remedy to make Allen behave in his robbery trial, and it is true that citing or threatening to cite a contumacious defendant for criminal contempt might in itself be sufficient to make a defendant stop interrupting a trial. If so, the problem would be solved easily, and the defendant could remain in the courtroom. Of course, if the defendant is determined to prevent *any* trial, then a court in attempting to try the defendant for contempt is still confronted with the identical dilemma that the Illinois court faced in this case. And criminal contempt has obvious limitations as a sanction when the defendant is charged with a crime so serious that a very severe sentence such as death or life imprisonment is likely to be imposed. In such a case the defendant might not be affected by a mere contempt sentence when he ultimately faces a far more serious sanction. Nevertheless, the contempt remedy should be borne in mind by a judge in the circumstances of this case.

Another aspect of the contempt remedy is the judge's power, when exercised consistently with state and federal law, to imprison an unruly defendant such as Allen for civil contempt and discontinue the trial until such time as the defendant promises to behave himself. This procedure is consistent with the defendant's right to be present at trial, and yet it avoids the serious shortcomings of the use of shackles and gags. It must be recognized, however, that a defendant might conceivably, as a matter of calculated strategy, elect to spend a prolonged period in confinement for contempt in the hope that adverse witnesses might be unavailable after a lapse of time. A court must guard against allowing a defendant to profit from his own wrong in this way.

The trial court in this case decided under the circumstances to remove the defendant from the courtroom and to continue his trial in his absence until and unless he promised to conduct himself in a manner befitting an American courtroom. As we said earlier, we find nothing unconstitutional about this procedure. Allen's behavior was clearly of such an extreme and aggravated nature as to justify either his removal from the courtroom or his total physical restraint. Prior to his removal he was repeatedly warned by the trial judge that he would be removed from the courtroom if he persisted in his unruly conduct, and, as Judge Hastings [of the Court of Appeals] observed in his dissenting opinion, the record demonstrates that Allen would not have been at all dissuaded by the trial judge's use of his criminal contempt powers. Allen was constantly informed that he could return to the trial when he would agree to conduct himself in an orderly manner. Under these circumstances we hold that Allen lost his right guaranteed by the Sixth and Fourteenth Amendments to be present throughout his trial. * * *

JUSTICE BRENNAN, concurring. * * *

I would add only that when a defendant is excluded from his trial, the court should make reasonable efforts to enable him to communicate with his attorney and, if possible, to keep apprised of the progress of his trial. Once the court has removed the contumacious defendant, it is not weakness to mitigate the disadvantages of his expulsion as far as technologically possible in the circumstances.

JUSTICE DOUGLAS. * * *

Our real problems of this type lie not with this case but with other kinds of trials. *First* are the political trials. They frequently recur in our history and insofar as they take place in federal courts we have broad supervisory powers over them. * * * In Anglo–American law, great injustices have at times been done to unpopular minorities by judges, as well as by prosecutors. I refer to London in 1670 when William Penn, the gentle Quaker, was tried for causing a riot when all that he did was to preach a sermon on Grace Church Street * * *. The panel of judges who tried William Penn were sincere, law-and-order men of their day. Though Penn was acquitted by the jury, he was jailed by the court for his contemptuous conduct [which consisted of repeatedly seeking to determine from the court "by what law it is you prosecute me, and upon what law you ground my indictment"]. Would we tolerate removal of a defendant from the courtroom during a trial because he was insisting on his constitutional rights, albeit vociferously, no matter how obnoxious his philosophy might have been to the bench that tried him? * * *

Second are trials used by minorities to destroy the existing constitutional system and bring on repressive measures. Radicals on the left historically have used those tactics to incite the extreme right with the calculated design of fostering a regime of repression from which the radicals on the left hope to emerge as the ultimate victor. The left in that role is the provocateur. The Constitution was not designed as an instrument for that form of rough-and-tumble contest. The social compact has room for tolerance, patience, and restraint, but not for sabotage and violence. Trials involving that spectacle strike at the very heart of constitutional government.

I would not try to provide in this case the guidelines for those two strikingly different types of cases. The case presented here is the classical criminal case without any political or subversive overtones. * * *

SECTION 2. THE RIGHTS OF CONFRONTATION AND COMPULSORY PROCESS

LILLY v. VIRGINIA

527 U.S. 116, 119 S.Ct. 1887, 144 L.Ed.2d 117 (1999).

JUSTICE STEVENS announced the judgment of the Court and delivered the opinion of the Court with respect to Parts I, II, and VI, and an opinion with respect to Parts III, IV, and V, in which JUSTICE SOUTER, JUSTICE GINSBURG, and JUSTICE BREYER join.

The question presented in this case is whether the accused's Sixth Amendment right "to be confronted with the witnesses against him" was violated by admitting into evidence at his trial a nontestifying accomplice's entire confession that contained some statements against the accomplice's penal interest and others that inculpated the accused.

I

On December 4, 1995, three men—Benjamin Lee Lilly (petitioner), his brother Mark, and Mark's roommate, Gary Wayne Barker—broke into a home and stole nine bottles of liquor, three loaded guns, and a safe. The next day, the men drank the stolen liquor, robbed a small country store, and shot at geese with their stolen weapons. After their car broke down, they abducted Alex DeFilippis and used his vehicle to drive to a deserted location. One of them shot and killed DeFilippis. The three men then committed two more robberies before they were apprehended by the police late in the evening of December 5.

After taking them into custody, the police questioned each of the three men separately. Petitioner did not mention the murder to the police and stated that the other two men had forced him to participate in the robberies. Petitioner's brother Mark and Barker told the police somewhat different accounts of the crimes, but both maintained that petitioner masterminded the robberies and was the one who had killed DeFilippis. * * * During both [of his] interviews [taped by the police], Mark continually emphasized how drunk he had been during the entire spree. When asked about his participation in the string of crimes, Mark admitted that he stole liquor during the initial burglary and that he stole a 12–pack of beer during the robbery of the liquor store. Mark also conceded that he had handled a gun earlier that day and that he was present during the more serious thefts and the homicide. The police told Mark that he would be charged with armed robbery and that, unless he broke "family ties," petitioner "may be dragging you right into a life sentence." Mark acknowledged that he would be sent away to the penitentiary. He claimed, however, that while he had primarily been drinking, petitioner and Barker had "got some guns or something" during the initial burglary. Mark said that Barker had pulled a gun in one of the robberies. He further insisted that petitioner had instigated the carjacking and that he (Mark) "didn't have nothing to do with the shooting" of DeFilippis. In a brief portion of one of his statements, Mark stated that petitioner was the one who shot DeFilippis.

The Commonwealth of Virginia charged petitioner with several offenses, including the murder of DeFilippis, and tried him separately. At trial, the Commonwealth called Mark as a witness, but he invoked his Fifth Amendment privilege against self-incrimination. The Commonwealth therefore offered to introduce into evidence the statements Mark made to the police after his arrest, arguing that they were admissible as declarations of an unavailable witness against penal interest. Petitioner objected on the ground that the statements were not actually against Mark's penal interest because they shifted responsibility for the crimes to Barker and to petitioner, and that their admission would violate the Sixth Amendment's Confrontation Clause. The trial judge overruled the objection and admitted the tape recordings and written transcripts of the statements in their entirety. The jury found petitioner guilty of robbery, abduction, carjacking, possession of a firearm by a felon, and four charges of illegal use of a firearm, for which offenses he received consecutive prison sentences of two life terms plus 27 years. The jury also convicted petitioner of capital murder and recommended a sentence of death, which the court imposed.

The Supreme Court of Virginia affirmed petitioner's convictions and sentences. As is relevant here, the court first concluded that Mark's statements were declarations of an unavailable witness against penal interest; that the statements' reliability was established by other evidence; and, therefore, that they fell within an exception to the Virginia hearsay rule. The court then turned to petitioner's Confrontation Clause challenge. It began by relying on our opinion in *White v. Illinois*, 502 U.S. 346, (1992), for the proposition that " '[w]here proffered hearsay has sufficient guarantees of reliability to come within a firmly rooted exception to the hearsay rule, the Confrontation Clause is satisfied.' " The Virginia court also remarked: "[A]dmissiblity into evidence of the statement against penal interest of an unavailable witness is a 'firmly rooted' exception to the hearsay rule in Virginia. * * * That Mark Lilly's statements were self-serving, in that they tended to shift principal responsibility to others or to offer claims of mitigating circumstances, goes to the weight the jury could assign to them and not to their admissibility."

II

As an initial matter, the Commonwealth asserts that we should decline to exercise jurisdiction over petitioner's claim because he did not fairly present his Confrontation Clause challenge to the Supreme Court of Virginia. We disagree. * * * [Petitioner's] arguments, particularly the reliance on our Confrontation Clause opinion in *Lee v. Illinois*, 476 U.S. 530 (1986), sufficed to raise in the Supreme Court of Virginia the constitutionality of admitting Mark's statements. Indeed, the court addressed petitioner's Confrontation Clause claim without mentioning any waiver problems.

III

In all criminal prosecutions, state as well as federal, the accused has a right, guaranteed by the Sixth and Fourteenth Amendments to the United States Constitution, "to be confronted with the witnesses against him." U.S. Const., Amdt. 6. * * * "The central concern of the Confrontation Clause is to ensure the reliability of the evidence against a criminal defendant by subjecting it to rigorous testing in the context of an adversary proceeding before the trier of fact." *Maryland v. Craig*, 497 U.S. 836 (1990). When the government seeks to offer a declarant's out-of-court statements against the accused, and, as in this case, the declarant is unavailable, courts must decide whether the Clause permits the government to deny the accused his usual right to force the declarant "to submit to cross-examination, the 'greatest legal engine ever invented for the discovery of truth.' "

In our most recent case interpreting the Confrontation Clause, *White v. Illinois*, supra, we rejected the suggestion that the Clause should be narrowly construed to apply only to practices comparable to "a particular abuse common in

16th- and 17th-century England: prosecuting a defendant through the presentation of ex parte affidavits, without the affiants ever being produced at trial." * * *
Because that restrictive reading of the Clause's term "witnesses" would have
virtually eliminated the Clause's role in restricting the admission of hearsay
testimony, we considered it foreclosed by our prior cases. Instead, we adhered to
our general framework, summarized in *Ohio v. Roberts*, 448 U.S. 56 (1980), that
the veracity of hearsay statements is sufficiently dependable to allow the untested
admission of such statements against an accused when (1) "the evidence falls
within a firmly rooted hearsay exception" or (2) it contains "particularized
guarantees of trustworthiness" such that adversarial testing would be expected to
add little, if anything, to the statements' reliability. * * * Before turning to the
dual *Roberts* inquiries, however, we note that the statements taken from petitioner's brother in the early morning of December 6 were obviously obtained for the
purpose of creating evidence that would be useful at a future trial. The analogy to
the presentation of ex parte affidavits in the early English proceedings thus brings
the Confrontation Clause into play no matter how narrowly its gateway might be
read.

IV

The Supreme Court of Virginia held that the admission of Mark Lilly's
confession was constitutional primarily because, in its view, it was against Mark's
penal interest and because "the statement against penal interest of an unavailable
witness is a 'firmly rooted' exception to the hearsay rule in Virginia." We assume,
as we must, that Mark's statements were against his penal interest as a matter of
state law, but the question whether the statements fall within a firmly rooted
hearsay exception for Confrontation Clause purposes is a question of federal law.
Accordingly, it is appropriate to begin our analysis by examining the "firmly
rooted" doctrine and the roots of the "against penal interest" exception. We have
allowed the admission of statements falling within a firmly rooted hearsay
exception since the Court's recognition in *Mattox v. United States*, 156 U.S. 237
(1895), that the Framers of the Sixth Amendment "obviously intended to ...
respec[t]" certain unquestionable rules of evidence in drafting the Confrontation
Clause. * * * We now describe a hearsay exception as "firmly rooted" if, in light
of "longstanding judicial and legislative experience," it "rest[s] [on] such [a] solid
foundatio[n] that admission of virtually any evidence within [it] comports with the
'substance of the constitutional protection.' " *Roberts*. This standard is designed
to allow the introduction of statements falling within a category of hearsay whose
conditions have proven over time "to remove all temptation to falsehood, and to
enforce as strict an adherence to the truth as would the obligation of an oath" and
cross-examination at a trial. In *White*, for instance, we held that the hearsay
exception for spontaneous declarations is firmly rooted because it "is at least two
centuries old," currently "widely accepted among the States," and carries "substantial guarantees of ... trustworthiness ... [that] cannot be recaptured even by
later in-court testimony." Established practice, in short, must confirm that
statements falling within a category of hearsay inherently "carr[y] special guarantees of credibility" essentially equivalent to, or greater than, those produced by
the Constitution's preference for cross-examined trial testimony.

The "against penal interest" exception to the hearsay rule—unlike other
previously recognized firmly rooted exceptions—is not generally based on the
maxim that statements made without a motive to reflect on the legal consequences of one's statement, and in situations that are exceptionally conducive to
veracity, lack the dangers of inaccuracy that typically accompany hearsay. The
exception, rather, is founded on the broad assumption "that a person is unlikely

to fabricate a statement against his own interest at the time it is made." * * * We have previously noted that, due to the sweeping scope of the label, the simple categorization of a statement as a " 'declaration against penal interest' . . . defines too large a class for meaningful Confrontation Clause analysis." In criminal trials, statements against penal interest are offered into evidence in three principal situations: (1) as voluntary admissions against the declarant; (2) as exculpatory evidence offered by a defendant who claims that the declarant committed, or was involved in, the offense; and (3) as evidence offered by the prosecution to establish the guilt of an alleged accomplice of the declarant. It is useful to consider the three categories and their roots separately.

Statements in the first category—voluntary admissions of the declarant—are routinely offered into evidence against the maker of the statement and carry a distinguished heritage confirming their admissibility when so used. * * * Thus, assuming that Mark Lilly's statements were taken in conformance with constitutional prerequisites, they would unquestionably be admissible against him if he were on trial for stealing alcoholic beverages. If Mark were a codefendant in a joint trial, however, even the use of his confession to prove his guilt might have an adverse impact on the rights of his accomplices. When dealing with admissions against penal interest, we have taken great care to separate using admissions against the declarant (the first category above) from using them against other criminal defendants (the third category). * * * Despite frequent disagreement over matters such as the adequacy of the trial judge's instructions, or the sufficiency of the redaction of ambiguous references to the declarant's accomplice, we have consistently either stated or assumed that the mere fact that one accomplice's confession qualified as a statement against his penal interest did not justify its use as evidence against another person. * * * See *Richardson v. Marsh* [infra this section] and [the *Bruton* and *Gray* opinions discussed in *Richardson*]. * * *

The second category of statements against penal interest encompasses those offered as exculpatory evidence by a defendant who claims that it was the maker of the statement, rather than he, who committed (or was involved in) the crime in question. In this context, our Court, over the dissent of Justice Holmes, originally followed the 19th-century English rule that categorically refused to recognize any "against penal interest" exception to the hearsay rule, holding instead that under federal law only hearsay statements against pecuniary (and perhaps proprietary) interest were sufficiently reliable to warrant their admission at the trial of someone other than the declarant. * * * *Donnelly v. United States*, 228 U.S. 243 (1913). Indeed, most States adhered to this approach well into the latter half of the 20th century. * * * As time passed, however, the precise *Donnelly* rule, which barred the admission of other persons' confessions that exculpated the accused, became the subject of increasing criticism. Professor Wigmore, for example, remarked years after *Donnelly* that: "The only practical consequences of this unreasoning limitation are shocking to the sense of justice; for, in its commonest application, it requires, in a criminal trial, the rejection of a confession, however well authenticated, of a person deceased or insane or fled from the jurisdiction (and therefore quite unavailable) who has avowed himself to be the true culprit. * * * "

Finally, in 1973, this Court endorsed the more enlightened view in *Chambers v. Mississippi*, 410 U.S. 284 (1973), holding that the Due Process Clause affords criminal defendants the right to introduce into evidence third parties' declarations against penal interest—their confessions—when the circumstances surrounding the statements "provid[e] considerable assurance of their reliability." Not surprisingly, most States have now amended their hearsay rules to allow the admission of such statements under against-penal-interest exceptions. But because hearsay statements of this sort are, by definition, offered by the accused, the admission of such statements does not implicate Confrontation Clause concerns. Thus, there is no need to decide whether the reliability of such statements is so inherently dependable that they would constitute a firmly rooted hearsay exception.

The third category includes cases, like the one before us today, in which the government seeks to introduce "a confession by an accomplice which incriminates a criminal defendant." The practice of admitting statements in this category under an exception to the hearsay rule—to the extent that such a practice exists in certain jurisdictions—is, unlike the first category or even the second, of quite recent vintage. This category also typically includes statements that, when offered in the absence of the declarant, function similarly to those used in the ancient ex parte affidavit system.

Most important, this third category of hearsay encompasses statements that are inherently unreliable. Typical of the groundswell of scholarly and judicial criticism that culminated in the Chambers decision, Wigmore's treatise still expressly distinguishes accomplices' confessions that inculpate themselves and the accused as beyond a proper understanding of the against-penal-interest exception because an accomplice often has a considerable interest in "confessing and betraying his cocriminals." Consistent with this scholarship and the assumption that underlies the analysis in our *Bruton* line of cases, we have over the years "spoken with one voice in declaring presumptively unreliable accomplices' confessions that incriminate defendants." * * *

It is clear that our cases consistently have viewed an accomplice's statements that shift or spread the blame to a criminal defendant as falling outside the realm of those "hearsay exception[s] [that are] so trustworthy that adversarial testing can be expected to add little to [the statements'] reliability." This view is also reflected in several States' hearsay law. Indeed, prior to 1995, it appears that even Virginia rarely allowed statements against the penal interest of the declarant to be used at criminal trials. That Virginia relaxed that portion of its hearsay law when it decided *Chandler v. Commonwealth*, 249 Va. 270, 455 S.E.2d 219 (1995), and that it later apparently concluded that all statements against penal interest fall within "a 'firmly rooted' exception to the hearsay rule in Virginia," is of no consequence. The decisive fact, which we make explicit today, is that accomplices' confessions that inculpate a criminal defendant are not within a firmly rooted exception to the hearsay rule as that concept has been defined in our Confrontation Clause jurisprudence.

V

Aside from its conclusion that Mark's statements were admissible under a firmly rooted hearsay exception, the Supreme Court of Virginia also affirmed the trial court's holding that the statements were "reliabl[e] ... in the context of the facts and circumstances under which [they were] given" because (i) "Mark Lilly was cognizant of the import of his statements and that he was implicating himself as a participant in numerous crimes" and (ii) "[e]lements of [his] statements were independently corroborated" by other evidence offered at trial. * * * The Commonwealth contends that we should defer to this "fact-intensive" determination. It further argues that these two indicia of reliability, coupled with the facts that the police read Mark his *Miranda* rights and did not promise him leniency in exchange for his statements, demonstrate that the circumstances surrounding his statements bore "particularized guarantees of trustworthiness," sufficient to satisfy the Confrontation Clause's residual admissibility test.[6]

The residual "trustworthiness" test credits the axiom that a rigid application of the Clause's standard for admissibility might in an exceptional case exclude a statement of an unavailable witness that is incontestably probative, competent, and reliable, yet nonetheless outside of any firmly rooted hearsay exception. When a court can be confident—as in the context of hearsay falling within a firmly rooted exception—that "the declarant's truthfulness is so clear from the surrounding circumstances that the test of cross-examination would be of marginal utility," the Sixth Amendment's residual "trustworthiness" test allows the admission of the declarant's statements.

Nothing in our prior opinions, however, suggests that appellate courts should defer to lower courts' determinations regarding whether a hearsay statement has particularized guarantees of trustworthiness. To the contrary, those opinions indicate that we have assumed, as with other fact-intensive, mixed questions of constitutional law, that "independent review is ... necessary ... to maintain control of, and to clarify, the legal principles" governing the factual circumstances necessary to satisfy the protections of the Bill of Rights. * * * We, of course, accept the Virginia courts' determination that Mark's statements were reliable for purposes of state hearsay law, and, as should any appellate court, we review the presence or absence of historical facts for clear error. But the surrounding circumstances relevant to a Sixth Amendment admissibility determination do not include the declarant's in-court demeanor (otherwise the declarant would be testifying) or any other factor uniquely suited to the province of trial courts. For these reasons, when deciding whether the admission of a declarant's out-of-court statements violates the Confrontation Clause, courts should independently review whether the government's proffered guarantees of trustworthiness satisfy the demands of the Clause.

The Commonwealth correctly notes that "the presumption of unreliability that attaches to codefendants' confessions ... may be rebutted." *Lee.* We have held, in fact, that any inherent unreliability that accompanies co-conspirator statements made during the course and in furtherance of the conspiracy is per se rebutted by the circumstances giving rise to the long history of admitting such statements. *See Bourjaily v. United States,* 483 U.S. 171 (1987). Nonetheless, the historical underpinnings of the Confrontation Clause and the sweep of our prior confrontation cases offer one cogent reminder: It is highly unlikely that the presumptive unreliability that attaches to accomplices' confessions that shift or spread blame can be effectively rebutted when the statements are given under conditions that implicate the core concerns of the old ex parte affidavit practice—that is, when the government is involved in the statements' production, and when the statements describe past events and have not been subjected to adversarial testing.

Applying these principles, the Commonwealth's asserted guarantees of trustworthiness fail to convince us that Mark's confession was sufficiently reliable as to be admissible without allowing petitioner to cross-examine him. That other

---

6. Although The Chief Justice contends that we should remand this issue to the Supreme Court of Virginia, it would be inappropriate to do so because we granted certiorari on this issue, and the parties have fully briefed and argued the issue. The "facts and circumstances" formula, recited above, that the Virginia courts already employed in reaching their reliability holdings is virtually identical to the *Roberts* "particularized guarantees" test, which turns as well on the "surrounding circumstances" of the statements. Furthermore, as will become clear, the Commonwealth fails to point to any fact regarding this issue that the Supreme Court of Virginia did not explicitly consider and that requires serious analysis.

evidence at trial corroborated portions of Mark's statements is irrelevant. We have squarely rejected the notion that "evidence corroborating the truth of a hearsay statement may properly support a finding that the statement bears 'particularized guarantees of trustworthiness.' " * * * *In Idaho v. Wright*, 497 U.S. 805 (1990), we concluded that the admission of hearsay statements by a child declarant violated the Confrontation Clause even though the statements were admissible under an exception to the hearsay rule recognized in Idaho, and even though they were corroborated by other evidence. We recognized that it was theoretically possible for such statements to possess " 'particularized guarantees of trustworthiness' " that would justify their admissibility, but we refused to allow the State to "bootstrap on" the trustworthiness of other evidence. "To be admissible under the Confrontation Clause," we held, "hearsay evidence used to convict a defendant must possess indicia of reliability by virtue of its inherent trustworthiness, not by reference to other evidence at trial."

Nor did the police's informing Mark of his *Miranda* rights render the circumstances surrounding his statements significantly more trustworthy. We noted in rejecting a similar argument in *Lee* that a finding that a confession was "voluntary for Fifth Amendment purposes . . . does not bear on the question of whether the confession was also free from any desire, motive, or impulse [the declarant] may have had either to mitigate the appearance of his own culpability by spreading the blame or to overstate [the defendant's] involvement" in the crimes at issue. By the same token, we believe that a suspect's consciousness of his *Miranda* rights has little, if any, bearing on the likelihood of truthfulness of his statements. When a suspect is in custody for his obvious involvement in serious crimes, his knowledge that anything he says may be used against him militates against depending on his veracity.

The Commonwealth's next proffered basis for reliability—that Mark knew he was exposing himself to criminal liability—merely restates the fact that portions of his statements were technically against penal interest. And as we have explained, such statements are suspect insofar as they inculpate other persons. * * * Similarly, the absence of an express promise of leniency to Mark does not enhance his statements' reliability to the level necessary for their untested admission. The police need not tell a person who is in custody that his statements may gain him leniency in order for the suspect to surmise that speaking up, and particularly placing blame on his cohorts, may inure to his advantage.

It is abundantly clear that neither the words that Mark spoke nor the setting in which he was questioned provides any basis for concluding that his comments regarding petitioner's guilt were so reliable that there was no need to subject them to adversarial testing in a trial setting. Mark was in custody for his involvement in, and knowledge of, serious crimes and made his statements under the supervision of governmental authorities. He was primarily responding to the officers' leading questions, which were asked without any contemporaneous cross-examination by adverse parties. Thus, Mark had a natural motive to attempt to exculpate himself as much as possible. * * * Mark also was obviously still under the influence of alcohol. Each of these factors militates against finding that his statements were so inherently reliable that cross-examination would have been superfluous.

VI

The admission of the untested confession of Mark Lilly violated petitioner's Confrontation Clause rights. Adhering to our general custom of allowing state courts initially to assess the effect of erroneously admitted evidence in light of substantive state criminal law, we leave it to the Virginia courts to consider in the first instance whether this Sixth Amendment error was "harmless beyond a reasonable doubt." *Chapman v. California* [Ch. 6, fn. a]. Accordingly, the judgment of the Supreme Court of Virginia is reversed, and the case is remanded for further proceedings not inconsistent with this opinion.

JUSTICE BREYER, concurring.

As currently interpreted, the Confrontation Clause generally forbids the introduction of hearsay into a trial unless the evidence "falls within a firmly rooted hearsay exception" or otherwise possesses "particularized guarantees of trustworthiness." *Ohio v. Roberts.* Amici in this case, citing opinions of Justices of this Court and the work of scholars, have argued that we should reexamine the way in which our cases have connected the Confrontation Clause and the hearsay rule. * * * The Court's effort to tie the Clause so directly to the hearsay rule is of fairly recent vintage, while the Confrontation Clause itself has ancient origins that predate the hearsay rule. * * * The right of an accused to meet his accusers face-to-face is mentioned in, among other things, the Bible, Shakespeare, and 16th and 17th century British statutes, cases, and treatises. * * * As traditionally understood, the right was designed to prevent, for example, the kind of abuse that permitted the Crown to convict Sir Walter Raleigh of treason on the basis of the out-of-court confession of Lord Cobham, a co-conspirator. * * * Viewed in light of its traditional purposes, the current, hearsay-based Confrontation Clause test, amici argue, is both too narrow and too broad. The test is arguably too narrow insofar as it authorizes the admission of out-of-court statements prepared as testimony for a trial when such statements happen to fall within some well-recognized hearsay rule exception. For example, a deposition or videotaped confession sometimes could fall within the exception for vicarious admissions or, in The Chief Justice's view, the exception for statements against penal interest. * * * But why should a modern Lord Cobham's out-of-court confession become admissible simply because of a fortuity, such as the conspiracy having continued through the time of police questioning, thereby bringing the confession within the "well-established" exception for the vicarious admissions of a co-conspirator? * * * Or why should we, like Walter Raleigh's prosecutor, deny a plea to "let my Accuser come face to face," with words (now related to the penal interest exception) such as, "The law presumes, a man will not accuse himself to accuse another"? * * * At the same time, the current hearsay-based Confrontation Clause test is arguably too broad. It would make a constitutional issue out of the admission of any relevant hearsay statement, even if that hearsay statement is only tangentially related to the elements in dispute, or was made long before the crime occurred and without relation to the prospect of a future trial. It is not obvious that admission of a business record, which is hearsay because the business was not "regularly conducted," or admission of a scrawled note, "Mary called," dated many months before the crime, violates the defendant's basic constitutional right "to be confronted with the witnesses against him." Yet one cannot easily fit such evidence within a traditional hearsay exception. Nor can one fit it within this Court's special exception for hearsay with "particularized guarantees of trustworthiness"; and, in any event, it is debatable whether the Sixth Amendment principally protects "trustworthiness," rather than "confrontation." * * *

We need not reexamine the current connection between the Confrontation Clause and the hearsay rule in this case, however, because the statements at issue violate the Clause regardless. * * * I write separately to point out that the fact that we do not reevaluate the link in this case does not end the matter. It may leave the question open for another day.

JUSTICE SCALIA, concurring in part and concurring in the judgment.

During a custodial interrogation, Mark Lilly told police officers that petitioner committed the charged murder. The prosecution introduced a tape recording of these statements at trial without making Mark available for cross-examination. In my view, that is a paradigmatic Confrontation Clause violation. See *White v. Illinois* (Thomas, J.,, concurring in part and concurring in judgment) ("The federal constitutional right of confrontation extends to any witness who actually testifies at trial" and "extrajudicial statements only insofar as they are contained in formalized testimonial material, such as affidavits, depositions, prior testimony, or confessions"). Since the violation is clear, the case need be remanded only for a harmless-error determination. I therefore join Parts I, II, and VI of the Court's opinion and concur in the judgment.

JUSTICE THOMAS, concurring in part and concurring in the judgment.

I join Parts I and VI of the Court's opinion and concur in the judgment. Though I continue to adhere to my view that the Confrontation Clause "extends to any witness who actually testifies at trial" and "is implicated by extrajudicial statements only insofar as they are contained in formalized testimonial material, such as affidavits, depositions, prior testimony, or confessions," *White v. Illinois*, (opinion concurring in part and concurring in judgment), I agree with The Chief Justice that the Clause does not impose a "blanket ban on the government's use of accomplice statements that incriminate a defendant." Such an approach not only departs from an original understanding of the Confrontation Clause but also freezes our jurisprudence by making trial court decisions excluding such statements virtually unreviewable. I also agree with the Chief Justice that the lower courts did not "analyz[e] the confession under the second prong of the *Roberts* inquiry," and therefore see no reason for the plurality to address an issue upon which those courts did not pass.

CHIEF JUSTICE REHNQUIST, with whom JUSTICE O'CONNOR and JUSTICE KENNEDY join, concurring in the judgment.

The plurality today concludes that all accomplice confessions that inculpate a criminal defendant are not within a firmly rooted exception to the hearsay rule under *Ohio v. Roberts.* * * * It also concludes that appellate courts should independently review the government's proffered guarantees of trustworthiness under the second half of the *Roberts* inquiry. I disagree with both of these conclusions, but concur in the judgment reversing the decision of the Supreme Court of Virginia.* * *

The confession of the accomplice, Mark Lilly, covers 50 pages in the Joint Appendix, and the interviews themselves lasted about an hour. The statements of Mark Lilly which are against his penal interest—and would probably show him as an aider and abettor—are quite separate in time and place from other statements exculpating Mark and incriminating his brother, petitioner Benjamin Lilly, in the murder of Alexis DeFilippis. * * * Thus one is at a loss to know why so much of the plurality's opinion is devoted to whether a declaration against penal interest is a "firmly rooted exception" to the hearsay rule under *Ohio v. Roberts.* Certainly, we must accept the Virginia court's determination that Mark's statements as a whole were declarations against penal interest for purposes of the Commonwealth's hearsay rule. Simply labeling a confession a "declaration against penal interest," however, is insufficient for purposes of *Roberts,* as this exception "defines too large a class for meaningful Confrontation Clause analysis." The plurality tries its hand at systematizing this class, but most of its housecleaning is unwarranted and results in a complete ban on the government's use of accomplice confessions that inculpate a codefendant. Such a categorical holding has no place in this case because the relevant portions of Mark Lilly's confession were simply not "declarations against penal interest" as that term is understood in the law of evidence. * * * This case therefore does not raise the question whether the Confrontation Clause permits the admission of a genuinely self-inculpatory statement that also inculpates a codefendant, and our precedent does not compel the broad holding suggested by the plurality today.

Nor do I see any reason to do more than reverse the decision of the Supreme Court of Virginia and remand the case for the Commonwealth to demonstrate that Mark's confession bears "particularized guarantees of trustworthiness" under *Roberts*. The Supreme Court of Virginia held only that Mark Lilly's confession was admissible under a state law exception to its hearsay rules and then held that this exception was firmly rooted for Confrontation Clause purposes. Neither that court nor the trial court analyzed the confession under the second prong of the *Roberts* inquiry, and the discussion of reliability cited by the Court, pertained only to whether the confession should be admitted under state hearsay rules, not under the Confrontation Clause. Following our normal course, I see no reason for this Court to reach an issue upon which the lower courts did not pass.

The lack of any reviewable decision in this case makes especially troubling the plurality's conclusion that appellate courts must independently review a lower court's determination that a hearsay statement bears particularized guarantees of trustworthiness. Deciding whether a particular statement bears the proper indicia of reliability under our Confrontation Clause precedent "may be a mixed question of fact and law," but the mix weighs heavily on the "fact" side. We have said that "deferential review of mixed questions of law and fact is warranted when it appears that the district court is 'better positioned' than the appellate court to decide the issue in question or that probing appellate scrutiny will not contribute to the clarity of legal doctrine." These factors counsel in favor of deference to trial judges who undertake the second prong of the *Roberts* inquiry. They are better able to evaluate whether a particular statement given in a particular setting is sufficiently reliable that cross-examination would add little to its trustworthiness. Admittedly, this inquiry does not require credibility determinations, but we have already held that deference to district courts does not depend on the need for credibility determinations. * * * It is difficult to apply any standard in this case because none of the courts below conducted the second part of the *Roberts* inquiry. I would therefore remand this case to the Supreme Court of Virginia to carry out the inquiry, and, if any error is found, to determine whether that error is harmless.

RICHARDSON v. MARSH

481 U.S. 200, 107 S.Ct. 1702, 95 L.Ed.2d 176 (1987).

JUSTICE SCALIA delivered the opinion of the Court.

In *Bruton v. United States,* 391 U.S. 123 (1968), we held that a defendant is deprived of his rights under the Confrontation Clause when his nontestifying codefendant's confession naming him as a participant in the crime is introduced at their joint trial, even if the jury is instructed to consider that confession only against the codefendant. Today we consider whether *Bruton* requires the same result when the codefendant's confession is redacted to omit any reference to the defendant, but the defendant is nonetheless linked to the confession by evidence properly admitted against him at trial.

Respondent Clarissa Marsh, Benjamin Williams, and Kareem Martin were charged with assaulting Cynthia Knighton and murdering her 4–year–old son, Koran, and her aunt, Ollie Scott. Respondent and Williams were tried jointly, over her objection. (Martin was a fugitive at the time of trial). At the trial, Knighton testified as follows: On the evening of October 29, 1978, she and her son were at Scott's home when respondent and her boyfriend Martin visited. After a brief conversation in the living room, respondent announced that she had come to "pick up something" from Scott and rose from the couch. Martin then pulled out a gun, pointed it at Scott and the Knightons, and said that "someone had gotten killed and [Scott] knew something about it." Respondent immediately walked to the front door and peered out the peephole. The doorbell rang, respondent opened the door, and Williams walked in, carrying a gun. As Williams passed respondent, he asked, "Where's the money?" Martin forced Scott upstairs, and Williams went into the kitchen, leaving respondent alone with the Knightons. Knighton and her son attempted to flee, but respondent grabbed Knighton and held her until Williams returned. Williams ordered the Knightons to lie on the floor and then went upstairs to assist Martin. Respondent, again left alone with the Knightons, stood by the front door and occasionally peered out the peephole. A few minutes later, Martin, Williams, and Scott came down the stairs, and Martin handed a paper grocery bag to respondent. Martin and Williams then forced Scott and the Knightons into the basement, where Martin shot them. Only Cynthia Knighton survived.

In addition to Knighton's testimony, the State introduced (over respondent's objection) a confession given by Williams to the police shortly after his arrest. The confession was redacted to omit all reference to respondent—indeed, to omit all indication that *anyone* other than Martin and Williams participated in the crime.[1] The confession largely corroborated Knighton's account of the activities of persons other than respondent in the house. In addition, the confession described a conversation Williams had with Martin as they drove to the Scott home, during which, according to Williams, Martin said that he would have to kill

---

1. The redacted confession in its entirety read:

"On Sunday evening, October the 29th, 1978, at about 6:30 p.m., I was over to my girl friend's house at 237 Moss, Highland Park, when I received a phone call from a friend of mine named Kareem Martin. He said he had been looking for me and James Coleman, who I call Tom. He asked me if I wanted to go on a robbery with him. I said okay. Then he said he'd be by and pick me up. About 15 or 20 minutes later Kareem came by in his black Monte Carlo car. I got in the car and Kareem told me he was going to stick up this crib, told me the place was a numbers house. Kareem said there would be over $5,000 or $10,000 in the place. Kareem said he would have to take them out after the robbery. Kareem had a big silver gun. He gave me a long barrelled [sic] .22 revolver. We then drove over to this house and parked the car across the big street near the house. The plan was that I would wait in the car in front of the house and then I would move the car down across the big street because he didn't want anybody to see the car. Okay, Kareem went up to the house and went inside. A couple of minutes later I moved the car and went up to the house. As I entered, Kareem and this older lady were in the dining room, a little boy and

another younger woman were sitting on the couch in the front room. I pulled my pistol and told the younger woman and the little boy to lay on the floor. Kareem took the older lady upstairs. He had a pistol, also. I stayed downstairs with the two people on the floor. After Kareem took the lady upstairs I went upstairs and the lady was laying on the bed in the room to the left as you get up the stairs. The lady had already given us two bags full of money before we ever got upstairs. Kareem had thought she had more money and that's why we had went upstairs. Me and Kareem started searching the rooms but I didn't find any money. I came downstairs and then Kareem came down with the lady. I said, 'Let's go, let's go.' Kareem said no. Kareem then took the two ladies and little boy down the basement and that's when I left to go to the car. I went to the car and got in the back seat. A couple of minutes later Kareem came to the car and said he thinks the girl was still living because she was still moving and he didn't have any more bullets. He asked me how come I didn't go down the basement and I said I wasn't doing no shit like that. He then dropped me back off at my girl's house in Highland Park and I was supposed to get together with him today, get my share of the robbery after he had counted the money. That's all."

the victims after the robbery. At the time the confession was admitted, the jury was admonished not to use it in any way against respondent. Williams did not testify.

After the State rested, respondent took the stand. She testified that on October 29, 1978, she had lost money that Martin intended to use to buy drugs. Martin was upset, and suggested to respondent that she borrow money from Scott, with whom she had worked in the past. Martin and respondent picked up Williams and drove to Scott's house. During the drive, respondent, who was sitting in the back seat, "knew that [Martin and Williams] were talking" but could not hear the conversation because "the radio was on and the speaker was right in [her] ear." Martin and respondent were admitted into the home, and respondent had a short conversation with Scott, during which she asked for a loan. Martin then pulled a gun, and respondent walked to the door to see where the car was. When she saw Williams, she opened the door for him. Respondent testified that during the robbery she did not feel free to leave and was too scared to flee. She said that she did not know why she prevented the Knightons from escaping. She admitted taking the bag from Martin, but said that after Martin and Williams took the victims into the basement, she left the house without the bag. Respondent insisted that she had possessed no prior knowledge that Martin and Williams were armed, had heard no conversation about anyone's being harmed, and had not intended to rob or kill anyone.

During his closing argument, the prosecutor admonished the jury not to use Williams' confession against respondent. Later in his argument, however, he linked respondent to the portion of Williams' confession describing his conversation with Martin in the car.[2] (Respondent's attorney did not object to this.) After closing arguments, the judge again instructed the jury that Williams' confession was not to be considered against respondent. The jury convicted respondent of two counts of felony murder in the perpetration of an armed robbery and one count of assault with intent to commit murder. The Michigan Court of Appeals affirmed in an unpublished opinion, and the Michigan Supreme Court denied leave to appeal.

Respondent then filed a petition for a writ of habeas corpus pursuant to 28 U.S.C. § 2254. She alleged that * * * introduction of Williams' confession at the joint trial had violated her rights under the Confrontation Clause. The District Court denied the petition. The United States Court of Appeals * * * reversed. The Court of Appeals held that in determining whether *Bruton* bars the admission of a nontestifying codefendant's confession, a court must assess the confession's "inculpatory value" by examining not only the face of the confession, but also all of the evidence introduced at trial. Here, Williams' account of the conversation in the car was the only *direct* evidence that respondent knew before entering Scott's house that the victims would be robbed and killed. Respondent's own testimony placed her in that car. In light of the "paucity" of other evidence of malice and the prosecutor's linkage of respondent and the statement in the car during closing argument, admission of Williams' confession "was powerfully incriminating to [respondent] with respect to the critical element of intent." Thus, the Court of

2. The prosecutor said: "It's important in light of [respondent's] testimony when she says Kareem drives over to Benjamin Williams' home and picks him up to go over. What's the thing that she says? 'Well, I'm sitting in the back seat of the car.' 'Did you hear any conversation that was going on in the front seat between Kareem and Mr. Williams?' 'No, couldn't hear any conversation. The radio was too loud.' I asked [*sic*] you whether that is reasonable. Why did she say that? Why did she say she couldn't hear any conversation? She said, 'I know they were having conversation but I couldn't hear it because of the radio.' Because if she admits that she heard the conversation and she admits to the plan, she's guilty of at least armed robbery. So she can't tell you that."

Appeals concluded, the Confrontation Clause was violated. We granted certiorari.
* * *

The Confrontation Clause of the Sixth Amendment, extended against the States by the Fourteenth Amendment, guarantees the right of a criminal defendant "to be confronted with the witnesses against him." The right of confrontation includes the right to cross-examine witnesses. Therefore, where two defendants are tried jointly, the pretrial confession of one cannot be admitted against the other unless the confessing defendant takes the stand.

Ordinarily, a witness whose testimony is introduced at a joint trial is not considered to be a witness "against" a defendant if the jury is instructed to consider that testimony only against a codefendant. This accords with the almost invariable assumption of the law that jurors follow their instructions, which we have applied in many varying contexts. For example, in *Harris v. New York*, 401 U.S. 222 (1971), we held that statements elicited from a defendant in violation of *Miranda v. Arizona* can be introduced to impeach that defendant's credibility, even though they are inadmissible as evidence of his guilt, so long as the jury is instructed accordingly. * * * In *Bruton*, however, we recognized a narrow exception to this principle: We held that a defendant is deprived of his Sixth Amendment right of confrontation when the facially incriminating confession of a nontestifying codefendant is introduced at their joint trial, even if the jury is instructed to consider the confession only against the codefendant. We said:

> "[T]here are some contexts in which the risk that the jury will not, or cannot, follow instructions is so great, and the consequences of failure so vital to the defendant, that the practical and human limitations of the jury system cannot be ignored. Such a context is presented here, where the powerfully incriminating extrajudicial statements of a codefendant, who stands accused side-by-side with the defendant, are deliberately spread before the jury in a joint trial * * *."

There is an important distinction between this case and *Bruton*, which causes it to fall outside the narrow exception we have created. In *Bruton*, the codefendant's confession "expressly implicat[ed]" the defendant as his accomplice. Thus, at the time that confession was introduced there was not the slightest doubt that it would prove "powerfully incriminating." By contrast, in this case the confession was not incriminating on its face, and became so only when linked with evidence introduced later at trial (the defendant's own testimony).

Where the necessity of such linkage is involved, it is a less valid generalization that the jury will not likely obey the instruction to disregard the evidence. Specific testimony that "the defendant helped me commit the crime" is more vivid than inferential incrimination, and hence more difficult to thrust out of mind. Moreover, with regard to such an explicit statement the only issue is, plain and simply, whether the jury can possibly be expected to forget it in assessing the defendant's guilt; whereas with regard to inferential incrimination the judge's instruction may well be successful in dissuading the jury from entering onto the path of inference in the first place, so that there is no incrimination to forget. In short, while it may not always be simple for the members of a jury to obey the instruction that they disregard an incriminating inference, there does not exist the overwhelming probability of their inability to do so that is the foundation of *Bruton*'s exception to the general rule.

Even more significantly, evidence requiring linkage differs from evidence incriminating on its face in the practical effects which application of the *Bruton* exception would produce. If limited to facially incriminating confessions, *Bruton* can be complied with by redaction—a possibility suggested in that opinion itself.

If extended to confessions incriminating by connection, not only is that not possible, but it is not even possible to predict the admissibility of a confession in advance of trial. The "contextual implication" doctrine articulated by the Court of Appeals would presumably require the trial judge to assess at the end of each trial whether, in light of all of the evidence, a nontestifying codefendant's confession has been so "powerfully incriminating" that a new, separate trial is required for the defendant. This obviously lends itself to manipulation by the defense—and even without manipulation will result in numerous mistrials and appeals. It might be suggested that those consequences could be reduced by conducting a pretrial hearing at which prosecution and defense would reveal the evidence they plan to introduce, enabling the court to assess compliance with *Bruton ex ante* rather than *ex post.* If this approach is even feasible * * *, it would be time consuming and obviously far from foolproof.

One might say, of course, that a certain way of assuring compliance would be to try defendants separately whenever an incriminating statement of one of them is sought to be used. That is not as facile or as just a remedy as might seem. Joint trials play a vital role in the criminal justice system, accounting for almost one third of federal criminal trials in the past five years. Many joint trials—for example, those involving large conspiracies to import and distribute illegal drugs—involve a dozen or more codefendants. Confessions by one or more of the defendants are commonplace—and indeed the probability of confession increases with the number of participants, since each has reduced assurance that he will be protected by his own silence. It would impair both the efficiency and the fairness of the criminal justice system to require, in all these cases of joint crimes where incriminating statements exist, that prosecutors bring separate proceedings, presenting the same evidence again and again, requiring victims and witnesses to repeat the inconvenience (and sometimes trauma) of testifying, and randomly favoring the last-tried defendants who have the advantage of knowing the prosecution's case beforehand. Joint trials generally serve the interests of justice by avoiding inconsistent verdicts and enabling more accurate assessment of relative culpability—advantages which sometimes operate to the defendant's benefit. Even apart from these tactical considerations, joint trials generally serve the interests of justice by avoiding the scandal and inequity of inconsistent verdicts.[4] The other way of assuring compliance with an expansive *Bruton* rule would be to forgo use of codefendant confessions. That price also is too high, since confessions "are more than merely 'desirable'; they are essential to society's compelling interest in finding, convicting, and punishing those who violate the law." *Moran v. Burbine,* 475 U.S. 412 (1986).

The rule that juries are presumed to follow their instructions is a pragmatic one, rooted less in the absolute certitude that the presumption is true than in the belief that it represents a reasonable practical accommodation of the interests of the state and the defendant in the criminal justice process. On the precise facts of *Bruton,* involving a facially incriminating confession, we found that accommodation inadequate. As our discussion above shows, the calculus changes when

4. The dissent notes that "all of the cases in this Court that involved joint trials conducted after *Bruton* was decided, in which compliance with the rule of that case was at issue, appear to have originated in a state court." It concludes from this that "*[f]ederal* prosecutors seem to have had little difficulty" in implementing *Bruton* as the dissent believes it must be implemented. Since the cases in question number only a handful, the fact that they happened to be state cases may signify nothing more than that there are many times more state prosecutions than federal. There is assuredly no basis to believe that federal prosecutors have been applying the dissent's interpretation of *Bruton.* Indeed the contrary proposition—as well as the harmfulness of that interpretation to federal law enforcement efforts—is suggested by the fact that the Solicitor General has appeared here as *amicus* to urge reversal for substantially the reasons we have given.

confessions that do not name the defendant are at issue. While we continue to apply *Bruton* where we have found that its rationale validly applies, we decline to extend it further. We hold that the Confrontation Clause is not violated by the admission of a nontestifying codefendant's confession with a proper limiting instruction when, as here, the confession is redacted to eliminate not only the defendant's name, but any reference to her existence.[5]

In the present case, however, the prosecutor sought to undo the effect of the limiting instruction by urging the jury to use Williams' confession in evaluating respondent's case. See n. 2. On remand, the court should consider whether, in light of respondent's failure to object to the prosecutor's comments, the error can serve as the basis for granting a writ of habeas corpus. See *Wainwright v. Sykes* [discussed in fn. b to *Herrera*, Ch. 18, § 4].

Justice Stevens, with whom Justice Brennan and Justice Marshall join, dissenting.

The rationale of our decision in *Bruton v. United States,* applies without exception to all inadmissible confessions that are "powerfully incriminating." Today, however, the Court draws a distinction of constitutional magnitude between those confessions that directly identify the defendant and those that rely for their inculpatory effect on the factual and legal relationships of their contents to other evidence before the jury. Even if the jury's indirect inference of the defendant's guilt based on an inadmissible confession is much more devastating to the defendant's case than its inference from a direct reference in the codefendant's confession, the Court requires the exclusion of only the latter statement. This illogical result demeans the values protected by the Confrontation Clause. Moreover, neither reason nor experience supports the Court's argument that a consistent application of the rationale of the *Bruton* case would impose unacceptable burdens on the administration of justice. * * *

[T]he Court * * * draws a line between codefendant confessions that expressly name the defendant and those that do not. The Court relies on the presumption that in the latter category "it is a less valid generalization that the jury will not likely obey the instruction to disregard the evidence." I agree; but I do not read *Bruton* to require the exclusion of *all* codefendant confessions that do not mention the defendant. Some such confessions may not have any significant impact on the defendant's case. But others will. If we presume, as we must, that jurors give their full and vigorous attention to every witness and each item of evidence, the very acts of listening and seeing will sometimes lead them down "the path of inference." Indeed, the Court tacitly acknowledges this point; while the Court speculates that the judge's instruction may dissuade the jury from making inferences at all, it also concedes the probability of their occurrence, arguing that there is no overwhelming probability that jurors will be unable to "disregard an incriminating inference." *Bruton* has always required trial judges to answer the question whether a particular confession is or is not "powerfully

5. We express no opinion on the admissibility of a confession in which the defendant's name has been replaced with a symbol or neutral pronoun.

[In *Gray v. Maryland,* 523 U.S. 185 (1998), the Court held that "*Bruton*'s protective rule" barred simply redacting the codefendant's confession "by substituting for the defendant's name a blank space or the word 'deleted'" where the confession (unlike that in *Richardson*) "refers directly to the 'existence of the nonconfessing defendant.'" In response to the question "who was in the group that beat [the victim]," the answer in the redacted confession had been read to the jury as: "Me, deleted, and a few other guys." The Court majority concluded that with such a redaction, "the jury will often realize that the confession refers directly to the defendant" and, indeed, "by encouraging the jury to speculate about the reference, the redaction may overemphasize the importance of the confession's accusation—once the jurors work out the reference."]

incriminating" on a case-by-case basis; they should follow the same analysis whether or not the defendant is actually named by his or her codefendant.

Instructing the jury that it was to consider Benjamin Williams' confession only against him, and not against Clarissa Marsh, failed to guarantee the level of certainty required by the Confrontation Clause. The uncertainty arose because the prosecution's case made it clear at the time Williams' statement was introduced that the statement would prove "powerfully incriminating" of the *petitioner* as well as of Williams himself. There can be absolutely no doubt that spreading Williams' carefully edited confession before the jury intolerably interfered with the jury's solemn duty to treat the statement as nothing more than meaningless sounds in its consideration of Marsh's guilt or innocence. * * *

The facts that joint trials conserve prosecutorial resources, diminish inconvenience to witnesses, and avoid delays in the administration of criminal justice have been well-known for a long time. It is equally well-known that joint trials create special risks of prejudice to one of the defendants, and that such risks often make it necessary to grant severances. See *Bruton*. The Government argues that the costs of requiring the prosecution to choose between severance and not offering the codefendant's confession at a joint trial outweigh the benefits to the defendant. Brief for United States as *Amicus Curiae*. On the scales of justice, however, considerations of fairness normally outweigh administrative concerns.

In the *Bruton* case the United States argued that the normal "benefits of joint proceedings should not have to be sacrificed by requiring separate trials in order to use the confession against the declarant." The Court endorsed the answer to this argument that Judge Lehman of the New York Court of Appeals had previously made:

"We still adhere to the rule that an accused is entitled to confrontation of the witnesses against him and the right to cross-examine them. * * * We destroy the age-old rule which in the past has been regarded as a fundamental principle of our jurisprudence by a legalistic formula, required of the judge, that the jury may not consider any admissions against any party who did not join in them. We secure greater speed, economy and convenience in the administration of the law at the price of fundamental principles of constitutional liberty. That price is too high."

The concern about the cost of joint trials, even if valid, does not prevail over the interests of justice. Moreover, the Court's effort to revive this concern in a state criminal case rests on the use of irrelevant statistics. The Court makes the startling discovery that joint trials account for "almost one-third of federal criminal trials in the past five years." In the interest of greater precision, the Court might have stated that there were 10,904 federal criminal trials involving more than one defendant during that 5 year period. The Court might have added that the data base from which that figure was obtained does not contain any information at all to show the number of times that confessions were offered in evidence in those 10,904 federal cases. The relevance of this data is also difficult to discern because all of the cases in this Court that involved joint trials conducted after *Bruton* was decided, in which compliance with the rule of that case was at issue, appear to have originated in a state court. *Federal* prosecutors seem to have had little difficulty, in conducting the literally thousands of joint trials to which the Court points, in avoiding "the great harm to the criminal justice system" that the Court speculates will occur if *Bruton*'s reasoning is applied to this case. Presumably the options of granting immunity, making plea bargains, or simply waiting until after a confessing defendant has been tried separately before trying to use his admissions against an accomplice have enabled the

Federal Government to enforce the criminal law without sacrificing the basic premise of the Confrontation Clause.

The Court also expresses concern that trial judges will be unable to determine whether a codefendant's confession that does not directly mention the defendant and is inadmissible against him will create a substantial risk of unfair prejudice. In most such cases the trial judge can comply with the dictates of *Bruton* by postponing his or her decision on the admissibility of the confession until the prosecution rests, at which time its potentially inculpatory effect can be evaluated in the light of the government's entire case. The Court expresses concern that such a rule would enable "manipulation by the defense," by which the Court presumably means the defense might tailor its evidence to make sure that a confession which does not directly mention the defendant is deemed powerfully incriminating when viewed in light of the prosecution's entire case. As a practical matter, I cannot believe that there are many defense lawyers who would deliberately pursue this high-risk strategy of "manipulating" their evidence in order to enhance the prejudicial impact of a codefendant's confession. Moreover, a great many experienced and competent trial judges throughout the Nation are fully capable of managing cases and supervising counsel in order to avoid the problems that seem insurmountable to appellate judges who are sometimes distracted by illogical distinctions and irrelevant statistics. I respectfully dissent.[8]

DAVIS v. ALASKA

415 U.S. 308, 94 S.Ct. 1105, 39 L.Ed.2d 347 (1974).

CHIEF JUSTICE BURGER delivered the opinion of the Court.

We granted certiorari in this case to consider whether the Confrontation Clause requires that a defendant in a criminal case be allowed to impeach the credibility of a prosecution witness by cross-examination directed at possible bias deriving from the witness' probationary status as a juvenile delinquent when such an impeachment would conflict with a State's asserted interest in preserving the confidentiality of juvenile adjudications of delinquency.

When the Polar Bar in Anchorage closed in the early morning hours of February 16, 1970, well over a thousand dollars in cash and checks was in the bar's Mosler safe. About midday, February 16, it was discovered that the bar had been broken into and the safe, about two feet square and weighing several hundred pounds, had been removed from the premises. Later that afternoon the Alaska State Troopers received word that a safe had been discovered about 26 miles outside Anchorage near the home of Jess Straight * * *. The safe, which was subsequently determined to be the one stolen from the Polar Bar, had been pried open and the contents removed. Richard Green, Jess Straight's stepson, told investigating troopers on the scene that at about noon on February 16 he had seen and spoken with two Negro men standing alongside a late-model metallic blue Chevrolet sedan near where the safe was later discovered. The next day * * * Green was given six photographs of adult Negro males. After examining the photographs for 30 seconds to a minute, Green identified the photograph of petitioner as that of one of the men he had encountered the day before * * *. Petitioner was arrested the next day, February 18. On February 19, Green picked petitioner out of a lineup of seven Negro males.

8. Except for Williams' confession, and the prosecutor's closing argument that will be separately considered on remand, there was a paucity of other evidence connecting respondent with the plan discussed in the car on the way to the victim's home. The Court of Appeals was thus unquestionably correct in concluding that the violation of the Confrontation Clause in this case was not harmless error.

At trial, evidence was introduced to the effect that paint chips found in the trunk of petitioner's rented blue Chevrolet could have originated from the surface of the stolen safe. Further, the trunk of the car contained particles which were identified as safe insulation characteristic of that found in Mosler safes. * * *

Richard Green was a crucial witness for the prosecution. He testified at trial that while on an errand for his mother he confronted two men standing beside a late-model metallic blue Chevrolet, parked on a road near his family's house. The man standing at the rear of the car spoke to Green asking if Green lived nearby and if his father was home. Green offered the men help, but his offer was rejected. On his return from the errand Green again passed the two men and he saw the man with whom he had had the conversation standing at the rear of the car with "something like a crowbar" in his hands. Green identified petitioner at the trial as the man with the "crowbar." The safe was discovered later that afternoon at the point, according to Green, where the Chevrolet had been parked.

Before testimony was taken at the trial of petitioner, the prosecutor moved for a protective order to prevent any reference to Green's juvenile record by the defense in the course of cross-examination. At the time of the trial and at the time of the events Green testified to, Green was on probation by order of a juvenile court after having been adjudicated a delinquent for burglarizing two cabins. Green was 16 years of age at the time of the Polar Bar burglary, but had turned 17 prior to trial.

In opposing the protective order, petitioner's counsel made it clear that he would not introduce Green's juvenile adjudication as a general impeachment of Green's character as a truthful person but, rather, to show specifically that at the same time Green was assisting the police in identifying petitioner he was on probation for burglary. From this petitioner would seek to show—or at least argue—that Green acted out of fear or concern of possible jeopardy to his probation. Not only might Green have made a hasty and faulty identification of petitioner to shift suspicion away from himself as one who robbed the Polar Bar, but Green might have been subject to undue pressure from the police and made his identifications under fear of possible probation revocation. Green's record would be revealed only as necessary to probe Green for bias and prejudice and not generally to call Green's good character into question.

The trial court granted the motion for a protective order, relying on Alaska Rule of Children's Procedure 23,[1] and Alaska Stat. § 47.10.080(g) (1971).[2]

Although prevented from revealing that Green had been on probation for the juvenile delinquency adjudication for burglary at the same time that he originally identified petitioner, counsel for petitioner did his best to expose Green's state of mind at the time Green discovered that a stolen safe had been discovered near his home. Green denied that he was upset or uncomfortable about the discovery of the safe. He claimed not to have been worried about any suspicions the police might have been expected to harbor against him, though Green did admit that it crossed his mind that the police might have thought he had something to do with the crime. * * * [After the defense counsel asked Green if he had "ever been questioned like that before by any law enforcement officers" and Green answered "No," the trial court cut off further questioning along this line on the prosecu-

1. Rule 23 provides: "No adjudication, order, or disposition of a juvenile case shall be admissible in a court not acting in the exercise of juvenile jurisdiction except for use in a presentencing procedure in a criminal case where the superior court, in its discretion, determines that such use is appropriate."

2. Section 47.10.080(g) provides in pertinent part: "The commitment and placement of a child and evidence given in the court are not admissible as evidence against the minor in a subsequent case or proceedings in any other court ...."

tion's objection that such questioning was "a carry-on with rehash of the same thing"].

Since defense counsel was prohibited from making inquiry as to the witness' being on probation under a juvenile court adjudication, Green's protestations of unconcern over possible police suspicion that he might have had a part in the Polar Bar burglary and his categorical denial of ever having been the subject of any similar law-enforcement interrogation went unchallenged. The tension between the right of confrontation and the State's policy of protecting the witness with a juvenile record is particularly evident in the final answer given by the witness. Since it is probable that Green underwent some questioning by police when he was arrested for the burglaries on which his juvenile adjudication of delinquency rested, the answer can be regarded as highly suspect at the very least. The witness was in effect asserting, under protection of the trial court's ruling, a right to give a questionably truthful answer to a cross-examiner pursuing a relevant line of inquiry; it is doubtful whether the bold "No" answer would have been given by Green absent a belief that he was shielded from traditional cross-examination. It would be difficult to conceive of a situation more clearly illustrating the need for cross-examination. The remainder of the cross-examination was devoted to an attempt to prove that Green was making his identification at trial on the basis of what he remembered from his earlier identifications at the photographic display and lineup, and not on the basis of his February 16 confrontation with the two men on the road.

The Alaska Supreme Court affirmed petitioner's conviction, concluding that it did not have to resolve the potential conflict in this case between a defendant's right to a meaningful confrontation with adverse witnesses and the State's interest in protecting the anonymity of a juvenile offender since "our reading of the trial transcript convinces us that counsel for the defendant was able adequately to question the youth in considerable detail concerning the possibility of bias or motive." Although the court admitted that Green's denials of any sense of anxiety or apprehension upon the safe's being found close to his home were possibly self-serving, "the suggestion was nonetheless brought to the attention of the jury, and that body was afforded the opportunity to observe the demeanor of the youth and pass on his credibility." The court concluded that, in light of the indirect references permitted, there was no error.

Since we granted certiorari limited to the question of whether petitioner was denied his right under the Confrontation Clause to adequately cross-examine Green, the essential question turns on the correctness of the Alaska court's evaluation of the "adequacy" of the scope of cross-examination permitted. We disagree with that court's interpretation of the Confrontation Clause and we reverse.

The Sixth Amendment to the Constitution guarantees the right of an accused in a criminal prosecution "to be confronted with the witnesses against him." * * * Confrontation means more than being allowed to confront the witness physically. "Our cases construing the [confrontation] clause hold that a primary interest secured by it is the right of cross-examination." *Douglas v. Alabama,* 380 U.S. 415 (1965). * * *

Cross-examination is the principal means by which the believability of a witness and the truth of his testimony are tested. Subject always to the broad discretion of a trial judge to preclude repetitive and unduly harassing interrogation, the cross-examiner is not only permitted to delve into the witness' story to test the witness' perceptions and memory, but the cross-examiner has traditionally been allowed to impeach, i.e., discredit, the witness. One way of discrediting the witness is to introduce evidence of a prior criminal conviction of that witness. By so doing the cross-examiner intends to afford the jury a basis to infer that the witness' character is such that he would be less likely than the average trustworthy citizen to be truthful in his testimony. The introduction of evidence of a prior crime is thus a general attack on the credibility of the witness. A more particular attack on the witness' credibility is effected by means of cross-examination directed toward revealing possible biases, prejudices, or ulterior motives of the witness as they may relate directly to issues or personalities in the case at hand. * * * We have recognized that the exposure of a witness' motivation in testifying is a proper and important function of the constitutionally protected right of cross-examination. *Greene v. McElroy,* 360 U.S. 474 (1959).

In the instant case, defense counsel sought to show the existence of possible bias and prejudice of Green, causing him to make a faulty initial identification of petitioner, which in turn could have affected his later in-court identification of petitioner. We cannot speculate as to whether the jury, as sole judge of the credibility of a witness, would have accepted this line of reasoning had counsel been permitted to fully present it. But we do conclude that the jurors were entitled to have the benefit of the defense theory before them so that they could make an informed judgment as to the weight to place on Green's testimony which provided "a crucial link in the proof * * * of petitioner's act." *Douglas v. Alabama.* The accuracy and truthfulness of Green's testimony were key elements in the State's case against petitioner. The claim of bias which the defense sought to develop was admissible to afford a basis for an inference of undue pressure because of Green's vulnerable status as a probationer, as well as of Green's possible concern that he might be a suspect in the investigation.

We cannot accept the Alaska Supreme Court's conclusion that the cross-examination that was permitted defense counsel was adequate to develop the issue of bias properly to the jury. While counsel was permitted to ask Green *whether* he was biased, counsel was unable to make a record from which to argue *why* Green might have been biased or otherwise lacked that degree of impartiality expected of a witness at trial. On the basis of the limited cross-examination that was permitted, the jury might well have thought that defense counsel was engaged in a speculative and baseless line of attack on the credibility of an apparently blameless witness or, as the prosecutor's objection put it, a "rehash" of prior cross-examination. On these facts it seems clear to us that to make any such inquiry effective, defense counsel should have been permitted to expose to the jury the facts from which jurors, as the sole triers of fact and credibility, could appropriately draw inferences relating to the reliability of the witness. Petitioner was thus denied the right of effective cross-examination which "would be constitutional error of the first magnitude and no amount of showing of want of prejudice would cure it." *Smith v. Illinois,* 390 U.S. 129 (1968).

The claim is made that the State has an important interest in protecting the anonymity of juvenile offenders and that this interest outweighs any competing interest this petitioner might have in cross-examining Green about his being on probation. The State argues that exposure of a juvenile's record of delinquency would likely cause impairment of rehabilitative goals of the juvenile correctional procedures. This exposure, it is argued, might encourage the juvenile offender to commit further acts of delinquency, or cause the juvenile offender to lose employment opportunities or otherwise suffer unnecessarily for his youthful transgression.

We do not and need not challenge the State's interest as a matter of its own policy in the administration of criminal justice to seek to preserve the anonymity of a juvenile offender. Here, however, petitioner sought to introduce evidence of Green's probation for the purpose of suggesting that Green was biased and, therefore, that his testimony was either not to be believed in his identification of petitioner or at least very carefully considered in that light. Serious damage to the strength of the State's case would have been a real possibility had petitioner been allowed to pursue this line of inquiry. In this setting we conclude that the right of confrontation is paramount to the State's policy of protecting a juvenile offender. Whatever temporary embarrassment might result to Green or his family by disclosure of his juvenile record—if the prosecution insisted on using him to make its case—is outweighed by petitioner's right to probe into the influence of possible bias in the testimony of a crucial identification witness. * * *

The State's policy interest in protecting the confidentiality of a juvenile offender's record cannot require yielding of so vital a constitutional right as the effective cross-examination for bias of an adverse witness. The State could have protected Green from exposure of his juvenile adjudication in these circumstances by refraining from using him to make out its case; the State cannot, consistent with the right of confrontation, require the petitioner to bear the full burden of vindicating the State's interest in the secrecy of juvenile criminal records. The judgment affirming petitioner's convictions of burglary and grand larceny is reversed and the case is remanded for further proceedings not inconsistent with this opinion.

JUSTICE STEWART, concurring.

The Court holds that, in the circumstances of this case, the Sixth and Fourteenth Amendments conferred the right to cross-examine a particular prosecution witness about his delinquency adjudication for burglary and his status as a probationer. Such cross-examination was necessary in this case in order "to show the existence of possible bias and prejudice * * *." In joining the Court's opinion, I would emphasize that the Court neither holds nor suggests that the Constitution confers a right in every case to impeach the general credibility of a witness through cross-examination about his past delinquency adjudications or criminal convictions.

JUSTICE WHITE, with whom JUSTICE REHNQUIST joins, dissenting.

As I see it, there is no constitutional principle at stake here. This is nothing more than a typical instance of a trial court exercising its discretion to control or limit cross-examination, followed by a typical decision of a state appellate court refusing to disturb the judgment of the trial court and itself concluding that limiting cross-examination had done no substantial harm to the defense. Yet the Court insists on second-guessing the state courts and in effect inviting federal review of every ruling of a state trial judge who believes cross-examination has gone far enough. I would not undertake this task, if for no other reason than that I have little faith in our ability, in fact-bound cases and on a cold record, to improve on the judgment of trial judges and of the state appellate courts who agree with them. I would affirm the judgment.

SECTION 3.   THE DEFENDANT'S RIGHT TO REMAIN SILENT—OR TO TESTIFY

GRIFFIN v. CALIFORNIA

380 U.S. 609, 85 S.Ct. 1229, 14 L.Ed.2d 106 (1965).

JUSTICE DOUGLAS delivered the opinion of the Court.

Petitioner was convicted of murder in the first degree after a jury trial in the California court. He did not testify at the trial on the issue of guilt, though he did testify at the separate trial on the issue of penalty. The trial court instructed the jury on the issue of guilt, stating that a defendant has a constitutional right not to testify. But it told the jury: [2]

"As to any evidence or facts against him which the defendant can reasonably be expected to deny or explain because of facts within his knowledge, if he does not testify or if, though he does testify, he fails to deny or explain such evidence, the jury may take that failure into consideration as tending to indicate the truth of such evidence and as indicating that among the inferences that may be reasonably drawn therefrom those unfavorable to the defendant are the more probable."

It added, however, that no such inference could be drawn as to evidence respecting which he had no knowledge. It stated that failure of a defendant to deny or explain the evidence of which he had knowledge does not create a presumption of guilt nor by itself warrant an inference of guilt nor relieve the prosecution of any of its burden of proof.

Petitioner had been seen with the deceased the evening of her death, the evidence placing him with her in the alley where her body was found. The prosecutor made much of the failure of petitioner to testify:

"The defendant certainly knows whether Essie Mae had this beat up appearance at the time he left her apartment and went down the alley with her.

"What kind of a man is it that would want to have sex with a woman that beat up if she was beat up at the time he left?

"He would know that. He would know how she got down the alley. He would know how the blood got on the bottom of the concrete steps. He would know how long he was with her in that box. He would know how her wig got off. He would know whether he beat her or mistreated her. He would know whether he walked away from that place cool as a cucumber when he saw Mr. Villasenor because he was conscious of his own guilt and wanted to get away from that damaged or injured woman.

"These things he has not seen fit to take the stand and deny or explain.

"And in the whole world, if anybody would know, this defendant would know.

"Essie Mae is dead, she can't tell you her side of the story. The defendant won't."

The death penalty was imposed and the California Supreme Court affirmed. The case is here on a petition for a writ of certiorari which we granted to consider the single question whether comment on the failure to testify violated the Self-Incrimination Clause of the Fifth Amendment which we made applicable to the States * * *.

If this were a federal trial, reversible error would have been committed. *Wilson v. United States,* 149 U.S. 60 (1893) so holds. It is said, however, that the *Wilson* decision rested not on the Fifth Amendment, but on an Act of Congress. 18 U.S.C. § 3481. That indeed is the fact, as the opinion of the Court in the

Wilson case states. * * * But that is the beginning, not the end of our inquiry. The question remains whether, statute or not, the comment rule, approved by California, violates the Fifth Amendment.

We think it does. It is in substance a rule of evidence that allows the State the privilege of tendering to the jury for its consideration the failure of the accused to testify. No formal offer of proof is made as in other situations; but the prosecutor's comment and the court's acquiescence are the equivalent of an offer of evidence and its acceptance. The Court in the *Wilson* case stated:

> "* * * the Act was framed with a due regard also to those who might prefer to rely upon the presumption of innocence which the law gives to every one, and not wish to be witnesses. It is not every one who can safely venture on the witness stand, though entirely innocent of the charge against him. Excessive timidity, nervousness when facing others and attempting to explain transactions of a suspicious character, and offenses charged against him, will often confuse and embarrass him to such a degree as to increase rather than remove prejudices against him. It is not every one, however honest, who would therefore willingly be placed on the witness stand. The statute, in tenderness to the weakness of those who from the causes mentioned might refuse to ask to be witnesses, particularly when they may have been in some degree compromised by their association with others, declares that the failure of a defendant in a criminal action to request to be a witness shall not create any presumption against him."

If the words "Fifth Amendment" are substituted for "Act" and for "statute" the spirit of the Self–Incrimination Clause is reflected. For comment on the refusal to testify is a remnant of the "inquisitorial system of criminal justice" which the Fifth Amendment outlaws. It is a penalty imposed by courts for exercising a constitutional privilege. It cuts down on the privilege by making its assertion costly. It is said, however, that the inference of guilt for failure to testify as to facts peculiarly within the accused's knowledge is in any event natural and irresistible, and that comment on the failure does not magnify that inference into a penalty for asserting a constitutional privilege. What the jury may infer given no help from the court is one thing. What they may infer when the court solemnizes the silence of the accused into evidence against him is quite another. * * *

We * * * hold that the Fifth Amendment, in its direct application to the federal government and its bearing on the States by reason of the Fourteenth Amendment, forbids either comment by the prosecution on the accused's silence or instructions by the court that such silence is evidence of guilt.

Reversed.[a]

JUSTICE STEWART, with whom JUSTICE WHITE joins, dissenting. * * *

We must determine whether the petitioner has been "compelled to be a witness against himself." Compulsion is the focus of the inquiry. Certainly, if any compulsion be detected in the California procedure, it is of a dramatically different and less palpable nature than that involved in the procedures which historically gave rise to the Fifth Amendment guarantee. When a suspect was brought before the Court of High Commission or the Star Chamber, he was commanded to answer whatever was asked of him, and subjected to a far-reaching and deeply probing inquiry in an effort to ferret out some unknown and frequent-

---

a. The Chief Justice took no part in the decision of the case. Harlan, J., concurred   "with great reluctance."

ly unsuspected crime. He declined to answer on pain of incarceration, banishment, or mutilation. And if he spoke falsely, he was subject to further punishment. Faced with this formidable array of alternatives, his decision to speak was unquestionably coerced.

Those were the lurid realities which lay behind enactment of the Fifth Amendment, a far cry from the subject matter of the case before us. I think that the Court in this case stretches the concept of compulsion beyond all reasonable bounds, and that whatever compulsion may exist derives from the defendant's choice not to testify, not from any comment by court or counsel. In support of its conclusion that the California procedure does compel the accused to testify, the Court has only this to say: "It is a penalty imposed by courts for exercising a constitutional privilege. It cuts down on the privilege by making its assertion costly." Exactly what the penalty imposed consists of is not clear. It is not, as I understand the problem, that the jury becomes aware that the defendant has chosen not to testify in his own defense, for the jury will, of course, realize this quite evident fact, even though the choice goes unmentioned. Since comment by counsel and the court does not compel testimony by creating such an awareness, the Court must be saying that the California constitutional provision places some other compulsion upon the defendant to incriminate himself, some compulsion which the Court does not describe and which I cannot readily perceive.

* * * No doubt the prosecution's argument will seek to encourage the drawing of inferences unfavorable to the defendant. However, the defendant's counsel equally has an opportunity to explain the various other reasons why a defendant may not wish to take the stand, and thus rebut the natural if uneducated assumption that it is because the defendant cannot truthfully deny the accusations made. * * *

The California rule allowing comment by counsel and instruction by the judge on the defendant's failure to take the stand is hardly an idiosyncratic aberration. The Model Code of Evidence, and Uniform Rules of Evidence both sanction the use of such procedures. The practice had been endorsed by resolution of the American Bar Association and the American Law Institute, and has the support of the weight of scholarly opinion. * * * [b]

ROCK v. ARKANSAS

483 U.S. 44, 107 S.Ct. 2704, 97 L.Ed.2d 37 (1987).

JUSTICE BLACKMUN delivered the opinion of the Court.

b. *United States v. Robinson*, 485 U.S. 25 (1988) recognized a "fair response" exception to the *Griffin* prohibition; where defense counsel argued that the government had never allowed defendant to tell his side of the story, the Fifth Amendment was not violated by the prosecutor's response that defendant could have "taken the stand." See also Mitchell v. United States, ch. 20, in which the majority extends *Griffin* to sentencing. Justice Scalia's dissent there not only opposes the extension but also questions the soundness of the *Griffin* ruling in an argument more extensive than the *Griffin* dissents.

Carter v. Kentucky, 450 U.S. 288 (1981), held that the accused had a constitutional right to a requested instruction informing the jury that the defendant had a constitutional right not to testify and that "the fact that he does not [testify] cannot be used as an inference of guilt and should not prejudice him in any way." The Court reasoned that, while "no judge can prevent jurors from speculating about why a defendant stands mute in the face of a criminal accusation, * * * a judge can, and must, if requested to do so, use the unique power of the jury instruction to reduce the speculation to a minimum." In *Lakeside v. Oregon*, 435 U.S. 333 (1978), the Court held that the trial court could insist upon giving a protective instruction even over objection of the defendant. Consider also the refusal to extend "the *Griffin* rationale" in *Portuondo v. Agard*, described in footnote a to *Rock v. Arkansas*, infra.

The issue presented in this case is whether Arkansas' evidentiary rule prohibiting the admission of hypnotically refreshed testimony violated petitioner's constitutional right to testify on her own behalf as a defendant in a criminal case.

Petitioner Vickie Lorene Rock was charged with manslaughter in the death of her husband, Frank Rock, on July 2, 1983. A dispute had been simmering about Frank's wish to move from the couple's small apartment adjacent to Vickie's beauty parlor to a trailer she owned outside town. That night a fight erupted when Frank refused to let petitioner eat some pizza and prevented her from leaving the apartment to get something else to eat. When police arrived on the scene they found Frank on the floor with a bullet wound in his chest. Petitioner urged the officers to help her husband, and cried to a sergeant who took her in charge, "please save him" and "don't let him die." The police removed her from the building because she was upset and because she interfered with their investigation by her repeated attempts to use the telephone to call her husband's parents. According to the testimony of one of the investigating officers, petitioner told him that "she stood up to leave the room and [her husband] grabbed her by the throat and choked her and threw her against the wall and * * * at that time she walked over and picked up the weapon and pointed it toward the floor and he hit her again and she shot him."

Because petitioner could not remember the precise details of the shooting, her attorney suggested that she submit to hypnosis in order to refresh her memory. Petitioner was hypnotized twice by Doctor Betty Back, a licensed neuropsychologist with training in the field of hypnosis. Doctor Back interviewed petitioner for an hour prior to the first hypnosis session, taking notes on petitioner's general history and her recollections of the shooting. Both hypnosis sessions were recorded on tape. Petitioner did not relate any new information during either of the sessions, id., at 78, 83, but, after the hypnosis, she was able to remember that at the time of the incident she had her thumb on the hammer of the gun, but had not held her finger on the trigger. She also recalled that the gun had discharged when her husband grabbed her arm during the scuffle. As a result of the details that petitioner was able to remember about the shooting, her counsel arranged for a gun expert to examine the handgun, a single action Hawes .22 Deputy Marshal. That inspection revealed that the gun was defective and prone to fire, when hit or dropped, without the trigger's being pulled.

When the prosecutor learned of the hypnosis sessions, he filed a motion to exclude petitioner's testimony. The trial judge held a pretrial hearing on the motion and concluded that no hypnotically refreshed testimony would be admitted. The court issued an order limiting petitioner's testimony to "matters remembered and stated to the examiner prior to being placed under hypnosis." At trial, petitioner introduced testimony by the gun expert, but the court limited petitioner's own description of the events on the day of the shooting to a reiteration of the sketchy information in Doctor Back's notes. The jury convicted petitioner on the manslaughter charge and she was sentenced to 10 years imprisonment and a $10,000 fine.

On appeal, the Supreme Court of Arkansas rejected petitioner's claim that the limitations on her testimony violated her right to present her defense. The court concluded that "the dangers of admitting this kind of testimony outweigh whatever probative value it may have," and decided to follow the approach of States that have held hypnotically refreshed testimony of witnesses inadmissible *per se.* * * * [I]t ruled that the exclusion of petitioner's testimony did not violate her constitutional rights. Any "prejudice or deprivation" she suffered "was minimal and resulted from her own actions and not by any erroneous ruling of the court."

Petitioner's claim that her testimony was impermissibly excluded is bottomed on her constitutional right to testify in her own defense. At this point in the development of our adversary system, it cannot be doubted that a defendant in a criminal case has the right to take the witness stand and to testify in his or her own defense. This, of course, is a change from the historic common-law view, which was that all parties to litigation, including criminal defendants, were disqualified from testifying because of their interest in the outcome of the trial. The principal rationale for this rule was the possible untrustworthiness of a party's testimony. Under the common law, the practice did develop of permitting criminal defendants to tell their side of the story, but they were limited to making an unsworn statement that could not be elicited through direct examination by counsel and was not subject to cross-examination.

This Court in *Ferguson v. Georgia,* 365 U.S. 570 (1961), detailed the history of the transition from a rule of a defendant's incompetency to a rule of competency. As the Court there recounted, it came to be recognized that permitting a defendant to testify advances both the " 'detection of guilt' " and " 'the protection of innocence,' " and by the end of the second half of the 19th century, all States except Georgia had enacted statutes that declared criminal defendants competent to testify.   * * *

The right to testify on one's own behalf at a criminal trial has sources in several provisions of the Constitution. It is one of the rights that "are essential to due process of law in a fair adversary process." *Faretta v. California.* [Ch. 17]. The necessary ingredients of the Fourteenth Amendment's guarantee that no one shall be deprived of liberty without due process of law include a right to be heard and to offer testimony.   * * *

The right to testify is also found in the Compulsory Process Clause of the Sixth Amendment, which grants a defendant the right to call "witnesses in his favor" * * *. Logically included in the accused's right to call witnesses whose testimony is "material and favorable to his defense," *United States v. Valenzuela–Bernal,* 458 U.S. 858 (1982), is a right to testify himself, should he decide it is in his favor to do so. In fact, the most important witness for the defense in many criminal cases is the defendant himself. There is no justification today for a rule that denies an accused the opportunity to offer his own testimony. Like the truthfulness of other witnesses, the defendant's veracity, which was the concern behind the original common-law rule, can be tested adequately by cross-examination.

Moreover, in *Faretta v. California,* the Court recognized that the Sixth Amendment "grants to the accused *personally* the right to make his defense." * * * Even more fundamental to a personal defense than the right of self-representation, which was found to be "necessarily implied by the structure of the Amendment," *Faretta,* is an accused's right to present his own version of events in his own words. A defendant's opportunity to conduct his own defense by calling witnesses is incomplete if he may not present himself as a witness.

The opportunity to testify is also a necessary corollary to the Fifth Amendment's guarantee against compelled testimony. In *Harris v. New York,* 401 U.S. 222 (1971), the Court stated: "Every criminal defendant is privileged to testify in his own defense, or to refuse to do so." Three of the dissenting Justices in that case agreed that the Fifth Amendment encompasses this right: "[The Fifth Amendment's privilege against self-incrimination] is fulfilled only when an accused is guaranteed the right "to remain silent unless he chooses to speak in the unfettered exercise of his own will.' * * * The choice of whether to testify in one's own defense * * * is an exercise of the constitutional privilege."

The question now before the Court is whether a criminal defendant's right to testify may be restricted by a state rule that excludes her post-hypnosis testimony. This is not the first time this Court has faced a constitutional challenge to a state rule, designed to ensure trustworthy evidence, that interfered with the ability of a defendant to offer testimony. In *Washington v. Texas,* 388 U.S. 14 (1967), the Court [struck down] * * * a state statute that prevented persons charged as principals, accomplices, or accessories in the same crime from being introduced as witnesses for one another. * * * By preventing the defendant from having the benefit of his accomplice's testimony, "the State *arbitrarily* denied him the right to put on the stand a witness who was physically and mentally capable of testifying to events that he had personally observed, and whose testimony would have been relevant and material to the defense." (Emphasis added.) * * * Just as a State may not apply an arbitrary rule of competence to exclude a material defense witness from taking the stand, it also may not apply a rule of evidence that permits a witness to take the stand, but arbitrarily excludes material portions of his testimony. In *Chambers v. Mississippi* [§ 2] the Court invalidated a State's hearsay rule on the ground that it abridged the defendant's right to "present witnesses in his own defense."

Of course, the right to present relevant testimony is not without limitation. The right "may, in appropriate cases, bow to accommodate other legitimate interests in the criminal trial process." *Chambers.* But restrictions of a defendant's right to testify may not be arbitrary or disproportionate to the purposes they are designed to serve. In applying its evidentiary rules a State must evaluate whether the interests served by a rule justify the limitation imposed on the defendant's constitutional right to testify.

The Arkansas rule enunciated by the state courts does not allow a trial court to consider whether posthypnosis testimony may be admissible in a particular case; it is a *per se* rule prohibiting the admission at trial of any defendant's hypnotically refreshed testimony on the ground that such testimony is always unreliable. Thus, in Arkansas, an accused's testimony is limited to matters that he or she can prove were remembered *before* hypnosis. This rule operates to the detriment of any defendant who undergoes hypnosis, without regard to the reasons for it, the circumstances under which it took place, or any independent verification of the information it produced.

In this case, the application of that rule had a significant adverse effect on petitioner's ability to testify. It virtually prevented her from describing any of the events that occurred on the day of the shooting, despite corroboration of many of those events by other witnesses. Even more importantly, under the court's rule petitioner was not permitted to describe the actual shooting except in the words contained in Doctor Back's notes. The expert's description of the gun's tendency to misfire would have taken on greater significance if the jury had heard petitioner testify that she did not have her finger on the trigger and that the gun went off when her husband hit her arm.

In establishing its *per se* rule, the Arkansas Supreme Court simply followed the approach taken by a number of States that have decided that hypnotically enhanced testimony should be excluded at trial on the ground that it tends to be unreliable. Other States that have adopted an exclusionary rule, however, have done so for the testimony of *witnesses,* not for the testimony of a *defendant.* The Arkansas Supreme Court failed to perform the constitutional analysis that is necessary when a defendant's right to testify is at stake.

Although the Arkansas court concluded that any testimony that cannot be proved to be the product of prehypnosis memory is unreliable, many courts have eschewed a *per se* rule and permit the admission of hypnotically refreshed testimony. Hypnosis by trained physicians or psychologists has been recognized as a valid therapeutic technique since 1958, although there is no generally accepted theory to explain the phenomenon, or even a consensus on a single definition of hypnosis. The use of hypnosis in criminal investigations, however, is controversial, and the current medical and legal view of its appropriate role is unsettled.

Responses of individuals to hypnosis vary greatly. The popular belief that hypnosis guarantees the accuracy of recall is as yet without established foundation and, in fact, hypnosis often has no effect at all on memory. The most common response to hypnosis, however, appears to be an increase in both correct and incorrect recollections. Three general characteristics of hypnosis may lead to the introduction of inaccurate memories: the subject becomes "suggestible" and may try to please the hypnotist with answers the subject thinks will be met with approval; the subject is likely to "confabulate," that is, to fill in details from the imagination in order to make an answer more coherent and complete; and, the subject experiences "memory hardening," which gives him great confidence in both true and false memories, making effective cross-examination more difficult. See generally M. Orne, et al., Hypnotically Induced Testimony * * *. Despite the unreliability that hypnosis concededly may introduce, however, the procedure has been credited as instrumental in obtaining investigative leads or identifications that were later confirmed by independent evidence.

The inaccuracies the process introduces can be reduced, although perhaps not eliminated, by the use of procedural safeguards. One set of suggested guidelines calls for hypnosis to be performed only by a psychologist or psychiatrist with special training in its use and who is independent of the investigation. See Orne, The Use and Misuse of Hypnosis in Court * * *. These procedures reduce the possibility that biases will be communicated to the hypersuggestive subject by the hypnotist. Suggestion will be less likely also if the hypnosis is conducted in a neutral setting with no one present but the hypnotist and the subject. Tape or video recording of all interrogations, before, during, and after hypnosis, can help reveal if leading questions were asked. Such guidelines do not guarantee the accuracy of the testimony, because they cannot control the subject's own motivations or any tendency to confabulate, but they do provide a means of controlling overt suggestions.

The more traditional means of assessing accuracy of testimony also remain applicable in the case of a previously hypnotized defendant. Certain information recalled as a result of hypnosis may be verified as highly accurate by corroborating evidence. Cross-examination, even in the face of a confident defendant, is an effective tool for revealing inconsistencies. Moreover, a jury can be educated to the risks of hypnosis through expert testimony and cautionary instructions. Indeed, it is probably to a defendant's advantage to establish carefully the extent of his memory prior to hypnosis, in order to minimize the decrease in credibility the procedure might introduce.

We are not now prepared to endorse without qualifications the use of hypnosis as an investigative tool; scientific understanding of the phenomenon and of the means to control the effects of hypnosis is still in its infancy. Arkansas, however, has not justified the exclusion of *all* of a defendant's testimony that the defendant is unable to prove to be the product of prehypnosis memory. A State's legitimate interest in barring unreliable evidence does not extend to *per se* exclusions that may be reliable in an individual case. Wholesale inadmissibility of a defendant's testimony is an arbitrary restriction on the right to testify in the absence of clear evidence by the State repudiating the validity of all posthypnosis recollections. The State would be well within its powers if it established guidelines to aid trial courts in the evaluation of posthypnosis testimony and it may be able to show that testimony in a particular case is so unreliable that exclusion is justified. But it has not shown that hypnotically enhanced testimony is always so untrustworthy and so immune to the traditional means of evaluating credibility that it should disable a defendant from presenting her version of the events for which she is on trial.

In this case, the defective condition of the gun corroborated the details petitioner remembered about the shooting. The tape recordings provided some means to evaluate the hypnosis and the trial judge concluded that Doctor Back did not suggest responses with leading questions. Those circumstances present an argument for admissibility of petitioner's testimony in this particular case, an argument that must be considered by the trial court. Arkansas' *per se* rule excluding all posthypnosis testimony infringes impermissibly on the right of a defendant to testify on his or her own behalf.[20]

The judgment of the Supreme Court of Arkansas is vacated and the case is remanded to that court for further proceedings not inconsistent with this opinion.

CHIEF JUSTICE REHNQUIST, with whom JUSTICE WHITE, JUSTICE O'CONNOR, and JUSTICE SCALIA join, dissenting.

In deciding that petitioner Rock's testimony was properly limited at her trial, the Arkansas Supreme Court cited several factors that undermine the reliability of hypnotically induced testimony. Like the Court today, the Arkansas Supreme Court observed that a hypnotized individual becomes subject to suggestion, is likely to confabulate, and experiences artificially increased confidence in both true and false memories following hypnosis. No known set of procedures, both courts agree, can insure against the inherently unreliable nature of such testimony. Having acceded to the factual premises of the Arkansas Supreme Court, the Court nevertheless concludes that a state trial court must attempt to make its own scientific assessment of reliability in each case it is confronted with a request for the admission of hypnotically induced testimony. I find no justification in the Constitution for such a ruling.

In the Court's words, the decision today is "bottomed" on recognition of Rock's "constitutional right to testify in her own defense." While it is true that this Court, in dictum, has recognized the existence of such a right, the principles identified by the Court as underlying this right provide little support for invalidating the evidentiary rule applied by the Arkansas Supreme Court.

As a general matter, the Court first recites, a defendant's right to testify facilitates the truth-seeking function of a criminal trial by advancing both the " 'detection of guilt' " and " 'the protection of innocence.' " Quoting *Ferguson v. Georgia*. Such reasoning is hardly controlling here, where advancement of the truth-seeking function of Rock's trial was the sole motivation behind limiting her testimony. The Court also posits, however, that "a rule that denies an accused the opportunity to offer his own testimony" cannot be upheld because, "[l]ike the truthfulness of other witnesses, the defendant's veracity * * * can be tested

20. This disposition makes it unnecessary to consider petitioner's claims that the trial court's order restricting her testimony was unconstitutionally broad and that the trial court's application of the order resulted in a denial of due process of law. We also need not reach petitioner's argument that Arkansas' restriction on her testimony interferes with her Sixth Amendment right to counsel. Petitioner concedes that there is a "substantial question" whether she raised this federal question on appeal to the Arkansas Supreme Court. Reply Brief for Petitioner 2.

adequately by cross-examination." But the Court candidly admits that the increased confidence inspired by hypnotism makes "cross-examination more difficult," thereby diminishing an adverse party's ability to test the truthfulness of defendants such as Rock. * * *

This Court has traditionally accorded the States "respect * * * in the establishment and implementation of their own criminal trial rules and procedures." *Chambers.* * * * One would think that this deference would be at its highest in an area such as this, where, as the Court concedes, "scientific understanding * * * is still in its infancy." * * * The Supreme Court of Arkansas' decision was an entirely permissible response to a novel and difficult question. M. Orne et al., Hypnotically Refreshed Testimony * * *. As an original proposition, the solution this Court imposes upon Arkansas may be equally sensible, though requiring the matter to be considered *res nova* by every single trial judge in every single case might seem to some to pose serious administrative difficulties. But until there is a much more general consensus on the use of hypnosis than there is now, the Constitution does not warrant this Court's mandating its own view of how to deal with the issue.[a]

SECTION 4. DUE PROCESS REQUIREMENTS

TAYLOR v. KENTUCKY

436 U.S. 478, 98 S.Ct. 1930, 56 L.Ed.2d 468 (1978).

JUSTICE POWELL delivered the opinion of the Court.

Only two Terms ago, this Court observed that the "presumption of innocence, although not articulated in the Constitution, is a basic component of a fair trial under our system of criminal justice." *Estelle v. Williams,* 425 U.S. 501 (1976). In this felony case, the trial court instructed the jury as to the prosecution's burden of proof beyond a reasonable doubt, but refused petitioner's timely request for instructions on the presumption of innocence and the indictment's lack of evidentiary value. We are asked to decide whether the Due Process Clause of the Fourteenth Amendment requires that either or both instructions be given upon timely defense motions.

Petitioner was tried for robbery in 1976, allegedly having forced his way into the home of James Maddox and stolen a house key and a billfold containing $10 to $15. During *voir dire* of the jury, defense counsel questioned the panel about their understanding of the presumption of innocence, the burden of proof beyond a reasonable doubt, and the fact that an indictment is not evidence. The prosecutor then read the indictment to the jury.

The Commonwealth's only witness was Maddox. He testified that he had known petitioner for several years and had entertained petitioner at his home on

a. In *Portuondo v. Agard*, 120 S.Ct. 1119 (2000), the prosecutor, in the course of a closing argument questioning the credibility of the defendant's testimony, pointed out that defendant, unlike other witnesses, had been present throughout the trial and was thus able to hear what other witnesses said before he testified. The Court rejected the contention that the "rationale of *Griffin*" should be extended to bar such comments as burdening the defendant's constitutional rights to be present at trial and to testify on his own behalf. It found *Griffin* to be a "poor analogue" for several reasons, including: (1) *Griffin* prohibited a prosecutor from urging a jury to do what it is not permitted to do, but it is "natural" and "appropriate" for a jury, "in evaluating the credibility of a witness who testifies last, to have in mind and weigh in the balance the fact that he heard the testimony of all those who preceded him"; and (2) "*Griffin* prohibited comments that suggest a defendant's silence is evidence of *guilt*," while the comment here challenges credibility, in accord with "the long-standing rule" that a defendant who takes the stand "may be impeached and his testimony assailed like that of any other witness."

several occasions. According to Maddox, petitioner and a friend knocked on his door on the evening of February 16, 1976, asking to be admitted. Maddox refused, saying he had to go to bed. The two left, but returned 15 minutes later. They forced their way in, hit Maddox over the head, and fled with his billfold and house key, which were never recovered.

Petitioner then took the stand as the only witness for the defense. He admitted having been at Maddox's home on other occasions, but denied going there on February 16 or participating in the robbery. He stated that he had spent that night with two friends sitting in a parked car, watching a rainstorm and a power failure. Defense counsel requested the trial court to instruct the jury that "[t]he law presumes a defendant to be innocent of a crime," and that the indictment, previously read to the jury, was not evidence to be considered against the defendant. The court declined to give either instruction, and did not convey their substance in its charge to the jury. It did instruct the jury as to the Commonwealth's burden of proving petitioner's guilt beyond a reasonable doubt. Petitioner was found guilty and sentenced to five years of imprisonment. The Kentucky Court of Appeals affirmed * * *, the Supreme Court of Kentucky denied discretionary review, and we granted certiorari.

"The principle that there is a presumption of innocence in favor of the accused is the undoubted law, axiomatic and elementary, and its enforcement lies at the foundation of the administration of our criminal law." *Coffin v. United States*, 156 U.S. 432, 453 (1895). The *Coffin* Court traced the venerable history of the presumption from Deuteronomy through Roman law, English common law, and the common law of the United States. While *Coffin* held that the presumption of innocence and the equally fundamental principle that the prosecution bears the burden of proof beyond a reasonable doubt were logically separate and distinct, sharp scholarly criticism demonstrated the error of that view. Nevertheless, these same scholars advise against abandoning the instruction on the presumption of innocence, even when a complete explanation of the burden of proof beyond a reasonable doubt is provided. * * * This admonition derives from a perceived salutary effect upon lay jurors. While the legal scholar may understand that the presumption of innocence and the prosecution's burden of proof are logically similar, the ordinary citizen well may draw significant additional guidance from an instruction on the presumption of innocence. Wigmore described this effect as follows:

> "[I]n a criminal case the term [presumption of innocence] does convey a special and perhaps useful hint over and above the other form of the rule about the burden of proof, in that it cautions the jury to put away from their minds all the suspicion that arises from the arrest, the indictment, and the arraignment, and to reach their conclusion solely from the legal evidence adduced. In other words, the rule about burden of proof requires the prosecution by evidence to convince the jury of the accused's guilt; while the presumption of innocence, too, requires this, but conveys for the jury a special and additional caution (which is perhaps only an implied corollary to the other) to consider, in the material for their belief, *nothing but the evidence*, i.e., no surmises based on the present situation of the accused. This caution is indeed particularly needed in criminal cases."

This Court has declared that one accused of a crime is entitled to have his guilt or innocence determined solely on the basis of the evidence introduced at trial, and not on grounds of official suspicion, indictment, continued custody, or other circumstances not adduced as proof at trial. And it long has been recognized that an instruction on the presumption is one way of impressing upon the jury the importance of that right. * * *

Petitioner argues that in the circumstances of this case, the purging effect of an instruction on the presumption of innocence was essential to a fair trial. He points out that the trial court's instructions were themselves skeletal, placing little emphasis on the prosecution's duty to prove the case beyond a reasonable doubt and none at all on the jury's duty to judge petitioner only on the basis of the testimony heard at trial.

Against the background of the court's rather Spartan instructions, the prosecutor's closing argument ranged far and wide, asking the jury to draw inferences about petitioner's conduct from "facts" not in evidence, but propounded by the prosecutor. For example, he described the reasonable-doubt standard by declaring that petitioner, *"like every other defendant* who's ever been tried who's in the penitentiary or in the reformatory today, has this presumption of innocence until proved guilty beyond a reasonable doubt." (emphasis added). This statement linked petitioner to every defendant who turned out to be guilty and was sentenced to imprisonment. It could be viewed as an invitation to the jury to consider petitioner's status as a defendant as evidence tending to prove his guilt. Similarly, in responding to defense counsel's rhetorical query as to the whereabouts of the items stolen from Maddox, the prosecutor declared that "[o]ne of the first things *defendants do after they rip someone off,* they get rid of the evidence as fast and as quickly as they can." (emphasis added). This statement also implied that all defendants are guilty and invited the jury to consider that proposition in determining petitioner's guilt or innocence.[14]

Additionally, the prosecutor observed in his opening statement that Maddox "took out" a warrant against petitioner and that the grand jury had returned an indictment, which the prosecutor read to the jury. Thus, the jury not only was invited to consider the petitioner's status as a defendant, but also was permitted to draw inferences of guilt from the fact of arrest and indictment. The prosecutor's description of those events was not necessarily improper, but the combination of the skeletal instructions, the possible harmful inferences from the references to the indictment, and the repeated suggestions that petitioner's status as a defendant tended to establish his guilt created a genuine danger that the jury would convict petitioner on the basis of those extraneous considerations, rather than on the evidence introduced at trial. That risk was heightened because the trial essentially was a swearing contest between victim and accused.

Against the need for a presumption-of-innocence instruction, the Commonwealth argues first that such an instruction is not required where, as here, the jury is instructed as to the burden of proof beyond a reasonable doubt. The trial court's truncated discussion of reasonable doubt, however, was hardly a model of clarity. It defined reasonable doubt as "a substantial doubt, a real doubt." This definition, though perhaps not in itself reversible error, often has been criticized as confusing. See, e.g., *United States v. Muckenstrum,* 515 F.2d 568 (1975). And even if the instruction on reasonable doubt had been more clearly stated, the Commonwealth's argument ignores both the special purpose of a presumption-of-innocence instruction and the particular need for such an instruction in this case.

The Commonwealth also contends that no additional instructions were required, because defense counsel argued the presumption of innocence in both his

---

14. We do not suggest that such prosecutorial comments, standing alone, would rise to the level of reversible error, an issue not raised in this case. But they are relevant to the need for carefully framed instructions designed to assure that the accused be judged only on the evidence.

opening and closing statements. But arguments of counsel cannot substitute for instructions by the court. Petitioner's right to have the jury deliberate solely on the basis of the evidence cannot be permitted to hinge upon a hope that defense counsel will be a more effective advocate for that proposition than the prosecutor will be in implying that extraneous circumstances may be considered. It was the duty of the court to safeguard petitioner's rights, a duty only it could have performed reliably. * * *

We hold that on the facts of this case the trial court's refusal to give petitioner's requested instruction on the presumption of innocence resulted in a violation of his right to a fair trial as guaranteed by the Due Process Clause of the Fourteenth Amendment. The judgment of conviction is reversed, and the case is remanded for further proceedings not inconsistent with this opinion.

JUSTICE BRENNAN, concurring.

I join the Court's opinion because in reversing petitioner's conviction it reaffirms that "the 'presumption of innocence, although not articulated in the Constitution, is a basic component of a fair trial under our system of criminal justice.'" It follows from this proposition, as is clear from the Court's opinion, that trial judges should instruct the jury on a criminal defendant's entitlement to a presumption of innocence in all cases where such an instruction is requested.

JUSTICE STEVENS, with whom JUSTICE REHNQUIST joins, dissenting.

In a federal court it is reversible error to refuse a request for a proper instruction on the presumption of innocence. *Coffin v. United States.* That is not, however, a sufficient reason for holding that such an instruction is constitutionally required in every criminal trial.

The function of the instruction is to make it clear that the burden of persuasion rests entirely on the prosecutor. The same function is performed by the instruction requiring proof beyond a reasonable doubt. One standard instruction adds emphasis to the other. Neither should be omitted, but an "omission, or an incomplete instruction, is less likely to be prejudicial than a misstatement of the law." *Henderson v. Kibbe,* 431 U.S. 145 (1977). In some cases the omission may be fatal, but the Court wisely avoids a holding that this is always so.

In this case the omission did not violate a specific constitutional guarantee, such as the privilege against compulsory self-incrimination. Nor did it deny the defendant his fundamental right to a fair trial. An instruction on reasonable doubt, admittedly brief, was given. The *voir dire* had made clear to each juror the defendant's right to be presumed innocent despite his indictment. The prosecutor's closing argument did not precipitate any objection from defense counsel who listened to it; it may not, therefore, provide the basis for a reversal. Although the Court's appraisal is not unreasonable, for this was by no means a perfect trial, I do not believe that constitutional error was committed. Accordingly, I respectfully dissent.[a]

a. *Kentucky v. Whorton,* 441 U.S. 786 (1979), reversed on prosecution appeal a Kentucky Supreme Court ruling that read *Taylor* as requiring a presumption of innocence instruction "in all criminal trials." The Court stressed that the *Taylor* ruling "focused on the failure to give the instruction as it related to the overall fairness of the trial in its entirety" and that the *Taylor* majority specifically limited its holding to "the facts of this case." The Court remanded to the Kentucky Supreme Court for reconsideration in light of the "total-ity of the circumstances—including all instructions to the jury, the arguments of counsel, whether the weight of the evidence was overwhelming and other relevant factors." Three Justices dissented, arguing that an instruction on the presumption of innocence should be "constitutionally required in every case where a timely request has been made," although the failure to give the instruction could constitute harmless error under the rule of *Chapman v. California* (see Ch. 11, fn. d).

DARDEN v. WAINWRIGHT

477 U.S. 168, 106 S.Ct. 2464, 91 L.Ed.2d 144 (1986).

JUSTICE POWELL delivered the opinion of the Court.

Petitioner was tried and found guilty of murder, robbery, and assault with intent to kill in the Circuit Court for Citrus County, Florida, in January 1974. Pursuant to Florida's capital sentencing statute, the same jury that convicted petitioner heard further testimony and argument in order to make a nonbinding recommendation as to whether a death sentence should be imposed. The jury recommended a death sentence, and the trial judge followed that recommendation. On direct appeal, the Florida Supreme Court affirmed the conviction and the sentence. Petitioner made several of the same arguments in that appeal that he makes here. With respect to the prosecutorial misconduct claim, the court disapproved of the closing argument, but reasoned that the law required a new trial "only in those cases in which it is reasonably evident that the remarks might have influenced the jury to reach a more severe verdict of guilt * * * or in which the comment is unfair." * * * It concluded that the comments had not rendered petitioner's trial unfair. * * *

Petitioner then sought federal habeas corpus relief, raising the same claims he raises here. * * * A divided panel of the Court of Appeals for the Eleventh Circuit affirmed. * * *

Because of the nature of petitioner's claims, the facts of this case will be stated in more detail than is normally necessary in this Court. On September 8, 1973, at about 5:30 p.m., a black adult male entered Carl's Furniture Store near Lakeland, Florida. The only other person in the store was the proprietor, Mrs. Turman, who lived with her husband in a house behind the store. Mr. Turman, who worked nights at a juvenile home, had awakened at about 5:00 p.m., had a cup of coffee at the store with his wife, and returned home to let their dogs out for a run. Mrs. Turman showed the man around the store. He stated that he was interested in purchasing about $600 worth of furniture for a rental unit, and asked to see several different items. He left the store briefly, stating that his wife would be back to look at some of the items.

The same man returned just a few minutes later asking to see some stoves, and inquiring about the price. When Mrs. Turman turned toward the adding machine, he grabbed her and pressed a gun to her back, saying "Do as I say and you won't get hurt." He took her to the rear of the store and told her to open the cash register. He took the money, then ordered her to the part of the store where some boxsprings and mattresses were stacked against the wall. At that time Mr. Turman appeared at the back door. Mrs. Turman screamed while the man reached across her right shoulder and shot Mr. Turman between the eyes. Mr. Turman fell backwards, with one foot partially in the building. Ordering Mrs. Turman not to move, the man tried to pull Mr. Turman into the building and close the door, but could not do so because one of Mr. Turman's feet was caught in the door. The man left Mr. Turman face-up in the rain, and told Mrs. Turman to get down on the floor approximately five feet from where her husband lay dying. While she begged to go to her husband, he told her to remove her false teeth. He unzipped his pants, unbuckled his belt, and demanded that Mrs. Turman perform oral sex on him. She began to cry "Lord, have mercy." He told her to get up and go towards the front of the store.

Meanwhile, a neighbor family, the Arnolds, became aware that something had happened to Mr. Turman. The mother sent her 16 year-old son Phillip, a part-time employee at the furniture store, to help. When Phillip reached the back door he saw Mr. Turman lying partially in the building. When Phillip opened the door to take Turman's body inside, Mrs. Turman shouted "Phillip, no, go back." Phillip did not know what she meant and asked the man to help get Turman inside. He replied, "Sure, buddy, I will help you." As Phillip looked up, the man was pointing a gun in his face. He pulled the trigger and the gun misfired; he pulled the trigger again and shot Phillip in the mouth. Phillip started to run away, and was shot in the neck. While he was still running, he was shot a third time in the side. Despite these wounds, Phillip managed to stumble to the home of a neighbor, Mrs. Edith Hill. She had her husband call an ambulance while she tried to stop Phillip's bleeding. While she was helping Phillip, she saw a late model green Chevrolet leave the store and head towards Tampa on state highway 92. Phillip survived the incident; Mr. Turman, who never regained consciousness, died later that night.

Minutes after the murder petitioner was driving towards Tampa on highway 92, just a few miles away from the furniture store. He was out on furlough from a Florida prison, and was driving a car borrowed from his girlfriend in Tampa. He was driving fast on a wet road. Petitioner testified that as he came up on a line of cars in his lane, he was unable to slow down. He attempted to pass, but was forced off the road to avoid a head-on collision with an oncoming car. Petitioner crashed into a telephone pole. The driver of the oncoming car, John Stone, stopped his car and went to petitioner to see if he could help. Stone testified that as he approached the car, petitioner was zipping up his pants and buckling his belt. Police at the crash site later identified petitioner's car as a 1969 Chevrolet Impala of greenish golden brown color. Petitioner paid a bystander to give him a ride to Tampa. Petitioner later returned with a wrecker, only to find that the car had been towed away by the police.

By the time the police arrived at the scene of the accident, petitioner had left. The fact that the car matched the description of the car leaving the scene of the murder, and that the accident had occurred within three and one-half miles of the furniture store and within minutes of the murder, led police to suspect that the car was driven by the murderer. They searched the area. An officer found a pistol—a revolver—about forty feet from the crash site. The arrangement of shells within the chambers exactly matched the pattern that should have been found in the murder weapon: one shot, one misfire, followed by three shots, with a live shell remaining in the next chamber to be fired. A specialist for the FBI examined the pistol and testified that it was a Smith & Wesson .38 special revolver. It had been manufactured as a standard .38; it later was sent to England to be rebored, making it a much rarer type of gun than the standard .38. An examination of the bullet that killed Mr. Turman revealed that it came from a .38 Smith & Wesson special.

On the day following the murder petitioner was arrested at his girlfriend's house in Tampa. A few days later Mrs. Turman identified him at a preliminary hearing as her husband's murderer. Phillip Arnold selected petitioner's picture out of a spread of six photographs as the man who had shot him.[1] * * *

---

1. There are some minor discrepancies in the eyewitness identification. Mrs. Turman first described her assailant immediately after the murder while her husband was being taken to the emergency room. She told the investigating officer that the attacker was a heavyset man. When asked if he was "neat in his appearance, clean-looking, clean-shaven," she responded "[a]s far as I can remember, yes, sir." Ibid. She also stated to the officer that she thought that the attacker was about her height, 5'6" tall, and that he was wearing a pullover shirt with a stripe around the neck. The first time she saw petitioner after the attack was when she identified him at the preliminary hearing. She had not read any

Petitioner * * * contends that the prosecution's closing argument at the guilt-innocence stage of the trial rendered his conviction fundamentally unfair * * *. It is helpful as an initial matter to place these remarks in context. Closing argument came at the end of several days of trial. Because of a state procedural rule petitioner's counsel had the opportunity to present the initial summation as well as a rebuttal to the prosecutors' closing arguments. The prosecutors' comments must be evaluated in light of the defense argument that preceded it, which blamed the Polk County Sheriff's Office for a lack of evidence,[5] alluded to the death penalty,[6] characterized the perpetrator of the crimes as an "animal," [7] and contained counsel's personal opinion of the strength of the state's evidence.[8]

The prosecutors then made their closing argument. That argument deserves the condemnation it has received from every court to review it, although no court has held that the argument rendered the trial unfair. Several comments attempted to place some of the blame for the crime on the Division of Corrections, because Darden was on weekend furlough from a prison sentence when the crime occurred.[9] Some comments implied that the death penalty would be the only guarantee against a future similar act.[10] Others incorporated the defense's use of the word "animal." [11] Prosecutor McDaniel made several offensive comments reflecting an emotional reaction to the case.[12] These comments undoubtedly were

newspaper accounts of the crime, nor had she seen any picture of petitioner. When she was asked if petitioner was the man who had committed the crimes, she said yes. She also repeatedly identified him at trial.

Phillip Arnold first identified petitioner in a photo line-up while in the hospital. He could not speak at the time, and in response to the written question whether petitioner had a mustache, Phillip wrote back "I don't think so." Phillip also testified at trial that the attacker was a heavyset man wearing a dull, light color knit shirt with a ring around the neck. He testified that the man was almost his height, about 6'2" tall.

A motorist who stopped at the scene of the accident testified that petitioner was wearing a white or off-grey button-down shirt and that he had a slight mustache. In fact, the witness stated that he "didn't know it was that [the mustache] or the raindrops on him or not. I couldn't really tell that much to it, it was real thin, that's all." Petitioner is about 5'10" tall, and at the time of trial testified that he weighed about 175 pounds.

5. "The Judge is going to tell you to consider the evidence or the lack of evidence. We have a lack of evidence, almost criminally negligent on the part of the Polk County Sheriff's Office in this case. You could go on and on about it." Record 728.

6. "They took a coincidence and magnified that into a capital case. And they are asking you to kill a man on coincidence." Record 730.

7. "The first witness you saw was Mrs. Turman, who was a pathetic figure; who worked and struggled all of her life to build what little she had, the little furniture store; and a woman who was robbed, sexually assaulted, and then had her husband slaughtered

before her eyes, by what would have to be a vicious animal." Record 717. "And this murderer ran after him, aimed again, and this poor kid with half his brains blown away. ... It's the work of an animal, there's no doubt about it." Record 731–732.

8. "So they come up here and ask Citrus County people to kill the man. You will be instructed on lesser included offenses. ... The question is, do they have enough evidence to kill that man, enough evidence? And I honestly do not think they do." Record 736–737.

9. "As far as I am concerned, there should be another Defendant in this courtroom, one more, and that is the division of corrections, the prisons. ... Can we expect him to stay in a prison when they go there? Can we expect them to stay locked up once they go there? Do we know that they're going to be out on the public with guns, drinking?" Record 749–750. "Yes, there is another Defendant, but I regret that I know of no charges to place upon him, except the public condemnation of them, condemn them." Record 750–751.

10. "I will ask you to advise the Court to give him death. That's the only way I know that he is not going to get out on the public. It's the only way I know. It's the only way I can be sure of it. It's the only way anybody can be sure of it now, because the people that turned him loose—" Record 753.

11. "As far as I am concerned, and as Mr. Maloney said as he identified this man as an animal, this animal was on the public for one reason." Record 749.

12. "He shouldn't be out of his cell unless he has a leash on him and a prison guard at the other end of that leash." Record 750. "I improper. But as both the District Court and the original panel of the Court of Appeals (whose opinion on this issue still stands) recognized, it "is not enough that the prosecutors' remarks were undesirable or even universally condemned." The relevant question is whether the prosecutors' comments "so infected the trial with unfairness as to make the resulting conviction a denial of due process." *Donnelly v. DeChristoforo,* 416 U.S. 637 (1974). Moreover, the appropriate standard of review for such a claim on writ of habeas corpus is "the narrow one of due process, and not the broad exercise of supervisory power." *DeChristoforo.*

Under this standard of review, we agree with the reasoning of every court to consider these comments that they did not deprive petitioner of a fair trial. The prosecutors' argument did not manipulate or misstate the evidence, nor did it implicate other specific rights of the accused such as the right to counsel or the right to remain silent. Much of the objectionable content was invited by or was responsive to the opening summation of the defense. As we explained in *United States v. Young,* 470 U.S. 1 (1985), the idea of "invited response" is used not to excuse improper comments, but to determine their effect on the trial as a whole. The trial court instructed the jurors several times that their decision was to be made on the basis of the evidence alone, and that the arguments of counsel were not evidence. The weight of the evidence against petitioner was heavy; the "overwhelming eyewitness and circumstantial evidence to support a finding of guilt on all charges," 329 So.2d, at 291, reduced the likelihood that the jury's decision was influenced by argument. Finally, defense counsel made the tactical decision not to present any witness other than petitioner. This decision not only permitted them to give their summation prior to the prosecution's closing argument, but also gave them the opportunity to make a final rebuttal argument. Defense counsel were able to use the opportunity for rebuttal very effectively, turning much of the prosecutors' closing argument against them by placing many of the prosecutors' comments and actions in a light that was more likely to engender strong disapproval than result in inflamed passions against petitioner.[14] For these reasons, we agree with the District Court below that "Darden's trial was not perfect—few are—but neither was it fundamentally unfair." 513 F.Supp., at 958.

JUSTICE BLACKMUN, with whom JUSTICE BRENNAN, JUSTICE MARSHALL, and JUSTICE STEVENS join, dissenting. * * *

The Court's discussion of Darden's claim of prosecutorial misconduct is noteworthy for its omissions. Despite the fact that earlier this Term the Court relied heavily on standards governing the professional responsibility of defense

wish [Mr. Turman] had had a shotgun in his hand when he walked in the back door and blown his [Darden's] face off. I wish I could see him sitting here with no face, blown away by a shotgun." Record 758. "I wish someone had walked in the back door and blown his head off at that point." Record 759. "He fired in the boy's back, number five saving one. Didn't get a chance to use it. I wish he had used it on himself." Record 774. "I wish he had been killed in the accident, but he wasn't. Again, we are unlucky that time." Record 775. "Don't forget what he has done according to those witnesses, to make every attempt to change his appearance from September the 8th, 1973. The hair, the goatee, even the moustache and the weight. The only thing he hasn't done that I know of is cut his throat." Record 779. After this, the last in a series of

such comments, defense counsel objected for the first time.

14. "Mr. McDaniel made an impassioned plea ... how many times did he repeat [it]? I wish you had been shot, I wish they had blown his face away. My God, I get the impression he would like to be the man that stands there and pulls the switch on him." Record 791.

One of Darden's counsel testified at the habeas corpus hearing that he made the tactical decision not to object to the improper comments. Based on his long experience with prosecutor McDaniel, he knew McDaniel would "get much more vehement in his remarks if you allowed him to go on." By not immediately objecting, he hoped to encourage the prosecution to commit reversible error. Supp.App. 46–47.

counsel in ruling that an attorney's actions did not deprive his client of any constitutional right, see *Nix v. Whiteside* [Ch. 17], today it entirely ignores standards governing the professional responsibility of prosecutors in reaching the conclusion that the summations of Darden's prosecutors did not deprive him of a fair trial.

The prosecutors' remarks in this case reflect behavior as to which "virtually all the sources speak with one voice," *Nix v. Whiteside*, that is, a voice of strong condemnation. The following brief comparison of established standards of prosecutorial conduct with the prosecutors' behavior in this case merely illustrates, but hardly exhausts, the scope of the misconduct involved:

1. "A lawyer shall not . . . state a personal opinion as to . . . the credibility [of] a witness . . . or the guilt or innocence of an accused." Model Rules of Professional Conduct, Rule 3.4(e). * * * Yet one prosecutor, White, stated: "I am convinced, as convinced as I know I am standing before you today, that Willie Jasper Darden is a murderer, that he murdered Mr. Turman, that he robbed Mrs. Turman and that he shot to kill Phillip Arnold. I will be convinced of that the rest of my life." And the other prosecutor, McDaniel, stated, with respect to Darden's testimony: "Well, let me tell you something: If I am ever over in that chair over there, facing life or death, life imprisonment or death, I guarantee you I will lie until my teeth fall out."

2. "The prosecutor should refrain from argument which would divert the jury from its duty to decide the case on the evidence, by injecting issues broader than the guilt or innocence of the accused under the controlling law, or by making predictions of the consequences of the jury's verdict." ABA Standards, The Prosecution Function, § 3–5.8(d). * * * Yet McDaniel's argument was filled with references to Darden's status as a prisoner on furlough who "shouldn't be out of his cell unless he has a leash on him." Again and again, he sought to put on trial an absent "defendant," the State Department of Corrections that had furloughed Darden. He also implied that defense counsel would use improper tricks to deflect the jury from the real issue. Darden's status as a furloughed prisoner, the release policies of the Department of Corrections, and his counsel's anticipated tactics obviously had no legal relevance to the question the jury was being asked to decide: whether he had committed the robbery and murder at the Turmans' furniture store. Indeed, the State argued before this Court that McDaniel's remarks were harmless precisely *because* he "failed to discuss the issues, the weight of the evidence, or the credibility of the witnesses."

3. "The prosecutor should not use arguments calculated to inflame the passions or prejudices of the jury." ABA Standards, § 3–5.8(c). Yet McDaniel repeatedly expressed a wish "that I could see [Darden] sitting here with no face, blown away by a shotgun." Indeed, I do not think McDaniel's summation, taken as a whole, can accurately be described as anything but a relentless and single-minded attempt to inflame the jury. * * * Almost every page contains at least one offensive or improper statement; some pages contain little else. The misconduct here was not "slight or confined to a single instance, but . . . was pronounced and persistent, with a probable cumulative effect upon the jury which cannot be disregarded as inconsequential." *Berger v. United States*.

The Court presents what is, for me, an entirely unpersuasive one-page laundry list of reasons for ignoring this blatant misconduct. First, the Court says that the summations "did not manipulate or misstate the evidence [or] . . . implicate other specific rights of the accused such as the right to counsel or the right to remain silent." With all respect, that observation is quite beside the point. The "solemn purpose of endeavoring to ascertain the truth . . . is the *sine qua non* of a fair trial," and the summations cut to the very heart of the Due Process Clause by diverting the jury's attention "from the ultimate question of guilt or innocence that should be the central concern in a criminal proceeding."

Second, the Court says that "[m]uch of the objectionable content was invited by or was responsive to the opening summation of the defense." The Court identifies four portions of the defense summation that it thinks somehow "invited" McDaniel's sustained barrage. The State, however, did not object to any of these statements, and, to my mind, none of them is so objectionable that it would have justified a tactical decision to interrupt the defense summation and perhaps irritate the jury.

The Court begins by stating that defense counsel "blamed" the sheriff's office for a lack of evidence. The Court does not identify which, if any, of McDaniel's remarks represented a response to this statement. I cannot believe that the Court is suggesting, for example, that defense counsel's one mention of the "almost crimina[l] negligen[ce] on the part of the Polk County Sheriff's Office," justified McDaniel's express and repeated wish that he could try the Department of Corrections for murder.

Next, the Court notes that defense counsel "alluded" to the death penalty. While this allusion might have justified McDaniel's statement that "you are merely to determine his innocence or guilt, nothing else," it could hardly justify, for example, McDaniel's expressions of his personal wish that Darden be "blown away by a shotgun."

Moreover, the Court says, defense counsel twice referred to the perpetrator as an "animal." It is entirely unclear to me why this characterization called for any response from the prosecutor at all. Taken in context, defense counsel's statements did nothing more than tell the jury that, although everyone agreed that a heinous crime had been committed, the issue on which it should focus was whether *Darden* had committed it.

Finally, the Court finds that Darden brought upon himself McDaniel's tirade because defense counsel gave his "personal opinion of the strength of the State's evidence." Again, the Court gives no explanation of how the statement it quotes—a single, mild expression of defense counsel's overall assessment of the evidence—justified the "response" that followed, which consisted, to the extent it represented a comment on the evidence at all, of accusations of perjury, and personal disparagements of opposing counsel. In sum, McDaniel went so far beyond "respond[ing] substantially in order to 'right the scale,'" *Young,* that the reasoning in *Young* provides no basis at all for the Court's holding today.

The third reason the Court gives for discounting the effects of the improper summations is the supposed curative effect of the trial judge's instructions: the judge had instructed the jury that it was to decide the case on the evidence and that the arguments of counsel were not evidence. But the trial court overruled Darden's objection to McDaniel's repeated expressions of his wish that Darden had been killed, thus perhaps leaving the jury with the impression that McDaniel's comments were somehow relevant to the question before them. The trial judge's instruction that the attorneys were "trained in the law," and thus that their "analysis of the issues" could be "extremely helpful," might also have suggested to the jury that the substance of McDaniel's tirade was pertinent to their deliberations.

Fourth, the Court suggests that because Darden enjoyed the tactical advantage of having the last summation, he was able to "tur[n] much of the prosecutors' closing argument against them." But the issue before the jury was whether

Darden was guilty, not whether McDaniel's summation was proper. And the question before this Court is not whether we agree with defense counsel's criticism of the summation but whether the jury was affected by it. Since Darden was ultimately convicted, it is hard to see what basis the Court has for its naked assertion that "[d]efense counsel were able to use the opportunity for rebuttal very effectively." * * *

Fifth, the Court finds, in essence, that any error was harmless: "The weight of the evidence against petitioner was heavy; the 'overwhelming eyewitness and circumstantial evidence to support a finding of guilt on all charges' reduced the likelihood that the jury's decision was influenced by argument." * * * I simply do not believe the evidence in this case was so overwhelming that this Court can conclude, on the basis of the written record before it, that the jury's verdict was not the product of the prosecutors' misconduct. The three most damaging pieces of evidence—the identifications of Darden by Phillip Arnold and Helen Turman and the ballistics evidence—are all sufficiently problematic that they leave me unconvinced that a jury not exposed to McDaniel's egregious summation would necessarily have convicted Darden.

Arnold first identified Darden in a photo array shown to him in the hospital. The trial court suppressed that out-of-court identification following a long argument concerning the reliability and constitutionality of the procedures by which it was obtained.

Mrs. Turman's initial identification was made under even more suggestive circumstances. She testified at trial that she was taken to a preliminary hearing at which Darden appeared in order "[t]o identify him." Instead of being asked to view Darden in a lineup, Mrs. Turman was brought into the courtroom, where Darden apparently was the only black man present. Over defense counsel's objection, after the prosecutor asked her whether "this man sitting here" was "the man that shot your husband," she identified Darden. * * * While the question whether the various in- and out-of-court identifications ought to have been suppressed is not now before the Court, my confidence in their reliability is nonetheless undermined by the suggestiveness of the procedures by which they were obtained, particularly in light of Mrs. Turman's earlier difficulties in describing the criminal.

Finally, the ballistics evidence is hardly overwhelming. The purported murder weapon was tied conclusively neither to the crime nor to Darden. Special Agent Cunningham of the FBI's Firearms Identification Unit testified that the bullets recovered at the scene of the crime "could have been fired" from the gun, but he was unwilling to say that they in fact had come from that weapon. He also testified, contrary to the Court's assertion, that rebored Smith & Wessons were fairly common. Deputy Sheriff Weatherford testified that the gun was discovered in a roadside ditch adjacent to where Darden had wrecked his car on the evening of the crime. But the gun was discovered the next day, and the ditch was also next to a bar's parking lot.

Darden testified at trial on his own behalf and denied any involvement in the robbery and murder. His account of his actions on the day of the crime was contradicted only by Mrs. Turman's and Arnold's identifications. Indeed, a number of the State's witnesses corroborated parts of Darden's account. The trial judge who had seen and heard Darden testify found that he "emotionally and with what appeared on its face to be sincerity, proclaimed his innocence." In setting sentence, he viewed the fact that Darden "repeatedly professed his complete innocence of the charges" as a mitigating factor.

Thus, at bottom, this case rests on the jury's determination of the credibility of three witnesses—Helen Turman and Phillip Arnold, on the one side, and Willie Darden, on the other. I cannot conclude that McDaniel's sustained assault on Darden's very humanity did not affect the jury's ability to judge the credibility question on the real evidence before it. Because I believe that he did not have a trial that was fair, I would reverse Darden's conviction; I would not allow him to go to his death until he has been convicted at a fair trial. * * *

HERRERA v. COLLINS

506 U.S. 390, 113 S.Ct. 853, 122 L.Ed.2d 203 (1993).

CHIEF JUSTICE REHNQUIST delivered the opinion of the Court.

Petitioner Leonel Torres Herrera was convicted of capital murder and sentenced to death in January 1982. He unsuccessfully challenged the conviction on direct appeal and state collateral proceedings in the Texas state courts, and in a federal habeas petition. In February 1992—10 years after his conviction—he urged in a second federal habeas petition that he was "actually innocent" of the murder for which he was sentenced to death, and that the Eighth Amendment's prohibition against cruel and unusual punishment and the Fourteenth Amendment's guarantee of due process of law therefore forbid his execution. He supported this claim with affidavits tending to show that his now-dead brother, rather than he, had been the perpetrator of the crime. Petitioner urges us to hold that this showing of innocence entitles him to relief in this federal habeas proceeding. We hold that it does not.

[On an evening in September 1981, a passerby found the body of police officer Rucker, who had been shot in the head, lying next to his patrol car on a highway outside Los Fresnos, Texas. At approximately the same time, Officer Carrisalez, traveling with passenger Hernandez, stopped a speeding vehicle on the same highway, which was headed toward Los Fresnos, and away from the place where the body was found. As Carrisalez approached the vehicle, the driver shot him in the chest and sped away. Carrisalez died from the wound nine days later.]

Petitioner Herrera was arrested a few days after the shootings and charged with the capital murder of both Carrisalez and Rucker. He was tried and found guilty of the capital murder of Carrisalez in January 1982, and sentenced to death. In July 1982, petitioner pleaded guilty to the murder of Rucker.

At petitioner's trial for the murder of Carrisalez, Hernandez, who had witnessed Carrisalez' slaying from the officer's patrol car, identified petitioner as the person who had wielded the gun. A declaration by Officer Carrisalez to the same effect, made while he was in the hospital, was also admitted. Through a license plate check, it was shown that the speeding car involved in Carrisalez' murder was registered to petitioner's "live-in" girlfriend. Petitioner was known to drive this car, and he had a set of keys to the car in his pants pocket when he was arrested. Hernandez identified the car as the vehicle from which the murderer had emerged to fire the fatal shot. He also testified that there had been only one person in the car that night.

The evidence showed that Herrera's Social Security card had been found alongside Rucker's patrol car on the night he was killed. Splatters of blood on the car identified as the vehicle involved in the shootings, and on petitioner's blue jeans and wallet were identified as type A blood—the same type which Rucker had. (Herrera has type O blood.) Similar evidence with respect to strands of hair found in the car indicated that the hair was Rucker's and not Herrera's. A handwritten letter was also found on the person of petitioner when he was arrested, which strongly implied that he had killed Rucker.[1]

Petitioner appealed his conviction and sentence, arguing, among other things, that Hernandez' and Carrisalez' identifications were unreliable and improperly admitted. The Texas Court of Criminal Appeals affirmed, and we denied certiorari. Petitioner's application for state habeas relief was denied. Petitioner then filed a federal habeas petition, again challenging the identifications offered against him at trial. This petition was denied, and we again denied certiorari.

Petitioner next returned to state court and filed a second habeas petition, raising, among other things, a claim of "actual innocence" based on newly discovered evidence. In support of this claim petitioner presented the affidavits of Hector Villarreal, an attorney who had represented petitioner's brother, Raul Herrera, Sr., and of Juan Franco Palacious, one of Raul Sr.'s former cellmates. Both individuals claimed that Raul Sr., who died in 1984, had told them that he— and not petitioner—had killed Officers Rucker and Carrisalez. The State District Court denied this application, finding that "no evidence at trial remotely sug- gest[ed] that anyone other than [petitioner] committed the offense." The Texas Court of Criminal Appeals affirmed, and we denied certiorari.

In February 1992, petitioner lodged the instant habeas petition—his second— in federal court, alleging, among other things, that he is innocent of the murders of Rucker and Carrisalez, and that his execution would thus violate the Eighth and Fourteenth Amendments. In addition to proffering the above affidavits, petitioner presented the affidavits of Raul Herrera, Jr., Raul Sr.'s son, and Jose Ybarra, Jr., a schoolmate of the Herrera brothers. Raul Jr. averred that he had witnessed his father shoot Officers Rucker and Carrisalez and petitioner was not present. Raul Jr. was nine years old at the time of the killings. Ybarra alleged that Raul Sr. told him one summer night in 1983 that he had shot the two police officers. Petitioner alleged that law enforcement officials were aware of this evidence, and had withheld it in violation of *Brady v. Maryland [see Bagley,* ch. 13, at note a].

* * * [T]he District Court granted petitioner's request for a stay of execution so that he could present his claim of actual innocence, along with the Raul Jr. and Ybarra affidavits, in state court. Although it initially dismissed petitioner's *Brady* claim on the ground that petitioner had failed to present "any evidence of withholding exculpatory material by the prosecution," the District Court also granted an evidentiary hearing on this claim after reconsideration * * *. The Court of Appeals [then] vacated the stay of execution. It agreed with the District Court's initial conclusion that there was no evidentiary basis for petitioner's *Brady* claim, and found disingenuous petitioner's attempt to couch his claim of actual innocence in *Brady* terms. Absent an accompanying constitutional viola- tion, the Court of Appeals held that petitioner's claim of actual innocence was not cognizable * * * under *Townsend v. Sain,* 372 U.S. 293 (1963). * * *

Petitioner asserts that the Eighth and Fourteenth Amendments to the United States Constitution prohibit the execution of a person who is innocent of the crime for which he was convicted. This proposition has an elemental appeal, as

---

1. The letter read: "To whom it may con- cern: I am terribly sorry for those I have brought grief to their lives. * * * What hap- pened to Rucker was for a certain reason. I knew him as Mike Tatum. He was in my business, and he violated some of its laws and suffered the penalty, like the one you have for me when the time comes. * * * The other officer that became part of our lives, me and Rucker's (Tatum), that night had not to do in this [sic]. He was out to do what he had to do, protect, but that's life. There's a lot of us that wear different faces in lives every day, and that is what causes problems for all. [Unintelligi- ble word]. * * *"

would the similar proposition that the Constitution prohibits the imprisonment of one who is innocent of the crime for which he was convicted. After all, the central purpose of any system of criminal justice is to convict the guilty and free the innocent. * * * But the evidence upon which petitioner's claim of innocence rests was not produced at his trial, but rather eight years later. In any system of criminal justice, "innocence" or "guilt" must be determined in some sort of a judicial proceeding. Petitioner's showing of innocence, and indeed his constitutional claim for relief based upon that showing, must be evaluated in the light of the previous proceedings in this case, which have stretched over a span of 10 years.

A person when first charged with a crime is entitled to a presumption of innocence, and may insist that his guilt be established beyond a reasonable doubt. *In re Winship,* 397 U.S. 358 (1970). Other constitutional provisions also have the effect of ensuring against the risk of convicting an innocent person. [The Court here cites a long line of illustrative cases, briefly describing the rights recognized there as: a "right to confront adverse witnesses"; a "right to compulsory process"; a "right to effective assistance of counsel"; a "right to jury trial"; an obligation of the prosecution to "disclose exculpatory evidence"; a "right to assistance of counsel"; and a "right to a fair trial in a fair tribunal."] In capital cases, we have required additional protections because of the nature of the penalty at stake. See, e.g., *Beck v. Alabama,* 447 U.S. 625 (1980) (jury must be given option of convicting the defendant of a lesser offense). All of these constitutional safeguards, of course, make it more difficult for the State to rebut and finally overturn the presumption of innocence which attaches to every criminal defendant. But we have also observed that "[d]ue process does not require that every conceivable step be taken, at whatever cost, to eliminate the possibility of convicting an innocent person." *Patterson v. New York,* 432 U.S. 197 (1977). To conclude otherwise would all but paralyze our system for enforcement of the criminal law.

Once a defendant has been afforded a fair trial and convicted of the offense for which he was charged, the presumption of innocence disappears. Here, it is not disputed that the State met its burden of proving at trial that petitioner was guilty of the capital murder of Officer Carrisalez beyond a reasonable doubt. Thus, in the eyes of the law, petitioner does not come before the Court as one who is "innocent," but on the contrary as one who has been convicted by due process of law of two brutal murders.

Based on affidavits here filed, petitioner claims that evidence never presented to the trial court proves him innocent notwithstanding the verdict reached at his trial. Such a claim is not cognizable in the state courts of Texas. For to obtain a new trial based on newly discovered evidence, a defendant must file a motion within 30 days after imposition or suspension of sentence. Tex.Rule App.Proc. 31(a)(1) (1992). The Texas courts have construed this 30–day time limit as jurisdictional.

Claims of actual innocence based on newly discovered evidence have never been held to state a ground for federal habeas relief absent an independent constitutional violation occurring in the underlying state criminal proceeding. Chief Justice Warren made this clear in *Townsend v. Sain,* 372 U.S. 293, (1963) (emphasis added):

"Where newly discovered evidence is alleged in a habeas application, evidence which could not reasonably have been presented to the state trier of facts, the federal court must grant an evidentiary hearing. Of course, such evidence must bear upon the constitutionality of the applicant's detention;

the existence merely of newly discovered evidence relevant to the guilt of a state prisoner is not a ground for relief on federal habeas corpus."

This rule is grounded in the principle that federal habeas courts sit to ensure that individuals are not imprisoned in violation of the Constitution—not to correct errors of fact.[a] * * *

Petitioner is understandably imprecise in describing the sort of federal relief to which a suitable showing of actual innocence would entitle him. In his brief he states that the federal habeas court should have "an important initial opportunity to hear the evidence and resolve the merits of Petitioner's claim." Acceptance of this view would presumably require the habeas court to hear testimony from the witnesses who testified at trial as well as those who made the statements in the affidavits which petitioner has presented, and to determine anew whether or not petitioner is guilty of the murder of Officer Carrisalez. Indeed, the dissent's approach differs little from that hypothesized here.

The dissent would place the burden on petitioner to show that he is "probably" innocent. Although petitioner would not be entitled to discovery "as a matter of right," the District Court would retain its "discretion to order discovery * * * when it would help the court make a reliable determination with respect to the prisoner's claim." And although the District Court would not be required to hear testimony from the witnesses who testified at trial or the affiants upon whom petitioner relies, it would allow the District Court to do so "if the petition warrants a hearing." At the end of the day, the dissent would have the District Court "make a case-by-case determination about the reliability of newly discovered evidence under the circumstances," and then "weigh the evidence in favor of the prisoner against the evidence of his guilt."

The dissent fails to articulate the relief that would be available if petitioner were to meets its "probable innocence" standard. Would it be commutation of petitioner's death sentence, new trial, or unconditional release from imprisonment? The typical relief granted in federal habeas corpus is a conditional order of release unless the State elects to retry the successful habeas petitioner, or in a capital case a similar conditional order vacating the death sentence. Were petitioner to satisfy the dissent's "probable innocence" standard, therefore, the District Court would presumably be required to grant a conditional order of relief, which would in effect require the State to retry petitioner 10 years after his first trial, not because of any constitutional violation which had occurred at the first trial, but simply because of a belief that in light of petitioner's new found evidence a jury might find him not guilty at a second trial. Yet there is no guarantee that the guilt or innocence determination would be any more exact. To the contrary, the passage of time only diminishes the reliability of criminal adjudications. * * *

This is not to say that our habeas jurisprudence casts a blind eye towards innocence. In a series of cases culminating with *Sawyer v. Whitley,* 507 U.S. 968 (1993), decided last Term, we have held that a petitioner otherwise subject to defenses of abusive or successive use of the writ may have his federal constitutional claim considered on the merits if he makes a proper showing of actual innocence.[b] This rule, or fundamental miscarriage of justice exception, is ground-

---

a. 28 U.S.C. § 2254(a) provides: "The Supreme Court, a Justice thereof, a circuit judge, or a district court shall entertain an application for a writ of habeas corpus in behalf of a person in custody pursuant to the judgment of a State court only on the ground that he is in custody in violation of the Constitution or laws or treaties of the United States."

b. This reference is to constitutional claims that ordinarily would be sufficient to gain habeas relief (i.e., the alleged constitutional violations are cognizable on habeas review and do ed in the "equitable discretion" of habeas courts to see that federal constitutional errors do not result in the incarceration of innocent persons. But this body of our habeas jurisprudence makes clear that a claim of "actual innocence" is not itself a constitutional claim, but instead a gateway through which a habeas petitioner must pass to have his otherwise barred constitutional claim considered on the merits.

Petitioner in this case is simply not entitled to habeas relief based on the reasoning of this line of cases. For he does not seek excusal of a procedural error so that he may bring an independent constitutional claim challenging his conviction or sentence, but rather argues that he is entitled to habeas relief because newly discovered evidence shows that his conviction is factually incorrect. The fundamental miscarriage of justice exception is available "only where the prisoner *supplements* his constitutional claim with a colorable showing of factual innocence." *Kuhlmann v. Wilson,* 477 U.S. 436 (1986). We have never held that it extends to freestanding claims of actual innocence. Therefore, the exception is inapplicable here.

Petitioner asserts that this case is different because he has been sentenced to death. But we have "refused to hold that the fact that a death sentence has been imposed requires a different standard of review on federal habeas corpus." *Murray v. Giarratano,* 492 U.S. 1 (1989) (plurality opinion). We have, of course, held that the Eighth Amendment requires increased reliability of the process by which capital punishment may be imposed. See, *e.g., McKoy v. North Carolina,* 494 U.S. 433 (1990) (unanimity requirement impermissibly limits jurors' consideration of mitigating evidence); *Eddings v. Oklahoma,* 455 U.S. 104 (1982) (jury must be allowed to consider all of a capital defendant's mitigating character evidence); *Lockett v. Ohio,* 438 U.S. 586 (1978) (plurality opinion) (same). But petitioner's claim does not fit well into the doctrine of these cases, since, as we have pointed out, it is far from clear that a second trial 10 years after the first trial would produce a more reliable result.

Perhaps mindful of this, petitioner urges not that he necessarily receive a new trial, but that his death sentence simply be vacated if a federal habeas court deems that a satisfactory showing of "actual innocence" has been made. But such a result is scarcely logical; petitioner's claim is not that some error was made in imposing a capital sentence upon him, but that a fundamental error was

not constitute harmless error), but have been procedurally defaulted because those claims either were not properly presented in the state proceedings or were not properly presented in an earlier petition for habeas review. The Supreme Court had held that such claims would not be considered upon habeas review unless the petitioner could show either (1) that there existed both "cause" excusing the failure to timely present the constitutional claim and "actual prejudice" resulting from the alleged constitutional violation, or (2) that allowing the conviction to stand would result in a "fundamental miscarriage of justice." This second, "fundamental miscarriage" exception to the general prohibition against considering procedurally defaulted claims was based on the premise that, notwithstanding the interests in finality, judicial economy, and timely factfinding that support the rules on which procedural defaults are based, habeas relief should still be available to remedy the "fundamentally unjust incarceration" which occurs when a constitu-

tional violation has resulted in the conviction and incarceration of a person who is "actually innocent." The Court had noted that a "fundamental miscarriage" was not established simply by showing that the defendant would have been acquitted except for the constitutional violation, as that violation may have been one that required an acquittal notwithstanding factual guilt (e.g., by excluding reliable evidence). The focus was on "actual" rather than "legal" innocence. *Smith v. Murray,* 477 U.S. 527 (1986).

In the *Sawyer* case cited above in the Court's opinion, the Supreme Court had held that the "fundamental miscarriage" exception also applied where a habeas petitioner in a capital case was "actually innocent" as to the imposition of capital punishment, although not as to the underlying offense. The post-*Herrera* decision of *Schlup v. Delo,* discussed infra in the Note following *Herrera,* further explored the content of "actual innocence" standard.

made in finding him guilty of the underlying murder in the first place. It would be a rather strange jurisprudence, in these circumstances, which held that under our Constitution he could not be executed, but that he could spend the rest of his life in prison.* * *

Petitioner also relies on *Johnson v. Mississippi,* 486 U.S. 578 (1988), where we held that the Eighth Amendment requires reexamination of a death sentence based in part on a prior felony conviction which was set aside in the rendering State after the capital sentence was imposed. There, the State insisted that it was too late in the day to raise this point. But we pointed out that the Mississippi Supreme Court had previously considered similar claims by writ of error *coram nobis.* Thus, there was no need to override state law relating to newly discovered evidence in order to consider Johnson's claim on the merits. Here, there is no doubt that petitioner seeks additional process—an evidentiary hearing on his claim of "actual innocence" based on newly discovered evidence—which is not available under Texas law more than 30 days after imposition or suspension of sentence. Tex.Rule App.Proc. 31(a)(1) (1992).

Alternatively, petitioner invokes the Fourteenth Amendment's guarantee of due process of law in support of his claim that his showing of actual innocence entitles him to a new trial, or at least to a vacation of his death sentence.[6] "[B]ecause the States have considerable expertise in matters of criminal procedure and the criminal process is grounded in centuries of common-law tradition," we have "exercis[ed] substantial deference to legislative judgments in this area." * * * Thus, we have found criminal process lacking only where it " 'offends some principle of justice so rooted in the traditions and conscience of our people as to be ranked as fundamental.' " "Historical practice is probative of whether a procedural rule can be characterized as fundamental." *Medina v. California,* 505 U.S. 437 (1992).

The Constitution itself, of course, makes no mention of new trials. New trials in criminal cases were not granted in England until the end of the 17th century. And even then, they were available only in misdemeanor cases, though the writ of error *coram nobis* was available for some errors of fact in felony cases. The First Congress provided for new trials for "reasons for which new trials have usually been granted in courts of law." Act of Sept. 24, 1789, ch. 20, § 17, 1 Stat. 83. This rule was early held to extend to criminal cases. * * * One of the grounds upon which new trials were granted was newly discovered evidence. * * *

The early federal cases adhere to the common-law rule that a new trial may be granted only during the term of court in which the final judgment was entered. Otherwise, "the court at a subsequent term has power to correct inaccuracies in mere matters of form, or clerical errors." In 1934, this Court departed from the common-law rule and adopted a time limit—60 days after final judgment—for filing new trial motions based on newly discovered evidence. Four years later, we amended Rule II(3) to allow such motions in capital cases "at any time" before

---

6. The dissent takes us to task for examining petitioner's Fourteenth Amendment claim in terms of procedural rather than substantive due process. Because "[e]xecution of an innocent person is the ultimate 'arbitrary impositio[n],' " the dissent concludes that "petitioner may raise a substantive due process challenge to his punishment on the ground that he is actually innocent." But the dissent puts the cart before the horse. For its due process analysis rests on the assumption that petitioner is in fact innocent. However, as we have discussed, petitioner does not come before this Court as an innocent man, but rather as one who has been convicted by due process of law of two capital murders. The question before us, then, is not whether due process prohibits the execution of an innocent person, but rather whether it entitles petitioner to judicial review of his "actual innocence" claim. This issue is properly analyzed only in terms of procedural due process.

the execution took place. * * * There ensured a debate as to whether this Court should abolish the time limit for filing new trial motions based on newly discovered evidence to prevent a miscarriage of justice, or retain a time limit even in capital cases to promote finality. In 1945, we set a two-year time limit for filing new trial motions based on newly discovered evidence and abolished the exception for capital cases. Federal Rule 33. We have strictly construed the Rule 33 time limits. * * * And the Rules's treatment of new trials based on newly discovered evidence has not changed since its adoption.

The American Colonies adopted the English common law on new trials. Thus, where new trials were available, motions for such relief typically had to be filed before the expiration of the term during which the trial was held. * * * Over time, many States enacted statutes providing for new trials in all types of cases. Some States also extended the time period for filing new trial motions beyond the term of court, but most States required that such motions be made within a few days after the verdict was rendered or before the judgment was entered. * * *

The practice in the States today, while of limited relevance to our historical inquiry, is divergent. Texas is one of 17 States that requires a new trial motion based on newly discovered evidence to be made within 60 days of judgment. One State adheres to the common-law rule and requires that such a motion be filed during the term in which judgment was rendered. Eighteen jurisdictions have time limits ranging between 1 and 3 years, with 10 States and the District of Columbia following the 2–year federal time limit. Only 15 States allow a new trial motion based on newly discovered evidence to be filed more than 3 years after conviction. Of these States, 4 have waivable time limits of less than 120 days, 2 have waivable time limits of more than 120 days, and 9 States have no time limits.

In light of the historical availability of new trials, our own amendments to Rule 33, and the contemporary practice in the States, we cannot say that Texas' refusal to entertain petitioner's newly discovered evidence eight years after his conviction transgresses a principle of fundamental fairness "rooted in the traditions and conscience of our people." This is not to say, however, that petitioner is left without a forum to raise his actual innocence claim. For under Texas law, petitioner may file a request for executive clemency. Clemency is deeply rooted in our Anglo–American tradition of law, and is the historic remedy for preventing miscarriages of justice where judicial process has been exhausted. * * *

Of course, although the Constitution vests in the President a pardon power, it does not require the States to enact a clemency mechanism. Yet since the British Colonies were founded, clemency has been available in America. The original States were reluctant to vest the clemency power in the executive. And although this power has gravitated toward the executive over time, several States have split the clemency power between the Governor and an advisory board selected by the legislature. * * * Today, all 36 States that authorize capital punishment have constitutional or statutory provisions for clemency. * * *

As the foregoing discussion illustrates, in state criminal proceedings the trial is the paramount event for determining the guilt or innocence of the defendant. Federal habeas review of state convictions has traditionally been limited to claims of constitutional violations occurring in the course of the underlying state criminal proceedings. Our federal habeas cases have treated claims of "actual innocence," not as an independent constitutional claim, but as a basis upon which a habeas petitioner may have an independent constitutional claim considered on the merits, even though his habeas petition would otherwise be regarded as successive or abusive. History shows that the traditional remedy for claims of innocence based on new evidence, discovered too late in the day to file a new trial motion, has been executive clemency.

We may assume, for the sake of argument in deciding this case, that in a capital case a truly persuasive demonstration of "actual innocence" made after trial would render the execution of a defendant unconstitutional, and warrant federal habeas relief if there were no state avenue open to process such a claim. But because of the very disruptive effect that entertaining claims of actual innocence would have on the need for finality in capital cases, and the enormous burden that having to retry cases based on often stale evidence would place on the States, the threshold showing for such an assumed right would necessarily be extraordinarily high. The showing made by petitioner in this case falls far short of any such threshold.

Petitioner's newly discovered evidence consists of affidavits. In the new trial context, motions based solely upon affidavits are disfavored because the affiants' statements are obtained without the benefit of cross-examination and an opportunity to make credibility determinations. * * * Petitioner's affidavits are particularly suspect in this regard because, with the exception of Raul Herrera, Jr.'s, affidavit, they consist of hearsay. Likewise, in reviewing petitioner's new evidence, we are mindful that defendants often abuse new trial motions "as a method of delaying enforcement of just sentences." *United States v. Johnson*, 327 U.S. 106 (1946). Although we are not presented with a new trial motion *per se*, we believe the likelihood of abuse is as great—or greater—here.

The affidavits filed in this habeas proceeding were given over eight years after petitioner's trial. No satisfactory explanation has been given as to why the affiants waited until the 11th hour—and, indeed, until after the alleged perpetrator of the murders himself was dead—to make their statements. * * * Equally troubling, no explanation has been offered as to why petitioner, by hypothesis an innocent man, pleaded guilty to the murder of Rucker.

Moreover, the affidavits themselves contain inconsistencies, and therefore fail to provide a convincing account of what took place on the night Officers Rucker and Carrisalez were killed. For instance, the affidavit of Raul Jr., who was nine years old at the time, indicates that there were three people in the speeding car from which the murderer emerged, whereas Hector Villarreal attested that Raul Sr. told him that there were two people in the car that night. Of course, Hernandez testified at petitioner's trial that the murderer was the only occupant of the car. The affidavits also conflict as to the direction in which the vehicle was heading when the murders took place, and petitioner's whereabouts on the night of the killings.

Finally, the affidavits must be considered in light of the proof of petitioner's guilt at trial—proof which included two eyewitness identifications, numerous pieces of circumstantial evidence, and a handwritten letter in which petitioner apologized for killing the officers and offered to turn himself in under certain conditions. That proof, even when considered alongside petitioner's belated affidavits, points strongly to petitioner's guilt.

This is not to say that petitioner's affidavits are without probative value. Had this sort of testimony been offered at trial, it could have been weighed by the jury, along with the evidence offered by the State and petitioner, in deliberating upon its verdict. Since the statements in the affidavits contradict the evidence received at trial, the jury would have had to decide important issues of credibility. But coming 10 years after petitioner's trial, this showing of innocence falls far short of that which would have to be made in order to trigger the sort of constitutional claim which we have assumed, *arguendo,* to exist. * * * The judgment of the Court of Appeals is Affirmed.

JUSTICE O'CONNOR, with whom JUSTICE KENNEDY, joins, concurring.* * *

Exercising restraint, the Court and Justice White assume for the sake of argument that, if a prisoner were to make an exceptionally strong showing of actual innocence, the execution could not go forward. Justice Blackmun, in contrast, would expressly so hold; he would also announce the precise burden of proof. * * * Resolving the issue is neither necessary nor advisable in this case. The question is a sensitive and, to say the least, troubling one. It implicates not just the life of a single individual, but also the State's powerful and legitimate interest in punishing the guilty, and the nature of state-federal relations. * * *

Nonetheless, the proper disposition of this case is neither difficult nor troubling. No matter what the Court might say about claims of actual innocence today, petitioner could not obtain relief. The record overwhelmingly demonstrates that petitioner deliberately shot and killed Officers Rucker and Carrisalez the night of September 29, 1981; petitioner's new evidence is bereft of credibility. Indeed, despite its stinging criticism of the Court's decision, not even the dissent expresses a belief that petitioner might possibly be actually innocent. Nor could it: The record makes it abundantly clear that petitioner is not somehow the future victim of "simple murder," (dissenting opinion), but instead himself the established perpetrator of two brutal and tragic ones. * * *

JUSTICE SCALIA, with whom JUSTICE THOMAS joins, concurring.

We granted certiorari on the question whether it violates due process or constitutes cruel and unusual punishment for a State to execute a person who, having been convicted of murder after a full and fair trial, later alleges that newly discovered evidence shows him to be "actually innocent." I would have preferred to decide that question, particularly since, as the Court's discussion shows, it is perfectly clear what the answer is: There is no basis in text, tradition, or even in contemporary practice (if that were enough), for finding in the Constitution a right to demand judicial consideration of newly discovered evidence of innocence brought forward after conviction. In saying that such a right exists, the dissenters apply nothing but their personal opinions to invalidate the rules of more than two thirds of the States, and a Federal Rule of Criminal Procedure for which this Court itself is responsible. If the system that has been in place for 200 years (and remains widely approved) "shocks" the dissenters' consciences, perhaps they should doubt the calibration of their consciences, or, better still, the usefulness of "conscience-shocking" as a legal test.

I nonetheless join the entirety of the Court's opinion, including the final portion—because there is no legal error in deciding a case by assuming *arguendo* that an asserted constitutional right exists, and because I can understand, or at least am accustomed to, the reluctance of the present Court to admit publicly that Our Perfect Constitution [1] lets stand any injustice, much less the execution of an innocent man who has received, though to no avail, all the process that our society has traditionally deemed adequate. With any luck, we shall avoid ever having to face this embarrassing question again, since it is improbable that evidence of innocence as convincing as today's opinion requires would fail to produce an executive pardon.

---

1. My reference is to an article by Professor Monaghan, which discusses the unhappy truth that not every problem was meant to be solved by the United States Constitution, nor can be. See Monaghan, Our Perfect Constitution, 56 N.Y.U.L.Rev. 353 (1981).

My concern is that in making life easier for ourselves we not appear to make it harder for the lower federal courts, imposing upon them the burden of regularly analyzing newly-discovered-evidence-of-innocence claims in capital cases (in which event such federal claims, it can confidently be predicted, will become routine and even repetitive). A number of Courts of Appeals have hitherto held, largely in reliance on our unelaborated statement in *Townsend v. Sain,* that newly discovered evidence relevant only to a state prisoner's guilt or innocence is not a basis for federal habeas corpus relief. * * * I do not understand it to be the import of today's decision that those holdings are to be replaced with a strange regime that assumes permanently, though only *"arguendo,"* that a constitutional right exists, and expends substantial judicial resources on that assumption. The Court's extensive and scholarly discussion of the question presented in the present case does nothing but support our statement in *Townsend,* and strengthen the validity of the holdings based upon it.

JUSTICE WHITE, concurring in the judgment.

In voting to affirm, I assume that a persuasive showing of "actual innocence" made after trial, even though made after the expiration of the time provided by law for the presentation of newly discovered evidence, would render unconstitutional the execution of petitioner in this case. To be entitled to relief, however, petitioner would at the very least be required to show that based on proffered newly discovered evidence and the entire record before the jury that convicted him, "no rational trier of fact could [find] proof of guilt beyond a reasonable doubt." *Jackson v. Virginia.* For the reasons stated in the Court's opinion, petitioner's showing falls far short of satisfying even that standard, and I therefore concur in the judgment.

JUSTICE BLACKMUN, with whom JUSTICE STEVENS and JUSTICE SOUTER join with respects to Parts I–IV, dissenting.[c]

Nothing could be more contrary to contemporary standards of decency, see *Ford v. Wainwright,* or more shocking to the conscience, see *Rochin v. California* [see (ch. 2, § 1, fn. a)], than to execute a person who is actually innocent.

I therefore must disagree with the long and general discussion that precedes the Court's disposition of this case. That discussion, of course, is dictum because the Court assumes, "for the sake of argument in deciding this case, that in a capital case a truly persuasive demonstration of 'actual innocence' made after trial would render the execution of a defendant unconstitutional." Without articulating the standard it is applying, however, the Court then decides that this petitioner has not made a sufficiently persuasive case. Because I believe that in the first instance the District Court should decide whether petitioner is entitled to a hearing and whether he is entitled to relief on the merits of his claim, I would reverse the order of the Court of Appeals and remand this case for further proceedings in the District Court.

The Court's enumeration of the constitutional rights of criminal defendants surely is entirely beside the point. These protections sometimes fail. We really are being asked to decide whether the Constitution forbids the execution of a person who has been validly convicted and sentenced but who, nonetheless, can prove his innocence with newly discovered evidence. Despite the State of Texas' astonishing protestation to the contrary, I do not see how the answer can be anything but "yes."

c. Part V of the dissent, referring to Justice Blackmun's previous opinions relating to the constitutionality of the death penalty as administered, is deleted. Justices Stevens and Souter concurred in all of the dissent reproduced here except the first two paragraphs.

The Eighth Amendment prohibits "cruel and unusual punishments." This proscription is not static but rather reflects evolving standards of decency. * * * I think it is crystal clear that the execution of an innocent person is "at odds with contemporary standards of fairness and decency." Indeed, it is at odds with any standard of decency that I can imagine. * * * [2]

The protection of the Eighth Amendment does not end once a defendant has been validly convicted and sentenced. In *Johnson v. Mississippi,* the petitioner had been convicted of murder and sentenced to death on the basis of three aggravating circumstances. One of those circumstances was that he previously had been convicted of a violent felony in the State of New York. After Johnson had been sentenced to death, the New York Court of Appeals reversed his prior conviction. Although there was no question that the prior conviction was valid at the time of Johnson's sentencing, this Court held that the Eighth Amendment required review of the sentence because "the jury was allowed to consider evidence that has been revealed to be materially inaccurate."* * *

The Court also suggests that allowing petitioner to raise his claim of innocence would not serve society's interest in the reliable imposition of the death penalty because it might require a new trial that would be less accurate than the first. This suggestion misses the point entirely. The question is not whether a second trial would be more reliable than the first but whether, in light of new evidence, the result of the first trial is sufficiently reliable for the State to carry out a death sentence. Furthermore, it is far from clear that a State will seek to retry the rare prisoner who prevails on a claim of actual innocence. * * *

Execution of the innocent is equally offensive to the Due Process Clause of the Fourteenth Amendment. The majority's discussion misinterprets petitioner's Fourteenth Amendment claim as raising a procedural rather than a substantive due process challenge. * * * Petitioner's claim falls within our [substantive] due process precedents. * * * The lethal injection that petitioner faces as an allegedly innocent person is certainly closer to the rack and the screw than the stomach pump condemned in *Rochin.* Execution of an innocent person is the ultimate " 'arbitrary impositio[n].' " *Planned Parenthood v. Casey,* 505 U.S. 833 (1992). It is an imposition from which one never recovers and for which one can never be compensated. Thus, I also believe that petitioner may raise a substantive due process challenge to his punishment on the ground that he is actually innocent.

Given my conclusion that it violates the Eighth and Fourteenth Amendments to execute a person who is actually innocent, I find no bar in *Townsend v. Sain,* to consideration of an actual innocence claim. Newly discovered evidence of petitioner's innocence does bear on the constitutionality of his execution. Of course, it could be argued this is in some tension with *Townsend*'s statement that "the existence merely of newly discovered evidence relevant to the guilt of a state prisoner is not a ground for relief on federal habeas corpus." That statement, however, is no more than distant dictum here, for we never had been asked to consider whether the execution of an innocent person violates the Constitution.

* * * The majority's discussion of petitioner's constitutional claims is even more perverse when viewed in the light of this Court's recent habeas jurisprudence. Beginning with a trio of decisions in 1986, this Court shifted the focus of

---

2. [transposed.] It also may violate the Eighth Amendment to imprison someone who is actually innocent. * * * On the other hand, this Court has noted that "death is a different kind of punishment from any other which may be imposed in this country * * *. From the point of view of the defendant, it is different in both its severity and its finality." *Beck v. Alabama,* 447 U.S. 625 (1980). We are not asked to decide in this case whether petitioner's continued imprisonment would violate the Constitution if he actually is innocent, and I do not address that question.

federal habeas review of successive, abusive, or defaulted claims away from the preservation of constitutional rights to a fact-based inquiry into the habeas petitioner's guilt or innocence. * * * The Court sought to strike a balance between the State's interest in the finality of its criminal judgments and the prisoner's interest in access to a forum to test the basic justice of his sentence. In striking this balance, the Court adopted the view of Judge Friendly that there should be an exception to the concept of finality when a prisoner can make a colorable claim of actual innocence. Friendly, Is Innocence Irrelevant? Collateral Attack on Criminal Judgments, 38 U.Chi.L.Rev. 142, 160 (1970). * * *

Having adopted an "actual innocence" requirement for review of abusive, successive, or defaulted claims, however, the majority would now take the position that "the claim of 'actual innocence' is not itself a constitutional claim, but instead a gateway through which a habeas petitioner must pass to have his otherwise barred constitutional claim considered on the merits." In other words, having held that a prisoner who is incarcerated in violation of the Constitution must show he is actually innocent to obtain relief, the majority would now hold that a prisoner who is actually innocent must show a constitutional violation to obtain relief. The only principle that would appear to reconcile these two positions is the principle that habeas relief should be denied whenever possible. * * *

The question that remains is what showing should be required to obtain relief on the merits of an Eighth or Fourteenth Amendment claim of actual innocence. I agree with the majority that "in state criminal proceedings the trial is the paramount event for determining the guilt or innocence of the defendant." I also think that "a truly persuasive demonstration of 'actual innocence' made after trial would render the execution of a defendant unconstitutional." The question is what "a truly persuasive demonstration" entails, a question the majority's disposition of this case leaves open. * * *

I would hold that, to obtain relief on a claim of actual innocence, the petitioner must show that he probably is innocent. This standard is supported by several considerations. First, new evidence of innocence may be discovered long after the defendant's conviction. Given the passage of time, it may be difficult for the State to retry a defendant who obtains relief from his conviction or sentence on an actual-innocence claim. The actual-innocence proceeding thus may constitute the final word on whether the defendant may be punished. In light of this fact, an otherwise constitutionally valid conviction or sentence should not be set aside lightly. Second, conviction after a constitutionally adequate trial strips the defendant of the presumption of innocence. The government bears the burden of proving the defendant's guilt beyond a reasonable doubt, but once the government has done so, the burden of proving innocence must shift to the convicted defendant. The actual-innocence inquiry is therefore distinguishable from review for sufficiency of the evidence, where the question is not whether the defendant is innocent but whether the government has met its constitutional burden of proving the defendant's guilt beyond a reasonable doubt. When a defendant seeks to challenge the determination of guilt after he has been validly convicted and sentenced, it is fair to place on him the burden of proving his innocence, not just raising doubt about his guilt.

In considering whether a prisoner is entitled to relief on an actual-innocence claim, a court should take all the evidence into account, giving due regard to its reliability. Because placing the burden on the prisoner to prove innocence creates a presumption that the conviction is valid, it is not necessary or appropriate to make further presumptions about the reliability of newly discovered evidence generally. Rather, the court charged with deciding such a claim should make a case-by-case determination about the reliability of the newly discovered evidence under the circumstances. The court then should weigh the evidence in favor of the prisoner against the evidence of his guilt. Obviously, the stronger the evidence of the prisoner's guilt, the more persuasive the newly discovered evidence of innocence must be. A prisoner raising an actual-innocence claim in a federal habeas petition is not entitled to discovery as a matter of right. 28 U.S.C. § 2254 Rule 6. The district court retains discretion to order discovery, however, when it would help the court make a reliable determination with respect to the prisoner's claim.

It should be clear that the standard I would adopt would not convert the federal courts into " 'forums in which to relitigate state trials.' " (opinion of the Court). It would not "require the habeas court to hear testimony from the witnesses who testified at the trial," though, if the petition warrants a hearing, it may require the habeas court to hear the testimony of "those who made the statements in the affidavits which petitioner has presented." * * *

* * * In one of the affidavits, Hector Villarreal, a licensed attorney and former state court judge, swears under penalty of perjury that his client Raul Herrera confessed that he, and not petitioner, committed the murders. No matter what the majority may think of the inconsistencies in the affidavits or the strength of the evidence presented at trial, this affidavit alone is sufficient to raise factual questions concerning petitioner's innocence that cannot be resolved simply by examining the affidavits and the petition.

I do not understand why the majority so severely faults petitioner for relying only on affidavits. It is common to rely on affidavits at the preliminary-consideration stage of a habeas proceeding. The opportunity for cross-examination and credibility determinations comes at the hearing, assuming that the petitioner is entitled to one. It makes no sense for this Court to impugn the reliability of petitioner's evidence on the ground that its credibility has not been tested when the reason its credibility has not been tested is that petitioner's habeas proceeding has been truncated by the Court of Appeals and now by this Court. In its haste to deny petitioner relief, the majority seems to confuse the question whether the petition may be dismissed summarily with the question whether petitioner is entitled to relief on the merits of his claim. * * *

NOTE: "Actual Innocence" and the 1996 Antiterrorism and Effective Death Penalty Act

1. In *Schlup v. Delo*, 513 U.S. 298 (1995), the Court commented further on *Herrera* and distinguished the "actual innocence" standard discussed in *Herrera* from that applied to a procedurally defaulted constitutional claim (see note b supra). In *Schlup*, the habeas petitioner, convicted of murder and sentenced to death, contended that significant exculpatory evidence had not been presented to his trial jury due to a due process violation by the prosecutor (see *Bagley*, ch. 13) and to the ineffective assistance of his counsel (see *Strickland*, ch. 17).[a] Both of

---

a. A recent study of post-trial dispositions of all state capital sentence cases from 1973–95 that reached the stage of final review found that these two claims constituted the most common grounds for reversals. See J. Liebman, J. Fagan, and V. West, A Broken System: Error Rates in Capital Cases, 19873–95, 5 (2000) (of state post-conviction reversals with opinions announcing grounds, ineffective assistance ac-counted for 37% of the reversals and *Bra-dy/Bagley* violations accounted for another 16–19%; in some instances the reversal related to the guilt determination, while in others it related to the capital sentencing proceeding). The overall percentage of reversals was dramatically higher than reversals in felony cases generally, which tend to fall in the 5–15% range. In capital punishment cases, on direct appellate those constitutional claims had been procedurally defaulted in prior proceedings, so the habeas petitioner, to gain relief, had to meet the "actual-innocence" standard discussed in note b supra. In discussing that standard, the Supreme Court explained why it imposed less of a burden upon a habeas petitioner than the standard discussed in *Herrera*. The Court (per Stevens, J.) noted:

> [A] court's assumptions about the validity of the proceedings that resulted in conviction are fundamentally different in Schlup's case than in Herrera's. In *Herrera*, petitioner's claim was evaluated on the assumption that the trial that resulted in his conviction had been error-free. In such a case, when a petitioner has been "tried before a jury of his peers, with the full panoply of protections that our Constitution affords criminal defendants," it is appropriate to apply an "extraordinarily high" standard of review. Id. (O'Connor, J., concurring). Schlup, in contrast, accompanies his claim of innocence with an assertion of constitutional error at trial. For that reason, Schlup's conviction may not be entitled to the same degree of respect as one, such as Herrera's, that is the product of an error-free trial. * * * Consequently, Schlup's evidence of innocence need carry less of a burden. In *Herrera* (on the assumption that petitioner's claim was, in principle, legally well founded), the evidence of innocence would have had to be strong enough to make his execution "constitutionally intolerable" *even if* his conviction was the product of a fair trial. For Schlup, the evidence must establish sufficient doubt about his guilt to justify the conclusion that his execution would be a miscarriage of justice *unless* his conviction was the product of a fair trial.

The *Schlup* Court concluded that the appropriate "actual innocence" standard in this context should be whether the habeas petitioner has shown that "it is more likely than not that no reasonable juror would have convicted him in light of the new evidence."

2. In 1996, Congress enacted the Antiterrorism and Effective Death Penalty Act. Title I of that Act contained several provisions that might be applicable today to habeas petitions of the type presented in *Herrera* and *Schlup*. These include: (1) a new chapter 154 of Title 28 of the United States Code, containing special provisions governing the timing and scope of habeas review in certain capital cases; (2) provisions imposing timing limits on habeas petitions not within chapter 154; (3) provisions limiting second or successive petitions; and (4) provisions limiting new evidentiary hearings. Each of these is briefly discussed below.

3. Chapter 154 consists of 28 U.S.C.A. §§ 2261–2266. This chapter applies only to federal habeas petitions filed by state prisoners sentenced to capital punishment in those states that meet prerequisites specified in § 2261 regarding the appointment of counsel in state postconviction proceedings. Such proceedings allow for collateral challenges to convictions after direct appellate review has been exhausted (see ch. 1, step 18). The Supreme Court has held that the indigent prisoner has no constitutional right to the appointment of counsel in such proceedings. See *Pennsylvania v. Finley*, 481 U.S. 551 (1987); *Murray v. Giarratano*, 492 U.S. 1 (1989) (a capital case). Chapter 154 offers to the state the

review, 41% of the cases were reversed either as to sentence or conviction. Nearly all of the cases not reversed were then reviewed in state postconviction proceedings, with a reversal rate there of 10%. Of those cases surviving state direct and postconviction review, 59% were reviewed on federal habeas corpus for constitutional error, with a reversal rate of 40%. Overall, of the more than 4,000 capital punishment cases followed in the study, 68% had been overturned at one of the three stages in the review process. Subsequent retrials were analyzed only as to cases reversed in state postconviction proceedings. Here, 75% (225 out of 301) resulted in a conviction with a sentence less than capital punishment and 7% resulted in a determination that the defendant was not guilty of the capital offense.

incentive of a short time limitation and restrictions on federal habeas review of issues not considered on the merits in state courts if the state is willing to adopt "a mechanism for the appointment, compensation and payment of reasonable litigation expenses of competent counsel in state postconviction proceedings brought by indigent prisoners whose capital sentences have been upheld on direct review." 28 U.S.C.A. § 2261.

Assuming that the state meets this prerequisite, any claim of actual innocence (or any other constitutional challenge) raised on federal habeas corpus would have to meet the time limit of § 2263. Whereas in *Herrera* there was no time limitation and the claim could be presented by a federal habeas petition filed 10 years after the prisoner's conviction, § 2263 requires that the claim ordinarily be filed within 180 days after "final state affirmance of the conviction and sentence on direct review" (although the 180 day period is tolled during the pendency of a petition for certiorari filed with the Supreme Court and the pendency of the state postconviction proceeding). Under § 2262, the 180 day period carries with it an automatic stay of execution and that remains in effect until there is a final disposition on the merits (with the district court required to rule within 180 days and the appellate court within 120 days of the respective filings in each). However, once that final decision is reached and the stay expires, no further stay may be granted unless the habeas petitioner meets the stringent requirement for successive petitions described in Note 6 below.

Assuming the "actual innocence" claim (or any other constitutional claim) is filed in a chapter 154 case within the prescribed time limit, there remains a further obstacle to gaining consideration of the claim where (as in *Herrera* and *Schlup*) that claim was not considered on the merits in the state courts because it was not presented in what the state courts considered to be a timely fashion. Under § 2264 the federal habeas court is directed to consider "only a claim or claims that have been raised and decided on the merits in the State courts, unless the failure to raise the claim properly is—(1) the result of State action in violation of the Constitution or laws of the United States; (2) the result of the Supreme Court's recognition of a new Federal right that is made retroactively applicable; or (3) based on a factual predicate that could not have been discovered through the exercise of due diligence in time to present the claim for State or Federal post-conviction review." No mention is made of an exception for a defaulted claim because of its relationship to actual innocence. Compare note 5 infra.

4. If the state prisoner's federal habeas petition does not come within chapter 154 because the challenge is to a noncapital conviction or to a capital conviction in a state that does not meet the counsel-appointment prerequisites of § 2261, it does not thereby escape Congress' efforts to "speed up" the postconviction review process. The Antiterrorism and Effective Death Penalty Act also included an amendment of § 2244(d) requiring that habeas petitions generally be filed within one year of the date on which the petitioner's judgment of conviction became final on direct appeal (excluding from the one-year period the time during which a properly filed collateral challenge was pending in the state courts). That provision does recognize three situations, however, in which the time limitation will be extended: (1) where the habeas applicant "was prevented from filing" by "state action in violation of the Constitution or laws of the United States"; (2) where the "factual predicate" of the constitutional claim could not have been discovered through due diligence prior to the time at which the conviction became final; and (3) where the claim relies on a new constitutional rule that the Supreme Court established and held applicable to collateral review after the prisoner's conviction became final (a rare circumstance since a new rule is given

retroactive effect only if it holds that the state lacks authority to criminalize particular conduct or imposes a "new watershed rule of criminal procedure").

5. Assuming that the habeas petition meets whichever timing requirement—§ 2244(d) or § 2263—is applicable to the case, § 2254(e) then presents another potential barrier to review should the claim be one that relies upon newly discovered evidence that the state courts refused to consider because they viewed it as not timely presented. As amended by the 1996 Act, § 2254(e) directs the federal habeas court not to hold an evidentiary on a claim as to which there was a "fail[ure] to develop the factual basis * * * in State court proceedings," unless two conditions are met—(1) "the claim relies on * * * a factual predicate that could not have been previously discovered through the exercise of due diligence" (or a "new rule" of constitutional law applied retroactively to collateral review) and (2) "the facts underlying the claim would be sufficient to establish by clear and convincing evidence that but for the constitutional error, no reasonable factfinder would have found the applicant guilty of the underlying offense."

In *(Michael) Williams v. Taylor*, 529 U.S. 420 (2000), the Court held that the limitations imposed by § 2254(e) apply only when the failure to develop the factual basis of the claim was the product of "a lack of diligence, or some greater fault, attributable to the prisoner or the prisoner's counsel." Applying this standard, the Court concluded that the habeas petitioner could not obtain a habeas hearing on a claim that the prosecution failed to disclose a psychiatric report concerning the state's main witness. The habeas petitioner's counsel on state postconviction proceedings had notice of the report, but did not read it. Due diligence would led counsel to read such a report and to consider its possible use as a grounding for a constitutional claim appropriately presented at that point.[a] Since § 2254(e) therefore was applicable and the petitioner admittedly could not meet the "actual-innocence" prerequisite of § 2254(e), he could not gain a hearing. However, a hearing was available as to another claim, where § 2254(e) did not apply because the failure to raise the claim was not the product of a lack of due diligence. The foreperson of the juror at the 1994 trial had fifteen years earlier divorced a key state witness and had been represented at that divorce by the prosecutor. None of this information was disclosed at trial when jurors were asked about any relationship to the state's witnesses or its attorneys. The information was discovered only after an investigator working on the federal habeas petition interviewed two other jurors who referred to the foreperson by her married name, leading the investigator to check the county's marriage records. Due diligence did not require defense counsel "to check public records containing personal information pertaining to each and every juror."

6. In both *Herrera* and *Schlup*, the decision being reviewed by the Supreme Court dealt with a second habeas petition raising a claim that had not been presented in the prisoner's first petition. The Antiterrorism and Effective Death Penalty Act amended § 2244(b) to impose new standards governing the consideration of "second or successive" petitions presenting claims not raised in earlier petitions. That section requires dismissal of such a petition unless the new claim is either based on a new constitutional rule applied retroactively to collateral review, or is based on a factual predicate that "could not have been discovered previously with due diligence" and presents facts "sufficient to establish by clear and convincing evidence that but for the constitutional error, no reasonable factfinder would have found the applicant guilty of the underlying offense." Moreover, the determination as to whether these exceptions are met is not to be

---

a. This failure could not provide the grounding for an ineffective assistance of counsel claim because the defendant had no constitutional right to the assistance of counsel at the state postconviction proceedings. See the introduction to chapter 17.

made by the District Court, but must be made by the Court of Appeals, which serves as the "gatekeeper" on the filing of a second or successive petition with the district court. Should the Court of Appeals decide that the § 2244(b) conditions are not met and deny leave to file, the prisoner cannot seek Supreme Court review by a petition for certiorari. The Supreme Court held in *Felker v. Turpin*, 518 U.S. 651 (1996), that a prisoner may still seek an original writ of habeas court from the Court, but warned that its consideration of such an application would be "inform[ed]" by the standards set forth in § 2244(b) and that original writs would continue to be "rarely granted."

Chapter 19

RETRIALS

788 – 835

Although it has some bearing on multiple punishments, the double jeopardy clause of the Fifth Amendment is concerned primarily with multiple trials. That concern extends to trials for both felonies and misdemeanors. The Court concluded, in its first major double jeopardy ruling, that the reference in the double jeopardy clause to "life and limb," when read against its common law background, was broad enough to encompass all criminal offenses without regard to the particular form of punishment that might be imposed. *Ex parte Lange*, 85 U.S. 163 (1873). The double jeopardy clause becomes applicable, however, only after the accused has been placed "in jeopardy", and that does not occur until (i) the jury is "empaneled and sworn" in a case involving a jury trial, or (ii) the first witness is sworn in a case involving a bench trial. *Crist v. Bretz*, 437 U.S. 28 (1978). Dismissals before jeopardy has attached, even where based on the ground that the prosecution's case is too weak to prevail, do not raise double jeopardy difficulties; since the defendant has not been placed in jeopardy at the point of dismissal, a reprosecution that results in a trial would not place him "twice" in jeopardy. Thus, double jeopardy does not bar returning a case to a grand jury after it has refused to indict, refiling charges and seeking a new preliminary hearing after the magistrate found a lack of probable cause at the first hearing, or refiling charges after a trial court dismissed the initial charges on some pretrial objection (e.g., an insufficiency of the pleading) that could be cured in a new indictment or information. So too, where a trial court dismisses charges before trial on grounds that would bar reprosecution (e.g., that the defendant had been denied his right to a speedy trial), no double jeopardy concerns are presented by allowing the state to appeal that dismissal and continue with the prosecution if it should win on appeal.

The principles described above are well established and fairly easy to apply. That is not true of all double jeopardy principles. Indeed, in *United States v. DiFrancesco*, 449 U.S. 117 (1980), Justice Blackmun's opinion for the Court, citing 21 double jeopardy cases decided by the Court over the previous decade, acknowledged that the application of the double jeopardy bar "has not proved to be facile or routine," as demonstrated by the various "changes in direction or in emphasis" found in the Court's rulings. The cases in this Chapter deal with the most significant of those double jeopardy principles that have proved troublesome in their definition or application.

SECTION 1: THE "SAME OFFENSE" LIMITATION

The double jeopardy clause states that no person shall twice be put in jeopardy for the "same offence." It was well established at common law that

788

prosecutions were not for the "same offense" where they involved the same statutory violation as to different victims, even when the violations occurred in the same incident. *Ashe v. Swenson,* the first case in this section, raises the question as to whether the double jeopardy bar places any limit on separate prosecutions in such situations. *Ashe,* through its adoption of the "collateral estoppel" doctrine, imposes such a limit, but it is restricted to instances in which the first prosecution results in an acquittal and that acquittal bears a special relationship to the offense charged in the second prosecution.

At common law, separate prosecutions involving the same incident and the same victim could be for "the same offense" even though alleging violations of different statutes. The second case in this section, *United States v. Dixon,* deals with the scope of the double jeopardy bar developed in this situation. Unlike the collateral estoppel doctrine of *Ashe,* the limitation imposed here does not depend upon the first prosecution having resulted in an acquittal. It should be kept in mind that state law may impose limitations beyond those mandated in *Ashe* and *Dixon.* Thus, some states require a single prosecution for all offenses arising from the same transaction, as urged by Justice Brennan in his concurring opinion in *Ashe,* and other states largely follow the standard of *Grady v. Corbin,* overruled in *Dixon.*

The third case in this section, *Heath v. Alabama,* deals with the possible application of the double jeopardy bar to multiple prosecutions by different sovereigns. The position taken by the Court here stands in contrast to the Court's interpretation of the Fifth Amendment's self-incrimination clause as extending to potential incrimination under the laws of a jurisdiction other than that compelling the witness to testify. See *Murphy v. Waterfront Commission* (discussed in the *Kastigar* opinion in Ch. 8). Multiple prosecutions for basically the same criminal activity by different jurisdictions (i.e., two states, or the federal government and a state) do occur, but are uncommon. The overlap of prosecutorial authority is most likely to arise between the federal government and a state, and here non-constitutional limitations restrict multiple prosecutions. The internal regulations of the Justice Department bar federal prosecution following a state prosecution "for substantially the same act" except upon the approval of an Assistant Attorney General, and many states have provisions that prohibit a state prosecution for any activity that has been the basis for a previous federal prosecution.

The last case in this section, *Hudson v. United States,* turns from the combination of separate prosecutions under different criminal statutes to the combination of a criminal prosecution and a proceeding designated as civil but which nonetheless may be seen as seeking to inflict "punishment" for the same violation as the criminal prosecution. The possible application of the double jeopardy bar to such a combination has great practical significance, as a wide range of criminal activity frequently leads not only to a criminal prosecution, but also to a "civil" proceeding brought by the government to gain a monetary or property award that is equal to (or exceeds) what may be obtained as part of the criminal sentence through a criminal fine or criminal forfeiture.

SECTION 2: ABORTED PROCEEDINGS

The two cases in this section, *Arizona v. Washington* and *Oregon v. Kennedy,* set forth the basic double jeopardy standards applicable to reprosecutions following a mistrial. The mistrial should be distinguished from the mid-trial dismissal, which is discussed in the *Scott* case in the next section. In contrast to dismissals of the type involved in *Scott,* a court ordering a mistrial does not find some fatal flaw in the prosecution that would present an absolute bar to conviction on the offense charged. Rather, the trial court rules that it would be inappropriate or impossible to continue with the trial and orders its termination without ending the prosecution. The judge ordering a mistrial assumes that a reprosecution can be brought, but as *Washington* and *Kennedy* indicate, that is not always the case.[9]

SECTION 3: REPROSECUTIONS FOLLOWING ACQUITTALS AND CONVICTIONS

The double jeopardy clause was derived in large part from the common law pleas of *autrefois acquit* (formerly acquitted) and *autrefois convict* (formerly convicted), and the two bedrock elements of the clause are the prohibitions against reprosecution for the same offense following an acquittal or a conviction. It is here, however, more so than in any other area of double jeopardy jurisprudence, that the Court has found the need to reevaluate applicable standards. In both of the cases in this section, *United States v. Scott* and *Burks v. United States,* the Court found it necessary to reassess the assumptions of earlier rulings.

Scott raises the basic question of what type of ruling should be viewed as an "acquittal." In particular, should a trial court dismissal that bars reprosecution be viewed as an acquittal without regard to the grounding of that ruling? The fact that the ending of the case in *Scott* (through dismissal) came from the judge rather than the jury was not critical; the Court had long held that the acquittal rule applied to acquittals by judges as well as by juries, a position reaffirmed in a case decided the same day as *Scott, Sanabria v. United States,* 437 U.S. 54 (1978).

Burks considers the proper scope of the "*Ball* exception" to the prohibition against reprosecution following a conviction. By allowing a reprosecution whenever a conviction was successfully overturned on a defense challenge, the *Ball* exception had basically limited that prohibition to the situation in which the defendant was willing to abide by his conviction (i.e. bring no challenge), but the state desired to prosecute again in the hopes of either raising the charge or obtaining a higher sentence. *Burks* recognizes an exception to the *Ball* exception, whereby the prohibition can have a bearing, under limited circumstances, even where the defendant successfully challenges the conviction.

SECTION 1. THE "SAME OFFENSE" LIMITATION

ASHE v. SWENSON

397 U.S. 436, 90 S.Ct. 1189, 25 L.Ed.2d 469 (1970).

poker robbery

JUSTICE STEWART delivered the opinion of the Court. * * *

Sometime in the early hours of the morning of January 10, 1960, six men were engaged in a poker game in the basement of the home of John Gladson at Lee's Summit, Missouri. Suddenly three or four masked men, armed with a shotgun and pistols, broke into the basement and robbed each of the poker players of money and various articles of personal property. The robbers—and it has never been clear whether there were three or four of them—then fled in a car belonging to one of the victims of the robbery. Shortly thereafter the stolen car was discovered in a field, and later that morning three men were arrested by a state trooper while they were walking on a highway not far from where the abandoned car had been found. The petitioner was arrested by another officer some distance away.

---

9. Where the court grants during trial a motion to dismiss based on a legal defect that is curable (and therefore assumes reprosecution), the applicable standards are the same as used for mistrials. See *Lee v. United States,* 432 U.S. 23 (1977) (prosecution dismissed during trial on a defense motion citing a defect in the charging instrument; the double jeopardy standard for defense requested mistrials held to govern the state's authority to reprosecute).

The four were subsequently charged with seven separate offenses—the armed robbery of each of the six poker players and the theft of the car. In May 1960 the petitioner went to trial on the charge of robbing Donald Knight, one of the participants in the poker game. At the trial the State called Knight and three of his fellow poker players as prosecution witnesses. Each of them described the circumstances of the holdup and itemized his own individual losses. The proof that an armed robbery had occurred and that personal property had been taken from Knight as well as from each of the others was unassailable. The testimony of the four victims in this regard was consistent both internally and with that of the others. But the State's evidence that the petitioner had been one of the robbers was weak. Two of the witnesses thought that there had been only three robbers altogether, and could not identify the petitioner as one of them. Another of the victims, who was the petitioner's uncle by marriage, said that at the "patrol station" he had positively identified each of the other three men accused of the holdup, but could say only that the petitioner's voice "sounded very much like" that of one of the robbers. The fourth participant in the poker game did identify the petitioner, but only by his "size and height, and his actions."

The cross-examination of these witnesses was brief, and it was aimed primarily at exposing the weakness of their identification testimony. Defense counsel made no attempt to question their testimony regarding the holdup itself or their claims as to their losses. Knight testified without contradiction that the robbers had stolen from him his watch, $250 in cash, and about $500 in checks. His billfold, which had been found by the police in the possession of one of the three other men accused of the robbery, was admitted in evidence. The defense offered no testimony and waived final argument.

The trial judge instructed the jury that if it found that the petitioner was one of the participants in the armed robbery, the theft of "any money" from Knight would sustain a conviction. He also instructed the jury that if the petitioner was one of the robbers, he was guilty under the law even if he had not personally robbed Knight. The jury—though not instructed to elaborate upon its verdict— found the petitioner "not guilty due to insufficient evidence."

Six weeks later the petitioner was brought to trial again, this time for the robbery of another participant in the poker game, a man named Roberts. The petitioner filed a motion to dismiss, based on his previous acquittal. The motion was overruled, and the second trial began. The witnesses were for the most part the same, though this time their testimony was substantially stronger on the issue of the petitioner's identity. For example, two witnesses who at the first trial had been wholly unable to identify the petitioner as one of the robbers, now testified that his features, size, and mannerisms matched those of one of their assailants. Another witness who before had identified the petitioner only by his size and actions now also remembered him by the unusual sound of his voice. The State further refined its case at the second trial by declining to call one of the participants in the poker game whose identification testimony at the first trial had been conspicuously negative. The case went to the jury on instructions virtually identical to those given at the first trial. This time the jury found the petitioner guilty, and he was sentenced to a 35-year term in the state penitentiary. * * *

"Collateral estoppel" is an awkward phrase, but it stands for an extremely important principle in our adversary system of justice. It means simply that when an issue of ultimate fact has once been determined by a valid and final judgment, that issue cannot again be litigated between the same parties in any future lawsuit. Although first developed in civil litigation, collateral estoppel has been an established rule of federal criminal law at least since this Court's decision more than 50 years ago in *United States v. Oppenheimer,* 242 U.S. 85 (1916). As Mr. Justice Holmes put the matter in that case, "It cannot be that the safeguards of the person, so often and so rightly mentioned with solemn reverence, are less than those that protect from a liability in debt." As a rule of federal law, therefore, "[i]t is much too late to suggest that this principle is not fully applicable to a former judgment in a criminal case, either because of lack of 'mutuality' or because the judgment may reflect only a belief that the Government had not met the higher burden of proof exacted in such cases for the Government's evidence as a whole although not necessarily as to every link in the chain."

The federal decisions have made clear that the rule of collateral estoppel in criminal cases is not to be applied with the hypertechnical and archaic approach of a 19th century pleading book, but with realism and rationality. Where a previous judgment of acquittal was based upon a general verdict, as is usually the case, this approach requires a court to "examine the record of a prior proceeding, taking into account the pleadings, evidence, charge, and other relevant matter, and conclude whether a rational jury could have grounded its verdict upon an issue other than that which the defendant seeks to foreclose from consideration." The inquiry "must be set in a practical frame, and viewed with an eye to all the circumstances of the proceedings." *Sealfon v. United States,* 332 U.S. 575 (1948). Any test more technically restrictive would, of course, simply amount to a rejection of the rule of collateral estoppel in criminal proceedings, at least in every case where the first judgment was based upon a general verdict of acquittal.

Straightforward application of the federal rule to the present case can lead to but one conclusion. For the record is utterly devoid of any indication that the first jury could rationally have found that an armed robbery had not occurred, or that Knight had not been a victim of that robbery. The single rationally conceivable issue in dispute before the jury was whether the petitioner had been one of the robbers. And the jury by its verdict found that he had not. The federal rule of law, therefore, would make a second prosecution for the robbery of Roberts wholly impermissible.

The ultimate question to be determined, then * * * is whether this established rule of federal law is embodied in the Fifth Amendment guarantee against double jeopardy. We do not hesitate to hold that it is. For whatever else that constitutional guarantee may embrace, it surely protects a man who has been acquitted from having to "run the gantlet" a second time. *Green v. United States,* 355 U.S. 184 (1957).

The question is not whether Missouri could validly charge the petitioner with six separate offenses for the robbery of the six poker players. It is not whether he could have received a total of six punishments if he had been convicted in a single trial of robbing the six victims. It is simply whether, after a jury determined by its verdict that the petitioner was not one of the robbers, the State could constitutionally hale him before a new jury to litigate that issue again. * * *

In this case the State in its brief has frankly conceded that following the petitioner's acquittal, it treated the first trial as no more than a dry run for the second prosecution: "No doubt the prosecutor felt the state had a provable case on the first charge and, when he lost, he did what every good attorney would do— he refined his presentation in light of the turn of events at the first trial." But this is precisely what the constitutional guarantee forbids. * * *

Reversed and remanded.[a]

Justice Brennan, whom Justice Douglas and Justice Marshall join, concurring.

a.   Separate concurring opinions of Justices   Harlan and Black are omitted.

I agree that the Double Jeopardy Clause incorporates collateral estoppel as a constitutional requirement and therefore join the Court's opinion. However, even if the rule of collateral estoppel had been inapplicable to the facts of this case, it is my view that the Double Jeopardy Clause nevertheless bars the prosecution of petitioner a second time for armed robbery. The two prosecutions, the first for the robbery of Knight and the second for the robbery of Roberts, grew out of one criminal episode, and therefore I think it clear on the facts of this case that the Double Jeopardy Clause prohibited Missouri from prosecuting petitioner for each robbery at a different trial. * * *

The Double Jeopardy Clause is a guarantee "that the State with all its resources and power [shall] not be allowed to make repeated attempts to convict an individual for an alleged offense, thereby subjecting him to embarrassment, expense and ordeal and compelling him to live in a continuing state of anxiety and insecurity ...." *Green v. United States*, 355 U.S. 184 (1957). This guarantee is expressed as a prohibition against multiple prosecutions for the "same offence." Although the phrase "same offence" appeared in most of the early common-law articulations of the double-jeopardy principle, questions of its precise meaning rarely arose prior to the 18th century, and by the time the Bill of Rights was adopted it had not been authoritatively defined.

When the common law did finally attempt a definition, in *The King v. Vandercomb* (Crown 1796), it adopted the "same evidence" test, which provided little protection from multiple prosecution:

> "[U]nless the first indictment were such as the prisoner might have been convicted upon by proof of the facts contained in the second indictment, an acquittal on the first indictment can be no bar to the second."

The "same evidence" test of "same offence" was soon followed by a majority of American jurisdictions, but its deficiencies are obvious. It does not enforce but virtually annuls the constitutional guarantee. For example, where a single criminal episode involves several victims, under the "same evidence" test a separate prosecution may be brought as to each. The "same evidence" test permits multiple prosecutions where a single transaction is divisible into chronologically discrete crimes. E.g., *Johnson v. Commonwealth*, 201 Ky. 314 (1923) (each of 75 poker hands a separate "offense"). Even a single criminal act may lead to multiple prosecutions if it is viewed from the perspectives of different statutes. Given the tendency of modern criminal legislation to divide the phases of a criminal transaction into numerous separate crimes, the opportunities for multiple prosecutions for an essentially unitary criminal episode are frightening. And given our tradition of virtually unreviewable prosecutorial discretion concerning the initiation and scope of a criminal prosecution, the potentialities for abuse inherent in the "same evidence" test are simply intolerable.

The "same evidence" test is not constitutionally required. It was first expounded *after* the adoption of the Fifth Amendment * * *. The "same evidence" test may once have been defensible at English common law, which, for reasons peculiar to English criminal procedure, severely restricted the power of prosecutors to combine several charges in a single trial. In vivid contrast, American criminal procedure generally allows a prosecutor freedom, subject to judicial control, to prosecute a person at one trial for all the crimes arising out of a single criminal transaction.

In my view, the Double Jeopardy Clause requires the prosecution, except in most limited circumstances, to join at one trial all the charges against a defendant that grow out of a single criminal act, occurrence, episode, or transaction. This "same transaction" test of "same offence" not only enforces the ancient prohibition against vexatious multiple prosecutions embodied in the Double Jeopardy Clause, but responds as well to the increasingly widespread recognition that the consolidation in one lawsuit of all issues arising out of a single transaction or occurrence best promotes justice, economy, and convenience. * * *

CHIEF JUSTICE BURGER, dissenting.

The Fifth Amendment to the constitution of the United States provides in part: "nor shall any person be subject for the same offence to be twice put in jeopardy of life or limb * * *." Nothing in the language or gloss previously placed on this provision of the Fifth Amendment remotely justifies the treatment that the Court today accords to the collateral-estoppel doctrine. Nothing in the purpose of the authors of the Constitution commands or even justifies what the Court decides today; this is truly a case of expanding a sound basic principle beyond the bounds—or needs—of its rational and legitimate objectives to preclude harassment of an accused. * * *

The concept of double jeopardy and our firm constitutional commitment is against repeated trials "for the *same offence*." This Court, like most American jurisdictions, has expanded that part of the Constitution into a "same evidence" test. *Blockburger v. United States*, 284 U.S. 299 (1932) * * *. Clearly and beyond dispute the charge against Ashe in the second trial required proof of a fact—robbery of Roberts—which the charge involving Knight did not. The Court, therefore, has had to reach out far beyond the accepted offense-defining rule to reach its decision in this case. What it has done is to superimpose on the same-evidence test a new and novel collateral-estoppel gloss. * * *

The collateral-estoppel concept—originally a product only of civil litigation—is a strange mutant as it is transformed to control this criminal case. In civil cases the doctrine was justified as conserving judicial resources as well as those of the parties to the actions and additionally as providing the finality needed to plan for the future. It ordinarily applies to parties on each side of the litigation who have the same interest as or who are identical with the parties in the initial litigation. Here the complainant in the second trial is not the same as in the first even though the State is a party in both cases. Very properly, in criminal cases, finality and conservation of private, public, and judicial resources are lesser values than in civil litigation. * * *

Some commentators have concluded that the harassment inherent in standing trial a second time is a sufficient reason for use of collateral estoppel in criminal trials. If the Court is today relying on a harassment concept to superimpose a new brand of collateral-estoppel gloss on the "same evidence" test, there is a short answer; this case does not remotely suggest harassment of an accused who robbed six victims and the harassment aspect does not rise to constitutional levels.

The essence of Justice Brennan's concurrence is that this was all one transaction, one episode, or, if I may so characterize it, one frolic, and, hence, only one crime. His approach, like that taken by the Court, totally overlooks the significance of there being *six entirely separate charges of robbery* against six individuals.

This "single transaction" concept is not a novel notion; it has been urged in various courts including this Court. One of the theses underlying the "single transaction" notion is that the criminal episode is "indivisible." The short answer to that is that to the victims, the criminal conduct is readily divisible and intensely personal; each offense is an offense against *a person*. For me it demeans the dignity of the human personality and individuality to talk of "a single transaction" in the context of six separate assaults on six individuals.

No court that elevates the individual rights and human dignity of the accused to a high place—as we should—ought to be so casual as to treat the victims as a single homogenized lump of human clay. I would grant the dignity of individual status to the victims as much as to those accused, not more but surely no less.

If it be suggested that multiple crimes can be separately punished but must be collectively tried, one can point to the firm trend in the law to allow severance of defendants and offenses into separate trials so as to avoid possible prejudice of one criminal act or of the conduct of one defendant to "spill over" on another.

What the Court holds today must be related to its impact on crimes more serious than ordinary housebreaking, followed by physical assault on six men and robbery of all of them. To understand its full impact we must view the holding in the context of four men who break and enter, rob, and then kill six victims. The concurrence tells us that unless all the crimes are joined in one trial the alleged killers cannot be tried for more than one of the killings even if the evidence is that they personally killed two, three, or more of the victims. Or alter the crime to four men breaking into a college dormitory and assaulting six girls. What the Court is holding is, in effect, that the second and third and fourth criminal acts are "free," unless the accused is tried for the multiple crimes in a single trial—something defendants frantically use every legal device to avoid, and often succeed in avoiding. This is the reality of what the Court holds today; it does not make good sense and it cannot make good law. * * *

UNITED STATES v. DIXON

509 U.S. 688, 113 S.Ct. 2849, 125 L.Ed.2d 556 (1993).

JUSTICE SCALIA announced the judgment of the Court and delivered the opinion of the Court with respect to Parts I, II, and IV, and an opinion with respect to Parts III and V, in which JUSTICE KENNEDY joins.

I

Respondent Alvin Dixon was arrested for second-degree murder and was released on bond. Consistent with the District of Columbia's bail law authorizing the judicial officer to impose any condition that "will reasonably assure the appearance of the person for trial or the safety of any other person or the community," Dixon's release form specified that he was not to commit "any criminal offense," and warned that any violation of the conditions of release would subject him "to revocation of release, an order of detention, and prosecution for contempt of court." See § 23–1329(a). While awaiting trial, Dixon was arrested and indicted for possession of cocaine with intent to distribute, in violation of D.C.Code Ann. § 33–541(a)(1). The court issued an order requiring Dixon to show cause why he should not be held in contempt or have the terms of his pretrial release modified. [Following] the show-cause hearing, * * * the court found Dixon guilty of criminal contempt under § 23–1329(c), [and sentenced him] to 180 days in jail. * * * He later moved to dismiss the cocaine indictment on double jeopardy grounds; the trial court granted the motion.

Respondent Michael Foster's route to this Court is similar. Based on Foster's alleged physical attacks upon her in the past, Foster's estranged wife Ana obtained a civil protection order (CPO) in Superior Court of the District of Columbia. * * * The order, to which Foster consented, required that he not " 'molest, assault, or in any manner threaten or physically abuse' " Ana Foster. * * * Over the course of eight months, Ana Foster filed three separate motions to have her husband held in contempt for numerous violations of the CPO. Of the

16 alleged episodes, the only charges relevant here are three separate instances of threats (on November 12, 1987, and March 26 and May 17, 1988) and two assaults (on November 6, 1987 and May 21, 1988). * * * After issuing a notice of hearing and ordering Foster to appear, the court held a 3–day bench trial. Counsel for Ana Foster and her mother prosecuted the action; the United States was not represented at trial, although the United States Attorney was apparently aware of the action, as was the court aware of a separate grand jury proceeding on some of the alleged criminal conduct. As to the assault charges, the court stated that Ana Foster would have "to prove as an element, first that there was a Civil Protection Order, and then [that] ... the assault as defined by the criminal code, in fact occurred." [T]he court granted Foster's motion for acquittal on various counts, including the alleged threats on November 12 and May 17, [but] found Foster guilty beyond a reasonable doubt of four counts of criminal contempt (three violations of Ana Foster's CPO, and one violation of the CPO obtained by her mother), including the November 6, 1987 and May 21, 1988 assaults. He was sentenced to an aggregate 600 days' imprisonment. * * *

The United States Attorney's Office later obtained an indictment charging Foster with simple assault on or about November 6, 1987 (Count I, violation of § 22–504); threatening to injure another on or about November 12, 1987, and March 26 and May 17, 1988 (Counts II–IV, violation of § 22–2307); and assault with intent to kill on or about May 21, 1988 (Count V, violation of § 22–501). Ana Foster was the complainant in all counts; the first and last counts were based on the events for which Foster had been held in contempt, and the other three were based on the alleged events for which Foster was acquitted of contempt. Like Dixon, Foster filed a motion to dismiss, claiming a double jeopardy bar to all counts, and also collateral estoppel as to Counts II–IV. The trial court denied the double-jeopardy claim and did not rule on the collateral-estoppel assertion.

The Government appealed the double jeopardy ruling in Dixon, and Foster appealed the trial court's denial of his motion. The District of Columbia Court of Appeals consolidated the two cases, reheard them en banc, and, relying on our recent decision in *Grady v. Corbin,* 495 U.S. 508 (1990), ruled that both subsequent prosecutions were barred by the Double Jeopardy Clause. * * *

II

To place these cases in context, one must understand that they are the consequence of an historically anomalous use of the contempt power. In both Dixon and Foster, a court issued an order directing a particular individual not to commit criminal offenses. (In Dixon's case, the court incorporated the entire criminal code; in Foster's case, the criminal offense of simple assault.) That could not have occurred at common law, or in the 19th–century American judicial system, [which followed a long-held "tradition against judicial orders prohibiting violation of the law."] * * * It is not surprising, therefore, that the double jeopardy issue presented here—whether prosecution for criminal contempt based on violation of a criminal law incorporated into a court order bars a subsequent prosecution for the criminal offense—did not arise at common law, or even until quite recently in American cases. * * *

The Double Jeopardy Clause, whose application to this new context we are called upon to consider, provides that no person shall "be subject for the same offence to be twice put in jeopardy of life or limb." U.S. Const., Amdt. 5. This protection applies both to successive punishments and to successive prosecutions for the same criminal offense. See *North Carolina v. Pearce,* 395 U.S. 711 (1969). It is well established that criminal contempt, at least the sort enforced through nonsummary proceedings, is "a crime in the ordinary sense." *Bloom v. Illinois,*

391 U.S. 194 (1968). We have held that constitutional protections for criminal defendants other than the double jeopardy provision apply in nonsummary criminal contempt prosecutions just as they do in other criminal prosecutions. See, e.g., *Gompers v. Bucks Stove & Range Co.,* 221 U.S. 418 (1911) (presumption of innocence, proof beyond a reasonable doubt, and guarantee against self-incrimination); *Cooke v. United States,* 267 U.S. 517 (1925) (notice of charges, assistance of counsel, and right to present a defense); *In re Oliver,* 333 U.S. 257 (1948) (public trial). We think it obvious, and today hold, that the protection of the Double Jeopardy Clause likewise attaches.

In both the multiple punishment and multiple prosecution contexts, this Court has concluded that where the two offenses for which the defendant is punished or tried cannot survive the "same-elements" test, the double jeopardy bar applies. See, e.g., *Brown v. Ohio,* 432 U.S. 161 (1977); *Blockburger v. United States,* 284 U.S. 299 (1932) (multiple punishment); *Gavieres v. United States,* 220 U.S. 338 (1911) (successive prosecutions). The same-elements test, sometimes referred to as the "*Blockburger*" test, inquires whether each offense contains an element not contained in the other; if not, they are the "same offence" and double jeopardy bars additional punishment and successive prosecution. * * * We recently held in *Grady* that in addition to passing the *Blockburger* test, a subsequent prosecution must satisfy a "same-conduct" test to avoid the double jeopardy bar. The *Grady* test provides that, "if, to establish an essential element of an offense charged in that prosecution, the government will prove conduct that constitutes an offense for which the defendant has already been prosecuted," a second prosecution may not be had.[a]

III

The first question before us today is whether *Blockburger* analysis permits subsequent prosecution in this new criminal contempt context, where judicial order has prohibited criminal act. If it does, we must then proceed to consider whether *Grady* also permits it.

We begin with *Dixon.* The statute applicable in Dixon's contempt prosecution provides that "[a] person who has been conditionally released ... and who has violated a condition of release shall be subject to ... prosecution for contempt of court." § 23–1329(a). Obviously, Dixon could not commit an "offence" under this provision until an order setting out conditions was issued. The statute by itself imposes no legal obligation on anyone. Dixon's cocaine possession, although an offense under D.C.Code Ann. § 33–541(a), was not an offense under § 23–1329 until a judge incorporated the statutory drug offense into his release order.

In this situation, in which the contempt sanction is imposed for violating the order through commission of the incorporated drug offense, the later attempt to prosecute Dixon for the drug offense resembles the situation that produced our judgment of double jeopardy in *Harris v. Oklahoma,* 433 U.S. 682 (1977) (per curiam). There we held that a subsequent prosecution for robbery with a firearm was barred by the Double Jeopardy Clause, because the defendant had already

---

a. The defendant in *Grady* was charged initially with the offenses of driving while intoxicated and crossing the median, to which he pleaded guilty. He was then charged with criminally negligent homicide, with the prosecution in a bill of particulars listing the driving while intoxicated and the median crossing as two of the acts of negligence. Justice Brennan wrote for a 5–4 majority, joined by Justices White, Marshall, Blackmun, and Stevens. The *Blockburger* test did not bar the second prosecution because neither the median crossing nor the driving while intoxicated were necessary elements of the homicide offense, but the double jeopardy still applied, the majority concluded, because the same conduct for which the defendant had already been prosecuted in the traffic offenses was now being used to prove the element of negligence on the homicide charge.

been tried for felony-murder based on the same underlying felony. We have described our terse per curiam in *Harris* as standing for the proposition that, for double jeopardy purposes, "the crime generally described as felony murder" is not "a separate offense distinct from its various elements." *Illinois v. Vitale*, 447 U.S. 410 (1980). So too here, the "crime" of violating a condition of release cannot be abstracted from the "element" of the violated condition. The *Dixon* court order incorporated the entire governing criminal code in the same manner as the *Harris* felony-murder statute incorporated the several enumerated felonies. Here, as in Harris, the underlying substantive criminal offense is "a species of lesser-included offense."

* * * Both the Government and Justice Blackmun contend that the legal obligation in Dixon's case may serve "interests ... fundamentally different" from the substantive criminal law, because it derives in part from the determination of a court rather than a determination of the legislature. That distinction seems questionable, since the court's power to establish conditions of release, and to punish their violation, was conferred by statute; the legislature was the ultimate source of both the criminal and the contempt prohibition. More importantly, however, the distinction is of no moment for purposes of the Double Jeopardy Clause, the text of which looks to whether the offenses are the same, not the interests that the offenses violate. And this Court stated long ago that criminal contempt, at least in its nonsummary form, "is a crime in every fundamental respect." *Bloom*, supra. Because Dixon's drug offense did not include any element not contained in his previous contempt offense, his subsequent prosecution violates the Double Jeopardy Clause.

The foregoing analysis obviously applies as well to Count I of the indictment against Foster, charging assault in violation of § 22–504, based on the same event that was the subject of his prior contempt conviction for violating the provision of the CPO forbidding him to commit simple assault under § 22–504. The subsequent prosecution for assault fails the *Blockburger* test, and is barred.[4]

* * * The remaining four counts in *Foster,* assault with intent to kill (Count V; § 22–501) and threats to injure or kidnap (Counts II–IV; § 22–2307), are not barred under *Blockburger*. As to Count V: Foster's conduct on May 21, 1988 was found to violate the Family Division's order that he not "molest, assault, or in any manner threaten or physically abuse" his wife. At the contempt hearing, the court stated that Ana Foster's attorney, who prosecuted the contempt, would have to prove first, knowledge of a CPO, and second, a willful violation of one of its conditions, here simple assault as defined by the criminal code. * * * On the basis of the same episode, Foster was then indicted for violation of § 22–501, which proscribes assault with intent to kill. Under governing law, that offense requires proof of specific intent to kill; simple assault does not. Similarly, the contempt offense required proof of knowledge of the CPO, which assault with intent to kill does not. Applying the *Blockburger* elements test, the result is clear: These crimes were different offenses and the subsequent prosecution did not violate the Double Jeopardy Clause. * * * Counts II, III, and IV of Foster's indictment are likewise not barred. These charged Foster under § 22–2307 (forbidding anyone to "threaten ... to kidnap any person or to injure the person of another or physically damage the property of any person") for his alleged

4. Justice White complains that this section of our opinion gives the arguments of the United States "short shrift," and treats them in "conclusory" fashion. * * * [A] part of Justice White's opinion that deals with this issue argues—by no means in conclusory fashion— that its practical consequences for law enforcement are not serious. He may be right. But we do not share his "pragmatic" view that the meaning of the Double Jeopardy Clause depends upon our approval of its consequences.

threats on three separate dates. Foster's contempt prosecution included charges that, on the same dates, he violated the CPO provision ordering that he not "in any manner threaten" Ana Foster. Conviction of the contempt required willful violation of the CPO—which conviction under § 22–2307 did not; and conviction under § 22–2307 required that the threat be a threat to kidnap, to inflict bodily injury, or to damage property—which conviction of the contempt (for violating the CPO provision that Foster not "in any manner threaten") did not. Each offense therefore contained a separate element, and the *Blockburger* test for double jeopardy was not met.

IV

Having found that at least some of the counts at issue here are not barred by the *Blockburger* test, we must consider whether they are barred by the new, additional double jeopardy test we announced three Terms ago in *Grady v. Corbin.* They undoubtedly are, since *Grady* prohibits "a subsequent prosecution if, to establish an essential element of an offense charged in that prosecution [here, assault as an element of assault with intent to kill, or threatening as an element of threatening bodily injury], the government will prove conduct that constitutes an offense for which the defendant has already been prosecuted [here, the assault and the threatening, which conduct constituted the offense of violating the CPO]."

We have concluded, however, that *Grady* must be overruled. Unlike *Blockburger* analysis, whose definition of what prevents two crimes from being the "same offence" has deep historical roots and has been accepted in numerous precedents of this Court, *Grady* lacks constitutional roots. The "same-conduct" rule it announced is wholly inconsistent with earlier Supreme Court precedent and with the clear common-law understanding of double jeopardy. We need not discuss the many proofs of these statements, which were set forth at length in the *Grady* dissent (Scalia, J., dissenting). We will respond, however, to the contrary contentions of today's pro-*Grady* dissents.

The centerpiece of Justice Souter's analysis is an appealing theory of a "successive prosecution" strand of the Double Jeopardy Clause that has a different meaning from its supposed "successive punishment" strand. We have often noted that the Clause serves the function of preventing both successive punishment and successive prosecution, see, e.g., *North Carolina v. Pearce,* 395 U.S. 711 (1969), but there is no authority, except *Grady,* for the proposition that it has different meanings in the two contexts. That is perhaps because it is embarrassing to assert that the single term "same offence" (the words of the Fifth Amendment at issue here) has two different meanings—that what is the same offense is yet not the same offense. Justice Souter provides no authority whatsoever (and we are aware of none) for the bald assertion that "we have long held that [the Government] must sometimes bring its prosecutions for [separate] offenses together." The collateral-estoppel effect attributed to the Double Jeopardy Clause, see *Ashe v. Swenson,* may bar a later prosecution for a separate offense where the Government has lost an earlier prosecution involving the same facts. But this does not establish that the Government "must ... bring its prosecutions ... together." It is entirely free to bring them separately, and can win convictions in both. Of course the collateral estoppel issue is not raised in this case.

Justice Souter relies upon four cases to establish the existence of some minimal antecedents to *Grady.* The fountainhead of the "same-conduct" rule, he asserts, is *In re Nielsen,* 131 U.S. 176 (1889). That is demonstrably wrong. *Nielsen* simply applies the common proposition, entirely in accord with *Blockburger,* that prosecution for a greater offense (cohabitation, defined to require proof of adultery) bars prosecution for a lesser included offense (adultery). * * * His second case comes almost a century later. *Brown v. Ohio,* 432 U.S. 161 (1977), contains no support for his position except a footnote that cites *Nielsen* for the proposition that "the *Blockburger* test is not the only standard for determining whether successive prosecutions impermissibly involve the same offense." *Brown,* at n. 6. Not only is this footnote the purest dictum, but it flatly contradicts the text of the opinion which, on the very next page, describes *Nielsen* as the first Supreme Court case to endorse the *Blockburger* rule. * * * The third case is *Harris,* which Justice Souter asserts was a reaffirmation of what he contends was the earlier holding in *Nielsen,* that the *Blockburger* test is "insufficient for determining when a successive prosecution [is] barred," and that conduct, and not merely elements of the offense must be the object of inquiry. Surely not. *Harris* never uses the word "conduct," and its entire discussion focuses on the elements of the two offenses. * * * Finally, [as to] *Vitale,* supra, * * * Justice Souter * * * elevates the statement in *Vitale* that, on certain hypothetical facts, the petitioner would have a "substantial" "claim" of double jeopardy on a *Grady*-type theory, into a holding that the petitioner would win on that theory. No Justice, the *Vitale* dissenters included, has ever construed this passage as answering, rather than simply raising, the question on which we later granted certiorari in *Grady.* * * * In contrast to the above-discussed dicta relied upon by Justice Souter, there are two pre-*Grady* (and post-*Nielsen*) cases that are directly on point. In both *Gavieres v. United States,* supra, and *Burton v. United States,* 202 U.S. 344 (1906), the Court upheld subsequent prosecutions after concluding that the *Blockburger* test (and only the *Blockburger* test) was satisfied. * * * Totally ignored by Justice Souter are the many early American cases construing the Double Jeopardy Clause, which support only an "elements" test. See *Grady* (Scalia, J., dissenting). * * *

But *Grady* was not only wrong in principle; it has already proved unstable in application. Less than two years after it came down, in *United States v. Felix,* 503 U.S. 378 (1992), we were forced to recognize a large exception to it. There we concluded that a subsequent prosecution for conspiracy to manufacture, possess, and distribute methamphetamine was not barred by a previous conviction for attempt to manufacture the same substance. We offered as a justification for avoiding a "literal" (i.e., faithful) reading of *Grady* "long-standing authority" to the effect that prosecution for conspiracy is not precluded by prior prosecution for the substantive offense. Of course the very existence of such a large and longstanding "exception" to the *Grady* rule gave cause for concern that the rule was not an accurate expression of the law. This "past practice" excuse is not available to support the ignoring of *Grady* in the present case, since there is no Supreme Court precedent even discussing this fairly new breed of successive prosecution (criminal contempt for violation of a court order prohibiting a crime, followed by prosecution for the crime itself).

A hypothetical based on the facts in *Harris* reinforces the conclusion that *Grady* is a continuing source of confusion and must be overruled. Suppose the State first tries the defendant for felony-murder, based on robbery, and then indicts the defendant for robbery with a firearm in the same incident. Absent *Grady,* our cases provide a clear answer to the double-jeopardy claim in this situation. Under *Blockburger,* the second prosecution is not barred—as it clearly was not barred at common law, as a famous case establishes. In *King v. Vandercomb,* 168 Eng.Rep. 455 (K.B.1796), the government abandoned, midtrial, prosecution of defendant for burglary by breaking and entering and stealing goods, because it turned out that no property had been removed on the date of the alleged burglary. The defendant was then prosecuted for burglary by breaking and entering with intent to steal. That second prosecution was allowed, because "these two offences are so distinct in their nature, that evidence of one of them will not support an indictment for the other." [15] * * *

Having encountered today yet another situation in which the pre-*Grady* understanding of the Double Jeopardy Clause allows a second trial, though the "same-conduct" test would not, we think it time to acknowledge what is now, three years after *Grady*, compellingly clear: the case was a mistake. We do not lightly reconsider a precedent, but, because *Grady* contradicted an "unbroken line of decisions," contained "less than accurate" historical analysis, and has produced "confusion," we do so here. *Solorio v. United States,* 483 U.S. 435 (1987). Although stare decisis is the "preferred course" in constitutional adjudication, "when governing decisions are unworkable or are badly reasoned, 'this Court has never felt constrained to follow precedent.'" *Payne v. Tennessee,* 501 U.S. 808, (1991). We would mock stare decisis and only add chaos to our double jeopardy jurisprudence by pretending that *Grady* survives when it does not. We therefore accept the Government's invitation to overrule *Grady*, and Counts II, III, IV, and V of Foster's subsequent prosecution are not barred.[17]

V

Dixon's subsequent prosecution, as well as Count I of Foster's subsequent prosecution, violate the Double Jeopardy Clause.[18] For the reasons set forth in Part IV, the other Counts of Foster's subsequent prosecution do not violate the Double Jeopardy Clause.[19] The judgment of the District of Columbia Court of Appeals is affirmed in part and reversed in part, and the case is remanded for proceedings not inconsistent with this opinion.

CHIEF JUSTICE REHNQUIST, with whom JUSTICE O'CONNOR and JUSTICE THOMAS join, concurring in part and dissenting in part.

* * * I do not join Part III of Justice Scalia's opinion because I think that none of the criminal prosecutions in this case were barred under *Blockburger*. I must then confront the expanded version of double jeopardy embodied in *Grady*. For the reasons set forth in the *Grady* dissent, supra, (Scalia, J., dissenting), and in Part IV of the Court's opinion, I, too, think that *Grady* must be overruled. I therefore join Parts I, II, and IV of the Court's opinion * * *.

In my view, *Blockburger*'s same-elements test requires us to focus not on the terms of the particular court orders involved, but on the elements of contempt of court in the ordinary sense. Relying on *Harris v. Oklahoma,* a three-paragraph

15. Justice Souter dislikes this result because it violates "the principles behind the protection from successive prosecution included in the Fifth Amendment." The "principles behind" the Fifth Amendment are more likely to be honored by following longstanding practice than by following intuition. But in any case, Justice Souter's concern that prosecutors will bring separate prosecutions in order to perfect their case seems unjustified. They have little to gain and much to lose from such a strategy. Under *Ashe v. Swenson,* an acquittal in the first prosecution might well bar litigation of certain facts essential to the second one—though a conviction in the first prosecution would not excuse the Government from proving the same facts the second time. Surely, moreover, the Government must be deterred from abusive, repeated prosecutions of a single offender for similar offenses by the sheer press of other demands upon prosecutorial and judicial resources. Finally, even if Justice Souter's fear were well founded, no double-jeopardy bar short of a same-transaction analysis will eliminate this problem; but that interpretation of the Double Jeopardy Clause has been soundly rejected, and would require overruling numerous precedents. * * *

17. We do not address the motion to dismiss the threat counts based on collateral estoppel, see *Ashe v. Swenson,* supra, because neither lower court ruled on that issue.

18. Justices White, Stevens, and Souter concur in this portion of the judgment.

19. Justice Blackmun concurs only in the judgment with respect to this portion.

per curiam in an unargued case, Justice Scalia concludes otherwise today, and thus incorrectly finds in Part III of his opinion that the subsequent prosecutions of Dixon for drug distribution and of Foster for assault violated the Double Jeopardy Clause. In so doing, Justice Scalia rejects the traditional view—shared by every federal court of appeals and state supreme court that addressed the issue prior to *Grady*—that, as a general matter, double jeopardy does not bar a subsequent prosecution based on conduct for which a defendant has been held in criminal contempt. * * *

At the heart of this pre-*Grady* consensus lay the common belief that there was no double-jeopardy bar under *Blockburger*. There, we stated that two offenses are different for purposes of double jeopardy if "each provision requires proof·of a fact which the other does not." Applying this test to the offenses at bar, it is clear that the elements of the governing contempt provision are entirely different from the elements of the substantive crimes. Contempt of court comprises two elements: (i) a court order made known to the defendant, followed by (ii) willful violation of that order. Neither of those elements is necessarily satisfied by proof that a defendant has committed the substantive offenses of assault or drug distribution. Likewise, no element of either of those substantive offenses is necessarily satisfied by proof that a defendant has been found guilty of contempt of court. * * * Our double jeopardy cases applying *Blockburger* have focused on the statutory elements of the offenses charged, not on the facts that must be proven under the particular indictment at issue—an indictment being the closest analogue to the court orders in this case. * * * By focusing on the facts needed to show a violation of the specific court orders involved in this case, and not on the generic elements of the crime of contempt of court, Justice Scalia's double-jeopardy analysis bears a striking resemblance to that found in *Grady*—not what one would expect in an opinion that overrules *Grady*. * * *

Close inspection of the crimes at issue in *Harris* reveals, moreover, that our decision in that case was not a departure from *Blockburger*'s focus on the statutory elements of the offenses charged. In *Harris,* we held that a conviction for felony murder based on a killing in the course of an armed robbery foreclosed a subsequent prosecution for robbery with a firearm. Though the felony-murder statute in *Harris* did not require proof of armed robbery, it did include as an element of proof that the defendant was engaged in the commission of some felony. We construed this generic reference to some felony as incorporating the statutory elements of the various felonies upon which a felony-murder conviction could rest. The criminal contempt provision involved here, by contrast, contains no such generic reference which by definition incorporates the statutory elements of assault or drug distribution.

Unless we are to accept the extraordinary view that the three-paragraph per curiam in *Harris* was intended to overrule sub silentio our previous decisions that looked to the statutory elements of the offenses charged in applying *Blockburger,* we are bound to conclude, as does Justice Scalia, that the ratio decidendi of our *Harris* decision was that the two crimes there were akin to greater and lesser included offenses. The crimes at issue here, however, cannot be viewed as greater and lesser included offenses, either intuitively or logically. A crime such as possession with intent to distribute cocaine is a serious felony that cannot easily be conceived of as a lesser included offense of criminal contempt, a relatively petty offense as applied to the conduct in this case. See D.C.Code Ann. § 33–541(a)(2)(A) (the maximum sentence for possession with intent to distribute cocaine is 15 years in prison). Indeed, to say that criminal contempt is an aggravated form of that offense defies common sense. * * *

Justice White with whom Justice Stevens joins, and with whom Justice Souter joins as to Part I, concurring in the judgment in part and dissenting in part.

I

The chief issue before us is whether the Double Jeopardy Clause applies at all to cases such as these. Justice Scalia finds that it applies, but does so in conclusory fashion, without dealing adequately with * * * the Government's arguments or the practical consequences of today's decision. Both, in my view, are worthy of more.

The position of the United States is that, for the purpose of applying the Double Jeopardy Clause, a charge of criminal contempt for engaging in conduct that is proscribed by court order and that is in turn forbidden by the criminal code is an offense separate from the statutory crime. The United States begins by pointing to prior decisions of this Court to support its view. * * * [But its strongest] decisions concern the power to deal with acts interfering directly with the performance of legislative functions, a power to which not all constitutional restraints on the exercise of judiciary authority apply. * * * [W]hatever application * * * [they] might have in the context of judicial contempt is limited to cases of in-court contempts that constitute direct obstructions of the judicial process and for which summary proceedings remain acceptable. Neither *Dixon* nor *Foster* is such a case.

The United States' second, more powerful, argument is that contempt and the underlying substantive crime constitute two separate offenses for they involve injuries to two distinct interests, the one the interest of the court in preserving its authority, the other the public's interest in being protected from harmful conduct. This position finds support in Justice Blackmun's partial dissent, and is bolstered by reference to numerous decisions acknowledging the importance and role of the courts' contempt power. * * * The fact that two criminal prohibitions promote different interests may be indicative of legislative intent and, to that extent, important in deciding whether cumulative punishments imposed in a single prosecution violate the Double Jeopardy Clause. See *Missouri v. Hunter,* 459 U.S. 359 (1983). But the cases decided today involve instances of successive prosecutions in which the interests of the defendant are of paramount concern. To subject an individual to repeated prosecutions exposes him to "embarrassment, expense and ordeal," violates principles of finality, and increases the risk of a mistaken conviction. That one of the punishments is designed to protect the court rather than the public is, in this regard, of scant comfort to the defendant. * * *

Both the Government and amici submit that application of the Double Jeopardy Clause in this context carries grave practical consequences. * * * It would, it is argued, cripple the power to enforce court orders or, alternatively, allow individuals to escape serious punishment for statutory criminal offenses. The argument, an offshoot of the principle of necessity familiar to the law of contempt, is that, just as we have relaxed certain procedural requirements in contempt proceedings where time is of the essence and an immediate remedy is needed to "prevent a breakdown of the proceedings," so too should we exclude double jeopardy protections from this setting lest we do damage to the courts' authority. * * *

Adherence to double jeopardy principles in this context, however, will not seriously deter the courts from taking appropriate steps to ensure that their authority is not flouted. Courts remain free to hold transgressors in contempt and punish them as they see fit. The government counters that this possibility will prove to be either illusory—if the prosecuting authority declines to initiate proceedings out of fear that they could jeopardize more substantial punishment for the underlying crime—or too costly—if the prosecuting authority, the risk notwithstanding, chooses to go forward. But it is not fanciful to imagine that judges and prosecutors will select a third option, which is to ensure, where necessary or advisable, that the contempt and the substantive charge be tried at the same time, in which case the double jeopardy issue "would be limited to ensuring that the total punishment did not exceed that authorized by the legislature." *United States v. Halper,* 490 U.S. 435 (1989).

Against this backdrop, the appeal of the principle of necessity loses much of its force. Ultimately, the urgency of punishing such contempt violations is no less, but by the same token no more, than that of punishing violations of criminal laws of general application—in which case, we simply do not question the defendant's right to the "protections worked out carefully over the years and deemed fundamental to our system of justice," including the protection of the Double Jeopardy Clause. "Perhaps to some extent we sacrifice efficiency, expedition, and economy, but the choice . . . has been made, and retained, in the Constitution. We see no sound reason in logic or policy not to apply it in the area of criminal contempt." *Bloom v. Illinois.*

Dixon aptly illustrates these points. In that case, the motion requesting modification of the conditions of Dixon's release was filed by the government, the same entity responsible for prosecution of the drug offense. Indeed, in so doing it relied explicitly on the defendant's indictment on the cocaine charge. Logically, any problem of coordination or of advance notice of the impending prosecution for the substantive offense was at most minimal. Nor, aside from the legitimate desire to punish all offenders swiftly, does there appear to have been any real need to hold Dixon in contempt immediately, without waiting for the second trial. * * *

More difficult to deal with are the circumstances surrounding Foster's defiance of the court order. Realization of the scope of domestic violence—according to the American Medical Association (AMA), "the single largest cause of injury to women,"—has come with difficulty, and it has come late. There no doubt are time delays in the operation of the criminal justice system that are frustrating; they even can be perilous when an individual is left exposed to a defendant's potential violence. That is true in the domestic context; it is true elsewhere as well. Resort to more expedient methods therefore is appealing, and in many cases permissible. Under today's decision, for instance, police officers retain the power to arrest for violation of a civil protection order. Where the offense so warrants, judges can haul the assailant before the court, charge him with criminal contempt, and hold him without bail. See *United States v. Salerno* [Ch. 9]. Also, cooperation between the government and parties bringing contempt proceedings can be achieved. The various actors might not have thought such cooperation necessary in the past; after today's decision, I suspect they will. * * *

II

If, as the Court agrees, the Double Jeopardy Clause cannot be ignored in this context, my view is that the subsequent prosecutions in both *Dixon* and *Foster* were impermissible as to all counts. I reach this conclusion because the offenses at issue in the contempt proceedings were either identical to, or lesser included offenses of, those charged in the subsequent prosecutions. Justice Scalia's contrary conclusion as to some of Foster's counts, which he reaches by exclusive focus on the formal elements of the relevant crimes, is divorced from the purposes of the constitutional provision he purports to apply. Moreover, the results to which this approach would lead are indefensible.

* * * Because in a successive prosecution case the risk is that a person will have to defend himself more than once against the same charge, I would have put to the side the CPO (which, as it were, triggered the court's authority to punish the defendant for acts already punishable under the criminal laws) and compared the substantive offenses of which respondents stood accused in both prosecutions. * * * Under Justice Scalia's view, the double jeopardy barrier is * * * removed because each offense demands proof of an element the other does not: Foster's conviction for contempt requires proof of the existence and knowledge of a CPO, which conviction for assault with intent to kill does not; his conviction for assault with intent to kill requires proof of an intent to kill, which the contempt conviction did not. Finally, though he was acquitted in the contempt proceedings with respect to the alleged November 12, March 26, and May 17 threats, his conviction under the threat charge in the subsequent trial required the additional proof that the threat be to kidnap, to inflict bodily injury, or to damage property. As to these counts, and absent any collateral estoppel problem, Justice Scalia finds that the Constitution does not prohibit retrial.

The distinction drawn by Justice Scalia is predicated on a reading of the Double Jeopardy Clause that is abstracted from the purposes the constitutional provision is designed to promote. To focus on the statutory elements of a crime makes sense where cumulative punishment is at stake, for there the aim simply is to uncover legislative intent. The *Blockburger* inquiry, accordingly, serves as a means to determine this intent, as our cases have recognized. But, as Justice Souter shows, adherence to legislative will has very little to do with the important interests advanced by double jeopardy safeguards against successive prosecutions. The central purpose of the Double Jeopardy Clause being to protect against vexatious multiple prosecutions, these interests go well beyond the prevention of unauthorized punishment. The same-elements test is an inadequate safeguard, for it leaves the constitutional guarantee at the mercy of a legislature's decision to modify statutory definitions. * * * Take the example of Count V in *Foster:* For all intents and purposes, the offense for which he was convicted in the contempt proceeding was his assault against his wife. The majority, its eyes fixed on the rigid elements-test, would have his fate turn on whether his subsequent prosecution charges "simple assault" or "assault with intent to kill." Yet, because the crime of "simple assault" is included within the crime of "assault with intent to kill," the reasons that bar retrial under the first hypothesis are equally present under the second: These include principles of finality, protecting Foster from "embarrassment" and "expense," and preventing the government from gradually fine-tuning its strategy, thereby minimizing exposure to a mistaken conviction. * * *

To respond, as the majority appears to do, that concerns relating to the defendant's interests against repeat trials are "unjustified" because prosecutors "have little to gain and much to lose" from bringing successive prosecutions and because "the Government must be deterred from abusive, repeated prosecutions of a single offender for similar offenses by the sheer press of other demands upon prosecutorial and judicial resources," [n. 15 of Justice Scalia's opinion], is to get things exactly backwards. The majority's prophesies might be correct, and double jeopardy might be a problem that will simply take care of itself. Not so, however, according to the Constitution, whose firm prohibition against double jeopardy cannot be satisfied by wishful thinking. * * *

Once it is agreed that the Double Jeopardy Clause applies in this context, the Clause, properly construed, both governs this case and disposes of the distinction between Foster's charges upon which Justice Scalia relies. I therefore see little need to draw *Grady* into this dispute. * * * The majority nonetheless has chosen to consider *Grady* anew and to overrule it. I agree with Justice Blackmun and Justice Souter that such a course is both unwarranted and unwise. Hence, I dissent from the judgment overruling *Grady.*

JUSTICE BLACKMUN, concurring in the judgment in part and dissenting in part.

I agree with Justice Souter that "the *Blockburger* test is not the exclusive standard for determining whether the rule against successive prosecutions applies in a given case." I also share both his and Justice White's dismay that the Court so cavalierly has overruled a precedent that is barely three years old and that has proved neither unworkable nor unsound. * * * If this were a case involving successive prosecutions under the substantive criminal law (as was true in *Harris v. Oklahoma, Illinois v. Vitale,* and *Grady*), I would agree that the Double Jeopardy Clause could bar the subsequent prosecution. But we are concerned here with contempt of court, a special situation. * * * The purpose of contempt is not to punish an offense against the community at large but rather to punish the specific offense of disobeying a court order. This Court said nearly a century ago: "[A] court, enforcing obedience to its orders by proceedings for contempt, is not executing the criminal laws of the land, but only securing to suitors the rights which it has adjudged them entitled to." *In re Debs,* 158 U.S. 564 (1895). * * * This fact is poignantly stressed by the amici: "Contempt litigators and criminal prosecutors seek to further different interests. A battered woman seeks to enforce her private order to end the violence against her. In contrast, the criminal prosecutor is vindicating society's interest in enforcing its criminal law. The two interests are not the same, and to consider the contempt litigator and the criminal prosecutor as one and the same would be to adopt an absurd fiction" (emphasis in original). Brief for Ayuda et al. as Amici Curiae 20.

Finally, I cannot so easily distinguish between "summary" and "nonsummary" contempt proceedings, for the interests served in both are fundamentally similar. It is as much a "disruption of judicial process," to disobey a judge's conditional release order as it is to disturb a judge's courtroom. And the interests served in vindicating the authority of the court are fundamentally different from those served by the prosecution of violations of the substantive criminal law. Because I believe that neither Dixon nor Foster would be "subject for the same offence to be twice put in jeopardy of life or limb," U.S. Const., Amdt. 5, I would reverse the judgment of the District of Columbia Court of Appeals.

JUSTICE SOUTER, with whom JUSTICE STEVENS joins, concurring in the judgment in part and dissenting in part.

While I agree with the Court as far as it goes in holding that a citation for criminal contempt and an indictment for violating a substantive criminal statute may amount to charges of the "same offence" for purposes of the Double Jeopardy Clause, I cannot join the Court in restricting the Clause's reach and dismembering the protection against successive prosecution that the Constitution was meant to provide. The Court has read our precedents so narrowly as to leave them bereft of the principles animating that protection, and has chosen to overrule the most recent of the relevant cases, *Grady v. Corbin,* decided three years ago. Because I think that *Grady* was correctly decided, amounting merely to an expression of just those animating principles, and because, even if the decision had been wrong in the first instance, there is no warrant for overruling it now, I respectfully dissent. * * *

In providing that no person shall "be subject for the same offence to be twice put in jeopardy of life or limb," the Double Jeopardy Clause protects against two distinct types of abuses. It protects against being punished more than once for a single offense, or "multiple punishment." Where a person is being subjected to more than one sentence, the Double Jeopardy Clause ensures that he is not receiving for one offense more than the punishment authorized. The Clause also protects against being prosecuted for the same offense more than once, or "successive prosecution." * * * The Clause functions in different ways in the two contexts, and the analysis applied to claims of successive prosecution differs from that employed to analyze claims of multiple punishment.

In addressing multiple punishments, "the role of the constitutional guarantee is limited to assuring that the court does not exceed its legislative authorization by imposing multiple punishments for the same offense." *Brown v. Ohio.* Courts enforcing the federal guarantee against multiple punishment therefore must examine the various offenses for which a person is being punished to determine whether, as defined by the legislature, any two or more of them are the same offense. Over 60 years ago, this Court [in *Blockburger*] stated the test still used today to determine "whether two offenses are sufficiently distinguishable to permit the imposition of cumulative punishment." * * * The *Blockburger* test "emphasizes the elements of the two crimes." *Brown.* Indeed, the determination whether two statutes describe the "same offence" for multiple punishment purposes has been held to involve only a question of statutory construction. We ask what the elements of each offense are as a matter of statutory interpretation, to determine whether the legislature intended "to impose separate sanctions for multiple offenses arising in the course of a single act or transaction." * * * The Court has even gone so far as to say that the *Blockburger* test will not prevent multiple punishment where legislative intent to the contrary is clear, at least in the case of state law. * * * *Missouri v. Hunter.* * * *

The interests at stake in avoiding successive prosecutions are different from those at stake in the prohibition against multiple punishments, and our cases reflect this reality. The protection against successive prosecutions is the central protection provided by the Clause. * * * Consequently, while the government may punish a person separately for each conviction of at least as many different offenses as meet the *Blockburger* test, we have long held that it must sometimes bring its prosecutions for these offenses together. If a separate prosecution were permitted for every offense arising out of the same conduct, the government could manipulate the definitions of offenses, creating fine distinctions among them and permitting a zealous prosecutor to try a person again and again for essentially the same criminal conduct. While punishing different combinations of elements is consistent with the Double Jeopardy Clause in its limitation on the imposition of multiple punishments (a limitation rooted in concerns with legislative intent), permitting such repeated prosecutions would not be consistent with the principles underlying the Clause in its limitation on successive prosecution. The limitation on successive prosecution is thus a restriction on the government different in kind from that contained in the limitation on multiple punishments, and the government cannot get around the restriction on repeated prosecution of a single individual merely by precision in the way it defines its statutory offenses. Thus, "the *Blockburger* test is not the only standard for determining whether successive prosecutions impermissibly involve the same offense. Even if two offenses are sufficiently different to permit the imposition of consecutive sentences, successive prosecutions will be barred in some circumstances where the second prosecution requires the relitigation of factual issues already resolved by the first." *Brown* at n. 6.

An example will show why this should be so. Assume three crimes: robbery with a firearm, robbery in a dwelling and simple robbery. The elements of the three crimes are the same, except that robbery with a firearm has the element that a firearm be used in the commission of the robbery while the other two crimes do not, and robbery in a dwelling has the element that the robbery occur in a dwelling while the other two crimes do not.

If a person committed a robbery in a dwelling with a firearm and was prosecuted for simple robbery, all agree he could not be prosecuted subsequently for either of the greater offenses of robbery with a firearm or robbery in a dwelling. Under the lens of *Blockburger,* however, if that same person were prosecuted first for robbery with a firearm, he could be prosecuted subsequently for robbery in a dwelling, even though he could not subsequently be prosecuted on the basis of that same robbery for simple robbery.[3] This is true simply because neither of the crimes, robbery with a firearm and robbery in a dwelling, is either identical to or a lesser-included offense of the other. But since the purpose of the Double Jeopardy Clause's protection against successive prosecutions is to prevent repeated trials in which a defendant will be forced to defend against the same charge again and again, and in which the government may perfect its presentation with dress rehearsal after dress rehearsal, it should be irrelevant that the second prosecution would require the defendant to defend himself not only from the charge that he committed the robbery, but also from the charge of some additional fact, in this case, that the scene of the crime was a dwelling. If, instead, protection against successive prosecution were as limited as it would be by *Blockburger* alone, the doctrine would be as striking for its anomalies as for the limited protection it would provide. Thus, in the relatively few successive prosecution cases we have had over the years, we have not held that the *Blockburger* test is the only hurdle the government must clear (with one exception). * * *

The recognition that a *Blockburger* rule is insufficient protection against successive prosecution can be seen as long ago as *In re Nielsen,* 131 U.S. 176 (1889), where we held that conviction for one statutory offense precluded later prosecution for another, even though each required proof of a fact the other did not. * * * In the past 20 years the Court has addressed just this problem of successive prosecution on three occasions. In *Harris v. Oklahoma,* we held that prosecution for a robbery with firearms was barred by the Double Jeopardy Clause when the defendant had already been convicted of felony murder comprising the same robbery with firearms as the underlying felony. * * * Subsequently, in *Illinois v. Vitale,* the Court again indicated that a valid claim of double jeopardy would not necessarily be defeated by the fact that the two offenses are not the "same" under the *Blockburger* test. In that case, we were confronted with a prosecution for failure to reduce speed and a subsequent prosecution for involuntary manslaughter. The opinion of the Illinois Supreme Court below had not made it clear whether the elements of failure to slow were always necessarily included within the elements of involuntary manslaughter by automobile, and we remanded for clarification of this point, among other things. We held that "if, as a matter of Illinois law, a careless failure to slow is always a necessary element of manslaughter by automobile, then the two offenses are the 'same' under *Blockburger* and *Vitale*'s trial on the latter charge would constitute double jeopardy...." Id., at 419–420. But that was not all. Writing for the Court, Justice White went on to say that, "in any event, it may be that to sustain its

---

3. Our cases have long made clear that the order in which one is prosecuted for two crimes alleged to be the same matters not in demonstrating a violation of double jeopardy. See *Brown v. Ohio* ("the sequence is immaterial").

manslaughter case the State may find it necessary to prove a failure to slow or to rely on conduct necessarily involving such failure.... In that case, because Vitale has already been convicted for conduct that is a necessary element of the more serious crime for which he has been charged, his claim of double jeopardy would be substantial under *Brown* [*v. Ohio*] and our later decision in *Harris v. Oklahoma.*"

Over a decade ago, then, we clearly understood *Harris* to stand for the proposition that when one has already been tried for a crime comprising certain conduct, a subsequent prosecution seeking to prove the same conduct is barred by the Double Jeopardy Clause.[7] * * * [But] even if this had not been clear since the time of *In re Nielsen,* any debate should have been settled by our decision three Terms ago in *Grady v. Corbin.* * * * As against this sequence of consistent reasoning from *Nielsen* to *Grady,* the Court's citation to two cases, *Gavieres v. United States,* and *Burton v. United States,* cannot validate its insistence that, prior to *Grady,* our exclusive standard for barring successive prosecutions under the Double Jeopardy Clause was the *Blockburger* test. * * * *Gavieres* is in fact the only case that may even be read to suggest that the Court ever treated a *Blockburger* analysis as the exclusive successive prosecution test under the Double Jeopardy Clause, and its precedential force is weak. * * * Whatever may have been the merits of the debate in *Grady,* the decision deserves more respect than it receives from the Court today. "Although adherence to precedent is not rigidly required in constitutional cases, any departure from the doctrine of stare decisis demands special justification. *Arizona v. Rumsey,* 467 U.S. 203 (1984).

HEATH v. ALABAMA

474 U.S. 82, 106 S.Ct. 433, 88 L.Ed.2d 387 (1985).

JUSTICE O'CONNOR delivered the opinion of the Court. * * *

In August 1981, petitioner, Larry Gene Heath, hired Charles Owens and Gregory Lumpkin to kill his wife, Rebecca Heath, who was then nine months pregnant, for a sum of $2,000. On the morning of August 31, 1981, petitioner left the Heath residence in Russell County, Alabama, to meet with Owens and Lumpkin in Georgia, just over the Alabama border from the Heath home. Petitioner led them back to the Heath residence, gave them the keys to the Heaths' car and house, and left the premises in his girlfriend's truck. Owens and Lumpkin then kidnaped Rebecca Heath from her home. The Heath car, with Rebecca Heath's body inside, was later found on the side of a road in Troup County, Georgia. The cause of death was a gunshot wound in the head. The estimated time of death and the distance from the Heath residence to the spot where Rebecca Heath's body was found are consistent with the theory that the murder took place in Georgia, and respondent does not contend otherwise.

Georgia and Alabama authorities pursued dual investigations in which they cooperated to some extent. * * * In November 1981, the grand jury of Troup County, Georgia indicted petitioner for the offense of "malice" murder. Georgia then served petitioner with notice of its intention to seek the death penalty, citing as the aggravating circumstance the fact that the murder was "caused and directed" by petitioner. On February 10, 1982, petitioner pleaded guilty to the

7. [Transposed footnote] In *Brown* we recognized that "[a]n exception may exist where the State is unable to proceed on the more serious charge at the outset because the addi-tional facts necessary to sustain that charge have not occurred or have not been discovered despite the exercise of due diligence."

Georgia murder charge in exchange for a sentence of life imprisonment, which he understood could involve his serving as few as seven years in prison.

On May 5, 1982, the grand jury of Russell County, Alabama, returned an indictment against petitioner for the capital offense of murder during a kidnaping. Before trial on this indictment, petitioner entered pleas of *autrefois convict* and former jeopardy under the Alabama and United States Constitutions, arguing that his conviction and sentence in Georgia barred his prosecution in Alabama for the same conduct. After a hearing, the trial court rejected petitioner's double jeopardy claims. It assumed, *arguendo*, that the two prosecutions could not have been brought in succession by one State but held that double jeopardy did not bar successive prosecutions by two different States for the same act. * * *

On January 12, 1983, the Alabama jury convicted petitioner of murder during a kidnaping in the first degree. After a sentencing hearing, the jury recommended the death penalty. * * * The judge accepted the jury's recommendation, finding that the sole aggravating factor, that the capital offense was "committed while the defendant was engaged in the commission of a kidnapping," outweighed the sole mitigating factor, that the "defendant was convicted of the murder of Rebecca Heath in the Superior Court of Troup County, Georgia, * * * and received a sentence of life imprisonment in that court." [The state appellate courts affirmed the conviction and sentence.]

Petitioner sought a writ of certiorari from this Court, raising double jeopardy claims and claims based on Alabama's exercise of jurisdiction. No due process objections were asserted. We granted certiorari limited to the question of whether Alabama's conviction was barred by this Court's decision in *Brown v. Ohio*, and requested the parties to address the question of the applicability of the dual sovereignty doctrine to successive prosecutions by two States.

Successive prosecutions are barred by the Fifth Amendment only if the two offenses for which the defendant is prosecuted are the "same" for double jeopardy purposes. Respondent does not contravene petitioner's contention that the offenses of "murder during a kidnaping" and "malice murder," as construed by the courts of Alabama and Georgia respectively, may be considered greater and lesser offenses and, thus, the "same" offense under *Brown v. Ohio*, absent operation of the dual sovereignty principle. See *Illinois v. Vitale*. We, therefore, assume *arguendo* that, had these offenses arisen under the laws of one State and had petitioner been separately prosecuted for both offenses in that State, the second conviction would have been barred by the Double Jeopardy Clause.

The sole remaining question upon which we granted certiorari is whether the dual sovereignty doctrine permits successive prosecutions under the laws of different States which otherwise would be held to "subject [the defendant] for the same offence to be twice put in jeopardy." Although we have not previously so held, we believe the answer to this query is inescapable. The dual sovereignty doctrine, as originally articulated and consistently applied by this Court, compels the conclusion that successive prosecutions by two States for the same conduct are not barred by the Double Jeopardy Clause.

The dual sovereignty doctrine is founded on the common law conception of crime as an offense against the sovereignty of the government. When a defendant in a single act violates the "peace and dignity" of two sovereigns by breaking the laws of each, he has committed two distinct "offences." * * *

In applying the dual sovereignty doctrine, then, the crucial determination is whether the two entities that seek successively to prosecute a defendant for the same course of conduct can be termed separate sovereigns. This determination turns on whether the two entities draw their authority to punish the offender from distinct sources of power. Thus, the Court has uniformly held that the States are separate sovereigns with respect to the Federal Government because each State's power to prosecute is derived from its own "inherent sovereignty," not from the Federal Government. See *Abbate v. United States*, 359 U.S. 187 (1959). * * * See also *Bartkus v. Illinois*, 359 U.S. 121 (1959).[a] * * *

The States are no less sovereign with respect to each other than they are with respect to the Federal Government. Their powers to undertake criminal prosecutions derive from separate and independent sources of power and authority originally belonging to them before admission to the Union and preserved to them by the Tenth Amendment. * * *

In those instances where the Court has found the dual sovereignty doctrine inapplicable, it has done so because the two prosecuting entities did not derive their powers to prosecute from independent sources of authority. Thus, the Court has held that successive prosecutions by federal and territorial courts are barred because such courts are "creations emanating from the same sovereignty." Similarly, municipalities that derive their power to try a defendant from the same organic law that empowers the State to prosecute are not separate sovereigns with respect to the State. These cases confirm that it is the presence of independent sovereign authority to prosecute, not the relation between States and the Federal Government in our federalist system, that constitutes the basis for the dual sovereignty doctrine. * * *

Petitioner invites us to restrict the applicability of the dual sovereignty principle to cases in which two governmental entities, having concurrent jurisdiction and pursuing quite different interests, can demonstrate that allowing only one entity to exercise jurisdiction over the defendant will interfere with the unvindicated interests of the second entity and that multiple prosecutions therefore are necessary for the satisfaction of the legitimate interests of both entities. This balancing of interests approach, however, cannot be reconciled with the dual sovereignty principle. This Court has plainly and repeatedly stated that two identical offenses are *not* the "same offence" within the meaning of the Double Jeopardy Clause if they are prosecuted by different sovereigns. If the States are separate sovereigns, as they must be under the definition of sovereignty which the Court consistently has employed, the circumstances of the case are irrelevant.

Petitioner, then, is asking the Court to discard its sovereignty analysis and to substitute in its stead his difficult and uncertain balancing of interests approach. The Court has refused a similar request on at least one previous occasion, see *Abbate v. United States*, and rightfully so. The Court's express rationale for the dual sovereignty doctrine is not simply a fiction that can be disregarded in difficult cases. It finds weighty support in the historical understanding and political realities of the States' role in the federal system and in the words of the Double Jeopardy Clause itself, "nor shall any person be subject for the same *offence* to be twice put in jeopardy of life or limb." * * *

a. These two cases combined held constitutionally permissible separate federal and state prosecutions for the same basic criminal conduct. *Bartkus* upheld a state conviction of defendant for bank robbery where the defendant had previously been tried and acquitted in federal court for the same robbery of the same bank (which was federally insured). *Abbate* upheld a conviction of defendants in federal court for conspiring to destroy communications facilities which were "essential and integral parts of systems * * * of communications operated and controlled by the United States", where defendants previously had "pleaded guilty to a charge in state court of conspiracy to destroy another's property" (the same telephone company facilities).

Justice Marshall, with whom Justice Brennan joins, dissenting. * * * b

Under the constitutional scheme, the Federal Government has been given the exclusive power to vindicate certain of our Nation's sovereign interests, leaving the States to exercise complementary authority over matters of more local concern. The respective spheres of the Federal Government and the States may overlap at times, and even where they do not, different interests may be implicated by a single act. See, e.g., *Abbate v. United States* (conspiracy to dynamite telephone company facilities entails both destruction of property and disruption of federal communications network). Yet were a prosecution by a State, however zealously pursued, allowed to preclude further prosecution by the Federal Government for the same crime, an entire range of national interests could be frustrated. The importance of those federal interests has thus quite properly been permitted to trump a defendant's interest in avoiding successive prosecutions or multiple punishments for the same crime. Conversely, because the States under our federal system have the principal responsibility for defining and prosecuting crimes, it would be inappropriate—in the absence of a specific congressional intent to preempt state action pursuant to the Supremacy Clause—to allow a federal prosecution to preclude state authorities from vindicating the historic right and obligation of the States to maintain peace and order within their confines. * * *

Where two States seek to prosecute the same defendant for the same crime in two separate proceedings, the justifications found in the federal-state context for an exemption from double jeopardy constraints simply do not hold. Although the two States may have opted for different policies within their assigned territorial jurisdictions, the sovereign concerns with whose vindication each State has been charged are identical. Thus, in contrast to the federal-state context, barring the second prosecution would still permit one government to act upon the broad range of sovereign concerns that have been reserved to the States by the Constitution. The compelling need in the federal-state context to subordinate double jeopardy concerns is thus considerably diminished in cases involving successive prosecutions by different States. Moreover, from the defendant's perspective, the burden of successive prosecutions cannot be justified as the *quid pro quo* of dual citizenship.

To be sure, a refusal to extend the dual sovereignty rule to state-state prosecutions would preclude the State that has lost the "race to the courthouse" from vindicating legitimate policies distinct from those underlying its sister State's prosecution. But as yet, I am not persuaded that a State's desire to further a particular policy should be permitted to deprive a defendant of his constitutionally protected right not to be brought to bar more than once to answer essentially the same charges. * * *

HUDSON v. UNITED STATES

522 U.S. 93, 118 S.Ct. 488, 139 L.Ed.2d 450 (1997).

Chief Justice Rehnquist delivered the opinion of the Court.

[Upon examination of two banks, the Office of the Comptroller of the Currency concluded several bank officers had used their positions to arrange loans to third parties in violation of federal banking statutes and regulations. The OCC took action to assess penalties against the bank officers, resulting in a consent order by which they would pay assessments of $16,500, $15,000, and $12,500, respectively, and agree not to "participate in any manner" in the affairs of any

b. Justice Brennan's separate dissent is   omitted.

bank without OCC authorization. A few years later, they were indicted on several criminal charges because of the same lending transactions; the district court dismissed the charges on double jeopardy grounds; the court of appeals reversed.]

The Double Jeopardy Clause provides that no "person [shall] be subject for the same offence to be twice put in jeopardy of life or limb." We have long recognized that the Double Jeopardy Clause does not prohibit the imposition of any additional sanction that could, " 'in common parlance,' " be described as punishment. The Clause protects only against the imposition of multiple criminal punishments for the same offense, and then only when such occurs in successive proceedings.

Whether a particular punishment is criminal or civil is, at least initially, a matter of statutory construction. A court must first ask whether the legislature, "in establishing the penalizing mechanism, indicated either expressly or impliedly a preference for one label or the other." *United States v. Ward,* 448 U.S. 242 (1980). Even in those cases where the legislature "has indicated an intention to establish a civil penalty, we have inquired further whether the statutory scheme was so punitive either in purpose or effect, as to" transfor[m] what was clearly intended as a civil remedy into a criminal penalty." In making this latter determination, the factors listed in *Kennedy v. Mendoza–Martinez,* 372 U.S. 144 (1963), provide useful guideposts, including: (1) "[w]hether the sanction involves an affirmative disability or restraint"; (2) "whether it has historically been regarded as a punishment"; (3) "whether it comes into play only on a finding of scienter"; (4) "whether its operation will promote the traditional aims of punishment-retribution and deterrence"; (5) "whether the behavior to which it applies is already a crime"; (6) "whether an alternative purpose to which it may rationally be connected is assignable for it"; and (7) "whether it appears excessive in relation to the alternative purpose assigned." It is important to note, however, that "these factors must be considered in relation to the statute on its face," and "only the clearest proof" will suffice to override legislative intent and transform what has been denominated a civil remedy into a criminal penalty.

Our opinion in *United States v. Halper,* 490 U.S. 435 (1989), marked the first time we applied the Double Jeopardy Clause to a sanction without first determining that it was criminal in nature. In that case, Irwin Halper was convicted of, inter alia, violating the criminal false claims statute based on his submission of 65 inflated Medicare claims each of which overcharged the Government by $9. He was sentenced to two years' imprisonment and fined $5,000. The Government then brought an action against Halper under the civil False Claims Act. The remedial provisions of the False Claims Act provided that a violation of the Act rendered one "liable to the United States Government for a civil penalty of $2,000, an amount equal to 2 times the amount of damages the Government sustains because of the act of that person, and costs of the civil action." Given Halper's 65 separate violations of the Act, he appeared to be liable for a penalty of $130,000, despite the fact he actually defrauded the Government of less than $600. However, the District Court concluded that a penalty of this magnitude would violate the Double Jeopardy Clause in light of Halper's previous criminal conviction. While explicitly recognizing that the statutory damages provision of the Act "was not itself a criminal punishment," the District Court nonetheless concluded that application of the full penalty to Halper would constitute a second "punishment" in violation of the Double Jeopardy Clause.

On direct appeal, this Court affirmed. As the *Halper* Court saw it, the imposition of "punishment" of any kind was subject to double jeopardy constraints, and whether a sanction constituted "punishment" depended primarily on whether it served the traditional "goals of punishment," namely "retribution and deterrence." Any sanction that was so "overwhelmingly disproportionate" to the injury caused that it could not "fairly be said *solely* to serve [the] remedial purpose" of compensating the government for its loss, was thought to be explainable only as "serving either retributive or deterrent purposes." (emphasis added).

The analysis applied by the *Halper* Court deviated from our traditional double jeopardy doctrine in two key respects. First, the *Halper* Court bypassed the threshold question: whether the successive punishment at issue is a "criminal" punishment. Instead, it focused on whether the sanction, regardless of whether it was civil or criminal, was so grossly disproportionate to the harm caused as to constitute "punishment." In so doing, the Court elevated a single *Kennedy* factor—whether the sanction appeared excessive in relation to its nonpunitive purposes—to dispositive status. But as we emphasized in *Kennedy* itself, no one factor should be considered controlling as they "may often point in differing directions." The second significant departure in *Halper* was the Court's decision to "asses[s] the character of the actual sanctions imposed," rather than, as *Kennedy* demanded, evaluating the "statute on its face" to determine whether it provided for what amounted to a criminal sanction.

We believe that *Halper*'s deviation from longstanding double jeopardy principles was ill considered. As subsequent cases have demonstrated, *Halper*'s test for determining whether a particular sanction is "punitive," and thus subject to the strictures of the Double Jeopardy Clause, has proved unworkable. We have since recognized that all civil penalties have some deterrent effect. See *Department of Revenue of Mont. v. Kurth Ranch*, 511 U.S. 767 (1994); *United States v. Ursery*, 518 U.S. 267 (1996).[a] If a sanction must be "solely" remedial (i.e., entirely nondeterrent) to avoid implicating the Double Jeopardy Clause, then no civil penalties are beyond the scope of the Clause. Under *Halper*'s method of analysis, a court must also look at the "sanction actually imposed" to determine whether the Double Jeopardy Clause is implicated. Thus, it will not be possible to determine whether the Double Jeopardy Clause is violated until a defendant has proceeded through a trial to judgment. But in those cases where the civil proceeding follows the criminal proceeding, this approach flies in the face of the notion that the Double Jeopardy Clause forbids the government from even "attempting a second time to punish criminally."

Finally, it should be noted that some of the ills at which *Halper* was directed are addressed by other constitutional provisions. The Due Process and Equal

---

a. *Kurth Ranch* departed from the specific analysis of *Halper* in assessing whether a tax constituted punishment under the double jeopardy clause, although stating that the Court adhered to *Halper*'s underlying premise "that only 'the character of the actual sanctions' can substantiate a possible double jeopardy violation." The Court there held that a tax on marijuana was invalid under the double jeopardy clause where the taxpayer had already been convicted of owning the taxed marijuana. In determining that the tax was "so punitive as to constitute punishment," the Court stressed that the tax was conditioned on the commission of a crime, and was imposed only after the taxpayer had been arrested, thus limiting its applicability only to a person charged with a crime. Also, the tax applied even though the taxpayer did not own or possess the taxed marijuana at the time the tax was imposed.

Ursery held that forfeitures were to be judged by a two-part test established long before *Halper*. Initially, the Court asked whether Congress intended the forfeiture to be criminal or civil. Second, it asked whether the forfeiture was "so punitive in fact as to 'persuade us that the forfeiture proceedings may not legitimately be viewed as civil in nature." Here Congress clearly intended the forfeiture to be civil. On the second question, the evidence fell far short of the "clearest proof" needed to overcome Congress' civil designation. Though the forfeiture had punitive aspects, it also had nonpunitive goals (encouraging property owners to take care to avoid the use of their property for illegal purposes), was not tied to scienter, and was imposed *in rem* (rather than *in personam*).

Protection Clauses already protect individuals from sanctions which are downright irrational. The Eighth Amendment protects against excessive civil fines, including forfeitures. The additional protection afforded by extending double jeopardy protections to proceedings heretofore thought to be civil is more than offset by the confusion created by attempting to distinguish between "punitive" and "nonpunitive"'" penalties.

Applying traditional double jeopardy principles to the facts of this case, it is clear that the criminal prosecution of these petitioners would not violate the Double Jeopardy Clause. It is evident that Congress intended the OCC money penalties and debarment sanctions * * * to be civil in nature. As for the money penalties, [the statutes] which authorize the imposition of monetary penalties * * * expressly provide that such penalties are "civil." While the provision authorizing debarment contains no language explicitly denominating the sanction as civil, we think it significant that the authority to issue debarment orders is conferred upon the "appropriate Federal banking agenc[ies]." That such authority was conferred upon administrative agencies is prima facie evidence that Congress intended to provide for a civil sanction.

Turning to the second stage of the * * * test, we find that there is little evidence, much less the clearest proof that we require, suggesting that either OCC money penalties or debarment sanctions are "so punitive in form and effect as to render them criminal despite Congress' intent to the contrary." First, neither money penalties nor debarment have historically been viewed as punishment. We have long recognized that "revocation of a privilege voluntarily granted," such as a debarment, "is characteristically free of the punitive criminal element." Similarly, "the payment of fixed or variable sums of money [is a] sanction which ha[s] been recognized as enforceable by civil proceedings since the original revenue law of 1789."

Second, the sanctions imposed do not involve an "affirmative disability or restraint," as that term is normally understood. While petitioners have been prohibited from further participating in the banking industry, this is "certainly nothing approaching the 'infamous punishment' of imprisonment." Third, neither sanction comes into play "only" on a finding of scienter. The provisions under which the money penalties were imposed allow for the assessment of a penalty against any person "who violates" any of the underlying banking statutes, without regard to the violator's state of mind. "Good faith" is considered by OCC in determining the amount of the penalty to be imposed, but a penalty can be imposed even in the absence of bad faith. The fact that petitioners' "good faith" was considered in determining the amount of the penalty to be imposed in this case is irrelevant, as we look only to "the statute on its face" to determine whether a penalty is criminal in nature. Similarly, while debarment may be imposed for a "willful" disregard "for the safety or soundness of [an] insured depository institution," willfulness is not a prerequisite to debarment; it is sufficient that the disregard for the safety and soundness of the institution was "continuing."

Fourth, the conduct for which OCC sanctions are imposed may also be criminal (and in this case formed the basis for petitioners' indictments). This fact is insufficient to render the money penalties and debarment sanctions criminally punitive, particularly in the double jeopardy context.

Finally, we recognize that the imposition of both money penalties and debarment sanctions will deter others from emulating petitioners' conduct, a traditional goal of criminal punishment. But the mere presence of this purpose is insufficient to render a sanction criminal, as deterrence "may serve civil as well as criminal goals." *Ursery.* For example, the sanctions at issue here, while intended to deter future wrongdoing, also serve to promote the stability of the banking industry. To hold that the mere presence of a deterrent purpose renders such sanctions "criminal" for double jeopardy purposes would severely undermine the Government's ability to engage in effective regulation of institutions such as banks. * * *

JUSTICE SCALIA, with whom JUSTICE THOMAS joins, concurring.

I wholly agree with the Court's conclusion that *Halper*'s test for whether a sanction is "punitive" was ill-considered and unworkable. * * * [In *Kurth Ranch,* I concluded] that the Double Jeopardy Clause prohibits successive prosecution, not successive punishment, and that we should therefore "put the *Halper* genie back in the bottle." Today's opinion uses a somewhat different bottle than I would, returning the law to its state immediately prior to *Halper*—which acknowledged a constitutional prohibition of multiple punishments but required successive criminal prosecutions. So long as that requirement is maintained, our multiple punishments jurisprudence essentially duplicates what I believe to be the correct double-jeopardy law, and will be as harmless in the future as it was pre-*Halper.* Accordingly, I am pleased to concur.

JUSTICE STEVENS, concurring in the judgment.

The maxim that "hard cases make bad law" may also apply to easy cases. * * * [T]his case could easily be decided by the straightforward application of well-established precedent. Neither such a disposition, nor anything in the opinion of the Court of Appeals, would require a reexamination of the central holding in *United States v. Halper,* or of the language used in that unanimous opinion. * * * The two proceedings at issue here involved different offenses that were not even arguably the same under *Blockburger.* * * *

Despite my disagreement with the Court's decision to use this case as a rather lame excuse for writing a gratuitous essay about punishment, I do agree with its reaffirmation of the central holding of *Halper* and *Department of Revenue of Mont. v. Kurth Ranch.* Both of those cases held that sanctions imposed in civil proceedings constituted "punishment" barred by the Double Jeopardy Clause. Those holdings reconfirmed the settled proposition that the Government cannot use the "civil" label to escape entirely the Double Jeopardy Clause's command, as we have recognized for at least six decades. That proposition is extremely important because the States and the Federal Government have an enormous array of civil administrative sanctions at their disposal that are capable of being used to punish persons repeatedly for the same offense, violating the bedrock double jeopardy principle of finality. * * *

* * * However the Court chooses to recalibrate the meaning of punishment for double jeopardy purposes, our doctrine still limits multiple sanctions of the rare sort contemplated by *Halper.* Today, as it did in *Halper* itself, the Court relies on the sort of multi-factor approach to the definition of punishment that we used in *Kennedy v. Mendoza–Martinez,* to identify situations in which a civil sanction is punitive. Whether the Court's reformulation of *Halper*'s test will actually affect the outcome of any cases remains to be seen. Perhaps it will not, since the Court recommends consideration of whether a sanction's " 'operation will promote the traditional aims of punishment—retribution and deterrence,' " and " 'whether it appears excessive in relation to the alternative [non-punitive] purpose assigned.' " *Ante* (quoting *Kennedy*). Those factors look awfully similar to the reasoning in *Halper,* and while we are told that they are never by themselves dispositive, they should be capable of tipping the balance in extreme cases. The danger in changing approaches midstream, rather than refining our established approach on an

incremental basis, is that the Government and lower courts may be unduly influenced by the Court's new attitude, rather than its specific prescribed test. * * *

JUSTICE SOUTER, concurring in the judgment.

I concur in the Court's judgment and with much of its opinion. * * * My acceptance of the *Kennedy-Ward* analytical scheme is subject to caveats, however. * * * While there are good and historically grounded reasons for using [the phrase "clearest proof"] to impose a substantial burden on anyone claiming that an apparently civil penalty is in truth criminal, what may be clear enough to be "clearest" is necessarily dependent on context * * *. I read the requisite "clearest proof" of criminal character, then, to be a function of the strength of the countervailing indications of civil nature (including the presumption of constitutionality enjoyed by an ostensibly civil statute making no provision for the safeguards guaranteed to criminal defendants). * * * I add further the caution to be wary of reading the "clearest proof" requirement as a guarantee that such a demonstration is as likely to be as rare in the future as it has been in the past. * * *

JUSTICE BREYER, with whom JUSTICE GINSBURG joins, concurring in the judgment.* * *

I agree with the majority and with Justice Souter that *United States v. Halper* does not provide proper guidance for distinguishing between criminal and noncriminal sanctions and proceedings. I also agree that *United States v. Ward* and *Kennedy v. Mendoza–Martinez* set forth the proper approach. * * * I do not join the Court's opinion, however, because I disagree with its reasoning in two respects. First, unlike the Court I would not say that " 'only the clearest proof' " will "transform" into a criminal punishment what a legislature calls a "civil remedy." I understand that the Court has taken this language from earlier cases. But the limitation that the language suggests is not consistent with what the Court has actually done. Rather, in fact if not in theory, the Court has simply applied factors of the *Kennedy* variety to the matter at hand. * * * The "clearest proof" language is consequently misleading, and I would consign it to the same legal limbo where *Halper* now rests.

Second, I would not decide now that a court should evaluate a statute only " 'on its face,' " rather than "assessing the character of the actual sanctions imposed." *Halper* involved an ordinary civil-fine statute that as normally applied would not have created any "double jeopardy" problem. It was not the statute itself, but rather the disproportionate relation between fine and conduct as the statute was applied in the individual case that led this Court, unanimously, to find that the "civil penalty" was, in those circumstances, a second "punishment" that constituted double jeopardy. Of course, the Court in *Halper* might have reached the same result through application of the constitutional prohibition of "excessive fines." But that is not what the Court there said. And nothing in the majority's opinion today explains why we should abandon this aspect of *Halper*'s holding. * * * It seems to me quite possible that a statute that provides for a punishment that normally is civil in nature could nonetheless amount to a criminal punishment as applied in special circumstances. And I would not now hold to the contrary.

That said, an analysis of the *Kennedy* factors still leads me to the conclusion that the statutory penalty in this case is not on its face a criminal penalty. Nor, in my view, does the application of the statute to the petitioners in this case amount to criminal punishment. I therefore concur in the result.

SECTION 2.   ABORTED PROCEEDINGS

ARIZONA v. WASHINGTON

434 U.S. 497, 98 S.Ct. 824, 54 L.Ed.2d 717 (1978).

JUSTICE STEVENS delivered the opinion of the Court.

In 1971 respondent was found guilty of murdering a hotel night clerk.   In 1973, the Superior Court of Pima County, Ariz., ordered a new trial because the prosecutor had withheld exculpatory evidence from the defense.   The Arizona Supreme Court affirmed the new trial order * * *.

Respondent's second trial began in January 1975.   During the *voir dire* examination of prospective jurors, the prosecutor made reference to the fact that some of the witnesses whose testimony the jurors would hear had testified in proceedings four years earlier.   Defense counsel told the prospective jurors "that there was evidence hidden from [respondent] at the last trial."   In his opening statement, he made this point more forcefully:

> "You will hear testimony that notwithstanding the fact that we had a trial in May of 1971 in this matter, that the prosecutor hid those statements and didn't give those to the lawyer for George saying the man was Spanish speaking, didn't give those statements at all, hid them.

> "You will hear that that evidence was suppressed and hidden by the prosecutor in that case.   You will hear that that evidence was purposely withheld. You will hear that because of the misconduct of the County Attorney at that time and because he withheld evidence, that the Supreme Court of Arizona granted a new trial in this case."

After opening statements were completed, the prosecutor moved for a mistrial.   In colloquy during argument of the motion, the trial judge expressed the opinion that evidence concerning the reasons for the new trial, and specifically the ruling of the Arizona Supreme Court, was irrelevant to the issue of guilt or innocence and therefore inadmissible.   Defense counsel asked for an opportunity "to find some law" that would support his belief that the Supreme Court opinion would be admissible.   After further argument, the judge stated that he would withhold ruling on the admissibility of the evidence and denied the motion for mistrial.   Two witnesses then testified.

The following morning the prosecutor renewed his mistrial motion.   Fortified by an evening's research, he argued that there was no theory on which the basis for the new trial ruling could be brought to the attention of the jury, that the prejudice to the jury could not be repaired by any cautionary instructions, and that a mistrial was a "manifest necessity."   Defense counsel * * * argued that his comment was invited by the prosecutor's reference to the witnesses' earlier testimony and that any prejudice could be avoided by curative instructions.   * * * Ultimately the trial judge granted the motion, stating that his ruling was based upon defense counsel's remarks in his opening statement concerning the Arizona Supreme Court opinion.   The trial judge did not expressly find that there was "manifest necessity" for a mistrial; nor did he expressly state that he had considered alternative solutions and concluded that none would be adequate. * * * [A federal district court, upon application for federal habeas corpus, granted the writ because of the absence in the record of such express findings.   The Court of Appeals affirmed.]

* * * The constitutional protection against double jeopardy unequivocally prohibits a second trial following an acquittal.   The public interest in the finality

of criminal judgments is so strong that an acquitted defendant may not be retried even though "the acquittal was based upon an egregiously erroneous foundation." If the innocence of the accused has been confirmed by a final judgment, the Constitution conclusively presumes that a second trial would be unfair.

Because jeopardy attaches before the judgment becomes final, the constitutional protection also embraces the defendant's "valued right to have his trial completed by a particular tribunal." The reasons why this "valued right" merits constitutional protection are worthy of repetition. Even if the first trial is not completed, a second prosecution may be grossly unfair. It increases the financial and emotional burden on the accused, prolongs the period in which he is stigmatized by an unresolved accusation of wrongdoing, and may even enhance the risk that an innocent defendant may be convicted. The danger of such unfairness to the defendant exists whenever a trial is aborted before it is completed. Consequently, as a general rule, the prosecutor is entitled to one, and only one, opportunity to require an accused to stand trial.

Unlike the situation in which the trial has ended in an acquittal or conviction, retrial is not automatically barred when a criminal proceeding is terminated without finally resolving the merits of the charges against the accused. Because of the variety of circumstances that may make it necessary to discharge a jury before a trial is concluded, and because those circumstances do not invariably create unfairness to the accused, his valued right to have the trial concluded by a particular tribunal is sometimes subordinate to the public interest in affording the prosecutor one full and fair opportunity to present his evidence to an impartial jury. Yet in view of the importance of the right, and the fact that it is frustrated by any mistrial, the prosecutor must shoulder the burden of justifying the mistrial if he is to avoid the double jeopardy bar. His burden is a heavy one. The prosecutor must demonstrate "manifest necessity" for any mistrial declared over the objection of the defendant.

The words "manifest necessity" appropriately characterize the magnitude of the prosecutor's burden. For that reason Mr. Justice Story's classic formulation of the test has been quoted over and over again to provide guidance in the decision of a wide variety of cases. Nevertheless, those words do not describe a standard that can be applied mechanically or without attention to the particular problem confronting the trial judge. Indeed, it is manifest that the key word "necessity" cannot be interpreted literally; instead, contrary to the teaching of Webster, we assume that there are degrees of necessity and we require a "high degree" before concluding that a mistrial is appropriate.

The question whether that "high degree" has been reached is answered more easily in some kinds of cases than in others. At one extreme are cases in which a prosecutor requests a mistrial in order to buttress weaknesses in his evidence. *IMPROPER* Although there was a time when English judges served the Stuart monarchs by exercising a power to discharge a jury whenever it appeared that the Crown's evidence would be insufficient to convict, the prohibition against double jeopardy as it evolved in this country was plainly intended to condemn this "abhorrent" practice. * * * Thus, the strictest scrutiny is appropriate when the basis for the mistrial is the unavailability of critical prosecution evidence, or when there is reason to believe that the prosecutor is using the superior resources of the State to harass or to achieve a tactical advantage over the accused.

At the other extreme is the mistrial premised upon the trial judge's belief that the jury is unable to reach a verdict, long considered the classic basis for a proper *PROPER* mistrial. The argument that a jury's inability to agree establishes reasonable doubt as to the defendant's guilt, and therefore requires acquittal, has been *→ Rejected!*

uniformly rejected in this country. Instead, without exception, the courts have held that the trial judge may discharge a genuinely deadlocked jury and require the defendant to submit to a second trial. This rule accords recognition to society's interest in giving the prosecution one complete opportunity to convict those who have violated its laws.

Moreover, in this situation there are especially compelling reasons for allowing the trial judge to exercise broad discretion in deciding whether or not "manifest necessity" justifies a discharge of the jury. On the one hand, if he discharges the jury when further deliberations may produce a fair verdict, the defendant is deprived of his "valued right to have his trial completed by a particular tribunal." But if he fails to discharge a jury which is unable to reach a verdict after protracted and exhausting deliberations, there exists a significant risk that a verdict may result from pressures inherent in the situation rather than the considered judgment of all the jurors. If retrial of the defendant were barred whenever an appellate court views the "necessity" for a mistrial differently from the trial judge, there would be a danger that the latter, cognizant of the serious societal consequences of an erroneous ruling, would employ coercive means to break the apparent deadlock. Such a rule would frustrate the public interest in just judgments. The trial judge's decision to declare a mistrial when he considers the jury deadlocked is therefore accorded great deference by a reviewing court.

We are persuaded that, along the spectrum of trial problems which may warrant a mistrial and which vary in their amenability to appellate scrutiny, the difficulty which led to the mistrial in this case also falls in an area where the trial judge's determination is entitled to special respect.

In this case the trial judge ordered a mistrial because the defendant's lawyer made improper and prejudicial remarks during his opening statement to the jury. * * * We recognize that the extent of the possible bias cannot be measured, and that the [federal] District Court was quite correct in believing that some trial judges might have proceeded with the trial after giving the jury appropriate cautionary instructions. In a strict, literal sense, the mistrial was not "necessary." Nevertheless, the overriding interest in the evenhanded administration of justice requires that we accord the highest degree of respect to the trial judge's evaluation of the likelihood that the impartiality of one or more jurors may have been affected by the improper comment. * * * The consistent course of decision in this Court in cases involving possible juror bias supports this conclusion. * * *

An improper opening statement unquestionably tends to frustrate the public interest in having a just judgment reached by an impartial tribunal. * * * The trial judge, of course, may instruct the jury to disregard the improper comment. In extreme cases, he may discipline counsel, or even remove him from the trial as he did in *United States v. Dinitz*, 424 U.S. 600 (1976). Those actions, however, will not necessarily remove the risk of bias that may be created by improper argument. Unless unscrupulous defense counsel are to be allowed an unfair advantage, the trial judge must have the power to declare a mistrial in appropriate cases. The interest in orderly, impartial procedure would be impaired if he were deterred from exercising that power by a concern that any time a reviewing court disagreed with his assessment of the trial situation a retrial would automatically be barred. The adoption of a stringent standard of appellate review in this area, therefore, would seriously impede the trial judge in the proper performance of his "duty, in order to protect the integrity of the trial, to take prompt and affirmative action to stop * * * professional misconduct." *Dinitz.*

There are compelling institutional considerations militating in favor of appellate deference to the trial judge's evaluation of the significance of possible juror bias. He has seen and heard the jurors during their *voir dire* examination. He is the judge most familiar with the evidence and the background of the case on trial. He has listened to the tone of the argument as it was delivered and has observed the apparent reaction of the jurors. In short, he is far more "conversant with the factors relevant to the determination" than any reviewing court can possibly be.

Our conclusion that a trial judge's decision to declare a mistrial based on his assessment of the prejudicial impact of improper argument is entitled to great deference does not, of course, end the inquiry. As noted earlier, a constitutionally protected interest is inevitably affected by any mistrial decision. * * * In order to ensure that this interest is adequately protected, reviewing courts have an obligation to satisfy themselves that, in the words of Mr. Justice Story, the trial judge exercised "sound discretion" in declaring a mistrial. * * * [I]f a trial judge acts irrationally or irresponsibly, his action cannot be condoned. But our review of this record indicates that this was not such a case. * * *

One final matter requires consideration. The absence of an explicit finding of "manifest necessity" appears to have been determinative for the District Court and may have been so for the Court of Appeals. If those courts regarded that omission as critical, they required too much. Since the record provides sufficient justification for the state-court ruling, the failure to explain that ruling more completely does not render it constitutionally defective.

Review of any trial court decision is, of course, facilitated by findings and by an explanation of the reasons supporting the decision. No matter how desirable such procedural assistance may be, it is not constitutionally mandated in a case such as this. The basis for the trial judge's mistrial order is adequately disclosed by the record, which includes the extensive argument of counsel prior to the judge's ruling. The state trial judge's mistrial declaration is not subject to collateral attack in a federal court simply because he failed to find "manifest necessity" in those words or to articulate on the record all the factors which informed the deliberate exercise of his discretion. * * *

JUSTICE BLACKMUN concurs in the result.

JUSTICE WHITE, dissenting.

I cannot agree with the Court of Appeals that the failure of a state trial judge to express the legal standard under which he had declared a mistrial is, in itself and without further examination of the record, sufficient reason to infer constitutional error foreclosing a second trial. * * * I would not, however, undertake an examination of the record here in the first instance. Rather, I would vacate the judgment of the Court of Appeals and direct that court to remand the case to the District Court to make the initial judgment, under the correct legal standard, as to whether the writ should issue.

JUSTICE MARSHALL, with whom JUSTICE BRENNAN joins, dissenting.

My disagreement with the majority is a narrow one. * * * I agree that, where a mistrial is declared over a defendant's objections, a new trial is permissible only if the termination of the earlier trial was justified by a "manifest necessity" and that the prosecution must shoulder the "heavy" burden of demonstrating such a "high degree" of necessity. Nor do I quarrel with the proposition that reviewing courts must accord substantial deference to a trial judge's determination that the prejudicial impact of an improper opening statement is so great as to leave no alternative but a mistrial to secure the ends of public justice. * * * Where I part ways from the Court is in its assumption that an "assessment of the prejudicial impact of improper argument," sufficient to support the need for a mistrial, may be implied from this record. * * *

Defense counsel's improper remarks occupied only one page of a lengthy opening statement. Despite the fact that the prosecutor had vigorously interrupted the opening statement at numerous points to assert various objections, he made no objection to the remarks that formed the basis for the mistrial. If the argument of defense counsel had had a visibly obvious impact on the jurors when uttered, it is hard to believe that this prosecutor would have waited until after the opening statement was finished and the luncheon recess concluded before making his objection known.

Although from this distance and in the absence of express findings it is impossible to determine the precise extent to which defense counsel's remarks may have prejudiced the jury against the State, the circumstances set forth above suggest that any such prejudice may have been minimal and subject to cure through less drastic alternatives. For example, the jury could have been instructed to disregard any mention of prior legal rulings as irrelevant to the issues at hand, and to consider as evidence only the testimony and exhibits admitted through witnesses on the stand. Were there doubt whether such instructions alone would suffice to cure the taint, the jury could have been questioned about the extent of any prejudice. Given the anticipated length of the trial (almost two weeks), it is not unlikely that, had the jury been appropriately instructed when the court first found defense counsel to have erred in his opening statement, any prejudice would have dissipated before deliberations were to begin. For these reasons, it is impossible to conclude that a finding of necessity was implicit in the mere grant of the mistrial. * * *

I do not propose that the Constitution invariably requires a trial judge to make findings of necessity on the record to justify the declaration of a mistrial over a defendant's objections. * * * What the "manifest necessity" doctrine does require, in my view, is that the record make clear either that there were no meaningful and practical alternatives to a mistrial, or that the trial court scrupulously considered available alternatives and found all wanting but a termination of the proceedings. * * * The record here * * * does neither. * * *

Had the court here explored alternatives on the record, or made a finding of substantial and incurable prejudice or other "manifest necessity," this would be a different case and one in which I would agree with both the majority's reasoning and its result. On this ambiguous record, however, the absence of any such finding—and indeed of any express indication that the trial court applied the manifest-necessity doctrine—leaves open the substantial possibility that there was in fact no need to terminate the proceedings. * * *

OREGON v. KENNEDY

456 U.S. 667, 102 S.Ct. 2083, 72 L.Ed.2d 416 (1982).

JUSTICE REHNQUIST delivered the opinion of the Court.

* * * Respondent was charged with the theft of an oriental rug. During his first trial, the State called an expert witness on the subject of Middle Eastern rugs to testify as to the value and the identity of the rug in question. On cross-examination, respondent's attorney apparently attempted to establish bias on the part of the expert witness by asking him whether he had filed a criminal complaint against respondent. The witness eventually acknowledged this fact, but explained that no action had been taken on his complaint. On redirect examination, the prosecutor sought to elicit the reasons why the witness had filed a complaint against respondent, but the trial court sustained a series of objections

to this line of inquiry.[1] The following colloquy then ensued:

> "Prosecutor: Have you ever done business with the Kennedys?
>
> "Witness: No, I have not.
>
> "Prosecutor: Is that because he is a crook?'"

The trial court then granted respondent's motion for a mistrial.

When the State later sought to retry respondent, he moved to dismiss the charges because of double jeopardy. After a hearing at which the prosecutor testified, the trial court found as a fact that "it was not the intention of the prosecutor in this case to cause a mistrial." On the basis of this finding, the trial court held that double jeopardy principles did not bar retrial, and respondent was then tried and convicted.

Respondent then successfully appealed to the Oregon Court of Appeals, which sustained his double jeopardy claim. * * * The Court of Appeals accepted the trial court's finding that it was not the intent of the prosecutor to cause a mistrial. Nevertheless, the court held that retrial was barred because the prosecutor's conduct in this case constituted what it viewed as "overreaching." * * *

Where the trial is terminated over the objection of the defendant, the classical test for lifting the double jeopardy bar to a second trial is the "manifest necessity" standard first enunciated in Justice Story's opinion for the Court in *United States v. Perez [22 U.S. 579 (1824)]*. * * * The "manifest necessity" standard provides sufficient protection to the defendant's interests in having his case finally decided by the jury first selected while at the same time maintaining "the public's interest in fair trials designed to end in just judgments." But in the case of a mistrial declared at the behest of the defendant, quite different principles come into play. Here the defendant himself has elected to terminate the proceedings against him, and the "manifest necessity" standard has no place in the application of the Double Jeopardy Clause. *United States v. Dinitz,* [424 U.S. 600, (1976)]. * * *

Our cases, however, have indicated that even where the defendant moves for a mistrial, there is a narrow exception to the rule that the Double Jeopardy Clause is no bar to retrial. See, e.g., *United States v. Dinitz.* The circumstances under which respondent's first trial was terminated require us to delineate the bounds of that exception more fully than we have in previous cases.

Since one of the principal threads making up the protection embodied in the Double Jeopardy Clause is the right of the defendant to have his trial completed before the first jury empaneled to try him, it may be wondered as a matter of original inquiry why the defendant's election to terminate the first trial by his own motion should not be deemed a renunciation of that right for all purposes. We have recognized, however, that there would be great difficulty in applying such a rule where the prosecutor's actions giving rise to the motion for mistrial were done "in order to goad the [defendant] into requesting a mistrial." *United States v. Dinitz.* In such a case, the defendant's valued right to complete his trial before the first jury would be a hollow shell if the inevitable motion for mistrial were held to prevent a later invocation of the bar of double jeopardy in all circumstances. But the precise phrasing of the circumstances which *will* allow a defendant to interpose the defense of double jeopardy to a second prosecution where the first has terminated on his own motion for a mistrial have been stated with less than crystal clarity in our cases which deal with this area of the law.

---

1. The Court of Appeals later explained that respondent's "objections were not well taken, and the judge's rulings were probably wrong." 49 Or.App. 415, 417, 619 P.2d 948, 949 (1980).

* * * The language [of *Dinitz* at points] would seem to broaden the test from one of *intent* to provoke a motion for a mistrial to a more generalized standard of "bad faith conduct" or "harassment" on the part of the judge or prosecutor. It was upon this language that the Oregon Court of Appeals apparently relied in concluding that the prosecutor's colloquy with the expert witness in this case amount to "overreaching."

The difficulty with the more general standards which would permit a broader exception than one merely based on intent is that they offer virtually no standards for their application. Every act on the part of a rational prosecutor during a trial is designed to "prejudice" the defendant by placing before the judge or jury evidence pleading to a finding of his guilt. Given the complexity of the rules of evidence, it will be a rare trial of any complexity in which some proffered evidence by the prosecutor or by the defendant's attorney will not be found objectionable by the trial court. Most such objections are undoubtedly curable by simply refusing to allow the proffered evidence to be admitted, or in the case of a particular line of inquiry taken by counsel with a witness, by an admonition to desist from a particular line of inquiry.

More serious infractions on the part of the prosecutor may provoke a motion for mistrial on the part of the defendant, and may in the view of the trial court warrant the granting of such a motion. The "overreaching" standard applied by the court below and urged today by Justice Stevens, however, would add another classification of prosecutorial error, one requiring dismissal of the indictment, but without supplying any standard by which to assess that error.[5]

By contrast, a standard that examines the intent of the prosecutor, though certainly not entirely free from practical difficulties, is a manageable standard to apply. It merely calls for the court to make a finding of fact. Inferring the existence or nonexistence of intent from objective facts and circumstances is a familiar process in our criminal justice system. When it is remembered that resolution of double jeopardy questions by state trial courts are reviewable not only within the state court system, but in the federal court system on habeas corpus as well, the desirability of an easily applied principle is apparent.

Prosecutorial conduct that might be viewed as harassment or overreaching, even if sufficient to justify a mistrial on defendant's motion, therefore, does not bar retrial absent intent on the part of the prosecutor to subvert the protections afforded by the Double Jeopardy Clause. A defendant's motion for a mistrial constitutes "a deliberate election on his part to forgo his valued right to have his guilt or innocence determined before the first trier of fact." *United States v. Scott* [§ 3 infra]. Where prosecutorial error even of a degree sufficient to warrant a mistrial has occurred, "[t]he important consideration, for purposes of the Double Jeopardy Clause, is that the defendant retain primary control over the course to be followed in the event of such error." *United States v. Dinitz.* Only where the governmental conduct in question is intended to "goad" the defendant into moving for a mistrial may a defendant raise the bar of double jeopardy to a second trial after having succeeded in aborting the first on his own motion.

5. If the Court were to hold, as would Justice Stevens, that such a determination requires an assessment of the facts and circumstances but without explaining how such an assessment ought to proceed, the Court would offer little guidance to the federal and state courts that must apply our decisions. Justice Stevens disagrees with this decision below be-cause his reaction to a cold record is different from that of the Oregon Court of Appeals. The Court of Appeals found "overreaching"; Justice Stevens finds none. Neither articulates a basis for reaching their respective conclusions which can be applied to other factual situations. We are loath to adopt such an essentially standardless rule.

Were we to embrace the broad and somewhat amorphous standard adopted by the Oregon Court of Appeals, we are not sure that criminal defendants as a class would be aided. Knowing that the granting of the defendant's motion for mistrial would all but inevitably bring with it an attempt to bar a second trial on grounds of double jeopardy, the judge presiding over the first trial might well be more loath to grant a defendant's motion for mistrial. If a mistrial were in fact warranted under the applicable law, of course, the defendant could in many instances successfully appeal a judgment of conviction on the same grounds that he urged a mistrial, and the Double Jeopardy Clause would present no bar to retrial. But some of the advantages secured to him by the Double Jeopardy Clause—the freedom from extended anxiety, and the necessity to confront the government's case only once—would be to a large extent lost in the process of trial to verdict, reversal on appeal, and subsequent retrial.

* * * We do not by this opinion lay down a flat rule that where a defendant in a criminal trial successfully moves for a mistrial, he may not thereafter invoke the bar of double jeopardy against a second trial. But we do hold that the circumstances under which such a defendant may invoke the bar of double jeopardy in a second effort to try him are limited to those cases in which the conduct giving rise to the successful motion for a mistrial was intended to provoke the defendant into moving for a mistrial. Since the Oregon trial court found, and the Oregon Court of Appeals accepted, that the prosecutorial conduct culminating in the termination of the first trial in this case was not so intended by the prosecutor, that is the end of the matter for purposes of the Double Jeopardy Clause of the Fifth Amendment to the United States Constitution. * * *

JUSTICE BRENNAN, with whom JUSTICE MARSHALL joins, concurring in the judgment.

I concur in the judgment and join in the opinion of Justice Stevens. However, it should be noted that nothing in the holding of the Court today prevents the state courts, on remand, from concluding that respondent's retrial would violate the provision of the Oregon Constitution that prohibits double jeopardy * * *.

JUSTICE POWELL, concurring.

I join the Court's opinion holding that the *intention* of a prosecutor determines whether his conduct, viewed by the defendant and the court as justifying a mistrial, bars a retrial of the defendant under the Double Jeopardy Clause. Because "subjective" intent often may be unknowable, I emphasize that a court—in considering a double jeopardy motion—should rely primarily upon the objective facts and circumstances of the particular case.

* * * [T]his would have been a close case for me if there had been substantial factual evidence of intent beyond the question itself. Here, however, other relevant facts and circumstances strongly support the view that prosecutorial intent to cause a mistrial was absent. First, there was no sequence of overreaching prior to the single prejudicial question. Moreover, it is evident from a colloquy between counsel and the court, out of the presence of the jury, that the prosecutor not only resisted, but also was surprised by, the defendant's motion for a mistrial. Finally, at the hearing on respondent's double jeopardy motion, the prosecutor testified—and the trial found as a fact and the appellate court agreed—that there was no " 'intention * * * to cause a mistrial.' " In view of these circumstances, the Double Jeopardy Clause provides no bar to retrial.

JUSTICE STEVENS, with whom JUSTICE BRENNAN, JUSTICE MARSHALL and JUSTICE BLACKMUN join, concurring in the judgment.

* * * The rationale for the exception to the general rule permitting retrial after a mistrial declared with the defendant's consent is illustrated by the situation in which the prosecutor commits prejudicial error with the intent to provoke a mistrial. * * * But the Court reaches out to limit the exception to that one situation, rejecting the previous recognition that prosecutorial overreaching or harassment is also within the exception.[22]

Even if I agreed that the balance of competing interests tipped in favor of a bar to reprosecution only in the situation in which the prosecutor intended to provoke a mistrial, I would not subscribe to a standard that conditioned such a bar on the determination that the prosecutor harbored such intent when he committed prejudicial error. It is almost inconceivable that a defendant could prove that the prosecutor's deliberate misconduct was motivated by an intent to provoke a mistrial instead of an intent simply to prejudice the defendant. The defendant must shoulder a strong burden to establish a bar to reprosecution when he has consented to the mistrial, but the Court's subjective intent standard would eviscerate the exception.

A broader objection to the Court's limitation of the exception is that the rationale for the exception extends beyond the situation in which the prosecutor intends to provoke a mistrial. There are other situations in which the defendant's double jeopardy interests outweigh society's interest in obtaining a judgment on the merits even though the defendant has moved for a mistrial. For example, a prosecutor may be interested in putting the defendant through the embarrassment, expense, and ordeal of criminal proceedings even if he cannot obtain a conviction. In such a case, with the purpose of harassing the defendant the prosecutor may commit repeated prejudicial errors and be indifferent between a mistrial or mistrials and an unsustainable conviction or convictions. Another example is when the prosecutor seeks to inject enough unfair prejudice into the trial to ensure a conviction but not so much as to cause a reversal of that conviction. This kind of overreaching would not be covered by the Court's standard because, by hypothesis, the prosecutor's intent is to obtain a conviction, not to provoke a mistrial. Yet the defendant's choice—to continue the tainted proceeding or to abort it and begin anew—can be just as "hollow" in this situation as when the prosecutor intends to provoke a mistrial.

To invoke the exception for overreaching, a court need not divine the exact motivation for the prosecutorial error. It is sufficient that the court is persuaded that egregious prosecutorial misconduct has rendered unmeaningful the defendant's choice to continue or to abort the proceeding. It is unnecessary and unwise to attempt to identify all the factors that might inform the court's judgment, but

22. The Court offers two reasons for cutting back on the exception. First, the Court states that "[t]he difficulty with the more general standards which would permit a broader exception than one merely based on intent is that they offer virtually no standards for their application." As I indicate in the text, however, some generality in the formula is a virtue and, in any event, meaningful and principled standards can be developed on a case-by-case basis that will not inhibit legitimate prosecution practices. Moreover, the general standards could hardly be more difficult to apply than the Court's subjective intent standard. * * *

Second, the Court is "not sure that criminal defendants as a class would be aided" by a broader exception. If a mistrial will more frequently constitute a bar to reprosecution, the Court supposes that trial judges will tend to refuse the defendant's mistrial motion and permit the error to be corrected on appeal of the conviction, in which event there would be no bar to reprosecution. This reasoning is premised on the assumption that an appellate court that concluded not only that the defendant's mistrial motion should have been granted but also that the prosecutor intended to provoke a mistrial would not be obligated to bar reprosecution as well as reverse the conviction. The assumption is "irrational." *Commonwealth v. Potter,* 478 Pa. 251, 386 A.2d 918 (1978) (Roberts, J.) (Pomeroy, J.).

several considerations follow from the rationale for recognizing the exception. First, because the exception is justified by the intolerance of intentional manipulation of the defendant's double jeopardy interests, a finding of deliberate misconduct normally would be a prerequisite to a reprosecution bar. Second, because the defendant's option to abort the proceeding after prosecutorial misconduct would retain real meaning for the defendant in any case in which the trial was going badly for him, normally a required finding would be that the prosecutorial error virtually eliminated, or at least substantially reduced, the probability of acquittal in a proceeding that was going badly for the government. It should be apparent from these observations that only in a rare and compelling case will a mistrial declared at the request of the defendant or with his consent bar a retrial.

No one case, of course, is a proper vehicle for identifying the limits of the exception. The Court repeatedly has shunned inflexible standards in applying the comparable "manifest necessity" exception to the general rule that a defendant is entitled to go to final judgment before the initial tribunal. The value of the overreaching standard, like "[t]he value of the [manifest necessity standard], thus lies in [its] capacity for informed application under widely different circumstances without injury to defendants or to the public interest." *Wade v. Hunter,* 336 U.S. 684 [(1949)]. The inexactitude of the standard used to protect defendants in the exceptional case surely should not concern the Court any more than the equally ill-defined formula used to protect prosecutors in the exceptional case. * * *

* * * The isolated prosecutorial error [here] occurred early in the trial, too early to determine whether the case was going badly for the prosecution. If anyone was being harassed at that time, it was the prosecutor who was frustrated by improper defense objections in her attempt to rehabilitate her witness. The gist of the comment that the respondent was a "crook" could fairly have been elicited from the witness, since defense counsel injected the respondent's past alleged improprieties into the trial by questioning the witness about his bias towards the defendant. The comment therefore could not have injected the kind of prejudice that would render unmeaningful the defendant's option to proceed with the trial. Because the present case quite clearly does not come within the recognized exception, I join the Court's judgment.

SECTION 3. REPROSECUTION FOLLOWING ACQUITTALS AND CONVICTIONS

UNITED STATES v. SCOTT

437 U.S. 82, 98 S.Ct. 2187, 57 L.Ed.2d 65 (1978).

JUSTICE REHNQUIST delivered the opinion of the Court.

On March 5, 1975, respondent, a member of the police force in Muskegon, Mich., was charged * * * with distribution of various narcotics. Both before his trial in the United States District Court and twice during the trial, respondent moved to dismiss the two counts of the indictment which concerned transactions that took place during the preceding September, on the ground that his defense had been prejudiced by preindictment delay. At the close of all the evidence, the court granted respondent's motion. * * *

The Government sought to appeal the dismissals of the first two counts to the United States Court of Appeals for the Sixth Circuit. That court, relying on our opinion in *United States v. Jenkins,* 420 U.S. 358 (1975), concluded that any further prosecution of respondent was barred by the Double Jeopardy Clause of the Fifth Amendment, and therefore dismissed the appeal. * * * We granted certiorari to give further consideration to the applicability of the Double Jeopardy Clause to Government appeals from orders granting defense motions to terminate a trial before verdict. We now reverse. * * *

A detailed canvass of the history of the double jeopardy principles in *United States v. Wilson,* 420 U.S. 332 (1975), led us to conclude that the Double Jeopardy Clause was primarily "directed at the threat of multiple prosecutions," and posed no bar to Government appeals "where those appeals would not require a new trial." We accordingly held in *Jenkins,* that, whether or not a dismissal of an indictment after jeopardy had attached amounted to an acquittal on the merits, the Government had no right to appeal, because "further proceedings of some sort, devoted to the resolution of factual issues going to the elements of the offense charged, would have been required upon reversal and remand." [a]

If *Jenkins* is a correct statement of the law, the judgment of the Court of Appeals * * * would in all likelihood have to be affirmed. Yet, though our assessment of the history and meaning of the Double Jeopardy Clause in *Wilson, Jenkins,* and *Serfass v. United States,* 420 U.S. 377 (1975), occurred only three Terms ago, our vastly increased exposure to the various facets of the Double Jeopardy Clause has now convinced us that *Jenkins* was wrongly decided. It placed an unwarrantedly great emphasis on the defendant's right to have his guilt decided by the first jury empaneled to try him so as to include those cases where the defendant himself seeks to terminate the trial before verdict on grounds unrelated to factual guilt or innocence. We have therefore decided to overrule *Jenkins,* and thus to reverse the judgment of the Court of Appeals in this case.

* * * At the time the Fifth Amendment was adopted, its principles were easily applied, since most criminal prosecutions proceeded to final judgment, and neither the United States nor the defendant had any right to appeal an adverse verdict. The verdict in such a case was unquestionably final, and could be raised in bar against any further prosecution for the same offense.

* * * It was not until 1889 that Congress permitted criminal defendants to seek a writ of error in this Court, and then only in capital cases. Only then did it become necessary for this Court to deal with the issues presented by the challenge of verdicts on appeal. And, in the very first case presenting the issues, *Ball v. United States,* 163 U.S. 662 (1896), the Court established principles that have been adhered to ever since. Three persons had been tried together for murder; two were convicted, the other acquitted. This Court reversed the convictions, finding the indictment fatally defective, whereupon all three defendants were tried again. This time all three were convicted and they again sought review here. This Court held that the Double Jeopardy Clause precluded further prosecution of the defendant who had been *acquitted* at the original trial but that it posed no such bar to the prosecution of those defendants who had been *convicted* in the earlier proceeding.

a. In *Wilson,* after the jury returned a verdict of guilty, the trial court reconsidered an earlier motion and dismissed the indictment on due process grounds. The Supreme Court concluded that no double jeopardy concerns were raised by an appeal of that ruling. An appellate court reversal of the dismissal would not require a new trial since the appellate court could simply reinstate the jury's verdict. In *Jenkins,* the dismissal was issued by the trial judge, sitting in a bench trial, before the judge reached a verdict. The trial judge's dismissal order was based on his interpretation of the substantive law, but the judge had not indicated what result he would have reached as the finder of fact if a contrary interpretation had been adopted. Thus, if the trial judge's order were reversed, further resolution of the facts relating to the elements of the offense would be required. The *Jenkins* opinion stressed this consequence of appellates reversal rather than the grounding of the trial court's ruling as a possible "acquittal."

* * * These then, at least, are two venerable principles of double jeopardy jurisprudence. The successful appeal of a judgment of conviction, on any ground other than the insufficiency of the evidence to support the verdict, *Burks v. United States* [§ 3, infra], poses no bar to further prosecution on the same charge. A judgment of acquittal, whether based on a jury verdict of not guilty or on a ruling by the court that the evidence is insufficient to convict, may not be appealed and terminates the prosecution when a second trial would be necessitated by a reversal. What may seem superficially to be a disparity in [these] rules governing a defendant's liability to be tried again is explainable by reference to the underlying purposes of the Double Jeopardy Clause. * * * [T]he law attaches particular significance to an acquittal. To permit a second trial after an acquittal, however mistaken the acquittal may have been, would present an unacceptably high risk that the Government, with its vastly superior resources, might wear down the defendant so that "even though innocent, he may be found guilty." *Green v. United States*, 355 U.S. 184 (1957). On the other hand, to require a criminal defendant to stand trial again after he has successfully invoked a statutory right of appeal to upset his first conviction is not an act of governmental oppression of the sort against which the Double Jeopardy Clause was intended to protect. * * *

Although the primary purpose of the Double Jeopardy Clause was to protect the integrity of a final judgment, this Court has also developed a body of law guarding the separate but related interest of a defendant in avoiding multiple prosecutions even where no final determination of guilt or innocence has been made. Such interests may be involved in two different situations: the first, in which the trial judge declares a mistrial; the second, in which the trial judge terminates the proceedings favorably to the defendant on a basis not related to factual guilt or innocence.

* * * In passing on the propriety of a declaration of mistrial granted at the behest of the prosecutor or on the court's own motion, this Court has [applied the *Perez* standard of manifest necessity]. * * * Where, on the other hand, a *defendant* successfully seeks to avoid his trial prior to its conclusion by a motion for mistrial, the Double Jeopardy Clause is not offended by a second prosecution. * * * Such a motion by the defendant is deemed to be a deliberate election on his part to forego his valued right to have his guilt or innocence determined before the first trier of fact. *United States v. Dinitz* [discussed in *Kennedy*, § 2 supra]. * * *

We turn now to the relationship between the Double Jeopardy Clause and reprosecution of a defendant who has successfully obtained not a mistrial, but a termination of the trial in his favor before any determination of factual guilt or innocence. Unlike the typical mistrial, the granting of a motion such as this obviously contemplates that the proceedings will terminate then and there in favor of the defendant. The prosecution, if it wishes to reinstate the proceedings in the face of such a ruling, ordinarily must seek reversal of the decision of the trial court. * * *

* * * It is quite true that the Government with all its resources and power should not be allowed to make repeated attempts to convict an individual for an alleged offense. This truth is expressed in the three common-law pleas of *autrefois acquit, autrefois convict,* and pardon, which lie at the core of the area protected by the Double Jeopardy Clause. As we have recognized in cases from *Ball* to *Sanabria v. United States*, 437 U.S. 54 (1978), a defendant once acquitted may not be again subjected to trial without violating the Double Jeopardy Clause.

But that situation is obviously a far cry from the present case, where the Government was quite willing to continue with its production of evidence to show the defendant guilty before the jury first empaneled to try him, but the defendant elected to seek termination of the trial on grounds unrelated to guilt or innocence. This is scarcely a picture of an all-powerful state relentlessly pursuing a defendant who had either been found not guilty or who had at least insisted on having the issue of guilt submitted to the first trier of fact. It is instead a picture of a defendant who chooses to avoid conviction and imprisonment, not because of his assertion that the Government has failed to make out a case against him, but because of a legal claim that the Government's case against him must fail even though it might satisfy the trier of fact that he was guilty beyond a reasonable doubt.

We have previously noted that "the trial judge's characterization of his own action cannot control the classification of the action." * * * [A] defendant is acquitted only when "the ruling of the judge, whatever its label, actually represents a resolution [in the defendant's favor], correct or not, of some or all of the factual elements of the offense charged." Where the court, before the jury returns a verdict, enters [an order entitled] a judgment of acquittal pursuant to Fed.Rule Crim.Proc. 29, appeal will be barred only when "it is plain that the District Court * * * evaluated the Government's evidence and determined that it was legally insufficient to support a conviction." *United States v. Martin Linen Supply Company*, 430 U.S. 564 (1977).

Our opinion in *Burks* [infra] necessarily holds that there has been a "failure of proof" requiring an acquittal when the Government does not submit sufficient evidence to rebut a defendant's essentially factual defense of insanity, though it may otherwise be entitled to have its case submitted to the jury. The defense of insanity, like the defense of entrapment, arises from "the notion that Congress could not have intended criminal punishment for a defendant who has committed all the elements of a proscribed offense," *United States v. Russell* [Ch. 4], where other facts established to the satisfaction of the trier of fact provide a legally adequate justification for otherwise criminal acts. Such a factual finding *does* "necessarily establish the criminal defendant's lack of criminal culpability," post, (Brennan, J., dissenting), under the existing law; the fact that "the acquittal may result from erroneous evidentiary rulings or erroneous interpretations of governing legal principles," ibid., affects the accuracy of that determination, but it does not alter its essential character. By contrast, the dismissal of an indictment for preindictment delay represents a legal judgment that a defendant, although criminally culpable, may not be punished because of a supposed constitutional violation. * * *

[I]n the present case, [defendant] successfully avoided a submission of [a part] * * * of the indictment [to the jury] by persuading the trial court to dismiss it on a basis which did not depend on guilt or innocence. He was thus neither acquitted nor convicted, because he himself successfully undertook to persuade the trial court not to submit the issue of guilt or innocence to the jury which had been empaneled to try him. * * * [Defendant] has not been "deprived" of his valued right to go to the first jury; only the public has been deprived of its valued right to "one complete opportunity to convict those who have violated its laws." *Arizona v. Washington*. No interest protected by the Double Jeopardy Clause is invaded when the Government is allowed to appeal and seek reversal of such a mid-trial termination of the proceedings in a manner favorable to the defendant. * * *

JUSTICE BRENNAN, with whom JUSTICE WHITE, JUSTICE MARSHALL, and JUSTICE STEVENS join, dissenting.

* * * While the Double Jeopardy Clause often has the effect of protecting the accused's interest in the finality of particular favorable determinations, this is not its objective. For the Clause often permits Government appeals from final judgments favorable to the accused. See *United States v. Wilson* (whether or not final judgment was an acquittal, Government may appeal if reversal would not necessitate a retrial). The purpose of the Clause, which the Court today fails sufficiently to appreciate, is to protect the accused against the agony and risks attendant upon undergoing more than one criminal trial for any single offense. * * * Society's "willingness to limit the Government to a single criminal proceeding to vindicate its very vital interest in enforcement of criminal laws" bespeaks society's recognition of the gross unfairness of requiring the accused to undergo the strain and agony of more than one trial for any single offense. *United States v. Jorn*, 400 U.S. 470 (1971). Accordingly, the policies of the Double Jeopardy Clause mandate that the Government be afforded but one complete opportunity to convict an accused and that when the first proceeding terminates in a final judgment favorable to the defendant any retrial be barred. The rule as to acquittals can only be understood as simply an application of this larger principle.

Judgments of acquittal normally result from jury or bench verdicts of not guilty. In such cases, the acquittal represents the factfinder's conclusion that, under the controlling legal principles, the evidence does not establish that the defendant can be convicted of the offense charged in the indictment. But the judgment does not necessarily establish the criminal defendant's lack of criminal culpability; the acquittal may result from erroneous evidentiary rulings or erroneous interpretations of governing legal principles induced by the defense. Yet the Double Jeopardy Clause bars a second trial. * * * The reason is not that the first trial established the defendant's factual innocence, but rather that the second trial would present all the untoward consequences the Clause was designed to prevent. Government would be allowed to seek to persuade a second trier of fact of the defendant's guilt, to strengthen any weaknesses in its first presentation, and to subject the defendant to the expense and anxiety of a second trial.

* * * The whole premise for today's * * * [decision] * * * is the Court's new theory that a criminal defendant who seeks to avoid conviction on a "ground unrelated to factual innocence" somehow stands on a different constitutional footing than a defendant whose participation in his criminal trial creates a situation in which a judgment of acquittal has to be entered. This premise is simply untenable. * * * [T]he reasons that bar a retrial following an acquittal are equally applicable to a final judgment entered on a ground "unrelated to factual innocence." The heavy personal strain of the second trial is the same in either case. So too is the risk that, though innocent, the defendant may be found guilty at a second trial. If the appeal is allowed in either situation, the Government will, following any reversal, not only obtain the benefit of the favorable appellate ruling but also be permitted to shore up any other weak points of its case and obtain all the other advantages at the second trial that the Double Jeopardy Clause was designed to forbid.

Moreover, the Government's interest in retrying a defendant simply cannot vary depending on the ground of the final termination in the accused's favor. I reject as plainly erroneous the Court's suggestion that final judgments not based on innocence deprive the public of "its valued right to 'one complete opportunity to convict those who have violated its laws,' " quoting *Arizona v. Washington,* and therefore differ from "true acquittals." The Government has the same "complete opportunity" in either situation by virtue of its participation as an adversary at the criminal trial.

Equally significant, the distinction between the two is at best purely formal. Many acquittals are the consequence of rulings of law made on the accused's motion that are not related to the question of his factual guilt or innocence: e.g., a ruling on the law respecting the scope of the offense or excluding reliable evidence. * * *

* * * A critical feature of today's holding appears to be the Court's definition of acquittal as "a resolution [in the defendant's favor], correct or not, of some or all of the factual elements of the offense charged," * * *. The language quoted from *Martin Linen Supply Co.*, was tied to the particular issue in that case and was never intended to serve as an all encompassing definition of acquittal for all purposes. Rather, *Martin Linen Supply* referred generally to "acquittal" as "a legal determination on the basis of facts adduced at trial relating to the general issue of the case," and this is the accepted definition. This * * * traditional definition of "acquittal" obviously is responsive to the values protected by the Double Jeopardy Clause. * * *

BURKS v. UNITED STATES

437 U.S. 1, 98 S.Ct. 2141, 57 L.Ed.2d 1 (1978).

CHIEF JUSTICE BURGER delivered the opinion of the Court.

We granted certiorari to resolve the question of whether an accused may be subjected to a second trial when conviction in a prior trial was reversed by an appellate court solely for lack of sufficient evidence to sustain the jury's verdict.

Petitioner Burks was tried in the United States District Court for the crime of robbing a federally insured bank by use of a dangerous weapon * * *. Burks' principal defense was insanity. To prove this claim petitioner produced three expert witnesses who testified, albeit with differing diagnoses of his mental condition, that he suffered from a mental illness at the time of the robbery, which rendered him substantially incapable of conforming his conduct to the requirements of the law. In rebuttal the Government offered the testimony of two experts, one of whom testified that although petitioner possessed a character disorder, he was not mentally ill. The other prosecution witness acknowledged a character disorder in petitioner, but gave a rather ambiguous answer to the question of whether Burks had been capable of conforming his conduct to the law. Lay witnesses also testified for the Government, expressing their opinion that petitioner appeared to be capable of normal functioning and was sane at the time of the alleged offense.

Before the case was submitted to the jury, the court denied a motion for a judgment of acquittal. The jury found Burks guilty as charged. * * * On appeal petitioner narrowed the issues by admitting the affirmative factual elements of the charge against him, leaving only his claim concerning criminal responsibility to be resolved. With respect to this point, the Court of Appeals agreed with petitioner's claim that the evidence was insufficient to support the verdict and reversed his conviction. * * * [It concluded that] the prosecution's evidence with respect to Burks' mental condition, even when viewed in the light most favorable to the Government, did not "effectively rebu[t]" petitioner's proof with respect to insanity and criminal responsibility.

At this point, the Court of Appeals, rather than terminating the case against petitioner, remanded to the District Court "for a determination of whether a directed verdict of acquittal should be entered or a new trial ordered." * * * [It indicated] that the District Court should choose the appropriate course "from a balancing of the equities," * * *. The Court of Appeals assumed it had the power to order this "balancing" remedy by virtue of the fact that Burks had explicitly requested a new trial. As authority for this holding the court cited, *Bryan v. United States,* 338 U.S. 552 (1950). * * *

Petitioner's argument is straightforward. He contends that the Court of Appeals' holding was nothing more or less than a decision that the District Court had erred by not granting his motion for a judgment of acquittal. By implication, he argues, the appellate reversal was the operative equivalent of a district court's judgment of acquittal, entered either before or after verdict. Petitioner points out, however, that had the District Court found the evidence at the first trial inadequate, as the Court of Appeals said it should have done, a second trial would violate the Double Jeopardy Clause of the Fifth Amendment. Therefore, he maintains, it makes no difference that the determination of evidentiary insufficiency was made by a *reviewing* court since the double jeopardy considerations are the same, regardless of which court decides that a judgment of acquittal is in order.

The position advanced by petitioner has not been embraced by our prior holdings. Indeed, as the Court of Appeals here recognized, *Bryan v. United States,* would appear to be contrary. * * * [The Court here discussed *Bryan* at length and noted that *Bryan* and similar rulings had as their "common ancestor, *Ball v. United States,* 163 U.S. 662 (1896).]

* * * *Ball v. United States* * * * [therefore] provides a logical starting point for unraveling the conceptual confusion arising from *Bryan* and the cases which have followed in its wake. This is especially true since *Ball* appears to represent the first instance in which this Court considered in any detail the double jeopardy implications of an appellate reversal.

Ball came before the Court twice, the first occasion being on writ of error from federal convictions for murder. On this initial review, those defendants who had been found guilty obtained a reversal of their convictions due to a fatally defective indictment. On remand after appeal, the trial court dismissed the flawed indictment and proceeded to retry the defendants on a new indictment. They were again convicted and the defendants came once more to this Court, arguing that their second trial was barred because of former jeopardy. The Court rejected this plea in a brief statement:

> "[A] defendant, who procures a judgment against him upon an indictment to be set aside, may be tried anew upon the same indictment, or upon another indictment, for the same offence of which he had been convicted."

The reversal in *Ball* was therefore based not on insufficiency of evidence but rather on trial error, i.e., failure to dismiss a faulty indictment. Moreover, the cases cited as authority by *Ball* were ones involving trial errors.

We have no doubt that *Ball* was correct in allowing a new trial to rectify *trial error:*

> "The principle that [the Double Jeopardy Clause] does not preclude the Government's retrying a defendant whose conviction is set aside because of an *error in the proceedings* leading to conviction is a well-established part of our constitutional jurisprudence." *United States v. Tateo,* 377 U.S. 463 (1964) (emphasis supplied).

As we have seen * * *, the cases which have arisen since *Ball* generally do not distinguish between reversals due to trial error and those resulting from evidentiary insufficiency. We believe, however, that the failure to make this distinction has contributed substantially to the present state of conceptual confusion existing in this area of the law. Consequently, it is important to consider carefully the respective roles of these two types of reversals in double jeopardy analysis.

Various rationales have been advanced to support the policy of allowing retrial to correct trial error, but in our view the most reasonable justification is that advanced by *Tateo*.

> "It would be a high price indeed for society to pay were every accused granted immunity from punishment because of any defect sufficient to constitute reversible error in the proceedings leading to conviction."

In short, reversal for trial error, as distinguished from evidentiary insufficiency, does not constitute a decision to the effect that the government has failed to prove its case. As such, it implies nothing with respect to the guilt or innocence of the defendant. Rather, it is a determination that a defendant has been convicted through a judicial process which is defective in some fundamental respect, e.g., incorrect receipt or rejection of evidence, incorrect instructions, or prosecutorial misconduct. When this occurs, the accused has a strong interest in obtaining a fair readjudication of his guilt free from error, just as society maintains a valid concern for insuring that the guilty are punished.

The same cannot be said when a defendant's conviction has been overturned due to a failure of proof at trial, in which case the prosecution cannot complain of prejudice, for it has been given one fair opportunity to offer whatever proof it could assemble.[10] Moreover, such an appellate reversal means that the government's case was so lacking that it should not have even been *submitted* to the jury. Since we necessarily afford absolute finality to a jury's *verdict* of acquittal—no matter how erroneous its decision—it is difficult to conceive how society has any greater interest in retrying a defendant when, on review, it is decided as a matter of law that the jury could not properly have returned a verdict of guilty.

The importance of a reversal on grounds of evidentiary insufficiency for purposes of inquiry under the Double Jeopardy Clause is underscored by the fact that a federal court's role in deciding whether a case should be considered by the jury is quite limited. Even the trial court, which has heard the testimony of witnesses firsthand, is not to weigh the evidence or assess the credibility of witnesses when it judges the merits of a motion for acquittal. The prevailing rule has long been that a district judge is to submit a case to the jury if the evidence and inferences therefrom most favorable to the prosecution would warrant the jury's finding the defendant guilty beyond a reasonable doubt. Obviously a federal appellate court applies no higher a standard; rather, it must sustain the verdict if there is substantial evidence, viewed in the light most favorable to the Government, to uphold the jury's decision. While this is not the appropriate occasion to re-examine in detail the standards for appellate reversal on grounds of insufficient evidence, it is apparent that such a decision will be confined to cases where the prosecution's failure is clear. Given the requirements for entry of a judgment of acquittal, the purposes of the Clause would be negated were we to afford the government an opportunity for the proverbial "second bite at the apple."

In our view it makes no difference that a defendant has sought a new trial as one of his remedies, or even as the sole remedy. It cannot be meaningfully said

---

10. In holding the evidence insufficient to sustain guilt, an appellate court determines that the prosecution has failed to prove guilt beyond a reasonable doubt. See *American Tobacco Co. v. United States*, 328 U.S. 781 (1946).

that a person "waives" his right to a judgment of acquittal by moving for a new trial. * * * Since we hold today that the Double Jeopardy Clause precludes a second trial once the reviewing court has found the evidence legally insufficient, the only "just" remedy available for that court is the direction of a judgment of acquittal. To the extent that our prior decisions suggest that by moving for a new trial, a defendant waives his right to a judgment of acquittal on the basis of evidentiary insufficiency, those cases are overruled. * * *

JUSTICE BLACKMUN took no part in the consideration or decision of this case.[a]

a. In Lockhart v. Nelson, 488 U.S. 33 (1988), the question presented was "whether the Double Jeopardy Clause allows retrial when a reviewing court determines that a defendant's conviction must be reversed because evidence was erroneously admitted against him, and also concludes that without the inadmissible evidence there was insufficient evidence to support a conviction." The Court concluded that the "logic of Burks requires the question to be answered in the affirmative." The Court reasoned that the situation presented here was "that * * * described in Burks as reversal for 'trial error'—the trial court erred in admitting a particular piece of evidence, and without it there was insufficient evidence to support a judgment of conviction. But clearly with that evidence, there was enough to support the sentence * * *. It is quite clear from our opinion in Burks that a reviewing court must consider all of the evidence admitted by the trial court in deciding whether retrial is permissible under the Double Jeopardy Clause * * *. The basis for the Burks exception to the general rule is that a reversal for insufficiency of the evidence should be treated no differently than a trial court's granting a judgment of acquittal at the close of all the evidence. A trial court in passing on such a motion considers all of the evidence it has admitted, and to make the analogy complete it must be this same quantum of evidence which is considered by the reviewing court."

Chapter 20

SENTENCING PROCEDURES

Sentencing procedures vary substantially from jurisdiction to jurisdiction. A state's sentencing procedures are determined in part by the structure of the state's sentencing system. That structure may vary both as to who has responsibility for sentencing and how much discretion is granted that sentencer. Apart from capital punishment (where jury sentencing is traditionally used), sentencing authority is usually vested in the judge. A small group of states, however, also employ jury sentencing for non-capital, felony sentencing. Such jury sentencing focuses largely on the nature of the crime. The jury imposes a sentence, within a maximum and minimum set by law, based on the evidence it has heard at trial. It does not have before it the information on the defendant's background that would be developed through the presentence report in a judicial sentencing system or through a sentencing hearing in a capital case. As with its decision on guilt, the jury announces its sentence without explaining its grounding. Moreover, in non-capital jury sentencing, ordinarily no attempt is made to guide the jury's exercise of discretion by offering illustrations of those factors that might justify the choice of one sentence or another within the range allowed by the legislature.

Judicial sentencing, like jury sentencing, starts with legislative direction as to the maximum and minimum sentences allowed. Under an indeterminate sentencing structure, where the sentence is to be incarceration, the legislature requires the court to impose a sentence consisting of both maximum and minimum periods of incarceration, with the parole board determining the actual length of the incarceration within those limits. In such jurisdictions, judges often are given no direction as to choice of sentence within the legislatively prescribed limits, except that there must be a certain gap between the maximum and minimum sentence (e.g., the minimum can be no more than half of the maximum). The judge need not set forth any reason for selecting any particular maximum and minimum nor, where probation is a legislatively allowable alternative, for choosing incarceration over probation.

In recent years, numerous states have moved away from indeterminate sentences, requiring judges choosing incarceration to select a specific term of years. In some of these states, the legislature sets a presumptive sentence that falls between the permissible high and low for the crime. The judge can move the sentence up or down from that presumptive sentence only upon finding that certain aggravating or mitigating circumstances exist. In other jurisdictions, administrative guidelines are used to guide the judge's choice of sentence within the range specified by the legislature. The guidelines take into consideration a variety of factors relating to both the crime and the offender. The judge must first determine which of those factors are present in the particular case so that the case can be placed in its proper category under the guidelines. If the judge then selects a sentence within the guidelines, no further explanation is required. The judge retains discretion, however, to go outside the guidelines, but here the judge must state the reasons for doing so.

Judicial sentencing under a structure calling for indeterminate sentences traditionally carried with it only limited procedural safeguards. The defense had the opportunity to present information that it believed to be relevant to sentencing and the defendant had a right to speak personally to the sentence (a right of "allocution"). The defense did not necessarily know, however, what other information the judge was considering or what factual assessments were being made by the judge in setting the sentence. That additional information came from a presentence report prepared by the probation department, and the defendant was given limited access, if any, to that report. The judge did not have to indicate what factors had been influential in setting the sentence, as the range of relevant considerations was thought to be too broad to require a sentencing judge to pinpoint the importance of any one factor or group of factors.

In recent years, there has been a movement toward more extensive disclosure of the presentence report to the defense, particularly in jurisdictions with presumptive or guideline sentencing. Also, as noted above, judges are required under guideline and presumptive sentencing structures to set forth the grounding of the sentence at least where it differs from the norm. Even here, however, the court's determination that a particular grounding exists is not a product of traditional trial procedures (such as the right of confrontation), and is not governed by traditional trial standards of proof.

Apart from the special setting of capital sentencing, the Supreme Court has spoken on relatively few occasions as to what the Constitution mandates in sentencing procedures. The first case in this chapter, *United States v. Grayson*, is the leading case of recent vintage considering the application of due process standards to non-capital sentencing. The second case, *Mitchell v. United States*, considers the applicability of the self-incrimination privilege in the sentencing context. The next case, *Apprendi v. New Jersey*, considers the limits that the constitution may impose upon the structuring of determinate sentencing. The last case, *McClesky v. Kemp*, involves capital sentencing, but discusses an issue (equal protection challenges to alleged discrimination in sentencing) that arises as well in non-capital sentencing, particularly under indeterminate sentencing schemes.

UNITED STATES v. GRAYSON

438 U.S. 41, 98 S.Ct. 2610, 57 L.Ed.2d 582 (1978).

CHIEF JUSTICE BURGER delivered the opinion of the Court.

We granted certiorari to review a holding of the Court of Appeals that it was improper for a sentencing judge, in fixing the sentence within the statutory limits, to give consideration to the defendant's false testimony observed by the judge during the trial.

In August 1975, respondent Grayson was confined in a federal prison camp under a conviction for distributing a controlled substance. In October, he escaped but was apprehended two days later by FBI agents in New York City. He was indicted for prison escape in violation of 18 U.S.C. § 751(a).

During its case in chief, the United States proved the essential elements of the crime, including his lawful confinement and the unlawful escape. In addition, it presented the testimony of the arresting FBI agents that Grayson, upon being apprehended, denied his true identity.

Grayson testified in his own defense. He admitted leaving the camp but asserted that he did so out of fear: "I had just been threatened with a large stick with a nail protruding through it by an inmate that was serving time at Allenwood, and I was scared, and I just ran." He testified that the threat was made in the presence of many inmates by prisoner Barnes who sought to enforce collection of a gambling debt and followed other threats and physical assaults made for the same purpose. Grayson called one inmate, who testified: "I heard [Barnes] talk to Grayson in a loud voice one day, but that's all. I never seen no harm, no hands or no shuffling whatsoever."

Grayson's version of the facts was contradicted by the Government's rebuttal evidence and by cross-examination on crucial aspects of his story. For example, Grayson stated that after crossing the prison fence he left his prison jacket by the side of the road. On recross, he stated that he also left his prison shirt but not his trousers. Government testimony showed that on the morning after the escape, a shirt marked with Grayson's number, a jacket, and a pair of prison trousers were found outside a hole in the prison fence.[1] Grayson also testified on cross-examination: "I do believe that I phrased the rhetorical question to Captain Kurd, who was in charge of [the prison], and I think I said something if an inmate was being threatened by somebody, what would * * * he do? First of all he said he would want to know who it was." On further cross-examination, however, Grayson modified his description of the conversation. Captain Kurd testified that Grayson had never mentioned in any fashion threats from other inmates. Finally, the alleged assailant, Barnes, by then no longer an inmate, testified that Grayson had never owed him any money and that he had never threatened or physically assaulted Grayson.

The jury returned a guilty verdict, whereupon the District Judge ordered the United States Probation Office to prepare a presentence report. At the sentencing hearing, the judge stated:

"I'm going to give my reasons for sentencing in this case with clarity, because one of the reasons may well be considered by a Court of Appeals to be impermissible; and although I could come into this Court Room and sentence this Defendant to a five-year prison term without any explanation at all, I think it is fair that I give the reasons so that if the Court of Appeals feels that one of the reasons which I am about to enunciate is an improper consideration for a trial judge, then the Court will be in a position to reverse this Court and send the case back for re-sentencing.

"In my view a prison sentence is indicated, and the sentence that the Court is going to impose is to deter you, Mr. Grayson, and others who are similarly situated. Secondly, *it is my view that your defense was a complete fabrication without the slightest merit whatsoever. I feel it is proper for me to consider that fact in the sentencing, and I will do so.*" (Emphasis added.)

He then sentenced Grayson to a term of two years' imprisonment, consecutive to his unexpired sentence.

---

1. The testimony regarding the prison clothing was important for reasons in addition to the light it shed on quality of recollection. Grayson stated that after unpremeditatedly fleeing the prison with no possessions and crossing the fence, he hitchhiked to New York City—a difficult task for a man with no trousers. The United States suggested that by prearrangement Grayson met someone, possibly a woman friend, on the highway near the break in the fence and that this accomplice provided civilian clothes. It introduced evidence that the friend visited Grayson often at prison, including each of the three days immediately prior to his penultimate day in the camp.

On appeal, a divided panel of the Court of Appeals for the Third Circuit directed that Grayson's sentence be vacated and that he be resentenced by the District Court without consideration of false testimony. * * * We reverse.

In *Williams v. New York,* 337 U.S. 241 (1949), Mr. Justice Black observed that the "prevalent modern philosophy of penology [is] that the punishment should fit the offender and not merely the crime," and that, accordingly, sentences should be determined with an eye toward the "[r]eformation and rehabilitation of offenders." But it has not always been so. In the early days of the Republic, * * * the period of incarceration was generally prescribed with specificity by the legislature. Each crime had its defined punishment. * * *

Approximately a century ago, a reform movement asserting that the purpose of incarceration, and therefore the guiding consideration in sentencing, should be rehabilitation of the offender, dramatically altered the approach to sentencing. A fundamental proposal of this movement was a flexible sentencing system permitting judges and correctional personnel, particularly the latter, to set the release date of prisoners according to informed judgments concerning their potential for, or actual, rehabilitation and their likely recidivism. * * * Indeterminate sentencing under the rehabilitation model presented sentencing judges with a serious practical problem: how rationally to make the required predictions so as to avoid capricious and arbitrary sentences, which the newly conferred and broad discretion placed within the realm of possibility. An obvious, although only partial, solution was to provide the judge with as much information as reasonably practical concerning the defendant's "character and propensities[,] * * * his present purposes and tendencies," and, indeed, "every aspect of [his] life." *Williams v. New York.* Thus, most jurisdictions provided trained probation officers to conduct presentence investigations of the defendant's life and, on that basis, prepare a presentence report for the sentencing judge.

Constitutional challenges were leveled at judicial reliance on such information, however. In *Williams v. New York,* a jury convicted the defendant of murder but recommended a life sentence. The sentencing judge, partly on the basis of information not known to the jury but contained in a presentence report, imposed the death penalty. The defendant argued that this procedure deprived him of his federal constitutional right to confront and cross-examine those supplying information to the probation officer and, through him, to the sentencing judge. The Court rejected this argument. It noted that traditionally "a sentencing judge could exercise a wide discretion in the sources and types of evidence used to assist him in determining the kind and extent of punishment to be imposed within limits fixed by law." "And modern concepts individualizing punishment have made it all the more necessary that a sentencing judge not be denied an opportunity to obtain pertinent information," indeed, "[t]o deprive sentencing judges of this kind of information would undermine modern penological procedural policies that have been cautiously adopted throughout the nation after careful consideration and experimentation." Accordingly, the sentencing judge was held not to have acted unconstitutionally in considering either the defendant's participation in criminal conduct for which he had not been convicted or information secured by the probation investigator that the defendant was a "menace to society."

Of course, a sentencing judge is not limited to the often far-ranging material compiled in a presentence report. "[B]efore making [the sentencing] determination, a judge may appropriately conduct an inquiry broad in scope, largely unlimited either as to the kind of information he may consider, or the source from which it may come." *United States v. Tucker,* 404 U.S. 443 (1972). Congress recently reaffirmed this fundamental sentencing principle by enacting 18 U.S.C. § 3577:

> "No limitation shall be placed on the information concerning the background, character, and conduct of a person convicted of an offense which a court of the United States may receive and consider for the purpose of imposing an appropriate sentence."

Thus, we have acknowledged that a sentencing authority may legitimately consider the evidence heard during trial, as well as the demeanor of the accused. *Chaffin v. Stynchcombe*, 412 U.S. 17 (1973). More to the point presented in this case, one serious study has concluded that the trial judge's "opportunity to observe the defendant, particularly if he chose to take the stand in his defense, can often provide useful insights into an appropriate disposition." ABA Sentencing Alternatives and Procedures § 5.1 (App.Draft 1968).

A defendant's truthfulness or mendacity while testifying on his own behalf, almost without exception, has been deemed probative of his attitudes toward society and prospects for rehabilitation and hence relevant to sentencing. Soon after *Williams* was decided, the Tenth Circuit concluded that "the attitude of a convicted defendant with respect to his willingness to commit a serious crime [perjury] * * * is a proper matter to consider in determining what sentence shall be imposed within the limitations fixed by statute." *Humes v. United States,* 186 F.2d 875 (1951). The Second, Fourth, Fifth, Sixth, Seventh, Eighth, and Ninth Circuits have since agreed. * * * Only one Circuit has directly rejected the probative value of the defendant's false testimony in his own defense. In *Scott v. United States,* 135 U.S.App.D.C. 377 (1969), the court argued that

> "the peculiar pressures placed upon a defendant threatened with jail and the stigma of conviction make his willingness to deny the crime an unpromising test of his prospects for rehabilitation if guilty. It is indeed unlikely that many men who commit serious offenses would balk on principle from lying in their own defense. The guilty man may quite sincerely repent his crime but yet, driven by the urge to remain free, may protest his innocence in a court of law."

The *Scott* rationale rests not only on the realism of the psychological pressures on a defendant in the dock—which we can grant—but also on a deterministic view of human conduct that is inconsistent with the underlying precepts of our criminal justice system. A "universal and persistent" foundation stone in our system of law, and particularly in our approach to punishment, sentencing, and incarceration, is the "belief in freedom of the human will and a consequent ability and duty of the normal individual to choose between good and evil." Given that long-accepted view of the "ability and duty of the normal individual to choose," we must conclude that the defendant's readiness to lie under oath—especially when, as here, the trial court finds the lie to be flagrant—may be deemed probative of his prospects for rehabilitation.

Against this background we evaluate Grayson's constitutional argument that the District Court's sentence constitutes punishment for the crime of perjury for which he has not been indicted, tried, or convicted by due process. A second argument is that permitting consideration of perjury will "chill" defendants from exercising their right to testify on their own behalf.

In his due process argument, Grayson does not contend directly that the District Court had an impermissible purpose in considering his perjury and selecting the sentence. Rather, he argues that this Court, in order to preserve due process rights, not only must prohibit the impermissible sentencing practice of incarcerating for the purpose of saving the Government the burden of bringing a separate and subsequent perjury prosecution but also must prohibit the otherwise *permissible* practice of considering a defendant's untruthfulness for the purpose of illuminating his need for rehabilitation and society's need for protection. He presents two interrelated reasons. The effect of both permissible and impermissible sentencing practices may be the same: additional time in prison. Further, it is virtually impossible, he contends, to identify and establish the impermissible practice. We find these reasons insufficient justification for prohibiting what the Court and the Congress have declared appropriate judicial conduct.

First, the evolutionary history of sentencing, set out [above] * * *, demonstrates that it is proper—indeed, even necessary for the rational exercise of discretion—to consider the defendant's whole person and personality, as manifested by his conduct at trial and his testimony under oath, for whatever light those may shed on the sentencing decision. * * * Second, in our view, *Williams* fully supports consideration of such conduct in sentencing. There the Court permitted the sentencing judge to consider the offender's history of prior antisocial conduct, including burglaries for which he had not been duly convicted.[a] * * * Third, the efficacy of Grayson's suggested "exclusionary rule" is open to serious doubt. No rule of law, even one garbed in constitutional terms, can prevent improper use of firsthand observations of perjury. The integrity of the judges, and their fidelity to their oaths of office, necessarily provide the only, and in our view adequate, assurance against that.

Grayson's argument that judicial consideration of his conduct at trial impermissibly "chills" a defendant's statutory right, 18 U.S.C. § 3481, and perhaps a constitutional right, to testify on his own behalf is without basis. The right guaranteed by law to a defendant is narrowly the right to testify truthfully in accordance with the oath—unless we are to say that the oath is mere ritual without meaning. This view of the right involved is confirmed by the unquestioned constitutionality of perjury statutes, which punish those who willfully give false testimony. Further support for this is found in an important limitation on a defendant's right to the assistance of counsel: Counsel ethically cannot assist his client in presenting what the attorney has reason to believe is false testimony. Assuming, *arguendo,* that the sentencing judge's consideration of defendant's

---

a. Should the defendant subsequently be prosecuted for other criminal conduct considered in sentencing the defendant for the offense in question, the separate sentence on that prosecution does not violate double jeopardy. This is so even under a determinate sentencing scheme that directs consideration of that other criminal conduct. In *Witte v. United States*, 515 U.S. 389 (1995), the defendant was initially charged with criminal liability for a planned 1991 shipment of marijuana. Under the federal sentencing guidelines for that offense, consideration was to be given to the total quantity of drugs involved in all conduct relevant to the charged offense, which encompassed all drug transactions "within the scope of the criminal activity that defendant jointly undertook" with others. Accordingly, in sentencing for the 1991 shipment, the sentencing judge added the quantity of narcotics to be shipped in a failed 1990 shipment that was part of the "same continuing conspiracy." This raised the defendant's offense-level score to 40, which produced a sentence of 144 months (within the statutory maximum of 40 years).

When defendant was subsequently prosecuted for the conspiring to import narcotics in 1990, based on the failed shipment, he argued that double jeopardy barred that prosecution because he already had been punished for that activity. Rejecting that contention, the Supreme Court noted that a court's consideration of other criminal behavior in sentencing for a particular offense simply guided sentencing on the offense charged within the statutory maximum, but did not impose punishment for the other behavior. This was not altered by guidelines that directed the sentencing court to take account of specific related conduct in determining the severity of the offense within the statutory maximum. In *United States v. Watts*, 519 U.S. 148 (1997), the Court added that "relevant conduct" considered in federal guideline sentencing could include criminal conduct that had resulted in acquittal. The acquittal only establishes the presence of a reasonable doubt and consideration for sentencing purposes generally is satisfied by a preponderance of the evidence proof standard.

untruthfulness in testifying has any chilling effect on a defendant's decision to testify falsely, that effect is entirely permissible. There is no protected right to commit perjury.

Grayson's further argument that the sentencing practice challenged here will inhibit exercise of the right to testify truthfully is entirely frivolous. That argument misapprehends the nature and scope of the practice we find permissible. Nothing we say today requires a sentencing judge to enhance, in some wooden or reflex fashion, the sentences of all defendants whose testimony is deemed false. Rather, we are reaffirming the authority of a sentencing judge to evaluate carefully a defendant's testimony on the stand, determine—with a consciousness of the frailty of human judgment—whether that testimony contained willful and material falsehoods, and, if so, assess in light of all the other knowledge gained about the defendant the meaning of that conduct with respect to his prospects for rehabilitation and restoration to a useful place in society. Awareness of such a process realistically cannot be deemed to affect the decision of an accused but unconvicted defendant to testify truthfully in his own behalf. * * *

Justice Stewart, with whom Justice Brennan and Justice Marshall join, dissenting.

The Court begins its consideration of this case with the assumption that the respondent gave false testimony at his trial. But there has been no determination that his testimony was false. This respondent was given a greater sentence than he would otherwise have received—how much greater we have no way of knowing—solely because a single judge *thought* that he had not testified truthfully.[1] In essence, the Court holds today that *whenever* a defendant testifies in his own behalf and is found guilty, he opens himself to the possibility of an enhanced sentence. Such a sentence is nothing more or less than a penalty imposed on the defendant's exercise of his constitutional and statutory rights to plead not guilty and to testify in his own behalf.

It does not change matters to say that the enhanced sentence merely reflects the defendant's "prospects for rehabilitation" rather than an additional punishment for testifying falsely. The fact remains that all defendants who choose to testify, and only those who do so, face the very real prospect of a greater sentence based upon the trial judge's unreviewable perception that the testimony was untruthful. The Court prescribes no limitations or safeguards to minimize a defendant's rational fear that his truthful testimony will be perceived as false. Indeed, encumbrance of the sentencing process with the collateral inquiries necessary to provide such assurance would be both pragmatically unworkable and theoretically inconsistent with the assumption that the trial judge is merely considering one more piece of information in his overall evaluation of the defendant's prospects for rehabilitation. But without such safeguards I fail to see how the Court can dismiss as "frivolous" the argument that this sentencing practice will "inhibit exercise of the right to testify truthfully." * * *

The minimal contribution that the defendant's possibly untruthful testimony might make to an overall assessment of his potential for rehabilitation, see n. 3, cannot justify imposing this additional burden on his right to testify in his own behalf. I do not believe that a sentencing judge's discretion to consider a wide

---

1. We know this only because of the trial judge's laudable explication of his reasons for imposing the sentence in this case. In many cases it would be impossible to discern whether a sentencing judge had been influenced by his belief that the defendant had not testified truthfully, since there is no requirement that reasons be given. But that fact does not argue against correcting an erroneous sentencing policy that is apparent on the face of the record. * * *

range of information in arriving at an appropriate sentence, *Williams v. New York,* allows him to mete out additional punishment to the defendant simply because of his personal belief that the defendant did not testify truthfully at the trial. Accordingly, I would affirm the judgment of the Court of Appeals.[b]

MITCHELL v. UNITED STATES

526 U.S. 314, 119 S.Ct. 1307, 143 L.Ed.2d 424 (1999).

JUSTICE KENNEDY delivered the opinion of the Court.

Two questions relating to a criminal defendant's Fifth Amendment privilege against self-incrimination are presented to us. The first is whether, in the federal criminal system, a guilty plea waives the privilege in the sentencing phase of the case, either as a result of the colloquy preceding the plea or by operation of law when the plea is entered. We hold the plea is not a waiver of the privilege at sentencing. The second question is whether, in determining facts about the crime which bear upon the severity of the sentence, a trial court may draw an adverse inference from the defendant's silence. We hold a sentencing court may not draw the adverse inference.

Petitioner Amanda Mitchell and 22 other defendants were indicted for offenses arising from a conspiracy to distribute cocaine * * *. According to the indictment, the leader of the conspiracy, Harry Riddick, obtained large quantities of cocaine and resold the drug through couriers and street sellers, including petitioner. Petitioner was charged with one count of conspiring to distribute five or more kilograms of cocaine and with three counts of distributing cocaine within 1,000 feet of a school or playground. In 1995, without any plea agreement, petitioner pleaded guilty to all four counts. She reserved the right to contest the drug quantity attributable to her under the conspiracy count, and the District Court advised her the drug quantity would be determined at her sentencing hearing.

Before accepting the plea, the District Court made the inquiries required by Rule 11 of the Federal Rules of Criminal Procedure. Informing petitioner of the penalties for her offenses, the District Judge advised her, "the range of punishment here is very complex because we don't know how much cocaine the Government's going to be able to show you were involved in." * * * By pleading guilty, the District Court [also] explained, petitioner would waive various rights, including "the right at trial to remain silent under the Fifth Amendment." After

---

b. In *United States v. Dunnigan,* 507 U.S. 87 (1993), the Court of Appeals had held unconstitutional a sentencing guideline for federal courts that treated a defendant's perjury at trial as conduct mandating enhancement of the guideline-specified sentence within the maximum provided for the offense of conviction. The Court of Appeals distinguished *Grayson* on the grounds that: (1) *Grayson* had relied on the perjury establishing a greater need for rehabilitation, but the federal sentencing guideline was aimed at punishment; and (2) the automatic character of the guideline enhancement constituted a "wooden or reflexive" response contrary to the admonition in *Grayson.* Reversing the Court of Appeals, a unanimous Supreme Court found *Grayson* controlling and neither of the above distinctions to be persuasive. While it was true that the rehabilitation was "no longer a goal of sentencing under the guidelines," the "lengthy discussion in *Grayson* of how a defendant's perjury was relevant to the potential for rehabilitation * * * was not meant to imply that rehabilitation was the only permissible justification for an increased sentence based on perjury." So too, the "cautionary remark" in *Grayson* regarding enhancement "in some 'wooden or reflexive fashion' did not invalidate the guideline." Under guideline procedures, where the enhancement is contested by the defendant, "the elements of perjury must be found by the district court [in independent factual findings] * * *, so the enhancement is far from automatic. And that the enhancement stems from a congressional mandate rather than from a court's discretionary judgment cannot be grounds, in these circumstances, for its invalidation."

the Government explained the factual basis for the charges, the judge, having put petitioner under oath, asked her, "Did you do that?" Petitioner answered, "Some of it." She indicated that, although present for one of the transactions charged as a substantive cocaine distribution count, she had not herself delivered the cocaine to the customer. The Government maintained she was liable nevertheless as an aider and abettor of the delivery by another courier. After discussion with her counsel, petitioner reaffirmed her intention to plead guilty to all the charges. * * *

In 1996, nine of petitioner's original 22 codefendants went to trial. Three other co-defendants had pleaded guilty and agreed to cooperate with the Government. They testified petitioner was a regular seller for ringleader Riddick. At petitioner's sentencing hearing, the three adopted their trial testimony, and one of them furnished additional information on the amount of cocaine petitioner sold. On cross-examination, the codefendant conceded he had not seen petitioner on a regular basis during the relevant period. * * * Petitioner put on no evidence at sentencing, nor did she testify to rebut the Government's evidence about drug quantity. Her counsel argued, however, that the three documented sales to Alvitta Mack [totaling two ounces] constituted the only evidence of sufficient reliability to be credited in determining the quantity of cocaine attributable to her for sentencing purposes.

After this testimony at the sentencing hearing the District Court ruled that, as a consequence of her guilty plea, petitioner had no right to remain silent with respect to the details of her crimes. The court found credible the testimony indicating petitioner had been a drug courier on a regular basis. Sales of 1 1/2 to 2 ounces twice a week for a year and a half put her over the 5–kilogram threshold, thus mandating a minimum sentence of 10 years. "One of the things" persuading the court to rely on the testimony of the codefendants was petitioner's "not testifying to the contrary." * * * The District Judge told petitioner: " 'I held it against you that you didn't come forward today and tell me that you really only did this a couple of times.... I'm taking the position that you should come forward and explain your side of this issue. Your counsel's taking the position that you have a Fifth Amendment right not to.... If he's—if it's determined by a higher Court that he's right in that regard, I would be willing to bring you back for resentencing. And if you—if—and then I might take a closer look at the [codefendants'] testimony.' " * * *

The District Court sentenced petitioner to the statutory minimum of 10 years of imprisonment, 6 years of supervised release, and a special assessment of $200. The Court of Appeals for the Third Circuit affirmed the sentence. According to the Court of Appeals, "By voluntarily and knowingly pleading guilty to the offense Mitchell waived her Fifth Amendment privilege." The court acknowledged other Circuits have held a witness can "claim the Fifth Amendment privilege if his or her testimony might be used to enhance his or her sentence," but it said this rule "does not withstand analysis." * * *

The Government maintains that petitioner's guilty plea was a waiver of the privilege against compelled self-incrimination with respect to all the crimes comprehended in the plea. We hold otherwise and rule that petitioner retained the privilege at her sentencing hearing. It is well established that a witness, in a single proceeding, may not testify voluntarily about a subject and then invoke the privilege against self-incrimination when questioned about the details. See *Rogers v. United States*, 340 U.S. 367, 373 (1951). The privilege is waived for the matters to which the witness testifies, and the scope of the "waiver is determined by the scope of relevant cross-examination," * * *. The justifications for the rule of waiver in the testimonial context are evident: A witness may not pick and choose what aspects of a particular subject to discuss without casting doubt on the trustworthiness of the statements and diminishing the integrity of the factual inquiry. As noted in *Rogers*, a contrary rule "would open the way to distortion of facts by permitting a witness to select any stopping place in the testimony." * * * The illogic of allowing a witness to offer only self-selected testimony should be obvious even to the witness, so there is no unfairness in allowing cross-examination when testimony is given without invoking the privilege.

We may assume for purposes of this opinion, then, that if petitioner had pleaded not guilty and, having taken the stand at a trial, testified she did "some of it," she could have been cross-examined on the frequency of her drug deliveries and the quantity of cocaine involved. The concerns which justify the cross-examination when the defendant testifies are absent at a plea colloquy, however. The purpose of a plea colloquy is to protect the defendant from an unintelligent or involuntary plea. The Government would turn this constitutional shield into a prosecutorial sword by having the defendant relinquish all rights against compelled self-incrimination upon entry of a guilty plea, including the right to remain silent at sentencing. * * * There is no convincing reason why the narrow inquiry at the plea colloquy should entail such an extensive waiver of the privilege. Unlike the defendant taking the stand, who "cannot reasonably claim that the Fifth Amendment gives him ... an immunity from cross-examination on the matters he has himself put in dispute," * * * the defendant who pleads guilty puts nothing in dispute regarding the essentials of the offense. Rather, the defendant takes those matters out of dispute, often by making a joint statement with the prosecution or confirming the prosecution's version of the facts. Under these circumstances, there is little danger that the court will be misled by selective disclosure. In this respect a guilty plea is more like an offer to stipulate than a decision to take the stand. Here, petitioner's statement that she had done "some of" the proffered conduct did not pose a threat to the integrity of factfinding proceedings, for the purpose of the District Court's inquiry was simply to ensure that petitioner understood the charges and that there was a factual basis for the Government's case.

Nor does Federal Rule of Criminal Procedure 11, which governs pleas, contemplate the broad waiver the Government envisions. * * * Of course, a court may discharge its duty of ensuring a factual basis for a plea by "question[ing] the defendant under oath, on the record, and in the presence of counsel about the offense to which the defendant has pleaded." Rule 11(c)(5). We do not question the authority of a district court to make whatever inquiry it deems necessary in its sound discretion to assure itself the defendant is not being pressured to offer a plea for which there is no factual basis. A defendant who withholds information by invoking the privilege against self-incrimination at a plea colloquy runs the risk the district court will find the factual basis inadequate. At least once the plea has been accepted, statements or admissions made during the preceding plea colloquy are later admissible against the defendant, as is the plea itself. A statement admissible against a defendant, however, is not necessarily a waiver of the privilege against self-incrimination. Rule 11 does not prevent the defendant from relying upon the privilege at sentencing.

Treating a guilty plea as a waiver of the privilege at sentencing would be a grave encroachment on the rights of defendants. At oral argument, we asked counsel for the United States whether, on the facts of this case, if the Government had no reliable evidence of the amount of drugs involved, the prosecutor "could say, well, we can't prove it, but we'd like to put her on the stand and cross-examine her and see if we can't get her to admit it." Counsel answered: "[T]he waiver analysis that we have put forward suggests that at least as to the facts surrounding the conspiracy to which she admitted, the Government could do that." Ibid. Over 90% of federal criminal defendants whose cases are not dismissed enter pleas of guilty or nolo contendere. * * * Were we to accept the Government's position, prosecutors could indict without specifying the quantity of drugs involved, obtain a guilty plea, and then put the defendant on the stand at sentencing to fill in the drug quantity. The result would be to enlist the defendant as an instrument in his or her own condemnation, undermining the long tradition and vital principle that criminal proceedings rely on accusations proved by the Government, not on inquisitions conducted to enhance its own prosecutorial power. * * *

The centerpiece of the Third Circuit's opinion is the idea that the entry of the guilty plea completes the incrimination of the defendant, thus extinguishing the privilege. Where a sentence has yet to be imposed, however, this Court has already rejected the proposition that "incrimination is complete once guilt has been adjudicated," *Estelle v. Smith*, 451 U.S. 454 (1981), and we reject it again today. * * * It is true, as a general rule, that where there can be no further incrimination, there is no basis for the assertion of the privilege. We conclude that principle applies to cases in which the sentence has been fixed and the judgment of conviction has become final. See, e.g., *Reina v. United States*, 364 U.S. 507 (1960). If no adverse consequences can be visited upon the convicted person by reason of further testimony, then there is no further incrimination to be feared.

Where the sentence has not yet been imposed a defendant may have a legitimate fear of adverse consequences from further testimony. As the Court stated in *Estelle*: "Any effort by the State to compel [the defendant] to testify against his will at the sentencing hearing clearly would contravene the Fifth Amendment." *Estelle* was a capital case, but we find no reason not to apply the principle to noncapital sentencing hearings as well. * * * The Government itself makes the implicit concession that the acceptance of a guilty plea does not eliminate the possibility of further incrimination. In its brief to the Court, the Government acknowledges that a defendant who awaits sentencing after having pleaded guilty may assert the privilege against self-incrimination if called as a witness in the trial of a codefendant, in part because of the danger of responding "to questions that might have an adverse impact on his sentence or on his prosecution for other crimes." * * *

The Government suggests in a footnote that even if petitioner retained an unwaived privilege against self-incrimination in the sentencing phase of her case, the District Court was entitled, based on her silence, to draw an adverse inference with regard to the amount of drugs attributable to her. The normal rule in a criminal case is that no negative inference from the defendant's failure to testify is permitted. *Griffin v. California* [Ch. 18, § 3]. We decline to adopt an exception for the sentencing phase of a criminal case with regard to factual determinations respecting the circumstances and details of the crime.

This Court has recognized "the prevailing rule that the Fifth Amendment does not forbid adverse inferences against parties to civil actions when they refuse to testify in response to probative evidence offered against them," *Baxter v. Palmigiano*, 425 U.S. 308 (1976), at least where refusal to waive the privilege does not lead "automatically and without more to [the] imposition of sanctions." In ordinary civil cases, the party confronted with the invocation of the privilege by the opposing side has no capacity to avoid it, say, by offering immunity from prosecution. The rule allowing invocation of the privilege, though at the risk of suffering an adverse inference or even a default, accommodates the right not to be a witness against oneself while still permitting civil litigation to proceed. Another reason for treating civil and criminal cases differently is that "the stakes are higher" in criminal cases, where liberty or even life may be at stake, and where the Government's "sole interest is to convict." *Baxter*, supra.

Baxter itself involved state prison disciplinary proceedings which, as the Court noted, "are not criminal proceedings" and "involve the correctional process and important state interests other than conviction for crime." Cf. *Ohio Adult Parole Authority v. Woodard*, 523 U.S. 272 (1998) (adverse inference permissible from silence in clemency proceeding, a nonjudicial post-conviction process which is not part of the criminal case). Unlike a prison disciplinary proceeding, a sentencing hearing is part of the criminal case—the explicit concern of the self-incrimination privilege. In accordance with the text of the Fifth Amendment, we must accord the privilege the same protection in the sentencing phase of "any criminal case" as that which is due in the trial phase of the same case, see *Griffin*, supra.

The concerns which mandate the rule against negative inferences at a criminal trial apply with equal force at sentencing. Without question, the stakes are high: Here, the inference drawn by the District Court from petitioner's silence may have resulted in decades of added imprisonment. The Government often has a motive to demand a severe sentence, so the central purpose of the privilege—to protect a defendant from being the unwilling instrument of his or her own condemnation—remains of vital importance. * * *

The rule against adverse inferences from a defendant's silence in criminal proceedings, including sentencing, is of proven utility. Some years ago the Court expressed concern that "[t]oo many, even those who should be better advised, view this privilege as a shelter for wrongdoers. They too readily assume that those who invoke it are either guilty of crime or commit perjury in claiming the privilege." *Ullmann v. United States*, 350 U.S. 422 (1956). Later, it quoted with apparent approval Wigmore's observation that "[t]he layman's natural first suggestion would probably be that the resort to privilege in each instance is a clear confession of crime." * * * It is far from clear that citizens, and jurors, remain today so skeptical of the principle or are often willing to ignore the prohibition against adverse inferences from silence. Principles once unsettled can find general and wide acceptance in the legal culture, and there can be little doubt that the rule prohibiting an inference of guilt from a defendant's rightful silence has become an essential feature of our legal tradition. This process began even before *Griffin*. When *Griffin* was being considered by this Court, some 44 States did not allow a prosecutor to invite the jury to make an adverse inference from the defendant's refusal to testify at trial. * * * The rule against adverse inferences is a vital instrument for teaching that the question in a criminal case is not whether the defendant committed the acts of which he is accused. The question is whether the Government has carried its burden to prove its allegations while respecting the defendant's individual rights. The Government retains the burden of proving facts relevant to the crime at the sentencing phase and cannot enlist the defendant in this process at the expense of the self-incrimination privilege. Whether silence bears upon the determination of a lack of remorse, or upon acceptance of responsibility for purposes of the downward adjustment provided in § 3E1.1 of the United States Sentencing Guidelines (1998), is a separate question. It is not before us, and we express no view on it. * * * By holding petitioner's silence against her in determining the facts of the offense at the sentencing hearing, the District Court imposed an impermissible burden on the exercise of the constitutional right against compelled self-incrimination.

JUSTICE SCALIA, with whom THE CHIEF JUSTICE, JUSTICE O'CONNOR, and JUSTICE THOMAS join, dissenting.

I agree with the Court that Mitchell had the right to invoke her Fifth Amendment privilege during the sentencing phase of her criminal case. In my view, however, she did not have the right to have the sentencer abstain from making the adverse inferences that reasonably flow from her failure to testify. I therefore respectfully dissent.

The Fifth Amendment provides that "[n]o person ... shall be compelled in any criminal case to be a witness against himself." As an original matter, it would seem to me that the threat of an adverse inference does not "compel" anyone to testify. It is one of the natural (and not governmentally imposed) consequences of failing to testify—as is the factfinder's increased readiness to believe the incriminating testimony that the defendant chooses not to contradict. Both of these consequences are assuredly cons rather than pros in the "to testify or not to testify" calculus, but they do not compel anyone to take the stand. Indeed, I imagine that in most instances, a guilty defendant would choose to remain silent despite the adverse inference, on the theory that it would do him less damage than his own cross-examined testimony.

Despite the text, we held in *Griffin v. California*, that it was impermissible for the prosecutor or judge to comment on a defendant's refusal to testify. We called it a "penalty" imposed on the defendant's exercise of the privilege. Ibid. And we did not stop there, holding in *Carter v. Kentucky*, that a judge must, if the defendant asks, instruct the jury that it may not sua sponte consider the defendant's silence as evidence of his guilt.

The majority muses that the no-adverse-inference rule has found "wide acceptance in the legal culture" and has even become "an essential feature of our legal tradition." Although the latter assertion strikes me as hyperbolic, the former may be true—which is adequate reason not to overrule these cases, a course I in no way propose. It is not adequate reason, however, to extend these cases into areas where they do not yet apply, since neither logic nor history can be marshaled in defense of them. The illogic of the *Griffin* line is plain, for it runs exactly counter to normal evidentiary inferences: If I ask my son whether he saw a movie I had forbidden him to watch, and he remains silent, the import of his silence is clear. Indeed, we have on other occasions recognized the significance of silence, saying that " '[f]ailure to contest an assertion ... is considered evidence of acquiescence ... if it would have been natural under the circumstances to object to the assertion in question.' " *Baxter v. Palmigiano*.

And as for history, *Griffin's* pedigree is equally dubious. The question whether a factfinder may draw a logical inference from a criminal defendant's failure to offer formal testimony would not have arisen in 1791, because common-law evidentiary rules prevented a criminal defendant from testifying in his own behalf even if he wanted to do so. That is not to say, however, that a criminal defendant was not allowed to speak in his own behalf, and a tradition of expecting the defendant to do so, and of drawing an adverse inference when he did not, strongly suggests that *Griffin* is out of sync with the historical understanding of the Fifth Amendment. Traditionally, defendants were expected to speak rather extensively at both the pretrial and trial stages of a criminal proceeding. The longstanding common-law principle, nemo tenetur seipsum prodere, was thought to ban only testimony forced by compulsory oath or physical torture, not voluntary, unsworn testimony.

Pretrial procedure in colonial America was governed (as it had been for centuries in England) by the Marian Committal Statute, which * * * [required the magistrate to "take the examination" of the arrested person not under oath and to record his response]. The justice of the peace [then] testified at trial as to the content of the defendant's statement; if the defendant refused to speak, this would also have been reported to the jury.

At trial, defendants were expected to speak directly to the jury. Sir James Stephen described 17th- and 18th-century English trials as follows: "[T]he prisoner in cases of felony could not be defended by counsel, and had therefore to speak for himself. He was thus unable to say ... that his mouth was closed. On the contrary his mouth was not only open, but the evidence given against him operated as so much indirect questioning, and if he omitted to answer the questions it suggested he was very likely to be convicted." * * * Though it is clear that adverse inference from silence was permitted, I have been unable to find any case adverting to that inference in upholding a conviction—which suggests that defendants rarely thought it in their interest to remain silent.

No one, however, seemed to think this system inconsistent with the principle of nemo tenetur seipsum prodere. And there is no indication whatever that criminal procedure in America made an abrupt about-face when this principle was ratified as a fundamental right in the Fifth Amendment and its state-constitution analogues. Justices of the peace continued pretrial questioning of suspects, whose silence continued to be introduced against them at trial. * * * If any objection was raised to the pretrial procedure, it was on the purely statutory ground that the Marian Committal Statute had no force in the new republic. * * * And defendants continued to speak at their trials until the assistance of counsel became more common, which occurred gradually throughout the 19th century. * * *

The *Griffin* question did not arise until States began enacting statutes providing that criminal defendants were competent to testify under oath on their own behalf. Maine was first in 1864, and the rest of the States and Federal Government eventually followed. Although some of these statutes (including the federal statute, 18 U.S.C. § 3481) contained a clause cautioning that no negative inference should be drawn from the defendant's failure to testify, disagreement with this approach was sufficiently widespread that, as late as 1953, the Uniform Rules of Evidence drafted by the National Conference of Commissioners on Uniform State Laws provided that "[i]f an accused in a criminal action does not testify, counsel may comment upon [sic] accused's failure to testify, and the trier of fact may draw all reasonable inferences therefrom." Uniform Rule of Evidence 23(4). See also Model Code of Evidence Rule 201(3) (1942) (similar).

Whatever the merits of prohibiting adverse inferences as a legislative policy, the text and history of the Fifth Amendment give no indication that there is a federal constitutional prohibition on the use of the defendant's silence as demeanor evidence. Our hardy forebearers, who thought of compulsion in terms of the rack and oaths forced by the power of law, would not have viewed the drawing of a commonsensical inference as equivalent pressure. And it is implausible that the Americans of 1791, who were subject to adverse inferences for failing to give unsworn testimony, would have viewed an adverse inference for failing to give sworn testimony as a violation of the Fifth Amendment. Nor can it reasonably be argued that the new statutes somehow created a "revised" understanding of the Fifth Amendment that was incorporated into the Due Process Clause of the Fourteenth Amendment, since only nine States (and not the Federal Government) had enacted competency statutes when the Fourteenth Amendment was adopted, and three of them did not prohibit adverse inferences from failure to testify.

The Court's decision in *Griffin*, however, did not even pretend to be rooted in a historical understanding of the Fifth Amendment. Rather, in a breathtaking act of sorcery it simply transformed legislative policy into constitutional command, quoting a passage from an earlier opinion describing the benevolent purposes of 18 U.S.C. § 3481, and then decreeing, with literally nothing to support it: "If the words 'Fifth Amendment' are substituted for 'act' and for 'statute,' the spirit of the Self–Incrimination Clause is reflected." Imagine what a constitution we would have if this mode of exegesis were generally applied—if, for example, without any evidence to prove the point, the Court could simply say of all federal procedural statutes, "If the words 'Fifth Amendment' are substituted for 'act' and for 'statute,' the spirit of the Due Process Clause is reflected." To my mind, *Griffin* was a wrong turn—which is not cause enough to overrule it, but is cause enough to resist its extension.

The Court asserts that it will not "adopt an exception" to *Griffin* for the sentencing phase of a criminal case. That characterization of what we are asked to do is evidently demanded, in the Court's view, by the very text of the Fifth Amendment: The phrase "any criminal case" requires us to "accord the privilege the same protection in the sentencing phase.... as that which is due in the trial phase of the same case." That is demonstrably not so.

Our case law has long recognized a natural dichotomy between the guilt and penalty phases. The jury-trial right contained in the Sixth Amendment—whose guarantees apply "[i]n all criminal prosecutions," a term indistinguishable for present purposes from the Fifth Amendment's "in any criminal case"—does not apply at sentencing. Nor does the Sixth Amendment's guarantee of the defendant's right "to be confronted with the witnesses against him." (The sentencing judge may consider, for example, reports of probation officers and psychiatrists without affording any cross-examination.) See *Williams v. New York*. Likewise inapplicable at sentencing is the requirement of the Due Process Clause that the prosecution prove the essential facts beyond a reasonable doubt. *McMillan v. Pennsylvania*, 477 U.S. 79, 92 (1986).

* * * Consistency with other areas of our jurisprudence points in the same direction. We have permitted adverse inferences to be drawn from silence where the consequence is a denial of clemency, and even deportation * * *. There is no reason why the increased punishment to which the defendant is exposed in the sentencing phase of a completed criminal trial should be treated differently— unless it is the theory that the guilt and sentencing phases form one inseparable "criminal case," which I have refuted above. Nor, I might add—despite the broad dicta that it quotes from *Estelle*—does the majority really believe that the guilt and sentencing phases are a unified whole, else it would not leave open the possibility that the acceptance-of-responsibility sentencing guideline escapes the ban on negative inferences.

Which brings me to the greatest—the most bizarre—inconsistency of all: the combination of the rule that the Court adopts today with the balance of our jurisprudence relating to sentencing in particular. "[C]ourts in this country and in England," we have said, have "practiced a policy under which a sentencing judge [can] exercise a wide discretion in the sources and types of evidence used to assist him in determining the kind and extent of punishment to be imposed within limits fixed by law." *Williams v. New York*. "[A] sentencing judge 'may appropriately conduct an inquiry broad in scope, largely unlimited either as to the kind of information he may consider, or the source from which it may come.' " "Few facts available to a sentencing judge," we have observed, "are more relevant to 'the likelihood that [a defendant] will transgress no more, the hope that he may respond to rehabilitative efforts to assist with a lawful future career, [and] the degree to which he does or does not deem himself at war with his society' " than a defendant's willingness to cooperate. *Roberts v. United States.* Today's opinion states, in as inconspicuous a manner as possible at the very end of its analysis (one imagines that if the statement were delivered orally it would be spoken in a very low voice, and with the Court's hand over its mouth), that its holding applies only to inferences drawn from silence "in determining facts of the offense." "Whether silence bears upon the determination of a lack of remorse, or upon acceptance of responsibility for purposes of the downward adjustment provided in § 3E1.1 of the United States Sentencing Guidelines (1998) is a separate question" on which the majority expresses no view. Never mind that we have said before, albeit in dicta, that "[w]e doubt that a principled distinction may be drawn between 'enhancing' the punishment imposed upon the petitioner and denying him the 'leniency' he claims would be appropriate if he had cooperated." *Roberts*, supra.

Of course the clutter swept under the rug by limiting the opinion to "determining facts of the offense" is not merely application of today's opinion to § 3E1.1, but its application to all determinations of acceptance of responsibility, repentance, character, and future dangerousness, in both federal and state prosecutions—that is to say, to what is probably the bulk of what most sentencing is all about. If the Court ultimately decides—in the fullness of time and after a decent period of confusion in the lower courts—that the "no inference" rule is indeed limited to "determining facts of the offense," then we will have a system in which a state court can increase the sentence of a convicted drug possessor who refuses to say how many ounces he possessed—not because that suggests he possessed the larger amount (to make such an inference would be unconstitutional!) but because his refusal to cooperate suggests he is unrepentant. Apart from the fact that there is no logical basis for drawing such a line within the sentencing phase (whereas drawing a line between guilt and sentencing is entirely logical), the result produced provides new support for Mr. Bumble's renowned evaluation of the law. Its only sensible feature is that it will almost always be unenforceable, since it will ordinarily be impossible to tell whether the sentencer has used the silence for either purpose or for neither.

If, on the other hand, the Court ultimately decides—in the fullness of time and after a decent period of confusion in the lower courts—that the extension of *Griffin* announced today is not limited to "determining facts of the offense," then it will have created a system in which we give the sentencing judge access to all sorts of out-of-court evidence, including the most remote hearsay, concerning the character of the defendant, his prior misdeeds, his acceptance of responsibility and determination to mend his ways, but declare taboo the most obvious piece of first-hand evidence standing in front of the judge: the defendant's refusal to cooperate with the court. Such a rule orders the judge to avert his eyes from the elephant in the courtroom when it is the judge's job to size up the elephant. * * *

The Court asserts that the rule against adverse inferences from silence, even in sentencing proceedings, "is of proven utility." Significantly, however, the only utility it proceeds to describe—that it is a "vital instrument" for teaching jurors that "the question in a criminal case is not whether the defendant committed the acts of which he is accused," but rather "whether the Government has carried its burden to prove its allegations"—is a utility that has no bearing upon sentencing, or indeed even upon the usual sentencer, which is a judge rather than a jury. * * *

Though the Fifth Amendment protects Mitchell from being compelled to take the stand, and also protects her, as we have held, from adverse inferences drawn from her silence at the guilt phase of the trial, there is no reason why it must also shield her from the natural and appropriate consequences of her uncooperative-ness at the sentencing stage. I respectfully dissent.

JUSTICE THOMAS, dissenting.

JUSTICE SCALIA's dissenting opinion persuasively demonstrates that this Court's decision in *Griffin v. California*, lacks foundation in the Constitution's text, history, or logic. * * * And, in my view, it also illustrates that Griffin and its progeny, including *Carter v. Kentucky*, should be reexamined. * * *

APPRENDI v. NEW JERSEY

530 U.S. 466, 120 S.Ct. 2348, 147 L.Ed.2d 435 (2000).

JUSTICE STEVENS delivered the opinion of the Court.

A New Jersey statute classifies the possession of a firearm for an unlawful purpose as a "second-degree" offense. Such an offense is punishable by imprison-ment for "between five years and 10 years." A separate statute, described by that State's Supreme Court as a "hate crime" law, provides for an "extended term" of imprisonment if the trial judge finds, by a preponderance of the evidence, that "[t]he defendant in committing the crime acted with a purpose to intimidate an individual or group of individuals because of race, color, gender, handicap, religion, sexual orientation or ethnicity." The extended term authorized by the hate crime law for second-degree offenses is imprisonment for "between 10 and 20 years." The question presented is whether the Due Process Clause of the Four-teenth Amendment requires that a factual determination authorizing an increase in the maximum prison sentence for an offense from 10 to 20 years be made by a jury on the basis of proof beyond a reasonable doubt.

At 2:04 a.m. on December 22, 1994, petitioner Charles C. Apprendi, Jr., fired several .22–caliber bullets into the home of an African–American family that had recently moved into a previously all-white neighborhood in Vineland, New Jersey. Apprendi was promptly arrested and, at 3:05 a.m., admitted that he was the shooter. After further questioning, at 6:04 a.m., he made a statement–which he later retracted–that even though he did not know the occupants of the house personally, "because they are black in color he does not want them in the neighborhood." A New Jersey grand jury returned a 23–count indictment charg-ing Apprendi with four first-degree, eight second-degree, six third-degree, and five fourth-degree offenses. The charges alleged shootings on four different dates, as well as the unlawful possession of various weapons. None of the counts referred to the hate crime statute, and none alleged that Apprendi acted with a racially biased purpose. * * * The parties entered into a plea agreement, pursuant to which Apprendi pleaded guilty to two counts (3 and 18) of second-degree possession of a firearm for an unlawful purpose, and one count (22) of the third-degree offense of unlawful possession of an antipersonnel bomb; the prosecutor dismissed the other 20 counts. Under state law, a second-degree offense carries a penalty range of 5 to 10 years, * * * As part of the plea agreement, however, the State reserved the right to request the court to impose a higher "enhanced" sentence on count 18 (which was based on the December 22 shooting) on the ground that that offense was committed with a biased purpose. Apprendi, correspondingly, reserved the right to challenge the hate crime sentence enhancement on the ground that it violates the United States Constitution. * * *

After the trial judge accepted the three guilty pleas, the prosecutor filed a formal motion for an extended term. The trial judge thereafter held an evidentiary hearing on the issue of Apprendi's "purpose" for the shooting on December 22. Apprendi adduced evidence from a psychologist and from seven character witnesses who testified that he did not have a reputation for racial bias. He also took the stand himself, explaining that the incident was an unintended consequence of overindulgence in alcohol, denying that he was in any way biased against African–Americans, and denying that his statement to the police had been accurately described. The judge, however, found the police officer's testimony credible, and concluded that the evidence supported a finding "that the crime was motivated by racial bias." Having found "by a preponderance of the evidence" that Apprendi's actions were taken "with a purpose to intimidate" as provided by the statute, the trial judge held that the hate crime enhancement applied. Rejecting Apprendi's constitutional challenge to the statute, the judge sentenced him to a 12–year term of imprisonment on count 18, and to shorter concurrent sentences on the other two counts.* * *

At stake in this case are constitutional protections of surpassing importance: the proscription of any deprivation of liberty without "due process of law," Amdt. 14, and the guarantee that "[i]n all criminal prosecutions, the accused shall enjoy the right to a speedy and public trial, by an impartial jury," Amdt. 6. Taken together, these rights indisputably entitle a criminal defendant to "a jury determination that [he] is guilty of every element of the crime with which he is charged, beyond a reasonable doubt." *United States v. Gaudin*, 515 U.S. 506, 510 (1995). * * * As we have, unanimously, explained, *Gaudin*, supra, the historical foundation for our recognition of these principles extends down centuries into the common law.* * *

Any possible distinction between an "element" of a felony offense and a "sentencing factor" was unknown to the practice of criminal indictment, trial by jury, and judgment by court as it existed during the years surrounding our Nation's founding. * * * [W]ith respect to the criminal law of felonious conduct, "the English trial judge of the later eighteenth century had very little explicit discretion in sentencing. The substantive criminal law tended to be sanction-specific; it prescribed a particular sentence for each offense. The judge was meant simply to impose that sentence (unless he thought in the circumstances that the sentence was so inappropriate that he should invoke the pardon process to commute it)." * * *This practice at common law held true when indictments were issued pursuant to statute. Just as the circumstances of the crime and the intent of the defendant at the time of commission were often essential elements to be alleged in the indictment, so too were the circumstances mandating a particular punishment. * * * "Where a statute annexes a higher degree of punishment to a common-law felony, if committed under particular circumstances, an indictment for the offence, in order to bring the defendant within that higher degree of punishment, must expressly charge it to have been committed under those circumstances, and must state the circumstances with certainty and precision. [2 M. Hale, Pleas of the Crown *170]." J. Archbold, Pleading and Evidence in Criminal Cases (15th ed. 1862).* * *

We should be clear that nothing in this history suggests that it is impermissible for judges to exercise discretion–taking into consideration various factors relating both to offense and offender–in imposing a judgment within the range prescribed by statute. We have often noted that judges in this country have long exercised discretion of this nature in imposing sentence within statutory limits in the individual case. See, e.g., *Williams v. New York*, 337 U.S. 241, 246 (1949).* * * As [noted] in *Williams*, our periodic recognition of judges' broad discretion in sentencing–since the 19th-century shift in this country from statutes providing fixed-term sentences to those providing judges discretion within a permissible range–has been regularly accompanied by the qualification that that discretion was bound by the range of sentencing options prescribed by the legislature.* * *

The historic link between verdict and judgment and the consistent limitation on judges' discretion to operate within the limits of the legal penalties provided highlight the novelty of a legislative scheme that removes the jury from the determination of a fact that, if found, exposes the criminal defendant to a penalty exceeding the maximum he would receive if punished according to the facts reflected in the jury verdict alone. * * * We do not suggest that trial practices cannot change in the course of centuries and still remain true to the principles that emerged from the Framers' fears "that the jury right could be lost not only by gross denial, but by erosion." But practice must at least adhere to the basic principles undergirding the requirements of trying to a jury all facts necessary to constitute a statutory offense, and proving those facts beyond reasonable doubt. * * * If a defendant faces punishment beyond that provided by statute when an offense is committed under certain circumstances but not others, it is obvious that both the loss of liberty and the stigma attaching to the offense are heightened; it necessarily follows that the defendant should not–at the moment the State is put to proof of those circumstances–be deprived of protections that have, until that point, unquestionably attached.* * *

Since In re *Winship*, 397 U.S. 358 (1970) [due process requires proof of "all facts necessary to constitute a statutory offense * * * beyond a reasonable doubt"], we have made clear beyond peradventure that *Winship's* due process and associated jury protections extend, to some degree, "to determinations that [go] not to a defendant's guilt or innocence, but simply to the length of his sentence." *Almendarez-Torres* v. *United States*, 523 U.S. 224, 251 (1998) (Scalia, J., dissenting).* * * It was in *McMillan v. Pennsylvania*, 477 U.S. 79 (1986), that this Court, for the first time, coined the term "sentencing factor" to refer to a fact that was not found by a jury but that could affect the sentence imposed by the judge. That case involved a challenge to the State's Mandatory Minimum Sentencing Act. According to its provisions, anyone convicted of certain felonies would be subject to a mandatory minimum penalty of five years imprisonment if the judge found, by a preponderance of the evidence, that the person "visibly possessed a firearm" in the course of committing one of the specified felonies. Articulating for the first time, and then applying, a multifactor set of criteria for determining whether the *Winship* protections applied to bar such a system, we concluded that the Pennsylvania statute did not run afoul of our previous admonitions against relieving the State of its burden of proving guilt, or tailoring the mere form of a criminal statute solely to avoid *Winship's* strictures.* * * We did not, however, there budge from the position that (1) constitutional limits exist to States' authority to define away facts necessary to constitute a criminal offense, and (2) that a state scheme that keeps from the jury facts that "expos[e] [defendants] to greater or additional punishment," may raise serious constitutional concern. As we explained: "Section 9712 neither alters the maximum penalty for the crime committed nor creates a separate offense calling for a separate penalty; it operates solely to limit the sentencing court's discretion in selecting a penalty within the range already available to it without the special finding of visible possession of a firearm ... The statute gives no impression of having been tailored to permit the visible possession finding to be a tail which wags the dog of the substantive offense." * * *

Finally, as we made plain in *Jones v. United States*, 526 U.S. 227 (1999), last Term, *Almendarez-Torres v. United States*, 523 U.S. 224 (1998), represents at best an exceptional departure from the historic practice that we have described. In that case, we considered a federal grand jury indictment, which charged the petitioner with "having been" "found in the United States ... after being deported," "in violation of 8 U. S. C. § 1326(a)–an offense carrying a maximum sentence of two years. 523 U.S., at 227. Almendarez–Torres pleaded guilty to the indictment, admitting at the plea hearing that he had been deported, that he had unlawfully reentered this country, and that "the earlier deportation had taken place 'pursuant to' three earlier convictions for aggravated felonies." The Government then filed a presentence report indicating that Almendarez–Torres offense fell within the bounds of § 1326(b) because, as specified in that provision, his original deportation had been subsequent to an aggravated felony conviction; accordingly, Almendarez–Torres could be subject to a sentence of up to 20 years. Almendarez–Torres objected, contending that because the indictment "had not mentioned his earlier aggravated felony convictions," he could be sentenced to no more than two years in prison.* * * Rejecting Almendarez–Torres' objection, we concluded that sentencing him to a term higher than that attached to the offense alleged in the indictment did not violate the strictures of *Winship* in that case. Because Almendarez–Torres had admitted the three earlier convictions for aggravated felonies–all of which had been entered pursuant to proceedings with substantial procedural safeguards of their own–no question concerning the right to a jury trial or the standard of proof that would apply to a contested issue of fact was before the Court. Although our conclusion in that case was based in part on our application of the criteria we had invoked in *McMillan*, the specific question decided concerned the sufficiency of the indictment. More important, as *Jones* made crystal clear, our conclusion in *Almendarez-Torres* turned heavily upon the fact that the additional sentence to which the defendant was subject was "the prior commission of a serious crime." 523 U. S., at 230; see also id., at 243 (explaining that "recidivism ... is a traditional, if not the most traditional, basis for a sentencing court's increasing an offender's sentence"); id., at 244 (emphasizing "the fact that recidivism "does not relate to the commission of the offense ...") * * *. Both the certainty that procedural safeguards attached to any "fact" of prior conviction, and the reality that Almendarez–Torres did not challenge the accuracy of that "fact" in his case, mitigated the due process and Sixth Amendment concerns otherwise implicated in allowing a judge to determine a "fact" increasing punishment beyond the maximum of the statutory range.

Even though it is arguable that *Almendarez-Torres* was incorrectly decided, and that a logical application of our reasoning today should apply if the recidivist issue were contested, Apprendi does not contest the decision's validity and we need not revisit it for purposes of our decision today to treat the case as a narrow exception to the general rule we recalled at the outset. Given its unique facts, it surely does not warrant rejection of the otherwise uniform course of decision during the entire history of our jurisprudence.

In sum, our reexamination of our cases in this area, and of the history upon which they rely, confirms the opinion that we expressed in *Jones*. Other than the fact of a prior conviction, any fact that increases the penalty for a crime beyond the prescribed statutory maximum must be submitted to a jury, and proved beyond a reasonable doubt. With that exception, we endorse the statement of the rule set forth in the concurring opinions in that case: "[I]t is unconstitutional for a legislature to remove from the jury the assessment of facts that increase the prescribed range of penalties to which a criminal defendant is exposed. It is equally clear that such facts must be established by proof beyond a reasonable doubt." 526 U.S., at 252–253 (opinion of Stevens, J.); see also id., at 253 (opinion of Scalia, J.).[16]

16. The principal dissent would reject the   Court's rule as a "meaningless formalism,"

The New Jersey statutory scheme that Apprendi asks us to invalidate allows a jury to convict a defendant of a second-degree offense based on its finding beyond a reasonable doubt that he unlawfully possessed a prohibited weapon; after a subsequent and separate proceeding, it then allows a judge to impose punishment identical to that New Jersey provides for crimes of the first degree, based upon the judge's finding, by a preponderance of the evidence, that the defendant's "purpose" for unlawfully possessing the weapon was "to intimidate" his victim on the basis of a particular characteristic the victim possessed. In light of the constitutional rule explained above, and all of the cases supporting it, this practice cannot stand.* * *[21]

Finally, this Court has previously considered and rejected the argument that the principles guiding our decision today render invalid state capital sentencing schemes requiring judges, after a jury verdict holding a defendant guilty of a capital crime, to find specific aggravating factors before imposing a sentence of death. *Walton v. Arizona*, 497 U.S. 639, 647–649 (1990). For reasons we have explained, the capital cases are not controlling: "Neither the cases cited, nor any other case, permits a judge to determine the existence of a factor which makes a crime a capital offense. What the cited cases hold is that, once a jury has found the defendant guilty of all the elements of an offense which carries as its maximum penalty the sentence of death, it may be left to the judge to decide whether that maximum penalty, rather than a lesser one, ought to be imposed ... The person who is charged with actions that expose him to the death penalty has an absolute entitlement to jury trial on all the elements of the charge." *Almendarez-Torres*, 523 U.S., at 257, n. 2 (Scalia, J., dissenting) (emphasis deleted).* * *

because it can conceive of hypothetical statutes that would comply with the rule and achieve the same result as the New Jersey statute. While a State could, hypothetically, undertake to revise its entire criminal code in the manner the dissent suggests extending all statutory maximum sentences to, for example, 50 years and giving judges guided discretion as to a few specially selected factors within that range–this possibility seems remote. Among other reasons, structural democratic constraints exist to discourage legislatures from enacting penal statutes that expose every defendant convicted of, for example, weapons possession, to a maximum sentence exceeding that which is, in the legislature's judgment, generally proportional to the crime. This is as it should be. Our rule ensures that a State is obliged "to make its choices concerning the substantive content of its criminal laws with full awareness of the consequence, unable to mask substantive policy choices" of exposing all who are convicted to the maximum sentence it provides. *Patterson v. New York*, 432 U.S., at 228–229, n. 13 (Powell, J., dissenting).* * * In all events, if such an extensive revision of the State's entire criminal code were enacted for the purpose the dissent suggests, or if New Jersey simply reversed the burden of the hate crime finding (effectively assuming a crime was performed with a purpose to intimidate and then requiring a defendant to prove that it was not, post), we would be required to question whether the revision was constitutional under this Court's prior decisions. Finally, the principal dissent ignores the distinction the Court has often recognized, see, e.g., *Martin v. Ohio*, 480 U.S. 228 (1987),

between facts in aggravation of punishment and facts in mitigation. If facts found by a jury support a guilty verdict of murder, the judge is authorized by that jury verdict to sentence the defendant to the maximum sentence provided by the murder statute. If the defendant can escape the statutory maximum by showing, for example, that he is a war veteran, then a judge that finds the fact of veteran status is neither exposing the defendant to a deprivation of liberty greater than that authorized by the verdict according to statute, nor is the Judge imposing upon the defendant a greater stigma than that accompanying the jury verdict alone. Core concerns animating the jury and burden-of-proof requirements are thus absent from such a scheme.

21. The principal dissent, in addition, treats us to a lengthy disquisition on the benefits of determinate sentencing schemes, and the effect of today's decision on the federal Sentencing Guidelines. The Guidelines are, of course, not before the Court. We therefore express no view on the subject beyond what this Court has already held. See, e.g., *Edwards v. United States*, 523 U.S. 511, 515, (1998) (opinion of Breyer, J., for a unanimous court) (noting that "of course, petitioners' statutory and constitutional claims would make a difference if it were possible to argue, say, that the sentences imposed exceeded the maximum that the statutes permit for a cocaine-only conspiracy. That is because a maximum sentence set by statute trumps a higher sentence set forth in the Guidelines").

JUSTICE SCALIA, concurring.

I feel the need to say a few words in response to Justice Breyer's dissent. It sketches an admirably fair and efficient scheme of criminal Justice designed for a society that is prepared to leave criminal justice to the State. (Judges, it is sometimes necessary to remind ourselves, are part of the State—and an increasingly bureaucratic part of it, at that.) The founders of the American Republic were not prepared to leave it to the State, which is why the jury-trial guarantee was one of the least controversial provisions of the Bill of Rights. It has never been efficient; but it has always been free.

As for fairness, which Justice Breyer believes "[i]n modern times," the jury cannot provide: I think it not unfair to tell a prospective felon that if he commits his contemplated crime he is exposing himself to a jail sentence of 30 years–and that if, upon conviction, he gets anything less than that he may thank the mercy of a tenderhearted judge (just as he may thank the mercy of a tenderhearted parole commission if he is let out inordinately early, or the mercy of a tenderhearted governor if his sentence is commuted). Will there be disparities? Of course. But the criminal will never get more punishment than he bargained for when he did the crime, and his guilt of the crime (and hence the length of the sentence to which he is exposed) will be determined beyond a reasonable doubt by the unanimous vote of 12 of his fellow citizens.

In Justice Breyer's bureaucratic realm of perfect equity, by contrast, the facts that determine the length of sentence to which the defendant is exposed will be determined to exist (on a more-likely-than-not basis) by a single employee of the State. It is certainly arguable (Justice Breyer argues it) that this sacrifice of prior protections is worth it. But it is not arguable that, just because one thinks it is a better system, it must be, or is even more likely to be, the system envisioned by a Constitution that guarantees trial by jury. What ultimately demolishes the case for the dissenters is that they are unable to say what the right to trial by jury does guarantee if, as they assert, it does not guarantee—what it has been assumed to guarantee throughout our history—the right to have a jury determine those facts that determine the maximum sentence the law allows. They provide no coherent alternative.

Justice Breyer proceeds on the erroneous and all-too-common assumption that the Constitution means what we think it ought to mean. It does not; it means what it says. And the guarantee that "[i]n all criminal prosecutions, the accused shall enjoy the right to ... trial, by an impartial jury" has no intelligible content unless it means that all the facts which must exist in order to subject the defendant to a legally prescribed punishment must be found by the jury.

JUSTICE THOMAS, with whom JUSTICE SCALIA joins as to Parts I and II, concurring.

I join the opinion of the Court in full. I write separately to explain my view that the Constitution requires a broader rule than the Court adopts.

Part I. This case turns on the seemingly simple question of what constitutes a "crime." * * * Several constitutional protections [notice of the accusation, prosecution by indictment, jury trial, and proof beyond a reasonable doubt] turn on determining which facts constitute the "crime"—that is, which facts are the "elements" or "ingredients" of a crime. In order for an accusation of a crime (whether by indictment or some other form) to be proper under the common law, and thus proper under the codification of the common-law rights in the Fifth and Sixth Amendments, it must allege all elements of that crime; likewise, in order for a jury trial of a crime to be proper, all elements of the crime must be proved to the jury (and, under *Winship*, proved beyond a reasonable doubt).

Sentencing enhancements may be new creatures, but the question that they create for courts is not. Courts have long had to consider which facts are elements in order to determine the sufficiency of an accusation (usually an indictment). The answer that courts have provided regarding the accusation tells us what an element is, and it is then a simple matter to apply that answer to whatever constitutional right may be at issue in a case—here, *Winship* and the right to trial by jury. A long line of essentially uniform authority addressing accusations, and stretching from the earliest reported cases after the founding until well into the 20th century, establishes that the original understanding of which facts are elements was even broader than the rule that the Court adopts today.

This authority establishes that a "crime" includes every fact that is by law a basis for imposing or increasing punishment (in contrast with a fact that mitigates punishment). Thus, if the legislature defines some core crime and then provides for increasing the punishment of that crime upon a finding of some aggravating fact—of whatever sort, including the fact of a prior conviction—the core crime and the aggravating fact together constitute an aggravated crime, just as much as grand larceny is an aggravated form of petit larceny. The aggravating fact is an element of the aggravated crime. Similarly, if the legislature, rather than creating grades of crimes, has provided for setting the punishment of a crime based on some fact—such as a fine that is proportional to the value of stolen goods—that fact is also an element. No multi-factor parsing of statutes, of the sort that we have attempted since McMillan, is necessary. One need only look to the kind, degree, or range of punishment to which the prosecution is by law entitled for a given set of facts. Each fact necessary for that entitlement is an element.

Part II. Cases from the founding to roughly the end of the Civil War establish the rule that I have described, applying it to all sorts of facts, including recidivism. As legislatures varied common-law crimes and created new crimes, American courts, particularly from the 1840's on, readily applied to these new laws the common-law understanding that a fact that is by law the basis for imposing or increasing punishment is an element.[2] [Justice Thomas here cites and discussed a series of state cases dealing with the failure to plead elements in indictments.].* * * Further evidence of the rule that a crime includes every fact that is by law a basis for imposing or increasing punishment comes from early cases addressing recidivism statutes. As Justice Scalia has explained, there was a tradition of treating recidivism as an element. See *Almendarez-Torres* 523 U.S., at 256–257, 261 (dissenting opinion). Courts treated the fact of a prior conviction just as any other fact that increased the punishment by law.

An 1872 treatise by one of the leading authorities of the era in criminal law and procedure confirms the common-law understanding that the above cases demonstrate. The treatise condensed the traditional understanding regarding the indictment, and thus regarding the elements of a crime, to the following: "The indictment must allege whatever is in law essential to the punishment sought to be inflicted." 1 J. Bishop, Law of Criminal Procedure 50 (2d ed. 1872)* * * In the half century following publication of Bishop's treatise, numerous courts applied his statement of the common-law understanding; most of them explicitly relied on his treatise. Just as in the earlier period, every fact that was by law a basis for

---

2. It is strange that Justice O'Connor faults me for beginning my analysis with cases primarily from the 1840's, rather from the time of the founding. As the Court explains, and as she concedes, the very idea of a sentenc-ing enhancement was foreign to the common law of the time of the founding. Justice O'Connor therefore, and understandably, does not contend that any history from the founding supports her position.* * *

imposing or increasing punishment (including the fact of a prior conviction) was an element. Each such fact had to be included in the accusation of the crime and proved to the jury. Courts confronted statutes quite similar to the ones with which we have struggled since *McMillan*, and, applying the traditional rule, they found it not at all difficult to determine whether a fact was an element.* * * Courts also, again just as in the pre-Bishop period, applied the same reasoning to the fact of a prior conviction as they did to any other fact that aggravated the punishment by law.

Without belaboring the point any further, I simply note that this traditional understanding–that a "crime" includes every fact that is by law a basis for imposing or increasing punishment–continued well into the 20th century, at least until the middle of the century. In fact, it is fair to say that *McMillan* began a revolution in the law regarding the definition of "crime." Today's decision, far from being a sharp break with the past, marks nothing more than a return to the status quo ante—the status quo that reflected the original meaning of the Fifth and Sixth Amendments.

Part III. The consequence of the above discussion for our decisions in *Almendarez-Torres* and *McMillan* should be plain enough, but a few points merit special mention.* * * First, it is irrelevant to the question of which facts are elements that legislatures have allowed sentencing judges discretion in determining punishment (often within extremely broad ranges). * * * Second, and related, one of the chief errors of *Almendarez-Torres*–an error to which I succumbed–was to attempt to discern whether a particular fact is traditionally (or typically) a basis for a sentencing court to increase an offender's sentence. For the reasons I have given, it should be clear that this approach just defines away the real issue. What matters is the way by which a fact enters into the sentence. If a fact is by law the basis for imposing or increasing punishment–for establishing or increasing the prosecution's entitlement–it is an element. One reason frequently offered for treating recidivism differently, a reason on which we relied in *Almendarez-Torres*, is a concern for prejudicing the jury by informing it of the prior conviction. But this concern, of which earlier courts were well aware, does not make the traditional understanding of what an element is any less applicable to the fact of a prior conviction.

Third, I think it clear that the common-law rule would cover the *McMillan* situation of a mandatory minimum sentence (in that case, for visible possession of a firearm during the commission of certain crimes). No doubt a defendant could, under such a scheme, find himself sentenced to the same term to which he could have been sentenced absent the mandatory minimum. The range for his underlying crime could be 0 to 10 years, with the mandatory minimum of 5 years, and he could be sentenced to 7. (Of course, a similar scenario is possible with an increased maximum.) But it is equally true that his expected punishment has increased as a result of the narrowed range and that the prosecution is empowered, by invoking the mandatory minimum, to require the judge to impose a higher punishment than he might wish.* * *

Finally, I need not in this case address the implications of the rule that I have stated for the Court's decision in *Walton v. Arizona*, 497 U.S. 639, 647–649 (1990). Walton did approve a scheme by which a judge, rather than a jury, determines an aggravating fact that makes a convict eligible for the death penalty, and thus eligible for a greater punishment. In this sense, that fact is an element. But that scheme exists in a unique context, for in the area of capital punishment, unlike any other area, we have imposed special constraints on a legislature's ability to determine what facts shall lead to what punishment–we have restricted the legislature's ability to define crimes. Under our recent capital-punishment juris-prudence, neither Arizona nor any other jurisdiction could provide–as, previously, it freely could and did–that a person shall be death eligible automatically upon conviction for certain crimes. We have interposed a barrier between a jury finding of a capital crime and a court's ability to impose capital punishment. Whether this distinction between capital crimes and all others, or some other distinction, is sufficient to put the former outside the rule that I have stated is a question for another day.[11]

* * *

JUSTICE O'CONNOR, with whom THE CHIEF JUSTICE, JUSTICE KENNEDY, and JUSTICE BREYER join, dissenting.

* * *Our Court has long recognized that not every fact that bears on a defendant's punishment need be charged in an indictment, submitted to a jury, and proved by the government beyond a reasonable doubt. Rather, we have held that the "legislature's definition of the elements of the offense is usually disposi-tive." *McMillan v. Pennsylvania*, 477 U.S. 79, 85 (1986).* * * Although we have recognized that "there are obviously constitutional limits beyond which the States may not go in this regard," and that "in certain limited circumstances *Winship's* reasonable-doubt requirement applies to facts not formally identified as elements of the offense charged," we have proceeded with caution before deciding that a certain fact must be treated as an offense element despite the legislature's choice not to characterize it as such. We have therefore declined to establish any bright-line rule for making such judgments and have instead approached each case individually, sifting through the considerations most relevant to determining whether the legislature has acted properly within its broad power to define crimes and their punishments or instead has sought to evade the constitutional require-ments associated with the characterization of a fact as an offense element.

In one bold stroke the Court today casts aside our traditional cautious approach and instead embraces a universal and seemingly bright-line rule limiting the power of Congress and state legislatures to define criminal offenses and the sentences that follow from convictions thereunder. The Court states: "Other than the fact of a prior conviction, any fact that increases the penalty for a crime beyond the prescribed statutory maximum must be submitted to a jury, and proved beyond a reasonable doubt." In its opinion, the Court marshals virtually no authority to support its extraordinary rule. Indeed, it is remarkable that the Court cannot identify a single instance, in the over 200 years since the ratification of the Bill of Rights, that our Court has applied, as a constitutional requirement, the rule it announces today.

According to the Court, its constitutional rule "emerges from our history and case law." None of the history contained in the Court's opinion requires the rule it ultimately adopts. The history cited by the Court can be divided into two categories: first, evidence that judges at common law had virtually no discretion in sentencing, and, second, statements from a 19th-century criminal procedure treatise that the government must charge in an indictment and prove at trial the elements of a statutory offense for the defendant to be sentenced to the punish-ment attached to that statutory offense.* * *

In his concurring opinion, Justice Thomas cites additional historical evidence that, in his view, dictates an even broader rule than that set forth in the Court's

11. It is likewise unnecessary to consider whether (and, if so, how) the rule regarding elements applies to the Sentencing Guidelines, given the unique status that they have under *Mistretta v. United States*, 488 U.S. 361 (1989). But it may be that this special status is irrele-vant, because the Guidelines "have the force and effect of laws." Id., (Scalia, J., dissenting).

opinion. The history cited by Justice Thomas does not require, as a matter of federal constitutional law, the application of the rule he advocates. To understand why, it is important to focus on the basis for Justice Thomas' argument. First, he claims that the Fifth and Sixth Amendments "codified" pre-existing common law. Second, he contends that the relevant common law treated any fact that served to increase a defendant's punishment as an element of an offense. Even if Justice Thomas' first assertion were correct–a proposition this Court has not before embraced–he fails to gather the evidence necessary to support his second assertion.* * * Rather, Justice Thomas divines the common-law understanding of the Fifth and Sixth Amendment rights by consulting decisions rendered by American courts well after the ratification of the Bill of Rights, ranging primarily from the 1840's to the 1890's. Whatever those decisions might reveal about the way American state courts resolved questions regarding the distinction between a crime and its punishment under general rules of criminal pleading or their own state constitutions, the decisions fail to demonstrate any settled understanding with respect to the definition of a crime under the relevant, preexisting common law.* * *

In contrast to Justice Thomas, the Court asserts that its rule is supported by "our cases in this area." That the Court begins its review of our precedent with a quotation from a dissenting opinion speaks volumes about the support that actually can be drawn from our cases for the "increase in the maximum penalty" rule announced today. See ante, (quoting *Almedarez-Torres*, 523 U.S., at 251 (Scalia, J., dissenting)).* * * The Court's reliance on *McMillan* is also puzzling, given that our holding in that case points to the rejection of the Court's rule.* * * Whether *Almendarez-Torres* directly refuted the "increase in the maximum penalty" rule was extensively debated in *Jones*, and that debate need not be repeated here. I continue to agree with Justice Kennedy that *Almendarez-Torres* constituted a clear repudiation of the rule the Court adopts today.* * * Of all the decisions that refute the Court's "increase in the maximum penalty" rule, perhaps none is as important as *Walton v. Arizona*, 497 U.S. 639 (1990). * * * Under Arizona law, the fact that a statutory aggravating circumstance exists in the defendant's case "increases the maximum penalty for [the] crime" of first-degree murder to death. If the judge does not find the existence of a statutory aggravating circumstance, the maximum punishment authorized by the jury's guilty verdict is life imprisonment. Thus, using the terminology that the Court itself employs to describe the constitutional fault in the New Jersey sentencing scheme presented here, under Arizona law, the judge's finding that a statutory aggravating circumstance exists "exposes the criminal defendant to a penalty exceeding the maximum he would receive if punished according to the facts reflected in the jury verdict alone." Even Justice Thomas, whose vote is necessary to the Court's opinion today, agrees on this point. If a State can remove from the jury a factual determination that makes the difference between life and death, as *Walton* holds that it can, it is inconceivable why a State cannot do the same with respect to a factual determination that results in only a 10–year increase in the maximum sentence to which a defendant is exposed.* * *

That the Court's rule is unsupported by the history and case law it cites is reason enough to reject such a substantial departure from our settled jurisprudence. Significantly, the Court also fails to explain adequately why the Due Process Clauses of the Fifth and Fourteenth Amendments and the jury trial guarantee of the Sixth Amendment require application of its rule. Upon closer examination, it is possible that the Court's "increase in the maximum penalty" rule rests on a meaningless formalism that accords, at best, marginal protection for the constitutional rights that it seeks to effectuate.* * *

For example, under one reading, the Court appears to hold that the Constitution requires that a fact be submitted to a jury and proved beyond a reasonable doubt only if that fact, as a formal matter, extends the range of punishment beyond the prescribed statutory maximum. A State could, however, remove from the jury (and subject to a standard of proof below "beyond a reasonable doubt") the assessment of those facts that define narrower ranges of punishment, within the overall statutory range, to which the defendant may be sentenced. Thus, apparently New Jersey could cure its sentencing scheme, and achieve virtually the same results, by drafting its weapons possession statute in the following manner: First, New Jersey could prescribe, in the weapons possession statute itself, a range of 5 to 20 years imprisonment for one who commits that criminal offense. Second, New Jersey could provide that only those defendants convicted under the statute who are found by a judge, by a preponderance of the evidence, to have acted with a purpose to intimidate an individual on the basis of race may receive a sentence greater than 10 years imprisonment.* * * The Court's proffered distinction of *Walton v. Arizona* suggests that it means to announce a rule of only this limited effect.* * *

Under another reading of the Court's decision, it may mean only that the Constitution requires that a fact be submitted to a jury and proved beyond a reasonable doubt if it, as a formal matter, increases the range of punishment beyond that which could legally be imposed absent that fact. A State could, however, remove from the jury (and subject to a standard of proof below "beyond a reasonable doubt") the assessment of those facts that, as a formal matter, decrease the range of punishment below that which could legally be imposed absent that fact. Thus, consistent with our decision in *Patterson v. New York*, 432 U.S. 197 (1977), New Jersey could cure its sentencing scheme, and achieve virtually the same results, by drafting its weapons possession statute in the following manner: First, New Jersey could prescribe, in the weapons possession statute itself, a range of 5 to 20 years imprisonment for one who commits that criminal offense. Second, New Jersey could provide that a defendant convicted under the statute whom a judge finds, by a preponderance of the evidence, not to have acted with a purpose to intimidate an individual on the basis of race may receive a sentence no greater than 10 years imprisonment.* * *

Given the pure formalism of the above readings of the Court's opinion, one suspects that the constitutional principle underlying its decision is more far reaching. The actual principle underlying the Court's decision may be that any fact (other than prior conviction) that has the effect, in real terms, of increasing the maximum punishment beyond an otherwise applicable range must be submitted to a jury and proved beyond a reasonable doubt.* * * The principle thus would apply not only to schemes like New Jersey's, under which a factual determination exposes the defendant to a sentence beyond the prescribed statutory maximum, but also to all determinate-sentencing schemes in which the length of a defendant's sentence within the statutory range turns on specific factual determinations (e.g., the federal Sentencing Guidelines). Justice Thomas essentially concedes that the rule outlined in his concurring opinion would require the invalidation of the Sentencing Guidelines. See n. 11 [of his opinion].* * *

Prior to the most recent wave of sentencing reform, the Federal Government and the States employed indeterminate-sentencing schemes in which judges and executive branch officials (e.g., parole board officials) had substantial discretion to determine the actual length of a defendant's sentence. Studies of indeterminate-sentencing schemes found that similarly situated defendants often received widely disparate sentences. Although indeterminate sentencing was intended to soften the harsh and uniform sentences formerly imposed under mandatory-sentencing systems, some studies revealed that indeterminate sentencing actually had the opposite effect.* * * In response, Congress and the state legislatures shifted to determinate-sentencing schemes that aimed to limit judges' sentencing discretion and, thereby, afford similarly situated offenders equivalent treatment. The most well known of these reforms was the federal Sentencing Reform Act of 1984, 18 U. S. C. § 3551 et seq. In the Act, Congress created the United States Sentencing Commission, which in turn promulgated the Sentencing Guidelines that now govern sentencing by federal judges.* * * Whether one believes the determinate-sentencing reforms have proved successful or not–and the subject is one of extensive debate among commentators–the apparent effect of the Court's opinion today is to halt the current debate on sentencing reform in its tracks and to invalidate with the stroke of a pen three decades' worth of nationwide reform, all in the name of a principle with a questionable constitutional pedigree. Indeed, it is ironic that the Court, in the name of constitutional rights meant to protect criminal defendants from the potentially arbitrary exercise of power by prosecutors and judges, appears to rest its decision on a principle that would render unconstitutional efforts by Congress and the state legislatures to place constraints on that very power in the sentencing context.

Finally, perhaps the most significant impact of the Court's decision will be a practical one–its unsettling effect on sentencing conducted under current federal and state determinate-sentencing schemes. As I have explained, the Court does not say whether these schemes are constitutional, but its reasoning strongly suggests that they are not. Thus, with respect to past sentences handed down by judges under determinate-sentencing schemes, the Court's decision threatens to unleash a flood of petitions by convicted defendants seeking to invalidate their sentences in whole or in part on the authority of the Court's decision today. Statistics compiled by the United States Sentencing Commission reveal that almost a half-million cases have been sentenced under the Sentencing Guidelines since 1989. * * * Because many States, like New Jersey, have determinate-sentencing schemes, the number of individual sentences drawn into question by the Court's decision could be colossal.

The decision will likely have an even more damaging effect on sentencing conducted in the immediate future under current determinate-sentencing schemes. Because the Court fails to clarify the precise contours of the constitutional principle underlying its decision, federal and state judges are left in a state of limbo.* * * The most unfortunate aspect of today's decision is that our precedents did not foreordain this disruption in the world of sentencing. Rather, our cases traditionally took a cautious approach to questions like the one presented in this case. The Court throws that caution to the wind and, in the process, threatens to cast sentencing in the United States into what will likely prove to be a lengthy period of considerable confusion.* * *

Because I do not believe that the Court's "increase in the maximum penalty" rule is required by the Constitution, I would evaluate New Jersey's sentence-enhancement statute by analyzing the factors we have examined in past cases. * * * See, e.g., *Almendarez-Torres*; *McMillan*. First, the New Jersey statute does not shift the burden of proof on an essential ingredient of the offense by presuming that ingredient upon proof of other elements of the offense.* * * Second, the magnitude of the New Jersey sentence enhancement, as applied in petitioner's case, is constitutionally permissible. Under New Jersey law, the weapons possession offense to which petitioner pleaded guilty carries a sentence range of 5 to 10 years imprisonment. The fact that petitioner, in committing that offense, acted with a purpose to intimidate because of race exposed him to a higher sentence range of 10 to 20 years imprisonment. The 10–year increase in the maximum penalty to which petitioner was exposed falls well within the range we have found permissible. See *Almendarez-Torres*, (approving 18–year enhancement). Third, the New Jersey statute gives no impression of having been enacted to evade the constitutional requirements that attach when a State makes a fact an element of the charged offense. For example, New Jersey did not take what had previously been an element of the weapons possession offense and transform it into a sentencing factor. See *McMillan*.* * *

JUSTICE BREYER, with whom CHIEF JUSTICE REHNQUIST joins, dissenting.

The majority holds that the Constitution contains the following requirement: "any fact [other than recidivism] that increases the penalty for a crime beyond the prescribed statutory maximum must be submitted to a jury, and proved beyond a reasonable doubt." This rule would seem to promote a procedural ideal–that of juries, not judges, determining the existence of those facts upon which increased punishment turns. But the real world of criminal justice cannot hope to meet any such ideal. It can function only with the help of procedural compromises, particularly in respect to sentencing. And those compromises, which are themselves necessary for the fair functioning of the criminal justice system, preclude implementation of the procedural model that today's decision reflects. At the very least, the impractical nature of the requirement that the majority now recognizes supports the proposition that the Constitution was not intended to embody it.

* * *[I]t is important for present purposes to understand why judges, rather than juries, traditionally have determined the presence or absence of such sentence-affecting facts in any given case. And it is important to realize that the reason is not a theoretical one, but a practical one. It does not reflect (Justice Scalia's opinion to the contrary notwithstanding) an ideal of procedural "fairness," (concurring opinion), but rather an administrative need for procedural compromise. There are, to put it simply, far too many potentially relevant sentencing factors to permit submission of all (or even many) of them to a jury. As the Sentencing Guidelines state the matter,

"[a] bank robber with (or without) a gun, which the robber kept hidden (or brandished), might have frightened (or merely warned), injured seriously (or less seriously), tied up (or simply pushed) a guard, a teller or a customer, at night (or at noon), for a bad (or arguably less bad) motive, in an effort to obtain money for other crimes (or for other purposes), in the company of a few (or many) other robbers, for the first (or fourth) time that day, while sober (or under the influence of drugs or alcohol), and so forth." Sentencing Guidelines, Part A, at 1.2.

The Guidelines note that "a sentencing system tailored to fit every conceivable wrinkle of each case can become unworkable and seriously compromise the certainty of punishment and its deterrent effect." To ask a jury to consider all, or many, such matters would do the same. At the same time, to require jury consideration of all such factors–say, during trial where the issue is guilt or innocence–could easily place the defendant in the awkward (and conceivably unfair) position of having to deny he committed the crime yet offer proof about how he committed it, e.g., "I did not sell drugs, but I sold no more than 500 grams." And while special postverdict sentencing juries could cure this problem, they have seemed (but for capital cases) not worth their administrative costs. Hence, before the Guidelines, federal sentencing judges typically would obtain relevant factual sentencing information from probation officers' presentence reports, while permitting a convicted offender to challenge the information's accuracy at a hearing before the judge without benefit of trial-type evidentiary rules. * * *

Finally, it is important to understand how a legislature decides which factual circumstances among all those potentially related to generally harmful behavior it should transform into elements of a statutorily defined crime (where they would become relevant to the guilt or innocence of an accused), and which factual circumstances it should leave to the sentencing process (where, as sentencing factors, they would help to determine the sentence imposed upon one who has been found guilty). Again, theory does not provide an answer. Legislatures, in defining crimes in terms of elements, have looked for guidance to common-law tradition, to history, and to current social need. And, traditionally, the Court has left legislatures considerable freedom to make the element determination.

By placing today's constitutional question in a broader context, this brief survey may help to clarify the nature of today's decision. It also may explain why, in respect to sentencing systems, proportionality, uniformity, and administrability are all aspects of that basic "fairness" that the Constitution demands. And it suggests my basic problem with the Court's rule: A sentencing system in which judges have discretion to find sentencing-related factors is a workable system and one that has long been thought consistent with the Constitution; why, then, would the Constitution treat sentencing statutes any differently?* * *

Legislatures have tended to address the problem of too much judicial sentencing discretion in two ways. First, legislatures sometimes have created sentencing commissions armed with delegated authority to make more uniform judicial exercise of that discretion.* * * Second, legislatures sometimes have directly limited the use (by judges or by a commission) of particular factors in sentencing, either by specifying statutorily how a particular factor will affect the sentence imposed or by specifying how a commission should use a particular factor when writing a guideline. Such a statute might state explicitly, for example, that a particular factor, say, use of a weapon, recidivism, injury to a victim, or bad motive, "shall" increase, or "may" increase, a particular sentence in a particular way.

The issue the Court decides today involves this second kind of legislation. The Court holds that a legislature cannot enact such legislation (where an increase in the maximum is involved) unless the factor at issue has been charged, tried to a jury, and found to exist beyond a reasonable doubt. My question in respect to this holding is, simply, "why would the Constitution contain such a requirement"? * * *The majority raises no objection to traditional pre-Guidelines sentencing procedures under which judges, not juries, made the factual findings that would lead to an increase in an individual offender's sentence. How does a legislative determination differ in any significant way? * * * With the possible exception of the last line of Justice Scalia's concurring opinion, the majority also makes no constitutional objection to a legislative delegation to a commission of the authority to create guidelines that determine how a judge is to exercise sentencing discretion. See also n.11. (Thomas, J., concurring) (reserving the question). But if the Constitution permits Guidelines, why does it not permit Congress similarly to guide the exercise of a judge's sentencing discretion? That is, if the Constitution permits a delegatee (the commission) to exercise sentencing-related rulemaking power, how can it deny the delegator (the legislature) what is, in effect, the same rulemaking power?

The majority appears to offer two responses. First, it argues for a limiting principle that would prevent a legislature with broad authority from transforming (jury-determined) facts that constitute elements of a crime into (judge-determined) sentencing factors, thereby removing procedural protections that the Constitution would otherwise require.* * * The majority's cure, however, is not aimed at the disease.* * * The same "transformational" problem exists under traditional sentencing law, where legislation, silent as to sentencing factors, grants the judge virtually unchecked discretion to sentence within a broad range. Under such a system, judges or prosecutors can similarly "transform" crimes, punishing an offender convicted of one crime as if he had committed another. A prosecutor, for example, might charge an offender with five counts of embezzlement (each subject to a 10–year maximum penalty), while asking the judge to impose maximum and consecutive sentences because the embezzler murdered his employer. And, as part of the traditional sentencing discretion that the majority concedes judges retain, the judge, not a jury, would determine the last-mentioned relevant fact, i.e., that the murder actually occurred.

This egregious example shows the problem's complexity. The source of the problem lies not in a legislature's power to enact sentencing factors, but in the traditional legislative power to select elements defining a crime, the traditional legislative power to set broad sentencing ranges, and the traditional judicial power to choose a sentence within that range on the basis of relevant offender conduct. Conversely, the solution to the problem lies, not in prohibiting legislatures from enacting sentencing factors, but in sentencing rules that determine punishments on the basis of properly defined relevant conduct, with sensitivity to the need for procedural protections where sentencing factors are determined by a judge (for example, use of a "reasonable doubt" standard), and invocation of the Due Process Clause where the history of the crime at issue, together with the nature of the facts to be proved, reveals unusual and serious procedural unfairness. Cf. *McMillan*, (upholding statute in part because it "gives no impression of having been tailored to permit the [sentencing factor] to be a tail which wags the dog of the substantive offense").

Second, the majority, in support of its constitutional rule, emphasizes the concept of a statutory "maximum." The Court points out that a sentencing judge (or a commission) traditionally has determined, and now still determines, sentences within a legislated range capped by a maximum (a range that the legislature itself sets). I concede the truth of the majority's statement, but I do not understand its relevance.* * * From a defendant's perspective, the legislature's decision to cap the possible range of punishment at a statutorily prescribed "maximum" would affect the actual sentence imposed no differently than a sentencing commission's (or a sentencing judge's) similar determination. Indeed, as a practical matter, a legislated mandatory "minimum" is far more important to an actual defendant. A judge and a commission, after all, are legally free to select any sentence below a statute's maximum, but they are not free to subvert a statutory minimum. And, as Justice Thomas indicates, all the considerations of fairness that might support submission to a jury of a factual matter that increases a statutory maximum, apply a fortiori to any matter that would increase a statutory minimum. To repeat, I do not understand why, when a legislature authorizes a judge to impose a higher penalty for bank robbery (based, say, on the court's finding that a victim was injured or the defendant's motive was bad), a new crime is born; but where a legislature requires a judge to impose a higher penalty than he otherwise would (within a pre-existing statutory range) based on similar criteria, it is not.

I certainly do not believe that the present sentencing system is one of "perfect equity," (Scalia J., concurring), and I am willing, consequently, to assume that the majority's rule would provide a degree of increased procedural protection in respect to those particular sentencing factors currently embodied in statutes. I nonetheless believe that any such increased protection provides little practical help and comes at too high a price.* * *

McCLESKEY v. KEMP

481 U.S. 279, 107 S.Ct. 1756, 95 L.Ed.2d 262 (1987).

JUSTICE POWELL delivered the opinion of the Court.

This case presents the question whether a complex statistical study that indicates a risk that racial considerations enter into capital sentencing determinations proves that petitioner McCleskey's capital sentence is unconstitutional under the Eighth or Fourteenth Amendment.

McCleskey, a black man, was convicted of two counts of armed robbery and one count of murder in the Superior Court of Fulton County, Georgia, on October 12, 1978. McCleskey's convictions arose out of the robbery of a furniture store and the killing of a white police officer during the course of the robbery. The evidence at trial indicated that McCleskey and three accomplices planned and carried out the robbery. * * * During the course of the robbery, a police officer, answering a silent alarm, entered the store through the front door. As he was walking down the center aisle of the store, two shots were fired. Both struck the officer. One hit him in the face and killed him. * * * At trial, the State introduced evidence that at least one of the bullets that struck the officer was fired from a .38 caliber Rossi revolver. This description matched the description of the gun that McCleskey had carried during the robbery. The State also introduced the testimony of two witnesses who had heard McCleskey admit to the shooting.

The jury convicted McCleskey of murder. At the penalty hearing, the jury heard arguments as to the appropriate sentence. Under Georgia law, the jury could not consider imposing the death penalty unless it found beyond a reasonable doubt that the murder was accompanied by one of the statutory aggravating circumstances. The jury in this case found two aggravating circumstances to exist beyond a reasonable doubt: the murder was committed during the course of an armed robbery, and the murder was committed upon a peace officer engaged in the performance of his duties, * * * The jury recommended that he be sentenced to death on the murder charge and to consecutive life sentences on the armed robbery charges. The court followed the jury's recommendation and sentenced McCleskey to death.

On appeal, the Supreme Court of Georgia affirmed the convictions and the sentences. This Court denied a petition for a writ of certiorari. The Superior Court of Fulton County denied McCleskey's extraordinary motion for a new trial. McCleskey then filed a petition for a writ of habeas corpus in the Superior Court of Butts County. After holding an evidentiary hearing, the Superior Court denied relief. The Supreme Court of Georgia denied McCleskey's application for a certificate of probable cause to appeal * * * and this Court again denied certiorari.

McCleskey next filed a petition for a writ of habeas corpus in the federal District Court for the Northern District of Georgia. His petition raised 18 claims, one of which was that the Georgia capital sentencing process is administered in a racially discriminatory manner in violation of the Eighth and Fourteenth Amendments to the United States Constitution. In support of his claim, McCleskey proffered a statistical study performed by Professors David C. Baldus, George Woodworth, and Charles Pulaski (the Baldus study) that purports to show a disparity in the imposition of the death sentence in Georgia based on the race of the murder victim and, to a lesser extent, the race of the defendant. The Baldus study is actually two sophisticated statistical studies that examine over 2,000 murder cases that occurred in Georgia during the 1970s. The raw numbers collected by Professor Baldus indicate that defendants charged with killing white persons received the death penalty in 11% of the cases, but defendants charged with killing blacks received the death penalty in only 1% of the cases. The raw numbers also indicate a reverse racial disparity according to the race of the defendant: 4% of the black defendants received the death penalty, as opposed to 7% of the white defendants.

Baldus also divided the cases according to the combination of the race of the defendant and the race of the victim. He found that the death penalty was assessed in 22% of the cases involving black defendants and white victims; 8% of the cases involving white defendants and white victims; 1% of the cases involving black defendants and black victims; and 3% of the cases involving white defendants and black victims. Similarly, Baldus found that prosecutors sought the death penalty in 70% of the cases involving black defendants and white victims; 32% of the cases involving white defendants and white victims; 15% of the cases involving black defendants and black victims; and 19% of the cases involving white defendants and black victims.

Baldus subjected his data to an extensive analysis, taking account of 230 variables that could have explained the disparities on nonracial grounds. One of his models concludes that, even after taking account of 39 nonracial variables, defendants charged with killing white victims were 4.3 times as likely to receive a death sentence as defendants charged with killing blacks. According to this model, black defendants were 1.1 times as likely to receive a death sentence as other defendants. Thus, the Baldus study indicates that black defendants, such as McCleskey, who kill white victims have the greatest likelihood of receiving the death penalty.

The District Court held an extensive evidentiary hearing on McCleskey's petition. * * * [That] court found that the methodology of the Baldus study was flawed in several respects.[6] * * * It dismissed the petition. The Court of Appeals for the Eleventh Circuit, sitting en banc, * * * assumed the validity of the study itself and addressed the merits of McCleskey's Eighth and Fourteenth Amendment claims. That is, the court assumed that the study "showed that systematic and substantial disparities existed in the penalties imposed upon homicide defendants in Georgia based on race of the homicide victim, that the disparities existed at a less substantial rate in death sentencing based on race of defendants, and

6. Baldus, among other experts, testified at the evidentiary hearing. The District Court "was impressed with the learning of all of the experts." Nevertheless, the District Court noted that in many respects the data were incomplete. In its view, the questionnaires used to obtain the data failed to capture the full degree of the aggravating or mitigating circumstances. The Court criticized the researcher's decisions regarding unknown variables. The researchers could not discover whether penalty trials were held in many of the cases, thus undercutting the value of the study's statistics as to prosecutorial decisions. In certain cases, the study lacked information on the race of the victim in cases involving multiple victims, on whether or not the prosecutor offered a plea bargain, and on credibility problems with witnesses. The court concluded that McCleskey had failed to establish by a preponderance of the evidence that the data was trustworthy. * * *

The District Court noted other problems with Baldus' methodology. First, the researchers assumed that all of the information available from the questionnaires was available to the juries and prosecutors when the case was tried. The court found this assumption "questionable." Second, the court noted the instability of the various models. Even with the 230-variable model, consideration of 20 further variables caused a significant drop in the statistical significance of race. In the court's view, this undermined the persuasiveness of the model that showed the greatest racial disparity, the 39-variable model. Third, the court found that the high correlation between race and many of the nonracial variables diminished the weight to which the study was entitled. * * * Finally, the District Court noted the inability of any of the models to predict the outcome of actual cases.

that the factors of race of the victim and defendant were at work in Fulton County." Even assuming the study's validity, the Court of Appeals found the statistics "insufficient to demonstrate discriminatory intent or unconstitutional discrimination in the Fourteenth Amendment context, [and] insufficient to show irrationality, arbitrariness and capriciousness under any kind of Eighth Amendment analysis." * * *

McCleskey's first claim is that the Georgia capital punishment statute violates the Equal Protection Clause of the Fourteenth Amendment.[7] He argues that race has infected the administration of Georgia's statute in two ways: persons who murder whites are more likely to be sentenced to death than persons who murder blacks, and black murderers are more likely to be sentenced to death than white murderers.[8] As a black defendant who killed a white victim, McCleskey claims that the Baldus study demonstrates that he was discriminated against because of his race and because of the race of his victim. In its broadest form, McCleskey's claim of discrimination extends to every actor in the Georgia capital sentencing process, from the prosecutor who sought the death penalty and the jury that imposed the sentence, to the State itself that enacted the capital punishment statute and allows it to remain in effect despite its allegedly discriminatory application. We agree with the Court of Appeals, and every other court that has considered such a challenge, that this claim must fail.

* * * [T]o prevail under the Equal Protection Clause, McCleskey must prove that the decisionmakers in *his* case acted with discriminatory purpose. He offers no evidence specific to his own case that would support an inference that racial considerations played a part in his sentence. Instead, he relies solely on the Baldus study. McCleskey argues that the Baldus study compels an inference that his sentence rests on purposeful discrimination. McCleskey's claim that these statistics are sufficient proof of discrimination, without regard to the facts of a particular case, would extend to all capital cases in Georgia, at least where the victim was white and the defendant is black.

The Court has accepted statistics as proof of intent to discriminate in certain limited contexts. First, this Court has accepted statistical disparities as proof of an equal protection violation in the selection of the jury venire in a particular district. * * * Second, this Court has accepted statistics in the form of multiple regression analysis to prove statutory violations under Title VII [employment discrimination].

But the nature of the capital sentencing decision, and the relationship of the statistics to that decision, are fundamentally different from the corresponding

---

7. Although the District Court rejected the findings of the Baldus study as flawed, the Court of Appeals assumed that the study is valid and reached the constitutional issues. Accordingly, those issues are before us. As did the Court of Appeals, we assume the study is valid statistically without reviewing the factual findings of the District Court. * * *

8. Although McCleskey has standing to claim that he suffers discrimination because of his own race, the State argues that he has no standing to contend that he was discriminated against on the basis of his victim's race. While it is true that we are reluctant to recognize "standing to assert the rights of third persons," this does not appear to be the nature of McCleskey's claim. He does not seek to assert some right of his victim, or the rights of black

murder victims in general. Rather, McCleskey argues that application of the State's statute has created a classification that is "an irrational exercise of governmental power," because it is not "necessary to the accomplishment of some permissible state objective." *Loving v. Virginia*, 388 U.S. 1 (1967). See *McGowan v. Maryland*, 366 U.S. 420 (1961) (statutory classification cannot be "wholly irrelevant to the achievement of the State's objective"). It would violate the Equal Protection Clause for a State to base enforcement of its criminal laws on "an unjustifiable standard such as race, religion, or other arbitrary classification." *Oyler v. Boles*, 368 U.S. 448 (1962). Because McCleskey raises such a claim, he has standing.

elements in the venire-selection or Title VII cases. Most importantly, each particular decision to impose the death penalty is made by a petit jury selected from a properly constituted venire. Each jury is unique in its composition, and the Constitution requires that its decision rest on consideration of innumerable factors that vary according to the characteristics of the individual defendant and the facts of the particular capital offense. Thus, the application of an inference drawn from the general statistics to a specific decision in a trial and sentencing simply is not comparable to the application of an inference drawn from general statistics to a specific venire-selection or Title VII case. In those cases, the statistics relate to fewer entities,[14] and fewer variables are relevant to the challenged decisions.[15]

Another important difference between the cases in which we have accepted statistics as proof of discriminatory intent and this case is that, in the venire-selection and Title VII contexts, the decisionmaker has an opportunity to explain the statistical disparity. Here, the State has no practical opportunity to rebut the Baldus study. "[C]ontrolling considerations of * * * public policy," dictate that jurors "cannot be called * * * to testify to the motives and influences that led to their verdict." Similarly, the policy considerations behind a prosecutor's traditionally "wide discretion" suggest the impropriety of our requiring prosecutors to defend their decisions to seek death penalties, "often years after they were made."[17] Moreover, absent far stronger proof, it is unnecessary to seek such a rebuttal, because a legitimate and unchallenged explanation for the decision is apparent from the record: McCleskey committed an act for which the United States Constitution and Georgia laws permit imposition of the death penalty.

Finally, McCleskey's statistical proffer must be viewed in the context of his challenge. McCleskey challenges decisions at the heart of the State's criminal justice system. "[O]ne of society's most basic tasks is that of protecting the lives of its citizens and one of the most basic ways in which it achieves the task is

---

14. We refer here not to the number of entities involved in any particular decision, but to the number of entities whose decisions necessarily are reflected in a statistical display such as the Baldus study. The decisions of a jury commission or of an employer over time are fairly attributable to the commission or the employer. Therefore, an unexplained statistical discrepancy can be said to indicate a consistent policy of the decisionmaker. The Baldus study seeks to deduce a state "policy" by studying the combined effects of the decisions of hundreds of juries that are unique in their composition. It is incomparably more difficult to deduce a consistent policy by studying the decisions of these many unique entities. It is also questionable whether any consistent policy can be derived by studying the decisions of prosecutors. The District Attorney is elected by the voters in a particular county. Since decisions whether to prosecute and what to charge necessarily are individualized and involve infinite factual variations, coordination among DA offices across a State would be relatively meaningless. Thus, any inference from state-wide statistics to a prosecutorial "policy" is of doubtful relevance. Moreover, the statistics in Fulton County alone represent the disposition of far fewer cases than the state-wide statistics. Even assuming the sta-

tistical validity of the Baldus study as a whole, the weight to be given the results gleaned from this small sample is limited.

15. In venire-selection cases, the factors that may be considered [i.e., the qualifications for jury service] are limited, usually by state statute. * * * These considerations are uniform for all potential jurors, and although some factors may be said to be subjective, they are limited and, to a great degree, objectively verifiable. While employment decisions may involve a number of relevant variables, these variables are to a great extent uniform for all employees because they must all have a reasonable relationship to the employee's qualifications to perform the particular job at issue. Identifiable qualifications for a single job provide a common standard by which to assess each employee. In contrast, a capital sentencing jury may consider *any* factor relevant to the defendant's background, character, and the offense. There is no common standard by which to evaluate all defendants who have or have not received the death penalty.

17. Requiring a prosecutor to rebut a study that analyzes the past conduct of scores of prosecutors is quite different from requiring a prosecutor to rebut a contemporaneous challenge to his own acts. See *Batson v. Kentucky* [Ch. 15, § 2].

through criminal laws against murder." Implementation of these laws necessarily requires discretionary judgments. Because discretion is essential to the criminal justice process, we would demand exceptionally clear proof before we would infer that the discretion has been abused. The unique nature of the decisions at issue in this case also counsel against adopting such an inference from the disparities indicated by the Baldus study. Accordingly, we hold that the Baldus study is clearly insufficient to support an inference that any of the decisionmakers in McCleskey's case acted with discriminatory purpose.

McCleskey also suggests that the Baldus study proves that the State as a whole has acted with a discriminatory purpose. He appears to argue that the State has violated the Equal Protection Clause by adopting the capital punishment statute and allowing it to remain in force despite its allegedly discriminatory application. * * * For this claim to prevail, McCleskey would have to prove that the Georgia Legislature enacted or maintained the death penalty statute *because of* an anticipated racially discriminatory effect. In *Gregg v. Georgia,* 428 U.S. 153 (1976), this Court found that the Georgia capital sentencing system could operate in a fair and neutral manner. There was no evidence then, and there is none now, that the Georgia Legislature enacted the capital punishment statute to further a racially discriminatory purpose.[20]

Nor has McCleskey demonstrated that the legislature maintains the capital punishment statute because of the racially disproportionate impact suggested by the Baldus study. As legislatures necessarily have wide discretion in the choice of criminal laws and penalties, and as there were legitimate reasons for the Georgia Legislature to adopt and maintain capital punishment, see *Gregg v. Georgia,* we will not infer a discriminatory purpose on the part of the State of Georgia. Accordingly, we reject McCleskey's equal protection claims.

McCleskey also argues that the Baldus study demonstrates that the Georgia capital sentencing system violates the Eighth Amendment. We begin our analysis of this claim by reviewing the restrictions on death sentences established by our prior decisions under that Amendment. [The Court here described a series of earlier decisions, starting with *Furman v. Georgia,* 408 U.S. 238 (1972). *Furman* held unconstitutional a death penalty statute which prescribed no standards for the imposition of the penalty, simply leaving the choice of that penalty to the unfettered discretion of the jury. In so ruling, the Court in *Furman* had "concluded that the death penalty was so irrationally imposed that any particular death sentence could be presumed excessive." In *Gregg v. Georgia,* 428 U.S. 153 (1976), the Court rejected the contention that the death penalty violated the Eighth Amendment "under all circumstances" and upheld the current Georgia statute, enacted after *Furman,* as having "met the concerns articulated in *Furman.*" That statute bifurcated guilt and sentencing proceedings, narrowed the class of murders subject to the death penalty to "cases in which the jury finds at least one statutory aggravating circumstance beyond a reasonable doubt," allowed the defense to introduce "any relevant mitigating evidence," required a "particularized inquiry into the circumstances of the offense together with the character and propensities of the offender," and provided for appellate review of the death sentence by the Georgia Supreme Court. Decisions after *Gregg* "im-

20. McCleskey relies on "historical evidence" to support his claim of purposeful discrimination by the State. This evidence focuses on Georgia laws in force during and just after the Civil War. Of course, the "historical background of the decision is one evidentiary source" for proof of intentional discrimination. *Arlington Heights v. Metropolitan Housing Dev. Corp.,* 429 U.S. 252 (1977). But unless historical evidence is reasonably contemporaneous with the challenged decision, it has little probative value. * * * Although the history of racial discrimination in this country is undeniable, we cannot accept official actions taken long ago as evidence of current intent.

posed a number of requirements on the capital sentencing process to ensure that capital sentencing decisions rest on the individualized inquiry contemplated in *Gregg.*"] * * *

In sum, our decisions since *Furman* have identified a constitutionally permissible range of discretion in imposing the death penalty. First, there is a required threshold below which the death penalty cannot be imposed. In this context, the State must establish rational criteria that narrow the decisionmaker's judgment as to whether the circumstances of a particular defendant's case meet the threshold. * * * Second, States cannot limit the sentencer's consideration of any relevant circumstance that could cause it to decline to impose the penalty. In this respect, the State cannot channel the sentencer's discretion, but must allow it to consider any relevant information offered by the defendant.

In light of our precedents under the Eighth Amendment, McCleskey cannot argue successfully that his sentence is "disproportionate to the crime in the traditional sense." See *Pulley v. Harris,* 465 U.S. 37 (1984). He does not deny that he committed a murder in the course of a planned robbery, a crime for which this Court has determined that the death penalty constitutionally may be imposed. *Gregg v. Georgia.* His disproportionality claim "is of a different sort." McCleskey argues that the sentence in his case is disproportionate to the sentences in other murder cases.

On the one hand, he cannot base a constitutional claim on an argument that his case differs from other cases in which defendants *did* receive the death penalty. On automatic appeal, the Georgia Supreme Court found that McCleskey's death sentence was not disproportionate to other death sentences imposed in the State. * * * Moreover, where the statutory procedures adequately channel the sentencer's discretion, such proportionality review is not constitutionally required. *Pulley v. Harris.*

On the other hand, absent a showing that the Georgia capital punishment system operates in an arbitrary and capricious manner, McCleskey cannot prove a constitutional violation by demonstrating that other defendants who may be similarly situated did *not* receive the death penalty. In *Gregg,* the Court * * * [rejected] the argument that "the opportunities for discretionary action that are inherent in the processing of any murder case under Georgia law," specifically the opportunities for discretionary leniency, rendered the capital sentences imposed arbitrary and capricious. * * *

Although our decision in *Gregg* as to the facial validity of the Georgia capital punishment statute appears to foreclose McCleskey's disproportionality argument, he further contends that the Georgia capital punishment system is arbitrary and capricious in *application,* and therefore his sentence is excessive, because racial considerations may influence capital sentencing decisions in Georgia. We now address this claim.

To evaluate McCleskey's challenge, we must examine exactly what the Baldus study may show. Even Professor Baldus does not contend that his statistics *prove* that race enters into any capital sentencing decisions or that race was a factor in McCleskey's particular case. Statistics at most may show only a likelihood that a particular factor entered into some decisions. There is, of course, some risk of racial prejudice influencing a jury's decision in a criminal case. There are similar risks that other kinds of prejudice will influence other criminal trials. The question "is at what point that risk becomes constitutionally unacceptable," *Turner v. Murray* [Ch. 15, § 2]. McCleskey asks us to accept the likelihood allegedly shown by the Baldus study as the constitutional measure of an unacceptable risk of racial prejudice influencing capital sentencing decisions. This we decline to do.

Because of the risk that the factor of race may enter the criminal justice process, we have engaged in "unceasing efforts" to eradicate racial prejudice from our criminal justice system. *Batson v. Kentucky* [Ch. 15, § 2]. Our efforts have been guided by our recognition that "the inestimable privilege of trial by jury * * * is a vital principle, underlying the whole administration of criminal justice," *Ex parte Milligan*, 4 Wall. 2 (1866). Thus, it is the jury that is a criminal defendant's fundamental "protection of life and liberty against race or color prejudice." Specifically, a capital sentencing jury representative of a criminal defendant's community assures a " 'diffused impartiality,' " in the jury's task of "express[ing] the conscience of the community on the ultimate question of life or death."

Individual jurors bring to their deliberations "qualities of human nature and varieties of human experience, the range of which is unknown and perhaps unknowable." The capital sentencing decision requires the individual jurors to focus their collective judgment on the unique characteristics of a particular criminal defendant. It is not surprising that such collective judgments often are difficult to explain. But the inherent lack of predictability of jury decisions does not justify their condemnation. On the contrary, it is the jury's function to make the difficult and uniquely human judgments that defy codification and that "buil[d] discretion, equity, and flexibility into a legal system."

McCleskey's argument that the Constitution condemns the discretion allowed decisionmakers in the Georgia capital sentencing system is antithetical to the fundamental role of discretion in our criminal justice system. Discretion in the criminal justice system offers substantial benefits to the criminal defendant. Not only can a jury decline to impose the death sentence, it can decline to convict, or choose to convict of a lesser offense. Whereas decisions against a defendant's interest may be reversed by the trial judge or on appeal, these discretionary exercises of leniency are final and unreviewable. Similarly, the capacity of prosecutorial discretion to provide individualized justice is "firmly entrenched in American law." As we have noted, a prosecutor can decline to charge, offer a plea bargain, or decline to seek a death sentence in any particular case. Of course, "the power to be lenient [also] is the power to discriminate," but a capital-punishment system that did not allow for discretionary acts of leniency "would be totally alien to our notions of criminal justice." *Gregg v. Georgia.*

At most, the Baldus study indicates a discrepancy that appears to correlate with race. Apparent disparities in sentencing are an inevitable part of our criminal justice system. The discrepancy indicated by the Baldus study is "a far cry from the major systemic defects identified in *Furman*," *Pulley v. Harris.* As this Court has recognized, any mode for determining guilt or punishment "has its weaknesses and the potential for misuse." Specifically, "there can be 'no perfect procedure for deciding in which cases governmental authority should be used to impose death.' " Despite these imperfections, our consistent rule has been that constitutional guarantees are met when "the mode [for determining guilt or punishment] itself has been surrounded with safeguards to make it as fair as possible." *Singer v. United States*, 380 U.S. 24 (1965). Where the discretion that is fundamental to our criminal process is involved, we decline to assume that what is unexplained is invidious. In light of the safeguards designed to minimize racial bias in the process, the fundamental value of jury trial in our criminal justice system, and the benefits that discretion provides to criminal defendants, we hold that the Baldus study does not demonstrate a constitutionally significant risk of racial bias affecting the Georgia capital-sentencing process.[37]

Two additional concerns inform our decision in this case. First, McCleskey's claim, taken to its logical conclusion, throws into serious question the principles that underlie our entire criminal justice system. The Eighth Amendment is not limited in application to capital punishment, but applies to all penalties. Thus, if we accepted McCleskey's claim that racial bias has impermissibly tainted the capital sentencing decision, we could soon be faced with similar claims as to other types of penalty.[38] Moreover, the claim that his sentence rests on the irrelevant factor of race easily could be extended to apply to claims based on unexplained discrepancies that correlate to membership in other minority groups,[39] and even to gender. Similarly, since McCleskey's claim relates to the race of his victim, other claims could apply with equally logical force to statistical disparities that correlate with the race or sex of other actors in the criminal justice system, such as defense attorneys, or judges. Also, there is no logical reason that such a claim need be limited to racial or sexual bias. If arbitrary and capricious punishment is the touchstone under the Eighth Amendment, such a claim could—at least in theory—be based upon any arbitrary variable, such as the defendant's facial characteristics, or the physical attractiveness of the defendant or the victim, that some statistical study indicates may be influential in jury decisionmaking. As these examples illustrate, there is no limiting principle to the type of challenge brought by McCleskey.[45] The Constitution does not require that a State eliminate any

37. Justice Brennan's eloquent dissent of course reflects his often repeated opposition to the death sentence. His views, that also are shared by Justice Marshall, are principled and entitled to respect. Nevertheless, since *Gregg* was decided in 1976, seven members of this Court consistently have upheld sentences of death under *Gregg*-type statutes providing for meticulous review of each sentence in both state and federal courts. The ultimate thrust of Justice Brennan's dissent is that *Gregg* and its progeny should be overruled. He does not, however, expressly call for the overruling of any prior decision. Rather, relying on the Baldus study, Justice Brennan, * * * questions the very heart of our criminal justice system: the traditional discretion that prosecutors and juries necessarily must have.

We have held that discretion in a capital punishment system is necessary to satisfy the Constitution. Yet, the dissent now claims that the "discretion afforded prosecutors and jurors in the Georgia capital sentencing system" violates the Constitution by creating "opportunities for racial considerations to influence criminal proceedings." The dissent contends that in Georgia "[n]o guidelines govern prosecutorial decisions * * *." Prosecutorial decisions necessarily involve both judgmental and factual decisions that vary from case to case. Thus, it is difficult to imagine guidelines that would produce the predictability sought by the dissent without sacrificing the discretion essential to a humane and fair system of criminal justice. Indeed, the dissent suggests no such guidelines for prosecutorial discretion. * * *

The dissent repeatedly emphasizes the need for "a uniquely high degree of rationality in imposing the death penalty." Again, no sug-

gestion is made as to how greater "rationality" could be achieved under any type of statute that authorizes capital punishment. * * * Given the * * * safeguards already inherent in the imposition and review of capital sentences, the dissent's call for greater rationality is no less than a claim that a capital-punishment system cannot be administered in accord with the Constitution. As we reiterate, the requirement of heightened rationality in the imposition of capital punishment does not "plac[e] totally unrealistic conditions on its use." *Gregg*.

38. Studies already exist that allegedly demonstrate a racial disparity in the length of prison sentences. * * *

39. In *Regents of the University of California v. Bakke*, 438 U.S. 265, 295 (1978) (opinion of Powell, J.), we recognized that the national "majority" "is composed of various minority groups, most of which can lay claim to a history of prior discrimination at the hands of the State and private individuals." * * *

45. Justice Stevens, who would not overrule *Gregg*, suggests in his dissent that the infirmities alleged by McCleskey could be remedied by narrowing the class of death-eligible defendants to categories identified by the Baldus study where "prosecutors consistently seek, and juries consistently impose, the death penalty without regard to the race of the victim or the race of the offender." This proposed solution is unconvincing. First, "consistently" is a relative term, and narrowing the category of death-eligible defendants would simply shift the borderline between those defendants who received the death penalty and demonstrable disparity that correlates with a potentially irrelevant factor in order to operate a criminal justice system that includes capital punishment. As we have stated specifically in the context of capital punishment, the Constitution does not "plac[e] totally unrealistic conditions on its use." *Gregg v. Georgia.*

Second, McCleskey's arguments are best presented to the legislative bodies. It is not the responsibility—or indeed even the right—of this Court to determine the appropriate punishment for particular crimes. It is the legislatures, the elected representatives of the people, that are "constituted to respond to the will and consequently the moral values of the people." *Furman v. Georgia* (Burger, C.J., dissenting). Legislatures also are better qualified to weigh and "evaluate the results of statistical studies in terms of their own local conditions and with a flexibility of approach that is not available to the courts," *Gregg v. Georgia.* Capital punishment is now the law in more than two thirds of our States. It is the ultimate duty of courts to determine on a case-by-case basis whether these laws are applied consistently with the Constitution. Despite McCleskey's wide ranging arguments that basically challenge the validity of capital punishment in our multi-racial society, the only question before us is whether in his case, the law of Georgia was properly applied. We agree with the District Court and the Court of Appeals for the Eleventh Circuit that this was carefully and correctly done in this case.

Justice Brennan, with whom Justice Marshall joins, and with whom Justice Blackmun and Justice Stevens join in all but Part I, dissenting.

I. Adhering to my view that the death penalty is in all circumstances cruel and unusual punishment forbidden by the Eighth and Fourteenth Amendments, I would vacate the decision below insofar as it left undisturbed the death sentence imposed in this case. * * * Even if I did not hold this position, however, I would reverse [for] petitioner McCleskey has clearly demonstrated that his death sentence was imposed in violation of the Eighth and Fourteenth Amendments. While I join [the parts] of Justice Blackmun's dissenting opinion discussing petitioner's Fourteenth Amendment claim, I write separately to emphasize how conclusively McCleskey has also demonstrated precisely the type of risk of irrationality in sentencing that we have consistently condemned in our Eighth Amendment jurisprudence.

II. At some point in this case, Warren McCleskey doubtless asked his lawyer whether a jury was likely to sentence him to die. A candid reply to this question would have been disturbing. First, counsel would have to tell McCleskey that few

those who did not. A borderline area would continue to exist and vary in its boundaries. Moreover, because the discrepancy between borderline cases would be difficult to explain, the system would likely remain open to challenge on the basis that the lack of explanation rendered the sentencing decisions unconstitutionally arbitrary.

Second, even assuming that a category with theoretically consistent results could be identified, it is difficult to imagine how Justice Stevens' proposal would or could operate on a case-by-case basis. Whenever a victim is white and the defendant is a member of a different race, what steps would a prosecutor be required to take—in addition to weighing the customary prosecutorial considerations—before concluding in the particular case that he lawfully could prosecute? In the absence of a current, Baldus-type study focused particularly on the community in which the crime was committed, where would he find a standard? Would the prosecutor have to review the prior decisions of community prosecutors and determine the types of cases in which juries in his jurisdiction "consistently" had imposed the death penalty when the victim was white and the defendant was of a different race? And must he rely solely on statistics? Even if such a study were feasible, would it be unlawful for the prosecutor, in making his final decision in a particular case, to consider the evidence of guilt and the presence of aggravating and mitigating factors? However conscientiously a prosecutor might attempt to identify death-eligible defendants under the dissent's suggestion, it would be a wholly speculative task at best, likely to result in less rather than more fairness and consistency in the imposition of the death penalty.

of the details of the crime or of McCleskey's past criminal conduct were more important than the fact that his victim was white. Furthermore, counsel would feel bound to tell McCleskey that defendants charged with killing white victims in Georgia are 4.3 times as likely to be sentenced to death as defendants charged with killing blacks. In addition, frankness would compel the disclosure that it was more likely than not that the race of McCleskey's victim would determine whether he received a death sentence: 6 of every 11 defendants convicted of killing a white person would not have received the death penalty if their victims had been black, while, among defendants with aggravating and mitigating factors comparable to McCleskey, 20 of every 34 would not have been sentenced to die if their victims had been black. Finally, the assessment would not be complete without the information that cases involving black defendants and white victims are more likely to result in a death sentence than cases featuring any other racial combination of defendant and victim. The story could be told in a variety of ways, but McCleskey could not fail to grasp its essential narrative line: there was a significant chance that race would play a prominent role in determining if he lived or died.

The Court today holds that Warren McCleskey's sentence was constitutionally imposed. It finds no fault in a system in which lawyers must tell their clients that race casts a large shadow on the capital sentencing process. * * *

III. It is important to emphasize at the outset that the Court's observation that McCleskey cannot prove the influence of race on any particular sentencing decision is irrelevant in evaluating his Eighth Amendment claim. Since *Furman,* the Court has been concerned with the *risk* of the imposition of an arbitrary sentence, rather than the proven fact of one. * * * This emphasis on risk acknowledges the difficulty of divining the jury's motivation in an individual case. In addition, it reflects the fact that concern for arbitrariness focuses on the rationality of the system as a whole, and that a system that features a significant probability that sentencing decisions are influenced by impermissible considerations cannot be regarded as rational.[1] * * *

The statistical evidence in this case * * * relentlessly documents the risk that McCleskey's sentence was influenced by racial considerations. This evidence shows that there is a better than even chance in Georgia that race will influence the decision to impose the death penalty: a majority of defendants in white-victim crimes would not have been sentenced to die if their victims had been black. In determining whether this risk is acceptable, our judgment must be shaped by the awareness that "[t]he risk of racial prejudice infecting a capital sentencing proceeding is especially serious in light of the complete finality of the death sentence" [and] that "[i]t is of vital importance to the defendant and to the community that any decision to impose the death sentence be, and appear to be, based on reason rather than caprice or emotion." In determining the guilt of a defendant, a state must prove its case beyond a reasonable doubt. That is, we refuse to convict if the chance of error is simply less likely than not. Surely, we should not be willing to take a person's life if the chance that his death sentence was irrationally imposed is *more* likely than not. In light of the gravity of the interest at stake, petitioner's statistics on their face are a powerful demonstration

---

1. Once we can identify a pattern of arbitrary sentencing outcomes, we can say that a defendant runs a risk of being sentenced arbitrarily. It is thus immaterial whether the operation of an impermissible influence such as race is intentional. While the Equal Protection Clause forbids racial discrimination, and intent may be critical in a successful claim under that provision, the Eighth Amendment has its own distinct focus: whether punishment comports with social standards of rationality and decency. * * *

of the type of risk that our Eighth Amendment jurisprudence has consistently condemned.

Evaluation of McCleskey's evidence cannot rest solely on the numbers themselves. We must also ask whether the conclusion suggested by those numbers is consonant with our understanding of history and human experience. Georgia's legacy of a race-conscious criminal justice system, as well as this Court's own recognition of the persistent danger that racial attitudes may affect criminal proceedings, indicate that McCleskey's claim is not a fanciful product of mere statistical artifice. * * *

[The dissent here noted that Georgia, at the time of the Civil War, had a "dual system" of criminal justice (distinguishing between crimes "committed by and against blacks and whites"). It noted further that Gunnar Myrdal's study of race relations in the United States (published in 1944) "mirrored McCleskey's evidence," that "the specter of race discrimination was acknowledged by the Court in striking down the Georgia death penalty statute in *Furman*," and that the Court in *Coker v. Georgia*, 433 U.S. 584 (1977), striking down the death penalty for rape, although "it did not explicitly mention race," had before it evidence "that black men who committed rape, particularly of white women, were considerably more likely to be sentenced to death."] * * * This historical review of Georgia criminal law is not intended as a bill of indictment calling the State to account for past transgressions. Citation of past practices does not justify the automatic condemnation of current ones. But it would be unrealistic to ignore the influence of history in assessing the plausible implications of McCleskey's evidence. * * *

* * * Our cases reflect a realization of the myriad of opportunities for racial considerations to influence criminal proceedings: in the exercise of peremptory challenges; in the selection of the grand jury; in the selection of the petit jury; in the exercise of prosecutorial discretion; in the conduct of argument; and in the conscious or unconscious bias of jurors. The discretion afforded prosecutors and jurors in the Georgia capital-sentencing system creates such opportunities. No guidelines govern prosecutorial decisions to seek the death penalty, and Georgia provides juries with no list of aggravating and mitigating factors, nor any standard for balancing them against one another. Once a jury identifies one aggravating factor, it has complete discretion in choosing life or death, and need not articulate its basis for selecting life imprisonment. The Georgia sentencing system therefore provides considerable opportunity for racial considerations, however subtle and unconscious, to influence charging and sentencing decisions.

IV. The Court cites four reasons for shrinking from the implications of McCleskey's evidence: the desirability of discretion for actors in the criminal-justice system, the existence of statutory safeguards against abuse of that discretion, the potential consequences for broader challenges to criminal sentencing, and an understanding of the contours of the judicial role. While these concerns underscore the need for sober deliberation, they do not justify rejecting evidence as convincing as McCleskey has presented.

The Court maintains that petitioner's claim "is antithetical to the fundamental role of discretion in our criminal justice system." It states that "[w]here the discretion that is fundamental to our criminal process is involved, we decline to assume that what is unexplained is invidious." Reliance on race in imposing capital punishment, however, is antithetical to the very rationale for granting sentencing discretion. Discretion is a means, not an end. * * *

The Court also declines to find McCleskey's evidence sufficient in view of "the safeguards designed to minimize racial bias in the [capital sentencing] process."

* * * It is clear that *Gregg* bestowed no permanent approval on the Georgia system. It simply held that the State's statutory safeguards were assumed sufficient to channel discretion without evidence otherwise. * * *

The Court next states that its unwillingness to regard the petitioner's evidence as sufficient is based in part on the fear that recognition of McCleskey's claim would open the door to widespread challenges to all aspects of criminal sentencing. Taken on its face, such a statement seems to suggest a fear of too much justice. Yet surely the majority would acknowledge that if striking evidence indicated that other minority groups, or women, or even persons with blond hair, were disproportionately sentenced to death, such a state of affairs would be repugnant to deeply rooted conceptions of fairness. The prospect that there may be more widespread abuse than McCleskey documents may be dismaying, but it does not justify complete abdication of our judicial role. * * *

In fairness, the Court's fear that McCleskey's claim is an invitation to descend a slippery slope also rests on the realization that any humanly imposed system of penalties will exhibit some imperfection. Yet to reject McCleskey's powerful evidence on this basis is to ignore both the qualitatively different character of the death penalty and the particular repugnance of racial discrimination, considerations which may properly be taken into account in determining whether various punishments are "cruel and unusual." Furthermore, it fails to take account of the unprecedented refinement and strength of the Baldus study. * * *

The Court also maintains that accepting McCleskey's claim would pose a threat to all sentencing because of the prospect that a correlation might be demonstrated between sentencing outcomes and other personal characteristics. Again, such a view is indifferent to the considerations that enter into a determination of whether punishment is "cruel and unusual." Race is a consideration whose influence is expressly constitutionally proscribed. We have expressed a moral commitment, as embodied in our fundamental law, that this specific characteristic should not be the basis for allotting burdens and benefits. * * *

Certainly, a factor that we would regard as morally irrelevant, such as hair color, at least theoretically could be associated with sentencing results to such an extent that we would regard as arbitrary a system in which that factor played a significant role. [However,] the evaluation of evidence suggesting such a correlation must be informed not merely by statistics, but by history and experience. One could hardly contend that this nation has on the basis of hair color inflicted upon persons deprivation comparable to that imposed on the basis of race. Recognition of this fact would necessarily influence the evaluation of data suggesting the influence of hair color on sentencing, and would require evidence of statistical correlation even more powerful than that presented by the Baldus study. * * *

Finally, the Court justifies its rejection of McCleskey's claim by cautioning against usurpation of the legislatures' role in devising and monitoring criminal punishment. The Court is, of course, correct to emphasize the gravity of constitutional intervention and the importance that it be sparingly employed. The fact that "[c]apital punishment is now the law in more than two thirds of our States," however, does not diminish the fact that capital punishment is the most awesome act that a State can perform. The judiciary's role in this society counts for little if the use of governmental power to extinguish life does not elicit close scrutiny. [The Court] fulfills, rather than disrupts, the scheme of separation of powers by closely scrutinizing the imposition of the death penalty, for no decision of a society is more deserving of the "sober second thought." * * *

The Court's decision today will not change what attorneys in Georgia tell other Warren McCleskeys about their chances of execution. Nothing will soften the harsh message they must convey, nor alter the prospect that race undoubtedly will continue to be a topic of discussion. McCleskey's evidence will not have obtained judicial acceptance, but that will not affect what is said on death row. However many criticisms of today's decision may be rendered, these painful conversations will serve as the most eloquent dissents of all.

JUSTICE BLACKMUN, with whom JUSTICE MARSHALL and JUSTICE STEVENS join and with whom JUSTICE BRENNAN joins in all but Part IV–B,[a] dissenting. * * *

In analyzing an equal protection claim, a court must first determine the nature of the claim and the responsibilities of the state actors involved to determine what showing is required for the establishment of a prima facie case. The Court correctly points out: "In its broadest form, McCleskey's claim of discrimination extends to every actor in the Georgia capital sentencing process, from the prosecutor who sought the death penalty and the jury that imposed the sentence, to the State itself that enacted the capital punishment statute and allows it to remain in effect despite its allegedly discriminatory application." Having recognized the complexity of McCleskey's claim, however, the Court proceeds to ignore a significant element of that claim. The Court treats the case as if it is limited to challenges to the actions of two specific decisionmaking bodies—the petit jury and the state legislature. This self-imposed restriction enables the Court to distinguish this case from the venire-selection cases and Title VII cases in which it long has accepted statistical evidence and has provided an easily applicable framework for review.

Considering McCleskey's claim in its entirety, however, reveals that the claim fits easily within that same framework. A significant aspect of his claim is that racial factors impermissibly affected numerous steps in the Georgia capital-sentencing scheme between his indictment and the jury's vote to sentence him to death. The primary decisionmaker at each of the intervening steps of the process is the prosecutor, the quintessential state actor in a criminal proceeding. * * * [M]y analysis in this dissenting opinion * * * concentrate[s] on the decisions within the prosecutor's office through which the State decided to seek the death penalty and, in particular, the point at which the State proceeded to the penalty phase after conviction. This is a step at which the evidence of the effect of the racial factors was especially strong, but is ignored by the Court.

A criminal defendant alleging an equal protection violation must prove the existence of purposeful discrimination. He may establish a prima facie case of purposeful discrimination "by showing that the totality of the relevant facts gives rise to an inference of discriminatory purpose." *Batson v. Kentucky* [Ch. 15, § 2]. Once the defendant establishes a prima facie case, the burden shifts to the prosecution to rebut that case. * * *

Under *Batson v. Kentucky* and the framework established in [the jury selection cases], McCleskey must meet a three-factor standard. First, he must establish that he is a member of a group "that is a recognizable, distinct class, singled out for different treatment." Second, he must make a showing of a substantial degree of differential treatment. Third, he must establish that the allegedly discriminatory procedure is susceptible to abuse or is not racially neutral.

There can be no dispute that McCleskey has made the requisite showing under the first prong of the standard. The Baldus study demonstrates that black persons are a distinct group that are singled out for different treatment in the

---

a. The reference here is to the last para-   graph of Justice Blackmun's dissent.

Georgia capital-sentencing system. The Court acknowledges, as it must, that the raw statistics included in the Baldus study and presented by petitioner indicate that it is much less likely that a death sentence will result from a murder of a black person than from a murder of a white person. * * * The raw figures also indicate that even within the group of defendants who are convicted of killing white persons and are thereby more likely to receive a death sentence, black defendants are more likely than white defendants to be sentenced to death.

With respect to the second prong, McCleskey must prove that there is a substantial likelihood that his death sentence is due to racial factors. * * * McCleskey demonstrated the degree to which his death sentence was affected by racial factors by introducing multiple-regression analyses that explain how much of the statistical distribution of the cases analyzed is attributable to the racial factors. * * * McCleskey produced evidence concerning the role of racial factors at the various steps in the decisionmaking process, focusing on the prosecutor's decision as to which cases merit the death sentence. McCleskey established that the race of the victim is an especially significant factor at the point where the defendant has been convicted of murder and the prosecutor must choose whether to proceed to the penalty phase of the trial and create the possibility that a death sentence may be imposed or to accept the imposition of a sentence of life imprisonment. McCleskey demonstrated this effect at both the statewide level, and in Fulton County where he was tried and sentenced. The statewide statistics indicated that black defendant/white victim cases advanced to the penalty trial at nearly five times the rate of the black defendant/black victim cases (70% vs. 15%), and over three times the rate of white defendant/black victim cases (70% vs. 19%). The multiple-regression analysis demonstrated that racial factors had a readily identifiable effect at a statistically significant level. The Fulton County statistics were consistent with this evidence although they involved fewer cases.

Individualized evidence relating to the disposition of the Fulton County cases that were most comparable to McCleskey's case was consistent with the evidence of the race-of-victim effect as well. Of the 17 defendants, including McCleskey, who were arrested and charged with homicide of a police officer in Fulton County during the 1973–1979 period, McCleskey, alone, was sentenced to death. The only other defendant whose case even proceeded to the penalty phase received a sentence of life imprisonment. That defendant had been convicted of killing a black police officer.

As to the final element of the prima facie case, McCleskey showed that the process by which the State decided to seek a death penalty in his case and to pursue that sentence throughout the prosecution was susceptible to abuse. Petitioner submitted the deposition of Lewis R. Slaton, who, as of the date of the deposition, had been the District Attorney for 18 years in the county in which McCleskey was tried and sentenced. As Mr. Slaton explained, the duties and responsibilities of that office are the prosecution of felony charges within the Atlanta Judicial Circuit that comprises Fulton County. He testified that during his years in the office, there were no guidelines informing the Assistant District Attorneys who handle the cases how they should proceed at any particular stage of the prosecution. There were no guidelines as to when they should seek an indictment for murder as opposed to lesser charges, when they should recommend acceptance of a guilty plea to murder, acceptance of a guilty plea to a lesser charge, reduction of charges, or dismissal of charges at the postindictment-preconviction stage, or when they should seek the death penalty. Slaton testified that these decisions were left to the discretion of the individual attorneys who then informed Slaton of their decisions as they saw fit.

Slaton's deposition proves that, at every stage of a prosecution, the Assistant District Attorney exercised much discretion. The only guidance given was "on-the-job training." * * * The sole effort to provide any consistency was Slaton's periodic pulling of files at random to check on the progress of cases. Slaton explained that as far as he knew, he was the only one aware of this checking. The files contained information only as to the evidence in the case, not any indication as to why an attorney made a particular decision. The attorneys were not required to record why they sought an indictment for murder as opposed to a lesser charge, or why they recommended a certain plea. The attorneys were not required to report to Slaton the cases in which they decided not to seek the death penalty, or the cases in which they did seek the death penalty * * *.

The above-described evidence, considered in conjunction with the other record evidence outlined by Justice Brennan, and discussed in opinions dissenting from the judgment of the Court of Appeals, gives rise to an inference of discriminatory purpose. * * * McCleskey's showing is of sufficient magnitude that, absent evidence to the contrary, one must conclude that racial factors entered into the decisionmaking process that yielded McCleskey's death sentence. The burden, therefore, shifts to the State to explain the racial selections. It must demonstrate that legitimate racially neutral criteria and procedures yielded this racially skewed result. * * *

The Court's explanations for its failure to apply this well-established equal protection analysis to this case are not persuasive. It first reasons that "each particular decision to impose the death penalty is made by a petit jury" and that the "application of an inference drawn from the general statistics to a specific decision in a trial and sentencing simply is not comparable to the application of an inference drawn from general statistics to a specific venire-selection or Title VII case." According to the Court, the statistical evidence is less relevant because, in the two latter situations, there are fewer variables relevant to the decision and the "statistics relate to fewer entities."

I disagree with the Court's assertion that there are fewer variables relevant to the decisions of jury commissioners or prosecutors in their selection of jurors, or to the decisions of employers in their selection, promotion, or discharge of employees. Such decisions involve a multitude of factors, some rational, some irrational. Second, I disagree with the comment that the venire-selection and employment decisions are "made by fewer entities." Certainly in the employment context, personnel decisions are often the product of several levels of decisionmaking within the business or government structure. The Court's statement that the decision to impose death is made by the petit jury also disregards the fact that the prosecutor screens the cases throughout the pretrial proceedings and decides to seek the death penalty and to pursue a capital case to the penalty phase where a death sentence can be imposed. McCleskey's claim in this regard lends itself to analysis under the framework we apply in assessing challenges to other prosecutorial actions. See *Batson v. Kentucky,* see also *Wayte v. United States* [Ch. 10, § 1].

The Court's other reason for treating this case differently from venire-selection and employment cases is that in these latter contexts, "the decisionmaker has an opportunity to explain the statistical disparity," but in the instant case the State had no practical opportunity to rebut the Baldus study. According to the Court, this is because jurors cannot be called to testify about their verdict and because policy considerations render it improper to require "prosecutors to defend their decisions to seek death penalties, 'often years after they were made.'"

I agree with the Court's observation as to the difficulty of examining the jury's decisionmaking process. * * * The Court's refusal to require that the prosecutor provide an explanation for his actions, however, is completely inconsistent with this Court's longstanding precedents. * * * Prosecutors undoubtedly need adequate discretion to allocate the resources of their offices and to fulfill their responsibilities to the public in deciding how best to enforce the law, but this does not place them beyond the constraints imposed on state action under the Fourteenth Amendment. Cf. *Ex parte Virginia,* 100 U.S. 339 (1880) (upholding validity of conviction of state judge for discriminating on the basis of race in his selection of jurors).

The Court attempts to distinguish the present case from *Batson v. Kentucky,* in which we recently reaffirmed the fact that prosecutors' actions are not unreviewable. I agree with the Court's observation that this case is "quite different" from the *Batson* case. The irony is that McCleskey presented proof in this case that would have satisfied the more burdensome standard of *Swain v. Alabama,* 380 U.S. 202 (1965), a standard that was described in *Batson* as having placed on defendants a "crippling burden of proof." As discussed above, McCleskey presented evidence of numerous decisions impermissibly affected by racial factors over a significant number of cases. The exhaustive evidence presented in this case certainly demands an inquiry into the prosecutor's actions.   * * *

One of the final concerns discussed by the Court may be the most disturbing aspect of its opinion. Granting relief to McCleskey in this case, it is said, could lead to further constitutional challenges. That, of course, is no reason to deny *McCleskey* his rights under the Equal Protection Clause. If a grant of relief to him were to lead to a closer examination of the effects of racial considerations throughout the criminal-justice system, the system, and hence society, might benefit. Where no such factors come into play, the integrity of the system is enhanced. Where such considerations are shown to be significant, efforts can be made to eradicate their impermissible influence and to ensure an evenhanded application of criminal sanctions.

Like Justice Stevens, I do not believe acceptance of McCleskey's claim would eliminate capital punishment in Georgia. Justice Stevens points out that the evidence presented in this case indicates that in extremely aggravated murders the risk of discriminatory enforcement of the death penalty is minimized. I agree that narrowing the class of death-eligible defendants is not too high a price to pay for a death-penalty system that does not discriminate on the basis of race.[b] Moreover, the establishment of guidelines for Assistant District Attorneys as to the appropriate basis for exercising their discretion at the various steps in the prosecution of a case would provide at least a measure of consistency. The Court's emphasis on the procedural safeguards in the system ignores the fact that there are none whatsoever during the crucial process leading up to trial. As Justice White stated for the plurality in *Turner v. Murray,* I find "the risk that racial prejudice may have infected petitioner's capital sentencing unacceptable in light of the ease with which that risk could have been minimized." I dissent.

b. In a third dissenting opinion, Justice Stevens, joined by Blackmun, J., described the majority's evident fear "that the acceptance of McCleskey's claim would sound the death knell for capital punishment in Georgia" as "unfounded": "One of the lessons of the Baldus study is that there exist certain categories of extremely serious crimes for which prosecutors consistently seek, and juries consistently impose, the death penalty without regard to the race of the victim or the race of the offender. If Georgia were to narrow the class of death-eligible defendants to those categories, the danger of arbitrary and discriminatory imposition of the death penalty would be significantly decreased, if not eradicated."

Although Justice Stevens would reverse, he believed that further proceedings were needed to determine whether McCleskey's death sentence should be set aside: "First, the Court of Appeals must decide whether the Baldus study is valid. I am persuaded that it is, but orderly procedure requires that the Court of Appeals address this issue before we actually decide the question. Second, it is necessary for the District Court to determine whether the particular facts of McCleskey's crime and his background place this case within the range of cases that present an unacceptable risk that race played a decisive role in McCleskey's sentencing."

Appendix A

SELECTED PROVISIONS OF THE UNITED STATES CONSTITUTION

ARTICLE I

Section 9. * * *

[2] The privilege of the Writ of Habeas Corpus shall not be suspended, unless when in Cases of Rebellion or Invasion the public Safety may require it.

[3] No Bill of Attainder or ex post facto Law shall be passed.

ARTICLE III

Section 1. The judicial Power of the United States, shall be vested in one supreme Court, and in such inferior Courts as the Congress may from time to time ordain and establish. The Judges, both of the supreme and inferior Courts, shall hold their Offices during good Behaviour, and shall, at stated Times, receive for their Services a Compensation, which shall not be diminished during their Continuance in Office.

Section 2. [1] The judicial Power shall extend to all Cases, in Law and Equity, arising under this Constitution, the Laws of the United States, and Treaties made, or which shall be made, under their Authority;—to all Cases affecting Ambassadors, other public Ministers and Consuls;—to all Cases of admiralty and maritime Jurisdiction;—to Controversies to which the United States shall be a Party;—to Controversies between two or more States;—between a State and Citizens of another State;—between Citizens of different States;—between Citizens of the same State claiming Lands under the Grants of different States, and between a State, or the Citizens thereof, and foreign States, Citizens or Subjects.

       * * *

[3] The trial of all Crimes, except in Cases of Impeachment, shall be by Jury; and such Trial shall be held in the State where the said Crimes shall have been committed; but when not committed within any State, the Trial shall be at such Place or Places as the Congress may by Law have directed.

Section 3. [1] Treason against the United States, shall consist only in levying War against them, or, in adhering to their Enemies, giving them Aid and Comfort. No Person shall be convicted of Treason unless on the Testimony of two Witnesses to the same overt Act, or on Confession in open Court.

[2]   The Congress shall have Power to declare the Punishment of Treason, but no Attainder of Treason shall work Corruption of Blood, or Forfeiture except during the Life of the Person attainted.

ARTICLE IV

Section 2.   [1] The Citizens of each State shall be entitled to all Privileges and Immunities of Citizens in the several States.

[2]   A Person charged in any State with Treason, Felony, or other Crime, who shall flee from Justice, and be found in another State, shall on demand of the executive Authority of the State from which he fled, be delivered up, to be removed to the State having Jurisdiction of the Crime.

ARTICLE VI

[2]   This Constitution, and the Laws of the United States which shall be made in Pursuance thereof; and all Treaties made, or which shall be made, under the Authority of the United States, shall be the supreme Law.

AMENDMENT I [1791]

Congress shall make no law respecting an establishment of religion, or prohibiting the free exercise thereof; or abridging the freedom of speech, or of the press; or the right of the people peaceably to assemble, and to petition the Government for a redress of grievances.

AMENDMENT II [1791]

A well regulated Militia, being necessary to the security of a free State, the right of the people to keep and bear Arms, shall not be infringed.

AMENDMENT III [1791]

No Soldier shall, in time of peace be quartered in any house, without the consent of the Owner, nor in time of war, but in a manner to be prescribed by law.

AMENDMENT IV [1791]

The right of the people to be secure in their persons, houses, papers, and effects, against unreasonable searches and seizures, shall not be violated, and no Warrants shall issue, but upon probable cause, supported by Oath or affirmation, and particularly describing the place to be searched, and the persons or things to be seized.

AMENDMENT V [1791]

No person shall be held to answer for a capital, or otherwise infamous crime, unless on a presentment or indictment of a Grand Jury, except in cases arising in the land or naval forces, or in the Militia, when in actual service in time of War or public danger; nor shall any person be subject for the same offence to be twice put in jeopardy of life or limb; nor shall be compelled in any criminal case to be a witness against himself, nor be deprived of life, liberty, or property, without due process of law; nor shall private property be taken for public use, without just compensation.

AMENDMENT VI [1791]

In all criminal prosecutions, the accused shall enjoy the right to a speedy and public trial, by an impartial jury of the State and district wherein the crime shall have been committed, which district shall have been previously ascertained by law, and to be informed of the nature and cause of the accusation; to be confronted with the witnesses against him; to have compulsory process for obtaining witnesses in his favor, and to have the Assistance of Counsel for his defence.

AMENDMENT VII [1791]

In Suits at common law, where the value in controversy shall exceed twenty dollars, the right of trial by jury shall be preserved, and no fact tried by jury, shall be otherwise re-examined in any Court of the United States, than according to the rules of the common law.

AMENDMENT VIII [1791]

Excessive bail shall not be required, nor excessive fines imposed, nor cruel and unusual punishments inflicted.

AMENDMENT IX [1791]

The enumeration in the Constitution, of certain rights, shall not be construed to deny or disparage others retained by the people.

AMENDMENT X [1791]

The powers not delegated to the United States by the Constitution, nor prohibited by it to the States, are reserved to the States respectively, or to the people.

AMENDMENT XIII [1865]

Section 1. Neither slavery nor involuntary servitude, except as a punishment for crime whereof the party shall have been duly convicted, shall exist within the United States, or any place subject to their jurisdiction.

Section 2. Congress shall have power to enforce this article by appropriate legislation.

AMENDMENT XIV [1868]

Section 1. All persons born or naturalized in the United States, and subject to the jurisdiction thereof, are citizens of the United States and of the State wherein they reside. No State shall make or enforce any law which shall abridge the privileges or immunities of citizens of the United States; nor shall any State deprive any person of life, liberty, or property, without due process of law; nor deny to any person within its jurisdiction the equal protection of the laws.

Section 5. The Congress shall have the power to enforce, by appropriate legislation, the provisions of the article.

AMENDMENT XV [1870]

Section 1. The right of citizens of the United States to vote shall not be denied or abridged by the United States or by any State on account of race, color, or previous condition of servitude.

Section 2. The Congress shall have power to enforce this article by appropriate legislation.

†